The Insider's Guide to the Colleges

The Insider's Guide to the Colleges

38th Edition

2012

Compiled and Edited
by the Staff of the
Yale Daily News

St. Martin's Griffin
New York

Visit *The Insider's Guide to the Colleges* Web site at www.yaledailynews.com/books.

The editors have sought to ensure that the information in this book is accurate as of press time. Because policies, costs, and statistics do change from time to time, readers should verify important information with the colleges.

THE INSIDER'S GUIDE TO THE COLLEGES, 2012 (thirty-eighth edition). Copyright © 2011 by The Yale Daily News Publishing Company, Inc. All rights reserved. Printed in the United States of America. For information, address St. Martin's Press, 175 Fifth Avenue, New York, N.Y. 10010.

www.stmartins.com

Previous editions copyright © 1997, 1998, 1999, 2000, 2001, 2002, 2003, 2004, 2005, 2006, 2007, 2008, 2009, 2010 by The Yale Daily News Publishing Company, Inc. Copyright © 1981, 1983, 1984, 1985, 1986, 1987, 1988, 1989, 1990, 1991, 1992, 1993, 1994, 1995, 1996 by The Yale Daily News Company, Inc. Copyright © 1971, 1972, 1973, 1974, 1975, 1978 by *The Yale Daily News*.

ISBN 978-0-312-67295-9

First Edition: July 2011

10 9 8 7 6 5 4 3 2 1

Contents

Contents

Preface

Welcome to the 2012 edition of *The Insider's Guide to the Colleges*! Choosing the right school and navigating through the application process may seem overwhelming, but you are beginning your search on the right foot simply by picking up this book. In the 38th edition of the *Insider's Guide*, we provide you with an accurate picture of day-to-day college life. For each school profile, we rely on hours of personal interviews with actual students to give you a true sense of the college and its student body.

We tell you what we wanted to know when we were in your shoes. College is going to be one of the most exciting and rewarding experiences of your life. It is about opening yourself up to new experiences, haphazardly putting together something edible in the dining hall when the lines are long and the food is bad, and making the kinds of friends who will skip class to give you a hand when you need it. It is about pulling all-nighters on papers due the next morning or talking to your roommates until the sun comes up. It is about driving halfway across the country to see your football team win, getting blasted for an opinion piece you wrote for the college newspaper, or volunteering at the local elementary school when you still have to do 300 pages of reading. College is gallons of coffee, stress, and laughter.

But first, you need to choose a school. Among the thousands of colleges that span the continent, you can apply to no more than a handful. Maybe you have a vague idea of what you want, but how do you begin to narrow your choices?

That is where the *Insider's Guide* comes in. For this 38th edition, we have revamped our entire book to ensure that it provides an accurate portrayal of college experience at each of the more than 300 institutions we feature. We give you the inside scoop directly from the students who attend these schools. We research each college by interviewing friends, friends of friends, and a selection of student leaders. These unique perspectives offer insights that you won't find on the glossy pages of admissions brochures or by browsing schools' Web sites. It also means that we are only as accurate as the opinions of our sources. After all, the college experience is unique for every individual. Indeed, one student's closet-sized dorm room may be another student's palace.

In addition to college profiles, the *Insider's Guide* includes a number of special features to help you in your search. "The College Finder" gives you a rundown on various schools according to key attributes, such as student body size and graduation rate. "Getting In" takes you step-by-step through the intricacies of the admissions process. In "The College Spectrum," we discuss some of the most important factors to consider when choosing between schools, as well as giving you a look at current trends in college life. "Introduction for International Students" provides tips on applying to American schools for those living outside of the United States, while "Students with Disabilities" informs those with learning or physical disabilities about issues they should consider when applying. "Study Abroad" gives you a peek at the overseas adventures that students undertake during their college years. The brand new "Summer Experiences" gives you a look at the many different ways to make the most of the summers of your college years, whether through an internship, community service project, or a study program. We have also included "Terms You Should Know," a glossary to help you decode the often-confusing college slang.

We have revised our "Insider's Packing List" and our "Insider's Quiz." Our editors have also added new items to the ever-popular "Editors' Choice" feature, a ranking of colleges in categories spanning from ugliest school colors to biggest rivalries. These lists are based on student interviews as well as our own research and assessment. We hope that this feature will offer you a new perspective or introduce you to a school you may not have otherwise considered.

We know how stressful the college selection process is for you. After all the hard work of preparing and applying, acceptances often appear to be offered randomly, with little regard to merit. You may not be able to attend your top college choice. Nevertheless, you should try not to worry, however difficult it may sound. Ultimately, the majority of students love their college experiences. In part, this is because they applied to schools that were right for them. But most importantly, every single college will provide you with new people to meet, new paths to explore, and new experiences to enjoy. Wherever you end up, just remember one thing: those four years fly by, so make the most of them!—*Michelle Yu*

Editor in Chief
Michelle Yu

Managing Editors
Hai Pham
Zoe Cheung

Executive Editor
Elizabeth Chrystal

Associate Editors
Connor Moseley

Statistics Editors
Zoe Cheung

Staff Writers
Akbar Ahmed
Susannah Albert-Chandhok
Anjali Balakrishna
Yvette Borja
Elizabeth Chrystal
Liliana Cousins
Max de la Bruyere
Jenny Dai
Charlotte Dillon
Madeline Duff
Lia Dun
Preetam Dutta
Julia Fisher
Andrew Giambrone
Jimin He
TaoTao Holmes
Christina Hull

Katerina Karatzia
McKenna Keyes
John Klement
Mason Kroll
Dashell Laryea
Margaret Lee
Larissa Liburd
James Lu
Clarissa Marzan
Lahn Matsumoto
Charlotte McDonald
Maddie McMahon
Connor Moseley
Senzeni Mpofu
Mitchell Murdock
Urvi Nopany
Edirin Okoloko
Cora Ormseth
Lauren Oyler
Sonja Peterson
Hai Pham
Iva Popa
Benjamin Prawdzik
Sharon Qian
Sijia Song
Arielle Stambler
Caroline Tan
Natasha Thondavadi
Liliana Varman
Iva Velickovic
Anna Wang
Antonia Woodford
Justine Yan
Sharon Yin

Acknowledgments

We would like to give particular thanks to Matt Martz, our editor at St. Martin's Press. Without his organizational and creative vision, the 2012 *Guide* would never have been published. To Emad Haerizadeh and Jeff Marsh, we give considerable thanks for their time and patience at *The Yale Daily News*. Thanks to the *Yale Daily News* business and editorial boards for their support through the entire project. We would also like to thank all the interviewees who were gracious enough to give us a peek into their lives and their colleges: Without you, this book would not have been possible. Finally, we are especially thankful to those Yalies who 40 years ago decided to devote their time and energy toward creating a helpful guide for high schoolers about to go to college. We hope you enjoy the book!

Graham Anderson	Ethan Greenspan	Claire Psarouthakis
Jourdan Aromin	Daniel Hauben	Ruth Rackover
Joe Babarsky	Amy Hernandez	Kaitlyn Ramsay
Ashley Barber	Danny Jimenez	Andrea Rectenwald
Kevin Baremore	Bree Ann Johnson	Samantha Rose
Colleen Bartman	David Johnson	Kenny Ryan
Katie Bartolotta	Jaleesa Joy	Elias Saber-Khiabani
Danny Berring	Danny Karp	McKinley Sayre
Caroline Berson	Dan Kaufman	Sara Schilling
Jennifer Bieznak	Roxanne Kierne	Eli Schmitt
Kyle Boylan	Marissa Lee	Bing Shao
Abby Cable	Erica Leslie	Stephanie Shapiro
Laura Cambruzzi	Andy Levine	Ryan Sigurdson
Steve Carmody	Tiffany Ling	Maninder Singh
Erica Carpenter	Madison Lipton	Justin Smith
Candice Cepeda	Boris Lipvetsky	Kathryn Steinhubl
Johanna Chong	Rochelle McConkie	Samara Still
Lindsay Clements	Andrew McCreary	Kyle Stokes
Kate Comaskey	Joe McDonald	Samantha Strack
Brad Cox	Crystal Mckenzie	Mike Stutes
Will Cullen	Maggie Melchiorre	Casey Super
Richard Dang	Alisa Miller	Matthew Sutter
Jonathan Patrick DeWeese	Amy Mokris	Esteban Tapetillo
Lauren Drozd	Molly Moody	Sarah Thurston
Asa Eisenhardt	Jenny Morrow	Rebecca Turkington
Dylan Elder	James Mulligan	Tim Vogeler
Jacob Eller	Simon Neely	Kelly Walsh
Maria Endsley	Zackery O'Connor	Katy Weaver
Kelly England	John Officer	Alexandra Weiss
Dana Rose Falcone	Krzysztof Pakula	Wendy Wilde
Ashkon Farmand	Dearon Panossian	Rhett Williamson
Michael Fennel	Bennett Parmington	Grace Wong
Marissa Ferber	Amanda Perez	Lisa Woo
Noam Finkelstein	Cat Pien	KaaBao Yang
Matt Foley	Anna Pitoniak	Alfred Young

How to Use This Book

How We Select the Colleges

O ne of the most difficult questions we wrestle with here at *The Insider's Guide* is which schools to include in the upcoming edition. From more than 2,000 four-year institutions nationwide, we only cover slightly over 300 colleges. We examine a number of criteria in deciding which colleges to select, but our first priority is always the quality of academics offered by the institution. Another key factor in our decision is the desire to offer a diversity of options in *The Insider's Guide*. Thus, we have included schools from all 50 states as well as several top institutions in Canada. In our school choices, we have also taken into account the range of extracurricular options available to students, including publications, teams, and ethnic organizations. Each year we review our list of schools, research potential additions, and try to include new colleges that have not been featured in the past. Our goal is to provide you with the latest and the most comprehensive insider information.

We have made a point to review the largest state-affiliated institutions because of the significant number of students who apply to and matriculate at their states' schools. These universities tend to offer a particularly wide range of opportunities. We have also made every effort to include a broad cross section of smaller colleges because of the unique education they offer. Many of these schools are liberal arts colleges, generally clustered in the Northeast, offering a broad but personalized education. To add to the diversity of schools reviewed by *The Insider's Guide*, we have also included selections from the most prominent technical schools and creative and performing arts schools. These institutions provide specialized education, combining general knowledge with a concentration in a particular field. The sampling of schools in this category is by no means comprehensive, and we encourage students interested in specialized institutions to explore their options more deeply through additional research.

In sum, this book covers the colleges we believe to be among the most noteworthy in both the United States and Canada. This se-lection does not imply in any way that you cannot get a good education at a school not listed in the *Guide*. We strongly encourage students to use strategies discussed within this book to explore the wide variety of schools that we did not have space to include here, including community colleges, state schools, international schools, and professional schools. In addition, it's not guaranteed that you will have a blissful four years if you attend one of the schools we feature! Rather, we believe that every school in the *Guide* offers students the raw materials for constructing an excellent education.

It's All Up to You

N ow that you have picked up a copy of *The Insider's Guide*, it's up to you how to use it. A few dedicated readers scrutinize the book from start to finish, determined to gain the most complete understanding of the college process and the schools that are out there. Others flip through the *Guide* for only a few minutes to look at **FYIs** from schools that interest them or to read funny quotes taken from nearby colleges. Another good strategy is to use the **College Finder**, **Editors' Choice lists**, and statistics that begin each article to learn more about colleges that you may not have heard of before. It might be worthwhile to read up on colleges that you wouldn't initially consider—you just may find yourself intrigued by the student perspectives. Take advantage of the opening features of the book—they are designed to help you zero in on schools that meet your search criteria. You can also explore these beginning sections to learn what is unique and important about schools you are already considering. We encourage all these approaches. Above all, we hope that the *Guide* is fun to read, educational, and a useful aid in helping to make the college selection process less stressful.

While our **Editors' Choice lists** use a mix of statistics and subjectivity to provide an alternative perspective on the schools we include, we have avoided the temptation to pigeon-hole the colleges with some kind of catch-all rating system, or worse, to numerically rank them from first to last. Our reason is that the "best" college for one person may come near the bottom of the list for another. Each student has his or her own particular set of wants and needs, so it would be impossible for us to objectively rank the schools from "best" to "worst." Whereas most rankings focus solely on academic factors, the college experience is a balance of academics, social life, extracurricular activities, and much more.

Even so, some may wonder why we don't rate the colleges solely on the basis of academic quality. We think that attempting to come up with such a ranking is both impossible and undesirable. There are too many variables—from the many factors that contribute to the quality of a department and school as a whole to the articulateness and accessibility of the professor who happens to be your academic advisor. Furthermore, it's useless to try to compare a college of 2,000 students with a university of 10,000 (or a university of 10,000 with a state school of 40,000 for that matter) on any basis other than individual preference. Despite these reasons not to, some reportedly reputable sources such as national magazines often insist on publishing numerical rankings of colleges. We advise you not to take these lists too seriously. Oftentimes the determining factor in the rankings is a statistic such as "percent of alumni who donate money," something that means very little to most college applicants.

For over 35 years, *The Insider's Guide* has been dedicated to the belief that the best rankers of schools are students themselves, not magazine writers. Our goal, therefore, is to help you train your eye so you can select the college that is best for you. Remember, we may describe, explain, interpret, and report— but in the end, the choice is always yours.

Getting In

Applying to college can seem as intimidating as reading through this thick book, but neither should be a chore. In the spring of your sophomore year of high school, your Aunt Doris, whom you have not seen in seven years, pinches your cheek and asks you where you are going to college. "How the heck should I know," you think to yourself. That fall, your mom tells you that the girl down the street with the 4.0 grade point average is taking the SAT prep course for the fifth time to see if she can get a perfect score and win thousands in scholarship money. You reply that you are late for school. You keep ducking the subject, but the hints come with increasing regularity. Not only has dinnertime become your family's "let's talk about Lauren's college options" hour, but friends at school are already beginning to leaf through college catalogs. Soon you find the guidance counselor's office crowded with your wide-eyed peers, and it's clear they aren't asking for love advice. Panicking, you decide to make an appointment with the counselor yourself.

When you first talk to your counselor, preferably in the early part of your junior year, you may not yet feel completely comfortable in high school, let alone prepared to think about college. The entire prospect seems far away, but choosing the right school for you takes a good amount of thought and organization—and a visit to your counselor is a solid start. You may even be wondering if college is the path you want to take after high school. And you're not alone. A good number of people choose to take a year or two off to work or travel before pursuing a college education.

One important resource in making a decision about any post-graduation plans is your counselor. College counselors have a wealth of information and experience from which to draw, and they can help you lay out a plan for whatever direction you wish to take. If you decide that college is your next step, you will have a lot of options. Although many schools are surveyed in this book, we have not included professional schools or community colleges, all of which also offer a wide variety of opportunities. With research of your own and the aid of your counselor, you should be able to find a school that will give you what you're looking for.

In your hunt for the best college, it is wise to do a little exploring of your own before sitting down with your counselor. Counselors can be invaluable advisors and confidants throughout the college admissions process, but sometimes counselors inadvertently limit your search by only recommending noncompetitive schools, or, conversely, by assuring you that you'll get into whichever school you want. A few may even try to dissuade you from applying to colleges that you are seriously considering. These cases aren't common, but they do happen. Regardless of your counselor's perspective, it is best if you already have an idea of what you are looking for, as it will help both you and your advisor sort out all the options. You can refer back to these initial goals as you learn more. In the end, always follow your instincts.

As you begin to wade through the piles of brochures, ask yourself questions. What factors about a school make a difference to you? What do you want in a college? A strong science department? A Californian landscape? A small student body? A great social life? Although each college is a mix of different features, it is wise to place your academic needs first. Check out the general academic quality of the school, as well as what kind of programs they offer. Please note: since many students change their majors repeatedly before finally settling down, it's a good idea to look for schools with programs in a number of areas that interest you.

Of course, it's impossible to think of all the angles from which you should approach your college search. You can't predict what your interests will be three or four years from now, or what things will prove most important to you at the college you attend. After all, those realizations are a big part of what the college experience is all about. But by taking a hard look at yourself now, and proceeding thoughtfully, you can be confident that you are investigating the right colleges for the right reasons.

As you begin the search, schools will start to seek you out as well. In the early winter of your junior year, you'll receive your PSAT scores, and unless you request otherwise, your mailbox will soon become inundated with letters from colleges around the country. The College Search Service of the College Board provides these schools with the names and addresses of students who show promise, and the schools crank out thousands of form letters to send, and often to students with backgrounds that they feel are underrepresented in their student population.

While sorting through these masses of glossy brochures, you'll probably notice that most of them contain lofty quotes and pictures of a diverse, frolicking student body. One of the best ways to find out if these ideals are actually truths is to visit the college. But before that, you can verify some of what you read by comparing it to nationally published articles and statistics. You will probably find the colleges that most interest you through your own research, and many of these schools wait for you to contact them before they send information. In that case, create a form letter that briefly expresses your interest in the college and requests materials. You'll get your name on their mailing lists, and they'll appreciate the fact that you took the initiative.

Throughout this process, make sure to listen to those who know you well and often have sound advice to share—namely, your parents and elder siblings. Besides having some ideas of schools you might enjoy attending, your parents also have great insight into how your education can and will be financed. If you come to an early understanding with your family about prospective colleges and financial concerns, things will move much more smoothly down the road. But be warned—the college search can be one of the most trying times in any parent-child relationship, and some parents become more or less involved in the process than students want. The best advice we can give is to remember that calm, patient discussions are a better tactic than yelling matches.

When consulting others about your college search, it is helpful to keep a few things in mind. Every piece of advice you receive will be a reflection of someone's own life experiences, and it is likely to be highly subjective. Most adults will suggest schools located in regions they know or colleges they have visited or attended themselves. Also, opinions are often based on stereotypes that can be false, outdated, or just misleading. Still, the more people you talk to, the better perspective you will gain on the colleges you are considering. Once you have a few outside ideas, this book can give you some inside information. If you like what you have heard about a particular school, follow up with some research and find out if it's still a place that calls to you.

As you approach the time when your final college list must be made, you will probably have visited college fairs and attended various college nights. Real-life representatives from the schools are always good to meet. Talking to current college students is an even more important step, as is visiting the schools that make it to your last list. During these encounters, ask the questions that are on your mind. Be critical and observant. When it's time for the final leg of the college selection process, you'll be calm and satisfied if you know you've really looked hard into yourself and all your options.

Visit

Whether your list of schools has been set for months or fluctuates on a daily basis, college visits are a great way to narrow down your choices and prioritize your list of options. Try to plan campus visits so you'll be finished by the fall of your senior year, especially if you are considering early application programs. Additionally, aim to see as many schools that interest you as possible—there's no better way to get a feel for where you'd like to spend the next four years of your life.

When you visit a campus, try to keep in mind why you are there. You have probably already seen the college viewbook with glossy pictures of green lawns and diverse groups of students in seminar-size classes. Now is the time to find out what the campus is really like. Is the student population truly that diverse? Do people really gather and play Frisbee on plush green lawns? What do the dorms actually look like? And most importantly, do you feel comfortable there?

If you are visiting a campus for an interview, make sure you schedule one in advance. Making the decision not to interview on campus may be a good one, however. While some schools require an on-campus interview, some insiders recommend that you request an alumni interview instead. Alumni interviews tend to be more convenient and less grueling than on-campus interviews. In any case, make sure you check a school's policy regarding interviews before you arrive, and schedule your visit accordingly.

While some prefer to visit colleges over summer vacation, we think the best time to visit is during the academic year, when regular classes are in session. During the summer months very few students are on campus, so it will be much more difficult to get a feel for the student culture and vibrancy (or lack thereof). Times of unusually high stress also will not give you a good idea of what ordinary life is like. For this reason, you'll also want to avoid exam periods and vacations. During the academic year, your questions about the campus are much more likely to be answered. You'll get a feel for the type of people at the school, and you'll get an idea of what it is like to be a student living on campus. It's important to get a good sense of what your daily life will be like if you end up attending the school.

Before you look at any college, take a little time to prepare. Perhaps you will want to come up with some kind of system to evaluate the schools you will visit. Putting together a list of characteristics that are important to you will make it easier to compare one school to the next, whether they be academics, the size of the campus, or the surrounding area's vibrancy and atmosphere. Make sure you jot down some notes on the schools during and after your trips. Although colleges may seem easy to differentiate at the time, your impressions of each may blur together when you are back at home, sitting in front of 10 seemingly identical applications.

An overnight stay with undergraduates can provide you with a more inside look at campus life. Most admissions offices have students on call who are happy to show you around campus, take you to some classes and parties, and let you crash in their dorms. If you have friends there, they are good resources as well. Either way, staying with students will help you see what an undergraduate's academic and social life is really like. One student said, "I found that it didn't matter much if I stayed over or not, as long as I got to talk to students. But if you do stay over, Thursday or Friday night is the best time." Sometimes it is hard to connect with students during a single day when everybody is rushing around to classes. Try to spend a night late in the week when students will have more time for you and the nightlife will be more vibrant. It is always possible that you will end up with hosts that are difficult to relate to or socially withdrawn. Don't let a bad hosting experience completely dictate your feelings about the college—just do everything you can to get out into the student body and explore what the school has to offer.

Keep in mind that college life doesn't consist entirely of classes. Sample the food, which is, after all, a necessity of life. Check

out the dorms. Take the campus tour. Although you are sure to be inundated with obscure facts about the college that may not interest you, it can be useful to have a knowledgeable guide to show you the buildings themselves and the campus as a whole. If you have any questions, do not hesitate to ask. Tour guides are often students and are a great resource for any information you want about the school.

Should you bring your parents along? Maybe. Some students prefer to leave them at home. Although parents don't mean any harm, they can sometimes get in the way. Your discomfort at having them around when you're trying to get along with new students may cloud your opinion of a school. However, most students do bring along at least one family member. If you go this route, don't completely discount the advice or opinions they may have about the school. Parents can be great resources to bounce ideas off of, particularly regarding the pros and cons of the various colleges you have seen. You might want to take the campus tour with them, and then break away to explore the campus on your own and talk with students one-on-one. When you enter college your parents will not be there with you, so it's a good idea to get a feel for what that will actually be like.

Most importantly, keep in mind your sense of the campus atmosphere. How does it feel to walk across the main quad? Does the mood seem intellectual or laid-back? Do T-shirts read "Earth Day Every Day" or "Coed Naked Beer Games"? Look for postings of events; some campuses are alive and vibrant while others seem pretty dead. Check your comfort level. Imagine yourself on the campus for the next four years and see how that makes you feel. Focus on these characteristics while you are on campus—you can read about the academic requirements when you get back home. Most of all, enjoy yourself! The campus visit is an exciting peek into a world that will soon be your own.

The Interview

Just about every college applicant dreads the interview. It can be the most nerve-wracking part of the college application process. But relax—despite the horror stories you might have heard, the interview will rarely make or break your application. If you are a strong candidate, don't be overly self-assured; if your application makes you look like a hermit, be lively and personable. Usually the interview can only help you, and at some schools it is nothing more than informational. "I was constantly surprised at how many questions they let me ask," one applicant reported.

Consider the interview your chance to highlight the best parts of your application and explain the weaker parts without being whiny or making excuses. Are your SAT scores on the low side? Does your extracurricular section seem a little thin? An interview gives you the opportunity to call attention to your successes in classes despite your scores, or explain that of the three clubs you listed, you founded two and were president of the third.

There are a few keys to a successful interview.

1. The first and most important is to stand out from the crowd. Keep in mind that the interviewer probably sees half a dozen or more students every day, month after month. If you can make your interviewer laugh, interest him or her in something unusual you have done, or somehow spice up the same old questions and answers, you have had a great interview. Don't just say that you were the president of something; be able to back up your titles with interesting and genuine stories. On the other hand, don't go overboard and shock your interviewer with spring break stories, for example. That will most likely work against you.

2. Do not try to be something you are not. Tell the truth and give the interviewer a feel for who you really are–your passions, your strengths, and your challenges. By doing so, you will be more relaxed and confident. Even if you feel that the "real you" isn't that interesting or amazing, take time to reflect on your high school experience–the stories that surface in your mind may just surprise you.

3. A few days before the actual interview, think about some of the questions you might be asked. Some admissions officers begin every interview by asking, "Why do you want to go to this school, and why should we let you in?" You should not have memorized speeches for every answer, but try not to get caught off guard. Make sure you really know why you want to attend this college. Even if you are not sure, think of a few plausible reasons and be prepared to give them.

Students often make the mistake of giving a canned answer, which is okay since most answers are similar, but admissions officers look to admit students who want to take advantage of all that is available at their school. Your answer must include the three essential elements of a good reply: your interests, whether academic or extracurricular; what you believe the school will provide; and how and why you are excited about the opportunity to take advantage of them. Other common questions include those about your most important activities, what you did with your summers, and what vision you may have for your future.

4. A note of caution: If your interview takes place after you have submitted your application, the interviewer might ask you questions about some of the things you included. One student wrote on his application that he read *Newsweek* religiously. During his interview, the admissions officer asked the student about a story in a recent issue of the magazine. The student had no idea what the interviewer was talking about. He was not accepted. While this was only one of many factors that the admissions officer had to consider, it is still important. So be ready to back up your claims. It is always an excellent idea to indicate that you have a special interest in something, but make sure the interest is genuine—you may wind up in an hour-long conversation on the topic. Do not start talking about how you love learning about philosophy if you have only dabbled in it once. An open, thoughtful manner can do as much as anything else to impress your interviewer, although an overly negative attitude will make just as much of an impression.

5. Being spontaneous in a contrived situation usually amounts to having a successful interview. If you are nervous, that's okay. Said one applicant, "I felt sick, and I didn't eat for a day before the interview." The most common misconception is that admissions officers are looking for totally confident individuals who know everything and have their entire future planned out. Almost the opposite is true. An admissions officer at a selective private college said, "We do not expect imitation adults to walk through the door. We expect to see people in their last year or two of high school with the customary apprehensions, habits, and characteristics of that time of life." Admissions offi-

cers know students get nervous. They understand. If everything in your life is not perfect, do not be afraid to say so when appropriate. For example, if the conversation comes around to your high school, there is no need to cover up if problems do exist. It is okay to say you did not think your chemistry lab was well equipped. An honest, realistic critique of your school or just about anything else will make a better impression than false praise ever could.

6. If something you say does not come out quite right, try to react as you would with a friend. If the interviewer asks about your career plans, it is alright to say that you are undecided. As a high school student, no one expects you to have all the answers—that is why you are going to college. Above all, remember that the admissions officer is a person interested in getting to know you as an individual. A person who may be a parent to someone, a friend of someone's, a sibling of someone's. They empathize. As one interviewer explained, "I'm not there to judge the applicants as scholars. I'm just there to get a sense of them as people."

7. Do not get so worried about saying all the right things that you forget to listen carefully to the interviewer. The purpose of the interview is not to grill you, but to match you with the school in the best interest of both. Sometimes the interviewer will tell you, either during the interview or in a follow-up letter, that you have little chance of getting in. If she says so or implies it, know that such remarks are not made lightly. On the other hand, if she is sincerely encouraging, listen to that, too. If an interviewer suggests other schools for you to look into, remember that she is a professional and take note. Besides, many interviewers appreciate a student's ability to listen as well as to talk.

8. Your interviewer might ask you whether you have a first choice, particularly if her college is often seen as a backup. If the school is really not your first choice, feel free to sidestep that question as gracefully as possible. Not only is it more than likely that you haven't made up your mind, but your first choice is your business, not theirs. If the school really is your first choice, though, feel free to say so, and give a good reason why. A genuine interest can be a real plug on your behalf.

9. Also know that you can direct the conversation. Do not worry about occasional

lapses as some interviewers wait to see how you will react to a potentially awkward situation. Take advantage of the pause to ask a question or bring up a relevant topic that really interests you. It is your job to present the parts of you and your background that you want noted.

10. Selective colleges need reasons to accept you. Being qualified on paper is not always enough. Think of the interviewer's position: "Why should we accept you instead of thousands of other qualified applicants?" The answer to that question should be evident in every response you give. Use the interview to play up and accentuate your most memorable qualities. Show flashes of the playful sense of humor that your English teacher cites in his recommendation; impress the interviewer with the astute eye for politics about which your history teacher raves.

11. Too many applicants are afraid to talk confidently about their accomplishments. If the interviewer is impressed by something, do not insist that it was not much, or he might believe you. If he is not impressed by something you think is important, tactfully let him know that he should be. But do not, under any circumstances, act like you are too good for the college. One well-qualified applicant to a leading college was turned down when the interviewer wrote, "It obviously isn't going to be the end of his world if he doesn't get in. And it won't be the end of our world, either." If there is any quality you want to convey, it is a sincere interest in the school.

12. Almost all interviewers will eventually ask, "Do you have any questions about our school?" Come to the interview armed with a couple of good questions, and not ones whose answers are easily found in the college's viewbook or on the school Web site. Do not ask if they have an economics department, for example, or ask the average class size in introductory economics courses. It may help to do some extra preparation ahead of time. Are you interested in studying abroad? If so, know what kind of programs the school offers and ask a few questions about them. If you are excited to learn more about the school and have already done some homework, it goes a long way in the eyes of the interviewer. Also, if the interviewer is an alumnus, a good question is to ask what they would have done differently during their time at the col-

lege. You can be sure that they will need a moment of reflection, and you'll have time to relax!

13. You will probably wonder what to wear. This is no life or death decision, but remember that your appearance is one of the first things the interviewer will notice about you. Wear something you will be comfortable in—a jacket and a tie or a nice dress is fine. Do not, however, be too casual. Faded jeans and a T-shirt will give the impression that you are taking the interview too lightly. But, if your interview is at Starbucks as opposed to someone's office building, take their choice in location as a cue for dress.

14. One crucial point: Keep your parents a thousand feet and preferably a thousand miles away from the interview session. It will be harder to relax and be genuine with an additional set of eyes on you, and you might hold back some interesting information. When parents sit in, interviews tend to be short, boring, and, worst of all, useless. If the interviewer feels you cannot handle an hour without your parents, she might be concerned about your ability to survive the pressures of college life. Take the risk of hurting your parents' feelings and ask them to wait outside.

    Once the interview is over, it is perfectly alright for your parents to ask any questions they may have if the interviewer walks with you back to the waiting room. Even if this makes you uncomfortable, do not let it show. Admissions officers can learn as much about you by the way you treat your parents as they do in the interview. The interviewer is not judging your parents. As long as you conduct yourself calmly and maturely, you have nothing to worry about.

15. It is a good idea to send a thank-you note after the interview. It doesn't need to be extensive, just let the interviewer know that you appreciate the time she or he spent with you and that you enjoyed learning more about the school. While it doesn't seem like much, a simple note can leave a lasting impression. Be sure to say something specific to your interview. If you shared a laugh or if the interviewer mentioned something about his or her job, try to slip something personal into the note. All of this advice applies for interviews given by alumni as well as those conducted by admissions staff. Alumni interviewers sometimes carry slightly less weight with the admissions office, but they are valuable contacts with the schools and should not be taken lightly. Expect on-campus interviews to be a bit more formal than alumni interviews.

What if you do not have an interview at all? Perhaps you live too far away, and you cannot get to the school itself. Or, perhaps you feel that your lack of poise is serious enough that it would work against you in any interview you had. Talk it over with your guidance counselor. In general, geographic isolation is a valid excuse for not having an interview, and most colleges will not hold it against you. Ask if they will allow a phone interview instead. Yet, if the college is fairly close and makes it clear that applicants should have an on-campus interview if at all possible, make the effort to go. Otherwise, the college will assume that for some reason you were afraid to interview, or worse, that you simply did not care enough to have one. If the prospect is genuinely terrifying, schedule your first interview for a safety school, or ask your guidance counselor to grant you a practice interview. You might discover that the process is not as horrible as you originally thought.

The Tests

Whether you are an Olympic hopeful, a musical prodigy, or a third-generation legacy, it doesn't matter. You cannot avoid taking standardized tests if you want to go to college. The 90 percent of all four-year institutions now require some type of admissions test. Certainly, tests do not tell the whole story—grades, recommendations, extracurricular activities, the application essays, and personal interviews round out the picture. However, standardized test scores are often the only uniform criteria available to admissions committees. They are meant to indicate the level of education you have had in the past, as well as your potential to succeed in the future. Unfortunately, while they aren't perfect, they are a necessary evil.

Virtually all of the nation's colleges require applicants to submit SAT Reasoning Test or ACT scores. In addition, many colleges will ask their applicants for SAT Subject Test scores. If you are an international student with a native language other than English (or recently moved from an education system using a foreign language), you may be required to take the TOEFL as well.

If you take AP tests or are in an IB program, your scores could help you earn college credit if they fulfill the score requirements of the college to which you are applying. Does all this seem overwhelming to you? Read this section and hopefully we can help you understand each test a little better.

The SAT Reasoning Test, formerly known as the Scholastic Aptitude Test (SAT), is the most widely chosen admissions test by college applicants. Administered by the Educational Testing Service (ETS) and created by the College Board, the SAT Reasoning Test currently has a math section, a critical reading section, and a writing section. A nearly four-hour test, there are a total of 10 sections; three are writing, three are verbal, three are math, and there is an unscored variable section (math or critical reading) thrown in somewhere to try out new question formats. The math section includes material up through Geometry and Algebra II, and, to your benefit, you are allowed to use calculators. It has five-choice multiple-choice questions and questions where you produce the answer yourself. In the critical reading section, you will find sentence completions and short and long passages with reading comprehension questions. The writing section involves an essay in response to a prompt and multiple choice questions that require you to identify grammar and usage errors and improve sentence and paragraph structure.

The SAT scores the math, critical reading, and writing sections separately on a 200 to 800 scale. Therefore, your combined score can be a minimum of 600 and a maximum of 2400. One disadvantage with the SAT is that you are penalized for wrong answers, so avoid guessing haphazardly. However, if you can eliminate a few answer choices, it is often better to guess than to leave the question blank. The average score for each section is a 500 based on the recentered scale that the ETS implemented starting in 1995. When the SAT was originally calibrated, it was done so that the average score for the math and verbal sections would each be 500. Over several decades, the average dropped—some say as a result of the declining American education system. However, others argue that the perceived "decrease" is not surprising considering that today's over two million SAT-takers are much more representative of American education as a whole than the 10,000 primarily affluent prep-school students who took the test when it was implemented in 1941. As a result, the scoring was recentered in 1995 in order to redistribute scores more evenly along the 200 to 800 scale. All colleges and scholarship institutions are aware of this new scoring calibration, so even though it may be easier to get that rare 800 section score, your percentile rank among other students who took the exam will not change.

There are five ways to register for the SAT. The two most common methods are to complete an online registration at www .collegeboard.com or mail in a registration form, which you can get from your high school counselor's office. If you've registered for an SAT Program test before, you can complete the registration over the phone. For those students living outside of the United States, U.S. territories, and Puerto Rico, there is an option to fax in your registration. International students have the option of registering through a representative found in the International Edition of the SAT Registration Bulletin. The SAT is administered seven times a year domestically, and six times a year overseas.

Before you take the test, be sure to take advantage of two services offered by the College Board upon registration. The first is called the Student Search Service. It allows universities, colleges, and scholarship programs to get general information about you, as well as what range your score falls into. You will receive a flood of information about different schools and scholarship programs in the mail in addition to information regarding financial aid opportunities. While you'll begin to see most of these letters as junk mail, some of them will help you come up with the list of colleges to which you intend to apply. As a second service, the College Board will mail your test scores to a maximum of four specified schools or scholarship programs for free. You can send additional score reports for a fee. Be aware that if you have taken the SAT more than once, all of your previous scores will be sent when reporting to schools and scholarship programs. If you have second thoughts and want to cancel your scores, you must do so by the Wednesday following your exam via e-mail, fax, or mail.

The American College Test (ACT) was required mostly by colleges in the southern and western regions of the country but is now accepted by most colleges across the nation. The exam covers English, reading, mathematics, and science reasoning in the format of 215 multiple-choice questions. It also offers an optional writing component. One distinguishing feature of the ACT is that it measures what you have learned in the high school curriculum rather than your aptitude.

The ACT, unlike the SAT, does not deduct any points for incorrect answers, so be sure to fill in a bubble for every question. You will receive a score on a scale of 1 to 36 for each of the four subject areas; your Composite score is just an average of the four scores rounded to the nearest whole number. Based on the over 1.3 million students who choose to take the test, the average Composite score is around 21. Registration is much like the SAT, with a mail-in option, online registration at www.act.org, or telephone preregistration. There is a stand-by registration option for those who forget to register. As far as score reporting goes, you can choose up to six schools or scholarship programs on your registration to have the scores sent to for free. The great thing about the ACT is that you can choose to send just one testing date's scores instead of having your whole history of scores sent, as is done with the SAT.

Many of the more selective colleges also require up to three SAT Subject Tests, formerly called SAT IIs. Available subjects include English, a variety of foreign languages, math, history, and several of the sciences. Due to the recent addition of the writing section to the SAT Reasoning Test, there is no longer a writing Subject Test available. One thing about the SAT Subject Tests is that you don't have to choose which tests you want to take until you're at the test center on the test date. The scores are reported on a 200 to 800 scale, with Score Choice as an option that allows students to not submit all of their scores. Score Choice has been controversial because students can choose to submit only their best scores, without revealing the total number of tests they have taken or the number of times they took each test.

The Test of English as a Foreign Language (TOEFL) is an English proficiency test provided for international students who want to study in the United States, Canada, or other English-speaking countries. It is administered by paper and pencil, on a test-center computer, or over the internet. The score scale for the test varies depending on which form of the test you choose to take. Furthermore, the essay is scored separately and has a separate scoring scale. The TOEFL will test your listening, structured writing, and reading skills—giving a better picture of your English to the schools you apply to.

Advanced Placement (AP) exams are another animal altogether since their purpose is not only to get you into college, but also to earn you credits once you get there. Administered in May, each test covers a specific subject area and scores your performance from 1 to 5. Different schools require different scores for granting college credit. Some will offer credit but still require you to take classes in a subject that you aced on the AP exams. Since the tests require in-depth knowledge of specific subjects, do not put off studying for them. The general practice is to take the exam in a particular subject the May right after you have finished (or are in the midst of finishing) a course in that area. Not only can you get college credit with a high score, but you can also help your college applications with AP exams taken before your senior year.

If you attend an International Baccalaureate (IB) school, you might be able to receive college credit for your coursework depending on your score. A score of 4 or 5 is the required minimum by a college for credit and/or placement, but many institutions require a score of 6 or 7. Although not as popularly embraced by colleges and universities across the nation for giving college credit, they will definitely recognize you for the rigorous work you have completed in the program and can enable you to take higher-level courses in certain subject areas.

You may have already taken the PSAT/NMSQT, which is usually administered to sophomores or juniors through their high school. This is a great practice exam for the SAT Reasoning Test because it has a lot of the same type of questions. It is also a good way to qualify for merit scholarships if you get a high score. The PSAT changed its format to incorporate writing skills in the fall of 2004 to complement the new SAT in 2005.

The most reliable way to keep up-to-date on test dates, testing sites, and registration deadlines is through your high school guidance office. After the PSAT, you will be on your own about when and where you take the tests. Find out way ahead of time which ones are required by the colleges you are interested in; deadlines have a way of sneaking up on you. It is a good idea to begin taking the tests by the spring of your junior year. If you take the SAT Reasoning Test in March or May of your junior year and do not do as well as you think you should, you will have a couple of other opportunities to improve your score. The required SAT Subject Tests should be taken by June of your junior year so that if you decide to apply to an early-action or early-decision program, you will have completed the required testing.

Avoid postponing required testing until November, December, or January of your senior year. One new college student, who put off his exams until the last minute, recalled his college freshman faculty advisor saying to him, "I just don't understand it . . . you went to one of the best high schools in Chicago and did very well. How could your SAT scores have been so low?" He told her how lucky he felt just getting into college; he had contracted a nasty flu and thrown up before, during, and after the test! On the other hand, do not repeat tests over and over. The ETS reports that students gain an average of 25 points on both the math and reading sections of the SAT Reasoning Test upon taking the test a second time. Two or three shots at the SATs should be sufficient. If you've got the time and money, you may want to consider taking a prep course given by a professional test-preparation service. National test-prep companies like Kaplan and the Princeton Review, as well as dozens of local companies, attempt to give helpful tips on how to take tests for those willing to shell out hundreds of dollars. If you do decide to take a prep course, take it seriously. You may have six or seven high school classes to worry about, but you cannot hope to get your money's worth if you do not attend all of the sessions and complete the homework in these prep courses.

Many people choose not to take practice courses. A good student who is confident about taking tests can probably do just as well studying on his or her own. Practice exams are available online and in commercially marketed practice books. Get acquainted with the tests you plan to take beforehand; you should not have to waste time during your exam rereading instructions and trying to figure out what to do. It's a good idea to even simulate an actual test by timing yourself with no interruptions on a real test that was previously administered.

The College Board puts out a book called *The Official SAT Study Guide* that proves to be one of the most effective ways to prepare for the SAT Reasoning Test. True to its title, the book has official SATs from the past, along with hints, test-taking strategies, and exercises to help you improve your test score. The ACT has a similar book called *The Real ACT Prep Guide* with three complete exams plus ACT's own analyses and explanations designed to help you with the test.

Getting the chance to practice exams in a real testlike situation (no phones, family, or friends to distract you) will help you to get a keener sense of the overall structure of the test and help you work faster during the actual exam. It might also help you calm down!

Do not cram the night before the exam. Get plenty of sleep and relax. "My teacher encouraged us to go out and have a good time the day before," recalled one first-year college student. "So I went to the movies as a distraction. I think it worked!" On the day of the test, eat a full breakfast that isn't too heavy, dress comfortably, and do not forget to bring two pieces of ID, a calculator, a couple of number two pencils and a pencil sharpener. Make sure you are up early and know where you will be taking the test as well as how to get there. The test center may be overcrowded, there may be no air-conditioning or heat, and a hundred construction workers may be drilling outside the nearest window—be prepared for anything!

The key to success on any of these exams is to keep calm. During the exam, keep track of how many problems there are and allot time accordingly. Read and attempt to answer every question since you do not get more credit for the hard ones than the easy ones. If you are stuck on a question, try to eliminate as many answers as possible and select from the remaining choices. Only if you really have no clue about the question should you leave it blank on the SAT.

A word of warning: Do not even think about cheating. It is not worth it, and your chances of getting caught and blackballed from college are high. To weed out cheaters, the ETS uses the mysterious K-index, a statistical tool that measures the chance of two students selecting the same answers. If your K-index is suspect, a form letter goes out to the colleges you are interested in, delaying your score until you retake the exam or prove your innocence. Know that looking at another person's test is not the only activity that the ETS considers cheating. Going back to finish work on a previous section is also against the rules. Do not tempt fate—a low score is better than no score at all.

At the beginning of this section, we stressed that standardized tests are important. How important? It varies depending on the school you are applying to. At many state schools, admission depends almost entirely on test scores and grades; if you score above the cutoffs, you are in. With the more selective schools, scores are usually only one of many important factors in the admissions process. According to the dean of admissions at Harvard University, "If scores are in the high 500 to low 700 range, they probably have a fairly small impact on our decisions." Each of the schools in this book lists a mean score range for the SAT. Remember that there are students who score below this range and above this range that were accepted to that college. Unless you score far below or far above the mean of your desired college, most likely your SAT Reasoning Test score will not make or break your chances of getting in. If you attended an inner-city school or a school in an area of the country where education standards are below the norm, your apparent deficit might, in fact, indicate a strength—as long as you are above the minimum levels.

Many students mistakenly believe that the SAT is the only test that "really matters" in competitive college admissions. In fact, SAT Subject Test scores taken as a whole are usually of equal importance. Colleges will often view these scores as a more accurate predictor of future performance than the SAT Reasoning Test. Aside from tests, it is important to remember that your high school record is weighed heavily. If you bomb your admissions tests, but have decent grades, there's a chance that your high school performance can outweigh the bad test scores. However, a poor GPA is hard to overlook, even if your scores are high. Remember that your admissions test scores are just a portion of the whole picture you present to the colleges. So try your best to make it advantageous to you, and don't worry if you don't get a perfect score!

The Application

It's the fall of your senior year of high school. You've done your research and found a few schools that you're interested in. You've taken the standardized tests, you've visited the campuses, and you may even have had some on-campus interviews. You still have one major hurdle ahead of you, however: The Application. Although the piles of paperwork may seem daunting, with some advance planning you can make the application process as painless as possible. As you go through the often challenging process, keep in mind that it's all worth it in light of your ultimate goal: acceptance.

First, you have to decide where you want to apply. You should have this done no later

than the first few weeks of your senior year. After talking to students and visiting campuses, try to narrow down your original list of colleges to somewhere between five and 15. Applying to any more schools than this is probably overkill. Not only is it a waste of time to apply to more schools than necessary, it is also a waste of money to apply to any school you won't be happy attending— application processing fees can be pricey. However, you want to apply to enough schools that you'll be sure to get accepted somewhere.

It's also important to think about the selectivity of the schools you apply to. Don't be scared to apply to your dream school even if your SAT score or GPA is a bit low. On the other hand, make sure to apply to at least one or two "safety schools," where you'll be both happy and stand an excellent chance of getting accepted. A good rule of thumb is to apply to at least one "reach" school, a school that may be a long-shot to get into, but one where you'd love to go, at least one "safety school," and a few "good fit" schools in between.

After you've listed the schools where you'll apply, get the applications and figure out when each of them is due. It may be a good idea to make a list of deadlines, both early and regular, and hang it somewhere in your room. Many schools allow you to download their applications from their Web sites. Others send them to you in the mail; if this is the case, make sure you request the application in plenty of time to fill it out carefully and send it in. Whatever you do, make sure you get your applications in on time. Many schools won't even look at applications they receive late, so make deadlines a priority.

Different schools accept applications in a variety of ways. A brief description of the major types of applications follows:

- *Rolling Admissions:* Most large public schools and many less-selective colleges accept "rolling applications," which means they process applications continuously, in the order they receive them. You hear back from the school a few weeks after you send in your application. Though these schools often accept applications into the spring, it is important to send in your application early because admittance often becomes more challenging as these schools accept more and more students. Try to send in applications to schools with rolling deadlines as early as you can.

- *Regular Decision:* Colleges that don't offer rolling admissions typically require all your application materials to be sent by a specific date, usually in December or early January. The applications are processed and evaluated all at the same time, so while it is still a good idea to send in your application materials early, there is no automatic advantage to applying as soon as you can, as there is with rolling admissions. Whereas with rolling admissions, you'll hear back from the college within a few weeks, with regular decision all applicants hear back from the school at the same time. Many schools have separate parts of the application with different deadlines, so be prepared to organize your calendar so as not to miss any deadlines. Acceptances and rejections get mailed in late March or early April.

- *Early Decision:* Some schools offer an early decision option as part of their regular decision program. However, a recent push by presidents of several top universities (including Harvard, Stanford, Yale, and others) is working to erode this option since it may hurt economically disadvantaged students who would need to compare financial aid packages in making their decision. Typically available at more selective colleges, the early-decision program allows you to apply to one school by mid-October or November. The school will then respond by mid-December either with an acceptance, rejection, or deferral. An acceptance to a school under an early decision program is binding. This means that when you apply early decision, you sign a contract stating that you absolutely commit to attending that school if you are accepted. Failure to comply with the agreement can lead to unpleasant consequences like being blackballed from other schools. Rejections are final. A deferral means that the admissions committee will wait to make a decision about your application until they see what the regular pool of applicants is like. If you are deferred from an early decision acceptance but are accepted with the regular pool, the contract is no longer binding, and you may choose to attend a different school.

  Early decision does have some advantages. By expressing a clear interest in one school, you may gain some advantage in admissions, and if accepted you'll already know where you're going to school in December. However, by no means feel that you need to apply to a school under an early decision commitment. You should not apply to a school early decision unless you are totally, completely, positively sure that the school is your first choice, and you should not apply early decision if you feel like your credentials will improve significantly during your first semester of your senior year. Rejections under early decision are final, so if you think your application will be stronger after another semester, you should wait until you can provide the best application possible.

- *Early Action:* Early action has become an increasingly common option at schools across the country. Like early decision, early action offers applicants a chance to find out in December if they've been admitted. However, the acceptance is not binding; if you get accepted to another school in April that you would prefer to attend, you're welcome to do so. This provides a convenient alternative for students who want to hear back from a school as soon as possible, but aren't ready to commit to attending a particular school right away. Some institutions, such as Stanford and Yale, now offer single-choice early action programs. Under these plans, acceptance is still nonbinding, but students may not submit an early application (early action or early decision) to any other institution. This allows early applicants to compare financial aid packages from the regular round of admissions before making a decision.

  Once you know when your applications will be due, it's time to start filling out the paperwork, either on actual paper or online. The latter is becoming increasingly common. There are a few general guidelines to follow. First, read the entire application carefully before you begin. Plan what you are going to say in each section before you write anything. It is a great idea to make a photocopy of the application to "practice" on before you fill out the official form, although applying online means you can go back and change your answers before the final submission. Always fill out or type the application yourself. If you're going to handwrite the application, try to use the same pen for the entire thing, to remain consistent in ink color and thickness. If you're going to use a printer, use a standard font like Times New Roman or Arial, and use the best printer you can find. Presentation and neatness count. If the application specifically suggests that you handwrite anything, be sure to do so, but draft exactly what you're going to write on scrap paper so that you don't have to make any corrections on the actual application.

More and more colleges nationwide are coming to accept the Common Application in lieu of applications specifically tailored for their schools. With a standard format and several general essays, you can fill out this application—online or on paper—once and submit it to any of the participating schools. It makes the application process somewhat less burdensome and time-consuming, although you may still want to consider tweaking essays to better fit the demands of each individual college. Some colleges will also have a Supplement to the Common Application specific to each college with additional questions.

Applications are usually divided up into several sections. All of them are important, and you should use all of them to your advantage. The following explanations of the application sections include some things you should remember when filling out your application:

- *Personal Information:* This section is fairly straightforward. It asks for general information about you, your school, and your family. Since all applications will ask for pretty much the same information, it's a good idea to keep it all on an index card so that you can easily reference it whenever you need to. This section often includes a question about race. Although this question is optional, you can go ahead and answer it; it won't hurt you, and the answer could help you. If you do answer, don't try to stretch the truth; answer it the way you would on a census form. Legal debates about affirmative action have gotten a lot of attention in recent years, but you still should not worry about answering this question.

- *Standardized Tests:* This is another relatively easy section to fill out. Most applications require you to fill in your test scores here, but also require you to have copies of your scores sent from the testing companies to the admissions offices. Make sure you do this in enough time for the test scores to arrive at the admissions office well before applications are due. Also, be sure you pay attention to which tests are required by your school. Some schools don't require test scores at all, others require either SAT Reasoning and Subject Tests or ACT scores, and still others specify which they want. Be sure your school receives all of the scores that it needs.

- *Extracurricular Activities:* This is the first section where your personality and accomplishments can shine through; be sure to make the most of it. Your extracurriculars allow the admissions office to see what you do when you're not studying. Sports, clubs, publications, student government, jobs, and volunteer positions are examples of some of the activities that fall into this category. Make sure to follow directions carefully when filling out this section. Some schools want you to write your activities directly on the form; others allow you to attach a typed list to the application instead. If you have the option to type a list, it's a good idea to do so, even if the rest of your application is handwritten. It looks neater, you'll have more space for all your activities, and you can just print out a copy of the list for each school that requests it. Just make sure to adapt the list to the particular requirements of the school. If the application instructs you to list your activities in chronological order, do so. Otherwise it is best to list activities in order of their importance to you.

  A few final words about extracurriculars—quality is more important than quantity. It is infinitely better to have long-term involvement and leadership positions in a few activities to which you devoted only an hour a month. Admissions officers can tell when you're just trying to pad your résumé with activities. They look more highly on passion and commitment to a few activities that reflect who you are and what interests you. You're also more likely to stand out to admissions officers if you have dedicated your time to an activity or subject that few others have explored. Admissions officers come across countless tennis captains and student-body presidents, but few national kayaking champions.

- *Transcript:* Your transcript is a window into your academic history. Admissions officers look at your grades and class rank, along with the types of classes you've taken. A high GPA is important, but so is the number of AP or Honors courses you've had. Colleges look for students who challenge themselves. At this point you can't go back and fix that C you got in freshman biology, but you can do a few things to make your transcript look as good as possible. First, make sure everything is accurate. Check that your grades are correct and that every honors class you have taken is listed as such. Second, remember that colleges will see your grades from senior year. Don't pad your schedule with blow-off courses; make sure to continue to take challenging classes. Try not to let yourself develop a serious case of "senioritis," because admissions committees will think that you don't take academics seriously. Also, if you received a poor grade in a particular class because of a certain situation, or you struggled all of sophomore year because someone you loved passed away, feel free to write an additional essay explaining any vast discrepancies. Lastly, request transcripts from your high school as soon as you can. They can take a while to print, and you don't want your application to be late because you did not get your transcript in time.

• Recommendations: Many schools request letters of recommendation from teachers, coaches, or other adults who know you well. These letters let the admissions officers see how others view you and your potential. Most people will be happy to write a good recommendation for you. If a teacher doesn't feel comfortable recommending you, he or she will most likely not agree to write a letter for you. So don't worry about a teacher trashing you behind your back; it probably won't happen.

Do think carefully about whom you choose to write these letters, though. You want to choose teachers who know you personally and with whom you have a good relationship. It's a good idea to choose teachers in your strong subjects, but it's also important to demonstrate some diversity of interest. For example, it is better to have your English teacher and your physics teacher write recommendations than it is to have two math teachers write them. Whomever you choose, make sure to provide them with plenty of time to write and revise a strong recommendation. You may even want to contact them before the summer of your senior year and let them know you'd like them to write on your behalf. That will give them ample time to write a shining letter! Many colleges want your teachers to send recommendations in separate from the rest of your application. If so, don't forget to give teachers a stamped and addressed envelope in which to send it. Be assertive; there's nothing wrong with re-

minding your teachers about the recommendation, and asking before the deadline if they'd gotten it done. Most teachers are careful about these deadlines, but it does not hurt to make sure. And don't forget to thank the people who have done such a big favor for you!

Additionally, most recommendation forms have a line asking you to waive your right to see the recommendation. You should probably sign it. Signing the waiver shows confidence that your teachers respect you and gives the recommendation more credibility. Finally, though most schools only require two recommendations from teachers, some allow you to send additional recommendations from others who know you well. Though by no means required or necessary, this is a good opportunity for students with significant activities outside of school-affiliated activities to get people like coaches, art tutors, or employers to say something helpful. Don't go overboard on these though; one extra recommendation is more than enough. Content is more important than the person who writes it. It's not impressive to get your state senator to write a recommendation for you if he's never met you before.

• *The Essay:* The college essay strikes fear in the hearts of high school seniors every fall, but you should not think about it as something scary. Instead, consider it an opportunity to show your wonderful, special, unique personality while telling the admissions officers a bit about yourself. If you give yourself plenty of time and have some fun with it, it can actually be the most enjoyable part of your application.

Think about your topic carefully, but do not kill yourself trying to come up with a topic that you think an admissions officer will like. It's always a good idea to write about something that is meaningful to you. If you feel strongly about the topic, it will show through in your writing, and that will catch an admissions officer's attention. Too many students write about a class project or winning the state championship—try to describe experiences that are less common. You want your personality and your passion to shine through. Though it might seem obvious, it's worth restating that you should be sure to answer whatever question the application asks. Sometimes you can reuse an essay for more than one school, but don't try to make an essay fit a topic just so you don't have to write another one. And be prepared to write several different essays if you're applying to a lot of schools.

Once your topic is chosen, give yourself enough time to write a good rough draft. It's sometimes intimidating to begin writing, but just put your pen to paper (or fingers to keyboard) and start. It doesn't matter what your draft looks like at first; you'll have plenty of time to correct and edit it later. Since the essay is the part of the application where you can be yourself, write in a way that feels natural to you, whether that's humorous, serious, or something completely different. Your essay should give colleges an idea of who you really are. Being honest with yourself and schools makes it more likely you'll end up somewhere that is a good fit. You should never submit a first draft to a college. Revise your essay a few times, both for style and for content. If the application gives you a word limit, stick to it.

Once you feel confident about the essay, it's a good idea to have a teacher, parent, older sibling, or counselor look over it for you. They can help you both find technical mistakes in spelling and grammar and point out places where you could be more clear in your content. By all means have others help you out with your essay in these ways, but under no circumstances should you ever, ever let anyone else write your essay for you. Not only is this dishonest, admissions officers read thousands of essays every year and have a good eye for essays that do not seem to be written by a particular student. While they probably won't be able to pinpoint why they're uncomfortable with a particular essay, they could be left with a negative feeling about your application. Once your essay has been drafted, revised, edited, and perfected, you can either handwrite it on the application form, or, if the school allows, you can attach a typed version to the form. However, almost all college applications are also available online, allowing you to simply insert the text into the online form or upload the document.

Once your application is complete, put a stamp on the envelope (or click that "submit" button that's been haunting you) and pat yourself on the back. Your application was honest, well-thought-out, neat, and will show the admissions committee who you are. Although you should make sure that the admissions office has received all of your materials, whether through a confirmation email or a phone call, there is not much left to stress out about. Once the application is in the mail, it's out of your hands, so kick back, relax, and enjoy the end of your senior year. After all that work, you deserve it.

The Wait

There is probably nothing anybody can say to you at this point to make you feel secure and confident regarding your applications. Your worries of the last few months about application deadlines and teacher recommendations are now petty concerns, replaced with the general unease that comes with the uncertain ground of your applications and your fate resting in the hands of various admissions offices across the state and country. You are finished with the applications but have only just begun the long road of anxiety.

Well, all is not lost. While it is nearly impossible to distract you from the near-constant pressure of the uncertainty regarding your future, we can at least let you know a little more about what is going on in the office.

Your application will arrive and most likely be put into an anonymous-looking, plain envelope. It will then be given to the admission officer who is in charge of your district or school. In some larger schools, you will not get much individual attention: There are often grade and SAT/ACT score cutoffs that they use to determine who gets admitted. With limitations on resources and thousands of applications pouring in, this is usually the only way they can manage the process in the given time frame. In smaller, private schools that can afford it, your application will be considered much more closely. Generally, your application will be read by up to three or four officers. Some schools use a numbering system to rate your academic record, your standardized test scores, and your extracurricular activities. There are some "bonus points" that you may end up with for uncontrollable variables such as your economic or racial background, or your relationship to an alumnus of the school.

Mostly, your application will speak for itself. While some schools weigh academics over extracurriculars, others might want to see high levels of community involvement or strong standardized test scores. This is where things are entirely out of your control. Each school is looking for a diverse group of students. The schools keep their academic standards relatively high, while looking for people from every possible background with every possible interest. If there happen to be 20 other students just like you from Houston, Texas, with 2100 SATs, a 3.5 GPA, roles in several school plays, and playing time on the varsity basketball team, all 20 will probably not be accepted. Likewise, if you happen to be the only student applying with a 1740 SAT, 2.8 GPA, and founded a nonprofit organization to help teach English to needy children in Africa, you would probably look more unique and attractive to the admissions officer. It is fantastically frustrating, but in the end much of this process is out of your control. You are not only competing to be good enough for a school, but you are competing against everybody else who is applying to the school. Admissions officers are quick to admit that they turn away an incredible number of qualified applicants every year; enough, in fact, to more than fill two separate classes of equal strength. The decision process, therefore, often seems arbitrary. You may end up on the wait list of one of your safety schools, and find yourself accepted at the strongest school you applied to. You simply cannot know what is going to happen until you receive the letters. Most schools are constantly adjusting their criteria in order to admit what they see as the most accomplished and vibrant student body possible.

When the decision has been made, the myth is generally true: Big, thick envelopes often have big admit letters inside. The thin ones often bring bad news. You will probably be receiving a mix of these, so don't let a poor first response get you down. You may end up knowing the decision before the envelope ever reaches your mailbox. Each year, more schools are letting students find out their acceptance status online.

The good news is that thin envelopes sometimes bring news of a place on the wait list. The last thing you want to do in this situation is anger the admissions office. Surely, a place on the wait list is disappointing. There are only two things that can help you get off, however. First and foremost, the best you can hope for is a lot of luck. Your eventual admission depends a lot on how many people reject their offers of admission. The second factor is how you act: Admissions offices like to see people eager to attend their school. A simple letter stating your excitement about the school and your eagerness to attend may help nudge things in your direction. Anything pestering or negative directed at the admissions office will

ensure you a rejection letter. In the end, you should choose the school where you feel most comfortable. The best advice we can offer you is to follow your instincts. If you get some kind of feeling about a school, go with it! There is no better reason out there to make a decision. For now, sit back and relax. It's your senior year, your very last semester in high school. While you can't start failing your classes now, there is plenty of room left for you to chill out. Do what you can to forget about your applications (and stress about work) and instead think about how you can make the most out of your last couple months of high school. Be proud that your applications are finished and go out and have some fun!

The Money

Best case scenario: you get into the college of your dreams. But what if you get into the college of your dreams only to realize you cannot pay for it. With many of the nation's most expensive colleges quickly passing the $35,000 annual tuition mark, adding up to $140,000+ for a four-year education (not to mention room and board), it is no wonder that many students are talking as much about finances as they are about SAT scores. Although few families can afford this expensive price tag, especially if there is more than one member of the family attending college, there are many resources to aid families in paying for college. You should never hesitate to apply to a college simply because of its "sticker price." Many colleges meet most, if not all, of a family's financial need with a combination of scholarships, grants, loans, and work-study programs.

The most important step you can take as a student is to openly discuss your family's financial situation at the outset of your college search. Talk about how much your family is able to pay for college, how much your parents are willing to take out in loans, and other financial topics. By initiating this discussion with your family, you are showing them that you are both responsible and sensitive to your family's financial situation.

Your biggest advantage in the financial aid game is to be organized. As you will find out, there are many forms that you must fill out in order to even begin applying for financial aid. Getting organized helps you to see exactly where you stand in the financial aid process. The money is not going to land on your doorstep, so you have to be proactive in looking for it. There are plenty of resources available to you, but you have to know where to look for them.

A good place to start is with your college guidance counselor. Counselors have knowledge and experience in helping students like yourself get into college and pay for college. Oftentimes, they receive information from colleges regarding scholarships and will post them around the school. Take note of these announcements and fill out the applications as soon as possible. The applications can be time-consuming, but if you are well-organized, there should be no problem. The following Web sites also provide useful information for students seeking financial aid: www.finaid.org and www.fastweb.com. The more persistent and diligent you are in your search, the better your chances will be for finding the resources you need.

The best sources for financial aid are the colleges themselves. Colleges oftentimes earmark large sums of money specifically for financial aid. Many colleges also receive money from federal and private sources for financial aid purposes. Scholarships come in a variety of forms, including need-based, merit, and achievement awards. You will need to look at what types of financial aid the schools that you are considering offer. Be aware of which colleges offer only need-based financial aid packages and which colleges offer merit and/or achievement scholarships. The policies and practices at each school can vary significantly, so it is important that you have the information you need.

Carefully read the bulletins provided by the colleges you are considering. If you have any questions, e-mail or call the admissions office or financial aid office right away. Find out what the colleges' admissions policies are regarding financial aid applicants. Some of the nation's wealthier schools have need-blind admissions, which means that you are considered for admission without taking into account your family's ability to pay. However, at some schools, financial need may play a part in the final admission decision, especially in borderline cases where preference may be given to those with the ability to pay. Even if you do not think you can afford it, apply to the school and for the financial aid. Then, just wait and see. You might be pleasantly surprised. Sometimes it is cheaper to attend a more expensive college because they often provide superior aid packages. Of course, this is not always the case, but it does prove that you should never

decide against a school because of money until you have a financial aid offer (or rejection) in your hand.

As a financial aid applicant, you will soon notice all that paperwork involved. Most schools require you to file a standardized need analysis form to determine an expected family contribution (EFC). Depending on the school, the form will either be the College Board's Profile form or the U.S. Department of Education's Free Application for Federal Student Aid (FAFSA), or in some cases, both. The school will also have its own financial form for you to fill out, which you have to send along with your family's income tax forms for verification. The school will determine a reasonable family contribution for one year. (The student is also usually expected to contribute at least $1,000 from summer earnings.) To come up with an estimate, a formula established by Congress is used. The formula takes into account family income, expenses, assets, liabilities, savings accounts, and other data. The cost of attendance minus this expected family contribution yields an approximate financial need. The school then designs a financial aid package that may consist of a low-interest, federally-guaranteed loan, a work-study job, and a combination of different types of grants. This would lead one to believe that all packages would be similar, yet this is not always the case. Even though all schools receive the same input data, they do not all use the same formula. The family contribution will thus vary slightly, but there should not be a big difference. The difference in aid packages comes mainly from the way the school issues money. Some schools may require you to get more loans, or they might give you more money.

Some schools will always make better offers than others. Some wealthier schools guarantee to meet the full "demonstrated" need of every applicant that they accept. At other colleges, however, the financial aid package may leave an "unmet" need that you will have to cover on your own. In unfortunate cases like these, students can bear the extra financial burden or choose a college that gives them a better offer.

There are a few things that you can do to improve your chances of receiving an adequate financial aid package from a school. First of all, be efficient in getting all of the forms in as early as possible. Some schools have a limited supply of funds available for financial aid, and the earlier they look at your application, the better your chance of receiving a larger share. Getting your forms in early shows a good-faith effort on your part, and schools are more likely to be cooperative with you if they feel you are being cooperative with them. Another thing you can do is write a letter to the financial aid office explaining any special family circumstances that are not reflected on the financial aid forms. These can include a recent death in the family or the need to support an aging relative. If you do not let the school know about such situations, there is no way they can take them into account.

If a school offers you a financial aid package that you consider inadequate despite your best efforts to let them know about your family situation, all is still not lost. After you have been accepted at the school, make a polite call to the school's financial aid office. If you noted any special circumstances either on the financial aid form or in a separate letter, ask if they took them into account when determining the award. Sometimes letters or comments get overlooked in the haste to get the aid awards out on time. If they say they took the circumstances into account, or if you did not mention any, tell them you would really like to attend the school but do not think it will be possible without more aid. If another school has offered you more aid, mention that, especially if the school is a competitor of the one you're talking to. Calling may not help, but they are not going to withdraw your acceptance once you are in.

If you are eligible for money on the basis of need, then the school may list some federal government assistance. The first of the types of federal government assistance are grants. Grants do not have to be paid back, unlike loans, but they are also harder to obtain. The federal government offers two grants: the Federal Pell Grant and the Federal Supplemental Education Opportunity Grants. You have to demonstrate "exceptional" financial need for either, but the latter is harder to obtain since the government does not guarantee as much. A Pell Grant is as high as $4,050, and the FSEOG is as high as $4,000 annually.

The federal government also offers lower-interest loans. If you demonstrate "exceptional" financial need, you may be eligible for a Perkins Loan, which can be loaned at 5 percent interest up to a maximum of $4,000. There are two types of Stafford Loans, one subsidized and the other unsubsidized. The subsidized Stafford Loan is only for people who demonstrate financial need, and it has a

fixed rate of 6.80 percent interest. The government pays for the interest while you are in school and during the grace period after you graduate. The unsubsidized loan is for those who do not demonstrate financial need, and they have to pay interest the whole time. There is also a new loan called the Federal Direct Student Loan which is just like the Stafford except that the lender is the federal government and not a bank.

There is also a federal government sponsored loan for parents called the PLUS loan. It is particularly valuable for those who qualify for little or no financial aid. Each year, parents are allowed to borrow the full amount of tuition less any financial aid the student receives. The loan requires good credit, repayment while the child is still in school, and interest rates that are not far from market rates. Still, it can help to ease the burden on middle-class families.

You will also probably be required to take a job through the federal work-study program. Many applicants worry that working part-time will detract from studying or, equally important, playtime. Yet, if you work on campus, you certainly will not be the only one: Most colleges report that about half of their students hold term-time jobs. It is possible to take a full load of courses, participate in extracurricular activities, and work 10 or 15 hours per week, all while maintaining a good grade point average. Although freshmen tend to get the least exciting jobs on campus, in later years you may well find yourself working on interesting research, in a lab, or in a library.

Many private colleges also provide scholarships based on academic, athletic, or artistic ability. As competition among colleges for the best students intensifies, more and more colleges are offering lucrative merit awards to well-qualified students. There are many excellent schools, including many state universities, that offer merit scholarships in ever-increasing numbers. The best sources for information are your high school counselor and state Department of Education.

Be sure not to overlook the millions of dollars of aid available from private sources. Organizations ranging from General Motors to the Knights of Columbus offer money for college, often as prizes to assist students from your community. Sometimes large companies offer scholarships to children of their employees, so have your parents find out if their employers have such programs. There are also several scholarships out there related to specific majors, religions, or even ethnic heritage. Or if you scored very high on the PSAT, you could be in the running for a National Merit Scholarship. There is often a catch to merit-based awards, however: If you qualify for awards from private sources, your school will often deduct some or all of the amount from any need-based aid you receive.

In the past two decades there has also been a revival of interest in ROTC (Reserve Officers Training Corps) programs. These scholarships from the four branches of the armed forces help pay for tuition, books, and room and board during college. When you graduate, you are committed to anywhere between four and eight years of reserve or active duty, depending on the program. As the supply of financial aid declines and the cost of college education continues to climb, more and more students are coming to see ROTC scholarships as worthwhile. However, be very thorough when investigating ROTC programs at different schools. Some colleges tend to be more antimilitary, and you may find yourself part of a controversial program. Even so, the benefits of the program can be substantial for a student who joins after careful consideration and research.

More and more, federal aid is being reserved exclusively for the very needy. Many families with incomes over $35,000 who qualify for PLUS loans must now pass a needs test to get Stafford Loans. Yet, if you play your cards right, your family should not have to undergo severe financial hardship to put you through school.

Advice for Transfers

If you are already in college and are thinking about transferring to another school, the preceding advice is mostly old news to you. Theoretically you know what to do now, but there are actually a number of new considerations that all potential transfers should keep in mind.

There are plenty of reasons students cite for transferring. Perhaps you don't feel comfortable in the social or political environment at your school. Maybe your academic interests have changed, and the programs available at your current college are not extensive enough. It could also be an issue of being too far from or close to home. Whatever the reason, it's important to figure out what it is about your college experience that doesn't work, so you can find one that does.

You're about to embark on a daunting and sometimes disappointing process, so be sure to think it through beforehand. It can be easy to blame your school if you are unhappy. But issues with the college experience itself, such as roommate problems or work overload, may be the real source of your dissatisfaction. If so, you may be able to work out these troubles without transferring.

Don't assume that you'll necessarily be happy at another university. One student left Stanford in search of "greener pastures." Instead, she found New England "cold, gray, and without pastures at all." According to another student, "It's a big risk. You have to really want to leave where you are or really want to go where you will be." There are no guarantees that you will be better off at another school, and the process itself may make things even less satisfactory for you. You might want to take a semester or two off to reevaluate your situation, or think about giving a more wholehearted effort at making your current situation work.

Most schools accept transfer students who have up to two years of credit at another university. It may be safer, however, to transfer after your first year, because your old university will be more likely to take you back if you change your mind. One student advised that it is better to take a leave of absence from your original school than to withdraw completely.

The application process is also slightly different for transfer students. Be aware that colleges tend to consider a transfer student in a different light from a high school senior. To your advantage, admissions officers tend to look upon transfer applicants as mature and motivated candidates who have the potential to make a significant impact on campus. However, few students tend to leave top private universities, so the acceptance rate for transfers at top schools is much, much lower than that for first-time applicants. The situation can be different at larger state schools.

Each school looks for different students, but grades, recommendations, and the essay that explains why you want to transfer are usually the three most important parts of the application. Make sure that you find classes with professors who will be able to write you good recommendations. Standardized test scores and extracurriculars are less important. One exception to this may be if you decide to take time off and do something exceptional during your time away from school. Keep in mind that your college transcript is incredibly important. As much as you might want to leave your school, do not ease up on your academics. If staying an extra semester will help boost your academic record, you may want to consider holding off on your move.

Because colleges will expect you to prove that you have developed during your first year or two of college and to show why you absolutely cannot stay at your old school, your essay (and interview if you can arrange one) is critical. Be definite and clear about your reasons for transferring and what you expect to find in a new environment. Academic reasons are best; personal ones are only as convincing as you can make them. It also helps if the department in which you want to major is undersubscribed at the new school.

Make sure you know a lot about the school you are applying to. Not only will this show through in your application, but you will also be much more prepared for the experience ahead. If what you need is an active, social campus in which to get involved,

then make sure that you will be guaranteed on-campus housing. If you are going to need financial aid, check and see that it will be available for transfer students. Also, be sure you look into how your credits will transfer at the new school. Will you get credit toward a major, or only toward graduation? If you don't have a major already picked out, it can be very difficult to graduate in four years.

Before submitting the paperwork, make sure that you are confident in your decision to transfer, and be ready for anything. It's important to have a backup plan for the upcoming year in case you don't get accepted. Come up with a plan for what you would do with a year off, or be prepared to make another run at getting the most out of your school. If everything does work out for you, make sure you have covered all of the bases before you commit to the new school. Making the decision to transfer is not a walk in the park, but you shouldn't let this deter you. If you are truly unhappy with your current situation, it can be a very rewarding and worthwhile route.

The College Spectrum

At first glance, the sheer number of colleges included in this book may seem a bit overwhelming—clearly you would never consider applying to over 300 schools. Since colleges and their student bodies vary in so many ways, it can be difficult to identify schools at which you would feel comfortable. One piece of advice is to be aware of the general social, political, and academic trends many schools are currently experiencing. Issues such as affirmative action, the fairness of standardized testing, expanding financial aid and early application programs have become heated topics of discussion on countless college campuses. It can be helpful to figure out where certain schools stand in terms of these trends. Another way to get some perspective on different colleges is to identify where they stand in terms of various criteria—to figure out where they fall on a continuum that we call the College Spectrum. Most importantly, it is not our place to judge which types of schools are best, but instead to present a variety of perspectives and observations that can help you with the decision-making process. Here are some of the many areas you can consider in comparing different schools.

Size

The total undergraduate enrollments of the schools in this book range from 26 at California's Deep Springs College to nearly 40,000 at Ohio State University. Considering the size of the campus you want to attend is helpful in the initial narrowing-down process; the feel of a school can be very dependent on the number of students around. There are two main parts of your experience that will be affected by the size of the school you choose: academics and social life.

Academically, class size and the accessibility of senior faculty are two important areas of comparison that tend to vary between large and small schools. In this case, smaller colleges decidedly have the advantage simply because a smaller population usually translates into smaller classes. Students at small schools have great opportunities for one-on-one student-faculty interaction. At large schools, students are more likely to complain of impersonal instruction and "being treated as a Social Security number."

To make up for this apparent disadvantage, many larger schools offer special programs intended to create a more intimate sense of community among professors and students. Different universities have different approaches. Some offer honors programs for a limited number of students, and some house all the students who are in special programs together. Generally, students in such programs all take the same or similar courses—most of which are small, discussion-oriented classes. Bear in mind that many honors and special programs are highly selective; do your best to make a realistic assessment of your chances to be accepted. Additionally, don't be taken in by the glossy pictures in admissions booklets: If you are considering a large university, take a close look at the quality of its special programs. If you are seriously considering one of these programs, try to speak with an undergraduate currently participating in the program—he or she may be able to paint a more accurate picture of what it is like. Another important factor to remember is that no matter how large a school is, not all of the classes it offers will be huge and overcrowded, and some of the bigger classes will break into smaller discussion groups. Thus, although most schools do have some very large classes, you can almost always find small ones of interest. But in this case, it is important to remember that in bigger schools, it is often difficult to get into small classes as an underclassman.

Also, pay attention to who teaches the classes. At most liberal arts colleges, only professors do. Many large universities pad their student-faculty ratios by including graduate students, or they advertise discussion classes that turn out to be taught by people who are still working toward a Ph.D. By reading guides such as this one and by talking to students, you can find out roughly how many graduate students teach and whether or not senior professors teach undergraduates at all. Keep in mind that having younger, less experienced professors teach is not always a bad thing. Many times, courses taught by graduate students allow for a rapport between teachers and students that does not develop with some of the stodgier old professors. However, if graduate students appear to dominate the teaching, even if only for the freshman year, you should definitely consider this as you make your decision. These facts will also give you a sense of how much personal attention the typical undergraduate student receives from the administration.

For highly specialized fields that require extensive facilities, the resources at small schools are generally limited. Larger universities usually have the funding to sponsor more expensive research facilities and to draw renowned professors to their specialized programs. For facilities not associated with academics, such as the gym or the library, size and showiness are not nearly as important as accessibility. You will not care how many racquetball courts the gym has as long as one is available when you want to play and it's not a three-mile walk away. Instead of asking how many volumes there are in the library, find out whether everyone has full access to all its resources, and if the library holds long hours. Since they cater to so many students with diverse interests, large universities most often offer a wide range of facilities.

Social life, too, is affected by the size of the school. Consider carefully what kind of social life you plan to have and which type of school would be more conducive to your interests. The setup of freshman housing will play a significant role in your social experience; your first-year roommates and hall-mates often become some of your closest friends. It's likely that the people you associate with will also be determined by your extracurricular interests—a sports team, a student newspaper, or student government. This tends to be especially true for universities that do not provide more than one year of campus housing.

The key is finding your own comfortable niche within any school. While there are usually more niches to be discovered in large colleges, finding yours may require some initiative. The larger the school, the more subgroups there are likely to be within the student body. Frats and sororities tend to be more abundant and popular on bigger campuses. An advantage to being a member

of a very large community is that the supply of new faces never runs out. If you get tired of one circle of friends, you can always find another. But it is also important to keep in mind that when you are on your own in the midst of all those unfamiliar people, it is also possible to feel very lonely. On the other hand, small environments can be more welcoming and friendly. Small schools often have a greater sense of community and people can find that making friends is easier. But some students find that small schools can be a little too small, because "everybody knows everybody else's business." In that case, you may want to consider studying at a school where you won't necessarily know everyone's name.

One common misconception about smaller schools is that they are inevitably more homogenous and have less school pride or spirit. On the contrary, many of them, especially the more selective ones, have just as many different types of people as do most large universities, only in smaller numbers. Although larger schools, especially those with a big emphasis on athletics, may have tremendous school spirit, smaller ones foster their own brand of pride, usually stemming from rich tradition and a strong sense of community.

Schools come in all different sizes. No matter how big or small a school is, make sure it prioritizes what is important to you. Be sure to keep in mind both academic and social consequences of the size of your school: Both have the potential to drastically change your college experience.

Location

At some point, if not right away, you will find yourself thinking about the towns in which each of your college choices is located. Can you see yourself living there for four years? What sounds more appealing to you—a college where your dorm is surrounded by towering oak trees, or a college with easy access to shops and malls? Before you answer these questions, be sure you really understand the difference between urban and rural settings, and more importantly, how this difference will impact your college experience.

Often, what some students perceive to be "city life," "suburban life," or "life on the farm" is not the reality of what living at a college in one of these areas would be like. Many factors need to be considered in order to get an accurate idea of how location will affect your whole college experience.

Whether you've found your way through cornfields for 18 years, or you've wandered around Times Square by yourself since you were 10, going away to college, while exciting and rewarding, can also be an intimidating experience. Many people arrive at school the very first day completely oblivious to the opportunities and the challenges of being out of their town, their state, or their region. If you are from a rural area and are considering the big move to the city, expect adjustment (to noise, traffic, people, crime, the hectic pace), but try not to make or accept any assumptions about "the horrors" of city life. If you are from an urban area and are considering the peace and quiet of a smaller school tucked in the woods somewhere, also expect adjustment (to relatively silent nights, no movie theater or department store, the slower pace), but also try not to make or accept any assumptions about "life with the cows." Your thoughts about the location of the school should be balanced by the fact that every school will inherently have some sort of community; is this community, along with the city the school is located in, right for you?

College is a great time to try new things, including a new location—a new city, a new state, maybe a whole new region of the United States or beyond. In general, you do need to be aware of certain broad characteristics of each type of campus. At a campus in a big city, for example, there is a greater chance that on-campus nightlife will be non-existent, as everyone will head to clubs and bars to relax. Yet after a week of academic work, extracurricular activities, dorm parties, visiting speakers, football games, and the multitude of other school-sponsored events, being in an urban environment means there is still the option of seeing a Broadway show or going to a world-renowned museum. As for a campus in a smaller town, the exact opposite may be true. Without anything to do around town, students will have all of their activities and create all of their own nightlife on campus. While you may sometimes wish you did have the major clubs and bars, the tight-knit community that forms among students at the school may very well more than compensate for those longings. Whichever setting you do end up choosing should depend on your own reflections on how you would feel in those surroundings.

Another point to consider is how comfortable you would be living so close to or so far away from home. Does leaving the Pacific Ocean for the Atlantic Ocean sound like a real adventure, or does being even two hours away from your family make your hands start to tremble? Are you at a point in your life where you still want to be with all of your friends going to the same school near your hometown, or can you not wait for all of your new friends and your "whole new life" far from home? Distance is one of those factors that require thinking about everything in context. Your life will change in college, whether you pack your bags to travel far away or keep your room at home. Anywhere you end up, even if you do stay close to home, your old relationships will change at least a little bit. Make sure you are honest with yourself about your reasons for choosing a particular school. It may be helpful to talk to current students at the school to get a sense of where they came from and what they think about the location. It may also be helpful to come up with a list of positive and negative aspects of the school's location. Include everything that will affect your life: the weather, the people, the travel expenses, and the homesickness, without forgetting to take into account the school's own community. Life at college will require at least some adjustment, but it may be that exact adjustment which completes your college experience.

Private vs. Public

The question of whether to attend a public or private school is best answered through a cost-benefit approach. Don't worry, we know you haven't had Econ 101, so consider this a free lesson. Let's first divide the universities in the United States into three categories: large private, public, and small private.

The most obvious distinction between a private and a public university is the price tag. As the cost of a private school education continues to climb, public school is becoming an increasingly attractive option. However, in recent years the tuition gap has significantly diminished for those who are eligible for financial aid, as private schools have allocated increasingly more funds to aid packages. These packages are almost always a combination of loans and grants, meaning that they do not always diminish the cost of college, but simply postpone it to a future date.

Most top-tier private institutions have adopted need-blind admissions policies which mean that they admit regardless of your ability to pay and then work with you to create a financial aid package that will allow you to attend. Princeton led the pack in this respect by announcing that it would replace loans with outright grants; soon many other colleges followed suit.

Smaller private schools, however, do not have the high-powered endowments necessary to fund such need-blind policies. In this area, public universities definitely have an advantage. Subsidized by state taxpayers, they offer an outstanding education at a fraction of its actual cost—everyone is basically a financial aid recipient.

If you do decide to break the bank and attend a private school, you will often be rewarded with smaller class sizes and greater student-teacher interaction. There is, however, a not-so-obvious advantage to small private colleges. At larger private or state universities much of the teaching duty has been increasingly placed on the shoulders of teaching assistants (graduate students). Additionally, at large private universities, professors must often devote a significant amount of time to research in order to stay ahead in their field. Small private colleges offer teaching environments in which the professors are not burdened with this dictum of publish or perish; they can devote all their time to teaching the material instead of contributing to it.

At college you will learn as much from your fellow students as you will from your professors, so it's important to consider the quality and diversity of the student body. This is an important consideration because at any good college, public or private, much of the valuable learning takes place outside of the classroom.

When deciding which type of school to attend, make sure you look beyond its label as either public or private. While some applicants consider attending a state university second-best when compared to an elite private school, others make a public institution their first choice. It is important to consider department-specific academic strengths along with the overall reputation of the university as a whole. Public schools such as UC Berkeley, UCLA, and University of Michigan rank among some of the top academic institutions, public or private, in the country. In the end, you should never be swayed too much by a school's private or public designation. Instead, try to choose the school that's best suited to you.

Coed or Single-Sex?

Since coeducation became the norm at American universities in the 1960s, the number of single-sex schools in the nation has dropped significantly. There are only four men's colleges remaining in this book: Deep Springs College, Hampden-Sydney College, Morehouse College, and Wabash College. The students here chose to attend mainly because of their belief that the absence of the opposite sex allows greater dedication to academics and a friendlier, more fraternal atmosphere. Tradition prevails at these all-male institutions, and men that work best in these atmospheres find themselves very content.

Women's colleges have similar reasons for existence as all-male colleges, but with a few twists. There are many more women's colleges, as the whole movement for women's education came later and is still firmly rooted in feminist beliefs. The most famous all-female schools are the Seven Sisters, a group of seven Northeastern colleges that self-organized in 1927 to promote single-sex education. The Seven Sisters—Barnard, Bryn Mawr, Mount Holyoke, Radcliffe (now folded into Harvard), Smith, Vassar (now coed), and Wellesley—hoped to compete with the image of the Ivy League schools.

Most women who attend single-sex colleges cite the supportive, nurturing environment as their college's greatest asset. In an arguably male-dominated culture, women's schools provide a learning environment where there is support for developing one's female identity, no academic competition with men, and numerous leadership opportunities. Women's colleges are usually very liberal, with focus on current events and debates on different points of view.

There is no debate, however, about the fact that life at a single-sex institution is very different from life at a coed one. Because single-sex schools tend to be smaller, there are often fewer academic programs and resources than at larger coed colleges. Also, the atmosphere is somewhat contrived, since one of the sexes is missing. There are always outlets through which students can find the opposite sex, such as "brother universities," but the social life and vivacity of the campus is usually at a much "calmer" level than coed schools. For students who want the best of both worlds, there are a few colleges that are part of coed consortia. Women at Mount

Holyoke and Smith can take classes at the neighboring Amherst and Hampshire Colleges and the University of Massachusetts; the women at Barnard are paired with the coed Columbia University; and Bryn Mawr allows its female students to explore academic offerings at Haverford and Swarthmore Colleges.

Besides the actual experience, another thing to keep in mind is a certain stigma attached to many single-sex schools. Since the majority of these schools are extremely liberal, they are generally known for strong activism in women's and gay rights. This reputation exists despite the more conservative nature of some of the top academic single-sex schools. Whether accurate or not, this is another factor to consider in your choice.

Single-sex atmospheres can be ideal for some students, but not everyone seeks out such a college experience. Most college-bound seniors end up enrolling in coeducational schools, an environment that requires little adjustment. Issues of coed bathrooms and dormitories may concern you, but there are many different housing options, including single-sex floors and Greek houses, and administrators work to make you comfortable. Most campuses also feature organizations that encourage members of the same sex to bond with each other, including fraternities and sororities as well as advocacy groups (usually female). So after choosing whether a single-sex or coed college is right for you, wait for your institution to send you information on handling all the details.

Advising and Tutoring

The first few weeks of college can be confusing. There are placement tests to take, forms to fill out, questions about AP credits to ask, and parents to kiss goodbye. Many freshmen are often unaccustomed to the breadth of courses from which to choose. Also, it's hard to plan your academic year when you're in the midst of meeting new friends, moving into your dorm room, trying to go to as many parties as possible, and asking out that cute girl from pre-orientation. However, do not be daunted.

Almost all colleges provide students with faculty advisors for at least the first year. Their function is twofold: they can both rubber-stamp your schedule and be used as reference for everything from course selection to general questions about the college. Though most students agree that faculty advisors are usually only good for placing their John Hancocks on your schedule, there are a few who are adamant that faculty advisors do have some value. If you do not know what you want to major in from day one, don't worry, your advisor can help you plan your schedule and think things through.

If you still have unanswered questions, ask upperclassmen (often the best source of good, quick information). They can point you toward interesting classes, often-overlooked majors, and talented professors—but remember their advice is very much based on their personal experience. For more detailed, department-specific questions about graduation/major requirements, ask a faculty member in that department.

Once you have chosen your classes, remember that this is only half the battle! Fortunately, most colleges and universities offer tutoring resources free of charge to help you succeed. If you find yourself in a large class with a professor who rushes through the most important points in the last five minutes of lecture or have a nervous or unhelpful TA, you should consider getting a tutor. Professors' office hours are usually insufficient for detailed explanations. Even the brightest students can benefit from going over the subject matter now and again.

Many times tutors are graduate students or particularly advanced undergraduates proficient in that specific academic discipline. Having recently learned the material, they can often make it more accessible than a professor who had taught it for decades. When exam time rolls around, look to upperclassmen for old study guides and more general insight into acing specific courses.

A Minority Perspective

As a minority student or a person of color, there might well be some additional factors to consider in your decision. You may, for example, be searching for a school with a high population of students from a particular background or for a school with high overall diversity. A school with a large minority population may prove to be more supportive and even more comfortable. Regardless of size, a strong minority community can be helpful during the next four years and can even help reduce ignorance on some campuses.

Another factor to consider is the general attitude of both the administration and the student body. Unfortunately, racism still exists in many parts of society, but do not assume a defensive attitude while visiting schools. Instead, be aware of possible situations and attitudes that may make you feel excluded and uncomfortable. What might have seemed like a diverse college in the brochures may not seem so open-minded after all. Take note of how integrated the minority community is and what the school does to recognize and support other cultures. Some schools may foster a pressure to conform; if the school has a large population of a certain race, there may be a distinct sense of separatism. For some this may provide a stronger sense of belonging, while for others it will only increase the stress of college life.

To determine the true attitude of the administration, look at how it attempts to support the minority communities. Some schools assign ethnic counselors to help minority students adjust to college life. Some students appreciate this; others resent it. One student reported that her school was doing so much to accommodate her minority status she felt separated rather than integrated. Many students, however, get used to the idea of special resources and ultimately find them supportive. Another thing to look at is the extracurricular life. What kinds of organizations are there for specific minority groups or minority students in general? The school may have cultural centers and politically-oriented associations that focus on the traditional arts and dances of their culture. Examples of popular organizations that foster a sense of community among minority students include Movimiento Estudiantil *Chicano* de Aztlán (MEChA) for Chicano students; Native American Student Associations at campuses around the country; and Asian American Student Associations.

Besides cultural centers and politically-oriented associations, many schools have Greek organizations centered on celebration of heritage. This category includes the predominantly Jewish fraternity Alpha Epsilon Pi, the Asian sorority Sigma Phi Omega, and African American fraternity Alpha Phi Alpha. Other minority students choose to organize themselves around professional aspirations (National Association of Black Journalists) or religion (Asian American Christian Fellowship).

For African American students, an important decision may be whether to attend a predominantly black college over another school. Despite the improving financial situations of most private black colleges, you are likely to find better facilities and larger academic departments at other schools. Unfortunately, the continuing decline of federal funding is likely to exacerbate this situation, since black colleges rely heavily on such resources. Nevertheless, many students choose to attend a predominantly black college for many of the same reasons other students choose to attend a single-sex school. Some black students find them a more congenial and accepting community that is more conducive to personal growth. Likewise, students often have a better chance to attain key leadership positions at a college where they do not have minority status. At a predominantly black school, the African American experience is one of the central issues on campus. What does it mean to be a black person in 21st century America? Of what importance is African American heritage? At predominantly black schools, these questions are addressed in a manner and with a commitment unrivaled by other institutions.

In this book, we include reports on five of the best-known predominantly black schools in the United States: Howard University in Washington, D.C.; Spelman and Morehouse Colleges in Georgia; Florida A&M University; and Tuskegee University in Alabama. For a more complete listing, we suggest you consult *The 100 Best Colleges for African American Students*, written by Erlene B. Wilson and published by Plume. An online resource under the name of Black Excel may also prove useful for African American students. Another school with an ethnic majority is the University of Hawaii, which is predominantly made up of Asian students.

Ultimately, you have to decide where you will feel most comfortable. Whatever your choice, it is important to remember that your ethnicity is an integral part of yourself and is not something you should have to compromise in choosing a school.

Sexual Minorities

The first question that a gay, lesbian, bisexual, or transgender student should ask when considering a college is the same one that straight students ask: where will I be the happiest and most comfortable for four years? Students planning on being openly gay at college will want to choose a campus where they can come out to their roommates, friends, and even professors without worrying about the consequences. But how can you tell after one or two trips to a college whether or not you'll get a positive reception?

The good news is that, as one transfer student put it, "there are sensitive people everywhere—at large schools and small ones." Another student said she sought out a campus with diversity, guessing that a diverse population "would create more understanding." But beyond these general guidelines, there are other aspects of campus life to observe. Check out a school's listing of organizations, for instance. A school with several gay alliances and clubs, for example, probably has a more accepting environment, even if you don't think you'll end up being active in any of them. One student pointed out that the surrounding community can be just as important. "Knowing that there were gay bars and events in the town made me more comfortable in my choice." The more town-gown interaction there is, the more important it is that a prospective student feels comfortable being gay in that city.

In looking for a school, all students search for a place with unlimited options. As a gay or lesbian student, the best college is going to be one where your opportunities are not constrained by your sexual orientation. As one gay member of a fraternity pointed out, "I wanted to join a frat in college, so it was important that I found a place where my sexuality wouldn't be as big a deal. . . ." In other words, there are countless schools where gay and lesbian students participate in every aspect of campus life—and fortunately it isn't too hard to track them down. This is not to say life for gay students is always perfect; gay students do risk running up against prejudices, but it is reassuring to know that gay and lesbian students at large and small schools, public and private, have managed to find their niche, be active members of the undergraduate community, and simply have a good time.

Politics

The level of political activism on a campus may affect how comfortable you are there. You will find that many schools have clubs of all alignments, and political journals of all bents as well, from the left-wing liberals to the Green Party to the ultraconservatives. Generally these partisan organizations are most active in presidential election years. If this is what interests you, you will have no trouble finding your political niche.

Forty years ago, political activism permeated college campuses. Today, the number of students strongly involved in politics on campus is generally a minority. One student remarked that a majority of her fellow students stay away from politics for social reasons: many people at her university look down on those with strong convictions because they assume them to be closed-minded. Instead of joining political organizations, many students channel their activism into volunteer programs that confront specific problems such as urban blight or environmental destruction. Usually, small liberal arts schools are the most politicized colleges. "At my school, you don't just put your name on name tags, you put your cause, your oppressor, your god, and your sexual orientation," said one student. Before selecting a school, you may want to see if it has a political forum that brings in outside speakers and organizes discussions and lectures.

Only ten years ago, campus activism was moving toward being institutionalized and domesticated. In recent years, however, concerns with the war in Iraq and Afghanistan, the controversy over the mosque to be built at the World Trade Center site, healthcare reform, and public transportation initiatives have since provoked an increasing amount of activity on behalf of students. Student protests, petitions, and marches have garnered much support as well as media recognition. Additionally, certain incidents and issues, particularly those involving racism and sexuality, receive community-wide attention. The gay- and lesbian-rights activists at some schools sponsor a kiss-in where same-sex couples cluster around the campus's central promenade and make out. Gay rights, AIDS awareness, and race-related issues are commonly on the collegiate slate of activist causes. Today, to be politically correct (PC)—manifested by a tolerance for others' ideas and political affiliations and an attempt to be inoffensive to any and all groups in speech as well as in print—is something of a secondary issue. Although PC was a hot topic on campuses in the nineties, the debates on the spelling of "woman" and whether your roommate is disabled or "differently-abled" seem to have faded.

However, the PC movement's focus on the implications of language has pushed people—particularly educators—to reconsider the lens through which academic disciplines are typically approached. Many schools now require students to take courses that focus on non-Western cultures, or courses aimed at raising sensitivity to minority issues and concerns. More and more schools have started classifying "Women and Gender Studies" as a major, as well as "Latin American Studies" and "African American Studies." Courses and programs exploring Native American Studies have also begun to emerge.

By visiting a college you can quickly pick up on how important politics are to the student body. Read posters and skim student newspapers to gauge whether or not the political climate on that campus is right for you. The best schools may be those that can absorb all viewpoints, so that no matter what you think, there will be others who will embrace your thoughts, challenge them, or respect your decision not to vocalize them.

Preprofessionalism vs. Liberal Arts

Preprofessionalism is a term you will see repeated throughout this book. Not all curriculums are the same, and whether you will receive either a preprofessional or liberal arts education is determined both by the school you attend and the major you choose there.

Majors that do not lead directly to a specific career fall into the liberal arts category. Even if a student plans to be an accountant, for example, he or she might get a liberal arts degree in philosophy or English, and then go on to study accounting at the appropriate professional school. The goal of a liberal arts education is to teach students how to think creatively and analytically, preparing them to pursue any career.

There are pros and cons to both tracks. Some argue that a liberal arts education is the key to a solid education and to becoming a well-rounded individual. Others believe that a liberal arts degree can be a waste of four years and thousands of dollars for those who already have their career plans mapped out. Students from a liberal arts background may also have a more difficult time securing a job immediately after graduating, as they tend to lack both experience and specific skills. Many preprofessional programs require students to take general education courses in liberal arts departments. In fact, almost all colleges insist that you take some courses outside your chosen field.

If you don't yet know your interests well enough to decide which option is for you, you may be pleased to learn that the largest colleges and universities have both liberal arts and preprofessional students. The University of Michigan, for example, has a strong undergraduate school of business; many students in Michigan's liberal arts school also plan to go into business eventually but are pursuing a B.A. in a more general field first. The case is similar with Cornell.

If you do know what you want from a school in terms of career preparation, then you may prefer to attend a preprofessional institution. But keep in mind that getting a liberal arts education and getting a good job are not mutually exclusive. Moreover many report that the learning environment at a preprofessional university is more competitive, and would therefore not be as enjoyable to a student who enjoys the intellectual exchange more common to liberal arts campuses.

Greek Life and Other Social Options

When choosing a college, you are choosing a place in which to live and learn. In this way the social life at colleges becomes a large factor in choosing your school and many people claim that when they visited colleges, the people they met made them love or hate the campus more than any other aspect. You will find that sometimes you just click with the students at a particular school. Although most schools are large enough to ensure you will find your social niche, it is also important to consider how the overall social atmosphere will affect you while you are there.

Collegiate life in the United States often conjures images of a social scene dominated exclusively by fraternities and sororities. While this is true of some schools, there are many schools where Greek life is either nonexistent or less central to college life than some would believe. Greek life can run the gamut from a dominating institution to a relatively unknown and tame element of college life. It is also true that while many fraternities and sororities have high levels of membership, some of the numbers are dropping across the country. This is due mostly to increasingly strict policies on campuses to curb hazing as well as alcohol abuse that has made Greek life so infamous in today's media.

Although the most widely publicized side of Greek organizations has to do with their partying habits, belonging to a Greek organization is not just for those who like to party. In fact, many organizations have reformed their policies to reduce or eliminate such practices as pledge hazing and many require that Greeks be dry at official functions (although that does not mean they cannot party together outside of meetings).

Beyond being a social group, Greek organizations offer many advantages to students including a nationwide network of alumni, community service opportunities and housing (which is often very difficult to find for upperclassmen). The emphasis on community service is particularly important to most Greek organizations and most chapters have an office dedicated specifically to organizing the chapter to participate in local charitable activities. On some campuses, the fraternities and sororities are the most active social-service organizations.

In terms of housing considerations, most organizations are on campus and thus are financially supported by the school, national chapter, and students. Because of this, Greek houses are often some of the nicest housing available, as freestanding buildings with manicured lawns and beautifully decorated interiors. However, an increasing trend among colleges is to kick Greek organizations off campus. This trend is especially marked among fraternities that gain the reputation of being unkempt and raucous. Without campus funding, many of the organizations lose large amounts of their financial support and thus cannot run as well as those that are on campus.

Whether Greek life appeals to you or not, it is essential to know just how influential the Greek organizations are at each school you are considering. At some campuses, not rushing could seriously limit your social options. On the other hand, there are many schools where fraternities and sororities are most certainly not part of campus life and are regarded as conformist. There are also schools, especially among the Ivy League, where although Greek life is present, there is a strong residence system that fills many of the social functions that Greek organiza-

tions occupy elsewhere. As a rule of thumb, Greek life is more dominant at the largest schools where practical concerns keep the organizations strong and smallest at the most specialized schools where campus life is intimate enough that smaller social organizations may prove stifling.

However, even at the most Greek-dominated campuses, there are always other social outlets. Your interests will largely determine who your friends are. Therefore, you should choose a school that has groups that represent your interests. Greek organizations, athletics, cultural organizations, or theater groups can all be part of your college experience. The people you meet in these organizations often become some of your closest friends. Ultimately, the best way to tell if a school's social scene is right for you is to visit the campus or talk to friends who go there. Most college applicants worry that they will not find people like themselves when they get to college, but, when they get there, they realize that making friends was much easier than expected. Find what you think will be the right combination of organizations, Greek or otherwise, and you will meet the right people.

Security

Students are in college to learn and to take advantage of what their schools have to offer, and campus security efforts are one reflection of a school's commitment to making that possible. Crime in general is increasing on campuses across the country, from recent tragedies that made students question the safety of their own classrooms to the rising number of sexual assaults. In response to this trend, federal legislation has made it mandatory for all colleges receiving federal aid (which is almost every one) to publish crime statistics in several categories. At your request, the appropriate office (usually the public relations or admissions offices) at any college or university should release to you the crime count for the last calendar year. Many colleges have also taken measures to beef up security. If you visit a campus and notice very stringent security measures (at the University of Pennsylvania, for example, you have to show your ID just to get into the quadrangle), remember that this means two things: there is a need for security measures, and the administration is responding to this need.

There are a number of features that any safety-conscious campus should have. Doors to individual dorm rooms and to the building entrances should be equipped with locks. All walkways should have bright lights, not only so that you yourself can see, but so friends and classmates would be able to see you from a distance in case of danger. Another important security measure is a safety phone system with one-touch access to an emergency line. Each safety phone should have a distinct light to make it easily recognizable at night. Ideally, there should be enough units so that you are never more than half a block from a phone. For getting around campus late at night, colleges should provide bus service or student safety escorts, free of charge. At least one of these services should be available 24 hours a day and should travel to every possible destination on campus. Every school should employ some type of security guard, whether unarmed monitors in or near the dorms or full-time police officers responsive solely to students and the affairs of the college. At the beginning of the year, make sure you enter these phone numbers into your cell, although they should be clearly posted as well.

Security problems are not limited to urban campuses. Some rural schools have crime rates as high as the urban ones. The sad truth is that most nonviolent crimes are committed by other students, not outsiders. Why is campus crime such an issue now? College students are ideal targets—they keep expensive stereo and computer equipment in poorly guarded areas, and they often walk alone across dark, seemingly safe campuses.

It is important to understand that you cannot judge the safety of a campus simply by eyeing it from the safe confines of a brochure. Yet, by using a little common sense and preventive measures, the security problems of a given school should not prevent you from attending. By making yourself aware of potential problems and following the school's security guidelines, you can improve your chances of enjoying a safe four years.

Computers

Whether you are an art major, a computer science major, or an expert procrastinator, computers will be an important part of your college experience. Looking up information for that re-

search paper due in 12 hours, searching for your classmate's e-mail address in the online directory, and downloading the next problem set from the class Web site are just a few examples of the countless ways that computers are a part of everyday life on campus. With that in mind, here are a few things to look for when evaluating a college's computing facilities:

24-Hour Computer Clusters: Make sure that there are at least a few accessible computer clusters to rely on when your computer or printer stops cooperating once you finally sit down to start your homework. Many people also like to work on their papers in computer clusters to get away from the distractions of their own room. Easily accessible clusters with numerous, fast computers are always a plus.

Macs vs. PCs: Although compatibility issues are largely a thing of the past, the networks at some schools may be preferentially built for Macs or PCs. If you are looking into bringing your computer, double-check that your school provides adequate support for your machine.

Support Staff: Another important thing to consider is the availability of technical assistance. Many schools hire students or other staff to troubleshoot the problems you may encounter with networking, hardware, or software licensed by the school. This can be especially helpful at the beginning of each semester when you have to register your computers with the school network and install the necessary software.

Internet and E-mail Access: Nearly every school now provides Ethernet access from dorm rooms and e-mail accounts that you can use during both the semester and your breaks. Another feature to look for is the availability of wireless Internet access at your school, which is also becoming more and more universal. In addition to getting rid of an extra wire on your desk, it also allows you to check your e-mail or chat with your roommate from anywhere on campus, including common rooms, labs, classrooms, and nearby coffee shops. But make sure you don't get too caught up in reading *The New York Times* online when you should be taking notes during a lecture!

Academic Usage of the Internet: Professors at most schools now use the Internet (in some form) as an important resource for their classes. Being able to find class notes, handouts, homework assignments, or even taped lectures posted on a Web site can be worth considering when choosing a class or a school. Although not every professor at every school is willing to put extensive course information online, finding a school where it is more common will help make your life slightly easier over the next four years.

A Final Note About Quality of Life

If you started at the first page and you've read up to here, you are probably thinking there are just way too many things to think about in choosing a college! Certainly, you already have many reasons why, right off the bat, you would add a college to, or eliminate a college from, your list. Perhaps the school has the best zoology program in the nation. Or maybe you have always wanted to be in the stands cheering as your school's basketball team wins the championship game. Either way, a final but crucial criterion for your decision is the overall quality of life you can expect to have at college.

Everyone goes to college to learn more, right? Yes, of course. Continuing your academic education will provide you with even more ways of thinking as well as more opportunities after graduation. You have to remember, though, college is someplace you will be for three or more years of your life. Academics are the most important reason to go to college, but when it comes down to everyday life, the college you choose will basically be your new world. Everything from extracurricular activities to housing, social life, and even weather will affect the way you eat, dress, study, and relax. Don't consider UMass if you can't stand the cold; and don't go to Florida State if the heat makes you miserable. Have you always thought about joining a fraternity or a sorority, and there just aren't any on campus? Or perhaps your favorite weekend activity is to curl up on a chair in a coffee shop; is the college in such a small town that there is no coffee shop? What about the housing situation? Could you see yourself coming "home" every day to that closet-sized room you share with three other students? Speaking of the other students, would you be comfortable being around them—or any of the people walking down the street? All of these factors can and will make a difference in how you feel about a school. The best way to really get an idea of what it would be like to be a student at the college is to visit the school, maybe stay over for a night or two, talk to the students around you, and browse through the student newspaper. Do you like what you see and how it feels to be there?

As you figure out what you like about a college, you may also want to check that those aspects of the school will still be there when you enroll. When the economy is doing poorly, an increasing number of schools, both public and private, face a shortage of funds; administrations at the schools have no choice but to make budget cuts. Without adequate funding, programs or even entire departments may be eliminated, the number of tenured professors may be reduced, campus renovations and additions may be delayed, extracurricular activities and sports teams may be cut, or worse yet, a combination of all of these possibilities may take place. If you are the star of your high school's varsity swimming team and want to continue swimming in college, check with the coach or the current swimmers to make sure the team is not rumored to be next on the list of programs to be cancelled. If you know that you want to major in biomedical engineering, make sure the department is big enough so that it is not one of the smaller and less popular departments that would be first to go. As recent newspaper headlines will tell you, even the best-endowed schools are tightening their purse strings.

We hope that we have given you a stronger sense as to what to think about and what to focus on as you continue to search for the college that's right for you. Just remember, in the end, you are the one who will be attending the college, so you should be the one who is happy. Best of luck!

Introduction for International Students

International students looking to apply to colleges in the United States may discover a daunting and unfamiliar path ahead of them. More so than in many other countries, admission to U.S. colleges depends not only on grades and scores, but on the whole package: what you have done outside of schoolwork, what your teachers have to say about you, and what you have to say about yourself. In addition to the typical trials of the application process, students from abroad may also have to deal with linguistic and cultural differences, scarce resources, and communication delays that their American counterparts do not. Yet you should not let yourself be deterred by these challenges—some basic planning can eliminate many potential obstacles and pave the way to a unique and rewarding college experience.

An "international student" formally refers to anyone who is applying to American universities from an address outside of the United States. This means U.S. citizens and permanent residents applying from abroad are still placed in the international category. Many colleges review this applicant pool differently from the domestic applicants—admissions committees might place less emphasis on SAT scores, for example. Many schools also look for geographical and cultural diversity, which could work in your favor if only a few students are applying from your country, or against you if there are many other applicants.

With these advantages and disadvantages in mind, here are some tips about the application process that might be especially helpful. You should also read the **Getting In** section of this book for more general information. The best advice is: get started early. Deadlines for American universities can be as early as October for fall admissions. As one student said, "make sure you take care of everything well ahead of time—last-minute surprises are harder to deal with abroad."

If you decide that you want to go to an American university, start getting involved. While extracurricular activities are not considered in the admissions processes for schools in many countries, American universities place emphasis on what you achieve outside of the classroom. Extracurricular experiences can include a variety of activities such as taking piano lessons, writing for the newspaper, doing volunteer work, or working part-time. These activities might highlight your leadership, talent, or determination. If your school does not offer many extracurricular activities, look for opportunities to get involved in the community or take the initiative to organize something yourself. When application time rolls around, be sure to list everything to which you have devoted your time.

Academically, international students might want to think about taking Advanced Placement (AP) tests and courses related to them if they are not already following the International Baccalaureate (IB) program. Although not required for college admission, AP exams measure the level of your knowledge in the subject as compared to American high school students. As an added bonus, high scores might let you bypass some classes in college or accelerate and graduate early. Arranging to take an AP test internationally might be difficult since testing sites are less ubiquitous than in the States; try to see if an American school in your area will arrange it. If you can take it and have recently completed a course corresponding to one of the tests, it would be a risk-free way to increase your chances at admission—students can choose whether to report individual AP scores. Students studying under the IB system, and even students who do not take either of these tests, might be able to negotiate for acceleration in their first year of college. Acceleration policies vary greatly, however, from college to college.

Deciding that you want to go to college in the United States and figuring out where to apply might be a rocky starting point for many international students because of the relative lack of information. But research is an essential part of the college application process and what many internationals said they wished they had spent more time doing. The United States is a huge country, and it will make a difference whether you are in California or Massachusetts, whether you are in a city or a rural area. There are also many schools with excellent programs, beyond the names that people outside of the United States would recognize. If you have a college guidance counselor at your school who is knowledgeable about admissions to U.S. schools, take advantage of the resource. However, many advisors are not. One international student, now a senior, warned, "don't trust your high school counselors too much; they probably don't know as much about the schools you're applying to as you might assume they do—including application deadlines."

If your advisor is unable to offer you the help you need, seek out a counselor outside of the school. You might also want to speak with someone who has recently gone through a similar decision-making process, or talk to an American expatriate. Libraries and the Internet are prime sources of information. College Web sites provide accurate, up-to-date information, and sometimes feature special application guidelines for international students. If possible, try to visit the colleges. It could make a big difference in your opinions.

You may also want to consider the size of the international population at the schools you are deciding between. Colleges with a larger number of students from abroad tend to have more organizations and activities geared toward international students. These schools will likely have more extensive resources available for you at the administrative level as well. However, this may not be an important factor in your decision, and it all depends on what kind of college environment you are looking for.

Testing

Most American colleges require international students to take the SAT Reasoning Test, a selection of SAT Subject Tests, and the TOEFL. The Educational Testing Service (ETS) has many international test sites, although the tests might still be hard to come by in certain countries. Students from such diverse countries as Israel, Japan, and Guatemala all said signing up was easy, particularly with online registration. However, some people might have to travel hours out of the way to get to the testing center. To avoid any unnecessary travel, register for these tests early before popular testing centers fill their seats. To find out where the nearest testing center is located, write to ETS or visit their Web site, www.ets.org.

Many colleges require the TOEFL (Test of English as a Foreign Language) if English is not your first language or the language of instruction in your high school. While taking another test might seem like a hassle, TOEFL is easier than the SAT and could work to your advantage since many schools will substitute a TOEFL score for the SAT Verbal score. If you are satisfied with your SAT Critical Reading scores, you should probably not bother taking TOEFL—although a near perfect score could never hurt. The recently instituted SAT Writing section's essay will pose a further hurdle to nonnative English speakers, and while colleges are likely to take your native abilities into account when making admissions decisions, the essay will most likely require more test preparation on the part of such students.

Application Package

In getting teachers to write recommendations for you, be sure to approach those who not only know your work but know you and are willing to write enthusiastically about you. International teachers tend to be more reluctant to award superlatives or write a personalized recommendation than their American counterparts. If you attended a school taught in a non-English language, you can ask the teachers to write you recommendations in English, have them translated, or send them to the colleges to have them translated. It is often better to have the recommendations translated in your own country than to send them to colleges to be translated by someone there. You might offer to work with your teacher to translate the letter into English, especially if you have a higher level of proficiency.

The essay is a personal reflection of yourself and an opportunity to have the different parts of your application come together. Think of what will be interesting to the admissions officers reading the essay, and allow for more creativity than might be acceptable in college applications in your own country. Many internationals choose to write about living in different countries or experiencing cultural differences, which might be more interesting than the fact that you won a national academic award—the latter point can be listed elsewhere in the application. You want to give the admissions officers a strong sense of who you are and how you will add to the college community.

Financial Aid and Visas

While some large and wealthy colleges can afford to be need-blind in their admission of international students, the consensus is that there is very little financial aid available for non–U.S. citizens and residents. If you will definitely need aid, you should research the financial aid policy of each college before applying. Depending on which country you are from, you might be able to look to sources in your home country for financial support. If, on the other hand, you are an American citizen applying from abroad, the financial aid process is the same as for any other American student.

As soon as you mail that final college application, most of your hard work will be over. Although regulations differ from country to country, you shouldn't have any problems obtaining a student visa once you are accepted to a U.S. school. The visa will allow you to work inside the university, but be forewarned that finding an outside job will be very difficult.

International students face a number of challenges when applying to U.S. universities, but some advance research and planning can help make the process as painless as possible. There are numerous benefits to pursuing an American education—you'll have a vast array of academic options, enjoy access to high-tech facilities, and be exposed to students with backgrounds quite different from your own. Attending a U.S. college is a chance to expand your horizons, and you shouldn't let the application obstacles hold you back. One international student summed it up by saying, "Although it is an endless process, it is worth it!"

Students with Disabilities

The college search process is a difficult one, but it can be even more so for students with disabilities. Whether the disability is physical or learning-related, the need for special resources means that, on top of evaluating academics and social life, students need to be certain that a school will help them learn and live as comfortably as any other student. Early preparation, along with careful planning for the transition from high school to college, will make life at college much easier.

Planning Is Key

Above all, students should choose a school for its merits. The director of the Resource Office on Disabilities at Yale said that her most important advice was to "check out the school first, but also consider the disability services office, as a second choice, very important." Even a high quality of services cannot remedy a school at which the student is unhappy—but weak or nonexistent disability services can be very detrimental to one's college experience.

High schools must accommodate students as fully as possible under the Individuals with Disabilities Education Act. However, colleges are classed under the Americans with Disabilities Act, which mandates that they provide "reasonable accommodations" for those in need; the definition of "reasonable" will vary from school to school. The best place to figure out what a school offers as "reasonable accommodation" is at the school's designated office for students with disabilities; the people there will be able to tell you what they have on hand and can arrange.

Before visiting the school, be sure to alert the admissions office. They can usually work with the disabilities office to make sure, for instance, that your tour has a sign interpreter or that it only visits wheelchair-accessible sites. When you visit, you will see how good a fit the school is for you in terms of accommodations. If at all possible, make time to visit the disabilities office while you are there. Have an honest discussion with the staff about the accommodations that are necessary for your disability; and get a feel from them about what they believe can be provided.

During the applications process, you can disclose or not disclose your disability at your discretion; admissions officers from multiple selective schools have made clear that "when we learn of an applicant with a disability, we check to make sure that our school has the resources available to accommodate the individual before we ask the traditional questions: Have they made the most of their high school career? Would they contribute to the school's community? And so on."

As soon as you decide on a school, you should contact the people at the school's disabilities office immediately, mid-May at the latest. The first thing they will need is documentation of the disability, and they will work from there. They will work with the housing department to provide necessary living accommodations, such as ground-floor rooms or flashing fire alarms. Often, the people in the disabilities office will ask more questions over the summer than you do to find out what you need and what other resources you can use. Don't be afraid to check back with them over the summer; working closely with the office will make it more likely that you're comfortable at the school in the fall.

Before coming to college, you should prepare yourself for the transition. Make sure that everything you need has been set up ahead of time. The first few weeks of college are such a whirlwind that dealing with small problems like malfunctioning hearing aids or mislaid walking sticks will take away from the experience of your new life away from home. And if things do not go as planned, the disabilities office will be one of your best resources for handling the unexpected.

If You Have a Physical Disability

For physical disabilities, the actual layout of the campus may matter most. If you are blind, you will want to make sure that the campus is easy to familiarize yourself with, and that there are multiple ways available to orient yourself. If you are in a wheelchair, you will need to know which buildings are accessible for you, including dorms, classroom buildings, and administrative buildings. Older campuses, especially those built in the eighteenth or nineteenth centuries, will need to be examined more thoroughly, and it may be necessary to ask the disabilities office to make sure that classes you have preregistered for are located in accessible buildings. One student pointed out that "schools that are truly committed to making their campuses accessible for wheelchair users will not only have many ramps available, but those ramps will be attractive and blend in naturally with the immediate environment." Elevators should be available when necessary. Many campuses will also provide special shuttle transport services for disabled students.

If You Have a Learning Disability

For learning disabilities, providing documentation starts with a diagnosis. If you don't have a formal diagnosis, check to see if the school of your choice offers diagnostic services; some even offer those services free. Given that information, the school will often work directly with the professors to make sure that those disabilities are accommodated. This might include extended testing time, typing rather than writing, or a private room for testing. These accommodations may also be available for students with temporary disabilities, such as severe recurrent migraine headaches or short-term injuries. The specific accommodations depend on the circumstances.

It is common for schools to offer alternate methods for course reading. Blind students might need the texts in Braille, while dyslexic students might prefer the text as an audio recording.

Note-taking services are offered at nearly every school. Because lectures can be fast-paced and seminars can be intensive, it may make more sense for students to receive notes from another person in the class. This option is also offered for those experiencing minor injuries: if a right-handed student breaks her right wrist, she will need a note-taker until she can write again.

Final Thoughts

Social life is an area in which students tend to be more independent: having a sign interpreter in class is common, but having a sign interpreter outside the academic sphere usually does not fall under "reasonable accommodation." Check, however, to see whether your school provides escort services if you are blind, or whether they will provide personal care assistants if you have a severe mobility disability; in that case, they may work with Vocational Rehabilitation services in your home state to help pay for those accommodations.

Usually, you will not have to pay for these services since they fall under "reasonable accommodations" mandated by the state. For specialized services, it will vary by school. Remember, it is entirely your decision whether or not to disclose your disability up front. Above all, you should find a school that is best suited to you individually, and *then* make sure that the school can help you and provide you with resources to be a successful student.

Essay: Study Abroad

Many people consider study abroad an important part of college education. Although the majority of students do not partake in these foreign ventures, many of those who took advantage of these opportunities tend to enjoy their overseas endeavors. In this section, we have three students, three countries, and three unforgettable experiences! The following students recount their time abroad in different parts of the globe.

Name: Elisabeth Wang Forsman
University/college: Mount Holyoke College
Major: English & Asian Studies Minor
Year of college you studied abroad: Junior (2008)
Place you studied abroad: Kunming, China
Subject/field studied: Chinese Language & Culture
Program name: Duke Study in China
Extremely random thing you most enjoyed about your experience: Chasing around monkeys in the mountains of southwestern China.

Upon deciding to go to China I realized that I didn't want to go to one of the major cities. I am of the opinion that all major cities are alike, only the language changes. Therefore, I travelled to Kunming, a city located in the mountains of Western China, with Duke University. Kunming is known as the "City of Eternal Spring" because of its consistently pleasant climate. The city has a population of five million people and is home to much of China's ethnic minority population.

Kunming may be a "smaller" city, with a laid-back atmosphere, but it is definitely not lacking in spirit. Given a food allowance of 350 Renminbi a week by the program, the equivalent of $50 at the time, my classmates and I were allowed to find our own way through the city. The majority of us were immediately drawn to the foreigners' district, just 10 minutes away from campus, where we would dine, shop and go dancing with foreigners and locals alike, and have regular run-ins with a wandering pig that we named Wu Tongchin after two of our classmates. Rarely did we spend more than what we were given. At Green Lake Park or Cui Hu we would lounge around, watching as people practiced t'ai chi or formed performing groups complete with instrumental sections.

For a two week period the program went on spring break. For the first week we all got onto a bus and travelled throughout Yunnan Province. We spent a week hiking, biking, horseback riding, teaching English to elementary school students, looking for monkeys and going out to the clubs. At night we stayed everywhere from Buddhist Temples and the homes of rural villagers to four-star hotels. We ate the strangest foods, like one dish made entirely of pig fat. For the second week we were given free rein. A group of us went to Beijing, Shanghai and Xi'an, even taking the 19-hour train from Shanghai to Xi'an, which was an experience in itself. Not at all like in the states.

As a part of the intensive total language immersion program we lived with Chinese roommates, spent two afternoons a week with a language tutor and every other weekend we would individually spend a day at the home of a local family. On other weekends we would take field trips to various locations outside of the city. At first it was tough to handle the workload and the requirement to speak only Chinese but over time we became well acclimated to it. The individualized attention was fantastic. My knowledge of Chinese increased exponentially. I came to China barely able to string phrases together and left being able to discuss even political issues with ease.

Name: Thi Ho
University/college: Brown University
Major: Literatures and Cultures in English
Year of college you studied abroad: Junior (2008)
Place you studied abroad: Paris, France
Subject/field studied: Literature, Art History, History
Program name: Brown in France, La Sorbonne

Extremely random thing you most enjoyed about your experience: I enjoyed Perle de Lait's coconut yogurt so much that I tried to have them ship it to me in the U.S. It didn't work.

Name: Molly Moody
University/college: University of California, Los Angeles
Major: Political Science, Minor: Spanish
Year of college you studied abroad: Junior (2007)
Place you studied abroad: Granada, Spain
Subject/field studied: Political Science, History, Spanish
Program name: Universidad de Granada, Centro de Lenguas Modernas
Extremely random thing you most enjoyed about your experience: Taking a weekly "movemiento" (aerobics) class with an overly-enthusiastic and overly-sculpted male instructor.

Paris, commonly perceived as the city of lights and love, regularly lives up to the hype. It is a gorgeous city. From major monuments like the Eiffel Tower to the Arc de Triomphe, Paris does not fail to impress you with the amount of beauty and history it possesses. I would definitely recommend visiting all the major tourist attractions, but this can be done in a day or two, depending on how fast you can walk and your tolerance for the crowds and sky-high prices. Personally, I preferred getting to know the city by simply strolling through the streets of the Latin Quarter and Montmartre, or by visiting the less well-known museums, like the Rodin Museum or the stunning St. Chapelle Cathedral.

Nevertheless, I have many conflicting opinions of Paris. For one, I studied abroad at a time when the exchange rate forced me to pay nearly twice as much for everything and I also lived alone in a tiny one-room studio with an oftentimes occupied and foul toilet down the hall. Still, I maintain that my experience in Paris was enlightening and enjoyable. Though prices were high, there are ways to budget, like going to the numerous open-air markets. The Bastille Market on the weekends stretches an entire street and has fresh ingredients and even jewelry. Bread, wine and chocolate can sometimes be cheaper than bottled water and of great quality. Monoprix, the French equivalent of Target, was my second home and has everything you need, from food to clothes to makeup. If you want a cheap meal, the bakeries on every block offer sandwiches and quiches with fresh-baked bread and fine cheese at very cheap prices. My personal favorite was the crepe stand across from the metro stop, Cluny-la-Sorbonne, which sold the cheapest crepes I found in the city.

One of the factors to consider before choosing Paris is whether city life is what you want for your study abroad experience. Cities can represent an extreme microcosm of the country as a whole, which can be a lot to take on all at once. Life is inevitably quicker and more expensive. It can also be eye-opening in many positive ways, like in familiarizing you with public transportation and life on a budget.

Southern Spain has one of the most hospitable cultures in the entire world—and I was lucky enough to experience this on a daily basis with my incredible Spanish family. One of the most loving individuals I have ever met, my Spanish mom, Conchi, became like a second mother to me. She would spend hours sitting talking to me in Spanish, teaching me about Granada's extraordinary culture, explaining her difficult experiences as a woman during the Franco era, exposing me to Spanish art, and making me some of the best authentic Spanish food imaginable.

Every day, I would wind through Granada's intricate cobblestone streets, in the shadows of the majestic Alhambra, on my way to the University of Granada. I took classes ranging from the Art History of Spain to the Politics of the European Union—and loved them all. Although all of my classes were in Spanish, I never felt overwhelmed by the language barrier. The enthusiastic professors were sensitive to the fact that their students were from different areas of the world who spoke Spanish as a second or even third language.

Granada is also an incredibly lively city at night with plenty of places to meet some of the 70,000 local and international students. There are discotecas underneath the "Plaza de Toros" where local Spaniards love to dance and bars where you feel like you are right back at home in the United States.

My experience abroad turned out to be one of the most defining times of my entire life, where every day presented a new challenge—be it understanding my host father's thick Andalucían accent, avoiding the Moroccan water on my excursion to Africa, or trying to plan a trip to Barcelona and Paris for less than 50 Euro. However, I grew more as an individual in this incredible country than I could have ever imagined. I learned to speak Spanish, I learned to be independent, I learned to be away from everything familiar—and I truly believe that I am a better person because of this magical city.

Terms You Should Know

Advanced Placement (AP)—College credit earned by students while still in high school. Many high schools offer specially designed AP courses that prepare students for the College Board's AP Exams. Administered in May, they can qualify students who score well for advanced standing when they enroll at certain colleges.

all-nighter—As in, "pulling an all-nighter." The process by which students attempt to learn a semester's worth of course material or crank out a paper of considerable length in a short period, often 24 to 48 hours. Soda, coffee, and/or caffeine pills are the staples of most all-night cramming sessions.

American College Test (ACT)—Test administered to high school juniors and seniors by the American College Testing Program. Traditionally it has been used as an admissions criterion primarily by Midwestern schools. Some Southern and Western schools use it as well.

American College Testing Program (ACTP)—The organization that produces the American College Test (ACT) and the Family Financial Statement (FFS). Many Midwestern universities use the ACT and the FFS in admissions instead of the SAT and the Financial-Aid Form (FAF). (See also "Family Financial Statement" and "Financial-Aid Form").

arts and sciences (also called liberal arts)—A broad term that encompasses most traditional courses of study, including the humanities, social sciences, natural sciences, mathematics, and foreign languages. A liberal arts college is also a college of arts and sciences. (See also "humanities" and "social sciences").

beer pong—A party game usually played with Solo cups and cheap beer. The 10 cups on each side of the table are arranged in a triangular formation, and attempts are made by the teams to direct ping pong balls into the other team's cups, either by a perfected toss or with a ping pong paddle. When the other team's ball lands in your cup, you must drink the contents. A frat house staple.

candidate's reply date—The May 1 deadline, observed by most selective colleges, by which the applicant must respond to an offer of admission, usually with a nonrefundable deposit of several hundred dollars. Colleges that require students to respond by May 1 in almost all cases notify them of their acceptance on or before April 15.

College Board—The organization that sponsors the SAT, the SAT Subject Tests, the Advanced Placement tests and the Financial-Aid Form (FAF). College Board admissions tests are developed and administered by the Educational Testing Service (ETS). (See also "Advanced Placement" and "Financial-Aid Form").

Common Application—A form produced by a consortium of over 300 colleges that may be filled out and sent to member colleges in lieu of each school's individual application. Colleges often require that a supplemental application specific to the particular school be submitted as well.

comprehensive exams (comps)—Also known as "generals," these tests, administered by some colleges (usually during the senior year) are designed to measure knowledge gained over a student's entire college career. Schools that give comps usually require students to pass the test in their major field in order to graduate.

computing assistant (CA)—A university employee, often an undergraduate, who helps students with all varieties of computing problems, from using a word processor to downloading games from the network.

consortium—A group of colleges affiliated in some way. The extent of the association can vary widely. Some consortiums–usually among colleges in close proximity–offer a range of joint programs that may include cross-registration, interlibrary loans, residential exchanges, and coordinated social, cultural, and athletic events.

co-op job—A paid internship, arranged for a student by his or her college, that provides on-the-job training, usually in an occupation closely related to the student's major.

core curriculum—A group of courses all students in a college must take in order to graduate. Core curricula are becoming widespread.

crew (rowing)—A sport, more familiar to those who live on or near either coast than to those from the South and Midwest, in which teams of two, four, or eight oarsmen or oarswomen race in long, narrow boats, usually on inland waterways. Crew is very "Ivy," quite popular at many schools, and usually requires no high school experience.

deferral—A college's postponement of the decision to accept or reject an early admissions applicant. The applicant's file is entered in with those of regular-action candidates in the spring and is reviewed once again, this time for a final decision.

discussion section—A smaller group of students who meet regularly with the guidance of a teaching assistant to discuss the material covered in a large lecture. Designed to make sure students do not get lost in large classes. The teaching assistant answers questions, fosters discussion, and usually grades assignments.

distribution requirements—Requirements stipulating that students take courses in a variety of broad subject areas in order to graduate. The number and definition of subject areas and the number of courses required in each varies from school to school. Typical categories include the humanities, social sciences, fine arts, natural sciences, foreign languages, and mathematics. Unlike a core curriculum, distribution requirements do not usually mandate specific courses that students must take. (See also "humanities," "social sciences," and "core curriculum").

drunk dial—To make a phone call to an old boyfriend or girlfriend, former hook-up (see below), or current love interest in an inebriated state.

dry—as in "dry campus." A school that does not allow alcohol for any students in its dorms or other campus facilities.

early action—A program that gives students early notification of a college's admissions decision. Unlike early decision, it does not require a prior commitment to enroll if accepted. Early action has become increasingly popular and is now available at many colleges covered in this book. Some institutions, including Stanford and Yale, offer "single-choice" early action programs. These plans work the same way as regular early action, except that students cannot apply early anywhere else. Deadlines for both types of early-action applications are usually in late fall, with notification in December, January, or February. An applicant accepted under early action usually has until May 1, the candidate's reply date, to respond to the offer of admission. (See also "early decision" and "candidate's reply date").

early decision—A program under which a student receives early notification of a college's admissions decision if the student agrees in advance to enroll if accepted. Students may apply early decision to only one college; it should be a clear first choice. Application deadlines for early decision are usually in November, with decision letters mailed by mid-December.

Ethernet—A direct, high-speed means of access to the Internet, as well as a way to keep in touch with friends via e-mail. Most campuses are "wired" with Ethernet.

Facebook—An online directory launched in 2004 that connects individuals through high school, college, and residential networks. Invaluable tool for procrastinators.

Facebookstalk—The process of "researching" the likes of a crush, former high school sweetheart, or ex-boyfriend's girlfriend through Facebook (See Facebook).

family contribution—The amount of money that a family can "reasonably" be expected to pay toward a student's education, as determined by one of the two standardized needs-analysis forms. (See also "Financial-Aid Form" and "Family Financial Statement").

Family Financial Statement (FFS)—The financial-needs analysis form submitted to the American College Testing Program (ACTP), which, like the FAF, determines the expected family contribution. Colleges that use the American College Test (ACT) for admissions purposes usually require a copy of the FFS report from students applying for financial aid. (See also "American College Testing Program," "family contribution," and "Financial-Aid Form").

fee waiver—Permission, often granted upon request, for needy students to apply for college admission without having to pay the application fee.

Financial-Aid Form (FAF)—The financial-needs analysis form submitted to the College Board by students applying for financial aid. Like the Family Financial Statement (FFS), it yields the expected family contribution. Colleges that require the Scholastic Assessment Test (SAT) for admission typically use the FAF as the basis for financial-aid awards. (See also "Family Financial Statement," "family contribution," and "College Board").

financial-aid package—The combination of loans, grants, and a work-study job that a school puts together for a student receiving financial aid.

five-year plan—The practice of completing a four-year degree program over a five-year period.

flex dollars—Miscellaneous credit, usually part of a purchased meal plan, that can be used at campus stores and sometimes restaurants on and off campus, rather than cash. Especially convenient for late-night snacking and study breaks.

four-one-four—An academic calendar consisting of two regular four-month semesters with a short "winter" or "January" term in between. Variations include four-four-one and three-three-two. In most cases, these numbers refer to the number of courses a student is expected to complete in each segment of the year, although at some schools they refer to the number of months in each segment.

freshman 15—A reference to the number of pounds students often gain during the freshman year. Usually caused by a combination of too little exercise, unlimited helpings in the dining hall, too many late-night runs for pizza, and overconsumption of alcoholic beverages.

gap year—The option of taking a year off between high school and college. Usually spent traveling, working, or volunteering.

government aid—Money that federal or state governments make available to students, most of which is administered through the colleges on the basis of need. Government aid can come in the form of grants, loans, and work-study jobs. Stafford Loans (formerly Guaranteed Student Loans) and PLUS parent loans are made available through commercial lending institutions. For further information on government aid programs, contact the state and federal departments of education.

grade inflation—A situation in which average work is consistently awarded a higher letter grade than it would normally earn. At most schools, the grade for average work is about B–/C+. But in classes or entire colleges with grade inflation, it can be as high as B or even B+.

Greek system—The fraternities and sororities on a particular campus. They are called "Greek" because most take their names from combinations of letters in the Greek alphabet.

gut—A course widely known to be very easy, often with enrollments well into the hundreds. Guts are traditionally favorites among second-semester seniors, but they can also help to balance a term that includes very difficult courses.

hipster—a member of the student body who appears to be more artsy, literary, emotionally attuned, and/or nicotine-addicted than the rest of the class. Known to sport vintage and/or ill-fitting clothing.

hook up—To enjoy a person's nonplatonic company, often used in reference to a one-night event. A very vague term that can range from an innocent kiss to sex, depending on usage.

humanities—Subjects in which the primary focus is on human culture. Examples include philosophy, language, and literature. (See also "social sciences").

independent study—A course, usually in a student's major field, in which he or she studies independently and meets one-on-one with a professor on a topic of the student's choosing. Some colleges require an independent study essay or research paper for graduation.

interdisciplinary major—A major that combines two complementary subjects from different fields, such as biology and psychology. Students completing these majors take courses in each area as well as courses that explicitly join the two.

International Baccalaureate (IB)—A high school program found across the world which, like AP courses, can earn a student advanced standing upon college enrollment.

intramurals—Athletic leagues informally organized within a college. Students are free from the burden of tryouts and play with and against fellow classmates.

jungle juice—A potent mix of liquor (often grain alcohol) and juice served at college parties out of a large water cooler or punchbowl. Freshmen who underestimate the juice's power due to its fruity taste, inevitably regret consumption the morning after.

language requirement—A rule at many colleges that requires students to study a foreign language before graduation. Two years on the college level are usually required, although credit from Advanced Placement or SAT Subject Tests often allows students to bypass the requirement.

legacy—An applicant whose mother or father is a graduate of a particular school. On occasion, students with legacy status are given extra consideration in admissions.

merit scholarship—A financial grant for some part of college costs, usually awarded for academic achievement or special skill in an extracurricular activity and not based on need. Private corporations and many colleges offer merit scholarships.

Natty Light—Cheap beer, a staple of college parties, sometimes referred to by its brand name, Natural Light. Often accompanied by its comrade "The Beast" (Milwaukee's Best), as well as a variety of inexpensive hard liquors.

need-based aid—Money awarded solely on the basis of need, usually administered through the colleges. Some schools agree to pay the difference between their total fees and the expected family contribution; others pay only part of it, leaving some "unmet" need. Most financial-aid packages consist of some combination of three components: grants, loans, and work-study jobs. Some of the money comes from the college's own resources, although part is financed by federal and state governments. (See also "government aid").

need-blind admissions—A policy in which the applicant's ability to pay does not affect the college's consideration of his or her application. Some schools with need-blind admissions also guarantee to meet the full demonstrated financial need of all accepted applicants as determined by one of the two standardized needs-analysis forms; others do not. (See also "family contribution," "Family Financial Statement," and "Financial-Aid Form").

office hours—A period during which a professor agrees to be available in his or her office for the purpose of talking with students about their coursework. Professors are not always required by their colleges to have office hours, but most do regardless.

open admissions—A policy under which any applicant with a high school diploma is accepted. State universities that have this policy usually limit open admission to state residents.

parietals—Regulations that govern the times when students of one sex may visit dorms or floors housing the opposite sex. Now usually found only at the most conservative schools.

pass/fail or CR/F or CR/D/F—An option offered by some schools in certain classes. A student may enroll in a class and simply receive credit or failure (or a D in "CR/D/F") for it on his or her transcript instead of a specific grade. While students often are not allowed to take required classes CR/D/F, the option allows them to take classes out of their comfort range without the fear of being punished with a bad grade for experimenting.

Phi Beta Kappa—An academic honor society to which students with the best grade point average in each class are elected. Less than the top 10 percent of a class, and usually far fewer, receive this honor.

PLUS parent loans—A component of the Stafford Loan, for parents. (See also "government aid").

pre-frosh—A visiting high school student, potential college recruit, or admitted student who has yet to enroll.

pregame—To prepare for a party, bar, show, or another event by imbibing beforehand. Saves time and money.

problem set—An annoying weekly assignment that is usually inevitable in science or quantitative classes. This thankless task will keep you up till 2 a.m. Sunday nights but can count for anywhere between 1/50 of your grade or one-half. Previously known as homework.

quad—An abbreviation for "quadrangle"; many dorm complexes are built in squares (quadrangles) with a courtyard in the middle. Quad can also refer to a suite of dormitory rooms in which four students live together.

quarter system—An academic calendar dividing the school year into four quarters, three of which constitute a full academic year. Less common than the semester system, it is most often used by large universities with extensive programs in agricultural and technical fields.

resident advisor/assistant (RA)—A student, usually an upperclassman, who lives in a dorm and helps to maintain regulations and enforce school policy, as well as offering advice and support to dorm residents. RAs receive compensation from the school for their services, usually in the form of free room and board.

rolling admissions—A policy under which a college considers applications almost immediately after receiving them. Decision letters are mailed within a month after the application is filed. Colleges with rolling admissions continue to accept applications only until the class is filled, so it is best to apply early.

Scholastic Aptitude Test (SAT)—Test administered to high school juniors and seniors by the College Board of the Educational Testing Service, with math, verbal, and written-language sections. Used as an admissions criterion at most colleges nationwide.

section all-star—A member of a discussion section who distinguishes him or herself by volunteering contributions in an excessively obnoxious or earnest manner. Sometimes encouraged by the TA, always reviled by other section members. Known for quoting from the original Greek and becoming belligerent during debates.

senior project—Many majors at many colleges require seniors to complete a special project during their senior year. This could involve a thesis (anywhere from 15 to 100 pages), a research project, some sort of internship, or all of the above. Some colleges offer seniors a choice between taking comps or doing a project. (See also "comps").

sexile—There are two people in the bedroom you share with your roommate, and you are not one of them. If you are lucky, you have a common room with a comfortable couch.

social sciences—Subjects that deal systematically with the institutions of human society, most notably economics and political science. The behavioral sciences, which include psychology, sociology and anthropology, are often included in this group as well.

Sophomore Slump—A period, usually the first semester of sophomore year, when students experience unprecedented levels of stress and angst. Often results from the disillusionment and increased workload following freshman year.

study break—An institutionalized form of procrastination involving food and talk. Often informally arranged–"I'm sick of calculus, let's take a study break at–(insert name of local hangout)"–but can be sponsored by RAs, cultural groups, or even school administrators. Some nights, study breaks can take more of your time than the actual studying.

teaching assistant (TA)—A graduate student who assists a professor in the presentation of a course. Usually the professor gives two to four lectures a week for all the students in the class; the TAs hold smaller weekly discussion sections.

three-two program (3–2)—A program that allows students to study for three years at one school, followed by two at another, more specialized school. Upon completion, many of these programs award both the bachelor's and the master's degrees.

town-gown relations—The contact between a college (students, employees, buildings) and its host town (citizens, businesses, local government) and the set of issues around which this contact revolves. Such issues include taxes, traffic, local employment practices, and government services such as road maintenance, sewage, and trash collection.

townie–A resident of a college town or city who is not enrolled in the college, but who might sit beside you at the local pub. Often involves a them-versus-us mentality.

trimesters—An academic calendar that divides the school year into three terms of approximately equal length. Schools on the trimester system generally have one term before the winter break and two after.

tutorial major (also self-designed or special major)—A program offered by many schools in which a student can plan his or her own major, combining the offerings of two or more traditional majors, usually in consultation with a faculty member. An example is Medieval Studies, in which the student might study the history, literature, philosophy, and art of the period, taking courses from a number of departments. (See also "interdisciplinary major").

waiting list—A list of students who are not initially accepted to a certain school, but who may be admitted later, depending on the number of accepted students who enroll. Most colleges ultimately accept only a fraction of the students on the waiting list, who are notified during the summer.

work-study—Campus jobs, for financial-aid recipients, that are subsidized by the federal government. Work-study jobs are a component of most need-based financial-aid packages. Students typically work 10 to 20 hours a week to help finance their education.

Editors' Choice

Biggest Jock Schools

University of Florida
University of Notre Dame
Ohio State University
Michigan State University
University of Iowa
University of Nebraska-Lincoln
University of Texas
University of Connecticut
Pennsylvania State University
University of North Carolina

"Sports are vital to the University because the teams bring in millions of dollars a year and create a sense of pride and tradition. The jocks get treated like the second coming of Christ."—Alexandria Butler, University of Connecticut

Easiest Course Load

Arizona State University
Seton Hall University
University of Alaska-Fairbanks
University of Hawaii
Salve Regina University
Hampshire College
Louisiana State University
University of Texas, Austin
Benedict College
University of California/Santa Cruz

"Hampshire is full of self-motivated kids with extraordinarily high goals. Hampshire does not have majors; you choose what to take. This creates a lot of pressure to choose the 'right' thing. We do have requirements, but they are just broader and include areas like multicultural perspectives and community service."—Jill Erwich, Hampshire College

Most Blondes

University of Southern California
University of Mississippi
Southern Methodist University
Pepperdine University
Arizona State University
University of California/Santa Barbara
Vanderbilt University
University of Notre Dame
Baylor University
Auburn University

Most Difficult Requirements

Columbia University
Claremont McKenna College
Stanford University
United States Air Force Academy
Colorado School of Mines
United States Military Academy
Harvey Mudd College
United States Naval Academy
Reed College
United States Coast Guard Academy

"I think it's completely true. Reed is ridiculously hard and truly belongs with the Harvards and Yales of the world. Going to Reed is like the Bataan Death March except we're not in the Philippines and the march never ends."—Alex Gersovitz, Reed College

Schools That Never Sleep

New York University
Arizona State University
University of Southern California
Hunter College
Columbia University
Tulane University
Yale University
Princeton University

University of Chicago
Parsons School of Design

"Contrary to popular belief, New York City sleeps . . . everywhere. Try taking the F train at 8 a.m.: it's all suits and snores. However, there's always a bunch of stuff you can busy yourself with so you can return home with pretty incredible stories for your friends stuck on those 'campus' things."—Jenna Rosenberg, New York University

Happiest Students

Stanford University
Brigham Young University
Yale University
University of Colorado
Clemson University
Bowdoin College
Whitman College
Claremont McKenna College
Brown University
Rice University

Most Behind the Times

College of William and Mary
Oral Roberts University
Bob Jones University
University of North Dakota
Union College
George Mason University
Davidson College
Brigham Young University
Washington and Lee University
Princeton University

"Princeton's attempt to spearhead a grade-deflation policy has received no followers among the Ivy League, which single-handedly puts us behind the times. Also, the obsession with both traditions and the creation of a Fitzgerald-era class of elitism and exclusivity definitely acts counter to the diversification efforts of most other institutions."—Ota Amaize, Princeton University

Strongest Undergraduate Focus

Princeton University
Carleton College
Grinnell College
Williams College
Yale University
Amherst College
Swarthmore College
Dartmouth College
Occidental College
Wellesley College

"Our professors are always available for office hours and spend significantly more time actually teaching than many others in the Ivy League. In addition, Yale has significant resources geared toward making undergraduate life as smooth and exciting as possible."—Ayibitari Owi, Yale University

Most Millionaire Graduates

Harvard University
University of Pennsylvania
Yale University
Massachusetts Institute of Technology
Dartmouth College
Princeton University
Stanford University
Northwestern University
Duke University
Brown University

Best Study Abroad Programs

University of Virginia
Baylor University
New York University
Tufts University
Georgetown University
American University
Middlebury College
Macalester College
Bates College
DePauw University

"There are a bunch of study abroad locations. I plan on going to Ghana junior year because I've heard some pretty wonderful things from upperclassmen. I'm excited for the great artist community and the food is supposed to be pretty incredible."—Jenna Rosenberg, New York University

Biggest Rivalries

Duke University/University of North Carolina
West Point/United States Naval Academy
Harvard University/Yale University
Stanford University/University of California/Berkeley
University of Florida/Florida State University
University of Washington/Washington State University
University of Texas/Austin/Texas A&M University
Ohio State University/University of Michigan
University of Southern California/University of California/Los Angeles
University of South Carolina/Clemson University

"Our rivalry with UNC is a great part of the Duke experience and quantifies the passion we bring to everything. There are some students that really bleed blue as they sleep in tents outside of Cameron Indoor Stadium for weeks on end in order to reserve seats for the big game."—Rajhai Wilson, Duke University

Place Most Likely to Find Your Spouse

Middlebury College
Connecticut College
Williams College
Princeton University
Brigham Young University
Clemson University
Florida State University
Wheaton College (Illinois)
University of Southern California
University of Mississippi

Best College Town

University of California/Berkeley (Berkeley)
University of Michigan (Ann Arbor)
University of Wisconsin (Madison)
Princeton University (Princeton)
Indiana University (Bloomington)
University of Florida (Gainesville)
North Carolina State (Raleigh)
University of Texas (Austin)
University of Miami (Oxford)
Boston College (Chestnut Hill)

"Chestnut Hill is a great college town because it combines the benefits of a big city with the feel of a suburban college campus. Just be sure to bring money, because Boston is expensive."—Gordon Bell, Boston College

Best Local Restaurants

Columbia University
New York University
University of Pennsylvania
Tulane University
University of California/Los Angeles
Boston University
Georgetown University
Harvard University
Yale University
University of Chicago

"New Haven's restaurants are fantastic. Even though it's a small city, New Haven possesses the diverse cuisines of a metropolis 10 times its size, including Japanese, Thai, Cuban, Italian, French, vegetarian, and even vegan."—JonPaul McBride, Yale University

Ugliest School Colors

Clemson University (Burnt Orange and Purple)
University of Oregon (Green and Yellow)
Bowling Green State University (Brown and Orange)
Rice University (Blue and Gray)
University of Washington (Purple and Gold)

Florida State University (Maroon and Dark Gold)

Rowan University (Brown and Yellow)

University of Tennessee (Bright Orange and White)

University of Wyoming (Brown and Gold)

Auburn University (Burnt Orange and Navy Blue)

Craziest Mascot

Xavier University (Blue Blob)

Evergreen State College (Geoducks)

University of Maryland (Terrapins)

University of California/Irvine (Anteaters)

University of California/Santa Cruz (Banana Slugs)

North Carolina School of the Arts (Fighting Pickles)

Rhode Island School of Design (Scrotie)

Whittier College (Poets)

University of Hawaii (Rainbow Warriors)

Connecticut College (Camels)

"An anteater is definitely a strange mascot because most people want a mascot to be intimidating. Instead, we have an anteater. At the same time, I guess it's cool because we always know that no one else will."

College Finder 2011

Regions

New England:
Connecticut
Maine
Massachusetts
New Hampshire
Rhode Island
Vermont
Eastern Canada

Mid-Atlantic:
Delaware
District of Columbia
Maryland
New Jersey
New York
Pennsylvania
West Virginia

Midwest:
Illinois
Indiana
Iowa
Kansas
Kentucky
Michigan
Minnesota
Missouri
Nebraska
North Dakota
Ohio
South Dakota
Wisconsin

Southeast:
Alabama
Arkansas
Florida
Georgia
Louisiana
Mississippi
South Carolina
North Carolina
Tennessee
Virginia

West:
Alaska
Arizona
California
Colorado

Hawaii
Idaho
Montana
New Mexico
Nevada
Oklahoma
Oregon
Texas
Utah
Washington
Wyoming
Western Canada

Schools with Fewer than 1500 Undergrads

New England:
College of the Atlantic
Marlboro College
Bennington College
United States Coast Guard Academy
Hampshire College
Bard College

Mid-Atlantic:
St. John's College
Trinity College
Haverford College
Bryn Mawr College
Swarthmore College
Goucher College
The Cooper Union for the
    Advancement of Science and Art
Sarah Lawrence College
The Juilliard School

Midwest:
Wabash College
Centre College
Cornell College
Earlham College
Knox College
Kalamazoo College
Alma College
Beloit College
Lake Forest College
St. Mary's College
Lawrence University
Principia College

Southeast:
New College of Florida
Randolph College
Sweet Briar College
Hollins University
Agnes Scott College
Milsaps College
Hampden-Sydney College
Wofford College
Birmingham-Southern College

West:
Deep Springs College
Harvey Mudd College
Mills College
California Institute of the Arts
Scripps College
California Institute of Technology
Pitzer College
Claremont McKenna College
Whitman College
Reed College
University of Dallas
Hendrix College
Whittier College

1500–5000 Undergrads

New England:
Amherst College
Babson College
Bates College
Bowdoin College
Clark University
Colby College
Connecticut College
College of the Holy Cross
Middlebury College
Mount Holyoke College
Rhode Island School of Design
Salve Regina University
Simmons College
Smith College
Trinity College
Wellesley
Wesleyan
Wheaton College
Williams College
Worcester Polytechnic Institute

Mid-Atlantic:
Alfred University
Allegheny College
Barnard College

Catholic University
Clarkson University
Colgate University
Dickinson College
Drew University
Franklin and Marshall College
Gettysburg College
Hamilton College
Hobart and William Smith Colleges
Lafayette College
Manhattanville College
Muhlenberg College
Skidmore College
St. Bonaventure University
St. Lawrence University
St. Mary's College of Maryland
Stevens Institute of Technology
Susquehanna University
Union College
Ursinus College
Vassar College

Midwest:
Albion College
Carleton College
College of Wooster
Denison University
DePauw University
Grinnell College
Gustavus Adolphus College
Kenyon College
Macalester College
Oberlin College
Ohio Wesleyan University
Rose-Hulman Institute of Technology
St. Olaf College
Wheaton College
Wittenberg University

Southeast:
Florida Southern University
Florida Institute of Technology
Furman University
Morehouse College
Rhodes College
Rollins College
Spelman College
Stetson University
Tuskegee University
University of Richmond
Washington and Lee University

West:
Colorado College
Colorado School of Mines
Lewis and Clark College
Occidental College
Pepperdine University
Pomona College

Rice University
St. Mary's University
Trinity University
University of Puget Sound
University of Redlands
University of Tulsa
Willamette University

Over 20,000 Undergrads

New England:
University of Toronto
University of Massachusetts/Amherst

Mid-Atlantic:
University of Maryland/College Park
Temple University
Penn State University

Midwest:
Indiana University
Iowa State University
Michigan State University
Ohio State University
Purdue University
University of Illinois/Urbana-Champaign
University of Iowa
University of Kansas
University of Michigan
University of Minnesota
University of Missouri/Columbia
University of Wisconsin/Madison

Southeast:
Florida State University
Louisiana State University
North Carolina State University
University of Florida
University of Georgia
University of South Florida
University of Tennessee/Knoxville
Virginia Polytechnic Institute

West:
Arizona State University
Brigham Young University
Texas A&M University
Texas Institute of Technology University
University of Arizona
University of California/Berkeley
University of California/Davis
University of California/Los Angeles
University of California/San Diego
University of Colorado/Boulder

University of Houston
University of Texas/Austin
University of Washington
University of Western Ontario

Single-Sex Schools

Female:
Mills College
Scripps College
Agnes Scott College
St. Mary's College
Mount Holyoke College
Spelman College
Barnard College
Smith College
Wellesley College
Trinity College (D.C.)
Bryn Mawr College
Sweet Briar College
Hollins University
Simmons College
Wells College

Male:
Deep Springs College
Wabash College
Hampden-Sydney College
Morehouse College

Predominantly Male Schools (>66%)

California Institute of Technology
Clarkson University
Colorado School of Mines
Florida Institute of Technology
Georgia Institute of Technology
Harvey Mudd College
Michigan Technological Institute
Rensselaer Polytechnic Institute
Rochester Institute of Technology
Rose-Hulman Institute of Technology
Stevens Institute of Technology
United States Military Academy
United States Naval Academy
United States Air Force Academy
United States Coast Guard Academy
Worcester Polytechnic Institute

Predominantly Female Schools (>66%)

Adelphi University
Bennington College
College of the Atlantic
Drew University
Eugene Lang College of The New School
　University
Goucher College
Howard University
Hunter College
Manhattanville College
Parsons The New School for Design
Rhode Island School of Design
Salve Regina University
Sarah Lawrence College
St. Mary's University
Wells College

High Minority Enrollment (>35%)

New England:
Amherst College
Babson College
College of the Atlantic
Dartmouth College
Harvard University
Massachusetts Institute of Technology
Mount Holyoke College
Rhode Island School of Design
Smith College
Trinity College (CT)
Wellesley College
Wesleyan University
Yale University

Mid-Atlantic:
Adelphi University
American University
City University of New York/City College
City University of New York/Queens
　College
Columbia University
The Cooper Union for the Advancement of
　Science and Art
Cornell University
Howard University
Hunter College
Johns Hopkins University
New York University
Princeton University
Rutgers/The State University of New Jersey

State University of New York/Stony Brook
Trinity University
University of Maryland/College Park

Midwest:
DePaul University
Loyola University
University of Chicago
University of Illinois/Chicago

Southeast:
Florida A & M University
Morehouse College
Spelman College
Tuskegee University
University of Miami
University of South Florida
University of Tampa

West:
California State University/Fresno
California Institute of Technology
Claremont McKenna College
New Mexico State University
Occidental College
Pepperdine University
Rice University
Scripps College
St. Mary's College of California
University of California/Riverside
University of California/Irvine
University of California/Los Angeles
University of California/Berkeley
Stanford University
University of California/Davis
University of California/San Diego
University of Alaska/Fairbanks
University of Hawaii/Manoa
University of Houston
University of New Mexico
University of Texas/Austin
University of Washington
University of Southern California
Whittier College

Schools Accepting <25% of Applicants

The Juilliard School
Yale University
United States Naval Academy
Harvard University
United States Military Academy
The Cooper Union for the Advancement of
　Science and Art
Stanford University

Princeton University
Columbia University
United States Air Force Academy
California Institute of the Arts
Massachusetts Institute of Technology
Brown University
Dartmouth College
Amherst College
Williams College
Pomona College
California Institute of Technology
University of Pennsylvania
Duke University
Washington University in St. Louis
Rice University
Claremont McKenna College
Georgetown University
United States Coast Guard Academy
University of California/Los Angeles
Middlebury College
Bowdoin College

Schools Accepting 25–40% of Applicants

University of California/Berkeley
Swarthmore College
University of South Carolina
Pepperdine University
Barnard College
Wesleyan College
Tufts University
Haverford College
Cornell University
Carleton College
Vassar College
Hunter College
Northwestern University
University of Notre Dame
Washington and Lee
Bates College
Boston College
Colgate University
Hamilton College
Bucknell College
Rhode Island School of Design
College of William and Mary
Connecticut College
Johns Hopkins University
New York University
Vanderbilt University
Oberlin College
Emory University
Trinity College

Bard College
Colby College
Wellesley College
Babson College
University of Virginia
Harvey Mudd College
California Polytechnic State University/
   San Luis Obispo
George Washington University
Kenyon College
Pitzer College
Macalester College
Brandeis University
University of Chicago
University of Richmond
Lehigh University
Carnegie Mellon University
City University of New York/Queens
   College
University of California/San Diego
University of Miami
Northeastern University
Elon University
State University of New York/Binghamton
Denison University
Colorado College
University of Tennessee, Knoxville
College of the Holy Cross
Sarah Lawrence College
Franklin and Marshall College
Reed College
Occidental College
Tulane University
University of Delaware
Wheaton College
Muhlenberg College
Gettysburg College
Spelman College
Howard University
Bryn Mawr College
Wake Forest University
Union College
University of Rochester
The College of New Jersey
Skidmore College
Kansas State University
Stevens Institute of Technology
Scripps College
Wabash College
University of Pittsburgh
Dickinson College
Rhodes College
University of Maryland/College Park
Fordham University
University of Connecticut
Whitman College
State University of New York/Stony Brook

Large Fraternity/ Sorority Systems (More than 30%)

Albion College
Birmingham-Southern College
Bucknell College
Case Western Reserve University
Centre College
Colgate University
Cornell College
Dartmouth College
Denison University
DePauw University
Emory University
Franklin and Marshall College
Furman College
Gettysburg College
Hamilton College
Hampden-Sydney College
Lehigh University
Millsaps College
Massachusetts Institute of Technology
Northwestern University
Ohio Wesleyan University
Rensselaer Polytechnic Institute
Rhodes College
Rollins College
Rose-Hulman Institute of Technology
Stevens Institute of Technology
Texas Christian University
Tulane University
University of Richmond
University of the South/Sewanee
University of Virginia
Ursinus College
Vanderbilt University
Wabash College
Wake Forest University
Washington and Lee University
Whitman College
Willamette University
College of William and Mary
Wofford College

Schools with No Fraternities or Sororities

Agnes Scott College
Alfred College
Amherst College
Antioch College

Bennington College
Boston College
Bowdoin College
Brandeis University
Brigham Young University
Bryn Mawr College
California Institute of Technology
California Institute of the Arts
Carleton College
Claremont McKenna College
Clark University
Colby College
College of the Atlantic
Connecticut College
Deep Springs College
DePaul University
Drew University
Earlham College
Eugene Lang College of The New School
    University
Evergreen State University
Fairfield University
Fordham University
Georgetown University
Goucher College
Hampshire College
Harvey Mudd College
Haverford College
Ithaca College
Lewis and Clark College
Macalester College
Marlboro College
Mills College
New College of South Florida
Pitzer College
Principia College
Rice University
Rhode Island School of Design
Sarah Lawrence College
Scripps College
Seton Hall University
Simmons College
Skidmore
Smith College
St. Bonaventure University
St. John's University/College of St. Benedict
St. Mary's College
St. Olaf College
Sweet Briar College
Trinity University
United States Air Force Academy
United States Coast Guard Academy
United States Military Academy
United States Naval Academy
University of Dallas
University of North Carolina/Chapel Hill
University of Notre Dame
University of Washington
Vassar College

Wellesley College
Wells College
Williams College

Schools with Very High Four-year Graduation Rates (>85%)

Amherst College
Bates College
Bucknell College
Carleton College
Claremont McKenna College
Columbia University
Dartmouth College
Davidson College
Duke University
Georgetown University
Harvard University
Haverford College
College of the Holy Cross
Johns Hopkins University
Lafayette College
Middlebury College
Muhlenberg College
Oberlin College
Oxford University
Pomona College
Princeton University
Principia College
St. Olaf College
Swarthmore College
Tufts University
University of Pennsylvania
United States Naval Academy
University of Notre Dame
United States Air Force Academy
United States Coast Guard Academy
University of Chicago
University of Michigan
University of Virginia
Vanderbilt University
Vassar College
Villanova University
Wake Forest University
Washington and Lee University
Washington University in St. Louis
Wellesley College
Whitman College
College of William and Mary
Williams College
Yale University

Under $10,000 (Out of State)

Brigham Young University
City University of New York/City College
Deep Springs College
Michigan State University
Millsaps College
Mississippi State University
New Mexico State University
Ohio University
Queen's University
Rutgers/The State University of New Jersey
United States Military Academy
United States Naval Academy
University of Arizona
University of Kansas
University of Michigan
University of Minnesota
University of South Alabama
University of South Dakota
University of Utah
University of Virginia
University of Waterloo
University of Western Ontario
United States Air Force Academy
United States Coast Guard Academy
West Virginia University
College of William and Mary

Under $10,000 (In State)

Arizona State University
Auburn University
Bowling Green State University
California Polytechnic State University/
   San Luis Obispo
California State University/Chico
California State University/Fresno
City University of New York/City College
Clemson University
Colorado School of Mines
Evergreen State University
Florida A & M University
Florida State University
George Mason University
Hunter College
Illinois State University
Indiana University, Bloomington
Iowa State University
Kansas State University
Louisiana State University
Marshall University

McGill University
Mississippi State University
New College of South Florida
New Mexico State University
Ohio State University
Oklahoma State University
Oregon State University
Southern Illinois University/Carbondale
State University of New York/Albany
State University of New York/Binghamton
State University of New York/Buffalo
State University of New York/Stony Brook
Texas A&M University
Texas Tech University
University of Connecticut
University of Massachusetts/Amherst
United States Military Academy
United States Naval Academy
University of California/Berkeley
University of California/Davis
University of California/Irvine
University of California/Los Angeles
University of California/Riverside
University of California/San Diego
University of California/Santa Barbara
University of California/Santa Cruz
University of North Carolina/Chapel Hill
University of Illinois/Urbana-Champaign
University of Alabama
University of Alaska/Fairbanks
University of Arkansas
University of Cincinnati
University of Colorado/Boulder
University of Delaware
University of Florida
University of Georgia
University of Hawaii/Manoa
University of Houston
University of Idaho
University of Illinois/Chicago
University of Iowa
University of Kansas
University of Kentucky
University of Maine/Orono
University of Maryland/College Park
University of Mississippi
University of Missouri/Columbia
University of Missouri/Kansas City
University of Montana
University of Nebraska/Lincoln
University of Nevada/Reno
University of New Mexico
University of North Dakota
University of Oklahoma
University of Oregon
University of Rhode Island
University of South Alabama
University of South Carolina
University of South Dakota

University of Tennessee/Knoxville
University of Texas/Austin
University of Washington
University of Wisconsin/Madison
University of Wyoming
United States Air Force Academy
United States Coast Guard Academy
Virginia Polytechnic University
Washington State
West Virginia University

Over $35,000

Amherst College
Bard College
Barnard College
Bennington College
Boston College
Boston University
Bowdoin College
Brandeis University
Brown University
Bucknell University
Carnegie Mellon University
Claremont McKenna College
Colgate University
Columbia University
Dickinson College
Franklin and Marshall College
George Washington University
Georgetown University
Hamilton College
Hampshire College
Haverford College
Kenyon College
Middlebury College
New York University
Pitzer College
Reed College
Sarah Lawrence College
Scripps College
St. John's University
St. Lawrence University
St. Olaf College
Stevens Institute of Technology
Swarthmore College
Trinity College
Tufts University
Tulane University
University of Pennsylvania
University of Richmond
Vassar College
Wheaton College
Whitman College

Insider's Quiz

Which high school stereotype would best describe you?
 a. Athlete
 b. Intellectual
 c. Hipster
 d. Prepster
 e. Emo or granola-loving Hippie

Which of the following statements do you best relate to?
 a. I want everyone to have heard of my college!
 b. It's okay if people haven't heard of my college before. I know it's a great school.
 c. In college I want to have the big city at my fingertips!
 d. I want my classmates to dress like me— classic and colorful with collars always up.
 e. I can't wait to go to school with people who understand me!

You wouldn't like a college that:
 a. Is too far away from home.
 b. Isn't in the quintessential college town.
 c. Isn't in a big city.
 d. Has too many students who don't summer in Nantucket or Martha's Vineyard.
 e. Doesn't care about political issues.

What do you expect walks to class will be like in college?
 a. I'll see lots of people that I have never met before.
 b. I'll see half my friends on the way and know almost all the people I see who are in my year.
 c. I'll be surrounded by the noises, people, and cars that fill a busy, buzzing city.
 d. It will look like a Ralph Lauren fashion show.
 e. I'll be almost too busy reading all the posters about political activism events that are going on around campus to walk!

You imagine that varsity athletics at your dream school will be:
 a. A huge draw.
 b. Not as popular as intramural sports.
 c. Not as well attended as the professional athletic events in the city.
 d. Important depending on the sport— lacrosse and crew will be bigger than football and basketball.
 e. What do you mean by varsity athletics?

Where do you see yourself meeting up with your college friends?
 a. At the student center, the hub of campus activity.
 b. On the quad, where people are hanging out on the lawn.
 c. At one of the zillion Starbucks that are on every corner.
 d. The squash court.
 e. At social activism meetings.

When you run into your professor outside of class, what do you think you'll discuss?
 a. Whether he/she saw the big game this weekend.
 b. The intense argument about Kant that took place between the 10 students who make up the class.
 c. Recommended local concert venues.
 d. The best conditions for yachting.
 e. Whether we could all just sit in a circle on the floor in the classroom and not at the desks.

You're running late to class, so you pull your tried-and-true wardrobe staple out of the closet:
 a. Your school sweatshirt.
 b. A sweater you permanently borrowed from your best friend.
 c. Skinny jeans.
 d. A Polo shirt.
 e. A hand-dyed scarf obtained in an obscure country.

What will your dream job be like?
 a. I'll be working at a big company with a dynamic atmosphere.
 b. I'll work at a smaller company where I can have a big influence.
 c. I'm not sure, but I know it will be in a big city.
 d. I'll either be a high-power consultant or a trophy wife/husband.

e. Who knows? I don't plan for the future. I just go with the flow.

What will you be doing in your free time 10 years after college graduation?
a. Cheering on my alma mater at home games.
b. Reading books in the local coffee shop.
c. Going to museums and cultural events during the day and clubbing at night.
d. Relaxing at my getaway home, sailing, and gossiping about my old classmates.
e. Going to rallies and protests.

Results

What kind of college is right for you?

If you answered mostly a's, a Big State School like University of Florida or Ohio State University.

If you answered mostly b's, a Small Liberal Arts school like Williams College or Vassar College.

If you answered mostly c's, an Urban School like New York University or Georgetown University.

If you answered mostly d's, a Preppy School like Washington and Lee University or Hamilton College.

If you answered mostly e's, an Alternative School like Wesleyan University or Reed College.

Insider's Packing List

Recreational

___Twister
___Deck of cards
___Dice
___A white T-shirt to write on
___Shot glass
___Magnetic poetry
___Board games
___Fan
___Feather boa
___Cowboy hat
___Picnic blanket
___Cute Facebook photo
___Bottle opener
___Corkscrew
___Water guns
___Water balloons
___Sexy underwear
___Bathing suit
___*US Weekly* subscription
___Hookah
___Frisbee
___DVDs
___A pair of aviators
___Volleyball/Basketball/Baseball (pretty
    much anything you can throw)
___Body paint
___Wig
___Game console (preferably a Nintendo
    Wii)

Practical

___Red cups
___Clorox wipes
___Airborne
___Shower shoes
___Febreze
___Tool kit
___iPod
___Duct tape
___Iron
___Layers
___Compact umbrella
___Brita

___Cough drops
___ATM card
___Checkbook
___Stamps
___Stationery
___Homemade cookies
___Sweatshirt blanket
___bleach pen
___Energy-saving lightbulbs
___Hand sanitizer
___Thai bowls
___Microwaveable mac & cheese
___One pair of shoes that you don't mind
    ruining
___One pair of shoes that you'd hate to ruin
___At least one nice outfit
___Social Security number (memorized)
___Best high school friends' e-mails and
    school addresses
___Markers
___Organized jewelry holder
___Lots of towels
___Hair straightener
___Plastic utensils
___Day planner
___Mirror
___Punch bowl
___Nalgene water bottle
___North Face fleece
___Ethernet cord
___Alarm clock
___Overnight bag
___As many pairs of socks and underwear as
    possible (to put off laundry day)
___Standing and/or desk lamp
___Hangers
___Scissors
___Digital camera
___Rechargeable batteries

Academic

Academic
___Laptop
___USB flash drive
___1-subject notebooks
___Index cards
___An endless supply of pens, highlighters,
    No. 2 pencils, etc.

Decorative

___Photos of your family
___Photos of your high school friends
___Christmas lights
___Sticky tack (for posters)
___Throw pillows
___Plastic hooks
___Corkboard
___Whiteboard

Things to Leave at Home

___Varsity jackets
___High school yearbooks
___Pleasure reading
___More than two stuffed animals
___A high school sweetheart
___SAT scores
___Trophies
___Stamp/baseball card/Absolut ad
    collections
___Overly descriptive Away messages
___Dry-clean-only clothes
___College T-shirts

A Word About Statistics

Do you want to narrow your search, size up a school quickly, or check out your chances of getting admitted? Statistics are a useful place to start when you are browsing colleges, and they are also helpful in creating that perfect list of reach, mid-range, and safety schools to which you will apply. A statistical profile precedes every college in The Insider's Guide. The colleges themselves typically provide the data. The letters "NA" (not available) either represent data that the school did not report, or those that could not be found on the school's Web site. For the most up-to-date information, as well as for all data not included in The Insider's Guide, you should contact the colleges directly.

As a rule, the statistics provided are from the most recent year for which the college has information. In most cases, this means either the 2008–2009 or the 2009–2010 academic year. In general, percentages have been rounded to the nearest whole-number percent. Statistically speaking, there is no significant difference between an acceptance rate of 30 percent and 30.4 percent; in fact, even a difference of 3 to 5 percent would hardly be noticeable.

Below the name of each school, the **address,** undergraduate **admissions phone number,** and undergraduate **admissions e-mail** address are listed; this is the contact information that a school's admissions office prefers applicants to use when corresponding.

A **Web site URL** is listed for each school, which we recommend you visit to get a quick sense of the school online.

Year Founded is the year that the school first accepted students.

The designation **private or public** refers to private schools versus publicly funded state schools. Tuition is often lower for public schools, especially for in-state students. This label cannot in any way be applied to refer to the quality of education.

Religious affiliation indicates whether a school is affiliated in any way with a particular religious establishment. This affiliation may vary—simply being a part of the school's history to being the religion predominantly practiced on campus.

Location describes the setting of the college, which is either rural, suburban, in a small city, or urban. This description gives only a general idea of the surroundings, and remember, like the rest of the statistics, it is given by the school itself.

Number of applicants is the number of completed first-year undergraduate applications received by the university.

The **percent accepted** figure is the number of applicants accepted for the most recent entering freshman class (in this case, usually the class of 2013) divided by the total number of applicants. This is an imperfect measure of a college's selectivity, and does not necessarily reflect academic quality, since many factors can influence acceptance rates. One example of this is that some schools with reputations for being easy after admission tend to attract larger numbers of applicants. For another example, public schools offer lower tuition to in-state residents, which is an attractive incentive for those applicants. Even winning sports teams can increase application numbers. There are many other factors that can influence the quality and size of the applicant pool even from year to year. Despite these caveats, the percent accepted figure is a revealing statistic. Colleges that accept relatively small numbers of applicants are usually in the best position to maintain high academic standards. When the acceptance rate is less than one-third, you can be assured that the school is one of the best around.

Percent accepted who enroll is the number of students who enroll divided by the number of students accepted. This figure, commonly called the "yield" by the admissions offices, is another way to assess how well a school attracts qualified applicants. Since many applicants have to decide between several schools, the yield is a good indicator of which schools are first-choice and which are "safety" schools. The latter usually have yields below 40 percent. The main use of yields is to compare colleges that have similar applicant pools. State universities tend to have high yields because some applicants are in-state students who do not apply elsewhere.

Number entering includes the total number of first-year students on campus at the beginning of the year.

Transfers reports the number of

students who were accepted for transfer to that institution each year. The transfers accepted is a better indication of an applicant's chances of gaining admission than the actual number of transfers matriculated, since often the number of transfers accepted is large compared to the number of matriculating transfer students. Keep in mind that "NA" here does not mean that there were no transfers, only that the schools did not report a number. Of course, not every school accepts transfer students, but those that do may restrict the number or have as many students leaving as transferring. Many big state schools are known for accepting lots of transfers from local community colleges. For these reasons, the number of transfers is not a good measure of a school's popularity.

The College Board prefers schools to use the **middle 50% SAT** range when discussing scores. This represents the range in which half of a particular school's new freshman students' scores fell. A mathematics range of 550 to 650 would mean that half the incoming freshmen had SAT mathematics scores between 550 and 650. The middle 50 percent range are the numbers between the twenty-fifth and seventy-fifth percentile boundaries; someone whose SAT score falls on the seventy-fifth percentile scored higher than 75 percent of the people who took that particular test. The same applies for someone whose score falls on the twenty-fifth percentile; the median is a score at the fiftieth percentile. Therefore, if your SAT score falls within the middle 50 percent range, you are on par with the SAT scores of last year's successful applicants. This does not mean that you have a 50–50 chance of getting in. Instead, view this figure as an indication of your own competitiveness against the overall applicant pool that the school evaluates.

Schools in the South and Midwest often prefer the American College Test (ACT). We report the **middle 50% ACT** in addition to the **middle 50% SAT** ranges for this reason. The scale for this test is 1 to 36, and the middle 50 percent range for this test means the same as it does for the SAT.

There has been a growing population of students applying early to college to demonstrate commitment or to increase chances of admission using **early decision** or **early action**. A school's policy for early admission may include "early action" (EA) or "early decision" (ED). Both programs have application due dates far in advance of regular admission, so check with the school to

make sure your application will arrive on time. Remember that while early action is advance acceptance with the option of applying and matriculating elsewhere, early decision requires a commitment to matriculate and to rescind all outstanding applications to other schools. The fact that these programs exist should not exert any pressure on an applicant to commit to an institution early.

The **EA and ED deadlines** are dates for the submission of early applications, while **Regular Deadline** is the final date for completed applications (except for second-term grade reports and late admissions tests) for freshman students. Early decision and early action programs have different deadlines, and rolling admissions may have priority deadlines after which an application is at a disadvantage. Transfer student applications usually are due one or two months after freshman applications. Nevertheless, submitting your application early gives the admissions committee more time to become familiar with your application and increases your chance of getting in.

The **application fee** is the processing fee for an application and is due at the same time as the other application materials. Check with individual schools to see if the application fee can be waived for economic reasons or for in-state applicants.

Full-Time undergraduate enrollment is the number of full-time undergraduate students for the most recent year available at the time of publication, whereas **Total enrollment** gives the total number of students, including part-time and full-time undergraduates, graduate students, and professional students. Often the ratio of undergraduate to graduate students gives an indication of the relative emphasis an institution places on each.

Percent male/female (M/F) gives the percentage of undergraduates of each sex.

Percent minority is the percentage of enrolled students who indicated on their applications that they consider themselves members of a minority group. This figure is broken down by percentages of students in four broad minority groups—**African American, Asian/Pacific Islander, Hispanic, and Native American**—to give a measure of the ethnic diversity of the school. **Other** includes any student who is a member of a minority group but not one of the four listed above. Many students of different ethnicities, such as international students and biracial students, are not included in this section. You may want to contact the college directly for more specific information.

Percent in-state/out-of-state is the percentage of enrolled undergraduates who are residents of the state in which the school is located. For Canadian schools, the percentage is that of students from within Canada. This figure gives an approximation of the regional diversity of the school. Obviously, the in-state numbers will usually be much higher for public schools than for private schools, although in most cases, states provide incentives for private schools to take in-state students.

Percent from public HS is, of course, the percentage of students whose secondary education took place in a public school.

The **Retention rate** is the percentage of first-year students who remain enrolled at a given institution for their second (sophomore) year. This statistic is an indicator of the quality of life, resources, and general satisfaction of the students at a particular college. Like the statistics on percent accepted who enroll, these numbers are most useful in comparisons between schools of the similar academic caliber, size, and student body.

The **Graduation rate** represents the percentage of students who graduate successfully over a certain time period. Schools were asked for both their **four-year** and **six-year** graduation rates. Many students take at least five years to obtain their bachelor's degree, and in this case the six-year graduation rate would be higher than the four-year rate. Contact a school directly to find out how long the average student takes to complete the requirements for his or her degree. Generally students are more likely to take over four years to graduate in public schools than private schools.

Percent Undergraduates in on-campus housing gives the portion of students living in school-controlled housing. Some smaller schools guarantee on-campus housing for all students if they choose to remain on campus. At most institutions, a large percentage of the freshman class lives on campus, while most of the rest of the student body lives off campus. There are often opportunities for upperclassmen to live on campus if they choose to do so, as Resident Assistants (RAs) or in other student leader positions. Be prepared to seek off-campus housing arrangements early if a school's housing percentage is less than 90 percent or if no figure is listed.

The **number of official organized extracurricular organizations** figure represents the number of extracurricular organizations recognized by the college administration. This is just another indicator of what student life is like outside of classes.

Three most popular majors lists the top programs of study among the seniors in the most recent graduating class for which the college has data. Remember, though, that popularity is not necessarily a measure of quality. Also, the exact number of students majoring in any given field can vary widely from year to year. Certain schools, however, are well-known for specific programs (e.g., criminology, biomedical engineering, government, journalism).

The **Student/Faculty** ratio indicates how many students there are in comparison to professors. While this statistic certainly varies by department, and has no real implication in the possibility of faculty-student interactions, many people like to know it. A more useful statistic is the **Average class size** for undergraduate classes, but beware, as often this includes small classes or sections not taught by a professor.

Percent of students going to grad school represents the percentage of students going on to graduate or professional school after graduation. Schools vary on whether this number represents those who go immediately after graduation, or after a few years. If you are interested in a particular graduate or professional degree, you may want to check with individual schools as to preparation programs they offer.

Tuition and fees and cost for **room and board** figures are given for the most recent year available. In cases where costs differ for **in-state** and out-of-state students, both figures are listed. Also, many public schools charge tuition that varies with the course load taken. Remember that these figures are meant as an estimate of the cost for a year at a given institution, and do not include travel, books, and personal expenses. These figures tend to increase every year. Use these figures as a relative index of how expensive one college is compared to another. For Canadian schools, these figures are reported in Canadian dollars.

For **percent receiving financial aid out of those who apply, first year**, schools are asked to report the percentage of the entering class receiving need-based financial assistance from the institution out of those applying for aid. This does not include students receiving only merit-based scholarships, federal loans not given out by the institution, and students who did not apply for aid. These figures are most relevant for comparing similar institutions. As to the **percent receiving financial aid among all students**, the number indicates the ratio of number of students receiving financial aid over undergraduate enrollment. Questions about schools' particular financial aid programs should be addressed directly to their financial aid offices.

Finally, **Canadian schools** report their statistical information in a very different manner from American schools, so some statistics such as average SAT scores are not reported. However, it is important to know that Canadian universities are familiar with applicants from the United States, since a large number of Americans do travel north for college education. As you get deeper into your search, it will be important to contact Canadian colleges directly since most schools in Canada also report their deadlines and statistics by individual program of study rather than for the college or university as a whole. Furthermore, admissions procedures, competitiveness, and tuition fees are often very different based on whether the student is a Canadian or international citizen, as well as the specific type of academic program. Our advice is to visit the schools' Web sites for detailed statistical information on the specific programs.

Alabama

Auburn University

Address: Quad Center
Auburn, AL 36849
Phone: 800-282-8769
E-mail address:
admissions@auburn.edu
Web site URL:
www.auburn.edu
Year Founded: 1856
Private or Public: Public
Religious Affiliation: None
Location: Suburban
Number of Applicants:
17,798
Percent Accepted: 69%
**Percent Accepted who
enroll:** 34%
Number Entering: 4,160
**Number of Transfers
Accepted each Year:** 1,980
Middle 50% SAT range:
M: 520–630, CR:
500–610, Wr: Unreported
Middle 50% ACT range:
22–27
**Early admission program
EA/ED/None:** None

**Percentage accepted
through EA or ED:** NA
EA and ED deadline: NA
Regular Deadline: Rolling
Application Fee: $40
**Full time Undergraduate
enrollment:** 19,812
Total enrollment: 23,187
Percent Male: 52%
Percent Female: 48%
**Total Percent Minority or
Unreported:** 15%
Percent African American:
9%
**Percent Asian/Pacific
Islander:** 2%
Percent Hispanic: 2%
Percent Native American:
<1%
Percent International: 1%
**Percent in-state/out of
state:** 69%/31%
Percent from Public HS: 86%
Retention Rate: 86%
Graduation Rate 4-year:
34%

Graduation Rate 6-year:
62%
**Percent Undergraduates
in On-campus housing:**
14%
**Number of official organized
extracurricular
organizations:** 300
3 Most popular majors:
Business, Education,
Engineering
Student/Faculty ratio: 18:1
Average Class Size: 25
**Percent of students going to
grad school:** 35%
Tuition and Fees: $18,260
**In-State Tuition and Fees if
different:** $6,500
Cost for Room and Board:
$8,260
**Percent receiving financial
aid out of those who apply,
first year:** 64%
**Percent receiving financial
aid among all students:**
54%

L ess than an hour's drive east of Montgomery, the plains of Alabama give rise to Auburn University. The school, whose athletics department has produced stars like Charles Barkley and Bo Jackson, boasts some of the region's top veterinary and engineering programs. But it is the student body that will most likely catch the eye of a passerby, especially if he or she hails from more northern lands. "Southern hospitality is alive and well here," students declare, and this charm mixed with fun and academics keeps Auburn students smiling.

Bed and Breakfast (and Lunch and Dinner)

Auburn students electing to live on campus can choose from four clusters of residence halls, but the housing is not guaranteed to

anyone, even freshmen. The more popular living areas are the Hill and the Quad, and dorms are either women-only or coed by floor. Many in-state students and upperclassmen choose to live off campus in one of the several apartment complexes near campus. Since many students opt not to live in dorms, Auburn provides an apartment guide and some helpful tips for students shopping the off-campus market. Tiger Transit is available to get students from point A to point B, and the Off Campus Association "gets you a good deal on utilities."

There is no shortage of food options on campus. The two main dining areas, Terrell Dining Hall and War Eagle Food Court, are located at the southern and northern ends of the campus, respectively. Both have an assortment of fast food and local restaurants that cater to students on the go. Auburn offers a variety of meal plans to meet a wide range of needs, and the Tiger Card can be used "like a debit card" at local eateries and grocery stores. Students deposit funds into the account and use the swipes until the balance dwindles down again.

Students choosing to eat on campus can get all the basic sandwiches and burgers, or they can go for a smoothie at Chillers in War Eagle Court. The town of Auburn offers the traditional fare of Ruby Tuesday and family dining along with some establishments appealing to the younger crowd. Students frequent the Mellow Mushroom for a more gourmet pizza and head to Moe's for "the best burritos in town."

Cracking the Books

Auburn University was the first land-grant college in the Southeast (a result of the Morrill Act), and to this day its engineering and agriculture departments remain strong. But the University has become more diverse in its faculty and currently offers undergraduate degrees in 12 schools—agriculture, architecture, business, education, engineering, forestry and wildlife, human sciences, liberal arts, nursing, pharmacy, science and mathematics and veterinary medicine. Moreover, the University recently began a Bachelor of Wireless Engineering program which represents the first degree of this type in the nation. Students select their majors at the end of the second year, but changing majors is not difficult with the help of Auburn's advising system.

> "Most professors are more than willing to help you out. All you have to do is ask."

The University offers plenty of options for study abroad. Auburn itself has a growing number of distinct programs, or students can participate in approved programs from other universities. One student who returned from a summer in Florence, a popular destination for art students, said "transferring credits was really easy."

While Auburn students put in their time in Draughton Library (open 24 hours a day during finals), they do not often complain of being tremendously overworked. "Some students skip classes and don't work that hard," but workload largely depends on the course of study. If an Auburn Tiger is having some difficulties in the classroom, he or she can usually find plenty of support. "Most professors are more than willing to help you out. All you have to do is ask."

Auburn professors have earned a reputation for being accessible and invested in their students' educations, but the same cannot always be said about teaching assistants, especially in math and science courses. Students said some TAs have problems speaking clear English, which can make learning more difficult.

In preparation for life after graduation, Auburn provides advice and information for students interested in graduate or professional school. A senior in the College of Sciences and Mathematics said her adviser has helped her not only navigate Auburn's undergraduate curriculum, but also apply to graduate schools. The University brings in representatives from schools throughout the region to speak to students about opportunities after graduation.

Frivolity, Fraternities, and Football

The social scene is alive and well at Auburn no matter what time of year, but students have different preferences for the seasons. During the fall, students don their best orange and blue to support their Tigers on the field at Jordan-Hare Stadium. The on-campus stadium is regularly filled to capacity of over 85,000 raucous fans screaming "War Eagle," and the surrounding areas are teeming with tailgates for each home game. Don't be surprised to see Auburn students dressed up for this Saturday afternoon affair. The game is a place to be seen as well as show school spirit. The fun continues, especially after a win, at Toomers Corner after the final snap.

The stadium is bursting at the seams when in-state rival the University of Alabama comes to town the Saturday before Thanksgiving for the Iron Bowl. Students must make sure they get their tickets early if they want a seat at this perennially sold-out event.

Many students hit the fraternity parties Friday and Saturday nights. A significant chunk of the student body is Greek, but "parties are open for the most part." In contrast to most other SEC schools, there are no sorority houses at Auburn. The sisterhoods have halls in dorms, mostly populated with sophomore members, and a chapter room. Greek organizations maintain a lively party environment with formal dances and band parties.

The Auburn police are usually present at larger organized events, but there is not a visible crackdown on underage drinking as long as students act responsibly. The police are strict on drunk driving. Since most students at Auburn come with cars and many live off campus, there is a volunteer designated-driver program to make sure every student makes it home safely.

In the spring semester, students focus their revelry on off-campus locales—apartments or downtown bars. College Park Apartments usually has something going on during the weekends. For good drink deals, of-age students head to Buffalo's for a brew and then to Quixote's, where "there is always a good band playing." While the town restaurants might let things slide, bars have no problem carding, and they can be quite difficult to get into at times.

Apart from the night life, students engage in many social activities and student groups on campus. Students can try their hand at radio broadcasting on WEGL, do community service through Habitat for Humanity or Kiwanis Club, partake in theater and singing groups, and do just about anything else that might be of interest.

Getting Your Bearings

Two important landmarks on campus for new students are the Foy Student Union and the Haley Center. These two buildings are the hubs of student life on campus. Foy contains the War Eagle Food Court, a CD and game store, study lounges, student organization offices, an ATM and a mail drop. The Haley Center houses a cafeteria, lecture halls and the campus bookstore. The one thing these buildings don't have is parking, which can be a "nightmare" on campus. Since most students are in-state or from surrounding areas, they drive to school from home, and having a car is "a big plus on the weekends for road trips to the beach."

Go to one football game, and it's easy to see the tradition that pervades the Auburn campus. Some students are third- or fourth-generation Tigers, but that should not scare away newcomers to the South. With pleasant weather and people, it is easy to understand why Auburn is one of the most popular universities in the region.—*Adam Weber*

FYI
If you come to Auburn, you'd better bring "your country music collection."
What's the typical weekend schedule? "Drink, drink, drink, go to a football game, drink, drink, and pass out."
If I could change one thing about Auburn, I'd "move it to a more metropolitan area."
Three things every Auburn student should do before graduating are "get every single flavor of milkshake at Cheeburger Cheeburger, participate in the cheesy 'Hey Day,' and run in the Cake Race."

Birmingham-Southern College

Address: 900 Arkadelphia Road, Birmingham, AL 35254
Phone: 800-523-5793
E-mail address: admission@bsc.edu
Web site URL: www.bsc.edu
Year Founded: 1856
Private or Public: Private
Religious Affiliation: United Methodist
Location: Urban
Number of Applicants: 2,227
Percent Accepted: 60%
Percent Accepted who enroll: 23%
Number Entering: 292
Number of Transfers Accepted each Year: 101
Middle 50% SAT range: M: 520–650, CR: 520–640, Wr: Unreported
Middle 50% ACT range: 22–28
Early admission program EA/ED/None: None

Percentage accepted through EA or ED: NA
EA and ED deadline: NA
Regular Deadline: Rolling
Application Fee: $40
Full time Undergraduate enrollment: 1,389
Total enrollment: 1,389
Percent Male: 59%
Percent Female: 41%
Total Percent Minority or Unreported: 16%
Percent African American: 9%
Percent Asian/Pacific Islander: 2%
Percent Hispanic: 2%
Percent Native American: <1%
Percent International: Unreported
Percent in-state/out of state: 67%/33%
Percent from Public HS: 65%
Retention Rate: 86%
Graduation Rate 4-year: 60%

Graduation Rate 6-year: 69%
Percent Undergraduates in On-campus housing: 77%
Number of official organized extracurricular organizations: 70
3 Most popular majors: Business Administration/Management, Health/Medical Preparatory Programs, Pre-Law Studies
Student/Faculty ratio: 10:1
Average Class Size: 15
Percent of students going to grad school: 50%
Tuition and Fees: $25,586
In-State Tuition and Fees if different: No difference
Cost for Room and Board: $8,595
Percent receiving financial aid out of those who apply, first year: 80%
Percent receiving financial aid among all students: 46%

B irmingham-Southern College prides itself on its reputation as a top-notch university, and the students here work hard to live up to BSC's expectations. Students manage the intense workload and credit the "loads of personal attention" to their success and survival.

"Life-long Learners"
As a four-year liberal arts college, Birmingham-Southern seeks to send out well-rounded, well-educated, and cultured leaders. As such, the academic requirements cover a broad range of subjects and interests. Freshmen have to take three "First-Year Foundations" courses in order to acclimate themselves to the college environment as well as to take their first steps as "life-long learners." Over the course of four years, students at BSC must accumulate at least one unit each of art, lab science, history, literature, a nonnative language, humanities, philosophy and religion, writing, math, and social science. After fulfilling these core courses, students must take two additional credits in humanities and one ad-

ditional credit in math or science. Although there are no pre-professional majors, many take a difficult course load aimed at medical or law school. English, Business, and Education are, not surprisingly, extremely popular majors. Math and Science majors are rarer but remain a presence on campus. A highly selective honors program is also available to the most motivated and qualified students at BSC. The program offers accelerated courses and small seminars with an interdisciplinary approach. Those interested in the program are encouraged to apply as early as spring of their senior year in high school.

BSC requires its students to go even farther above and beyond the minimal requirements, and make use of its unique "interim term." The interim term, the "1" portion of Birmingham-Southern's 4-1-4 year, is a month-long period between the school's two four-month semesters in which students are free to explore one specific interest. One student used one of her four interim terms to design a course as a teaching assistant in an urban school environment. The student explained, "I decided how long I was in the classroom, what types of activities I would do, how I would be graded . . . all of that." Although some students think the interim term can be a "pain," many say it also provides the opportunity to travel abroad without worrying about falling off a four-year track.

With all that Birmingham-Southern requires, "the workload can be tough"; however, students have advisors at their disposal and a strong support system. Professors are generally described as "great" and "absolutely approachable." Classes with good reputations may be tricky to obtain for freshmen (it's not easy getting that first-choice class), but amazing classes are definitely available. "[My professor] set up a fake crime scene . . . roped it off, had a chalk outline of the body, fake blood everywhere . . ." said a student about his Forensic Science course. "We had to walk around, take it apart . . . all the way to conviction." The bottom line remains: people at BSC take academics pretty seriously, and as one student affirmed, "people do what they've got to do."

Outside the Classroom: Like Wonder Bread?

Despite the high academic expectations, BSC students know how to balance the books with some much-needed down time. With Birmingham in their backyard and a variety of clubs and activities to choose from, students have a wide array of weekend options. Prospective students should be aware, however, that Birmingham-Southern has a definite Greek feel. "The frat scene is definitely the dominant social scene here . . . the rush process starts during the summer," a freshman explained, "but the formal rush doesn't happen until the third week of school or so." The downside of having such a close-knit and supporting Greek system is that "what Greek organization you belong to has a large impact on who you're going to be friends with." As one student remarked, "It's sad in my opinion that in the cafeteria, people still sit at certain tables based on what fraternity, sorority, or sports team he/she is on." Still, students are quick to point out that the Greek life isn't for everybody at BSC—and that's okay. The Student Government Association sponsors movie-nights out, for example, and clubs such as "Chaos" and "Platinum" are a short drive away. And as most students have cars on campus—"if you don't, you can always mooch off someone else," according to one student—transportation is usually not a huge issue.

Big annual activities include the Greek-sponsored "Philanthropy Party" as well as the Entertainment Festivals (E-Fest in BSC vernacular) where local talents are showcased each semester. Students also note attempts by administration and other students to broaden the cultural offerings on campus. Although diversity at Birmingham-Southern may prove a disappointment to some (minority enrollment has been documented at around 20 percent, but students generally deemed geographic and class diversity to be somewhat lacking), clubs such as the BSC Step Team are giving a different feel to the pervasive—as one student termed it, "Wonderbread—white and rich"—culture of the school.

"We know how to do things: be it academics, partying, or whatever: right here."

Another extracurricular option is intramurals, also known as IMs. Flag football, inner tube water polo, and dodgeball are just a few examples of available intramural activities. "People play [IMs] and they can get pretty competitive, but everybody realizes it's just IMs and we're all out of shape," one BSC student said. In addition to IMs, students can cheer for their school's teams. While Birmingham-Southern does not have a football team, they "live vicariously through [University of] Alabama and Auburn [University]." The basketball and baseball games are well-attended, and "it's a face-painted, T-shirt-wearing, screaming, jumping good time." One student summed it up saying, "We know how to do things—be it academics, partying, or whatever—right here."

Living and Dining

"Dorms are . . . well, dorms" one junior explained, "you can't expect too much." Freshmen guys live in New Men's, while freshmen girls live in either Cullen Daniel or Margaret Daniel. A student revealed that "New Men's is pretty nasty, but it's a cool experience." The freshmen dorms have two people to a room and communal bathrooms. Other options include a four room-four person suite, a four room-eight person suite, or two doubles connected by a bathroom. Housing situations improve with both seniority and GPA—those with seniority and higher GPAs pick first. Residential Advisors (RAs) are on each floor of the freshmen dorms, ready to

6   Alabama

help with any problems. However, RAs are also meant to enforce the rules: "Level of strictness varies from person to person . . . they're there to enforce the rules through fines mostly." Students sometimes choose to forgo dorm life for student apartments on campus or the Sorority Townhouses and Fraternity Row. Other notable buildings and locations on campus include the science building (which was remodeled in 2003), the humanities building, and the United Methodist Center. The Center recently built a new facility on the former Frat Row. "The [Frats] are a hangout area . . . as well as the Caf, and the Cellar." The Cellar, a coffee house, is a popular place for both relaxing and studying. The cafeteria, or "Caf" as BSC students call it, was recently revamped and

is "a definite improvement" over the old cafeteria, and now boasts a Subway, a KFC, a soul food bar, a grille and a salad stand. Students living on campus have to purchase a meal plan; the choices range from light, medium, and hearty, which differ in numbers of meals provided.

Coming to Birmingham-Southern is coming into a great tradition of excellence. With its mixture of Division I sports, academics, and bridges into the business world, Birmingham promises to provide not only an unforgettable college experience, but connections for life. "We produce the best and the brightest—but not only that, once you're a part of the BSC family, those ties never die. [That] sounds so sappy, but it's true."—*Melody Pak*

FYI
If you come to BSC, you'd better bring "your leg muscles, it's hilly."
The typical weekend schedule includes: "Friday: some sort of party Friday night, Saturday: football games, sports, party on Saturday night, Sunday: really low key."
If I could change one thing about BSC, I'd "bring more diversity."
Three things every student at BSC should do before graduating are "spend half of your day trying to figure out what you did the night before, make love, and still pass with a 3.5 or higher."

Tuskegee University

Address: 120 Old Administration Building Tuskegee, AL 36088
Phone: 334-727-8500
E-mail address: adm@tuskegee.edu
Web site URL: www.tuskegee.edu
Year Founded: 1881
Private or Public: Private
Religious Affiliation: None
Location: Rural
Number of Applicants: 2,692
Percent Accepted: 58%
Percent Accepted who enroll: 51%
Number Entering: 795
Number of Transfers Accepted each Year: 378
Middle 50% SAT range: M: 380–490, CR: 390–500, Wr: Unreported
Middle 50% ACT range: 16–21
Early admission program EA/ED/None: None

Percentage accepted through EA or ED: NA
EA and ED deadline: NA
Regular Deadline: 15-Jul
Application Fee: $25
Full time Undergraduate enrollment: 2,514
Total enrollment: 2,701
Percent Male: 44%
Percent Female: 56%
Total Percent Minority or Unreported: 99%
Percent African-American: 86%
Percent Asian/Pacific Islander: <1%
Percent Hispanic: <1%
Percent Native-American: <1%
Percent International: Unreported
Percent in-state/out of state: 30%70%
Percent from Public HS: Unreported
Retention Rate: Unreported
Graduation Rate 4-year: 25%

Graduation Rate 6-year: 50%
Percent Undergraduates in On-campus housing: 55%
Number of official organized extracurricular organizations: 36
3 Most popular majors: Electrical, Electronics and Communications Engineering, Veterinary Medicine
Student/Faculty ratio: 12:1
Average Class Size: Unreported
Percent of students going to grad school: 23%
Tuition and Fees: $15,450
In-State Tuition and Fees if different: No difference
Cost for Room and Board: $7,130
Percent receiving financial aid out of those who apply, first year: 72%
Percent receiving financial aid among all students: Unreported

Tuskegee University has historically been home to many generations of African American men and women searching for an outstanding academic experience in addition to a unique cultural enrichment. Tuskegee's close-knit student community lives and studies in one of the country's most historic African American universities.

Changing Tradition

Tuskegee affords its undergraduates the opportunity to pursue a true liberal arts education through the College of Liberal Arts and Education. Although it was founded with the intention of giving African Americans a more technical, career-specific education to give them an edge in specific job markets, the curriculum has gradually changed to ally Tuskegee with other liberal arts schools. Still, some traditions remain: all freshmen are required to take an orientation course, which consists of University history, including the mandatory reading of Booker T. Washington's *Up from Slavery*, and advice for adapting to college life. Freshmen will also discover that their other basic requirements include physical education and English courses.

The University includes five colleges in total: the College of Agriculture, Environmental and Natural Sciences; the College of Business and Information Science; the College of Engineering, Architecture and Physical Sciences; the College of Veterinary Medicine, Nursing and Allied Health; and the College of Liberal Arts and Education. Thus, despite the shift toward a more liberal arts–oriented academic environment, many Tuskegee students are engineering or science majors. The school often receives acclaim for its pre-vet, pre-med and nursing programs, and students confirm high numbers of enrollees in each of these disciplines. Lower level lectures tend to enroll between 40 and 50 students, but the average class size overall is about 20 students. Students like the class sizes, and report that "whatever class size you prefer, you can usually pick accordingly." The smaller class sizes and minimal use of TAs keep student-faculty interaction high. Students generally give Tuskegee's academics a high rating. There were those who disagreed, remarking that "it can be easy to feel lost in the larger classes that don't have TAs," but on the whole, many agreed that the school is "demanding but rewarding." Tuskegee's history is clearly visible around its campus. A senior

commented that "It's very cool, some of the brick buildings were built by students when the school was founded."

Still Living in the Past

The residential life on campus is one of students' more frequent complaints. In addition to being "ancient" and "without much furniture," dorms are not coed and students are required to live on campus both freshman and sophomore years. The older dorm buildings have a reputation for being in poor physical condition, and one student called the dorms "older than rocks." "You had better bring things that make you feel at home," said one undergrad, because "there's no real cozy feeling." The on-campus apartment situation is slightly better; the Commons apartments offer students the amenities of a kitchen in addition to rooms that they can make their own with decorations. Students' biggest problem, however, is with the University housing regulations. Because of the school's conservative nature, men's and women's dorms are separated by a 10-minute walk to prevent students from visiting those of the opposite gender. The University staff also keeps a close eye on dorms; students are not allowed to be on the "wrong" side of campus after 11 p.m. and, if caught, face punishment.

> "The town of Tuskegee offers nothing except seclusion from the modern world, but you learn a lot trapped in the wilderness."

Many upperclassmen choose to move off campus. One student said of the coed policies, "I love my campus, but I had to leave it because of the rules." Students tend to meet in the student union, which contains a movie theater, a grill, a game room and offices for student organizations. The student cafeteria is another popular meeting place, and serves as a place where Tuskegee's many clubs and organizations can meet to bring students together. Some of the biggest clubs are the state clubs, which unite students hailing from the same state to plan activities relating to their home turf. African-American groups like the National Society of Black Engineers and several prominent fraternities and sororities are also present on campus. There is an active chapter of ROTC, which helps some students to fund their education. Students are active in community service, and the nearby hospital employs a number of Tuskegee students.

Football and basketball games generate great excitement at Tuskegee. In particular, the rivalries with Morehouse College and Alabama State University tend to draw the largest crowds to sporting events. Homecoming is one of the biggest social events of the year. The weeklong tradition incorporates performances by student groups, the Miss Tuskegee Gala and a number of pep rallies to boost school spirit. In the spring, the school hosts "Springfest," an event drawing many students together for shows, concerts and a dance.

The Typical Tuskegee Student

While the Greek system is a visible presence on campus, students report that they do not feel an urge to rush. There is little animosity between the fraternities, but they reportedly have a "friendly rivalry." Officially, alcohol is prohibited on campus and students who are caught with it face fines or other penalties. As a result, drinking generally tends to oc-

cur off campus. Students said they considered the town of Tuskegee "slow," but most agree that it has most of the things necessary for college life. And, as one student put it, "Tuskegee has a lot of potential to grow," adding, "but you come for the school, not the town." Tuskegee students also added that their campus is safe, with a large body of security officers and a closely monitored electronic keycard system.

Tuskegee is more than just an academic college experience; it is also one of cultural and historical enrichment. The school's fundamental mission remains an avid part of why students attend, and the school's community and tradition are enough to overcome some of its more conservative and comparatively strict policies. The experience tends to bind people in a lasting way. As one student said, "There are a lot of good people here and you can meet a lot of great minds—not to mention we're friends for life. People might complain about things here, but in the end, you don't want to leave."—*Melissa Chan and Staff*

FYI
If you come to Tuskegee, you'd better bring "a car to survive here because the nearest mall is 20 minutes away. The town of Tuskegee offers nothing except seclusion from the modern world, but you learn a lot trapped in the wilderness."

What's the typical weekend schedule? "Go to a football game if we're playing at home and then party at a fraternity at night."

If I could change one thing about Tuskegee I'd "change the administration. It seems to have no respect or regard for the students, the registration process takes three days, and the dorms are really run-down."

The three things every student should do before graduating from Tuskegee are "try the food at the Chicken Coop, go to Homecoming, and visit the George Washington Carver Museum on campus."

University of Alabama

Address: P.O. Box 870132
Tuscaloosa, AL 35487-0132
Phone: 205-348-5666
E-mail address:
admissions@ua.edu
Web site URL: www.ua.edu
Year Founded: 1831
Private or Public: Public
Religious Affiliation: None
Location: Suburban
Number of Applicants:
18,500
Percent Accepted: 60%
**Percent Accepted who
enroll:** 45%
Number Entering: 5,034
**Number of Transfers
Accepted each Year:** 2,006
Middle 50% SAT range:
M: 500–610, CR:
490–600, Wr: Unreported
Middle 50% ACT range:
21–27
**Early admission program
EA/ED/None:** None

**Percentage accepted
through EA or ED:** NA
EA and ED deadline: NA
Regular Deadline: 1-Feb
Application Fee: $35
**Full time Undergraduate
enrollment:** 22,341
Total enrollment: 26,318
Percent Male: 48%
Percent Female: 52%
**Total Percent Minority or
Unreported:** 16%
Percent African-American:
11%
**Percent Asian/Pacific
Islander:** 1%
Percent Hispanic: 2%
Percent Native-American:
<1%
Percent International: 1%
**Percent in-state/out of
state:** 73%/27%
Percent from Public HS: 90%
Retention Rate: 86%
Graduation Rate 4-year: 35%

Graduation Rate 6-year:
62%
**Percent Undergraduates in
On-campus housing:** 30%
**Number of official organized
extracurricular
organizations:** 294
3 Most popular majors:
Elementary Education,
Finance, Nursing
Student/Faculty ratio: 20:1
Average Class Size: 12
**Percent of students going to
grad school:** 24%
Tuition and Fees: $18,000
**In-State Tuition and Fees if
different:** $6,400
Cost for Room and Board:
$6,430
**Percent receiving financial
aid out of those who apply,
first year:** 64%
**Percent receiving financial
aid among all students:**
61%

An institution that survived the devastation of the Civil War, the University of Alabama is one of the most prominent research universities in the state of Alabama. It is the largest member of the state's public university system and presents an array of academic, social, and professional opportunities for nearly 25,000 students from around the world. Perhaps better known to sports enthusiasts as a school with an outstanding football program, Alabama provides a very good education to its students and ranks among the nation's top public universities. Furthermore, the scope of the school allows students to pursue a great variety of research topics, thus making the academic experience at Alabama highly rewarding.

Programs for Everyone

Alabama has eight colleges that grant degrees to undergraduates: Arts and Sciences, Commerce and Business Administration, Communication and Information Sciences, College of Education, Engineering, Human Environmental Sciences, Nursing, and Social Work. Each school has its own charac-

teristics, but over the course of his or her stay at Alabama, each student is likely to have taken courses for two or more of those colleges to broaden the scope of study. At the same time, the presence of law and graduate schools also allows capable students to undertake the challenge of experiencing a few graduate courses, which can be valuable for all those aiming to be admitted to graduate programs after college. "We have so many interesting classes," said one student. "I wish I had more time to take them all."

The school has more than 200 fields of study, most of which are dedicated to undergraduate students. The majors range from the traditional liberal arts degrees that focus on providing students with a broad assortment of skills and the pre-professional curriculums, such as health care management, which helps train students for a specific career. As in many large-scale public universities, a large number of students are pre-professional, and students agree that the programs tend to be effective in providing transferable knowledge and skills to jobs. "I really like my program in design," said one student. "I think I learned a lot of practical things that will be definitely useful in the future."

Alabama is known for a program called New College. It is used to create an interdisciplinary approach to learning. Originally an independent college, it has since then been integrated into the College of Arts and Sciences. Students enrolled in New College work with a group of advising committees to create their best programs of study, which include a number of integrative seminars that aim to improve analytical and writing skills. At the same time, each student must design and complete a depth study, an independent research program used to ensure that the students are proficient in a specific field and capable of conducting projects without much guidance. Another option for those looking for a challenge is the Honors College, where students take small seminars and often have easier access to personal attention from faculty members.

Another advantage of attending Alabama is that it is one of the state's main research consortiums. It has over 30 different research centers and institutes, thus providing undergraduates with a large number of opportunities to enrich their experience either by conducting research there or simply working in the labs and facilities to learn more about the works of some of the nation's top academics.

For most students, the coursework is manageable. It certainly depends on the majors and professors. Some students, such as those in engineering, do feel that some of their classes can be very difficult and time-consuming. "Some of the introductory classes are used to weed out people who are not qualified enough," said one student. For the most part, however, students are able to complete their schoolwork and participate in a number of extracurricular activities or simply find part-time employment around campus.

According to *U.S. News and World Report*, Alabama is positioned within the 100 best universities in the country. It is also among the top 55 public institutions. This distinction also means that acceptance into the university does require some strong qualifications. "There are a lot of really smart people," said one student. "Some of them will just blow you away with their knowledge and intelligence." Clearly, for all those who are intellectually curious, Alabama provides a very good education for students.

Tuscaloosa

The university is also the engine of Tuscaloosa, a small city in central Alabama. The city has its share of retail stores, restaurants, and bars surrounding the university's campus. After all, with the large population of students, the school is at the center of the city's economy. Furthermore, Tuscaloosa is also considered a strong manufacturing base, attracting a large number of companies to establish factories and plants around the area. Nevertheless, the city does not have anything special to be particularly exciting for incoming students. "Tuscaloosa is pretty boring," said one student. "But this is such a big university that you can simply stay on campus and find all the activities you want."

All freshmen are required to live on campus. This helps students to become familiar with al the facilities offered by Alabama as well as meeting new people. At the same time, some students do believe that living on campus actually helps them focus on academics. The residential halls vary greatly, and there are both coeducational and single-sex buildings. "The dorms are decent, but nothing special," said one student. The dining services also offer a large array of options, and all freshmen must sign up for one of the Freshmen Year Experience plans, which encourage students to eat in dinning halls so that they can meet more people and become more involved within the campus. One of the popular dining locations is the Ferguson Center, which offers a large number of fast-food chains to satisfy students' cravings.

> "We have so many interesting classes. I wish I had more time to take them all."

Alabama has 56 fraternities and sororities, thus encompassing a large percentage of the student body. The Greek life is certainly important to organize the weekend activities, as well as the off-campus houses and apartments where many upperclassmen live after their first year. For some students who are not interested in the Greek life, there are also assortments of bars where students can socialize and relax during weekends.

Crimson Tide

The football program at Alabama was founded in 1892, making it one of the oldest in the country. The popularity of the football team, one of the most prestigious in the nation, can be best demonstrated by its stadium, which seats more than 90,000 fans. It is in fact one of the largest venues in the world. During the fall semester, football brings students together as an important social venue. The competition against in-state powerhouse Auburn is one of the most intense rivalries in collegiate sports, and many of Alabama's games are nationally televised, demonstrating the fervor of the students' support for their team.

For many people, the memory of George Wallace in 1963 standing at the university to prevent entrance of black students remains one of the darker periods of Alabama. Today, people of all ethnic groups are accepted into the university. Nevertheless, the minority student body remains small. The university, of course, is working to increase diversity, but it may take some time before it can greatly raise the percentage of minorities on campus. Nevertheless, students agree that the school has become very tolerant and sensitive to diversity issues. Given the strong academics and the great school spirit, Alabama should be a very good college choice for everyone.—*Xiaohang Liu*

FYI

What is the typical weekend schedule? "Parties start at nights. But make sure you get to the football games on time."

If I could change one thing about Alabama, I'd "get more parking spaces."

Three things every student at Alabama should do before graduating are "go to Iron Bowl, join a frat or sorority, and remember that four years can be really short."

University of South Alabama

Address: 307 University Boulevard, North Mobile, AL 36688-0002
Phone: 251 460-6101
E-mail address: admiss@usouthal.edu
Web site URL: www.southalabama.edu
Year Founded: 1963
Private or Public: Public
Religious Affiliation: None
Location: Suburban
Number of Applicants: 3,089
Percent Accepted: 88%
Percent Accepted who enroll: 53%
Number Entering: 1,457
Number of Transfers Accepted each Year: 1,750
Middle 50% SAT range: M: 460–580, CR: 440–570, Wr: Unreported
Middle 50% ACT range: 19–24
Early admission program EA/ED/None: None

Percentage accepted through EA or ED: NA
EA and ED deadline: NA
Regular Deadline: 10-Sep
Application Fee: $35
Full time Undergraduate enrollment: 10,690
Total enrollment: 13,500
Percent Male: 45%
Percent Female: 55%
Total Percent Minority or Unreported: 37%
Percent African-American: 24%
Percent Asian/Pacific Islander: 4%
Percent Hispanic: 2%
Percent Native-American: 1%
Percent International: 3%
Percent in-state/out of state: Unreported
Percent from Public HS: 92%
Retention Rate: 70%
Graduation Rate 4-year: 13%

Graduation Rate 6-year: 31%
Percent Undergraduates in On-campus housing: 16%
Number of official organized extracurricular organizations: 185
3 Most popular majors: Health Professions, Business/Marketing, Education
Student/Faculty ratio: 13:1
Average Class Size: Unreported
Percent of students going to grad school: Unreported
Tuition and Fees: $9,922
In-State Tuition and Fees if different: $5,512
Cost for Room and Board: $5,308
Percent receiving financial aid out of those who apply, first year: Unreported
Percent receiving financial aid among all students: Unreported

Located in Mobile, Alabama, the University of South Alabama—"USA" or "South" to students—combines the conservative hospitality of the South with the warm sunny climate of the Gulf Coast. Mobile itself is a historic port city and boasts wildlife-rich deltas and estuaries, antebellum homes with hanging Spanish moss, its own popular Mardi Gras celebration and of course, 21 golf courses and a variety of nearby beaches. The University, located in the heart of the city, caters to both traditional and nontraditional students alike and offers a variety of degree options for adults of any age returning to earn their bachelors' degrees.

Academics: Something for Everyone

The University of South Alabama offers a variety of special programs to accommodate the diverse groups that comprise its student body. Those maintaining at least a 3.5 GPA in high school can apply for the university Honors Program, which includes participation in small honors seminars and the completion of an Honors Senior Project. Each honor student is assigned a faculty mentor from the department of his or her major; these mentors offer advice on everything from course selection to future careers within the field, and both mentor and student participate in group community service projects. New students jump into college life through USA's First Year Experience Program, in which all freshmen living in the dorms are required to participate. The program includes a mandatory freshman seminar designed to teach "effective study skills, exam preparation, college level research skills, writing effectively and student health issues," among other topics, as well as providing tutors, a campus meal plan, and access to student RAs who can offer advice and counsel about campus life. In addition, many USA courses in a variety of disciplines are offered online, allowing students to attend class from home and submit homework in their pajamas.

A branch campus of the University in Fairhope, Alabama, located in Baldwin County—USABC—also offers undergraduate, graduate, and nondegree courses and opportunities for public service involvement for students who, for a variety of reasons, might prefer a different location. This branch campus primarily supports undergraduate majors in business, both elementary and secondary education, nursing and adult interdisciplinary studies. USABC is not a residential campus—students enrolling here generally commute from their homes in Baldwin County—and boasts its own computer lab and performance center but shares the libraries and other research resources

with the main University campus across Mobile Bay.

> "The university, located in the heart of the city, caters to both traditional and nontraditional students alike."

All students must fulfill the core curriculum before graduation, which requires taking several courses in each of the major academic disciplines—humanities and fine arts; natural sciences and mathematics; and history, social and behavioral sciences—as well as two classes in written composition. South is divided into nine different colleges encompassing a variety of fields of study. Those related to healthcare—the Colleges of Medicine, Nursing and Allied Health Professions—are considered to be particularly strong and rigorous. The joint BS/MS degree programs in these majors are popular, but to gain admission, students must have GPAs in the 3.8 range and apply during their junior year.

BYOB

South's architecture is fairly nondescript like many college campuses built in the late twentieth century. One student described it as "nothing fancy . . . built to last, not to look pretty." Few students live in the dorms all four years, but for those who do, it can be a rewarding experience and provide the opportunity to meet many new friends quickly. "Living in dorms is a terrific way to meet people," enthused one junior. "Most of the people I hang out with now I met freshman year in dorms." The residence halls offer various rooming options in the form of suites and apartments; for first-time students, the most popular options are the Epsilon and Delta two-person suites with private baths. All students living on campus are required to purchase a meal plan, but limited weekend operating hours for the on-campus eateries can reportedly cause frustration. USA also offers married students housing in the form of unfurnished single-family houses in the neighborhood of Hillsdale Heights.

Most of South's 11,400 undergraduate students come from nearby cities and towns in Alabama, making the University primarily a commuter school in which much of the student body drives to class every day. Many clubs, for example, hold meetings in the afternoons to accommodate members who

Alabama

13

leave campus in the evening. Because of this, the campus activities and night life can be somewhat lacking; as one student complained, "there is no campus life at South!" However, the University is taking steps to correct this problem, and programs such as the Freshman Year Experience help new students to make friends and connections. The RAs in each dorm occasionally sponsor activities to foster a community spirit, and interested students can join intramural sports and other organizations to stay involved.

The social scene that does exist at USA revolves around the Greek system, and most events that take place on campus are sponsored by one of the college's 19 fraternities and sororities. Although total membership is not huge, the Greeks have a strong presence on campus, due mainly to their widespread involvement in other clubs and organizations. Because South's campus is officially dry (although, as one student put it, this is true "in name only"), the frats do not usually supply alcohol at their parties, so Greek and non-Greek partiers alike are encouraged to bring their own beverages.

The Jaguar Life

The University recently approved the addition of a football team to the school's athletic offerings; it is scheduled to start play in the fall of 2013. In the past, many students have lamented the lack of school spirit that results from not having a football team. In the sport's absence, the crowd-pleasing sports to watch are men's and women's varsity basketball; die-hard Jaguar fans can also watch these games live via Internet streaming. Students can also indulge their competitive sides in an assortment of intramural sports based out of USA's state-of-the-art Intramural Field Complex, including inner tube water polo, soccer, flag football, basketball, volleyball, and softball. The Student Recreation Center is home to two basketball courts, a weight-lifting room, a track and a game room containing table tennis and a pool table as well as free SouthFit aerobics and dance classes. The University has also recently announced plans to build a brand-new recreation center with additional facilities.

South also boasts a sizeable Student Center that hosts lounge areas, a computer lab, office space for student groups, a big-screen TV, a variety of small eateries located in the Market area, and a large ball room that can be reserved for student use. Jaguar Productions, the Student Activities Board, meets here as well, and provides a relatively popular way for students to become involved with the university and help to plan campuswide concerts, film screenings, lectures, vacation trips, and more. Over 200 clubs and organizations also offer a chance to meet fellow students and include everything from pre-professional organizations to groups for sports, music, meteorology, and video gaming enthusiasts. Jag TV, USA's student-run television station, is broadcast in all of the residence halls and other buildings throughout the campus.

The University of South Alabama offers numerous benefits to its many students, from its location in the welcoming Deep South city of Mobile to its variety of special degree and enrichment programs. Non-traditional students especially find its continuing education programs to be accommodating and flexible, while those living in the residential dorms appreciate the social atmosphere and the friendly RAs. The University's shortcomings, most notably a lack of school spirit, can be overcome through a determination to stay involved, and South's recent efforts to this end have made strides in improving the sense of community.—*Kristin Knox*

FYI
If you come to USA, you better bring "a desire to get involved and make the most of the college experience."
What is the typical weekend schedule? "Go to a frat party at night, catch up on work during the day."
If I could change one thing about USA, it would be "the lack of a football team."
Three things every student at USA should do before graduating are "play oozeball (volleyball in a knee-deep mud pit), go to an event in the Mitchell Center, and take advantage of the fine-arts offerings."

Alaska

University of Alaska/Fairbanks

Address: PO Box 757480
Fairbanks, AK 99775-7480
Phone: 907-474-7500
E-mail address:
admissions@uaf.edu
Web site URL: www.uaf.edu
Year Founded: 1917
Private or Public: Public
Religious Affiliation: None
Location: Suburban
Number of Applicants:
1,758
Percent Accepted: 78%
Percent Accepted who
enroll: 58%
Number Entering: 793
Number of Transfers
Accepted each Year: 667
Middle 50% SAT range:
M: 450–590, CR:
450–600, Wr: Unreported
Middle 50% ACT range:
18–25
Early admission program
EA/ED/None: None

Percentage accepted
through EA or ED: NA
EA and ED deadline: NA
Regular Deadline: 1-Aug
Application Fee: $40
Full time Undergraduate
enrollment: 7,568
Total enrollment: 8,627
Percent Male: 42%
Percent Female: 58%
Total Percent Minority or
Unreported: 40%
Percent African-American:
3%
Percent Asian/Pacific
Islander: 3%
Percent Hispanic: 3%
Percent Native-American:
20.0%
Percent International: 2%
Percent in-state/out of
state: 87%/13%
Percent from Public HS:
Unreported
Retention Rate: 74%

Graduation Rate 4-year: 8%
Graduation Rate 6-year: 30%
Percent Undergraduates in
On-campus housing: 31%
Number of official organized
extracurricular
organizations: 93
3 Most popular majors:
Biology, Business,
Psychology
Student/Faculty ratio: 10:1
Average Class Size: 16
Percent of students going to
grad school: Unreported
Tuition and Fees: $14,248
In-State Tuition and Fees if
different: $4,828
Cost for Room and Board:
$7,190
Percent receiving financial
aid out of those who apply,
first year: 44%
Percent receiving financial
aid among all students:
55%

Originating as a federal Agricultural and Forestry Experiment Station in the northernmost frontier of the United States, the University of Alaska at Fairbanks today continues its legacy of cutting-edge research in a unique arctic environment. Through the gradual accumulation of government grants and support, Alaska's largest university has developed into an institution that prides itself on its ability to teach specialized skills to students in a very distinctive setting.

Scientific Significance
Since its founding in 1917, the University of Alaska at Fairbanks has acquired an array of resources from the government in order to further its progress in the world of research. After its humble beginnings as a land-grant institute, UAF eventually gained sea-grant and space-grant status—signs of the importance of its scientific polar research. Additionally, its unique location in the middle of Alaska led Congress in 1948 to establish the Geophysical Institute, which is renowned for its studies of the geological world in polar regions and which also maintains the Poker Flat Research Range, the world's largest land-based rocket range. Indeed, for the brave souls that can withstand the bitterly cold winters in this harsh arctic tundra, UAF provides excellent opportunities for students to interact with the exceptional environment surrounding them.

Arctic Adventures
One of the main factors that differentiates UAF from other schools is its setting just 200 miles south of the Arctic Circle. UAF does not joke when it boasts about its "360-

million-acre classroom." Many of the majors that are offered make use of the University's vast environmental resources: Geophysics majors may find themselves measuring tectonic plate motions in Denali National Park; Oceanography majors might conduct research on the R/V *Alpha Helix*, one of the Seward Marine Center's research vessels; a Natural Resources Management student could end up developing and promoting Alaska's reindeer industry—the list goes on. Above this, one of the most unique opportunities students have is the ability to work right alongside the world's brightest scientists at any of the top-notch research institutes that call UAF home. In fact, many professors are "from all over the country, including Ivy League schools, since the research here is not available in science programs elsewhere."

The educational route that students take is in large part framed by the Baccalaureate Core, which requires a range of credits in six different areas: communication, perspectives on the human condition, mathematics, natural sciences, library and information research, and upper-division communication. Although most students agree that the Core provides the foundation upon which students begin to build their knowledge, some find it a little bit strict (38–39 core credits are needed). The classes can get quite large, and sometimes it is hard to get into your first-choice course. In the end, though, UAF's eight schools and colleges—Engineering and Mines, Liberal Arts, Natural Science and Mathematics, Rural and Community Development, Education, Fisheries and Ocean Sciences, Management, Natural Resources and Agricultural Sciences—still manage to provide flexibility by covering a broad spectrum of fields, offering 167 degrees and 28 certificates in over 122 disciplines. The professors will assist students "as long as you communicate with them one on one."

All Bundled Up

The most obvious shared trait evident amongst the student body is their similar taste in fashion: everyone wears winter hats, scarves, and jackets. Although one student opined that the culture is "very bad because we're always late to get all the latest trends in clothing and music," another countered that at least all the students have the latest in winter-weather clothing. The typical student can be as variable as the arctic weather. On one hand, there are a handful of traditional party-types, who scour the campus for the

liveliest events. One student believes that "because it is dark most of the winter, a lot of people drink more than usual." On the other hand, "a lot of people [at UAF] do not drink—but instead are outdoorsy and down-to-earth." The drinking that does occur usually takes place in the many student apartments on campus. Freshmen are required to live in dorms for their first year.

> "The characteristic student can be as variable as the arctic weather."

Though UAF was founded in the 20th century, it already has a number of traditions that continue their legacy each year. "Starvation Gulch," started in 1923 by the founding president, Charles Bunnell, involves a ceremony with the building of very large bonfires—"some of the piles the size of a small house"—that signify the "passing of knowledge" from upperclassmen to the incoming freshmen. Many campus groups fight over the possession and control of the "Tradition Stone," a block of concrete with a sign that was placed on a pile of beer bottles in defiance of an alcohol ban instituted in the 50s.

Close-knit Community

Though many of the campus buildings may be aesthetically unappealing, one student quaintly characterizes the campus as "90s meets Gotham." Filled with a mix of "square/blah" and more-modern buildings, the tight layout of the campus—one student posits that it might be to "increase the 'warmth' of the community"—contains a number of wonderful structures. The Elmer E. Rasmuson Library now holds more than 1.75 million volumes and contains a specialized collection of "Alaska and Polar Regions" materials. The Wood Campus Center, created "as a solution to cabin fever," serves as the center of the student community. Housing a ballroom, adjoining conference rooms, an eight-lane bowling alley ("Polar Alley"), and a number of eateries, the facility is frequented by many students. Pizza Piazza, in particular, is a popular hangout spot for students. Additionally, the Upper Campus views of the stunning Brooks Mountain Range more than make up for any lack of architectural beauty.

Polar Pastimes

Though the thermometer can hit extremely low readings during the winter, students try to take advantage of what they can. Within heated buildings, the Alaska Gravity Works juggling club spends time "throwing things in the air and periodically letting them hit the ground." The Space and Robotics clubs cater toward the many students that have a passion for science. Students can also participate in a video game tournament sponsored by the VICE Club. In the great Alaskan outdoors, students take advantage of the ski slopes and trails, which the University Trails Club maintains.

Athletes make the most of the fairly limited varsity-level athletic offerings. The UAF "Nanooks" (polar bears) have had particular success in cold-weather sports such as skiing and hockey. Even the more traditional basketball team has had its successes: it won the Division I Top of the World Classic in 2002. Alone in national prominence, however, is the Nanook rifle team, which dominates the national circuit with 10 NCAA titles in the past 15 years. As a testament to the team's success, UAF hosted the 2007 NCAA Championships for the first time ever. Most students, however, rally around the hockey team as they compete each season. Of course, for those looking for a more leisurely experience, the UAF intramurals program offers 19 sports ranging from two-person volleyball to hoop shooting to the IM classic, broomball.

Northern Nuance

The single-most important factor that UAF students emphasize is Alaska's beautiful arctic landscape and natural resources. With gorgeous summer days filled with 24 hours of sunshine, and winter nights dazzled by the flashing of the Aurora Borealis in the sky, UAF's setting in rural Alaska provides its students with an outstanding learning environment. The biggest complaint one might have of the University of Alaska at Fairbanks, however, is the extreme cold and harsh winters. At times, the thermometer readings can hit as low as −65. But as one student declared, "Don't let that scare you out of the experience, because it's sure to be one you'll never forget." Indeed, UAF students take the climate in stride; it is a testament to the hearty character of the student body that you can always find a scantily clad student posing alongside a time/temperature sign that flashes 40 below zero.—*Wookie Kim*

FYI
If you come to UAF, you'd better bring "lots of entertainment and no clothing; the only quality winter clothes are sold here."
What's the typical weekend schedule? "Each night starts out with calling or MySpacing friends to see where the parties are. Bowling, sledding, bonfires, cabin parties, clubbing, concerts, drag shows . . ."
If I could change one thing about UAF, I'd "make it less cold!"
Three things every student at the University of Alaska at Fairbanks should do before graduating are "sled at midnight under the Northern Lights, eat moose meat, and join the 40-below club."

Arizona

Arizona State University

Address: PO Box 870112
Tempe, AZ 85287
Phone: 480-965-7788
E-mail address:
admissions@asu.edu
Web site URL: www.asu.edu
Year Founded: 1885
Private or Public: Public
Religious Affiliation: None
Location: Suburban
Number of Applicants:
27,089
Percent Accepted: 95%
**Percent Accepted who
enroll:** 35%
Number Entering: 8,458
**Number of Transfers
Accepted each Year:**
5,258
Middle 50% SAT range:
M: 480–610, CR:
470–600, Wr:** Unreported
Middle 50% ACT range:
20–26
**Early admission program
EA/ED/None:** None

**Percentage accepted
through EA or ED:** NA
EA and ED deadline: NA
Regular Deadline: Rolling
Application Fee: $25
**Full time Undergraduate
enrollment:** 53,298
Total enrollment: 65,804
Percent Male: 48%
Percent Female: 52%
**Total Percent Minority or
Unreported:** 35%
Percent African-American:
5%
**Percent Asian/Pacific
Islander:** 6%
Percent Hispanic: 15%
Percent Native-American:
2%
Percent International: 2%
**Percent in-state/out of
state:** 78%/22%
Percent from Public HS:
Unreported
Retention Rate: 80%
Graduation Rate 4-year: 29%

Graduation Rate 6-year:
54%
**Percent Undergraduates
in On-campus housing:**
78%
**Number of official organized
extracurricular
organizations:** 512
3 Most popular majors:
Journalism, Multidisciplinary
Studies, Psychology
Student/Faculty ratio: 22:1
Average Class Size: 15
**Percent of students going to
grad school:** Unreported
Tuition and Fees: $17,949
**In-State Tuition and Fees if
different:** $5,661
Cost for Room and Board:
$8,790
**Percent receiving financial
aid out of those who apply,
first year:** 70%
**Percent receiving financial
aid among all students:**
66%

Located in Phoenix, Arizona, the nation's fifth largest city, Arizona State University (ASU) educates more than 67,000 students on four differentiated campuses. These four campuses are unified by their goal being centers for academic excellence and innovative research. Under the leadership of one of *Time* magazine's "10 Best College Presidents," Michael Crow, ASU has been shedding its reputation as of one of America's top party schools and evolving into a research institution that attracts a diverse, motivated student body. The students are responding positively towards the change. As one student states, "I'd like to change the stereotype/reputation that ASU has maintained over the years designating it *only* as a party school with low education standards." While the "play hard"

culture at ASU is still an option to those who desire it, Arizona State is moving toward an environment that is lauded for its advances in academia rather than a university defined by the popularity of weekend parties.

Study like a Sun Devil

Within the undergraduate degree program, ASU offers over 250 academic majors on its four campuses: Downtown Phoenix, Polytechnic, Tempe, and West campus. According to one student, "There's such a wealth of opportunities available because we are so large. Anything you want to do, you can do it at Arizona State. Any major, any organization, any research project, any study abroad program—literally anything, you can make it happen here."

Students declare a major when they apply

and are admitted to one of the fifteen different schools. The largest schools are the College of Liberal Arts and Sciences and the W.P. Carey School of Business. Professor Edward Prescott, the 2004 Nobel Prize winner in Economic Sciences, teaches classes at the business school while the former executive editor of the *Washington Post*, Professor Len Downie, educates students at the Walter Cronkite School of Journalism and Mass Communication. Students studying at the renowned Cronkite School receive valuable hands-on experience through numerous internship opportunities in the nation's 12th largest media market. This school is located at the new Downtown Phoenix Campus and is easily accessible by the recently constructed Light Rail.

Barrett, the Honors College at ASU, enjoys the reputation of being one of the nation's premier undergraduate honors colleges. Barrett students live in a 130-million-dollar residential community that was opened in fall of 2009. Students seem to love the ability to experience the small college feel in Barrett while still being able to enjoy the resources and athletic programs of a large university. A well-liked Honors class is Human Event. A mandatory freshman course for honors students, this class focuses on "tracing the written word from the beginning to the present day across various cultures and disciplines."

Of the 277 different academic fields, "marketing, political science, communication, business, sustainability (ASU's School of Sustainability is the first degree-granting institution of sustainability in the entire country), and journalism" are some of the most popular majors at ASU. With all of these options, students agree that it is "not really" difficult to enroll in classes at Arizona State, especially given the fact that most classes are "huge." According to one student, "Some classes that have a famous professor or a class that pertains to a special topic may fill up fast, but there is usually a variety of class sections offered." Popular classes at ASU include Professor Matt McCarthy's Computer Applications and Information Technology course and Professor David Capco's Biology and Chinese Medicine course. Another student raves, "American Political Thought and Political Ideologies were the most fun classes for me personally because I'm a political science major!"

Arizona State University has attracted a wide array of prominent visitors in the past few years. As one student states, "Because we are such a large campus, we always have great speakers and cultural events happening. We have dozens of off-Broadway shows and famous symphonies." ASU also hosts a wide variety of guest lecturers. According to one Sun Devil, "In the last few years, we've had dozens of famous people make stops here—Nancy Pelosi, Jonathan Alter, Bill Clinton, Al Gore, and Ron Paul. President Barack Obama has visited ASU numerous times, most recently when he was our commencement speaker." Additionally, Professor Donald Johanson, the founder of the Institute of Human Origins at Arizona State who found the skeleton known as "Lucy," has given talks about his discovery.

Social Life of Sun Devils

Students at ASU love their university's size. Making friends is easy because "there is ALWAYS something going on around campus and friendly faces everywhere." As one Sun Devil states, "I don't think there's any bad part about going to a school [ASU's] size because it's easy to find smaller communities and to make connections with other students and professors."

> "Any major, any organization, any research project, any study abroad program—literally anything—you can make it happen here."

On the weekend, students enjoy hanging out with their friends at parties hosted by the different Greek houses. According to one student, Greeks comprise a "small percentage of the population but are a very visible and active one, so they have a dominant presence on campus. Greeks have such a large presence on campus because they're usually always doing some sort of community service, holding leadership positions in other organizations, and making themselves visible. It's different than at other schools because most chapters have untraditional housing (no sorority houses, just dormlike housing)." About "nine percent" of the undergraduates are in fraternities or sororities. According to one student, "Recruitment for ASU's 13 pan Hellenic sororities and rush for ASU's 22 fraternities begins around Labor Day. Spring rush is only for fraternities and some houses."

For those who want to escape the Greek scene, students can spend time on Mill Avenue during the weekends. Sun Devils also flock to Tempe Marketplace. Both are popular spots for nightlife, shopping, and dining. Another popular destination is Old Towne Scottsdale, which contains shopping, entertainment, arts, and dining attractions. Many students have cars, although Sun Devils agree that parking is difficult and often expensive. Students love the ability to take road trips, and many travel to Las Vegas, California, or Mexico during their four years as an ASU student.

At Arizona State, "most students live on campus their freshman year and then live off campus." Students agree that it is not really difficult to find housing. As one student described it, "Housing at ASU is solid." Students rave about the new residence halls, especially the new Honors complex designed exclusively for honors students to live in throughout their junior and senior years. According to one Sun Devil, "It's changing the way students live on campus."

If students live on campus, they are required to be on a meal plan. Students at ASU find that the dining hall options are good. However, there are complaints about the cost of meal plans and the dining hall hours. One student states, "The quality is ok, but the variety gets old fast."

Sun Devil Spirit

ASU students have a wide variety of ways to become involved in campus life. The oldest student organization on campus is Devils' Advocates, a group of students who talk to high school students about the opportunities and benefits of attending ASU. Other prominent groups on campus include the Undergraduate Student Government, the Resident Hall Association, and the Programming and Activities Board. The Greek community and the Sports Club Association also attract a sizeable number of students.

When students at Arizona State are asked about what sets their university apart from other schools, they generally reply with the three Ss: "size, social scene, and sports." Sun Devils love being a part of the Pac-10.

Although one student laments, "If I could change one thing about ASU, we would have a better football team."

School spirit runs high during the "Duel in the Desert." Since 1899, Arizona State and the University of Arizona have been battling it out on the football field the Saturday after Thanksgiving. During this time, students at ASU participate in Lantern Walk, the school's oldest tradition. At this homecoming event, "thousands of students take lighted candles and walk up to the "A" mountain (a mountain with the big gold A on it)." The ceremony is accompanied by a big pep rally. Other fun traditions at ASU include: Oozeball—a campus wide mud volleyball tournament, Undie Run—a tradition where students take off their clothes, donate them to charity, and run around campus half naked to celebrate the end of classes, and the whitewashing "A" Mountain—a part of Freshman Orientation when the newest class of Sun Devils hikes to the mountain and whitewashes the coveted letter gold to ring in the new school year.

Without a doubt, Sun Devils love their school. According to one student, "I love that ASU was founded by the people of Arizona—we were literally established by a ballot initiative. I think that fuels our desire to be the best public university. We were established by the citizens of Arizona, and we open our doors to people who want to learn." Students truly feel like ASU is setting the standards for any public educational institution. Even though the university can be characterized as "fast-moving and untraditional," students appreciate the culture at ASU. As one Sun Devil states, "The culture really differentiates our school from others. Administration, students, and faculty are pretty laid back relative to traditional schools on the East Coast." Students truly love studying under the bright Arizona sun, and they appreciate the new direction their institution has taken. "There are so many new and innovative ideas coming out of ASU. I think that we are constantly growing and achieving, and we are not slowing down."—*Alexa Sassin*

FYI

If you come to ASU you'd better bring: "sunscreen, maroon and gold, and flip flops."

What's the typical weekend schedule: "People begin going out Thursday evenings. Students typically visit the different house and frat parties. Class fills up Friday afternoons until the evening when the partying picks up again. Saturdays are spent at the pool or an ASU athletic event, followed by a night on Mill Avenue. On Sundays, students spend the day catching up on homework."

If I could change one thing about ASU I would: "have it by the beach."

Three things a student should do before graduating: "Climb "A" mountain, Attend Sigma Chi's Hallowrave party, Have a meal at the Chuckbox."

University of Arizona

Address: PO Box 210040
Tucson, AZ 85721-0040
Phone: 520-621-3237
E-mail address:
appinfo@arizona.edu
Web site URL:
www.arizona.edu
Year Founded: 1885
Private or Public: Public
Religious Affiliation: None
Location: Urban
Number of Applicants:
25,449
Percent Accepted: 77%
**Percent Accepted who
enroll:** 43%
Number Entering: 8,426
**Number of Transfers
Accepted each Year:** 2,846
Middle 50% SAT range:
M: 500–630, CR:
490–600, Wr: Unreported
Middle 50% ACT range:
20–26
**Early admission program
EA/ED/None:** None

**Percentage accepted
through EA or ED:** NA
EA and ED deadline: NA
Regular Deadline: 1-May
Application Fee: $50
**Full time Undergraduate
enrollment:** 29,070
Total enrollment: 35,940
Percent Male: 46%
Percent Female: 54%
**Total Percent Minority or
Unreported:** 32%
Percent African-American:
3%
**Percent Asian/Pacific
Islander:** 6%
Percent Hispanic: 17%
Percent Native-American:
4%
Percent International: 3%
**Percent in-state/out of
state:** 69%/31%
Percent from Public HS:
90%
Retention Rate: 80%
Graduation Rate 4-year: 57%

Graduation Rate 6-year:
Unreported
**Percent Undergraduates in
On-campus housing:** 20%
**Number of official organized
extracurricular
organizations:** 504
3 Most popular majors:
Cellular and Molecular
Biology, Political Science and
Government, Psychology
Student/Faculty ratio: 18:1
Average Class Size: 15
**Percent of students going to
grad school:** 42%
Tuition and Fees: $16,058
**In-State Tuition and Fees if
different:** $4,824
Cost for Room and Board:
$7,812
**Percent receiving financial
aid out of those who apply,
first year:** 60%
**Percent receiving financial
aid among all students:**
35%

The University of Arizona Wildcats spend their four years living the ideal of "fun in the sun." Located in the desert oasis of Tucson, Arizona (an hour from the Mexican border), students bask in 300 days of sunshine as they scurry between sporting events and classes. Quality academics and a large student body provide for nearly every degree and extracurricular interest.

If You Want It, You Got It

A student would be hard pressed to find something he or she didn't love among the more than 150 undergraduate degree programs offered at Arizona. Majors like accounting and theatre arts provide a mere glimpse at the incredible variety of academic options available to Wildcats. Taming the freedom of the student body is the notorious "Gen. Ed." requirement. Gen. Ed. is made up of three tiers of classes, including Traditions and Cultures, Individuals and Societies, and the feared Natural Sciences. Gen. Ed. classes can be annoying and packed with 150 to 300 students, but students say that they fulfill the requirements with minimal discomfort.

Psychology, communications, political science and government, and cellular and molecular biology are the most popular majors. Students wishing to take a more rigorous academic route subscribe to the engineering department's five-year program. One student warned, however, that "as a general rule it seems that all of the hard science classes and engineering courses are the toughest on campus."

Arizona boasts one of the nation's top business schools, the Eller College of Management. One student proudly stated, "The Eller School is one of the most well-known departments in the country and is perennially one of the top business schools in the country." Brainy Wildcats enjoy a special Honors College that demands no lower than a 3.5 GPA. Competition for admission is fierce, but the select few enjoy smaller classes, a support structure of 90 advisors and 11 staff members, private residence halls, and $40,000 annually for student research projects. Although for the majority of Wildcats the classes can be large and the student-teacher ratio overwhelming, students agree that, "grading is done fairly and the professors are always willing to listen if you have a question."

Going Greek

Outside of the classroom, most Wildcats spend time at the restaurants and bars located on University and Fourth Avenue. Students report that they value their fake IDs, but those without still have ample opportunity for underage drinking at Tucson house parties and along Frat Row.

Arizona administrators can be tough, however, on those caught drinking, as one student revealed. "There is no tolerance for underage drinking on campus, and if caught there is a mandatory program that all students must attend." Worse still is the Red Tag Policy, which declares that for six months post party-breakup students must hang a red tag in the window and limit visitors to the number of housemates. Luckily, students report that "the Student Senate is currently trying to amend the situation" and Wildcats have plenty of opportunities for good clean fun.

Greek life is "the dominant social scene on campus," consisting of 50 sororities and fraternities. Undergrad Greeks agree that Arizona Greek life offers members a support system, a community service group, and a post-grad network system, not to mention a full calendar of mixers and socials. Nearly 1,500 men and women rush, and getting a bid can be stressful. Yet, as one sorority girl advised, "Don't worry about everything. If it's right, it will happen."

Where'd Everybody Go?

With all that sunshine, students freely frolic about the entire campus. But the most popular spot is the student union. "The union is the main place people go if they have time. There are restaurants and rooms for people to sit and study or sleep." The newly built Student Union Memorial Center on the west side of campus is a $60-million-dollar, 450,000-square-feet structure, with amenities including a bookstore, a post office, and even an arcade. Although everyone frequents the unions, University Drive, "a street right next to campus with restaurants, bars and shopping," is another hot spot for student activity. The campus is safe and full of friendly Wildcats, but students are warned to retain common sense as they travel around.

Dorms at Arizona vary significantly from "some really nice ones to some really bad dorms." The housing system offers students coed dorms, women-only dorms, sorority and fraternity housing, apartments for single students, special housing for disabled students, and even special housing for international students. For the adventurous, the Coronado dorm is "the biggest dorm on campus and every year it leads all the other dorms in evictions." The RAs at Arizona are described as "cool." "Their major role," one student explained, "is to make sure nothing horrible happens . . . and they usually organize activities to let everyone get to know each other."

Although the insides of dorms vary, students report that the architecture is exactly the same: "everywhere you go, brick red buildings, everywhere." The most famous building on campus is the Old Main, built upon the University's founding in 1885. But one student noted that, "there is always construction of some kind on campus and new buildings are always popping up," leaving hope for a campus mini-makeover in the near future.

In terms of food, students can choose from a variety of meal plans offering fast food and restaurant fare. When describing student union food, one student reported that, "there are several different meal plans to choose from, but the food generally stinks." In response to whether the dining hall is better or worse than other schools, a student offered, "There is only one. So there isn't much choice in the matter."

> "A big city, Tucson can still be looked at as a college town."

Perhaps the bad dining is the reason "there is a huge off-campus life." "The majority of upper classmen live in the neighborhoods surrounding campus," one student explained. Whatever the reason, students are well received by the nearby towns. "The University is one of the largest employers in town, and it seems that the population supports the university as much as it can. . . . A big city, Tucson can still be looked at as a college town."

Wildcat Fever

Sports rule at the University of Arizona, and basketball is king. One student reported that, "Yesterday, there was a basketball game against North Carolina. The game started at 11, and there were students lining up at 10 the night before to get in." But all those denied basketball tickets have football, baseball and softball games, not to mention numerous intramurals, to attend. Wildcats are an active bunch, so if they're not outside enjoying the sun, they're sweating it out at the student recreation center, which one student said is "nice, but it is always packed." In true Arizona fashion, plans to expand the popular rec center are already in progress.

The University of Arizona offers every student opportunities for academics, extracurricular activities, and socializing. School spirit permeates every aspect of life—school pride, sports, student organizations and popular events like Spring Fling and Homecoming make life at Arizona unforgettable. With so much to offer, a wise Wildcat advised, "Make the most of your time here." —*Eliza Crawford*

FYI
If you come to Arizona, you'd better bring "suntan lotion."
What is the typical weekend schedule? "Friday nights you usually go out [and party], Saturdays are sporting events and more partying, and Sundays are usually recovery days [when] you get all your work for the week done."
If I could change one thing about Arizona, I'd "lower the faculty to student ratio; some of the lower-level class sizes are pretty big."
Three things every student at Arizona should do before graduating are "attend a Wildcat basketball game, sunbathe in January, make the most of your time here."

Arkansas

Hendrix College

Address: 1600 Washington Avenue, Conway, AR 72032
Phone: 501-450-1362
E-mail address: adm@hendrix.edu
Web site URL: www.hendrix.edu
Year Founded: 1876
Private or Public: Private
Religious Affiliation: Methodist
Location: Rural
Number of Applicants: 1,420
Percent Accepted: 94%
Percent Accepted who enroll: 32%
Number Entering: 433
Number of Transfers Accepted each Year: 41
Middle 50% SAT range: M: 550–660, CR: 580–690, Wr: Unreported
Middle 50% ACT range: 25–31
Early admission program EA/ED/None: None

Percentage accepted through EA or ED: NA
EA and ED deadline: NA
Regular Deadline: 1-Jun
Application Fee: $40
Full time Undergraduate enrollment: 1,342
Total enrollment: 1,342
Percent Male: 45%
Percent Female: 55%
Total Percent Minority or Unreported: 6%
Percent African-American: 4%
Percent Asian/Pacific Islander: 3%
Percent Hispanic: 4%
Percent Native-American: <1%
Percent International: 2%
Percent in-state/out of state: 49%/51%
Percent from Public HS: 71%
Retention Rate: 85%
Graduation Rate 4-year: 62%

Graduation Rate 6-year: 68%
Percent Undergraduates in On-campus housing: 84%
Number of official organized extracurricular organizations: 80
3 Most popular majors: Biology/Biological Sciences, General English Language and Literature, General Psychology
Student/Faculty ratio: 12:1
Average Class Size: 18
Percent of students going to grad school: 92%
Tuition and Fees: $25,780
In-State Tuition and Fees if different: No difference
Cost for Room and Board: $7,950
Percent receiving financial aid out of those who apply, first year: 100%
Percent receiving financial aid among all students: 100%

Located in Conway, Arkansas, Hendrix College is a tiny, Methodist-affiliated liberal arts school with an openly liberal student body. Yet despite the elitism you might expect at an "oasis of liberalism" in the middle of conservative Arkansas, Hendrix is a down-to-earth college where "the atmosphere is just awesome, and the people are so friendly." Don't pass over this Southern school without a closer look—the outstanding academics and intimate size make Hendrix a perfect fit for many.

Journeys and Explorations

Universally, students are delighted with the quality of Hendrix academics, the hallmark of which is the faculty-student interaction permitted by its small student body (about 1,350 undergraduates and no graduate school). "The academic life," one sophomore said, "is by far my favorite aspect of Hendrix. I'm a pretty big fan of the faculty. I haven't had a bad teacher yet, and I've had some amazing ones."

A small college, of course, means that there are fewer majors available (31) and fewer course options. Yet students are satisfied with the trade-off, reporting that their classes are intimate (the average class size being 17) and they know their professors well. One sophomore said that her classes have been evenly split between lectures and seminars, but that even her lectures are no larger than 30 students. In all classes, active student participation is emphasized. "One of the things I've noticed about my classes," a freshman said, "is that there's a lot more open discussion than in what most people would consider a college environment."

Though there are no noticeably weak academic programs here, Hendrix's strong suits are traditional fields such as English, politics, and biology, with pre-med being a popular choice. Hendrix has many core requirements that it believes constitute a broad liberal arts education. But as one sophomore said, "While a lot of students at other schools dread core requirements, students often have fun here taking core classes no matter how unrelated to their major they are. I'm currently in a natural history lab where we take fun field trips to forests." Plus, because the school is so small, many upper-level courses are available to freshmen and sophomores.

Hendrix places heavy emphasis on integrating freshmen into the social and academic life of the college immediately upon arrival. A mandatory course for all freshmen, "Journeys," introduces students to important works by Plato, Confucius and other philosophers all in one year. Less popular is the required orientation "Explorations," which focuses on introducing freshmen to the campus by creating small groups led by a faculty member and a sophomore guide.

The college welcomes freshmen to Hendrix life in more ways than just academics. Every student participates in an orientation trip before even arriving on campus; one freshman described his trip up to the Buffalo River, where his group went canoeing for two days with upperclassmen, who "kind of showed us the ropes." Indeed, because Hendrix is so small, college life thrives on interaction between upperclassmen and freshmen.

"Hippies and Gays"?

One junior described a "weird kind of dual stereotype" about the Hendrix student body. On the one hand, he said, Hendrix is the most academically challenging school in the state and the object of many Arkansans' aspirations, but on the other, "there is the image of Hendrix as an out-of-control party school with hippies and gays running rampant." Students say neither stereotype is truly accurate, though they do agree that many diverse opinions and beliefs are expressed openly on the Hendrix campus.

The school's Methodist background and religious life play an important part in many students' lives at Hendrix. One freshman described "countless religious groups at Hendrix, lots of Catholics and other religions who have their organizations on campus." And though political leanings here are "predominantly liberal," one student assures that "you'll find your conservatives and socialists and other groups there too."

Still, there isn't much geographic diversity, and students who are from out-of-state sometimes find themselves isolated. "There's a lot of southerners, a fair amount from Little Rock and Arkansas," a sophomore said. "All the non-southern people sort of clump together. It's a very regional school in that sense."

Partying Under Strict Scrutiny

Hendrix may have a miniscule student body and lack fraternities or sororities, but students repeatedly emphasized that they still manage to have a bustling social life. Residential dorm parties are the major attraction on weekend nights. Each dorm has its own personality and reputation, and in a fake rush week every year they mimic fraternities and pretend to recruit new "taps." "There's definitely one spot—Martin Hall, one of the dorms—where every Wednesday, Friday and Saturday you can pretty much guarantee there will be people drinking," one student said.

Students frequently complain about the way the Hendrix administration deals with partying. "In recent years, there's been a very notable and organized effort by the administration to crack down on parties," one student said. As part of its efforts, the administration has attempted to cloister all student partying in one house, the Cottage, or in the Brick Pit, an open space in the middle of campus where college police can easily manage students. Other Hendrix-approved social events include a dance competition called Shirttails Serenade at the end of the first week of school, for which all the male freshmen "do this sort of dance, usually a little raunchy, where they're just wearing their boxer shorts and an Oxford shirt. They perform it in front of these judges, and the winners get a pizza party."

The insularity and closeness of Hendrix social life—and the jumping through hoops required to throw parties on campus—lead a number of students to escape campus on the weekends, usually to Little Rock, the closest major city. Conway offers up a few movie theatres and restaurants near campus, and Hendrix puts on some concerts and theatrical productions throughout the year, but partying seems to be the central focus of student social lives.

Beyond complaints about the administration's alcohol policies, students also cited inflexible and difficult housing regulations and poor access to health services as further problems. In fact, a number of students mentioned the uncaring administration as their biggest gripe with Hendrix. "I was lucky, and housing flowed for me," a sophomore said, "but there's a Facebook group about getting screwed over by the administration." "The president is highly unpopular, as well as the new dean of students," another sophomore noted. "The students aren't afraid to speak up and try to do something about it, but it is very hard to get pro-student laws passed as the board of trustees is a bunch of conservative Methodists."

An Unusual School Spirit

Although extracurricular involvement varies widely among students, there are several influential organizations on campus. The Student Senate deals with campus issues and gives students a voice. "They struggle with the administration every once in a while," a freshman said. But despite occasional problems, they "really do care about the students and try to get stuff done."

Another popular activity is writing for and editing the student newspaper, *The Profile*, which has a regular staff of 50 and an editorial staff of 10–15. For a small school, Hendrix boasts an impressive array of other extracurricular options, from political groups such as the Young Democrats and the Progressive Student Alliance to musical ensembles such as the jazz band, pep band, and wind ensemble.

At Hendrix, approximately 200 students are athletes, on nine men's teams and 10 women's teams. Students say that they show a great deal of school spirit, but winning is not necessarily important to Hendrix culture. "We're not going to be real upset if the basketball team doesn't do that well this year. We care because our friends might be on it, but we don't care because we want Hendrix to win—we care about the people and not about the competition," one student said. Describing the easygoing nature of Hendrix athletics, one junior said, "We're probably best known for our Ultimate Frisbee team, the Flying Squirrels."

A Close Community

The sense that every Hendrix student knows everyone else constitutes a great deal of the school's appeal, but also its drawbacks. Several students said they felt claustrophobic after being on campus a year. "Last year, I found that a lot of my friends, one way or another, thought about leaving," a sophomore said. "But the feeling is that this year, my friends are more settled in. It's just anxiety over change."

> "Whatever bias or opinions or preconceived notions you have about anything will be challenged at Hendrix."

Many students come to Hendrix for financial reasons, citing its strong financial aid package as a major appeal. But once they've arrived on campus and have gotten over some of its problems, most thrive in its intimate atmosphere. "I don't think twice when I meet new people," a sophomore said. "I almost think, well, they're at Hendrix, they have to be good people."

Above all, Hendrix prizes an active academic life and personal, social, and academic development. As one student put it, "Whatever bias or opinions or preconceived notions you have about anything will be challenged at Hendrix."—*Yotam Barkai*

FYI

If you come to Hendrix, you'd better bring "flip-flops, a Ryan Adams CD, and a healthy appreciation for mob flicks."

What is the typical weekend schedule? "Friday, there's usually some sort of party going on, and the campus usually tries to have some other activity going on (a play at the theater or a movie). Saturdays are pretty much up in the air—unless there's a soccer game, there's usually not that much on campus. We do a lot of studying."

If I could change one thing about Hendrix, I'd "loosen the rules regarding partying and social life and alcohol."

Three things every student at Hendrix should do before graduating are "break into the greenhouse, check out the Ozarks, and get thrown into the fountain for your birthday."

University of Arkansas

Address: 232 Silas Hunt Hall
   Fayetteville, AR 72701
Phone: 479-575-5346
E-mail address:
   uofa@uark.edu
Web site URL: www.uark.edu
Year Founded: 1871
Private or Public: Public
Religious Affiliation: None
Location: Urban
Number of Applicants:
   12,045
Percent Accepted: 58%
Percent Accepted who
   enroll: 43%
Number Entering: 2,979
Number of Transfers
   Accepted each Year:
   1,686
Middle 50% SAT range:
   M: 520–650, CR:
   510–630, Wr: Unreported
Middle 50% ACT range:
   23–29
Early admission program
   EA/ED/None: EA

Percentage accepted
   through EA or ED:
   Unreported
EA and ED deadline: 15-Nov
Regular Deadline: 15-Aug
Application Fee: $40
Full time Undergraduate
   enrollment: 14,948
Total enrollment: 18,245
Percent Male: 50%
Percent Female: 50%
Total Percent Minority or
   Unreported: 15%
Percent African-American:
   5%
Percent Asian/Pacific
   Islander: 3%
Percent Hispanic: 3%
Percent Native-American:
   2%
Percent International: 3%
Percent in-state/out of
   state: 67%/33%
Percent from Public HS: 84%
Retention Rate: 83%
Graduation Rate 4-year: 32%

Graduation Rate 6-year: 56%
Percent Undergraduates
   in On-campus housing:
   29%
Number of official organized
   extracurricular
   organizations: 238
3 Most popular majors:
   Finance, Journalism,
   Marketing/ Marketing
   Management
Student/Faculty ratio: 17:1
Average Class Size: 25
Percent of students going to
   grad school: Unreported
Tuition and Fees: $15,279
In-State Tuition and Fees if
   different: $6,399
Cost for Room and Board:
   $7,422
Percent receiving financial
   aid out of those who apply,
   first year: 62%
Percent receiving financial
   aid among all students:
   71%

For it's A-A-A-R-K-A-N-S-A-S for Arkansas! Fight! Fight! Fi-i-i-ght!" Don't even think about setting foot in Fayetteville, Arkansas, without knowing the words to the Razorback fight song. Athletics aren't just for the jocks at this Southern university. If you are looking for a community with school pride, are unsure if you want to rush Pi Beta Phi or just go to their parties, and are interested in anything from engineering to agriculture, the University of Arkansas is calling your name.

Welcome to Fayetteville

Located in the Ozark Mountains, Fayetteville is the home of 345 acres of University of Arkansas campus. The city has a population of about 73,600 people for now, but Northwest Arkansas is considered one of the fastest-growing regions in the United States, according to the U.S. Census.

Upon arrival in Fayetteville, freshmen are introduced to their academic advisers, who "really know what they're doing," according to one senior. During orientation period, freshmen are clued in to all university poli-

cies and academic requirements. "It's hard to fall through the cracks freshman year," students said. "There are advisers and older students who really take pride in helping the younger ones." Make sure you ask about Advanced Placement status in classes, or how to "CLEP-out" of the University's second-language requirement by taking proficiency tests or foreign language classes. Oftentimes high school AP credits can cut down your "core" course load. The completion of core classes is required for graduation, and according to a senior, the readily accessible advisers are helpful in "letting us know exactly what we need" in order to graduate on time.

By sophomore year undergrads are usually enrolled in a specific college at the University of Arkansas. Students may choose between the Dale Bumpers College of Agricultural, Food & Life Sciences, the School of Architecture, the Fulbright College of Arts & Sciences, the Sam M. Walton College of Business, the College of Education and Health Professions, and the College of Engineering, depending on the student's academic interests. With over 200 academic degree programs, UA covers virtually all academic bases.

Most students are quick to say that the professors are all easy to reach, and hold convenient office hours, often meeting students for coffee on campus. However, as the freshmen core courses (such as Chemistry and Communications) are usually numbered at around 200 or 300 students, they are mostly taught by Teaching Assistants, not actual professors. One senior business major explained, "Once you get more into your major by junior and senior year, you get more of the professors, and people who actually wrote the books you are reading."

Deemed the hardest major at Arkansas by a number of students, engineering is only a hair less harrowing than molecular biology. Nonetheless, students claim that the difficulty of the subjects really shouldn't deter any undergrads from taking them. "Help is really just around the corner," one sophomore said. "I have tutors in a few subjects, and they are really flexible, and helpful around midterms and finals especially."

Life as a Razorback
While students are required to live on campus their freshman year, this is certainly not viewed as a bad thing. The dorms are described as "traditional" and "spacious" but beware: they are not all created equal. Humphreys (aka "the Hump-Dump") is coed and in the middle of campus. However, it has no air-conditioning and is "miserable" at the beginning of school because "it can get pretty hot here in Arkansas." A better dorm is Pomfret, which "everyone who lives there loves" and "they have a lot of fun." Its location isn't as convenient, however, as it sits at the "very bottom of a great big hill." (Don't come to Fayetteville without good walking shoes; students say "we have a ton of huge hills!")

By sophomore year many students choose to live off campus in any of Fayetteville's many apartment complexes. The city is "overflowing" with them, and the crowding in the city has also created a huge parking problem. Students call the city parking "awful" and "downright impossible." Luckily for future classes, the city just built the biggest parking deck in the state of Arkansas, which holds more than 500 automobiles.

Greeks and Non-Greeks
Sophomore year is also the first year that students who choose to "Go Greek" can live in their fraternity and sorority houses. While Greek life is a large part of the Arkansas social scene, it is certainly not something that students feel pressured to join. "If you do it, great, but if you don't want to do it, that's great too," one Razorback senior commented. Greek or not, students can still attend frat parties, where the serving of alcohol to minors is reportedly "not a problem whatsoever." Students who live in off-campus apartments and houses often open up their houses for parties and keggers, and offer a stress-free night for students who are underage.

The Greek houses are also all on campus, making party-hopping very convenient. With Sorority Row on Maple Street and Fraternity Row on Stadium Drive, undergrads don't have to look far for a "typical huge, beautiful, southern-style Greek house" offering plenty of cold beer and Southern hospitality.

Students are quick to add that there are no lines drawn between dorm-dwellers and off-campus renters. UA offers over $100 million of financial aid each year, and many students receive this in the form of free room and board. The cafeterias received mixed reviews from Razorback undergrads. While some students lived on campus for four years and "never got tired of it" others don't think they will "step foot into a dining hall" for a whole year, even if they live in the dorms.

On campus or off, students mix and mingle the nights away on Fayetteville's Dickson Street. Running straight through campus, the street offers so many bars and clubs that "it's hard to keep up with the new names and owners," explains one seasoned senior. Go to George's Majestic Lounge and rub elbows with University of Arkansas alums recounting the nights they spent at the waterhole 50 years ago. Gypsy, Alligator Ray's and Grubb's are just a few of the places that shouldn't be missed during an educational stint in Razorback Country. Even underage students can party with the rest of them on certain nights. Clubs and bars often offer 18-and-over nights, and on big weekends (think Homecoming Weekend versus South Carolina, or 'Bama and Texas games) the whole street is closed off.

"Suuuey, Hogs"
A University of Arkansas education is incomplete without the inclusion of Arkansas athletics. Their unstoppable track program, which is known to have won 17 consecutive indoor titles (though the last championship traces back to 2006), and their powerhouse

football and basketball teams, are just a few examples of nationally dominant Razorbacks sports. "The weekends are all about sporting events," students explain. "You have to get real geared up for the game, and no matter what, you MUST know the fight songs."

> **"Arkansas sporting events are huge, women's or men's, it's just a culture."**

With no professional sports teams to root for in the area, the entire Fayetteville community supports their hogs on game day. From the parquet in the Bud Walton Arena to the green grass of the Donald W. Reynolds Razorback Stadium, the thrill of victory (and the stench of keg beer) lingers in the sweet Southern air. Arkansas sports aren't simple weekend entertainment for UA Students. Students reported that "Arkansas

sporting events are huge. Women's or men's, it's just a culture."

If a Division I athletic career isn't a personal option, undergrads can still quench their competitive spirits within the confines of HPER (the UA Health, Physical Education, and Recreation building). The $14 million facility is the largest in the area and features 10 racquetball courts, four basketball gyms, an indoor track, an Olympic-size swimming pool, a climbing wall, men's and women's saunas, a computer lab, thousands of lockers, and a human performance lab.

Greek or non-Greek, on campus or off, athlete or academic, Razorbacks are all about one thing: having one hell of a time. If you are looking for a school with tons of school pride nestled in a true Southern college city, then University of Arkansas is the place to be. When you are leaving home, don't forget to pack your Razorback football jersey. You won't regret it.—*Meredith Hudson*

FYI
If you come to Arkansas, you'd better bring "your car or enough money to buy one."
What's the typical weekend schedule? "Friday: hit up a frat party; Saturday: go crazy at the football game, head to the bars at night; Sunday: sleep in, catch up on studying."
If I could change one thing about the University of Arkansas, I would "send more funds to the science department instead of to athletics. Sometimes we lack a sufficient amount of chemicals to perform chemistry experiments."
Three things every student should do before graduating are "attend a Razorback football game and 'call the hogs,' take a class that is taught in Old Main, and eat at Herman's restaurant."

California

California Institute of Technology

Address: 1200 East California Boulevard, Pasadena, CA 91125
Phone: 626-395-6341
E-mail address: ugadmissions@caltech.edu
Web site URL: www.caltech.edu
Year Founded: 1891
Private or Public: Private
Religious Affiliation: None
Location: Urban
Number of Applicants: 3,597
Percent Accepted: 17%
Percent Accepted who enroll: 38%
Number Entering: 231
Number of Transfers Accepted each Year: 11
Middle 50% SAT range: M: 770–800, CR: 700–780, Wr: 680–770
Middle 50% ACT range: 32–35
Early admission program EA/ED/None: EA

Percentage accepted through EA or ED: Unreported
EA and ED deadline: 1-Nov
Regular Deadline: 1-Jan
Application Fee: $60
Full time Undergraduate enrollment: 913
Total enrollment: 2,126
Percent Male: 59%
Percent Female: 41%
Total Percent Minority or Unreported: 44%
Percent African-American: 1%
Percent Asian/Pacific Islander: 38%
Percent Hispanic: 5%
Percent Native-American: <1%
Percent International: 9%
Percent in-state/out of state: 35%/65%
Percent from Public HS: Unreported
Retention Rate: 98%
Graduation Rate 4-year: 80%

Graduation Rate 6-year: 87%
Percent Undergraduates in On-campus housing: 90%
Number of official organized extracurricular organizations: 148
3 Most popular majors: Mathematics, Mechanical Engeneering, Physics
Student/Faculty ratio: 3:1
Average Class Size: 14
Percent of students going to grad school: Unreported
Tuition and Fees: $31,437
In-State Tuition and Fees if different: No difference
Cost for Room and Board: $10,146
Percent receiving financial aid out of those who apply, first year: 60%
Percent receiving financial aid among all students: 60%

M any people across the nation just think of football and New Year's parades when they think of Pasadena, but this sunny Southern California suburb is home to more than just the Rose Bowl. For those who are familiar with science, they know that Caltech is home to one of the world's premier research institutions. And for students who are serious about math and science, and looking for opportunities for world-class research, they'll find what they're looking for in the small, close-knit community of Caltech. At this school, students take their education seriously, but they also have fun in an off-beat way, all while sharing the campus with Nobel Prize winners and professors who are the leaders in their fields.

Not for the Faint of Heart

To be blunt, Caltech is not for everyone, and students don't pretend otherwise. Caltech students say that the academics are rigorous and a love for learning and science is definitely necessary. The core curriculum required of all students includes five terms each of math and physics, in addition to classes in chemistry and biology. But don't think students can get through without taking any English classes—although Caltech places an obvious emphasis on math and science, it also requires students to take 12 courses in the humanities and social sciences. For many, making the transition from high school to Caltech's level of academics may be a bit challenging; students describe classes as especially hard. Luckily, students take all classes pass/fail for their first two terms to help them transition and, beyond freshman year, collaboration is always a big part of Caltech life. People typically work in small groups for homework, and exchange answers between groups. "You wouldn't pass if you didn't work with other people," one sophomore said.

Students say most of the work involves lots of problem-solving as opposed to just plug-and-chug with numbers. One student described freshman classes as very intellectual—calculus is proof-based and chemistry classes go beyond the typical high school approach. "I expected that I would be one of the people left behind, since there are so many smart people, but everyone really starts off in the same place," one freshman said. "Most people haven't seen the new material covered since we basically start from scratch—it's much more of a theoretical approach."

Students admit that Caltech's academics can get overwhelming, but that help is readily available for those who seek it, whether it's from friends, classmates, RAs, or free tutors. "You can get help in whatever class you need and if you're sick and can't finish a set, you can get an extension from the health department," one student said. "People are glad to help and it's mutual because even if you're one of the few people who know how to do a problem, you're going to need help on other ones."

A big part of Caltech's academic community is the Honor Code, which in effect makes almost all exams take-home and trusts undergraduates to time themselves and be honest. One student said, "Undergrads are given a lot of free range and people take it pretty seriously." Students say the honor code is designed not to punish, but to eliminate unfair advantage. "I really like the honor code because it goes into all aspects of Caltech life," said one freshman, who hadn't had any proctored tests yet. "There are open kitchens, and you can leave your door unlocked because people won't steal your stuff unless it's for a prank, but then you'll get it back." And it's exactly this kind of trust that builds a small, close-knit undergraduate community.

Ditching the Books for the Stacks

Sleep deprivation due to late-night problem sets is a regular part of Caltech culture, but don't think that Caltech students skip out on fun. Pranks are very much a part of Caltech culture, and they happen very often. But these go beyond your typical college pranks. A classic example of Caltech fun is the annual Pumpkin Drop, where students use liquid nitrogen to freeze pumpkins and drop them off the tallest building on campus. One of the most popular days on campus is Ditch Day, when school essentially stops—professors even extend set deadlines so that everyone can participate in the fun. The senior class plays hooky for a day, and in order to prevent underclassmen from ransacking their rooms, they block their doors with "stacks." Originally, these were physical blocks made of plywood and concrete intended to prevent anyone from entering, but they've since become complex sets of puzzles planned months or years in advance, intended to occupy the underclassmen's attentions while the seniors are away.

> **"It's a lot of hard work, in not very much time, but it's fun."**

Students say that Ditch Day consists of people running around solving problems—essentially high-tech, brainy scavenger hunts. "Last year, I worked on a stack that involved rearranging electrical circuits," one sophomore said. "There was one stack where undergrads were given a reprogrammed TI-83 [calculator] to plug in numbers and get clues to run around campus."

Houses Are Where the Heart Is

Caltech's social scene is dominated by houses, which students describe as a cross between frats and dorms. All students go through Rotation during their first days at Caltech, a process when every freshman eats a meal in each of the eight houses. After getting a feel for the houses, which each have different personalities, the freshmen rank their top three choices and get assigned to the house where they will live for the rest of their time at Caltech. Students say they meet many if not most of their friends through their houses—living in the same dorm and having family-style dinners every day creates a strong bond. "The house system is great because it gives you an instant sense of connection," one student said. "It's not so great for people who don't like the houses they're in, but it works for almost everyone, and you can switch house affiliation."

And at the heart of the housing system are the students of Caltech. Although students admit Caltech has a much higher density of nerds and geeks than your typical school, and that there is an uneven mix of genders, they say that the students make the close-knit community very comfortable. "It's an exceptional group of students," one sophomore said. "People are really interested in science, but you can typically talk to people about any topic and they'll be knowledgeable." Students say there are a certain number of students who stay in their rooms and study all day, but that most people are very outgoing and willing to help out with house events. In response to the stereotype of awkward nerds, one freshman said, "If anything, that helps us bond better, because if there's someone just like you, you're more likely to bond." Even if they're working, most students will leave their doors open and many leave messages on dry-erase whiteboards, keeping the small community connected.

Under Construction

"Our idea of fun is definitely different from most colleges," one freshman said. Students say that partying in the typical college sense of the word isn't very prevalent on campus, but when Caltech students party, they go all out—in an off-beat way, of course. Students don't just go to the local store for red Solo cups; they go to Home Depot to buy two-by-fours for major construction. For all large parties, the houses spend two to three weeks building elaborate structures in their courtyards. One freshman described her house's courtyard: "We built a dance floor about five feet off the floor, and then flooded the entire courtyard two to three feet. We also had fountains and waterfalls." For

Interhouse, one of the biggest parties of the year, all the south houses build similarly elaborate structures in their courtyard, and if students aren't happy with one party, they can hop on over to another party close by. On other days of the year, there are camping trips and pool games and even margarita Mondays.

But despite the fun, students are brought back by the reality of the demands of school. Students point out the high rate of 5–6 year graduations, dropouts and transfers, and say that students need to be able to perform under high pressure. "Even if you're the best, you can still not do well here," one sophomore said. "Being smart and working hard don't guarantee success, and you can't let that drag you down." But if students can get beyond the challenges of hard classes, they'll find a rewarding experience and will have some fun along the way. In fact, they may become one of the many famous physicists, engineers or scientists who have graduated from Caltech and gone on to make a name for themselves in science-related fields, whether in academia, industry or research. Students have the opportunity to sample the big leagues as part of professors' research projects, or by getting hands-on experience at the famous Jet Propulsion Laboratory, which Caltech operates for NASA.

Summing up the Caltech experience, one sophomore said, "It's a lot of hard work, in not very much time, but it's fun." This sunny Southern California school may not be for everyone, but if you're dedicated to math and science, willing to work really hard, and can persevere with a sense of humor, then this just might be the school for you. Caltech is a unique experience and, upon graduation, students enjoy the unique benefit of a world-class education and the respect of anyone familiar with the fields of math and science. One student said, "It's not for everyone, but anyone can come here and be accepted, no matter who you are."—*Della Fox*

FYI
If you come to Caltech, you'd better realize "it's not so much what you bring, but what you take out, and how you stay through in the middle."
What's the typical weekend schedule? "Saturday is typically relaxed: playing Frisbee and maybe catching up on sleep a bit. Sunday you work until midnight when you order pizza, and then you work more."
If I could change one thing about Caltech, I'd "make the classes easier so we would have more time to engage in extracurricular activities. And make pass/fail last longer than two terms."
Three things every student at Caltech should do before graduating are "participate in Ditch Day, do SURF (Summer Undergraduate Research Fellowship), and explore the tunnels underneath the campus, which help you get into buildings you wouldn't normally be able to get into."

California Institute of the Arts

Address: 24700 McBean Parkway, Valencia, CA 91355
Phone: 661-255-1050
E-mail address: admiss@calarts.edu
Web site URL: www.calarts.edu
Year Founded: 1961
Private or Public: Private
Religious Affiliation: None
Location: Suburban
Number of Applicants: 1,186
Percent Accepted: 32%
Percent Accepted who enroll: 40%
Number Entering: 151
Number of Transfers Accepted each Year: 188
Middle 50% SAT range: Unreported
Middle 50% ACT range: Unreported
Early admission program EA/ED/None: None
Percentage accepted through EA or ED: NA

EA and ED deadline: NA
Regular Deadline: 4-Jan
Application Fee: $70
Full time Undergraduate enrollment: 820
Total enrollment: 1,317
Percent Male: 54%
Percent Female: 46%
Total Percent Minority or Unreported: 30%
Percent African-American: 9%
Percent Asian/Pacific Islander: 9%
Percent Hispanic: 12%
Percent Native-American: <1%
Percent International: 8%
Percent in-state/out of state: 66%/44%
Percent from Public HS: Unreported
Retention Rate: Unreported
Graduation Rate 4-year: 57%
Graduation Rate 6-year: Unreported

Percent Undergraduates in On-campus housing: 40%
Number of official organized extracurricular organizations: 5
3 Most popular majors: Acting; Film, Video and Photographic Arts; Visual Performing Arts
Student/Faculty ratio: 7:1
Average Class Size: 12
Percent of students going to grad school: Unreported
Tuition and Fees: $32,860
In-State Tuition and Fees if different: No difference
Cost for Room and Board: $5,236
Percent receiving financial aid out of those who apply, first year: Unreported
Percent receiving financial aid among all students: 38%

C alifornia Institute of the Arts, a school self-contained in a single building, was supposed to be a haven for artists in the middle of nowhere. Besides the fact that a strip-mall town grew up around it, Cal Arts is pretty much just that: a place for artists to gather and work on their skills. Students who go to Cal Arts love it, but more importantly, they love what they do, making the focused nature of the school perfect for self-motivated artists.

Math and Science? Not really . . .

The nearly 900 undergraduates enrolled in Cal Arts are members of one of six schools, in a range of highly selective BFA programs. One student said that the music technology program accepts around six to eight students each year. Cal Arts only has Bachelor of Fine Arts and Master of Fine Arts programs. To graduate, students not only need to take a certain number of classes within their "métier," what the students interviewed called their discipline, but also need to complete a Critical Studies requirement. Critical Studies are academic subjects, spread over a number of distributional requirements. There are also core classes required of students: a Writing Arts course, which discusses the relationship between art and society, and Foundation courses, which could be on a number of topics. The Foundation courses are geared specifically toward a certain discipline. One photography and media major said that the Foundation course required of all fine arts majors entitled "What Makes it Art," was "kind of a lame class," and featured the only teacher he did not like.

The categories for distributional requirements, the Breadth requirements, include humanities, social sciences, cultural studies, natural sciences, quantitative, métier studies in the student's métier and métier studies in a separate métier. Yes, there is even a quantitative requirement. "But it's art school math, so it's pretty friendly," one student said. Even in the Critical Studies classes, which students take on Wednesdays, there is usually an art bent, the same student said. She said that her paper topic for her philosophy class was to pick three pieces of art and "philosophize about them." Another student said Critical Studies is "kind of the fun way to do something that is out of your métier."

While the classes within the métiers are usually capped around eight to 10 students, Critical Studies classes can have up to about 30. Despite this, students said that there are no 800-student lectures, and all classes are taught with students sitting "in a round," emphasizing student participation. One student, who transferred to Cal Arts from NYU's Tisch School of the Arts, said she preferred the Critical Studies classes at Cal Arts as opposed to the distributional requirements at NYU. The student, who is in the School of Theater's BFA Acting program, said that it was hard to be in classes at NYU with majors in non-art subjects. "The academics are set up for artists and they are very artist friendly," she said. That being said, students agreed that the Critical Studies classes are not particularly challenging. "I can definitely say it is not as challenging as it could be and sometimes I do find myself a little bored," one student said.

"You have to love what you do, because that is basically all you do."

For students at Cal Arts, most of their time, both inside and outside of the classroom is spent concentrating on their métier. "I'm a violin performance major and for my major all I do is focus on music," one student said. Most students interviewed said that the classes within their métier are challenging and require a lot of work outside the classroom. One student stressed that to succeed in métier classes one has to be self-motivated. "The department classes are going to be challenging," the student in the acting program said. "You are going to work really hard. It's easy to sit back, but the kids who do that don't last very long."

Each student is given a mentor in his or her field, and, since the student body is relatively small, that professor only has a small number of students he or she is mentoring, which makes relationships quite casual. Students always call their instructors by their first names. Students praise the instructors, who for the most part are all working professionals. "They have great insight," one student in the dance program said. "It's really different than having someone who has

sort of had their career that is sort of over and is teaching. Another student said he liked the fact that while you are showing a teacher your work, that teacher will often turn around and show you theirs as well.

No ABCs

Students at Cal Arts are graded on a pass/fail basis. Upon finishing a course students receive a mark of High Pass, Pass, Low Pass, No Credit or NX (insufficient attendance). No credit is essentially the equivalent of failing. If a student chooses to take the class in which he or she received a No Credit again, the previous class will go off their record. Additionally, if a student receives an "Incomplete," he or she is required to finish that class at some point in time. One student, who came to Cal Arts from a high-stress-level private school said she appreciates the system of grading. "I take so much more pride in my work because I feel like I am getting positive feedback as opposed to feeling like there is someone out to get me in the grading."

Let's put on a show!

Students at Cal Arts in the performing arts are required to be involved in performances outside of their classroom work, and the facilities are state of the art. The student in the acting program raved about the Disney Modular Theater. The theater—there is only one other like it in the entire world—can transform into anything a production wants it to be. The stage can be raised if that is necessary, or a production can even have a waterfall, like one recent show did. There are also smaller and more casual ways for students to perform. Most students interviewed mentioned the Coffee House, which puts on performances that are student-run, directed, produced and performed. At Cal Arts students interviewed said the focus is interdisciplinary. One student described an instance in which a student in the world music program helped out his friend who is a dance major.

An artists' commune in a conservative town

There are two dorm complexes, one for undergraduates and one for grad students. In Ahmanson, the dorm for graduate students, most of the residents are older, and many have families. Every freshman is required to have a meal plan, but some students end up cooking in their dorm rooms. Since there is no guaranteed housing for undergraduates, many students live off campus. But that doesn't mean they spend a lot of time in Valencia. While students love the Cal Arts campus, the surrounding town of Valencia receives less than rave reviews. "The town of Valencia is like one giant strip mall," one student said. "Basically everything is a chain." She added that students go to Abbey Lane Café, one of the few restaurants that is not a chain in the neighborhood. Cal Arts remains isolated from the town. "The town never knows what is going on," another student said. "It's like the house on the hill in *Edward Scissorhands*."

> **"All of the action happens at Cal Arts. It's like the Vatican."**

Despite the fact that Valencia is a suburb of Los Angeles, one student said he does not get the opportunity to go there often since transportation is difficult. There is no easy form of public transportation to get to the city, and once there it is hard to get around without a car. While some students have cars, others who don't often don't want to feel like they are begging rides off of them. "If you don't have a car you can feel like you are in a bubble," he said. "All of the action happens at Cal Arts," another student said. "It's like the Vatican."

The Red Cup Rule

Even though there are not a lot of the big parties that come with Greek life, there is a fair amount of alcohol and drug use on and off campus among students. Most students interviewed agreed that school policy on drug and alcohol use is fairly lax. One student mentioned what she knows as the "red cup rule." The "red cup rule" is an unspoken rule between school security and students. The rule implies that as long as the liquid is protected in a plastic red cup, students can drink anything. "If a security guard sees you with a red cup they can't tell you to throw it away," she said. Another student said, "there is obviously a lot of pot." While there is a lot of pot, harder drugs are rare, although one student said you will hear about the isolated instances of a student going to rehab.

While most students socialized with others in their métier, art gallery openings on Thursdays are a chance for all students to get together. At the gallery openings there is wine and beer for students over 21 years old, and sometimes live music or a DJ. There are also a few famed parties that most students at the school attend, such as the Halloween party. Despite the popularity of the art gallery openings and the Halloween party, one student said that most of the "hardcore parties" are off-campus.

The place for artists

Most students interviewed had trouble finding things to complain about at Cal Arts. For students who really care about their art and want to pursue it as their career, Cal Arts seems to be the perfect place. While there are so many opportunities for artists that one student said a "workaholic" tendency can take over, she emphasized that "it's a really good school if you are self-motivated." —*Esther Zuckerman*

FYI
If you come to Cal Arts, you'd better bring "receptivity, a willingness to work. If you aren't willing to do the work then you are not going to do very well."
What is the typical weekend schedule? "If I were in a show there would be rehearsal on Saturday and rehearsal on Friday night. Sundays would be off and your free time is your free time. I'd rehearse at some point for a scene in my acting class. At night it's a social hour or it's work."
If I could change one thing about Cal Arts, I'd "have online class sign-ups. Everyone just runs for it."
Three things every student at Cal Arts should do before graduating are "put on your own show, live in the dorms for one year and make sure to chill on the hill a lot."

California State University System

The California State system boasts that it comprises the largest and most diverse universities in America. It offers the chance to study everything from marine navigation and technology to mathematics and engineering among its 23 campuses. Geographically too, the University spans from San Diego State—just 18 miles from the Mexican border, to Humboldt State, 774 miles north in Eureka, Calif.

Founded in 1960 and administered by a governor-appointed 25-member Board of Trustees, the CSU system coexists with the University of California system and California Community Colleges to form a trifecta of higher education in the Golden State.

Where to go

With so many options in regards to location, the third-largest state may seem a bit intimidating. To help out, www.csumentor.com eases the application and decision process for prospective undergrads. Each campus offers different programs and has different sized student bodies. Along with the UCs and Community Colleges, the three systems allow a place for every California resident to pursue a degree. Financing an education is easy too—tuition ranges from $4,000 to $21,000 depending on living situation and campus and financial aid opportunities are plentiful.

The wide array of campuses, along with their geographical differences offers prospective students enough choice to satisfy even the most fickle of tastes.

In the Classroom

Though the UC system retains the spotlight, Cal States are no slouch in academics. The system maintains a focus on undergraduate education, as opposed to the larger universities' research-oriented approach.

California Polytechnic—San Luis Obispo's College of Engineering, for example, was ranked No. 1 by *U.S. News and World Report* for public undergrad engineering schools. One of the first Cal State universities, San Francisco State, offers a world-class cinema department. Cal-Maritime Academy offers the opportunity to study Coast Guard and Naval operations without the requirement of military service.

The Cal State system offers a variety of academic opportunities boasting, "We prepare graduates who go on to make a difference in the workforce."

Sunshine and Sports

All 23 campuses, except CSU–Channel Islands, have either a Division I or Division II sports program. Recently, Cal State Dominguez Hills sent their No. 9 ranked men's soccer team to the national semifinals before the Toros' championship run was cut short in a 3-2 double overtime defeat to Tampa. CSU–Northridge, affectionately known as cee-sun, boasts a long sports tradition. The Matadors men's basketball squad finished second in the Big West to UC–Santa Barbara.

Many CSU schools compete in the Big West league while six campuses participate in the Mountain Pacific Sports Federation. With the sun shining year-round, IM and club sports are also popular.

With the draw of a diverse student body, numerous options in location and academic course of study, the California State University system retains a vital role to California's higher education.—*Brittany Golob*

California Polytechnic State / San Luis Obispo

Address: Admissions Office
San Luis Obispo, CA 93407
Phone: 805-756-2311
E-mail address:
admissions@calpoly.edu
Web site URL:
www.calpoly.edu
Year Founded: 1901
Private or Public: Public
Religious Affiliation: None
Location: Suburban
Number of Applicants:
33,352
Percent Accepted: 34%
Percent Accepted who
enroll: 31%
Number Entering: 3,501
Number of Transfers
Accepted each Year:
1,623
Middle 50% SAT range:
M: 570–680, CR:
530–630, Wr: Unreported
Middle 50% ACT range:
24–29
Early admission program
EA/ED/None: ED

Percentage accepted
through EA or ED:
Unreported
EA and ED deadline: 31-Oct
Regular Deadline: 30-Nov
Application Fee: $55
Full time Undergraduate
enrollment: 18,516
Total enrollment: 19,777
Percent Male: 56%
Percent Female: 44%
Total Percent Minority or
Unreported: 24%
Percent African-American:
1%
Percent Asian/Pacific
Islander: 11%
Percent Hispanic: 11%
Percent Native-American:
<1%
Percent International: 1%
Percent in-state/out of
state: 96%/4%
Percent from Public HS:
Unreported
Retention Rate: 90%
Graduation Rate 4-year: 23%

Graduation Rate 6-year:
70%
Percent Undergraduates
in On-campus housing:
29%
Number of official organized
extracurricular
organizations: 375
3 Most popular majors:
Engineering, Business,
Agriculture
Student/Faculty ratio: 19:1
Average Class Size: 24
Percent of students
going to grad school:
20%
Tuition and Fees: $15,213
In-State Tuition and Fees if
different: $5,043
Cost for Room and Board:
$9,369
Percent receiving financial
aid out of those who apply,
first year: 43%
Percent receiving financial
aid among all students:
Unreported

S an Luis Obispo, one of the oldest cities in California, is home to one of the most prestigious institutions of the California State University system, California Polytechnic State, also known as Cal Poly. A large land-grant university of nearly 20,000 students, Cal Poly is a prominent research institution that focuses on engineering and agriculture, even though it also offers an array of liberal arts programs of study. As a technical school, research is also an important part of the university. In addition, the affordability of the school for Californian residents means that it is a highly desirable destination for many students from the Golden State.

Engineering and Beyond

Although the College of Engineering is recognized across the country, Cal Poly includes five other divisions: Agriculture, Food, and Environmental Sciences; Architecture and Environmental Design; Business, Liberal Arts; and Sciences and Mathematics. Given the

university's name, it is clear what topics are the most important to Cal Poly. Students generally agree that engineering and architecture are particularly prestigious. It shows with the enrollment. In fact, the engineering school accounts for nearly one-third of the undergraduate student body. The College of Liberal Arts, however, only has 3,000 students, which is less than one-sixth of the student population. "We are definitely a technical school," said one student. "Compared to other schools, we don't have that many liberal arts majors."

An important distinction in the application process for Cal Poly is that it requires students to declare their majors on their applications. Therefore, most students going into the school have a specific career in mind. Each major has its own high school requirements to ensure that all students have the basic skills to succeed in the field. The school has over 60 majors from which the students can choose when they apply. The admissions office then selects the best candidates from the application pools of each major. To prevent people from applying to easy majors and then changing them during the course of their study at Cal Poly, the university has very strict standards in transferring from one major to another. "Most people here know exactly what they want to do, and they are really focused," said one student. Indeed, given the technical nature of the university, Cal Poly is best for prospective students who have mapped out their next few years both academically and professionally.

Despite the technical aspect of the university and the specialized nature of many majors, students are required to take a number of general education courses in order to ensure that they have some knowledge of other academic fields. "The required courses can be annoying because you have to take them," said one student. "But after you have taken them, you are glad because you always learn something new in those classes." The general education classes are divided into communication, science and mathematics, arts and humanities, society and individual, and technology. The requirements are also different for students depending on their college. For example, those in the College of Engineering have to take fewer classes in humanities than those who are in the College of Liberal Arts.

The coursework at Cal Poly can be difficult, especially for those who are not ready to work hard. Given the large number of engineering students and the mathematical proficiency needed for technical majors, many students can face some difficulties at the beginning. However, as they become more familiar with college living, students generally make enough adjustments to manage their workload. "I had a hard time in freshman year," said one student. "But I have been doing well since then because I found better work methods." Furthermore, the engineering and science majors can be difficult and competitive, while some business and agriculture programs of study are more relaxed.

Over the years, Cal Poly has been highly regarded as one of the best technical schools in the country. Among western universities for which the highest program offered is the master's degree, Cal Poly is consistently ranked in the top-10 by the *U.S. News and World Report*. It is also consistently recognized as having a top engineering program, not to mention an outstanding architecture school. All of this means that the application process is highly competitive. The acceptance rate has recently fallen under 40 percent.

A Historic City

San Luis Obispo traces its current settlement to 1772 with the beginning of a Spanish mission in the area. Today, the city remains relatively small, with a population of only 44,000, and much of the activity in the city is centered on Cal Poly. The town is small, but, given the scope of the university, it offers a number of restaurants and bars close to campus to serve and entertain students. The natural location of the city is very convenient for all those enjoying the outdoors. The Los Padres National Park is only five miles to the east, while the Pacific Ocean is less than 10 miles to the West. Big cities, however, are less accessible, since San Luis Obispo is almost at the midpoint between San Francisco and Los Angeles. "I enjoy living here," said one student. "But you won't find too many interesting places to go to during weekends."

> "Most people here know exactly what they want to do, and they are really focused."

The housing at Cal Poly is highly limited. Most of the on-campus residential halls are reserved for freshmen. There is a special arrangement of six freshmen residences called Living-Learning Program halls. The idea is for the university to combine living with academics. Therefore, students of the same college live together. This way, they can support each other in their academics and make useful connections for future endeavors. For all those who are interested in bringing alcohol to the dorms, it might not be a very good idea, as the university is strict about the usage and possession of alcohol. Freshmen in dorms must purchase a meal plan. The campus has 19 different food venues for students, though many of them are quite small and limited. More than half of the student body live off campus after their first year. It is generally easy to find reasonable housing around the campus area in San Luis Obispo.

Given the small number of students living on campus and the dry dorm policy, most parties and weekend socializing opportunities happen in off-campus housing, Greek houses, or local restaurants and bars. Although the Greek life certainly exists, it is only one small portion of the social scene. Despite all of this, given the size of the university, students agree that they can no doubt find many interesting events to attend during the weekends.

Diversity and Festivity

While the school has a mix of students from all ethnic groups, it is not particularly as diverse as many other universities within the California public education system. Nevertheless, most people are happy with the makeup of the student body. One issue, however, is that more than 90 percent of the students are from within California. After all, it is a public university designed to serve

Californians. Nevertheless, students do not believe that this aspect of the school has any effect on their college experience.

For students who have a clear vision of what they want to do during their college years and who are willing to work hard, Cal Poly certainly represents a very good destination. Many of its technical programs are highly prestigious, and it can be relatively affordable for residents of California. Therefore, if you don't mind living in a small, historic town away from big cities, Cal Poly is certainly a great college option.—*Xiaohang Liu*

FYI
If you come to Cal Poly, you'd better bring "a car."
What is the typical weekend schedule? "Parties! What else?"
If I could change one thing about Cal Poly, I'd "build more dorms."
Three things every student at Cal Poly should do before graduating are "go hiking, swimming, and study hard."

California State University / Chico

Address: 400 West First Street, Chico, CA 95929-0722
Phone: 530-898-4428
E-mail address: INFO@csuchico.edu
Web site URL: www.csuchico.edu
Year Founded: 1887
Private or Public: Public
Religious Affiliation: None
Location: Urban
Number of Applicants: 15,069
Percent Accepted: 87%
Percent Accepted who enroll: 21%
Number Entering: 2,765
Number of Transfers Accepted each Year: 3,082
Middle 50% SAT range: M: 460–570, CR: 450–550, Wr: Unreported
Middle 50% ACT range: 19–24
Early admission program EA/ED/None: None

Percentage accepted through EA or ED: NA
EA and ED deadline: NA
Regular Deadline: 30-Nov
Application Fee: $55
Full time Undergraduate enrollment: 15,804
Total enrollment: 17,034
Percent Male: 48%
Percent Female: 52%
Total Percent Minority or Unreported: 22%
Percent African-American: 2%
Percent Asian/Pacific Islander: 6%
Percent Hispanic: 13%
Percent Native-American: 1%
Percent International: 2%
Percent in-state/out of state: 98%/2%
Percent from Public HS: Unreported
Retention Rate: 79%
Graduation Rate 4-year: 15%

Graduation Rate 6-year: 52%
Percent Undergraduates in On-campus housing: 1%
Number of official organized extracurricular organizations: 192
3 Most popular majors: Business Administration, Liberal Arts, Psychology
Student/Faculty ratio: 22:1
Average Class Size: 23
Percent of students going to grad school: Unreported
Tuition and Fees: $14,178
In-State Tuition and Fees if different: $4,008
Cost for Room and Board: $8,718
Percent receiving financial aid out of those who apply, first year: 88%
Percent receiving financial aid among all students: 87%

A member of the California State University system, the largest system of higher education in the United States, California State University, Chico has an enrollment of nearly 17,000 students, the great majority of whom come from the Golden State. Founded in 1889 as Northern Branch State Normal, Chico State has now become a major educational institution in California, offering both bachelor's and master's programs. The school is especially popular with Californian students who are able to receive a solid education at relatively low costs and enjoy the college town atmosphere offered by Chico.

A Research Institution

Chico is divided into nine colleges, covering all major academic and professional areas. The schools include Agriculture, Business, Behavioral and Social Sciences, Communication and Education, Engineering, Humanities and Fine Arts, Natural Sciences, Graduate Studies, and Continuing Education. This means a large selection of academic programs for students. "We are a pretty big state school," said one student. "We have people of diverse interests, and I think Chico does a good job in having something for everyone in terms of academics."

The university offers nearly 150 undergraduate majors in more than 50 departments, which is a very large number for any academic institution. Some of the unique majors include Recreation Administration, Kinesiology, and Applied Computer Graphics, which are hard to find in most other universities. The specialized nature of many majors means that a high percentage of students at Chico State are focused on career preparation when they enter the school. "There are always a lot of people who don't know what they want to do even when they are seniors," said one student. "But there are also a lot of people who came in here to focus on specific professions." According to students, the classes at Chico State are mostly "pretty good" in preparing students for future careers.

For the most part, students do not complain about workload. "You always meet a bunch of professors who give us a lot of work and grade really harshly," said one student. "But from my experience, as long as you don't fall too far behind, you will do just fine in most of your classes." Ultimately, the difficulties of classes depend on the students' choices. Similar to many other colleges, a number of classes in engineering can be particularly challenging, especially for those who do not have strong backgrounds in mathematics.

As in most universities, Chico State has a list of general education requirements for all undergraduates. They are designed to expose students to a number of important disciplines so that they will have a wide range of knowledge and skills. The first part of the requirements ensures that students have basic abilities in communications, mathematics, and logic, three topics that are highly valuable for undergraduates in any majors. The rest of the requirements focus on knowledge, meaning that all graduates of Chico State must have some understanding of social sciences, natural sciences, and humanities. Although many students may find some of the classes rather interesting and enlightening, others believe that it can be burdensome and boring. "I didn't like the required classes," said one student. "I will never use some of the stuff that they teach in those classes."

The lectures at Chico State can be very large. However, compared to many other large institutions, the university is very good at ensuring a number of small classes. "I think the professors and the students do get to know each other," said one student. "And I never think the classes are too big." One of the best ways to have a small, more intimate academic experience is through the honors program, which ensures that its members will be able to attend classes with less than 25 students. Other benefits include living in Honors House during freshmen year and priority registration for classes, which can be valuable for students to enroll in some of the more popular courses. There are even opportunities for some upper-level classes to have two professors per course, so that students can hear different viewpoints on subjects.

The City of Roses

Chico, also known as the City of Roses, is at the foot of the Sierra Nevada Mountains. It is surrounded by a few other midsized towns and cities, but for the students at Chico State, the city is rather small and not too interesting. The location, however, is highly appreciated by outdoors enthusiasts who are able to take advantage of the different expeditions to the surrounding parks, creeks, and hills. Chico is also home to Bidwell Park, the largest municipal park in the United States. "I am not bored by Chico," said one student. "But if you are, you can get out of here and go hiking and rafting."

The dormitory system is mostly occupied by freshmen. In fact, the dorms provide housing to slightly over 1,200 students. Besides the traditional housing facilities, the university also provides a number of themed houses. Most of them are based on the academic programs of students. For example, there is one program for students in agriculture and another for those in engineering. Alcohol policy is very strict, as alcohol is generally forbidden from university facilities. The meal plans provide sit-down dining services in two locations as well as a number of coffee shops and convenience stores. Of course, given the size of Chico State, there are few dining locations. It does not disturb most students, however, as they generally live off campus anyway.

> "On the weekends, you can definitely find places where you can have a good time."

The reason for the large number of students living off campus is that the apartments and houses around the area can be found at reasonable prices. In addition, the university's housing office also provides resources to students in their search for dwellings. The great majority of upperclassmen move off campus, which also allows for a greater degree of freedom. One student said, "I prefer living off campus because you feel more like you are on your own."

The parties at Chico State are generally found in the fraternities and sororities, as well as in off campus houses. Furthermore, even though the city is relatively small, it still offers a number of bars, restaurants, and clubs for late-night entertainment, especially during the weekend. "We have some really cool parties here," said one student. "On the weekends, you can definitely find places where you can have a good time."

Enjoying Life

Chico State does have a very good athletic program. Most teams compete in NCAA Division II, and the men's baseball team has made several appearances in the championship series during the last two decades. One drawback, however, is that the football program was disbanded in 1997 as a way to cut costs.

Chico State is primarily an institution of Californians, as most students are from the state. However, as one student pointed out, "it's not like everybody looks at you differently when you say you are not from California." For students from anywhere, the university provides a very good education with hundreds of options. At the same time, despite being located in a relatively small city, the social aspect of Chico State is still highly inviting, making it a very good destination for students.—*Xiaohang Liu*

FYI
If you come to Chico State, you'd better bring "hiking boots."
What is the typical weekend schedule? "Parties are on Thursday, Friday, and Saturday. If you want to go outdoors, you should probably go on Saturday."
If I could change one thing about Chico State, I'd "get more people to live on campus."
Three things every student at Chico State should do before graduating are "go hiking, enjoy the weekends, and just have fun."

California State University / Fresno

Address: 5150 North Maple Ave. M/S JA 57 Fresno, CA 93740-8026
Phone: 559-278-2261
E-mail address: admissions@csufresno.edu
Web site URL: www.csufresno.edu
Year Founded: 1911
Private or Public: Public
Religious Affiliation: None
Location: Urban
Number of Applicants: 14,537
Percent Accepted: 70%
Percent Accepted who enroll: 27%
Number Entering: 2,823
Number of Transfers Accepted each Year: 2,798
Middle 50% SAT range: M: 410–540, CR: 400–510, Wr: Unreported
Middle 50% ACT range: 16–22
Early admission program EA/ED/None: None

Percentage accepted through EA or ED: NA
EA and ED deadline: NA
Regular Deadline: 1-Feb
Application Fee: $55
Full time Undergraduate enrollment: 19,245
Total enrollment: 21,728
Percent Male: 43%
Percent Female: 57%
Total Percent Minority or Unreported: 56%
Percent African-American: 6%
Percent Asian/Pacific Islander: 16%
Percent Hispanic: 34%
Percent Native-American: <1%
Percent International: 1%
Percent in-state/out of state: Unreported
Percent from Public HS: 99%
Retention Rate: 82%
Graduation Rate 4-year: 15%

Graduation Rate 6-year: 46%
Percent Undergraduates in On-campus housing: 6%
Number of official organized extracurricular organizations: 250
3 Most popular majors: Health Sciences, Liberal Arts, and Sciences
Student/Faculty ratio: Unreported
Average Class Size: 25
Percent of students going to grad school: Unreported
Tuition and Fees: $13,857
In-State Tuition and Fees if different: $3,687
Cost for Room and Board: $8,590
Percent receiving financial aid out of those who apply, first year: 80%
Percent receiving financial aid among all students: Unreported

I f you come to the city of Fresno on a typical Saturday afternoon, you might be engulfed in a sea of red. "The whole town comes out" for University tailgates and football games, taking over the campus and celebrating their successful team. But California State University, Fresno, or "Fresno State," has even more to offer than great athletics. The student body invests pride in not only its strong agriculture programs, but a wide range of popular academic offerings, ranging from criminology and education to preparation for jobs in the health profession. Students looking for a state school that provides diversity, a "laid-back but ambitious" atmosphere, and plenty of opportunities for involvement in the heart of California should give Fresno State a closer look.

Not Just an Ag School

Students at Fresno State are required to take a wide range of specific classes over their first two years to fulfill their General Education credits. These courses, which are classified as Foundation, Breadth, Integration and Multicultural/International, are designed to give undergraduates a broad base of knowledge along with their specialized areas of study. Foundation covers oral and written communication, critical thinking, and quantitative reasoning; Breadth includes physical and life sciences and arts and humanities. Integration courses are upper-division versions of these offerings, and the Multicultural/International requirements provide insights into international relations and countries around the world. Some students say that, as far as GE classes are concerned, "If you show up and do your work, you'll be fine," but others complain that the requirements "are a real pain—I feel like I'm wasting my time taking so many of these courses when I would rather have more focus on my interests."

Students feel that Fresno State offers a good liberal arts background—the most popular majors include teaching and business. On the other hand, one senior griped that "the sciences are not well developed or taken care of—the humanities are more straightforward." One of the school's most distinguishing features is its agriculture program; Fresno is perfectly situated in the richly cultivated San Joaquin Valley and includes a 1,022-acre University Farm. In particular, students mention the viticulture program, which teaches participants about winemaking in the school's very own vineyard. Overall students report that, while grading is fair and people don't do much work on the weekends, "A lot of people get really stressed out around midterms and finals, maybe because they skip classes during the semester."

Underclassmen also complained about being able to sign up for their courses, saying that "seniors are given top priority, and freshmen are last, which can really make it difficult getting into some of the courses you want." However, few had problems with inordinately large class sizes, since many classes are capped at 30, and the occasional large lecture class has around 200 members. Students praised their professors for being "helpful and available," although many feel people don't take as much advantage of office hours as they should. One senior stated, "My professor was really surprised when I came to his office—apparently, it doesn't happen that often." The school also offers many tutoring options, such as a writing lab, that struggling students use to keep their grades up.

Variety of Social Options

A great deal of Fresno's social scene centers around the football team. Weekend games are elaborate events that entail rowdy tailgates in the campus parking lots, cheering yourself hoarse in the stands, and usually after-parties in the frats. The frats and sororities have a "pretty big presence on campus, and their parties are popular." They often have themed parties, such as "Pimps and Hos" and toga parties. In general, "the police don't shut them down unless things are really out of control."

Another big party sector at Fresno State is present in the apartments near campus, where many students choose to live. One freshman girl who lives in the apartments said that "on the weekends, no one sleeps." Students say that, in general, "everyone drinks—from what I've seen, maybe two people don't," and smoking is not uncommon, but anything harder than that is rare. There have been a few binge-drinking inci-

dents, but "people are usually just social drinkers, not drinking to get hammered."

There are "tons of places around campus to eat or go shopping—I think every major store or restaurant on the West Coast is present here," a junior girl said. Some students venture farther off campus to areas like the Tower District, which offers a more unique experience with its thrift stores and clubs, even though it "isn't as advertised as it should be."

Fresno State's University Student Union (USU) also provides students with entertainment a little closer to home, including a food court, a post office, a lounge, and a recreation center complete with bowling, billiards, video games, and more. The University also puts on a number of events throughout the year. The new Save Mart Center often hosts concerts, counting Prince and Britney Spears among its recent attractions. Big annual events include Vintage Days, when the University invites local bands and offers activities like wine tasting, and the Top Dog Alumni Awards, when students are recognized for contributions to the school and community. However, "the sad thing is that few students really care that much about these events. The school needs to step it up and get better attractions if they want a lot of people to come."

While "it's difficult to describe a typical Fresno student because there's so much diversity," many people are from the Fresno County area, and nearly everyone is from California. Guys are "usually into sports" and girls are a "happy medium between really fashionable and laid-back." In general, "people here are really cool and chill," and there aren't problems with making friends. Students feel that there is a very strong feeling of diversity on campus, in part because it has a large Hispanic population, as well as many Asian-Americans and African-Americans.

Living in Fresno

Students who choose to live in the dorms can decide between the community and the suite options. In the community-style dorms, there is a guys' side and a girls' side to each floor, separated by a common lounge area, with two bathrooms and two RAs. In the suites, six people share a common room and a bathroom. All the rooms are doubles, often with bunk beds. The dorms are dry, and "the RAs are very strict if they catch you with alcohol." On the other hand, "they will take care of you if you're in bad shape after a night of partying, so you shouldn't be afraid of going to them for help." People "spend a lot of time hanging out in the dorms," where "they leave their doors open and people can just walk in and talk if they want to." But, if you want on-campus housing, you'd better be on top of the applications, because "they fill up very quickly—in fact, some people are still living in a hotel because there were more people who wanted to live in the dorms than the school anticipated."

A lot of students choose to move off campus into apartments, which are plentiful, close to campus and affordable. One girl said enthusiastically that "it gives me more freedom, plus the social scene out here is great." However, students caution against discounting the dorms right away, since that's where many of them met their friends. It's also easy to move off campus into Greek housing, which is another popular option.

A meal plan is not required, but there are quite a few options if you choose to purchase one. There is one central dining hall, the Residence Dining Facility, which some students not-so-affectionately nickname "RD-Barf." However, others say the food "isn't that bad—I was expecting much worse, but I eat the same thing every day." Meal plans can include flex points which students use to buy food at the Student Union restaurants, which include Panda Express, Subway and Taco Bell.

> **"Fresno State is the city of Fresno!"**

The dominant theme of the campus architecture is "old and brick," but there are new buildings scattered around as well. Students say proudly that "a lot goes into campus maintenance," resulting in picturesque lawns and greenery. Fresno State has been undergoing a lot of renovation recently, including the expansion of the Henry Madden Library.

Students say that "just about everyone has a car, and if you don't have one, you're probably getting one next semester." A lot of people make weekend trips to Cal Poly San Luis Obispo, which is about an hour and a half away, and others even drive north to the Bay Area or south to Los Angeles, since Fresno is directly in between the two locations. Cars are also useful since a sizeable portion of the student body (students estimate as much as 25 percent) commute from their homes in the Fresno area. While it doesn't mean that the campus is dead on the weekends, "it can get kind of quiet sometimes." Fresno State offers a good opportunity for students looking for an education close to home.

All in all, "Fresno State *is* the city of Fresno," since both have developed together. The school is such a dominant presence in the area, providing jobs and opportunities for the community, that "although Fresno is not really a college town, the city really does a lot to make things nicer for college kids." Students report feeling safe walking around campus and the surrounding area, as well as enjoying the support of the many local businesses, which "always have Fresno State posters and paraphernalia up."

Go Bulldogs

If you haven't noticed already, "Sports are huge here!" The football team's successes have "really boosted school spirit," encouraging the school and "what seems like everyone who lives in Fresno County" to come out to the games and support the Bulldogs. Other popular sports are basketball and baseball. The school supports its athletic teams with stunning facilities, such as the new Save Mart Center, two gyms, and a new two-story fitness center that includes an indoor track and pool. You don't have to be a stellar athlete to get in on the action, though, because "intramural sports are also really popular," encouraging many students to play everything from inner-tube water polo to ultimate Frisbee.

Fresno State also boasts a large number of student organizations, which range from the Bulldogger Rodeo Club to the Meat Science Club. Some of the most popular include the Campus Crusade for Christ, the Salsa Club, and various cultural organizations. Generally, "people are very committed to their extracurricular activities, and there are a ton to choose from!" In addition, "almost everyone has a job because so many of us are paying our own college tuition." Competition for on-campus jobs can be tough, but there are so many businesses in the surrounding area that "if you want a job, you'll be able to find one somewhere." Students don't report much of a problem balancing their jobs with schoolwork on the whole.

If you're a California student looking for a school not too far from home that will offer myriad opportunities for your next four years, Fresno State may be the perfect school for you. Along with its strong agricultural tradition, Fresno also provides its students with good preparation in other disciplines, giving them a wide field of experience with which to face the world after college. Just don't forget your Bulldog spirit!—*Kimberly Chow*

FYI

If you come to Fresno State, you'd better bring "all of your red clothing to show your Bulldog spirit!"

What's the typical weekend schedule? "College Night on Thursday, going to bars, a football or basketball game, chilling."

If I could change one thing about Fresno State, I'd "make the nightlife better: there isn't a lot for people under 21, and frat parties get old."

Three things every student at Fresno should do before graduating are: "Go to a football game, go to the Tower District, and go snowboarding or tubing at Sierra Summit."

The Claremont Colleges

The Claremont Colleges consist of five small independent liberal arts colleges and two graduate schools found in the tree-lined streets of Claremont, California. Claremont McKenna, Harvey Mudd, Pitzer, Pomona and Scripps form the 5-Cs, the undergraduate liberal art colleges while the graduate institutions are the Claremont Graduate University and the Keck Graduate Institute, which are separated from the undergraduate institutions/colleges. While each of the 5-Cs is independent the close proximity of the other colleges of the consortium enables students to enjoy both the resources of a large university and the intimacy of a small liberal arts college.

Academic Unity

The colleges are distinct in the sense that students receive their degrees from their own college and the colleges' administration and admissions departments are independent from each other. However, partly due to the highly specialized nature of each of the colleges, raging from the humanities and the social sciences to engineering and math, students from individual institutions can take classes in colleges other than their own. Cross-registration is very common and students can even take most of their classes in colleges other than their own. Due to the high degree of specialization in the colleges,

students might even choose to do an off campus major and major in a different college, if they find that their own college's emphasis no longer satisfies their academic interests.

The colleges also share many programs and academic departments such as the Women's Union, the Intercollegiate Department of Media Studies, and the Five-College Theater Department. Shared facilities include counseling centers and the Libraries of the Claremont Colleges, all of the dining halls and the campus bookstore.

Campus interests

In addition to academic integration, the colleges also share many athletic and social activities. Pitzer and Pomona make up an NCAA Division III team while the other three colleges form another. At the same time, all undergraduates can use most of the 5-Cs athletic facilities.

The schools' social scene is quite integrated in the sense that students often attend parties in other colleges. Many times however, their dorms function as the students' social circles with parties inside rooms although there are often all-college parties hosted by the colleges.

Many of the students organizations are integrated in the sense that their membership draws from all five colleges.—*Katerina Karatzia*

Claremont McKenna College

Address: 890 Columbia
Avenue, Claremont, CA
91711
Phone: 909-621-8088
E-mail address:
admission@claremont
mckenna.edu
Web site URL:
www.claremontmckenna.edu
Year Founded: 1946
Private or Public: Private
Religious Affiliation: None
Location: Suburban
Number of Applicants:
3,670
Percent Accepted: 22%
**Percent Accepted who
enroll:** 40%
Number Entering: 320
**Number of Transfers
Accepted each Year:** 86
Middle 50% SAT range:
M: 660–750, CR:
630–740, Wr: Unreported
Middle 50% ACT range:
Unreported

**Early admission program
EA/ED/None:** ED
**Percentage accepted
through EA or ED:** 28%
EA and ED deadline: 15-Nov
Regular Deadline: 2-Jan
Application Fee: $60
**Full time Undergraduate
enrollment:** 1,211
Total enrollment: 1,211
Percent Male: 54%
Percent Female: 46%
**Total Percent Minority or
Unreported:** 28%
Percent African-American:
4%
**Percent Asian/Pacific
Islander:** 12%
Percent Hispanic: 11%
Percent Native-American:
<1%
Percent International: 6%
**Percent in-state/out of
state:** 46%/54%
Percent from Public HS:
Unreported

Retention Rate: 97%
Graduation Rate 4-year: 90%
Graduation Rate 6-year: 94%
**Percent Undergraduates in
On-campus housing:** 98%
**Number of official organized
extracurricular
organizations:** 280
3 Most popular majors:
Economics, International
Relations, Political Science
Student/Faculty ratio: 8:1
Average Class Size: 17
**Percent of students going to
grad school:** Unreported
Tuition and Fees: $37,060
**In-State Tuition and Fees if
different:** No difference
Cost for Room and Board:
$11,930
**Percent receiving financial
aid out of those who apply,
first year:** 45%
**Percent receiving financial
aid among all students:**
51%

For any students who wish they could have the nurturing, close-knit environment of many liberal arts schools on the East Coast but balk at the thought of New England weather, Claremont McKenna College offers the best of both coasts. Located at the foot of the San Gabriel Mountains in the suburban town of Claremont, California, the College is roughly three hours from Las Vegas and less than an hour away from Los Angeles. Somewhat closer, however, are the four other schools that comprise the Claremont consortium. This close proximity to other colleges gives Claremont McKenna the feel of a larger university, despite its relatively small undergraduate enrollment of just over 1,200 students. In addition, students have the chance to utilize the resources—from dining halls to parties—of their neighboring institutions. Whether to take advantage of that larger community or to remain within the cozy campus of Claremont McKenna is the personal choice of each student; every "CMC-er" can attend a college that is truly whatever size they wish.

Academics on Lockdown

Claremont McKenna's academic requirements, on the other hand, are somewhat less fluid. Students must fulfill eleven General Education (GE) requirements that include taking required classes in four disciplines—including science and mathematics, literature, social sciences and humanities—as well as show proficiency in a foreign language and satisfy a physical education requirement. The nine or ten additional requirements for each major leave underclassmen with relatively little freedom of choice when it comes to their course loads. One freshman lamented, "It's stricter than I'd like it to be. As a freshman, you're pretty much locked in because you have to get these requirements out of the way. It's frustrating not being able to take some of the really good courses that you know are out there."

The upside to the broad range of mandated classes, however, is that by the end of their sophomore year, when it is recommended that GE requirements be completed, CMC students have a rich educational base from which to select their major. "They really emphasize a liberal arts education here. They want you to be grounded in a wide range of things before you decide what you want to study. You really have to test everything out," said one student who is a fan of the broad range of requirements. The college is known for its exceptional programs in government, international relations, and economics. According to one student, the government professors are "the most well-known on campus," while another added that "the economics professors are notoriously the most difficult." The strength of those three programs also leads to a semiserious stereotype among the students at the Claremont Colleges that Claremont McKennans are "capitalist, conservative, power-hungry maniacs."

"We aren't so big in the sciences," remarked one student. "At least half the people I know are majoring in econ." Nonetheless, students who pursue the pre-med course of study still perform well above the national average; recently, 70 percent of them were accepted to medical school. Other programs have a strong pre-professional focus; the newspaper editor-in-chief remarked that "It's a school-wide event when top consulting and investment banker firms come in for recruitment."

Before students can choose a major or a career, however, they must register for classes. The process has just been switched over from a manual to online system and can seem fairly arbitrary, with students being assigned a time to register for classes and sometimes finding themselves at the mercy of their scheduled time slot. "The people who get the times earlier in the day definitely benefit from that," one student said. "Class sizes are also kept small, which can be a problem." Yet perseverance, combined with the friendly atmosphere for which the school is known, can often overcome the inconvenience of registration. "If you really want to take a class, you can," one freshman said. "I just showed up to all the classes I wanted to take and the professors were willing to let me in."

Additionally, students may take advantage of programs, classes and majors offered at the other four colleges. Undergraduates have the ability to cross-register for off-campus courses, and if they choose an off-campus major from another school's department they may submit their required senior thesis to the sponsoring college's department in lieu of writing their CMC thesis.

While cross-registering can give Claremont McKenna the feel of a larger college, students agree that the school's small size usually makes for a decidedly intimate and personal classroom experience. "My largest class has 20 students, and we're really on a family member basis with our teachers. We go to dinner with them pretty often," said one student. In addition to forming friendships outside the classroom, faculty members and students have generally good academic relationships. One freshman observed that while much of the grading for his classes is done on a curve, his teachers are not unreasonable when it comes to distribution of A's. "The teachers really want you to do well. No one is out to trick you, but there also are no easy teachers. It's really up to the student." Professors really work to make themselves accessible beyond their standard office hours, with some even handing out their cell phone numbers.

No Frats? Who Cares?

While CMC's lack of Greek life sets it apart from many other college campuses, the social scene hardly suffers as a result. In fact, with four other schools close by, students say that people who are eager to go out are never at a loss for a party—in fact, they have five different campus party scenes to choose from. "When one campus is hosting an especially big or good party, everyone else from the Five C's will go there too. There's a lot of interaction between schools," said one student.

"Every Thursday, there's a huge themed party," explained another. "We've had a resort theme, rock star night, a black and white party. Harvey Mudd even threw a foam party—and they made their own foam." These theme parties are organized by the upperclassmen in individual dorms but are usually held outside. Dorms even have funds earmarked for buying alcohol for such events, a practice that is indicative of the administration's view towards alcohol on campus. One student says, "The alcohol policy is very, very lax. Officially the school doesn't condone it, but it's certainly very lax. The school provides a keg to anyone over the age of 21 who wants to host a party, and they are then responsible for carding at parties. But that rarely happens."

The general consensus on campus is that the campus security staff is primarily there to protect students rather than break up parties or arrest anyone who's underage and imbibing. In fact, the campus has what is known as "a red cup policy"—as long as students carry their alcohol around campus in a cup rather than a bottle, they run into very few problems with the administration. While students feel that "the social scene does center around drinking," Claremont McKenna makes an extra effort to plan social events like movie nights for non-drinkers. "There's an entire committee set up on campus that plans weekly sober activities. I mean, drinking is a big part of being at CMC. But if you don't, it's no big deal."

Sticking to "The Five C's"

In general, the school's social scene extends only as far as the campuses of the other Five C's; students report trips to Claremont, or "the Village," as relatively rare—especially for anyone looking to go out. "We don't really go to bars in Claremont. I don't know if there are any bars here," one student commented.

While the relations between town residents and students are thought to range from "non-existent" to "fine," students sometimes spot "townies" or "drunk Claremont high school kids" at campus parties. In general, however, students have limited but cordial contact with Claremont residents and choose to stick close to home; this sentiment is supported by the overwhelming majority of students, about 97 percent, who opt to live on campus all four years.

Despite the popularity of campus living arrangements, not every student is as enthusiastic about the campus itself. As one student said, "Everything is in really good shape, but I just can't stand the architecture. It's all stucco, and the campus is made up of all these one- or two-story buildings. It's really different in that regard from East Coast schools."

Even so, many students are content to stay on campus as much as possible, though one student deemed a car (or at least a friend with one) as "definitely a necessity." This campus-centric outlook applies to many aspects of student life. Rather than eat at restaurants in Claremont itself, most students opt to swipe at one of any of the five colleges' dining halls—Harvey Mudd has Steak Night every Sunday, "the best dining halls are at Scripps and Pomona," and free snacks are served each night at 10:30 p.m. While the student center, ironically called "The Hub," is not a very popular gathering spot, many students enjoy hanging out on the school's social North Quad, which is also home to dorms. "People spend a lot of time out there, which makes life for people that live there kind of tough." In comparison, Mid Quad dorms are known as the slightly more

subdued social areas and South Quad, comprised of three towers, is "generally pretty quiet." Students who do not drink have the option to live in a substance-free dorm, Stark Hall. One upperclassman shared a very unusual fact: "Although CMC offers a cleaning service, it is by no means conventional. Many students develop lasting relationships with those staff, as with all other branches of service work at the school. CMC is a community for not only students, but also faculty and staff on every level."

For those nights when the standard dining hall fare becomes bland, the Athenaeum is a viable option. Every weeknight, there will be "a distinguished speaker who gives a presentation over a gourmet meal. Recent Athenaeum speakers include Salman Rushdie, Justice Antonin Scalia, and Anderson Cooper. However, speakers are not limited to the big names. From artists to historians, student-debated panels to top political analysts, the Athenaeum is a true incarnation of the liberal arts experience," said a former Student Government participant.

Dorms are assigned via a lottery system, with some students having the option to retain their room from year to year. Each year, the Dean of Students chooses seniors to live in each dormitory as resident assistants. While students did not report having especially close relationships with these RAs, they are generally well-liked by their advisees. "They're cool people," one freshman said. "We don't really hang out with them, but it's not like they pop in to our rooms every few hours to make sure we aren't doing anything bad."

"We're the frat boys with no frats, according to the kids at the other Five C's."

Claremont McKenna students often branch out from their dorms and make the trip "literally across the street" to their neighboring schools for social events like the aforementioned foam party. "It's really like one huge campus. If your school is too small for you, you can always expand it to include any of the others."

"Our football team sucks," as an upperclassman put it. Pomona College is Claremont McKenna's main rival, which often leads to the sentiment that the competition can be extreme at times due to proximity. Indeed, even students who claim to see a lack of diversity in their student body had a difficult time identifying the "stereotypical" Claremont McKenna student. "We're the frat boys with no frats, according to kids at the other Five C's," one student ultimately decided. "And the stereotypical CMC girl? Well, we don't know. We don't date the girls

from CMC." Ultimately, whatever their background, Claremont McKenna students have come to their school to take part in world-class academics while also reaping the benefits of a vibrant party scene. And the California sunshine doesn't hurt either.
—*Angelica Baker*

FYI
If you come to CMC, you'd better bring "an air-conditioning unit, a red cup, and a skateboard—that seems to be the preferred method of transportation on-campus."
The typical weekend schedule includes "a theme party on Thursday night, studying on Friday, going to whatever 5C is hosting the main party for the night, and spend Sunday recovering and studying."
If I could change one thing about CMC, I'd "make it a little bit bigger. The campus can get small really quickly."
Three things every student at CMC should do before graduating are "get thrown in 'the pond' on your birthday, win a beer pong tournament, and learn how to skateboard."

Harvey Mudd College

Address: 301 Platt Boulevard Claremont, CA 91711
Phone: 909-621-8011
E-mail address: admission@hmc.edu
Web site URL: www.hmc.edu
Year Founded: 1955
Private or Public: Private
Religious Affiliation: None
Location: Suburban
Number of Applicants: 2,493
Percent Accepted: 28%
Percent Accepted who enroll: 31%
Number Entering: 219
Number of Transfers Accepted each Year: 5
Middle 50% SAT range: M: 740–820, CR: 690–760, Wr: 680–760
Middle 50% ACT range: Unreported
Early admission program EA/ED/None: ED

Percentage accepted through EA or ED: 21%
EA and ED deadline: 15-Nov
Regular Deadline: 2-Jan
Application Fee: $60
Full time Undergraduate enrollment: 735
Total enrollment: 735
Percent Male: 66%
Percent Female: 34%
Total Percent Minority or Unreported: 50%
Percent African-American: 1%
Percent Asian/Pacific Islander: 21%
Percent Hispanic: 8%
Percent Native-American: 1%
Percent International: 4%
Percent in-state/out of state: 50%/50%
Percent from Public HS: 74%
Retention Rate: 96%
Graduation Rate 4-year: 83%
Graduation Rate 6-year: 89%

Percent Undergraduates in On-campus housing: 99%
Number of official organized extracurricular organizations: 109
3 Most popular majors: Computer Science, Engineering, Math
Student/Faculty ratio: 8:1
Average Class Size: 9
Percent of students going to grad school: 43%
Tuition and Fees: $36,635
In-State Tuition and Fees if different: No difference
Cost for Room and Board: $11,971
Percent receiving financial aid out of those who apply, first year: 83%
Percent receiving financial aid among all students: 59%

Harvey Mudd College is one of the five prestigious Claremont Colleges located in sunny southern California. Although many may not have heard of this small college, which only enrolls about 200 students per class, Harvey Mudd is one of the best math, science, and engineering colleges in the nation—all while maintaining its

identity as a liberal arts college. Harvey Mudd is home to some of the brightest and quirkiest students in the country.

The List of Majors: Short and Sweet
At Harvey Mudd, there are only nine majors: biology, biology/chemistry, chemistry, com-

puter science, engineering, mathematics, mathematics/computer science, mathematical biology and physics. In addition, there is the Independent Program of Study and the Off-Campus Major. The limited number of majors demonstrates how serious Harvey Mudd is in its commitment to teaching math, science, and engineering, but the students there do not find themselves restricted. Students at Harvey Mudd are free to take humanities classes either at Harvey Mudd or at any of the other four Claremont colleges. The core requirements required of all Harvey Mudd students are four semesters of math, three semesters of physics and physics lab, two semesters of chemistry and chemistry lab, two semesters of humanities and social sciences, an engineering course, a biology class and a computer science class.

Since there really is no such thing as a gut class at Harvey Mudd, no particular major is considered harder than the others. Getting into classes for one's major is quite easy; one student noted, "I have never *not* gotten into a class I wanted to be enrolled in." Just as the list of majors is short, classes are likewise very small. Classes are at the most 200 students for freshmen core lecture classes, and upper division classes tend to be around 30 students at the most. An engineering major said, "Upper division classes tend to weed people out and have smaller class sizes." In fact, there are certain engineering classes known as "weed-out" classes, intended to determine which students *really* want to major in that field.

Once students get through these most difficult courses, however, they are rewarded. Mudd offers a Clinic program, which gives upperclassmen the opportunity to work on real-world industrial projects in teams of four or five under the guidance of a student team leader, a faculty advisor, and a liaison from a sponsoring organization. While other schools have engineering senior projects, Mudd "actually gets companies to pay something like $40,000 to have a few Mudd students do a project for them, so it's cool to get that real world experience before graduating."

A Liberal Arts/Math and Science School

On top of the classes required for their major, Mudd students are required to take 10 additional humanities and social sciences classes, which students fondly call "hum/ soc classes" (pronounced hum-sock). They must also pick a concentration in the humanities as well, which ensures that Harvey Mudd students aren't knowledgeable only about numbers and equations. Even though they are at a math and science school, students tend to be quite well rounded. A sophomore said, "We get to take a lot of really cool humanities classes from the other Claremont colleges."

Students agree that, although Harvey Mudd is the best of the five Claremont Colleges, it is definitely nice to have the other colleges around. With four other colleges in such close proximity, students are offered countless opportunities. One student listed the classes he took outside of Harvey Mudd: "I've taken voice lessons, music theory and Chinese at some of the other colleges."

All My Professors Know My Name

Because classes tend to be so small, students are usually very close to their professors and professors are very involved in their students' academic pursuits and personal lives. Professors want students to achieve academic excellence, but at the same time believe in personal development. First-semester freshmen do not have grades for their classes but receive either high pass, pass or fail marks. If a freshman "high passes" all or too many of their classes, they are promptly sent a good-natured letter from their dean: "We are very happy with your academic achievement but, please, get a life!" The Dean's words are humorous, but true. Professors and deans truly want their students to be happy and have fun—Mudd throws famous annual parties funded by the school such as "Tequila Night."

In addition, professors are provided with a financial fund to take students out for lunch or dinner. One student noted that her professor was "in competition" with another professor to see who could take out the most students for a meal. Opportunities like these encourage interaction and foster relationships between students and professors outside of the classroom. Students say professors tend to be "down to earth" and very accessible for help or questions. Students agree that professors truly want to help their students and will often seek out those who are not doing well in their classes to help them. Nonetheless, even though professors are kind and good-natured, they still are hard graders. One student said, "Getting A's is hard and there is definitely grade deflation at our school."

So What Do You Do Outside of Studying?

Outside of studying and doing endless problems for their five or more classes, Mudd students play as hard as they study. They may be some of the brightest students in the nation, but Mudd students do many of the same things any college student would do: "hang out with people, play guitar, procrastinate." The people that Mudd students tend to hang out with are determined on proximity—the dorms that Mudd students are assigned to often function as their social circles as well. Because dorms are considered "extremely spacious," pretty much everyone lives on campus, even as upperclassmen.

Dorm life is exciting and packed with personality. North dorm folk, or "Northies," know how to party and will often have a game or two of beer pong going. The school is strict on underage drinking, but often "turns a blind eye" and cares more about their students' well-being. West dorm folk have their own traditions: "Their courtyard often has broken electronics, appliances, who-knows-what lying around, and often a fire going on at night." East dorm is quieter and composed mainly of CS majors, and one can always join them for a competitive video game or two. The South dorm is also considered quieter, although they are quite a musical bunch; one can often find a few Southies in the courtyard playing guitar together. Across the street from Mudd is Scripps College, which is a small, all-girls liberal arts college. Students comment that there is definitely a lot of interaction between the schools, "enough to make the Mudd girls jealous sometimes."

Mudd also throws some pretty wicked parties which are kindly funded by the school. Parties that all students must attend at least once include the LTG (Long Tall Glasses), a formal party hosted in the North dorms. Suds is another popular party open to all the Claremont colleges involving foam generating machines and a lot of partying.

Besides partying, Mudd students are very active and involved in their extracurricular activities. For those who are artistically inclined there is a jam society that maintains a jam room with a drum set and other musical equipment. There is also a Mudd art club which exhibits a lot of student artwork. Mudd students can also join organizations at other Claremont colleges as well. For the physically active, there is the "Foster's Run," which is an annual nine-mile unicycle ride to a local donut shop which gives students free strawberry donuts "which are quite tasty." Overall, Mudd students are a diverse and involved group of people who seem to find their niche in the school pretty quickly.

The Joke's on You

Harvey Mudd may not have a Greek scene or a football team, but it does have some of the nation's best pranksters. Pranks play a huge role on campus and myths are passed on from upperclassmen to underclassmen about past accomplishments. However, there are rules to pulling a prank such as the "24-hour reverse rule" in which the prank must be reversible in 24 hours. Therefore, a student fondly noted, "you can't shave off someone's eyebrows while they're sleeping because it won't grow back in 24 hours."

Individuals enjoy pranking each other, but there is also a rivalry between Mudd, Caltech, and MIT. Mudd was the first college to steal Caltech's campus cannon, followed by MIT. Perhaps due to the nature of their pranks, Mudd students are not allowed to prank other Claremont colleges. Despite the prankster nature of students, the administration trusts students and there is a school-wide honor code. Students are given 24-hour access to the academic buildings, including labs and machine shops. The campus is filled with unlocked bikes, skateboards and scooters because students respect each other's property and well-being.

"Although school and work can get hard, it's good to know that everyone's working as hard as you. Everyone is doing something amazing."

Mudd students all learn to accept the fact that they are nerds. In fact, they are proud of it. A sophomore remarked that her physics professor "quacks when he's lecturing" because he uses penguins to describe special relativity. Professors and students alike are quirky, but friendly. Freshmen are encouraged to find their interests immediately on campus and dorm with upperclassmen, who often help them integrate into the campus. Students agree that "although school and work can get hard, it's good to know that everyone's working as hard as you. Everyone is doing something amazing."—*Emily Chen*

FYI

If you come to Harvey Mudd, you'd better bring "a Brita water filter, since the tap water isn't too good to drink."

What is the typical weekend schedule? "Slack off as much as possible on Friday and Saturday, and then do pretty much all my weekend work on Sunday. It seems to work pretty well. I think many manage to not even have classes on Friday, so their weekend probably starts a bit earlier."

If I could change one thing about Harvey Mudd, I'd "make studying abroad easier."

Three things every student at Harvey Mudd should do before graduating are "learn to unicycle, explore the random basements in the academic buildings, and pull a prank on someone."

Pitzer College

Address: 1050 North Mills Avenue, Claremont, CA 91711

Phone: 909-621-8129

E-mail address: admission@pitzer.edu

Web site URL: www.pitzer.edu

Year Founded: 1963

Private or Public: Private

Religious Affiliation: None

Location: Suburban

Number of Applicants: 4,031

Percent Accepted: 22%

Percent Accepted who enroll: 29%

Number Entering: 268

Number of Transfers Accepted each Year: 20

Middle 50% SAT range: M: 590–680, CR: 590–670, Wr: Unreported

Middle 50% ACT range: 26–30

Early admission program EA/ED/None: ED

Percentage accepted through EA or ED: Unreported

EA and ED deadline: 15-Nov

Regular Deadline: 1-Jan

Application Fee: $50

Full time Undergraduate enrollment: 1,025

Total enrollment: 1,025

Percent Male: 41%

Percent Female: 59%

Total Percent Minority or Unreported: 59%

Percent African-American: 6%

Percent Asian/Pacific Islander: 11%

Percent Hispanic: 15%

Percent Native-American: <1%

Percent International: Unreported

Percent in-state/out of state: 48%/52%

Percent from Public HS: Unreported

Retention Rate: 92%

Graduation Rate 4-year: 74%

Graduation Rate 6-year: Unreported

Percent Undergraduates in On-campus housing: 65%

Number of official organized extracurricular organizations: 120

3 Most popular majors: Psychology, Media Studies, Sociology

Student/Faculty ratio: Unreported

Average Class Size: 12

Percent of students going to grad school: Unreported

Tuition and Fees: $37,870

In-State Tuition and Fees if different: No difference

Cost for Room and Board: $10,930

Percent receiving financial aid out of those who apply, first year: 77%

Percent receiving financial aid among all students: 42%

P itzer, one of the five Claremont Colleges, is known as the most liberal of colleges within the consortium. An intimate community located a world from the cold New England winter, Pitzer is a breeding ground for creative and adventurous young people determined to make a change. Students very much march to the beat of their own drum, and enjoy the freedom and creativity of academic life at Pitzer. As one student said, "Pitzer students aren't looking for a formula, they're looking to create their own."

Creative Academics

Along the grassy mounds of Pitzer, the words "academic requirements" and "department" are conspicuously absent. Instead, students are discussing how they'll meet their "objectives" and which "field group" they plan on majoring in. Pitzer students have the ability to choose from and combine a variety of majors, and many design their own. Some student-created majors include Theater for Social Change, Media Studies and Gender Studies, and Visual Pragmatics. For students focused on the humanities and social justice, the possibilities are endless. As one student put it, "Pitzer has made me think of academics as something that's creative. They are so much your own."

Pitzer's unique academic philosophy and strong programs in the behavioral sciences set it apart from the other Claremont colleges. Its most popular programs include Psychology, Sociology, and Media Studies. The school's mission statement requires that students commit themselves to the pursuit of social justice, intercultural understanding, and environmental sensitivity in academic life. Pitzer's strong sense of community and social responsibility gives it a special flavor. "I don't know anyone who's not passionate about what they're learning," said a Sociology major.

> **"Pitzer students aren't looking for a formula, they're looking to create their own."**

Students rave about interactive classes in which they are able to engage with different communities. "A lot of the professors were or are activists in the community. Because of that, classes are very geared towards how to make social changes," observed one student. At Pitzer, a Sudanese Lost Boy teaches a class on African politics. A community organizer takes his Rural and Urban Social Movements class to La Paz, where the Farm Movement's union headquarters are located, and students meet the leaders who they had learned about in the classroom. A creative writing course collaborates with a juvenile detention facility, and culminates in a joint poetry reading on campus. Pitzer students agree that the courses are student driven, and that the small class sizes allow for these sorts of opportunities.

Because the school is so heavy on the humanities and behavioral sciences, Pitzer students are grateful for the opportunities provided by the five-college consortium. It's very easy to take classes at the other schools, which include Pomona, Harvey Mudd, Claremont McKenna, and Scripps. "I have a friend who's majoring at Pomona because they didn't have the major at Pitzer. It's very flexible," explained a sophomore. "It's possible to take all of your courses at another 5-C if you want to," said another student.

While the resources of the consortium are available, don't think of Pitzer as an acade-mic "backdoor" to the other Claremont Colleges. Pitzer admissions have become increasingly competitive. One student on the academic advisory council noted that, "the most recent freshmen and sophomores are more academically competitive than in years past. More and more you're seeing Pitzer kids studying in the library on Friday nights along with students from the other 5-C's." However, the students are not competing with one another. "I don't know how my friends do in school, but I know what they're interested in and involved in."

Hipsters—Not Hippies

There is the old stereotype of Pitzer as the hippie, pot smoking Claremont College, a product of its conception in the ultraliberal era of the sixties. While the student body is certainly creative, and there is a laid-back, liberal feel to campus, don't expect to see peace signs, pot, and tie-dye everywhere you look. "There are a lot of HIPSTERS—not hippies," joked one student. She added that Pitzer students are "very passionate and very independent. They're also usually pretty quirky."

While you won't find students pre-gaming for a wild frat party, the social life is definitely active and also more intimate than at other schools. "Because the school is so small, it's hard not to be friends with and know who everyone is," said one sophomore, "and everyone's always hanging out and down to do something." When not at relaxed dorm parties, Pitzer students will go to dance parties and concerts at the Grove House, a unique old house built in 1902 and transported to campus that now serves as a center of social life. Grove House "is my favorite place on the planet," gushed one student. Aside from "Groove at the Grove," there are 5-C events every weekend, and for those who are worried about the small size of Pitzer, students say that it is not an issue. "You have the other schools if you feel claustrophobic or want a new scene," said a student. Overall, "Pitzer kids like to have a good time, but it's more laid-back fun," said another.

Some other major events on campus include Kohoutek, a giant music festival that occurs every spring and is a highlight of the year. A smaller festival, called Reggae Fest, happens in the fall. Students also enjoy hiking and skiing at Baldy Mountain, and throw themselves into the 120 on-campus extracurricular activities. At Pitzer, students are more likely to cheer for their friends playing intramural sports than the Sagehens, the official mascot of the joint Pomona-Pitzer athletic program. Internships in the surrounding area during the school year are also very popular. Through the Ontario program, students can design an independent study project in a local community in conjunction with a class. Students also play a role in all of the college's decisions as voting members of Pitzer's governing bodies.

And as for that stereotype? "Yea, there's the idea that we're all pot smoking hippies," said one student. "But if you look at the extra-curriculars on campus, and what students are doing, the reality doesn't mesh with the old stereotype."

Dorm Life

Pitzer's campus grounds consist of grassy mounds and cacti amidst a gorgeous backdrop of the San Gabriel mountains. California weather is certainly an appeal. On campus, student murals containing political and social messages, approved by a student committee, adorn some of Pitzer's building walls. The nearest town is a sleepy suburb containing little shops and restaurants that primarily cater to residents.

Most students stay on campus all four years in one of five residence halls. Three of Pitzer's newest halls are certified gold standard—recognized by the U.S. Green Building Council as some of the leading sustainable buildings in the United States. Upperclassmen typically live in Meade, and enjoy common rooms and suites of eight. Freshmen dorms are horseshoe shaped, making it "easy to know what people are up to." During a student's first year, he or she will live in a double joined to another double by a common bathroom. Each hall has a mentor and an RA. Mentors help the students feel comfortable and hold small bonding events, whereas RA's monitor the halls. As for the prevalence of drugs and alcohol on campus, one student said, "I don't know if there's more here than at other schools, but alcohol and pot are definitely present."

The Gold Center is another central feature of campus. It holds a fitness center, a gallery, and multi-purpose rooms. Students frequent the Center's Shakedown café, an organic eatery run by creative student chefs. The center also holds various events that bring students together, ranging from hosting speakers on campus to holding "snackysnack time," when they bring restaurant food to students at 10 pm Tuesday nights.

While students have the luxury of being able to get anywhere on campus within five minutes of walking, they also benefit from the unique student-run Green Bike Program. The program allows students to enter a lottery system, and winners enjoy a free bike, repairs included, for the rest of the year. Pitzer students founded the Green Bike Program as an eco-friendly way to travel between the Claremont Colleges.

Pitzer and the World

Pitzer's small student population certainly lends itself to a nurturing and "comforting" environment. With the amenities of the five-college consortium, personalized academic attention, and idyllic California weather, Pitzer students are living in the perfect college bubble. Yet, students are constantly stretching themselves, engaging with different communities and designing hands-on projects. Students are able to enjoy the support of a personal community as they explore academia and the world beyond. One student said, "While Pitzer is its own world, it makes an effort to show how you can fit into the bigger picture."—*Raphaella Friedman*

FYI

If you come to Pitzer, you'd better bring "a sense of initiative so you can take control of your own education and ideals."

What's the typical weekend schedule? "Parties at the other 5-C's on Thursday and Friday nights, a musical event, playing Frisbee, maybe going into L.A., and studying on Sunday."

If I could change one thing about Pitzer, I would change "the level of student apathy—I really wish the average student would care more about the environment and stop sinking into the Southern California lifestyle."

Three things every student at Pitzer should do before graduating are: "Go to the hot springs, have an internship with a social justice group in L.A., and go on a Pitzer Outdoor Adventures trip."

Pomona College

Address: 333 N College Way
   Claremont, CA 91711
Phone: 909-621-8134
E-mail address:
   admissions@pomona.edu
Web site URL:
   www.pomona.edu
Year Founded: 1887
Private or Public: Private
Religious Affiliation: None
Location: Suburban
Number of Applicants: 6,293
Percent Accepted: 16%
Percent Accepted who
   enroll: 39%
Number Entering: 396
Number of Transfers
   Accepted each Year:
   Unreported
Middle 50% SAT range:
   M: 690–780, CR:
   700–780, Wr: 680–770
Middle 50% ACT range: 30–34
Early admission program
   EA/ED/None: ED I, ED II

Percentage accepted
   through EA or ED: 29%
EA and ED deadline: 1-Nov,
   28-Dec
Regular Deadline: 2-Jan
Application Fee: $65
Full time Undergraduate
   enrollment: 1,532
Total enrollment: 1,532
Percent Male: 49%
Percent Female: 51%
Total Percent Minority or
   Unreported: 39%
Percent African-American:
   8%
Percent Asian/Pacific
   Islander: 18%
Percent Hispanic: 11%
Percent Native-American: 1%
Percent International:
   Unreported
Percent in-state/out of
   state: 33 %/67%
Percent from Public HS: 69%
Retention Rate: 97%

Graduation Rate 4-year:
   90%
Graduation Rate 6-year: 95%
Percent Undergraduates in
   On-campus housing: 98%
Number of official organized
   extracurricular
   organizations: 227
3 Most popular majors:
   Economics, English, Politics
Student/Faculty ratio: 8:1
Average Class Size: 14
Percent of students going to
   grad school: 80%
Tuition and Fees: $35,318
In-State Tuition and Fees if
   different: No difference
Cost for Room and Board:
   $12,220
Percent receiving financial
   aid out of those who apply,
   first year: 81%
Percent receiving financial
   aid among all students:
   52%

Pomona College might not be the most recognizable of names outside the state, but it has an appeal all its own. This small liberal arts college tucked into Southern California boasts "very curious and passionate" students and a location that's "one hour from snow, one hour from the beach, and one hour from Disneyland." As one of the members of the Claremont College Consortium, the college is able to have the benefits of an undergraduate focus without sacrificing the resources of a large research university. Combining strong academics, an idyllic setting, and an intimate atmosphere, Pomona boasts some of the happiest students in the country. One student summed up Pomona's unique appeal: "Pomona gives you a liberal arts education as good as anything on the East Coast, but I think the people here are a lot more cheerful, a lot friendlier, and just really happy."

A Truly Liberal Education

Students at Pomona say their classes are "demanding," but that they ultimately have a lot of freedom to design their own educations. To graduate, Pomona requires all students to take thirty-two courses and fulfill the Breadth of Study Requirements, which one junior described as "take five classes you like and then, done." Every student takes at least one course in each of five disciplines: Creative Expression; Social Institutions and Human Behavior; History, Values, Ethics and Cultural Studies; Physical and Biological Sciences; and Mathematical Reasoning. In addition, students have to participate in physical education and take an intermediate language class or its equivalent. While upperclassmen can pick any of forty-five different majors to concentrate in, freshmen start out by taking a required first-year seminar. These Critical Inquiry classes, with unique topics ranging from "Facebook, Fairness, and Forgery" to "The Heart of a Doctor," have a capped enrollment of 15 students and are "writing-intensive."

Although the most popular majors at Pomona are said to be in the social sciences and humanities, especially politics and economics, many students focus on the natural sciences, which are notoriously difficult. "It's a big jump place for medical school, and there are lots of premeds," said one freshman.

But non-science majors need not fear; Pomona offers a variety of science courses that are relatively easier and more interdisciplinary, such as geology classes and "Physics and Music." In general, students are interested in a range of areas and are easily able to find classes to fulfill their requirements: "Here, you can really like religious studies even if you're a chemistry major," one senior said.

Students at Pomona frequently mentioned having casual meals with their professors, getting advanced research opportunities as underclassmen, and learning about their professors' quirkier sides. "Classes are small enough that you get to know your professors as people," a junior said. In addition to having accessible professors, Pomona students can take advantage of small discussion-based classes that are taught seminar-style. According to one student, a "big" class consists of thirty students, and "most of them are small enough that they can be definitely interactive." While upperclassmen have priority in picking classes, a freshman said that he hadn't had problems registering for the courses he wanted.

One of Pomona's most distinctive features is its membership in the Claremont Colleges consortium (Pomona even shares athletic teams and a mascot, the Sagehen, with Pitzer College), which gives Pomona students the option of registering in courses offered by the other colleges—Claremont McKenna, Harvey Mudd, Pitzer, and Scripps. Many students sample the rigorous science courses at Harvey Mudd, the media studies program at Pitzer, and the business program at Claremont McKenna. "If it were just Pomona, I would feel a little limited by class options," said one girl. However, freshmen aren't allowed to cross-register, and even upperclassmen must take at least two courses at Pomona every semester. Popular courses at Pomona itself include the English seminar "Obscure and Eclectic Fiction" and "The U.S. Congress," in which students participate in simulations of the U.S. legislature along with other Claremont students. In general, students say the workload is intense but "open-ended," with much more collaboration than competition. "It's definitely challenging, but it's never too much. You get a lot of collaboration here," said one. Another added, "There's almost nonexistent competition between students here. Individually, they are really high-achieving, they are motivated, they have goals in life, and they work really hard, but it's not like if you get an A, I can't get an A."

Surfing, Skiing, and Partying

"The smart and personable people you will meet at Pomona and love for the rest of your life—that's really the best thing about it," declared a senior. Students say Pomona does an excellent job of welcoming its freshmen right from the beginning and continues to support them for the rest of their undergraduate years. Before classes start, freshmen go on student-led Orientation Adventure trips throughout California. Freshmen say they "really start to bond" with their classmates over four days of hiking around Yosemite, surfing in Santa Barbara, or just exploring Southern California while doing community service. But one of the most praised features of freshman year is the sponsor group program, in which freshmen are divided into groups of ten to twenty. Guided and mentored by two sophomores who are "like their brothers and sisters," these groups live in the same hall together and become "like family."

The consortium system offers Pomona students not only academic options, but also a variety of social scenes. "There definitely is a big party scene, but there are basically no frats," said a freshman. "Parties are usually inside the rooms, or there's always a big party at the other colleges." In addition, Pomona students receive a daily "student digester e-mail" listing all of the day's events and activities, including official college-sponsored parties, shows, movie screenings, and even "politics talks," in which politics professors and students gather to drink wine, eat cheese, and discuss current events. Although "the alcohol scene is definitely present," and "pretty much everyone" drinks, students have the option of choosing substance-free housing. A sophomore said, "I've generally found that there are more nondrinkers than one would think and it's not hard to find stuff to do without drinking heavily."

Pomona's alcohol policy is considered "not super-rigid." Drinks are allowed everywhere on campus; however, no hard liquor is allowed on South Campus, where underclassmen live. RAs are known to be stricter on South Campus, but are mostly there to make sure students understand how to handle alcohol responsibly, and "if there's an emergency they'd know how to respond to it."

The college often sponsors parties, and when it comes to big annual events, "the administration treats students like royalty." These events are a large part of Pomona's quirky culture and lore, or "Pomoniana." Along with traditional parties like the "screw your roommate dance," in which students set up their roommates on blind dates, Pomona organizes an annual "Death by Chocolate" event on the last day of classes before fall semester finals. "Basically, they just fill one of our auditorium rooms with chocolate—fondue, cocoa, cake, everything," explained a junior. On Snow Day, another pre-finals event, the college hires a snow machine to fill the quad with snow, so students can enjoy snowball fights and snowmen in the middle of Southern California. Of course, ski resorts aren't that far from Pomona, and one of the college's most beloved traditions is Ski-Beach Day: "In the morning, Pomona pays for us to go skiing and snowboarding in the mountains, and in the afternoon, we drive down to the beach and hang out in the sun." Despite its closeness to both beaches and mountains—not to mention that it's just an hour away from L.A.—most students stay on campus. That's because there's plenty to do at Pomona itself, students say, but for those who would like to venture off campus, there's a Metrolink station a few blocks away, and "people will drive or ride up to go see games and concerts."

Students say that hall life is very social, with residents keeping their doors open most of the time. "The students here are pretty easygoing and pretty content and smiley," said a junior. "People will go out all the time and do homework in the sun on the lawn or on the 'beach,' which is this sandy area with a beach volleyball court." While some students praised the feel of a small, intimate community—"everyone knows everyone else, everyone knows where everyone else lives"—one freshman said he already felt that the community was "too small." Even in this small community, students have a wide variety of passions and come from a variety of ethnic backgrounds and states. However, most students are considered "really liberal" and middle- to upper-class.

A Sagehen's Habitat

Housing at Pomona is guaranteed for all four years, and only a few seniors live off-campus. About two-thirds of freshmen are in doubles, and the rest are in singles. Most underclassmen live on South Campus in hall-style dorms, but housing improves with seniority. North Campus, where upperclassmen live, has many two-room doubles, which are two singles connected by a small entryway and a door. Juniors and seniors generally have singles or even suites, and

"one of our nicest dorms has fireplaces and balconies, with really spacious rooms."

In addition, students can also choose to live in a few themed dorms, including substance-free housing, and "Unity Dorm," which consists of one floor of students who "really actively want to be engaged in their dorm, so they do barbecues and field trips and stuff together." Students who want to immerse themselves in a foreign language can live in one of six special language halls in Oldenborg, the language center. For example, if you live in the Spanish hall, "you don't have to talk in Spanish all the time, but if you're doing Spanish work there's always someone to help you," a junior explained. Oldenborg's dining hall—one of three at Pomona—offers language tables where students can practice conversing over lunch.

Since meal plans can be used at any of the other Claremont campuses' dining halls, students have a total of eight dining halls to choose from. The different meal plans offer either a set number of meals per week or meals plus "flex dollars," which are accepted at the "Coop Fountain," a student-run snack and smoothie shop and convenience store. For a nicer, sit-down meal, students can visit the Sagehen Café. One of Pomona's most popular dining features is "Snack," a weeknight study break, in which the dining halls reopen at 10:30 p.m. and students can enjoy free snacks. "We come at the end of the day to just kind of run into each other, sum up our days, relax, eat, and talk. It's great because I always get hungry at night," said a junior. In general, students say they are really satisfied with the food.

The meal plan's flex dollars can't be applied off-campus, but Pomona does offer a "Claremont Cash" card, which works like a debit card at campus stores and about half of the stores in "the Village," which is what students call the surrounding town of Claremont. The Village "is a little bit on the small side" and "a little sleepy," with not much nightlife, according to students. About a third of the town's population consists of retirees, and students describe it as "such a safe, nice, quaint little town; we feel completely comfortable walking around, even at night."

Pomoniana and More

Activities outside the classroom aren't just limited to exploring the Village. Pomona students can join clubs not just on their own campus, but also those at any of the other campuses. One of Pomona's most popular clubs is "On the Loose," which rents out outdoors equipment, sponsors several outdoors trips every week and trains students to lead trips. Favorite destinations include Death Valley and Joshua Tree.

Also, "it's really easy to get a job if you want a job. Students mentioned jobs at the libraries and other campus facilities, as well as positions as volunteer coordinators and interns in the Pomona College internship program. Under this program, students can take normally unpaid internships in the L.A. area, but still receive wages from Pomona.

> "The smart and personable people you will meet at Pomona and love for the rest of your life: that's really the best thing about it."

Although Pomona fields a variety of Division III teams, athletics don't dominate other campus activities. "I wouldn't say our school is the greatest on athletic spirit," said one student. The Pitzer-Pomona Sagehens' biggest rivals are the neighboring Claremont McKenna-Scripps-Harvey Mudd teams, especially in basketball, which can get "pretty heated." Coaches at Pomona understand that students' focus is on academics, so "it's nice for people who want to continue playing sports in college, but not dedicate their lives to sports," said a sophomore.

In keeping with Pomona's sunny, carefree atmosphere, campus traditions are often more quirky and fun than steeped in history and legend. All of the fountains on campus are chlorinated because on students' birthdays, "it's a tradition to dump them into the fountains." Possibly the oddest bit of Pomona lore is the campus' fascination with the number 47. From Pomona's highway exit (47) to the founding date of Claremont McKenna (1947) to the number of students in Pomona's first graduating class (47), the number seems to be everywhere, and one student even wrote a thesis on all the different places 47 occurs in nature. Alum Joe Menosky '79, a writer and co-producer for *Star Trek*, has also inserted the number into episode after episode of the series.

With academic rigor and opportunities comparable to that of any liberal arts college and a relaxed, intimate atmosphere, Pomona is home to happy students, caring faculty, and a sunny "California attitude." As one senior said, "I feel like we are on the one hand selecting bright students, but they're not just smart students who study a lot; we choose people who are really decent. There are so many instances where I've had a conversation with someone and they've surprised me in so many ways and made me realize how good people can be."—*Vivian Yee*

FYI
If you come to Pomona College, you'd better bring "sunblock and sunglasses, innovativeness and inventiveness."
What is the typical weekend schedule? "Get out of class on Friday, do a little work or go into town, play a game of basketball or volleyball, go to a dorm party at one of the 5-Cs, sleep in Saturday, work and hang out, go to events or concerts or lectures, go out to dinner in the village and party again. Sunday, people work."
If I could change one thing about Pomona, I'd "expand the college a little: it's too small."
Three things every student at Pomona should do before graduating are "break into the pool after hours, watch the sun set at Joshua Tree National Park, and leave with a really great group of friends."

Scripps College

Address: 1030 N. Columbia Avenue, Claremont, CA 91711
Phone: 909-621-8149
E-mail address: admission@scrippscollege.edu
Web site URL: www.scrippscollege.edu
Year Founded: 1926
Private or Public: Private
Religious Affiliation: None
Location: Suburban
Number of Applicants: 1,931
Percent Accepted: 43%
Percent Accepted who enroll: 30%
Number Entering: 260
Number of Transfers Accepted each Year: 55
Middle 50% SAT range: M: 620–710, CR: 640–730, Wr: 650–730
Middle 50% ACT range: 28–32

Early admission program EA/ED/None: ED I, ED II
Percentage accepted through EA or ED: 15%
EA and ED deadline: 1-Nov, 1-Jan
Regular Deadline: 1-Jan
Application Fee: $50
Full time Undergraduate enrollment: 944
Total enrollment: 944
Percent Male: 0%
Percent Female: 100%
Total Percent Minority or Unreported: 25%
Percent African-American: 4%
Percent Asian/Pacific Islander: 13%
Percent Hispanic: 7%
Percent Native-American: 1%
Percent International: Unreported
Percent in-state/out of state: 41%/59%
Percent from Public HS: 59%
Retention Rate: 95%

Graduation Rate 4-year: 74%
Graduation Rate 6-year: 80%
Percent Undergraduates in On-campus housing: 96%
Number of official organized extracurricular organizations: 50
3 Most popular majors: Psychology, Politics and International Relations, Media Studies
Student/Faculty ratio: 11:1
Average Class Size: 15
Percent of students going to grad school: 60%
Tuition and Fees: $37,950
In-State Tuition and Fees if different: No difference
Cost for Room and Board: $11,500
Percent receiving financial aid out of those who apply, first year: 70%
Percent receiving financial aid among all students: 11%

O ne of the first things that come to students' minds when describing Scripps College is its intimate community, coupled with a great location outside of Los Angeles. Scripps is the only single-sex school among the Claremont Colleges, offering a highly reputable education to about 950 female students. Although, students are quick to point out that they chose Scripps because of the great education and numerous opportunities it offers, not because of its all-female student body. So if you want to spend four years in a college that has perfect weather, Mediterranean architecture, a proximity to a large city and reputable academics, maybe take a closer look at Scripps.

An All-Female School
One of the advantages of going to an all-female school is its "very warm, friendly atmosphere." According to one student, "A lot of kids here went to high schools with as many or even more people. That's why we didn't feel at the beginning that college life was so overwhelming." Her sentiments are echoed by other members of the student pop-

ulation. "The small student body makes it a great and really close community," added one.

Despite the small enrollment, however, Scripps is located right next to the other four Claremont Colleges, all of which are co-educational. As a result, being an all-female school does not mean that there is no inter-action with male students. In fact, since students often register for classes in the other colleges, there are plenty of opportunities to make friends with people in the other colleges, both male and female. "Scripps is like part of a much larger campus. You get to go to other colleges all the time, so you don't have to worry about Scripps being an all-female college," said a student. One undergrad pointed out that, as a single-sex school, Scripps receives "differing, condescending attitudes from other colleges in the consortium," but most people agree that the consortium system works very well for Scripps' social atmosphere.

The City of Trees and PhDs
As an upscale suburb of Los Angeles, Clare-mont is also known as the "City of Trees and

PhDs," thanks to a high concentration of professors working in the city's universities. The older neighborhoods of Claremont take pride in their shade-covered streets, making Scripps "a delightful place to live in."

The primary shopping center is at the Village, a collection of small shops and restaurants located at walking distance of the Claremont Colleges. Some students complain about the overpriced shopping, but they generally agree that, "the Village is indispensable for college life." Whenever they crave a little more excitement than the Village, students can jump on a train and visit Los Angeles. Although downtown Los Angeles is still about 30 miles away, it only takes ten minutes for Scripps students to walk to the MetroLink station, a railway system that connects directly to Los Angeles Union Station.

Within the Claremont Colleges, Scripps' own campus is very small. It extends over about three blocks and is only built around one single quad, the Jaqua Quadrangle. Nevertheless, the small campus adds even more to the College's intimacy, and according to the students, "the Mediterranean Revival architecture that dominates the campus feels very welcoming to us."

Sharing Is Fun!

Scripps is generally ranked among the top 30 liberal arts colleges by *US News and World Report*. It is a relatively selective college, accepting less than 50 percent of the applicant pool. "Above all else, people come to Scripps because it has a strong academic program," said a student.

By sharing facilities with the other colleges of the consortium, Scripps, despite its small size, offers its students the level of resources and opportunities of a large university. "The departments here are often interrelated to the same departments of the other colleges," said one junior. "For example, Scripps College has a Joint Science Department with Pitzer and Claremont McKenna." This close relationship between the colleges maximizes the resources of the consortium, letting the students explore a greater number of opportunities.

Just like most other liberal arts colleges, Scripps has an interdisciplinary Core Program, which focuses on critical thinking. The Core is divided into three different courses. Core I teaches the students about the relationship between knowledge and cultures. Core II lets the students choose between different courses that offer in-depth studies of topics introduced in Core I. Core III focuses on innovation and requires the students to come up with a self-designed project as part of the course. According to a student, "Core I is important. It builds the foundations for future undergraduate work. Core II is not as beneficial, as it is too narrow. My section, at least, did not seem to end up anywhere. Core III is a wonderful experience. It makes one feel potent and encourages applying what you've learned."

In addition, the students are also required to fulfill the general requirements, which include one class each in fine arts, letters, writing, natural science, social science, race and ethnic studies and mathematics. Students also have to take three semesters of a foreign language. These rather extensive requirements enable the students to acquire knowledge and skills in a variety of fields, an important goal of the College.

Scripps' classes are generally small, having less than 20 students, which lets students interact frequently with their professors. Since there are no teaching assistants, the professors devote a significant part of their time to office hours in order to help their students. "I interact a lot with professors outside of class," one undergrad explained. "I go to office hours frequently, have done an internship with one professor, and have gone to conferences with some others."

Kicking it with the Consortium

Scripps provides its students with great dorm rooms. "The average dorm room is spacious, elegantly furnished, and clean." Each dorm also has a browsing room, a small quiet library that forbids male entrance.

"During Friday and Saturday, there are generally several parties going on in different colleges, but if you just restrict yourself to Scripps, you might not find anything interesting during the weekends."

Scripps athletes participate in competitions with Claremont McKenna and Harvey Mudd as one single team. Scripps does have its own clubs, but many larger organizations draw members from the entire consortium.

The weekend life is similarly conjoined with that of the other colleges. Students usually go to parties in any of the Claremont Colleges, since Scripps' small size usually does not make for extremely exciting parties.

According to one student, "During Friday and Saturday, there are generally several parties going on in different colleges, but if you just restrict yourself to Scripps, you might not find anything interesting during the weekends." But lack of social life said, one student still cited the biggest disadvantage of being at Scripps as being that "they make you leave after four years." —*Xiaohang Liu*

FYI

If you come to Scripps, you'd better bring "a stapler!"

What is the typical weekend schedule? "Friday: party. Saturday: party, L.A. Sunday: work, work, and work."

If I could change one thing about Scripps, I'd "have more diversity."

Three things every student at Scripps should do before graduating are "to play glow-in-the-dark Frisbee on the lawn at midnight, attend candlelight dinners, and participate in the Humanities Institute."

Deep Springs College

Address: HC 72, Box 45001 Dyer, NV 89010-9803	**Percentage accepted through EA or ED:** NA	**Graduation Rate 6-year:** Unreported
Phone: 760-872-2000	**EA and ED deadline:** NA	**Percent Undergraduates in On-campus housing:** Unreported
E-mail address: apcom@deepsprings.edu	**Regular Deadline:** 15-Nov	
Web site URL: www.deepsprings.edu	**Application Fee:** $0	**Number of official organized extracurricular organizations:** Unreported
Year Founded: 1917	**Full time Undergraduate enrollment:** 26	
Private or Public: Private	**Total enrollment:** 26	**3 Most popular majors:**
Religious Affiliation: None	**Percent Male:** 100%	Liberal Arts and Sciences,
Location: Rural	**Percent Female:** 0%	General Studies, and
Number of Applicants: 186	**Total Percent Minority or Unreported:** Unreported	Humanities
Percent Accepted: 7%	**Percent African-American:** Unreported	**Student/Faculty ratio:** 4:1
Percent Accepted who enroll: 92%	**Percent Asian/Pacific Islander:** Unreported	**Average Class Size:** 9
Number Entering: 12	**Percent Hispanic:** Unreported	**Percent of students going to grad school:** 96%
Number of Transfers Accepted each Year: Unreported	**Percent Native-American:** Unreported	**Tuition and Fees:** $0
Middle 50% SAT range: M: 700–800, Cr: 750–800, Wr: 750–780	**Percent International:** Unreported	**In-State Tuition and Fees if different:** No difference
Middle 50% ACT range: Unreported	**Percent in-state/out of state:** 20%/80%	**Cost for Room and Board:** $0
Early admission program EA/ED/None: None	**Percent from Public HS:** 50%	**Percent receiving financial aid out of those who apply, first year:** NA
	Retention Rate: 100%	**Percent receiving financial aid among all students:** NA
	Graduation Rate 4-year: Unreported	

Deep Springs College is absolutely unique. Founded in 1917, this two-year, all-male, tuition-free, 26-student educational institution remains an anachronism in the landscape of higher education. Whether it's because of Deep Springs' precious isolation, its drug and alcohol-free student body, its commitment to training young men for lives of service, or the fact that it's situated on a working farm and cattle ranch, every Deep Springer will agree that there is no college like it. Students at Deep Springs give up the amenities and resources of a normal college campus to live, study and work hard in an isolated desert valley in Eastern California. While graduates from other universities may reminisce about their time in college, there's a reason why Deep Springs' alumni always refer back to their "Deep Springs experience."

Don't Let Me Out!

The first thing any visitor to Deep Springs will notice is its isolation. An hour's drive from the closest town (Bishop, CA) and five hours from the closest cities (Las Vegas and Los Angeles), Deep Springs is a little speck of green in the middle of a high desert valley. This isolation is made even more intense by the students' self-imposed "isolation policy" which states that students cannot leave the valley or have visitors while school is in session. It may seem excessive, but this policy does have its benefits. "We never meet new people at Deep Springs, but we meet the same people over and over again, each time with more intensity and understanding," one second-year student commented. The students also uphold a policy against the use of drugs and alcohol during term which, like the isolation policy, is self-imposed and self-regulated. These rules are a part of the Self-Governance process which allows the students to effectively own and run the college while they are enrolled. "Students hold each other accountable for upholding rules, completing all of their tasks, and generally running the college," one recent graduate explained. "Rarely are young people given so much responsibility and so many opportunities."

Each student at Deep Springs sits on a committee (Applications, Curriculum, Communications, or Review and Reinvitation Committee) and each committee is responsible for running a part of the college. Whether they're reading essays and accepting the incoming class, interviewing and hiring faculty, or writing and publishing the college brochure, every student has a hand in making the place run. The student body also gathers every Friday night for a collective meeting where committees give reports, legislation is discussed, and issues are debated. During the winter these meetings are held in the dorm or the boarding house, though in the summer students often drive out to remote spots in the desert to meet around a campfire, under the stars. Meetings often run late into the night, only ending when all the business has been completed, or when the cows need to be milked.

The Self-Governance process is also a way for students to hold positions of responsibility. Some of the positions include: student body president, labor commissioner, secretary, annual giving representative and committee chair. "You are a political member before you are a social member of this community," one first-year student noted, and most students do hold an elected position in the Self-Governance process before they graduate.

Home On the (Gas) Range

At the same time that students at Deep Springs run the administrative side of the college, they also provide nearly all the labor for the school, farm and cattle ranch. Though they pay no tuition, students are required to work an average of 20 to 30 hours per week in various jobs. Labor positions are assigned by the student Labor Commissioner and change often, so students get to experience a lot of different kinds of work before they graduate. "One term you might be cooking dinner for the community every night, and the next you're building fences or herding cows." The one job that every Deep Springer is required to do is BH duty, which includes washing dishes, mopping floors, and cleaning up after meals. Other labor positions include butcher, gardener, farm assistant and dairy boy.

Many students enjoy the labor program because of the practical skills that they learn, like cooking, carpentry or welding, but even the work they'll probably never do again, like slaughtering or milking cows, has its benefits. "Deep Springs is first and foremost about learning to put the needs of the community and of the farm and ranch on which you live above yourself, and coming to cherish yourself as a piece in the puzzle," said one second-year student. Deep Springers also use the time during work to talk or think about intellectual issues. Four hours of painting a wall or digging post-holes in the desert is a good amount of time to think about an upcoming paper or discuss a reading with another student. Most students come to appreciate the labor program as an important part of their education, and not as a distraction from academics. "With so much physical work to do all the time, academic work begins to seem like a privilege and a kind of relaxation. It really makes you appreciate your education."

Will This Class Ever End?

Classes at Deep Springs are comparable to courses at top level institutions, except that you'll never have to sit in a lecture hall with 300 other students. Most classes have enrollments between four and 10 students, and nearly all of them are seminars. The only two required courses are composition and public speaking, the latter taken every semester. Class discussions can get very intense, since the students all know each other perhaps too well. "Classes here are intense, and students often expect more of each other than professors are able to expect of students in other, more traditional environments," said one second-year student. "At Deep Springs, if a peer doesn't prepare well and class discussion suffers as a result, you have both a right and a responsibility to confront him about it." Though this kind of intensity can be daunting for new students straight out of high school, the general atmosphere in class is one of deep concern and engagement with issues. "Classes at Deep Springs are like a cross between a big family meal and a trial in court: personal, rigorous, intense, and deeply enjoyable."

Since students and their professors live within a few steps of each other, classroom discussions often continue after class is over. It's not uncommon for students to continue debating an issue in the dining hall at lunch and through their afternoon work. "I don't think that 'the way people think' could be more important at another school than Deep Springs," as students are always engaging each other's beliefs and thought processes inside and outside of class. Professors often open their homes to students at night to continue discussions, help edit papers, or just to have coffee. "The most common social activity is talking. Simply talking," and Deep Springers certainly do a lot of it: with their professors, each other, and the families and kids that make up the community.

The majority of the courses at Deep Springs are in the humanities or literary arts, though a number of math and science courses are always offered. To keep the curriculum balanced, Deep Springs employs three long-term professors in Humanities, Social Sciences, and Math and Natural Sciences. Along with these three, the student body hires a handful of visiting professors each semester to teach anything from "Figure Drawing" to "Wittgenstein's *Philosophical Investigations*."

Dance It Off

Whatever diversity Deep Springs may lack in its small and somewhat homogeneous student body, it makes up for in the larger campus community. Though only around 50 people live in the valley, they range in age from very young to very old, and come from all over the country and the world. Professors often bring their spouses and kids along, and everyone takes part in the greater community of Deep Springs. The one obvious thing lacking is female students, though the issue is formally debated every year and is a constant topic of discussion. "Most students' feelings about going to a single-sex school change radically, in all kinds of directions, once they've actually been at Deep Springs," said a recent graduate. But the lack of girls doesn't stop the boys from having their fun. "Of course we dance (boogie)," explained a second-year. "An hour of heavy boogie-ing provides enough exercise and catharsis to last a week or so."

> **"Students who are looking for a challenging academic environment should look into Deep Springs."**

The valley provides great opportunities for hiking, running and climbing, and even though Deep Springs has no sports program, students will often organize games of soccer or basketball in the free half-hour before dinner. But as any Deep Springer will tell you, free time is hard to come by. Often weekends are filled with extra work projects, slaughters, cattle drives or music practice. "There isn't much free time, but dance parties, shooting guns, making paintings, and reading groups occupy the little that there is." Often, because of the amount of work and responsibility every student must take on, relaxation feels just like procrastination. But then again, every student signed on to push themselves and take on a challenge. One graduate summed it up nicely: "Attending Deep Springs is like running a marathon. While you're in it you can only think about how hard it is, but once it's over you can look back and see what an amazing thing you just did."—*Jesse Bradford*

FYI

If you come to Deep Springs, you'd better bring "a toothbrush. Almost everything else you need can be found in the bonepile (communal clothing stockpile)."

What is a typical weekend schedule? "Cooking a meal for the community, preparing for a Heidegger reading group, doing committee work, a game of soccer, working on a couple essays, a quick boogie, then a few hours of solid reading."

If I could change one thing about Deep Springs, "I'd add a couple of hours to each day."

Before graduating, every Deep Springer should "cook an elaborate meal without enough help, stay up all night writing a paper then go for a swim in the upper reservoir at dawn, and punch a charging bull in the face."

Mills College

Address: 500 MacArthur
Boulevard, Oakland, CA
94613
Phone: 510-430-2135
E-mail address:
admission@mills.edu
Web site URL: www.mills.edu
Year Founded: 1852
Private or Public: Private
Religious Affiliation: None
Location: Suburban
Number of Applicants: 2,129
Percent Accepted: 57%
**Percent Accepted who
enroll:** 17%
Number Entering: 208
**Number of Transfers
Accepted each Year:** 189
Middle 50% SAT range:
M: 490–590, CR:
520–650, Wr: 520–620
Middle 50% ACT range: 20–27
**Early admission program
EA/ED/None:** EA
**Percentage accepted
through EA or ED:** 67%

EA and ED deadline:
15-Nov
Regular Deadline: 1-Aug
Application Fee: $50
**Full time Undergraduate
enrollment:** 930
Total enrollment: 1454
Percent Male: 0%
Percent Female: 100%
**Total Percent Minority or
Unreported:** 57%
Percent African-American:
9%
**Percent Asian/Pacific
Islander:** 8%
Percent Hispanic: 14%
Percent Native-American:
<1%
Percent International: 3%
**Percent in-state/out of
state:** 80% /20%
Percent from Public HS:
80%
Retention Rate: 74%
Graduation Rate 4-year:
54%

Graduation Rate 6-year:
60%
**Percent Undergraduates
in On-campus housing:**
56%
**Number of official organized
extracurricular
organizations:** 47
3 Most popular majors:
English, Political Science,
Psychology
Student/Faculty ratio: 11:1
Average Class Size: 15
**Percent of students going to
grad school:** 20%
Tuition and Fees: $35,190
**In-State Tuition and Fees if
different:** No difference
Cost for Room and Board:
$10,550
**Percent receiving financial
aid out of those who apply,
first year:** 86%
**Percent receiving financial
aid among all students:**
72%

Mills College, an all-female liberal arts college in Oakland, California, has been committed to women's education for over 150 years. In fact, Mills made news in 1990 when the board of trustees voted to admit males to the undergraduate program. Students, outraged, immediately adopted the slogan "Better Dead than Coed." They mounted protests, officially shutting down the campus, and they refused to resume their normal lives until the board of trustees reversed their decision. Eventually, the trustees conceded, and Mills reinforced its position as a school dedicated to women's education. That take-charge spirit is characteristic of Mills students, who remain a group of empowered women committed to making the most of their education.

Blaze Your Own Trail
Historically, Mills has been a school of "firsts": the first women's college to the west of the Rockies, the first women's college to offer a computer science major and a 4+1 MBA degree, and even one of the first liberal arts colleges to offer a modern dance degree. Mills students agree that their academic experience is completely "what you make of it." One student noted that it's possible to "slack" through a semester with easy classes, but said that it is equally possible to have a hard semester by taking classes from hard professors—it's all up to the individual.

The general education requirement at Mills consists of 36 credits in what the school calls three "outcome categories": skills, perspectives, and disciplinary experiences. The skills category includes classes in written communication, quantitative reasoning, and information technology skills. Perspectives courses include women and gender, multicultural, and interdisciplinary studies. Classes in arts criticism, historical perspectives, natural sciences, and human behavior comprise the disciplinary exercises category. Despite the variety of academic requirements at Mills, many students complain about the lack of diversity in the choice of classes, saying they wish there were "more fun and random classes."

Fortunately, for those seeking classes outside the box, UC Berkeley and other Bay Area schools welcome Mills students to cross-register in some of their programs.

Some of the most popular Mills majors are English, psychology, and Political, Legal, and Economic Analysis. Several students complained about the school's recent loss of the theater major. "The theater department was dropped because there weren't enough people majoring in it," one student explained. And although there's still a theater club on campus, those looking to major in theater arts may be disappointed. For those Mills women anxious to get a head start on advanced degrees, the school has seven dual degree programs, in which students can get master's degrees in Business Administration, Public Policy, Infant Mental Health, Interdisciplinary Computer Science, Engineering, Mathematics, or they can get a Credential in Teacher Education. Another specialized degree program at Mills is its Nursing Leadership Program, which consists of two years of liberal arts followed by two years of nursing school.

The Hills of Mills

Living at Mills is like, as one student put it, living in a "gorgeous oasis" with "beautiful architecture." The campus has recently completed a significant amount of renovations, such as a new environmentally friendly "green" science building. Mills women agree that their dorms are "very nice." Freshmen live in singles or doubles in two residences right in the middle of campus, and their housing is not too shabby. "One of our buildings, Orchard Meadow, is considered one of the nicest dorms on campus," one freshman boasted. There are a total of five residence halls at Mills. Upperclass women can choose among on-campus apartments, townhouses, or house co-ops.

> "Most Mills women are usually feminists and interested in women's rights—or at least, they become so after four years here!"

The main dining hall at Mills is called Founders Commons, and it is set atop a hill. Students generally agree that the food is "fairly good for a college." The cafeterias are independently owned, and, to the relief of many Californians, "there are always vegetarian and vegan options." In addition to dining halls, Mills has a teashop that serves hot breakfast and "quick meals like hamburgers," along with a popular coffee shop, Café Susie's.

Unfortunately, Oakland has no real "college-town feel." In fact, some students even go so far as to say that, "the area around campus does not feel very safe." Nonetheless, Mills has its own shuttle system and even a bus stop outside its front gate, making it easy to get on and off campus. There are several restaurants and shops off campus that are popular with Mills women, especially the Italian favorite, La Fiesta Pizza. And, for those looking to escape from Oakland entirely, San Francisco and all its distractions are just a car or shuttle ride away.

Friendly Feminists

Outside of the classroom, Mills women are famous for being friendly and sociable. One freshman enthused that, "On the first day of college, I sat down at tables at the cafeteria where I didn't know anyone, and was warmly welcomed!" The student body of Mills is notoriously diverse, both ethnically and culturally. One Caucasian woman even went so far as to joke that "sometimes I feel like a minority."

The women of Mills also have their own unique take on age diversity: about a quarter of the undergraduate population is made up of "resumers," or students over the age of 23. Resumers are usually students who have taken time off from their studies to pursue careers or raise families. Resumers have their own apartments on campus that welcome spouses and children. Yet, far from being secluded from the rest of the population, students universally proclaim that there is no real division on campus between resumers and regular undergraduates. Friendships form between women of all ages.

The integration of resumers into the community is just one aspect of Mills' openness and tolerance of differences. These include sexual orientation as well. "There is a lesbian stereotype," one student said, "but although there are many lesbians on campus, it is often hard to tell whose toast is buttered which way." No matter one's sexual preference, "most Mills women are usually feminists and interested in women's rights—or at least, they become so after four years here!"

Partying Without Guys?

Mills women agree that their school is not, by any means, a party school. Most students go out on weekend nights, and because many students don't have classes on Fridays, weekends tend to include Thursdays. There are a few popular campus-wide parties, including the Fetish Ball, which discourages clothing. Alcohol has little presence on campus. One freshman noted that she has seen "very little drinking in the freshman dorms." Even once you hit the age of 21, "even then it has to be done behind closed doors," one student explained. Students do note that drugs, mostly pot, are a lot more prevalent on campus than alcohol.

Be warned, Mills women don't often get a chance to mingle with members of the opposite sex. In fact, most couples around the school are female-female. Mills allows men to stay overnight in the dorms for up to seven nights each month, which is good news for students with boyfriends at other schools. Mills' graduate school, on the other hand, *is* coed, and Berkeley and Stanford are not too far away, so students say that if you're really looking for men, they're not too hard to find if you're willing to make a small trek.

Fun and Games

Athletics are admittedly not Mills' main focus, and, not surprisingly, the school doesn't have a football team. However, as a Division III school, Mills has seven varsity sports: cross country, crew, soccer, swimming, tennis, volleyball, and track and field. Students generally seem happy that more inexperienced athletes are allowed to participate since some of the pressure is off. As one Mills woman put it, "We take pride in what we've got." If varsity sports aren't your thing, you can get a workout by playing club sports, or by taking yoga and swimming classes at the gym.

Off the field, there are a plethora of student clubs and organizations, some favorites of which are the Animé Club, Horror Movie Club, Superhero Club, and the Gay/Lesbian Alliance. Mills women say that there is definitely something for everybody to be involved in, and if not, students are encouraged to start new organizations. Many students also get on-campus jobs, like serving food in the campus cafeteria.

A Tradition of Empowerment

In a school rooted in tradition, Mills students say that one of their favorite rites of passage is Paint Night. Students assign a color to each class, and on Paint Night—which takes place in the spring—seniors storm the campus and paint surfaces the color of their class. This tradition, fun and silly as it is, ties into Mills' continual emphasis on fostering strong women, ready to use their education to make a difference in the world around them. Still stubbornly single-sex, Mills continues to be a place where students and administration both remain believers in the power of all-women's schools.—*Becky Bicks*

FYI
If you come to Mills you'd better bring "an open mind."
What's the typical weekend schedule? "Enjoying weekend brunch, relaxing during free time, and evening on-campus activities."
If I could change one thing about Mills, I'd "make the campus more accessible, offering a shuttle to and from the airport at break time."
Three things every student at Mills should do before graduating are "explore the whole campus, get an on-campus job, eat the dining hall waffles for breakfast."

Occidental College

Address: 1600 Campus Road Los Angeles, CA 90041
Phone: 800-825-5262
E-mail address: admission@oxy.edu
Web site URL: www.oxy.edu
Year Founded: 1887
Private or Public: Private
Religious Affiliation: None
Location: Urban
Number of Applicants: 5,790
Percent Accepted: 39%
Percent Accepted who enroll: 21%
Number Entering: 519
Number of Transfers Accepted each Year: 60
Middle 50% SAT range: M: 590–680, **CR:** 590–690, **Wr:** 590–690
Middle 50% ACT range: 26–30
Early admission program EA/ED/None: ED
Percentage accepted through EA or ED: 11%

EA and ED deadline: 15-Nov
Regular Deadline: 10-Jan
Application Fee: $60
Full time Undergraduate enrollment: 1,846
Total enrollment: 1,868
Percent Male: 44%
Percent Female: 56%
Total Percent Minority or Unreported: 36%
Percent African-American: 6%
Percent Asian/Pacific Islander: 15%
Percent Hispanic: 14%
Percent Native-American: 1.2%
Percent International: Unreported
Percent in-state/out of state: 49%/51%
Percent from Public HS: 60%
Retention Rate: 94%
Graduation Rate 4-year: 82%

Graduation Rate 6-year: 86%
Percent Undergraduates in On-campus housing: 80%
Number of official organized extracurricular organizations: 104
3 Most popular majors: Economics, Diplomacy and World Affairs, Psychology
Student/Faculty ratio: 10:1
Average Class Size: 17
Percent of students going to grad school: Unreported
Tuition and Fees: $37,071
In-State Tuition and Fees if different: No difference
Cost for Room and Board: $10,270
Percent receiving financial aid out of those who apply, first year: 76%
Percent receiving financial aid among all students: 27%

If living on a hilltop close to mountains, deserts, and beaches sounds like a pretty good deal, Occidental College in Los Angeles might be the perfect fit for you. This small school boasts a population of only 2,102 students who are both high achievers and very laid-back, in a climate that couldn't be much nicer. Oxy, as it is more commonly known, was one of the first schools to include the word "diverse" in its mission statement, and the community lives up to that goal. Although it is a very small school, Oxy provides diversity not only in the student body, but also in the breadth of academic options, the expansive extracurricular opportunities, and the great resources of Los Angeles that make the school unique.

The Core of it All

The school may be small, but the educational requirements certainly are not. The distributional core at Oxy requires all students to take three courses in math and lab sciences, study two out of four time periods and world areas, achieve the 102 level of a foreign language, and take two art credits. Although students are generally expected to

have completed these core courses by the end of junior year, "that isn't strictly enforced." The freshman year Cultural Studies Program (CSP) is another part of Oxy's dedication to bringing students a well-rounded educational experience, and it takes advantage of all the resources Los Angeles has to offer. One freshman said that her CSP took her around to concerts in LA in addition to on campus, which allowed her to get off campus while bonding with members of her class. For the most ambitious students, the Oxy Honors Program requires a certain GPA within a given department, "usually around 3.5," and also mandates a more complex senior project than the ones that are required for the rest of the student body.

The school definitely does not skimp on the academics, and students say that small classes play a large role in the effectiveness of the classes at Oxy. While one student said that class size "depends on the department and class level," he also noted that his classes this semester "range from four to 10 people." Even introductory science courses, which at larger schools can fill auditoriums, only have about 20 to 30 students each at Oxy. The small size gives great access to all professors, whom one student said are "very flexible and accommodating." A sophomore said that he has "gotten together with professors over lunch, sometimes to discuss class-related issues, and sometimes just to get to know them better." This relaxed relationship between students and professors contributes a great deal to the learning environment at Oxy, and it allows for students to learn not from imposing figures, but from "actual human beings."

Living and Breathing Oxy

Despite the "beastly, steep hill" that divides the campus into upper and lower components, students say that "most of the stuff you need" is fairly conveniently located on the small campus, including two dining halls. Because classroom buildings are on lower campus, students do not need to go to upper campus often. In fact, "unless you can fly," the amount of stairs makes it a pretty big commitment to go up there. Still, upper campus houses some of the nicest dorms as well as Keck Theater, where performances occur all the time. Lower campus is still the center of community life, as the two all-freshman dorms are located there along with two housing all upperclassmen. Students agree that most of the dorms are essentially the same, but they disagree about the nicest. One freshman mentioned that "Haines has all four years and a really nice porch," while a sophomore highlighted the brand new Rangeview Hall, which is "very fancy. All the rooms have private bathrooms, there's a weight room, and a bunch of posh lounges. The only problem is that it's pretty far away." Another particularly distinctive dorm is Pauley, which "places a special emphasis on bringing together students of different cultures," although the student added, "really, that could be said of any dorm." Wherever they happen to live, generally it is on campus. Although "a few upperclassmen live in houses within walking distance from campus," the vast majority live in dorms and "very few commute by car."

The Ins-N-Outs of Oxy Social Life

"People mostly stay on campus during the weekends. If they leave, it's usually just during the day to go to the beach or late night In-N-Out runs or concerts." With a location that makes it "hard to get off campus without a car," Oxy encourages students to stay on the hill and make the most of the college. There is "a good sushi place within walking distance" as well as the rest of the Eagle Rock community that directly surrounds the college. Students describe the partying as "low key" and "not very organized," especially since there is very little Greek presence on campus. Although students admit that the party scene is "mostly centered on drinking," they are quick to point out that "it's unfair to lump all drinkers together. Many people are very reasonable" and do not overdo the partying. Oxy students also have excellent access to concerts and performances, both on campus and in the LA area. One student noted that there is little pressure to go out at all. "There is a little kitchen in the dorm and you can stay in, bake a cake, and watch a movie—it all depends on who you hang out with." Even within such a small community, there are many different options for the levels of partying students feel comfortable with, but it is certainly "small scale." One student summed it up well by saying, "If partying is your scene, you can definitely find it, but people also spend a lot of time just hanging out with small groups of close friends."

Fun in the Sun

During the day, there are "lots of clubs" which are "really easy to get involved in." Extracurriculars are a main focus of most students, and there are plenty to choose from even though the school itself is small. Students clearly find plenty of activities to suit any interest, as one student mentioned "yoga and political groups" as some of the most popular clubs on campus, whereas another student emphasized orchestra, a cappella, Glee Club, and Dance Production as big draws on campus, both for people involved and for the students who "show up to their shows in big numbers." Though students may find their niche in very different places, one sophomore said that "Oxy's a small enough community that there isn't really one main social scene; they all kind of overlap."

> "Professors make themselves available to students both during and outside of class. Many times I have gotten together with professors over lunch, sometimes to discuss class-related issues and sometimes just to get to know them better."

In addition to the student clubs, "lots of people have on-campus jobs." Students emphasize that Oxy is very good at supplying these jobs and making them available for anyone. Popular jobs include working at the Cooler, which is one of the dining halls, driving the Oxy Bus, which transports students around campus, researching, doing grounds work, and helping in the financial aid office. The countless opportunities for work and play at Oxy really set it apart from other colleges of its size.

Oxy-gen Bonds

"The Oxy community is really open and friendly," said one freshman, and a sophomore added, "It's a small enough community that even with total strangers you're almost guaranteed to have mutual friends, and there's a lot of overlapping in social circles." Although with such a small school, students are likely to "see a lot of the same people," the students generally appreciate the closeness of the campus and the comfortable environment that creates. "Students are very vocal" and they are "very accepting of what other people have to say." In addition to the niceness of the students, the environment itself is conducive to a pleasant experience. When asked about the climate, one student paused before saying, "well . . . it rained twice, and forest fires made my asthma go to town. Otherwise it's sunny." With LA in their backyard and a small community of open, happy students, it's no surprise that "people love Oxy."—*Hannah Jacobson*

FYI

If you come to Occidental, you'd better bring "sunscreen!"

What is the typical weekend schedule? "Thursday night is the beginning of the weekend, but most people just stay up late and do some low-key hanging out and sleeping in, then go to Stewie Hall, the party dorm, on Friday and Saturday nights."

If I could change one thing about Occidental, I'd "make it easier to leave large musical instruments on upper campus rather than having to lock them in a broom closet."

Three things every student at Occidental should do before graduating are "take a class with Simeon Pillich, go to an a cappella and orchestra concert, and find the Taco Truck at three in the morning."

Pepperdine University

Address: 24255 Pacific Coast Highway, Malibu, CA 90263
Phone: 310-506-4392
E-mail address: admission-seaver@pepperdine.edu
Web site URL: www.pepperdine.edu
Year Founded: 1937
Private or Public: Private
Religious Affiliation: Church of Christ
Location: Suburban
Number of Applicants: 6,661
Percent Accepted: 35%
Percent Accepted who enroll: 33%
Number Entering: 753
Number of Transfers Accepted each Year: Unreported
Middle 50% SAT range: M: 570–680, CR: 560–670, Wr: 560–670
Middle 50% ACT range: 24–29
Early admission program EA/ED/None: None

Percentage accepted through EA or ED: NA
EA and ED deadline: NA
Regular Deadline: 15-Nov, 15-Jan
Application Fee: $65
Full time Undergraduate enrollment: 3,398
Total enrollment: 6,877
Percent Male: 45%
Percent Female: 55%
Total Percent Minority or Unreported: 41%
Percent African-American: 7%
Percent Asian/Pacific Islander: 10%
Percent Hispanic: 10%
Percent Native-American: 1%
Percent International: 7%
Percent in-state/out of state: 50%/50%
Percent from Public HS: Unreported
Retention Rate: 88%

Graduation Rate 4-year: 72%
Graduation Rate 6-year: Unreported
Percent Undergraduates in On-campus housing: 67%
Number of official organized extracurricular organizations: 50
3 Most popular majors: Business, Communication, Social Sciences
Student/Faculty ratio: 13:1
Average Class Size: 21
Percent of students going to grad school: 53%
Tuition and Fees: $36,770
In-State Tuition and Fees if different: No difference
Cost for Room and Board: $10,480
Percent receiving financial aid out of those who apply, first year: 57%
Percent receiving financial aid among all students: 35%

At a glance, Pepperdine University might look like a party school. Almost every point on its scenic Malibu, California campus has views of the Pacific Ocean, and it is a short drive to Los Angeles. But Pepperdine bills itself as a Christian university committed to the highest standards of academic excellence and Christian values. It seeks to educate students devoted to excellence and motivated by their belief in God. The school tries to accomplish this through its religious devotion, extensive emphasis on international experience, general education program that all students must complete. Pepperdine seeks to create individuals with a solid grasp of both their duties to the world and their duties to themselves.

Focusing on religion

Pepperdine's spiritual commitment is based on its affiliation with the Church of Christ. George Pepperdine, who founded the university in 1937, was a devout member of the church who was alarmed at the rate at which college students lost their faith. He founded the university that bears his name in order to provide the best education possible while supporting its student's belief. The university accepts students from all faiths, and tries to extend its ideals of religious devotion and tolerance to its students. But the university also asks all students "to open their minds to be introduced to the Christian faith." It carries out that request by requiring three total courses on the Bible and Christianity. Perhaps because of those requirements, religious diversity mostly exists only in terms of different Christian denominations. There were no Jews, Muslims, or Buddhists in the 2010 freshman class. That bothers some students. "There's some diversity, but mostly you'll just meet blonde Republican Christians," said one.

God's people

Pepperdine might not have religious diversity, but it does advertise a student body that has a majority of minorities. Moreover, students agree, the brand of Christianity on campus is progressive and as welcoming as the school's publications advertise. "This is a very accepting campus because its full of progressive young Christians who are sick of the old school religion they heard from their parents' generation," said a sophomore. That progressiveness means that some students can be more open than might be expected of a Christian school — especially about their sexuality. "It's a problem," said a junior. "The boys are gorgeous and the girls are stunning, but all the cute guys are gay."

The people and location might be gorgeous, but that doesn't translate into Pepperdine being a laid back party school. The campus is dry and there are no residences for the fraternities and sororities that count a third of the student body as members, so one student says, "We don't go to a party school. Here you're going to be learning sober." But not totally sober, argue other students with access to cars. Many of those students have given up the dorms they all praise for off campus housing for precisely that reason, as well as the high cost of the meal plan. "Because Pepperdine has such a strict no tolerance drinking policy and it can hit you even after you turn 21, most students move off campus after freshman year," said a sophomore natural science major.

To live off campus or to access the bulk of social life on campus, those same students say that cars are a necessity. The school's campus may be suburban, but Hollywood and Los Angeles are just a short drive away. "If you're a partier, you'll need to be willing to drive off campus and drink," said a senior, "Nothing happens on campus."

Wait, This is College

Although Pepperdine boasts a beautiful campus, its academic reputation was not heavily praised in previous years. But, that may no longer be the case. In 2005, it had one of its largest applicant pools, with over 7,800 applicants and 837 freshmen and transfer students enrolled. "I think Pepperdine is getting more and more academically ambitious students," one senior said. "Good thing for the reputation, maybe not so much for the people who have to compete with them."

Students can complete their studies in 38 different fields of study to receive their bachelor's degrees. Motivated students can choose to complete a master's degree in one of seven areas. To promote a well-rounded education, Pepperdine encourages students to take courses in new areas, which they have not previously explored or experienced. In accordance with their founder's ambitions, students are required to take three terms of religious classes. "This [mandatory religion courses] is the biggest downside for me as a student because I respect the religion, but would not like to be forced to take those courses," one student said.

Pepperdine has structured their courses in a way that allows a close relationship between the instructor and the student by having small class sizes. "When I was in high school, I hated classes where there were a huge number of people," one student said. "I get a better opportunity to learn, ask questions, and interact with other students in the smaller environment."

However, students are not limited to stay in California all four years. At some point in their academic career at Pepperdine, a student may choose to take one or more semesters abroad in a country such as Germany, England, Italy, and various other countries. It is this educationally diverse opportunity that separates Pepperdine from other Christian Universities. Students can either go during the regular semester or over the summer. Studying abroad can also help fulfill the language requirement. "You should never miss out on being able to study abroad," one student said. "It is unlike any other experience because we are so used to how things are in the United States and this puts everything into perspective. I definitely appreciate many things I previously took for granted more now and the people were all really nice."

Blue All Around

Complain about whatever you want, but the picturesque campus is unparalleled and students rarely deride the excellent on-campus housing available to all students. "The dorms are unlike anything I have seen at any school I visited and this makes the university even more appealing," one visiting student noted. At no time are students given mediocre housing unlike other universities that typically bestow the less appealing living arrangement to freshmen. However, it should be noted that some students choose to live off campus despite the comfortable living arrangements. "It's about having the space and the freedom to move around," one off-campus student said.

The student body disagrees that the only beautiful element of the campus is the majestic blue waters. "We have the best-looking student population of the entire United States," one student boasted. It is not rare to see this self esteem common among students, many of which can be seen wearing bathing suits and tanning in the pristine beaches. When asked why she would like to attend Pepperdine, a female student responded, "Well, the guys are so cute!"

However, a key downside to the serene, beach milieu is the fact that Pepperdine is not a college town. Students will need to have a car to go off campus if the beach is not their primary source of entertainment. The idea of traveling to nearby Santa Monica, Westwood, and Los Angeles is not that easy given the heavy Southern California traffic.

Athletics

The emphasis placed on religion and faith is present in the Athletic realm as well as the academic. Pepperdine follows the principles set forth by their founder George Pepperdine, "Therefore, as my contribution to the well-being and happiness of this generation and those that follow, I am endowing this institution to help young men and women prepare themselves for a life of usefulness in this competitive world and to help them build a foundation of Christian character and faith which will survive the storms of life."

There's some diversity, but mostly you'll just meet blond Republican Christians.

Despite the small size of the undergraduate class, Pepperdine can boast an unparalleled level of success in national championships. "We are a small school that has had great success and a number of the teams are nationally ranked," the Director of Sports Information added. At the end of the day, Pepperdine places its priority on the Christian faith and much of the athletic mindset stems from being a devout Christian university. According to the Director of Sports Information, "Pepperdine tries to develop student athletes that will be leaders with a service based mindset and become well rounded people."

For students committed to their faith as well as to academics, Pepperdine is the place to be. It would be difficult to convince anyone to leave the stunning campus and palatial dorms, but the school's top-of-the-line study abroad opportunities might just do the trick. So might the absence of a typical college social scene on campus. Students say they're happy and you will be too — this is Malibu we're talking about, after all.
—*Preetam Dutta and Max de la Bruyere*

FYI
Most everyone in the school is Christian.
What can you do if you don't want to go to the beach? Party.
The guys and girls on campus are hot.
People here actually study when they're not at the beach.

St. Mary's College of California

Address: 1928 Saint Mary's Road, Moraga, CA 94556
Phone: 925-631-4224
E-mail address: smcadmit@stmarys_ca.edu
Web site URL: www.stmarys-ca.edu
Year Founded: 1863
Private or Public: Private
Religious Affiliation: Roman Catholic
Location: Suburban
Number of Applicants: 3,929
Percent Accepted: 82%
Percent Accepted who enroll: 19%
Number Entering: 611
Number of Transfers Accepted each Year: 293
Middle 50% SAT range: M: 480–590, CR: 480–590, Wr: Unreported
Middle 50% ACT range: Unreported
Early admission program EA/ED/None: EA

Percentage accepted through EA or ED: Unreported
EA and ED deadline: 15-Nov
Regular Deadline: 1-Feb
Application Fee: $55
Full time Undergraduate enrollment: 2,402
Total enrollment: 2,685
Percent Male: 39%
Percent Female: 61%
Total Percent Minority or Unreported: 42%
Percent African-American: 5%
Percent Asian/Pacific Islander: 11%
Percent Hispanic: 21%
Percent Native-American: 1%
Percent International: 2%
Percent in-state/out of state: 85%/15%
Percent from Public HS: 58%
Retention Rate: 77%
Graduation Rate 4-year: 53%

Graduation Rate 6-year: 61%
Percent Undergraduates in On-campus housing: 58%
Number of official organized extracurricular organizations: 42
3 Most popular majors: Business Administration, Management and Operations, Other Communication and Media Studies
Student/Faculty ratio: 11:1
Average Class Size: 26
Percent of students going to grad school: 48%
Tuition and Fees: $33,250
In-State Tuition and Fees if different: No difference
Cost for Room and Board: $11,680
Percent receiving financial aid out of those who apply, first year: 72%
Percent receiving financial aid among all students: 69%

Amidst the big-city bustle of both San Francisco and Berkeley, St. Mary's College lies nestled in the picturesque town of Moraga, California. The surrounding woody scenery and majestic green hills give the campus a tranquil vibe that one student describes as "beautiful for its small-town-lazy feel." While the campuses' location may at times feel isolated and lonely, particularly on the weekends when many students travel to the surrounding large cities in the Bay Area, the school makes sure to provide a variety of activities for students to participate in such as Saturday rock climbing and laser tag adventures. This small private college provides a well-balanced mix of strong academic programs, a solid Christian foundation based on the teachings of the De La Salle brothers, and a formidable athletic program whose basketball team often contends in the NCAA's "March Madness."

Something for Everyone

Students are quick to boast about the variety of unique career specific programs that St. Mary's offers including the nursing program, engineering program, and the "Teachers for Tomorrow" program. The nursing and engineering programs are unique in that the initial undergraduate years are spent at St. Mary's and the final undergraduate years are spent at a partner school. Students in the nursing program spend two years at St. Mary's and then later transfer to Samuel Merritt University in Oakland, California. The engineering program also has a similar system with students spending three years at St. Mary's and then transferring to the University of Southern California to complete the degree in two years. The "Teachers for Tomorrow" program also attracts many students to St. Mary's because it allows them to attain their bachelor's degree and teaching credential in five years.

Students also have the option of taking three additional courses in order to also attain a Master of Arts degree in teaching. For those who are understandably unsure of their post-graduation plans, the Integral Program of Liberal Arts offers a solution. The program takes a liberal arts approach to learning and has been described by students as "basically its own college" because of the fact that classes featured in the program can only be taken by Integral students. The program focuses on a broad spectrum of subjects but all are taught in seminar style. The classes are all based on discussion. One student noted that the program was interesting because even in science and math classes, students are still pushed to "talk about what those things mean." Some students joke about those in the program saying, "all they do is talk referring to the Integral system of no tests. A panel of professors presents students with their final grades by evaluating the student as they sit in front of them. The Integral program is also beneficial for anyone interested in entering a career that will require proficient public-speaking skills because students are forced to regularly participate in class as part of their grade. One student noted that this system "forces those who are shy to come out of their shell."

Unique Opportunities
St. Mary's academic calendar is based on the "4-1-4" system in which there are two semesters in which students take four credits, and one month in the middle, dubbed "Jan-term" during which students focus intensively on one class only. The off-kilter classes offered during the month of January include "You can't make me do this," "Transmission, translation, and transformation: astronomical ideas in the Islamic world," and "Tool or Trade: Bicycle History." Classes meet for two and a half hours, four days a week. There are no classes on Wednesdays, which gives students a much-appreciated mid-week break for students to unwind. Some students treat the midweek break as a quasi-weekend and an opportunity to make Friday come a little earlier. Students also have the opportunity to go off-campus during Jan-term through study abroad programs in countries such as Brazil and Rome. Students do not have to travel far to have a memorable experience, however. One example of this is the course called "Live Sen-

tence" during which students travel to San Quentin prison to speak with the inmates about their experiences. Despite some classes having heavy reading assignments, for the most part, students regard Jan-term as "a good time to catch up and take a little breather."

Social Scene
While students admit that St. Mary's is "not a party school" and it is not unusual to find students "just hanging out in someone's room watching a movie" on a Saturday night, they also say that there is a party scene present for those who want it. On-campus parties are generally smaller because they are hosted in people's dorm rooms and are also therefore likely to be shut down by Public Safety, the campus police, quickly. Most students agree that the best parties are those hosted off-campus at upperclassmen houses. Although others point out that loud off-campus parties contribute to the strained town-gown relations. "Moraga is mostly old people and families. They don't want to have to deal with rowdy students, so they call the police for noise violations," one student explained. Upperclassmen feel that the best parties to attend are those in the townhouses, the upperclassmen on-campus housing, because it is less likely for those parties to get shut down. "The older you get, the less strict the rules are," one student explained. Aside from drinking, students also state that there is a fairly large marijuana presence on campus, "but not more than any other Northern California school."

> "I love walking to class and being able to run into and say hi to at least ten people."

Housing: The Luck of the Draw
While St. Mary's is known for its small size, in recent years the number of students enrolling as freshmen has increased. The entering freshman class of 2014 is the largest in St. Mary's history to date. Unfortunately for freshmen, this led to forced doubles and triples in rooms that were originally designed to be singles and doubles. Not all complain about their freshman housing, however. Many students are content with their dorms, particularly those that live suite-style. "Basically, it's all about luck. Some freshmen get

rooms with in-suite bathrooms. Others get forced triples," one student explained. While some describe the lottery system as fair, others complain about the fact that everyone pays the same amount for housing, despite the fact that some rooms are clearly bigger than others. Housing at St. Mary's improves by year, however, and by the time students become upperclassmen, they get to enjoy the campus townhouses, which are all designed apartment-style with their own living room, kitchen, and bathroom. Not all upperclassmen are guaranteed housing, however, which forces students to live in the neighboring cities of Moraga, Lafayette, and Orinda.

Small Colleges: A Double-Edged Sword

Most St. Mary's students can agree that the college's small size is extremely beneficial in the classroom. The class size, which is generally around twenty students, allows for in-depth discussions and for students to get to know their professors very well. At the same time, some students feel that the size can be a hindrance to the social scene, particularly on weekends when many students go home or off-campus. While one student "can't imagine the classes being any bigger" she also admits that "the school feels almost lonely" on the weekends. Others embrace the size. "I love walking to class and being able to run into and say hi to at least ten people" one student gushed. Most St. Mary's students can agree that the campus's small size and surrounding greenery give it a serene feel; despite its size, there is plenty to do: from going to a basketball game, to taking part in a school-sponsored Saturday trip, to watching a movie in a friend's room. At St. Mary's, students are taught based on both a liberal arts philosophy and the beliefs of the De la Salle Christian brothers, which gives for a very well-balanced community overall.
—*Yvette Borja*

FYI

What is the typical weekend schedule? "Friday night: go to an off-campus party, come back to drink in your room or chill with friends and watch a movie. Saturday: go to Walnut Creek to go shopping or go to San Francisco and sight-see. Sunday: get a late lunch with friends, relax, do homework, optional Church service on Sunday nights.

If I could change one thing about St. Mary's I'd "make it so that not as many people went home on the weekends."

Stanford University

Address: 355 Galvez Street
Stanford, CA 94305-6106
Phone: 650-723-2091
E-mail address:
admission@stanford.edu
Web site URL:
www.stanford.edu
Year Founded: 1885
Private or Public: Private
Religious Affiliation: None
Location: Suburban
Number of Applicants:
30,428
Percent Accepted: 8%
**Percent Accepted who
enroll:** 70%
Number Entering: 1,700
**Number of Transfers
Accepted each Year:** 23
Middle 50% SAT range: M:
680–780, CR: 660–760,
Wr: 670–760
Middle 50% ACT range:
30–34
**Early admission program
EA/ED/None:** EA

**Percentage accepted
through EA or ED:** 14%
EA and ED deadline: 1-Nov
Regular Deadline: 1-Jan
Application Fee: $90
**Full time Undergraduate
enrollment:** 6,565
Total enrollment: 18,498
Percent Male: 51%
Percent Female: 49%
**Total Percent Minority or
Unreported:** 52%
Percent African-American:
11%
**Percent Asian/Pacific
Islander:** 22%
Percent Hispanic: 15%
Percent Native-American:
4%
Percent International: 8%
**Percent in-state/out of
state:** 44%/56%
Percent from Public HS: 60%
Retention Rate: 98%
Graduation Rate 4-year:
79%

Graduation Rate 6-year: 93%
**Percent Undergraduates in
On-campus housing:** 88%
**Number of official organized
extracurricular
organizations:** >600
3 Most popular majors:
Biology/Biological Sciences,
General Economics, General
Political Science and
Government
Student/Faculty ratio: 6:1
Average Class Size: 19
**Percent of students going to
grad school:** 52%
Tuition and Fees: $37,881
**In-State Tuition and Fees if
different:** No difference
Cost for Room and Board:
$11,463
**Percent receiving financial
aid out of those who apply,
first year:** 75%
**Percent receiving financial
aid among all students:**
78%

L azy palm trees, gorgeous weather, luscious Spanish-style architecture, happy students—if you're looking for a preeminent research institution with the quintessential West Coast vibe, Stanford University is the school for you. Home to some of the nation's most innovative entrepreneurs and brilliant students, especially in the sciences and engineering, Stanford does an excellent job of entwining superlative academics with a diverse array of extracurricular and pre-professional opportunities to satisfy every student's needs, enfolding the experience in a spirit of cooperation and noncompetitiveness that causes its student body to be ranked consistently as one of the happiest in the country.

Studying was Never So Much Fun

Stanford is famous for its seemingly laid-back students and relaxed pace of life, but do not let the easy-going atmosphere deceive you: Stanford academics are no walk in the park. "Most students here are actually quite Type-A;" and the hefty 180 units re-

quired for graduation and the unique quarter-system calendar make for a challenging experience. The average course load is 15 to 16 units per quarter, and because of the shorter length of the quarter, this translates into a virtually unremitting series of midterms from the second week to "Dead Week" before exams.

All students are required to fulfill General Education Requirements (GERs), in three categories: "Introduction to the Humanities"— "honestly, it's a waste of time, uselessly time-consuming"; "Disciplinary Breadth"— these are simply courses in each of five major areas of study "that essentially fulfill themselves;" and "Education for Citizenship"— encompassing classes on "really cool topics like gender studies and globalization." Most students praise their academic experience, citing "attentive professors" and "an amazing advising system" as reasons for their contentment. Indeed, although especially freshman introductory classes can become quite large—"my linear algebra class exceeded maybe 300 students," stated one freshman— professors are still extremely accessible and hold "extensive office hours" to motivate students to visit them.

Students are especially enthusiastic about Stanford's myriad interdisciplinary majors: human biology; science, technology, and society; modern thought and literature; and urban studies are only a few examples of the bountiful opportunities the university presents for combining disparate interests. However, biology and economics remain the most popular majors. Prospective humanities majors should expect a slightly easier experience: one student majoring in the sciences averred, "The fuzzier majors have a much easier time garnering an A and maintaining a high GPA than the rest of us." Although a Stanford education is not immediately associated with the humanities, the quality of scholarship in those subjects is by no means inferior. Indeed, another student emphasized, "professors in those departments are even more supportive of and accessible to dedicated students."

Life Beyond the Classroom

From the leather easy chairs in the Lane reading room of the Green Library to the sparkling labs of the Clark Center, students are immersed in a variety of rich learning experiences during the day. The Haas Center for Public Service is particularly popular among students, sporting over 600 volunteer, internship, and research opportunities. "The opportunities are extremely accessible and multifarious—there is something for everyone," one student commented. There are also more than 650 clubs and organizations, and each of these is supported by the Student Activities and Leadership division of Stanford's Student Affairs office. SAL staff and student peer advisers take responsibility for guiding students to the opportunities and organizations that best befit their interests.

> "The opportunities are extremely accessible and multifarious—there is something for everyone."

Stanford's support of student's extracurricular intellectual exploration does not end with the school year. Rather than merely relax after a grueling three quarters, the majority of students use their summer quarter to acquire real-world experience through internships, research, or study-abroad programs like the Bing Overseas Program or Summer Research College that Stanford

sponsors. Stated one sophomore, "Study abroad, especially in non-English-speaking countries, is a big deal: about 50 percent of students go abroad, and there are many resources to do so. Research is also a huge deal, and students who are interested start as early as their freshman year."

Living at Camp Stanford

Stanford offers one of the most diverse housing systems of any university, sporting the standard dormitories of 60 to 200 people; self-operated houses of 25 to 50 residents; and independent co-ops, which require complete student control over cooking and cleaning. The incredible variety of options, ranging from academic and theme houses to Greek houses to university-owned apartments, inevitably leads to some disappointment and some euphoria, and it is Stanford's lottery system, "The Draw," that seals students' fate. Most students seem to agree on one point, that "the most popular dorms are those either on The Row, where all the frat houses are, or as near The Row as possible, because that's where the social scene is." Yet a small number of freshmen choose to participate in the Program in Structured Liberal Education, an intensive residential community that provides freshmen only with a comprehensive introduction to the liberal arts in an intimate living and learning environment. And although there are 16 fraternities and 12 sororities on campus, less than 15 percent of students feel the need to go Greek. It seems that whether students are blessed with palatial three-room suites accompanied by a masterful chef, or condemned to cramped one-room triples, by and large, they are quite content.

Students' biggest complaint about living at Stanford, besides the "terrible forced doubles," is the mandatory expensive meal plan, in which all students must participate as long as they reside in a dorm. The average yearly cost for the meal plan exceeds $5,000, a considerable fee for standard dining hall fare. "I'm not at all impressed with Stanford Dining; the meal plan should definitely be more flexible," grumbled one student. Those students who do tire of the cafeteria food— "trust me, you won't eat more than 14 meals in a week"—usually go out with friends to one of the myriad restaurants in the area or on campus. The CoHo coffeehouse, Treehouse, Subway, and Peet's Coffee are popular campus eateries, but many students who seek to venture farther bemoan the exorbitant prices of surrounding Palo Alto. Thus, although Palo

Alto is elegant and affluent—"a treat to occasionally indulge in"—it is no college town, and this fact tends to foster what some call the "Stanford bubble." However, there is never a lack of things to do: theater performances, a cappella concerts, cultural shows, Row house parties always keep students busy. And for the entrepreneurially minded, the proximity of Silicon Valley and the slew of venture capital firms on nearby Sand Hill Road create incredible opportunities.

There is a reason students fondly refer to their school as "Camp Stanford:" the sunny skies and grassy fields, Frisbee-throwing students and flip-flop-wearing professors, stellar athletics and powerful sense of school pride all create an exhilarating and richly rewarding experience. One student summed up life on the "Farm" nicely: "Amazing academics, check. Top-notch sustainability report card, check. Diversity, check. Groundbreaking research, check. Successful entrepreneurs, check. The most brilliant students of the world, check. And a superlative record in football, check. I love you, Stanford!"—*Sejal Hathi*

FYI
If you come to Stanford, you'd better bring: "the desire to explore, a Frisbee, a bike, and your workout clothes."
What's the typical weekend schedule? "Chill Friday nights, party Saturdays, hit the books Sunday."
If I could change one thing about Stanford, I'd change: "the meal plan schedule."
Three things every student at Stanford should do before graduating are: "attend an Entrepreneur Thought Leader seminar, go to the Big Game, and hike the Dish."

University of California System

Students from California undoubtedly will have heard of the University of California, the state's leading public university system for high-achieving high school students. But the UC system stands out not only in California, but across the country, and even the world. A model for public institutions across the United States, eight of its undergraduate campuses rank in the top 100, six in the top 50, and two in the top 25 universities in the country. With more than 191,000 students, 1,340,000 living alumni and an overall endowment of $9.6 billion as of 2007, students looking to enter the UC system will be joining good company. Counting 32 Nobel laureates and 254 members of the National Academy of Sciences within their faculty, UC students are able to get a world-class education without the hefty price tag that comes with private colleges.

So Many Choices

The UC system counts nine campuses among its members, along with a tenth school, San Francisco, which is limited to graduate study in the health sciences. As the charter campus, Berkeley is still regarded by some as the system's flagship school, leading the other campuses with its tradition of academic excellence. But the University of California, Los Angeles, and UC San Diego are not far behind. UCLA's admission rate is comparable to Berkeley's in competitiveness—both hover around 20 percent—and UCSD has already made a name for itself both in the U.S. and abroad for its excellence in the sciences. Irvine boasts an ideal campus location in sunny Orange County, just miles from the beach, not to mention its technological and scientific instruction. Davis is a leading university known for its premier agricultural research as well as strengths in math and sciences. Santa Barbara is quickly proving itself as a rising star in the academic world for its active research, which includes 11 national research centers. Santa Cruz can find pride in its physics, math and astronomy programs, as well as its political science and art departments, not to mention its convenient location right outside beautiful Monterey Bay, just a short trip away from San Francisco and San Jose. Back down south near the greater Los Angeles area, Riverside maintains its reputation for pioneering citrus research and entomology, as well as well-known programs in science fiction and photography. Finally, last but not least, is Merced, founded in 2005 as the newest addition to the UC family. Although it is located in a rural area associated with agriculture (it's just miles from

Yosemite National Park), it emphasizes cutting edge research in the fields of natural science, math, and engineering.

Something for Everyone

While each school handles its admissions separately, students only need to use one application for all the UC's, thereby simplifying the process for students. All eligible students from California are guaranteed a spot in the UC system, though admissions to their top choice of campuses is not necessarily guaranteed. Through statewide admissions, the UC system automatically accepts students among the top eighth of California public school graduates, as well as the top four percent of any given high school. If eligible students are not granted admissions to their top choices, they are then referred to other UC campuses which still have open space. Because several UC campuses have fairly competitive admissions policies, some students will inevitably be disappointed, but even those who end up at their second, third or even fourth choice colleges generally find themselves satisfied with their experience. As one student said about UC Irvine, "The people that come to this school are friendly and the atmosphere is welcoming and comfortable. This was not my first choice school, but when I came here, I grew to like it a lot."

The UC system no longer uses affirmative action policies after the passing in 1996 of California's Proposition 209, which prohibits public institutions such as the UC schools from considering race, sex and ethnicity in their selection processes. As a result, underrepresented minorities and students from underprivileged backgrounds have had a more difficult time enrolling at UC schools, especially those in the proverbial top tier. As such, issues of racial imbalance have arisen, but the UC system has named representing California's diversity in its schools as one of its priorities. Riverside itself can boast of a student body that draws its strength from diversity—the school has topped national rankings in ethnic and socioeconomic diversity, third and fifteenth in the nation, respectively.

All in all, the University of California offers a variety of opportunities among its many campuses and within each campus, the benefits of a huge array of strong academic departments. Students who are looking for a quality education but don't want to graduate with significant debt will certainly be able to find the rewarding experience they seek in the UC system. With so many campuses and a wide range of strengths in research and departments, the UC system is bound to have something for everyone.—*Della Fok*

University of California / Berkeley

Address: 110 Sproul Hall, #5800 Berkeley, CA 94720-5800

Phone: 510-642-3175

E-mail address: Visit Web site to submit questions

Web site URL: www.berkeley.edu

Year Founded: 1868

Private or Public: Public

Religious Affiliation: None

Location: Urban

Number of Applicants: 43,983

Percent Accepted: 23%

Percent Accepted who enroll: 41%

Number Entering: 4,204

Number of Transfers Accepted each Year: 3,311

Middle 50% SAT range: M: 630–760, CR: 590–710, Wr: 600–720

Middle 50% ACT range: Unreported

Early admission program EA/ED/None: None

Percentage accepted through EA or ED: NA

EA and ED deadline: NA

Regular Deadline: 30-Nov

Application Fee: $60

Full time Undergraduate enrollment: 24,636

Total enrollment: 33,903

Percent Male: 45%

Percent Female: 55%

Total Percent Minority or Unreported: 70%

Percent African-American: 3%

Percent Asian/Pacific Islander: 45%

Percent Hispanic: 12%

Percent Native-American: <1%

Percent International: 3%

Percent in-state/out of state: 90%/10%

Percent from Public HS: 85%

Retention Rate: 97%

Graduation Rate 4-year: 60%

Graduation Rate 6-year: Unreported

Percent Undergraduates in On-campus housing: 35%

Number of official organized extracurricular organizations: 300

3 Most popular majors: Computer Engineering, English Language and Literature, Political Science and Government

Student/Faculty ratio: 15:1

Average Class Size: 12

Percent of students going to grad school: Unreported

Tuition and Fees: $28,264

In-State Tuition and Fees if different: $7,656

Cost for Room and Board: $14,494

Percent receiving financial aid out of those who apply, first year: 63%

Percent receiving financial aid among all students: 49%

Students at the University of California at Berkeley enjoy the University's challenging and stimulating academic environment combined with its constant access to beautiful California Bay Area. Considered the top public university in the nation, UC Berkeley—affectionately known as "Cal"—commands an impressive 1,232 acres of campus and a thriving urban city life, only minutes away from San Francisco.

4.0 GPA: Hard to Get, Harder to Keep

UC Berkeley offers six different colleges for undergraduate students: the College of Letters and Science, College of Environmental Design, College of Chemistry, College of Natural Resources, College of Engineering and the Haas School of Business. Each college has its own graduate requirements although UC Berkeley requires a fulfillment of seven "breadth" courses that cover a wide range of the humanities and sciences. According to one freshman in the College of Chemistry, "As a chemical engineering major, we have few humanities requirements, but a *lot* of technical science and engineering courses that we have to take." Although requirements differ from college to college, all students must take specific requirements in order to receive their Bachelor's degree, including Entry Level Writing, American History and American Institutions. "The curriculum is designed to inspire students to become actively interested and knowledgeable about subjects outside the scope of their particular major," said one freshman in the College of Letters and Sciences. "For example, due to the breadth program, I've taken courses that have discussed ancient Greek philosophical views, a subject that fascinated me and that I wouldn't have otherwise been exposed to if it wasn't for the breadth requirement."

UC Berkeley currently offers more than 100 majors, and among its popular majors are typically Molecular and Cell Biology, Electrical Engineering and Computer Science,

Psychology, Business Administration and Economics. Students wishing to enroll in the Haas School of Business must apply for the two-year program during the fall of their sophomore year and, if accepted, begin taking business classes their junior year. Although enrollment in the Haas is limited to 700 students, one aspiring Haas freshman noted, "It's possible for underclassmen who have not yet been admitted to Haas to also take upper division courses."

Average class sizes range from 20 to over 200 students, depending on the structure of the class (discussion-based or lecture) and the material covered; some popular classes, such as Political Science 179, may have as many as 700 students. Berkeley offers a range of different courses, from advanced physics courses to "Physics for Future Presidents," which focuses on the hands-on side of physics instead of mathematical and quantitative aspect. As a large public university, students at Berkeley are often placed on wait-lists for course registration. According to one student, however, "the horror stories about students having to commit more years to finishing their degree are often both over-exaggerate and misunderstood. If a student is diligent and attends his or her classes, he or she is almost always accepted into the class."

While students agree that grading at Berkeley can be tough with terrible curves, most concede that the system is fair and enjoy the challenging environment. "At Berkeley, it's decently easy to get B's but exponentially difficult, almost impossible, to get A's ," said one freshman, who added that she did at least enjoy "the bonding experience over the extremely difficult midterms and finals." According to one sophomore in the College of Engineering, "course grades are curved so that there is a balance distribution of grades, even if the raw scores are abysmal."

Living in an Urban City

Students at Berkeley are guaranteed housing for two years. Prior to arriving on campus, students rank dorm preferences and, if they do not specify a roommate, fill out a housing application to determine a compatible roommate. All but two dorms at Berkeley are co-ed, although most buildings do set aside one floor only for women; Stern Hall is only for women, while Bowles Hall is exclusively for men. Although there are no dorms specifically for freshmen, most upperclassmen tend to move off campus by their sophomore or junior year anyway. Each student has an RA who lives on cam-

pus, guides incoming freshmen and enforces dorm rules. According to one sophomore, "RAs are friendly undergraduate students who organize events for their floors, such as Christmas parties or dinner get-togethers." One student added, "My own RA planned frequent excursions to SF, Oakland, and the movie theatre for our floor."

Berkeley's architecture ranges from the "old and distasteful to regal and modern." According to one student, "Sproul Hall (the main administrative building) looks like a grand Greek building, while Wurster Hall (the architecture building, ironically enough) is infamous for being rather unattractive—supposedly to inspire architecture students to do much better."

There are four dining halls, known as "dining commons" or "DCs" at Berkeley, each of which are located near or inside a dorm building. Although the food is "decently good," students unsatisfied with DC food may choose to eat out instead. There are also on-campus cafes and minimarkets where students can spend meal points in lieu of eating at a dining hall. According to one student, "The dining commons are buffet-styled with many different cuisines available every night with frequent themed nights—the meals leading up to Thanksgiving, for example, all included turkey as a main dish."

Golden Bears and the Golden Gate Bridge

With San Francisco just across the Bay, Berkeley students frequently find their weekend schedules packed with trips to "San Fran," parties at fraternities and sororities, football games, and a cappella performances. On Thursday, Friday, and Saturday nights, students enjoy going to apartment parties or clubbing in San Francisco. Because most upperclassmen move off campus by their sophomore or junior year, underclassmen and upperclassmen generally do not mingle over the weekends. Nonetheless, students easily make friends at Berkeley. According to one freshman, "my floor itself is a great community of people that I've bonded very closely with. As a result, I have a wide social net at Berkeley that I can hang out with."

Although alcohol and binge drinking is not a problem on campus, marijuana is a common presence. One student noted that Berkeley is considered the country's "marijuana capital," and students have easy access to pot. While alcohol and drugs are not technically allowed in dorms, "the amount of enforcing really depends on the RA, and even then, alcohol and drugs are not strongly enforced at all outside of dorms."

> "There's such a wide range of people to interact and meet with that one is never short of fun. This turns the size of Berkeley from being one of its detractors to being one of its strong suits."

There is also a variety of social opportunities for students uninterested in alcohol or marijuana, including weekend concerts, musical performances, cheap movies, and multiple dining options such as Blondie's Pizza or Crepes-a-Go-Go. Students can also go shopping in one of Berkeley's many thrift shops or discover their musical preferences at Rasputin Records, a large records store in walking distance. Although most students do not own cars because "parking at Berkeley is a nightmare," most commute using the free bus service or the BART transrail, making transportation easy and accessible.

More to Love

Berkeley students are as intense about their extracurricular activities as they are about their academics, and students have the opportunity to join an enormous variety of organizations. "Berkeley is HUGE in all ways," said one freshman. "There are lots of frats, sororities, a cappella teams, great sports teams, many intramural sports, and clubs for basically any interest." Professional fraternities and organizations are especially popular, and clubs such as the Asian Business Association or Circle K (a community service organization) are among the larger clubs on campus. Moreover, Berkeley also offers its fair share of unusual organizations, including a Quidditch team and the Cal Hawaii Club, for students looking for a unique college experience.

Students at Berkeley are intensely proud of being Bears and their shared pride is manifested most strongly during the Big Game, the annual football game between Berkeley and its southern rival Stanford University. Every evening before the Big Game, students on the Berkeley rally team organize a blazing bonfire rally at the Greek theater to encourage school spirit. Generally, however, students don't need extra encouragement to take pride in their school. According to one freshman, "I had initially expected the worst, but found the best. Once I discovered my own niche in Berkeley, all those cautionary tales against the school because of its size disappeared." Another sophomore agreed, adding, "There have been times when I was treading academic rough waters, but upon hindsight, I think these past semesters have been rather rewarding. Given a second chance, I would choose Berkeley again."—*Caroline Tan*

FYI
If you come to Berkeley, you'd better bring "all your attention, focus, motivation, creativity, brains, and willpower to work your butt off."
If I could change one thing about Berkeley, I'd "change the attitude of people who place so much concentration on getting good grades instead of learning."
The biggest college-wide tradition/event at Berkeley is "the Big Game Day. Everyone dresses up and gets pumped for it."

University of California / Davis

Address: 178 Mrak Hall, One Shields Avenue, Davis, CA 95616
Phone: 530-752-2971
E-mail address: undergraduateadmissions@ucdavis.edu
Web site URL: www.ucdavis.edu
Year Founded: 1905
Private or Public: Public
Religious Affiliation: None
Location: Suburban
Number of Applicants: 35,148
Percent Accepted: 59%
Percent Accepted who enroll: 24%
Number Entering: 4,955
Number of Transfers Accepted each Year: 5,466
Middle 50% SAT range: M: 540–660, CR: 490–630, Wr: 500–630
Middle 50% ACT range: 20–27

Early admission program EA/ED/None: None
Percentage accepted through EA or ED: NA
EA and ED deadline: NA
Regular Deadline: 30-Nov
Application Fee: $60
Full time Undergraduate enrollment: 23,499
Total enrollment: 27,593
Percent Male: 44%
Percent Female: 56%
Total Percent Minority or Unreported: 65%
Percent African-American: 3%
Percent Asian/Pacific Islander: 41%
Percent Hispanic: 12%
Percent Native-American: 1%
Percent International: 2%
Percent in-state/out of state: 97%/3%
Percent from Public HS: 84%
Retention Rate: 90%

Graduation Rate 4-year: 42%
Graduation Rate 6-year: 80%
Percent Undergraduates in On-campus housing: 81%
Number of official organized extracurricular organizations: 364
3 Most popular majors: Biology, Economics, Psychology
Student/Faculty ratio: 19:1
Average Class Size: 16
Percent of students going to grad school: 40%
Tuition and Fees: $29,243
In-State Tuition and Fees if different: $8,635
Cost for Room and Board: $11,978
Percent receiving financial aid out of those who apply, first year: 58%
Percent receiving financial aid among all students: 75%

Just minutes away from Sacramento and San Francisco Bay, UC Davis is cozily set in the lush green surroundings of California's Central Valley. The school continues its legacy as a top-notch public research institution and maintains its commitment to excellence through rigorous liberal arts academic programs, research experience, and diverse extracurricular activities. With over 500 athletes in 23 varsity sports and nearly $800 million in research funding, the largest UC campus creates an atmosphere of achievement and opportunity.

Size Matters

UC Davis is one of the larger public schools in the country, a fact with both positive and negative impacts on student life. With over 100 undergraduate majors, 88 graduate programs, and more than 30,000 enrolled students, over 24,500 of which are undergraduates, UC Davis provides unparalleled variety for study. Despite its large size, students say it is relatively easy to get into their desired courses. While upperclassmen do seem to have prior-

ity in choosing some of the more popular and entertaining classes, there are no complaints most of the time. As one student explained, "Classes aren't really large, but they aren't so small as to not be able to accommodate people's requirements for their majors."

Introductory courses are taught in lecture hall settings with PowerPoint slides as a primary tool for professors. Such classes meet in small sections of 10–20 students with teaching assistants as instructors. During such discussion sections, students are encouraged to ask for clarifications and help on material that they are having difficulties with. A few students claim that it is occasionally hard to understand TAs whose first language is not English, but most students find it beneficial to attend sections, even if they are not mandatory. Regardless of the size of lecture, most professors are easily accessible either after class or during office hours and are eager to converse with students.

UC Davis is composed of four colleges that differ in general coursework and interdisciplinary resources: Agricultural and

Environmental Sciences, Biological Sciences, Letters and Science, and Engineering. The College of Letters and Science is the largest and most diverse of the four colleges, including instruction in the natural sciences, social sciences, humanities, arts, and cultural studies. Potential undergraduates apply to specific college programs when applying to Davis, each with unique general requirements. Although students are allowed to change majors after the first quarter, some find it tedious switching to another college.

The school year at Davis runs on a quarter system, which is made up of three quarters during the traditional academic year and one during the summer. This is similar to that of most high schools, so most students have little problem in the transition process. The quarter system induces a fast-paced learning environment in which work for classes is concentrated. One freshman stated that "there is no time to slack off since it is difficult to anticipate upcoming exams." As an upside, she said, "Students can get out of a class they dislike in as short as nine to 10 weeks."

Luxurious Living

All incoming freshmen are guaranteed spots in on-campus residence halls, and approximately 90 percent of them end up in on-campus housing. Consequently, on-campus housing is mostly occupied by freshmen. There are a wide variety of options including single-sex, coed, and theme housing. Floor plans illustrate single room arrangements, double room arrangements, cluster-style four-person arrangements, and suite-style four-person arrangements. The three undergraduate residence locations on campus are Segundo, Tercero, and Cuarto. All these residence halls have certain features in common: high-speed internet, cable television, study space, laundry rooms, kitchenettes, and lounges.

Dining commons are present at all four residence halls, and students are free to eat at any one. Students select one of three meal plans, each with a number of "points," with one point swiped per meal. The dining halls put on theme dinner nights throughout the year, so there is no need to worry about eating the same foods everyday. The Segundo dorm has a relatively new dining commons, and an overwhelmingly high proportion of students compliment it. One Cuarto resident said, "In general, the dining hall in Segundo provides more variety and food of better quality." Midnight snackers may add "late-night points" to purchase pizza, cookies, and snack foods sold in the commons until midnight each night.

Sophomores also have the choice to live in dorms, but most decide to live off campus since they receive lowest priority in housing. Students described the process of finding off-campus housing as very easy, with "a lot of beautiful neighborhoods to choose from" and a "very tight relationship between Davis and the community." From apartments to townhouses to condos, the city of Davis has options to match any lifestyle. People moving in from large metropolises experience pleasant surprises from the affordability of off-campus arrangements. Generally, off-campus housing is more than significantly cheaper than on-campus housing. Average rental rates for unfurnished apartments range from $867/month for a one-bedroom to $2738/month for a five-bedroom. Living prices are major factors to consider for some people who are somewhat dissatisfied with their current living arrangements. But, as one freshman complained, "a negative side to on-campus housing is that students are randomly assigned rooms inside their resident halls, and everyone pays the same price regardless of room size."

The Davis campus offers a number of facilities, such as the popular MU Games Area, which features old-time favorites like bowling, pool, and air hockey. One student said, "The MU arcade is a nice place to relax, especially during events where iPods are given away." Other students enjoy spending time at the Quad in their spare time, where various extracurricular organizations congregate and advertise. Davis also recently constructed the Activities and Recreation Center (REC), a large, modern gym. A student who is currently taking a pilates class in the REC praises it for the diversity of activities that are offered, such as yoga and the "*300* Spartan Training Class," a program teaching warrior-like philosophy and exercises to its participants. Professional academic and leadership coordinators are on-hand at each of the housing areas to work with residents individually or through programs and events.

Campus Culture

Thursday, Friday, and Saturday nights represent the zenith of undergraduate social life, as fraternities and sororities frequently throw parties. Responsible drinking is expected of students. University alcohol permits can be easily attained as long as event coordinators demonstrate good judgment. To reduce binge drinking, the university has implemented a "0–3" campaign in an effort to limit student alcohol to three drinks or fewer.

As parties aren't frequent on campus, the Mondavi Center provides an alternative way to enjoy the weekend through exploration of the full range of performing arts. Students may come to Mondavi to enjoy international music, dance, and theater. The university hosts events like Picnic Day and Open House for Davis, designed to showcase recreational activities and the achievements of UC Davis students and alumni. People come to wander through the more than 150 events throughout the day, sampling delicious food and grabbing informational pamphlets along the way.

Whether you're a spectator or competitor, UC Davis won't disappoint your athletic needs. With 23 varsity sports, 33 club sports, and 14 intramural sports ranging from ultimate Frisbee to water polo, there will be plenty to cheer for and play in. With UC Davis's entrance into NCAA Division I come phenomenal new recreational facilities including the Activities and Recreation Center, Equestrian Center, Hockey Pool, Recreation Fields, and Rec Pool. One student noted, "While athletics aren't as large as they are at Berkeley or UCLA, school spirit is large and obvious—you can always spot someone in a school sweatshirt."

The city of Davis is a great small city, devoid of cinderblock superstores like Wal-mart and Target. But those looking for a "small town" feel need not panic. As one student remarked, the Target still takes a 15-minute bike ride away from central campus. Davis is also quite strict about its recycling policies, which keeps the area green and lush. Cleanliness makes the town a perfect location for a sunny afternoon snack at Fuji Café's sushi buffet or a $4 movie screening at the local theater. Downtown Davis features student hangouts like Ciocalat, a great place to study while soaking in the sun and enjoying a cup of tea. Sophia's Thai Restaurant features a casual dining environment and includes a Thai room where one has the option of sitting on the floor in traditional Thai style. This is also the place to get enough free refills of Thai tea to satisfy anyone's appetite.

> "While athletics aren't as large as they are at Berkeley or UCLA, school spirit is large and obvious: you can always spot someone in a school sweatshirt."

No matter where you go in Davis, you'll find something to enjoy. One freshman summed up her experience: "Davis is a welcoming community. Everyone always smiles and everyone is accepting. I feel like I belong. I feel like I can get to know people better. There's a feeling of innocence. Davis is a home away from home."—*Bing Han*

FYI
If you come to UC Davis, you'd better bring "a bicycle with locks, because that's the most efficient way to get around."
The typical weekend schedule at UC Davis "involves a combination of doing homework, spending time with friends, and occasional partying."
If I could change one thing about UC Davis, I'd "construct a Chinatown in its vicinity, so that there would be better Chinese food."
Three things every UC Davis student should do before graduating are "get a free tire fill-up at the Bike Barn located in the Silo Student Union, join the Aggie Pack in support of the athletic department's 75 percent home winning record, and check out the Cross Cultural Center."

University of California / Irvine

Address: 204 Aldrich Hall
Irvine, CA 92697-1075
Phone: 949-824-6703
E-mail address:
admissions@uci.edu
Web site URL: www.uci.edu
Year Founded: 1965
Private or Public: Public
Religious Affiliation: None
Location: Suburban
Number of Applicants:
34,531
Percent Accepted: 60%
Percent Accepted who
enroll: 21%
Number Entering: 4,314
Number of Transfers
Accepted each Year:
5,939
Middle 50% SAT range:
M: 570–680, CR:
540–630, Wr: Unrepoted
Middle 50% ACT range:
Unreported
Early admission program
EA/ED/None: None

Percentage accepted
through EA or ED: NA
EA and ED deadline: NA
Regular Deadline: 30-Nov
Application Fee: $60
Full time Undergraduate
enrollment: 19,930
Total enrollment: 24,283
Percent Male: 50%
Percent Female: 50%
Total Percent Minority or
Unreported: 74%
Percent African-American:
2%
Percent Asian/Pacific
Islander: 49%
Percent Hispanic: 12%
Percent Native-American:
<1%
Percent International: 2%
Percent in-state/out of
state: 97%/3%
Percent from Public HS:
Unreported
Retention Rate: 93%
Graduation Rate 4-year: 57%

Graduation Rate 6-year:
79%
Percent Undergraduates in
On-campus housing: 82%
Number of official organized
extracurricular
organizations: 378
3 Most popular majors:
Biology, Computer and
Information Sciences,
Economics
Student/Faculty ratio: 19:1
Average Class Size: 16
Percent of students going to
grad school: 30%
Tuition and Fees: $28,654
In-State Tuition and Fees if
different: $8,046
Cost for Room and Board:
$10,527
Percent receiving financial
aid out of those who apply,
first year: 44%
Percent receiving financial
aid among all students:
64%

H alfway between Los Angeles and San Diego lies the sunny campus of UC Irvine. With beaches, restaurants and shopping destinations within close reach, students at this school can enjoy strong academics without a stressful atmosphere. Taking a peek at this low-key campus will reveal college staples such as supportive freshman dorms, as well as the bonuses of great meal options and a budding hip hop scene.

Break out those calculators
At UC Irvine, math and science are kings. Students agreed that their school is more math, science and engineering based and stronger in these fields than in the humanities. This is reflected in the popular majors on campus—biology (in which the school has a very strong department), chemistry, and engineering; psychology and social sciences are also popular. Despite the science-leaning tendencies of the school, UC Irvine makes sure that its students get a well-rounded education through the Breadth Requirements, which require students to take

classes across a variety of academic disciplines including social sciences, humanities and math.

On the whole, classes at UC Irvine tend to be on the large size, though "it depends on your major and the class you're taking," one junior explained. Writing or art classes typically have a max of 20–30 students, while lower-division bio classes can have up to 450 students. A psychology major said, "In the classes I have been in, the average number is about 150 to 200 students." Students said classes begin to get smaller in upper-division courses specifically in the major. To get into classes, students register according to how many units they have completed, so upperclassmen have first dibs. Students said certain classes—writing classes, labs, popular major/minor classes, and GE's—are hard to get into because so many are competing for the same spots. However, students in the Campus-Wide Honors Program are one of the first to register for classes regardless of units taken, which is one of the major perks of the program. First-years get accepted into this program while they are still in high school (no additional application necessary), but current and transfer students must apply.

Grading at UC Irvine varies, depending on the professor's choice or the department. The more competitive classes such as biology, chemistry and mathematics are curved down so that a certain amount of A's, B's, C's, D's, and F's are set in advance. For other classes such as language courses, they are curved in the sense that only the maximum amount of students that can receive A's is 15 percent and the rest receive a B+ and lower. One junior explained, "It is definitely possible to get A's, but there are those teachers that make it hard to get them. The older professors are usually the ones that don't curve in their classes." But despite the occasional competitive curve and difficulty in getting into popular courses, "the academic life is very rewarding due to the prominent and notable professors that teach here," a Social Ecology major said.

Living in Irvine

For incoming freshmen, there are three main housing options—Middle Earth, Mesa Court, and Arroyo Vista. The first two are dorming communities, whereas students who live in Arroyo Vista need to take a shuttle to get to class since it is located off of the main campus. The application for first-year housing is very specific on helping students find the right people to live with, and according to upperclassmen, the freshman dorms are very comfortable and fit the needs of students living away from their parents for the first time. "It's recommended for first-years. You meet a lot of new people and learn a lot about each other," one student said.

The dorm community is composed of a variety of small buildings, each with specific themes that fit the students' interests, though some dorm rooms are nicer than others, depending on which hall you get. The general rule is, "The newer the hall, the bigger your room," as one junior put it. UC Irvine guarantees two years of on-campus housing, and most people move into on-campus apartments their second year after living in dorms as freshmen. In their third year, students move off-campus to the many apartments near campus.

Each hall in the dorms has its own RA, but students say that they usually aren't that strict about policies because they are students themselves and thus, more lenient. In addition, a senior commented, "RA's for the dorms are really nice people and they act as mentors, friends, and teachers for freshmen—they

help make living on campus fun and easy." Students praised Irvine for its safety, overwhelmingly citing Irvine as "one of the safest cities to live in" and being known as "the safest city in California."

As for food, there is a plethora of options in restaurants, both on- and off-campus. Even among the dining halls, there are distinctions—Mesa Court has one dining hall while Middle Earth has two. Students living in Mesa Court or Middle Earth have three meal plans to choose from, and one junior advised, "People usually never finish their meals so it's better to choose the cheapest one." She added, "The food seems to be getting better every quarter, and you can even choose from organic foods." In addition to dorm dining halls, there is also an on-campus food court which offers a variety of choices, including Chinese food, pasta, Quizno's, and Wendy's. For those who need their caffeine fix, there are two coffee shops on campus—Starbucks and Cyber A Cafe. UC Irvine also has its own pub and three other "restaurants" on different parts of the campus. Meal options include the option of flex dollars, which is money you can use at any of these places. Of course, the Southern California experience wouldn't be complete without In-N-Out, the quintessential California fast-food chain that serves fresh burgers and fries. Students can find one literally on their doorstep, as there is one right across the street from campus at the University Town Center, which also features a Yogurtland. In addition, you can find sandwiches, Mexican food and Japanese food, just to mention a few.

Feel the Beat

UC Irvine offers many clubs that fit specific interests and culture. One student noted, "Clubs are run by very enthusiastic members who are willing to give the time to making the club prosper and letting students feel comfortable." But another student added, "How much a person commits to their club/organization really depends on the person." Many people are involved in culture clubs such as Chinese Association, Korean-American Student Association, and Tomo No Kai (Japanese Club), to name a few. Due to the school's student population, which students describe as not very diverse, these culture clubs tend to be Asian-American-oriented.

A school in the suburbs of Orange County with a majority of Asian students may not seem like it would have this reputation, but the campus features prominent hip-hop dance teams. "A lot of people know UCI as the 'hip hop dance' university," a junior said. The school has four hip-hop teams, the most famous of which is Kaba Modern, which was featured on MTV's "America's Best Dance Crew." As a result, "a lot of hip-hoppers want to go to UCI," a student explained.

Students say there are many social scenes on campus, including the aforementioned cultural clubs and dance teams, in addition to academic clubs, a cappella groups, and sports teams. But fraternities and sororities are by far the most dominant, students say. During the first two weeks or so of every quarter, the Greek society takes over the campus to promote their fraternities and sororities. One junior described the experience: "At the beginning of the school year, there will be booths set up at the club fair, as well as on Ring Road. You will get bombarded with flyers to rush for their fraternity/sorority. Panhellenic frats and sororities have a different rushing process than Asian fraternities and sororities." Thursdays are usually when fraternities and sororities have clubbing events, and conveniently, there are usually buses taking people to the club so they don't have to worry about drinking and driving. Students say that not everybody drinks ("Those who go to parties usually drink; those who don't go to parties don't drink."), but alcohol, hookah and pot are popular around campus. Dorm policies are the same as anywhere else—Students can't get drunk in the dorms (no alcohol or drugs are allowed in the dorms), but students can be drunk in the dorms. One student added, "I would say that the people who drink the most are those who are involved in sorority and frat events."

On other nights, students say they usually just hang out at each other's apartments or dorm rooms, or attend club events and meetings. Other low-key weekend options include going out to eat and shopping at Fashion Island in Newport Beach or South Coast Plaza and the Irvine Spectrum, which are popular malls nearby. In addition, students said many people have Disneyland passes and sometimes hang out and eat at Downtown Disney or go watch fireworks at night. One student said, "On the weekends, a lot of people stay or go home every other weekend, but usually, on the weekends there isn't really much to do in Irvine." On the whole, though, a junior summed up social life at UC Irvine as "It's what you make of it."

> **"A lot of hip-hoppers want to go to UCI."**

Students who end up at Irvine can expect to dress to impress, even to class. A Film and Media Studies major said, "People at school are definitely into fashion, and our school is good on keeping up with the latest fashion trends." However, he added, "There are also a lot of people who have their own style/attitude. Unlike high school, it's okay to dress the way you want and not be judged for it."

UC Irvine may not be as high-profile as its counterparts in Berkeley or Los Angeles, but the experience can be just as positive. As one senior reflected, "The people that come to this school are friendly and the atmosphere is welcoming and comfortable."
—*Della Fok*

FYI
If you come to UC Irvine, "you'd better bring money and a swimsuit."
What's the typical weekend schedule? "Most SoCal people leave on the weekends, which leaves all the NorCal people alone in Irvine."
If I could change one thing about UC Irvine, "I'd put on-campus apartments within walking distance of class. Why are off-campus apartments closer to classes than on-campus apartments?"
Three things every student at UC Irvine should do before graduating are: "make a lot of friends, join a club, and learn the area because there are so many restaurants around campus!"

University of California / Los Angeles

Address: 1147 Murphy Hall, Box 951436, Los Angeles, CA 90095-1436
Phone: 310-825-3101
E-mail address: ugadm@saonet.ucla.edu
Web site URL: www.ucla.edu
Year Founded: 1919
Private or Public: Public
Religious Affiliation: None
Location: Urban
Number of Applicants: 50,755
Percent Accepted: 24%
Percent Accepted who enroll: 38%
Number Entering: 4,515
Number of Transfers Accepted each Year: 5,330
Middle 50% SAT range: M: 700–760, CR: 660–720, Wr: 670–720
Middle 50% ACT range: 28–31
Early admission program EA/ED/None: None

Percentage accepted through EA or ED: NA
EA and ED deadline: NA
Regular Deadline: 30-Nov
Application Fee: $60
Full time Undergraduate enrollment: 25,928
Total enrollment: 36,899
Percent Male: 45%
Percent Female: 55%
Total Percent Minority or Unreported: 66%
Percent African-American: 3%
Percent Asian/Pacific Islander: 38%
Percent Hispanic: 15%
Percent Native-American: <1%
Percent International: 4%
Percent in-state/out of state: 96%/4%
Percent from Public HS: 78%
Retention Rate: 97%
Graduation Rate 4-year: 64%

Graduation Rate 6-year: 87%
Percent Undergraduates in On-campus housing: 92%
Number of official organized extracurricular organizations: 774
3 Most popular majors: Biology, Political Science and Government, Psychology
Student/Faculty ratio: 16:1
Average Class Size: 15
Percent of students going to grad school: Unreported
Tuition and Fees: $28,162
In-State Tuition and Fees if different: $7,551
Cost for Room and Board: $12,891
Percent receiving financial aid out of those who apply, first year: 49%
Percent receiving financial aid among all students: 82%

S trolling on UCLA's sunlit Bruin Walk in the middle of the day, one is surrounded by faces representing countless different nationalities, races, academic inclinations, and extracurricular interests. But one thing is for certain on this Southern California public school campus in a city that advertises 329 days of sun per year: the Bruin spirit courses through its large, diverse student body, making them proud of their nationally renowned sports, academics, and West Coast culture.

Studying among the Stars

UCLA is situated on 419 acres in the picturesque Los Angeles district of Westwood, bordering Beverly Hills and Bel-Air. But the school's proximity to the glamour of Hollywood doesn't mean the students don't put in their work. The schools open to undergraduate enrollment are the College of Letters and Science, the School of the Arts and Architecture, the Henry Samueli School of Engineering and Applied Science, the School of Nursing, and the School of The-

ater, Film, and Television. Students in the College of Letters and Science must fulfill General Education requirements in three foundational areas: three courses in the arts and humanities, three in society and culture, and four in scientific inquiry. Possible subgroups of these areas include visual and performance arts analysis and practice, historical analysis, and physical sciences. In addition, there are writing, quantitative reasoning, and foreign language requirements, but these can be fulfilled with test scores or high school credit. Students say that the GE requirements aren't too much of a pain; in fact, there is the option of taking a GE cluster, which is a group of classes across disciplines that allows them to get several GEs out of the way in one fell swoop.

UCLA is on the quarter system, meaning that there are three segments during the academic year and one in the summer. While one female student said that this system lets her finish courses she dislikes fairly quickly, she complained that "it's midterm season all the time!" Classes are geographically split, for the most part, between South Campus—the sciences—and North Campus—humanities—with rare crossover. Although some students pointed to a psychological divide between the two, saying that there is often mutual distrust or the feeling that one side is more challenging than the other, a junior said that "at the end of the day, it's not going to stop you from being friends with people from the other side." Students did generally agree that the atmosphere on South Campus is "more cutthroat," especially since more and more freshmen are coming to UCLA intending to be pre-med. Recent additions to scientific research and health buildings on campus reflect this growing trend.

Besides biology and other sciences, popular majors at UCLA include psychology, political science, economics, and communications. South Campus grading is more curve-based because the classes are larger, while North Campus grading is reportedly more subjective, but less stressful. The system by which students sign up for classes, while "imperfect and sometimes more stressful than it should be" because of the high demand for many classes, seems to be working for now. Signups occur online, and the order is determined by class year and honors status. Students generally take three or four courses per quarter, ranging from 13 to 19 units per quarter, with 180 units needed to graduate. Most students are able to graduate within four years, but if you choose your major late, it's less likely that you'll be able to pull the credits together, at least without summer school. But the academic offerings are impressive: professors include Nobel laureates, Rhodes scholars, and countless other famous researchers. But somehow, the focus on undergraduate education is maintained, even in this large public university. Students report developing close relationships with professors—one sophomore gushed about a seminar leader she invited to her sorority's professor dinner.

Luckily, studying isn't all about work. Every finals week, on Wednesday at midnight, students run through campus to Royce Hall, doing the UCLA cheers, and jump in the fountain—in their underwear. "Undie Run is one of those experiences that makes a big school smaller," a junior said.

Living in LaLa Land

Living accommodations earn mixed reviews, but with more than 25,000 undergraduates crammed into housing, that's to be expected. The four high-rise residence halls in which freshmen are housed are Dykstra, Hedrick, Rieber, and Sproul. These are "typical college dorms," with between 100 and 200 students per coed floor. A girl explained that, on her floor, 50 girls shared a bathroom, and most people were in one-room triples with bunk beds. The "res halls" are currently being renovated one at a time, but the plazas are less than five years old, featuring triples as well but with the convenience of sharing a bathroom between only two rooms. The suites have private bathrooms and two bedrooms, each with two or three people living in them. While the latter two options may be less hectic and cramped, most students recommended living in the res halls because of the social component. Those who choose to live off campus can move into their sororities and fraternities or rent apartments in Westwood close to campus. The rent is expensive in the area, getting cheaper farther away from the University, but a junior said that "it's worth it to have a nice apartment."

The food gets stellar reviews. Students are given a certain amount of "swipes" for the quarter, which they can use at various times of the day at the four main dining halls—Covel, De Neve, Hedrick, and Rieber—and at the three cafes: Bruin, Crossroads, and Puzzles. "Compared to the average dining hall experience, UCLA is excellent," a history major said. "Everyone who moves out of the dorms always tries to bribe people into giving them a swipe," commented a junior political science major, going on to describe the variety of cuisines available at the main dining facilities, including Italian, American, Thai, and just plain healthy.

The striking campus features a variety of architectural styles, predominantly brick and Spanish Mediterranean, and sometimes Gothic. When they venture into the surrounding area, Bruins find themselves with a wealth of opportunities for play, and even work. The bus system easily (and inexpensively) takes them around the city, from the beach at Santa Monica to downtown Hollywood. Cars, which are off-limits for first-years, are more difficult to manage simply because the parking is "limited and inconvenient," but those who have jobs and internships elsewhere in the city find them worth the effort. Just walking down to the shops in Westwood opens up a variety of shopping, eating, and bar-hopping possibilities. Even trips to Las Vegas or Mexico are not unusual.

A perk, according to one sophomore, is the University's proximity to Hollywood.

Many directors who want to screen their films before releasing them to wider audiences gives sneak previews to UCLA students, she said.

Socializing in the Sun

An awareness that has arisen over the past few years at many UC campuses, UCLA in particular, is that the student body is becoming more diverse—or is that less so? It's true that Asian-American students make up nearly 40 percent of the student body, while black students account for less than three percent. As the stereotype of "University of Caucasians Lost among Asians" becomes increasingly pervasive, the school's administration is working hard establishing initiatives that will supposedly ensure that the sense of diversity is maintained. Keeping with the Southern California feel, though, there is a significant Latino presence.

Students' geographical origins may be likewise deceptively diverse—all 50 states and more than 100 countries are represented, although only two percent of the student body is from outside California—but politics, while heavily weighted toward liberal viewpoints, are by no means homogenous. The Bruin Republicans are reported to be "pretty vocal." People come from "every background imaginable," because of the University's public school availability, though the upper-middle class is well-represented. The relatively casual nature of the campus, with many simply sporting sweatpants or semi-preppy outfits, contributes to the laid-back feel.

Fraternities and sororities are a big part of social life on campus, whether you belong to a Greek organization or not. The houses host many events, although non-Greek girls have an easier time gaining access than their male counterparts. For those who belong, the array of date parties, formals, theme parties, and spirit events means there is no lack of a social life. But for those who are reluctant to join the 13 percent of students who go Greek, fear not: "It's just another outlet— some people choose it, and some people don't," a non-Greek junior explained. "It's not necessarily exclusive." "If you aren't in it, there are plenty of other ways to fit in on campus," added a sorority girl, who indicated the superior housing as a reason she chose to pledge.

Superfluous Spirit

There are countless ways to get involved at UCLA. More than 700 registered organizations attract the motivated each year, from Unicamp, through which Bruins volunteer to hold a summer camp for underprivileged LA kids, to *The Daily Bruin*, the student newspaper. Some of the most visible groups on campus include the Student Alumni Organization, which organizes some of the biggest events each year, the Undergraduate Students Association Council, and Tours, the tour guide group. The SAA puts on Spring Sing and Homecoming Week events, among others. Welcome Week, held each year on the Sunday before the first week of class, kicks off with BruinBash, usually featuring a star-studded concert. Previous performers include T.I. and Rooney. The annual Dance Marathon raises money for the Elizabeth Glaser Pediatric AIDS Foundation— over the past seven years, the event has raised almost a million dollars for the cause.

> "Our athletics are unparalleled, and our school spirit definitely shows it."

Although school spirit is evident in these activities, it is truly apparent when Bruins are backing their sports teams—especially when they come head-to-head with the crosstown rival, University of Southern California. "Our athletics are unparalleled, and our school spirit definitely shows it," said a sophomore, pointing out UCLA's consistently strong showing in the NCAA Division 1-A Pac-10 conference. As of 2007, UCLA had racked up 121 national championships across the many teams it fields, including 11 NCAA championships, exceeding the totals of all other universities. The Rose Bowl and Pauley Pavilion are usually packed for competitions, and tailgates are especially intense, with full body paint a common sighting. The school has ticket packages for the football and basketball seasons, and many loyal fans take them up on the offer.

And it's not only the students who are feeling the draw of the vibrant, involved campus. "To say celebrities like to get involved at UCLA is an understatement," a political science major said, rattling off a list of recent visitors that included Bill Clinton, Al Gore, Stevie Wonder, Julie Andrews, and Oprah. The students may not ever get used to bumping into the rich and famous as they walk their dogs or jog in Westwood, but the shock of the large university setting does wear off, as most can attest to. "I thought I'd get lost here, but not a day goes by where I don't see someone I know every 10 seconds," a sophomore said. "By joining different clubs and organizations, you create communities within communities." Don't let the six campus pools and plentiful opportunities for sunbathing fool you—Bruins take their academics as seriously as their leisure. A junior put it suc-cinctly: "Everyone here is really good at having fun, but also getting stuff done." If you think the LA mentality might be for you, or if you're good at focusing on your studies even when the weather is beautiful year-round, you might find that four years in Southern California are right for you.—*Kimberly Chow*

FYI

If you come to UCLA, you'd better bring "face paint and your jersey; the spirit here on campus is awesome."

What is the typical weekend schedule? "On Saturday, sleep in, then go head to the pool or a football game or hang out in Westwood with friends, then at night go to parties in the apartments or the frats. Sunday, have brunch in Westwood, do some reading, and have club meetings at night."

If I could change one thing about UCLA, I'd "have more counseling and more of an ability to contact academic advisors so you can figure out classes."

Three things every student at UCLA should do before graduating are "spot a celebrity in Westwood, do Undie Run, and go to a basketball game in Pauley Pavilion and sit in the Den."

University of California / Riverside

Address: 1120 Hinderaker Hall, Riverside, CA 92521
Phone: 951-827-3411
E-mail address: discover@ucr.edu
Web site URL: www.ucr.edu
Year Founded: 1954
Private or Public: Public
Religious Affiliation: None
Location: Suburban
Number of Applicants: 20,126
Percent Accepted: 82%
Percent Accepted who enroll: 22%
Number Entering: 3,701
Number of Transfers Accepted each Year: 4,086
Middle 50% SAT range: M: 470–610, CR: 450–560, Wr: 450–560
Middle 50% ACT range: 18–23
Early admission program EA/ED/None: None

Percentage accepted through EA or ED: NA
EA and ED deadline: NA
Regular Deadline: 30-Nov
Application Fee: $60
Full time Undergraduate enrollment: 14,973
Total enrollment: 17,138
Percent Male: 48%
Percent Female: 52%
Total Percent Minority or Unreported: 82%
Percent African-American: 7%
Percent Asian/Pacific Islander: 42%
Percent Hispanic: 26%
Percent Native-American: <1%
Percent International: 2%
Percent in-state/out of state: 99%/1%
Percent from Public HS: 88%
Retention Rate: 83%

Graduation Rate 4-year: 39%
Graduation Rate 6-year: 63%
Percent Undergraduates in On-campus housing: 71%
Number of official organized extracurricular organizations: 251
3 Most popular majors: Biology, Business, Psychology
Student/Faculty ratio: 18:1
Average Class Size: 27
Percent of students going to grad school: Unreported
Tuition and Fees: $28,453
In-State Tuition and Fees if different: $7,846
Cost for Room and Board: $10,850
Percent receiving financial aid out of those who apply, first year: 63%
Percent receiving financial aid among all students: 80%

The orange groves and botanical gardens lining University of California-Riverside serve as vestiges of its past as the UC Citrus Experiment Station. The university opened in 1954, and because of its proximity to the Box Springs Mountains, commonly called the Highlands, became known as home of the Highlanders. As an ode to the Highlands of Scotland, UCR's mascot Scotty the bear soon donned a kilt, and an impressive bagpipe team assembled.

U.S. News and World Report recently ranked UCR the fourth most racially diverse campus in the nation. With a student body that is 40 percent Asian, 30 percent Latino, 17 percent Caucasian, and 8 percent African American, UCR offers a cultural learning experience outside of the classroom. A freshman recalled a time when, unable to find a free table in the crowded lunch area, she sat in a random seat and struck up a conversation with two people who happened to be from Britain and Afghanistan. "Whenever a group of students comes out of a lecture hall, I see Asians, Caucasians, African-Americans . . . It makes the UCR community as a whole more open to new ideas and less biased towards others," said one undergrad.

Sibling Rivalry

Let's take a moment to confront the elephant in the room. Every UC has an acronym: there's University of Caucasians Lost among Asians (UCLA), UC Socially Dead (US San Diego), University of Casual Sex and Beer (UC Santa Barbara), and then there's UC Rejected. UCR has a reputation as a safety school because of its higher admittance rate, 77.4 percent, compared to that of its older UC sister schools. "I just wish UCR had a better name," noted one freshman who turned down offers from UC Berkeley and UCSD to matriculate at UCR. And UCR certainly deserves more than what its reputation suggests. The university boasts an impressive faculty, keynote speaker events, and a modern, hip campus, qualities that have contributed its growing number of applicants, and it will not be long before UCR outgrows its nickname.

Students at UCR characterized the university as having more of a humanities emphasis and noted the university's strong business administration program. For those interested in medicine, a selective UCR/UCLA Thomas Haider Program in Biomedical Science consisting of 24 undergrads are guaranteed admission to UCLA's medical school. Students enrolled in UCR's honors program take extra workshops on top of their regular course load.

Classes fill up quickly, with lectures usually consisting of more than 150 students and discussion sections consisting of 20 to 30. UCR is home to such influential faculty members as Susan Straight, a Riverside native and professor in the creative writing department,

who has won numerous awards for her novels. "The faculty keeps us up to date and goes out of their way to help us," said one student, who remembers a time in chemistry lecture when the professor was so inspirational that his class stood up, cheering.

Meet me at the HUB

On-campus housing is clean, albeit cramped. Some freshmen are forced to live in triples meant to be doubles. But the close comfort of the dorms, arranged by floors and halls, provides for late-night bonding. "There will always be people walking around and awake even at 4 a.m.," said a resident of East Lothian, one of the four freshman dorms. True to Highlander spirit, most buildings on campus are named after places in Scotland: Pentland Hills, Aberdeen, Stone Haven, etc. After freshman year, many students ditch their faux-Scottish abodes and move off campus into apartments, making UCR a major commuter school.

The place to be at UCR is the HUB, the Highlander Union Building. The three-story structure houses meeting rooms, lounges, restaurants, the school newspaper, and various administrative facilities. The focal point of the campus is the Bell Tower, which chimes on the hour, signaling the start and end of classes. On some days, a professional carillonneur can be heard, and Wednesdays at noon feature the aptly named "Nooners," small concerts at the tower that liven up the HUB.

R-Side

Located about 50 miles east of Los Angeles, the inland city of Riverside is nicely situated so that weekend excursions to LA or the beach are just a quick trip away. It helps to have a car while studying at UCR, although the parking situation is woefully lacking. As a result, parking has become both an art form and an exercise in stealth. "They'll follow students back to their cars, inching slowly behind them. Some will even give students a ride back to their car in return for their parking space. Others fail to find parking, skip class, and just head home," said one junior. For the locomotive challenged, the University Village beckons just a 10-minute walk away with theatres, restaurants, and shops. And for an instant getaway, just cross the street to Getaway Café, a sports bar where one senior said she met many of her friends.

Riverside is a nice town, but areas around it in San Bernardino County can be sketchy. "The police keep us too informed," said one student, who has since taken to carrying around pepper spray. Daily reports of all the robberies in nearby areas freak out the student body, making them extra vigilant.

TGIF

According to one junior, at UCR "there is no sign of human life on the weekends." Because so many students are from the SoCal region, the vast majority of the school heads home once class is out. Only a few special occasions keep undergrads on campus for the weekend: Block Party, Heat, and Spring Splash. The Associated Students Program Board (ASPB) coordinates these free concerts that take place during fall, winter, and spring quarter, respectively. Headliners such as Estelle, Common, Taking Back Sunday, Shiny Toy Guns, Far East Movement, Steve Aoki, and Nas have all performed in recent years. But devoid of this star power, students stay on campus only if they need to get work done in the ghost town that UCR provides over the weekend.

That is not to say that UCR doesn't know how to have fun. On Wednesdays, the frats and sororities congregate at the Bell Tower, and the atmosphere is "really social and lively," said one frat pledge. While Greek life plays a major role in the campus party scene, one need not be a member to partake in the revelry. ASPB planned a Homecoming Bonfire featuring fireworks, laser tag, a mechanical bull, and quintessential California cuisine: In-N-Out. But be forewarned—as in most colleges, alcohol is omnipresent. "Every party has alcohol, even a pajama party," said one markedly disappointed

freshman who was startled by students' openness about drinking, drugs, and sex.

Here Comes the Sun

Seasonal affective disorder is not an issue at UCR, where the sun shines year round. And when the weather gets sweltering, the clothes come off. The beginning of fall term saw a daily uniform of tank tops, shorts, and sandals. "That was literally the least amount of clothing I could wear without people giving me weird looks, and I was still sweating," said one male undergrad.

> "Whenever a group of students comes out of a lecture hall, I see Asians, Caucasians, African-Americans . . . It makes the UCR community as a whole more open to new ideas and less biased towards others."

The sunshine that bathes UCR reflects the university's generally sunny disposition. It is a young, open, growing campus that offers abundant resources for those who wish to seek them out and an ethnic melting pot that is a learning experience in itself. But be sure to either have a car, friends with cars, or especially loving parents willing to double as chauffeurs, because come Friday, you'll want to be cruising down PCH or heading home for your mom's cooking. While UCR is alive and well five days a week, when it comes to the weekend, it knows there's no place like home.—*Cora Ormseth*

FYI
If I could change one thing about UCR, I'd *add a parking structure for undergrads.*
What surprised me most when I arrived at UCR was *that everyone was from SoCal.*
If you come to UCR, you'd better leave your *microwave and mini-fridge. They're provided in the dorms.*

University of California / San Diego

Address: 9500 Gilman Drive, 0021, La Jolla, CA 92093-0021
Phone: 858-534-4831
E-mail address: admissionsinfo@ucsd.edu
Web site URL: www.ucsd.edu
Year Founded: 1959
Private or Public: Public
Religious Affiliation: None
Location: Suburban
Number of Applicants: 45,073
Percent Accepted: 43%
Percent Accepted who enroll: 22%
Number Entering: 4,141
Number of Transfers Accepted each Year: 6,408
Middle 50% SAT range: M: 590–700, CR: 540–660, Wr: 550–670
Middle 50% ACT range: 23–29
Early admission program EA/ED/None: None

Percentage accepted through EA or ED: NA
EA and ED deadline: NA
Regular Deadline: 30-Nov
Application Fee: $60
Full time Undergraduate enrollment: 22,048
Total enrollment: 22,048
Percent Male: 48%
Percent Female: 52%
Total Percent Minority or Unreported: 72%
Percent African-American: 1%
Percent Asian/Pacific Islander: 43%
Percent Hispanic: 12%
Percent Native-American: <1%
Percent International: 3%
Percent in-state/out of state: 97%/3%
Percent from Public HS: Unreported
Retention Rate: 95%
Graduation Rate 4-year: 55%

Graduation Rate 6-year: 83%
Percent Undergraduates in On-campus housing: 92%
Number of official organized extracurricular organizations: 405
3 Most popular majors: Economics, Microbiology, Political Science and Government
Student/Faculty ratio: 19:1
Average Class Size: 26
Percent of students going to grad school: 30%
Tuition and Fees: $28,670
In-State Tuition and Fees if different: $8,062
Cost for Room and Board: $10,787
Percent receiving financial aid out of those who apply, first year: 49%
Percent receiving financial aid among all students: 69%

The University of California, San Diego, is one of 10 colleges in the University of California system and is located in La Jolla, California. The school was founded in 1960 as a science and engineering research institution in hopes of becoming the next CalTech. Today, UCSD is ranked one of the top public universities in America, known for excellence not only in scientific research but also in undergraduate academics and student life.

Get the GE out of the way!

The undergraduate program at UCSD is separated into five divisions. These include the Arts and Humanities, Biological Sciences, Physical Sciences, Social Sciences and the Jacobs School of Engineering. Students may take classes from any of these divisions, provided they complete their General Education (GE) Requirements. Depending on the residential college into which you are placed, your GE requirements can vary greatly. Some find the GE requirement a way

to explore areas of interests outside of their major, while others find it a nuisance. One junior International Studies Majors complains, "I'm in Revelle which has the most GE requirements. I've had three quarters of chem, one of bio and physics, while other colleges have less!" There are six of these colleges and on top of designating your GE requirements they also serve as residential halls. Muir College is known to have very loose requirements and the most recently established Sixth College has requirements focusing on culture, art and technology. When applying, each student indicates which colleges they would like to study and live in, and for the most part "you end up where you're supposed to," said one senior.

Classes tend to be larger during freshman and sophomore years—many have up to 500 students in one lecture hall, with alternate times offered during the day. Upper division classes taken during the junior and senior years tend to be smaller and more intellectually stimulating. However, UCSD also offers

Freshman Seminars to freshmen who miss the intimacy of high school classrooms. The offerings are unique, from French New Wave Cinema to Psychology of Humor.

Studying is a must and UCSD students make it a major priority. Students say that in general they take academics very seriously and many classes at UCSD are very competitive, in particular the science and engineering courses. "If one does not keep up with their work, they will lag behind for sure," said one junior. Another factor that makes academics fast-paced and intense for students is the quarter system. Rather than switching classes in the middle of the year like most colleges, UCSD adopted the unconventional quarter system. Most students claim to enjoy this rapid turnover "because you get to take a variety of subjects during one year."

The Jewel
While school takes up a majority of time for the UCSD kids, they still manage to get involved on campus, partake in festivities and kick back and relax. The name of the city La Jolla comes from the Spanish "la joya" meaning "jewel," and most students would agree that it's a gem of a city. It is primarily a suburban area known for its high-class neighborhoods and expensive rent. One student says of La Jolla, "The area is definitely pretty, the beach is right there, the air is clean, and we're so close to Sea World and the San Diego Zoo." However, the high cost of living and lack of parking space for cars can be a problem for students. But another junior claims, "Despite what others may say, there is a lot to do in La Jolla [without spending money]. My advice is . . . go on random adventures!" A senior in Warren College says, "I love La Jolla because of the climate. You can't beat sunny, high 60, low 50, every day of the year!"

> **"You can't beat sunny, high 60, low 50 every day of the year!"**

During the weekend, when they aren't studying, UCSD students can find a plethora of activities to engage in. The going-out crowd is rather small at UCSD and many of those that go out on the weekends are involved in Greek life. There are 10 fraternities and nine sororities on campus and some are known for throwing "insane" parties. Those who choose not to go Greek still have weekend options. San Diego and La Jolla have nightclubs and the campus is close to other college-populated towns at Mission Beach and Pacific Beach. An experienced senior added, "Also, it's only a 30-minute drive to Mexico where hundreds of underage students go to party."

Campus Traditions
While normal weekends are usually pretty tame, students go crazy during the annual Sun God festival, named for one of a dozen public art pieces on campus which together comprise the Stuart Collection. The Sun God is a winged structure by the artist Niki de Saint Phalle located near the Faculty Club. But the Sun God is also an all-day extravaganza with concerts, games, and "a lot of drinking." Although music aficionados complain that "they don't get very good performers or big names often," the majority agree that "it's great. You get to see all of your friends from all the colleges, enjoy a fun night with a free concert, and then head over to OVT (a late night café) and grab a midnight snack."

Another anticipated campus tradition is the Pumpkin Drop in the fall and the Watermelon Drop during the spring. The Watermelon Drop comes from a physics exam question in 1965 involving the velocity of a dropped object. The event today involves the dropping of a large watermelon from the top floor of Revelle College's Urey Hall and a beauty pageant resulting in a Watermelon King and Queen. One student cites this event as the "weirdest thing I've seen on campus." The Pumpkin Drop is similar but involves a large pumpkin filled with candy instead of a watermelon.

College Spirit?
Student life on campus is defined also by the various extracurricular activities that UCSD-ers take part in. Due to the high percentage of Asian-Americans on campus, there are many cultural and political groups for various Asian-American interests such as the Japanese American Student Organization. Also, student-run papers are widely circulated. *The Koala*, a somewhat controversial, satirical humor paper, and the *UCSD Guardian*, the campus newspaper, are both read extensively on campus. Such enthusiasm is not universal, however. Despite UCSD's 23 varsity sports teams, most students agree that there isn't much support for the Tritons. "I wouldn't say UCSD is very school spirited. The lack of a football team probably makes it worse. I myself haven't been to any sports games" said one junior.

The aforementioned residential college system is by far the most significant aspect of student life at UCSD. "I personally like the college system," one junior in Muir College remarked. "It gives you that small campus feel within a larger university. I didn't understand the benefit of it going into school, but now it's one of my favorite features of UCSD. It allows you to meet more people and gives you a much more accessible administrative office and faculty." In fact, the college system is so ingrained into the students that some feel they have more spirit and pride toward their residential college than to the University itself. "I'm from Muir, the best college EVER!" exclaimed one senior.—*Lee Komeda*

FYI

If you come to UCSD, you'd better bring "a surfboard, a bike to get around the huge campus, and a willingness to find a club that interests you."

What's the typical weekend schedule? "Usually, I have to put some time away for studying since UCSD is a quarter system and it moves quickly. We usually play a little beer pong, go out to eat, relax from the school week and just meet up with friends and socialize."

If I could change one thing about USCD, I'd "add more parking spaces. Parking on campus SUCKS!"

Three things every student at UCSD should do before graduating are "visit the cliffs of Black's Beach on a full moon, spray paint the stairwell at Mandeville and experience Mexico (the overrated-ness of Tijuana)."

University of California / Santa Barbara

Address: 1210 Cheadle Hall, Santa Barbara, CA 93106-2014
Phone: 805-893-2881
E-mail address: admissions@sa.ucsb.edu
Web site URL: www.ucsb.edu
Year Founded: 1909
Private or Public: Public
Religious Affiliation: None
Location: Suburban
Number of Applicants: 40,933
Percent Accepted: 54%
Percent Accepted who enroll: 19%
Number Entering: 4,324
Number of Transfers Accepted each Year: 5,622
Middle 50% SAT range: M: 540–660, CR: 530–650, Wr: 530–650
Middle 50% ACT range: 23–29
Early admission program EA/ED/None: None

Percentage accepted through EA or ED: NA
EA and ED deadline: NA
Regular Deadline: 30-Nov
Application Fee: $60
Full time Undergraduate enrollment: 18,415
Total enrollment: 21,410
Percent Male: 45%
Percent Female: 55%
Total Percent Minority or Unreported: 47%
Percent African-American: 3%
Percent Asian/Pacific Islander: 16%
Percent Hispanic: 19%
Percent Native-American: 1%
Percent International: 1%
Percent in-state/out of state: 96%/4%
Percent from Public HS: 86%
Retention Rate: 91%
Graduation Rate 4-year: 62%

Graduation Rate 6-year: 81%
Percent Undergraduates in On-campus housing: 94%
Number of official organized extracurricular organizations: 508
3 Most popular majors: Biology, Economics, Psychology
Student/Faculty ratio: 17:1
Average Class Size: 19
Percent of students going to grad school: Unreported
Tuition and Fees: $28,994
In-State Tuition and Fees if different: $8,386
Cost for Room and Board: $12,485
Percent receiving financial aid out of those who apply, first year: 46%
Percent receiving financial aid among all students: 68%

Imagine a warm, sunny Saturday afternoon spent lounging on the beach with your friends and planning for another night out together. If you are a student at the University of California Santa Barbara, this isn't a dream Spring Break vacation, but is, instead, a typical day of living and learning on the southern California coast.

Life's a Beach, but School is School

The 17,000 undergraduates, called Gauchos, who call UCSB home quite literally live on the beach, something in which most students take great pride. It's no surprise that the presence of their very own beach only adds to the laidback, West Coast culture UCSB embodies. In fact, while the architecture of UCSB is not particularly noteworthy, with a "hodgepodge of buildings that are concrete 60s institutional style, while others are ultramodern," as one student described, students feel that the abundant natural beauty of the campus more than makes up for what is lacking. Students' favorite places on campus were, appropriately, "Campus Point", where the campus meets the sea, and the lagoon walk.

Academics at UCSB, however, is no vacation. The school has a stellar reputation in the sciences and engineering, and the Bren School of Environmental Science is nationally renowned. While such science majors are highly regarded, students admit that "there is a definite lack of respect toward the "easy" majors," with a zoology major adding, "Here it's like, 'Oh, you're a communications major? How is tanning and drinking with no homework?'" Some classes, on the other hand, are appreciated by both science and humanities students as being easy and fun. Several students interviewed said that some of their favorite classes had been theater classes. "I've taken all the theater and film classes I can without having to declare it as a major," explained a sophomore math major.

Some new, state-of-the-art science facilities parallel these departments' strengths. A particular highlight is the Marine Biology building, with one side of the building designed to look like a lighthouse and a room at the top with windows that offer a 360-degree view of the surrounding area, including the Pacific Ocean and the Santa Ynez Mountains. Even more impressive than the facilities are the professors who teach in them: five UCSB faculty members are Nobel Laureates.

A universal complaint about the university's academic atmosphere is the effects of severe budget cuts due to the state government's recent financial crisis. With fewer classes offered and fewer faculty members to teach these classes, it is often difficult for students to enroll in popular or required courses. "It took me two quarters of 'crashing' classes to get into general chemistry!"

griped the zoology major. Students "crash" a course when they are unable to enroll during registration and employ various strategies in an attempt to eventually land a spot on the roster. Many UCSB students are all too familiar with this process.

While it may be difficult to secure a spot in these popular introductory courses, the classes are large, sometimes reaching 800 students. This contributes to an "anonymous" type of academic experience, said a biology major. "Our professors don't know us past our student I.D. numbers. Nobody will hold your hand in anything." Many students agreed that it is the responsibility of the student to make personal connections with professors during office hours, through which faculty make themselves "easily accessible," according to a math major. She added that when students do attend office hours, they find that "UCSB's faculty is extremely nice".

I.V., D.P. and UCSB

When the weekend finally rolls around, UCSB proudly lives up to its party school reputation. Every weekend, you'll find the ragers in Isla Vista. The name is simply shortened to "I.V." by Gauchos and Santa Barbara City College students, who live— and party—in the area as well. I.V. is a tight-knit community right off campus, in which 50 percent of the residents are students. Their apartments, packed in next to each other over the span of a few blocks, are also home to some serious revelry at night. "It's pretty wild, pretty crazy," said a political science major attempting to explain the party scene to an outsider. The craziest, and most popular, of these parties are usually to be found on the beach front street Del Playa (called "D.P") in student apartments with prime ocean views. The most famous night of debauchery is on Halloween, "a ridiculous, multiday orgy that people from all over California attend." Another revered UCSB party occurs right on the beach, and more specifically in the ocean itself. For Floatopia, held each spring, "everyone brings floaties and booze and then makes giant drinking rafts!" Recently, however, the police have been cracking down on Floatopia, and last year they closed the beaches altogether to prevent the students from celebrating. Students cleverly changed the name of the event that year to "No-topia".

It's Not All Greek to Me

With such a vibrant party scene, it might surprise people to know that Greek Life, while certainly present, does not dominate the social scene as it is at many other large state schools. A freshman member of a sorority explained, "The Greek system is not a large part of UCSB social life", saying that only 2 of her closest friends are also involved. Still, she said, "I love being Greek because it makes such a large school smaller". While the parties in the few weeks after sorority and fraternity rushes "could compete with *Old School* and *Animal House*, they mellow out from then out and consist of parties called TG's (themed gatherings)," says the sorority member. As a non-Greek student explained, "People will sometimes go to frats for parties, but mostly they stay on D.P. Ocean views beat puke filled yards any day!" Prospective students will be happy to know that there is, in fact, no dominant social group at UCSB. As the same non-Greek student described it, "everybody indiscriminately parties regardless of "group". A freshman added that, when it comes to nightlife, "There is really no single group you could award all the fame to. There are always random parties enjoying life and partying large".

Sailing the Not-So-Sober Seas
And when these groups party together, they drink together. While students agree that most people drink, they also say there are students who do not. A Greek member said, "There is a large population of people who sail the sober seas. I personally don't know them that well, but they are there!" That being said, when students are partying in I.V., drinking has a strong presence. When asked if there are problems with binge drinking, a biology major responded, "I like to count the amount of ambulances I hear heading to D.P. on the weekends. Does that answer your question?" Overall, however, most students manage to party responsibly. In terms of drug usage, marijuana is most common. "Marijuana is more popular than cigarettes here," said one student. All students agreed that harder drugs, while they can be found, are not seen very often. Students who choose not to imbibe still have options for having fun on the weekends. State Street is a shopping district in Santa Barbara with movie theaters and restaurants as well, and is a popular hang-out destination for students. Students also insist that the best things to do at UCSB don't even involve drinking. One freshman explained, "There are so many active things to do besides drink. You can go to the beach, play volleyball, play in the sun, and so on. I believe that

is the best way to make friends." Another student added that, while parties are fun, "my best times at UCSB are spent watching the sunset with my closest friends while someone plays the guitar".

Who Are We, Anyways?
Students overwhelmingly enjoy the social scene their school has to offer, but all are quick to point out that their parties do not define UCSB and its student population. "We party a lot, but we study a lot too. People somehow manage to do it all," argues a senior. Another student added that her fellow Gauchos aren't simply party lovers. When describing the student population, she offered, "There's a multitude of democrats, hippies, free spirits, and beach lovers, but all students are intelligent and have motivation and goals. As the school gets harder to get into, I believe UCSB will be characterized with more respect!" Still, one student had a less enthusiastic view of the student population. "Our school is not that diverse. There are a lot of bro surfer dudes and bleach blonds with the occasional Asian." Other students believe that these ideas of "typical" surfer bros and ditzy blondes are just stereotypes. One freshman said, "I was surprised to meet so many genuine, academically driven people. It is not a shallow environment. It's a beautiful place to learn and make lifelong friendships."

Get Involved
What do Gauchos do when they're not studying, partying or at the beach? Plenty. While one student complained that, "people aren't that involved—I feel like they are either busy partying or busy studying," other students had different views, saying their classmates were "very committed" to extracurricular activities. Some students like to cheer on their sports teams, just not the typical ones. One student observed, "Our soccer games get sold out pretty quickly!" That's not surprising, considering the UCSB men's soccer team is very competitive and won the NCAA championship in 2006. It is important to note, however, that UCSB lacks a football team, which some students saw as a negative feature, in that there is not much school spirit on campus. Varsity sports don't have a large presence, but students are often found being active themselves at the gym. The athletic facilities received high marks from students. "They are like a temple for working out! We even have an indoor rock climbing wall," said a

sophomore. Other students prefer to stay active in alternative ways, such as through the Excursion Club. The Excursion Club, one of UCSB's best-known student groups, goes on outdoor adventures throughout the year, including hiking, skiing, rock-climbing, and even skydiving! Luckily, with UCSB's location in southern California, all of these activities are possible within relative proximity to the campus.

For students seeking extracurricular involvement through less adrenaline-rushing means, options still abound. The daily campus newspaper, *The Daily Nexus*, is the only entirely student-run daily newspaper in California, and all students interviewed agreed that it is the most popular student publication at UCSB. Still, opinions were mixed. One student said, "It is really only a source of sudoku and crosswords during lecture". That's better than Facebook, at least.

When they're not in class, students can also become involved with the UCSB Student Entrepreneurship Association (SEA). SEA is a group for business-minded students to engage in networking and a resource for transitioning into the job world after graduation. One student interviewed said his friend was a member who, in true Santa Barbara fashion, designs his own surfboards.

Sweet Home Santa Barbara

Students find meeting new people is easy at UCSB, and those interviewed said the freshman year dorms are most conducive to making new friends. One student explained, "It is so easy to become close with people you live with and see around often," and all students interviewed said that living in the dorms are an essential—and fun—part of the freshman experience at UCSB. There are seven dorms for freshmen only, one dorm for all classes, and one exclusively for upperclassmen. Most students seem satisfied with on-campus housing, noting that three of the dorms even have ocean views. After freshman year, most students decide to move into apartments in Isla Vista, but the university is currently adding more dorms so that 50 percent of the student population will be able to live on campus. Even upperclassmen in Isla Vista nostalgically think back to their time living on campus as freshmen. "The dorms are very nice and clean, and they are probably the most social places anyone will ever live!" said one sophomore.

> My best times at UCSB are spent watching the sunset with my closest friends while someone plays the guitar.

It is clear that most students feel at home at their school, whether they are studying in the library, partying in Isla Vista, or enjoying the California sunshine on the beach. While Gauchos may have to deal with budget cuts and large class sizes, they are still able to graduate with a highly respected—and memorable—college education. When asked if she would choose UCSB again if she had to do it all over, one student affirmed, "Yes. We don't have a small-school feel or a football team, but we compromise. UCSB is truly unique."—*McKenna Keyes*

FYI
If you come to UCSB, you'd better bring "a bike lock, a bikini, and maybe a pen."
What's the typical weekend schedule? Going out at night, going to the beach when it's warm during the day and reading in the afternoon.
If I could change one thing about UCSB, "I'd make everyone just a bit more studious to increase our reputation. Instead of being "the party school," being the school that "parties and works hard".

University of California / Santa Cruz

Address: Cook House, 1156 High Street, Santa Cruz, CA 95064
Phone: 831-459-4008
E-mail address: admissions@ucsc.edu
Web site URL: www.ucsc.edu
Year Founded: 1965
Private or Public: Public
Religious Affiliation: None
Location: Suburban
Number of Applicants: 24,453
Percent Accepted: 82%
Percent Accepted who enroll: 19%
Number Entering: 3,717
Number of Transfers Accepted each Year: 3,374
Middle 50% SAT range: M: 520–630, CR: 500–620, Wr: 500–620
Middle 50% ACT range: 21–29

Early admission program EA/ED/None: None
Percentage accepted through EA or ED: NA
EA and ED deadline: NA
Regular Deadline: 30-Nov
Application Fee: $60
Full time Undergraduate enrollment: 14,403
Total enrollment: 15,825
Percent Male: 47%
Percent Female: 53%
Total Percent Minority or Unreported: 49%
Percent African-American: 3%
Percent Asian/Pacific Islander: 21%
Percent Hispanic: 16%
Percent Native-American: 1%
Percent International: 1%
Percent in-state/out of state: 97%/3%
Percent from Public HS: 85%
Retention Rate: Unreported

Graduation Rate 4-year: 45%
Graduation Rate 6-year: 66%
Percent Undergraduates in On-campus housing: 99%
Number of official organized extracurricular organizations: 141
3 Most popular majors: Art, Business, English
Student/Faculty ratio: 19:1
Average Class Size: 24
Percent of students going to grad school: Unreported
Tuition and Fees: $28,808
In-State Tuition and Fees if different: $8,200
Cost for Room and Board: $13,038
Percent receiving financial aid out of those who apply, first year: 47%
Percent receiving financial aid among all students: 67%

Famous for once employing the pass/fail grading system and known by many as a "hippie" school, the University of California at Santa Cruz offers an exciting, though somewhat alternative college experience. Located in a redwood forest on the coast of Northern California and with around 15,000 undergraduates and 1,500 graduate students, UC Santa Cruz provides students with a liberal arts education in a relaxed environment.

Pass/Fail? Not quite.

Although Santa Cruz no longer employs its infamous pass/fail, many students still describe academics at Santa Cruz as laid back and not too intense. Although students seem satisfied with academics, some wish they were more rigorous. "It'd be nice if it were more challenging," said a student. Freshmen usually take large intro lectures, which many students say they do not feel they need to attend. Distribution requirements are easy to fulfill. Students love the mandatory core and writing classes. Based on his or her interests, each student picks a residential college before arriving at Santa Cruz, and the core classes are smaller seminars with around twenty students that center around the college's theme; for example, Porter College's theme is Arts in a Multicultural Society and one of its core classes is called "Arts Practicum." Even for the larger lectures, students feel professors are accessible and easy to get to know because of the small number of graduate students. "All of my professors and TA's have office hours twice a week," said a student, "so it's easy to get help if you need it."

Although Santa Cruz is known for being less academically prestigious and easier to get into than the other UC's, it is also famous for many of its science departments, including astronomy, engineering, and other sciences. "It's a very science-related school," said a student. "A lot of kids here are majoring in some kind of science." Many students, however, major in the humanities and social sciences, with economics as one of the most popular majors. There are many research opportunities for undergraduate research because of the small number of graduate students.

Where are all the parties?

Santa Cruz provides a unique college experience. Though it exists, Greek life does not have a large presence on campus. There are five fraternities, but they are not housed. Santa Cruz also does not have a lot of school spirit when it comes to sports, and there isn't much turnout for athletic events. Most of the partying takes place off campus because alcohol and drug policing is strict. "The social life is pretty laid back," said a student. For those looking for the traditional college social life, UC Santa Cruz may not be the right place for them. "It doesn't feel like the college experience, " said one student. "People are stuck in their dorms a lot." Santa Cruz does, however, provide students with other opportunities to socialize. One of the most popular clubs is the Ski and Snowboard Club. Intramural sports are also popular. Many students also love the communities within their residential colleges. "The RA's plan a lot of events for freshmen in their colleges," said one student. "I made most of my friends in the dorms."

Students love the school's location. The campus is located in a redwood forest about a fifteen-minute bus ride away from the beach. "It feels like your hiking when you walk to class," said one student. "In a good way. It's beautiful." Students also frequent the downtown Santa Cruz area, which like the campus has an alternative vibe. "They don't like chains in Santa Cruz," said a student, "so there are a lot of little independent shops and restaurants. Really unique stuff." Since Santa Cruz doesn't have a traditional party scene, many students, especially freshmen who are not allowed to have cars, come to the downtown for the weekends for off-campus parties at upperclassmen's houses or just to hang out and watch a movie.

The quality of on-campus varies between residential colleges. Freshman dorms can be anything from cramped to comfortable with lots of space. Building types also vary by college; for example, College 8 is like "a Victorian house" but is "crappy inside," while students in Stevenson live in a series of smaller houses. Most sophomores live in on-campus apartments that students describe as being spacious with a kitchen, living room, dining room, and bedrooms upstairs. There is a two-year housing guarantee, so many juniors and seniors move off campus into houses in Santa Cruz, though these houses are "really expensive" because they cater more to the wealthier inhabitants of Santa Cruz than to students. Food also varies between residential colleges, and there are some popular on-campus cafes like Oaks Café and Tacos Moreno, where students can use their meal plan "flexis."

Nudity?

Santa Cruz has a number of quirky traditions that define the UCSC experience. "No one should leave Santa Cruz without doing at least one naked run," said a student.

"The first rain in a year, students run through campus naked." In addition to naked run, "4/20" is an important Santa Cruz tradition when on April 20 students take to a part of campus called East Field and spend the day smoking pot. "It's a total weed school," said one student. Indeed, Santa Cruz has a reputation for being a weed-hippy school, but what is the Santa Cruz student body really like?

The student body is ethnically diverse but not as diverse as other California schools with about 50 percent of students identifying as Caucasian. About 97 percent come from within California, but in terms of the type of people that go to UC Santa Cruz, there seems to be a range. "People can be too laid back," said one student. "So laid back that they don't want to do anything." Still, others say it's impossible to categorize. "Everyone here is so different," said one student. "You really can't call the people as hippy or prep or those kinds of things."

> "Santa Cruz students are laid back. It's not too intense here."

For students who want a college experience a bit different from the norm, UC Santa Cruz would be a good prospect. The campus is beautiful, located in a redwood forest next to the beach. Those who are not concerned with Greek life and sports would do well to consider UC Santa Cruz.—*Lia Dun*

FYI
If you come to Santa Cruz, you'd better bring "pot."
If you come to Santa Cruz, you'd better leave "Your bike. The hills are devilish."
Three things every student at Santa Cruz should do before graduating are "naked run, 4/20, hike."

University of Redlands

Address: 1200 East Colton Avenue, Redlands, CA 92373-0999
Phone: 909 748-8074
E-mail address: admissions@redlands.edu
Web site URL: www.redlands.edu
Year Founded: 1886
Private or Public: Private
Religious Affiliation: None
Location: Suburban
Number of Applicants: 3,757
Percent Accepted: 67%
Percent Accepted who enroll: 25%
Number Entering: 604
Number of Transfers Accepted each Year: 230
Middle 50% SAT range: M: 540–620, CR: 520–620, Wr: Unreported
Middle 50% ACT range: 21–27
Early admission program EA/ED/None: None

Percentage accepted through EA or ED: NA
EA and ED deadline: NA
Regular Deadline: 1-Apr
Application Fee: $45
Full time Undergraduate enrollment: 2,354
Total enrollment: 4,269
Percent Male: 45%
Percent Female: 55%
Total Percent Minority or Unreported: 17%
Percent African-American: 3%
Percent Asian/Pacific Islander: 5%
Percent Hispanic: 12%
Percent Native-American: <1%
Percent International: 1%
Percent in-state/out of state: 61%/39%
Percent from Public HS: Unreported
Retention Rate: 86%
Graduation Rate 4-year: 54%

Graduation Rate 6-year: 66%
Percent Undergraduates in On-campus housing: 72%
Number of official organized extracurricular organizations: 106
3 Most popular majors: Liberal Arts, Business/Marketing, Social Sciences
Student/Faculty ratio: 12:1
Average Class Size: 19
Percent of students going to grad school: 15%
Tuition and Fees: $32,294
In-State Tuition and Fees if different: No difference
Cost for Room and Board: $10,122
Percent receiving financial aid out of those who apply, first year: 80%
Percent receiving financial aid among all students: 63%

Boasting an enviable location in the midst of Southern California, the Univeristy of Redlands lays at the base of the magnificent San Bernardino Mountains. The desert landscape is indicative of the great weather year-round, but also serves as a reminder that a Redlands experience without a car can quickly turn into a very isolated one. Most students find a way to get around the small city and many say they appreciate the college's small size, citing the 720-student entering class size and the 12:1 student-faculty ratio as proof that they are more than just numbers here. "Coming from a small high school, I feel like Redlands has helped make the transition a very smooth one," said one junior. "Almost all of my professors know my name and I often see them outside of class." With a beautiful campus, small classes, and professors who are interested in teaching, Redlands seems to offer a good deal; that is if you're willing to pick up the tab.

When Nature Calls: Being Aware of Your Surroundings

The Redlands campus has been used as a set for recent films such as "Rules of Attraction" and "Joy Ride," but even if the college grounds are attractive, it's the surroundings that stand out the most, for they offer great opportunities for students to interact with nature. Students recognize their surroundings as full of opportunities for wildlife observation, rock climbing, hiking, mountain biking, photography or just camping out. To this end, Redlands helps organize "Outdoor Programs" which may last from as short as a weekend afternoon to a month during the summer. "Going out on the hot air balloon was the coolest experience ever!" recalled one student. Other available excursions include bungee jumping, skiing, snowboarding, skydiving and surfing.

For those who wish to take their own initiative, Redlands has everything the casual outdoorsman needs: tents, sleeping bags, backpacks and rain gear are all available to students for free. Although a credit card is required as deposit, students generally agree that the rental shop is very accessible. "As long as you plan a few days in advance, you can usually get what you need."

Unfortunately, while its surroundings may be a paradise for the outward bound, the small city of Redlands (population approximately 75,000) does not have much to offer. The town is a little far from central campus, but almost everyone either owns a car or knows someone who does. The trolley system that operates during the mornings and afternoons doesn't run during the nights, but it's usually easy to catch a ride. Downtown Redlands boasts many of the most popular fast food shops, as well as some fancier Italian restaurants and coffee shops, which students and townspeople frequent. Besides going downtown, students use their cars to "catch a late-night snack or go shopping at the nearby outlet malls." One student agreed that "Redlands will definitely get dull very quickly if you don't get out often." He commented that he and his friends often go into downtown Los Angeles or San Diego, which are only about an hour away. Some upperclassmen also go to Las Vegas—about five hours away.

Making Service a Way of Life

Although students often reveal their concern for the lack of economic diversity at Redlands, one thing that can be said about the kids here is that they know how to get their hands dirty to serve others. Community service is integrated into the curriculum and students must complete a combination of service instruction and outreach requirements. While some students serve at the local high schools, others use their summers or May terms to go as far as Africa. One senior recalled her experience with helping victims of Hurricane Katrina as "one of the most enriching experiences of my entire life." She added, "I felt like I was really making a difference in people's lives and I really want to go back." The same student agreed that Redlands seems to attract a more service-oriented crowd, "but it's not like a huge deal for everyone."

A Bold Academic Experiment

The flagship of the Redlands academic experience is the Johnston Center for Integrative Studies. Requiring a supplemental application, the center admits a limited number of the incoming freshman class. Students in the Johnston Center have unparalleled control over their education. Students may create their own major and choose their own courses. They are also allowed to write contracts for individual courses, leaving it to the students to decide how they will go about meeting their educational needs and which requirements they will fulfill. Quizzes may be substituted for longer tests or papers, and vice-versa. It's also possible to increase or decrease the credits for many courses by contracting to do more or less work.

> **Redlands has everything the casual outdoorsman needs . . . for free.**

However, as is true of many things, there's a catch: each contract must be negotiated between the student and the professor, and complete academic freedom is more of an aspiration than a reality. All Redlands students are also expected to graduate with sufficient "depth" and "breadth" in their studies. "The distributional requirements are complex and pretty burdensome," a freshman pointed out. "I think it's a little easier for the Johnston kids because they don't have to take any particular courses, but for those in the LAF [Liberal Arts Foundation], there's not that much freedom because you have to be worrying about your requirements so much."

Unlike large research universities, Redlands is focused on teaching. Students express a lot of respect for their faculty and really like the individualized attention. "My expectations have been surpassed over and over again," said one student. Another student added: "Having such small classes helps me keep motivated. I feel like I know my professors and my professors know me. I also know who I'm working with and that makes me feel much more comfortable. I don't think I'd be as motivated if I were taking larger classes at a bigger school." Most people refer to their peers as "competent" or "smart," but generally agree that the school "does not attract the biggest minds. Most kids care about their classes and study, but their interest rarely goes beyond the classes they're taking. This is not the kind of place where you'll find people discussing philosophy all day, although politics seem to be a common dinner table topic."

One aspect of Redlands that is appreciated by almost everyone in the community is the strong emphasis that is placed on study abroad. Although the focus is often on European countries to the exclusion of other regions of the world, there are ample opportunities for Redlands students to study a semester or a whole year abroad through a university-approved program. The most popular study abroad destination is Salzburg, Germany. Credit and financial aid are easily transferable. Students hoping to spend less time abroad may also opt to take one of the courses during the "May term." The May term refers to one month of intensive study, usually undertaken abroad. Courses during the May term include "Japanese Gardens" and "Economics in Buenos Aires."

Housing for All Tastes

Redlands doesn't approach housing in a "one-size-fits-all" fashion. While all undergraduates are guaranteed a room on-campus, every year, students can choose to live in one of the dozen or so different halls. Each of these housing complexes has its own perks and advantages. Some of them, like East Hall, are for freshmen only, while Cortner Hall and Melrose Hall tend to have more upperclassmen. Melrose, with its extended quiet hours, is also seen as a good fit for the more studious. On the other hand there's North Hall, the closest to the gymnasium and thereby host to many of Redlands' jocks. Some of the halls are same-sex, but most are coed.

"Most people seem to be happy with their living conditions," one junior said. "The most common complaint about housing is that some halls are not air-conditioned and it can get extremely hot during the summer." Students are advised to bring a fan—or several. "It was pretty bad the first few weeks of the fall semester," noted a freshman. "However, for most of the year the weather was just perfect." Still, those who hail from colder weather may often be less excited. SNOW (Students in Need of Winter) is a student group that brings together all those who are interested in following the ski season in the nearby Rockies.

Besides the regular housing options, students may also elect to live at one of the fraternity or sorority houses. Although there are several Greek organizations around campus, they don't seem to dominate the social scene. "Generally, there are a few guys who are really into it, but Greek life just isn't as big as you would expect." Students estimate that less than 10 percent of their peers have donned Greek letters.

It's Not Just About the Academics

Redlands offers a fairly wide variety of extracurricular activities and student groups. Opportunities for giving back to the community are plentiful through volunteer groups and there are many student-run religious and cultural organizations as well. The University also has an outstanding debate society, often placing among the top in the country. In fact, debate is valued so much at Redlands that the University offers merit scholarships for outstanding debaters.

Everyone has an opportunity to play sports—at some level—at Redlands. "It's fairly easy to be a walk-on at Redlands if you played in high school," said one junior who plays for the basketball team. "Some kids certainly get recruited, but some sports membership may be almost half walk-ons." The most popular club sports include golf, lacrosse, ultimate Frisbee and ice hockey. There is also an equestrian club.

While many find Redlands too small by the end of their four years, most enjoy the tight-knit community it affords. Within that community, some complain of "a total lack of diversity," and one student remarked that the stereotypical Redlands student was "your average intellectual rich white kid from the West Coast." This does seem to be changing, as Redlands has been recruiting more widely and applications have been increasing significantly in recent years. For all its insularity, Redlands seems to be about unexpected surprises. Whether students enjoy uncovering these hidden treasures will dictate whether they survive their four years out in the oasis of the Californian desert.
—*Gerardo Giacoman*

FYI

If you come to Redlands, you'd better bring: "a car or a friend who has one; also, bring a fan: or several in case your housing unit is not air-conditioned."

What's the typical weekend schedule? "Fraternity parties are prevalent during the weekends, but with the recent crackdown on alcohol consumption, weekend nights usually involve hanging out with friends, or getting out of Redlands to find a real party."

If I could change one thing about Redlands, I'd "move it closer to Las Vegas and fight the formation of social cliques."

Three things that every student should do before graduating are: "attend the festival of lights, make a 2 a.m. Del Taco run, drive to Mexico for Spring Break."

University of Southern California

Address: 700 Childs Way
Los Angeles, CA
90089-0911
Phone: 213 740-2311
E-mail address:
admitusc@usc.edu
Web site URL: www.usc.edu
Year Founded: 1880
Private or Public: Private
Religious Affiliation: None
Location: Suburban
Number of Applicants:
33,760
Percent Accepted: 25%
**Percent Accepted who
enroll:** 35%
Number Entering: 2,963
**Number of Transfers
Accepted each Year:**
1,784
Middle 50% SAT range:
M: 650–750, CR:
620–720, Wr: 640–730
Middle 50% ACT range:
28–32
**Early admission program
EA/ED/None:** None

**Percentage accepted
through EA or ED:** NA
EA and ED deadline: NA
Regular Deadline: 10-Jan
Application Fee: $65
**Full time Undergraduate
enrollment:** 16,384
Total enrollment: 30,703
Percent Male: 48%
Percent Female: 52%
**Total Percent Minority or
Unreported:** 59%
Percent African-American:
6%
**Percent Asian/Pacific
Islander:** 25%
Percent Hispanic: 13%
Percent Native-American:
<1%
Percent International: 11%
**Percent in-state/out of
state:** 58%/42%
Percent from Public HS:
55%
Retention Rate: 96%
Graduation Rate 4-year:
68%

Graduation Rate 6-year:
86%
**Percent Undergraduates
in On-campus housing:**
41%
**Number of official organized
extracurricular
organizations:** 642
3 Most popular majors:
Business/Marketing, Social
Sciences, Visual and
Performing Arts
Student/Faculty ratio: 9:1
Average Class Size: 15
**Percent of students going to
grad school:** Unreported
Tuition and Fees: $37,890
**In-State Tuition and Fees if
different:** No difference
Cost for Room and Board:
$11,298
**Percent receiving financial
aid out of those who apply,
first year:** 67%
**Percent receiving financial
aid among all students:**
36%

To find a Trojan, you don't have to go back to Greek mythology; in fact, you can find more than 16,000 of them right here in the heart of sunny Southern California. USC students, just like the warriors for which they were named, are filled with pride and tradition. And unlike other schools that may have reputations for being "nerd schools" or "party schools," USC students say their school has the best of both worlds. As one senior said, "USC is becoming more focused on academics, which is reflected in its increasing national and international standings, but the great thing about this campus is that the social atmosphere has not taken a backseat to the greater focus on academics." From the time students step onto the beautiful campus that forms a backdrop for many a Hollywood movie, to the many years students have after graduation, USC students are and will always be Trojans.

Nuts and Bolts of the Classroom

Class sizes at USC vary, and depend on what type and level of classes you're looking for. As one junior explained, "USC boasts about having smaller class sizes, but that's not necessarily true. Just because it's a private school doesn't mean the ratios get any smaller." Average lecture halls can run up to 300 students in one room, but writing classes, which everyone has to take, are usually limited to only 12–15 students. Students say that getting into core classes isn't competitive since there are more available seats than students, but spots for interesting elective classes, such as Ballroom Dancing 101, can fill up pretty fast, especially with juniors and seniors who have priority. Both class sizes and grading usually vary between departments—popular majors on campus are Business, Biological Sciences, and Communications, and majors known for being particularly difficult are Architecture, Engineering and the sciences in general.

Grading at USC, while not super generous, is fair, students say. "Since I'm a pre-med major, my workload is immense compared to other majors. Being a science major is competitive already, but being a pre-med is even more competitive," said a student majoring in Biological Sciences. Good thing competitive core science classes are curved, then. This system saves a lot of students—students who get B's or B+'s on exams will still probably end up with an A-, or even an A, by the end of the semester. One senior added, "Most classes are curved and there also many professors who don't mind giving A's to everyone who deserves them." Smaller classes like business and language classes usually aren't curved, but the general rule of thumb is that if it's a class with a lot of people, it will be curved.

Professors, however, can be a mixed bag. While most instructors are accessible and easy to talk with during their office hours, others are less open. Professors who are here for research—since USC is a research school—are required to teach as well, so those who would rather bury themselves in work don't try to make themselves accessible to students. Luckily, Trojans have other means of finding academic support in the form of study groups, which students readily form to help each other out and create study groups. "I like that the atmosphere isn't generally a cutthroat competition. The school really wants us to do well so they make a lot of resources available to students like supplemental instruction and free tutors," a junior said.

Trojans Gone Greek

It's no coincidence that USC has a dominant Greek scene—after all, their Greek nature is practically written in their Trojan name. A freshman noted, "Everyone knows not to make plans with a frat/sorority member on a Monday night because they have to go to Monday night dinners." Greek life is evident all throughout campus, but the core is off-campus on West 28th Street, more commonly known as The Row. With a fifth of the total student population involved with Greek life, and many more involved in service and ethnic Greek communities outside Panhellenic and Interfraternal councils, it's no surprise that much of the partying that goes on at USC happens out on The Row. However, good times are not just limited to frat parties—students often also hit up the 9-0

Bar, a local favorite, and house parties hosted in apartments. And with the City of Angels in their backyard, USC students also have the opportunity to go clubbing in the hot streets of Downtown Los Angeles.

While not everyone at USC drinks, a large majority do—one student guessed that upwards of 80 percent of the students on campus drink. While binge drinking is not so big a problem that the University needs to address it, students recognize they have peers who regularly drink at unhealthy levels. But beyond drinking and partying, USC also offers many other opportunities to kick back and enjoy the Southern California sun. Students say having a car is nice, but not necessary since it's easy to find other friends who have cars for exploring the area. Even students who live nearby stay on campus over the weekends. It's easy to get into the heart of L.A., and there's always something fun to do. Places to explore range from Little Tokyo and Chinatown to the fashion district, and they're all within a few miles of each other. One junior enthusiastically, and simply, described USC's social life as "Great!" as she went on to explain, "I like USC because the people there are smart, but they still know how to have fun. I guess it's just the atmosphere of being in Southern California and how it's always so chill."

The social scene at USC is a dynamic one. One senior reflected on his experiences at USC and said, "There is a niche for everyone. If you are into the arts scenes, then you can find that. If you are into partying, then you can find that. There is something for everyone. It is up to the student to find the right fit."

Diversity at USC is present, but at the same time, also lacking. Students say that the typical USC student is rich—indeed, "University of Spoiled Children" is a common nickname for the school. There are frat boys and sorority girls who tend to be rich because going Greek requires a fair amount of money, but there are also many students who are on financial aid, so not necessarily everyone is loaded. "A typical USC student is a white trust fund baby, but there are also a lot of students here from a modest background," one student said. Students say there are a lot of preps, jocks, and band geeks like in high school, but that USC is less cliquish. Despite diversity in interests and geography, to name two facets, students said their peers tend to hang out within their own ethnic groups. But at the end of the day, as one junior noted, "I find that USC is really diverse and many 'groups' are just chill, down-to-earth kinds of people."

Pimp My Housing, Please?
To be frank, housing at USC is not great. Underclassmen have priority in on-campus housing, but even then, students usually move out by the time they are sophomores. This is because of USC's rather limited geographical area—the campus is right in the middle of South Central Los Angeles, so there isn't much room for expansion. "Freshmen and sophomores get priority in choosing University housing, so if you're a senior, I would say good luck in trying to find a place to live," a junior said.

Most off-campus apartments are about a block or more away from campus, and the farther away from campus you get, the more dangerous it is. While USC may get a bad reputation for being in the middle of South Central, students say the campus is safe at night, if you stay conscious about it. "They always tell us to walk in groups and not to be alone at night. The dumb students are the ones who walk home alone at 3 a.m. after a party—they're the ones who get robbed," a senior explained. Students say housing at USC needs to be improved, and the school has started what it calls a Master Plan and has already started buying property and building new housing complexes near campus.

> "I felt like I was able to ease into college comfortably because the campus makes a huge effort to get people involved and people really fall in love with USC."

As for meal options, one student described them as "kind of sucky." USC has two cafeterias—EVK and Parkside, the latter of which serves more international foods and is generally regarded as the better dining hall. There is the Commons area, which is kind of small, but is in the process of getting renovated. There's also Café 84 which is "alright;" one student summed up USC's dining options as "Most are mediocre." Students can also go out to the 9-0, which is a bar near campus, or stay on campus and go to Traddie's, which is short for Traditions Bar.

Hope You Like Football!
While housing and food may leave students wanting more, USC's extracurricular activity

opportunities just might be the thing to fulfill a Trojan's appetite. One aspect of USC that is extremely important is students' dedication to extracurricular activities. With more than 700 student organizations, there is definitely something for everyone. One popular extracurricular is community service. "Our geographic location near Downtown Los Angeles allows us to become deeply involved in community service. I love that USC encourages community service and the strong sense of family is a strong plus," said one student who is the president of a service fraternity.

The most visible outside-the-classroom activity is one in which only a small fraction of the student population directly participates. But while the number of students on the field as football players and cheerleaders is quite small, practically the entire school makes it out to the stadium for football games. With pre-games, tailgates, and post-parties, football at USC is everything you've seen on national television and more. "We're practically defined by our football team. If you don't buy a spirit card, which allows you to go to football games and more, you are probably crazy for not doing so," one junior said. Even students who aren't into sports find themselves among the most hardcore of USC football fans. "There's a huge football culture on this campus. There is extreme pride and everyone from students to alumni goes all out. On game days, every single inch of the main campus is filled with people and everyone is wearing red," a senior said.

Join the Family
This dedication to USC Football reflects something larger, which is the dedication to the school as a whole. Students say they are part of "the Trojan Family" and that a strong sense of pride and tradition is instilled in them from the first day they step onto campus. "I felt like I was able to ease into college comfortably because the campus makes a huge effort to get people involved and people really fall in love with USC," a junior said. Partly because networking is so important at USC, relationships are strong within the school and outside of it. Alumni come back for career fairs and workshops looking specifically to hire fellow Trojans, and it is these lasting ties that form the core of what it means to go to USC. One student explained, "Whenever I see a fellow Trojan outside of school, even if they are a stranger, there's already a connection because of the school. Sometimes we may exchange a few words or a 'Fight On!' sign while passing by. It sounds kind of cheesy, but it's true."

Reflecting upon her time as a Trojan, one senior said, "I think that a lot of people have a misconception that USC is just a school full of rich kids, and that students basically buy their diploma. I also used to believe this before I entered, but I was surprised that most of the people I've met come from middle-class families, and most wealthy students do not flaunt their wealth." So if you're ready to challenge yourself, and have your preconceptions challenged as well, get ready to immerse yourself in the Trojan family and make friendships and connections that will last a lifetime.—*Della Fok*

FYI

If you come to USC, you'd better bring "An open attitude to different types of people and personalities because you never know who you will end up becoming friends with here at USC."

What's the typical weekend schedule? "Thursday is the big party night because many people don't have classes on Fridays: they call it 'Thirsty Thursday.' People have small parties every night, though, and a lot of people go to Hollywood or Westwood on the weekends."

If I could change one thing about USC, "I'd change its location to an area with more shops and restaurants so there would be more things to do."

Three things every student at USC should do before graduating are "join a club, fraternity or sorority, go to at least one football game, definitely, and eat at Chano's, which is this old Mexican drive-through place that looks dirty, but it's really good Mexican food!"

Whittier College

Address: 13406 Philadelphia Street, Whittier, CA 90608
Phone: 562-97-4238
E-mail address: admission@whittier.edu
Web site URL: www.whittier.edu
Year Founded: 1887
Private or Public: Private
Religious Affiliation: None
Location: Urban
Number of Applicants: 2,196
Percent Accepted: 67%
Percent Accepted who enroll: 19%
Number Entering: 282
Number of Transfers Accepted each Year: 120
Middle 50% SAT range: M: 480–602, CR: 480–600, Wr: 480–590
Middle 50% ACT range: 20–27
Early admission program EA/ED/None: EA

Percentage accepted through EA or ED: Unreported
EA and ED deadline: 1-Dec
Regular Deadline: Rolling
Application Fee: $50
Full time Undergraduate enrollment: 1,259
Total enrollment: 1,369
Percent Male: 45%
Percent Female: 55%
Total Percent Minority or Unreported: 43%
Percent African-American: 3%
Percent Asian/Pacific Islander: 8%
Percent Hispanic: 30%
Percent Native-American: 1%
Percent International: 3%
Percent in-state/out of state: 73%/27%
Percent from Public HS: Unreported
Retention Rate: 78%

Graduation Rate 4-year: 52%
Graduation Rate 6-year: 52%
Percent Undergraduates in On-campus housing: 60%
Number of official organized extracurricular organizations: 68
3 Most popular majors: Biology, Business, Psychology
Student/Faculty ratio: 13:1
Average Class Size: 15
Percent of students going to grad school: 28%
Tuition and Fees: $31,950
In-State Tuition and Fees if different: No difference
Cost for Room and Board: $9,050
Percent receiving financial aid out of those who apply, first year: 92%
Percent receiving financial aid among all students: 89%

Whittier College, a small, diverse liberal arts college, is spread out over 75 acres in California, only about 18 miles southeast of the city of Los Angeles. Originally a Quaker institution, Whittier is now a secular school, but some of its original Quaker values, like emphasis on the individual and the diversity of the student body, remain an integral part of the Whittier experience.

Founding 'Friends'

Whittier College began as a Quaker academy established by the Religious Society of Friends in 1887, the same year that they founded the town of Whittier itself. Although the Quaker heritage is visible in such things as the name of the weekly student newspaper, the *Quaker Campus*, there does not seem to be a large focus on the legacy of the founding Friends. One student even went so far as to say that, despite the school's reputation as a former Quaker haven, "They don't force much onto us about Quakers."

Fewer Students, More Options

With such a small student body, Whittier is able to offer smaller, more intense classes. The average class size is about 19, which fosters the development of real relationships between students and professors. As one student said, "It's nice to be able to get to know your teachers." However, limiting the number of students in each classroom does create other issues. "Some of the classes are hard to get in to because of how small they are and the order of how [students] register," a junior complained.

Besides regular classes, students at Whittier can design their own major in the Whittier Scholars Program (WSP). Members of the WSP work closely with professors and other students to build their own curriculums, whether by creating their own major or fashioning a course of study around an existing one. Students can even incorporate off-campus experiences like study abroad and internships into their course of study, a large academic draw to Whittier.

Another way for students to expand their academic horizons is Whittier's one-month term in January. The courses offered for the "Jan Term" often cover more "fun" and interesting subjects, including classes that even integrate travel or other types of hands-on experiences into the session. Some of the most popular options include a class on death and dying, involving a trip to the morgue, or a trip to help clean up New Orleans. Students generally enjoy these more unconventional opportunities. "I love the Jan Term classes!" one Whittier student enthused.

Splendid Spectrum: Sports, Societies, and Student Groups

From small-town charm to the bustling activity of nearby Los Angeles, Whittier's 75-acre campus has no shortage of ways to stay busy outside of the classroom. There are tons of extracurricular activities to get involved in, from editing the *Quaker Campus*, to working on the Whittier College Radio station. And, if you can't find the club for you, never fear—the Whittier Office of Student Activities specializes in helping students create their own clubs or groups.

> **"I love the Jan Term classes!"**

On a typical weekend, a lot of people spend time partying with societies, special fraternity-type organizations unique to Whittier. The societies host numerous social events and remain an important part of Whittier's history and traditions. Founded in the 1920s, the societies are behind most of the biggest parties on campus. If that's not your scene, never fear—students also report that there are plays, movies and concerts on campus to entertain them. And, for the more adventurous, L.A. has a whole world of restaurants, museums and shopping to amuse even the pickiest of procrastinators.

In terms of sports, Whittier has 21 Division III varsity teams on which students keep busy, the most popular of which is definitely lacrosse. Aside from the varsity teams, students can choose from a multitude of intramural sports, often played outside in the region's year-round temperate climate.

Overall, students agree that they can find whatever they want in Whittier's diverse campus. Although students may venture to downtown Los Angeles or the nearby Pacific coastline, they need not look beyond their own community for exciting opportunities among familiar faces.—*Suzanne Salgado*

FYI
If you come to Whittier, you'd better bring "pictures, posters, decorations and anything that gives you a sense of comfort from home."
What's the typical weekend schedule? "Get up at noon or so, do whatever you can on Saturday, and then Sunday is homework day."
If I could change one thing about Whittier it would be "make smaller classes easier to get into."
Three things every student at Whittier should do before graduating are "study abroad, get involved, and take advantage of the free services and fun events provided for students."

Colorado

Colorado College

Address: 14 East Cache la Poudre Street, Colorado Springs, CO 80903
Phone: 719-389-6344
E-mail address: admission@coloradocollege.edu
Web site URL: www.coloradocollege.edu
Year Founded: 1874
Private or Public: Private
Religious Affiliation: None
Location: Urban
Number of Applicants: 4,089
Percent Accepted: 34%
Percent Accepted who enroll: 33%
Number Entering: 524
Number of Transfers Accepted each Year: 72
Middle 50% SAT range: M: 620–700, CR: 620–700, Wr: 660–730
Middle 50% ACT range: 27–30

Early admission program EA/ED/None: EA and ED
Percentage accepted through EA or ED: 27%
EA and ED deadline: 15-Nov
Regular Deadline: 15-Jan
Application Fee: $50
Full time Undergraduate enrollment: 2,053
Total enrollment: 2,075
Percent Male: 41%
Percent Female: 59%
Total Percent Minority or Unreported: 21%
Percent African-American: 2%
Percent Asian/Pacific Islander: 4%
Percent Hispanic: 7%
Percent Native-American: 1%
Percent International: 2%
Percent in-state/out of state: 27%/73%
Percent from Public HS: 58%

Retention Rate: 92%
Graduation Rate 4-year: 77%
Graduation Rate 6-year: 83%
Percent Undergraduates in On-campus housing: 76%
Number of official organized extracurricular organizations: 92
3 Most popular majors: Economics, English, Biology
Student/Faculty ratio: 10:1
Average Class Size: 9
Percent of students going to grad school: Unreported
Tuition and Fees: $33,972
In-State Tuition and Fees if different: No difference
Cost for Room and Board: $8,498
Percent receiving financial aid out of those who apply, first year: 92%
Percent receiving financial aid among all students: 35%

If Colorado College had a mantra it would be something along the lines of to to be yourself is to fit in; it's a good thing we can all manage that. And the Block Plan, its heart and soul, is not too shabby itself, especially against the rugged Colorado backdrop. With the school's geographic paradise, structural freedom, and one-of-a-kind student body, your years at Colorado College can be whatever you want them to be.

Block Plan

Colorado College is the Block Plan. An alternative to the classic three-to-four-classes-at-once term, blocks allow students to really zoom in on one subject that especially sparks their fancy. The academic recipe: step one—give a topic your undivided attention for eighteen days; step two—repeat eight times. Note: even if you get tired of whatever it is that you're learning, remember to pour in your all. While the structure stipulates that students soak in a whole course of information in less than a month, it also allows for more hands-on creative ways of acquiring knowledge that are unlike those of the anonymous lecture. If you don't want to be stuck in a classroom, you don't have to be. Another step in the recipe—sprinkle on some real-world experience. According to one junior, at Colorado College, "geology classes can study geology in the Rocky Mountains [and] Homer's epic poems can be taught in the Mediterranean." The whole experience can be a whirlwind, though; don't expect to have hours and hours of time to yourself. In the face of so much stress, "quirky dressing is a must," one senior says.

The school's statistics themselves are impressive. Classes cannot have more than twenty-five people per instructor, meaning that students learn in smaller groups, a stimulating method channeling cooperation, participation, and preparedness. This also allows for stellar relationships between professors and their students; each teacher is more than happy to sit down with a pupil to discuss whatever it is that may be of interest. This always-present availability of help balances out any difficulties that could arise from all that there is to do. In a survey of favorite professors, the most commonly mentioned was history scholar Dennis Showalter, but so were teachers from most departments; in reality, each member of the faculty has strengths, it just depends on with whom students decide to develop connections. Students describe grading as reasonable; there is no hyper-curving. The most intricate process seems to be that of choosing classes, though it has its good and its bad—one must make the best use of his or her 80 points each year. As one sophomore says, "it just depends on how good of a gambler you are."

Cracking Conventionality

With Colorado College's cozy-sized student body, a cold shoulder is never turned—not in the classroom, and especially not in the community. A categorization of Colorado College students: uncategorizable. There is every kind of person on the campus expressing him or herself in every way. A senior remarked that "the only way of dressing that isn't commonplace is the 'preppy' look." And a group of individuals comes with a guaranteed open-mindedness, at least to a certain extent. The block system makes for a pretty interesting group of people, too; because everyone has chosen to dedicate themselves so wholeheartedly to one subject matter, there is always something to talk about with soon-to-be friends and oh so many different intellectual thirsts. A sophomore assures that she has "learned to look deeper within the meaning of diversity," for while there may be a "lack of ethnic diversity . . . people who seem the same as you by looks are very different."

> "People who seem the same as you by looks are very different."

A junior describes the "variety of annual parties, such as Halloween, XXXmas, Winter Ball, Drag Ball, and Llamapalooza," some with musicians, some with activities, and some with both. If anything rules the party scene it is the festivities of the sport teams, not the Greek life that sometimes defeats all other kinds of life; parties are accessible—there really is no sense of the exclusivity that is sometimes integral in college merry-making. Because students want to party together, if you want to get in somewhere, you can. While athletes are known for hosting fun events, they are in no way unapproachable. The earthen Colorado hills make it difficult to not love being outside; sports-related endeavors are a large part of students' experiences—not in a cliquey sense, per se, but in an appreciating-your-surroundings way. Treks through the wilderness that is Colorado never get old—don't forget your tent!

Daily Details

Students' experiences with the dorms can be sculpted by their specific needs. While, for the most part, freshmen live alongside one another, sophomores, juniors, and seniors are given more of a choice. If you enjoy a certain subject or hope to pursue a certain lifestyle, there may be a specific house to satisfy that need. Seniors can choose to leave the traditional dorm for their own places, however many opt out, preferring to stay close to those with whom they have grown up on campus. Students feel safe going out at night; an alarmingly high rate of crime is certainly not a pertinent problem. If any issue should arise, Resident Advisors' ears are open, without fail. Food is prepared for every eater, always with a healthy swing; the central dining hall, Rastall, is cushioned by smaller eateries, more specialized in their dishes. As for the presence of illegal substances, those most consumed are alcohol and drugs, of which the most popular is marijuana. There is no especially restricting alcohol policy—just don't make an intoxicated fool out of yourself. If you look, you can definitely find harder things, but there is no pressure to use them.

After Class?

Whatever it is that Colorado College students gain through the trials and tribulations of their arduous curriculum without a doubt transfers to other facets of their lives. Sports are a huge part of the lifestyle, especially with such a conducive setting. While hockey and soccer are the most well-known, hype-worthy sports, most students use their free time to play intramurals, whether on campus or around it. These games are huge community builders—multitudes gather at games. Others are involved in whatever their specific interests are—theater, sculpture, music; if you like something you will be encouraged to pursue it. And whatever that is, there is genuine student support—students love to see what their peers have created.

If your search for the perfect school is at least partly shaped by the idea of a place where freedom comes with all of the other classic marks of an A+ institution, you're not going to get much closer. Colorado College is that place, surrounded by organic earthly beauty, intellectually explorative students, and—of course—the Block Plan. It really does never get old.—*Liliana Cousins*

FYI

Three things every student at Colorado College should do before graduating "are 1) the incline [a grouping steps that seem to go on forever] 2) Bombs and Wings 3) DU-CC Hockey game." The biggest college-wide event at Colorado College "is Psychedelic Bowling." If you come to Colorado College, "you'd better leave your high heels behind."

Colorado School of Mines

Address: 1500 Illinois Street Golden, CO 80401
Phone: 303-273-3200
E-mail address: admit@mines.edu
Web site URL: www.mines.edu
Year Founded: 1874
Private or Public: Public
Religious Affiliation: None
Location: Suburban
Number of Applicants: 3,142
Percent Accepted: 61%
Percent Accepted who enroll: 29%
Number Entering: 776
Number of Transfers Accepted each Year: 128
Middle 50% SAT range: M: 600–690, CR: 540–640, Wr: Unreported
Middle 50% ACT range: 25–30
Early admission program EA/ED/None: None

Percentage accepted through EA or ED: NA
EA and ED deadline: NA
Regular Deadline: 1-Jun
Application Fee: $45
Full time Undergraduate enrollment: 3,456
Total enrollment: 4,488
Percent Male: 79%
Percent Female: 21%
Total Percent Minority or Unreported: 25%
Percent African-American: 2%
Percent Asian/Pacific Islander: 5%
Percent Hispanic: 6%
Percent Native-American: 1%
Percent International: 4%
Percent in-state/out of state: 78%/22%
Percent from Public HS: 90%
Retention Rate: 84%
Graduation Rate 4-year: 27%

Graduation Rate 6-year: 63%
Percent Undergraduates in On-campus housing: 43%
Number of official organized extracurricular organizations: 126
3 Most popular majors: Chemical Engineering, Mathematics, Mechanical Engineering
Student/Faculty ratio: 15:1
Average Class Size: 16
Percent of students going to grad school: 14%
Tuition and Fees: $25,248
In-State Tuition and Fees if different: $11,238
Cost for Room and Board: $7,626
Percent receiving financial aid out of those who apply, first year: 91%
Percent receiving financial aid among all students: Unreported

The name of the University may be slightly misleading. Yes, the Colorado School of Mines does place a great deal of importance on mining, but that is only a small portion of what it does. In fact, the University is considered to be among the best engineering schools in the country. Lo-

cated in Golden, Colorado, a town originally built to serve miners, the School of Mines was founded in 1873 and even operated its own experimental excavations to teach students about the intricacies of mining. Today, it is home to more than 4,000 students and represents one of the most important research institutions in Colorado and a top destination for engineering students.

Not Just Mining

Given the name of the University, it is obvious that not too many humanities majors attend the school. Of course, CSM does offer some social sciences programs, but they are mostly limited to a bachelor of science in economics or a number of minors in subjects such as humanities and international economy. As a result, the focus of the University is on applied sciences, engineering, and geology, the three main academic divisions of the university. "Our school is obviously an engineering school," said one student. "It is a public school, but we are really prestigious and we receive some of the best technical training you will find anywhere." Furthermore, the school is mostly focused on undergraduate education, as less than one-quarter of the student body are postgraduates.

Given the specialized nature of the University, CSM only has 13 academic departments, ranging from economics to metallurgy. There are less than 30 majors offered at the school, and only one—Economics—is not science and engineering related, although it is important to point out that a bachelor of science in economics also requires a great deal of training in mathematics. For those interested in liberal arts, a select number of minors are also available to broaden the students' knowledge in humanities and social sciences. "We have programs in things like humanities," said one student. "But think about it: when you go to a college called the School of Mines, not too many people are going to take those kinds of classes."

The academics at CSM are vigorous. An example of the demands of the coursework is the long list of required classes at the school. CSM, like most other schools, has a core sequence of classes that must be taken by all students to ensure that everyone has the skills necessary to succeed in college. Unlike other institutions, however, the required classes at CSM are very specific. For example, everyone must take Calculus I, II, and III, Differential Equations, and a number of physics and chemistry classes. While students at many other schools can choose among a variety of classes often vaguely related to numbers to fulfill their requirements in mathematics, students at CSM undergo very intense and specific training. "The core courses are important because you are going to need them anywhere," said one student. Indeed, given that almost everyone is

in a field related to engineering, the calculus classes are essential for the rest of their stay at the university.

Given the academic vigor, it is not surprising that students do feel the pressure from the classes. "People say that introductory engineering classes are supposed to overwhelm people who are not fit to major in engineering so that they can go and choose other things," said one student. "I don't think it is that way, but you definitely have to work to keep up with classes." While the classes can be difficult and the professors sometimes very demanding, students also sense that they do have easy access to their instructors. "The school is not that big," said one student. "That's why we do get to meet and talk to professors very often. It's great because you don't get that in many other schools."

> "The city is not big, but it has everything I need as a college student."

One other advantage of attending CSM is that it is a research university, thus presenting students the opportunity to experience real-life applications of what they learn in the classrooms. The different engineering labs and institutions provide the more entrepreneurial students with a head start in their future academic pursuit or simply allow them to see what the top scientists and engineers do in their jobs.

The University is ranked among the top 100 national universities by the *U.S. News & World Report*. It accepts more than half of the applicants, but entering the university is no easy task. It has a very selective process. After all, given the academics of the school, it is important for prospective students to have the ability to follow the course load of CSM as well as have the quantitative skills demanded by many of the school's classes.

Not So Fun but Plenty of Beer

Besides the presence of CSM, the city of Golden is perhaps best known for being home to one of the largest breweries in the world, the Coors Brewery, which offers tours and, sometimes, access to an enormous amount of beer at a discounted price. Besides the brewery, the city is relatively small, and the economy greatly dependent on the university. It is located in the foothills of the Rocky Mountains and is only 15 miles away from Denver. Therefore, even though it has a population fewer than 20,000 people, Golden does have easy access to other parts of Colorado, not to mention a great view of the mountains from the university's campus. "The city is not big, but it has everything I need as a college student," said one junior.

No one is required to live on campus. However, the school strongly recommends students live in University residences at least for the duration of freshman year, which is often considered an essential part of college experience. The majority of first-year students do choose to live in dorms. Furthermore, living on campus gives students different benefits, such as tutoring, which can be much more difficult to access when living off campus. "The residence halls are not great," said one student. "But you definitely meet more people, so you should stay on campus during your freshman year. After that, most people find apartments elsewhere." In fact, the majority of upperclassmen choose to live away from CSM's campus. Some people do choose apartments at Mines Parks, which are unfurnished and close to campus, thus allowing students better accessibility to the university's facilities while being able to live off campus.

The party scene at CSM, however, is relatively uninteresting. The Greek life exists but is not particularly vibrant. Students do hold parties during weekends, but it is clear that CSM is not a party school. "You will find some things to do during weekends, but there is not much variety," said one student. "If you want, you can also go to Denver, which is not that far if you have a car," added another student.

A School for the Future
In recent years, CSM found great success in its athletic programs, which mostly compete in Division II. The football team has received some recognition in the national media for being a very good program, but the most successful athletic program is cycling. In fact, given the location of the University, it is not surprising that the school is a mountain bike powerhouse, finishing in the top three in the nation several times during the last few years.

For students willing to work hard during their college years and looking for a top-notch engineering degree at the price of a public university, look no further than CSM. Of course, Golden is not the busiest city in the world, and the party scene may leave students with some small disappointments. Nevertheless, it is clear that the school offers a very good education, not to mention a great deal of interactions between professors and students. It is a widely recognized institution with a number of research opportunities even for undergraduates. Therefore, do not let the name School of Mines make you believe that it is only a school about digging up coal from mountains. It is much, much more than that.—*Xiaohang Liu*

FYI
If you come to CSM, you'd better bring a "work ethic."
What is the typical weekend schedule? "Some studying and hanging out with friends."

Colorado State University

Address: 1062 Campus Delivery, Fort Collins, CO 80523-8020
Phone: 970-491-6909
E-mail address: admissions@colostate.edu
Web site URL: www.welcome.colostate.edu
Year Founded: 1870
Private or Public: Public
Religious Affiliation: None
Location: Suburban
Number of Applicants: 12,494
Percent Accepted: 86%
Percent Accepted who enroll: 42%
Number Entering: 4,392
Number of Transfers Accepted each Year: 2,012
Middle 50% SAT range: M: 500–620, CR: 500–600, Wr: 560–660
Middle 50% ACT range: 22–26
Early admission program EA/ED/None: None

Percentage accepted through EA or ED: NA
EA and ED deadline: NA
Regular Deadline: 1-Feb
Application Fee: $50
Full time Undergraduate enrollment: 20,765
Total enrollment: 27,030
Percent Male: 48%
Percent Female: 52%
Total Percent Minority or Unreported: 16%
Percent African-American: 2%
Percent Asian/Pacific Islander: 3%
Percent Hispanic: 6%
Percent Native-American: 2%
Percent International: 1%
Percent in-state/out of state: 79%/21%
Percent from Public HS: Unreported
Retention Rate: 83%
Graduation Rate 4-year: 35%

Graduation Rate 6-year: 65%
Percent Undergraduates in On-campus housing: 25%
Number of official organized extracurricular organizations: 330
3 Most popular majors: Constructing Engineering Technology, Kinesiology and Exercise Science, Psychology
Student/Faculty ratio: 18:1
Average Class Size: 24
Percent of students going to grad school: Unreported
Tuition and Fees: $18,858
In-State Tuition and Fees if different: $5,418
Cost for Room and Board: $7,382
Percent receiving financial aid out of those who apply, first year: 71%
Percent receiving financial aid among all students: 62%

Colorado State University is nestled between the edge of the Great Plains and the foothills of the Rocky Mountains in the mid-size city of Fort Collins, Colorado. Enjoying an average of 300 sunny days per year and ranked as one of the "Best Places to Live" in the western U.S. by *Money Magazine*, Fort Collins is home to vast green spaces coupled with low stress and lower crime rates, and the students of CSU are well aware of the advantages of living in this "outdoor lovers' paradise." Besides enjoying the beauty of their surroundings, under- and upperclassmen alike appreciate their school's rigorous academics at a reasonable cost as well as the numerous opportunities to get involved in a wide array of extracurricular and athletic activities.

Decisions, Decisions

When applying to CSU, students must apply for acceptance into one of eight colleges—Agricultural Sciences, Applied Human Sciences, Business, Engineering, Liberal Arts, Forestry and Natural Resources, Veterinary Medicine and Biomedical Sciences—and select their major before arriving on campus. However, as many as a third of the freshman class opts to take advantage of the "open option" programs that postpone the choice of a major until the beginning of sophomore year. Various individual departments offer this alternative in addition to the university-wide program that allows undecided freshmen to take courses in a variety of subject areas before committing to only one. The school also offers an honors program that provides enrichment for 340 students and features smaller honors sections in key courses within each major, priority housing in the honors dormitory, early class registration, and research opportunities with members of the faculty.

Class registration at CSU can easily be done online, but students unable to reach their computers early enough on registration day might find themselves shut out of some necessary courses and rearranging their schedules to take them the next year instead. The most frequent class size is between 20 and 29. Smaller classes naturally fill up more quickly and the competition to gain entrance can be quite fierce; larger classes are generally quite easy to get into. These larger lectures can offer frustrations of their own, however, as many of the freshman introductory classes must accommodate upwards of 200 to 300 students. While the amount of work assigned in any class can pile up, most of these introductory 100-level classes are known for being relatively easy. One of the most popular courses offered—and one that fills up very quickly on registration day—is "Psychology of Human Sexuality," which hosts a "porn day" during which the entire class watches a pornographic video for an hour in order to study and discuss its psychological implications. In order to graduate, all CSU students must take a course in English composition, although it is possible to test out of this requirement by scoring well on an AP or departmental exam. A wide variety of course options is available for fulfilling the other areas of the core curriculum, and students generally agree that it is relatively painless to do so.

At the Foot of the Mountains

Freshmen at CSU are required to live on campus, and the school does honor housing requests on a first-come, first-serve basis, so submitting dorm preferences early is a good idea. Each of the 13 residence halls has its own theme and offers related "Living Learning Communities" that provide tutoring and study groups in its focus academic area: Ingersoll, for example, is the science dorm, Academic Village, the honors dorm, and Edwards serves the pre-veterinarians and agricultural sciences. There are also dorms with non-academic reputations: Corbett is the "Party Dorm," and most of the athletes live in The Towers. In spite of the fact that many students consider on-campus living to be enjoyable, "The food is pretty terrible and the rooms are not good," and so most move into off-campus housing after their first or second year. Huge apartment complexes such as Ram's Pointe and Ram's Village are located conveniently close to campus and cater primarily to sophomores, as upperclassmen tend to "realize that those places aren't much better than the dorms were and find a house or a better apartment." The architecture of the dorms and other buildings at CSU tends to vary in aesthetics; the older part of campus seems built in the design of the old Spanish Mission style, while other

areas call to mind classical revivalist or "some kind of nasty 70s non-style," although these latter buildings have been undergoing recent renovations to improve their appearance. The Lory Student Center is a popular place to hang out for CSU students and boasts restaurants, student lounges featuring video arcades, TVs, and pool tables, a ballroom, a theater and the campus box office, and stores offering everything from textbooks and school supplies to haircuts and bicycle repairs. When this monolithic facility was renovated several years ago, *The New York Times* ranked it as one of the 10 best student centers in the country.

CSU has a firm alcohol policy and the on-campus dorms are strictly dry, but even so, alcohol often makes its way onto school property and into students' bedrooms. There are RAs on every hall to watch over their student charges, but most are not terribly severe and instead favor a policy of general oversight to stringently enforcing every rule. Binge drinking indeed is somewhat of a problem at CSU, and "at least one frat per year gets shut down for getting an underage girl sent to the hospital." With the exception of marijuana, which is somewhat popular, recreational drugs do not make much of an appearance here, and the use of harder substances is very rare.

> Fort Collins's 300 days of sunshine keep students—particularly those who love the outdoors—smiling.

Fort Collins offers a particularly vibrant bar scene, which tends to attract many CSU students. There are bars with specials every night of the week, although the most popular evenings for bar hopping tend to be Tuesdays and Thursdays, and seniors frequent these establishments more often than the underclassmen, who often prefer the party scene offered by the frats. As one student summed up, "You can see herds of freshmen walking off campus at night looking for parties, but the older classes usually just stay home or go to friends' houses."

Freshmen and upperclassmen living on campus can choose from one of three different meal plans that offer a great deal of flexibility and include the option of eating at the all-you-can-eat residence hall dining center as well as any of the restaurants housed in the Lory Student Center. Nevertheless, students are lukewarm in their enthusiasm for the food quality in the on-campus retail facilities and often end up traveling beyond the campus borders to find a satisfying meal.

Most students, particularly those from nearby towns and cities, bring their cars to campus, and those who do not have a vehicle are definitely in the minority. Although the majority do remain at CSU during the weekends, a notable minority use their cars to go home or visit nearby Denver, sixty-five miles away, for a couple of days.

Indeed, most of CSU's 21,000 undergraduates do come from within the state and are well used to Colorado's chilly winters, which in Fort Collins can reach a low of 15°F in January. Nevertheless, there are still plenty of girls who wear "mini skirts and fuzzy boots" around campus as they attempt to strike a compromise between fashion and warmth. The student body stereotypically tends to be "upper middle class and white" and sports perhaps a lower level of diversity than might be common at other universities. The Greek scene remains prevalent and drives much of the party scene, and in the weeks before rush, advertisements for the various fraternities and sororities flood the campus.

Ram-ping Up the Involvement

Football is the major player in the CSU sports arena and much of the University's sense of school spirit derives from it, although as one student admits, "The team isn't very good." Spirit organizations—the cheerleading squad, the marching band and Cam the Ram, the University's costumed mascot—support the team on game days and pull the crowd into the action. On the other hand, the varsity volleyball and lacrosse teams boast a great deal of talent but lack the attention given to football. Intramural sports are extremely popular, especially among freshmen and upperclassmen living on campus, and can become quite competitive depending on the level of ability. Everything from football to soccer to inner-tube water polo is offered, and students who want to play a sport that has not been organized are encouraged to start a new league for it. The Campus Rec center provides basketball courts, exercise rooms, a racquetball court, a pool and spa, a track and a boxing area, among many other facilities, and is popular among athletes and non-athletes alike. The only disadvantage to this altar to exercise is that it often becomes very busy and overly crowded.

Outside of athletics, CSU hosts over 300 recognized clubs, organizations and performance groups, and as with IMs, any student who finds that his or her interests are not already represented can found a new one. The student government—Associated Students of Colorado State University (or ASCSU)—is a popular extracurricular activity that makes it easy to become involved with the University through voluntary committees and associate positions as well as running for office in campus-wide elections. Both the college radio station, KCSU, and the student-run TV channel, Campus Television, attract their share of the University audience, and the *Rocky Mountain Collegian* keeps undergraduates informed about recent news. In addition, the Curfman Gallery at the Lory Student Center offers several rotating art exhibits every year, and undergraduates can become involved in choosing and displaying the works. Volunteering off campus is also a popular pastime for CSU students, and opportunities abound to become involved with many different projects in Fort Collins and beyond. A bi-annual event called the Involvement Expo allows campus organizations to showcase themselves and man informational displays while interested students browse their options for extracurricular involvement.

Here Comes the Sun

Students at Colorado State University benefit from the multitude of offerings presented by their college, from the abundance of in-depth courses to the wide variety of extracurricular options, and although the food may not be gourmet or the architecture artistic, CSU undergraduates are generally quite positive about their experience. From the Lory Student Center to the themed dorms to the popular gymnasium, the amenities available on campus compare favorably with those of other universities, and Fort Collins's 300 days of sunshine keep students—particularly those who love the outdoors—smiling.—*Kristin Knox*

FYI

If you come to CSU, you'd better bring "a car - students who don't have them are definitely in the minority."

What's the typical weekend schedule? "Sleep till noon, go skiing or biking, have dinner with friends, go out."

If I could change one thing about CSU, it would be "the food options in the dining halls."

Three things every student at CSU should do before graduating are "hang out in the student center, hike to the Aggies sign above Fort Collins and go into the Old Town on Friday night."

United States Air Force Academy

Address: HQ USAF/RRS, 2304 Cadet Drive, Suite 2300 USAF Academy, CO 80840

Phone: 719-333-2520

E-mail address: rr_webmail@usafa.edu

Web site URL: www.usafa.edu

Year Founded: 1954

Private or Public: Public

Religious Affiliation: None

Location: Suburban

Number of Applicants: 9,001

Percent Accepted: 18%

Percent Accepted who enroll: 81%

Number Entering: 1,336

Number of Transfers Accepted each Year: Unreported

Middle 50% SAT range: M: 620–700, CR: 600–680, Wr: 560–660

Middle 50% ACT range: 25–29

Early admission program EA/ED/None: None

Percentage accepted through EA or ED: NA

EA and ED deadline: NA

Regular Deadline: 31-Jan

Application Fee: $0

Full time Undergraduate enrollment: 4,537

Total enrollment: 4,537

Percent Male: 81%

Percent Female: 19%

Total Percent Minority or Unreported: 23%

Percent African-American: 5%

Percent Asian/Pacific Islander: 9%

Percent Hispanic: 7%

Percent Native-American: 2%

Percent International: 1%

Percent in-state/out of state: 15%/85%

Percent from Public HS: 99%

Retention Rate: 93%

Graduation Rate 4-year: 70%

Graduation Rate 6-year: 72%

Percent Undergraduates in On-campus housing: 100%

Number of official organized extracurricular organizations: 77

3 Most popular majors: Aerospace, Aeronautical and Astronautical Engineering, Business, Social Studies

Student/Faculty ratio: 9:1

Average Class Size: 16

Percent of students going to grad school: 7%

Tuition and Fees: $0

In-State Tuition and Fees if different: No difference

Cost for Room and Board: $0

Percent receiving financial aid out of those who apply, first year: NA

Percent receiving financial aid among all students: NA

The United States Air Force Academy demands both academic and physical excellence, a challenge that many find difficult to meet. The first challenge one meets in becoming a cadet is being admitted. Subsequently, cadets are constantly tested both in and outside of the classroom with strict rules and harsh reprimands. Although the environment is intense, the benefits of attending such a university are incalculable. Cadets are paid to attend school, become part of a closely knit squad, live in beautiful Colorado and learn how to fly.

Not an Easy Transition

When a new freshman enters the Air Force Academy compound for the very first time, the transition from high school to college takes on a new meaning. Known to the upperclassmen as "doolies," the freshmen have to adjust to many lifestyle changes. The USAFA imposes a strict daily regimen for all cadets, but freshmen experience fewer privileges and less space to live in. The beginning of a freshman's career as a cadet begins with mandatory Basic Cadet Training during the summer. This five-week long program teaches future cadets basic military skills and serves as a preliminary "weeding out" of prospects. Not everyone is able to endure such an intense lifestyle, even at the beginning.

Cadets are divided randomly into 36 squadrons of 120 each. Each squadron includes students from all four years and determines where a cadet will live. Although everyone lives in the squadrons, the living arrangements differ according to class. Freshmen live in the most crowded rooms with three roommates, while sophomores and juniors live with two, and seniors live with just one roommate. This squadron system provides smaller groups within the academy for cadets to bond.

At USAFA, hierarchy and experience are very highly valued. With each year, cadets are given more freedom and privileges. Only seniors are allowed to have a car at school, and are thus more likely to get the opportunity to party at neighboring colleges such as Colorado College and Colorado University in Colorado Springs. For freshmen, the Academy institutes strict prohibitions against underage drinking, where getting caught with alcohol can lead to expulsion. The most treasured forms of freedom are leave and phone privileges. As a first-year, cadets may only receive phone calls during the weekends and cannot leave the premises other than when on break. After the first year, cadets may leave the campus and visit local areas. Therefore, it's definitely better to be an upperclassman, but the fact of the matter is that every cadet has to go through freshman year.

The cadet dining facilities are akin to other military schools within the US. Mitchell Hall is the largest dining hall where the entire cadet wing assembles to eat family-style breakfast and lunch everyday. This type of dining means preparing and serving 12,000 meals per day. Because of this, specialized dining is very rare and many cadets view the food as "getting old very fast."

Studying Among the Best

The USAFA is ranked as the number one Baccalaureate Program in the West, according to *U.S. News & World Report*'s "America's Best Colleges 2010," making it clear that academics are taken very seriously. The average class size is small, ranging from 15 to 20 students, allowing for a more personalized form of learning. In addition to taking courses that fulfill one's major, all cadets are required to take several military courses.

Many find the academic scene highly rigorous and competitive. Once a cadet is admitted, they compete with the other students for grades as everything is graded on a curve.

Cadets usually study about 20 hours a week usually during the mandated study periods scheduled during the day when not in class. Otherwise, cadets are expected to study in their rooms or in the library during Academic Call to Quarters (ACQ). This highly regulated studying time is implemented to ensure academic success and contributes to the overall goal of efficient use of time.

Students are required to have at least 132 credit hours to graduate, but most end up having far more due to the mixture of military and major courses offered. Most cadets either major in engineering or management and each have their own reputations. One cadet said, "The engineering majors are geeks, the computer science majors don't even bother looking for dates, and the management majors don't bother doing homework because it is more of a recommendation than a requirement." The engineering major regardless of its specification is considered the hardest, where the management major is considered the easiest and most flexible major available.

EXTRAcurriculars

All cadets are required to participate in the athletic program the Air Force offers, which includes both physical education courses and competitive sports. If a cadet does not participate in a varsity sport, then he or she is expected to participate in at least one intramural sport. These sports range from Ultimate Frisbee to soccer and are very competitive.

> "There truly is nothing better than to compete for the Academy."

Varsity sports are prevalent at the academy, with about one fourth of all cadets participating in them. And the teams are known to take a lot of pride in what they do. All athletes are expected to participate in their sport and fulfill all other requirements, an obligation that can prove to be difficult at times. One swimmer remarked, "Being an athlete here at the Air Force is like doubling the military requirements. It literally is like another job. However, all varsity athletes are very respected and there truly is nothing better than to compete for the Academy."

Because of the required involvement in extracurricular activities and the highly enforced regimen, cadets don't have a lot of free time. Luckily, they don't have to worry about making money, for every cadet is paid a salary monthly. A variety of scholarships is also offered to many cadets. Although they are banned from outside employment, the student salary and lack of tuition and rooming and board expenses clearly make up for

it. Overall the USAFA is one of the best colleges out there for those who want to make a difference. For many cadets, being able to serve one's country and gain an education is an honor. You learn the skills you need to survive both on the battlefield and in the workplace. The highly accomplished staff, class offerings, emphasis on leadership skills, and the networking opportunities available make the Air Force an incredible experience. However, be warned that this school is not for the weak.—*Taylor Ritzel*

FYI

If you come to the Air Force Academy, you'd better bring "an ability to stick it through freshman year; it gets better from there!"

What's the typical weekend schedule? "Training classes and study hours during the weekend, however most of the time is free time."

If you could change one thing about the Air Force Academy, "I would get rid of noncommissioned officer (NCO) presence here. The AFA is training cadets to be commissioned officers, and NCOs have no part in the training of cadets."

Three things every cadet should do before graduating: "Remain standing and cheering for the football team even though it's the fourth quarter and the team is losing by over three touchdowns, use your uniform to pick up the opposite sex, deploy overseas to see what you are getting into."

University of Colorado / Boulder

Address: 552 UCB Boulder, CO 80309-0552
Phone: 303-492-6301
E-mail address: apply@colorado.edu
Web site URL: www.colorado.edu/prospective
Year Founded: 1876
Private or Public: Public
Religious Affiliation: None
Location: Suburban
Number of Applicants: 19,857
Percent Accepted: 82%
Percent Accepted who enroll: 34%
Number Entering: 5,520
Number of Transfers Accepted each Year: 1,973
Middle 50% SAT range: M: 540–650, CR: 520–630, Wr: 540–630
Middle 50% ACT range: 23–28

Early admission program EA/ED/None: None
Percentage accepted through EA or ED: NA
EA and ED deadline: NA
Regular Deadline: 15-Jan
Application Fee: $50
Full time Undergraduate enrollment: 26,155
Total enrollment: 30,945
Percent Male: 54%
Percent Female: 46%
Total Percent Minority or Unreported: 22%
Percent African-American: 2%
Percent Asian/Pacific Islander: 6%
Percent Hispanic: 6%
Percent Native-American: 1%
Percent International: 2%
Percent in-state/out of state: 69%/31%
Percent from Public HS: Unreported

Retention Rate: 83%
Graduation Rate 4-year: 41%
Graduation Rate 6-year: 65%
Percent Undergraduates in On-campus housing: 94%
Number of official organized extracurricular organizations: 300
3 Most popular majors: English, Physiology, Psychology
Student/Faculty ratio: 16:1
Average Class Size: 16
Percent of students going to grad school: 21%
Tuition and Fees: $26,756
In-State Tuition and Fees if different: $7,278
Cost for Room and Board: $9,860
Percent receiving financial aid out of those who apply, first year: 42%
Percent receiving financial aid among all students: 52%

Situated in the foothills of the Rocky Mountains, the University of Colorado at Boulder presents students with unbounded opportunities to explore every aspect of college life. "CU-Boulder" simply has it all. Passionate outdoors-types can take advantage of the hundreds of miles of trails for running, biking and hiking that surround the campus. Or, daredevils can hit the slopes at over 20 ski resorts located in the vicinity. Such limitless exploration goes far beyond the outdoors, however. With over 3,400 courses in 150 fields of study, the University offers students endless ways to pursue their academic interests. The presence of four Nobel Prize winners and seven MacArthur Fellowship recipients among the faculty further reinforces CU-Boulder's high standard of academics. The unique "hippie" flavor of the town of Boulder entertains students with its laid-back but fun atmosphere. In short, CU-Boulder combines the best of many worlds, offering rigorous academic discipline in a free-spirited environment.

Open-Ended Opportunity

The first thing that students mention when referring to CU-Boulder is its freedom. With a plethora of course offerings, students may choose from thousands of courses to satisfy their intellectual desires. To help students streamline their interests, the University is divided into seven different colleges. While most take the common Arts and Sciences track, many students also enroll in the Leeds School of Business and the School of Engineering and Applied Science. The other colleges are in Architecture and Planning, Education, Journalism and Mass Communication, and Music. Students' majors vary widely, but the three most popular majors from the Fall 2008 term were psychology, integrative physiology, and English.

Without a doubt, accommodating more than 30,000 students at CU-Boulder is no small task. Although the average class size is 10–19 students, many express a frustration with the size of some classes. "I hate the big lectures!" a sophomore exclaimed. Another frequent complaint is the core curriculum requirement. The curriculum is divided between "skills acquisition" (foreign language, quantitative reasoning, writing, and critical thinking) and "content areas of study" (history, diversity, United States, literature, natural science, contemporary society, and values). Nonetheless, as at most colleges, the requirements "lessen as you progress through the years."

While finding a niche at such a large institution might seem intimidating to many incoming freshmen, CU-Boulder does provide opportunities for personalized attention. One unique aspect of the University is the presence of RAPs (Residential Academic Programs) that allow undergraduates to share experiences with others who have common interests. The sense of community engendered by the RAPs is bolstered by the fact that select relevant courses are located in the respective halls, and special events are planned just for the program. RAPs are centered on numerous concepts, including, but not limited to: Environmental Science (Baker), Diversity (Hallett), Liberal Arts (Farrand), Honors (Kittredge), American West (Sewall), and the Arts (Libby).

Beyond the RAPs, CU-Boulder offers an Honors Program for exceptionally motivated students, providing specialized curriculum and advising from faculty members. Also, the Norlin Scholars Program, a merit-based award of $3,000 per year, helps talented students achieve their goals with individual guidance.

> "Everyone's really laid-back."

For those looking for diverse experiences outside of Colorado, the University offers an extensive study-abroad program in locations ranging from Perugia, Italy, to Valparaiso, Chile, to Cape Town, South Africa, to Ulaanbaatar, Mongolia.

Adventuresome Architecture

With over 200 "architecturally pleasing" rural-Italian-style buildings, students have plenty to gape at besides the Rocky Mountains. A common "hotspot" on campus is Norlin Quadrangle, a broad grassy area where students can go to study, meet up with friends, or simply relax and enjoy the nice weather. One student comments that Norlin Quad is "nice and open, has lots of sunshine, and is simply a nice place where you can just lie down and see the Flatirons." Slacklining—tightrope walking across climbing ropes, usually tied between two trees— is an interesting pastime commonly seen on the Quad. Other often-frequented buildings on campus include Macky Auditorium and the Norlin Library, which, with five million volumes, boasts the "largest library collection in the Rocky Mountain region." Charles Z. Klauder designed most of the buildings on campus in a distinctive rural North Italian fashion. The red-tiled roofs and rough walls evoke an impression of being in the mountainous regions of Northern Italy—a particularly relevant ambiance for a university placed at the base of the Rockies.

Hippie Heaven
"Everyone's really laid-back," explained one student, referring to the student body. When asked about the basic composition of the general population, most people name "Hippie" and "frat guy" as the common student types that exist at CU-Boulder. In terms of music and culture, many students list the Grateful Dead and Phish among their favorite bands. In addition, there is a recognizable presence of marijuana on campus, albeit amongst a smaller group of people.

Drinking is ubiquitous. Though the University's stated policy disallows drinking in the dorms, enforcement of the rules is characteristic of the school as a whole—laid-back. The "two-strikes" policy comes as a result of CU-Boulder's campaign as one of the first schools in the nation to systematically address student alcohol abuse. Nonetheless, drinking provides much entertainment for CU-Boulder students, especially at the fraternities and sororities that are located on "The Hill," a favorite district for students.

Recreational Respites
Located on the Eastern slope of the Rocky Mountains at an altitude of 5,400 feet, the University has the natural rocky formations as its backyard. The miles and miles of trails allow students to hike, bike, climb, or snowshoe for hours on end. During the warmer months of the year, students can opt to go whitewater rafting or kayaking on the Colorado River.

But for those who aren't willing to make the trek out to the mountains, there is plenty to do on campus. The Colorado Buffaloes football team is a source of shared pride for nearly all CU-Boulder students. Playing in Folsom Stadium, the football team draws huge crowds during games against perennial opponents such as the Nebraska Cornhuskers. The Colorado Buffaloes also boast a strong cross-country running team, and they have produced world-class runners such as Adam Goucher and Dathan Ritzenhein.

For students who are less competitive, the intramurals program offers an array of exciting and relaxed sports to play. Among the many options, the Ultimate Frisbee team is generally regarded as a highly competitive and successful group. Other IMs include whiffleball, broomball, and inner-tube water polo.

Free Future
As successful as it has been thus far, CU-Boulder still desires to improve as an institution. In August of 2006, the stunning $31-million, 66,000-square-foot ATLAS (Alliance for Technology, Learning, and Society) Center opened, heralding a new age of advanced technological resources for student use. In September of 2006, the dedication of the new Wolf Law Building occurred. With a gigantic new law library and two high-tech courtrooms, the Law Building will be a landmark building for generations to come.

In general, CU-Boulder looks towards the future. Faculty members have won four Nobel Prizes in the last 2 decades, and have advanced the scientific knowledge of mankind in many respects. In fiscal year 2008, the school received $280 million in sponsored research awards from organizations such as the National Sciences Foundation, NASA, and the Department of Health and Human Services. With its strong, forward-looking academic program and an environment that promotes the freedom to explore, CU-Boulder provides the perfect experience for students looking to excel in new and old frontiers.—*Wookie Kim*

FYI
If you come to CU, you better bring "a tent and a beer funnel."
What's the typical weekend schedule? "Go camping, watch the football game, and drink beer."
If I could change one thing about CU, "I'd make the campus less hilly."
Three things that every student should do before graduating from CU are "hike the Flatirons, attend a frat party, and go to a CU football game."

University of Denver

The "oldest independent university in the Rockies" is undergoing a face-lift. Students agree that the focus of the school has shifted noticeably in the past several years. The existing emphasis on community leadership and involvement is being matched by a set of construction projects aimed at centralizing and modernizing the campus. The administration has also cracked down on the wild Greek scene. The result? A mellow, focused, and more academically oriented feel pervades the school that once was known only for its traditions of good times, great skiing and rousing school events.

Personalized Academics

To start off their time at DU, freshmen are required to take a medley of courses, including a foreign language, oral communication, math, computer science, and English. Most students are in agreement that the core curriculum lets them explore the school's strengths before choosing a major. "My favorite class to date was definitely my freshman year Spanish class, no question," one sophomore said. The student-to-faculty ratio is an impressive 10 to 1, and many commented on the personal attention received from teachers. The result is that students enjoy very small class sizes and foster "interactive" relationships with professors. TAs are a concept foreign to DU students, except in a few science courses. DU also boasts a freshman-mentoring program, which assigns all entering freshmen a faculty mentor to see them through the major decisions of the first year. After freshman year, students split their range of studies in various directions, from Arts and Literature to Creative Expression.

Popular majors include business, reflecting DU's impressive Business School; psychology, and marketing. Science majors are generally considered more difficult, and include killer courses in organic chemistry and cellular biology.

For all majors, DU makes an effort to foster a merit-based academic feel on campus from the very start. Freshmen can apply to be in the Pioneer Leadership Program the summer before they arrive. This highly selective program fits into their curriculum as a minor, applicable to any primary major later on. Equally selective is the Honors Program, which offers students with a 3.5 GPA or higher who apply to the program access to special lectures and seminars. The Pioneer Leadership and Honors Program students live on special, separate floors in freshman housing.

Another popular offering is the Interterm Program, which provides students with intensive programs between the formal academic quarters, both based at DU and abroad. Past Interterm opportunities, which are available in the fall, winter and spring recesses, have included An Economic History of the Caribbean taught on St. Kitts and Nevis in the West Indies, Religious and Social Justice in Vienna on location in Austria, and a course on gaming and gambling taught from the casinos of Las Vegas.

Students at DU generally like the academic term system, which divides the school year into quarters. Some complain that it is a bit fast-paced at times, leaving "no room for screwing up." The daily workload is manageable, and having more than two or three classes per day is rare.

DU students are motivated and engaged, but not over-the-top intense. One student describes academics as "strong, but nothing I can't handle. I'm challenged, but not killing myself over work on a daily basis."

Central and Modern

"Copper is big here," commented one DU student when describing the campus. A nice blend of fresh, modern architecture and older structures makes for a very pleasant campus feel. The red brick tower of University Hall meets the low lines of Penrose Library, while pathways snake through manicured lawns and green open spaces. The wide Colorado sky and view of the Rockies add to the picturesque feel of the campus. The University prides itself on its accomplishments in enhancing the beautiful surroundings as well, with additions such as the beautiful Humanities Gardens near the center of campus. Students call the campus "very central and modern," and praise the large capital project devoted to the recently completed residence hall and science center. Recent construction projects are part of the University's efforts to move much of DU's satellite campus, Park Hill, closer to the action on the central grounds. The Ritchie Center for Sports and Wellness is another highly visible landmark, as well as a state-of-the-art athletic facility for varsity athletes and gym-rats alike.

The campus is manageably sized, so that "It never takes more than 10 or so minutes to get to class, at the extreme," one student said. Freshmen and sophomores are required to live on campus. Freshmen are housed in two dormitories, Johnson-McFarlane, or J-Mac, and Centennial Halls. Both buildings are air-conditioned and made up of suites with kitchenettes. Centennial Halls is the home of Special Interest floors, which group students by interests such as substance-free, business, math/science, all male or all female, and the Honors Program. Members of the Pioneer Leadership Program and others live in J-Mac, generally regarded as the "dorkier" of the two freshman residences. The dorms are variously described as "decent" and "kinda gross." Freshmen live with RAs on each floor, who keep tabs on alcohol, which is forbidden, and noise violations. A new residence hall, Nagel Hall, opened in 2008. Designed to keep more upperclassmen on campus, it features singles, doubles and apartments.

Students eat in cafeterias located in both of the freshman dorms, and the upperclassman dorm. After freshman year, many sophomores choose to eat in their fraternity or sorority, and there are few upperclassmen in the cafeterias at all. DU offers a "point system" allowing students extra meal points with which they can eat in local restaurants and "get a Starbucks fix."

Greek Festivities

The area around campus is "residential and cute," made up of mostly student houses. There is a small, "adequate" commercial area a few blocks from campus, and downtown Denver is only a 10-minute drive from campus. A majority of students have cars on campus, and they are permitted for freshmen. The social life at DU has many ties to the Greek system, and more than 20 percent of students are members of the nine fraternities and five sororities. As the campus continues with renovations, many of the Greek facilities will be among those revamped. Those inside the Greek system say that "It does not entirely dominate the social scene, but it is strong," and say that there are "tons of alternative, non-Greek weekend options," though some are more adamant that the Greek system "is the social scene." Students lament the increased frequency with which house parties are broken up, and say that the party scene has begun to shift towards "bar parties," where a group will rent a bar, and allow anyone over 18 (those over 21 get a wristband) to enter and enjoy dancing and drinking. Traditional fraternity events at the ever-popular SAE, Lambda Chi Alpha, and Sigma Chi fraternities include annual theme parties, such as Western, Pajama, and Principals and Schoolgirls. All formal events are Greek-based. One of the major non-Greek events is the yearly Winter Carnival, a hugely popular campus-wide event in January.

Involved and Evolving

Like all universities of its size, DU has a long list of interesting extracurricular possibilities, from public service organizations to professional honors societies and dance troupes. The student newspaper, *The Clarion*, is a popular involvement, and the Alpine Club is known for organizing frequent outdoor excursions.

> **"Those who don't ski can feel a little excluded."**

The student body at DU is "not extremely diverse," and one student commented that with regards to breaking the stereotype that it's a school of rich kids, "They try but it's pretty white, fairly preppy, not a lot of punks." The 20 percent of the student body of minority background does not fail to make an impression on campus, however, forming a strong community within a community through ethnic clubs and organizations.

One student remarked that arts opportunities have not been at the forefront at DU, but that with the recent completion of the Newman Center for the Performing Arts, which includes a larger theater space, students no longer "need to be in the know to hear about the arts."

Winter Sports Rule

Skiing is a huge campus pastime and "Those who don't ski can feel a little excluded," as many students hit the slopes every weekend throughout the winter. Aside from skiing, DU offers many athletic choices to the sports-minded. Club sports are popular. They do not make any cuts and are "a lot of fun" for all involved. DU also fosters strong varsity sports teams, the most popular of which is its successful hockey team, followed by the lacrosse, soccer and swim teams. There is generally "good turnout" to games, though hockey is unquestionably king. Division I hockey games take the place of football games, as DU has no football team, and the annual game against rival Colorado College is "not to be missed."

Traditions such as the enthusiasm for the hockey team unify DU as it continues to establish itself as a rising academic institution. Students are as relaxed and ready to take advantage of its opportunities to hit the slopes and fraternity row as they are to hit the books.—*Charlotte Taft*

FYI
If you come to the University of Denver, you'd better bring "a fake ID."
What is the typical weekend schedule? "Rest up, go out, squeeze in the homework."
If I could change one thing about DU, "I'd change the rules about social activities: make them less anal about breaking up house parties."
Three things that every student should do before graduating from the University of Denver are "travel around the area because Colorado is beautiful, realize what downtown has to offer, and go to the Colorado College-DU hockey game."

Connecticut

Connecticut College

Address: 270 Mohegan Avenue, New London, CT 06320
Phone: 860-439-2200
E-mail address: admission@conncoll.edu
Web site URL: www.conncoll.edu
Year Founded: 1911
Private or Public: Private
Religious Affiliation: None
Location: Suburban
Number of Applicants: 4,316
Percent Accepted: 38%
Percent Accepted who enroll: 30%
Number Entering: 492
Number of Transfers Accepted each Year: 65
Middle 50% SAT range: M: 610–700, CR: 620–720, Wr: 670–720
Middle 50% ACT range: 25–29
Early admission program EA/ED/None: ED

Percentage accepted through EA or ED: Unreported
EA and ED deadline: 15-Nov
Regular Deadline: 1-Jan
Application Fee: $60
Full time Undergraduate enrollment: 1,996
Total enrollment: 2,026
Percent Male: 40%
Percent Female: 60%
Total Percent Minority or Unreported: 27%
Percent African-American: 4%
Percent Asian/Pacific Islander: 4%
Percent Hispanic: 5%
Percent Native-American: 1%
Percent International: 6%
Percent in-state/out of state: 27%/73%
Percent from Public HS: 55%
Retention Rate: 91%
Graduation Rate 4-year: 82%

Graduation Rate 6-year: 86%
Percent Undergraduates in On-campus housing: 99%
Number of official organized extracurricular organizations: 60
3 Most popular majors: English, Political Science, Psychology
Student/Faculty ratio: 10:1
Average Class Size: 15
Percent of students going to grad school: Unreported
Tuition and Fees: $46,675 comprehensive fee
In-State Tuition and Fees if different: No difference
Cost for Room and Board: Included
Percent receiving financial aid out of those who apply, first year: 77%
Percent receiving financial aid among all students: 41%

C onnecticut College is a liberal arts institution in southeastern Connecticut, overlooking the Thames River and just minutes from the Long Island Sound. With its manageable size and small student body, ConnColl has a cozy and cohesive feel. The school's honor code is an important tradition and source of pride for students, and its effects can be seen in many different aspects of college life.

Academics and Administration
With a student to teacher ratio of just 10:1, the teachers are generally very accessible, and classes are small and intimate learning environments. "One thing I really liked was the advising I received as a freshman," said one sophomore. "If you make the effort to approach them, teachers can really learn a

lot about you as a student and make your transition into college that much easier." Students must fulfill general education requirements spanning seven different core areas, but few find these to be limiting. In addition, all incoming students choose from a selection of freshman seminars, giving them an opportunity to experience some of the best available courses in their first year.

The honor code allows students unique levels of comfort with their studies not found at other institutions, in particular when it comes to final exams, which are self-scheduled and not proctored.

Perhaps the most impressive college program is CELS (Career Enhancing Life Skills) through which students complete workshops to receive funding for internships. This is an incredible opportunity for students at a "small school," especially for those who would for financial reasons be less inclined to take unpaid internships in fields they enjoy. One veteran of CELS went so far as calling it "the best-run office on campus. Most who do it say it is the best thing that ever happened to them."

A point of particular interest at ConnColl is campus celebrity Leo Higdon, the College President who took office following the 2005–2006 school year. Young, energetic and student-friendly, the president can often be seen walking around campus and asking students for their input on various campus issues. Not the tallest head administrator around, he has earned such nicknames as "Big Hig" and "Higgie Smalls," according to one student who proudly claims to have a T-shirt with his face on it.

Campus

Students at ConnColl are "a pretty homogenous group of preppy white kids, most of whom are from 'right outside Boston,'" according to one interviewee. "We're not all totally preppy, though. We've got our fair share of hippies and artsy fartsy kids," said another. The student body is small enough that most faces are familiar by sophomore year, giving the campus a tight, family feeling. This unity is reinforced by campus-wide events such as "Camelympics," an inter-dorm competition organized by students that happens every fall and lasts for 48 fun-filled hours. Events range from midnight volleyball games to scavenger hunts to Scrabble.

> "My experience has been that, once you find something you like to do, the College opens up a world of opportunities."

Extracurricular activities are widely available as there are numerous clubs, organizations, volunteering opportunities, and sports teams at the varsity, club, and intramural level. Nearly all campus groups are run by students, allowing a deep level of involvement. According to one student, "My experience has been that, once you find something you like to do, the College opens up a world of opportunities."

The campus is actually comprised of several hundred acres, although "for the part you walk around on a day-to-day basis, it would take you only 10 minutes to go from the tip of south to the tip of north," said one

junior. The rest of campus is an arboretum managed by the College. Another unusual feature of the campus is that soccer and lacrosse games are played on a field situated in the middle of a cluster of dorms known as south campus, making them very convenient locations for socializing.

Some students complain about a lack of variety in the dining halls, particularly when it comes to healthy options, but the dining services work hard to take student feedback into account when preparing their menus. The meal plan is included in the comprehensive tuition, room and board fee, and is unlimited. Students can eat as much as they want and enter any dining hall on campus as many times as they want. Despite this apparent flexibility, some feel that the availability of food is too restricted due to hour constraints and the fact that only one dining hall is open on the weekends.

Housing

The campus is unofficially divided into three areas: north, central and south. South has older dorms and is loud, whereas north is newer and quieter. Central campus is less defined, but conveniently located. There is no Greek life at ConnColl, but south campus picks up the slack as far as parties are concerned. Said one admittedly biased south campus stalwart: "North has A/C and nicer rooms, but it's boring and more anti-social . . . south is way more fun."

There are no RAs at ConnColl, in keeping with the honor code and the amount of trust the administration puts in the students to behave appropriately. Instead, there is one "house fellow" in charge of each dorm, as well as SAs (student advisors) who are generally sophomores and who do not serve a disciplinary function, but rather help ease the transition into college life for freshmen.

"I know zero people who live off campus," said one sophomore. There are options for off-campus housing, but 99% of students choose to stay in the dorms, which helps draw the various years together and create a stronger feeling of campus unity. While first-year rooms are typically "nothing to write home about," the housing provided for upperclassmen is a big incentive for staying on campus. Juniors and seniors are guaranteed comfortably sized singles if they want them and many sophomores can get them as well.

New London

According to one sophomore, "It's very important to have a car or a good friend who does, although parking sucks for freshmen, and campus safety loves to ticket." The College does, however, have a free bus service that brings students from campus to downtown New London. In addition, the College sponsors monthly trips to New York City for various events, and many students take advantage of these opportunities.

The city itself receives mixed reviews from interviewed students. "Like any city, it has its bad areas; it also has beautiful areas. There are some great restaurants and also good beaches only 15 minutes away by car," said one student. Shopping opportunities are limited, but there are a Target and a Walmart close by for essentials. The average student leaves campus at least once a week to eat out.

Weekend

The weekend scene at ConnColl is quite lively, especially considering the lack of a Greek scene or a true urban downtown close by. Very few students have class on Fridays, so ConnColl weekends start Thursday afternoon. Drinking is definitely the focus of most students' weekends, and there are often keg parties in the south campus dorms. Any keg on campus must be signed for by two students who have taken a one-day class called Keg 101. One sophomore resident of south campus described the

weekends as "loud. South campus is loud on Saturday because of soccer games, but the night life is just as loud."

Enforcement of drinking laws is not strict, in keeping with the honor code, and Campus Safety is generally lenient with drinking; its first responsibility is making sure students are safe, not getting them into trouble. The lack of a Greek system tends to make for a much more inclusive weekend scene at ConnColl. "I love that. I feel like everyone is equal as far as social life is concerned," one student said.

Aside from drinking, the administration makes a great effort to provide alternative activities on the weekends. FNL (Friday Nights Live) is a weekly concert on campus. In addition there are weekly Thursday Night Events, ranging from dances to comedians to movie nights to tie-dye. These events are typically more popular among freshmen, and one older student described them as "kind of lame, and definitely repetitive after a year or two." New London itself does not provide many nightlife alternatives in terms of cultural enrichment, a cause of complaint for non-drinkers.

Coming to Connecticut College, one will find a quaint, beautiful campus filled with prepsters who know how to have a good time, as well as one of the better liberal arts curricula available.—*David Allen*

FYI
If you come to Connecticut College, you'd better bring "a car, the latest copy of the J. Crew catalog and a Red Sox hat or something else related to Boston."
What is the typical weekend schedule? "Thursdays are parties, Fridays are pretty chill, and Saturdays are parties with lots of kegs in south campus."
If I could change one thing about Connecticut College, I'd "change the 'average' Conn student so it's not hard to fit in if you aren't decked out in Vineyard Vines. Oh, and also I'd get rid of the coed bathrooms. Those freak me out sometimes."
Three things every student at Connecticut College should do before graduating are "participate in Camelympics, live in south campus and ring the gong."

Fairfield University

Address: 1073 N. Benson Rd
Fairfield, CT 06824
Phone: 203-254-4100
E-mail address:
admis@mail.fairfield.edu
Web site URL:
www.fairfield.edu
Year Founded: 1942
Private or Public: Private
Religious Affiliation: Roman
Catholic-Jesuit
Location: Suburban
Number of Applicants: 8,732
Percent Accepted: 59%
**Percent Accepted who
enroll:** 17%
Number Entering: 927
**Number of Transfers
Accepted each Year:** 75
Middle 50% SAT range: M:
540–630, CR: 520–610,
Wr: 540–630
Middle 50% ACT range: 23–27
**Early admission program
EA/ED/None:** EA

**Percentage accepted
through EA or ED:** 58%
EA and ED deadline: 15-Nov
Regular Deadline: 15-Jan
Application Fee: $60
**Full time Undergraduate
enrollment:** 3,469
Total enrollment: 5,128
Percent Male: 42%
Percent Female: 58%
**Total Percent Minority or
Unreported:** 15%
Percent African-American:
3%
**Percent Asian/Pacific
Islander:** 3%
Percent Hispanic: 8%
Percent Native-American:
<1%
Percent International:
Unreported
**Percent in-state/out of
state:** 23%/77%
Percent from Public HS: 55%
Retention Rate: 90%

Graduation Rate 4-year: 74%
Graduation Rate 6-year: 77%
**Percent Undergraduates in
On-campus housing:** 85%
**Number of official organized
extracurricular
organizations:** 100
3 Most popular majors:
Finance, Marketing,
Psychology
Student/Faculty ratio: 13:1
Average Class Size: 24
**Percent of students going to
grad school:** 20%
Tuition and Fees: $36,075
**In-State Tuition and Fees if
different:** No difference
Cost for Room and Board:
$10,850
**Percent receiving financial
aid out of those who apply,
first year:** 70%
**Percent receiving financial
aid among all students:**
48%

Also known as "J Crew University" due to its almost homogenous "preppy" population, Fairfield University is a college in Connecticut characterized by strong academics, a vibrant social scene and a myriad of extracurricular activities. The campus is warm, pretty and inviting. It is also free from the gothic architecture that characterizes some of New England schools and most students find its suburban setting "convenient."

Education for the Mind, Body and Spirit

Fairfield University's Jesuit approach to education sets it apart from other tertiary institutions in that it provides to those enrolled therein, a holistic college experience that seeks to educate the mind, body and spirit. At undergraduate level, students choose amongst courses offered by the College of Arts and Sciences, School of Business, School of Nursing, School of Engineering and the College of Continuing Studies. Hence, in addition to a liberal arts education, Fairfield students are provided with a platform on

which they can explore their career options and apply in-class education to prospective career pathways.

Furthermore, for academically motivated freshmen and sophomores, there is the option of being a part of the prestigious Honors program. This is a program into which only fifty freshmen are admitted each year. Amongst many other things, it seeks to nurture an ability to question and analyze information as well as to stimulate an insatiable quest for knowledge of Western traditions, heritage, history and culture. Those who have had the privilege of being a part of this program describe it as "culturally enriching" and "insightful."

Fairfield University students never talk about academics without mentioning the enormous amount of support that they receive from faculty members. The small class ratio of 13:1 gives professors enough proximity to identify the academic strengths and weaknesses of their students and to build upon or help mitigate them. The library staff is also famous for its enthusiasm to help; and in addition, there exists a myriad of tutoring programs and special support groups such as the Women in Mathematics, Science, Technology, and Engineering that provides academic assistance to women in science. As a female prospective Chemistry major put it, "I chose Fairfield University because it has a high med-school acceptance rate and there is just the right amount of support for me to excel in my major."

Situated Exactly Where I Want It

"Fairfield is close to everywhere!" one student pointed out excitedly. Fairfield University is an hour from New York, ten minutes from the beach, and five minutes from both the Fairfield train station and the Fairfield public library. In addition, Fairfield is close to Stamford where one can go deal hunting at the mall and is served by numerous restaurants. Some students find this setting particularly advantageous as it allows them easy access to internships and volunteer opportunities in local hospitals, businesses and in organizations where they can gain invaluable work experience.

Fairfield University's generous financial aid package is particularly attractive as it can provide up to full funding throughout the four years of college. Despite the flailing economy (or maybe because of it), Fairfield University increased its financial aid package by 13%. For many students, this was the major factor that they considered when they chose to matriculate at Fairfield.

Diversity, Religious and Otherwise

Fairfield University is a very inclusive place where anyone can easily fit in. "You can be as religious as you want to be, if you want to be religious at all." For the devout, the school goes out of its way to incorporate all religions. In December, the time of Kwanzaa, Hanukah and Christmas, the school runs activities that encourage the inclusion of everyone, such as competitions in which students are required to decorate their rooms according to the three holidays.

However, Fairfield University still has a long way to go in addressing ethnic diversity on its campus. "If I could change anything about Fairfield, I would definitely make it more diverse," one student lamented. Fairfield is a predominantly preppy college (hence the nickname J Crew University) and a vast majority of its student population is white and comes from the rich New England suburbs.

Life in General

Undergraduates have the option of living in eight of the residence halls, in townhouses or in beach houses. Each residence hall has an easily accessible kitchen where one can cook up a storm or just make a cup of tea. For many students, this is a plus as it provides a break from the monotony of the food that is offered at the dining hall.

The townhouses and beach houses are generally occupied by upperclassmen and are famous for huge gigs and parties. While many sophomores and freshmen can host parties in their dorm rooms, most of the big parties are held in the townhouses or the beach houses. There is always something going on every night and drinking and hookups are predominant. However, recent developments and conflicts between non-University beach house inhabitants and Fairfield University beach house inhabitants have led to stricter police supervision of the beach area and speculation over whether or not Fairfield University will still hold its position as one of the Top Party Schools on the Princeton Review list.

During the day, Fairfield students engage themselves in the numerous extracurricular activities that the school has to offer. These include musical groups such as the jazz ensemble and the glee club, ethnic societies, writing publications and political organizations. "You can even form your own organization too!"

> "Fairfield has just the right amount of support for me to excel in my major."

Fairfield is not very dominant on the sports scene and does not have a varsity football team. However, it has a strong men's basketball team that is known and revered throughout the state.

If you are looking for a place to explore spirituality while challenging yourself academically, Fairfield is definitely worth considering. The upbeat social tempo encourages interaction among students and its curriculum has produced graduates who are well equipped both socially and intellectually to enter the world.—*Senzeni Mpofu*

Quinnipiac University

Address: 275 Mount Carmel Avenue, Hamden, CT 06518
Phone: 203-582-8600
E-mail address: admissions@quinnipiac.edu
Web site URL: www.quinnipiac.edu
Year Founded: 1929
Private or Public: Private
Religious Affiliation: None
Location: Suburban
Number of Applicants: 14,994
Percent Accepted: 45%
Percent Accepted who enroll: 22%
Number Entering: 1,484
Number of Transfers Accepted each Year: 540
Middle 50% SAT range: M: 560–630, CR: 540–610, Wr: Unreported
Middle 50% ACT range: 23–27
Early admission program EA/ED/None: None

Percentage accepted through EA or ED: NA
EA and ED deadline: NA
Regular Deadline: Rolling
Application Fee: $45
Full time Undergraduate enrollment: 5,870
Total enrollment: 7,036
Percent Male: 40%
Percent Female: 60%
Total Percent Minority or Unreported: 12%
Percent African-American: 3%
Percent Asian/Pacific Islander: 2%
Percent Hispanic: 5%
Percent Native-American: <1%
Percent International: 1%
Percent in-state/out of state: 30%/70%
Percent from Public HS: 70%
Retention Rate: 90%
Graduation Rate 4-year: 69%

Graduation Rate 6-year: 73%
Percent Undergraduates in On-campus housing: 75%
Number of official organized extracurricular organizations: 78
3 Most popular majors: Business, General Physical Therapy, Psychology
Student/Faculty ratio: 12:1
Average Class Size: 16
Percent of students going to grad school: 37%
Tuition and Fees: $31,100
In-State Tuition and Fees if different: No difference
Cost for Room and Board: $12,520
Percent receiving financial aid out of those who apply, first year: 70%
Percent receiving financial aid among all students: 68%

At only 2 hours from Boston, 90 minutes from New York, and 10 minutes from New Haven, Quinnipiac University in Hamden, CT, is perfectly situated to let its students experience both the excitement of urban nightlife and the comfort of the suburban day. And students don't miss out on either experience—every student interviewed said that a "must-do" for any QU student is a nighttime visit to New Haven. Yet despite their frequent trips to the city, QU students claim that there is little lacking on their 212-acre campus.

This Is Who We Are

Students at Quinnipiac hail largely from Connecticut and the surrounding areas (according to statistics put out by the university, of this year's enrolling freshmen, 1,371 came from Connecticut, Massachusetts, New York, or New Jersey). But QU isn't a commuter school by any means; though one member of the class of 2012 worried that people would go home on the weekends, she claims that she soon discovered that the opposite is true. Another sophomore explains that "I don't feel like I live 30 minutes away; QU is its own world."

Learning New and Old

For students interested in following a liberal arts curriculum that leads down a less-than-traditional path, QU may be the way to go. Quinnipiac requires all its students to take an intensive core curriculum consisting of 46 credits, including three "University Seminars": "The Individual and the Community," "National Community," and "Global Community."

The reward for completing this rigorous course of study lies in the chance to graduate with a degree in one of 52 diverse majors, ranging from the typical English and Economics degrees to the far less common Diagnostic Imaging and Interactive Digital Design degrees.

Yet students at QU are more interested in their classes than their degrees. Most students claim that professors are dedicated to their students, and that class sizes are small. One public relations major explained that, coming from a small high school, she was concerned about not getting the attention she needed but found that "not only do I have great relationships with my professors, but what's great is that many of them are still working in their field." With a student-to-faculty ratio of 16:1, classes are rarely bigger than 25 students. Even the marketing major who disliked the campus, the food, and the social life praised QU's professors.

One of the most exciting parts of a QU curriculum is its study abroad program. One senior estimates that over 80% of QU students study abroad at some point during their four years. One junior, who is currently studying abroad, praises the program, explaining that it costs no extra money beyond typical Quinnipiac tuition. Though students claim that it is easy to get into a study abroad program, they say that the easiest route to an approved program is to attend QU's sister school in Ireland.

Room and Board

Students at QU are guaranteed three years of housing, and many move off-campus during their junior year to live in apartments in surrounding towns. Housing consists of a mixture of dorms and suites, with, best of all, free wireless. "The dorms are all well maintained; they have a lot of new buildings and they are enjoyable to live in," says one sophomore marketing major. "And wireless internet is good to have."

Students also enthusiastically talk about the beauty of the campus and its closeness to Sleeping Giant Park, a state park with over 30 miles of hiking trails. "Campus is absolutely beautiful, especially in the fall with all of the foliage and the mountains," says one freshman. Students enjoy the compact size of the campus, although some lament

that upperclassman housing is not located on Main Campus and that shuttles are therefore used to get to class. Overall though, most students agree that "the campus is absolutely BEAUTIFUL."

> "Campus is absolutely beautiful, especially in the fall with all of the foliage and the mountains."

By contrast, there is distinct lack of enthusiasm for the food. Though one student admits that the grilled cheese is pretty good, this is not exactly a screaming compliment for a campus where one student claims "they give us no money for food, and the quality is awful." QU students are served on an "a la carte" basis, paying per food item, and many students admit that the amount of food on the meal plan is not enough for a hungry student to get by. At least not if that student doesn't want to be hungry anymore.

It's (Not) All Here

For many QU students, Thursday and Saturday nights are spent in New Haven. Though the university attempts to make this commute easier, by offering a shuttle to the nearby city, students complain that the service takes far longer than it should. "It's only twenty minutes away," says one sophomore, "but because it stops in so many different places it takes an hour to get there." A junior majoring in Psychology adds, though, that she thinks the shuttle system is important because it keeps students from drinking and driving.

On-campus weekend life is a mixture of school-hosted events, clubs and sports, and parties. "Drinking laws are enforced more than they should be for a university," says a sophomore marketing major. "Security abandons their role of protecting students and decides to police them instead." But not all students are unhappy with the school's policies; one student explains that, even though there is a lot of drinking on campus, no one gets in serious trouble for alcohol violations unless they are causing disruptions. And despite the prevalence of drinking on the QU campus, students claim that you don't need to drink to have fun. "There is a lot of drinking," says one student, "but you don't have to drink to have fun, because there are so many other things to do."

As far as clubs and organizations go, Greek life has been growing, says one member of the class of 2011, though there are only four sororities and three frats on campus and no Greek houses. Students not interested in Greek life can find their niche in any one of the over 70 organizations that QU offers, ranging from "anime club to Irish club," according to one sophomore. Students are also encouraged by the University to form their own clubs if they find that already existing ones don't meet their needs.

The University and its RAs host a number of events every month. One sophomore in the public relations major praises the school for making it so easy to have fun and make friends: "I'm really shy," she explains, "but

they had a lot of great programs to help us make friends, and I did the first day. The RAs are also great, and definitely helped make the transition easier."

Finally, sports make up a major part of life at Quinnipiac. With 19 NCAA Division-1 sports teams, Quinnipiac is a school loaded with athletic pride, especially when it comes to hockey. "Since we're a D1 school," says one student, "sports are pretty big, even though you don't get people going to much else other than hockey. Hockey is really big here." Students at hockey games often proudly sport QU gear, creating a sea of "Boomer the Bobcat" sweatshirts.—*Heather Robinson*

FYI

If you come to Quinnipiac, you'd better bring: "LOTS OF MONEY FOR NEW HAVEN! You better bring a lot of Easy Mac also—our café sucks so you need to make sure you have food in the dorms to keep yourself alive."

What's the typical weekend schedule? "People go out hard (to New Haven) on Thursdays, and usually Saturdays. Friday nights are more house parties or dorm parties."

If I could change one thing about Quinnipiac, I'd: "change how big the school is. They let more and more freshmen in each year, and we are going to change from being a 'medium' size school to 'large' pretty quickly."

Three things to do before you graduate: "Go to Toads, attend a Yale vs. Quinnipiac Hockey game, and climb Sleeping Giant State Park Mountain."

Sacred Heart University

Address: 5151 Park Avenue, Fairfield, CT 06825-1000
Phone: 203-371-7880
E-mail address: enroll@sacredheart.edu
Web site URL: www.sacredheart.edu
Year Founded: 1963
Private or Public: Private
Religious Affiliation: Catholic
Location: Suburban
Number of Applicants: 7,568
Percent Accepted: 65%
Percent Accepted who enroll: 20%
Number Entering: 980
Number of Transfers Accepted each Year: 328
Middle 50% SAT range: M: 490–580, CR:460–570, Wr: Unreported
Middle 50% ACT range: Unreported
Early admission program EA/ED/None: ED

Percentage accepted through EA or ED: Unreported
EA and ED deadline: 1-Dec
Regular Deadline: Rolling
Application Fee: $50
Full time Undergraduate enrollment: 4,274
Total enrollment: 6,023
Percent Male: 39%
Percent Female: 61%
Total Percent Minority or Unreported: 10%
Percent African-American: 4%
Percent Asian/Pacific Islander: 2%
Percent Hispanic: 6%
Percent Native-American: 0%
Percent International: 1%
Percent in-state/out of state: 29%/71%
Percent from Public HS: Unreported
Retention Rate: 81%
Graduation Rate 4-year: 62%

Graduation Rate 6-year: Unreported
Percent Undergraduates in On-campus housing: 70%
Number of official organized extracurricular organizations: Unreported
3 Most popular majors: Business, Psychology, Health Professions
Student/Faculty ratio: 12:1
Average Class Size: 21
Percent of students going to grad school: Unreported
Tuition and Fees: $28,790
In-State Tuition and Fees if different: No difference
Cost for Room and Board: $11,330
Percent receiving financial aid out of those who apply, first year: 58%
Percent receiving financial aid among all students: 79%

Sacred Heart University is one of the country's largest Catholic universities, second only to Boston College. Located in suburban Fairfield, Connecticut, the school has a student body numbering about 6,000 with degrees offered in 40 programs of study. This university offers a breadth of study combined with a distinctive Catholic tradition of education. With new majors and programs being continually developed and added, the curriculum at Sacred Heart offers challenging and diverse academics for students. The university campus situated on 67 beautiful acres in the town of Fairfield is in the shadow of big metropolitan areas such as New York and Boston while still maintaining a distinctive suburban atmosphere.

Contemporary Education, Catholic Tradition

Sacred Heart offers a good selection of majors from which to choose while emphasizing a lot on the vocational pathways of its students. Well-known programs include the combined Physical Therapy and Occupational Therapy programs where students are able to obtain their bachelor's and professional degrees in less time than usual. Other health professions such as the undergraduate program in nursing and the pre-professional tracks are very popular among students. The College of Health Professions is distinguished with having the best physical therapy program in Connecticut and one of the top five in New England. Students at Sacred Heart can study anything from business economics to religious studies with numerous opportunities to obtain an accelerated master's degree in five years instead of the standard six. "There are a lot of options," says a sophomore. The honors program at Sacred Heart University allows exceptionally prepared students to challenge themselves further with more student-oriented small lectures and presentations as well as more access to resources and academic and social advising. Students in the honors program are required to take more courses and more rigorous courses in addition to standard requirements that culminate in an Honors Portfolio or research presentation in the annual Honors conference.

Students in all programs complete the required core curriculum to be eligible for the bachelor's degree. The core is broken down into three areas of concentration: foundational, common, and elective. The foundational core is fulfilled by classes in the humanities, arts, social science, natural science, religion, and philosophy. This is aimed at developing more socially minded students in a global world. The common core, focusing on The Human Journey, is distinct in a Sacred Heart education that sharpens ethical thinking and moral decision making. "It makes you not only a better student, but a better person," remarks a senior. This part of the core curriculum is grounded in the Catholic traditions of the University with classes including The Human Journey, Literary Expression of the Human Journey, The Human Community, and The Human Community and Science Discovery. This portion of the core is capped off with The Search for Human Truth, Justice, and Common Good. The final portion of the core is completed with elective courses in a chosen major.

> **"[Sacred Heart] makes you not only a better student, but a better person."**

With new programs being added every day, Sacred Heart aims to keep students' educations relevant in the real world. The University itself is split into the College of Arts and Science, John F. Welch College of Business, College of Education and Health Professions, and University College as the four constituent undergraduate schools. University College, owing to the University's aim to maintain relevance, is a unique school catering to adult learner and non-traditional students with evening, weekend, and accelerated classes. Whatever your goal, Sacred Heart has a program that will cater to it.

Campus Life

Life at Sacred Heart is typical of many suburban universities; lush green turf and lots of open space. The main campus itself is located in Fairfield, CT, with satellite campuses in cities around the state including Trumbull, Stamford, and Griswold. The University also maintains international campuses in Luxembourg and Ireland. The majority of students here hail from the New England area with New York, New Jersey, Connecticut, and Massachusetts as the top feeder states.

One thing that many students seem to notice is the lack of diversity on campus. The student body is overwhelmingly white at

85% of the total population. "It seems like everyone here comes from the same background with the same experiences," recounts a freshman. The lack of diversity may be offset by the plethora of activities available to students on campus and in the surrounding area. Making friends and finding one's niche at Sacred Heart seems to be less of a problem as many people are friendly and welcoming. "People seem to be nice here," says a freshman. The lack of diversity does not mean social isolation. From day one, entering freshman have access to special services in adjusting to college life. Additionally, every freshman is provided with a laptop computer as part of Sacred Heart's mission to incorporate technology into the classroom.

Residential life has evolved greatly since the school's founding in 1963 as a mainly commuter school. With the inception of residential life and on-campus living in 1991, over 70% of the undergraduate population now live on campus. Freshmen are housed mainly in Seton, Merton, and Roncalli Halls while sophomores are almost exclusively in the Commons. Rooms are generally very nice since most buildings are fairly new, being less than 20 years old. Upperclassmen may also choose to live in off-campus university-owned housing in apartment and townhouse style arrangements. Most resident halls are within close proximity to class buildings and other on-campus amenities with the exception of some off-campus housing. The one University dining hall on campus is not operated by the actual University but a secondary food-service provider. "The food is so-so," says a sophomore. "You definitely need to pick and choose," cautions another student. With residential life relatively new to the university's history, it's to be expected that some services are not as developed as at other older, more-established universities.

The Spectrum

Social life on campus revolves around the University focus on service and learning. Each year over 1,200 students and faculty log in over 30,000 hours of community service on campus and surrounding areas. The Sacred Heart chapter of Habitat for Human-

ity, for example, has gained recognition as one of the top 10 chapters in the nation for their work. However, community service is not the only way students get involved around campus. Athletics offer another way for everyone, not just athletes, to get involved. The Pioneers compete with 31 Division I teams and 800 athletes but the school also has a thriving club sports scene with over 500 students participating in 23 club sports each year. In addition, there are over 85 clubs and organizations to keep students occupied. Anything from the American Chemical Society chapter of Sacred Heart to cheerleading to ministry clubs can be found on campus. "There's something for everybody here," reminisces a freshman.

The social life doesn't stop there though. Greek life is notable on campus with sororities outnumbering fraternities 2 to 1. The six sororities and three fraternities provide campus with the typical frat party scene seen on most college campuses. Greek life doesn't dominate the scene here, but their presence can be felt. The fraternity and sorority life here is not as widespread because it doesn't need to be. Students have easy access to one of the busiest and exciting cities in the world: New York City. Less than an hour away by train, students at Sacred Heart can inexpensively frolic in the Big Apple, and many do. Boston, the other big metropolitan area, is about 150 miles away and accessible by bus.

Pioneer Life

All in all, Sacred Heart students come here because they want a traditional Catholic education that can maintain relevance in today's ever changing world. Classes prepare students not only for a vocation through their professional studies, but also to be lifelong learners and thinkers. Academics are fairly rigid with multiple core curriculums but that's the exact reason why some students choose Sacred Heart: for the core. Social life is not limited but rather is centered around the school's Catholic traditions. The school offers a unique educational experience that will delight those looking for a traditional education with Catholic traditions in a modern-day suburban university.—*Hai Pham*

FYI
If you come to Sacred Heart, you should bring: "a car. It will make everything so much easier."
What would you change about Sacred Heart? "More diversity and more dining options."
What should every Sacred Heart student do before they graduate? "Join a community service club, visit NYC, and sit out on the lawn."

Trinity College

Address: 300 Summit Street
Hartford, CT 06016
Phone: 860-297-2180
E-mail address:
admissions.office@trincoll.
edu
Web site URL:
www.trincoll.edu
Year Founded: 1823
Private or Public: Private
Religious Affiliation: None
Location: Urban
Number of Applicants:
5,950
Percent Accepted: 34%
**Percent Accepted who
enroll:** 28%
Number Entering: 576
**Number of Transfers
Accepted each Year:** 24
Middle 50% SAT range:
M: 620–710, CR:
620–710, Wr: 630–720
Middle 50% ACT range:
27–31
**Early admission program
EA/ED/None:** ED

**Percentage accepted
through EA or ED:** 68%
EA and ED deadline: 15-Nov
Regular Deadline: 1-Jan
Application Fee: $60
**Full time Undergraduate
enrollment:** 2,388
Total enrollment: 2,566
Percent Male: 50%
Percent Female: 50%
**Total Percent Minority or
Unreported:** 38%
Percent African-American:
7%
**Percent Asian/Pacific
Islander:** 6%
Percent Hispanic: 6%
Percent Native-American:
<1%
Percent International: 4%
**Percent in-state/out of
state:** 17%/83%
Percent from Public HS:
47%
Retention Rate: 91%
Graduation Rate 4-year:
81%

Graduation Rate 6-year:
85%
**Percent Undergraduates in
On-campus housing:** 95%
**Number of official organized
extracurricular
organizations:** 105
3 Most popular majors:
Economics, English
Language and Literature,
Political Science and
Government
Student/Faculty ratio: 10:1
Average Class Size: 16
**Percent of students going to
grad school:** 19%
Tuition and Fees: $38,733
**In-State Tuition and Fees if
different:** No difference
Cost for Room and Board:
$9,900
**Percent receiving financial
aid out of those who apply,
first year:** Unreported
**Percent receiving financial
aid among all students:**
39%

E ven though Trinity College was founded in 1823 and boasts some of the earliest examples of Gothic architecture in America, this college is not afraid of innovation. With a fresh curriculum and a large handful of renovated buildings, Trinity students enjoy constant improvements in both facilities and academics. Located in Hartford, Connecticut's capital, Trinity offers a small community feeling in an urban setting, where friendliness is a common attribute. As one sophomore said, "I was surprised in a good way, because it is so easy to fit in; you can always find a group of friends."

Small Class Conundrum

Trinity offers a wide range of classes and attracts students with a variety of interests. Though Trinity is one of the best liberal arts schools in the country, students are not deterred from pursuing science majors. Students must fulfill their distribution requirements by taking classes from five general areas: humanities, the arts, natural sciences, social sciences, and numerical and symbolic reasoning. Within each area, students are free to choose whichever classes interest them. As one sophomore declared, "I took an environmental studies course for a requirement, which I never would have chosen myself, and ended up loving it!" Students find that the requirements improve their academic experience and give just enough freedom for finding classes.

Part of Trinity's close-knit community feeling stems from the seminar classes each freshman is required to take. First-years take a seminar and live with the same group of students, fostering strong relationships and forming a comfortable environment from the very beginning of their Trinity experience. One junior commented, "these seminars are not traditional classes; they focus on unique topics and have a budget to plan activities like going to the Bushnell Theater for a show or eating out at a local restaurant." Trinity can be characterized by this focus on small classes and close student-faculty relationships.

Among the popular majors on campus are history, economics and political science, which offer more classes than smaller majors such as classics or computer science. Trinity also started a new Human Rights Program and has unique classes under such disciplines as Women, Gender, and Sexuality and Community Action. Though students are pleased with the range of courses, they comment that competition for entry into the most popular classes such as philosophy of sports or fitness classes severely limits their availability, especially to underclassmen. A current freshman moaned, "There is a lot of competition to get into classes. Most people settle for classes in their major that they need to take; only a few get to take the ones they really want."

> "Professors will even give you their cell phone number. They are willing and eager to help you with anything."

Regardless of the classes' popularity, students universally agree that the small-class environment has made for a wonderful academic experience. Students regularly eat dinner with their professors and one claimed that "Professors will even give you their cell phone number. They are willing and eager to help you with anything." Yes, the academic experience fulfills students' expectations of rigor, but students say that is just "part of what they do here; there is still plenty of time to socialize." Though some students strive to make the dean's list, others find that academics are not a dominant part of life. Professors are fair with grading, and as a savvy junior remarked, "School is just about as hard as you make it."

Community of Bantams
After freshmen year, when the students all live together in a quad, they have the ability to choose their roommates and even request themed housing. Housing for upperclassmen is integrated with a variety of buildings, including the coveted Praxis dorm. A sophomore insisted that "Dorms get bigger after freshman year with a little more to choose from, like the option of having a living room."

The RA system provides yet another way for students to form relationships with figures of authority and guidance. Though RAs are responsible for students following dorm policies and act as mediators between students and the administration, students praise the system and are happy about the bond forged between them and their RAs. "We have fantastic RAs. They are trusting and make sure you are safe, but are not an overbearing presence. They want to keep you out of trouble with authority." The college prohibits alcohol in rooms with underage students and restricts everyone from possessing hard alcohol, but students claim that the policies are not strictly enforced.

Among old Gothic architecture, a beautiful chapel, and a Victorian-style English Department building, Trinity students find new modern facilities that add even more to the college's character. Recently, students have been able to enjoy the addition of an entirely new dorm complex and a community hockey rink. When the weather is nice, students flock to the quad to socialize or play frisbee with their friends between classes and, when it's crunch time, students take advantage of quiet study spots such as Gallows Hill with comfy couches and free coffee.

The main dining hall, where most students eat on the weekdays, provides another place to meet students and socialize. There are two places available to eat other than the main dining hall, which serve a variety of sandwiches and burgers and fries. Students pay a fee, choosing from five levels, at the beginning of the year and budget from that set amount of money. The food receives neither great praise nor terrible complaints and is occasionally surpassed by those venturing to restaurants in West Hartford or looking for a cheap meal at Trinity, a local favorite.

Party If You Please
Trinity students agree that the social scene on campus revolves around Vernon Street, the home of the college's rowdy fraternities. A male freshman cautioned that "Some are hard to get into if you don't have girls, but you can always find a party on the weekend." The frats also host annual themed parties such as Tropical, a party ranked in *Playboy* magazine, where the students bring in sand, and Foam, where a frat house is filled with—believe it or not—foam. Some other favorite party spots include the football house or one of the cultural houses. Students usually party from Thursday through Saturday, and drinking remains a very prominent part of the campus social life.

If these parties aren't enticing enough to relieve students' weekday stresses, they may find themselves at one of the student-run coffeehouses or attending an event hosted by "The Fred." The Fred Pfeil Community Project is a group of students who host daily events such as comedians or arts shows as an alternative to drinking. Although Trinity is a small school and most of the social scene is integrated, most upperclassmen can be found in The Tap, while underclassmen search for local bars that don't card. Drinking may be a part of campus culture, but "not in the absence of other options," claimed a well-rounded sophomore.

One student rejoiced that "Though there are school policies regulating alcohol consumption, everyone drinks; it happens in everyone's room." Pot is also fairly common on campus, though the harder drugs are scarce. Luckily, regardless of students' preferences of how to have fun, all rave about the general friendliness and ease of finding their own comfort zone.

Change of Heart-Ford

Students disagree about the role the surrounding city of Hartford plays in their educational and social experience at Trinity. All students either own cars or have access to a friend's for shopping trips to the Westfarms Mall or food runs down the Berlin Turnpike. One junior warned, "I would never walk around campus at night alone" and that the surrounding area can either be "really nice or really sketchy." Others comment about living in the "Trinity bubble," where it's really easy to forget the city and only use campus resources.

The administration and student-run volunteer groups strive to close the gap between the college "bubble" and the Hartford community. An involved sophomore described taking a class called Child Development, where students design a public policy project: "We had to identify a problem relating to child development in Hartford, speak to community members, formulate a solution, and present proposals to the community that were later implemented." The school also offers classes on Hartford to further familiarize the students with the city and perhaps inspire them to invest time in promoting its growth.

Squashing Opponents

Step aside, football; the 11-time national championship squash team draws the largest crowd on this campus. Though both sports enjoy support from their dedicated fans, squash remains Trinity's true claim to fame. A spirited senior said that "Around campus you can sense the Trinity pride," which carries over into other extracurricular activities as well. Everyone is involved on this campus, whether a student competes as a varsity athlete, on the intramural fields, or just cheers on a friend.

In addition to sports, Trinity students participate in a variety of clubs, from the student newspaper, *The Tripod*, to student government, a wide range of volunteer groups, and even a cat alliance, which cares for cats roaming the campus. Do It Day, a campus-wide volunteer initiative, provides another outlet for students to get involved in the community by participating in activities such as painting a nursing home or planting flowers outside hospitals. There is an activity here for all interests, and as one sophomore explained, "People here are so over-involved, you hardly find anyone who only has one commitment."

Students at Trinity brag about their close relationships with amazing, compassionate professors, show their Bantam spirit through devotion to myriad activities, and save their best tropical attire to debut for weekend revelry. With so much to do, schedules are usually packed, but most students wouldn't have it any other way.—*Cara Dermody*

FYI
If you come to Trinity, you'd better bring "a pair of Uggs, a car, and a high squash IQ."
What is the typical weekend schedule? "Most spend the afternoon watching movies or playing sports, followed by pregaming for a long night at a frat or attending a concert with friends."
If I could change one thing about Trinity, "I'd bring back a dating scene."
Three things every student at Trinity should do before graduating are "Go to a squash game, volunteer in Hartford, and go to Tropical."

United States Coast Guard Academy

Address: 31 Mohegan Avenue
New London, CT
06320-8103
Phone: 860-444-8503
E-mail address:
admissions@uscga.edu
Web site URL: www.uscga.edu
Year Founded: 1876
Private or Public: Public
Religious Affiliation: None
Location: Suburban
Number of Applicants: 1,633
Percent Accepted: 24%
**Percent Accepted who
enroll:** 70%
Number Entering: 274
**Number of Transfers
Accepted each Year:**
Unreported
Middle 50% SAT range:
M: 600–680, CR:
570–665, Wr: Unreported
Middle 50% ACT range:
25–29
**Early admission program
EA/ED/None:** EA

**Percentage accepted
through EA or ED:** 29%
EA and ED deadline: 1-Nov
Regular Deadline: 1-Feb
Application Fee: $0
**Full time Undergraduate
enrollment:** 973
Total enrollment: 973
Percent Male: 72%
Percent Female: 28%
**Total Percent Minority or
Unreported:** 14%
Percent African-American:
3%
**Percent Asian/Pacific
Islander:** 5%
Percent Hispanic: 5%
Percent Native-American:
<1%
Percent International:
1%
**Percent in-state/out of
state:** 6%/94%
Percent from Public HS:
81%
Retention Rate: 86%

Graduation Rate 4-year:
59%
Graduation Rate 6-year:
62%
**Percent Undergraduates in
On-campus housing:** 100%
**Number of official organized
extracurricular
organizations:** Unreported
3 Most popular majors:
Engineering, Oceanography,
Political Science
Student/Faculty ratio: 9:1
Average Class Size: 15
**Percent of students going to
grad school:** Unreported
Tuition and Fees: $0
**In-State Tuition and Fees if
different:** No difference
Cost for Room and Board:
$0
**Percent receiving financial
aid out of those who apply,
first year:** NA
**Percent receiving financial
aid among all students:** NA

The United States Coast Guard Academy provides its students with the discipline and skills useful for all tracks of life, turning its cadets into the leaders of the future. With military employment following graduation and several opportunities for development while in the Academy, cadets receive much more than a four-year education. The USCGA holds firm to its rigorous academic curriculum, strong athletics programs, and varied extracurricular offerings. Each graduate leaves the Academy with a sense of accomplishment that inevitably leads to post-graduation success.

Core Values

The United States Coast Guard Academy boasts much more than a commanding name and intimidating reputation. Founded as the Revenue Cutter School of Instruction in 1876, the USCGA offers an impressive combination of tradition, rigor, and discipline that has shaped leaders of America for over a century. In fact, the leadership skills developed during the four years at USCGA are what many cadets refer to as the best aspect of the Academy. The USCGA's set of core values is threefold, emphasizing honor, respect and devotion to duty. These values form the foundation for all programs in the Academy. The lofty reputation of the Academy often intimidates potential students, discouraging them from applying to the undergraduate program. However, prospective candidates should be encouraged "to consider the broad range of opportunities that the Academy has to offer, and acknowledge the diverse student body that enjoys the benefits of the USCGA."

The USCGA draws a student body that is about 72 percent male and 28 percent female. All cadets receive equal treatment with respect to academics, housing, and athletic training. The promise of equal opportunities at the Academy is one of the most treasured aspects of the institution, as reported by many cadets. The USCGA provides an equal playing field whether a cadet is male or female, first-class or fourth-class. You might ask: What is the difference between a first-class and a fourth-class cadet? How can delineating classes exist within a system of fair play?

All freshmen at the Academy are called fourth-class cadets, and each year students climb one rung on the ladder. Each class has special roles and duties at the Academy; this reflects the hierarchical structure of military life and prepares cadets for post-graduation military employment. Fourth-class cadets can be compared to understudies, learning the ropes of military life and closely following examples of the more experienced. Third-class cadets are assigned to advise one or two fourth-class cadets, while second-class cadets assume the responsibility of Assistant Division Officers, leading the younger cadets during training. Finally, first-class cadets have the opportunity to become Regimental Staff Officers, Company Commanders, Department Heads, and Division Officers. This specific regimentation at the Academy prepares cadets for the structured system of military duty and creates a progressive path towards increased responsibility, learning, and opportunity. At the end of four years, first-class cadets have had the experience of being followers, mentors, assistant leaders, and commanders. Each of these roles provides a wide range of opportunities for growth and enrichment unique to the mission of the Academy.

The Typical Day

With such a close parallel to military structure and core values, it is hardly surprising that discipline plays a tremendous role in the lives of cadets at the USCGA. Although cadets' names and roles change from year to year, the typical weekday schedule "falls equally upon all cadets alike." The wake-up alarm sounds at "0600" and breakfast quickly follows. Academic instruction begins promptly at 0800 and ends at 1200 for lunch. Classes then resume after lunch and end for the day at 1600. The Academy's curriculum offers a Bachelor of Science degree for all students. Classes are often competitive, though many cadets enjoy the academic challenges laid before them. The classroom setting encourages cadets to think quickly, observe objectively, and analyze deeply. Most classes do not exceed 40 students, and this fosters close relationships between students and professors, as well as interactive learning. The Academy has set core requirements, which students often complete during their first two years.

The USCGA ensures the well-roundedness of its cadets, whether they are in the classroom or on the field. Sports period runs from 1600 to 1800, and the school encourages all of its cadets to pursue athletics. The majority of students play for a varsity team, though some cadets take sports less seriously and wish there was less emphasis on it at the Academy. In addition to intramural and varsity sports, a cadet may choose from 18 other clubs and activities. These range "from glee club to aviation club to ski club to pep band." Cadets may develop a wide variety of talents and delve into many of their special interests.

> **"The friends you meet here will be the ones you keep for the rest of your life."**

Sports period doesn't end the day for cadets. Buffet dinner follows from 1700 to 1900. Then, 1900 marks the beginning of military period, and from 2000 until 2200 is study hour. Sleep becomes an option only at 2200, and all cadets must be in bed by 2400. Cadets must stay on the base during the week, and the Academy requires its students to live on the base all four years. Cadets say that living "on base" gives them a strong sense of unity with the whole student body, and this is valued very highly. Cadets report that homesickness does not often occur because of the strong bonds that cadets form while living, training, and learning together. One sophomore cadet reports that "The best thing about the Academy is the people you are surrounded by. The friends you meet here will be the ones you keep for the rest of your life."

Life Beyond the Coast

Cadets need not apply for jobs after graduation, since the Academy assures them of a career with the United States Coast Guard. Immediately following graduation, cadets receive positions as Deck Watch Officers or Engineers in Training for their first two-year tour. This embarks them on a military journey that further develops their minds, bodies, and spirits. The work ethic taught at the USCGA prepares cadets for a successful life within the military or in civilian surroundings.

Alumni of the Academy also make their mark on the outside world, often receiving honors in fields such as medicine, business and law. They attribute much of their success to the training at the USCGA and often come back to the Academy for lectures and conferences. A strong alumni network really kindles the spirit at the Academy and illustrates the fact that the Academy's core values continue to thrive in the minds of its cadets long after graduation.

The job security that the USCGA offers is one of the most attractive features of the Academy. After the first tour, cadets can apply for advanced-degree programs financed by the U.S. Coast Guard. Flight school is another appealing option for many graduates. Pay and benefits, including full medical and dental plans, continue during any tenure of employment with the Coast Guard. Cadets admit that many of them choose the USCGA because it ensures them job security when they finally embark into the world.

Graduating from the USCGA is not the end for cadets, but rather the beginning of a fruitful career of military life and much more. The USCGA asks a lot of its students but gives back just as much, if not more. —*Aleksandra Kopec*

FYI

If you come to the U.S. Coast Guard Academy, you'd better bring "a sense of humor for the many disciplining challenges you will encounter."

What is the typical weekend schedule? "Live large while freedom reigns. Leisure time increases as cadets get closer to graduation, but getting off the base is something most cadets try to do during the weekend. Maybe a little bit of studying on Sunday would ease the workload for the rest of the week, but it is important to get outside the gates and enjoy yourself."

If I could change one thing about the U.S. Coast Guard Academy, I'd "give cadets the option to get into bed before 10 p.m."

Three things every student at the U.S. Coast Guard Academy should do before graduating are "go to the Caribbean for five weeks on a 300-foot sailboat, experience swab summer: a rigorous orientation program prior to the beginning of freshman year, and become part of an athletic team."

University of Connecticut

Address: 2131 Hillside Road, Unit 3088, Storrs, CT 06268-3088
Phone: 860-486-3137
E-mail address: beahusky@uconn.edu
Web site URL: www.uconn.edu
Year Founded: 1881
Private or Public: Public
Religious Affiliation: None
Location: Rural
Number of Applicants: 21,105
Percent Accepted: 49%
Percent Accepted who enroll: 30%
Number Entering: 3,179
Number of Transfers Accepted each Year: 1,107
Middle 50% SAT range: M: 560–660, CR: 530–630, Wr: 540–640
Middle 50% ACT range: 23–28
Early admission program EA/ED/None: EA

Percentage accepted through EA or ED: 72%
EA and ED deadline: 1-Dec
Regular Deadline: 1-Feb
Application Fee: $70
Full time Undergraduate enrollment: 16,348
Total enrollment: 22,773
Percent Male: 49%
Percent Female: 51%
Total Percent Minority or Unreported: 33%
Percent African-American: 5%
Percent Asian/Pacific Islander: 7%
Percent Hispanic: 5%
Percent Native-American: <1%
Percent International: 1%
Percent in-state/out of state: 77%/23%
Percent from Public HS: 87%
Retention Rate: 93%
Graduation Rate 4-year: 56%

Graduation Rate 6-year: 75%
Percent Undergraduates in On-campus housing: 97%
Number of official organized extracurricular organizations: 303
3 Most popular majors: Business, Political Science and Government, Psychology
Student/Faculty ratio: 17:1
Average Class Size: 15
Percent of students going to grad school: 30%
Tuition and Fees: $24,050
In-State Tuition and Fees if different: $9,338
Cost for Room and Board: $9,300
Percent receiving financial aid out of those who apply, first year: 50%
Percent receiving financial aid among all students: 64%

With a history dating back to 1881, University of Connecticut is a large public school with the tradition of more famous private universities, and recent years have seen UConn prove itself to be one of the most academically and athletically prominent public universities in the Northeast.

The University

Four-fifths of UConn's almost 22,000 undergraduates live and study on the main campus in Storrs, Connecticut, and the rest attend one of UConn's five regional campuses located all about the state. Most of the student body hails from the state, but the lack of geographic diversity has little effect on the intellectual diversity.

> "There's always someone you can make friends with, whether you want to drink or you want to study. There are so many people here that it's unavoidable."

UConn offers its undergraduates over 100 programs of study for 7 different undergraduate degrees among these different campuses. The academic core of the university is the College of Liberal Arts and Sciences, located on the main Storrs campus, which graduates about half of UConn's baccalaureate students. The College requires students to complete 120 credits worth of classes, each usually worth three credits, including general education requirements for Writing Competency, Quantitative Competency, Second Language Competency, Arts and Humanities, Social Sciences, Science and Technology, and Multiculturalism and Diversity. The classes most commonly used to fulfill these requirements "are usually pretty large, just like any intro class," said one student. UConn offers an honors program for students looking for a greater challenge with smaller class sizes. Of course students are not limited to the College of Liberal Arts and Sciences, but even those who enroll in the College can apply to one of the University's specialized schools—such as the Business School, Pharmacy School, or School of Education—by their junior year.

Some of UConn's more popular majors include Business and Psychology, but even more difficult majors such as "the plentiful forms of Engineering still have quite a large student base among scientifically-minded people," one student said.

Parties and Apartments

Of course, UConn students are always ready to take their well-deserved break from classes each weekend, and while the school alleges its anti-drinking policies are strictly enforced, UConn is popularly seen as a party school where "whether or not you get in trouble depends on whether or not you get written up by the RA, who really couldn't care less," said one freshman, and another student agreed that "people make 'Thirsty Thursday' a very big deal in the residence halls and none of the RAs really care." Most students take the trip to the off-campus Carriage House or to the Celeron Square Apartments to get their partying done on the weekends. Students explain that "the walk is kind of long, but it's definitely safe and can be a bonding experience for fellow travelers." On Saturdays, "everyone tends to go out (and it's especially easy for the girls to get into frat parties all located along Huntington Lodge Rd)," said one male student, "but if you have connections, you'll be fine." The frat scene at UConn is not very large, but it is always noticeable. "It helps to rush a frat to make friends, but it is in no way necessary," said another student. UConn students see their school as a place where "you can party with literally thousands of people at once during Spring Weekend or sit in your dorm with a few good friends. There's always someone you can make friends with, whether you want to drink or you want to study. There are so many people here that it's unavoidable."

The Housing Jungle

Freshman moving on to UConn's Storrs campus are guaranteed housing, which is definitely a luxury at a university with such a large number of students and, recently, an unexpectedly high percent of admitted students matriculating. Aside from those who, for example, live in honors housing, live in the EcoHouse, or live with fellow members of the WiMSE (Women in Math, Science & Engineering) Learning Community, most freshmen will move into one of the eleven dorm buildings on North Campus or one of the seven dorms on Northwest Campus when they begin their college career. While those who live on Northwest get a relatively new and nice dorm, "freshmen in North live in 'The Jungle'; it's pretty old and until recently were very loud and crowded party spaces," according to one student who described North's dorm rooms, which usually hold up to three people.

After one or two years on campus, students commonly move into apartments of their own, but students say that these apartments aren't often very close to classes and "they are sometimes as hard to find as it is to find a room in the dorms." Unfortunately, housing has been a struggle for UConn administration and students for several years now.

The Storrs campus offers its students eight dining halls, which one student said "[range] from 'Gross, they put mayonnaise on our pizza'-disgusting to 'Holy moly, they got pad thai!'-awesome." These dining halls are spaced throughout the campus, but students recognize that "people living on Northwest get the best freshman housing and also the best dining hall."

Since almost four-fifths of UConn's student body hail from Connecticut, returning home on weekends is rather common. However, one student said that this is not a large problem at all: "Although I originally expected most people to leave on the weekends as a typical state 'suitcase-school,' there's plenty to do on the weekends when others aren't around, and you're never alone."

Huskymania

UConn is well known for its sports teams, and this is totally unsurprising given their perennial success. Both the women's and men's basketball teams have established dominance, as yearly they compete for national championships, with the women's team recently winning a much-publicized 90 games in a row, the longest winning streak of any NCAA men's or women's college basketball team. Tickets to watch the Huskies dominate in the on-campus Gampel Pavillion and the XL Center in nearby Hartford are so popular they sometimes become rather scarce, but "if you're lucky you can snag a ticket" and enjoy a really exciting game on a Friday night in the winter.

The football team, playing at home in the 40,000-seat Rentschler Field, also has become quick to rise to fame. The Connecticut Huskies football team became a full-fledged member of Division I-A in the first two years of the millennium, and in the same decade as its membership, has reached a ranking high enough to compete in the Bowl Championship Series. Keeping up with this high level of excellence, the soccer teams and field hockey team have proven their mettle, going far in several NCAA tournaments in recent years.

For those who are not varsity quality (a high standard in such an athletically successful university), UConn also offers its students plenty of intramural sports ranging from the standard football and basketball to others such as dodgeball. The IM games are very much for fun, but in a school with such athletic prowess and pride, they also result in "some seriously fierce competition." Students say that this competitive nature is something to be expected, and feel that their Husky pride is well-deserved.—*Connor Moseley*

FYI

What's the typical weekend schedule? "Basketball game, party, or maybe an intramural football game with some friends, catch up on work and maybe some sleep."

What differentiates UConn the most from other colleges is "the ridiculous amount of school and team spirit."

If I could change one thing about UConn, I'd change "the fact that many people like to leave on the weekends."

Wesleyan University

Address: 70 Wyllys Avenue, Middletown, CT 06459
Phone: 860-685-3000
E-mail address: admission@wesleyan.edu
Web site URL: www.wesleyan.edu
Year Founded: 1831
Private or Public: Private
Religious Affiliation: None
Location: Suburban
Number of Applicants: 8,250
Percent Accepted: 27%
Percent Accepted who enroll: 32%
Number Entering: 715
Number of Transfers Accepted each Year: 110
Middle 50% SAT range: M: 660–740, CR: 640–740, Wr: 640–740
Middle 50% ACT range: 27–33
Early admission program EA/ED/None: ED

Percentage accepted through EA or ED: 43%
EA and ED deadline: 15-Nov
Regular Deadline: 1-Jan
Application Fee: $55
Full time Undergraduate enrollment: 2,796
Total enrollment: 3,222
Percent Male: 50%
Percent Female: 50%
Total Percent Minority or Unreported: 27%
Percent African-American: 7%
Percent Asian/Pacific Islander: 11%
Percent Hispanic: 8%
Percent Native-American: 1%
Percent International: 6%
Percent in-state/out of state: 8%/92%
Percent from Public HS: 57%
Retention Rate: 94%

Graduation Rate 4-year: 84%
Graduation Rate 6-year: 93%
Percent Undergraduates in On-campus housing: 99%
Number of official organized extracurricular organizations: 200
3 Most popular majors: English, Government, Psychology
Student/Faculty ratio: 9:1
Average Class Size: 19
Percent of students going to grad school: 70%
Tuition and Fees: $38,634
In-State Tuition and Fees if different: No difference
Cost for Room and Board: $10,636
Percent receiving financial aid out of those who apply, first year: 79%
Percent receiving financial aid among all students: 44%

Named the "Most Annoying Liberal Arts College" by the gossip blog Gawker in 2007, Wesleyan University has a strong reputation for being an ultra-liberal school where political correctness is not just commendable but necessary. While this image of Wesleyan certainly rings true to many students, the University has seen a gradual shift towards a new identity. Situated in Middletown—nearly halfway between Boston and New York—Wesleyan provides a refined breeding ground for the expression of diverse perspectives for its multifaceted students.

Sincere and Studious Students

The academic atmosphere at Wesleyan can be described as being extremely genuine. Students consider learning to be an intrinsically valuable endeavor, and tend to push themselves to learn as much as they can. Although there are some people who are GPA-conscious—"You have to work hard for an A, but it's not impossible"—students "work hard because they like what they do: they're not all mindless drones." According to one sophomore, there are a good number of "ide-ologically driven classes with political perspectives," especially within feminine, gender, and sexuality studies, in which "young activists are being taught by the wise, old activists." However, another student mentioned that while there is an abundance of politically motivated courses, standard "objective" classes do exist at Wesleyan. Indeed, Wesleyan's science program is one of the strongest amongst the small liberal arts colleges: it receives the largest amount of National Science Foundation grants and also recently built a $12.5-million science center.

The Wesleyan education focuses on developing in each student "10 essential capabilities"—including writing, speaking, interpretation, intercultural literacy, and effective citizenship. In the liberal arts tradition, students are expected to meet Gen Ed Expectations, although these are somewhat less stringent than at other comparable institutions. There are two special academic programs that Wesleyan students can enter during their sophomore year. The College of Social Studies (CSS) is a rigorous interdisciplinary program that integrates economics, political science, history, and government through colloquia, tutorials, and seminars. CSS has a reputation as being a program "for people who want to run the world." The other alternative is the humanities-oriented College of Letters (COL)—also known as the "College of Love." Both programs involve a number of courses without grades, with written evaluations in their stead. According to one student, admitted students tend to be somewhat insular and host parties on Mondays, since they have group assignments due on Sunday nights. The CSS and COL tend to be in the student body's general consciousness, as everyone knows about the programs, and most people have probably considered applying at one time or another.

Among the academic departments, the Department of Film Studies, led by the renowned film critic Jeanine Basinger, is regarded as particularly strong. The numerous alumni have a very successful track record and have penetrated the ranks of the Hollywood elite through the achievements of the group known as the "Wesleyan mafia," which includes Michael Bay (director of *Transformers*, *Armageddon*, and *The Rock*), Joss Whedon (creator of *Buffy the Vampire Slayer*), and Laurence Mark (producer of *Jerry Maguire*). The Film Studies program attempts to integrate "history and theory with practice" and emphasizes the analysis of film over merely its production. Most of the program takes place in the state-of-the-art Center for Film Studies, which also houses a vast and unique film archive.

The academics at Wesleyan are as intimate as they are sincere. Students find that the small size of the school lends to the ease with which students can interact and eventually befriend their professors. For example, one student noted that apart from a "few arrogant professors" most of his professors had gotten to know him better, typically through relationships beyond the classroom: "Our professor took [our class] to his house and had a BBQ, where we also played croquet in his yard." The ability to get really close to a professor is a distinct benefit at a small liberal arts college such as Wesleyan. In the end, small class size and a passionate, vocal student body allow classes to "get some really great conversations going," where students pay serious attention to each other while furiously scribbling notes.

Lively Liberalism
The political climate at Wesleyan has always been—and continues to be—very liberal. One student, while speculating on the presence of conservative-leaning students on campus, remarked, "Even if there were conservative people, they're probably hiding it." Students on the right of the political spectrum seem to have trouble finding space to express themselves openly and honestly without being ostracized.

Without a doubt, Wesleyan has played a key part in many of the country's most progressive movements. According to one student, Wesleyan was a frontrunner in the civil rights movement. For example, a number of professors traveled down to Mississippi and demonstrated alongside Dr. Martin Luther King. This sort of historical precedent has affected Wesleyan's contemporary political culture. One student mentioned that the countercultural movement's lifeblood in part lies in the "sense of history that exists [at Wesleyan], a sense of Wesleyan as countercultural—even before the sixties—a sense that has extended until now."

On campus, the "social activist" groups maintain a very active presence. For example, according to one junior, the "Transgender/gay/lesbian community [and their associated clubs] host viewings of pornographic films on a regular basis." Beyond the socially aware, the assertive presence of "hipsters"—not to be confused with "hippies," although they also exist on campus—at Wesleyan elicit reactions such as "pretentious wannabes" or "elitist crowd." Without fail, a large portion of Wesleyan students draw on the lifestyle made famous by residents of Williamsburg, Brooklyn. Of all the organizations on campus, the Eclectic Society, a fraternity, provides Wesleyan's social glue: its hipster members host many of the more well-attended parties on campus.

> "Wesleyan is a very experimental place, which is a fun thing to be as a college—it's fun to have people who aren't afraid of doing something abnormal."

Although it is clear that Wesleyan's student body represents a broad spectrum of ethnic, geographic, and cultural backgrounds, some students question the extent of interactions that occur between people from different comprehensive worldviews. One student cautioned that one's understanding of the diversity of the student body "depends on what kind of angle you're coming from." While he appreciated the multitude of viewpoints, he pointed out that "There are a bunch of people who don't branch out and try to meet people with fresh views." Another student mentioned that "There is a pretty clear segregation that sort of naturally happened. You wouldn't want to say that in public though—there's a lot of political correctness." Although it may look as though Wesleyan is an ideal "melting pot" of unique individuals coming together to form the Wesleyan identity, there is certainly a share of the student body that remains skeptical of the tolerance of its peers.

In a nutshell, according to one junior, Wesleyan students can best be characterized as "socially aware and offbeat people with a variety of tastes." The student body is composed of people with a range of personalities and perspectives from all walks of life. Students place a high emphasis on the discovery of one's own identity, and the ability to express and enact such an identity with minimal restraint. The lifestyle of the inhabitants of West College ("WestCo") serves as a testament to this theme. Inhabitants of the so-called "naked dorm" make their own rules on how they should live and behave in their residence. That clothing is optional should be readily apparent; in addition, meetings are planned at odd times such as 9:13 p.m. as a way to break the norm in society that events must occur on the hour or at 10- or 15-minute intervals. WestCo's inhabitants—and, more broadly, Wesleyan students—are constantly pushing their creative abilities to the limit in an attempt to better expose their interests to the world around them: Wesleyan students are not afraid to confidently live their lives as they see fit.

Freedom on Foss Hill

Students find that living at Wesleyan is remarkably easy. This begins with the wide range of campus living options available to students. Freshmen usually begin their Wesleyan experience in freshman dorms, where they are paired up with other new students. As they become upperclassmen, students have the opportunity to live in normal dorms.

"Program housing," where small groups of students can live in houses with unique mission statements (e.g. community service house) are available, as well as senior houses, which are semi-off-campus and wood-frame. The sprawl of the campus is very manageable and the campus living situation meets every student's needs.

Another way in which students live easier lives comes from the fact that the administration—intentionally or not—turns a blind eye toward the pervasive drug culture that exists on campus. Students tend to favor marijuana and the psychedelic effects of occasional shroom and acid trips. A number of students confirmed that a majority of the student body smokes weed. In fact, Wes Fest weekend—when accepted high school seniors come visit Wesleyan—is always scheduled to include April 20th (an important day for marijuana lovers), on which day the student body congregates en masse on Foss Hill. One student proudly asserted that Foss Hill was a "legendary place on 4/20, where literally 1,500 people with bongs meet on the Hill." Foss Hill is widely regarded as both the central location and favorite hang-out spot on campus. Students pass by it between classes and agree that "it's a place to go on the nice, sunny days for a nice game of Ultimate Frisbee."

An Experimental Experience

Upon comparing their pre-matriculation expectations to post-matriculation realities, most students seem to agree that Wesleyan does lie on the frontier of political activism. One student said the political atmosphere "surprised me, because I didn't realize just how political the school was." Above all, however, the school is about experimentation, and a number of students agree with this description. One sophomore praised the benefits of testing out new things: "Wesleyan is a very experimental place, which is a fun thing to be as a college—it's fun to have people who aren't afraid of doing something abnormal." But then again, it's okay to be "normal" too, because, at the end of the day, "If you're fine with being normal, you can still find your crowd."—*Wookie Kim*

FYI
If you come to Wesleyan, you'd better bring "weed: you'll make lots of friends."
What is the typical weekend schedule? "Wake up for brunch on Saturday, work a bit, hang out under the sun on Foss Hill, go to a performance event (like Samsara), head to Eclectic or Fountain Street. Work all of Sunday."
If I could change one thing about Wesleyan, I'd "change the repressive remnants of political correctness that actually make people self-censoring and make conversations less interesting."
Three things every student at Wesleyan should do before graduating are "do shrooms in the graveyard, go to an Eclectic party, and see Prometheus (a fire-throwing group) at the base of Foss Hill."

Yale University

Address: PO Box 208234
New Haven, CT
06520-8234
Phone: 203-432-9300
E-mail address:
undergraduate.admission@
yale.edu
Web site URL: www.yale.edu
Year Founded: 1701
Private or Public: Private
Religious Affiliation: None
Location: Urban
Number of Applicants:
26,003
Percent Accepted: 8%
**Percent Accepted who
enroll:** 69%
Number Entering: 1,307
**Number of Transfers
Accepted each Year:** 28
Middle 50% SAT range:
M: 700–790, CR:
700–800, Wr: 700–790
Middle 50% ACT range:
30–34

**Early admission program
EA/ED/None:** EA
**Percentage accepted
through EA or ED:** 18%
EA and ED deadline: 1-Nov
Regular Deadline: 1-Jan
Application Fee: $75
**Full time Undergraduate
enrollment:** 5,311
Total enrollment: 10,206
Percent Male: 50%
Percent Female: 50%
**Total Percent Minority or
Unreported:** 32%
Percent African-American:
9%
**Percent Asian/Pacific
Islander:** 14%
Percent Hispanic: 9%
Percent Native-American: 1%
Percent International: 9%
**Percent in-state/out of
state:** 6%/94%
Percent from Public HS: 55%
Retention Rate: 99%

Graduation Rate 4-year: 97%
Graduation Rate 6-year: 99%
**Percent Undergraduates in
On-campus housing:** 87%
**Number of official organized
extracurricular
organizations:** 350
3 Most popular majors:
Economics, History, Political
Science
Student/Faculty ratio: 6:1
Average Class Size: 15
**Percent of students going to
grad school:** 50%
Tuition and Fees: $35,300
**In-State Tuition and Fees if
different:** No difference
Cost for Room and Board:
$10,700
**Percent receiving financial
aid out of those who apply,
first year:** 81%
**Percent receiving financial
aid among all students:**
46%

When Yale's newly renovated Bass Library reopened at midnight in October 2007, the event seemed more like a late-night blowout than the opening of a library. But as students raced through the underground stacks, admiring the new shelves and sampling the café's organic fare, the library extravaganza tied together the aspects of Yale life that its students cherish. With love of learning at the center of the Yale experience, students still find ways to create fun and new traditions in the unlikeliest of ways, all within the context of a university that continues to grow and reshape itself while maintaining centuries of tradition.

A Community of Scholars

Founded in 1701 by Congregationalist ministers, Yale has maintained a commitment to academic excellence ever since. But don't let the world-renowned professors intimidate you—the University is well-known for its strong focus on undergraduate education, which means that faculty members are not so pressured to publish and conduct research that they fail to throw themselves wholeheartedly into teaching their under-

graduates. One sophomore said she has found that there is a "robust dialogue between students and faculty." And while entering an academic institution filled with thousands of other motivated high-achievers may seem daunting as well, Yalies—who are known as both Bulldogs and Elis—find that their fellow students provide a supportive rather than cutthroat environment and are usually more than willing to study and brainstorm together.

As part of its liberal arts curriculum, Yale requires students to fulfill 36 credits—as opposed to the 32 mandated by the other Ivy League schools—including courses to fulfill a major and two course credits each in the humanities and arts, the sciences, the social sciences, quantitative reasoning and writing. The additional foreign language requirement may be completed with between one and three courses, depending on previous language study. While these rigorous requirements contribute to an intense academic environment, students said, rather than oppressive, they found the challenge to be more of an opportunity to thrive. One junior remarked that he felt "acceptably overwhelmed."

One reason that many students feel overwhelmed is the 2,000 courses from which to choose. During the first two weeks of each semester, students take advantage of "shopping period" by attending as many classes as they wish—and sometimes as many as they can fit into a day—and deciding whether they like the professor and course material before officially enrolling. And when the time comes to enroll in courses, students report little trouble in gaining access to the ones they want, with the exception of some competitive seminars with caps of 15 to 18 participants, and even then "talking to the professor and making your case usually does the trick." Most courses have between 15 and 30 students, though some introductory lectures host more than 100. While the most popular majors are continuously history, economics, and political science, there is a lot of interest in psychology and the pre-med track, particularly biology. Professors and courses that students highly recommended included Introduction to Psychology with either Paul Bloom or Marvin Chun, History of Modern China with Jonathan Spence, Sex, Evolution, and Human Nature with Laurie Santos, and Constitutional Law with Akhil Amar.

For those looking to fulfill the distributional requirements, there are a variety of gut courses, including Philosophy of Science, and Computers and the Law, although some students warned that while there may be less work, these supposedly easy classes are not guaranteed A's. Humanities-oriented students who take gut classes instead of opting to hike up "Science Hill" early each morning are often ridiculed by the more scientifically inclined, and a mechanical engineering major said he and his friends do debate the relative difficulty of the sciences and the humanities. Other students said while classrooms in the different disciplines are separated geographically by the Hill, residential life and extracurriculars bring everyone together seamlessly. An English major said she enjoys that Yale's academic life "really helps stimulate interesting conversations outside the classroom. People aren't afraid to admit that they're really passionate about a subject."

The All-Important Sorting Ceremony

Many of these intimate dialogues in dining halls or dorm rooms are fostered by the residential college system, which Yalies across the board identify as one of the most distinctive, rewarding features of life as a Bulldog.

Students are randomly sorted into one of the 12 colleges, which serve as a living community, social environment, intramural sports base, and source of unique pride and loyalty. That almost 90 percent of Yale students choose to live on campus for all four years is a testament to the strong bonds that are formed among those that share a college. While the 12 differ architecturally—Jonathan Edwards is Gothic, Davenport is Georgian, and Morse and Stiles are 60s-era Saarinen designs, for example—and they offer different amenities, the random assemblage of students is representative of the University at large. While Yale, with around 5,400 students, is mid-sized, the colleges help to make the school more personal. A Morse College student described the residential college system as "An amazing opportunity to escape the major college campus. It's a community within a community, with a master and dean and so many resources, like a library and buttery." Along with cheap late-night food from the buttery and the convenience of the nearby library, colleges also offer a variety of facilities, including gyms, movie theaters, performance spaces, and woodworking areas.

Old Campus houses freshmen from 10 of the 12 colleges, allowing members of the same class to get to know each other before moving into their respective colleges. Students in the larger Timothy Dwight and Silliman may live there all four years. The colleges also provide both academic and general support, from the freshman counselors who live on Old Campus to masters and deans, who live in the colleges and are enthusiastic about getting to know students. The University has almost completed the renovation of the 12 colleges, which has transformed suite arrangements, added new facilities, and beautified, all while retaining the traditional architecture and atmosphere. Each year, students in the college being renovated live in "Swing Space," a recently constructed dorm that features long hallways of suites with common rooms, kitchenettes, and private bathrooms. Students said that while Swing is less centrally located than many of the colleges, its living arrangement is a refreshing alternative from the norm, which consists of separate entryways and complex suites of between two and 10 residents, rather than the hallways common at other schools.

With the "Hogwarts-style" Commons, a dining hall in each of the 12 colleges, plus additional eateries in the University's professional and graduate schools, Yalies seem to have a lot of dining options. But some said they feel constrained by the requirement that on-campus students purchase a meal plan, even though they can exchange meals for flex dollars to be used at the convenience store. The benefit of eating in the dining halls, in spite of the sometimes monotonous food, is the knowledge that you will almost always have someone you can sit with, and a strong sense of community develops. The Sustainable Food Project, which brings local-grown and organic food to dining halls, may be "often healthier but not always tastier," although students said they gave the spirit of the project high marks.

Not Too Busy to Have Fun

Even as the residential colleges provide a social foundation, students raved about the many opportunities to "find your scene." Although students said there are definitely some distinct social groups—such as athletes and hipsters—a film major said he has "always felt that one can easily move throughout groups as long as you have the right disposition and outlook." Extracurricular activities are a common method of meeting new people. In terms of drinking, students estimated that about two-thirds of Yale students drink, but it is "perfectly acceptable" for someone to choose not to and still hang out with people who imbibe. Yale's policy towards alcohol consumption is fairly lenient, despite recent Connecticut laws that strengthened adherence to restrictions. A JE junior commented that "The policy of Yale has always been to give us a lot of respect in that regard, and they're not going to strongly enforce us on drinking . . . but they do take care of us when we over-drink and need help." As for drugs, the junior's perception of on-campus use was that "It's probably mostly just pot and maybe some cocaine, but I don't think too many people do really hardcore drugs."

In any case, students take advantage of campus events as well as parties, ensuring that alcohol does not by any means dominate University socializing. The myriad campus groups devoted to putting on dance, theater, comedy, and musical productions guarantee that there will always be something happening in the evenings, and periodic residential college council-sponsored dance parties and special events add to the fun. Morse and Stiles's Prohibition, previously Casino Night, in November regularly draws more than 2,000 students, JE pulls out all the stops for the Spider Ball in April, and neon-clad stu-

dents dance the night away to Duran Duran at Silliman's 80's-themed Safety Dance in October. During the day, the residential colleges' "Master's Teas" are well-known for bringing interesting and prominent figures to campus for intimate talks with groups of students—recent visitors include children's folk singer Raffi, the editor of the *Harry Potter* books and the pop group Hanson, while past guests include former Supreme Court justice Sandra Day O'Connor and author Kurt Vonnegut.

The majority of Yale students are politically liberal, and those that self-identify as moderates tend towards the left as well, but there is a strong contingent of conservative students who do find a voice on campus amongst all the Yale Dems activities. When it comes to clothing, Elis know how to dress well, as befitting the New England private school stereotype, but while it's not uncommon to see guys wearing button-downs and slacks to class, sweatpants are accepted as well. Yalies are perceived as being predominantly middle-class, students said, and approximately 56 percent of the student body receives some form of financial aid. The campus is racially and ethnically diverse, and student organizations dedicated to celebrating unique cultural heritages are prominent fixtures on campus. A sizable 10 percent of the student body hails from outside the United States, but the rest "come from New York or California, and not often in between." The openly gay community at Yale—which is often labeled the "gay Ivy"—is a testament to the high level of acceptance on campus; a gay junior remarked that "You can't really be openly prejudiced or comfortably prejudiced here because you just won't fit in." Moreover, a senior in Branford explained that labels do not have to be all-encompassing: "It's okay to be gay and not to be defined by being gay here."

Out in the Elm City

When they arrive on campus, Yalies immediately face the question of how the University integrates with the surrounding city. While New Haven still retains some of its reputation for crime and racial tension, the city is on the upswing, having undergone major efforts at revitalization over the past two decades. One area near campus that students mentioned as indicative of how the city is changing is Ninth Square, located a few blocks from campus. Formerly a district of abandoned storefronts, Ninth Square has been overhauled by a city commission. Several restaurants, including Indian, French bistro and Malaysian cuisine, have opened in the area. Older standbys near campus include Yorkside, a multitude of Thai restaurants and "the burrito cart" for meals, while Rudy's, Hot Tomato's, and Viva's are popular nighttime stops.

But even as new businesses multiply close to campus, students still point out the University's problems integrating with the New Haven community. Occasional incidents of crime on campus, usually muggings, have students conscious of taking big-city precautions, such as not walking alone at night. One student remarked, "I think people feel safe but also realize they need to be responsible and aware." Some panhandlers are such fixtures that they have acquired quasi-affectionate monikers, such as the "Flower Lady" and the "Shakespeare Lady." The surrounding area does provide myriad opportunities for community involvement, including tutoring and canvassing for local political candidates. Furthermore, all the excitement of New York City is less than two hours away by train.

Quirky or Cultish? You Decide.

It's hard to go wrong with 350 registered undergraduate organizations. There are the campus favorites, such as political groups, publications, cultural groups, community service organizations, and a cappella groups. And then there are the quirkier niche groups, such as the Society for the Exploration of Campus Secrets, whose members sneak around campus looking for access to hidden Yale locales, and the Anti-Gravity Society, which draws the school's jugglers. The Yale College Council provides opportunity for student government involvement. Some of the organizations, including the Yale Political Union, the *Yale Daily News*, and a cappella groups, have reputations for being "cultish," but students will tell you that most undergraduates are very committed to their extracurricular activities. A good number of students have jobs as well, mostly on campus.

The Yale men's hockey team has recently risen to the top of national rankings and now

regularly draws full attendance at Ingalls Rink. Otherwise, however, except at the epic Harvard-Yale football game every November, school athletic pride doesn't surface very often. Few undergraduates regularly attend other sporting events, even though the rowing and sailing teams are of international caliber. The Bulldogs' home, the Yale Bowl, holds more than 64,000 spectators, and Payne Whitney Gymnasium is the second-largest gym in the world. The Harvard-Yale game is almost better known for its tailgating, alumni reunions and pranks pulled by each school than for the football game itself.

> "People aren't afraid to admit that they're really passionate about a subject."

The Harvard-Yale rivalry certainly encompasses athletics, but it also extends into good-natured competition over which student body enjoys better quality of life, which school is ranked higher in a particular year, and other quibbles. While the jury is still out on a scientific conclusion, the emphatic Yale refrain persists: "Harvard sucks!"

And a unique Yale pride does follow students not only through their four "bright college years" in New Haven (as the school song goes), but into their later years as well, through the alumni community. While a junior affirmed, "I think there are more spectacular, friendly, and interesting people here than I thought possible," a sophomore happily pointed out that "Students didn't choose Yale to get a 4.0—they chose it because it's a genuinely intellectual place to be." Even as Yale looks to the future—for example, through globalization initiatives that connect the University intimately to China—it manages to retain an atmosphere of tradition, both in academics and fun. Any undergraduate studying grand strategy with the bells of Harkness Tower playing Britney Spears in the background can tell you that.—*Kimberly Chow*

FYI

If you come to Yale, you'd better bring "a coffeemaker and a big mug to go with it!"

What's the typical weekend schedule? "On Thursday night, go to a bar like Rudy's; try to get errands done during the day on Friday, then go out to a play, room party, organization-sponsored dance party, a cappella concert, improv show, or some combination thereof on Friday and Saturday nights; go to a late brunch and cram in as much studying as possible on Sunday, and go to bed too late."

If I could change one thing about Yale, I'd "work on the sometimes tense relationship between Yale and the city of New Haven."

Two things every college student at Yale should do before graduating are "climb Harkness Tower and go to a naked party."

Delaware

University of Delaware

Address: 116 Hullihen Hall
Newark, DE 19716-6210
Phone: 302-831-8123
E-mail address:
admissions@udel.edu
Web site URL:
www.udel.edu
Year Founded: 1743
Private or Public: Public
Religious Affiliation: None
Location: Suburban
Number of Applicants:
21,930
Percent Accepted: 47%
Percent Accepted who
enroll: 31%
Number Entering: 3,202
Number of Transfers
Accepted each Year: 802
Middle 50% SAT range:
M: 560–660, CR:
540–640, Wr: 540–650
Middle 50% ACT range:
23–28
Early admission program
EA/ED/None: None

Percentage accepted
through EA or ED: NA
EA and ED deadline: NA
Regular Deadline: 15-Jan
Application Fee: $60
Full time Undergraduate
enrollment: 15,211
Total enrollment: 18,616
Percent Male: 39%
Percent Female: 61%
Total Percent Minority or
Unreported: 17%
Percent African-American:
5%
Percent Asian/Pacific
Islander: 4%
Percent Hispanic: 4%
Percent Native-American:
<1%
Percent International: <1%
Percent in-state/out of
state: 40%/60%
Percent from Public HS:
80%
Retention Rate: 90%
Graduation Rate 4-year: 67%

Graduation Rate 6-year:
77%
Percent Undergraduates
in On-campus housing:
93%
Number of official organized
extracurricular
organizations: 200
3 Most popular majors:
Biology, Education,
Psychology
Student/Faculty ratio: 12:1
Average Class Size: 15
Percent of students going to
grad school: 55%
Tuition and Fees: $21,126
In-State Tuition and Fees if
different: $8,646
Cost for Room and Board:
$8,478
Percent receiving financial
aid out of those who apply,
first year: 42%
Percent receiving financial
aid among all students:
55%

At once known for its party scene and its academic rigor, the University of Delaware provides the proverbial balance of work and play. With abounding extracurricular options and a welcoming, involved student body, UDel students can quickly find their niche and create their own unique college experience.

Personal Attention and Flexibility at a Large School

Despite the size of the school, with nearly 16,000 undergraduates, students said, "UDel is big, but not too large to get lost." Students say there is no need to worry about a lack of personal attention. As one freshman stated, "I was really surprised by how friendly and welcoming the upperclassmen are to us freshmen, and even the teachers are really available and eager to talk whenever." Students agree they never have a problem getting extra help when they need it.

Another benefit of the size of the school is the range of choice and flexibility students have in their courses. As might be expected, some majors, especially the chemical engineering, biology and nursing programs, have more difficult requirements to fulfill than others do, and, as a result, course loads do vary greatly from student to student. But the consensus among students is that UDel's requirements leave them with enough flexibility in their schedules so that "As long as you pick your classes well, you'll find a load you can deal with." Students also have the core curriculum in common, though students are able to place out of some of the requirements through advanced high school courses.

UDel offers 125 majors and 100 minors—enough options to give students the ability to study exactly what they want. Many students choose to have a minor in addition to their major. The University features a prominent agriculture department, whose full-fledged farm is accessible to students of all majors. And if that is not enough, there is a special Dean's Scholar Program that allows especially motivated students to essentially design their own major and undergraduate program. There is also the Honors College at UDel, to which students may be admitted when they are accepted to the university, offering smaller class size, more student-faculty interaction and personal attention and even special dorms.

Work Hard . . .

When asked about what made UDel stand out from other schools, an undergraduate offered, "It's the classic football-frats-parties college, but has a great academic foundation as well." UDel is notorious for its intense party scene on top of its intense academic programs. With such a lively social atmosphere around them, students said, "It can be easy to let yourself start struggling if you don't keep up with the work."

> "It's the classic football-frats-parties college, but has a great academic foundation as well."

A distinctive feature of UDel is its academic calendar. The Winter Session, a two-month break from mid-December to mid-February, was designed to give students the option of studying abroad for a semester during the winter. During that time, students who do not go abroad or choose to stay on campus to take additional courses are able to go home and relax for a long winter break.

. . . And Party Hard

While UDel is known for its parties and the dominance of drinking and Greek life in the social lives of students, many students agreed with one student who noted, "Yeah, it's a party school, but only if you want it to be." It is easy to find and join parties, many of which are the typical frat parties where alcohol abounds. The University is very strict, however, regarding alcohol abuse among its undergraduates on campus. Its rules include a "three-strikes-and-you're-out" policy for alcohol violations in the dorms. As a result, parties are usually taken off-campus and away from possible crack-downs by the University.

There are also always many dry events for students who choose not to drink. The student social committee organizes a variety of events, from weekend movies and concerts to having prominent speakers on campus. One student said about UDel, "It offers all of the opportunities for you to choose exactly what you want from your college life." During the 2008 presidential election, for example, 7,000 undergraduates flocked to see vice presidential candidate and UDel alumnus Joe Biden and his wife speak at a campaign rally on campus.

Abundant Extracurricular Options

UDel students can frequently be found cheering on their school's 23 varsity sports teams, including the successful Fightin' Blue Hens football team. The UDel football team has a huge following in part due to its long history of success, and the games and tailgates are a classic part of the undergraduate experience there. Thousands of students show up at every game to support the team, and games against rival Villanova draw an attendance of over 20,000 every year.

With 200 student organizations on campus, as one student remarked, "You're a fool to not get involved. There are so many options available and everyone is so welcoming." The "Hen Zone" in the Perkins Student Center is a gathering place for students of all skill levels to play a round of billiards, ping-pong, air hockey or foosball. Many UDel students are involved in sports, and there are always many activities going on around campus: a freshman aptly summarized, "Whatever you want, someone is probably doing it."

Campus Living

While many students complain about the living situation at UDel, one student remarked, "It's not a five-star hotel, but I have no complaints." Taking into consideration that there is only so much one can expect from a college dorm, another student said, the dorms are "a little on the small side, but very functional." While over 90 percent of students do stay in on-campus housing, it is fairly easy to find off-campus housing. The University also helps students to find good housing, including a Web site where students can post ads or search for local apartments.

When it comes to the food, a freshman said, "The dining halls get old fast. You learn quickly which dining halls are better. For dining halls, they're good, but get a meal plan with more points and less meals." Most students seemed to agree with going with more of UD's points when selecting a mandatory meal plan, which can be used towards purchases at any dining retail location on campus. While many students complain about the food at UDel, there is such a wide array of food on and around campus that it is difficult to not find something, though it usually is slightly more expensive than dining hall food.

Diversity?

As a state university, UDel attracts students mainly from Delaware and the states surrounding it—namely Maryland, Pennsylvania, New Jersey and New York. In terms of diversity, students expressed that UDel is a bit lacking in both geographic and ethnic diversity. "Not everyone at UDel is white, but some groups are definitely poorly repre-sented," one student said. She added, "I would say half of my dorm is white, with more African-Americans and Hispanics than Asians or other minorities." Despite the relatively small minority population at UDel, student cultural groups like the Chinese Cultural Student Association (CCSA) often host events like the Lunar New Year Celebration that magnify the presence of minorities on campus.

In terms of campus safety, students agreed that there is really nothing to be scared of around UDel's suburban campus. Crimes are rare and "I feel very safe on campus, no matter what the time," a freshman said. Overall, students not only feel safe, but happily at home and welcome at UDel. With so much going on and seemingly endless opportunities for students to get involved on campus, students insist that it is nearly impossible to stay bored for long at UDel.
—*Michelle Yu*

FYI

If you come to UDel, you'd better bring "your UDel gear for football games and maybe rain boots."

What is the typical weekend schedule? "Parties, movies, sleep. Whatever you want, someone is probably doing it."

If I could change one thing about UDel, I'd "make classes later. Everyone I know has an 8 a.m. class."

Three things every student at UDel should do before graduating are "eat at Grotto Pizza, go to the farm, and, of course, go to a football game. Also, take advantage of the great concert opportunities."

District of Columbia

Address: 4400 Massachusetts Avenue, NW, Washington, D.C. 20016-8001
Phone: 202-885-6000
E-mail address: admissions@american.edu
Web site URL: www.american.edu
Year Founded: 1893
Private or Public: Private
Religious Affiliation: Methodist
Location: Urban
Number of Applicants: 15,847
Percent Accepted: 53%
Percent Accepted who enroll: 15%
Number Entering: 1,284
Number of Transfers Accepted each Year: 910
Middle 50% SAT range: M: 580–670, **CR:** 590–690, **Wr:** 580–690
Middle 50% ACT range: 25–30

Early admission program EA/ED/None: ED
Percentage accepted through EA or ED: 55%
EA and ED deadline: 15-Nov
Regular Deadline: 15-Jan
Application Fee: $45
Full time Undergraduate enrollment: 6,042
Total enrollment: 9,967
Percent Male: 37%
Percent Female: 63%
Total Percent Minority or Unreported: 37%
Percent African-American: 5%
Percent Asian/Pacific Islander: 5%
Percent Hispanic: 5%
Percent Native-American: <1%
Percent International: 6%
Percent in-state/out of state: 21%/79%
Percent from Public HS: Unreported

Retention Rate: 86%
Graduation Rate 4-year: 62%
Graduation Rate 6-year: 69%
Percent Undergraduates in On-campus housing: 75%
Number of official organized extracurricular organizations: 180
3 Most popular majors: Business, International Relations, Communications
Student/Faculty ratio: 14:1
Average Class Size: 15
Percent of students going to grad school: Unreported
Tuition and Fees: $33,283
In-State Tuition and Fees if different: No difference
Cost for Room and Board: $12,418
Percent receiving financial aid out of those who apply, first year: 61%
Percent receiving financial aid among all students: 69%

Founded in 1893, American University has since grown and expanded with its Washington D.C. setting to provide unique opportunities to its students. From government internships to special events, students are able to take advantage of the opportunities provided by the university's surroundings, all while enjoying the resources of a prestigious university.

No Curve . . . Just Hard Work

Six different schools are housed within American University: College of Arts and Sciences, Kogod School of Business, School of Communication, School of International Service, School of Public Affairs, and Washington College of Law. Undergraduates are able to attend all the schools except for Washington College of Law. American is well-known for its international studies and business programs, but interaction with professors seems to vary from school to school. A student in the College of Arts and Sciences said her professors were easy to find and to get along with. In addition, she added that a perk of her college was that her professors knew her name, whereas students in other schools said they had to work to get professors to know who they were. Although biochemistry is seen by most people as being the hardest major, one student says it really "depends on the caliber of the person." For instance, while some would consider sciences difficult, some science students view the political science or literature majors as difficult due to the large quantities of reading required for those courses. Even though American University is more well-known for its humanities programs (particularly international studies), one student said that "students in each department pretty much think that the others have it harder. I think biochem is easier that stats or micro. They think vice versa. We're all nice to each other, even if we're in different schools." That said, the classes typically deemed as the hardest are ones in the chemistry and biology departments, as well as microeconomics and macroeconomics. Classes at American are generally worth 3 credits each, but language classes and science classes including labs can be worth up to 4 or 5 credits each.. A College of Arts and Sciences student said, "I get mostly A's. A lot of people make the Dean's list for the college. The harder you work, the greater the rewards. I don't think any of my teachers so far curve."

> "We're all nice to each other, even if we're in different schools."

Social Life What You Make of It

As far a social life goes, the experience seems to vary from person to person. People usually go out on Friday and Saturday. Options include going out to eat, attending frat parties, going to clubs or visiting monuments and museums. Cars are not seen as a necessity, as the metro station is close to campus and the university provides shuttles for transportation; however, upperclassmen are known to have cars. Both upperclassmen and underclassmen alike attend frat parties, but upperclassmen tend to have more private parties than the younger students. "People party on campus nightly," a student said. The Greek scene was described by a student as "there, but avoidable." Some people don't attend frats, whereas other rush and enjoy the experience. Drinking is a personal choice, as is drug use. American University is a dry campus, and the rules are enforced when seen,

so some students "hide things well," as one student described it.

Hangout Spaces Galore

The living experience, like the social scene, varies from student to student. RA's live on each floor and are supposed to handle disputes and promote floor unity. Some are strict, but others are more lax. Even though dorms get better with seniority, a lot of people tend to move off campus as they get older, and most are living off-campus by senior year so that they can do internships. As far as campus hangouts go, The Tavern is a popular dining venue that provides a relaxing atmosphere. At nighttime, a good place to hang is The Perch, a coffeehouse, or the Davenport Lounge. A unique building on campus is the Katzen Arts Center, which houses the American University Museum, the Studio Theatre, a recital hall and the departments of arts and performing arts. The campus is safe at night, as is the surrounding area, which consists of fairly wealthy neighborhoods. "Homeland security is down the street. NBC is too," one student said. The surrounding area has good hangout places as well, such as Chipotle, Z-burger, Starbucks, Robeks, as well as bars and clubs. Metro Center and Dupont are also popular places.

One City, Infinite Opportunities

American University has well over 100 student organizations, but some of the most prominent ones are a capella groups, dance teams, cheer teams, crew and RHA. RHA, or Residence Hall Association, is the student government for each residential hall whose goal is to improve the quality of life for each residential hall as well as build a greater sense of community among American University students. Some members are very committed to their extracurricular activities, particularly members of RHA, but the amount of student involvement in organizations depends on the student. Publications are also a fairly popular form of extracurricular participation, with the AU Eagle in particular being popular. Sports don't seem to really have a major presence on campus, but basketball games and volleyball matches are known to draw crowds. "The bleachers are filled, but not everyone goes," one student remarked about these events. Overall, the distinguishing factor of American University seems to be its D.C. location, which gives students access to opportunities unavailable to those at other universities, such as hearing President Obama speak. No matter what opportunities present themselves, students agree that having downtown Washington D.C. close to cam- pus allows students to use the city's offerings to enrich their college experiences. —*Liliana Varman*

FYI
Three things every student at American should do before graduating are see a play, go to a game, take a class with Professor Patrick Jackson.
What differentiates American the most from other colleges is the ability to do interesting double majors and minors (i.e., Biochemistry and theater).
What surprised me the most about American was the beauty of the campus itself.

Catholic University of America

Address: Cardinal Station Washington, D.C. 20064
Phone: 202-319-5305
E-mail address: cua-admissions@cua.edu
Web site URL: www.cua.edu
Year Founded: 1887
Private or Public: Private
Religious Affiliation: Roman Catholic
Location: Urban
Number of Applicants: 5,180
Percent Accepted: 81%
Percent Accepted who enroll: 22%
Number Entering: 901
Number of Transfers Accepted each Year: 202
Middle 50% SAT range: M: 500–610, CR: 510–610, Wr: Unrepoted
Middle 50% ACT range: 21–27
Early admission program EA/ED/None: EA

Percentage accepted through EA or ED: Unreported
EA and ED deadline: 15-Nov
Regular Deadline: 15-Feb
Application Fee: $55
Full time Undergraduate enrollment: 3,326
Total enrollment: 5,470
Percent Male: 45%
Percent Female: 55%
Total Percent Minority or Unreported: 14%
Percent African-American: .5%
Percent Asian/Pacific Islander: 3%
Percent Hispanic: 7%
Percent Native-American: <1%
Percent International: 3%
Percent in-state/out of state: 1%/99%
Percent from Public HS: Unreported
Retention Rate: 82%

Graduation Rate 4-year: Unreported
Graduation Rate 6-year: Unreported
Percent Undergraduates in On-campus housing: 68%
Number of official organized extracurricular organizations: 100
3 Most popular majors: Architecture, Nursing, Political Science
Student/Faculty ratio: 11:1
Average Class Size: 20
Percent of students going to grad school: Unreported
Tuition and Fees: $30,670
In-State Tuition and Fees if different: No difference
Cost for Room and Board: $11,320
Percent receiving financial aid out of those who apply, first year: 91%
Percent receiving financial aid among all students: 88%

Don't let the name scare you! Although CUA is a Roman Catholic institution, not everyone goes to church all the time (or at all, for that matter). Most students are "Catholics from New England, Philly and New Jersey," but people of all faiths are not only tolerated but are also encouraged to come. With D.C. as its playground, CUA is a great place to be a student: "You have no reason to be bored!" one senior said.

Not Just for Catholics
Students at CUA are required to complete a number of core courses, including "Intro to Religion," but most people don't mind it. There is a wide variety of difficulty in the course work offered at CUA, ranging from the easier political science major (after all, you are right at the heart of the American political process) to the more challenging engineering and architecture majors that students say "really set CUA apart from

other universities." There is also a one-year master's program in engineering for students who completed their undergraduate work at CUA. Students interested in social work should also take note of the opportunities CUA affords in that area—a field placement class takes you outside the classroom and puts you in a social work agency for 16 hours a week. Talk about a hands-on experience! Drama is a popular major at CUA, and the Drama School (for graduate work) is a very well-respected part of the institution. For those with a more scientific mind, the School of Nursing at CUA is an excellent school, consistently ranked in the top 10 nursing schools in the country.

Some of the best classes for undergrads are Dynamics of Christian Spirituality, World Religions, Introduction to Peace Studies, and Greek Literature in Translation. For the students not looking to work too hard there are easier classes (like Social Work 101, Anthropology, or Astronomy) but there are definitely opportunities for CUA kids to challenge themselves. Difficult courses like Fluid Dynamics make people work for their grades more than other classes. Students say that grading "depends on the professor, but it's usually fair." The workload at CUA definitely depends on the student, but many kids work and play sports while still taking a full (or more than full) course load.

Studying at CUA is a must, and there are plenty of places to work. Some students prefer to stay in the city after work at an off-campus job, working in coffee shops around D.C., while others enjoy the quiet rooms of Mullen, the main library. If you can't find your books there, have no fear: CUA is a member of the Washington Research Library Consortium, which also includes Howard, George Washington and American universities. "Pretty much any research material you need, you can find." Furthermore, the largest library in the United States, the Library of Congress, is only a few metro stops away from campus.

Gotta Eat Somewhere . . . Just Not on Campus!
Living arrangements at CUA make other universities look like they came from the Stone Age. Incoming freshmen can look forward to two of the greatest luxuries offered on a college campus—air-conditioning and cable. Furthermore, CUA provides a number of different housing choices for students. The University offers suite-style dorms, apartments, singles, and even trailers (yes, trailers—but

only during renovation). There are also typical dorms where students share a bathroom down the hall from their rooms. All of the different styles of living "makes for a great change of pace over the four years," students say. And don't let the seemingly strict administration fool you—CUA kids know how to have a good time, even on campus.

As for food on campus, students at CUA (like at most schools) say it's not worth the money they're paying for it. One senior however said: "There has been a huge improvement over the four years I've been here. Since our new student center opened up, the dining halls have better hours and more options." There are not always choices available to vegetarian students, and some believe the University could "cater to the more health-conscious eaters better." Students describe food prices on campus as "ridiculous," but there are always other options. Fortunately CUA is so close to downtown D.C. that you can find "any kind of food you want within 10 to 25 minutes . . . ANY kind of food."

Such proximity to a major city might make some parents nervous about their student's safety, but a modern blue-light system coupled with regularly patrolling police make students feel safe. "I've never been scared and walk alone at night without worrying," one girl said. Common sense does, however, always pay off. "I would never walk off campus in the neighborhood alone at night, though." Smart advice for just about anywhere.

It's a Party in the City
"My favorite part of CUA is the student body: they know how to party and have fun, but also how to deal with life!" Despite a reportedly "very closed-minded" administration that "cares more about the 'image' of the school than meeting students' needs," CUA is a great place to spend four years. Located right in the District of Columbia, students take full advantage of city life. There are endless numbers of museums and national monuments to visit in the city, not to mention the exciting social life an urban center provides. Although the school policy is "strict about citing underage drinkers" (there are no kegs allowed), one student pointed out that "It's a big campus." Since the school has its own Metro stop—and D.C. has an extremely well-run public transportation network—students tend to go out in the city rather than on campus. Bars dominate the social scene on party nights (generally Thursday through

Saturday). Fado Irish Pub has "a great local band" on Thursdays, and Brooks and Johnny K's are popular bars for the freshmen to check out. Fortunately, drinking isn't the only thing to do around D.C. "Because we have a big Catholic identity going on, there are actually quite a number of people who don't drink at all," one student notes.

> "Because we have a big Catholic identity going on, there are actually quite a number of people who don't drink at all."

Though there isn't a significant Greek presence on campus, students "find their niche pretty easily." People at CUA love that the school is small and say that everyone is "really close," "approachable" and "friendly." One thing that incoming students should definitely know, however, is that CUA is not a place where aspiring athletes thrive. "Don't come here if you want basketball or football games to be the highlight of your weekend," says one student. CUA is a Division III school, but school pride doesn't center on athletics. There are workout facilities for health-conscious students, including a new fitness center for non-athletes. "It has great equipment, but not enough to keep up with the demand on peak-use hours," one student said.

Student life at CUA is busy—many upperclassmen get internships in the city, and student organizations are large. The Campus Ministry "has a lot to offer to one's faith life, including mass, adoration, community service, prayer groups and more," one female student said. Drama is also a popular activity for the student body. With a prestigious Drama School at the University, it's no surprise that CUA attracts aspiring actors and actresses. There are also club sports teams (including Ultimate Frisbee, soccer, and crew) and a Division I rugby team that routinely performs well. All in all there is really something for everyone at CUA. Let's not forget, of course, student-run political groups that attract students from both ends of the spectrum. What else would you expect from a school in D.C.?—*Emily Cleveland*

FYI

If you come to Catholic, you'd better bring "a passion for politics."

What is the typical weekend schedule? "Friday: go clubbing in D.C.; Saturday: spend time with friends and party at night; Sunday: go to church and study."

If I could change one thing about Catholic, I'd "make the administration better at dealing with financial issues."

Three things every student at Catholic should do before graduating are "spend a late night at Johnny K's, walk around the monuments at night, and go to a protest."

George Washington University

Address: 2121 I Street, NW, Suite 201, Washington, D.C. 20052
Phone: 202-994-6040
E-mail address: gwadm@gwu.edu
Web site URL: www.gwu.edu
Year Founded: 1821
Private or Public: Private
Religious Affiliation: None
Location: Urban
Number of Applicants: 19,606
Percent Accepted: 37%
Percent Accepted who enroll: 30%
Number Entering: 2,123
Number of Transfers Accepted each Year: 980
Middle 50% SAT range: M: 600–690, CR: 600–690, Wr: 600–690
Middle 50% ACT range: 26–29
Early admission program EA/ED/None: ED

Percentage accepted through EA or ED: Unreported
EA and ED deadline: 10-Nov
Regular Deadline: 10-Jan
Application Fee: $65
Full time Undergraduate enrollment: 10,701
Total enrollment: 22,710
Percent Male: 45%
Percent Female: 55%
Total Percent Minority or Unreported: 40%
Percent African-American: 7%
Percent Asian/Pacific Islander: 10%
Percent Hispanic: 6%
Percent Native-American: <1%
Percent International: 5%
Percent in-state/out of state: 2%/98%
Percent from Public HS: 70%
Retention Rate: 90%

Graduation Rate 4-year: 72%
Graduation Rate 6-year: 77%
Percent Undergraduates in On-campus housing: 64%
Number of official organized extracurricular organizations: 220
3 Most popular majors: Social Sciences, Business, Psychology
Student/Faculty ratio: 13:1
Average Class Size: 18
Percent of students going to grad school: 20%
Tuition and Fees: $40,437
In-State Tuition and Fees if different: No difference
Cost for Room and Board: $9,920
Percent receiving financial aid out of those who apply, first year: 74%
Percent receiving financial aid among all students: 37%

Going to school in the nation's capital certainly has its advantages. Just a few blocks from the White House, and a mere Metro ride from the National Archives and Capitol Hill, the GW campus is a hub of activity for its students. At GW, lazy afternoons easily turn into historical and political adventures, and even an early morning run has the unique appeal of boasting the Washington Monument and the Jefferson Memorial as backdrops. The Supreme Court is nearby, as is Embassy Row and the Smithsonian Museums. In fact, it's possible to spend four years at GW and not have enough time to explore all of the many options available. Located in the nation's political center and one of the world's most beautiful cities, George Washington University stands out for the opportunities it gives students for learning both inside and beyond the classroom. Whether you're a politics buff or not, it's certainly an exciting place to be.

One Part Academia, One Part Politics

George Washington University is comprised of six individual schools, each with its own requirements, to which aspiring freshmen apply directly: The Columbian College of Arts and Sciences, The School of Media and Public Affairs, The School of Business, The School of Public Health and Health Services, The Elliot School of International Affairs, and the School of Engineering and Applied Science. Although the six schools may seem to have a narrow focus, each student must fulfill general liberal arts requirements, and students are permitted and encouraged to take classes outside of their specific school. (Students warn, however, that it is important to be on top of your own classes and requirements, because it is surprisingly easy to "fall through the cracks" here.) In addition, GW offers a number of specialized programs including an eight-year Integrated Engineering/M.D. program, a seven-year B.A./M.D. program, and an Integrated Engineering and Law Program. The University Honors Program is a smaller, more selective college within the university that allows students a four-year, multidisciplinary, interschool undergraduate experience. Acceptance to the Honors Program is also sweetened with a significant merit-based scholarship.

The GW faculty and classes receive solid reviews, though students are careful to warn that "It really varies based on your school, major, and professor." Most students are "happy with the accessibility of the faculty and the quality of the teaching," though students emphasize the need for their peers to make the effort to engage their professors. The workload is described as "pretty average" by most students, with some emphasizing the rigor of first-year/introductory classes. "They try to weed you out," one senior remarked. Grades are "fairly accurate," and there isn't too much "grading on a curve." Double majoring is fairly common, and not too difficult. Class sizes vary, with introductory lectures being the largest. Other classes are usually smaller, with an average of 20 to 50 students. Small discussion groups led by TAs are a popular way to master the material discussed in larger lectures.

Because of GW's central location, academics tend to go hand-in-hand with taking advantage of the opportunities available in Washington, D.C. Many students are able to intern and work during the school year, with government agencies being a popular job option. "Getting an internship or a job in government or politics may be easier during the school year," one student noted, "because fewer students are looking for work than in the summer, when tons of undergrads want to work and live in D.C." Other advantages of GW's location include the fact that professors will frequently bring notable speakers and politicians in to speak to their classes, and field trips to museums and other attractions are often part of course work.

A World of Social Possibilities

"Because we're in a city, people spread out a lot on weekends," said one senior. Many students head to bars or dance clubs in D.C., and while they complain about the cover charges, they generally agree that there's little to do on campus at night. "Sometimes freshmen party on campus," said one sophomore. "But as you get older, I think the bars and clubs are more of a draw. You can't re-

ally come to GW without a fake ID." That said, partying on campus can be difficult—there is officially no alcohol allowed in campus housing if you are under 21, and students caught three times with alcohol are forced to relinquish their campus housing. Any student found with an illegal substance must move off-campus at the first strike. Community Facilitators (CFs) are GW's answer to residential advisers, and while many students reported "becoming friends with" their CFs, Community Facilitators are more than willing to write up students on alcohol charges when necessary. Despite this, drinking seems to be a large part of social life at GW. Upperclassmen gravitate toward the bars in Adams Morgan, a notoriously fun part of the city, and bars closer to home, like McFadden's on New Hampshire Ave. The meal plan, called GWorld, can be used at certain local restaurants, which students reported to be a nice feature of GW dining. Students generally say that the meal plan is "good, though nothing to brag about," and are likely to dine out on the weekends, noting the restaurants on Georgetown's M Street and in Dupont Circle as particularly good options.

Drinking may be a big part of social life at GW, but fraternities and sororities are not. Greek life is an option for students that are interested, but many GWers think it unnecessary and a hindrance to enjoying all that Washington, D.C., has to offer. While students report that their peers are "pretty friendly," they also acknowledge that "The University isn't particularly helpful in helping people meet each other." Overall, being in such a great city provides a lot of opportunity, but also causes GW to lack a sense of community spirit. Most students meet their friends through their majors or extracurricular activities, even though few people feel defined by these groups. The administration attempts to foster a greater sense of community spirit by hosting events like Fall Fest and Spring Fest, and increasing the number of formal balls.

Students at GW think of themselves as "fit," and most take part in intramurals and take advantage of the beautiful Washington scenery by frequently running around the city. Many athletic teams are in the Atlantic 10 Conference as well as NCAA Division I. Students tend to show their (limited) school spirit by attending basketball games, as basketball is by far "the most popular sport on campus." Extracurricular activities are also popular, and most students get involved in at least one organization. "There are tons of options," said one student, "especially in the realm of political and cultural organizations." Students take advantage of their surroundings by joining clubs that take them to the National Gallery of Art and the Capitol, among other locales. Students tend not to feel categorized by the clubs they join, and enjoy the fact that "It always seems like you can meet someone new."

Location, Location, Location

The location of the George Washington University is its greatest draw to students, although particular departments are also very attractive. The main Foggy Bottom Campus (there is a smaller campus called Mount Vernon) is composed of four-by-four square city blocks. "It is definitely an urban, city campus," said one student, "and it is often hard to tell if someone you pass is a GW student or a government employee." While students complain about a lack of grassy space, they are always quick to realize how lucky they are to live in such a beautiful and vibrant city. Students generally feel very safe on campus, though "Of course, we're in a major city, so you have to be careful." Security measures have been increased with the threat of terrorism in recent years, and most students seem to feel that the school is doing all it can to protect their well-being.

> "It is often hard to tell if someone you pass is a GW student or a government employee."

Freshmen and sophomores are required to live on campus, and freshmen are usually split between Thurston (affectionately called "the tenements" by residents) and about four other dorms. Thurston is the largest freshman dorm on campus, and like all on-campus locations, offers apartment-style or suite living (some have kitchens, some do not). Juniors and seniors are not guaranteed on-campus housing, and may take their chances in a lottery that works on the basis of seniority. Mitchell Hall is one of the most sought after, offering attractive living conditions: all single dorms and a veranda. Many upperclassmen opt for apartments in the city (which are "SO EXPENSIVE!" warns one student) and some choose to live in the suburbs of Maryland or Virginia. For others, sorority and fraternity houses are the way to go.

The Marvin Center—the school's student union—is largely regarded as the center of campus life. The Marvin Center houses the headquarters and offices of student organizations, as well as a few fast-food and chain restaurants. Meals can be eaten in the Marvin Center or in standard dining halls, where food is described as "good but unhealthy." The center is a hub for students, a place where "Lots of kids hang out, do their work, and get meals." The center also houses a grocery store and travel agency. The Marvin Center is considered a great convenience, especially for freshmen who don't yet know their way around the city. "If you need something, chances are you can get it there."

Official school statistics show a geographically and racially diverse student population, but students tend to think the school is too dominated by the wealthy. Students complain that people at GW are ostentatious about their wealth. "People here are well-off, and they let you know it." While there are definitely stereotypes about well-dressed, BMW-driving students, others claim that it really depends on where you choose to hang out, and with whom. "A stereotype is just that," said one articulate senior, "it under-represents the variety of student 'types' on campus."

With a prime location in the hub of the political world, George Washington University provides an education in academics, politics, and real-life, city living. With so much to see, do, and learn, students are more than happy with their choice to come here. "I love GW," said one senior, "and I don't know many people who feel otherwise."—*Erica Ross*

FYI

If you come to GW, you'd better bring "a coffee mug for the Starbucks on every corner in D.C.!"

What is the typical weekend schedule? "Wake up late, do some work, go out all night, and wake up late again the next day!"

If I could change one thing about GW, I'd "make the administration more accessible to students."

Three things every student at GW should do before graduating are "go to the monuments at night, get a Manuche dog, and party in Georgetown."

Georgetown University

Address: 37th and O Streets, NW, Washington, D.C. 20057-1270
Phone: 202-687-0100
E-mail address: guadmiss@georgetown.edu
Web site URL: www.georgetown.edu
Year Founded: 1789
Private or Public: Private
Religious Affiliation: Roman Catholic-Jesuit
Location: Urban
Number of Applicants: 16,163
Percent Accepted: 21%
Percent Accepted who enroll: 47%
Number Entering: 1,579
Number of Transfers Accepted each Year: 368
Middle 50% SAT range:
M: 650–740, CR: 650–750, Wr: Unreported
Middle 50% ACT range: Unreported
Early admission program EA/ED/None: EA

Percentage accepted through EA or ED: 8%
EA and ED deadline: 1-Nov
Regular Deadline: 15-Dec
Application Fee: $65
Full time Undergraduate enrollment: 7,038
Total enrollment: 11,979
Percent Male: 45%
Percent Female: 55%
Total Percent Minority or Unreported: 30%
Percent African-American: 7%
Percent Asian/Pacific Islander: 11%
Percent Hispanic: 5%
Percent Native-American: <1%
Percent International: 8%
Percent in-state/out of state: 2%/98%
Percent from Public HS: 49%
Retention Rate: 96%
Graduation Rate 4-year: 90%

Graduation Rate 6-year: 92%
Percent Undergraduates in On-campus housing: 71%
Number of official organized extracurricular organizations: 103
3 Most popular majors: English, International Relations, Political Science and Government
Student/Faculty ratio: 11:1
Average Class Size: 26
Percent of students going to grad school: 31%
Tuition and Fees: $37,947
In-State Tuition and Fees if different: No difference
Cost for Room and Board: $12,753
Percent receiving financial aid out of those who apply, first year: 72%
Percent receiving financial aid among all students: 40%

Nestled in a distinct residential neighborhood of Washington, D.C., Georgetown University encompasses the charms of both city and suburban life. Yet, given its tremendous wealth of resources, dynamic population, and sometimes-controversial stances, the political noise generated on this campus makes for a college experience that is by no means pastoral.

Friendly Internal Rivalries

The undergraduate experience at Georgetown is markedly diverse, with four primary schools: Georgetown College, The Edmund A. Walsh School of Foreign Service, The Robert Emmett McDonough Business School, and the School of Nursing and Health Studies. Although students live, work, and play together, prospective Hoyas apply for admission to one of the four colleges, becoming affiliated with that school upon matriculation. Of the internal divisions, students said the differences only manifest themselves during mock competition, and one University tour guide described the practice as "Harry Potter-esque." In a similar vein, students admitted to the presence of some inter-school tension, but were quick to add that the tension was not strongly palpable. "We have a lot of University pride, but a lot of school pride too," said one senior.

As always, there are stereotypes about students in each of the schools. One junior explained: "There's the idea that business school kids are only there to make money; that SFS students are arrogant, conceited, naïve, and think they're the most intelligent people on campus; and that the College kids don't know what they want to do with their lives since all 900 of them come in here undeclared. The Nursing kids don't really have a reputation since there are only around 80 of them per year."

The "Georgetown Paradox"

The "Georgetown Paradox" is the understanding that "Everyone wants you for your internship, but you have no way to get to that internship," explained a sophomore. The inaccessibility of Georgetown is the primary gripe among its students. Although the University provides a bus system, many students complain about its irregularity and unreliability. "Things would be better if we had a Metro stop," said one freshman. "But I think it's because Jackie Onassis, who owned four homes in the neighborhood over the course of her lifetime, didn't want Georgetown to be accessible to just anyone." With the Georgetown stamp of approval on their resumes, most students have no problem securing competitive internships throughout the D.C. area. "Anything that I've applied for, I've gotten," said one McDonough student. "It's a matter of deciding between what you've been offered. For example, Ameriprise Financial almost exclusively recruits Georgetown students." It seems that for a Hoya the only real problem is getting there.

A Hoya Halloween

Founded alongside the country, Georgetown stands as America's oldest Catholic and Jesuit university. And with over 200 years of history, it is one with its fair share of unique traditions spanning the traditional and the innovative. Not only do Georgetown students ceremoniously steal the clock handles from Healy Clock Tower and mail them to the Vatican to be blessed by the Pope, they also dance in the Dahlgren Fountain, evoking the opening credits of the television show *Friends*.

Another Georgetown staple is the nightly 11:15 p.m. candlelight Catholic mass, held in the major University chapel, Dahlgren Chapel of the Sacred Heart, and most frequented on Sunday nights. On a Hoya's 21st birthday, it is practically mandated that they celebrate at "The Tombs." And around the holidays, students are known to climb up and sit in the lap of the statue of their founder (Archbishop John Carroll) and tell him what they want for Christmas.

Basketball games are another Hoya institution. As one McDonough student put it, "Attending a Georgetown basketball game will change your life." Students described the scene as a mass of gray-clad Hoyas (the school colors are gray and blue) roaring with applause each time the team scores. "Of course, some people Georgetown it up and wear a popped collar underneath," said

one sophomore. The respect for Georgetown basketball extends even to the band. One New Jersey native said, "Our pep band gets more respect than any other pep band in the country." But this immense fan base lacks a football counterpart. Some students said that the football team is so bad that "People pretend we don't have a football team." With basketball characterized by a self-described "cult of followers," it is clear that Hoya pride is expressed most intensely on the court, not on the field.

The biggest campus tradition is undeniably Halloween night. The 1973 William Friedkin film, *The Exorcist*, was filmed almost entirely on Georgetown's campus. This fact adds fuel to the eerie fire driving the renowned Hoya Halloween. Students generally agreed with one senior's conclusion that "Halloween is the biggest thing on campus." That night, students dress up and proceed to the main assembly hall, where they watch the film on a jumbo screen, then go down to the intersection of M Street and Wisconsin to dance in the street. One student bragged that the Hoya holiday tradition was rated among the top towns featuring fun Halloween celebrations.

The Jesuit Influence

Students report that there are a lot of Jesuit professors, but that the Jesuit influence was only very strong around Christmas when "mangers pop up around campus." A freshman who said he was initially apprehensive of attending a Catholic-affiliated school said that his fears of "a Jesuit behind [his] back" were quickly allayed when he found their presence was not overwhelming. "The Jesuit tradition is a very welcoming and open one. There is some restriction, but they're very accommodating and open to hearing things," he said. However, other students pointed to the facts that the pro-choice group on campus is not allowed to table like other campus organizations and that, though they are permitted to flyer, anyone offended by their literature can tear them down. They also noted that none of the on-campus stores can sell condoms, though they admitted there is an unrestricted CVS just four blocks away from campus. Students further explained that Red Square is a free speech zone, where one can "pretty much say anything" without repercussions.

Not Your Average Greek

Georgetown University does not officially recognize traditional fraternities and sororities. But there are some illegitimate on-campus Greek organizations in addition to recognized professional and service organizations. "It's not your typical college Greek life; it's more of the resume-building than boozing-up kind," explained one junior. On-campus parties are not centered around Greek life, but are popular in the University townhouses, of which there are roughly 70 within a one-block radius of the front gates, populated by upperclassmen. However, recent changes to drinking policies and restrictions on parties have made on-campus fiestas almost extinct. "All it's done is push alcohol use into the surrounding areas," said one senior. Despite the enormous backlash from students and months of publications devoted to criticizing the new crackdowns, Georgetown's prime social life now exists primarily along the town's bar-lined streets.

What's in the Salad?

Georgetown students consistently commented on the University's widespread culture of looking good. "We're always ranked among the fittest campuses, and I think that's a function of the fact that when Georgetown selects its well-rounded students, a lot of them happen to be varsity athletes and come from a culture of being fit," explained one female freshman. Other students, however, were more skeptical, and sometimes sarcastic, in their justifications of the University's fit reputation. "There's a rumor that they spray carbs on the salad to get the kids to gain weight," stated one junior. "Actually, I think eating disorders are another Georgetown tradition."

> "For the most part, I feel a real sense of community here, but if you want to see a split on Georgetown's campus, come visit around election time."

"There is a lot of competition in terms of who can put on the biggest show of carrying the largest Louis Vuitton bag without breaking a bone," said a male Marketing major. Others elaborated on the student body's fashion choices as conclusively preppy. "We do have a large preppy contingency and that's going to happen at any higher-level school that feeds from higher-level prep schools, but Georgetown does seem to take it to an extreme," commented one freshman male. "I do feel outnumbered as a public

school grad." Other students commented on the same phenomenon. "Some of the things you wonder if people do in real life, they happen here. People are playing croquet on the front lawn; kids go quail hunting," said an SFS female. Students described the overall atmosphere as reflecting "the two p's—pearls and polos," and said that the prep level increases when people go out. One senior said, "The preppy look is definitely noticeable, but not universal."

Class, Clinton, Class . . .

Georgetown's capital location ensures proximity to a great deal of political events, an all-star faculty, various specialized courses, and famous speakers. "When people are in D.C. and want to give a speech, they come to us, we don't go to them," said a female Finance major. Students remembered instances of famous speakers coming to campus and commented on the choice between seeing Bill Clinton speak or going to class. "It was pretty funny that when Bill Clinton came to town, I remember his motorcade was blocking my path, and I actually got annoyed," recalled one senior. "The idea of choice in that situation is ridiculous, but sometimes class wins out."

It comes as no surprise that this choice would be difficult for Georgetown students who are at once notoriously studious and politically active. Hoyas are known to take it to the streets when bothered by, well, anything. Students have even mobilized to protest Wal-Mart representatives speaking on corporate responsibility. Recently, students mobilized against a series of assaults on individuals identified as homosexual, critiquing the University's position on the matter and raising the difficult issue of what a Catholic institution's position should be on such a sensitive topic. Students did, however, note that the mood at Georgetown is typically one of unity. "For the most part, I feel a real sense of community here, but if you want to see a split on Georgetown's campus, come visit around November," said a junior, referencing election time.

Popular Georgetown majors include pre-med, finance, culture and politics, comparative studies and economics. The school is noted for rigorous requirements, like "Map of the Modern World." All SFS students must pass this course in order to graduate, and in order to pass this course, they must successfully distinguish and name every country in the world, its capital, population, religion, and political system. Another requirement is

"The Problem of God," fulfilled with one of 24 sections that, depending on the professor, can range from getting a comparative religion approach to a psychological one to general theology. On Georgetown's general requirements, a senior said, "You're going to love them or hate them, but the fact that they're requirements means there are a lot of ways to get them done."

Georgetown students appear well-versed in working within established frameworks to accomplish their goals. They succeed at holding down impressive internships while handling full course loads, protesting for gay rights at a Catholic university, demolishing the competition on the basketball court and becoming scholars, while having a great deal of fun.—*Nicholle Manners*

FYI

If you come to Georgetown, you'd better bring "a pastel Polo."

What is the typical weekend schedule? "Friday: go to classes, if you have any, do work for a while in the library, go out to dinner, come back to campus to party or study, depending on the weekend; Saturday: go out to the city during the day, party at night; Sunday: spend the entire day in the library."

If I could change one thing about Georgetown, I'd "overhaul the dining hall food; it's horrendous and every prospective student should be warned."

Three things every student at Georgetown should do before graduating are "go to a basketball game, go to a performance at the Kennedy Center, and protest in Red Square."

Howard University

Address: 2400 Sixth Street, NW, Washington, D.C. 20059

Phone: 202-806-2700

E-mail address: AskEM@howard.edu

Web site URL: www.howard.edu

Year Founded: 1867

Private or Public: Private

Religious Affiliation: None

Location: Urban

Number of Applicants: 7,603

Percent Accepted: 54%

Percent Accepted who enroll: 35%

Number Entering: 1,443

Number of Transfers Accepted each Year: 250

Middle 50% SAT range: M: 440–650, CR: 460–660, Wr: 410–650

Middle 50% ACT range: 20–28

Early admission program EA/ED/None: EA

Percentage accepted through EA or ED: Unreported

EA and ED deadline: 1-Nov

Regular Deadline: 15-Feb

Application Fee: $45

Full time Undergraduate enrollment: 6,988

Total enrollment: 6,988

Percent Male: 33%

Percent Female: 67%

Total Percent Minority or Unreported: 32%

Percent African-American: 67%

Percent Asian/Pacific Islander: 1%

Percent Hispanic: 0%

Percent Native-American: <1%

Percent International: 5%

Percent in-state/out of state: 23%/77%

Percent from Public HS: 80%

Retention Rate: 84%

Graduation Rate 4-year: 43%

Graduation Rate 6-year: 63%

Percent Undergraduates in On-campus housing: 55%

Number of official organized extracurricular organizations: 150

3 Most popular majors: Biology/Biological Sciences, Journalism, Radio and Television

Student/Faculty ratio: 8:1

Average Class Size: 9

Percent of students going to grad school: 60%

Tuition and Fees: $13,215

In-State Tuition and Fees if different: No difference

Cost for Room and Board: $6,976

Percent receiving financial aid out of those who apply, first year: 96%

Percent receiving financial aid among all students: 96%

Washington, D.C., one of the most diverse cities in the United States, is home to one of the oldest historically black colleges, Howard University. A private, federally funded institution, of nearly 7,000 students, Howard University is an up and coming research institution. Known as the "Black Harvard," Howard offers degrees through doctoral and professional levels, various extracurricular opportunities, and traditions, making Howard an excellent school in an exciting city.

The Mecca

Self-known as the "Mecca of Black education," Howard University is the richest black educational institution in America, and one of the country's top research schools. Howard has always been synonymous with either medicine or law studies; and, although these areas are still popular and prestigious aspects of the school, many different colleges have grown significantly in the past few years. Students choose from one of several different colleges to focus on during their time at Howard (Arts and Sciences, Communications, etc.). Though, recently, the University has taken initiatives to "revamp the curriculum" and "reach higher ground" according to President Sidney A. Ribeau, Ph.D. in order to "maintain the highest standards of academic and administrative excellence." Howard University plans to reduce the number of majors and graduate programs. Among those on the chopping block: classics and African studies, Old World language majors such as Russian, and philosophy. Students will still be able to take courses such as African-American Philosophy and Slavery in the Ancient World. The changes have met criticism but the leadership feels it necessary to formulate a curriculum that will not only challenge its students but also prepare them for a changing world. Ribeau commented, "I feel a tremendous sense of responsibility to those who came before me, and an even greater responsibility to those who come after me," he says. "One challenge is to continue to convince our community that if you attend Howard University, your child has a full opportunity to be successful, both in terms of human growth and potential, and professional growth and potential in this society."

In conjunction with one's major, many students take on a subsequent minor and fulfill an undergraduate requirement termed "practical education," manifested in areas such as the required physical education classes. Though some of these classes are large, classes are usually intimate (8:1 teacher ratio). The total undergraduate enrollment is around 7,000 and freshmen enrollment is around 1,500 students. According to one senior, "Because of the small class sizes, teachers develop strong relationships with their students. They are constantly supplying them with opportunities for internships and ways to utilize being in Washington, D.C." It is because of these great teachers that there are certain must-take classes at Howard such as Literature of Love and Pan-Africanism. With readings that vary from Toni Morrison to William Shakespeare, Literature of Love is a class that encourages students to seek to understand human interaction through famous literary works. Well-known professors such as Dr. Gregory Carr and John Davis are integral parts of life at Howard and are constantly seen at functions all around campus.

The Whose Who?

With a thriving social scene, Howard has opportunities for all different types of people to get involved with student activities. HUSA, Howard University Student Association, is one of the biggest groups on campus. Howard students serve on the Board of Trustees and on University-wide committees. They can express their views through student organizations, as well as *The Hilltop* student newspaper—rated "The Best Campus Newspaper" by the *Princeton Review*—and the *Bison Yearbook*. Howard University invites you to visit their newly redesigned Newsroom that helps you stay connected with the University, its students, faculty, staff and alumni. Other students are involved in a wide variety of extracurriculars, including everything from putting on pageants to joining step groups. *The Hilltop* is very highly regarded and has won numerous accolades both nationally and at the yearly Historically Black Colleges & Universities conference. Mock Trial is also highly acclaimed at Howard. Howard University was the first team to win two national championships in the same year, both the 1997 National Silver Flight Tournament and the 1997 National Championship. In accordance with the international student population, the African Student Association and the Caribbean Student Association are also huge forces on campus. Along with chapters of national organizations such as the NAACP and NSCS (National Society of Collegiate Scholars), Howard boasts a unique system of clubs for each of the fifty states. These clubs are known to host activities and gatherings such as the well-attended yearly party thrown by the Louisiana and Texas Clubs. There are other school-wide activities such as "ResFest" where different dormitories divide into teams and compete against other dorms in competitions such as dance contests and sporting events.

Although there are lots of different social scenes around campus, none is more dominant than Greek life. One student said "Part of the reason the Greek scene here is so prominent is because of its legacy on campus. Greeks have a responsibility that goes beyond partying." Fraternity and sorority members hold positions of power around campus and have a very prominent place at Howard. The groups strive to be more than just social groups, emphasizing both community service and African-American unity.

In addition to evolving living situations and eating habits, the social scene, too, changes, as students get older. The clubbing scene begins to fade and instead of heading out to clubs like H2O, FUR, and Love, as they did as freshman and sophomores, upperclassmen tend to socialize at bars, house parties, and more sophisticated places such as The Diner, which is a coffee-shop-like place to hang out. As the workload increases and the realization dawns that professional life is quickly approaching, many seniors spend weekend time differently than they did their first few years at Howard.

Coming Home to Howard

The annual homecoming is a definite must see. One student said, "some say it's the vibe, while others say it's the events. Some say it's the people and others say it's the hype. No matter what is said, the fact remains that people have always talked about Howard University's homecoming. With homecoming, students are thinking back to past experiences in anticipation of what's to come." People from all over the world come to gather together and share in special activities and events that last all week long. From the moment that guests arrive on campus on Sunday, they have the option of attending chapel services, talent shows, concerts, and more. One of the most famous events is the step show that takes place at the yard, where each fraternity has its own section from which to observe the events. Although the weekend is technically centered on sports, the hype is more about the gathering of all different people in a single venue. When asked about homecoming, one sophomore said, "The fact that you can meet so many people from so many different regions and backgrounds, all with the same goal in mind,

is a beautiful thing." For those who doubt the importance of the event: Homecoming was even mentioned in a Ludacris song. Besides the events that characterize homecoming, alumni and other prominent members of the African-American community who return to Howard are reminded of the time they spent at the gorgeous, hilly campus lined with old, New England–style buildings.

> "We come from diverse backgrounds and circumstances and share a unique heritage, but what we all have in common is that we're HERE, right where we belong, both with something to gain and something to give."

No matter what type of background a person comes from or what activities he or she participates in, Howard is a place where students can build on their potential and grow into future leaders. A student best explained, "We come from diverse backgrounds and circumstances and share a unique heritage, but what we all have in common is that we're HERE, right where we belong, both with something to gain and something to give." Howard has awarded more than 95,000 degrees. In fact, Howard produces more African-American Ph.D.s and MDs than any other university in the world. And with more than 3,000 faculty members, it has the largest concentration of African-American scholars in the world. Notable Howard alumni include Nobel Laureate Toni Morrison, Emmy Award-winning actress Phylicia Rashad, singer Jessye Norman, actress-producer Debbie Allen, Dr. LaSalle Leffall, Jr., Thurgood Marshall, L. Douglas Wilder, and former United Nations Ambassador Andrew Young.

The Capitol

Washington, D.C., is considered to be one of the liveliest metropolitan areas in America and the over 16 colleges in the city definitely have something to do with that. The different colleges have established particular cultures for their surrounding areas.

Howard is often referred to as the Mecca, or the center, of every Historically Black College, or, even, the University of the nation. The unified pride that the students have in the school's history and what it represents is real and substantial. This shared legacy is felt and strongly exuded whether it be in academics, sports, or extracurriculars. Howard University is moving forward, constantly striving to become better and more competitive with each passing year. More importantly, most students understand that *their* legacy will be their contribution to the upward trajectory of their beloved University. For a student who wants legacy, pride, and a voice at an institution, a pilgrimage to the Mecca is a clear choice.—*Dashell Laryea*

FYI

Typical weekend schedule? Go to a house party on Friday night, relax outside during the day on Saturday, head to Adams Morgan or a bar on Saturday night, and then recover and relax on Sunday, take a shuttle to church in the morning and catch up on work the rest of the day.

Stay for Homecoming, it's a must.

Take in a free performance at The Kennedy Center's Millennium Stage every evening at 6pm. Acts include everything from performances by the National Symphony Orchestra to gospel groups to jazz musicians to poetry slams.

Trinity Washington University

Address: 125 Michigan Avenue, NE, Washington, D.C. 20017
Phone: 202-884-9400
E-mail address: admissions@trinitydc.edu
Web site URL: www.trinitydc.edu
Year Founded: 1897
Private or Public: Private
Religious Affiliation: Roman Catholic
Location: Urban
Number of Applicants: 441
Percent Accepted: 75%
Percent Accepted who enroll: 48%
Number Entering: 182
Number of Transfers Accepted each Year: Unreported
Middle 50% SAT range: Unreported
Middle 50% ACT range: Unreported
Early admission program EA/ED/None: EA

Percentage accepted through EA or ED: Unreported
EA and ED deadline: 1-Dec
Regular Deadline: Rolling
Application Fee: $40
Full time Undergraduate enrollment: 1,047
Total enrollment: 1,449
Percent Male: 0%
Percent Female: 100%
Total Percent Minority or Unreported: 98%
Percent African-American: 70%
Percent Asian/Pacific Islander: 1%
Percent Hispanic: 10%
Percent Native-American: <1%
Percent International: Unreported
Percent in-state/out of state: 50%/50%
Percent from Public HS: Unreported
Retention Rate: Unreported
Graduation Rate 4-year: 29%

Graduation Rate 6-year: 44%
Percent Undergraduates in On-campus housing: 22%
Number of official organized extracurricular organizations: 34
2 Most popular majors: Communications Studies, Speech Communication and Rhetoric
Student/Faculty ratio: 11:1
Average Class Size: Unreported
Percent of students going to grad school: Unreported
Tuition and Fees: $18,960
In-State Tuition and Fees if different: No difference
Cost for Room and Board: $8,450
Percent receiving financial aid out of those who apply, first year: Unreported
Percent receiving financial aid among all students: Unreported

Founded in 1897 by the Sisters of Notre Dame de Namur as one of the nation's first Catholic women's liberal arts colleges, Trinity has been attracting focused but fun-loving women ever since. And after becoming a university in 2004 with the addition of two professional schools, Trinity has even more resources to offer its small female population.

"At Trinity, everything is tradition. It's a very traditional school," one junior said. And indeed, the Trinity campus does abide by deep-seated social and moral standards. But with its location in the heart of Washington, D.C., the campus provides plenty of opportunity to create a mix between old and new, fun and serious.

A Foundation for Leadership

With just over 1,000 undergraduates Trinity is a tight-knit community, with many specialized programs to meet the needs of its students. Trinity students complete the Foundation for Leadership Curriculum (FLC), an interdisciplinary program with a professional focus that combines courses from five areas of study: Communication Skills, Traditions and Cultural Expression, Search for Ultimate Meanings, Scientific and Mathematical Exploration, and Perspectives on Self and Society.

Some of the most popular majors at Trinity are, understandably, politically focused, with political science as a perennial favorite, trailed by communications, business, psychology and international affairs. Trinity's political science department has graduated such political stars as California state representative and Democratic Leader of the House of Representatives Nancy Pelosi, Kansas governor Kathleen Sebelius, and several upper-level judges.

Thanks in part to its small size, and also its comfortable all-female dynamic, Trinity fosters an intimacy and camaraderie in the classroom that students cannot stop raving about. "At Trinity, you're a name, not a social security number," one student said. Another commented, "You definitely walk away with everyone pushing for you."

Students and professors are very close at Trinity, and students say it is not unusual to have a professor's home or cell phone number—or even to have class dinners at the homes of professors during the semester. "The professors at Trinity are amazing," one junior said. "They love teaching and sharing their lives and all that they have learned with their students." Another student put it more succinctly: "Trinity's professors rock!"

On the honor system since 1913, Trinity students are diligent and supportive about their work. Help abounds at Trinity, with the Academic Support and Career Services (ASCS) offering one-on-one tutoring throughout the four-year education and also the Future Focus Program offering help specifically targeted to freshman year.

And while Trinity's academics are sufficient—with classes from Human Sexuality to Political Lives of Women to Civil Rights and Liberties on offer—the University is also part of a consortium of schools in the D.C. area, allowing students to take classes at any number of other colleges and universities, and also bringing in other students (even men!) to Trinity. Washington, D.C., is also the perfect area for professional internships, and Trinity students take advantage of their connections throughout the academic year with internships at anywhere from the White House and the Department of State to the Washington Mystics and the National Zoo.

National Government and Student Government

At Trinity, extracurriculars often take a backseat to academics and internships, but they do play a part in campus life. An NCAA Division III school, Trinity is a founding member of the Atlantic Women's College conference, and competes at the varsity level in basketball, crew, field hockey, lacrosse, soccer, softball, swimming, tennis, track and field, and volleyball. Students also play a wide variety of intramural sports, but most students seem to spend their time doing individual workouts in Trinity's $20-million state-of-the-art athletic complex, the Trinity Center for Women and Girls in Sports.

Beyond athletics, Trinity extracurriculars run the gamut of usual clubs and organizations, particularly focused on the political and the journalistic. Student government is big at Trinity, as are the College Democrats and the College Republicans. Students run three publications: the literary magazine *The Record*, the yearbook *Trinilogue*, and the newspaper *The Trinity Times*. The Latina American Caribbean Student Association (LACASA) is especially active on campus.

There are no sororities allowed on the Trinity campus, though students are free to join sororities at other schools in the D.C. Consortium. "I think one of the reasons why sororities are not recognized on our campus is that there is not really a need for them," one student explained. "Being an all women's institution necessarily connects us into a sisterhood or community that I can appreciate."

Off-Campus Life

Part of the reason why extracurriculars are not a primary focus of Trinity life is that so many students live off campus. Although the dorms themselves are considered fine, though not by any means spectacular, the University's housing crunch combined with the abundant housing in the D.C. area means that many students commute, especially after freshman year. Trinity is a dry campus, and the dorms are "very restrictive"—"It holds up to all the stereotypes of a private, Catholic women's college," one junior said— so many students also move off campus to get a bit more freedom.

The campus itself, while restrictive, is quite beautiful, sitting on 26 wooded acres. The original Main Building, completed in 1909, contains all administrative offices, most classrooms and faculty offices, the computer center, the post office, the campus bookstore, and a residence hall. In addition to the Main Building, there are two more residence halls—Cuvilly and Kerby—as well as the Science Building, the Sister Helen Sheehan Library, the Trinity Center for Women and Girls in Sports, the award-winning Notre Dame Chapel, and the Alumnae Hall, which houses the campus dining facilities.

Since most students live off campus, they don't rely heavily on the meal plan, though students say Trinity has a "wonderful catering service," which is the same company that contracts for the government and provides food for the House of Representatives and the Senate.

An Emphasis on Diversity

Trinity students' social lives also take place primarily off campus, especially because of Trinity's strict no-alcohol policy and the easy transportation into the city or to surrounding schools. Drinking and drugs are very uncommon on the Trinity campus, with most socializing taking place in D.C. itself—an easy metro ride away. Besides the strict liquor policy, the Trinity lifestyle simply does not lend itself to tons of free time for socializing. "The student organizations fight to create community on campus and have decent success," one student said. "However, Trinity women are typically extremely busy."

The dating scene on campus is, of course, "quite non-existent." Many women, however, date men from area universities and from the D.C. area, and everyone is very enthusiastic about the all-woman atmosphere. "I would say it's comfortable," a junior said. "Many of the distractions that are found on large coed campuses are non-factors at Trinity. I am in college for an education and that is what I get."

> "Many of the distractions that are found on large coed campuses are non-factors at Trinity. I am in college for an education and that is what I get."

But just because only a few men from the Consortium ever enter Trinity's campus does not mean Trinity is not diverse. The school is actually amazingly diverse—less so geographically, but with incredible racial and socioeconomic diversity. Also, because of its continuing education programs, it is not unusual for older women to be in class with the more typical twenty-somethings, lending a viewpoint that the younger students appreciate.

Constantly Evolving Traditions

As busy as they are, Trinity women always find the time to participate in Trinity traditions. "We're very into keeping up those traditions." Ultimately, these traditions are not just important to the Trinity experience, but symbolic of it: holding on to the past, but always moving forward into the future.

The many long-standing traditions at Trinity include the First Year Medal Ceremony, Sophomore Pin Ceremony, Junior Ring Ceremony, Convocation, Cap and Gown Weekend, Founders' Day, Family Weekend, and "Well Sings."

But the most important Trinity tradition, and the one that speaks most to the strong community and legacy that is a Trinity education, is the class colors. The first four graduating classes each chose a color: red, blue, green and gold. Now, at the end of the year, graduating seniors give their color to the incoming first-year class, to create a common bond between every fourth class. This is what it means to be part of a true sisterhood.—*Claire Stanford*

FYI
If you come to Trinity, you'd better bring "a well-polished résumé because you never know who you're going to meet, walking shoes, your own social life."
What's the typical weekend schedule? "Go out on Friday, protest on Saturday, sleep on Sunday."
If you could change one thing about Trinity, I'd "make the school have a bigger budget for more classes."
Three things every student at Trinity should do before graduating are "go on a midnight monument tour, go paddle-boating at the Cherry Blossom festival in the Spring, and see fireworks at the National Mall on the Fourth of July."

Florida

Address: Suite G-9, Foote-Hilyer Administration Center, Tallahassee, FL 32307
Phone: 850-599-3796
E-mail address: ugrdadmissions@famu.edu
Web site URL: www.famu.edu
Year Founded: 1887
Private or Public: Public
Religious Affiliation: None
Location: Urban
Number of Applicants: 4,708
Percent Accepted: 61%
Percent Accepted who enroll: 60%
Number Entering: 1,705
Number of Transfers Accepted each Year: 605
Middle 50% SAT range: M: 440–550, CR: 440–550, Wr: Unreported
Middle 50% ACT range: 19–22
Early admission program EA/ED/None: None

Percentage accepted through EA or ED: NA
EA and ED deadline: NA
Regular Deadline: 9-May
Application Fee: $20
Full time Undergraduate enrollment: 9,591
Total enrollment: 10,124
Percent Male: 43%
Percent Female: 57%
Total Percent Minority or Unreported: 97%
Percent African-American: 94%
Percent Asian/Pacific Islander: 1%
Percent Hispanic: 1%
Percent Native-American: <1%
Percent International: 1%
Percent in-state/out of state: 73%/27%
Percent from Public HS: 85%
Retention Rate: 89%
Graduation Rate 4-year: 41%

Graduation Rate 6-year: Unreported
Percent Undergraduates in On-campus housing: 75%
Number of official organized extracurricular organizations: 10
3 Most popular majors: Business, Health Professions, Security and Protective Services
Student/Faculty ratio: 17:1
Average Class Size: 9
Percent of students going to grad school: 33%
Tuition and Fees: $15,513
In-State Tuition and Fees if different: $3,572
Cost for Room and Board: $6,508
Percent receiving financial aid out of those who apply, first year: Unreported
Percent receiving financial aid among all students: Unreported

Tallahassee, Florida, is known as a great college town. Since the city has two major universities, students who matriculate at Florida A&M (FAMU) can expect that something is always going on. In addition, as the State University System's only historically black university, FAMU has a long tradition of separating itself from the pack and retaining its individuality.

Structured Study

Undergraduates at FAMU have their pick of 62 majors in 11 different colleges. Much of the educational activity that goes on at FAMU is geared toward professional or pre-professional studies. In particular, the University's strongest programs are reputed to be in the School of Business and Industry, the College of Education, the School of Architecture, and the College of Pharmacy. The College of Engineering, which is shared with Florida State University, is also popular and well respected.

Students sometimes complain that the education they receive is a little too structured. "My academic program is way too narrowly defined," one freshman said. "There is little room for personal exploration." On the whole, however, students say the academics are "reasonable" and "manageable" if, like most FAMU students, one enters the school with a clearly defined notion of one's professional goals.

One aspect of FAMU's pedagogical goals

that distinguishes the University from its State University System peers is its commitment to undergraduates. While FAMU is trying to expand its graduate program enrollment across disciplines, most of the school's energies are geared toward its undergrads. All classes are taught by professors, who as a general rule interact often and individually with their students. TAs are hired only to assist with labs and occasionally to substitute for faculty. This focus on undergraduates has always been a hallmark of the FAMU education.

Chilling at the Set
Housing headaches have long been considered a part of life at FAMU, though this may be changing for the better in the near future. Most students have traditionally lived off campus, but there are residence halls as well. The University requires all freshmen whose families live 35 or more miles away to live in the dorms. In order to create a more tight-knit community, the University has been trying to make its housing options more attractive to all students. To date, those in the dorms tend to be ambivalent about their living conditions. "[It's] fine—nothing great, nothing awful," one student said. Meal plans are required of those who do live in on-campus housing.

For those who choose their own accommodations, Tallahassee offers a wealth of housing options that cater to college students. Apartments are generally available, and local places to shop and grab a bite to eat (including two malls) are abundant. Clubs and restaurants are also popular destinations. FAMU's campus is very near downtown, which offers not only practical and social advantages but also great educational and professional-development opportunities, given Tallahassee's status as the capital of Florida. FAMU has several established internship programs with local institutions, such as the popular program that places journalism majors at the *Tallahassee Democrat*, the local daily newspaper, for a summer or more.

There is plenty to do on campus as well. One popular hangout is "the Set," which is a common area near the Student Union. It contains the post office, the bookstore, a market and a TV room. Such shared spaces give off-campus residents a great excuse to hang out with on-campus friends. "It is great to have the Set so that off-campus people like myself can still stay connected with the rest of the student body," one sophomore said.

Never a Dull Moment
Popular activities among students include the Student Government Association, fraternities and sororities, musical events, pre-professional societies, journalism, theater and sporting events. With so much going on, it goes without saying that FAMU students are an active, spirited group.

One of the challenges of the student government has been to keep off-campus students involved in the larger campus life. According to most accounts, they have succeeded admirably. "They do a terrific job," one student said. One popular annual event is "Be Out Day," which brings the student body out to the athletic fields for a day of food, partying and games. Another SGA-run event that "we all look forward to each year" is Homecoming.

The Greek system is another big draw for students. According to the Office of Student Union and Activities, all of the national historically black fraternities and sororities have chapters at FAMU. In addition to these more traditional college Greek houses, there are also numerous community-service organizations and honor societies.

> "I am going out into the real world with not only solid academic training, but a host of life experiences that I won't soon forget."

Music is also an important part of life at FAMU. The gospel choir is very popular, and the marching band, known as the Marching 100, has achieved an international reputation. The second largest college marching band in the world, the Marching 100 has been featured in a Bastille Day parade in Paris and played at President Clinton's second inauguration. Several predominantly black high-school bands in North Florida and other areas intentionally imitate the flamboyant, show-boating style and discipline of the Marching 100.

FAMU Rattler sports are a pretty big deal in Tallahassee, even though they are often in the shadow of the larger and better-known teams of Florida State University. Students show their school spirit by decking themselves in orange and green and attending NCAA Division I sporting events, especially football, which is in Division I-AA. Intramural sports are also popular and are described as "fierce and fun."

A Close Community

With most schools in the country focusing their recruiting efforts on increasing diversity, FAMU has bucked the trend. The school is very proud of its status as Florida's only public historically black university, and has made the recruitment of high-achieving black students its No. 1 priority. At times, FAMU has performed as well as or better than such universities as Harvard, Yale and Stanford in recruiting National Achievement Scholars.

Students say that although they wish there were more diversity on campus, they do appreciate and enjoy the community they have. "I love this community, but . . . there is much to be desired in terms of creating a more diverse student body," one senior said. "I look outside and everyone is so much like me." Of course, the students do have diversity when it comes to their backgrounds and interests (although around 75 percent are from Florida). There is considerable political diversity, but strikingly uniform is the students' take on homosexuality. The small community of gay students isn't organized, and students say they're "not very open-minded when it comes to that."

FAMU has been a traditional top choice for many black students from Florida because of its respected pre-professional and professional academic programs, its warm environment (in more ways than one), and its commitment to undergraduate education. As one senior put it, "I am going out into the real world with not only solid academic training, but a host of life experiences that I won't soon forget."—*Jay Buchanan*

FYI
If you come to FAMU, you'd better bring "sunglasses."
What is the typical weekend schedule? "Friday, catch up on sleep; Saturday, go out and party; Sunday, do all the work from the previous week."
If I could change one thing about FAMU, "I'd improve the landscape. There are too many bushes around here."
Three things that every student at FAMU should do before graduating are "chill at the Set, volunteer in Tallahassee and attend Homecoming."

Florida Institute of Technology

Address: 150 West University Boulevard, Melbourne, FL 32901-6975
Phone: 321-674-8030
E-mail address: admission@fit.edu
Web site URL: www.fit.edu
Year Founded: 1958
Private or Public: Private
Religious Affiliation: None
Location: Suburban
Number of Applicants: 3,168
Percent Accepted: 82%
Percent Accepted who enroll: 25%
Number Entering: 635
Number of Transfers Accepted each Year: 338
Middle 50% SAT range: M: 540–640, CR: 500–610, Wr: Unreported
Middle 50% ACT range: 22–28
Early admission program EA/ED/None: None
Percentage accepted through EA or ED: NA

EA and ED deadline: NA
Regular Deadline: Rolling
Application Fee: $50
Full time Undergraduate enrollment: 2,594
Total enrollment: 5,118
Percent Male: 61%
Percent Female: 39%
Total Percent Minority or Unreported: 65%
Percent African-American: 8%
Percent Asian/Pacific Islander: 3%
Percent Hispanic: 6%
Percent Native-American: <1%
Percent International: 17%
Percent in-state/out of state: 55%/45%
Percent from Public HS: 56%
Retention Rate: 73%
Graduation Rate 4-year: 42%
Graduation Rate 6-year: 58%

Percent Undergraduates in On-campus housing: 37%
Number of official organized extracurricular organizations: 99
3 Most popular majors: Aerospace/Aeronautical Engineering, Aviation Management, Mechanical Engineering
Student/Faculty ratio: 13:1
Average Class Size: 16
Percent of students going to grad school: 20%
Tuition and Fees: $30,190
In-State Tuition and Fees if different: No difference
Cost for Room and Board: $10,250
Percent receiving financial aid out of those who apply, first year: Unreported
Percent receiving financial aid among all students: Unreported

Nestled in a tropical, lush environment and boasting a challenging curriculum with unique research opportunities, the Florida Institute of Technology stands apart from other technical universities. Indeed, this small technical school, located five minutes from the beach, offers more than just an education: Florida Tech prepares its students for life.

Challenging Courses

Despite the appeal of relaxing on the beach, students at Florida Tech take academics seriously. Many said they find the academics to be difficult, but rewarding. As one student said, "Classes are challenging. They really put you to the test."

Students say that one of the best aspects of academics at Florida Tech is the small size of a typical class. Since many classes enroll less than 20 people, students have the chance to actively engage in classroom discussions and interact with the professor. As one sophomore said, "You're not just a number. Professors get to know your name, and you get to know a lot about them too. It's a really nice relationship, but they keep it very challenging."

On top of their classes, many students take advantage of the excellent hands-on research opportunities available at Florida Tech. From manatee preservation and beach erosion studies to working at NASA or Lockheed Martin, every student can plug into Florida Tech's extensive research program.

Along with the requirements for each major, most students have to complete core classes, which include Physics I and II, Calculus I and II, Civilization I and II, and Differential Equations and Linear Algebra. Students must also complete various communication classes, including Composition and Rhetoric, Writing about Literature, and Science and Technical Communication.

Although Florida Tech offers numerous majors through its Colleges of Engineering, Science, Aeronautics, Business, and Psychology and Liberal Arts, two popular majors are Aerospace Engineering and Marine Biology.

"Everything Under the Sun"

Student organizations and clubs exist for "everything under the sun," as one sophomore said. Indeed, with many registered student organizations on campus, "There's something here for everyone," and students have little trouble finding organizations that interest them. Popular organizations range from bowling and sport fishing to math and skydiving. Many students also get involved with community service. Florida Tech has its own organization for Habitat for Humanity as well as a program for working with local elementary school students.

Students at Florida Tech participate in 14 intercollegiate sports at the Division II level. While Florida Tech may not be known for its varsity athletics, students said that the soccer and basketball teams have recently been particularly successful. One sophomore commented that "Athletic spirit could be better, although it has improved in the last couple of years." For those not as eager to indulge in athletics at such a high level, Florida Tech also offers many opportunities to get involved with intramural sports.

Social Life

General friendliness seems to abound at Florida Tech. According to one student, "People will bend over backwards to help you." And, because Florida Tech has a small student body, "Everyone really gets a chance to get to know all the students."

> **"It wasn't what I was expecting . . . it was a lot better."**

On campus, "There's always something going on," as one sophomore said. The student-run Residential Hall Association and the Campus Activities Board set up popular campus events, including comedy shows, concerts and an International Fair, which allows students to explore the traditions of people from different cultures across the world.

Off campus, most students spend their free time hanging out on the beach. While there, people enjoy a range of water activities, including surfing, boating, kayaking or simply relaxing in the sun. Students can also drive less than an hour to get to Disney World.

Greek fraternities and sororities attract a large number of students and are a dominant presence on campus. Some students complain about a lack of on-campus parties, though they acknowledge that parties do take place off campus. Florida Tech tends to have a strict policy against alcohol, although students do not always follow it—"We still drink, of course," one sophomore commented.

Florida Tech's uneven male-female ratio of 65:35 affects social life on campus. Male students joke that, "If you don't find a girlfriend in the first couple of weeks in freshmen year, you won't ever find a girlfriend." However, such sentiment is not pervasive throughout the entire student body. As one male student said, "It doesn't bother me too much. I probably have more female friends on campus than male friends."

Around Campus

Students live in one of six campus residential halls and two apartment complexes. Campbell and Wood Halls offer housing primarily to freshmen, although their convenient locations draw many upperclassmen to share these residencies as well. Roberts Hall is the largest residence facility on campus and houses only freshmen. Women may choose to live in Shaw Hall, a female-only residence. Outside of the residence halls, students love the Columbia Village Suites and Southgate Apartments. The Southgate Apartments, which come with in-suite amenities and an outdoor pool, are so popular that "people wait outside and sleep in tents for a week to get in," said one student. All freshmen are required to live on campus, while about half of the remaining students choose to live off campus.

Residence halls are watched over by student RAs. One sophomore mentioned, "RAs are pretty strict compared to other schools."

Students tend to find the food at Florida Tech to be decent. As one student said, "When I come back from break, I'm excited to eat the food. But after three weeks, I'm kind of tired of it." Students often socialize at "The RAT," an eatery and pub on the lower level of Evans Hall that also features a big-screen TV, game room, and computer cluster. Off campus, students enjoy eating at local restaurants such as Carrabba's Italian Grill, City Tropics Bistro and Outback Steakhouse.

Not Typically Techie

Despite its name, Florida Tech offers much more than an education in technology. From the lush botanical gardens on campus to the beautiful beaches just miles from campus, from scuba diving to watching shuttle launches at Kennedy Space Center, from graphs to Greek life, Florida Tech offers the

complete college experience. One student put it best, "I wasn't sure what I was getting into. It just blew me away. It wasn't what I was expecting...it was a lot better."
—*David Flinner*

FYI

If you come to Florida Tech, you'd better bring "a calculator."
What's the typical weekend schedule? "Friday: Get out of class as early as possible and take a nap; Saturday: hang out at the beach; Sunday: study."
If I could change one thing about Florida Tech, I'd "lower tuition."
Three things every student at Florida Tech should do before graduating are "help out with some community service projects, watch the shuttle lift off, and make many trips to the beach!"

Florida Southern College

Address: 111 Lake Hollingsworth Drive, Lakeland, FL 33801-5698
Phone: 863-680-4131
E-mail address: fscadm@flsouthern.edu
Web site URL: www.flsouthern.edu
Year Founded: 1883
Private or Public: Private
Religious Affiliation: Methodist
Location: Urban
Number of Applicants: 2,559
Percent Accepted: 58%
Percent Accepted who enroll: 28%
Number Entering: 424
Number of Transfers Accepted each Year: 148
Middle 50% SAT range: M: 470–600, CR: 480–600, Wr: 460–570
Middle 50% ACT range: 20–25
Early admission program EA/ED/None: ED

Percentage accepted through EA or ED: 14%
EA and ED deadline: 1-Dec
Regular Deadline: 1-Mar
Application Fee: $30
Full time Undergraduate enrollment: 1,693
Total enrollment: 1,801
Percent Male: 40%
Percent Female: 60%
Total Percent Minority or Unreported: 20%
Percent African-American: 7%
Percent Asian/Pacific Islander: 1%
Percent Hispanic: 6%
Percent Native-American: <1%
Percent International: 4%
Percent in-state/out of state: 75%/25%
Percent from Public HS: 79%
Retention Rate: 71%
Graduation Rate 4-year: 37%

Graduation Rate 6-year: 52%
Percent Undergraduates in On-campus housing: 74%
Number of official organized extracurricular organizations: 70
3 Most popular majors: Biology, Marketing, Psychology
Student/Faculty ratio: 13:1
Average Class Size: 14
Percent of students going to grad school: 27%
Tuition and Fees: $22,145
In-State Tuition and Fees if different: No difference
Cost for Room and Board: $7,850
Percent receiving financial aid out of those who apply, first year: 82%
Percent receiving financial aid among all students: 62%

Finding a pleasant atmosphere to enjoy the Florida sun is never hard at Florida Southern College. Located in the town of Lakeland, the Moccasins boast a championship-caliber women's golf team, proximity to some of the most beautiful beaches in the world, and by all accounts one of the most hospitable institutions in the South. "I would definitely choose to go here

again. There are tons of great people and great professors," said one proud student.

Rockin' the Classroom

Florida Southern is known across the country for its scholastic excellence. It consistently ranks as one of the best academic colleges in the Southeast. Undoubtedly one cause for FSC's educational acumen is its small class sizes. Most classes average around 15 students, with popular lectures being the only courses where you might get lost in a crowd. One student commented that "It's a nice learning environment because classes are smaller and more intimate. The professors know you by name." Florida Southern also offers a wide variety of courses from guts like Jogging, Waterskiing, and Physical Education, to more challenging fare such as New and Old Testament, Classical and Medieval Philosophy, and Human Genetics. Students also report that being rejected from a class you really want to take is virtually a non-issue. "If you need to get into a certain course, just talk to the professor."

Party like a Mocc-star

During the day, a plethora of leisure activities is available to your average Moccasins. They can enjoy the beautiful Florida weather on the shores of Lake Hollingsworth, hop in the car and take a 35-minute drive down the road to enjoy that same weather at Clearwater Beach, or shop at the new outdoor mall at Lakeside Village, which boasts over 100 stores. When the sun sets, however, Lakeland doesn't really offer too many party options for Florida Southern students. The scene usually starts on Thursday evenings, and begins with a trip to traditional crowd-pleasers like Chili's, Bennigan's, or Applebee's. For students who don't want to go too far, the local club scene is dominated by Kau Kau Korner, a legendary bar just off Florida Southern's campus. Students who don't mind traveling pile into their cars on the weekends to sample the sizzling nightlife of nearby Orlando and Tampa's Ybor City.

For those not into that scene, the Association of Campus Entertainment (ACE) has worked in recent years to make life in Lakeland more exciting. "The school made a concerted effort to plan weekend activities to keep students on campus," said one student. These dogged efforts have paid off. ACE has even managed to lure some comedians that have been prominently featured on networks like Comedy Central.

If you are looking for illegal drugs or a school whose drug policy is pretty lax, then Florida Southern is not the campus for you. One student reported that "the drug rules are pretty strictly enforced, especially for the freshmen." Florida Southern is also a dry campus, but the drinking restrictions are much less strict than those on drugs. Florida Southern does have Resident Assistants, who vary in temperament. "It depends on

the person: some are laid-back, some not so much. Some are more involved than others." Strict RA or not, a Florida Southern senior said that "If you want to find a place to drink, you'll definitely be able to."

Oh Those Generous Greeks!

Greek life is pretty important at Florida Southern. One student estimated the Greek population to be even higher than the official statistics. Frats and sororities are quite vocal and involved on campus. Despite this, "Lakeland does not allow sorority and fraternity houses, so certain dorm rooms are considered fraternity or sorority areas," explained one sorority member. Though these dorms are set aside for Greek use, the connection is informal and no one fraternity lays claim to a whole dormitory. Also, these frats aren't all about partying and debauchery; many students report that Greeks at Florida Southern have to be well-rounded. "We're really big on philanthropy, and are also really involved in student government and other leadership roles on campus," said one fraternity member.

Doin' It Big in Lakeland

There are many students who move off campus into cheaper housing close to school after their freshman year. On the other hand, many Moccasins enjoy staying on campus for the four years they'll be there. "At this small school, if I didn't live on campus, I would really be out of the loop," said one student. Students described their campus as "pretty diverse" with "A lot of students from Florida, but also people from up north and out west. However, there are more East Coast students."

One common complaint among FSC's pupils is the mediocre food in the dining hall. There are also concerns about the limited hours the dining hall is open. Fortunately, beneath the dining hall there is a 24-hour café to satisfy all the late-night hungers from working out, partying, or just hanging with your friends. If you prefer your meals over a good book, then you can head to the cybercafé where Moccasins stay up late nights fueled by Starbucks coffee, typing away furiously on their laptops. In addition, there is also a yogurt stand that serves smoothies for those days when the sun beats down particularly hard.

Get Up, Get Out, and Do Something

Anyone who wants to sit on their duff for their college career had better not apply to

Florida Southern; students usually have their hands in a lot of pots. "We're usually pretty committed to different activities. There are lots of student athletes," explained one Moc. Florida Southern competes in Division II of the NCAA in all of its sports. The Mocs lay claim to 27 national championships. Residing in gorgeous central Florida, it comes as no surprise that FSC is home to some of the best golfers at the college level with 11 men's golf championships and four women's golf championships, including one in 2007.

> "Our location, history, and the fun stories behind the school differentiate us from other colleges."

Despite the consistent excellence of the golf team, baseball and softball are by far the most popular sports on campus. The men's baseball team has even played exhibitions with MLB's Detroit Tigers. However, in an effort to increase student participation in the school's other stellar athletics programs, a Sports Management Club has recently been founded. Also, on weekday afternoons the intramural warriors take advantage of the extensive IM fields. Moccasins are just as active off the field, too. Since Florida Southern was originally founded as a Methodist college, theology and church do play a role in the day-to-day activities on the college grounds.

"Campus ministry is also a large part of the campus life," reports one student. Other students, however, don't feel pressured into taking part in the various religious activities.

Everything Is All-Wright

Florida Southern's most famous attribute is its bond with one of the most renowned architects of the 20th century. "We have the largest collection of Frank Lloyd Wright architecture in the world on our campus," bragged one student. One of the most popular Wright works are the underground tunnels he built for the Cold War. "Lots of kids try to get in there." There is also the recently reconstructed Water Dome, which was a part of FSC's campus as early as 1948 but has now been built to Wright's original specifications. Consisting of a huge pool surrounded by fountains cascading together at the monument's center, the Water Dome is the crowning piece of a paean to the daring mind and bold spirit that Frank Lloyd Wright represented.

Florida Southern is also a haven for the supernatural. It seems that the residents of a particular freshman dorm have spotted a ghost. "It's [former] President Spivey's son. You'll hear a basketball bouncing, and then you have to say 'No, Allen, I don't want to play,' and he'll go away." Students enjoy the color that comes with living in a place like Lakeland. "Our location, history, and the fun stories behind the school differentiate us from other colleges," said one sophomore. —*JonPaul McBride*

FYI
If you come to Florida Southern you'd better bring "a Frisbee, a car, and an open mind."
What's the typical weekend schedule? "Go see a comedy show, grab dinner at Lakeside Village, run around Lake Hollingsworth, and chill at the beach on Sunday."
If I could change one thing about Florida Southern, I would "change how different our breaks are from other schools, especially spring break."
Three things every student at Florida Southern should do before graduating are "go to Kau Kau Korner, take funny pictures with the statues, and take a religion class."

F l o r i d a   S t a t e   U n i v e r s i t y

Address: PO Box 3062400
Tallahassee,
FL 32306
Phone: 850-644-6200
E-mail address:
admissions@admin.fsu.edu
Web site URL: www.fsu.edu
Year Founded: 1851
Private or Public: Public
Religious Affiliation: None
Location: Urban
Number of Applicants:
25,485
Percent Accepted: 47%
**Percent Accepted who
enroll:** 42%
Number Entering: 4,992
**Number of Transfers
Accepted each Year:** 3,118
Middle 50% SAT range:
M: 560–650, CR:
550–640, Wr: Unreported
Middle 50% ACT range:
23–28
**Early admission program
EA/ED/None:** None

**Percentage accepted
through EA or ED:** NA
EA and ED deadline: NA
Regular Deadline: 21-Jan
Application Fee: $30
**Full time Undergraduate
enrollment:** 31,595
Total enrollment: 39,434
Percent Male: 44%
Percent Female: 56%
**Total Percent Minority or
Unreported:** 28%
Percent African-American:
10%
**Percent Asian/Pacific
Islander:** 3%
Percent Hispanic: 12%
Percent Native-American:
1%
Percent International: 1%
**Percent in-state/out of
state:** 88%/12%
Percent from Public HS: 84%
Retention Rate: 89%
Graduation Rate 4-year:
70%

Graduation Rate 6-year:
Unreported
**Percent Undergraduates in
On-campus housing:** 21%
**Number of official organized
extracurricular
organizations:** 500
3 Most popular majors:
Criminal Justice, English,
Finance
Student/Faculty ratio:
20:1
Average Class Size: 26
**Percent of students going to
grad school:** 42%
Tuition and Fees: $18,243
**In-State Tuition and Fees if
different:** $3,799
Cost for Room and Board:
$8,178
**Percent receiving financial
aid out of those who apply,
first year:** 50%
**Percent receiving financial
aid among all students:**
32%

L ocated in the heart of Tallahassee, Florida State University offers its nearly 40,000 students a beautiful campus, a plethora of extracurricular opportunities, and a variety of fun social venues. With excellent athletic teams and a unique sense of pride in the Seminole community, FSU is known for its students' passionate school spirit. Given its well-rounded liberal arts program and enjoyable campus environment, FSU is certainly worth considering for all those looking for a good education at a large and lively university.

Going North to Get to the South

The vast majority of FSU's students are Floridians. Yet Tallahassee's atmosphere is likely to surprise many of the state's natives. Located in the northern panhandle of Florida, Tallahassee actually seems more like the South to the Floridian freshmen than many of their hometowns. One new student proclaimed her surprise that "Everything about Tallahassee felt completely different from Florida, including the buildings,

the people, and even the trees." The weather is quite different from the rest of the state. A freshman remarked that "As long as it's not August," the weather is "not bad, and high temperatures even dip into the 70s and 60s as early as October." Aside from the temperature differences, students are often pleasantly surprised that Tallahassee has less humidity and rain than the rest of Florida. As one senior said, "The weather here makes the campus feel more like Georgia or Alabama, in a really good way."

FSU's location also makes it an ideal school for both the studious scholars and collegiate socialites. As one freshman put it, "Tallahassee is a great mix between a large college town and a vibrant Southern capital." Within walking distance is the Florida Capitol Building, where students can learn about politics firsthand. For those interested in the social scene, the Strip, a commercial district located right across from FSU, is a good place to enjoy free time. The Strip includes Chubby's and Potbelly's, two infamous Tallahassee hangouts that double as nightclubs, and a good number of shops and restaurants. As one freshman explained, "The unique mix of intellectually stimulating venues and upbeat social centers in this city makes Tallahassee a truly incredible college town."

A True Liberal Arts Experience

Students at Florida State University tout their well-rounded academic programs. Popular majors include business, political science, and international studies. "Business administration seems to be the most popular major here," said one sophomore. "But, being in Tallahassee, a lot of students also choose the political science and international studies tracks." However, unlike most other state schools, Seminoles can wait until their junior year to declare a major. Many take advantage of this by trying a variety of courses. One freshman schedule included such courses as "Multicultural Film, Mythology, American Government, and German I," while another included "Chemistry I, Biology I, and General Psychology." Students at FSU find this freedom in selecting classes one of FSU's greatest academic assets.

FSU also has an excellent Honors Program with high scholastic standards and great academic rewards. Students in FSU's Honors Program receive many perks, including "really nice dorms" and "early registration for classes." In addition, FSU Honors students are allowed to live in the Honors building (Landis Hall) for more than a year, take Honors classes throughout their college years, and receive registration benefits, making this program a very desirable option.

FSU students can also choose from several other great programs. Two highly regarded alternatives include creative writing and film studies. Students brag that FSU has one of the best creative writing programs in the country. It offers a great variety of classes and, as one sophomore claimed, "FSU has world-class writing professors." Students can also take film studies as a major, if they are in The College of Motion Picture, Television, and Recording Arts. According to one junior, this is a "phenomenal program" that shows students "how to make their own cinematographic works of art, while also learning to understand other classic and contemporary works."

Though FSU's academic programs are a great fit for many students, some do see important drawbacks. Students have found that the mathematics and engineering programs are quite small, with smaller faculty and facilities. Students admit that many of their classes are lecture-based and place little emphasis on individual attention. One freshman bemoaned the "lack of availability of TAs" and also complained that professors at times were "virtually inaccessible." However, many students found that, with "persistent emailing" and "diligent planning," they were usually able to receive the help they needed. Indeed, despite these drawbacks, for a large public university FSU fosters a great learning environment with which most students are very satisfied.

A Customized, Newly Renovated Campus Life

The majority of freshman at FSU live on campus, and most have found FSU's dorms and facilities to be comfortable, easily accessible, and in great condition. Recent renovations have led the newly renovated dorms such as Wildwood and Degraff to be the dorms of choice. One freshman noted that most dorms are "small but comfortable" and was also very pleased to find that most of FSU's dorms are "conveniently located near the center of campus." Special housing in Landis Hall is also available for Honors students. As one freshman Honors student noted, "Rooming with other Honors students makes the Honors program at FSU that much more enjoyable and gives you a tight-knit group of friends."

College life on campus also offers a variety of fun places for students to hang out with friends or relax. Students cite Landis Green as a major on-campus hangout. "Landis Green is a beautiful courtyard area and is a huge part of what makes FSU the school it is. We play football or Frisbee there, talk with friends, or study, and students can even sunbathe in the Florida heat while doing homework, which is very cool." Westcott Fountain also offers a place for students to cool off, and birthday swims in the Fountain are a major part of FSU tradition. Students also relax at the Suwannee Room, where they can "eat good food and have good conversation with friends." FSU's Oglesby Union Center is also a great place to find fast food: students can choose from a local Chinese food venue, a Hardee's, and a Pollo Tropical, among others. To work off those extra calories, students spend many afternoons at the Leach Center, FSU's three-story on-campus workout facility, and students are also very active in FSU's intramural sports programs.

If students at FSU wish to leave campus most find they are actually within walking distance of a vibrant social scene. Though Seminoles feel that their college is more than just a party school, they are very proud of the notorious party scene that can be found at the many nightclubs of the Strip and the fraternity and sorority houses nearby. Alcohol is "a must have" for most social events, but students are strictly forbidden to bring alcohol on campus, so most partying takes place in off-campus apartments and dance parties at Chubby's or other nightclubs on the Strip. Hook-ups are also frequent at such events. As one freshman bragged (to the concurrence of several others), "FSU takes great pride in the beauty of its women. FSU girls are by far among the prettiest you will ever see."

Most upperclassmen choose to live off campus. "That is actually for the best," said one freshman, "since FSU's dorms are already crowded, and apartments are actually cheaper." In addition, many freshmen concede that RAs here can be a problem. One freshman noted that her RA was "very unsociable and not very helpful" and that many of her friends also had problems with RAs. Also, parking at FSU, said one freshman, is "Abysmal . . . after the first two weeks I brought my car back home. It was too much of a hassle." FSU students also lament that there is not enough racial diversity on campus. However, despite these concerns, most students enjoy their on-campus living experience.

Seminole Pride and Success in Athletics and Beyond

Though FSU is known for its party scene, it is even better known for its prized football team and fan base. "Football at FSU is a religion. The Florida State Seminoles are its holy ministers, and the fans and alumni are its loyal, devout followers," one sophomore proclaimed. The FSU Seminoles boast a fan base in the hundreds of thousands both in Tallahassee and around the state. The Student Boosters sponsor massive pep rallies such as the Downtown Getdown and huge tailgating events. Tradition is also important for Seminole football games. As one sophomore explained, "Each game starts with the Seminole mascot, the Osceola, galloping onto the field with a flaming spear that is thrown into the center of the field to rile up the fans." Indeed, football at FSU is a significant source of school pride, especially during match-ups with FSU's two major rivals, the University of Florida and the University of Miami.

Though football is the major sport of choice, FSU also has a variety of excellent varsity and intramural sports. College basketball and baseball are very popular at FSU. According to one sophomore, the school has "an awesome baseball team, possibly one of the best in the country." For FSU's more casual athletes, intramural sports are an essential element of life. "FSU has an intramural league for almost every sport you can imagine," explained one freshman. "Flag football actually has over 500 participants this year." In addition, the Leach Center's athletic facilities are state-of-the-art and include two floors of workout equipment, an indoor track, and an Olympic-sized swimming pool. Yoga, spinning, and aerobic exercise classes are also offered there for free, so students of all athletic inclinations can enjoy working out.

> "Football at FSU is a religion. The Florida State Seminoles are its holy ministers, and the fans and alumni are its loyal, devout followers."

In addition to athletics, FSU has a strong set of extracurricular activities. Greek life is the predominant activity at FSU. One freshman said, "Almost everyone I know is pledging for a fraternity or sorority." Greek organizations give students leadership opportunities and can be more party-oriented or career-based depending on the chapter. FSU's Student Government Association also hosts a variety of events, including Parents' Weekend festivities and weekly movie nights. Also, students can apply to intern for the Florida State Legislature at the Capitol Building, which, as one senior noted, "is life-changing, if you have the time and the discipline to do it."

Finally, a unique and valuable gem in FSU's treasury of school pride rests in the excellent study-abroad program. One junior said that FSU "has one of the best study-abroad programs in the country." For the program in England, "It's right in the heart of London, and had so many different courses. It gave me so much cultural knowledge, was great for my political science major, and was a blast." FSU also offers programs in other locations, including Panama, Spain, France, China, Australia, Italy, and Costa Rica. Indeed, FSU's study-abroad program is something that truly distinguishes FSU from other universities.

FSU is a well-rounded academic institution that offers students unique academic opportunities and a lively atmosphere of social events. As one student said, "FSU is a place where students party hard, Seminole pride and history is celebrated, valuable lessons are learned, and life-changing opportunities are found."—*Andrew Pearlmutter*

FYI

If you come to Florida State University, you'd better bring "good walking shoes. You do a lot of walking at FSU."

What is the typical weekend schedule? "Friday nights are spent partying at a friend's apartment or clubbing at the Strip. On Saturdays, most go to the football game after tailgating and then party. Sundays are spent sleeping in and studying."

If I could change one thing about FSU, I'd "add more parking garages and bring a better variety of food to the campus."

Three things every student at FSU should do before graduating are "tour the Florida Capitol Building, study abroad with FSU's amazing study-abroad program, and go to a Florida State Seminoles football game."

New College of Florida

Address: 5800 Bay Shore Road, Sarasota, FL 34243-2109
Phone: 941-487-5000
E-mail address: admissions@ncf.edu
Web site URL: www.ncf.edu
Year Founded: 1964
Private or Public: Public
Religious Affiliation: None
Location: Small city
Number of Applicants: 1,221
Percent Accepted: 58%
Percent Accepted who enroll: 32%
Number Entering: 239
Number of Transfers Accepted each Year: 27
Middle 50% SAT range: M: 590–670, CR: 630–730, Wr: 600–690
Middle 50% ACT range: 27–31
Early admission program EA/ED/None: None
Percentage accepted through EA or ED: NA

EA and ED deadline: NA
Regular Deadline: 15-Feb, 15-Apr
Application Fee: $30
Full time Undergraduate enrollment: 785
Total enrollment: 785
Percent Male: 38%
Percent Female: 62%
Total Percent Minority or Unreported: 16%
Percent African-American: 2%
Percent Asian/Pacific Islander: 3%
Percent Hispanic: 10%
Percent Native-American: 1%
Percent International: Unreported
Percent in-state/out of state: 82%/18%
Percent from Public HS: 80%
Retention Rate: 82%
Graduation Rate 4-year: 45%

Graduation Rate 6-year: 63%
Percent Undergraduates in On-campus housing: 80%
Number of official organized extracurricular organizations: 35
3 Most popular majors: Biology, Psychology, Political Science
Student/Faculty ratio: 10:1
Average Class Size: 18
Percent of students going to grad school: 17%
Tuition and Fees: $26,940
In-State Tuition and Fees if different: $5,338
Cost for Room and Board: $7,464
Percent receiving financial aid out of those who apply, first year: 58%
Percent receiving financial aid among all students: 39%

Imagine a college with 825 students, a laid-back atmosphere, a beach-side location, and no grades. This is no cushy finishing school; this is New College of Florida, the state's public honors college. Formerly the honors college of the University of South Florida, New College has only recently been able to stand alone in the State University System as one of Florida's, and the nation's, most unique institutions of higher learning.

Free-Form Academics

One of the most oft-cited facts about New College's academic program is its absence of formal grades. For each class, students receive from their professor a detailed evaluation of their performance that term. A common misconception is that this decreases students' motivation to do their best work. In reality, this system is a great compliment to the culture of self-motivation that is so pervasive at the school. (It's also a great boost to applications to graduate school.)

"The best education demands a joint search for learning by exciting teachers and able students," claims the college's Web site. Though this may sound idealistic, at New College these words are put into practice. "High-caliber" faculty and an eclectic, self-selected group of high-achieving students create for each other the "constructive pressure to succeed," in the words of one sophomore. In elaborating on this "constructive pressure," one art major cites not only the close relationships she has developed with the faculty in her department, but also the various student-run art shows that she and her friends have organized. Another student described the typical student-professor relationship: "You'll definitely have professors who know you well—some will probably cook your whole class dinner." Students work especially closely with their professors on their senior thesis, which is a universal graduation requirement.

In general, the academic requirements are not considered very strict. The distribution requirements are minimal at most, and many students elect to design their own major. There are, however, traditional majors available, with literature, anthropology and the sciences tending to be among the most popular. Marine biology is also particularly strong, a fact enhanced by the college's proximity to the Gulf of Mexico.

An Open Atmosphere: Thanks to the "Walls"

New College has a deserved reputation as being a hotbed of activism. An overwhelming majority of its students consider themselves liberal, and radicalism—including anarchism—tends to be the rule rather than the exception. But rather than identifying themselves based on such labels, students would prefer to be seen as open-minded. Perhaps one student put it best in stating that Novo Collegians are better at "theorizing about activism" than practicing it.

But there are certainly other things to do. One of students' favorite New College traditions is "the Walls." These parties are usually held multiple times a week in the school's main courtyard, the Palm Court. Students sign up to host the college-sponsored event, and the whole school is always invited. One sophomore found it hard to describe, other than that the Walls are much more "open and comfortable" than parties at other schools. "If you're not comfortable dancing," she said, "come to New College and you'll soon become a great dancer." Other popular school-wide dance parties include the Palm Court Parties (PCPs), which are more organized and happen on special occasions, such as Valentine's Day and Halloween.

> **"You'll definitely have professors who know you well—some will probably cook your whole class dinner."**

Complementing this open party atmosphere is a widely accepted culture of drugs and alcohol. Marijuana and alcohol are prevalent and widely available, and it is common knowledge that the few law enforcement officials on campus are there to protect students against outsiders, not to break up social gatherings. "Cops look the other way most of the time," one student said. However, most students agree that there is little pressure on those who do not wish to participate in illicit activities.

One aspect of New College's setting that draws complaints is the town of Sarasota. Wealthy retirees are the average residents of this town, which is "a community with aspirations of being cultural and artsy." But the weather gets high marks, as do the tourist attractions: the beach and the Ringling Museum. The latter is gaining more popularity with students because of its efforts to build new student centers and libraries close to campus. And if one is desperate to get out of Sarasota for a while, there's always Tampa, which is less than an hour away by car.

There is plenty to do on campus as well. Many students are involved in such extracurriculars as *The Catalyst*, the weekly student-run newspaper; student government; and activist groups. Sports are admittedly a smaller part of life than at larger universities. New College has no varsity programs, but racquetball and soccer are popular choices for pickup games.

Beds and Bread

Dorm life receives positive reviews from most students. Lucky students are assigned to a Pei dorm or the newer Dort, or Goldstein Hall. The former are apparently the most spacious and best designed overall (originally designed as hotels by I.M. Pei), whereas the latter is more modern in all aspects and has suite-style living arrangements. The Pei dorms are reputedly the most social. "You will see your friends when you enter and leave the building, and hang out outside talking a lot," one resident said. The main drawback is that since New College is working on increasing the size of its student body, many of the rooms that were designed as doubles are suddenly becoming triples.

Campus residents are required to be on the meal plan, which is not considered a bonus. The food leaves something to be desired: "There's a reason we were ranked as the worst college food in the South," one student explained. There is one central cafeteria, but alternatives abound, including the Four Winds, a student-run cafe.

A One-of-a-Kind Experience

New College is not known to be an incredibly diverse place, as most students are white, middle-class, liberal and suburban. Other aspects of diversity, however, are present on campus. For example, the school has what one sophomore called "gender diversity." The school is very gay-friendly, and all sorts of lifestyles find acceptance at New College. Overall, the students self-select to a large extent; while this is great for creating and sustaining a unique culture, it has the downside of perpetuating the school's homogeneity.

If you are a Florida resident, you won't find a much better education for the money than New College, as many in-state students are eligible for the state's generous scholarship programs and don't have to pay a dime to go to school. But everyone, both Florida residents and out-of-state students, shares the uniqueness of the New College experience: a non-competitive, high-quality academic program with laid-back, intelligent students in an ideal campus setting.—*Jay Buchanan*

FYI
If you come to New College, you'd better bring "your stamina and social skills."
What is the typical weekend schedule? "Friday, relax and get ready for the party in Palm Court; Saturday, relax and play some sports; Sunday, nothing else but studying."
If I could change one thing about New College, "I'd make the student population more diverse."
Three things that every student should do before graduating are: "go to a Wall or PCP, walk around barefoot, and write a thesis."

R o l l i n s   C o l l e g e

Address: 1000 Holt Avenue #1502, Winter Park, FL 32789
Phone: 407-646-2161
E-mail address: admission@rollins.edu
Web site URL: www.rollins.edu
Year Founded: 1885
Private or Public: Private
Religious Affiliation: None
Location: Suburban
Number of Applicants: 3,485
Percent Accepted: 53%
Percent Accepted who enroll: 25%
Number Entering: 464
Number of Transfers Accepted each Year: 97
Middle 50% SAT range: M: 555–650, **CR:** 555–650, **Wr:** Unreported
Middle 50% ACT range: 24–29
Early admission program EA/ED/None: ED

Percentage accepted through EA or ED: 41%
EA and ED deadline: 15-Nov
Regular Deadline: 15-Feb
Application Fee: $40
Full time Undergraduate enrollment: 1,785
Total enrollment: 1,785
Percent Male: 44%
Percent Female: 56%
Total Percent Minority or Unreported: 29%
Percent African-American: 4%
Percent Asian/Pacific Islander: 4%
Percent Hispanic: 10%
Percent Native-American: <1%
Percent International: 4%
Percent in-state/out of state: 47%/53%
Percent from Public HS: 55%
Retention Rate: Unreported

Graduation Rate 4-year: 59%
Graduation Rate 6-year: 68%
Percent Undergraduates in On-campus housing: 69%
Number of official organized extracurricular organizations: 112
3 Most popular majors: Economics, Business, Psychology
Student/Faculty ratio: 10:1
Average Class Size: 15
Percent of students going to grad school: 41%
Tuition and Fees: $34,520
In-State Tuition and Fees if different: No difference
Cost for Room and Board: $10,780
Percent receiving financial aid out of those who apply, first year: 70%
Percent receiving financial aid among all students: 70%

Set in idyllic Winter Park, Florida, Rollins College is "like a vacation every single day." Whether sunning by the outdoor pool, enjoying scenic Lake Virginia, or partying in nearby Orlando, Rollins students know how to have fun, and they do it in style.

Steady Studies
Academics at Rollins are "above average but not too difficult." Students who want to do well can work towards a more intense schedule, but others opt to get by in less demanding majors such as education. Science, business and foreign language majors are "competitive and demanding," requiring a minimum of several hours work every night, but well worth the professors they feature. "I know a lot of them wrote the textbooks they teach with . . . several famous politicians graduated from Rollins, too."

Rollins students have one complaint in the academic department—thick bureaucracy. It's tough to get into the classes you want, and as one freshman complained, "It's difficult to switch/drop/add classes. I spent two weeks trying to fix my schedule." But such pains are made up for with exceptionally hands-on class options. As one student raved, "Rollins offers a course that allows students to get credit by tutoring elementary kids."

High-Class Frats
For the more action-oriented, the party scene at Rollins is packed. "Everyone drinks in the dorm rooms," frat parties are frequent, and Orlando, less than ten minutes away, is packed with bars and clubs. That's a lot to handle in one weekend, especially when combined with a prevalent drug scene. "The drug scene is definitely big," one student said. "Coke is huge."

About thirty percent of the student body is part of the Greek community. One freshman said that "It isn't hard to rush and I haven't heard of any bad stories. It's expensive, but there are really fun theme parties. Golf Pro's Tennis Hoes was my favorite." ATO and Chi Psi are the "best frats," but "TKE has good parties." Kappa Delta and Kappa Kappa Gamma are the most popular sororities.

Even when they aren't going out, Rollins students dress to impress. "Many people are very preppy," a sophomore commented. "Everyone here owns a Lacoste shirt and many girls wear Lilly Pulitzer dresses and have Gucci and Louis Vuitton bags." Although diversity is lacking at Rollins, beauty is big. One girl said that "The student body is like no other. I've had several friends come and visit and they were all in shock. Everyone wears ridiculously expensive clothing, drives ridiculously nice cars and tries to outdo everyone else." And the old Spanish-style campus tends to be as perfectly manicured as the undergrads themselves. The Rollins campus is "absolutely beautiful" and "covered in gorgeous foliage." And it's also a safe haven for students seeking alone time. One student said, "You can always find a place to hide down by the lake" or go running outside at night. "I love that I don't ever have to worry about anything happening."

Dumpy Dorms
For all the good-looking people and places in Winter Park, the student dorms don't quite match up. "For the price of Rollins, the dorms are disgusting. They're always filthy and covered in vomit, empty beer cans and cockroaches." "McKean is probably the worst dorm because it's always so dirty. We have a pretty big issue with cockroaches and stray cats right now. It's pretty gross." Air-conditioning is about the only perk. And interestingly enough, Florida law prohibits coed bathrooms. Considering the on-campus housing options, it is no surprise that many students opt to move off. "The apartments and houses in Winter Park are all very adorable so most people want to live close by."

Luckily, the food fares a bit better. "The meal plan is great at Rollins" one undergrad said. Students get $1,700 per semester to use at dining halls and neighborhood restaurants, including Domino's pizza. There is also a deli counter and food store for kids on the run. However, "The dining hall is defi-

nitely a social scene," so students try to make time to go there and "talk with friends." When in the mood for a night on the town, Winter Park offers "amazing" restaurants, bars, and shops.

Tars Take It Slow
Extracurricular activities at Rollins "aren't huge" and "not many students work." "They're more likely to be found by the pool," one junior commented. Sports aren't very popular either, but as one student pointed out, "The baseball boys have good parties." Baseball games also attract the highest attendance, along with men's soccer (perhaps all its European recruits make it hard for even a Florida girl to resist the accents). Overall, though, "There is little team spirit," which bothers some students, especially since the Tars house a conference-leading men's basketball team.

> "Being on a sports team here isn't really a big deal. It's probably better to join a frat or sorority."

Those students who choose to participate in extracurricular activities are well respected—particularly the members of the SGA, Rollins' Student Government Association. For theater buffs, the Annie Russell Theatre is quite the attraction. One seat is kept empty at all times for the ghost of Annie Russell, said to haunt the building. There are even students who claim to have seen and heard Annie there at night. When students aren't at a practice or in a meeting, they hit the gym. "Many people wakeboard on the lake in their free time," one student said. There is also an outdoor swimming pool and golf course nearby for athletes at heart. "Being on a sports team here isn't really a big deal. It's probably better to join a frat or sorority."—*Lauren Ezell*

FYI
If you come to Rollins, you better bring "a designer handbag, bathing suit and Lilly Pulitzer dress (for girls) and a Lacoste polo shirt, a ton of cash and a BMW (for guys)."
What is a typical weekend schedule? "Party at night, lay by the pool during the day, possibly get some homework done and do it all over again the next night."
If I could change one thing about Rollins, I'd "change the cost of tuition. It's not worth the $42,000 plus."
Three things every student at Rollins should do before graduating are: "Go to Disney World at least once, take a trip to Cocoa Beach and party at Club Paris."

Stetson University

Address: 421 N Woodland Boulevard, DeLand, FL 32723
Phone: 800-688-0101
E-mail address: admissions@stetson.edu
Web site URL: www.stetson.edu
Year Founded: 1883
Private or Public: Private
Religious Affiliation: None
Location: Rural
Number of Applicants: 4,119
Percent Accepted: 54%
Percent Accepted who enroll: 28%
Number Entering: 697
Number of Transfers Accepted each Year: 100
Middle 50% SAT range:
M: 500–600, CR: 500–610, Wr: 480–580
Middle 50% ACT range: 21–26
Early admission program EA/ED/None: ED

Percentage accepted through EA or ED: Unreported
EA and ED deadline: 1-Nov
Regular Deadline: 15-Mar
Application Fee: $40
Full time Undergraduate enrollment: 2,143
Total enrollment: 3,696
Percent Male: 43%
Percent Female: 57%
Total Percent Minority or Unreported: 18%
Percent African-American: 5%
Percent Asian/Pacific Islander: 3%
Percent Hispanic: 10%
Percent Native-American: <1%
Percent International: Unreported
Percent in-state/out of state: 80%/20%
Percent from Public HS: 75%
Retention Rate: 77%

Graduation Rate 4-year: 55%
Graduation Rate 6-year: 67%
Percent Undergraduates in On-campus housing: 72%
Number of official organized extracurricular organizations: 100
4 Most popular majors: Business, Psychology, Political Science and English, Communication Studies
Student/Faculty ratio: 12:1
Average Class Size: 18
Percent of students going to grad school: 60%
Tuition and Fees: $30,216
In-State Tuition and Fees if different: No difference
Cost for Room and Board: $8,436
Percent receiving financial aid out of those who apply, first year: 22%
Percent receiving financial aid among all students: 15%

It's tough to deny the allure of packing swimsuits and tanning lotion instead of snow pants and boots in preparation for college. But Stetson University, in sunny DeLand, Florida, isn't just any laid-back, rural Florida school. It's known for solid academics—including several well-respected professional programs—and a vibrant campus atmosphere.

Academics

According to *U.S. News & World Report*, Stetson consistently ranks among the best regional schools in the Southeast. There is a lot to choose from when it comes to academics: with over 60 major and minor fields available to undergraduates in the College of Arts and Sciences, the School of Business Administration and the School of Music, students can study anything from digital arts (a collaboration between the departments of Art and Computer Science and the School of Music) to chemistry to business law.

In addition to completing the require-ments for a major, undergraduates in the College of Arts and Sciences must fulfill a stringent set of distributional requirements, which encompass the areas of "Founda-tions" (basic courses such as English, math and foreign language), "Breadth of Knowl-edge" (natural and social science), "Bases of Ethical Decision Making" (ethics courses), and a non-academic requirement, "Cultural Attendance," which entails attending ap-proved cultural events every semester. Some academic requirements can be waived with AP scores, but either way, the fact remains that you will get a well-rounded education at Stetson. "All the requirements can be irritat-ing," one junior said. "But . . . if you're an En-glish major, at least you have the experience of having taken some science."

There are also several programs that en-courage Stetson's brightest to go beyond the curricular minimum. The Honors Program, for example, gives students the opportuni-ties to take a Junior Honors Seminar and de-sign their own major, as well as encouraging them to study abroad. Although any entering student may apply, most accepted students have had SAT scores in the 50 percent range of 1490 and 1800 and 41 percent have been in the top 10 percent of their high-school class.

As one might expect from a school with such a variety of academic disciplines and such a small student body, classes at Stetson are small, and professors are accessible. With relatively few classes within each division, majors often encompass broad areas of study. Students change their majors often, a process that is apparently neither difficult nor stigmatized. But having small class sizes—even in such traditionally impersonal disciplines as business—can make all the difference for some. "You do tend to bond with your professors, whether you like it or not," said one senior, a marketing major. "I have not been in a class with more than 50 students."

Once students have experienced the ease of getting into their desired classes and the delight of having the professor know their names from Day One, there's the actual class work to consider. More difficult subjects are rumored to be biology, chemistry and music. At one point, "Music Theory" had the highest failure rate on campus. Communications and education, according to students, are easier majors.

Dorm Life

Since freshmen, sophomores and juniors are all required to live on campus, "dorm life" at Stetson is often synonymous with "campus life." "The dorms aren't particularly nice," one sophomore said, "but they are amazing places to meet people and really learn how to live on your own." Students praised the location of the dorms—they are all within walking distance of central campus.

Other facilities are certainly not lacking. The college gymnasium and pool received high marks. The gym offers classes during the semester, and the pool is "very spacious and a good place to relax," presumably since most of the year is bathing-suit weather.

The dining halls are also decent. The main eating facility is Commons, which is apparently "fair" in terms of food and seating arrangements. Known as a social place, Commons is an area where "You can just pick up a conversation with anyone really." Stetson's flexible dining plan allows students to cash in unused meals for purchases at other eateries close by, such as the popular grill Hat Rack, Einstein Bros. Bagels, and the nearby smoothie shop.

Campus Life

Though Stetson features a variety of clubs and activities for students, the Greeks, with their six fraternities and five sororities, tend to be the biggest force on campus. They often host large parties and events in their mostly off-campus venues. Most of these events are nonexclusive.

Two other prominent groups on campus are the Council for Student Activities (CSA) and the Student Government Association (SGA). They have been responsible in the past for bringing in such big-name acts as Less Than Jake and Busta Rhymes. In addition, Stetson hosts a variety of speakers every year. "If you want to hear a speaker every week at Stetson, you definitely can," one senior said. There are, of course, a variety of smaller organizations that cater to more specific groups; these, however, tend to be less active.

Athletics are also a big part of campus life. Although the school lacks the draw of a football team, students report that the other varsity teams' events are well-attended and popular. While the teams themselves "tend to keep together," according to a senior nonathlete, this doesn't keep the rest of the student body from going to games and cheering them on. The basketball and soccer teams receive the most attention. Intramural sports are also popular.

Outside the Bounds of Campus Grounds

The town of DeLand is not generally known as a fun place to hang out, but it has its advocates. This minority says that the town fulfills all "basic needs" with a Wal-Mart and several chain restaurants, that the historic downtown area provides a nice walk, and that "You couldn't ask for a safer place to have a school."

> "You couldn't ask for a safer place to have a school."

But those who seek a setting that includes more than McDonald's, picturesque promenades and a sense of security flock instead to Daytona or Orlando, each of which is less than an hour away. Popular destinations include malls, clubs, bars, theme parks and anything else the rural town just can't provide. To this end, many students do bring cars to campus, but—as with most colleges—the limitations of on-campus parking can make owning a car more of a burden than anything. Many students use their cars to drive home to other Florida cities on a regular basis.

For those who choose to stay on campus or in DeLand, there is certainly not a dearth of things to do. The most popular parties, thrown by the Greeks, are generally held off campus, but there are large on-campus parties as well. These tend to be contained by Public Safety, Stetson's security detail. Drinking is prevalent at all of these parties, but there are alternatives. Many groups, particularly various Christian ones, host dry events on a regular basis. Drug use does occur at Stetson, but it is easy to avoid and by no means popular. According to students, alternatives to "traditional" college partying include bowling, ice skating, going to the movies, and listening to live music.

Conclusion

So why choose Stetson? For many, the appeal is that the college is "a small school close to home." Around 80 percent of the students are Floridians; it's tough for any Florida native to consider going anywhere farther north for school. But the year-round sun is not the only draw: Stetson features high-quality academics on a gorgeous campus. Although it is located in a rural town, Orlando and Daytona are close enough that students don't feel stranded. Add to that the small classes, accessible professors, school spirit and general commitment to excellence, and you've got a school that would be hard for anyone to pass up.— *Jay Buchanan*

FYI

If you come to Stetson, you'd better bring "a bathing suit, because we have a nice pool and people take trips to the beach very often."

What is the typical weekend schedule? "Friday, drive to Daytona; Saturday, spend the afternoon in Daytona and hang out with friends; Sunday, relax in DeLand."

If I could change one thing about Stetson, "I would bring a better selection of food during the weekends."

Three things that everyone should do before graduating from Stetson are "go to all the beaches, join a club or Greek organization and get involved, and enjoy it!"

University of Florida

Address: 201 Criser Hall, Box 114000, Gainesville, FL 32611-4000
Phone: 352-392-1365
E-mail address: ourwebrequests@registrar.ufl.edu
Web site URL: www.ufl.edu
Year Founded: 1853
Private or Public: Public
Religious Affiliation: None
Location: Suburban
Number of Applicants: 24,126
Percent Accepted: 42%
Percent Accepted who enroll: 63%
Number Entering: 6,390
Number of Transfers Accepted each Year: 2,150
Middle 50% SAT range: M: 580–690, **CR:** 560–670, **Wr:** Unreported
Middle 50% ACT range: 25–29
Early admission program EA/ED/None: None

Percentage accepted through EA or ED: NA
EA and ED deadline: NA
Regular Deadline: 1-Nov
Application Fee: $30
Full time Undergraduate enrollment: 35,189
Total enrollment: 47,390
Percent Male: 47%
Percent Female: 53%
Total Percent Minority or Unreported: 36%
Percent African-American: 10%
Percent Asian/Pacific Islander: 8%
Percent Hispanic: 14%
Percent Native-American: <1%
Percent International: 1%
Percent in-state/out of state: 96%/4%
Percent from Public HS: 81%
Retention Rate: Unreported
Graduation Rate 4-year: 82%

Graduation Rate 6-year: Unreported
Percent Undergraduates in On-campus housing: 77%
Number of official organized extracurricular organizations: 500
3 Most popular majors: Finance, Political Science and Government, Psychology
Student/Faculty ratio: 13:1
Average Class Size: 20
Percent of students going to grad school: Unreported
Tuition and Fees: $20,640
In-State Tuition and Fees if different: $3,790
Cost for Room and Board: $7,150
Percent receiving financial aid out of those who apply, first year: 39%
Percent receiving financial aid among all students: 63%

Swish. Gurgle. Gulp. Ahhhh. Refreshing isn't it? Light, tangy, and just a little salty, Gatorade is cherished as an electrolyte-replenishing elixir for athletes around the world. Where'd this wondrous creation come from? Why the University of Florida of course! It was the blistering summer of '65 . . . little did UF physicians realize that their secret brew would become the official sports drink of the NFL—a title it holds to this day. One of the most influential schools in the South, UF excels in academics and athletics. With A+ students, UF consistently graduates at the top of its class.

Is It In You?

UF, is, like, *the* school to get into in the state of Florida. Meaning, it gets a mind-boggling, incredible amount of in-state applicants every year. In the state of Florida, the Bright Futures scholarship covers approximately 80% of in state students' expenses. However, the acceptance rate has been dropping as more and more students clamber for entrance into Gator Land. Acceptances are mailed out in late February, but unlike most private schools, UF lets students fend for themselves in terms of finding a place to stay. With its overwhelming incoming class size, often students prefer to live off campus. Gainesville is overflowing with student apartment complexes that allow students to have the freedom of owning a car and taking care of their own apartment while sharing it with a few friends from high school. However, of course, with luxury come risks. Good luck finding a parking spot during rush hour.

For those that manage to snatch a dorm on campus, there is an Internet system in the late spring where students essentially advertise themselves and hope that their match finds their ad. This pick-your-own-roomie system is risky at times. There are chances that one could find their life long best bud, but as another freshman put it, "It can be a nightmare. My roommate and I absolutely did not get along. I wish I'd just chosen someone from my high school to room with me." While not all cases are this extreme, it is recommended that prospective roommates chat a bit, and get to know each other's sleeping habits and such before proceeding.

Take It Off
That's right. Hello, Sunshine State, where the weather's always balmy. Chilly at times, but still better than the climates of other northern schools. This smart school is a mix of all kinds of extracurricular activities. Social life is everywhere. Whether one joins a tennis club, a robotics team, or a horticulture club, people at UF know how to work hard and play hard.

There is no stereotypical UF gator. One student said that, "We're a super diverse student body who all know how to have a good time." UF has students from all over the world as well. South Africa, Korea, China, Japan, Mexico—and all feel welcomed." With an undergraduate body that spills over 30,000, this comes as no surprise.

> "We're a super diverse student body who all know how to have a good time."

Play the piccolo? The oboe? Don't even know what these instruments look like? No problem! If one is, in any shape or form, a music-addict, UF's band program will welcome you with open arms. Marching band students travel to every football game and get perks like precious tickets in the best sections of the stadiums. For the true paint brush wielding, charcoal stained, turpentine reeking art lover, museums and galleries surround UF's campus. For instance, the Samuel P. Ham Museum of Art has a permanent collection of over 6,000 original pieces that consist of prints, ceramics, photographs, paintings, and sculptures. The artwork displayed there represents areas from all around the globe: the South Pacific, Europe, Africa, and Asia. Best of all? 'Tis free to visit.

Most students also get jobs in their spare time. Locally, a student can pick from a variety of employers. From being a store clerk at the local Gainesville Mall, to volunteering at the local teaching hospital, opportunities abound. The UF Center for Leadership and Service oversees dozens of student organizations. Gator Teen Mentors is a program that pairs UF undergrads with "at risk" high school students and aims to provide these students with the resources and skills to successfully pursue a furthered education. Another group, called the Women's Leadership Council, is a group of undergraduate women at UF who try to empower women with the skills that prepare them to lead in the diverse and ever-changing settings of the 21st century. It doesn't take too much looking to find a club or organization that will suit one's taste at this school, for sure.

It's Such a Rush, She's Such a Crush
Yep, UF is one in a million. Especially, when the sun goes down. Greek life plays a huge role in the social scene. You've got your Tri-Delt's, your Kappa's, your Sigma-whatever's, the list goes on and on. Drinking is highly prevalent, but mind you—these Floridian reptiles can hold their liquor. If you wanna roll with them, you better start practicing. Don't think that their straight-A grades mean that they can't play a nasty game of beer pong.

Tailgating. Huge deal? Understatement. Hear, Hear! Welcome to the UF-FSU game. At the biggest game of the year Gators size up Florida State Seminoles in an all-out tailgating war. Die-hard gator fans start drinking at 8 am. No joke. Get ready for some hyped-up screaming, shouting, and yelling about Gator dominance. The stadium vibrates with thousands upon thousands of students painted over in royal blue and zesty orange.

Not so into the prospect of blowing your eardrums? Check out Gator Nights hosted by the Reitz Union! Funded by the Student Government group on campus, it's the leading late night program in the Southeast and takes place every Friday night of Fall and Spring semesters. It offers free first-run movies, comedians, interactive lectures, improv shows, novelties, cultural events, dances, artists and even video game tournaments. Forget late night coffee, Gator Nights even provide a free midnight breakfast! No matter where you choose to go, the nocturnal creature inside will most definitely be satisfied at the University of Florida.

We Canz Read Good?
Aside from the memorable parties, the great friends, the excitement of athletic games—there is schoolwork. Luckily UF prides itself

in holding to a high level of academic excellence. Some of the popular majors are political science, business, and engineering. However, in a school this size, there are indeed challenging courses that force students to reconsider their majors. Worry not, for UF does provide freshmen with plenty of such as academic advisors. The great thing about this state school, one freshman pointed out, is that "AP credits are accepted and can really speed you through." If a student truly excelled through high school and took say 10 AP courses, then they can graduate in three years—or less! Though, most students simply take their time and just use the AP credits to waive out of prerequisite courses.

Summer Session is an option that many students also take to get some credits out of the way. This is most common for pre-meds. Since UF has no strict defined pre-med major, most students that dream of wearing a white lab coat and responding to the sweet sound of "Doctor (fill in the blank)" feel that taking some courses over the summer can help boost GPA. Summer classes usually have fewer students and give students a chance to focus more on their classes due to an overall smaller course load. A junior once recounted a horror story about his physics class that had a class average of a "D." However, when he retook the class over the summer, he triumphantly returned with a B.

Keep that in mind, dear pre-meds. Swamp dangers lurk in the land of the Gator. Without a doubt, Summer Sessions A, B, and C ensure that the campus stays a bustling place of activity all year round.

One problem with the size of the classes at UF is that some students find it easier to just stay in their dorm and watch the class lectures online. UF's extended open courseware program hopes to remedy the difficulties that students face when going to such a large public institution. A freshman noted that her Intro to Political science class had "over 700 kids. I even see some kids go to class, struggle to find a seat, turn on their laptops, and watch the lecture online, while in the building! Like, they need binoculars to see the board!" Incredible, isn't it? Nevertheless, if one is not afraid of waves of people, UF could be a perfect fit.

Beer, bros, bands, and books. If one can handle the crowd surfing and is willing to keep up with the university's ambitious academic goals, then UF should be at the top of their college application list. UF is a stronghold in the South—a school filled with Gators that live by the "party-hard, work-hard" philosophy. A plethora of activities exist, and the social scene is both engaging and varied. It's an absolutely stunning campus, dripping with Spanish moss and scattered with ancient oaks. Truly, UF is a vibrant place to be. Go Gators!—*Anna Wang*

FYI

If you come to the University of Florida, you'd better bring: "something orange, something blue, something old, and something new."

If I could change one thing about the University of Florida, I'd "create more on-campus dorms . . . with air-conditioning!"

What's the typical weekend schedule? "Go out and party! And then worry about Monday's physics test . . ."

Three things every UF student should do before graduating are: "Go to the game! Go to the game! Go to the game!"

University of Miami

Address: PO Box 248025
Coral Gables, FL
33124-4616
Phone: 305-284-4323
E-mail address:
admission@miami.edu
Web site URL:
www.miami.edu
Year Founded: 1925
Private or Public: Private
Religious Affiliation: None
Location: Suburban
Number of Applicants:
19,676
Percent Accepted: 38%
**Percent Accepted who
enroll:** 27%
Number Entering: 1,980
**Number of Transfers
Accepted each Year:** 1,392
Middle 50% SAT range:
M: 600–690, CR:
580–680, Wr: 560–650
Middle 50% ACT range:
28–31
**Early admission program
EA/ED/None:** EA and ED

**Percentage accepted
through EA or ED:**
EA: 45.3%; ED: NA
EA and ED deadline: 1-Nov
and 1-Nov
Regular Deadline: 15-Jan
Application Fee: $65
**Full time Undergraduate
enrollment:** 10,379
Total enrollment: 13,370
Percent Male: 48%
Percent Female: 52%
**Total Percent Minority or
Unreported:** 55%
Percent African-American:
8%
**Percent Asian/Pacific
Islander:** 5%
Percent Hispanic: 22%
Percent Native-American:
0%
Percent International: 7%
**Percent in-state/out of
state:** 50%/50%
Percent from Public HS:
Unreported
Retention Rate: 90%

Graduation Rate 4-year:
64%
Graduation Rate 6-year:
Unreported
**Percent Undergraduates in
On-campus housing:** 44%
**Number of official organized
extracurricular
organizations:** 217
3 Most popular majors:
Business/Marketing, Visual
and Performing Arts, Biology
Student/Faculty ratio: 11:1
Average Class Size: 25
**Percent of students going to
grad school:** 35%
Tuition and Fees: $34,834
**In-State Tuition and Fees if
different:** No difference
Cost for Room and Board:
$10,254
**Percent receiving financial
aid out of those who apply,
first year:** 78%
**Percent receiving financial
aid among all students:**
48%

W e've got some 'Canes over here! Whoosh! Whoosh!" Loud cheers erupt throughout the Orange Bowl Stadium as thousands of fans gather to witness the annual University of Miami vs. Florida State University football showdown. Clad in orange and green paraphernalia, the enthusiastic spectators show vibrant support for their team. But Hurricane pride is hardly limited to the athletic field. University of Miami students have their whole school to be proud of: top academic programs, a wide array of student activities, and a beautiful campus located in sunny South Florida.

Work Hard, Play Hard

The University of Miami distinguishes itself from other schools in that it focuses heavily on both academics and athletics. What other school can lay claim to both hosting a Presidential Debate and being home to numerous championship athletic teams? In terms of academics, UM students have over 180 un-

dergraduate programs to choose from, offered through eight colleges: Architecture, Arts and Sciences, Business, Communication, Education, Engineering, Music, and Nursing. Freshmen accepted into the University as "undecided" majors are admitted through the College of Arts and Sciences.

The academic requirements differ depending on your college. Nevertheless, "Students have very diverse interests and are encouraged to take classes in other fields and departments," one psychology major said. The most popular majors at the College of Arts and Sciences at UM include Biology, Psychology and Political Science. Students generally agree that the "hardest majors tend to be in the science and engineering fields," such as Biology, Neuroscience, Biomedical Engineering, Physics and Genetics. Most students say that introductory courses, which generally contain between 100 and 200 students, are relatively easy. But upper-level courses, including "Organic Chemistry," "Experimental Psychology," "Ancient

Greek" and "Politics of the Middle East" are known for being particularly tough. UM also offers several unique courses, including "Dance Therapy," "Horror Literature" and "Videogame Systems."

The majority of classes are taught by professors, not TAs. One junior notes, "I've had some really amazing professors here who are scarily brilliant and very approachable." Professors tend to be available and "encourage students to take advantage of their office hours."

Extending invitations to only the top 10 percent of the entering class, the University's Honors Program is considered one of the most prestigious academic tracks for incoming freshmen. Students must have a minimum SAT Math and Reading score of 1360 or ACT score of 31 and be ranked in the top five percent of their high school graduating class to be admitted. The Honors Program offers over 200 courses and course sections per semester, and classes are generally small seminars that foster intimate class discussion and interactive learning. In addition, the University of Miami has a highly selective Honors Program in Medicine, in which students can earn both a Bachelor of Science and a Doctor of Medicine degree in seven to eight years. Dual Degree Honor Programs in Biomedical Engineering, Marine Geology, Physical Therapy, Latin American Studies and Law are also available. Overall, the academic life is described as "pretty balanced," and "There's room for fun if you break up your time well."

Fun in the Florida Sun
University of Miami students have tons of social options on weekends, both on and off campus. There are frequent activities on campus such as concerts, movie screenings at the free campus cinema, and invited guest comedians and musicians. Frats also regularly sponsor parties where "everyone's welcome." Moreover, club-sponsored socials, such as the Hispanic Heritage Month Gala, are popular weekend options that "cater to everyone." Homecoming is another big event on campus and even includes a parade and fireworks. As one sophomore noted, "Now the school is starting to hold more events on campus on Saturdays and Sundays so that people stay more on campus." Drinking is prevalent on campus and the general feeling is that "almost everyone drinks." Nevertheless, students who do not drink say that they do not feel excluded.

Despite the active on-campus social scene, many UM students venture off to enjoy the Miami nightlife on weekends. As one student put it, "That's the beauty of being in Miami—on any given night there is something to do." Typical weekend hangouts include clubs in Coconut Grove, the Design District, South Beach and Bayside Marketplace. Usually, the minimum age for admittance into clubs is 21. On Thursdays, however, Coconut Grove has a "College Night," when students 18 and over are allowed to get into its clubs. During the day on weekends, many students catch movies or go shopping at The Shops at Sunset Place, a popular mall near campus. Of course, UM students can always be found hanging out and tanning in South Beach.

> "That's the beauty of being in Miami—on any given night there is something to do."

Although many University of Miami students have cars on campus, the school offers several transportation options to get around Miami. The Hurry 'Canes shuttle takes students to Coconut Grove and The Shops at Sunset Place, as well as areas on campus. Also, the Metrorail is a convenient way to get to Bayside Marketplace, downtown Miami and Dadeland, a huge shopping mall.

Living in Paradise
Covered with palm trees and beautiful foliage, the University of Miami is frequently praised for its beauty and described by students as "our own tropical paradise." The buildings on campus are built in modern style, and many, such as Hecht College, have been recently renovated.

The University of Miami has several central gathering areas for students. One of the most popular campus locations is the University Center (UC), which contains comfortable sofas, an arcade, a café with pool tables, a convenience store, a food court, and the offices of student organizations. The Rathskeller, nicknamed "the Rat" is another popular social area, where students can play pool, watch one of the widescreen TVs, or sit outside in the tropical warmth at swinging picnic tables. The "Rat" is also a venue for campus entertainment and frequently features live bands and dance parties. Students enjoy hanging out around the pool area to enjoy the Florida sun.

University of Miami students who choose to live on campus are assigned to one of five residential colleges—Eaton, Hecht, Mahoney, Pearson and Stanford. The dorms are described as "relatively nice" and all are air-conditioned. As freshmen, students are randomly assigned to the dorms. Students have the option of being placed on "quiet floors," where there are stricter rules about noise. Unlike typical college dorms, a faculty master and his or her family live alongside students in each residential college. The residential colleges are also staffed by Residential Coordinators (RCs) and Residential Advisors (RAs). According to students, most RAs are "pretty strict," and "getting caught drinking or doing drugs will get people in trouble." Alcohol is only allowed in the dorm rooms of students who are 21 and over, and if they are drinking, they must keep their door closed.

The University of Miami also has a large number of commuters, some of whom belong to organizations such as the Association for Commuter Students. Upperclassmen generally decide to live off campus in apartments or houses that rent out to students in the Coral Gables neighborhood. Additionally, UM completed the University Village in 2006; the complex consists of apartments housing only upperclassmen and graduates.

Go 'Canes!

Students at the University of Miami have incredible school spirit. The University's Division One athletic teams dominate collegiate sports and have won more than 20 national championships. Sports such as football, basketball and baseball have "a huge presence on campus," and football is generally considered the most popular sport. As one student put it, "Football season gets crazy down here . . . tailgates start at least four hours before a game."

Aside from varsity sports, students are encouraged to participate in club and intramural teams. The athletic facilities for both athletes and non-athletes are "amazing." The University's multi-million-dollar Wellness Center is a top-notch fitness, recreation, and wellness facility open to all students. The activities offered at the Wellness Center include intramural sports, exercise classes, and wellness programs.

University of Miami students are also pas-sionate about extracurricular activities. Greek life is very popular, with over 1,000 undergraduate members of UM's 31 sororities and fraternities. During Canefest, the organization fair at the beginning of fall semester, students are able to choose from a wide variety of clubs. Some popular organizations include Student Government, Council for Democracy, College Democrats, College Republicans, Committee on Student Organizations (COSO), and Hurricane Productions.

There are also a number of honor societies, clubs for specific majors, and community service groups. Moreover, multicultural organizations, such as La Federacion de Estudiantes Cubanos (FEC), are very prominent. Several unique activities exist on campus, such as Salsa Craze, Swing Club, and Adrian Empire, which is a Medieval/Renaissance reenactment group. And as one student remarked, "If there's something you want to do that UM doesn't have, it's pretty easy to start it up." Most students are fairly committed to their extracurricular activities. One sophomore stated, "Getting involved . . . has made it so much better because that's how you make friends and gain experience and knowledge that will help you in the future."

'Cane Spirit

Despite a common stereotype that University of Miami students are "rich" and "snobby," most students claim otherwise. Students note that "The majority of people are pretty down-to-earth" and "really friendly." The University also has a great deal of diversity, with students from "all over the world and all around the U.S." A recent graduate said that the prevalent diversity on campus was a "unique, educational and rewarding experience."

Students praise the University's commitment to both academics and athletics and attribute the University's growing prestige to President Donna Shalala, who is doing "so many things to get our school's name out there." The tropical climate, beautiful campus, and diverse and nurturing student atmosphere are all factors that draw students to the University of Miami. But what really distinguishes the school for most students is "The fact that people actually really care about their school and are proud to go to UM." Go 'Canes!—*Eileen Zelek*

FYI

FYI
If you come to the University of Miami, you'd better bring "your bathing suit, flip-flops, shorts, and sunscreen."

What is the typical weekend schedule? "For the most part it consists of lots of homework during the day and partying at night. The weekend starts on Thursday with 'College Night' in Coconut Grove and the rest of the time is usually spent tanning or clubbing in South Beach."

If I could change one thing about the University of Miami, "I'd add more parking garages and make the restaurants and dining halls on campus stay open longer."

Three things every student at the University of Miami should do before graduating are "go to a football game at the Orange Bowl, spend time at South Beach, and hang out at the Rat."

University of South Florida

Address: 4202 East Fowler Avenue, Tampa, FL 33620-9951
Phone: 813-974-3350
E-mail address: admissions@admin.usf.edu
Web site URL: www.usf.edu
Year Founded: 1956
Private or Public: Public
Religious Affiliation: None
Location: Suburban
Number of Applicants: 27,017
Percent Accepted: 50%
Percent Accepted who enroll: 30%
Number Entering: 3,664
Number of Transfers Accepted each Year: 7,549
Middle 50% SAT range: M: 530–630, CR: 510–610, Wr: 490–580
Middle 50% ACT range: 23–28
Early admission program EA/ED/None: None

Percentage accepted through EA or ED: NA
EA and ED deadline: NA
Regular Deadline: 15-Apr
Application Fee: $30
Full time Undergraduate enrollment: 34,897
Total enrollment: 44,395
Percent Male: 42%
Percent Female: 58%
Total Percent Minority or Unreported: 35%
Percent African-American: 12%
Percent Asian/Pacific Islander: 6%
Percent Hispanic: 14%
Percent Native-American: 1%
Percent International: 1%
Percent in-state/out of state: Unreported
Percent from Public HS: 95%
Retention Rate: 81%
Graduation Rate 4-year: Unreported

Graduation Rate 6-year: Unreported
Percent Undergraduates in On-campus housing: 13%
Number of official organized extracurricular organizations: 507
3 Most popular majors: Biomedical Sciences, Business, Psychology
Student/Faculty ratio: 4:1
Average Class Size: 14
Percent of students going to grad school: 19%
Tuition and Fees: $16,623
In-State Tuition and Fees if different: $3,906
Cost for Room and Board: $8,080
Percent receiving financial aid out of those who apply, first year: 69%
Percent receiving financial aid among all students: 76%

I f you are searching for a college with a fun campus environment, a warm, sunny location, and great academic programs in business, engineering, and science, the University of South Florida is a school worth considering. In addition to enjoying USF's excellent sports teams and numerous nearby social scenes, students there take advantage of the many perks associated with being college kids in Tampa, Florida. Indeed, whether it is spending a day at the beach (only half an hour away), visiting one of the two nearby major theme parks, or enjoying exciting Division I football games, USF students always have something fun to do while they receive an excellent education.

Getting the Sunshine State Experience

Located in suburban Tampa, USF presents its students numerous benefits, creating an environment that students at other colleges only experience during spring break. Living in Florida is "a blast" according to one sophomore from out of state, who added, "Winters at USF are fantastic, since they are virtually nonexistent." The weather in Tampa is ideal during the winter and spring months, when high temperatures fall comfortably between 60 and 80 degrees, and low temperatures rarely dip below the mid-30s. Most students find the winter months to be enjoyable, and they can frequently be seen lounging about in the many green areas on campus. However, some students did complain about Florida's heat and humidity in the summer and fall months. If you play outdoor sports, be advised, "It is very, very easy to get dehydrated, especially with the high heat and humidity. The Florida heat in August, September, October, and May can be intense."

Students also find that USF is an ideal location within the city itself. One freshman noted, "Two incredible Florida theme parks, Busch Gardens and Adventure Island, are only about five minutes away from campus." In addition, USF is located "about 10–15 minutes north of downtown Tampa, which has Ybor City and Channelside as two major entertainment districts." Channelside has a variety of entertainment venues, including a movie theatre with an IMAX screen, a state-of-the-art bowling alley, and a great variety of clubs and restaurants. Ybor City not only has numerous nightclubs but also a Gameworks, a movie theatre, a line of shops, and a lot of restaurants. The beach is only a 30-minute drive away; students typically recommend Clearwater Beach as a great, year-round hangout place. The many sports teams in the area are also popular venues for students. They frequent both the Tampa Bay Buccaneers football games and the Lightning hockey games. The New York Yankees also conduct their spring training in Tampa. Furthermore, USF's football team, the Bulls, attracts massive crowds weekly, making the University a virtual Mecca for sports enthusiasts. However, one student did advise against watching one specific team. "Even though they practically give away the tickets," one junior noted, "it's just not worth seeing the Devil Rays play baseball."

USF's Academic Trifecta

USF has a strong academic program, especially in the areas of business, engineering, and pre-med. It also has all the benefits of a large university while placing emphasis on personal attention. Incoming freshmen can take a class called "The University Experience" which helps them get acclimated to college life while instructing them in the research techniques and study habits that they

will need to be successful. Students report that USF's business program is very popular on campus. "Most of the people I know are enrolled in at least some type of business-oriented class," one freshman explained, "and many of my friends have already decided to take business administration as their major."

For students not interested in a business-related major, there are lots of excellent options. USF's pre-med program is quite reputable. USF's campus includes the Moffitt Cancer Center, which is one of the top cancer research institutions in the nation and a place where many students volunteer. USF's engineering program is also noteworthy for its great faculty. One student bragged that her professor in the robotics department, Ms. Robin Murphy, missed the first day of class to deploy her robotic technology at the Crandall Canyon Mine to search for mining accident victims underground. This happens to be "just one of many examples in which USF faculty members make a difference."

While USF's academics are very strong in many aspects, students admit that it is not an ideal school for those pursuing math or humanities majors. One freshman criticized the mathematics department for having professors and teaching assistants that "do not speak English very well, are hard to understand, and not very able to help the students." The humanities department, many students complain, needs more classes and does not have enough majors from which they can choose. Despite these drawbacks, however, USF has a solid academic record overall that continues to improve each year.

Living the Good Life, On or Off Campus

A sizable number of students at USF are commuters who live nearby. Most of these students, however, cite financial concerns for this choice. One junior noted that it was much cheaper for him to stay in an apartment nearby and that most students who opt to stay off campus do so for similar reasons. Campus living at USF is generally quite enjoyable. "I made most of my friends here by hanging out in dorms and watching movies together," noted one sophomore. "The dorms are tiny but conveniently located, and the University tries to pair you up with people you will be compatible with, so nightmare roommates are rare." Most students cite the Marshall Center as the best hangout location on campus. One freshman boasted that the Marshall Center includes "lots of pool tables, a big-screen TV, video games, a food court, and live bands that play every week." Students report that the food at USF is also quite good. In addition to a cafeteria-style meal plan, students can choose from Burger King, Subway, Einstein's Bagels, and Ben and Jerry's, among others. The library is also a great place to get together for academic and social purposes; it has a Starbucks on the first floor and is centrally located. Students also frequent the school's many courtyards and greeneries, which "have plenty of shade and are great places to study or talk to friends."

If students want to get off campus for some fun but do not have money for a night downtown or a day at Busch Gardens, the Gator Dockside is known as a good place to get together with friends. One student noted that "Gator nuggets and watching sports are a must" at this restaurant. USF students also frequent the nearby University Mall, which has a variety of shops and restaurants less than five minutes away from campus. The numerous athletic events held on campus each week, which students can get into for free, are also popular.

When on campus, students report that safety is not a major issue; in fact, "aside from the occasional bike thief," students feel safe. However, some lament that parking is an issue. While new parking lots are being constructed, "parking is terrible" at USF, and commuters complain at "having to arrive up to an hour early at times" to secure a spot close to class and that they "park really far away, which can be annoying."

A Social Scene with Something for Everyone

USF has a unique combination of athletic, Greek, and service organizations. Athletics (participating in or watching) are at the forefront of such activities. As one student noted, "Club-level and intramural sports are always fun" and are "easy to join and stay active in." By far the most popular sport at USF is football, and two major student organizations hold tailgating parties at every home game. The Student Bulls Club is probably the more universal athletic booster organization, as it is open to all students and sets up events at both home and away games for football, basketball, volleyball, soccer, and other Bulls sports. The Beef Studs is the other major athletic booster organization on campus. One freshman stated, "The Beef Studs are a one-of-a-kind, die-hard

group of fans that wear body-paint at every event, always keep the crowd pumped, and travel to just about every game. I'm not even sure if they ever remove the body paint, even during the week." There are plenty of reasons for cheering on the USF Bulls: students tout the fact that their football team is having a phenomenal season and, in October 2007, was ranked number 5 in the SEC.

> "The Beef Studs are a one-of-a-kind, die-hard group of fans that wear body-paint at every event, always keep the crowd pumped, and travel to just about every game. I'm not even sure if they ever remove the body paint, even during the week."

For those not as enthusiastic about sports, USF has a variety of other organizations. One freshman said, "Joining student government is a great way to become involved." Student government organizes school-wide social events and runs the Campus Activities Board, which oversees the funding and administration of student-run organizations on campus. The 42 fraternities and sororities represent the Greek life that plays a major but not dominant role in USF's social scene. While USF has its fair share of fun parties, students there are proud that drinking and drugs "are not a major problem." As one freshman put it, "No one really feels pressured to drink if they go to parties here."

For the more altruistic students, community service organizations and events are also thriving parts of campus life. Students work with Metropolitan Ministries, Habitat for Humanity, and other local non-profits. USF even hosts the region's Special Olympics competition every March. Indeed, as one student said, "USF has an endless number of activities that continue to grow with the interests of the student body. So even if students can't find something they are interested in, they can easily start it up and get funding from the school."

Mixing Business with Pleasure

Finally, students at USF place unique emphasis on career preparation. Alpha Kappa Psi, one of USF's coed professional business fraternities, prepares its members for successful careers in the corporate world. They frequently hold workshops, coach each other for interviews, host speakers from business-related fields, and visit the offices of major companies in the area. Furthermore, students at USF become involved in fields where they have a personal, life-long interest. One particularly driven freshman with a keen interest in hockey secured a marketing internship with the Tampa Bay Lightning, an "incredible, life-shaping experience" in which he has been able to combine "a love for hockey with a career interest in marketing and management." For him, this "has opened the door for a whole new world of opportunities." A host of similar career-oriented internships are available through the Moffitt Cancer Center and in the surrounding community. As the same freshman noted, "USF has a well-known career fair each year and is uniquely adept at helping interested students get quality internships in areas that they are really passionate about. USF really values a well-rounded education."

Overall, the University of South Florida is a strong, up-and-coming large state university that allows its students to enjoy their college experience filled with Florida-style fun, lots of school spirit, and numerous academic and career-oriented opportunities. As one student aptly and enthusiastically put it, "USF is a place where great individuals come for a great, fun experience in a great place where there are great academic programs and opportunities."—*Andrew Pearlmutter, special thanks to Steven Marsicano*

FYI

If you come to the University of South Florida, you'd better bring "something green. School spirit is big here."

What is the typical weekend schedule? "Fridays are spent hanging out with friends near campus or at someone's dorm. On Saturday, most go to a football game or some other type of athletic event, and then party or hang out that night. On Sunday, students start studying and preparing for the next week of classes."

If I could change one thing about USF, I'd "add more parking garages."

Three things every student at USF should do before graduating are "visit local landmarks such as Busch Gardens and Clearwater Beach, spend an evening at the Dockside and eat gator nuggets, and go to all the home football games. Go Bulls!"

Georgia

Address: 141 East College Avenue, Atlanta/Decatur, GA 30030-3797
Phone: 404-471-6285
E-mail address: admission@agnesscott.edu
Web site URL: www.agnesscott.edu
Year Founded: 1889
Private or Public: Private
Religious Affiliation: Presbyterian
Location: Suburban
Number of Applicants: 1,595
Percent Accepted: 48%
Percent Accepted who enroll: 30%
Number Entering: 218
Number of Transfers Accepted each Year: 29
Middle 50% SAT range: M: 500–610, CR: 550–680, Wr: 550–660
Middle 50% ACT range: 22–29
Early admission program EA/ED/None: EA

Percentage accepted through EA or ED: Unreported
EA and ED deadline: 15-Nov
Regular Deadline: Rolling
Application Fee: $35
Full time Undergraduate enrollment: 757
Total enrollment: 885
Percent Male: 0%
Percent Female: 100%
Total Percent Minority or Unreported: 46%
Percent African-American: 21%
Percent Asian/Pacific Islander: 5%
Percent Hispanic: 4%
Percent Native-American: <1%
Percent International: 5%
Percent in-state/out of state: 54%/46%
Percent from Public HS: 80%
Retention Rate: 82%

Graduation Rate 4-year: 63%
Graduation Rate 6-year: 67%
Percent Undergraduates in On-campus housing: 87%
Number of official organized extracurricular organizations: 80
3 Most popular majors: Economics, English, Psychology
Student/Faculty ratio: 9:1
Average Class Size: 15
Percent of students going to grad school: 25%
Tuition and Fees: $39,955
In-State Tuition and Fees if different: No difference
Cost for Room and Board: $9,850
Percent receiving financial aid out of those who apply, first year: 99%
Percent receiving financial aid among all students: 71%

F rom its origins in 1889 as a seminary for women to its recent renovations featuring a three-story rendering of Agnes Scott's DNA, Agnes Scott College has had an incredible history as a women's college famed for its liberal arts education and its warm atmosphere. Located just outside of Atlanta, the weather provides a welcoming home for students year-round. But above all, strong academics with a focus on leadership and a thriving social life complete the beauty of a hip and enthusiastic women's campus.

Professors and Credits and Homework, Oh My!

Many students have said that the amount of work is "crazy," but all are quick to point out that many professors will "give extensions if you need them and will always work through things with you." Scotties do mention that their professors tend to become notorious with the Classics department taking the cake. One sophomore described how her Roman Civilization teacher came to class and conducted it in the persona of Gaius Sempronius Gracchus. "For a day or so afterwards, he signed all his e-mails to us 'GSG.'"

There are few academic requirements—approximately one per discipline, along with two PE classes and several others for a total of 128 credits across 8 semesters. These requirements can be fulfilled through a variety of unique classes; in short, there are enough options that artsy students need not fear the math requirement. One undergrad explained that she was "Immensely grateful that I was so challenged to learn and broaden my horizons."

Students agree that Agnes Scott is difficult. "There are 'marginally less difficult' majors and then there is biochemistry. Our creative writing department is fairly competitive; any of the science majors are challenging," joked one Scottie. However, the atmosphere is collaborative rather than aggressive, so "People won't sabotage you or anything."

Since there are less than 1,000 undergraduates, the atmosphere at Agnes Scott is incredibly cozy. Class sizes range from three or four students to a maximum of 42, but with such a small student body, "They rarely fill to that point." In accordance with the liberal mindset of the school, assignments tend to be fairly innovative. One student recalled designing "a giant kids' book about a scientific experiment done with fear genes" and another professor "gave us our daily quiz one day by asking us to line up appropriately in a phalanx—spears and shields included—and we marched on Agnes Scott." And for those who want a study-abroad experience without having to undergo separation anxiety, Global Connections allows students to take "a 'trip' class and then go on a mini-study abroad trip with that class."

Working Hard, Playing like Crazy

Beyond homework and classes, Agnes Scott students keep busy. School nights tend to be set aside for homework and other extracurriculars, peppered with some trips to neighboring Georgia Tech to meet guys. Sports are very low key, with calmer fans on the sidelines. However, when asked, a student exclaimed, "Football! We have been undefeated for the last hundred years" and promised to send out shirts to anybody who asked. As at any other college campus, Frisbee is a popular pick-up game. Extracurricular groups include WAVE (the feminist group), the Anime Club, the Asian Studies Department (because the academic department does not exist), Latinas Unidas, Classics Club, Witkaze, Arabic Lunch Table, Scottie Social Dance, and many more.

The upperclassmen tend to split between the Mortar Club, which is very conservative and traditional, and the significantly more lax Pestle Club, which "just sets out to be the diametric opposite of Mortar Board." Freshmen tend to mix and mingle at larger and more organized functions, like the Red Light Green Light party, swing dance nights, movie nights and other on-campus events, while upperclassmen tend to gravitate to Georgia Tech for the coed environment. Describing Greek life on campus, a junior joked that "Our Greek system is limited to my Theocritus class. We don't have sororities. We are a sorority."

As part of the feminist environment, people do respect personal preferences. Many students joked that first-years go in believing "Agnes will turn you gay" but in reality, people just become more supportive of the atmosphere around them. The campus is complimented for being very open and diverse. A Caucasian woman from the Midwest rattled off a list of groups with high profiles at Agnes Scott, including "Dems, Republicans, Libs, Pagans, Christians, Jews, Muslims, lesbians, transgenders, straight women, girls who look like men, girls who look very fem, black, brown, Indian, Native American, Hispanic, white and paler than white" before trailing off.

Amazing Atlanta

The campus is very calm, thanks to its scenic location just outside Atlanta. One upperclassman could not stop gushing: "It's very quaint and small and Gothic. The dining hall looks like 'The Great Hall' of Harry Potter." Just a few miles on MARTA, Atlanta's metropolitan rail system, gets you into the city, which offers incredible sports venues, nightlife, zoos, and much more.

> "We don't have sororities. We are a sorority."

The campus residences are extraordinarily varied. The freshmen are put in two dorms, Winship and Walters. Students in each consider the other their rival, although a couple of years of perspective blurs the two. Not many students live off campus, which makes the student body that much closer and intimate. And as such, there are a great number of traditions, as one student listed: "Ringing the bell in the tower when you get a job or are accepted to grad school, getting thrown in the alumnae pond if you're engaged, running around mostly naked at Black Cat, capping the spring of your junior year for Pestle Board, and, of course, the campus ghosts . . ."

Agnes Scott, more than any other women's

college, offers an incredible opportunity for community as well as education. When asked if she would go back to Agnes Scott, a soon-to-graduate student said, "I'd be here in a heartbeat. I've grown up and learned both emotionally and academically. I feel like I could function in the world after being here, as a person rather than a 'woman.'" And, of course, it's just plain beautiful! —*Jeffrey Zuckerman*

FYI

What's the typical weekend schedule? "Chill. And then panic about homework. Some people do more of the homeworking. We party or see movies or watch reruns of Project Runway. LOTS of Project Runway."

If I could change one thing about Agnes Scott, I'd "try to get just a little less homework."

Three things every student at Agnes Scott should do before graduating are "chill at Java Monkey, spend the night in the light lab, and visit the health center with a headache to see how long it takes them to give you a pregnancy test."

Emory University

Address: Boiseuillet Jones Ctr Atlanta, GA 30322
Phone: 404-727-6036
E-mail address: admiss@learnlink.emory.edu
Web site URL: www.emory.edu
Year Founded: 1836
Private or Public: Private
Religious Affiliation: Methodist
Location: Urban
Number of Applicants: 12,865
Percent Accepted: 32%
Percent Accepted who enroll: 30%
Number Entering: 1,235
Number of Transfers Accepted each Year: 152
Middle 50% SAT range: M: 660–740, CR: 640–730, Wr: 660–740
Middle 50% ACT range: 29–33
Early admission program EA/ED/None: ED

Percentage accepted through EA or ED: 31%
EA and ED deadline: 1-Nov
Regular Deadline: 15-Jan
Application Fee: $50
Full time Undergraduate enrollment: 6,546
Total enrollment: 9,300
Percent Male: 42%
Percent Female: 58%
Total Percent Minority or Unreported: 31%
Percent African-American: 9%
Percent Asian/Pacific Islander: 19%
Percent Hispanic: 3%
Percent Native-American: 1%
Percent International: 8%
Percent in-state/out of state: 29%/71%
Percent from Public HS: 64%
Retention Rate: 94%
Graduation Rate 4-year: 83%

Graduation Rate 6-year: 87%
Percent Undergraduates in On-campus housing: 66%
Number of official organized extracurricular organizations: 282
3 Most popular majors: Business, Economics, Psychology
Student/Faculty ratio: 7:1
Average Class Size: 14
Percent of students going to grad school: 65%
Tuition and Fees: $33,900
In-State Tuition and Fees if different: No difference
Cost for Room and Board: $10,220
Percent receiving financial aid out of those who apply, first year: 80%
Percent receiving financial aid among all students: 53%

With distinguished faculty members such as Former U.S. President Jimmy Carter and His Holiness the XIV Dalai Lama, Emory offers a rigorous curriculum to "enable students to develop individual expertise and values, expressed in service to others." This top 20 research university has a motto of "A wise heart seeks knowledge" and its small classes and high quality of professors reflect their philosophy. Emory encourages its students to pursue their interests and to be inquisitive. Even though it leans towards math and science, its liberal arts college is recognized internationally.

Rigorous Academics without Competition

Emory offers a diverse and wide selection of courses to its undergraduate students. With 70 majors and more than 55 minors, Emory covers a wide range of subjects. Popular majors on campus include Biology, Chemistry, and Neuroscience and Behavioral Biology (NBB) and many students are on the pre-med, pre-law or pre-business track. Emory is a known leader in HIV research and has the longest-running program to integrate sustainability into the educational curriculum. Although Emory offers a lot of opportunities to those who are interested in sciences, Emory does not leave the humanities behind. The multitude of courses that Emory has offers an even blend of math, science and humanities classes, and the General Education Requirements (GERs) are more centered on the humanities than math or science.

For undergraduates, Emory offers four schools, each with its own application: Emory College of Arts and Sciences, Oxford College, Goizueta Business School and Nell Hodgson Woodruff School of Nursing.

Students in Emory College must satisfy the recently updated General Education Requirements. This includes one course in First-Year Seminar Classes (FSEM), one course in the First-Year Writing Requirement (FWRT), three courses in Continuing Writing Requirement (WRT), one course in Math & Quantitative Reasoning (MQR), two courses in Science, Nature and Technology (SNT), two courses in History, Society, Cultures (HSC), four courses in Humanities, Arts, Performance (HAP) & (HAL), one one-hour course in Personal Health (HTH), and three one-hour courses in Physical Education and Dance (PED). While this list may look daunting, many of these requirements can be satisfied with a score of four or five on AP tests.

Emory offers two special programs to its undergraduates after their second year. During their sophomore year, students can apply to Goizueta Business School or Nell Hodgson Woodruff School of Nursing. After spending junior and senior year in these schools, they can receive either a bachelor's degree in business administration or a bachelor's of science degree in nursing.

Even though Emory is a prestigious university with high academic standards, the lack of a bell curve in most classes makes Emory a place where students focus on working together and in groups. Students find that there is a lack of competition among students because of the lack of a rigid bell curve. "We don't work against each other. [The classes] focus on study groups and working with other students," says a pre-med freshman. One exception is the classes in the Goizueta Business School, or the "B-School" as it is more commonly known. The bell curve is applied in business classes and these classes can be extremely rigorous. However, the difficulty and amount of workload do not deter the B-School students.

> "I'm honored to learn from professors who are experts within their fields, and their passion helps to make lectures more engaging."

Class size is definitely one of Emory's many strengths. The average is 14 students. Students praise the "accessibility" and the "high caliber" of professors. One student stated, "They really try their best to be available for students and put their best effort into helping the students." Another exclaimed, "I'm honored to learn from professors who are experts within their fields, and their passion helps to make lectures more engaging." Emory's dedication to its students encourages them to pursue their passions and continue to seek knowledge.

No Football . . . But There's Dooley!

Emory University began with the help of a one-million dollar donation from Asa Candler, the founder of The Coca-Cola Company. However, the one rule was that Emory could never have a football team. Over 100 years later, Emory has honored Candler's wishes and doesn't have a football team. However, Emory does have the unofficial mascot Dooley who safeguards Emory's school spirit. Dooley began as a lab skeleton in an 1899 biology lab and started writing his own column, Dooley's Column, in the school newspaper. Now, he shows up around campus wearing a cape surrounded by bodyguards. It is commonly known that secret societies have the obligation of keeping Dooley's identity safe and maintaining the campus tradition every year. One of the biggest traditions on campus is Dooley's Week and Dooley's Ball, the culmination of Dooley's Week. During one week in March, events such as comedy shows, concerts, food samplings and movie screenings are open to students and the community. During this week, Dooley frequently appears and causes mischief on campus. He can dismiss any class with his water gun and successfully increases school spirit. The week ends with Dooley's Ball, the most attended social event of the year.

Geeks and Greeks

Social life, especially on the weekend, is centered off campus unless Emory is hosting a major event. However, without the use of a car, many freshmen find the need of public transportation to get into Atlanta a hassle and costly. However, there are many options to socialize on campus. If students are not in the mood to party, Starbucks and Yogli Mogli, the frozen yogurt place near campus, are popular places to hang out that are close by. If students are in the party mood, there are many options on and off campus. The most popular option on campus is the fraternities on "Frat Row." There are 15 fraternities and 13 sororities. The sororities are not allowed to have parties, so many people congregate around the frats, which are not discriminatory. "It's free for everyone—girls and guys, and you can generally get in with or without an invite," one freshman remarked. Frats are also right next to freshmen dorms so they are easy to get to, especially for people without cars. Sports teams also have parties but an invitation is necessary.

Emory is not a party school. "I can probably say that a lot of students stay in their dorms on the weekends, because most of the students are not from the Atlanta area," notes one student. However, "It's pretty common to find students drinking—it's rare that there's nothing to do," one freshman stated. The party scene at Emory benefits from the laidback attitude of the police. Even though there are police cars stationed on Frat Row, students can walk past them carrying Solo cups full of beer without any reaction or complaint from the police. Students at Emory also have medical amnesty, which serves as a "free pass" for any misdemeanor related to alcohol. If something happens, friends can call 911 and nothing will go on the record on the first offense.

Nerdy, Athletic and Engaged

When questioned about the typical Emory student, many students could not find a label. "We have students who spend most of their free time in the books, students consid-

ered preppy, students who are really involved in sports, and students who like to get involved with dancing and the arts," stated a Pre-Med student.

However, some students said that most people come into Emory as prospective science majors and there is a "slight division between students of difference focus." Most people at Emory seem to fit into categories of Pre-Business, Pre-Med, or Pre-Law and one of the first questions usually asked is "Well, what's your focus?" However, this slight rift does not completely separate the groups and many students are able to make friends in many different groups. While the Emory student body is diverse in interests, some students felt that the majority of Emory students are nerdy. "There are definitely a lot of nerds but I feel like everyone has a bit of nerd in them at Emory to deal with the rigor," stated a freshman.

But Emory's "nerdiness" does not stop its student body from being athletic. Even though Emory is a Division III school, it does not mean that Emory students are not athletic. In fact, most students participate in intramural sports and clubs.

Other popular clubs on campus are the a cappella groups. One of the traditions in Emory is that all the a cappella groups perform in front of the dining hall the first Friday of every month. Even though many Emory students share their love of music and a cappella, many students say that Emory students have very diverse extracurricular activities and one club is not more popular than the next.

Amazing Accommodations in Atlanta

Even with the large number of clubs and volunteer activities on campus, most students find that the number one way to make friends is getting to know your hall mates. And with hall bonding traditions such as SongFest where freshmen write and perform songs as a hall, many people find that dorms are a quick and easy way to make friends.

Freshmen and sophomores are required to live on campus and they have beautiful newly renovated dorms to choose from. For freshmen, there are eight air-conditioned dorms with choices of rooms from singles to suite-style. Students can even choose three dorms with themes of Global Cultures, Living Green, and Citizenship. For upperclassmen, there is the opportunity to live in the much-desired Clairmont Tower apartments. All the sophomores try to get dorms in Clairmont and with good reason. Each apartment is air-conditioned, has a kitchen, a bathroom and laundry room. Most of the apartments also have balconies. Coupled with the gor-geous Georgian weather, it's hard to find a student with a campus-related complaint. What's better than getting a degree in a "five-star hotel"?—*Sharon Qian*

FYI

If you come to Emory, you'd better leave "any preconceived notions behind."

The typical weekend schedule: "Thursday night is frat or club night; Friday night is frat or dorm party night; Saturday is homework and frat and any other party night; Sunday is doing the work you put off until then."

If I could change one thing about Emory, I'd "make sports more popular. It'd be fun to have more school spirit and teams to cheer on."

Georgia Institute of Technology, Atlanta

Address: 225 North Avenue NW Atlanta, GA 30332-0320
Phone: 404-894-4154
E-mail address: admission@gatech.edu
Web site URL: www.gatech.edu
Year Founded: 1885
Private or Public: Public
Religious Affiliation: None
Location: Urban
Number of Applicants: 9,664
Percent Accepted: 63%
Percent Accepted who enroll: 43%
Number Entering: 2,626
Number of Transfers Accepted each Year: 448
Middle 50% SAT range: M: 650–730, CR: 590–690, Wr: 580–670
Middle 50% ACT range: 27–31
Early admission program EA/ED/None: None

Percentage accepted through EA or ED: NA
EA and ED deadline: NA
Regular Deadline: 15-Jan
Application Fee: $50
Full time Undergraduate enrollment: 12,565
Total enrollment: 18,742
Percent Male: 68%
Percent Female: 32%
Total Percent Minority or Unreported: 45%
Percent African-American: 5%
Percent Asian/Pacific Islander: 18%
Percent Hispanic: 5%
Percent Native-American: <1%
Percent International: 5%
Percent in-state/out of state: 70%/30%
Percent from Public HS: Unreported
Retention Rate: 92%
Graduation Rate 4-year: 31%

Graduation Rate 6-year: 76%
Percent Undergraduates in On-campus housing: 59%
Number of official organized extracurricular organizations: 311
3 Most popular majors: Business Administration, Industrial Engineering, Mechanical Engineering
Student/Faculty ratio: 14:1
Average Class Size: 19
Percent of students going to grad school: 41%
Tuition and Fees: $25,182
In-State Tuition and Fees if different: $6,040
Cost for Room and Board: $7,694
Percent receiving financial aid out of those who apply, first year: 44%
Percent receiving financial aid among all students: 32%

Georgia Institute of Technology is a college name with a certain gritty, metallic taste at the end. Images of short circuit wires, helter-skelter reading glasses, and test tubes abound. Often short-ened to just GTech, this school embodies your typical "Insert-Letter-Here-Tech" school. But it's got more to offer than a dedication to advanced science and technology. And it's more than a pretty brick campus snuggled away in downtown Atlanta.

We Get It, We're Engineers.

The vast majority of the undergraduate students at GTech major in the sciences. Typically, the word "engineering" appears somewhere in the official name. However, GTech houses six different departments: the

Colleges of Architecture, Engineering, Sciences, Computing, Management, and the Ivan Allen College of Liberal Arts. A freshman Yellow Jacket cautioned that "You should expect to work a lot. A lot. It's all about time management."

Students note that classes are usually "challenging," but not impossible in that there are strong support networks available. For Biomeds specifically, BROS will always be there to lend a hand. BROS stands for Biomedical Research and Opportunities Society and it helps students network with upperclassmen and graduates to find tips for success and opportunities for greater involvement.

Georgia Tech is lauded nationally for some of its more specialized engineering majors. Not only is it a blue ribbon winner in prestigious fields such as industrial engineering and biomedical engineering, this school has consistently ranked in the top ten in aerospace, biomedical, nuclear, and radiological engineering over the past couple of years. Rest assured, GTech will continue to be a pack leader for years to come.

Regarding core curriculum, all majors must take at least one introductory calculus class, English Composition I and II, two lab-intensive sciences, and several courses in the humanities, fine arts, and social sciences. Students feel that this core recipe has certain advantages and disadvantages. At the very least, they contribute to a better-rounded student upon graduation.

Normally, classes in the humanities such as English garner a smaller class size when compared to intro-level calc. English classes often only have around 20 students.

One student noted that many intro-level science and math courses serve as "weed-out" classes that cause many students to lose hope in certain subjects. Chemistry I, Physics I, and Calculus II in particular have low pass rates and harsh curves. Rumors of the "Four Horsemen of Calc II" even drift across campus. Success, thus, depends greatly on high school preparation and self motivation.

Slurp. Fizzy. I Heart CO_2.

Scientific research is the name of the game at GTech. The school has an Undergraduate Research Opportunities Program that provides students with a list of labs for in school and summer research with professors to gain insight on scientific explorations and discoveries. It also has a Cooperative Education Program that gives undergrads

the chance to attend school for five years. During these five years, students would alternate semesters of full-time work with semesters of full-time study. It is one of the largest of its kind in the United States.

Here's where GTech's location in the midst of Atlanta comes into play. Industry leaders such as NASA, Coca-Cola, and General Electric often turn to picking the brains of Georgia's brightest and most dedicated.

I Say Yellow, You Say Jacket!

As a public institution, a majority of the students are Georgia residents. However, there is a very diverse representation of states and countries such as India, South Korea, and Germany. Social life is usually tossed in with red Solo cups, crumbling buildings, and beer-stained floors. Fraternities. The cumbersome and unequal gender distribution within the student body, along with difficult course loads, opens the doors for Greeks to take first place. Approximately one-fourth of the freshman class pledges to one of the 40-plus chapters on campus. The usual menu of mixers, punch pong, and "liquor treating" is heartily served.

However, for those who prefer to avoid self-induced memory loss and value their liver, GTech offers a plethora of student-run and school-sponsored clubs. Activities range from cultural as in the Indian Club to technical such as the Robotics Team. Musicians flock to join the Georgia Tech Band programs. Members of the 300 plus member marching band travel to every football game and invite students from nearby universities without football programs to participate. It's an amalgam of talented performers from all over Georgia. If you can't toot a horn, but can belt "My Heart Will Go On" with frightening enthusiasm, GTech offers several a capella groups who will welcome you with open arms. Some of the most popular ones are "Nothin' but Treble" and "Infinite Harmony." There's even an "Under Water Hockey Club," if the daredevil inside isn't satisfied.

The dating scene at the school is easily remedied by the campus's closeness to other North Georgia colleges, including Spelman and Emory. Students thus mingle and gain opportunities to explore the rest of Atlanta and its surrounding suburbs.

Looking to remedy nightmares of last week's physics test? Try soaking in some city sights. MARTA (Metro Atlanta Rapid Transit Authority) has you covered. The Georgia Aquarium, a stone's throw away, is famous for being the only aquarium in the United States to house bus-sized whale sharks. South African diamond, Nandi, attracts waves of tourists from all over the world with her 13 foot manta ray wing span. If peaceful giants are not what one is looking for, the Atlanta Symphony Orchestra is another option. Nearby eateries such as Mellow Mushroom, The Varsity, and Chipotle are sure to keep ravenous students well-fed.

Buzz Buzz Sting

It's summer, the be-...jackets are, well... swarming. Regardless, it's luminous and temperate on GTech's sprawling emerald landscapes. Rustling trees tickle students with shade, while shielding them from the concrete jungle meters away from the edge of campus. Nestled snuggly between two major highways, the campus is indeed a southern jewel. Georgian architecture dots dormitory buildings and nearby Greek houses on East campus. West campus is newer and more spread out, inviting long relaxing walks. All one needs is their own picnic basket—a freshman warned against the rather drab dining hall pickings.

There's no doubt that GTech has a passionate student body that isn't so easily clique-ified. Students proudly consider themselves "crazy," but most definitely know how to have a good time. Donning brazen yellow and bold black during school games is second nature to the student body. Screaming school pride comes off as instinct. Nowhere else do "TI-89 wielders" roar alongside "basketball jocks," high five with "Mac wizards" and bump elbows with "acid-stained lab rats."

Churning out some of the most talented engineering masters in the country, this school has a lot to offer. It should never be thought of as just your typical "Insert-Letter-Here-Tech" school.—*Anna Wang*

FYI
If you come to Georgia Tech, you'd better "leave sleep behind."
If I could change one thing about Georgia Tech, I'd "make out-of-state tuition cheaper!"
What's the typical weekend schedule? "Friday night: something fun (i.e. party); Saturday: club related activities, sometimes sleeping in and sometimes homework; Sunday: homework and laundry."

Morehouse College

Address: 830 Westview Drive, SW, Atlanta, GA 30314
Phone: 404-215-2632
E-mail address: admissions@morehouse.edu
Web site URL: www.morehouse.edu
Year Founded: 1867
Private or Public: Private
Religious Affiliation: None
Location: Urban
Number of Applicants: 2,277
Percent Accepted: 67%
Percent Accepted who enroll: 46%
Number Entering: 700
Number of Transfers Accepted each Year: 127
Middle 50% SAT range: M: 480–590, CR: 480–580, Wr: Unreported
Middle 50% ACT range: 20–24
Early admission program EA/ED/None: EA

Percentage accepted through EA or ED: Unreported
EA and ED deadline: 15-Oct
Regular Deadline: 15-Feb
Application Fee: $45
Full time Undergraduate enrollment: 2,810
Total enrollment: 2,810
Percent Male: 100%
Percent Female: 0%
Total Percent Minority or Unreported: >99%
Percent African-American: 95%
Percent Asian/Pacific Islander: <1%
Percent Hispanic: 1%
Percent Native-American: <1%
Percent International: 3%
Percent in-state/out of state: 28%/ 72%
Percent from Public HS: 80%
Retention Rate: 84%

Graduation Rate 4-year: 32%
Graduation Rate 6-year: 49%
Percent Undergraduates in On-campus housing: 55%
Number of official organized extracurricular organizations: 34
3 Most popular majors: Business & Commerce, Computer & Informational Sciences
Student/Faculty ratio: 15:1
Average Class Size: 9
Percent of students going to grad school: 25%
Tuition and Fees: $20,358
In-State Tuition and Fees if different: No difference
Cost for Room and Board: $8,648
Percent receiving financial aid out of those who apply, first year: 100%
Percent receiving financial aid among all students: 100%

Nothing illuminates the excellence of the Morehouse College education better than its impressive crop of graduates. Martin Luther King, Jr., Spike Lee, Samuel L. Jackson, countless distinguished professors, lead researchers, CEOs, and Rhodes scholars are examples of the "Morehouse Men" that graduate from this premier, private, historically black liberal arts college for men. Just 10 minutes from downtown Atlanta, Morehouse offers students an array of opportunities that parallels the diversity of talents and interests in its students.

Fashioning a Morehouse Man

Morehouse College, originally founded as the Augusta Institute, was established just two years after the Civil War to prepare students to be educators or enter the ministry. Under the leadership of visionaries, Morehouse became one of the leading Historically Black Colleges and Universities (HBCUs) by expanding its curriculum and acquiring the resources necessary to prepare African-American males for the challenges they face inside and outside of the classroom. Morehouse soon left the bottom of a church's basement for the now 61-acre campus in Atlanta.

Over 140 years later, Morehouse provides a quality liberal arts education with 26 majors from which students may choose. Although some students call the course offerings "standard and conservative," many find the variety of courses interesting, unlike those of many liberal arts colleges, and at nearly half the price. The students also report difficulties dealing with the administration, though they admit the educational opportunities far outweigh any shortcomings.

True to its mission, Morehouse's General Education requirements develop the talents necessary to graduate "empowered, informed, and responsible" men. In accordance with its goal of providing a structured learning environment, Morehouse mandates that freshmen enroll in a year-long academic and social orientation to college life. Orientation meets on a weekly basis and is on a "Pass/Fail" system that students said "would require a student to never attend" to fail. Most students find the topics, like safe sex and personal finance, useful and interesting.

The Crown Forum is another favorite among students. Receiving its name from a famous quotation encouraging Morehouse men to grow tall enough to wear their crown, the Crown Forum helps mold students' characters and cultural competency. Students are required to attend a minimum of six events per semester for six semesters, though many say they have attended more. Overall, students are happy with the requirements because they help them "discover unknown interests and talents" that can guide them towards their majors, and say there is flexibility in the timing of scheduling some of the less popular requirements like religion.

Nearly one-third of the students at Morehouse eventually major in Business Administration. Other popular majors are Biology and Computer Science. Even though students find Morehouse to be a "supportive and encouraging" environment to grow academically, they acknowledged that "Business general requirement classes can be very competitive, with students contending for Fortune 500 internships." In addition, the Morehouse course load is considered intense for any student majoring in the natural sciences. However, students feel that their advisors are a "great resource," as evidenced by students' successful applications for research internships and medical school. Students reported an average of 9 students per class, which made professors accessible and "genuinely interested in their students' success."

Opportunities to Branch Out

Students searching for a greater challenge than the curriculum provides can enter the Morehouse College Honors Program (HP) during their first year, if they meet certain criteria. The HP provides students with smaller classrooms and more advanced course offerings than the regular courses, and is taught by distinguished professors. Army ROTC is also available to Morehouse students through Georgia Institute of Technology. The college also offers a plethora of internships, on-site learning opportunities, and community service projects in which roughly three-fourths of the student body participates. Through the Bonner Office of Community Service, which has partnerships with numerous organizations like the NFL YET Boys & Girls Club and Hands on Atlanta, students can easily make substantial contributions to their city. Many students also find additional service and mentoring opportunities on their own.

Morehouse's location and prestige affords its students many opportunities to learn off campus. Since they are a part of many academic consortiums, the men of Morehouse may spend a semester or academic year at universities such as Stanford and New York University, enroll in classes at colleges at Spelman, or participate in the Georgia Institute of Technology's Dual-Degree Engineering Program. These opportunities are highly recommended by students because they help Morehouse men "develop contacts, learn in unique environments, and meet women."

Life in the "A"

The single-sex education and living arrangements allow Morehouse students to "focus when it is time to focus, and party when it is time to party." "The well-known and active students" are usually leaders of popular campus organizations like student government and the NAACP. Since freshmen are required to live on campus, "class unity" quickly develops and most students become active upon their arrival. Many students meet classmates with similar interests while working on projects for science competitions or in organizations like the Morehouse Business Association.

> "Morehouse was a nurturing environment; I fell in love with the College and developed into a responsible and cognizant citizen."

After their first year, many students opt to live in the many affordable off-campus apartments near the college. Many upperclassmen have cars. "House parties and the clubs on Peachtree Street" are where students from all local colleges and universities congregate. Students report a "relatively easy time for Morehouse Men to meet other students, especially girls from other colleges in Atlanta." Greek life also attracts many Morehouse undergraduates, but problems with hazing have kept many of the "Divine Nine" National Pan-Hellenic Conference fraternities officially "off the yard."

Despite the varying interests and talents students from across the world bring to

Morehouse, "a true brotherhood develops" with the men recognizing each other's talents and desiring to better not only themselves, but also their surrounding community. As one student aptly summarized his experience,

"Morehouse was a nurturing environment; I fell in love with the College and developed into a responsible and cognizant citizen. In other words, I became a man of Morehouse College."—*Ayibatari Owi*

FYI

If you come to Morehouse, you'd better bring "a suit, a nice tie, and a white dress shirt."

What's the typical weekend schedule? "Most students get off work on Friday, then head to happy hour and house parties. Students study during the day on Saturday and go out to the clubs on Saturday night, sleep late, and then start the grind again on Sunday."

If I could change one thing about Morehouse I'd "change the religious foundation requirement."

Three things every student at Morehouse should do before graduating are "join extracurricular groups, mature and grow, and learn the history of the school."

Spelman College

Address: 350 Spelman Lane SW, Atlanta, GA 30314
Phone: 404-270-5193
E-mail address: admiss@spelman.edu
Web site URL: www.spelman.edu
Year Founded: 1881
Private or Public: Private
Religious Affiliation: None
Location: Urban
Number of Applicants: 5,656
Percent Accepted: 35%
Percent Accepted who enroll: 30%
Number Entering: 553
Number of Transfers Accepted each Year: 101
Middle 50% SAT range: M: 490–570, CR:500–580,
Wr: Unreported
Middle 50% ACT range: 21–25
Early admission program EA/ED/None: ED and EA

Percentage accepted through EA or ED: Unreported
EA and ED deadline: 1-Nov, 15-Nov
Regular Deadline: 1-Feb
Application Fee: $35
Full time Undergraduate enrollment: 2,270
Total enrollment: 2,270
Percent Male: 0%
Percent Female: 100%
Total Percent Minority or Unreported: 100%
Percent African-American: 92%
Percent Asian/Pacific Islander: 0%
Percent Hispanic: 0%
Percent Native-American: 0%
Percent International: <1%
Percent in-state/out of state: 31%/69%
Percent from Public HS: 84%
Retention Rate: 88%

Graduation Rate 4-year: 67%
Graduation Rate 6-year: 77%
Percent Undergraduates in On-campus housing: 43%
Number of official organized extracurricular organizations: 17
3 Most popular majors: Political Science and Government, Psychology, Biology
Student/Faculty ratio: 12:1
Average Class Size: 14
Percent of students going to grad school: Unreported
Tuition and Fees: $20,281
In-State Tuition and Fees if different: No difference
Cost for Room and Board: $9,734
Percent receiving financial aid out of those who apply, first year: Unreported
Percent receiving financial aid among all students: 75%

Spelman College in Atlanta, Georgia, offers the intimacy of a women's college without the seclusion—all-male Morehouse College, which is also an historically black institution, sits directly across the street. Spelman has just over 2,300 women enrolled which, according to students, makes the experience extremely personal.

Interdisciplinary Offerings

Spelman is a liberal arts college, so students are required to take a large variety of classes before graduating. There are requirements in English, math, the humanities, women's studies/international relations, fine art, and physical education. Students say the most popular majors are Political Science and

Government and Psychology but things may change with the recent introduction of a new major, African Diaspora in the World. The ADW major is interdisciplinary and focuses on the study of black people and culture throughout the world.

Class sizes are small, with an average of 14 students in each. The workload is also reasonable, as one student said she does about eight hours of studying a week. Spelman boasts many accomplished scholars and professors, including Pearl Cleage, a well-known author, and Dr. Christine King Ferris, the only living sibling of Dr. Martin Luther King, Jr. Both women are active professors at the College and teach classes on a regular basis. Some Spelman students expressed concern that the school's close, personal atmosphere leads professors to expect too much and to be too hard on the students, but many seniors said they were grateful for the personal attention they had received throughout the years. One student said, "They feel responsible for your success—that's why they are so hard on us. But I think it's worth it in the end."

Getting Along with the Girls

Like many women's colleges, Spelman students are constantly fighting the myth that there are no opportunities for interaction with the opposite sex. This just isn't true, says one Spelman sophomore: "We do everything with Morehouse—we can cross-register for classes, their football team is essentially our football team, and most social events are jointly organized."

> "They feel responsible for your success—that's why they are so hard on us. But I think it's worth it in the end."

Students say social activities at Spelman are strongly dominated by fraternities and sororities. The city of Atlanta offers many options as well—students said their weekend activities are often centered around clubs and events located downtown. Thursdays, Fridays, and Saturdays are the most popular nights to go out, but Spelman is a dry campus, meaning no alcohol can be consumed on school grounds. Consequently, nearly all parties take place off-campus. The annual Battle of the Bands contest is one of the biggest parties of the year for Spelman students, attracting students from historically black colleges all over the country.

Atlanta offers decent public transportation, but the majority of upperclassmen still bring cars to campus. Parking is "absolutely horrible," according to one junior. Many students said MARTA, the Metropolitan Atlanta Rapid Transport Authority, is inexpensive and an excellent alternative for getting around in the city.

Spelman students come from all over the country, but in a racial sense the College is not particularly diverse. One sophomore said there are less than five non-black undergraduates enrolled at the school, though this is to be expected considering its reputation as an historically black college.

Southern Comfort

Spelman is not the kind of campus where students live in school housing all four years—most live off campus by junior year. It might have something to do with the dorms themselves. A sophomore student said the dorms "Don't have air-conditioning, they are very small, and the buildings are really old." Despite this, students feel the exteriors of the dorms are aesthetically pleasing and "very pretty." Freshmen are required to live on campus, and freshman dorms are staffed by residential advisors. RAs are not generally strict, according to one freshman, but she said they are very involved in a student's freshman experience.

According to most students, dining at Spelman leaves something to be desired. There are essentially two options for meal-plan dining—Jaguar Underground Grill and Alma Upshaw Dining Hall. Both serve the typical cafeteria fare, though the Underground Grill is arranged food-court style. One junior said the décor of the dining locations is very nice, but the food is simply bad.

To earn extra cash, many Spelman students work in retail—at the mall or in local shopping centers. There are not any particularly prominent student groups on campus, but most students interviewed said most Spelman Jaguars are heavily involved in at least one activity.

Running with the Jaguars

This all-female historically black college (HBC) is all about tradition—freshmen and seniors have celebrated Founders Day for decades. During the event, held every year in April, the freshman and senior classes must wear white dresses and are joined by various alumni to celebrate Spelman's "birthday." Additionally, the Spelman campus features a grassy area known as "The Oval" which is the location of an arch that students are not allowed to walk under until after graduation.

Students said interactions between the Atlanta community and Spelman are "nonexistent" and occasionally hostile. They said that, when help is offered by the College, the community generally rejects it and all in all Spelman and the local community do not have the "best relationship." While Spelman students say they feel safe on campus, the surrounding area has significant crime rates

like any other metropolitan area. One sophomore offered this advice: "The area outside of campus is definitely not that safe at night; you should always walk with someone else if it's late." Spelman's security force includes state-certified policemen who retain the same powers (arrest, etc.) as any member of the Atlanta Police Department.

So what is it like to go to an all-women's college? A senior student said, "Going to an all-girls school has only enhanced my college experience. I think guys and girls add a different dynamic than all one sex. With just girls, we have a more intimate setting and discussions are more productive."—*Samantha Broussard-Wilson*

FYI

If you come to Spelman, you'd better bring "a skirt."
What's the typical weekend? "Going into the city to shop, eat, and maybe going to a club at night."
If I could change one thing about Spelman, I'd "improve the administration: they are very unorganized and don't generally like students."
Three things every student should do before graduating are "cross-register at Morehouse, take MARTA into the city, and go to a sporting event."

University of Georgia

Address: Terrell Hall, Athens, GA 30602
Phone: 706-542-8776
E-mail address: undergrad@admissions.uga.edu
Web site URL: www.uga.edu
Year Founded: 1785
Private or Public: Public
Religious Affiliation: None
Location: Suburban
Number of Applicants: 17,022
Percent Accepted: 54%
Percent Accepted who enroll: 51%
Number Entering: 4,696
Number of Transfers Accepted each Year: 1,524
Middle 50% SAT range: M: 570–650, CR: 560–660, Wr: 560–640
Middle 50% ACT range: 25–29
Early admission program EA/ED/None: EA

Percentage accepted through EA or ED: Unreported
EA and ED deadline: 15-Oct
Regular Deadline: 15-Jan
Application Fee: $50
Full time Undergraduate enrollment: 25,335
Total enrollment: 32,282
Percent Male: 43%
Percent Female: 57%
Total Percent Minority or Unreported: 18%
Percent African-American: 6%
Percent Asian/Pacific Islander: 6%
Percent Hispanic: 2%
Percent Native-American: <1%
Percent International: 1%
Percent in-state/out of state: 79%/11%
Percent from Public HS: 81%

Retention Rate: Unreported
Graduation Rate 4-year: 51%
Graduation Rate 6-year: 79%
Percent Undergraduates in On-campus housing: 98%
Number of official organized extracurricular organizations: 352
3 Most popular majors: Art, Biology, Psychology
Student/Faculty ratio: 18:1
Average Class Size: 26
Percent of students going to grad school: 22%
Tuition and Fees: $22,343
In-State Tuition and Fees if different: $6,031
Cost for Room and Board: $7,528
Percent receiving financial aid out of those who apply, first year: 31%
Percent receiving financial aid among all students: 49%

A bit over one-hundred miles northeast of Atlanta lies Georgia's flagship university—the University of Georgia. Established in 1801, the University has deep ties with the surrounding area of Athens, a city with a vibrant music, restaurant and bar scene. Within the past twenty years, UGA has transformed from a regional school known mainly for its parties to a renowned academic institution.

HOPEing for an "A"

Created as a lure in the early 1990s so that Georgia students stay in-state, the HOPE Scholarship Program provides free tuition to all Georgia residents who maintain a 3.0 GPA throughout high school and college. In doing so, admission to upper-tier state schools, including the University of Georgia, has become much more difficult in recent years because of high-performing Georgian students' decisions to stay in-state. As the Georgia tax base continues to shrink, however, state representatives have called for HOPE to be restricted to a need-based program, a highly divisive move.

The University of Georgia is comprised of sixteen colleges—including a recent satellite campus of the Medical College of Georgia to which incoming freshman may apply. These range from the Franklin College of Arts and Sciences, the general "catch-all" school, to the specialized College of Agriculture and Environmental Sciences. Students typically apply to the highly coveted pre-professional schools, such as the Terry College of Business and the Grady School of Journalism, in the spring of their sophomore year.

Popular majors include Art, Psychology, Biology and Chemistry, housed in the Franklin College of Arts and Sciences, and any variety of "pre-anything." Students also note that the Genetics—the only such major available at a public school in the South—and Biochemistry and Molecular Biology majors are increasingly desired by students. Students note grading as a whole to be difficult, with the notion of a curve being virtually nonexistent. Surprisingly, students note that though the Chemistry department is the most difficult by far, the History and Philosophy departments "aren't a piece of cake either," though no department has an easier reputation than the engineering department—since none exists. Led by the current president, efforts have been made to establish an Engineering school, but, as for now, that is a realm dominated by academic and sports rival Georgia Tech.

Yet, according to one current freshman, "at times, it can seem like sixty to seventy percent of the student body is pre-professional." However, many students drop their ambitions for Medical School after enduring the "weed-out" class in general or organic chemistry. Curriculum requirements vary by both college and major, but all students are required to complete two semesters of English, two of math and one of physical education in order to graduate from the University, in addition to a class on Georgia history.

Though class sizes vary widely for department and course level, the University boasts its fair share of classes numbering more than three hundred. In addition, students can participate in First-Year Seminars, one-hour per week, more intimate classes focusing on relatively obscure topics such as "The hobbits: fact or fiction?" or "Bob Dylan." Nonetheless, the faculty is praised for being easily accessible, with mandatory office hours each week and a sincere desire to help students. Notable professors include Darroll Batzer of the entomology department who students note as being "incredibly enthusiastic."

Athens: A Quintessential College Town

Located 1.5 hours away from the metropolitan capital of Atlanta, Athens, the home to the University of Georgia, caters largely to the taste of the University's students. A city of slightly over 100,000, Athens can boast of over one hundred bars, most of which are open to the 18-and-up crowd. As such, a student typically ends up downtown to finish up a night of "going out." With the weekend beginning on Thursday evening, one student commented that they wish that the festivities occurred a bit less frequently.

"I like going out maybe once a week, but three or four times is too much," she said.

On-campus entertainment options also exist, driven mainly by the Greek life system on Thursdays. With over twenty-five percent of the campus participating and 1500 out of 2400 freshman girls participating in sorority rush, students admit that the scene is "big, but is far from being dominant." Rush process occurs mainly during the first weeks of fall semester and consumes the entire day. A recent inductee said that the process was "Crazy for Sororities. It's five-days, going from house to house to house, from 6 AM to 6-7 PM." And though the prevalence of a heavy bar and Greek Life scene could signify a lax attitude toward alcohol, the administration strictly enforces a zero-tolerance policy. Even as ranked the number one party school by the Princeton Review, one alcohol-related offense results in probation, an immediate loss of any financial aid (including the HOPE scholarship for Georgia residents) and can end in a transfer to a local university.

The RAs, though widely regarded as kind and chill, particularly concerning administrative issues (i.e. a leaking ceiling), strictly prohibit alcohol in all rooming situations –even for students who are twenty-one— and punishment for storing alcohol is equitable to that of drinking.

However, a large percentage of students walk out of the "hallowed arch" (which, according to university lore, if students pass through before graduation, they will not graduate from the University), a black arch present on North Campus, during the weekends. Some visit home, but some students, particularly freshman, lack cars, citing high fees and hassle for parking spaces. More upperclassmen retreat to their off-campus apartments, becoming less involved in campus life as they gain credit-hours. The vast majority of upperclassmen have a job on campus, and substitute extracurricular activities on campus for extra hours working.

Nevertheless, some students claim that UGA exemplifies the "white, preppy, upper-middle class student" stereotype with little diversity otherwise, but other students attest to the prevalence of international students as a source of diversity. "It almost doesn't faze me anymore to hear others speaking in another language or wearing the garbs of their native country," a freshman said. And "no one really judges if you go to class dressed to the 9's or in gym shorts and a T-shirt."

Although the high ratio of in-state students, approximately seventy-nine percent, can impede students from forming new friendships, the students report that both the Greek Life system and other extracurriculars function as ways to break out of one's pre-formed social circle.

Living as a 'Dawg

All UGA freshmen are required to live on campus, barring extenuating circumstances, and are typically segregated into three "high-rise" dorms, each having nine floors: Russell and Creswell, which are both coed, and Brumby, an all-girls dorm known for its high concentration of future members of sororities. Students apply for dormitories online immediately after they are admitted.

Some luckier freshman apply early enough for housing to gain a spot in the Oglethorpe, or "O-house," which is coveted for its central location on campus and non-communal bathrooms—and its Georgian architectural style, reminiscent of North Campus, and contrasting with the institutionalism of the other dorms.

Students can also choose to reside in a language-immersion community, or an Oxford-like residential college. Those who qualify for the honors program, requiring a separate application process before or during their years at Georgia, can live in the envied Myers dorm, known for its spaciousness.

Upperclassmen also have the opportunity to dorm in East Campus Village, a series of upper-scale quasi-apartment housing which the University leases to students. Freshman varsity athletes also share in that privilege. However, most upperclassmen tend to secure off-campus housing after their freshman year, typically using the large amount of apartment housing that abuts the university. A current sophomore cites the inexpensive relative cost, lack of guaranteed on-campus housing for sophomores and a sense of "freedom" as reasons for moving off campus.

A universally adored area of the University is North Campus, featuring grand classical architecture and grassy fields and a plethora of buildings which house most of the humanities departments. Contrastingly, south campus, playing host to the science buildings, should not be considered whatsoever for its architectural charm, looking like an industrial plant. Other parts include east campus, which includes the new forty-million-dollar Lamar Dodd School of Art, and west campus, where the majority of freshmen reside. In addition, the newly renovated Tate Student Center, costing thirty million dollars to reconstruct and LEED certified gold, lies centrally located on campus.

Students rave about UGA's four dining halls, all having their general perks, with some continuously serving breakfast and others being continuously open. Meal plans come in two denominations, a five-day plan and a seven-day plan. Both plans allow unlimited swipes on the days specified by the plan. But all dining halls close at two PM on Sunday, leaving students left to fend for themselves for dinner. However, some students see this as a distinct advantage.

"It gives you a reason to explore Athens, and learn more about the local eateries," one student said.

In fact, UGA dining is so popular among students that the infinitive "to snellibrate" is used, a combination of Snellings, a popular dining hall, and to celebrate, after a "rainy day" or a high score on an exam or some other personal victory or defeat, typically late at night.

> "It was pretty much what I expected: large amount of students, tons of classes to choose from, and lots of activities to partake in."

After "Snellibrating" to the greatest extent possible, taking advantage of the fact that the dining halls are unlimited cafeteria style, a student will head to Ramsey Student Center, a 420,000 square foot athletic facility, to avoid gaining the "freshman fifteen."

While the most popular student organizations are the philanthropic UGA Hero and Miracle for Life, students assign prestige to the debate societies, including the Desmothian Literary society and the Phi Kappa Literary society.

"They're almost like fraternities," one freshman said. The most well-read student publication is the independent newspaper, with a relatively liberal tilt, *The Red and Black*.

However, virtually all students agree that the biggest extracurricular of the students is tailgating. Though recently barred by the administration from doing so on historic North Campus due to beautification concerns, students sacrifice their sleep deficit so that they can support the "Bulldawgs" in the red and black, the school's colors, on the ball field. For the football games most girls wear a dress on Game Day. And while the football team has suffered a recent lack of playoff success, both the basketball and gymnastics teams have surged in popularity. Sports remain a valued tradition at the University of Georgia. A freshman claims that each time she walks past Sanford Stadium, the football stadium of the University and often called the 'Dawghouse: "Almost as if I now feel like I belong, it's hard to describe."—*John Klement*

FYI
Three things every student at UGA should do before graduating are: "see the Dog Walk" (a series of painted bulldog statues in downtown Athens), "take a picture with Uga," and "ring the chapel bell."
If you come to UGA, you'd better bring "your pair of Chaco sandals."
What differentiates UGA the most from other colleges is "our awesome UGA pride."

Hawaii

University of Hawaii at Mānoa

Address: 2600 Campus Road Honolulu, HI 96822
Phone: 800-823-9771
E-mail address: ar-info@hawaii.edu
Web site URL: www.hawaii.edu/admrec
Year Founded: 1907
Private or Public: Public
Religious Affiliation: None
Location: Urban
Number of Applicants: 7,196
Percent Accepted: 67%
Percent Accepted who enroll: 39%
Number Entering: 1,879
Number of Transfers Accepted each Year: 2,751
Middle 50% SAT range: M: 440–490, CR: 440–500, Wr: Unreported
Middle 50% ACT range: 17–24
Early admission program EA/ED/None: None

Percentage accepted through EA or ED: NA
EA and ED deadline: NA
Regular Deadline: 2-Jan
Application Fee: $50
Full time Undergraduate enrollment: 11,283
Total enrollment: 20,051
Percent Male: 45%
Percent Female: 55%
Total Percent Minority or Unreported: 67%
Percent African-American: 1%
Percent Asian/Pacific Islander: 64%
Percent Hispanic: 2%
Percent Native-American: <1%
Percent International: Unreported
Percent in-state/out of state: 75%/25%
Percent from Public HS: 69%
Retention Rate: 78%

Graduation Rate 4-year: 15%
Graduation Rate 6-year: 55%
Percent Undergraduates in On-campus housing: 19%
Number of official organized extracurricular organizations: 150
3 Most popular majors: Biology, Art, Hospitality
Student/Faculty ratio: 13:1
Average Class Size: 33
Percent of students going to grad school: Unreported
Tuition and Fees: $16,608
In-State Tuition and Fees if different: $5,952
Cost for Room and Board: $7,564
Percent receiving financial aid out of those who apply, first year: 41%
Percent receiving financial aid among all students: Unreported

The benefits of attending the University of Hawaii at Mānoa go far beyond the beautiful nature that makes Hawaii a top destination for tourists from around the world. As the flagship institution of the state's public education system, the University is also the primary research body of Hawaii. Furthermore, UH is not just a college for in-state students. In fact, over 20% of the student body hail from outside of Hawaii, demonstrating that the school offers a good education and a great quality of life that are able to attract students from not only continental United States, but also foreign countries.

Study of the Pacific

UH is divided into 19 different colleges and schools, including several specialized ones

that are pertinent to Hawaii, such as the College of Tropical Agriculture and Human Resources and the School of Hawaiian Knowledge. The University also places strong emphasis on the study of the Pacific region, particularly East Asia. In fact, some of the best programs by UH are in the School of Pacific and Asian Studies. Furthermore, the business school is also known to provide very good undergraduate programs to students. Given the location of the university, the different marine programs are also highly acclaimed.

The University offers nearly 90 undergraduate majors and slightly fewer than 40 minors. The academic programs are notable for the availability of ethnic and regional studies centered on Hawaiian history and culture. Given the large selection of courses, students generally agree that UH has sufficient variety of programs to satisfy almost any types of academic pursuit. "It is a pretty big school," said one student. "We are the biggest university in Hawaii, and we have a really complete set of classes from engineering to liberal arts." In addition, it is worth noting that more than 6,000 graduate students also study at UH, thus giving the more ambitious undergraduates the opportunity to take a graduate class, if only for the experience.

As in most universities, UH has a lengthy list of core requirements, which are classes that must be taken by all students regardless of majors. They are used to ensure that all graduates have the necessary skills in a wide range of professions. The core is divided into two categories: the foundation and the diversification requirements. The classes in foundation are used to give students basic skills in writing, mathematics, and logic. It also has a multicultural component, in which students learn about cross-cultural interactions. The diversification requirements are simply classes in other majors that students must take to be exposed to other academic fields. "You never know," said one student. "You might find out that you really like arts even if you always thought that you wanted to study engineering."

The pressure of academic life at UH is considered easily manageable by most students. "As long as you don't fall behind too much," said one student. "You will not have too much trouble in classes." Of course, the difficulty can vary depending on the topic as well as the professor who teaches the class.

> "I have some professors who really encourage people to go ask questions in their offices."

As is often the case in a large public university, the introductory lectures can be very big and not very interactive. However, for upperclassmen, it is much easier to find smaller classes where students have greater access to professors. "If you like small classes, eventually you will have the chance to be in them," said one student. As to the availability of instructors to answer students' questions and offer advice, most people agree that professors at UH are generally happy to see students outside of classes. "I have some professors who really encourage people to go ask questions in their offices because so few people actually bother to show up," said one student.

Although UH is not considered a particularly selective school during the admissions process, students agree that people on campus are generally talented people. "I feel that most people here have some unique talent or skill," said one student.

Paradise Island

Of course, in the United States, it is difficult to find a school with weather like that of UH. For many people, that is certainly part of the reason to attend the University. "I had a choice to go to New England, but it is just so much more comfortable here," said one student. The University is located in Mānoa, a residential neighborhood of Honolulu and only three miles from the downtown. Surrounding the university are beautiful mountain ranges, since Mānoa is situated in a valley. Nevertheless, one can also spot the high rises of downtown Honolulu. Some people who have not been to UH may expect to see the Pacific Ocean when they are on campus; unfortunately, the campus is not actually on the seashore. Nevertheless, students still have easy access to the ocean as well as beautiful sandy beaches fewer than two miles south of the campus.

The immediate surrounding of the university is relatively disappointing for students. Since it is located in a residential area, the campus and its surrounding blocks do not have too much to offer in terms of restaurants, bars, and clubs. "You will not find much around the school," said one student. "The good news is that we are so close to downtown Honolulu." Indeed, with the center of Hawaii only a few miles away, students looking for fun weekend activities, shopping, or good eateries can simply go to the city. "I really like Honolulu," said an out-of-state student. "It has this really relaxed, warm atmosphere. It makes you feel you are on vacation all the time."

Since the school is located in a residential neighborhood, housing options outside of the college are widely available, and the majority of students opt to stay off campus. The university certainly has its own residential program, largely divided into two different kinds of living arrangements. The majority of on-campus housing is in the form of traditional residential halls. Most students live in doubles, and each room is furnished. All students in residential halls must also participate in the board program, which includes meal plans. For upperclassmen seeking more independence, several apartment buildings are also available, and each unit contains a kitchen, living room, and bedrooms, all of which are already furnished.

Given the large number of off-campus students, the partying scene within the boundaries of the University can be limited. However, given the proximity to Honolulu and the ocean, students generally travel a few miles to the seashore and enjoy the numerous activities there. As expected, the beaches are certainly one of the most popular spots for the students, not to mention the downtown clubs. "The thing about going away from campus is that you can have a lot of fun," said one student. "But if you want to hang out just with college kids, then you may be disappointed, because in clubs, you find people from everywhere."

A Southern Environment

Since the school is in Hawaii, the majority of students are Asian or Pacific Islanders and multicultural. "The school is mostly Asian or Asian-descent, but you find people of all ethnic groups, and what is special about here is that we are all very tolerant and enjoy the diversity," said one student. Ultimately, UH simply offers a great quality of life. It is friendly, fun, and not too stressful, thus providing a great, memorable college experience.
—*Xiaohang Liu*

FYI

If you come to UH, you'd better bring "a swimsuit."

What is the typical weekend schedule? "Some partying and enjoy all the outdoor activities we have."

If I could change one thing about UH, I'd "move it a couple of miles down the road."

Three things every student at UH should do before graduating are "enjoy every minute while you can, go to other islands, and go hiking."

Idaho

University of Idaho

Address: PO Box 444264
Moscow, ID
83844-4264
Phone: 208-885-6326
E-mail address:
admissions@uidaho.edu
Web site URL: www.uihome
.uidaho.edu/uihome
Year Founded: 1889
Private or Public: Public
Religious Affiliation: None
Location: Rural
Number of Applicants: 4,577
Percent Accepted: 77%
Percent Accepted who
enroll: 46%
Number Entering: 1,623
Number of Transfers
Accepted each Year: 966
Middle 50% SAT range:
M: 480–600, CR:
480–600, Wr: 450–570
Middle 50% ACT range:
20–25
Early admission program
EA/ED/None: None

Percentage accepted
through EA or ED: NA
EA and ED deadline: NA
Regular Deadline: 1-Aug
Application Fee: $40
Full time Undergraduate
enrollment: 9,018
Total enrollment: 11,309
Percent Male: 55%
Percent Female: 45%
Total Percent Minority or
Unreported: 17%
Percent African-American:
1%
Percent Asian/Pacific
Islander: 2%
Percent Hispanic: 5%
Percent Native-American: 1%
Percent International: 2%
Percent in-state/out of
state: 62%/38%
Percent from Public HS:
90%
Retention Rate: Unreported
Graduation Rate 4-year:
21%

Graduation Rate 6-year:
54%
Percent Undergraduates in
On-campus housing:
Unreported
Number of official organized
extracurricular
organizations: 190
3 Most popular majors:
Education, Mechanical
Engineering, Psychology
Student/Faculty ratio: 16:1
Average Class Size: 15
Percent of students going to
grad school: Unreported
Tuition and Fees: $14,712
In-State Tuition and Fees if
different: $4,632
Cost for Room and Board:
$6,762
Percent receiving financial
aid out of those who apply,
first year: 56%
Percent receiving financial
aid among all students:
75%

The University of Idaho provides a lot of things promised of a small town in land-locked America, including friendly people and a focus on agriculture. While the U of I is no mainstay of diversity, and a sometimes disconnected administration means that students do a lot of their own degree-planning legwork, students looking for an intimate campus with the social benefits of a large university will find their promised land at the University of Idaho.

Academics
Students say that the academic frontier at the University of Idaho—notable alumni of which include the first-ever female, Republican vice-presidential nominee Sarah Palin and Jack Lemley, construction manager of the Chunnel—can be really hard or really easy—it's all up to them. The University is well-known for the close relationship it has with the Idaho National Laboratory (INL), a governmental science and engineering laboratory that focuses on environmental, energy and nuclear technology. As a result, programs in engineering and the life sciences are well-funded and popular. That being said, students are quick to list engineering and chemistry classes at the University among the most difficult. Agricultural and food sciences programs are also popular choices, and feed graduates into Idaho's flourishing farming and dairy industries. U of I partners with Washington State University in nearby Pullman, Wash., in many of these departments, which contributes to the availability of equipment and talented fac-

ulty and graduate students, who often serve as TAs for large lectures. Communications is understood to be the easiest major possible. The school's Business department, while generally considered markedly less demanding than anything in the sciences, is a place where many students find common ground—"Everyone has a Business minor," notes one.

As is often the case at large universities, lecture classes required early in a student's curriculum tend to be very large and can be weed-out classes, with less-generous grading than upper-level classes. Students in every major are required to take at least one math and one science course, but most have no trouble finding an easy way around their requirements, with classes like Math 123, "Mathematics Applied to the Modern World," and Geography 100, "Physical Geography." Other favorite, unusual classes include Business 103, "Introduction to Professional Golf Management," and Psychology 330, "Human Sexuality," affectionately known as "Dirty 330."

Students note that a department's level of funding has a meaningful effect on the undergraduate experience in that department. Funding is largely a function of donation by graduates, so engineering and business-oriented disciplines are the most cash-flush on campus. One obvious way in which this disparity manifests itself is in the frequency of course offerings, even those required for the major. One French major noted such a required class that is only offered every other year, and only in the fall—it isn't uncommon that students in such situations must extend their time at the University by a semester or a year for the sake of access to that single class. That's to say nothing of what happens when students wait the semester or year, and then can't get into the class because of capped enrollment or registration bottlenecks, a circumstance for which the University administration has little sympathy.

All of which might not be so bad, if the University devoted resources to helping students plan their track to degree completion, but advising is a sore point for many students. While general advising is available for freshmen unsure about their choice of major, "As soon as you get into your department, advising goes downhill fast." The system is very decentralized, students say, with department advisors changing almost every semester and the role often filled by the newest members of the department, who may have less expertise navigating the system than the students themselves. Appointments with advisors can be hard to make, and many students remember taking classes that could have counted for more than one requirement, or which counted for no requirements at all, despite their advisors' information to the contrary.

Professors, fortunately, are another matter. Students are enthusiastic about the faculty they work with and find them accessible. Smaller departments are most intimate, and students find it possible to develop close relationships with their professors. Some even have favorite members of professors' supporting administration: "The secretary of the history department has probably saved my life multiple times."

To Greek or Not to Greek?
The course of University of Idaho students' social lives is charted early and depends a lot on their decision whether or not to go Greek. Wherever they end up, social life at U of I can be rather segmented. Greek life is prominent on campus, and frat brothers and sorority sisters tend to associate with one another, to the exclusion of students outside the circle. "I really wish there wasn't such a huge delineation between the Greek system and everything else," said one student. "I have friends in the Greek system that I really don't hang out with, and that's lame." The alternative to the Greek system for most freshmen is living in the dorms, where they make the friends they'll have for the rest of college. Even within the dorms, athletes often separate into cliques and move off campus within their first semester, and "the music kids stick together."

U of I students have a bone to pick with their reputation as a party school: "Not everyone is an alcoholic." Moscow is a small town and social life can revolve around the bar scene, but that's true even for students who aren't serious drinkers. Theirs is a nominally dry campus, and the administration makes a proactive attempt to catch offenders and educate students; punishment often centers around classes on drinking responsibly. "They're not necessarily condoning it [alcohol consumption], but they're trying to make sure people are safe." Some fraternities are expressly dry as well. Bars take the legal drinking age seriously, and fake IDs are traditionally unsuccessful, so the social world opens up a lot when students turn 21. Popular bars include John's Alley, The Plantation, The Corner Club, and Garden Lounge;

Casa Lopez and The Alehouse are restaurant bars with good drink specials. One student sums up the party scene this way: "You don't have to look too hard to find a party, but it's not like the dorms are going crazy with drunk kids hanging out every door." There is a prominent coffeehouse subculture on the campus, with strongholds at Bucer's, The Sisters' Brew Café and The One World Café, "a bastion of liberal thinking," in one student's words.

Moscow is fairly isolated, so most students stay in the area on weekends. A car isn't a necessity in town, and can sometimes be a hassle, since parking around campus is limited and parking enforcement very stringent. A free bus system runs all over the campus and the town of Moscow, so students without cars have no trouble getting around. That said, many students keep cars, and they're necessary to get away. The nearest big-city experience is in Seattle, about a five-hour trip by car. That opportunity for escape is important to students who struggle with the small-town pace and feel of Moscow. The university system supports the town in many ways, especially the many bars, restaurants and coffeehouses. Moscow hasn't forgotten it, and town-gown relations are symbiotic and pleasant. The town is small, but there is no shortage of things to do for the motivated student—the well-known Lionel Hampton School of Music supports a healthy culture of live performance, especially of jazz; the Arboretum and nearby Moscow Mountain make for nice walking and hiking; the Kenworthy Theater is a historic way to enjoy a movie; and Elizabethan enthusiasts will enjoy the Kiva Theatre, which puts plays up regularly and seats in the round.

Campus Living

Two main options exist for University of Idaho freshmen making housing plans: the Greek system, which rushes at the very beginning of the fall semester, and the residence halls. Residence hall living is perfect for the student who enjoys structure, doesn't want to deal with paying bills, and enjoys a social atmosphere, since there are always people around. Some halls are explicitly restricted to first-years, most notable is the Tower, which boasts 11 stories of coed (by floor) housing. Another large residence is Wallace Hall, also coed by floor. Some housing is in the single- or double-bedroom-in-a-long-hallway tradition, and some is suite-style, but whatever the organization,

the University administration is very flexible and reasonable about students interested in making changes in their housing at any time in the year, for any reason. "If things aren't working out with your roommate, or anything else, they ask you to wait it out for two weeks, and if you still want to switch, you can." Different residence halls have different personalities. Examples are a hall for students in agriculture (characterized by flannel outerwear and cowboy boots), an engineering hall, and a hall for students in the education departments. Single-sex housing is also available; Graham Hall is all-male, Houston Hall and Hayes Hall are all-female. For sophomores who choose not to move off campus or go Greek in their second opportunity to rush, there is the Living and Learning Community, a hall dedicated to second-year students. Most students on the dorm track spend one year in a residence hall before moving off-campus. Many cite RAs as a reason to escape dorm living as soon as they have friends with whom they'd like to find an apartment. While some RAs can be cool, they say, dorm living usually feels more like a police state, with strict University alcohol and furnishings policy enforcement: "Unless you get a good RA, you're going to be dealing with someone trying to catch you with an illegal candle."

Dining options on campus are dismal, which may account for the thriving restaurant business in Moscow. The largest, best-known dining halls are Bob's Café and Commons. A fair variety of foods is available, including pasta dishes, a salad bar and ever-present hamburgers, hot dogs and grilled cheese sandwiches, but the menu never changes, and as one student puts it, "You can get tired of pasta." Dining halls also keep odd hours—Commons, for example, closes at 4 p.m.—but students on a meal plan can use their Vandal Card at a variety of smaller coffee-shop venues around campus, so food is always available somewhere. Favorite off-campus dining options include The Pita Pit, with varied Greek offerings, and The Breakfast Club, which does a brisk business in brunch and lunch specials.

The U of I-campus is beautiful, and students appreciate it. Composed of mostly brick buildings, it's an ivy-covered haven in the woods of northern Idaho. The campus was designed by Frederick Law Olmstead, the landscape architect responsible for Central Park in New York City, and a favorite location for many is the lawn in front of the administration building. The campus is intimate, and students feel it's a factor that distinguishes their school from other, more commuter campuses in the state.

Extracurriculars

Athletics and the Greek system are major drivers in extracurricular activities at the University of Idaho. Vandal pride is strong, although students are candid about the disappointing performance of their teams. Football and men's basketball are the most popular varsity sports on campus. The former has shown especially weak performance in recent years, but game attendance remains strong and historic moments of domination over rival Boise State University are fresh in the minds of die-hard fans. An aggressive anti-BSU T-shirt campaign takes place every year leading up to the schools' annual football face-off. In addition to varsity sports, intramural activities are going on all the time, and students love the University's recently opened Student Recreation Center. Students of every level of athletic ability have access to the climbing wall—the largest of any university in the United States—massage services and "Every kind of free-weight, cardio machine or court you could ever want."

> "Not everyone is an alcoholic."

The Greek system, by design, requires a great deal of community service activity, and philanthropic pursuits are going on all the time on campus. Student government at U of I is good at organizing large events like speaking engagements or campus-wide community service trips, but students say that involvement in the voting and planning process is low. Many students have jobs for 10 to 20 hours a week, either on campus in help-desk or library services or off campus in restaurant work.

Extracurricular activities are an important way for students to experience diversity on campus, which is far from extensive, but is developing. Students characterize the campus as predominantly white and middle- to upper-middle-class, although socioeconomic perceptions are skewed downward by the proximity of Washington State University, recognized in the area as a very wealthy campus. U of I students are primarily natives of Idaho, and those not from Idaho tend to come from other Pacific-Northwestern states. Scholarships offered to multicultural students, especially those from Alaska, are improving the campus' diversity score, and the campus is adapting to broader horizons with recent introductions of multicultural fraternities and sororities. There are also a growing number of groups on campus for gay, lesbian, and transgender students.

Students considering the University of Idaho should, in short, be prepared to be intrepid if they want to be challenged, and will experience four or five years of relative homogeneity in demography and opportunities for socializing. Still, students will find their classmates friendly and willing to try new things, and the community formed at the University of Idaho will likely be a lasting one.—*Elizabeth Woods*

FYI
If you come to the University of Idaho, you'd better bring "your party pants."
What is the typical weekend schedule? "Party Friday and Saturday nights, and spend all day Sunday working; and maybe, depending on the season, do something adventurous during the day on Saturday, like go for a hike or see a football game."
If I could change one thing about the University of Idaho, I would "want a Target somewhere nearby."
Three things every student should do before graduating are "go to a drag show in Pullman, WA, take advantage of the VandalCard by renting an Xbox or a laptop from the University, and sing great karaoke at the otherwise terrible CJ's Nightclub."

Illinois

DePaul University

Address: 1 East Jackson Boulevard, Chicago, IL 60604
Phone: 312-362-8300
E-mail address: admitdpu@depaul.edu
Web site URL: www.depaul.edu
Year Founded: 1898
Private or Public: Private
Religious Affiliation: Roman Catholic
Location: Urban
Number of Applicants: 10,294
Percent Accepted: 70%
Percent Accepted who enroll: 35%
Number Entering: 2,522
Number of Transfers Accepted each Year: 2,512
Middle 50% SAT range: M: 510–620, Cr: 510–630, Wr: 590–670
Middle 50% ACT range: 21–26
Early admission program EA/ED/None: EA and ED

Percentage accepted through EA or ED: 59%
EA and ED deadline: 15-Nov
Regular Deadline: 1-Feb
Application Fee: $40
Full time Undergraduate enrollment: 15,024
Total enrollment: 22,377
Percent Male: 44%
Percent Female: 56%
Total Percent Minority or Unreported: 29%
Percent African-American: 8%
Percent Asian/Pacific Islander: 8%
Percent Hispanic: 11%
Percent Native-American: 1%
Percent International: 1%
Percent in-state/out of state: 84%/16%
Percent from Public HS: 74%
Retention Rate: 85%

Graduation Rate 4-year: 39%
Graduation Rate 6-year: 64%
Percent Undergraduates in On-campus housing: 19%
Number of official organized extracurricular organizations: 170
3 Most popular majors: Accounting, Communications, Finance
Student/Faculty ratio: 14:1
Average Class Size: 26
Percent of students going to grad school: Unreported
Tuition and Fees: $22,365
In-State Tuition and Fees if different: No difference
Cost for Room and Board: $9,801
Percent receiving financial aid out of those who apply, first year: 75%
Percent receiving financial aid among all students: 62%

I f you take the Brown Line to the Fullerton Stop on the Chicago El, you'll exit onto a bustling street in the Lincoln Park neighborhood of Chicago. But just hang a left and in a few minutes you'll be in the tree-lined heart of DePaul University. DePaul offers its students the best of both worlds: a school committed to the life and study of its undergraduates and a wealth of opportunities to be involved in the "real world" in Chicago. With about 22,000 students and the whole city open to exploration, few people at the University have a chance to be bored. Although it has been known as a commuter school in the past, DePaul is rapidly attracting students from all over while maintaining its uniquely Midwestern warmth and sense of community both inside the University and within Chicago through service and active learning.

Domains of Learning

DePaul takes its commitment to integrating into the surrounding urban environment very seriously. In fact, the first choice freshmen must make when they are accepted is whether to take the Discover Chicago or Explore Chicago class. In Discover, freshmen arrive at school a week early to participate in weeklong orientation programs that allow students to "totally immerse themselves in one aspect of the city's culture." These programs run the gamut from "Poverty Amidst Plenty," which gives students the opportunity to visit homeless shelters and participate in community service activities, to "Biking in Chicago," which allows students to go on bike trips that help orient them to the traffic patterns while taking in the sights. Much like Discover, but expanded to cover the entire first quarter, Explore allows students to get a "more in-depth view of the inner workings of Chicago." This includes everything from a class titled Understanding Beauty in Chicago to a quarter devoted to studying the Chicago Cubs.

DePaul does not stop initiating service learning after the first quarter. The University offers many opportunities for "experiential learning," which covers study abroad, internship, and service learning areas. In fact, DePaul's Center for Community-Based Learning focuses on volunteer work and sponsors such popular classes as Peace, Social Justice, Conflict Resolution, and Psychology outreach programs that allow students to work in area clinics and get credit for it. Given the number of outside resources available, it doesn't come as much of a surprise that many students double-major and/or double-minor in applied fields such as Peace Studies and Political Science-International Relations. This interdisciplinary approach to learning permeates the atmosphere of the school, and students say that many people are very politically engaged as a result.

This sense of active engagement also extends to the rest of the academic environment, as students say the "Focus of classes is more on practice than just study." For example, art history classes often come with a studio art component, just as English majors will frequently get a teaching certification in addition to their liberal arts degree. That extends in particular to the School of Commerce, which boasts "a lot of ties to accounting firms," say students, as well as a "business mindset as opposed to a pure learning mindset."

Potential Blue Demons take note: the classroom is front and center in a DePaul education, and prospective students should be prepared for a broad range of requirements that encourage active thinking and participation. The core curriculum, called the Liberal Studies Program, is comprised of a set of "learning domains," which involve completion of arts and literature, philosophical inquiry, religion, scientific inquiry, Self and the Modern World, and Understanding the Past requirements. Each of these broad-based areas allows for a great deal of free-

dom in choosing the classes that most interest the student, which "brings a lot more individualism into the program," say students. The Honors Program also works to tailor the broader school requirements to individual students. A member of the Honors Student Government noted that while the required classes are more specific in the honors program, "All honors classes are capped at 20, which means that they might be a little harder to get into, but in the end, it's worth it for the close engagement with the professors." In fact, one student's "Biggest class had forty-five people in it . . . actually, there are only two or three places on campus that will even hold more than fifty people."

That closeness is also manifested in the love-it or hate-it quarter system that DePaul uses as opposed to the traditional semester. Summers are a little shorter, with school ending in late June, but students enjoy a six-week winter break. Students typically take classes three out of four quarters, as the fourth quarter is summer vacation. Students give the system mixed reviews, mentioning that "You never get bored or feel like you've wasted a semester if you end up taking a class you're not that into." A sophomore agreed, saying, "You can sample things more and experience lots of classes, and you can focus more on each one while you're taking it." And one senior hit upon a very important factor for most students, noting, "One class can't mess up your GPA because you have so many to pad any not-so-great grades."

Students also appreciate the fact that DePaul is not a research university— "Professors are very present in their fields in terms of writing and peer-reviewing, [but] the focus is clearly on teaching and coming up with new ways to present material and get students engaged."

Hit That High(Rise)

One of the hallmarks of DePaul student life is the exodus from on-campus living after freshman and sophomore year. Students are quick to say that prospectives shouldn't be turned off by this: "You stay friends with most of your friends from freshman year, and even though you don't see people congregating to go out as much, the upperclassmen are the ones who have the parties . . . so you'll see people no matter what." One junior noted that freshman year "Feels like a smaller community because you see the same people and develop a real sense of camaraderie, [but] living in an apartment becomes completely natural." Although students readily admit it is a "different lifestyle," one that includes "being independent and paying your own bills," they also say that it is "very freeing" and "exciting to live on your own with your friends." Because of the culture of living in neighborhood apartments, the campus "isn't as hoppin' on the weekends," but students insist that "Lincoln Park is a lively neighborhood, so it never feels like a dead corn town."

And never fear: there's still plenty to do, both off campus and on. When asked about the biggest party day, one junior responded, "Um, every day?" While it's clear that DePaul students are not shy about letting loose, students say that partying comes down to "less of a woo-hoo, we're in college, let's drink" atmosphere and more of a "hanging out with friends or go to a bar" environment. Students admit that many of their peers have fake IDs and that drinking is fairly prevalent on campus, but they also note that the college has a safety-first policy. DePaul provides a public safety escort from 6 p.m. to 6 a.m. every day.

For students who find that the drinking scene isn't their thing, there are plenty of events on and around campus to keep them busy. One of DePaul's most striking qualities is the diversity of its student body. As a result, there are "tons and tons of different cultural events going on all the time." Everything from the Black Student Union to a Spanish dance group to Hillel holds activities on the weekends. This is true of the diversity of the campus in general as well—as one senior said, "You definitely see people from a lot of different backgrounds."

> "A lot of people here worked really hard to be the first in their family to go to college, and it gives a very diverse perspective in class when there are people with those experiences right there: it's not just a hypothetical."

Although there are admittedly "a lot of people from Illinois and Ohio," students think there is "true diversity" at DePaul in the sense that you can "Come as you are—there is somewhere you'll fit in here." While students note that there is still separation among groups, they laud the school's particular efforts to broaden the scope of diversity by accepting students who are diverse not only in race, but also in socioeconomic status, state and country of origin, ideas, and belief systems. One junior also noted that there are "many first-generation college students at DePaul. You don't usually think about this in terms of diversity, but it really gives you perspective."

The Windy Campus

With the Chicago skyline serving as the main campus attraction, students at DePaul should never be worried about being stuck behind gates or locked into exclusively meeting people from the 18–22 set. When "the whole city is your campus," students recommend preparing for "interaction with *real people* every day." While Chicago is certainly different from many college towns, students really appreciate the cultural and community-oriented opportunities it provides. In fact, one senior noted that the "community comes into life a lot more than at other places." As an example, she pointed to the relatively large number of people from the community who come in and take classes at DePaul as well as the very large number of students who perform community service, both through DePaul and on their own initiative. On an academic level, "Things don't have to be as abstract as they are in the classroom because you can go out and experience them." This extends to the internship and work opportunities. This is particularly useful for the large number of business majors, as it gives them concentrated networking contacts from which to draw and plenty of alums who are happy to help out a fellow Blue Demon.

However, students do warn prospectives that they should prepare for a very different college experience. "It does take something away from the college experience," admitted one junior, and another student added that the whole perspective on college changes "when you're not walking across a campus to get home." Still, they note that the Student Center, the gym, the coffee shop, and study tables at the Schmidt Academic Center, known by students as SAC, tie the DePaul community together. One sophomore said, "We're definitely not separated completely, and the ways that DePaul are different are mostly really good, and add another level to the college experience."

The DePaul "Thing"

"It's not really our motto . . . and it's not really a slogan . . ." One student tried hard to describe it, but the best she could think of was "the DePaul Thing." This three-tiered saying perfectly encapsulates DePaul, students say, and it goes something like this. DePaul is: "1) Catholic—in the true root meaning of oneness, 2) Urban—in the commitment to the urban community, 3) Vincentian—in the goal of serving and loving each other." Although it may not have an overarching name, the DePaul credo, of sorts, really brings together the aspects of the school that separate it from other large,

urban universities. DePaul's deep commitment to the community that surrounds it permeates every aspect of student life, and this creates a bond between students that keeps them together even in the midst of a busy city. One student captured this sense perfectly when she said: "DePaul feels real. We have all the resources and cultural opportunities of the city, but in the end, Chicago attracts down-to-earth kids from the Midwest. It's real."—*Hannah Jacobson*

FYI

If you come to DePaul, you'd better bring "a fully loaded iPod (kids are really into music here)," "a bike lock (a bike is really useful for getting around the city)," and "warm boots!"

What is the typical weekend schedule? "Thursday, go out to the bars, meet some new people, and get great drunk food; Friday, sleep in, have a class or a club meeting, go shopping, and go to the beach if it's nice out; Saturday, do some community service, like the AIDS Walk, during the day, then at night go to a bar, go to a party, go see a show, or go to one of the tons of concert venues around Chicago; and Sunday, grab the brunch buffet at the Student Center: it's crucial for curing hangovers!"

If I could change one thing about DePaul, I'd "make it easier to get on-campus housing and streamline the bureaucracy so it would be easier to get answers from the higher-ups."

Three things every student at DePaul should do before graduating are "go on a service immersion trip to experience something outside DePaul and Chicago, get to know the city by visiting neighborhoods that are off the beaten path, and sit in the arms of the Father Egan statue!"

Illinois State University

Address: Admissions, Campus Box 2200, Normal, IL 61790-2200

Phone: 800-366-2478

E-mail address: admissions@ilstu.edu

Web site URL: www.ilstu.edu

Year Founded: 1857

Private or Public: Public

Religious Affiliation: None

Location: Suburban

Number of Applicants: 13,671

Percent Accepted: 67%

Percent Accepted who enroll: 35%

Number Entering: 3,182

Number of Transfers Accepted each Year: Unreported

Middle 50% SAT range: Unreported

Middle 50% ACT range: 22–26

Early admission program EA/ED/None: None

Percentage accepted through EA or ED: NA

EA and ED deadline: NA

Regular Deadline: 15-Nov, 1-Feb

Application Fee: $40

Full time Undergraduate enrollment: 16,959

Total enrollment: 20,799

Percent Male: 43%

Percent Female: 57%

Total Percent Minority or Unreported: 11%

Percent African-American: 5%

Percent Asian/Pacific Islander: 2%

Percent Hispanic: 4%

Percent Native-American: <1%

Percent International: Unreported

Percent in-state/out of state: 99%/1%

Percent from Public HS: 88%

Retention Rate: 83%

Graduation Rate 4-year: 41%

Graduation Rate 6-year: 70%

Percent Undergraduates in On-campus housing: 30%

Number of official organized extracurricular organizations: 250

3 Most popular majors: Elementary Education, Marketing, Criminal Justice Sciences

Student/Faculty ratio: 19:1

Average Class Size: 25

Percent of students going to grad school: Unreported

Tuition and Fees: $16,444

In-State Tuition and Fees if different: $9,814

Cost for Room and Board: $7,458

Percent receiving financial aid out of those who apply, first year: 60%

Percent receiving financial aid among all students: 46%

The oldest public university in Illinois, Illinois State University boasts a diverse student body of over 18,000 undergraduates. Located two hours south of Chicago in Normal, Illinois—yes, the city is really called "Normal"—the school certainly is anything but a normal state school.

Big School, Small Class

Students at Illinois State University have to complete a minimum of 120 credit hours to graduate, about one-third of which are for general education requirements. However, with over 167 fields of study and a 312-page course catalog, there are many ways for students to fulfill those hours. For example, among the University's many courses is one that allows finance majors to manage a $400,000 portfolio their senior year.

Students say that, despite the University's size, class sizes average around 25 students, with almost all classes taught by professors, and students praised the variety of professors at the school and their accessibility. As one student said, "I like how there are many different ways of teaching in one school. You'll be able to find teachers who teach to the way you learn." Grading is straightforward, most said, and tests rarely have to be curved; students who work hard generally earn As and Bs.

ISU was founded as a teaching school, and its teacher education program remains its flagship course of study, ranking among the top 10 teacher education programs in the nation. Students say ISU's strength as a teaching school has pushed the school to be stronger overall in the humanities.

Illinois State University also boasts the oldest laboratory schools in the nation. Thomas Metcalf Laboratory School and University High School, both part of ISU, teach students from nursery school through 12th grade, and education students spend much of their time at the schools. They are required to have 100 hours of work with K-12 students. However, as one senior advised, "Don't be frightened by that number [100 hours]. There are so many things that qualify for the hours; they are very easy to rack up. Personally, I already had my 100 hours by the end of my freshman year."

One of the most striking features of ISU's campus is its new College of Business building. Opened in 2005, the building has drawn more students and faculty to the program, the University claims. Perhaps even more striking than the new building, however, is the Marketing department's dress code. Students are required to wear business casual dress to their marketing classes. The policy change elicited mixed reactions from students and faculty alike. As one junior put it, "I think it's good and bad. I have a struggle every morning with what I'm going to wear . . . but it gives the class a more professional feel."

Life on a Breezeway

Although most upperclassmen live off campus, underclassmen at Illinois State University have a wide variety of residence halls from which to choose—10, to be exact. As one sophomore put it, "The dorms as a whole are a blast to live in because . . . there always seems to be something going on."

At 28 stories, Watterson Towers is the tallest residence hall in the world. It holds 10 "houses," each considered an individual residence hall. Because of Watterson's design, the central elevator only stops at each house, and students take a breezeway from the center elevator to their respective house, from where they take the stairs to their room. Student comments about Watterson, unsurprisingly, focus on the building's size—some like the close proximity to 2,000 other students, while others felt that the bustle made it harder to make friends.

> "The dorms as a whole are a blast to live in because . . . there always seems to be something going on."

Athletes generally live in Tri-Towers on the west side of campus due to its proximity to the athletic facilities, though the recently renovated rooms pull even non-athletes from the centrally located dorms. Because of that proximity to the athletic facilities, students say it has a "fun atmosphere on game days for football and basketball." Although they say that athletics haven't been too big a deal on campus, in recent years school spirit has increased largely due to the success of the men's basketball team.

The rest of the residence halls border the campus's east and west sides, and all are scheduled for renovation as part of a 15-year plan.

On-campus students are required to enroll in a meal plan, and each residential complex has a dining hall. The University recently switched from an a la carte to an all-you-care-to-eat system, which has upset some students who were used to picking up small snacks throughout the day. In general, students were very satisfied with the dining options available, which range from fast food to traditional cafeteria fare.

Students say the Resident Advisors are generally relaxed. As one freshman put it, "They are basically just there if you have any questions and to make sure you don't break the rules too much." With the exception of one floor in one residence hall for students of age, alcohol is prohibited in the dorms, and the University's stringent drinking policies mean that underage students caught with alcohol on campus may be fined. However, perhaps worse than the fine is the alcohol education class that underage students caught drinking have to take at 8:00 a.m. on a Saturday morning.

Though the school is not terribly diverse—11 percent of students identify as a minority, a statistic congruous with the demographics of the surrounding area—students say that they feel the school's atmosphere is very inclusive. Additionally, they say that the convergence of rural, suburban and urban (read: Chicago) students adds a unique mix to the student body.

The Normal Life
As one junior put it, "When the weather is nice, the quad is always packed." Whether students are doing homework, playing football, or, occasionally, reassuring their professor that it was, in fact, a good idea to move class outside, student life happens on the quad (which, for fans of foliage, also happens to be a registered arboretum). Most academic buildings are on the main quad, so it is rarely a long walk between classes, and pedestrian over- and underpasses mean that, even when traveling to buildings off the main quad, students rarely have to cross more than one street.

To the east of the University lies uptown Normal, which has a number of local restaurants, bars and stores that cater to students. Many of these businesses are open late at night. The area is currently undergoing a major facelift that is bringing a new hotel and train/bus terminal to the area. Trains make the two-hour trip between Normal and Chicago many times each day, and tickets cost about $12 each way. Further east lies Normal's twin city, Bloomington, which offers even more restaurants and shopping.

Because of University policies, most partying occurs off campus. According to one senior, "The Greek scene is pretty dominant; however, there are many other social opportunities, as well." Underclassmen tend to go to organized parties hosted by either fraternities or individual students living off campus, while upperclassmen flock to the bars in nearby uptown Normal and downtown Bloomington. One popular destination is Pub II in uptown Normal, which one junior called "THE ISU bar." Pub II is famous for its food, and finding a parking spot there any time of day is tough. Unfortunately for underclassmen, bars in the area only admit those over 21. As such, some underage students will make the 45-minute trip to the University of Illinois campus in Champaign-Urbana, where the minimum age for bars is 19.

True Midwestern Living
True to its roots in the fields of Illinois, Illinois State University simultaneously offers students Midwestern hospitality and a 21st-century curriculum. Its solid academics, enthusiastic faculty, and central location make for a great environment. As one freshman said, "It has a small-town feel . . . it just has a really friendly atmosphere," as she affirmed her satisfaction with her choice to come to ISU.—*Rustin Fakheri*

FYI
If you come to ISU, you'd better bring "notecards, because you're gonna be doing a lot of studying."
What is the typical weekend schedule? "Wake up at 11, study until about 5, eat dinner at The Rock . . . [then] go out for a couple hours to apartment parties."
If I could change one thing about ISU, "I'd make the meal plan change back to when you chose your items and your meal card was like a debit card and deducted money."
Three things every student at ISU should do before graduating are "sit in the big bowl-shaped fountain outside Stevenson Hall," "go to Pub II, THE ISU bar," and "live in a friendly dorm like Hewett or Tri-Towers to make lots of friends."

Illinois Wesleyan University

Address: PO Box 2900
  Bloomington, IL
  61702-2900
Phone: 309-556-3031
E-mail address:
  iwuadmit@iwu.edu
Web site URL: www.iwu.edu
Year Founded: 1850
Private or Public: Private
Religious Affiliation: None
Location: Urban
Number of Applicants:
  2,963
Percent Accepted: 57%
Percent Accepted who
  enroll: 32%
Number Entering: 538
Number of Transfers
  Accepted each Year: 27
Middle 50% SAT range:
  M: 590–690, **CR:**
  540–680, **Wr:** Unreported
Middle 50% ACT range:
  26–30
Early admission program
  EA/ED/None: None

Percentage accepted
  through EA or ED: NA
EA and ED deadline: NA
Regular Deadline: Rolling
  through April
Application Fee: $0
Full time Undergraduate
  enrollment: 2,125
Total enrollment: 2,125
Percent Male: 42%
Percent Female: 58%
Total Percent Minority or
  Unreported: 7%
Percent African-American:
  5%
Percent Asian/Pacific
  Islander: 4%
Percent Hispanic: 3%
Percent Native-American:
  <1%
Percent International: 3%
Percent in-state/out of
  state: 87%/13%
Percent from Public HS:
  84%
Retention Rate: 92%

Graduation Rate 4-year: 77%
Graduation Rate 6-year: 82%
Percent Undergraduates in
  On-campus housing: 77%
Number of official organized
  extracurricular
  organizations: 170
3 Most popular majors:
  Biology/Biological Sciences,
  Business/Commerce,
  Psychology
Student/Faculty ratio: 13:1
Average Class Size: 16
Percent of students going to
  grad school: 35%
Tuition and Fees: $32,260
In-State Tuition and Fees if
  different: No difference
Cost for Room and Board:
  $7,350
Percent receiving financial
  aid out of those who apply,
  first year: 95%
Percent receiving financial
  aid among all students:
  91%

"Everybody here is so nice," one Illinois Wesleyan senior said, and she would probably know. With an enrollment of about 2,100 undergraduates, IWU is smaller than many public high schools, allowing students to quickly form a common identity. Studying in Bloomington, students reap the rewards of the school's unique academic offerings, including the Gateway Colloquium seminars for first-years, an annual student research conference and May Term, which allows undergrads to explore non-traditional learning experiences. And if anything can be gleaned from the school's strong record of alumni giving, it is that IWU's unique programs and tight-knit community make a lasting impact on the students who step through its doors.

Challenging and Welcoming Work

Professors are very accessible to IWU students, who often develop meaningful relationships with faculty outside of class. Because the school is entirely undergraduates, most students are lavished with attention. Classes range from largish lectures (50–100 people) to very intimate seminars (less than 10 people), and come in varying levels of difficulty. "For the most part," said one sophomore, "the classes are as challenging as you make them."

Certain programs are developing a reputation for particular excellence, with the expectations for students in these majors rising accordingly. Biology and Business are the hot majors, and produce some of the school's top graduates. "A 3.0 in the bio program would translate to a 3.8 almost anywhere else," said one Biology major. Additionally, many science majors cite the value of being able to do research under the guidance of their professors.

The Business program boasts its own unique learning experience. "We have more discussion, more hands-on experience," one Business major said. The Business department has a successful record of placing stu-

dents in summer internships in Bloomington, Chicago, or elsewhere in the country.
Despite the recent prevalence of these two
programs, IWU still offers strong liberal arts
programs true to its founding at 1850.

Today, most upperclassmen agree that the
younger classes are smarter and more interesting every year. "I don't think I would still
get in if I had to apply now," noted one senior. First-years who do make the cut benefit from the Gateway Colloquium, a series of
small, discussion-oriented classes that focus on writing skills. Students also enjoy
the John Wesley Powell Undergraduate Research Conference, a yearly event at which
students present their research to the rest of
the campus community. "You shouldn't miss
it," exhorted a senior female.

Campus Culture and Living Arrangements
If there is a stereotype of IWU students, it
centers on their background. "As much as
the administration tries to push diversity,
everyone comes from the same kind of suburb," said one transfer student. "To some extent, everybody here is a little bit of a nerd,"
added a physics major.

Stereotypes aside, IWU students are
generally hard-working, smart, and from an
upper-middle-class higher economic background. "As such," noted one student from
the Chicago suburbs, "the students demand
a relatively high level of living."

> "To some extent, everybody here is a
> little bit of a nerd."

Integral to the "high life" at IWU is gaming. Video and computer gaming are popular
pastimes in the dorms, especially for the
guys, with the majority of rooms linked to
facilitate multi-player tournaments. "College is the ultimate gaming experience," declared one male student. Intramural sports
are also an option, but casual sports, such as
Frisbee on the quad, are more prevalent.
One sophomore, however, disagreed, saying
that the political side of university life was
more interesting.

Most students applaud the on-campus
housing, and though a few live off campus,
all are in assigned dorms during freshman
year. "I was surprised to have gotten a really
cool roommate," one freshman noted. The
school has a fairly successful method for
putting roommates together and, according

to one sophomore, it really "encourages
everyone to get to know each other."

A Small Student Body Congregates
The size of the student body doesn't limit its
spirit, especially on the few occasions that a
large group congregates. All students agree:
"Basketball is big." The team is ranked in Division III, and a home basketball game
draws more than half of the student body.
Other varsity teams are well-regarded, but
definitely not as well-supported as basketball. In balancing the athletic experience
with his academic load, one varsity swimmer emphasized the accommodation of his
professors, "They are very willing to give me
make-up tests." An athlete could do much
worse than the facilities he will be able to
use at IWU. The Shirk Center is the large
athletic complex and, according to one student, "Everything is kept up very well."

The Student Senate also gathers large
amounts of attention on campus, as it is the
primary liaison between the school administration and the students. "The administration is genuinely receptive to student input,"
noted one student who worked in the admissions office.

Finally, weekend afternoons and early evenings, much of the student body congregates
at the student center, which screens films,
brings comedians and other live acts to campus, and acts as a simple meeting point for
students before the night's activities.

Food and Drink
"The food is really good," exclaimed one excited sophomore. Still, a freshman noted
that "A lot of upperclassmen claim it gets
old really fast." So, if the students get tired
of "Saga," the main dining hall on campus,
they can go to a few on-campus alternatives
or take their hunger into Bloomington. Nevertheless, "You have not had the full experience," one sophomore explained, "until you
are yelled at by this crazy old lady in the dining hall."

After being chewed out by the elderly, students like to party on the weekends. The fraternities and sororities provide a large
majority of the options, though there are invariably other parties on many occasions, if
not on every night. Additionally, for those
with ID, there are a number of bars in Bloomington that become frequent destinations.

Student opinion regarding the Greeks is
mixed. Some think that the parties could be
better, while others praise the generally

strong social scene given the size of the student body. The truth, however, is that "If you are in the mood for a party, you'll definitely be able to find one."

Extra Opportunities

The experience at IWU would not be complete without "the monkey pit." Beneath a bridge next to the science offices, one can often see students lounging in a space that looks similar to a monkey habitat at a zoo, prompting its nickname.

But the final distinguishing element of the IWU educational experience is May Term. Students finish second semester at the end of April, but almost all continue with a three-week term immediately thereafter called May Term. During May Term, each student takes one class, which meets

once a day for a few hours. While it is possible to take normal classes to satisfy major or graduation requirements, most students take advantage of various exciting opportunities.

Students take courses on campus that are offered according to a professor's hobby or special interest. Particularly popular are travel classes. During May term, students can study biology in Costa Rica or Australia, theater in New York City, international politics in the European Union, or classical music in Italy, among other options.

Yet the essence of Illinois Wesleyan remains the opportunities that await students when they leave the school. One senior said, "I feel like I will take the knowledge that I learn here into the real world."—*Peter Johnston*

FYI

If you come to IWU, you'd better bring "Mountain Dew to stay up late."

A typical weekend at Illinois Wesleyan consists of "sleeping late, partying, studying, and playing video games."

If I could change one thing about IWU, I would change "the math department."

Three things every student at IWU should do before graduating are "get yelled at by the crazy old lady at the dining hall, go to a basketball game, and play in the monkey pit."

Knox College

Address: Box K-148 Galesburg, IL 61401
Phone: 309-341-7100
E-mail address: admission@knox.edu
Web site URL: www.knox.edu
Year Founded: 1837
Private or Public: Private
Religious Affiliation: None
Location: Suburban
Number of Applicants: 2,419
Percent Accepted: 61%
Percent Accepted who enroll: 21%
Number Entering: 307
Number of Transfers Accepted each Year: 42
Middle 50% SAT range: M: 580–670, CR: 610–710, Wr: 580–670
Middle 50% ACT range: 26–31
Early admission program EA/ED/None: EA

Percentage accepted through EA or ED: Unreported
EA and ED deadline: 1-Dec
Regular Deadline: 1-Feb
Application Fee: $40
Full time Undergraduate enrollment: 1,371
Total enrollment: 1,371
Percent Male: 42%
Percent Female: 58%
Total Percent Minority or Unreported: 9%
Percent African-American: 4%
Percent Asian/Pacific Islander: 6%
Percent Hispanic: 5%
Percent Native-American: <1%
Percent International: 6%
Percent in-state/out of state: 52%/48%
Percent from Public HS: 83%
Retention Rate: 91%

Graduation Rate 4-year: 64%
Graduation Rate 6-year: 74%
Percent Undergraduates in On-campus housing: 94%
Number of official organized extracurricular organizations: 102
3 Most popular majors: Anthropology, Economics, Political Science
Student/Faculty ratio: 12:1
Average Class Size: 13
Percent of students going to grad school: 24%
Tuition and Fees: $30,180
In-State Tuition and Fees if different: No difference
Cost for Room and Board: $6,726
Percent receiving financial aid out of those who apply, first year: 95%
Percent receiving financial aid among all students: 94%

Knox College welcomes students from the minute they set foot on campus. "Other schools just sort of tolerated me when I visited," one current Knox student recalled. "But Knox professors and students alike seemed to take a genuine interest in me." Students come to Knox, located in Galesburg, Illinois, from around the globe to experience the intense academics and the strong community spirit that the college has built. For many, Knox offers the best of both worlds: "Knox students know how to get it done during the week and know how to relax on the weekends."

No Tests in the Bathroom

The academic year at Knox is run on what is commonly known as a "3-3" calendar. Effectively, this breaks the year into three trimesters in which students take three classes at a time in 10-week blocks, leaving a full six weeks for winter break. While this may, on paper, appear to be an easy schedule to maintain, students at Knox know better. As one current French and Creative Writing double major asserted, "We'd die if we took any more than three classes at Knox. [Courses] are very intense and fast-paced, since we have to pack in 16 weeks of material." Furthermore, students appreciate the frequent change of classes. As one pointed out, "You never get bored of anything you take."

All freshmen are required to take a course entitled First-Year Preceptorial (according to some, also known as "How To Be A Knox Student 101"). Beyond that, there is a wide variety of directions students can take, depending on their interests. But even the introductory classes at Knox receive rave reviews. "They have a broad scope to begin with," one student explained, "but each professor I've had has created a way for the student to do a project that allows them to work on something they find interesting about the subject." In fact, the popularity of the faculty in general is undeniable. "The staff here is incredible," a current sophomore raved. "It's a great situation to be in and I am absolutely convinced that it is what makes Knox so laid-back."

When classes get really challenging, students tend to form study groups and cooperate rather than compete. "There are so many other things to worry about in college that I'm glad academic competition isn't one of them," one anthropology major said. The unique approach to academics is epitomized in the school's Honor Code. Professors do not proctor exams, so students have their choice of where to take them. In other words, according to one student, "Sometimes, we get to take our tests anywhere we want in the building except for bathrooms and stairwells."

Theme Houses and T-shirts

The unique Knox experience extends beyond the classroom. As one history major who recently spent a spring break working in New Orleans with college funding explained, "Knox realizes that you don't just learn in the classroom . . . you need to experience the real world. And they will assist you in any way to achieve that."

In no way is this point better illustrated than through the study-abroad program that Knox offers. In addition to three college-sponsored programs in Buenos Aires, Barcelona, and Besançon, France, Knox students have a wealth of study-abroad options to choose from and are strongly encouraged to go. In fact, since a period of "experimental learning" (such as study abroad or an internship) is required for graduation, many students find the program to be an integral part of their college experience. "There are plenty of domestic study programs that are very popular here such as the D.C. semester at American University and the Arts semester at the University of Chicago," added a freshman. And to top it off, the trimester system makes it easy for students to spend a semester abroad and still be back at Knox for two full terms.

Although some students may opt to move off campus, on-campus housing varies. Dorms aside, upperclassmen have a number of different options, including the rare case of theme housing. Only three or four exist at any given time, but essentially students come together as a group to apply for a theme house, explaining both what their theme is and how it could enhance life on the Knox campus. While the types of theme houses vary every year, some current favorites include the Red House (giving its residents a taste in Communist living), and the Do-it-Yourself house.

The food, while every so often drawing predictable student complaints, is reportedly satisfying overall. One of the most popular additions to the dining hall has been stir-fry, with two chefs ready to cook whatever students put together for them. For caffeine and sugar runs on campus, students head for the Gizmo, a coffeehouse that is open until one in the morning.

But campus life does not end with dorms, houses, and food. In fact, it barely begins there. With more than 100 clubs and activities on campus, Knox has something to offer everyone. Best of all, the community spirit that is fostered on campus encourages many to try something new. One student, for example, came to campus with no musical background and soon found herself taking harp lessons. "Knox is so inclusive. Everyone does all that they can to help people get involved with new things and make them feel comfortable in what they choose to do," she explained.

In terms of nightlife, there is a wide variety of groups—fraternities, sororities, theme houses, and even private suites—that throw parties. And when they do, students tend to get creative. For example, the fraternity TKE hosts "Graffiti Night," during which everyone wears a white T-shirt and sports a washable marker that they are handed at the door. "There are always parties to suit any occasion," a current sophomore noted. And partying at Knox does not necessarily mean getting drunk. "There are a lot of parties that I go to where I just want to dance and not drink and there is no pressure whatsoever," one student explained. "It's definitely a personal choice here and people both acknowledge and respect that."

Pumphandle and Flunk
Among the many campus traditions at Knox, there are two that especially stand out. The first, "Pumphandle Day," occurs on the day before classes start. Everyone who is on campus that day (students, faculty, even family members!) gathers to shake everyone else's hands. As one current senior described, "People dress weird and write strange things on their name tags. It's definitely memorable." "This year we had a giant gorilla, a giant ba-

nana, a Catwoman and a Superman!" another student noted.

The second can't-miss tradition is "Flunk Day," which takes place every spring. When it arrives (the exact date is always kept a secret), the campus is woken up by fog horns in the early morning hours. Classes and meetings are canceled. In their place, a spring carnival awaits students and faculty alike. And while many students try to describe the various activities of the day, one sophomore asserted, "It's really something you just have to experience. I've never heard a description of Flunk Day that really did it justice."

> **"[When students] have a paper due, they'll work on the paper for a while and THEN go to the game."**

Both of these events are evidence of Knox's strong school spirit. This pride extends both to the school in general (as one student claimed, "Everyone has at least two things emblazoned with 'Knox'") and to sports, in particular. "Basketball and football are most popular by far," one current varsity basketball player noted, and most students agree. Even so, many keep academics as their first priority. "[When students] have a paper due, they'll work on the paper for a while and THEN go to the game."

From collaborative efforts in the classroom to dinners at professors' houses, students get to know the people around them in ways that might not be possible at other schools. Looking back, one senior noted that, "I never visited Knox before enrolling, but I felt at home from the moment I stepped on campus." Knox gives students the confidence and comfort they need to enjoy their college experience to the fullest.—*Stephanie Brockman*

FYI
If you come to Knox, you'd better bring: "sweatpants and social skills."
What is the typical weekend schedule? "Lots of work! In general, studying the whole time except for Friday and Saturday night, when there are theme and frat parties, bands, comedians, movies, performances, etc."
If I could change one thing about Knox, I'd "get a few mountains put in nearby . . . The prairie is really hard to get used to!"
Three things every student at Knox should do before graduating are: "Go sledding in the Knox Bowl (our football field), go abroad ANYWHERE, get Roger (our president) to remember your name."

Lake Forest College

Address: 555 North Sheridan Road, Lake Forest, IL 60045
Phone: 847-735-5000
E-mail address: motzer@lakeforest.edu
Web site URL: www.lakeforest.edu
Year Founded: 1857
Private or Public: Private
Religious Affiliation: None
Location: Suburban
Number of Applicants: 2,203
Percent Accepted: 61%
Percent Accepted who enroll: 26%
Number Entering: 356
Number of Transfers Accepted each Year: 50
Middle 50% SAT range: M: 540–660, CR: 560–660, Wr: 540–640
Middle 50% ACT range: 24–29
Early admission program EA/ED/None: EA and ED
Percentage accepted through EA or ED: Unreported

EA and ED deadline: 1-Dec
Regular Deadline: 15-Feb
Application Fee: $40
Full time Undergraduate enrollment: 1,381
Total enrollment: 1,381
Percent Male: 41%
Percent Female: 59%
Total Percent Minority or Unreported: 8%
Percent African-American: 4%
Percent Asian/Pacific Islander: 5%
Percent Hispanic: 6%
Percent Native-American: <1%
Percent International: 8%
Percent in-state/out of state: 48%/52%
Percent from Public HS: 65%
Retention Rate: 82%
Graduation Rate 4-year: 65%
Graduation Rate 6-year: 68%

Percent Undergraduates in On-campus housing: 80%
Number of official organized extracurricular organizations: 90
3 Most popular majors: Communication Studies/Speech Communication and Rhetoric, English Language and Literature, Psychology
Student/Faculty ratio: 13:1
Average Class Size: 15
Percent of students going to grad school: Unreported
Tuition and Fees: $30,600
In-State Tuition and Fees if different: No difference
Cost for Room and Board: $7,326
Percent receiving financial aid out of those who apply, first year: 88%
Percent receiving financial aid among all students: 91%

Lake Forest College, often referred to as "Chicago's National Liberal Arts College," is a small school located in the quaint suburb of Lake Forest, Illinois, 30 miles north of Chicago. With a diverse, spirited, and enthusiastic student body of approximately 1,400 students representing 47 states and 72 countries, Lake Forest College promotes a liberal arts education within a cohesive student-faculty environment. As one student put it: "[Lake Forest] is a community of interesting, motivated, and most of all FUN people!"

Academics

Academic requirements at Lake Forest are not excessively rigorous. One student explained, "Graduation requires a 2.0 and certain foundational requirements that are typical of small liberal arts schools (two math or science classes, a culturally diverse class, and so on)." This flexibility allows students to explore multiple programs: "Gen-

eral education requirements are light, so it's easy for people to double major and minor." One disillusioned student complained that, although "grading is relatively fair," it is somewhat inflated, and that the academics are not as challenging as some would like. However, another student pointed out that programs have become increasingly rigorous over the past few years: "The workload is getting heavier because LFC is becoming a better school. It's challenging, but doable."

The University offers a variety of popular majors such as communications, psychology, business, art history, economics and politics, as well as some more challenging majors like education, chemistry and other math- and science-oriented subjects. In general, majors in the humanities are considered much easier and more popular, while the science and math departments are more highly accredited and recognized—in particular the economics department. While there is not a large selection of course offerings in these majors, students greatly enjoy the quality of instruction and accessibility of the professors: "I love the fact that the professors who teach at LFC could teach at Northwestern or the University of Chicago as well (lots of them used to actually), but they come here because they like teaching to undergrads in a small environment." One student went so far as to say, "I can call or e-mail professors whenever! They are very concerned with helping you do well." Specific professors mentioned were Robert Baade, Carolyn Tuttle, and Robert Lemke in the Economics Department, Les Dlabay in Business, DeJuran Richardson in the Math Department, and Spanish professor Lois Barr. James Marquardt's "World Politics" was also noted as a "key class."

> "I can call or e-mail professors whenever! They are very concerned with helping you do well."

Students who apply to Lake Forest College can also seek acceptance into the Richter Program, a competitive freshman research program. Accepted students remain on campus for the summer to pursue research with a professor.

Social Life

The social life on campus is dominated by sports teams, fraternities, and sororities. Lake Forest College boasts 14 varsity sports teams, in addition to various intramural and club sports. The most popular sports are hockey, football, and rugby. A large portion of the student body is involved in sports in some way. Although the facilities are often described as "inadequate," this doesn't stop the spirited and enthusiastic student body from enjoying them. A student-run organization led by the University's mascot, Boomer, supports the varsity sports teams. For a small fee, a student can join the "Athletic Council," more commonly known as the "Forest Fanatic," and take advantage of a free Fanatic T-shirt, VIP seating at home games, free food at select games, reduced bus fare to away games, e-mail notifications of upcoming events and behind-the-scenes updates and highlights.

As for Greek life, there are seven fraternities and sororities (some of which are international). One member of Delta Kappa Epsilon said, "The sororities are strong and fraternities are lacking numbers. However, I have absolutely no regrets about joining a fraternity at Lake Forest College. It has been an amazing experience for me." A member of Delta Delta Delta described the Greek scene as "relaxed, small, personal, and authentic." Another student pointed out that, while Greeks tend to be the "most involved" at Lake Forest and often secure top positions in student government, "You don't have to be a Greek to be integrated in the school. Non-Greeks are friends with Greeks."

As the surrounding town of Lake Forest isn't exactly thriving, the overall social scene at LCF is largely campus-based. While most upperclassmen have cars, the majority stay in the area. There are a few campus-wide parties, typically hosted by the fraternities, as well as semi-formals for various student organizations. The annual "Winter Ball," held in the botanical garden, the "Mr. Casanova Contest," and the "DKE Rampant Lion March Party," are particularly popular. The University has recently tightened up its alcohol policies, but the majority of the campus drinks. As for drugs, one student explained, "They are common but not socially acceptable. They are used behind closed doors (even hidden from other students)." Another stated that drugs are not common at all. As for those who are of drinking age, some venture into the city on the weekends and hit up Chicago's bars. The city of Chicago also offers many alternatives to a typical college social scene such as Navy Pier, museums like the Field Museum, an aquarium and planetarium, two major league baseball teams, a hockey team, an NFL football team and fabulous shopping on Michigan Avenue.

The University takes pride in community service activities. Although Lake Forest itself doesn't offer many opportunities, Chicago, which is only a 45-minute drive or 90-minute train ride away, provides many unique community service opportunities. The Big Brothers/Sisters program of Lake County is one such group. Located in Gurnee, a suburb about 20 minutes north of Lake Forest, this group has been around since 1904. Many Lake Forest College students volunteer for the program, which focuses primarily on mentoring throughout the Chicago community. Other activities include literary groups such as Collage, as well as political organizations including the League for Environmental Awareness, College Democrats and College Republicans. Art and performance groups exist, and the University boasts a number of additional religious, cultural, academic, and business-orientated groups.

Campus Life

Although the social scene is somewhat constrained by the general attitude and environment of the town itself, Lake Forest provides nice, on-campus living arrangements. Freshmen are assigned dorms, while upperclassmen pick through a random lottery system. There are some specialized dorms—an all-girls dorm, an international dorm, four substance-free dorms—while the remainder of the dorms are mixed. Alcohol is allowed in a select number of the dorms and only if the inhabitants of the rooms are 21. Gregory is known as the party dorm.

One girl explained, "A large majority of students live on campus because no one can afford a home in Lake Forest." The town itself is described as "very high class," "an affluent neighborhood" in a "very safe community—the safest in Illinois." One perk this exclusivity offers is the availability of high-paying babysitting jobs. However, one student noted the homogenizing effect of the school's setting: "The campus looks like a country club, the town is one of the richest in the United States, and this environment tends to influence the students; in some ways, I think, the environment 'preppifies' everyone."

There have been a few recent additions to the campus, like the brand-new library and student center. As for on-campus food, one girl described it as "excellent for cafeteria food!" On-campus living includes three meals per day Monday through Friday and two meals per day on the weekend. Miramar, The Lantern, Teddy O's, The Grill and The Wooden Nickel are popular local eateries among students.

In general, this small, somewhat secluded university is able to differentiate itself from other universities through its personable professors and enthusiastic social life. One specific reason not to overlook this university, as one student put it: "It is a small liberal arts school close to a big city; it is not located in the middle of nowhere!"—*Caroline Kaufman*

FYI

If you come to Lake Forest, you'd better bring "a hat and mittens because it gets cold, an empty stomach because the cafeteria food is awesome, and a hard-working, positive attitude."

What's the typical weekend schedule? "After class on Friday, take a nap and then get ready to go out . . . South Campus is where the parties are; sleep in late on Saturday and head to the cafeteria in your PJs, watch movies, and then get ready to go out all over again! Sunday: get your work done . . . Occasionally there are All-Campus Parties that everyone attends . . . they are really fun."

If I could change one thing about Lake Forest, I'd "make the Education Major less difficult! The classes are demanding and tons of work, but it is all worth it in the end because they have a history of 100 percent job placement after graduation."

Three things every student at Lake Forest should do before graduating are "eat at the cafeteria, get involved with on-campus organizations, and study abroad: we have great programs."

Loyola University Chicago

Address: 820 North Michigan Avenue, Chicago, IL 60611-9810
Phone: 312-915-6500
E-mail address: admission@luc.edu
Web site URL: www.luc.edu
Year Founded: 1870
Private or Public: Private
Religious Affiliation: Roman Catholic-Jesuit
Location: Urban
Number of Applicants: 17,671
Percent Accepted: 60%
Percent Accepted who enroll: 20%
Number Entering: 2,060
Number of Transfers Accepted each Year: 1,830
Middle 50% SAT range: M: 520–640, CR: 540–640, Wr: 510–628
Middle 50% ACT range: 23–28
Early admission program EA/ED/None: None

Percentage accepted through EA or ED: NA
EA and ED deadline: NA
Regular Deadline: Rolling
Application Fee: $25
Full time Undergraduate enrollment: 10,124
Total enrollment: 15,951
Percent Male: 33%
Percent Female: 67%
Total Percent Minority or Unreported: 30%
Percent African-American: 3%
Percent Asian/Pacific Islander: 11%
Percent Hispanic: 9%
Percent Native-American: <1%
Percent International: 1%
Percent in-state/out of state: 55% / 45%
Percent from Public HS: 66%
Retention Rate: 84%
Graduation Rate 4-year: 56%

Graduation Rate 6-year: 65%
Percent Undergraduates in On-campus housing: 40%
Number of official organized extracurricular organizations: 175
3 Most popular majors: Biology, Nursing, Psychology
Student/Faculty ratio: 14:1
Average Class Size: 16
Percent of students going to grad school: Unreported
Tuition and Fees: $29,486
In-State Tuition and Fees if different: No difference
Cost for Room and Board: $10,490
Percent receiving financial aid out of those who apply, first year: 84%
Percent receiving financial aid among all students: 72%

The largest Jesuit University in the nation, Loyola University in Chicago, aims to provide its nearly 16,000 students with opportunities and experiences that are unique and different from all other leading universities in the nation. Combining core Jesuit values with the diversity that a city like Chicago boasts, Loyola University in Chicago challenges each student, undergraduate and graduate, to expand their minds through service, stimulating classroom settings, and interactions with a variety of interesting people.

Remembering Their Past

Loyola University in Chicago makes a promise to each student who steps on its campus—students will be prepared to "lead extraordinary lives" in the future. Loyola expects its graduates to be the leaders of tomorrow, and it looks to the 5 core principles of a Jesuit Education to achieve this goal. There must be a commitment to excellence. Loyola students are expected to seek knowledge and bask in the classroom. The Jesuit

relationship to God is equally important. Loyola promotes maintaining a strong and well-developed belief system so that one may help others to deepen their own relationships to God. Loyola also stresses a strong commitment to service and global awareness. Loyola students should demonstrate a well-rounded understanding of the world and its people, and then they must use their knowledge and awareness to serve their communities and seek justice for all. The final characteristic of a Jesuit Education ensures a consistent focus on values and justice that create a strong but fair leader in whatever field. One student recognized the value of the Jesuit foundation of Loyola: "The Jesuit mission is *huge*. Service learning is required for graduation. People who come to Loyola want to make a difference and are very driven and passionate."

Hard to the Core?

Loyola University in Chicago, probably more than any of its other characteristics, takes pride in its unique academic system.

Illinois237

Students are encouraged to "learn broadly" by choosing from more than 70 undergraduate majors and taking full advantage of the 14:1 student/faculty ratio. Classes are small, unless they are a major lecture, with only 15 students per class. Loyola is well known for its humanities, but there is also a strong premed program. Students name political science, social work, business, education, and communications other popular majors.

The faculty is kind, and eager to impart some of their vast knowledge on their students. Professors are extremely willing to meet students outside of the classroom to talk about, well, anything! "The teachers that I have had are very agreeable and . . . one of my favorite aspects of the academic life at Loyola," one student said. Even more impressive about Loyola's staff is that professors have almost always worked in their respective fields before coming to the Windy City. "All of my favorite professors have worked for major companies before teaching so they have incredible experience that lends to a very hands-on teaching style. I feel like they have a lot more to offer than simply reciting the textbook," said one sophomore.

> "All of my favorite professors have worked for major companies before teaching so they have incredible experience that lends to a very hands-on teaching style."

Indeed, Loyola focuses on real experience as a valuable and necessary tool for the classroom. Students, in their path to "extraordinary lives," must first possess the real life skills that naturally accompany such futures. Given its incredible location in a major city, Loyola University in Chicago encourages its students to take advantage of the many academic opportunities that Chicago has. There are numerous research and fieldwork opportunities at many of the city's major institutions. Among the long list are the Lincoln Park Zoo, Field Museum, and Adler Planetarium. One student exclaimed, "I'm in an events planning class right now that is amazing! I am a . . . double major, and I have already had a ton of hands-on classes. My advanced advertising class this semester is recreating an entire ad campaign and presenting it to a firm in Chicago."

But, perhaps one of the most unique aspects about Loyola's academic structure is its strict core curriculum. The Core includes 15 required courses that span 10 knowledge-area learning outcomes. This naturally results in a high number of credits required for the core curriculum. Each student is expected to take one writing seminar, one art course, one quantitative analysis course, and two courses each of history, literature, philosophy, science, social science, and theology. The courses aim to create a unique, well-rounded education that encourages students to further develop and pursue the ultimate goals of leadership and unparalleled intellectual skill in the field of their choice.

Life on the Water & in the Windy City

Loyola University of Chicago's campus has 3 distinct Chicago area campuses: the Maywood Campus, the Water Tower Campus, and the Lake Shore Campus. The Maywood Campus is home to Loyola's medical center, while the other two campuses house most of the undergraduate students. The Lake Shore Campus, as its name suggests, overlooks Lake Michigan from its location right next to the water. The Water Tower Campus is located in the middle of downtown Chicago's most famous shopping strip on Michigan Avenue. Students can easily get from one part of the campus to the other with special passes that provide unlimited access to the University's shuttle service and Chicago's aboveground metro, the El. The student body generally likes the effect of two main campuses. "My favorite part of campus is anything along the water, especially the IC because it is 3 stories of glass windows and absolutely beautiful. I also love having a downtown campus because I can experience the best of both worlds," one student remarked. Another student agreed that the Michigan Avenue campus was equally as important as the scenic Lake Water campus: "I love spending time at the downtown campus because it is in the middle of the city and I can truly grasp the fact that I am living in one [of] the greatest cities in America."

Of course, living in a major urban area has its downsides. Loyola has a commitment to exposing its students to a variety of new experiences and people that go along with a city like Chicago. However, Loyola, even more so, values its students' safety and well-being. "Safety is sometimes an issue in the area surrounding Loyola but the Campus Police has been handling the situation well.

We have a transportation system that will drive you anywhere near campus so that you do not have to walk alone at night. Sometimes I feel unsafe at night but mainly it is not a concern of mine," said one sophomore.

Perhaps, this, in part, led to the requirement that undergraduate students live on campus in dorms for the first two years. Living in the dorms for the first couple years allows students to ease into the experience of living in a major city. Freshmen live in freshmen-only dorms, and sophomores live in sophomore-only dorms. Freshmen dorms vary greatly, but sophomores live in apartment style dorms complete with individual kitchens. All residential buildings are relatively nice (though some, of course, are smaller), but there is a lottery that students enter which decides their actual room assignments. One student looked back on her experience with fondness. "I got a really good one [with] 3 bedrooms, 2 bath, kitchen, living room with 4 other girls. I loved it!" After the first two years, students are given the option of living off-campus and most eventually do so. There is always a push to further immerse oneself in Loyola's rich surroundings.

Loyola knows how to have fun!
Although Loyola's social scene is not centered around the same kinds of things and activities as many other schools, the student body certainly has no trouble finding things to do. Sports are not as big at Loyola as they are at other schools. For example, there is no football team so basketball, soccer, and hockey are the most popular sports. There is also, therefore, not a great deal of social energy that centers around athletic events. Greek life is also not as present as at some other schools; one student described the breakdown of student social groups as such: "8.9% Greek, some athletes, the kids who aren't Greek or athletes but hang out with them and then a lot of hipsters."

But this is not to say that Loyola students do not go out. Quite the opposite, in fact! There are two main bars by campus that students frequent because "everyone has a fake." And, once students turn 21, they usually head to Lincoln Park or downtown. Still, it is absolutely not a problem if one does not want to drink. "I think a majority of people drink," said one sophomore, "but not to the excess that is seen on other campuses. A lot of girls on my honors floor last year didn't drink." There are also a number of off-

campus and on-campus parties that are somewhat smaller in size but "just as fun as frat parties." One student described a typical weekend at Loyola: "The typical weekend schedule is Thursday Night partying for some and homework for others. Friday night, there is usually a party somewhere or the bars are always a good option. Saturday during the day usually consists of sleep, homework and sometimes exploring the city of Chicago. Saturday night there are more parties and a lot of people usually end up at a bar near campus to end the night."

Popular Extracurriculars
As was stated earlier, Loyola's varsity sport scene is not as popular as it sometimes is on other campuses, but students are still often involved in some kind of athletic or physical activity. Intramural sports are a nice, stress-free alternative to competing at the varsity level in various sports. One student described intramurals as "very relaxed, but also very fun" because "there usually aren't many games, so it doesn't take as much of a commitment."

Really, the amount of time each extracurricular takes is unique to each club. It definitely depends on the extracurricular when judging dedication and commitment. Said one student, "I am in a sorority, and most people are very involved. I am also on the club swim team and there is much less involvement. However, those who are involved really love it. There are so many options that people usually get pretty excited once they find the club that is right for them." There are so many different organizations on campus, like the student said, that it is hard to determine which clubs are generally the most popular. However, it is pretty universally accepted that *The Phoenix*, Loyola's newspaper, has a great staff that successfully "cover all the current events around campus and the changes that happen within the administration of the college." This is also the case for the college's literary magazine, *The Diminuendo*, which is published twice a year and selectively accepts submissions from all students.

Aside from the two main campus publications, students generally agree that employment plays a big role in their lives as students at Loyola. Many students have jobs, both on and off-campus, that provide both an interesting pastime and a source of funds. "A lot of people have jobs. Loyola is expensive so many people need to make some extra money to help with tuition. Internships are also a requirement for graduation for many majors," explained one student.

In general, Loyola University in Chicago provides its students with opportunities and experiences that are not easily found on other campuses. For one student, this uniqueness is exemplified by the two campuses, one right on the lake and the other in the heart of the city. "This opens [up] so many opportunities. Somehow though, the campuses are very connected and I never feel alienated or like I'm missing out because we are split up." For another student, the Loyola student's one-of-a-kind experience is a product of the Jesuit traditions

upon which the school is founded: "What surprised me the most about Loyola when I arrived was how nice all the students were . . . [and the] focus on helping others and . . . serving the community." Naturally, the things that set this institution apart vary by student but one thing all Loyola students *can* agree on—they are confident that they made the right decision. When asked if she would choose Loyola if she had the chance to change or stay, one student responded whole-heartedly, "If I could do the whole applying to College process again I would definitely pick Loyola without a doubt."—*Edirin Okoloko*

FYI

If you come to Loyola, "you'd better leave your car behind because Chicago traffic can be pretty bad."

What's your classic weekend schedule: "Class, Workout, Nap, Fun activity (downtown or exploring somewhere), Pregame with close friends, head to a larger party or the bar, go to bed or post party . . . Sleep in Sat (unless you have tests/work), lounge with friends or do something fun in the city/campus, repeat Friday night . . . Sleep in Sunday, homework, homework, homework, laundry!

Three things every student should do at Loyola: "skinny dip in Lake Michigan, sample every Chicago pizza place, and go shopping on Michigan Ave during Christmas Time."

Northwestern University

Address: PO Box 3060, 1801 Hinman Avenue, Evanston, IL 60204-3060

Phone: 847-491-7271

E-mail address: ugadmission@northwestern.edu

Web site URL: www.northwestern.edu

Year Founded: 1851

Private or Public: Private

Religious Affiliation: None

Location: Suburban

Number of Applicants: 21,930

Percent Accepted: 27%

Percent Accepted who enroll: 33%

Number Entering: 1,981

Number of Transfers Accepted each Year: Unreported

Middle 50% SAT range: M: 680–770, CR: 670–750, Wr: 660–750

Middle 50% ACT range: 30–34

Early admission program EA/ED/None: ED

Percentage accepted through EA or ED: Unreported

EA and ED deadline: 1-Nov

Regular Deadline: 1-Jan

Application Fee: $65

Full time Undergraduate enrollment: 8,476

Total enrollment: 16,932

Percent Male: 48%

Percent Female: 52%

Total Percent Minority or Unreported: 41%

Percent African-American: 6%

Percent Asian/Pacific Islander: 17%

Percent Hispanic: 7%

Percent Native-American: 0%

Percent International: 5%

Percent in-state/out of state: 25%/75%

Percent from Public HS: 73%

Retention Rate: 97%

Graduation Rate 4-year: 86%

Graduation Rate 6-year: Unreported

Percent Undergraduates in On-campus housing: 65%

Number of official organized extracurricular organizations: 415

3 Most popular majors: Economics, Engineering, Journalism

Student/Faculty ratio: 7:1

Average Class Size: 19

Percent of students going to grad school: 23%

Tuition and Fees: $37,125

In-State Tuition and Fees if different: No difference

Cost for Room and Board: $11,295

Percent receiving financial aid out of those who apply, first year: 77%

Percent receiving financial aid among all students: 40%

N orthwestern University, the only private university of the Big Ten, is a top-tier university located in Evanston, Illinois. Bordering Lake Michigan and only an hour away from Chicago, students there have easy access to both the excitement of the city as well as peacefulness of the suburbs.

Six Colleges, One University

Northwestern students appreciate the academic experience, commenting on the diverse course options and range of requirements, the fast pace of the quarter system, and the ability to find a comfortable workload.

Requirements depend on which college the student is in, and there are six different colleges at Northwestern University. The Weinberg College of Arts and Sciences, the most popular, requires proficiency in a foreign language and two courses in each of the following: natural sciences, the social/behavioral department, quantitative category, ethics and values, and history. While

these requirements seem strict, one freshman said that she welcomes the broad distribution of her course load. "There's just a lot of really interesting courses, and because of the distributional requirements, I don't feel guilty taking courses that don't really relate to my major."

While the broad range of classes in the College of Arts and Sciences is liberating for some, many students speak of an entirely different lifestyle for engineers and math majors. "If you're an engineer here, it's very, very, very difficult," said one freshman girl in the School of Communications.

The dynamic between students in different areas of study is generally one of mutual respect, according to a Weinberg student. "I tell my friend that I have to go read 100 pages of *Anna Karenina*, and he's like 'oh my God!'" At the same time, however, humanities students appreciate the difficulty that engineering students face.

The amount of work also depends largely on your major, and can vary from person to person within a major. "I feel like the engineers and people who are pre-med tend to be busy, while those in other majors tend to be sporadically busy," said one freshman.

That said, most Northwestern students, regardless of major, remark that the quarter system does not allow time to settle down and get too comfortable. "It feels like you're always studying for midterms," said one student, "but this can be a blessing in disguise. If you're taking a class you don't like, it's over quickly, and over my four years, I'll take eight more classes than the semester student."

Northwestern students also appreciate the line-up of special classes and noteworthy professors at their University. In a class called Human Sexuality, the professor brings in homosexuals, bisexuals, transsexuals, and sexual offenders throughout the semester to speak about their experiences in a guest lecture.

Students also laud the faculty at Northwestern. Among the star-studded staff, Dale Mortenson, a Northwestern economics professor, won the Nobel Prize in 2010 for "analysis of markets with search frictions." Despite the accomplishments of the faculty, students find their professors generally accessible, saying that "if you want to meet up with them, just shoot them an email."

Dancing with Wildcats

Northwestern students, known affectionately as "wildcats," say that there are plenty of social opportunities, ranging from annual events like Dance Marathon to the standard Friday night at a fraternity. While the social component is what you make it, students say that most people they know are pretty socially engaged.

Much of the weekend revolves around the Greek scene, but the diverse student body finds equally diverse outlets for activity. One sophomore girl said that the party scene fits most people's interest and comfort level. "If that's what you're into, you won't have a problem finding parties and drinking, but if you don't want to drink, it's easy to find other things to do." Northwestern is an officially dry campus, so the drinking regulations are strict, but this doesn't stifle the partying as much as it shapes people's drinking habits. The dry campus rules "force people who want to drink, especially those underage, away from the public eye." But one freshman says that drinking is "not like a big problem. People are pretty responsible."

The typical going-out schedule consists of Monday night at the Keg of Evanston, Thursday at the Deuce (another bar), and Friday and Saturday mostly frat parties, though some motivated students organize trips into Chicago with friends.

The Greek scene is a strong presence. Rush is in January, and "boys have Sunday Night Dinners for all of fall quarter, but girls' contact with sororities begins with rush," according to one freshman girl.

The student body is hard to characterize simply; one junior said that "'educated' is the only real defining characteristic that fits." The students are generally friendly, a fact that a sophomore attributed to the school's location. "It is the Midwest, after all." Another student said, "I've been told that you can categorize all of Northwestern as 'closet nerds.'"

Nerdy as they may be, Northwestern students easily make friends. Dorm life, pre-orientation trips, extracurricular activities, and classes provide opportunities to get socially involved. "I know a lot of people who live in my dorm. My floor is like a family now," said one freshman.

While some students describe the population as pretty homogeneous, they acknowledge the presence of diversity as well. "It's pretty white bread, but they're trying to diversify," said one sophomore. According to one freshman, though, the campus is incredibly diverse. "I just remember walking down Sheridan Road and I heard conversation in four different languages in a ten minute walk. There are people coming from all across the world to this school."

Where Modern Meets Historic

Northwestern's campus is beautiful and quaint, displaying a variety of different architectural styles. Some buildings, such as Deering Library, are "typical ivy-covered Harry Potter-esque," while others "look like prisons." Nonetheless, Northwestern students love their campus and particularly its close proximity to both the city and nature. Bordering Lake Michigan and only an hour away from Chicago, students enjoy a combination of both scenic and city life. The Lakefill, a man-made pond by Lake Michigan, is a favorite campus spot for Northwestern students. As described by one junior, "being able to walk to the edge of the water and just sit for a while listening to the waves hit the rocks is a very nice luxury."

Campus dorm options include residential halls, which are generally larger and just a "regular dorm," or residential colleges, which generally "have a theme and a tighter knit community." Residential colleges—assigned based on academic interests, gender, or cultural ethnicity—require interested students to fill out an application, although the process is "not very intense." Incoming freshmen rank their top five housing options in the spring, while upperclassmen are assigned a priority number and choose their rooms on that basis. Dorms generally carry their own stereotypes: Jones attracts theater and performance majors, while Bobb appeals to hardcore partygoers. As one freshman put it, "Bobb is the rage dorm. If you want to come home drunk and throw the trash around, you should live in Bobb." The North-South divide also play into dorm stereotypes. "North campus dorms are more hard-partying, and filled with more athletes. South campus tends to be artsier, with theater and film kids," said one sophomore, who added that housing "is not like living in a luxury hotel, but it's pretty good, and being close to your classes is worth it when it's 10 degrees."

Northwestern has six dining halls which offer the same types of food but on different rotations. Although the food is described as "pretty good," one sophomore admits that it's "not out of this world," instead enjoying his favorite meals outside of campus. According to one freshman, "Evanston has many restaurants, coffee shops, and bars. It's a whole mecca of entertainment on food right outside campus," including Thai food, deep-dish pizza, and the always-popular Burger King.

Work Hard, Play Hard

Students at Northwestern are "involved to a fault" in campus extracurricular activities, ranging from traditional organizations such as Model United Nations and mock trial to more unconventional ones, including the Happiness Club and Dance Marathon Committee, which organizes the University's annual 30-hour dance competition for charity. Campus jobs are similarly popular, and qualifying students are eligible for the Work-Study Program, which guarantees underprivileged students a job on campus. Some of Northwestern's more unique jobs include making calls for the Phone-athon or driving for SafeRide, a shuttle service for students at night.

Organizations on campus advertise events and send messages to the student body by painting "The Rock," a large boulder that sits between University and Harris Hall on Northwestern's campus. Student groups interested in painting the boulder must guard it for 24 hours, from sunrise to early morning the next day. Painting "The Rock" is one of the biggest traditions on campus and, according to one sophomore, "there are even people that propose by painting The Rock." Other traditions include the Primal Scream, an annual event on the Sunday before finals when students "scream as loud[ly] as they can to let out their stress," and the "Wildcat growl," in which students make wildcat claws with their hands during football games and growl at the other team.

Northwestern's many traditions unify the student population and give them an enriching and memorable college experience. According to one sophomore, "I think what makes Northwestern different from other schools is that almost everyone at Northwestern is very smart, trying to save the world, double majoring with a minor, and involved in 30 different activities, but they're pretty down to earth about it." One freshman added that if given the chance to choose colleges again, not only would she choose Northwestern again, but she would also "probably apply early."—*Caroline Tan, John Stillman*

FYI
If you come to Northwestern, you'd better bring "a bike, a down comforter, and a purple scarf."
What is the typical weekend schedule? "Dinner at Elder, Party at The Keg, study all day Sunday."
If I could change one thing about Northwestern, I'd change the "library. It's a labyrinth, there are practically no windows, and it's an ugly cement block in the middle of campus. It's an uncomfortable place to study."
Three things every student at Northwestern should do before graduating are "skinny dip in Lake Michigan, get lost in the Technological Institute (one of the biggest academic buildings in the country!), and participate in the Primal Scream."

Principia College

Address: 1 Maybeck Place
Elsah, IL 62028
Phone: 618-374-5181
E-mail address:
enroll@prin.edu
Web site URL: www.prin.edu
Year Founded: 1898
Private or Public: Private
Religious Affiliation:
Christian Science
Location: Rural
Number of Applicants:
221
Percent Accepted: 87%
**Percent Accepted who
enroll:** 61%
Number Entering: 117
**Number of Transfers
Accepted each Year:**
Unreported
Middle 50% SAT range:
M: 500–620, CR:
510–650, Wr: Unreported
Middle 50% ACT range:
21–30
**Early admission program
EA/ED/None:** EA

**Percentage accepted
through EA or ED:**
Unreported
EA and ED deadline: 15-Nov
Regular Deadline: 1-Mar
Application Fee: $0
**Full time Undergraduate
enrollment:** 542
Total enrollment: 542
Percent Male: 48%
Percent Female: 52%
**Total Percent Minority or
Unreported:** 19%
Percent African-American:
1%
**Percent Asian/Pacific
Islander:** 1%
Percent Hispanic: 1%
Percent Native-American:
0%
Percent International: 13%
**Percent in-state/out of
state:** 12%/88%
Percent from Public HS: 61%
Retention Rate: 79%
Graduation Rate 4-year:
72%

Graduation Rate 6-year:
Unreported
**Percent Undergraduates in
On-campus housing:**
99%
**Number of official organized
extracurricular
organizations:** 29
3 Most popular majors:
Business, Fine Arts, Mass
Communication
Student/Faculty ratio: 8:1
Average Class Size:
Unreported
**Percent of students going to
grad school:** 27%
Tuition and Fees: $22,950
**In-State Tuition and Fees if
different:** No difference
Cost for Room and Board:
$8,730
**Percent receiving financial
aid out of those who apply,
first year:** Unreported
**Percent receiving financial
aid among all students:**
Unreported

As the only exclusively Christian Scientist college in the world, Principia College attracts followers of its faith from all over the globe. Located high above the bluffs in Elsah, Illinois, over the Mississippi River, the small liberal arts school affectionately known as Prin, is a small, tight-knit community dedicated to both academic excellence and devotion to the Christian Scientist faith.

An Academic Haven
Since Principia's founding in 1898, its academic mission has evolved, placing an increased emphasis on developing students' analytical thinking, problem solving and communication skills. In order to address the specific academic needs of freshmen, Principia instituted its First Year Experience (FYE) program in 1998. Upon arrival, each freshman enrolls in FYE, which consists of two or three courses to be taken during one's freshman year. Each program of courses has a unique theme and incorporates several

classes from different departments, and the variety of programs allows freshmen to choose a theme that appeals to their personal academic interests. After FYE, students choose from 32 majors and four minors, or they may design and petition for a special major not already offered by the school.

No matter what they major in, Prin students will have a hard time skipping class or dozing off during lectures. As one junior explained, "Most of the classes are 20 students or less, and attendance is a part of the grade in most classes." The upside is that the small classroom size and campus environment make professors very accessible. "Most of them list their home phone or cell phone numbers on the course syllabus," said one student.

Live by the Code
Outside the classroom, Principia students are held to an additional standard of integrity known as the honor code. The school's

honor code is based on the principles set forth by Mary Baker Eddy, the Discoverer and Founder of Christian Science, and by Mary Kimball Morgan, who founded Principia. While most secular liberal arts schools have some sort of general honor code loosely regulating the basics—i.e. no plagiarism and no stealing—Principia's code addresses its students' more personal and spiritual activities. It outlines specific requirements for social conduct, academic integrity and performance, financial integrity and spiritual reliance. In following the code, students agree to abstain from alcohol, tobacco, drugs and premarital sex, as well as rely exclusively on Christian Science for healing. Principia's administration finds that following these guidelines is vital in fulfilling Principia's original mission and keeping in line with the Christian Scientist faith. Enforcement of the code is taken very seriously.

Party, Prin Style
Do not be fooled by Principia's claim to be a "small" liberal arts college—its campus spans 2,500 acres. Since the nearest town is 20 minutes away, Prin has its own social committee that "provides a wide range of activities both on and off campus for the students and ways to get to them." Special events include live music courtesy of on- and off-campus bands, weekly movies screened on a large movie screen and regular parties hosted by dorms. In fact, there's so much going on at Prin that people often forget that the bustling city of St. Louis, with its restaurants, sports teams, and famous zoo, is a mere 40-minute drive from campus. Although students admit that "There is some drinking that goes on, both on campus and off," it's definitely against the code, and undergrads caught drinking can get suspended.

Feels Like Home
Nearly all students live on campus in one of 10 house-like residences, many of which were designed by the renowned architect Bernard Maybeck. In fact, Principia was designated a National Historic Landmark to honor Maybeck's exceptional architecture. All new freshmen live on campus in two dorms: Anderson House and Rackham Court. Each freshman dorm houses eight upperclassmen who serve as resident assistants (RAs). And the living ain't shabby. One Principia student even went so far as to say that ". . . Anderson House is enormous and beyond beautiful . . . we are all spoiled. I could

not have asked for a better place to live my first year in college."

> "I could not have asked for a better place to live my first year in college."

After freshman year, almost all students move to another house where they reside their sophomore, junior and senior years. Some students, referred to as non-traditional students, or "non-trads" (generally those students older than traditional college age), live in Hitchcock, one of three "cottages" designed by Maybeck, or in off-campus housing. Yet, most Prin students reside on campus and enjoy Maybeck's architecture and the campus's great facilities. All residences are equipped with computer labs, laundry rooms and kitchens—and there are Christian Science and academic study rooms available in each building that are open at all times. Students agreed that houses serve as smaller communities where people make friends and become involved in extracurricular activities. Each house has its own student government and board members who plan social functions, coordinate intramural athletics and lead student orientations. Aside from planning activities within the house, the board members coordinate annual campus-wide activities in each residence. Rackham House kicks off the first weekend of the fall with an annual toga party, and Ferguson has a popular haunted house during Halloween. Later in winter the Sylvester House holds an 80s dance in their rec room. Members of each residence come together each year to throw some fun co-house parties, and everyone on campus gets to enjoy activities planned by all of the other houses throughout the year, which, as one junior put it, is "not a bad deal!"

Get Involved!
The combination of Principia's small and motivated student body and the college's vast resources makes it a great place to cultivate leadership roles in extracurricular activities. In terms of sports, Principia is a Division III school and has 10 varsity sports teams for men and women, not to mention a variety of IMs. There are multiple opportunities to get involved in theater and musical groups as well, including the winter dance production and the spring play. Prin students can write for the campus newspaper, edit the yearbook, host a radio show on

Principia's FM-radio station (WTPC), or even help to coordinate the annual Public Affairs Conference (PAC), which tackles questions like, "Is Democracy the Global Solution?" Getting back to basics, the Christian Science Organization (CSO) offers undergraduates a chance to further the study of their common faith. In short, Principia offers a multitude of activities and opportunities for its students, while furthering its mission to instill in its students the values of the Christian Scientist Church.—*Suzanne Salgado*

FYI

If you come to Principia, you'd better bring "an open mind."

What's a typical weekend schedule? "Football, volleyball, or basketball game Saturday afternoon, a movie or trip into town Saturday night, church Sunday morning and homework Sunday afternoon."

If I could change one thing about Principia, I'd "change the strictness . . . Prin is fairly reasonable for why it has the rules it does, but some of them seem a bit ridiculous."

Three things everyone should do before graduating Principia are: "travel abroad, be part of a dance or theater production, and go to the City Museum with all your buds!"

Southern Illinois University / Carbondale

Address: Carbondale MC 4710, Carbondale, IL 62901-4512

Phone: 618-536-4405

E-mail address: admrec@siu.edu

Web site URL: www.siuc.edu

Year Founded: 1869

Private or Public: Public

Religious Affiliation: None

Location: Suburban

Number of Applicants: 11,785

Percent Accepted: 69%

Percent Accepted who enroll: 33%

Number Entering: 2,660

Number of Transfers Accepted each Year: 3,727

Middle 50% SAT range: M: 440–590, CR: 420–570, Wr: 410–520

Middle 50% ACT range: 19–24

Early admission program EA/ED/None: None

Percentage accepted through EA or ED: NA

EA and ED deadline: NA

Regular Deadline: Rolling

Application Fee: $30

Full time Undergraduate enrollment: 14,313

Total enrollment: 15,980

Percent Male: 43%

Percent Female: 57%

Total Percent Minority or Unreported: 32%

Percent African-American: 18%

Percent Asian/Pacific Islander: 2%

Percent Hispanic: 4%

Percent Native-American: <1%

Percent International: 2%

Percent in-state/out of state: 94%/6%

Percent from Public HS: Unreported

Retention Rate: Unreported

Graduation Rate 4-year: 46%

Graduation Rate 6-year: Unreported

Percent Undergraduates in On-campus housing: 30%

Number of official organized extracurricular organizations: 402

3 Most popular majors: Criminal Justice, Elementary Education, Trade and Industrial Teacher Education

Student/Faculty ratio: 16:1

Average Class Size: 14

Percent of students going to grad school: 58%

Tuition and Fees: $20,276

In-State Tuition and Fees if different: $9,813

Cost for Room and Board: $7,137

Percent receiving financial aid out of those who apply, first year: 78%

Percent receiving financial aid among all students: 81%

Southern Illinois University at Carbondale, among its claims to fame, boasts one of the most unusual mascots of any American university—the Saluki, an Egyptian hunting dog. The connection between the Saluki and SIU (originally a small teacher's college founded in 1869 with a mere 143 students enrolled) remains mysterious. Nevertheless, Salukis take pride in their mascot and love their school, which has grown from humble beginnings into one of the largest and most affordable universities in the country—not to mention one of the most famous party schools in the Midwest.

Southern Illinois, Southern Hospitality

Approximately three-fourths of SIU students come from Illinois, and as many students explained, there is a common misconception that all Salukis are just "southern Illinois hicks." But despite an apparent lack of geographic diversity, the student body is composed of individuals with a variety of backgrounds and interests. One student noted, "There are students here of all ages, varying from the traditional fresh-out-of-high school student to the parent of three trying to get a better job. People here come from all different backgrounds and tend to mesh together very well." The large number of students at SIU makes it easy to make friends. "There are all sorts of opportunities to meet people," explained one student. "For the most part, everyone on campus is friendly. Whether you meet them in class or out at the bars, chances are you'll be friends on Facebook before the day is over."

Home Sweet Home

With such a large student body, SIU provides four main undergraduate housing areas: University Park, Brush Towers, Thompson Point, and University Hall. Each housing area has its own laundry facility and dining hall. Students are only required to live on campus during their freshman year. Salukis typically describe the on-campus housing as "pretty nice . . . besides the cinder block walls." University Park has the smallest rooms, but is located in a picturesque, wooded part of campus. Students who live in Brush Towers enjoy it particularly because of its private bathrooms and small, suite-shared kitchenettes, but some say that it can be chaotic living in a large complex of apartment-like towers. Thompson Point, said to be the "prettiest," is located on nearby Thompson Lake. University Hall is a bit farther away from the other three, but it offers the same amenities. All of the residential facilities have RAs. Students say that usually RAs are easy to talk to and helpful with problems, although some can reportedly be strict disciplinary figures. Most ju-

niors and seniors at SIU choose to live off campus, which is where most of the famed SIU partying takes place.

There are three meal plans to choose from at SIU, and they can be used at any of the four on-campus dining halls. The meal plan is based on a points system, and any unused points at the end of the week can be used to purchase snacks and other food and drink items from the on-campus market. Unfortunately, despite the variety of options offered by the meal plan, the food at SIU is not something students brag about. Descriptions of SIU food ranged from "It is disgusting" to "It sucks!" Luckily, there are many restaurants near campus. Some student favorites are Buffalo Wild Wings, Applebees, Lonestar Steakhouse and Quatros.

Work Hard . . .

As such a large research university, plenty of academic opportunities abound at SIU. And most Salukis agree that having a variety of resources allows them lots of opportunity for hands-on work, whether on a farm for agricultural studies majors or in a broadcast station for radio and TV majors. The University has a core liberal arts curriculum that must be completed by all students before graduation. Although core classes tend to be the largest, students say that even the professors in the big lecture classes are accessible, and there are plenty of opportunities to take small classes or seminars. SIU students' general opinion with regard to the University's professors is that they are relatively easy. As one student said, "The grading scale varies from teacher to teacher, but is generally pretty lenient." Another added, "All of my professors are really easy."

> "For the most part, everyone on campus is friendly. Whether you meet them in class or out at the bars, chances are you'll be friends on Facebook before the day is over."

In terms of majors, different ones require different workloads. In particular, science classes like engineering and aviation prove to be especially challenging. The most popular major at SIU is Criminal Justice, followed by Elementary Education and Teaching and Trade and Industrial Teacher Education.

Students are asked to declare a major when they are admitted to SIU, but if they are unsure of what they want to do, they are admitted to the pre-major program with a pre-major advisor. Salukis in the pre-major program must declare a major before the end of their sophomore year.

Most students at SIU are satisfied with their overall academic experience and try to take advantage of the University's resources. "Academically we are a great school," one sophomore assured. "Departments and professors provide very hands-on learning and are willing to work with students to see that we all succeed."

. . . Play Hard

Not only is it easy to make friends at SIU, but Salukis agree that it is easy to have a good time. SIU lives up to its reputation as being a party school, but many students say that the stereotype is blown way out of proportion. One male student explained that "Underage drinking is definitely an issue here, but just as it is everywhere else." Most students agree that the drinking at SIU seems about comparable to that of any other state school, but admit that the social scene does revolve around alcohol. People go out Wednesday through Saturday nights, but "There is a party somewhere every night if you want one." Bars on "the strip" in Carbondale are popular, and although the legal drinking age is 21, it is not hard to obtain drinks if you're underage. Furthermore, the SIU administration is relatively easygoing about alcohol monitoring. They "try to look the other way," one student explained.

Saluki Spirit

Without doubt, SIU students are definitely proud of their Division I sports teams. Among the plethora of varsity sports, football and basketball are among the most popular. Students say that club sports are competitive—especially softball—but that they're all fun to play. SIU boasts a large Rec Center where Salukis can enjoy basketball and racquetball courts, as well as an Olympic-sized swimming pool. The Rec Center also rents out sports equipment and camping supplies to students. Non-athletes will be glad to know that there are about 400 clubs and RSOs (Registered Student Organizations) on campus. Students say the most popular RSO is "definitely the skydiving club." For some fun closer to the ground, The Student Programming Committee plans student events like dances, concerts, and movies. Greek life at SIU is relatively small, with seven sororities and 20 fraternities. Some students complain that "People here do not really understand [Greek life] because it is so small" while others say that they enjoy the minimal Greek presence on campus. Whatever their preference, Salukis can always find an organization to join during their time at SIU.

Most Salukis say they feel relatively safe on campus and very welcomed by the residents of Carbondale. Many hail Carbondale as "the perfect college town." The majority of students live on campus and do not have cars, but a lack of wheels doesn't prevent Salukis from taking advantage of a vast amount of resources and Carbondale's collegiate charm. Salukis just know how to have fun while keeping busy.—*Becky Bicks*

FYI

If you come to SIU, you'd better bring: "clothes for all seasons—the weather changes every five minutes."

What's the typical weekend schedule? "Sleeping in, drinking at night, and working on homework."

If I could change one thing about SIU, I'd "improve the parking policy and build another lot or two without unfair regulations."

Three things every Southern student should do before graduating are "join an RSO, go to Saluki football and basketball games, and have LOTS and LOTS of fun."

University of Chicago

Address: 1101 E 58th Street, Rosenwald Hall Suite 105 Chicago, IL 60637
Phone: 773-702-8650
E-mail address: collegeadmissions@ uchicago.edu
Web site URL: www.uchicago.edu
Year Founded: 1891
Private or Public: Private
Religious Affiliation: None
Location: Urban
Number of Applicants: 13,564
Percent Accepted: 27%
Percent Accepted who enroll: 36%
Number Entering: 1,335
Number of Transfers Accepted each Year: 54
Middle 50% SAT range: M: 730, CR: 735, Wr: 715
Middle 50% ACT range: 30
Early admission program EA/ED/None: EA

Percentage accepted through EA or ED: 30%
EA and ED deadline: 1-Nov
Regular Deadline: 2-Jan
Application Fee: $65
Full time Undergraduate enrollment: 5,066
Total enrollment: 12,332
Percent Male: 51%
Percent Female: 49%
Total Percent Minority or Unreported: 30%
Percent African-American: 6%
Percent Asian/Pacific Islander: 15%
Percent Hispanic: 9%
Percent Native-American: 0%
Percent International: 9%
Percent in-state/out of state: 18%/82%
Percent from Public HS: 64%
Retention Rate: 98%
Graduation Rate 4-year: 85%

Graduation Rate 6-year: 91%
Percent Undergraduates in On-campus housing: 56%
Number of official organized extracurricular organizations: 300
3 Most popular majors: Economics, Political Science, Biological Science
Student/Faculty ratio: 6:1
Average Class Size: 15
Percent of students going to grad school: 20%
Tuition and Fees: $38,550
In-State Tuition and Fees if different: No difference
Cost for Room and Board: $11,697
Percent receiving financial aid out of those who apply, first year: Unreported
Percent receiving financial aid among all students: Unreported

---

T he University of Chicago is the kind of school that embraces its "nerdy" population and revels in creating enjoyable events that mirror the quirkiness of its students. Their annual scavenger hunt has been the basis of two documentaries and has prompted the arrival of CIA agents looking for the creators of a breeder reactor, all far more exciting than a game of beer pong at a frat.

Not "The Place Where Fun Comes to Die"

As the saying goes, "you can't spell UChicago without 'Chicago.'" Located in Hyde Park, the University is a short ride on the El from the city. While the area surrounding the school is not entirely student-friendly, security efforts put the population at ease, and students quickly learn how to act in a safe manner. The average student travels to the city a few times a month, providing a nice escape from the intense academic life on campus. Chicago is recognized as the improv capital of the world, and is home to nu-

merous jazz clubs and bars. In short, it's a cleaner version of New York, but with worse bagels.

While the city gives students great options in terms of weekend plans, most undergrads choose to remain on campus, favoring social functions and the occasional frat party. A junior tour guide stated, "I came to U of C because I wanted to go to the nerdiest school possible, while having an average social life." Some students would like to think that there is a standard "face of UChicago," but there are sharp divisions among the undergrads that make it impossible to stereotype it as a geek school. One student said, "The school doesn't have a social identity in an explicit sense; I'd be tentative in even saying that everybody is going to be smart." There are plenty of jocks and "bros" mixed in with future Noble Laureates and library junkies. As one undergrad put it, "There really are no unifying social factors."

In terms of admissions, undergrads credit high acceptance rates to self-selection among high school seniors and ill-advised guidance counselors. One student stated, "I know dozens of people from my high school who would have applied had it not been for 'that crazy application.'" In order to avoid scaring away applicants, UChicago switched to the Common App from the quirky "Uncommon App" to increase the number of applicants. A visit to UChicago will often provide potential applicants with a better understanding of what the school has to offer, indicating that it is not "the place where fun comes to die." Any obstacle to class diversity may be a result of the University's efforts to not reject an applicant based on "type."

Get 'er Done

UChicago is not recognized for its gorgeous students. In fact, some characterize it as the place "Where the squirrels are more attractive than the girls, and more aggressive than the guys." In UChicago students' defense, it's hard to look good and effuse machismo when classes cover a semester's worth of work in a rapid 10 weeks. Students quickly become accustomed to the massive workload, and subsequently struggle to understand how some college students "don't actually do their work." With easy access to "remarkable award-winning professors" it is no surprise that students are very academically motivated. One student remarked, "All courses have a learning-for-the-sake-of-learning twist."

> **"The squirrels are more attractive than the girls, and more aggressive than the guys."**

The professors are not only accomplished (winning Pulitzer Prizes, MacArthur Fellowships, and everything in between), but accessible and uncharacteristically inviting. It is not uncommon for professors to hold wine and cheese office hours, or take time out of their home schedules to accommodate a student. Courses taught by TAs are few in number and well advertised so as not to provide any surprises. This is not to say that the TAs are not qualified teachers, as one student remarked that "some of the most interesting courses" she had taken were taught by graduate students.

UChicago's Common Core is mandatory for all students, and is meant to instill a liberal arts education within the framework of a large research institution. The core requires students to take courses on every-

thing from the humanities and civilization studies to physical education. While this may seem like a controlling environment, students remark that if given the choice they would still opt to take core classes. Although humanities-oriented students may dread the mathematics requirement, and mathletes may fear the humanities requirement, the variety of core courses ensures that the stereotypical "black-sweatered cigarette-smoking jazz enthusiast" won't have to struggle through a semester of multivariable calculus. This is not to say that the core is easy; in fact, some students have expressed the desire to have a pass/fail "get out of jail free card" protecting GPAs from the inevitable "disastrous core class." The core provides every student with a solid foundation for upper-level classes, with the necessary "reading and analytical skills" for brilliant class discussions.

Economics and biology remain the two most popular majors amongst UChicago students. The Economics department is regarded as the "best in the nation," featuring multiple Nobel Laureates (including Gary Becker and Robert Fogel), and Steven Levitt, the brains behind *New York Times*–bestseller *Freakonomics*. There is an extensive variety of majors offered, including non-degree programs such as the popular Human Rights program. Staying true to its liberal arts foundation, the U of C steers clear of most preprofessional majors, including engineering.

Living in Chi-Town

UChicago has 10 different residence halls, ranging from brand-new orange buildings, to converted luxury hotels of the past. Two residence halls, Blackstone and Stony Island, are strictly for upperclassmen and transfers, and feature such amenities as computer rooms and solariums. Other than Blackstone and Stony Island, residence halls are not separated by year. Each residence hall is broken down into anywhere from one to eight "houses." There are 35 houses in total, with the average house size being 70 students. Each house has one or more Resident Heads, who work as counselors to students, while coordinating social events and forming intramural teams for sports like broomball and inner-tube water polo.

The house system puts help with math problem sets and essay editing within an arm's reach. Students will usually eat dinner, watch movies, talk politics and have small in-suite parties with fellow house members.

Some are known for wacky traditions and small singles, while others are known for their prowess in intramurals marked by the assumption of the Maroon Cup. Max Palevsky, home to eight houses, is the newest residence hall and is regarded for its proximity to everything good, including "the Regenstein library, the academic quad, and recreation and music rooms." Given that Max-P is so new, it features great amenities such as air-conditioning and a meal plan with Bartlett commons, otherwise known as the best of the three campus dining halls. In fall of 2009, the University unveiled its new South Campus Residence Hall and Dining Commons which added eight additional houses and is home to 811 residents. Regardless of accommodations, most students develop a great deal of house pride, and form bitter rivalries with other houses: "People in May House struggle to even talk with those in Alper." The only noted flaw with the house system is that students are not guaranteed that they will remain in their freshman house. For this reason, many students end up moving off campus with former housemates.

UChicago students meet their future housemates at O-Week (Orientation week). The U of C structures O-Week in a manner that encourages in-house mingling, as housemates are forced to eat together and talk about controversial matters regarding college students. The only events that students seem to find more enjoyable are the Polar Bear run, Shake Day and the infamous Scavenger Hunt. One sophomore remarked that his most memorable UChicago night involved "Dean of Admissions Ted O'Neil wearing his 'I admitted your mom last night' T-shirt and posting it on YouTube for [Scavenger Hunt] points."

Campus food is regarded as anywhere from "passable" to "better than my mom's cooking." The dining halls are organized in stations where students have a variety of choices charting all different types of cuisine. No matter the time, there is always a place where students can use their dining points. Students often turn to the Reynolds Club in place of a formal student union. The club is home to several eateries and shops, and serves as the headquarters for multiple organizations, including the radio station and weekly news. Even if students get tired of events and food on campus, there is a variety of great restaurants and entertainment venues in Hyde Park and downtown.

Dead Greek and Sports Life

Intercollegiate sports are not viewed as very important at UChicago, to say the least. One student remarked, "Apparently one of our teams is pretty good. I don't know which one though." An upperclassman remarked, "I don't even know where the fields are." The blatant disconnect between the athletes and the academic majority is not necessarily detrimental to the school population. The athletes still manage to find a good social scene, either by joining frats or going to bars, while other students manage to find good athletics through intramural sports. In addition to the number of male students who join frats, there are a slew of females who decide to join the two sororities on campus. Similar to their knowledge of sporting facilities, a lot of students have no idea where the fraternities are. One freshman noted, "I only know where the frats are because they're so close to my dorm."

More or less, UChicago provides an option for every type of person. Not everyone who attends is a turtleneck-wearing bookworm. The best description of UChicago lies not in its stereotypical nerdy student, but in its reputation as a great liberal arts college within a massive research university, a short train ride away from downtown Chicago. With a plethora of Nobel Laureates on staff, the "best economics department in the country," and the nation's best scavenger hunt, the school is worth any hardworking student's consideration.—*Zachary Fuhrer*

FYI
If you come to UChicago, you'd better bring "a laptop. Campus is incredibly wired."
What's the typical weekend schedule? "Go out Thursday night . . . don't remember anything else. Study sometime. (That's a joke.)"
If I could change one thing about UChicago I would "allow students to take one core course pass/fail."
Three things every student should do before graduating are "scare first-years about classes, play intramural broomball and hook up in the Regenstein Library."

University of Illinois / Chicago

Address: Box 5220 m/c 018, Chicago, IL 60680-5220
Phone: 312-996-4350
E-mail address: uicadmit@uic.edu
Web site URL: www.uic.edu
Year Founded: 1965
Private or Public: Public
Religious Affiliation: None
Location: Urban
Number of Applicants: 13,595
Percent Accepted: 64%
Percent Accepted who enroll: 38%
Number Entering: 3,272
Number of Transfers Accepted each Year: 2,686
Middle 50% SAT range: Unreported
Middle 50% ACT range: 21–26
Early admission program EA/ED/None: None

Percentage accepted through EA or ED: NA
EA and ED deadline: NA
Regular Deadline: 15-Jan
Application Fee: $40
Full time Undergraduate enrollment: 15,672
Total enrollment: 23,390
Percent Male: 48%
Percent Female: 52%
Total Percent Minority or Unreported: 55%
Percent African-American: 9%
Percent Asian/Pacific Islander: 23%
Percent Hispanic: 16%
Percent Native-American: <1%
Percent International: 2%
Percent in-state/out of state: 98%/2%
Percent from Public HS: Unreported
Retention Rate: 79%

Graduation Rate 4-year: 20%
Graduation Rate 6-year: 46%
Percent Undergraduates in On-campus housing: 47%
Number of official organized extracurricular organizations: 348
3 Most popular majors: Biology, Business, Psychology
Student/Faculty ratio: 16:1
Average Class Size: 25
Percent of students going to grad school: 33%
Tuition and Fees: $24,100
In-State Tuition and Fees if different: $11,710
Cost for Room and Board: $8,774
Percent receiving financial aid out of those who apply, first year: 57%
Percent receiving financial aid among all students: 74%

Founded in 1965, the University of Illinois at Chicago (UIC) is one of the youngest campuses in the Illinois public university system. Located in one of America's most vibrant metropolitan areas, UIC is known for its strong ties with the city and energetic atmosphere. If you dream of going to a school in the middle of a large city filled with extracurricular distractions, you should definitely consider UIC as a potential college choice.

The Blessing of Chicago

All students live on or near the two UIC campuses (East and South) in the heart of a city known to some as one of the premier business, cultural, and entertainment centers of America. "The great thing about UIC is that you are so close to the city," explained one student. Although the school itself offers a relatively quiet learning environment, its prime location offers plenty of activities just outside the confines of its walls. Despite the fact that there are few activities organized by the University during the weekends, it is obvious that UIC students are never bored.

Since UIC has one of the lowest tuition costs amongst four-year universities, students can afford to spend more money than many other college students in the country on recreational activities.

UIC and Chicago are closely connected. UIC students frequent the countless eateries, stores, theaters, bars, and malls around the campus, while many residents of the city visit the campus to, as one student put it, "take a tour and experience the college life." On the downside, being so close to the city also means greater exposure to the city's crime, making student safety a concern.

Understated Academia

Of all the University of Illinois schools, the campus at Chicago is one of the most unknown. However, this lack of reputation does not mean the school offers little in terms of academics. "Despite what other people say, people come here to study," said one senior.

One strong feature of UIC is its science departments. "Our science departments are very hard. Classes are generally very competitive," said another student. The humanities and social science classes are also known for their rigor. Most students agree that UIC has excellent faculty in a variety of fields. Classes are based on semester hours. Most classes are four hours per week, and the students need 120 semester hours to graduate; therefore, people generally take four to five classes per semester.

"The great thing about UIC is that you are so close to the city."

One of the distinctive elements of UIC is that it has graduation requirements in almost all subjects offered in the school in order to help students "achieve a more rounded education." There are requirements in the humanities, the natural sciences, and the social sciences. There is also an English composition requirement and one in cultural diversity that allows students to "study the culture, social and political institutions, and value systems of social groups, regions, or nations different from those present in the dominant American culture." Students are also required to take a few of the many seminar courses offered in a variety of disciplines to supplement the large lecture courses that make up the bulk of their schedules.

The students at UIC choose their majors among the 75 different bachelor's degrees ranging from Movement Science to Social Work. Among the popular majors at UIC are business management, engineering, and psychology. Students can also make their own major if they can justify having their own course of study with faculty approval and supervision.

UIC students describe the course load as challenging. According to one student, "UIC has one of the largest work loads for any class whether it be sciences, social sciences, humanities, etc. All areas are challenging and UIC encourages their students to try them all."

Living in the City
It is often very difficult for UIC students to connect with their professors because of UIC's tendency to have mainly large lecture classes. The average class size of 25 is misleading because the classes tend to be extremely large or extremely small, and it is often very difficult to get into the tiny seminars. "The only professor I actually got to know in person led my psychology seminar. I don't think my other professors even know my name," one female student complained. Even though most professors have office hours, some students still complain about the lack of opportunities to interact with professors.

The majority of UIC students don't live in dorms; 75 percent of the students live in the greater Chicago area and commute to class every day from home or from off-campus apartments. In the recent years, however, the administration has worked to expand their campus and to decrease the number of commuters. As of the end of the South Campus expansion, 3,800 students, including over half of all freshmen, live in one of UIC's 10 residential halls. Those students who do live on campus describe their housing as being more like apartments than the typical idea of a dorm. Since many students immediately leave campus after class and Chicago is so dynamic, on-campus activities are limited. Fraternities and sororities do not have a heavy influence on the social scene. Instead, students prefer to party off campus in Chicago's bars and clubs. One student remarked, "Going to parties is a chance to mingle with the locals and students from other colleges in the area." Many reported that some bars and clubs are lenient about letting in underage students, making alcohol an important factor in UIC social life.

UIC is a diverse college. Minorities combined to make up more than half of the college population, with 30 percent of the total population being non-native speakers of English. Also, 52 percent of the UIC population is female—a dynamic unique from other University of Illinois campuses.

Overall, students have a good opinion about their school. UIC students love their city and their fellow students, and are for the most part satisfied with the education they are receiving.—*Xiaochen Su*

FYI
If you come to UIC, you'd better bring "wind-resistant clothing."
What is the typical weekend schedule? "Go shopping and party at clubs in the city."
If I could change one thing about UIC, I'd "lower the noise level around campus."
Three things every student at UIC should do before graduating are "go to downtown Chicago, go watch a White Sox or Cubs baseball game, and take a few seminar classes."

University of Illinois / Urbana-Champaign

Address: 901 West Illinois Street, Urbana, IL 61801
Phone: 217-333-0302
E-mail address: admissions@illinois.edu
Web site URL: www.illinois.edu
Year Founded: 1867
Private or Public: Public
Religious Affiliation: None
Location: Suburban
Number of Applicants: 21,645
Percent Accepted: 71%
Percent Accepted who enroll: 45%
Number Entering: 6,948
Number of Transfers Accepted each Year: 1,148
Middle 50% SAT range: M: 630–740, CR: 540–670, Wr: Unreported
Middle 50% ACT range: 26–31
Early admission program EA/ED/None: EA

Percentage accepted through EA or ED: Unreported
EA and ED deadline: 10-Nov
Regular Deadline: 2-Jan
Application Fee: $40
Full time Undergraduate enrollment: 30,895
Total enrollment: 41,316
Percent Male: 54%
Percent Female: 46%
Total Percent Minority or Unreported: 34%
Percent African-American: 7%
Percent Asian/Pacific Islander: 13%
Percent Hispanic: 7%
Percent Native-American: <1%
Percent International: 6%
Percent in-state/out of state: 93%/7%
Percent from Public HS: 75%
Retention Rate: 93%
Graduation Rate 4-year: 62%

Graduation Rate 6-year: 80%
Percent Undergraduates in On-campus housing: 99%
Number of official organized extracurricular organizations: 1000
3 Most popular majors: Cell and Molecular Biology, Political Science and Government, Psychology
Student/Faculty ratio: 17:1
Average Class Size: 25
Percent of students going to grad school: 26%
Tuition and Fees: $26,024
In-State Tuition and Fees if different: $12,240
Cost for Room and Board: $8,764
Percent receiving financial aid out of those who apply, first year: 42%
Percent receiving financial aid among all students: 65%

L ocated between two small towns in southern Illinois, the University of Illinois at Urbana-Champaign offers the quintessential large university experience. Known for its excellent academics, Illinois is also home to a dominant sports culture, abundant Greek life, and a lively campus atmosphere.

United by a passion for learning.

Students at Illinois are divided into different academic colleges from the time of application, each with its own set of graduation requirements. Illinois' engineering programs are world-renowned and not surprisingly, classes in mathematics and the sciences are supposed to be much more demanding. "Humanities is considered easier," one engineering student said. "Students who are in my math and science classes sometimes joke about switching into some random humanities major when it gets really hard." Students also note that few science classes are curved, and those that are sometimes de-

flate grades rather than ease the coursework. Nonetheless, students at Illinois are motivated about learning and appreciate the opportunities granted by a strong engineering school despite the increased workload. Another engineering student praised the research being conducted by his professors. "The progress being made in engineering, physics, and math is something that really sets Illinois apart," a sophomore engineering major said. Moreover, the enthusiasm that attracts applicants to a competitive school like Illinois leads them to appreciate the passion of their classmates. Students are known for helping each other, often studying in groups and working on homework assignments together. "I love my engineering classes because I've met so many people as interested as I am in studying and learning," said one freshman.

The love of learning unites students at Illinois across the academic schools. Each college selects James Scholars for an honor program based on grades and test scores. Along with several other honors programs that recognize applicants for different sets of academic criteria, this distinction allows students to have an earlier selection of classes and gives them the opportunity to work on special projects or participate in smaller seminars. Illinois also offers "discovery courses," for freshmen, which are really small and feature close interaction with a professor. One freshman said, "I took a course called Science and Pseudoscience. It was surprisingly interesting and the small class size made it a lot easier to get to know the professor." For the most part, however, classes at Illinois are relatively large and impersonal. Several students remarked that the lack of student-teacher interaction was their least favorite discovery about Illinois. One freshman complained, "Sometimes you just feel like a number in your classes." Regardless, Illinois offers classes on all sides of the spectrum, with an outstanding engineering program and numerous and varied opportunities to excel in the humanities and social sciences.

Fighting Illini.

Students at the University of Illinois at Urbana-Champaign almost universally agree that varsity athletics have an incredibly notable presence on campus. The teams are competitive, especially the basketball team. "Football and basketball season are huge here," one student said. "Everyone watches or goes to the games, and there is definitely a lot of school pride for our sports teams." School pride organizations are popular, giving devoted fans a channel for organized spirit. Intramurals are also popular. According to one student, "There is a giant intramural sports program that is run through the university. Some, like flag football, are even extremely competitive." Even students not involved in sports have the luxury of incredibly nice athletic facilities, which many take advantage of. "The fitness centers are busy literally all hours of the day," one student remarked. "They offer really cool workout and dance classes too." More whimsical Illini even participate in quasi-athletic activities like "Falling Illini," the skydiving club, and broomball, a sport invented by college students.

Due to its large size, Illinois offers countless extracurricular activities beyond sports as well. The passion held by students for their pursuits outside the classroom is fervent, and this has led to the large number and prevalence of student organizations. "Everyone I know is really committed to their activities," one student said. "Even if it takes a lot of work it's worth it because people are usually able to find some extracurricular they really care about." Ethnic clubs are popular, as is the campus newspaper, the *Daily Illini*. Generally, Illinois students show the same devotion out of the classroom as they do in their academics, both on and off the field.

Got Greek?

Illinois is known for its dominant fraternity and sorority culture. "It's basically the biggest Greek scene in the country," one junior noted. Weekend social life is filled with frat parties, and many people move off campus to live in the houses of their fraternity or sorority after freshman year. Regardless of participation in frat culture, drinking is commonplace at Illinois. Alcohol is technically not allowed in the dorms, one of the reasons for Greek life's popularity, but students, especially freshmen, still seem to drink in the dorms. The commercial area of town also boasts a variety of bars, which are popular hang-outs for students, often with certain bars serving as "haunts" for various social circles. "I love going to bars here because they admit anyone over nineteen even if they can't drink," one underage student said. "I like being able to go dance and chill with my friends without alcohol being an issue."

> **"I've met so many people as interested as I am in studying and learning."**

Though it may not be a popular choice at Illinois, many students still choose to abstain from alcohol. Freshmen have the option of living in Snyder, a substance-free dormitory. While all the dorms at Illinois discourage alcohol usage, students who live in Snyder have a mutual understanding to respect the choices of their peers. "I like having the option to go out and party if I want to, but not having to live with it all the time," one freshman living in Snyder said. "It's nice having the choice."

Snyder is one of many dorms at Illinois that have a theme, explicit or implicit. The "six pack," a group of dorms, is known as the home of partiers, while other dorms are known for embracing foreigners. Engineering students tend to cluster in dorms closer to their academic buildings due to the large size of campus, leading to a somewhat polarized living dynamic. This doesn't last long, however, as most people move off campus sophomore or junior year. "The off-campus housing here is great because it can be just as cheap as the better on-campus housing and you don't have to deal with strict RAs or sticking to the meal plan," said a senior.

At the end of the day, Illinois students have active social lives despite their commitment to academic excellence, lending itself to well-rounded students and a balanced environment. The incredibly strong engineering program, combined with honors options in the humanities, provides students with a world-class education—on the budget of a public university. If you think living in a town with thousands of other college students sounds like a good time and don't mind putting in the hard work, the University of Illinois at Urbana-Champaign may be the place for you to spend your next four years.—*Natasha Thondavadi*

FYI

Before graduating everyone should "go to an Illinois basketball game and take a nap in the student union."

If I could change one thing about Illinois "I'd make it easier to get around campus."

The biggest college tradition at Illinois is "the Oskee Wow Wow song."

Wheaton College

Address: 501 College Avenue, Wheaton, IL 60187

Phone: 800-222-2419

E-mail address: admissions@wheaton.edu

Web site URL: www.wheaton .edu

Year Founded: 1860

Private or Public: Private

Religious Affiliation: Interdenominational Christian

Location: Suburban

Number of Applicants: 2,083

Percent Accepted: 62%

Percent Accepted who enroll: 45%

Number Entering: 581

Number of Transfers Accepted each Year: 102

Middle 50% SAT range: M: 610–690, CR: 600–700, Wr: 600–719

Middle 50% ACT range: 27–31

Early admission program EA/ED/None: EA

Percentage accepted through EA or ED: 48%

EA and ED deadline: 1-Nov

Regular Deadline: 10-Jan

Application Fee: $50

Full time Undergraduate enrollment: 2,365

Total enrollment: 2,915

Percent Male: 49%

Percent Female: 51%

Total Percent Minority or Unreported: 18%

Percent African-American: 9%

Percent Asian/Pacific Islander: 3%

Percent Hispanic: 3%

Percent Native-American: <1%

Percent International: 1%

Percent in-state/out of state: 22%/78%

Percent from Public HS: 61%

Retention Rate: 94%

Graduation Rate 4-year: 77%

Graduation Rate 6-year: 84%

Percent Undergraduates in On-campus housing: 95%

Number of official organized extracurricular organizations: 75

3 Most popular majors: Economics, English, Psychology

Student/Faculty ratio: 12:1

Average Class Size: 15

Percent of students going to grad school: 34%

Tuition and Fees: $22,540

In-State Tuition and Fees if different: No difference

Cost for Room and Board: $7,040

Percent receiving financial aid out of those who apply, first year: 69%

Percent receiving financial aid among all students: 67%

Wheaton College isn't just another small liberal arts college with a picturesque campus, excellent professors and rather unsuccessful sports teams: it is above all a Christian college. Students come to Wheaton hoping for something more than a degree in music or mathematics. They seek knowledge of "how to better serve God." Wheaton students also point to the strong sense of community on campus as something that sets Wheaton apart.

Integrating Faith and Learning

Students say classes at Wheaton are very challenging but manageable. Science majors are known to be particularly difficult, but students say there are challenging classes in almost every department. "There isn't an honors program—I think if there was everyone would be in it," said one freshman. Students say Wheaton seems to attract perfectionists, leading to a somewhat competitive atmosphere at times.

> "There isn't an honors program—I think if there was everyone would be in it."

Like most students at liberal arts colleges, students at Wheaton are required to fulfill general education requirements with courses in subjects such as English literature, history and natural sciences. More unique to Wheaton are the numerous requirements in theological and biblical studies. All students take a course on both the Old and New Testament as well as courses on Christian thought and culture.

Academic standards are high at Wheaton, "but professors are very helpful and focused on teaching," according to one sophomore. Wheaton encourages close relationships with professors through its "Dine with a Mind" program. Students are given five meal cards to pay for a professor's meal in the dining hall. It's a chance to continue a discussion from class, ask for spiritual guidance, or see pictures of their grandkids–or maybe all three. Students say that Wheaton professors are religious as well as academic guides. Wheaton's commitment to Christian education means that every class, not just the ones in the Theology department, is based in a Christian worldview.

Another important component of Wheaton academics is its music program. Calling someone at Wheaton a 'Conservie' isn't a comment about their political views—it's a nickname for students in the Conservatory of Music. The Conservatory offers six different majors, including performance, music education and music and ministry. While one Conservatory student said at times it feels like there is "a Conservie bubble," Conservatory students are still integrated with the rest of the college, living in the same housing and mixing with other students in general education classes.

Living by the Covenant

Asked about drugs and drinking on campus, a freshman said that for the most part, "it's just not there." All students sign a Community Covenant, pledging not to use alcohol or drugs while they are at Wheaton and they stick to their word. Most students who choose Wheaton are fully aware that it's far from a party school. For some, it's an attraction. "It's nice not to have the pressure," said one sophomore. Students say there is a very small percentage of students who break the rules, known as the Wheaton Underground, but most students have very little contact with this group unless they try to seek them out.

Wheaties still love to have fun. The College Union organizes various parties, a popular Talent Show, and live music nights. Dorm floors and on-campus houses host theme parties. Ever since a ban on social dancing was lifted in 2003, there have been several college sponsored dances every year. And for those who feel a little suffocated by the small campus, Chicago is less than an hour away by train. Most students stay on campus during the weekends. Freshmen are not allowed to have cars on campus, though many upperclassman have them.

Most Wheaton students seem satisfied by housing, and nearly all students live on-campus. On-campus housing options include four residence halls, as well as 13 college-owned houses and several college-owned apartment complexes. Freshman will meet many of their first college friends on their floors. Floors are single-sex, but each floor has a brother or sister floor, and "bro-sis" get-togethers are popular. Fischer, a co-ed dorm for freshmen and sophomores, is considered the most social on campus, while Traber is "the jock dorm," according to one freshman. Upperclassmen tend to try for the campus-owned apartments and avoid Saint and Elliot apartments.

In underclassmen dorms, members of the opposite sex can only visit each other's floors during a few hours two days per week, or during special "open hours." Guys and girls are free to hang out together in dorm lounges and lobbies, and in most dorms students can be found in the lobby at almost any time. "Lobby couples" take advantage of these spaces by spending all their free time there "being obnoxiously couple-y," said one student, but generally lobbies are fun places to socialize or study together. The regulations for upperclassmen are less strict, though overnight visits are still technically forbidden.

These strict regulations on how guys and girls interact, along with a gossipy small campus atmosphere and student attitudes towards dating can make casual dating a little difficult, though students say it improves over time. There are plenty of single people on campus who want to date, but guys are hesitant to ask girls on dates. In a place where seniors worry about having a "ring by spring," an invitation to a movie is seen as the first step towards a marriage proposal. As a result, most relationships at Wheaton are serious relationships, even though many students say they would like to see more casual dating.

Proud to be a Wheatie

Wheaton students have school pride: "you see about 20 Wheaton t-shirts in a row," said one freshman. This pride shows when Wheaties turn out to support football and soccer teams, which do well in Division III competition. Intramural sports are also very popular, with opportunities for fairly intense competition as well as laid-back goofing around with friends. Wheaton students tend to be in good shape. Almost all are active in some way, whether as members of a varsity, club or intramural team or as a dedicated gym goer.

Wheaties admit that campus diversity isn't fantastic, but the school does try to attract a diverse group of students. There is some ethnic diversity and socioeconomic diversity but the average Wheaton student is still a middle to upper class white kid. One diverse group that Wheaton attracts are students from missionary families. These bring with them stories of childhoods spent in Zambia or Zimbabwe and unique perspectives developed in their time away from the U.S. There are few to no openly gay students on campus. Politically, Wheaton students lean right but some say they've become less conservative during college. Wheaton students are united by their Christian faith, but the college is interdenominational. Most students identify with some variety of evangelical Protestantism, though not all.

Part of being a Wheatie is taking part in its many school traditions. For example, Wheaton students may adhere faithfully to the Community Covenant as far as drinking goes, but for the sake of a seven-foot long concrete slab, they've been known to break a law here and there. The slab in question is known as the Bench—erected in the 1920's and placed outside Blanchard Hall for the exclusive use of seniors. The juniors first stole the bench around 1950, and since then juniors and seniors have waged a bitter war for possession of the bench. In 1959, the seniors suspended the bench from a helicopter and flew over the football field during the homecoming game to taunt the junior class. More recently, in 2005, a high speed car chase for the Bench resulted in several speeding tickets.

Another Wheaton tradition is ringing the tower bell in Blanchard Hall to announce an engagement. Wheaton seems to have more of these to announce than other colleges, though some students say that might be a stereotype: "I feel like Wheaton has a rep for people getting married, but it's exaggerated," said one student.

Attending Wheaton is a unique college experience. While most students who choose Wheaton seem very satisfied with their decision, they also admit that they know their school wouldn't be right for everyone. Some students also worry that four years at Wheaton might leave them unprepared for "the real world," where not everyone will share or understand their beliefs. But for the most part, Wheaton students seem to deeply value the way Wheaton has shaped them intellectually and spiritually. "After my first semester, I know I would definitely choose Wheaton again," said one freshman.—*Sonja Peterson*

FYI
If you come to Wheaton College, you'd better bring "lots of crazy clothes for theme parties."
Three things every student should do before graduating are "explore Chicago, play IMs and have a snowball fight."
What differentiates Wheaton most from other colleges is "the amazing community."

Indiana

DePauw University

Address: 101 E. Seminary
 Greencastle, IN 46135
Phone: 765-658-4006
E-mail address:
 admission@depauw.edu
Web site URL:
 www.depauw.edu
Year Founded: 1837
Private or Public: Private
Religious Affiliation:
 Methodist
Location: Surburban
Number of Applicants:
 4,439
Percent Accepted: 68%
Percent Accepted who
 enroll: 22%
Number Entering: 664
Number of Transfers
 Accepted each Year: 23
Middle 50% SAT range:
 M: 570–660, Cr: 560–660,
 Wr: 620–690
Middle 50% ACT range:
 25–29
Early admission program
 EA/ED/None: EA and ED

Percentage accepted
 through EA or ED:
 Unreported
EA and ED deadline: 1-Nov
Regular Deadline: 1-Feb
Application Fee: $40
Full time Undergraduate
 enrollment: 2,276
Total enrollment: 2,276
Percent Male: 44%
Percent Female: 56%
Total Percent Minority or
 Unreported: 16%
Percent African-American:
 6%
Percent Asian/Pacific
 Islander: 3%
Percent Hispanic: 3%
Percent Native-American:
 1%
Percent International: 2%
Percent in-state/out of
 state: 54%/46%
Percent from Public HS:
 83%
Retention Rate: 92%
Graduation Rate 4-year: 79%

Graduation Rate 6-year:
 81%
Percent Undergraduates
 in On-campus housing:
 99%
Number of official organized
 extracurricular
 organizations: 119
3 Most popular majors:
 Economics, English,
 Communications
Student/Faculty ratio:
 10:1
Average Class Size: 15
Percent of students going to
 grad school: 31%
Tuition and Fees: $29,300
In-State Tuition and Fees if
 different: No difference
Cost for Room and Board:
 $8,100
Percent receiving financial
 aid out of those who apply,
 first year: Unreported
Percent receiving financial
 aid among all students:
 Unreported

A t DePauw University, the students' sense of fun and the college's unique traditions more than compensate for the Midwestern chill. With a flourishing Greek life scene and a tight-knit population of "casual and accepting" students, this small but proud private liberal arts college offers a welcoming atmosphere. Through its distinctive combination of a strong liberal arts education and pre-professional opportunities, DePauw encourages its students to apply their intellects to the working world. As one senior put it, "DePauw really emphasizes putting yourself out there, getting involved, and getting everything out of the time you have in college."

Challenge, Freedom, and Excitement: All in a Day's Work

The classes and academic standards at DePauw "definitely require you to work," but there is plenty of freedom to choose courses, and there are several "exciting" options for learning outside of the classroom, a freshman said. Depending on the type of bachelor's degree being pursued, students need to take either 31 or 33 course credits: 31 for normal Bachelor of Arts, Bachelor of Music, and Bachelor of Musical Arts degrees, and 33 for a Bachelor of Music Education degree at DePauw's well-known music school. All students except those in the music school must take courses that fulfill three skill areas: expository writing, quantitative reasoning, and oral communication. They also have to take classes in six distributional areas: natural science and mathematics; social and behavioral sciences; literature and the arts; historical and philosophical understanding; foreign language, and self-expression through performance and participation (which can involve physical activity, the arts, or participation in a campus extracurricular activity). Students agree that these requirements hardly restrict their college experiences at all. "It's possible to get out of taking subjects you hated in high school and just take classes you're interested in," a junior said.

Meanwhile, DePauw's unusual academic calendar, which includes a month-long Winter Term in addition to the traditional fall and spring semesters, gives students the option of having adventurous, flexible learning experiences. Since Winter Term projects are graded on a "satisfactory/unsatisfactory" basis, one senior described them as "a lot of fun and not that stressful." Students can choose among dozens of short, on-campus courses ranging from EMT certification to wildlife management to campanology (the history and practice of bell ringing). They can also study at another college, do research, take an internship to build up their professional experience, or go on special study projects in different countries. One sophomore said she traveled to Morocco on a study trip just to tour the country and learn about its cultural offerings.

Yet another academic opportunity offered by DePauw is the set of five programs of distinction, which allow top students to experience "enhanced study." Students can apply to become Honor Scholars, Management Fellows, Media Fellows, Science Research Fellows or Information Technology Associates. Each program comes with its own set of benefits and hands-on experiences: while Management Fellows can enroll in special seminars and take paid semester-long internships during their junior year, Science Research Fellows are able to receive graduate-level science research opportunities.

Inside the classroom, the learning environment is both intimate and challenging. A sophomore said she had never been in a class larger than 50 people, and average class sizes hover around 15, according to students. Although the intimate, personal setting does ensure that no student slips through the cracks—"I'm afraid of sleeping in class or skipping class because my professor actually knows me," a freshman

said—students said they enjoy the personal bonds they develop with professors, who tend to be "dynamic" and liberal-leaning. In addition to high-quality teaching and mentoring, professors at DePauw will also invite students over for dinner or ask students to babysit, students said. All in all, it makes for fairly demanding academic work: classes at DePauw are challenging but not impossible.

DePauw's focus on academics is complemented by its state-of-the-art campus technology; the campus is known for being one of the most "connected" and "wireless" in the country. Professors can hold online office hours and give out exams and homework online, and the campus boasts comprehensive wireless Internet. To ensure that students can take advantage of the campus's technology, all freshmen are required to bring laptops to DePauw.

It's (Almost) All Greek to Me
Almost three-quarters of DePauw students are involved in the University's large, active Greek life scene, which dominates DePauw social life and makes for a unique party scene. With 14 fraternities and 11 sororities, including two of the oldest fraternity chapters in the country, it's "rush or be rushed," as one sophomore put it: even the minority of students who decide not to join a fraternity or sorority end up having a large circle of Greek friends and often attend parties in Greek houses. But the Greek scene is far from intimidating. Because so many students rush, "It's really easy to get into a fraternity or sorority if you want to," a senior said, adding that the Greek system is not competitive at all. Instead, it provides many traditions, great housing, and a plentiful, fun party scene. Although Greek parties do involve "a lot of drinking," students say no one is pressured to drink at DePauw.

However, some pressure still exists to join the Greek scene because so many students rush, and "independents," as students who choose not to join fraternities or sororities are called, sometimes feel ostracized. A senior said he had to work harder to meet new people and establish connections at first because he chose not to rush. Several students, both Greek and independent, criticized the Greek party scene, saying parties on campus are "hot, crowded, drunken messes that get old after sophomore year." On-campus parties are limited to the Greek houses, although organizations and the university itself often organize events such as concerts and movie screenings.

Upperclassmen often skip the Greek party scene altogether in favor of Greencastle, the surrounding town, which has several bars that are popular with both townies and college students—favorite haunts include the Duck, Topper's, and Third Degree. One bar, Moore's, even features karaoke. "You can actually hear yourself talk and you don't have to drink that much in bars, but at the frats, everyone drinks a lot," a senior said. Other than the bars, however, Greencastle has little entertainment to offer, students say; it is a small, "pretty dull" rural town. Still, students frequent Marvin's, a classic American diner that stays open later than most other Greencastle restaurants and also employs students. Marvin's special garlic cheeseburger, or "GCB," has even become part of campus culture. Nearby Indianapolis, Indiana's largest city, is a popular destination for short road trips, since many students have cars and "Indy" is only an hour away from Greencastle.

Greencastle may lack the excitement of a big city, but it is certainly safe, and features a small-town atmosphere with typical Midwestern picturesque scenery. A freshman said he felt "completely safe" at DePauw—and added that "Wherever I leave it, my stuff is completely safe too." Students regularly walk around at night and usually leave their doors unlocked. Meanwhile, students take advantage of Greencastle's "peaceful, green, and pretty" Bowman Park to just hang out and relax. The campus itself is full of greenery and attractive, classic brick buildings, such as East College, which is the oldest building at DePauw and is listed on the National Register of Historic Places.

Living on campus is required for all four years, so students live in one of eleven residence halls, with their fraternities or sororities, or in University-owned apartments. As freshmen, students all live in dorms, which usually feature coed floors and communal bathrooms as well as "small but nice and well-kept" rooms. Upperclassmen can continue to live in the dorms, move into Greek "mansions," or enter an apartment lottery for juniors and seniors. The apartments are furnished, cost about the same as living in the residential halls, and do not require their inhabitants to be on the University meal plan. Although a junior said DePauw's campus dining "isn't terrible," students agree that eating in fraternity or sorority houses or off campus in Greencastle offers better quality and more variety.

A Bell Worth Fighting For

DePauw varsity teams compete in NCAA Division III, and its women's golf, softball, and basketball teams have been especially successful in recent years. The women's basketball team has won several conference championships and one Division III national title. Still, DePauw games are not especially well-attended; students say they rarely have enough time in their busy schedules to go to games. But many students participate in intramural sports, which "are fun and keep us fit, but aren't too big of a time commitment," a sophomore said.

> "DePauw really emphasizes putting yourself out there, getting involved, and getting everything out of the time you have in college."

The one reliably popular game at DePauw is the Monon Bell Classic—simply known as "the Game"—in which the DePauw Tigers take on the rival Wabash College in football. One of the nation's oldest college football rivalries, the Game regularly attracts many current students as well as alumni, who will "pay through the nose" to get seats, according to a junior. Since the two schools are only 27 miles apart, many of the players and students on both sides are friends, relatives, or former classmates, making the Game even more heated. The teams battle for the Monon Bell trophy, a 300-pound locomotive bell that was first introduced in 1932—to keep Wabash students from stealing it when DePauw wins the trophy, the University seals the bell in a glass case.

Fun Traditions and an Easygoing Atmosphere Await

Students say DePauw's student body tends to be from the Midwest, especially Indiana, and moderate to conservative-leaning, with few minority students. However, DePauw's atmosphere is anything but dull and homogenous. Not only are the students friendly and outgoing, they also eagerly participate in a rich variety of traditions, from Boulder Run to an annual bike race in late April to a game known as "campus golf." In Boulder Run, students streak from their dorms to the Columbia Boulder, a campus landmark, while in campus golf, students dress in traditional golf attire and use golf clubs to hit tennis balls around campus courses. Although there are no actual holes, students attempt to hit their balls against specific targets while walking around student-designed unofficial golf courses.

Not only are DePauw students active in campus life, they are also generally easygo-ing and accepting, creating a casual, pleasant atmosphere. At DePauw, a junior said, "Everyone is definitely different, but most people still get along and manage to have a good time and get a good education at the same time."—*Vivian Yee*

FYI

If you come to DePauw, you'd better bring "a car and golf clothes for campus golf!"

What is the typical weekend schedule? "Friday is the day to hang out and go party-hopping at the frat houses or the bars; you still party on Saturday, but it's a little more laid-back. On Sunday, study, do work and hang out."

If I could change one thing about DePauw, I'd "add more minority students and more out-of-state students."

Three things every student at DePauw should do before graduating are "take a road trip to Indianapolis, eat a GCB at Marvin's, and rush a fraternity or sorority."

Earlham College

Address: 801 National Road West Richmond, IN 47374	**Percentage accepted through EA or ED:** 96%	**Graduation Rate 4-year:** 62%
Phone: 765-983-1600	**EA and ED deadline:** 1-Jan	**Graduation Rate 6-year:** 70%
E-mail address: admission@earlham.edu	**Regular Deadline:** 15-Feb	**Percent Undergraduates in On-campus housing:** 87%
Web site URL: www.earlham.edu	**Application Fee:** $30	**Number of official organized extracurricular organizations:** 70
Year Founded: 1847	**Full time Undergraduate enrollment:** 1,200	**3 Most popular majors:**
Private or Public: Private	**Total enrollment:** 1,300	History, Psychology,
Religious Affiliation: Quaker	**Percent Male:** 43%	Economics
Location: Suburban	**Percent Female:** 57%	**Student/Faculty ratio:** 12:1
Number of Applicants: 6,205	**Total Percent Minority or Unreported:** 11%	**Average Class Size:** 14
Percent Accepted: 69%	**Percent African-American:** 7%	**Percent of students going to grad school:** 22%
Percent Accepted who enroll: 27%	**Percent Asian/Pacific Islander:** 2%	**Tuition and Fees:** $28,600
Number Entering: 1,156	**Percent Hispanic:** 2%	**In-State Tuition and Fees if different:** No difference
Number of Transfers Accepted each Year: 43	**Percent Native-American:** 1%	**Cost for Room and Board:** $6,200
Middle 50% SAT range: M: 540–660, Cr: 570–690, Wr: 560–680	**Percent International:** Unreported	**Percent receiving financial aid out of those who apply, first year:** 90%
Middle 50% ACT range: 24–29	**Percent in-state/out of state:** 31%/69%	**Percent receiving financial aid among all students:** 56%
Early admission program EA/ED/None: EA and ED	**Percent from Public HS:** 68% **Retention Rate:** 82%	

E arlham College, located in the heart of Middle America, is a Quaker school, a fact that colors every aspect of campus life. Even the sports teams are called the Quakers. Advisory committees, comprised of both students and faculty, make the decisions that govern both the current state and future direction of the college—all reached by consensus, of course. Everyone is referred to by his or her first name—the current president, Douglas Bennett, is affectionately referred to as "Dougie B." The school's Quaker heritage contributes to its overall emphasis on fostering individual growth. As one third year explained, "The education here is geared towards individual learning, and if you expect to be spoon-fed a degree and then feel accomplished, you'll be sadly mistaken."

From India to Indiana

Through different study-abroad programs, to numerous small classes and seminars taught by professors who are actively interested in their students, Earlham offers countless academic opportunities that are there for the taking. All freshmen (or first years, as they are called at Earlham) must take two reading and writing intensive seminars. The topics of each class vary from year to year, but they often are, as one student put it, "whatever the professor is passionate about." And with class size capped at 15, there is plenty of room for professors to pass this enthusiasm on to their students. "You leave the class and everyone's still discussing the topic," recalls one second year. With subjects such as the History of Sexuality in the Nineteenth and Twentieth Centuries to Religion: For or Against the Common Good, these courses work to provide first years with an introduction to the ins and outs of Earlham academic life.

Another defining emphasis of an Earlham education is its international focus. Earlham not only attracts a large number of international students, but the college also boasts a great number of its own programs run by Earlham professors in countries around the globe. The travel opportunities offered by such programs (some remain in one city, while others take students on guided tours throughout specific areas) in conjunction with the expertise of professors, largely accounts for the popularity of studying abroad for Earlhamites.

> "[Professors] are always available to answer questions individually and personally connect with students. I don't even know what a T.A. is."

Whether they are in India or in Indiana, Earlham professors are always more than willing to work and learn with their students. "They are always available to answer questions individually and personally connect with students. I don't even know what a T.A. is," one senior asserted. Through their "enlightening discussion-based classes," professors are able to work closely with their students. "I came planning to be a journalist and pretty quickly changed to politics mostly because of my professor . . . many professors here are inspiring and completely change the direction people go," one student said.

Hymnals and "Hash"

Outside the classroom, Earlham students can immerse themselves in a variety of extracurricular activities and sports. And, if there is a part of campus life or the Earlham administration that does not satisfy students, they can join a committee that addresses that particular issue. One popular committee is the Admissions and Financial Aid Advisory Committee, which recently redrafted the Earlham application. Another popular student group is the International Education Committee, which focuses on revising and expanding Earlham's international focus. As members with positions equal to the faculty that also serve on these committees, students have a great impact in creating their own college experience.

Earlham is, in the words of one student, "not a jock school." But even though "Our teams suck, we are still really proud of them." Soccer, for example, never fails to draw a crowd of enthusiastic Earlhamites who sing "uproaringly funny fight songs at sports games." More often than not, students (lovingly) poke fun at their school through these cheers. In fact, the cheers themselves have been printed into a "hymnal," so that generations after generations can use them to reflect their own quirky sense of school spirit.

Although students at Earlham seem to be more than content with their choice of school, one common complaint concerns the surrounding town of Richmond. But as one student put it, "Indiana is what you make of it." Luckily, there are a number of cities within driving distance that can keep students entertained when not busy on campus.

In fact, the on-campus activities at Earlham often make students reluctant to leave, even when they have the chance. And with few other alternatives, there is a high turnout for many of the larger events sponsored by Earlham. "This makes for a good sense of campus cohesion," one senior noted. "Everyone gets to know everyone." Furthermore, the creativity of students, when it comes to finding ways to entertain themselves, is second to none. Many rave about the "quirky theme parties" that are thrown on the weekends, with some past favorites including, "Come As Your Favorite Lesbian" and "Seventh Grade."

Even though Earlham is a dry campus, one junior claimed that, "Earlham tacitly accepts and does not punish many of the known drinking gatherings that occur on a regular basis." One of the most popular of these events is an off-campus party known as "the Hash." "People gather together at two or three on a Saturday afternoon . . . they [sing] a little song while holding hands," a freshman explained. After that, students follow a long and winding flour path around campus that eventually ends at the keg provided somewhere in the 600-acre "back campus." This unconventional approach to partying is undoubtedly characteristic of the adventurous nature of the Earlham student body.

Home Away from Home

Earlham housing offers a variety of options from which students can choose. All first years live in dorms, but after that, students can choose to stay in the dorms, or move into on-campus houses (usually theme houses dedicated to a particular culture or concept). For the truly adventurous, there is an opportunity to live and work on Earlham's Miller Farm. "It has a three story treehouse with a fire pole!" one junior exclaimed.

And for those who are thinking about venturing to off-campus housing (the majority of which is owned by Earlham itself), be wary. Many students have suffered from a small sense of regret. As one student explained, "As mushy as it is to say, we have a wonderful campus community . . . I often feel that I miss out on some of that by being off campus."

Earlham's international focus, combined with the creativity of its students and its Quaker roots, enables the college to offer an unforgettable educational experience, in and out of the classroom. "In the residence halls, classes, dining halls and everywhere else on campus, I am constantly engaged," one senior said. "I am challenged in my assumptions and beliefs almost everywhere I go."—*Stephanie Brockman*

FYI
If you come to Earlham, you'd better bring a "sense of independence and willingness to find things out for yourself."
What is the typical weekend schedule? "A concert, dirt-cheap beer, a theme party, reading, and papers."
If I could change one thing about Earlham, I'd "put it closer to a big city, or have more things of interest in a closer radius."
Three things every student at Earlham should do before graduating are "go off campus for a semester, take a random class outside of your major and interest area and serve on Earlham Student Government in some way."

Indiana University / Bloomington

Address: 300 North Jordan Avenue, Bloomington, IN 47405-1106
Phone: 812-855-0661
E-mail address: iuadmit@indiana.edu
Web site URL: www.indiana.edu
Year Founded: 1820
Private or Public: Public
Religious Affiliation: None
Location: Suburban
Number of Applicants: 29,059
Percent Accepted: 70%
Percent Accepted who enroll: 35%
Number Entering: 7,181
Number of Transfers Accepted each Year: 629
Middle 50% SAT range: M: 520–640, CR: 510–620, Wr: Unreported
Middle 50% ACT range: 23–28
Early admission program EA/ED/None: None

Percentage accepted through EA or ED: NA
EA and ED deadline: NA
Regular Deadline: 1-Aprl
Application Fee: $50
Full time Undergraduate enrollment: 30,394
Total enrollment: 31,626
Percent Male: 49%
Percent Female: 51%
Total Percent Minority or Unreported: 8%
Percent African-American: 4%
Percent Asian/Pacific Islander: 4%
Percent Hispanic: 2%
Percent Native-American: <1%
Percent International: 5%
Percent in-state/out of state: 67%/33%
Percent from Public HS: Unreported
Retention Rate: 89%
Graduation Rate 4-year: 50%

Graduation Rate 6-year: 71%
Percent Undergraduates in On-campus housing: 36%
Number of official organized extracurricular organizations: 300
3 Most popular majors: Business/Commerce, Communication, Journalism
Student/Faculty ratio: 18:1
Average Class Size: Unreported
Percent of students going to grad school: Unreported
Tuition and Fees: $12,778
In-State Tuition and Fees if different: $3,196
Cost for Room and Board: $5,714
Percent receiving financial aid out of those who apply, first year: 79%
Percent receiving financial aid among all students: 71%

Bloomington, Indiana, is the quintessential college town. The only unusual thing about it is that the college it surrounds has almost 32,000 total students. IU may seem like the typical big state school, but its students say that it's much more than that. It has a Midwestern warmth that brings the large campus together as a community and, despite the size, IU students are connected in school spirit and true friendliness. With unique academic programs and endless opportunities to get involved, IU is full of motivated students who want to make the most of their college experience inside the classroom and beyond.

Inside IU Academics

If reading about a big state school conjures the image of huge auditoriums seating 5,000 people and professors who probably have no idea who half the students are, fear not, say students. "My first semester was full of interactions with each of my professors on an individual basis, and I had classes ranging from 20 students to 300." The range of class sizes is normal for this University, where flexibility in the educational program is key. One junior said, "The core education differs for every major, which means I never have to take math again!" The ability to take classes that interest students on a personal level is a trademark of the Indiana education. IU encourages students to enter under the "exploratory" option, which allows them to fully experiment with a broad range of classes before settling on a major. One student said, "I think this keeps people loving school; education should be about pursuing your passions, not about a random guess as to what profession you will have at the age of forty." This focus on the individual and the awareness that each student is different sets IU apart.

With the same philosophy of exploration and a broad educational spectrum, IU offers some unique major programs that many students enjoy immensely. LAMP is the Liberal Arts and Management Program, which allows a student to double-major in business and liberal arts. Students say that this program consistently gets rave reviews for its creative seminars and flexible approach to learning. One student explained the appeal of the program in terms of the students themselves: "The business school at IU, Kelley, is very prestigious but often students get frustrated with the thought of giving up liberal arts classes for the sake of a successful future. The clear understanding that students have more than just one interest comes through strongly with this program." Similarly, a minor in LESA, the Leadership, Ethics, and Social Action program, gives students the opportunity to explore a variety of fields while still having some direction.

> "Everyone finds something to do here. People can sit in their rooms and play Halo, but there's also a club for that."

The prestige of the Kelley School of Business, the sociology department, and the Jacob School of Music draw students to IU. But students say that what makes the academic environment truly special is the high caliber and approachability of the professors. One student said, "I think IU is unique because the professors are all well-known scholars with impressive backgrounds, yet they are down to earth and really love to teach." Although students admit that it "takes individual effort" to get to know professors in such a large environment, they also say that "IU across the board makes it easy to get one-on-one attention."

Ancient Greece

With 45 fraternities and sororities to choose from, many students at IU do decide to go through the rush process. Although officially only about 17 percent of students are involved in Greek life, students say that the campus undeniably feels the Greek presence. While one student said, "You're not missing out if you're not in a frat," he also commented that frats "bring the campus together." Because on-campus housing almost exclusively contains freshmen, upperclassmen need other places to go. Students say that there is "good housing around campus," but one student also mentioned that this is one reason to go Greek. Most people who join a fraternity or sorority end up living in the frat or sorority house, which are governed by the school even though they are not technically located on campus.

Saturday Night Fever

Fraternities and sororities clearly preside over partying, but one student asserted that "IU is too large to have a dominant social scene. There is truly a niche for everyone." Still, weekends on campus do revolve around drinking for most students. There are six bars within walking distance of central campus, and upperclassmen tend to center their partying on those. Underclassmen are "less likely to have the means to get into the bars, so they party at the frats or go to dorm and house parties." Regardless of how people decide to let loose, one student pointed out that "People hardly ever leave campus because we all want to be with the family we've formed at school." Cars are allowed, but students agree that they are more of a hassle than anything, since "IU tickets more than the entire city of Cincinnati." With downtown Bloomington only "ten steps away" from campus, students don't need to go far to find entertainment. One student summed up the weekend experience with the statement, "People here really know how to party."

On-Campus at IU

"The campus as a whole is very kind and friendly," one junior said, while a freshman agreed, "IU has such a friendly campus!" This extends to the wide range of political views that comes from a fairly equal number of liberals and conservatives on campus. Both parties are "very vocal," students say, and it "makes for great debates in political science classes!" The involvement in politics is only one way in which students can get involved. One student said, "Sports are huge here, especially the basketball team, which has been ranked in the top twenty-five." The same student also said that there are many opportunities for club and intramural sports for those not quite of the varsity caliber. For those more musically inclined, the a cappella scene is prominent, with the all-male Straight No Chaser and the women's group Ladies First. Even if those particular activities don't sound particularly exciting, "Everyone finds something to do here. People can sit in their rooms and play Halo, but there's also a club for that." Another student said, "It's impossible not to get involved." IU recognizes that, just as students have more than one interest in the classroom, their extracurricular passions are varied. As such, the school makes it possible to explore many different areas, from club sports to a cappella and everything in between. "Anything you want to do, there's a way to do it."

IU in Focus
."It's fun here all the time—there's always something to do." This sense that opportunities are limitless comes through in the academics, the extracurriculars, and in the students themselves. The school creates an

environment in which students are not only allowed but also positively encouraged to explore a diverse curriculum and take advantage of all the resources of a large university. IU recognizes that every student is different, and as a result the school is set up so that each person has the chance to get what he or she wants and needs out of the college experience. As one student put it, "Investigate IU! There's a lot more beneath the surface."—*Hannah Jacobson*

FYI
If you come to IU, you'd better bring "a fake ID."
What's the typical weekend schedule? "Thursday night: go out, Friday night: go out, Saturday night: go out, and Sunday do homework."
If I could change one thing about IU, I'd "make it warm all year round."
Three things every student at IU should do before graduating are "swim in Showalter Fountain, see an IU basketball game, and go to a Straight No Chaser concert!"

Purdue University

Address: 475 Stadium Mall Drive, West Lafayette, IN 47907
Phone: 765-494-1776
E-mail address: admissions@purdue.edu
Web site URL: www.purdue.edu
Year Founded: 1869
Private or Public: Public
Religious Affiliation: None
Location: Suburban
Number of Applicants: 30,707
Percent Accepted: 65%
Percent Accepted who enroll: 32%
Number Entering: 6,459
Number of Transfers Accepted each Year: Unreported
Middle 50% SAT range: M: 540–660, CR: 490–610, Wr: 490–600
Middle 50% ACT range: 23–29
Early admission program EA/ED/None: None

Percentage accepted through EA or ED: NA
EA and ED deadline: NA
Regular Deadline: 1-Mar
Application Fee: $30
Full time Undergraduate enrollment: 30,468
Total enrollment: 40,090
Percent Male: 58%
Percent Female: 42%
Total Percent Minority or Unreported: 12%
Percent African-American: 3%
Percent Asian/Pacific Islander: 5%
Percent Hispanic: 3%
Percent Native-American: <1%
Percent International: 14%
Percent in-state/out of state: 59%/41%
Percent from Public HS: Unreported
Retention Rate: 86%
Graduation Rate 4-year: 40%

Graduation Rate 6-year: 71%
Percent Undergraduates in On-campus housing: 35%
Number of official organized extracurricular organizations: 815
3 Most popular majors: Mechanical Engineering, Management, Aero and Astro Engineering
Student/Faculty ratio: 13:1
Average Class Size: 24
Percent of students going to grad school: Unreported
Tuition and Fees: $23,224
In-State Tuition and Fees if different: $8,638
Cost for Room and Board: $8,500
Percent receiving financial aid out of those who apply, first year: 38%
Percent receiving financial aid among all students: 6%

Purdue University is known for being a leading engineering and agriculture school in the US. So, it's no surprise that 23 of Purdue's alumni have become (or are in the process of becoming) astronauts. The university is home to over

30,000 undergraduates who in addition to its excellent academics, are legacies of a long tradition in athletic dominance.

If you want to be an astronaut . . .

Originally founded to instruct men and women to lead productive and utilitarian careers, Purdue University remains true to its roots with its renowned engineering, aerospace and physics departments. However, the university also has strong programs in the pharmaceutical sciences, veterinary medicine and computer science.

Despite Purdue's acclaim in the sciences, the university also has reputed humanity and social science departments. One of the most prominent executed by the Krannert School of Management, whose undergraduate program was recently ranked #19 by the *U.S.News & World Report*. Regardless of the breadth of educational opportunities, almost a fifth of undergraduates major in engineering.

Students can register in a plethora of subjects. The university offers courses in over 210 major areas of study and students may choose to enroll in the Undergraduate Studies Program which permits undergraduates to try out the options available at Purdue for up to four semesters before selecting a major. Notwithstanding, some of the colleges, such as the College of Engineering, significantly limit the students' ability to explore a variety of different subjects due to vigorous predetermined academic curricula.

The alma mater of 23 astronauts, Purdue has excellent aviation and aerospace departments. As a matter of fact, because of the emphasis on these subjects, the campus has an airport. Used primarily by the aviation technology department, the establishment enables aerospace engineering students to test their constructions while at the same time offers them the option of obtaining their own flight licenses.

A unique opportunity offered by the same department is Design/Build/Fly. Admitted students attend to aeronautical projects in teams to construct their own aircrafts and enter them in the Design/Build/Fly competition held by the American Institute of Aeronautics and Astronautics. One aeronautical engineering student said of the program, "Purdue gives me the tools needed to create a better future, helping me fulfill not only my dreams but also to encourage others to do so."

Further emphasis on creative approaches on research is instigated by the university's "Discovery Park" which is essentially a multidisciplinary research park that provides students with useful practical work experience.

Purdue's 30,000 undergraduates comprise the second largest student body in Indiana. This fact more or less could dictate large classes. Most students interviewed have said that they are not daunted by this fact, as there is extensive use of technological aids, which span from microphones to effective screen placements in lecture halls. Although lectures are normally larger, class size averages to around 24 students and size typically decreases for more advanced and specialized courses.

Although the university uses curves, getting A's can be difficult. According to a freshman, "[grades] depend on the major but C-B are normal." Although all of Purdue's courses are considered challenging, math and science courses are generally considered harder than humanity courses.

Where Greeks don't drink

As Purdue is a state school, a significant percentage of the undergraduates are Indiana residents. This statistic significantly influences campus social life as many locals choose to leave campus on weekends to visit their families—which triggers a remarkable decrease of the campus population. This fact also denotes that a notable percentage of students have cars, something that expands the undergrads outing possibilities as it permits them to visit large nearby metropolises such as Indianapolis and Chicago more easily.

Greek life is prominent and influential on campus. Statistics estimate that approximately 5,000 students are members of fraternities or sororities, which amounts to about 17% of the student body. Many greek organizations provide housing and meal services and involve their members in various ways, from intramural athletic competitions to community service activities. The organizations host various social functions which often enable members to interact with other campus organizations. Most Greeks also abide by Purdue's very strict undergraduate no-alcohol policy, as organizations that refuse to do so are severely penalized by the university.

Different policies have been enforced, and many Greek organizations have been placed on suspension in the past as a result of alcohol abuse. Alcohol abuse is treated as a serious threat to student health and so the university tries to enforce alcohol education throughout the year in order to avoid any unwelcome situations.

On weekends, many students that remain on campus choose to go out to bars or cafés. Widely attended bars include Harry's Chocolate Café and Where Else? Harry's Chocolate Café although originally a soda shop, is now a favorite bar. Alternatively, students might choose to casually hang out in dorms.

Popular university-wide events include Homecoming and Halloween. During Homecoming, students can attend the Boilermaker Night Train Parade—which features marching band displays and a march to the stadium for the Homecoming football game. Football is important for what is one of Purdue's most distinct traditions, the "Breakfast Club." While this is not aimed for underclassmen due to the potential for alcohol abuse, participating students dress up in costumes before home games. The students, who wake up at 6am to attend, go to local bars and drink before going to the game.

X-Tra sporty

An institution that has three school mascots is bound to have strong school spirit and the athletic merit to match up to it.

Out of the three Purdue mascots, the "Boilermaker Special," a Victorian-era railroad locomotive, is the only official university mascot. The train design symbolizes the strength of the university's engineering programs. There have been various versions of the mascot in the past, the current one being the "Boilermaker Special V." The locomotive is maintained by the student members of the Purdue Reamer Club, and is available for free rides on Fridays and can be rented for private events. A smaller version of the mascot, the Boilermaker Special VI, is affectionately known as the X-Tra Special. This mascot often appears in home games and some indoor functions—places where the Boilermaker Special V cannot go to due to its massive size.

The other two mascots are an example of, albeit fictional, Purdue potential legacies. Purdue Pete, a mascot that first appeared in the '60s, is portrayed to be an ardent boilermaker that holds a hammer in one hand and always sports a hard hat. His younger brother, Rowdy, aspires that one day he too will become a Boilermaker.

A founding member of the Big Ten Conference, the oldest Division I athletic conference in the US, Purdue athletics are first-rate. Currently, the university has 18 Division I/I-A teams and its football and bas-

ketball are among the best in the nation. The men's and women's basketball teams have won more Big Ten Championships than any other university and Purdue is traditionally called the "Cradle of Quarterbacks" as it has produced a large number of NFL stars.

There is a wide variety of sports and this enables students to take part in those that suit them the most. In addition to traditional ones such as tennis, swimming and—of course—football, there are some more unconventional sports students can compete in such as Quidditch and Ultimate Frisbee.

The university owns a wide range of athletic amenities that are at the students' disposal. Currently, Purdue is undertaking a multimillion-dollar renovation and expansion of RSC, the Purdue Student Fitness and Wellness Center. The center is expected to be completed by fall 2012 but in the meantime, students can still use many of the available facilities. Additionally, there are many intramural sports where students can participate for fun that do not require the skills, experience or commitment that varsity sports do.

Other than the individual gym resources at the RSC like weights and treadmills, the center offers an abundance of group courses. Group Exercise, or "Group X," offers a multitude of programs students can choose from ranging from cardio workouts and aqua aerobics to Zumba—a workout program that fuses Latin and international music and accompanies it with dance. "Learn to Play" is another fitness program offered by the university that fosters progressive learning where classes gradually expand in their complexity and require increasing acquisition of skills. The university also provides the students with the option to hire instructors for classes outside the complex for an additional fee.

Purdue in the prairie

While in Purdue you get a feeling of vastness and openness. When walking across the Purdue terrain, you are surrounded by a profusion of trees that are inhabited by squirrels and other small arboreal fauna. In the warmer months, you are in the midst of green brilliance and during the cold winters you are encircled by mountains of snow. The campus is decorated with statues and fountains and you cannot fail to admire the consistency of the red brick layout.

The majority of the campus is built in classic red brick. Exceptions to this pattern are observed in Rawls Hall and the Krannert

Building which are primarily made out of limestone. Another building with significantly reduced use of red brick in its structure is the Neil Armstrong Hall of Engineering, that is primarily made out of glass although it too uses red brick in parts of the structure. The building was dedicated/completed in 2007 and on the front porch has a statue of the astronaut. It appears that although engineering students love the building, they come to significantly dislike it as soon as they "have an all-nighter in it" said an engineering student. The Hall among other things features a replica of the Apollo 1 command module which hangs from the ceiling of the building's atrium.

Another structure favored by the students is the Steven C. Beering Hall of Liberal Arts and Education which is a preferred place for study of many students across the disciplines, although it primarily houses several departments of Purdue's College of Liberal Arts and Purdue's School of Education.

Many students opt for dorm housing as the prices are "reasonable" said a freshman, although this is mostly the case with underclassmen. Housing prices depend on room size, occupancy and amenities. Some dorms are considered to be better than others; First Street Towers, a hall that first opened in July 2009, is considered to be among the nicest and most expensive ones. Others, as for example Earhart Hall which is favored by engineering students, have their own character and often consist of different "learning communities."

Although the university does not have its own private transit, students can use City-Bus which is operated by the municipality free of charge as it is subsidized by the university. There are specific routes which are designed for the students' use and stop at most of the widely used campus buildings. CityBus is also used by locals.

> **"Purdue gives me the tools needed to create a better future, helping me fulfill not only my dreams but also to encourage others to do so."**

The city of West Lafayette and the university are heavily interdependent. West Lafayette is primarily a university city so most businesses thrive thanks to the university, a fact that leads to city-wide Purdue Pride. According to a student, you can see people wearing Purdue apparel in many off-campus locations, even if these people are not officially affiliated with the university.

Diversity Overload

Purdue is dominated by students who succeed in various fields. While it's predominately an agricultural and engineering school, it also has strong programs in the humanities and the social sciences. The university has vast resources for all of its students which range from a brand new Fitness Center to an airport. The balance of academics, social activities and athletics make Purdue a place where everyone can find something they are passionate about.—*Katerina Karatzia*

FYI
If you come to Purdue, you'd better bring "Warm gear and boots"
If you come to Purdue, you'd better leave "your Indiana University apparel" behind.
The biggest college-wide tradition/event at Purdue is "becom[e] an astronaut after graduation"

Rose-Hulman Institute of Technology

Address: 5500 Wabash Avenue, Terre Haute, IN 47803
Phone: 812-877-8213
E-mail address: admissions@rose-hulman.edu
Web site URL: www.rose-hulman.edu
Year Founded: 1874
Private or Public: Private
Religious Affiliation: None
Location: Rural
Number of Applicants: 3,088
Percent Accepted: 70%
Percent Accepted who enroll: 17%
Number Entering: 474
Number of Transfers Accepted each Year: 40
Middle 50% SAT range: M: 630–710, CR: 560–680, Wr: Unreported
Middle 50% ACT range: 27–31
Early admission program EA/ED/None: None

Percentage accepted through EA or ED: NA
EA and ED deadline: NA
Regular Deadline: 1-Mar
Application Fee: $40
Full time Undergraduate enrollment: 1,832
Total enrollment: 1,923
Percent Male: 80%
Percent Female: 20%
Total Percent Minority or Unreported: 11%
Percent African-American: 2%
Percent Asian/Pacific Islander: 4%
Percent Hispanic: 2%
Percent Native-American: <1%
Percent International: 2%
Percent in-state/out of state: 42%/58%
Percent from Public HS: 83%
Retention Rate: Unreported
Graduation Rate 4-year: 72%

Graduation Rate 6-year: 81%
Percent Undergraduates in On-campus housing: 60%
Number of official organized extracurricular organizations: 87
3 Most popular majors: Biomedical Engineering, Chemical Engineering, Mechanical Engineering
Student/Faculty ratio: 12:1
Average Class Size: 25
Percent of students going to grad school: 20%
Tuition and Fees: $30,243
In-State Tuition and Fees if different: No difference
Cost for Room and Board: $8,343
Percent receiving financial aid out of those who apply, first year: 100%
Percent receiving financial aid among all students: 99%

Rose-Hulman Institute of Technology is a small technology/specialty school of about 1,800 students located amidst trees and rolling hills on the fringes of Terre Haute, Indiana. Rose is a utopia for those students who value a quality education over a name-brand university. It offers a more relaxed environment than its rivals, as cutthroat competition is unheard of. Because of this balance between rigor and relaxation, students are genuinely happy to be at Rose-Hulman.

Tough as Nails

Most Rose students were accustomed to getting As in high school, but things quickly change for them at Rose, where Bs are only feasible for those who work hard. Indeed, students don't exaggerate the work load when they claim "Straight As are really rare." On the other hand, if the rumors are true, no student who attends every class has ever failed a course either.

There are few easy routes to a diploma, though students agree that certain majors such as civil engineering aren't as demanding as others. The most popular majors are "anything engineering," such as mechanical engineering, electrical engineering, chemical engineering, or computer engineering. Regardless of a student's major, one sure bet is that "Most students are lucky if they get five hours of sleep a night because they are doing homework all night." Despite Rose students' work ethic, "Students here don't tend to compete with each other. We work cooperatively. Rose really stresses group projects and practical experience."

The first two years are considered the most difficult, but luckily, the workload improves after that. The sophomore curriculum is known to be brutal because it consists of classes that teach the basics for all the disciplines. Students can count on help from their professors, since they have "very good relationships." Professors often give students their home phone numbers in case they ever need help outside of office hours and professors "will help students with work for other classes as well." They are clearly "willing to put in extra hours to help students and [they] make an effort to get to know the students, and really care about us," says one student. One notorious professor, Dr. John Rickert, "can solve two different math problems at the same time on the board—solving one with each hand. This is true." He also races against the computer math program, Maple, and wins sometimes. Moreover, all classes at Rose are taught by professors, though TAs are also available to help students with questions.

In spite of the workload, students are truly happy and say that the school is all they expected. One student says, "The teachers are nice, the work is challenging, and I have made a lot of new friends." Also impressive is Rose's record of nearly 100-percent job placement rate for graduating seniors and its rank in *U.S. News & World Report* as the top college in math, science, and engineering for the last ten years running, proving that the hard work is definitely worth the trouble. As one student puts it, "Rose-Hulman has given me opportunities that I could never have found anywhere else. Its supportive environment has helped me grow to become the person I am today."

When They Aren't Studying

Rose-Hulman has nearly 90 clubs and organizations, and students are encouraged to create a club if they can't find one that suits their needs. Apparently, "The Gun Club" has a high membership, though students are "not sure if that's to relieve stress or what." Drama, WMHD radio, student government, the student newspaper, yearbook, and other major-related clubs are also very popular, and people are dedicated to their organizations "but classwork comes first."

Intramurals are also competitive; students compete in tennis, Ultimate Frisbee, indoor soccer and flag football—regardless of their skill level. Since Rose is a Division III school, it can't give athletic scholarships and this enhances the all-around feeling that classes take precedence in life at Rose. Varsity football and basketball games, however, still manage to draw fairly big crowds. Rose is also not without its own traditions. Each year during Homecoming the freshmen build a huge bonfire and guard it all week from the sophomores who try to knock it down. In past years, the bonfire has been enormous and required air-traffic monitors, but the fire department has started enforcing stricter rules.

Beautiful, Safe Campus Living

Half of Rose's buildings have a modern feel: "The campus is cozy and pretty, with two lit-tle ponds in the center, some woods and lots of deer and squirrels." Rose has a small campus and everything is within walking distance. Those students less concerned about their appearance can roll out of bed 10 minutes before class and still make it there on time. Students are described as "geeky—few people make time to dress up, and some people wear pajamas to morning classes."

> "One of the janitors took about 45 minutes to give me a tour of the buildings, show me classrooms, and explain how to keep from getting lost."

The campus is generally considered beautiful and it is improving every day. Recent renovations include the multimillion-dollar Sports and Recreation Center, the observatory, the technology center, and new residence halls. "The school is always building something new, and our SEC [Sports and Recreation Center] is amazing and a great place to relieve stress." Apartments, affectionately called "Sammy Suites" by students and opened in 2004, provide apartment-style living for upperclassmen.

Rose is described as "very safe since there is zero crime on campus." The campus is far enough away from the city of Terre Haute that safety isn't much of an issue. To further deter crime, emergency phones are located all over campus. Despite these efforts, most students feel comfortable enough to leave their dorm doors open all the time and say they "have never felt threatened on campus."

Dorm Life

Students have few complaints about the dorm system at Rose. Freshmen have normal dorm rooms, sophomores have suite-style ones, and juniors and seniors on campus have apartment-style dorms. The dorms are big, come with nice oak furniture, and most are air-conditioned. While freshman floors are segregated by sex, the halls are not, and upperclassmen can live on coed floors. Rooms improve each year, and dorms help foster unity among the students, especially during freshman year. "The facilities themselves are pretty good, but it's the atmosphere and staff that make them great. RAs and sophomore advisors (SAs) are really great people and help make the transition to college pretty seamless," claims one student. Each freshman has one RA and two SAs, and "You can ask anyone on campus and they see their RA as a friend more than a rule enforcer." This advising system is quite unique to Rose.

Another perk of Rose's on-campus living is that a housekeeper cleans the rooms once a week. The garbage is taken out, beds are made with fresh sheets, and the floors are vacuumed. "The housekeeping ladies are wonderfully motherly and the building janitors all take a lot of pride in their work and show good feelings toward the student body." Students say that the people who work for Rose are treated well and as a result are happy and helpful. One student describes how, during her freshman orientation, she was wandering through the academic buildings trying to find classes, and "One of the janitors took about 45 minutes to give me a tour of the buildings, show me classrooms, and explain how to keep from getting lost. He still says hi to me in the halls." Clearly, Rose has an altogether friendly atmosphere among its students, faculty, and staff.

Engineered Food

Rose-Hulman has one dining hall and food can be found on-campus until midnight. The food is described as "edible," but students warn, "Don't come here for the food." The campus has recently added a Subway, which has spurred improvement in the dining services: "Either Subway will take over campus or the cafeteria food will have to get better."

In addition to the main dining hall and Subway, "The Worx" in the basement serves burgers, chicken nuggets, French fries, and salads after dining hall hours. There are also restaurants off-campus such as Moggers, which serves sandwiches, an Italian restaurant, Mexican restaurants, and lots of steakhouses and chains. As one can see, "Terre Haute is packed with restaurants."

Nerds Have Fun Too

Terre Haute is not exactly an amusement mecca; Rose students must be adventurous in creating their own fun. On campus are nine fraternities and four sororities, and the school is small enough that Greek life domi-

nates the social scene. Approximately half of the student body is involved. There is a frat on campus for every type of person, but "We are not the stereotypical Greeks because we are all nerds underneath." Rushing is a six-week dry process. It is a great way to meet people and is described as very non-committal. "We say that fraternities rush you because they take guys out to eat, have lots of events at their houses, and generally drop a lot of money on rush."

Since there aren't a lot of women at Rose-Hulman, guys tend to hang out with girls from Indiana State University, which is right down the road. As one student said, "Coming in I figured it would be a bunch of nerds in their rooms on weekends, but it's definitely not like that." Each fraternity has its own annual parties and students typically go out on weekends and Tuesday nights (if they don't have a lab due the next day). Each year the annual Camp Out party transforms a frat house into the wilderness, completely filled with leaves and a 25-foot-tall tree.

Diversity?

Rose-Hulman might not offer an ideal setting for those students wanting culture and diversity, since most of the student body is described as white, upper-middle-class males from the Midwest. However, while there's limited diversity, there's definitely no discrimination. "People who aren't Caucasian stick out. There is also a strong gender imbalance, but I don't think people are intolerant."

Rose has only been coed since 1995, and this contributes to the huge imbalance of males to females. Rose is about 80 percent male and 20 percent female, but one girl said that instead of feeling part of the minority, "I feel appreciated for being a girl, which is a nice feeling." Along with Indiana State University, Rose men also look for girls at nearby St. Mary-of-the-Woods College to counteract the imbalance. Despite this imbalance, Rose-Hulman offers an incredible undergraduate education that is quite balanced when it comes to working hard, as students here still maintain a strong sense of fun and relaxation.—*Terren O'Reilly*

FYI

If you come to Rose-Hulman, you'd better bring "an eagerness to learn in an educational yet relaxed environment."

What's the typical weekend schedule? "A trip to Indiana State University or St. Mary-of-the-Woods College if you're a guy (not enough women at Rose-Hulman Institute of Technology, suck it up if you're a girl.)"

If I could change one thing about Rose-Hulman, I would "find lots more girls or make it easier."

Three things every student at Rose-Hulman should do before graduating are "hours of homework on a Friday night, go through rush/recruitment, and get to know everybody (at least in your major)."

St. Mary's College

Address: Le Mans Hall, Notre Dame, IN 46556
Phone: 574-284-4587
E-mail address: admission@saintmarys.edu
Web site URL: www.saintmarys.edu
Year Founded: 1844
Private or Public: Private
Religious Affiliation: Roman Catholic
Location: Suburban
Number of Applicants: 1,422
Percent Accepted: 80%
Percent Accepted who enroll: 40%
Number Entering: 455
Number of Transfers Accepted each Year: 47
Middle 50% SAT range: M: 520–620, CR: 520–620, Wr: 530–630
Middle 50% ACT range: 23–27
Early admission program EA/ED/None: ED
Percentage accepted through EA or ED: 90%

EA and ED deadline: 15-Nov
Regular Deadline: None/ Priority Application deadline: 1-Mar
Application Fee: Regular fee: $30; Online: No application fee
Full time Undergraduate enrollment: 1,601
Total enrollment: 1,628
Percent Male: None
Percent Female: 100%
Total Percent Minority or Unreported: 16%
Percent African-American: 1%
Percent Asian/Pacific Islander: 3%
Percent Hispanic: 7%
Percent Native-American: <1%
Percent International: Unreported
Percent in-state/out of state: 28%/72%
Percent from Public HS: 43%
Retention Rate: 79%
Graduation Rate 4-year: 70%

Graduation Rate 6-year: Unreported
Percent Undergraduates in On-campus housing: 82%
Number of official organized extracurricular organizations: 70
3 Most popular majors: Business/Commerce, General Elementary Education and Teaching, Nursing/Registered Nurse
Student/Faculty ratio: 10:1
Average Class Size: 16
Percent of students going to grad school: 30%
Tuition and Fees: $28,212
In-State Tuition and Fees if different: No difference
Cost for Room and Board: $8,938
Percent receiving financial aid out of those who apply, first year: 94%
Percent receiving financial aid among all students: 91%

Nestled in South Bend, Indiana, minutes from the University of Notre Dame, is one of the nation's best-kept secrets in women's colleges. In addition to offering top-notch academic programs, St. Mary's College provides a welcoming environment for women with ambition, individuality, and faith. While "It isn't the school for everyone," current students, or "Belles," sing the College's praises—when asked if she could go through the application process again, one student gushed "I would choose St. Mary's 20 times over." Though many are not familiar with the small women's College in South Bend, those seeking strong academic programs, as well as a focus on spirituality and self-expression, might want to give St. Mary's a second glance.

Getting the W

St. Mary's strong academic programs are a key draw for applicants. The school offers a liberal arts education, and students are required to take a wide range of courses in areas such as the sciences, religion and liter-ature to satisfy their General Education requirements. Most students do not consider the requirements a hindrance, and some are even grateful for the requirements—one mathematics and economics major stressed the benefit of the liberal arts background they provide. But the same student also recommends spreading out the GEs over four years, to avoid being stuck with a semester full of classes in one discipline as an upperclassman. Those seeking a wider range of options to choose from can pursue a co-exchange program with Notre Dame, which involves taking two classes a semester at the campus across the street.

In addition to fulfilling their GEs, students must satisfy an extensive writing requirement by getting their Ws. General writing proficiency must be achieved as a first-year and again within the major as a junior and a senior—but students describe the requirement as a plus. "I feel more confident writing papers now that I have the W," one sophomore said. Writing portfolios are graded by professors from all departments and include work done in disciplines other than English. In combination with the typical course load, the writing requirement ensures that "You learn how to write and how to communicate your ideas" during your four years at St. Mary's.

Academics at St. Mary's are not for the weak-willed—the workload is described as "heavy" and "intimidating" but "definitely manageable." Students take around five courses, or 16–18 credits, a semester. Those seeking a laid-back academic atmosphere be warned—there is a decent amount of competition for honor societies and internship opportunities. "The college is small, all the students are women, and women can be really competitive," as one student explains. However, another described the atmosphere as encouraging rather than cutthroat: "We're all helping each other out, but we're all pushing each other at the same time." While all areas of study are demanding, some say communications majors enjoy a bit less work than others. Strong advising systems established through the Academic Affairs and First Year Studies office help students chart out their academic plans.

Benefits of the college's small size—there are only about 1,500 undergraduates on campus—include intimate class settings and tight relationships with professors. The average class size is 16 and upperclassmen report that they have had few classes with more than 20 students. Art students call instructors by their first names and math students share Memorial Day picnics with professors and their families. Professors typically list their home and cell phone numbers on syllabi and students have been known to dial them as late as 1 a.m. with questions on the homework. This one-on-one attention also means professors are more than willing to provide career guidance, research opportunities and valuable graduate school recommendations for their students.

A Packed Social Calendar

While St. Mary's students devote themselves tirelessly to their studies, they also find time to unwind. The Student Activities Board keeps Belles busy with a host of campus activities. Two of the biggest events are the SMC Tostal and the Twilight Tailgate; others include Jamaica Shaka (a freshman orientation mixer with Notre Dame students), pumpkin carving and Sundaes on Sundays. Dalloway's, a student-run coffeehouse, is a popular venue for those seeking a diversion from their studies. The organization offers karaoke, bands, dating games and other activities throughout the week.

Weekends at SMC are described as fairly low-key; students often stay in to watch movies with their friends or catch up on work. One of the benefits of SMC's proximity to the University of Notre Dame is the extra set of activities the school offers. Notre Dame's film screenings draw large crowds from St. Mary's as do school-sponsored activities such as laser tag. While St. Mary's permits dorm parties for those over 21, many head across the street for a more lively night life. "We go to Notre Dame if we want to go to a party," said one SMC student. A non-drinking club between the two schools, Flipside, hosts at least one activity each weekend for those who prefer to abstain. *The Observer*, a publication that serves St. Mary's, Notre Dame, and the College of the Holy Cross, keeps students on all three campuses up to date on what's happening each weekend. As one student said, "Within this five-mile sphere, there is never a dull moment!"

The University of Notre Dame also provides a nice outlet from the same-sex environment at SMC. "You don't realize you're missing men in classes, but on the weekends, you do," confessed one student. A trolley runs back and forth between the two colleges, making intercollegiate dating a definite possibility.

Those seeking a break from the on-campus nightlife gravitate toward nearby bars and restaurants but one student confessed that "South Bend is sort of rundown, not the kind of place you want to hang out." Liquor locales in the surrounding area include Bookmakers, Fever, The Linebacker and Rum Runners. Trips to Chicago are also popular for those seeking respite from campus life. For those lacking a car, the school sponsors a few bus trips to the city each year.

The Facts of Life

Freshmen are placed within one of the four residence halls on campus: Le Mans, Holy Cross, Regina and McCandless. LeMans Hall, designed by a Notre Dame architecture student, is one of the more sought after dormitories. Once a building for both classrooms and dorms, it features marble in the bathrooms and chalkboards in some of the bedrooms. In general, students are pleased with the size of the rooms: "You don't feel like you're getting the shaft." Suites in McCandless even include a separate carrel for studying, because "St. Mary's believes you should separate study from sleep."

Roommates are assigned freshman year. If the relationship becomes less than idyllic, students can seek mediation at the Counseling Center, which offers help for everything from roommate troubles to stress management to depression. Resident Advisors serve on hall floors or sections to provide guidance for underclassmen. There are also Hall Directors, who tend to be recent college graduates. Upperclassmen, on the other hand, opt to move off campus.

SMC recently revamped both the student center and the dining hall. Students cite a significant improvement in the food since the reopening. In addition to soup, salad and cereal, students can choose from six food stations which offer pizza, hamburgers, Asian, vegetarian and home-style options. While some say the meals are "really, really good," they are also eager for more options. "I've never eaten anything that's bad, I just sometimes wish there would be more variety," said one student. Praise for the dining hall manager abounds; students who request certain goodies or recipes from home find their cravings answered within a few weeks. Some meal plans include "munch money," which can be used at the convenience store, Dalloway's, the Cyber Café, or on-campus restaurants.

> "It is just a very empowering environment to be immersed in as a female college student."

St. Mary's was founded by the Sisters of the Holy Cross in 1844, and is still sponsored by the organization today. The GE requirements include two courses in religion, but the focus on religion extends beyond the classroom. Prayer groups and intercultural groups are common. Overall, students describe their peers as open-minded when it comes to religion on campus, so students who don't practice Catholicism should not be deterred from applying. "It's not looked down upon if you don't go [to church]," explained one student. However, those who do attend services can expect to see a large number of their fellow classmates in the pews, especially on Sunday nights. "It's like a social event to go to church," said one sophomore.

While students said they were more than pleased by most facets of the St. Mary's experience, they were unanimous in their concern for the lack of diversity on campus. In particular, they emphasized the lack of racial diver-

sity on campus: "We need more diversity—the majority of St. Mary's is Caucasian," said one junior. The school has made a concerted effort in recent years to address the issue, but as one student pointed out, recruitment can be difficult given the current student body makeup: "It's kind of intimidating because you have this white, conservative, Catholic student body."

Despite the lack of visual diversity on campus, a broad range of socioeconomic backgrounds is represented. A large portion of the student body receives financial aid. In addition, women come to SMC from across the country—at least 47 states are represented in a typical class.

A League of Their Own
Tight relationships exist both inside and outside the classroom at St. Mary's. Students describe their peers as "welcoming" and "friendly," which can help ease the transition freshman year. There are no sororities on campus but that may be because they aren't needed—a running joke is that the whole school is a sorority. Annual T-shirts supporting "SMC" say "no rush required" and "the most exclusive sorority." Indeed students are quick to describe the sense of sisterhood that develops among women at the college.

Overall, SMC students don't seem to lament the dearth of Y chromosomes on campus. While some freshmen list the same-sex atmosphere as one of their least favorite things about St. Mary's, upperclassmen often report just the opposite. The guy-free environment has been known to bring out the more assertive sides of some students and women can find themselves pursuing positions and activities they wouldn't have considered in a coed environment.

St. Mary's offers students an exceptional academic experience on a campus brimming with a "strong sense of community and pride." As one transfer student said, "I was completely caught off guard. . . . I fell in love with the school, the professors, classes and student body immediately." Women hesitant to embrace four years without men should not be deterred from applying to St. Mary's; the Notre Dame campus sits less than a mile away, and a same-sex learning environment does offer a host of benefits. As one SMC senior said, "all the leadership positions are held by women, our president is a woman . . . it is just a very empowering environment to be immersed in as a female college student."—*Christen Martosella*

FYI

If you come to St. Mary's, you'd better bring "something that reminds you of your faith, your family, your friends."

What's the typical weekend schedule? "Friday: stay in for girls' night and watch a movie; Saturday: work during the day, go to Notre Dame for a film screening or party at night; Sunday: go to brunch, study, go to church."

If I could change one thing about St. Mary's I'd "increase diversity."

Three things every student should do before graduating are: "Learn how to ask questions, go through the haunted tunnels, and participate in midnight madness (a series of competitions between classes held in the athletic facility, followed by a huge all-night blow-out party)."

University of Notre Dame

Address: 220 Main Building Notre Dame, IN 46556
Phone: 574-631-7505
E-mail address: admissions@nd.edu
Web site URL: www.nd.edu
Year Founded: 1842
Private or Public: Private
Religious Affiliation: Roman Catholic
Location: Suburban
Number of Applicants: 14,503
Percent Accepted: 25%
Percent Accepted who enroll: 56%
Number Entering: 1,989
Number of Transfers Accepted each Year: 191
Middle 50% SAT range: M: 630–720, CR: 640–750, Wr: 630–720
Middle 50% ACT range: 31–34
Early admission program EA/ED/None: EA

Percentage accepted through EA or ED: 48%
EA and ED deadline: 1-Nov
Regular Deadline: 31-Dec
Application Fee: $65
Full time Undergraduate enrollment: 8,371
Total enrollment: 11,134
Percent Male: 54%
Percent Female: 46%
Total Percent Minority or Unreported: 24%
Percent African-American: 4%
Percent Asian/Pacific Islander: 7%
Percent Hispanic: 9%
Percent Native-American: 1%
Percent International: 3%
Percent in-state/out of state: 8%/92%
Percent from Public HS: 50%
Retention Rate: Unreported
Graduation Rate 4-year: 96%

Graduation Rate 6-year: Unreported
Percent Undergraduates in On-campus housing: 76%
Number of official organized extracurricular organizations: 265
3 Most popular majors: Business/Commerce, Engineering, Pre-Medicine/ Pre-Medical Studies
Student/Faculty ratio: 13:1
Average Class Size: 15
Percent of students going to grad school: 31%
Tuition and Fees: $36,847
In-State Tuition and Fees if different: No difference
Cost for Room and Board: $9,828
Percent receiving financial aid out of those who apply, first year: 67%
Percent receiving financial aid among all students: 47%

J ust to the north of unexciting South Bend, Indiana, is the lush campus of the University of Notre Dame. But the campus is not this university's only selling point: academics, athletics and faith are entwined in an energetic suburban setting, Notre Dame is justifiably regarded highly in the region and around the country. This regard manifests itself locally in the passionate school spirit that suffuses everything; one senior, soon to graduate, said that "if there's one thing I'll miss when I leave is just how much everyone loves the place." Whether at Mass or in the 80,000-person capacity football stadium, Notre Dame's just-over 11,000 undergraduates know just how lucky they are to be there.

A Right to Choose

Notre Dame's academic spirit incorporates both depth and breadth, preparing students for all manner of future options. All entering Freshman join the First Year of Studies, a program that allows them to not only take a broad range of arts and science courses, but also to take advantage of an academic advisor who can counsel students about prospective majors and suggest courses to take. In addition to all this, Notre Dame offers academic support for writing, reading and basic mathematics, ensuring students get a good foothold when they begin the college journey. One sophomore said of First Year of Studies that she "would not have had it any other way".

At the conclusion of freshman year, students are confronted with a choice between five undergraduate colleges, in which they will spend their next three years. Each of these colleges focuses on a specific curriculum: the college of arts and letters (the most popular), the college of science, the school of architecture, the college of engineering and the Mendoza College of Business. The choice, naturally, is not easy; one sophomore summarized his choice as "trying to find the best out of a lot of good options." Each college has their own requirements that must be fulfilled in the sophomore year before a major can be declared.

Still, once the difficult of choosing classes has been overcome, students at Notre Dame generally enjoy their classes, which typically have fewer than 40 students. While one junior reported taking an introductory science class with over 200 students, she also said her more recent classes, which had as few as 8 students, were "intimate chats with wonderful professors." Others agreed about the quality of professors, who by university requirements need to hold at least 4 office hours a week to engage with students. These hours can be more productive than class time; one student said that "in office hours the professor would run through the problems as if a personal tutor, while in class [the professor] was a machine." Student-faculty interaction is further enhanced by the free access professors have to the dining halls, allowing productive discussion to take place in and out of the classroom.

And the workload? The consensus among interviewed students was decidedly "manageable," though one senior said that in her time at Notre Dame she had faced several periods with homework that "took more hours than [there were] available in a day." Nevertheless, students entering Notre Dame are aware of the demanding coursework, and are ultimately free to choose how much of a challenge to make their education.

An Upright Institution

Notre Dame is at heart a Catholic institution, and few prospective students are unaware of the fact. Over 90 percent of students identify as Christian, with around 80 percent of them being Catholic. The high self-reported figures, however, may not necessarily be reflected in reality. One student described the religious feeling on campus as "definitely there, but it's not overwhelming at all." Unsurprisingly, theology is a requirement for all students, though it need not be Catholic theology.

Students are assigned dorms when they enter Notre Dame, and are generally expected to remain there all four years, though many move off-campus in their senior year. Each has its own distinct identity—a senior still living on-campus said each dorm has it's own "reputation, a sort of flavor of life"—and combined with structural features like mascots and hall governments, ensures most students identify strongly with where they live. Moreover, in the absence of Greek life, the closest relationships tend to be formed by the dorm system. A sophomore, who said his best friend at the college was his roommate from freshman year, suggested that while roommates are randomly assigned, "chance is on your side" when it comes to being matched with relatable roommates.

Each dorm has a chapel in which Mass is held every day except Saturday. Given the high attendance rate, some students suggest that faith is another unifying factor on campus, strengthening community values and evoking a feeling of extended family among students.

But Notre Dame's Catholic affiliation affects dorm life beyond individual faith. All dorms are officially single sex and the university enforces a visitation policy, known as "parietals," that specify certain times members of the opposite sex are allowed to visit. These are generally unpopular, and at least one student described them as "inconvenient," though none said it ought to be a deterrent to coming to Notre Dame. And better still, to compensate for the stringency of the policy, all residence halls have 24-hour social spaces in which parietals are not enforced, allowing students to socialize.

On and Off the Field

Notre Dame students are busy on and off the field. Partying—whether at local bars including Corby's, the Linebacker, and the Fever, or on-campus—routinely takes place from Thursday to Sunday. While enforcement of ID laws has been getting stricter in recent years, according to students alcohol is still accessible and drinking is by no means a prerequisite for having fun. Indeed, hard alcohol is banned on campus and punishments can be severe.

Throughout the fall, weekends feature rambunctious tailgates for football games involving Notre Dame's team, the Fighting Irish. While its performance in recent years has not matched the team's storied past, almost every student buys season tickets and "the shirt," whose color changes each year, making student supporters instantly recognizable. "It's just an amazing show—both by the boys on the field and us in the stands," one student said when asked to describe a home game. Friday night pep rallies are boisterously attended, with bagpipes played around midnight; on Saturday morning, the campus is "electric" with excitement as everyone with any relationship to the university packs into the stadium, according to one student.

And football is not the only sport big on campus—"you'll find people into pretty much all sports here," one student says. He said virtually all students participate in dorm sports, which can get very serious, and many students take advantage of the university's excellent training facilities.

Of course, a university of Notre Dame's caliber is not without myriad other extracurricular offerings. Clubs and organizations exist to satisfy almost every taste and interest, and one student was quick to point that "if something doesn't exist, it isn't difficult to start it up." Theater, community service, and music groups are among the most popular extracurricular activities on campus.

A Tradition—And Loving It

A common complaint is the lack of diversity among the student body. One student suggested that the homogeneity of students arose because of "how traditional Notre Dame is," though he was quick to add that he knew many interesting non-white and non-Catholic students and counted many as his friends. There is definitely a conservative slant to things on campus, ranging from politics to social life, but progressivism and other liberal ideologies are not absent from the workings of campus, most students report.

The sense of tradition carries over to the city Notre Dame is situated in, South Bend, Indiana, which features all manner of chains near campus, including J.Crew, Urban Outfitters, Burger King, and Starbucks. "It can be hard to find exciting options after a while," one senior commented, but students generally said they were happy with the university's location in the city and more broadly, as cold as the area might get at times.

> "Notre Dame is about commitment—to academics, football, and faith."

And why wouldn't they be happy? The opportunity to learn, grow and have fun at a place so steeped in tradition is something "you realize you'll probably never get again," according to one senior. Another student described the university thus: "Notre Dame is about commitment—to academics, football, and faith." The rewards of this commitment make Notre Dame a university thoroughly worth committing to.—*James Lu*

FYI
If you come to Notre Dame, you'd better bring "Fighting Irish apparel."
What is the typical weekend schedule? "Tailgating, tailgating, tailgating. And of course parties, rest, and a little study slotted in somewhere."
If I could change one thing about Notre Dame, I'd "improve integration with the city."

Valparaiso University

Address: 1700 Chapel Drive
Valparaiso, IN 46383
Phone: 219-464-5000
E-mail address:
undergrad.admissions@valpo
.edu
Web site URL: www.valpo.edu
Year Founded: 1859
Private or Public: Private
Religious Affiliation:
Lutheran
Location: Suburban
Number of Applicants: 2,932
Percent Accepted: 90%
Percent Accepted who
enroll: 27%
Number Entering: 715
Number of Transfers
Accepted each Year: 201
Middle 50% SAT range:
M: 500–630, CR:
490–600, Wr: 480–590
Middle 50% ACT range: 22–28
Early admission program
EA/ED/None: EA

Percentage accepted
through EA or ED: 93%
EA and ED deadline: 1-Nov
Regular Deadline: 15-Jan
Application Fee: $30
Full time Undergraduate
enrollment: 2,917
Total enrollment: 3,874
Percent Male: 48%
Percent Female: 52%
Total Percent Minority or
Unreported: 22%
Percent African-American: 7%
Percent Asian/Pacific
Islander: 2%
Percent Hispanic: 6%
Percent Native-American:
<1%
Percent International: 3%
Percent in-state/out of
state: 35%/65%
Percent from Public HS:
Unreported
Retention Rate: 85%
Graduation Rate 4-year: 75%

Graduation Rate 6-year:
Unreported
Percent Undergraduates in
On-campus housing: 70%
Number of official organized
extracurricular
organizations: Unreported
3 Most popular majors:
Business/Marketing, Social
Sciences, Engineering
Student/Faculty ratio: 18:1
Average Class Size: 17
Percent of students going to
grad school: 23%
Tuition and Fees: $26,950
In-State Tuition and Fees if
different: No difference
Cost for Room and Board:
$7,620
Percent receiving financial
aid out of those who apply,
first year: 83%
Percent receiving financial
aid among all students:
77%

N estled in the small Midwestern town of Valparaiso, slightly over 3,000 students can be found studying, cheering at a basketball game, or organizing the latest charity extravaganza. Maybe a few freshmen are reconnoitering the "haunted" dorm, or lounging in the new student union Harre Union. It's a typical weekday evening at Valparaiso University, a modest Lutheran college where almost 80 percent of the students are affluent, conservative Caucasians, nearly all united in a common faith and a dedication to hard work and social justice. This spirit of integrity and dedication pervades all of campus life, guiding students both in their studies and in their extracurricular activities.

The Valparaiso Core of Success

All freshmen are required to take the Valparaiso Core, a year-long interdisciplinary course titled "The Human Experience" that is equivalent to general education requirements at other schools. "The Human Experience" is organized into five units, each a discussion of texts on real-life issues: Creation and Birth, Coming of Age and Educa-

tion, Citizenship and Service, Love, Work and Vocation, and Life and Death. "It's a really great way to meet other students and gain a solid foundation and wide base of knowledge for the rest of a student's academic experience at Valparaiso," one senior noted.

Those students desiring a more challenging academic environment can choose to apply for "Christ College," Valpo's four-year honors college. Study begins with a two-semester course sequence freshman year called "Texts and Contexts: Traditions of Human Thought," which seeks to stimulate critical reading of, persuasive writing about, and focused debate on great works of literature. Christ College is an opportunity for students to amplify their own potential as well as capitalize on the best that Valparaiso academics can offer. "Christ College has probably been the most valuable experience I have had here: I have grown as an individual and together with my class in ways I never could have conceived as a freshman."

Meteorology and Engineering are among the popular areas of study, "so the campus can seem a little nerdy sometimes," a humanities major admitted; but students can take courses in any of Valparaiso's four colleges: Arts and Sciences, Nursing, Engineering, and Business Administration. The workload, especially for science majors, can exceed 20 to 30 hours per week, "but this is hardly bad," assured one student: "I still had enough time to maintain three part-time jobs." And the professors are always considerate and eager to offer their advice and support to those students who ask for it. Indeed, across the board, students agree that Valpo's greatest strength is the intimate class size, usually 20 to 25 students at most, and the incredible accessibility of all of their professors. One chemistry major shared proudly, "I have the cell phone numbers of all of my professors," while another concurred, "If I need help with anything, I can approach my professors right away and be sure of prompt assistance." No Teaching Assistants lecture or oversee the classes, functioning in more of an auxiliary than a primary role. Additionally, the advising system receives high praise, as students are offered a smorgasbord of mentors, tutors, and counselors, the latter including pre-professional as well as major and minor advisers.

Rules, Religion, and Social Justice

Outside of the classroom, students are engaged in a slew of activities, though the most popular are religious associations, Greek life, and intramural sports. There are several academic clubs—Chemistry Club, the English Society, the Society of Physics Students are just a few—and "almost every club is affiliated with a missionary trip." If students are not attending a club meeting or working in Valpo's solitary Christopher Center Library, they are probably at a party, a social fundraiser, or a basketball game. Basketball is the one sport guaranteed to attract throngs of students, for when there is a game, visitors can expect a campus starkly deserted except for the packed stadium: "Very few clubs even attempt to hold productive meetings on game nights," laughed one student.

Greek life is also prominent on campus, with about a fifth of the student body belonging to a fraternity or a sorority. Such student involvement in Greek life gives fraternities and sororities formidable clout in student government, as a student's probability of winning election and successfully passing legislation can arguably be solely determined by his membership in a Greek organization. Still, one student states, "Greek organizations are incredibly inclusive: there is little separation between Greek students and non-Greek students, and several Greek events are open to the entire campus." And if Greek life doesn't sound appealing, there are myriad other groups to join. For example, social justice groups like the Social Action Leadership Team (SALT) are always looking for passionate underclassmen to organize service events, philanthropic dance parties, or campus-wide humanitarian campaigns.

> "One of the reasons I decided to come to this school was the incredible friendliness of the students. Although people are fairly set in their views, Valpo is very relaxed and welcoming."

Only a small, brazen contingent of students can be found partying hard, however, because Valpo is a dry campus, and freshmen in particular have a separate curfew for the first month. All Valparaiso students are not permitted on opposite-sex floors in the dorms later than 1 a.m. on weekdays and 2 a.m. on weekends, and rules are strictly enforced. One student put it bluntly: "It sucks." Every dorm elects a group of students called the Judicial Board to mete out punishments for noise and curfew violations, alcohol use, and door propping, although the J-Boards are notorious for their leniency. Much more stringent is the Valparaiso University Police Department, which often works collaboratively with the city police to punish students for alcohol and drug use.

Freshmen through juniors are required to live in dorms on campus, unless they belong to a fraternity or sorority. There is a reason for this rule, for "the best part of living in the dorms is the openness of community, especially freshman year." Most of the nine residence halls have double rooms and community bathrooms, and the University's two upperclassmen apartments offer suite-style living with private bedrooms, a common room, and a shared bathroom. And the University is planning to renovate the dorms even further and build larger and more plush residences for upperclassmen. Despite the fairly comfortable accommodations, 30 percent of undergraduates choose to eschew the strict campus life by living on their own.

Pushing Boundaries

But even then, there is only so much more they can do in the immediate area. Valparaiso is a small Midwestern town, usually dormant, but intermittently stirred to a tepid liveliness for the annual Popcorn Festival and the county fair. Most students don't patronize bars, although the few that do mention Brewski's and Northside Tap as favorites. The town's redeeming point seems to be its proximity to other, more enticing locales. One student explained, "The best thing about Valpo is that you can always hop onto one of the free buses the University provides and travel to the beach 30 minutes away, or to Chicago just an hour away." Most students will take advantage of this opportunity a few times a month, although sometimes, of course, their studies can keep them busy for weeks.

Overall, students praise their Valparaiso experience as all that they could ask for. "You get from it as much as you invest in it: if you utilize all of the University's resources, you're set for a rewarding four years in college." Another student shares, "One of the reasons I decided to come to this school was the incredible friendliness of the students. I would be walking around as a prefrosh and people would just stop and hold the door open for me. Although people are fairly set in their views, Valpo is very relaxed and welcoming." Thus, if you are searching for a friendly peer group, accessible professors, and a small-town atmosphere, Valparaiso may be just the place for you.—*Sejal Hathi*

FYI

If you come to Valparaiso, you'd better bring: "rain boots, a Frisbee, a beach towel to go to the Dunes, and expectations for a small room."

What's the typical weekend schedule? "Sleeping in, waking up late, doing homework, hanging out with friends, and indulging Sunday."

If I could change one thing about Valparaiso, "I'd get rid of the 'dry school' rule and place air-conditioning in the freshman dorms."

Three things every student at Valparaiso should do before graduating are "running down the hill behind Guild-Memorial Hall; attending at least one Midnight Madness event, the first basketball practice of the season; and eating at El Amigo, a late-night Mexican restaurant."

Wabash College

Address: 301 W. Wabash Avenue, Crawfordsville, IN 47933
Phone: 765-361-6225
E-mail address: admissions@wabash.edu
Web site URL: www.wabash.edu
Year Founded: 1832
Private or Public: Private
Religious Affiliation: None
Location: Suburban
Number of Applicants: 1,419
Percent Accepted: 47%
Percent Accepted who enroll: 37%
Number Entering: 250
Number of Transfers Accepted each Year: 31
Middle 50% SAT range: M: 520–630, CR 540–660, Wr: 500–610
Middle 50% ACT range: 21–27
Early admission program EA/ED/None: ED

Percentage accepted through EA or ED: Unreported
EA and ED deadline: 15-Nov
Regular Deadline: Rolling
Application Fee: $30
Full time Undergraduate enrollment: 917
Total enrollment: 1,827
Percent Male: 100%
Percent Female: 0%
Total Percent Minority or Unreported: 14%
Percent African-American: 6%
Percent Asian/Pacific Islander: 2%
Percent Hispanic: 5%
Percent Native-American: 0%
Percent International: 5%
Percent in-state/out of state: 76%/24%
Percent from Public HS: 91%
Retention Rate: 88%
Graduation Rate 4-year: 64%

Graduation Rate 6-year: 64%
Percent Undergraduates in On-campus housing: 91%
Number of official organized extracurricular organizations: 64
3 Most popular majors: English, History, Psychology
Student/Faculty ratio: 10:1
Average Class Size: 15
Percent of students going to grad school: 47%
Tuition and Fees: $25,900
In-State Tuition and Fees if different: No difference
Cost for Room and Board: $7,200
Percent receiving financial aid out of those who apply, first year: 93%
Percent receiving financial aid among all students: 88%

As one of America's few remaining all-male institutions, Wabash College students benefit from the school's rich tradition of excellence, impressive endowment, small class sizes and academic rigor. From the long-held football rivalries to the major Greek presence on campus, Wabash offers a unique college experience for highly focused young men.

Small Classes, Personal Experience

Class sizes at Wabash tend to be much smaller than at competing institutions. "The largest size I have ever heard of for a class at Wabash is around 35," one student reported. When classes attract larger volumes, the school generally responds by offering several sections, rather than limiting those who can enroll. The intimate classroom environment provides students with the opportunity to foster relationships with professors, who students say "encourage individual thought and contribution in class" and are "almost uniformly excellent." After completing courses, students frequently visit and maintain lasting relationships with professors. One senior noted, "Students can build strong relationships with their professors here at Wabash, and these contacts will later be valuable resources for recommendations and help in finding a career." All this personal attention seems to pay strong dividends to Wabash's graduates. In the years after graduation, approximately 47 percent of students attend graduate or professional school, and a remarkable 80-plus percent of premed students are accepted to medical school, a percentage much higher than the national average.

The academic standards at Wabash are high. Wabash requires all freshmen to participate in the Freshman Tutorial program. This set of introductory courses concentrates on everything from sculpture to nanotechnology, providing freshmen with the opportunity to critically interpret and discuss topics of interest. Many enjoy the tutorials and find them to be a great way to "get freshmen used to the college way of thinking." Another requirement, somewhat less heralded than its freshman-year counterpart, is the year-long course entitled "Cultures and Traditions," a world humanities survey offered for sophomores. Students are also required to demonstrate proficiency in writing and a foreign language. To graduate, seniors must complete "comps." These comprehensive exams, taken over the course of a week, cover every course taken in the student's given major. Some at Wabash compare this period of extensive examination to graduate school defense boards.

Life at Wabash

Wabash students generally find living without women fairly easy to get used to; however, some feel that the academic and social scenes are lacking without members of the opposite sex. One student explains the college's obligation to remain all-male: "Unfortunately (or not, depending on how you look at it), Wabash relies on alumni for our proportionally gigantic endowment, and none of the alumni want to see 'Wabash tradition' destroyed by going coed." Despite the occasional complaints about the lack of female presence, many say they feel less pressure to conform to fashion trends and are able to avoid relationship-related drama.

> "Students can build strong relations with their professors here at Wabash, and these contacts will later be valuable resources for recommendations and help in finding a career."

In terms of social life, the Greek system dominates at Wabash, with 10 nationally recognized chapters and more than half of students choosing to live in frat houses. Incoming freshmen often move into fraternities prior to the start of classes, and pledge different frats after having lived with the brothers. Alternatives to this unorthodox Greek system are, however, plentiful. Other housing options include living on campus in Martindale, College, Morris or Wolcott halls, as well as in college-owned off-campus housing.

Every fall, near the end of September, the fraternity pledges compete against one another in singing—or what has become screaming—the Wabash school song, "Old Wabash," at an event dubbed "Chapel Sing." The freshmen are judged by the Sphinx Club, an upperclassmen leadership group with fraternity-affiliated members. These seniors

ultimately decide the winning house. In recent years, the students have been required to tone down this tradition as many were adversely affected by the yelling. One student described the administration's reasoning behind regulating the festivities, "[Chapel Sing] had sort of degenerated over the years into a big screaming mass of hoarse, painted, shirtless men. And we're talking bleeding-throat, can't-talk-for-a-week-screaming."

Most students complain that the social offerings of Crawfordsville, the small town of about 15,000 that's near to Wabash, aren't exactly thrilling. One student described it as a "Nowhereville along the side of I-74." Commercial outlets are few and far between, with little beyond a Wendy's, Wal-Mart, a bowling alley, and a theater. For most students, however, the limitations of Crawfordsville don't stand in the way of a good time. With regular parties and activities on campus, most deem venturing into town unnecessary. On weekends, many students also elect to travel to Indianapolis, only an hour away by car, or Lafayette, hometown of Purdue, to "sample the real college-town atmosphere." In addition, juniors and seniors have made a tradition of frequenting the Cactus Bar, a Lafayette establishment.

While students are generally "pretty satisfied—not complaining too loud" with housing and the social scene, they are less than thrilled with the food selection. As is the case at almost every college and university, the food at Wabash can be less than stellar, especially considering its high cost. Dining options at the Sparks Center have been described as "really scandalously bad." The food prepared by fraternity-hired cooks tends to be of a similarly mediocre quality, negating the perceived advantage of "living in-frat."

Athletics but No Cheerleaders

One student describes the athletic presence on campus as "pretty huge." One student reported that "Wabash has a top-notch athletics facility and is very focused on athletics, even though it is a Division III college." For over a hundred years Wabash has taken on DePauw University in one of the Midwest's longest-standing football rivalries: the Monon Bell Game. The winning team is awarded possession of the Monon Bell, a former fixture on the regular train running between Greencastle, home of DePauw, and Crawfordsville, and holds on to it until the following meeting. This trophy has historically been highly prized, with students from both schools making repeated theft attempts over the years. While Wabash places a major emphasis on football, many other athletic programs on campus are also quite popular. Wabash track and field coach Robert Johnson offered world-class athletes his expertise as an assistant coach at the 2000 Summer Olympics held in Sydney, Australia; he was the first Division III coach ever to work in that capacity. Wabash students take advantage of the great athletic resources available to them, with 40 percent of students participating in one of 10 varsity sports, and nearly 65 percent partaking in one of 23 intramural activities ranging from canoe racing to volleyball. Whether it's on the athletic field or in seminar, Wabash men are determined to get the most out of the college experience.—*Natalie Hale*

FYI

If you come to Wabash, you'd better bring "a car for all the weekend travel you'll want to do."

What's the typical weekend schedule? "Hang out with friends at frats and dorms at night, and work out or do laundry during the day."

If I could change one thing about Wabash, I would "change the town; it's boring here."

Three things every student at Wabash should do before graduating are "hang out at the Silver Dollar Bar, attend the Wabash/DePauw game, and branch out and go to a social event at a neighboring school."

Iowa

Address: 600 1st St. SW, Mt. Vernon, IA 52314
Phone: 319-895-4000
E-mail address: communications@cc.edu
Web site URL: www.cornellcollege.edu
Year Founded: 1853
Private or Public: Private
Religious Affiliation: Methodist
Location: Rural
Number of Applicants: 3,791
Percent Accepted: 39%
Percent Accepted who enroll: 24%
Number Entering: 354
Number of Transfers Accepted each Year: 39
Middle 50% SAT range: M: 540–670, CR: 560–670, Wr: 620–710
Middle 50% ACT range: 24–29
Early admission program EA/ED/None: EA and ED

Percentage accepted through EA or ED: 25%
EA and ED deadline: 1-Nov
Regular Deadline: 1-Mar
Application Fee: $30
Full time Undergraduate enrollment: 1,115
Total enrollment: 1,115
Percent Male: 47%
Percent Female: 53%
Total Percent Minority or Unreported: 16%
Percent African-American: 3%
Percent Asian/Pacific Islander: 1%
Percent Hispanic: 3%
Percent Native-American: 1%
Percent International: 3%
Percent in-state/out of state: 30%/70%
Percent from Public HS: 85%
Retention Rate: 85%

Graduation Rate 4-year: 60%
Graduation Rate 6-year: 66%
Percent Undergraduates in On-campus housing: 87%
Number of official organized extracurricular organizations: 76
3 Most popular majors: Economics, English, Psychology
Student/Faculty ratio: 11:1
Average Class Size: 14
Percent of students going to grad school: Unreported
Tuition and Fees: $26,100
In-State Tuition and Fees if different: No difference
Cost for Room and Board: $6,970
Percent receiving financial aid out of those who apply, first year: 79%
Percent receiving financial aid among all students: 68%

No, Cornell College is not an Ivy-League university in Ithaca. Despite its small size and rural setting, however, it does attract some top talent from across the country—and it was founded 12 years earlier than that other Cornell in upstate New York. At Cornell College in Mount Vernon, Iowa, students have the opportunity to enroll in only one course at a time, join "social groups" and participate in one of the country's few college steel drum ensembles.

One-Course-At-A-Time

For students who prefer concentrating on only one subject as opposed to juggling four or five per semester, Cornell's unique One-Course-At-A-Time, or OCAAT, scheduling system is a big attraction. All courses are scheduled in blocks, with each year consisting of nine, three-and-a-half week blocks. Most courses meet for morning and afternoon sessions every day of the week, with courses requiring labs often running longer sessions than other courses. Overall students tend to give OCAAT very positive reviews. As one student described, "it allows students to focus and also to be more intense."

Additionally, students said they appreciate OCAAT for the strong student-faculty relationships it fosters as well as for the flexibility it provides. Because professors, too, have only one course at a time to focus on, they can devote all their energy and resources to the students of that particular course. Students described their professors as "awesome" and "totally dedicated" to teaching and advising. And, since so many professors live right in the small town of Mount Vernon, casual meetings outside of the classroom are very common.

Furthermore, class sizes tend to be fairly small, since all are capped at 25 students (some are even capped at 18), including introductory-level courses. The combination of small classes and block scheduling thus gives students more opportunities to attend field trips, take advantage of their own classrooms—which are not shared during the block period, and get one-on-one attention from professors.

Of course, as any student will tell you, OCAAT has its drawbacks, too—aside from the fact that taking an uninteresting course will only be that much worse when one has to go to it every day for a month. Students also acknowledged that while OCAAT works well for most classes, it can be problematic for certain areas of study. For example, it might be difficult to cram certain technical- or memorization-intensive courses, such as an introductory language course or mathematics class, into such a short period of time. But students also said Cornell is in the process of trying to adjust OCAAT slightly to better accommodate these differences. Possibilities include combining harder courses into two-block courses, or grouping some classes for interdisciplinary purposes.

Cornell also allows for a decent amount of academic flexibility. Students said they appreciated OCAAT because it allows them to take a "vacation block" if they so desire. During that time, they might decide to go on a trip, do some community service, relax, or get an early start on a summer internship. The college also makes it relatively easy for students to double-major, or to add a minor to their major. One student, who had planned on majoring in biomedical engineering before coming to Cornell, said she decided to take advantage of the school's flexibility and create her own tailor-made biophysics major. "There's a big emphasis on independence," she explained.

Not Just Another Cornfield in Iowa

Due in part to Cornell's unique academic offerings, students said the school is surprisingly not as homogenous as one would expect. "For being a small school in the middle of a cornfield in Iowa, it's really diverse," noted one junior. Although racial diversity is perhaps not as strong as in some other colleges—"it's predominantly white middle-class"—Cornell's 1,100 students do hail from all over the country, with only about 20 percent coming from Iowa. Students also said that while the campus is often described as "very liberal," voices from a broad political spectrum are heard as well. "We lean to the left, but there's room for discussion and there's a lot of it that goes on," remarked one student.

In addition to OCAAT, Cornell's diverse base of students might also be attracted to the school for its beautiful campus and lively atmosphere. "I know a lot of people who made their decision to come here solely based on the campus—we're located on a hill, one of the few in Iowa," one student joked. The architecture, too, is noteworthy. Mt. Vernon, a town of just over 4,000, boasts three National Historic Districts. "The campus is often described as a 'slice of New England hilltop in the Midwest,'" noted one student, "and I think it's kind of corny but also kind of true." Though many of the buildings on and around campus do tend to be old, they are also well-preserved and often newly renovated.

The students who live on campus also tend to live in older buildings, although one newly built senior dorm features a more modern suite-style setup. While the dorms may not be "as lavish as some other places," they do the trick and suit students "just fine."

Unfortunately, the quality of the food is not quite as impressive as the campus scenery and architecture. Students are required to purchase meal plans, with either 14 or 20 meals per week, and even students living off campus must still purchase a partial meal plan of seven meals a week. Although students said the quality of the food and the setup of the college's single cafeteria were "improving," they also said having a meal plan can get tiresome. "We're a 'Tier II' school when it comes to food," noted one senior. "There's even worse and I can't imagine what that would be."

Getting Involved

Cornell students also take advantage of the many extracurricular organizations available. About 80 different student organizations exist, but if there's not a group that strikes a student's fancy, he or she is easily able to start one independently. The Student

Senate is in charge of doling out funds to the various organizations, which range from the Medieval Renaissance Club to the Union of Progressive Students to *The Cornellian*, the college newspaper. One of the more popular activities at Cornell is Pandemonium, a steel drums ensemble comprised of about 20 people performing a wide variety of traditional and contemporary music on four different kinds of drums.

> **"Because we're so small and isolated, it really pulls our campus together."**

Athletics are also very popular at Cornell, with several intramural activities offered during each block period. Though traditional sports, like basketball and volleyball, tend to be the most popular, students also participate in intramural watermelon seed-spitting contests, indoor Wiffle ball games, and dodgeball tournaments. While many also participate in varsity sports, students noted that there are definitely athletic and nonathletic crowds on campus. Interest in athletics is "not campus wide," but games for football, as well as for basketball and volleyball, tend to get "pretty decent" turnouts, particularly for such a small college. Wrestling also tends to be popular, as Cornell is in one of the toughest Division III wrestling conferences in the country.

Going Social
Unlike at larger institutions, much of the social interaction at Cornell tends to take place on a smaller scale—a characteristic many students said they appreciated. "It's a small town so it's a much smaller scene, but I'm the type of person who's okay with that," explained one senior. Another noted that "because we're so small and isolated, it really pulls our campus together." The Performing Arts and Activities Council at Cornell also hosts a number of popular activities, bringing popular comedians, bands, or speakers to campus for all to enjoy on the weekends.

However, Cornell students are still able to enjoy large campus-wide parties, with "social groups" frequently hosting some of the larger off-campus gatherings. Social groups act similarly to fraternities and sororities elsewhere—but while they have Greek names, they are not nationally-affiliated and so are unique to Cornell. Some of the groups are service-based, like the Taus and Rhozes, and others are more "party-oriented," like the Delts, Owls and Phi-Os. About half of all students are members of a social group, but parties are often open to the entire University. Although events including the Delts' St. Patty's Day party and the Gamma's pig roast are popular, the social groups also host formals and semiformals every year, too.

If the pub scene is more fitting to a party-goer's interest, there are several bars within Mount Vernon, "each of which usually has a different crowd on a given weekend night." For a wider array of entertainment options, a lot of students also travel to Cedar Rapids or Iowa City (where the University of Iowa is located), both of which are a mere 20-minute car ride away. Students said that while alcohol is popular and easily accessible, there is "no more or less of a problem than at any other college."

Testing the Waters
Students suggested that potential Cornell applicants might consider spending a night or going to classes for a day or two to feel out the One-Course-At-A-Time schedule. "You either love it or hate it," remarked one student, adding that a fair number of students realize upon entering Cornell that one course at a time may not suit them as well as they thought. Regardless, incoming freshman should look forward to taking advantage of small class sizes and professor accessibility. "Professors are here because they like to teach, and the interactions we can have with them are just priceless." And, of course, they might also want to check out Cornell's social groups, scenery, and historic landmarks. One student said, "If you're looking for a good time here, you'll find it."—*Kendra Locke*

FYI

If you come to Cornell College, you'd better bring "a lot of warm clothing, because it gets pretty windy here."

What is the typical weekend schedule? "Go to social group parties, bars, or Iowa City or Cedar Rapids on Friday and Saturday nights, and relax with friends or study on Sunday."

If I could change one thing about Cornell College, I'd "put it somewhere warmer, maybe by a beach somewhere."

Three things every student should do before graduating are: "Go sledding down Pres Hill in downtown, go camping at Palisades-Kepler State Park, and take a block off and spend it however you want."

Grinnell College

Address: 1103 Park Street	**EA and ED deadline:** 15-Nov	**Percent Undergraduates**
Grinnell, IA 50112	**Regular Deadline:** 2-Jan	**in On-campus housing:**
Phone: 641-269-3600	**Application Fee:** $30	87%
E-mail address:	**Full time Undergraduate**	**Number of official**
askgrin@grinnell.edu	**enrollment:** 1,678	**organized extracurricular**
Web site URL:	**Total enrollment:** 1,678	**organizations:** 300
www.grinnell.edu/admission	**Percent Male:** 47%	**3 Most popular majors:**
Year Founded: 1846	**Percent Female:** 53%	Political Science,
Private or Public: Private	**Total Percent Minority or**	Psychology, Economics
Religious Affiliation: None	**Unreported:** 19%	**Student/Faculty ratio:**
Location: Rural	**Percent African-American:**	9:1
Number of Applicants: 3,217	5%	**Average Class Size:**
Percent Accepted: 43%	**Percent Asian/Pacific**	18
Percent Accepted who	**Islander:** 8%	**Percent of students**
enroll: 34%	**Percent Hispanic:** 6%	**going to grad school:**
Number Entering: 468	**Percent Native-American:**	Unreported
Number of Transfers	<1%	**Tuition and Fees:** $35,428
Accepted each Year: 25	**Percent International:** 11%	**In-State Tuition and Fees if**
Middle 50% SAT range: M:	**Percent in-state/out of**	**different:** No difference
620–710, CR: 610–740,	**state:** 12%/88%	**Cost for Room and Board:**
Wr: Unreported	**Percent from Public HS:**	$8,272
Middle 50% ACT range:	65%	**Percent receiving financial**
28–32	**Retention Rate:** 94%	**aid out of those who apply,**
Early admission program	**Graduation Rate 4-year:**	**first year:** 81%
EA/ED/None: ED	84%	**Percent receiving financial**
Percentage accepted	**Graduation Rate 6-year:**	**aid among all students:**
through EA or ED: 69%	86%	Unreported

G rinnell College is a small school in a small town, but size hasn't stopped it and, in many ways, has defined its tightly knit intellectual and social community. Founded in 1846, Grinnell has since become a top choice for students thanks to its challenging academic program, quirky student body, and numerous—though often unconventional—extracurricular opportunities. Named the "Best All-Around College" in *Newsweek*'s "Hot Schools of 2004" list and ranked eighteenth on the *U.S. News & World Report*'s list of best liberal arts colleges for 2011, Grinnell, though located "basically in the middle of a cornfield," is a renowned institution that will provide students with an excellent education and a unique social experience.

Small Classes, Large Workload

Classes at Grinnell are small. Even popular introductory classes remain at under 30 students, which allows for close interactions with professors starting on the first day of class in freshman year. On the downside, it also means that it is difficult to slack off or blend in.

A new system of course selection has eliminated competition for most popular classes, and students get into their top choices without a fight. "I got all my first-choice classes, even as a freshman," boasted one student.

Sociology is generally considered the easiest major on campus, and the sciences are thought to be the hardest. Weekdays "are pretty much exclusively for studying" due to a large workload with significant amounts of reading. Grinnell students, though, don't mind. Coursework is usually interesting. "We read primary documents, not textbooks about those documents. It is not about memorizing facts and regurgitating them, it is about analyzing everything yourself," said one student. "Your teachers want you to challenge them. You're not supposed to accept what is given," said another. This, in combination with small class sizes, allows students to develop close relationships with professors.

The only academic requirement at Grinnell is the first-year tutorial, in which groups of 12 students develop their writing skills on a wide range of topics, ranging from serious classes on "Russia in Revolution" to amusing courses like "The Onion, Sarah Silverman, and Flatulence: Why Are Funny Things Funny?"

Grinnell also offers students the chance to create their own courses via the Mentored Advanced Project program (MAP). It allows students to work with a member of the faculty on "scholarly research or the creation of a work of art." Another option is to take ExCo, or Experimental College, which is a number of informal, often student-taught classes on a range of topics that interest students, townspeople, and staff alike.

Sound Body, Sound Mind

To study, students retreat to the Burling Library or either of the two student centers, Harris Center and Joe Rosenfield Center. Students rave about the library's study gym, which is essentially "a playscape for studying. You can climb ladders to get to where you want to work," said one student. Traditional seating, of course, is also available. The recently renovated Harris and the brand-new JRC boast not only places to study but also an assortment of recreational facilities such as game rooms and a concert hall. Many students also choose to spend time in the lounges of their dorms.

Grinnell's new gym is popular, as are the newer dorms on East Campus, which boast air-conditioning and new furniture. Students live in East, South, or North Campus. East Campus is the quietest, North Campus has many athletes, and South Campus has the most parties. Though off-campus housing is often more affordable than on-campus housing, most students choose to live on campus.

Dining at Grinnell is "pretty good," with enough selection for a student to claim that "there's definitely something for everybody." A pastry chef on staff makes "absolutely amazing" desserts. However, there are many popular dining options off campus, including AJ's Steakhouse, La Cabana, and Pizza Hut.

Not a Bunch of Dirty Hippies

Grinnell students boast about their self-governance policy, which is a variation of the honor code for everyday living to hold students accountable. In practice, this means the administration "lets you do what you want, as long as you're not dumb about it. It's pretty sensible," said one student. There are also Student Advisors, volunteers who live with undergraduates. They do not function as police or traditional residential advisors, but rather as community builders who are under no obligation to report illicit activities, such as substance abuse.

> "We joke about being a bunch of dirty hippies. Everyone showers at least once a month, whether they need it or not."

Partying includes weekly dance parties, with themes like '80s, Fetish and Cross Dress. The small campus and student body allow different cliques to socialize on the weekends and on Wednesdays, which is "a big party night, if you don't have a ton of work to get done," said one student. For nondrinkers, there is no pressure to imbibe. However, for the most part, students drink, and a large number smoke pot, which can "really overwhelm the campus social scene sometimes." The presence of marijuana on campus is what leads some students to characterize themselves self-deprecatingly as "a bunch of dirty hippies," but as one student explained, "We are aware of it, and it's not really true. We joke that people here will always shower once a month, whether they need it or not."

In their free time, students also explore the town of Grinnell, which is "the stereotypical Midwestern town with stereotypical Midwestern chain stores," commented one student. Town-gown relations are peaceful, perhaps because "there really isn't much" in Grinnell. Wal-Mart is a frequented resource, and "if you don't like Wal-Mart, you're screwed," said one student.

Work-study programs are also popular. Most participants are assigned to Dining Services, which "can be a drag," but there are other options. "I was able to find a job playing with babies in the child-care center," one freshman said.

United by Procrastination

There are "way too many different things to do" at Grinnell. No experience is needed to join extracurricular activities, which include a theater program that freshmen can "actually get into." Also bountiful are community service opportunities, publications, and singing groups. A large number of famous people, bands and speakers also travel to Grinnell. "Even though it is in Iowa, Ashton and Demi were here a while back, and I could see them from my dorm window," one student said.

Sports do not draw large crowds at Grinnell. "We're good in our division, I think," said one student. Another believed that if Ultimate Frisbee were a sport, Grinnell would be ranked first in the nation "for enthusiasm at least." Some gripe about the students lacking athletic spirit, instead dedicating themselves to nontraditional sports like the Quidditch team rather than more traditional athletics.

What students love about Grinnell athletics, however, is that "the jocks here are smart." Indeed, "everyone defies stereotypes here." One student recalled how the quiet football player in her psychology class turned out to be a "huge fan of Japanese and Chinese culture and wanted to study there in the future." Another explained, "You can't make any assumptions about anyone. Every single person is enormously different." A common trait for all students is said to be "the ability to procrastinate. We're all really good at it, and it's probably one of the things that link us all together."

Most students also love the idea of going to a small school. There "is such a sense of community," and "everyone wants you to be here." Grinnell's large endowment means not only good financial aid but also good quality of life. "Everything you could possibly want is here at Grinnell," said one student. The rigorous academic experience in combination with an eclectic community of intellectuals makes life at Grinnell College truly a "one-of-a-kind experience."—*Erica Rothmam*

FYI

What is the typical weekend schedule? "Go to a free Grinnell-sponsored event during the day, watch a movie with some friends, hit a few dorm parties, and wake up the next morning to go to the library."

If I could change one thing about Grinnell, I'd "move it out of Iowa."

Three things every student at Grinnell should do before graduating are "get to know a professor well, play a game of Ultimate, and climb on the study gym."

Iowa State University

Address: 100 Alumni Hall
Ames, IA 50011-2011
Phone: 515-294-5836
E-mail address:
admissions@iastate.edu
Web site URL:
www.iastate.edu
Year Founded: 1858
Private or Public: Public
Religious Affiliation: None
Location: Suburban
Number of Applicants:
11,058
Percent Accepted: 89%
**Percent Accepted who
enroll:** 44%
Number Entering: 4,335
**Number of Transfers
Accepted each Year:**
1,527
Middle 50% SAT range: M:
530–680, CR: 510–640,
Wr: Unreported
Middle 50% ACT range:
22–27
**Early admission program
EA/ED/None:** None

**Percentage accepted
through EA or ED:** NA
EA and ED deadline: NA
Regular Deadline: 1-Jul
Application Fee: $30
**Full time Undergraduate
enrollment:** 21,004
Total enrollment: 25,668
Percent Male: 57%
Percent Female: 43%
**Total Percent Minority or
Unreported:** 7%
Percent African-American:
3%
**Percent Asian/Pacific
Islander:** 3%
Percent Hispanic: 3%
Percent Native-American:
<1%
Percent International: 4%
**Percent in-state/out of
state:** 79%/21%
Percent from Public HS:
93%
Retention Rate: 85%
Graduation Rate 4-year:
33%

Graduation Rate 6-year: 65%
**Percent Undergraduates in
On-campus housing:** 39%
**Number of official organized
extracurricular
organizations:** 699
3 Most popular majors:
Management Science,
Marketing/Marketing
Management, Mechanical
Engineering
Student/Faculty ratio: 16:1
Average Class Size: 25
**Percent of students going to
grad school:** 17%
Tuition and Fees: $16,514
**In-State Tuition and Fees if
different:** $231 per Credit-
Hour
Cost for Room and Board:
$6,715
**Percent receiving financial
aid out of those who apply,
first year:** 87%
**Percent receiving financial
aid among all students:**
79%

L ying between rolling fields of corn and the small city of Ames, Iowa, the campus of Iowa State University is known as one of the most beautiful in America. A vast twenty-acre central lawn includes a fountain sculpted by Dutch artist Christian Petersen, Lake LaVerne (home to resident swans Sir Lancelot and Elaine) and the Reiman Gardens. While both a major research university and a member of the Big 12 Conference, the school prides itself on creating a supportive atmosphere and a small-community feel.

A relaxed, friendly Midwestern attitude characterizes the student body, which a freshman described as "really laid-back and down-to-earth." She went on to marvel, "My first day here, I was wandering around, looking lost, and a number of people just walked up to me and offered to help me out!" Most students tend to wear jeans and a sweatshirt, often featuring Cy the Cyclone, voted "Most Dominant College Mascot on Earth" by CBS sports fans in 2007. "You see cyclone stuff everywhere," noted one student. Al-

though much of the student body may fit the white, farm-kid stereotype, a growing number of minority students, especially Asian students, are bringing increased diversity to campus. "For Iowa, it's diverse," a freshman declared.

Hitting the Books

Iowa State offers more than 100 majors and pre-professional programs, which are organized among the seven colleges of the University: Agriculture and Life Sciences, Business, Design, Engineering, Human Sciences, Liberal Arts and Sciences, and Veterinary Medicine. Students enter one of these colleges sorted according to their major. Undecided students are automatically placed in the College of Liberal Arts and Sciences, where they take a range of classes to help them decide what to study. While graduation requirements depend on major, Engineering and Veterinary Medicine are known for being especially rigorous programs. "Engineering is really tough," one student affirmed, perhaps unsurprising for a school that was the home of the world's first computer. Agricultural programs are also well regarded.

Some students complained about large class sizes, especially in introductory courses, but added that classes get much smaller once students get more advanced in their majors. Professors were unanimously described as helpful and open. "It's just up to the student to take the initiative," said one freshman. "If you just go to their office hours or ask to speak with them before or after class, they're usually really happy to talk with you." While the classes were described as "challenging," students commended the school for its academic support network, saying that ISU "does a good job of helping students." All freshmen are assigned faculty advisors, and supplementary instruction is offered for general education classes. Learning communities, small groups of students who take a few classes together and may also live on the same floor in their dorms, also help students with academics.

Where to Call Home

While students are not required to live on campus, the vast majority of incoming freshmen choose to live in the dorms. "It's a great way to meet people," said one recently arrived freshman. "People generally leave their doors open and you can say hi just walking down the hall." Resident advisors create a sense of community by holding weekly floor meetings and often scheduling special activities. There are a number of different residential buildings on campus, which vary in size, age, and amenities. Although some dorm rooms were described as "kind of small," many have been recently renovated and feature such comforts as wall-to-wall carpeting and air-conditioning. Two gyms near the dorms were also praised as "state-of-the-art." Several major dining centers as well as retail locations accepting Dining Dollars, food money saved on students' ID cards, ensure that students stay well fed.

Upperclassmen often take advantage of the new University-owned apartments, which were described as "really new and modern." Others choose to take advantage of apartments in surrounding Ames, although the longer walk to classes in chilly Iowa winter weather deters some. Fraternities and sororities also serve as housing for upperclassmen.

Boring Cornfields? No Way!

Although Iowa may not be known as a mecca of activity and cosmopolitan flavor, students say that "there's plenty going on, you just

have to go find it." Comedians, lectures, and concerts abound on campus, and Student Union Board (SUB) films are popular events on Friday nights. Nearby Campustown features several convenience stores, bars, and restaurants. Those in search of more action tend to go into Ames or Des Moines. Although many students have cars, the bus system, known as CyRide, offers an easy and free option for getting around. "The bus system is great," gushed one freshman. "It takes you close or right next to every class, and it always runs on schedule." On weekend evenings, the Moonlight Express (or, as it's nicknamed, "the drunk bus") ensures students a safe journey home from a night on the town.

> "I love walking around the campus here—it's so beautiful!"

Greek life also serves as a popular form of social activity, although it is described as "not dominant." "While most people on campus do drink," said one student, "there are things going on if you don't want to." Fraternities and sororities also pride themselves on philanthropic involvement, and often perform community service in Ames. Those looking for a lower-key weekend often take advantage of offerings at the Memorial Union, which includes art exhibits, a food court, and bookstore. On a lower level there is even a bowling alley, billiards, and arcade. Beware, though—legend dictates that if you step on the zodiac symbols on the floor near the entrance, you'll fail your next test!

From Campaniling to VEISHEA

Campaniling, one of Iowa State's oldest and best-loved traditions, is a classic rite of passage for Iowa State students. On the Friday night of homecoming, hundreds or even thousands of students gather under the old clock tower on central campus to kiss their significant other at the stroke of midnight. Those particularly enamored might even walk around Lake LaVerne three times without talking, which supposedly destines them to be together forever. Homecoming week also features barbeques, fireworks, concerts, a pep rally, and tailgating.

The other major event of the year is VEISHEA, an entirely student run event held each spring. The initials represent the five original colleges of Iowa State: veterinary medicine, engineering, industrial science, home economics, and agriculture. Events include a huge parade with floats built by student groups, a talent show, concerts, and booths and open houses open to the community. Ames families and parents mingle with ISU students while browsing the hundreds of activities and displays. "VEISHEA is one of the most fun events of the year," one student excitedly proclaimed.

All About Cy

For a school whose football team was described as "pretty average this year," Iowa State students are a spirited bunch. School sports games, especially wrestling, basketball, volleyball—and, of course, football—all receive good showings. Intramurals are also "incredibly popular," with tournaments every week, sometimes featuring competitions between dormitory floors or teams. Options include such traditional sports as ice hockey and softball, as well as more unusual options like broomball, dodgeball, and even card games.

Other popular extracurricular activities include volunteer programs, cultural groups, and clubs. Many organizations are centered around students' majors, such as the Advertising Club or the Agricultural Business Club. No matter what their activity, ISU students are characterized as spending a lot of time on extracurriculars. "I would say that most people do four to five clubs," one student asserted. "People enjoy being involved."
—*Elizabeth Chrystal*

FYI

If you come to ISU, you'd better bring "a camera to take a picture of the beautiful campus, and an umbrella for getting across it when it's wet!"

What's the typical weekend schedule? "Some people leave on Friday afternoon to go home for the weekend. People staying on campus usually catch a film or go out with friends. Saturday, study or go to the football game if there is one and tailgate, party all night. Sunday, catch up on work and maybe go to club meetings in the evening."

If I could change one thing about ISU, I'd "make the walk to classes shorter in the winter and in the rain. The campus is nice, but it's a pain when the weather's bad!"

Three things every student at ISU should do before graduating are "go to VEISHEA, share a kiss under the Campanile (the bell tower on campus), and attend a home football game."

University of Iowa

Address: 107 Calvin Hall,
Iowa City, IA 52242
Phone: 319-335-3847
E-mail address:
admissions@uiowa.edu
Web site URL:
www.uiowa.edu
Year Founded: 1847
Private or Public: Public
Religious Affiliation:
None
Location: Urban
Number of Applicants:
15,060
Percent Accepted: 83%
**Percent Accepted who
enroll:** 33%
Number Entering: 4,063
**Number of Transfers
Accepted each Year:**
>2,000
Middle 50% SAT range: M:
560–690, CR: 500–640,
Wr: Unreported
Middle 50% ACT range:
23–28

**Early admission program
EA/ED/None:** None
**Percentage accepted
through EA or ED:** NA
EA and ED deadline: NA
Regular Deadline: 1-Apr
Application Fee: $40
**Full time Undergraduate
enrollment:** 20,574
Total enrollment: 28,987
Percent Male: 48%
Percent Female: 52%
**Total Percent Minority or
Unreported:** 10%
Percent African-American:
2%
**Percent Asian/Pacific
Islander:** 4%
Percent Hispanic: 3%
Percent Native-American:
<1%
Percent International: 4%
**Percent in-state/out of
state:** 51%/49%
Percent from Public HS:
90%

Retention Rate: 83%
Graduation Rate 4-year: 40%
Graduation Rate 6-year: 63%
**Percent Undergraduates in
On-campus housing:** 29%
**Number of official organized
extracurricular
organizations:** 500
3 Most popular majors:
Business, Communication
Studies, Psychology
Student/Faculty ratio: 15:1
Average Class Size: 30 or less
**Percent of students going to
grad school:** Unreported
Tuition and Fees: $22,198
**In-State Tuition and Fees if
different:** $6,824
Cost for Room and Board:
$8,004
**Percent receiving financial
aid out of those who apply,
first year:** 51%
**Percent receiving financial
aid among all students:**
72%

Settled in the middle of vibrant Iowa City and split by a river running through campus, the University of Iowa offers a small-town community feel at a large Big Ten school. In a town where people bleed black and gold, Iowa students find their home a "gorgeous, fun, and homey location," as an enthusiastic sophomore noted. With newly renovated athletic facilities, hundreds of student organizations, and classes such as the World of the Beatles, the University of Iowa leaves little room for complaints. Students agree: the Hawkeye spirit is unmatched, the academics are challenging and the social scene will not disappoint.

Wide Variety, Extensive Requirements

With the University of Iowa's General Education Program, most students spend their first two years completing requirements in distributional areas such as rhetoric, foreign language, interpretation of literature, historical perspectives, natural sciences, quantitative or formal reasoning, social sciences and distributed general education. If reading that list leaves you exhausted, you're not alone. Iowa students agree that the requirements are excessive. Though most students apply to another college within the University, such as Iowa's business or education schools, after two years, the requirements provide a wide base with eclectic classes.

Iowa offers fun freshman seminars that liven such a requirement-centric schedule with choices like The Age of Dinosaurs, Elementary Psychology, and Stars, Galaxies, and the Universe. Students agree that physical education options such as pilates, yoga and weight training provide a welcoming break to the monotony, though they fill up quickly. After freshman year, popular majors include communication and business; while more challenging—or "unusually hard," as one savvy junior warned—tracks include engineering, nursing, and dentistry. In addition, Iowa boasts an impressive Creative Writing department, with alumni such as Kurt Vonnegut.

With an enrollment of over 20,000 undergraduate students, majors and departments vary in both degree of difficulty and number of required courses. Despite being a large school, students insist that professors make themselves accessible and possess a genuine interest in students' experiences. As a senior explained, "I feel we have a diverse staff and that there is really a professor out there that will touch each and every student who comes through the University." Students rave about professors eager to reach out, regardless of the lecture size. With larger lecture classes, however, comes students' control over the heaviness of their workload. Each department looks to interest students by moving them out of the classroom, and students generally appreciate the faculty's effort to instill a passion in students to pursue their interests both in school and the community.

Whether studying business management or the era marked by John Lennon and Paul McCartney's catchy lyrics, Iowa students guarantee that everyone will meet passionate professors who truly enjoy teaching. From nationally recognized writing programs to competitive nursing schools, the Iowa curriculum provides students with enough choices within requirements and chosen areas of study to form a well-rounded education.

From the Dirty Burge to the Palatial Pentacrest

Split by the scenic Iowa River, the University's campus offers a range of architecture from the east to the west side of the river. Dorms are located on either side of the river, brewing pride and a covert rivalry between those who live on either side. While one side facilitates sleeping in and the pajamas-to-class look by being closer to all the classroom buildings, the other allows a welcome break from school and the academic environment. On the west side of the river students may live in the Mayflower or Parklawn dorm, while the east side offers dorms such as Currier and the so-called "Dirty Burge." With underclassmen comprising an overwhelming majority of on-campus inhabitants, some dorms earn themselves reputations, such as the notorious "Dirty Burge," a dorm recognized in *Playboy* magazine as one of the top 10 places to get lucky. Some reputations, however, are less sexy—everyone knows Hillcrest is for athletes and Daum is for the "smart kids," as a sophomore noted.

Regardless of living on the east or west side, in the athletic or honors dorm, all students love the community feeling on-campus housing provides to underclassmen. Specific floors, in some cases, are even designated for fields like "Women in Science and Engineering" or "Writers' Communities." Each floor also has its own RA who fosters and develops dorm communities as well as enforces dorm regulations. Though RAs must monitor their respective floors, most students enjoy their relationship with a neighboring upperclassman.

After sophomore year, the majority of students live off campus in apartments that are all within a mile of campus. Parking spots are limited around campus, but the University offers a bus from residential areas to the center of campus. Without dorms to conveniently hang out with friends, students often stop by the Iowa Memorial Union (IMU) between classes and relax in the Hawk Lounge. On warmer days, students socialize on Hubbard Park's grassy fields or enjoy the beautiful surroundings of the historic Pentacrest buildings. The five oldest buildings sit in the center of campus, most noticeably the old capitol building that can be easily recognized by its gold dome. New and renovated facilities, such as the business school's state-of-the-art Pappajohn building, join Iowa's historic Pentacrest buildings to form a mix of architecture marked by both tradition and innovation.

The meal plan elicits few complaints, offering three options for the number of meals per week and a dining hall on the east and west side of campus. The food is served buffet style, with as much food as you want for each card swipe. Overall, Iowa's campus features a strong community, a variety of architectural styles and numerous food options under the meal plan. As one junior explained about having such a close-knit campus in a city, "The residents of Iowa City have as much pride in the University as the students, making the institution and the town seemingly one."

The Greeks and Athletes

Starting with freshman year's on-campus housing, meeting people at the University of Iowa is the least of students' worries. Students love being a Hawkeye and different social groups don't stifle the overriding pride of attending Iowa. Athletics, the Greek system, and downtown Iowa City dominate the social scene, but at Iowa, "people are friends with people from different groups. The cliques disappear at this school. Everyone is supportive of others," claimed a Hawkeye senior.

The University prohibits alcohol in dorms,

but the Greek scene, consisting of 19 fraternities and 18 sororities, compensates with popular parties. Vitos, an Iowa City bar, is a popular Thursday night destination, while outgoing freshmen are found at Summit. Luckily, bars admit students who are 19 or over, leaving little divide between the underclassmen's and upperclassmen's social spheres. Though the University may have a strong reputation for drinking—as one student bragged, "Iowa is definitely a huge party school"—drinking is optional and only one part of Iowa's social scene. The school's numerous student clubs and organizations plan annual events that are well attended. Students within specific disciplines, such as engineering, enjoy close relationships with peers they lived with or recognize from class. Athletic events and celebrations, fraternity parties and local bars earn high marks from students, but by no means exclusively make up the social scene.

Midwestern Charm

Behind each student's praise of the University of Iowa and the beautiful campus lies the backbone of Iowa's Midwestern charm. Though about 51 percent of the student body is from Iowa, students agree that the University strives to admit a diverse group of students from those regions. Once students reach Iowa City, they immediately fall in love with the welcoming, vibrant community with its Midwestern charm trademark. As a nostalgic senior reminisced, "Iowa is a large school that feels small: the campus is compact, the people are friendly, and the school spirit is like no other—that I will truly miss. The residents are extremely supportive of the Hawkeyes and the students of the University."

The Iowa River, a University of Iowa staple, also adds to the University's unique environments. As one west side native described, "I enjoy the west side because you have a separation of school and home. Walking across the river everyday gives me a chance to clear my head and get some thinking done." Few American campuses can offer such stunning

scenery in the heart of their campus, and Iowa students do not take that for granted.

Harkey's Nest

Everyone loves the school's mascot Harkey the Hawkeye and students live for Iowa football. Regardless of a winning season or playing in a bowl game, every game day the Iowa City streets are a sea of black and gold. Football, basketball and Iowa's acclaimed wrestling program draw the largest crowds, but everyone on Iowa's campus is somehow involved in promoting the College and representing its student body.

> "Iowa is a large school that feels small: the campus is compact, the people are friendly, and the school spirit is like no other."

Athletes enjoy perks such as the newly renovated Kinnick Stadium and their own private building for studying, but intramurals, clubs and volunteer organizations also receive campus funding with very high participation levels. Intramurals provide a great outlet to meet new people and can become very competitive. Popular intramurals include basketball, flag football, sand volleyball, rock climbing and Texas hold 'em. The University has 500 student organizations and clubs such as the 24-hour Dance Marathon, the largest organization on campus that raises money for children with cancer, and the 10,000 Hour Show, where students receive a concert ticket for every 10 hours of volunteering completed.

An experienced junior said it best: "I thought Hawkeye pride was about athletics; it's about so much more than that." From daylong dance marathons to Thursday nights at Vitos and a sold-out game at Kinnick Stadium, the University of Iowa is anything but boring. Iowa graduates leave college with a cemented love for the Midwest and unrelenting Hawkeye pride.—*Cara Dermody*

FYI
If you come to the University of Iowa, you'd better bring "a good pair of walking shoes, your Iowa apparel, and 19-year-old ID for Iowa City bars."
What is the typical weekend schedule? "Attend a football or basketball game on Saturday, drink with friends that night, and spend Sunday hanging out at the Coralville mall or finishing up some work."
If I could change one thing about the University of Iowa, I'd "flatten the hills on campus."
Three things every student at the University of Iowa should do before graduating are "participate in the dance marathon, go for a run along the Iowa River, and go to a Hawkeye football game!"

Kansas

Kansas State University

Address: 119 Anderson Hall
Manhattan, KS 66506
Phone: 785-532-6011
E-mail address:
k-state@k-state.edu
Web site URL:
www.k-state.edu
Year Founded: 1863
Private or Public: Public
Religious Affiliation: None
Location: Rural
Number of Applicants: 6,658
Percent Accepted: 95%
**Percent Accepted who
enroll:** 50%
Number Entering: 3,128
**Number of Transfers
Accepted each Year:**
1,017
Middle 50% SAT range:
Unreported
Middle 50% ACT range:
27–31
**Early admission program
EA/ED/None:** None

**Percentage accepted
through EA or ED:** NA
EA and ED deadline: NA
Regular Deadline: Rolling
Application Fee: $30
**Full time Undergraduate
enrollment:** 18,545
Total enrollment: 23,081
Percent Male: 52%
Percent Female: 48%
**Total Percent Minority or
Unreported:** 20%
Percent African-American:
4%
**Percent Asian/Pacific
Islander:** 2%
Percent Hispanic: 4%
Percent Native-American:
<1%
Percent International: 7%
**Percent in-state/out of
state:** 86%/14%
Percent from Public HS: 81%
Retention Rate: 79%
Graduation Rate 4-year: 24%

Graduation Rate 6-year:
Unreported
**Percent Undergraduates in
On-campus housing:** 37%
**Number of official organized
extracurricular
organizations:** 594
3 Most popular majors:
Animal Sciences, Journalism,
Mechanical Engineering
Student/Faculty ratio: 10:1
Average Class Size: 15
**Percent of students going to
grad school:** 18%
Tuition and Fees: $15,360
**In-State Tuition and Fees if
different:** $5,625
Cost for Room and Board:
$6,084
**Percent receiving financial
aid out of those who apply,
first year:** 53%
**Percent receiving financial
aid among all students:**
80%

As one of the nation's first land-grant schools, Kansas State University has always been known for its top-notch agriculture programs. However, it also boasts several of the leading academic departments in the nation. Four of its nine colleges are ranked in the top ten in the United States: the College of Agriculture, College of Human Ecology, College of Architecture and College of Veterinary Medicine. Among the state's high school seniors and community college transfers, K-State is ranked as the No. 1 choice of university.

Real-World Preparation

Students have the opportunity to begin taking courses in their college of choice as early as freshman year. As the backbone of the University, the College of Arts and Sciences has the largest student enrollment, with about 7,000 undergraduates. But with more than 250 majors available and 50 minors to choose from, many students tend to mix degree programs to match their specific interests. For example, K-State has the largest Leadership Studies program in the country, with over 1,200 students earning a minor in that program.

Each department has its own general education requirements that students must meet before graduation. The requirements vary from college to college, but they can include English, math, foreign language and even public speaking courses. Though some students complain that requirements are a nuisance, others recognize that such courses help provide a "broad, well-rounded education," even though they may not be related at all to one's major.

Each student is assigned a faculty member who serves as their academic adviser at the beginning of freshman year. Students said advisors have been known to be helpful not only for providing academic assistance, but for providing "real-world" guidance as well, such as finding part-time jobs or internships in a student's field of interest. According to one student, the K-State faculty is committed to "instructing students so that we walk away with the traits needed to be successful."

Students noted that the relationship between students and professors at K-State is "pretty good," and that professors on the whole are perhaps more receptive and dedicated to the undergraduate's education than at other similarly large research universities. One sophomore remarked that the faculty has "been good as far as making undergraduates feel like they're important." He said the majority of professors are interested in interacting with their students, and receptive to speaking with anyone during designated visiting hours. While introductory classes tend to be quite large—often enrolling several hundred students at a time—upper-level courses tend to be much smaller, sometimes with as few as 10 students in the more advanced ones.

K-State also provides its students with a good learning environment. All of the University's general classrooms are currently being renovated to serve state-of-the-art technology, and the campus is completely wireless. Students described their buildings as "very beautiful," with fairly uniform architecture throughout, accented by limestone and ivy.

An At-Home Atmosphere

Despite the fact that K-State boasts more than 23,000 undergraduates, it "has the sort of atmosphere that makes everyone feel comfortable." In fact, many students enjoy studying at K-State because it has "such a friendly campus." One student noted that the administration "bends over backwards to help you out," adding that such guidance was one of the main reasons she decided to attend the University in the first place. While the majority of students are from Kansas, the quality of academic programs and the school's out-of-state affordability also make it an attractive place for students from all over. All 50 states are represented in the student population, but most out-of-staters come from Missouri, Nebraska, Texas and Colorado.

Students agreed that most people feel very comfortable on-campus, no matter what their background is. Others, however, noted that Kansas is a conservative state and characterized the University, too, as somewhat of a "closed and conservative place." One foreign student remarked that even though the majority of people on campus and in the surrounding town are "very nice to outsiders," sometimes he got the sense that many are "just not used to dealing with people from different cultures." Still, students at K-State tend to be more moderate in their political views than one might expect, and overall the campus is "very receptive" to different opinions and backgrounds.

The Little Apple

One hundred and twenty-five miles west of Kansas City and populated by just over 50,000 residents, Manhattan, Kansas, is definitely known as a college town. Yet it is also home to Fort Riley, a large military base, so its residents are accustomed and welcoming to large amounts of people moving in and out of town.

> "[K-State] has the sort of atmosphere that makes everyone feel comfortable."

Students agreed that the University's relationship with Manhattan is a very good one—the community is involved in University activities, and students are also involved in the community. For example, the student government sends liaisons to attend all city commission meetings and some have even been elected to the city commission, so that a line of communication is maintained between the city and the student body, while the town's residents often attend many of the athletic and cultural events held on campus. Students said that residents are "generally really supportive" of the University, beyond the standard occasional complaints about things like parking, traffic congestion and noise during large events.

Some K-State students complain of a lack of activity and shopping options in Manhattan, since it's primarily a college town. However, they also noted that it is an extremely affordable place to live, and in the words of one student, "you can concentrate here pretty well." Furthermore, residents on the whole are very "nice and kind" to students who are new to the area. Some even noted that Manhattan is experiencing quite a bit of growth, and that several new retail and housing opportunities are being developed as well.

Housing provided by the University is separated from the city, but most students do decide to live off campus. While freshmen are not required to live on campus, it is highly encouraged and about 90 percent choose to do so. By sophomore year, students begin moving into apartment buildings, townhomes or houses, and by junior year the majority of students choose to live away from campus. The University is currently in the process of completing a $100 million housing project to be completed in 2015 that will include more townhouses and apartments to supplement the existing suites and residence halls.

Kicking Back in Aggieville

Despite its location in the "Little Apple," K-State campus and surrounding area provide plenty of options for students looking to have a good time. Aggieville, an approximately four-block district of bars, cafes, restaurants and nightclubs within walking distance of campus, is a popular place for crowds to gather both during the week and on the weekends. While it may not be filled with tons of "trendy, hip lounges" for students to hang out in, students said the bar scene is "great," and that there are plenty of fun places to meet up with friends.

With a fairly sizable portion of the student body deciding to join fraternities or sororities, some students considered K-State to be a "huge Greek school." As one student noted, "If you decide to go to the Greek system, your life pretty much revolves around that stuff." Though drinking is a big part of the social scene, particularly for students in the Greek system, "there's still a lot of stuff to do if you don't drink." And for students not involved in fraternity or sorority life, there's also a fairly sizable house party system.

One student described the social scene at K-State as an "at-home atmosphere that's really laid-back and accented by great nightlife." Yet for those not as interested in the bar or frat scene, there are plenty of other options as well. A union programming council coordinates activities several nights each week, while other student groups sponsor their own events. The student union, for example, puts on concerts, free movies and poker nights, among other programs.

Rooting for the Wildcats

As a member of the Big 12 Athletic Conference, K-State boasts championship football and basketball teams. Football games in the fall are an extremely popular activity with students and the Manhattan community alike, who also enjoy attending away games every once in a while. The school has big rivalries with the state's other big public school, the University of Kansas, but also competes heavily with Nebraska and Oklahoma. The Homecoming game is a fairly strong tradition at K-State, during which fraternities, sororities and other student groups create giant floats and parade around town with the marching band.

Beyond the Wildcats, students have the opportunity to participate in almost 600 student clubs and organizations on campus encompassing a broad range of interests, including academics, politics and religion. Groups like the Future Financial Planners, Entrepreneurs Club and Pre-Veterinary Medicine Club also emphasize career interests. Club sports are popular as well, and include water polo, lacrosse, softball and even skydiving teams. Students said campus involvement is a strong tradition at K-State, and one added that the University does a "pretty good job of getting students interested and active in student organizations."

Students recommended that incoming freshmen get involved in some sort of student organization when they arrive on campus. Many agreed that they developed a strong sense of camaraderie working with their peers in various organizations, and that they tended also to interact socially with their groups on the weekends as well. Athletics, in particular, are a good way for students to get to know the University a little better—whether it is joining a club team, playing an intramural sport or just cheering on the Wildcats at a football game. The large number of clubs is also conducive to helping students develop leadership skills, which is something that K-State emphasizes heavily. As one student commented, "the University really empowers students to do great things if they come with an open mind and a positive attitude."—*Kendra Locke*

FYI
If you come to K-State, you'd better bring "school spirit and a love of football!"
What's the typical weekend schedule? "The bar scene is big on Thursday nights, students go out
  with friends on Fridays and Saturdays, and relax around town or study in the library on Sundays."
If I could change one thing about K-State, I'd "improve the transportation situation by adding some
  parking garages and developing a mass-transit system."
Three things every student should do before graduation are "go to an away football game, spend a
  summer in Manhattan to get to know the town a little better when there aren't so many students
  around, and check out the outdoor opportunities in the Konza Prairie Preserve, which is owned
  by the University."

University of Kansas

Address: 1502 Iowa Street Lawrence, KS 66045
Phone: 785-864-3911
E-mail address: adm@ku.edu
Web site URL: www.ku.edu
Year Founded: 1866
Private or Public: Public
Religious Affiliation: None
Location: Urban
Number of Applicants: 10,367
Percent Accepted: 92%
Percent Accepted who enroll: 42%
Number Entering: 4,034
Number of Transfers Accepted each Year: 1,963
Middle 50% SAT range: Unreported
Middle 50% ACT range: 22–27
Early admission program EA/ED/None: None

Percentage accepted through EA or ED: NA
EA and ED deadline: NA
Regular Deadline: 1-Apr
Application Fee: $30
Full time Undergraduate enrollment: 20,298
Total enrollment: 25,619
Percent Male: 51%
Percent Female: 49%
Total Percent Minority or Unreported: 19%
Percent African-American: 4%
Percent Asian/Pacific Islander: 4%
Percent Hispanic: 4%
Percent Native-American: 1%
Percent International: 3%
Percent in-state/out of state: 77%/23%
Percent from Public HS: Unreported
Retention Rate: 79%

Graduation Rate 4-year: 34%
Graduation Rate 6-year: 58%
Percent Undergraduates in On-campus housing: 22%
Number of official organized extracurricular organizations: 515
3 Most popular majors: Accounting, Biology/Biological sciences, Psychology
Student/Faculty ratio: 19:1
Average Class Size: 25
Percent of students going to grad school: 28%
Tuition and Fees: $18,909
In-State Tuition and Fees if different: $7,725
Cost for Room and Board: $6,474
Percent receiving financial aid out of those who apply, first year: 48%
Percent receiving financial aid among all students: 36%

With three campuses in Lawrence, Kansas City, and Overland Park, University of Kansas is considered the flagship institution of higher learning in the state. Founded in 1866, KU is a comprehensive research university that serves more than 20,000 undergraduates. More than three quarters of the student body comes from within the state, in large part due to the relatively low tuition for Kansans. Nevertheless, given that thousands of students from other States as well as foreign countries also come to KU for their undergraduate education, it is clear that the University certainly has a number of qualities that would attract out-of-state students. Indeed, KU has a strong academic tradition with a large selection of majors and a commitment to improve student life, making the University an attractive place to spend four years of undergraduate study.

In the Classrooms

Prospective students must choose a specific undergraduate school when they submit an application to KU. There are 12 schools, and all except the Medical School are open to undergraduate enrollment. However, only four units within the University are open to freshmen. The others have significant prerequisites that must be completed before admissions. First-year students have access to the College of Liberal Arts and Sciences, Engineering, Music, and Architecture. Upperclassmen can eventually enroll in other parts of the University such as Business, Journalism, and Pharmacy. Overall, the undergraduate program is very complete, satisfying the pursuits of those who are interested in liberal arts studies and those who are more focused on career preparation.

The University offers more than 190 majors. While there are the traditional chemistry, economics, and history, KU also has much more specialized fields of study, such as cytotechnology, which is the examination and detection of cancer cells. "What is great about KU is that you can be as specific as you want in your major or as broad as you want," said one student.

> "What is great about KU is that you can be as specific as you want in your major or as broad as you want."

The University offers an honors program that offers smaller classes oriented toward discussions and research. Honor students also have better access to faculty support and priority enrollment to courses that may otherwise be filled up during the regular sign-up periods. Both incoming and current students can apply to the honors program, but an application is required. For admission into honors, students must have good standardized test scores and strong performances in high school in both receiving high grades and taking challenging classes. "The Honors Program is really useful when you want to get into the classes you want," said one student.

The general education requirements, which are obligatory classes for all students, vary from school to school. After all, people in the engineering school should generally have much better mathematics training than those studying history; therefore, it would be foolish to require the mathematics classes for both engineers and historians. In the College of Liberal Arts and Sciences, students must complete a long list of courses in English, foreign language, western and non-western cultures, sciences, and mathematics. Most of the classes are finished within the first two years of study because they can help pinpoint students into the specific majors as well as provide the necessary general skills necessary in all high-level classes.

"The requirements can sometimes get complicated, but I like them because you are exposed to a variety of topics instead of just your major," said one student.

As to the classes, they are generally manageable. "There are a few professors who are out there to get you," said one student. "But I think most of them are pretty lenient." The class sizes vary from a dozen students to several hundred. For freshmen, it tends to be difficult to get into many of the oversubscribed courses, particularly smaller ones. "It can be frustrating when you are a freshman," said one student. "However, you will eventually get your chance as you get more seniority." Ultimately, for a school considered one of the top 50 public universities in the country by different rankings, the overall assessment of KU academics is quite positive.

Mount Oread

The KU main campus rests on Mount Oread of Lawrence, Kansas, though the name "mount" may be a little misleading. After all, the hill on which KU is located is only 200 feet above the city. Lawrence is the sixth largest metropolitan area in Kansas, which translates into a population of fewer than 100,000. It is mostly considered a college town, and much of the city's activities evolve around KU. However, students do not find Lawrence particularly exciting. "It is a nice, pretty town, but there is just not much to do here," said one student. "The biggest attraction in town is KU, so there is nothing exciting outside of the campus."

The University offers two female-only residences and six coed dorm buildings. The accommodations are quite nice compared to many other universities. The furnishing is simple but sufficient. Like most state universities, on-campus housing is mostly catered to freshmen and sophomores. Juniors and seniors often get a group together and find either apartments or houses in nearby areas. Going off campus is, for many students, a sign of growth and maturity, not to mention the fact that careful budgeting can save students money by moving off campus.

The dining services are responsible for over 20 locations spread across campus. However, there are only three residential dining halls. Others are different cafes, convenience stores, or small retails. Students are mostly happy with the dining options, at least for a short amount of time. After all, most people do not eat on campus for all four years, since off-campus students often have meals elsewhere.

The party scene often evolves around Greek life. As in most universities, no one feels extremely pressured to join a fraternity or sorority, but they certainly represent good socializing opportunities. Most events by Greek houses are open to everyone. In addition, people also host parties in different locations hosted by off-campus students. "You will find nice parties to have fun every weekend, but they can get repetitive, and then you might want to find other things to do, like going to some on-campus shows or just trying to find something interesting in Lawrence," said one student.

Basketball and the Rest

For all those interested in sports, KU must be one of the most heard of universities on television, in large part due to its highly successful basketball program. Historically, KU men's basketball ranks third among all collegiate teams and is tied fourth for the total number of national championships. KU is not only one of the most storied teams in the sport. Its first head coach, James Naismith, was in fact the inventor of basketball. The team also once featured all-time greats in professional basketball, such as Wilt Chamberlain and Larry Brown. Due to all these reasons, KU basketball games are not only packed, sometimes the tickets can be extremely difficult to find. "I think we have really strong school spirit because our basketball program dominates almost every year," said one student. KU's location may leave some wanting more, but its solid academics and an ardent school spirit make it a good choice.—*Xiaohang Liu and Paul Treadgold*

FYI

If you come to KU, you'd better bring "a bike. It can be really useful."

What is the typical weekend schedule? "You have to go to basketball games and party the rest of the weekend."

If I could change one thing about KU, I'd "make it easier to sign up for classes."

Kentucky

Centre College

Address: 600 West Walnut Street, Danville, KY, 40422
Phone: 859-238-5350
E-mail address: admission@centre.edu
Web site URL: www.centre.edu
Year Founded: 1819
Private or Public: Private
Religious Affiliation: Presbyterian
Location: Rural
Number of Applicants: 2,176
Percent Accepted: 63%
Percent Accepted who enroll: 25%
Number Entering: 345
Number of Transfers Accepted each Year: 25
Middle 50% SAT range: M: 570–670, CR: 560–700, Wr: 550–680
Middle 50% ACT range: 26–30
Early admission program EA/ED/None: EA

Percentage accepted through EA or ED: 40%
EA and ED deadline: 1-Dec
Regular Deadline: 1-Feb
Application Fee: $40
Full time Undergraduate enrollment: 1,236
Total enrollment: 1,241
Percent Male: 45%
Percent Female: 55%
Total Percent Minority or Unreported: 9%
Percent African-American: 3%
Percent Asian/Pacific Islander: 2%
Percent Hispanic: 2%
Percent Native-American: 1%
Percent International: Unreported
Percent in-state/out of state: 60%/40%
Percent from Public HS: 70%
Retention Rate: 94%
Graduation Rate 4-year: 84%

Graduation Rate 6-year: Unreported
Percent Undergraduates in On-campus housing: 98%
Number of official organized extracurricular organizations: Unreported
3 Most popular majors: Social Sciences, English, Biology
Student/Faculty ratio: 11:1
Average Class Size: 18
Percent of students going to grad school: 40%
Tuition and Fees: $29,600
In-State Tuition and Fees if different: No difference
Cost for Room and Board: $7,400
Percent receiving financial aid out of those who apply, first year: 60%
Percent receiving financial aid among all students: 60%

Situated in the middle of the Bluegrass State, Danville, Kentucky, is the home to Centre College, a top-50 liberal arts college of around 1,200 students. Founded in 1819, Danville is an hour or two away from big city attractions while maintaining a small town feel with Southern charm. Centre provides its students an education that is rich in depth and width while offering an intimate environment suitable for social and personal growth.

Harvard of the South

Centre has been called the Harvard of the South, and students there agree with the sentiment behind the moniker. "But since Centre has more Rhodes scholars per capita than Harvard, we really think that Harvard should be referred to as the 'Centre of the North.'" The pride is not unfounded. The average student to teacher ratio is 11:1 and 97% of the professors have earned their doctoral degrees. One student called academics at Centre "well-rounded," adding that the intense workload and strict grading is backed up by an opportunity for growth and a diverse array of options.

Undergraduate students must fulfill Basic Skills Requirements in three areas deemed essential: expository writing, foreign language, and mathematics. In addition to that, students must also earn a total of 12 convocation credits every year for a grade of A on their transcripts. Convocation credits can be fulfilled by attending events ("convos") that are designed to help students become more cultured; students choose from around 40 theater shows, academic talks, music shows, and art exhibitions, among others. In the realm of regular classes, Centre offers a huge variety. There is everything from organic chemistry—which is considered one of the harder classes in the college—and Classics of Ethnography to Glass Blowing, Basketball as a Religion, and The Crusades. The Crusades is a class students can take during "Centre Term" which is a short January term that lasts about three weeks between the fall and spring semesters. In the class, students must make a 45 minute documentary on the Crusades, complete with advertisements and jokes. Students dress up and pillage all around campus, armed with fake swords and a video camera.

Taking advantage of Centre's variety is a cinch. Students report no real difficulties in getting into classes, noting that the college has a very streamlined process of registering kids. One student said that despite her major in the sciences, she is able to take upper-level dramatic and visual arts classes. And teaching these captivating classes are great professors and an average class size of 18. One student calls professors "the life of academics at Centre" and it is undeniable that Centre professors are particularly dedicated, available, and friendly, in addition to being excellent scholars. "I am really going to miss the many conversations I've had with professors about so many different topics," one student said. "They have not only been my teachers, but also good friends, parental figures, and great mentors for my own personal success." In line with the spirit of the professors, Centre offers students "The Centre Commitment"—if a student meets academic and social requirements, they are guaranteed an internship, a study abroad experience, and graduation in four years. If Centre fails to meet these requirements, the student gets an additional, tuition-free year.

Frat Row and Diversity
Danville is no big city, and that is no secret. Its population is around 15,000 and social options off-campus are limited. Campus life and festivities, however, offer a traditional Southern school social life coupled with a diverse array of new and exciting options. Greek life is a prominent figure in social life at Centre, where rushing is a big deal, and frat parties are the center of party life. But one member of a sorority at Centre explained that it is in no way exclusive or demanding. "I've never felt that being in a sorority has affected my reputation or inhibited my friend group in any way," she said.

Party nights are Wednesday, Friday, and Saturday. Wednesday is for the "hardcore partiers," while Friday is suitable for freshmen and Saturday is the biggest party night of the week. The frats are known for throwing annual parties like Phi Kappa Tau's "Air Guitar," a huge deal on campus which includes a dance competition. Sigma Alpha Epsilon's "Paddy Murphy" and Sigma Chi's "Derby Days" are other big parties. If a student is not too immersed in Greek life, there are other options: there are parties in dorms and apartments, homecoming, and Carnival, a one-day festival and party hosted by the Student Activities Council, featuring astrojumps, rock-climbing walls, and bands. And because of Centre's liberal alcohol policy, drinking is a common (but certainly not universal) activity on campus. "Strawberry Andre champagne, Kentucky bourbon, Natty Lights," one student remarked, "are the most popular on campus." While alcohol is prevalent, there is no pressure to drink and many can choose not to because a variety of campus parties are designated as dry. Centre's strict drug policy, however, prevents a drug scene from forming. "I feel like if drugs are used, no one knows about it," one student said.

As for the diversity of the student body, Centre does pretty well despite its location in a small, rural town in Kentucky. Students explain that while Centre is not divided into clear cliques, there is evidence of segregation. There are the athletes, the artsy kids, the nerds, the World of Warcraft kids, "the J.Crew and Brooks Brothers crowd," and the "Lilly Pulitzer hoard." In the past, Centre has received applications from 48 states, but 60% of the students enrolled come from Kentucky. Socioeconomic diversity is not something that Centre talks about extensively, but one student is assured that it exists, despite preconceived notions. "There is no such thing as the rich, white stereotype at Center—there is the fun, outgoing, helpful stereotype." It is important to note, nonetheless, that the student body is mostly white, Southern, and upper-middle class.

Campus Strolls
Centre's campus is a beautiful one, filled with buildings that are modern and old, and with trees and greens to satisfy a need for refreshment. Old Centre is a "historic and beautiful" building on campus that students like to pride themselves on. The Greek Revival structure stands on a slight hill, and a tree with a rope for swinging attracts students on lazy afternoons. Campus Centre is a favorite hangout spot. It features the din-

ing hall, Everyday Cafe, which offers an alternative to traditional dining halls, with fireplaces, and a game room upstairs, complete with billiards, ping-pong, foosball, and multiple video gaming systems.

> "Centre is different because its number one priority is its students. Everything is personalized."

Dormitories are, apparently, nothing special. Freshmen dorms are known to promote cross-class and cross-gender bonding and often define a student's group of friends. Because of Centre's Dorm, conditions tend to improve with seniority; Pearl Hall is Centre's newest and hottest housing option and has been certified LEED GOLD for its environmentally friendly design. There are very few themed housing options at Centre, and most dorms are randomly assigned freshman year and beyond. But every year, the administration assigns a residence hall to the "artsy, international, nerdy" types who are into art, theater, or dance. There is also a substance-free hall for those who request it, and RAs to make sure things are in order in every residence hall on campus. "The RAs exist, but they don't make a huge difference," one student said. "You either don't care about them, or you're their friend."

Two prominent landmarks on campus serve as the center of two Centre traditions. The college seal, which is set in the sidewalk in front of Old Centre, is the home to a romantic myth. Legend has it that if two students kiss on top of the seal, they will end up married (which isn't too big of a stretch—a large number of Centre alums are married to each other). Another is a statue called "The Flame" which was originally donated by an alumnus. The tradition is called "running the flame" and can be witnessed during Rush Week or after big athletic victories. One student explained that "it involves stripping naked in your dorm, running to The Flame, circling it three times and returning, often chased by the Department of Public Safety, also known as campus police."

Like most other colleges in the South, Centre is home to frats, sororities, preps, and Natty Lights. But both the administration and student body are working towards creating an environment that is more open, more international, and more cultured. And so far, it has been working. A wide diversity of students will feel at home there. Socially and academically, Centre offers a rich experience.—*Margaret Lee*

FYI
If you come to Centre, you'd better bring boat shoes.
If I could change one thing about Centre, I'd get better restaurants in town.
What surprised me the most about Centre when I arrived was how frickin' awesome it was.

University of Kentucky

Address: 100 Funkhouser Building, Lexington, KY 40506
Phone: 859-257-2000
E-mail address: admisso@uky.edu
Web site URL: www.uky.edu
Year Founded: 1865
Private or Public: Public
Religious Affiliation: None
Location: Urban
Number of Applicants: 10,024
Percent Accepted: 81%
Percent Accepted who enroll: 51%
Number Entering: 4,118
Number of Transfers Accepted each Year: Unreported
Middle 50% SAT range: M: 500–630, CR: 490–610, Wr: 470–590
Middle 50% ACT range: 21–26
Early admission program EA/ED/None: None

Percentage accepted through EA or ED: NA
EA and ED deadline: NA
Regular Deadline: 15-Feb
Application Fee: $40
Full time Undergraduate enrollment: 18,770
Total enrollment: 24,324
Percent Male: 49%
Percent Female: 51%
Total Percent Minority or Unreported: 12%
Percent African-American: 5%
Percent Asian/Pacific Islander: 2%
Percent Hispanic: 1%
Percent Native-American: 0%
Percent International: 1%
Percent in-state/out of state: 83%/17%
Percent from Public HS: Unreported
Retention Rate: 78%
Graduation Rate 4-year: 29%

Graduation Rate 6-year: 57%
Percent Undergraduates in On-campus housing: 22%
Number of official organized extracurricular organizations: 348
3 Most popular majors: Business/Marketing, Communications/Journalism, Social Sciences
Student/Faculty ratio: 17:1
Average Class Size: 25
Percent of students going to grad school: Unreported
Tuition and Fees: $15,884
In-State Tuition and Fees if different: $7,736
Cost for Room and Board: $5,887
Percent receiving financial aid out of those who apply, first year: Unreported
Percent receiving financial aid among all students: Unreported

A school with almost 19,000 undergraduates, University of Kentucky boasts a wide variety of courses and majors, accessible faculty, and a basketball team with the "most ridiculous and hardcore fan base ever."

Book Learnin'

Students appreciate the wide variety of majors and courses offered, but they cringe when it comes time to register for classes; one senior Spanish major lamented that "unless you have early registration benefits, it can sometimes be very difficult to get into classes that you want" and said that some of the classes are too big. The problem is especially salient for science majors in popular departments like biology and chemistry; indeed, another student estimated that the average class size for a science course was around 200 students. Still, one senior says, "Many students start off being pre-med but quit later on."

At such a large school, students say that they initially expected professors to be inaccessible but were pleasantly surprised to discover the opposite was true. While one senior sociology major advises that "it's up to students to forge ties with professors," students agree that professors are very approachable and willing to help students if asked. Several students recommend courses taught by Kim Woodrum, UK's director of General Chemistry, and Dr. Alan DeSantis, a popular communications professor. Nevertheless, one student who switched her major from biology to Spanish reveals, "I've found that my English and Spanish professors are much more approachable than when I was a Biology major and tried to visit those professors' office hours."

This divide between the sciences and the humanities extends beyond their faculties; students feel strongly that studies in the humanities are considered far easier than studies in math and sciences. Still, the University offers a variety of courses and majors in both areas. In the humanities, students rave about Human Sexuality courses and unique minor programs, like Folklore and Mythology, Indian Culture, and Appalachian Studies.

On the flip side, UK's engineering programs are lauded by students, and the school's medical center offers plenty of opportunities for research.

For many, the financial benefits for in-state students outweigh the disadvantages of attending such a large university. Indeed, many students cite scholarships as their primary reason for coming to UK; the University offers many awards to incoming freshmen ranging from the full-ride Otis A. Singletary Scholarship to the Flagship Scholarship, which automatically awards $1,500 to freshmen who score a 26–27 on the ACT and maintain a 3.30 unweighted GPA.

For advanced students, UK also offers an Honors Program that grants them advanced registration privileges and small seminar courses in the Program. Honors students must take four interdisciplinary colloquia that each concentrate on an era in the history of the Western world. Students are also required to complete an independent project either with a member of the Honors faculty or in the department of the student's major.

"It was one of the best academic experiences I had at UK. The faculty is engaging, and some of the students are very motivated to learn," says a sophomore Sustainable Agriculture major of the Honors Program. "All of my honors classes were fascinating." As a bonus, the colloquia courses also satisfy UK's distributional requirements, which include classes in humanities, sciences, writing, mathematics, foreign languages, and non-Western cultures.

Another unique program that the University offers is the Discovery Seminar Program for freshmen. These courses are small seminars with fewer than 25 students that often satisfy University requirements and focus on topics like comparative geology and ecocentrism.

Off Campus, On the Ball

Students coming to the University of Kentucky don't expect to stay there for long. At least, not in the dorms.

"Mainly freshmen live in dorms," says one junior. For this reason, many students say that housing does not improve with seniority because it doesn't really matter. "Sophomores, juniors, and seniors live in off-campus apartments or Greek housing," says one senior. Students say that one reason that people move off campus so soon is that it is more cost-effective. Meal plans are a particular area that needs improvement according to many students, who complain that they are not flexible enough and overpriced. Popular on-campus spots include Ovid's Café and Blazer Café, but students are more excited about Lexington's off-campus restaurants and bars. Students also feel safe in Lexington, which one sophomore described as a "bike-able city," which also contributes to the high number of students who move off campus. In addition, students highly recommend experiencing Keeneland, a thoroughbred horse racetrack.

Another reason for such a large off-campus population? The campus maintains a very strict policy on alcohol; the entire campus is dry, and if caught with alcohol, students face UK's three-strike policy, in which punishments increase with each infraction until the student is eventually expelled. However, one freshman says, "These policies aren't enforced equally around campus. It depends on where you live and who catches you."

Go Wildcats!

But the dry policy melts on game day. Renowned for its winning basketball team, the University of Kentucky takes pride in the Wildcats, who hold the record for the most all-time victories in the history of college basketball. Students and alumni alike get seriously pumped for games, and according to one junior, "Basketball is like a religion at UK." Another student says, "I have never, ever seen people that into any sports team."

"Basketball is like a religion at UK."

With such a large fan base, it's natural that athletics take up a lot of room in students' social activities. Only slightly less important to the student body? Greek life.

Making up nearly 20% of the student population, those students involved in Greek life praise it gratuitously, but students on the outside say "it is a very exclusive group whose events and parties are not open to everyone." Although one Tri-Delta sorority member claims that there exists no hatred between sororities and that "everyone hangs out," one senior not in a fraternity or sorority says of the social scene at UK, "If you are not in a frat or a sorority, you are left to fend for yourself."

One advantage students believe that Greek life has is that the very formal rush week that takes place before classes begin in the fall gives participants a chance to "meet new people and get involved before school even starts!"

Still, for students not interested in either of these pursuits adjusting to UK might be difficult. Although another favored activity among the student body is involvement in religious organizations, those students who join religious organizations are often the same ones who participate in Greek life and regularly attend athletic events. "Sometimes I feel like I'm the only one in the world without season tickets and Greek letters," says one freshman anthropology major.

Home Is Where the Heart Is

The students who do love the University of Kentucky love it without hesitation. Students say that the atmosphere is friendly and supportive—not what you'd expect from a large research university. Despite its shortcomings, the University of Kentucky has that special something for many students, whether it's a community of die-hard basketball fans or the Sustainable Agriculture program. Says one sophomore biology major, "I decided to go to UK because as soon as I set foot on campus, it felt like home."—*Lauren Oyler*

FYI

If you come to University of Kentucky, you'd better bring "your drinking shoes and a healthy obsession with UK athletics."

What's the typical weekend schedule? "Go out with your fraternity or sorority on Friday, sleep in until it's time for tailgating on Saturday, go out with your fraternity or sorority again on Saturday, and do homework all day on Sunday."

If I could change one thing about UK, I'd "make cooking facilities more available for all students."

Three things every student at UK should do before graduating are "experience Keeneland, go to a basketball game, and try to get into the 18th floor of the Patterson Office Tower."

Louisiana

As the largest institution of higher learning in the state, Louisiana State University is also the flagship school for Louisiana. Located in Baton Rouge, LSU may be best known among sports fans as the home of the Tigers, a college football powerhouse. Nevertheless, in the academic world, the University is also well known for its topnotch graduate programs and research projects. Home to more than 20,000 undergraduates, LSU offers a large variety of opportunities to students in both academics and research. Opened as an institution focused on military training, LSU now ranks among the nation's top-tier universities and attracts students from around the world.

Plenty of Choices

LSU is a large university. In fact, it is composed of 17 different schools and colleges, ranging from the traditional College of Arts and Sciences to the School of Library and Information Science. However, the present scheme of academic organization is under review. The University is working to make the system work more efficiently. "It does not make much difference which school you are in," said one student. "Besides your major, you probably will end up taking classes outside of your school anyway because there are extra requirements that you have to fulfill."

LSU has majors in over 70 fields of study. Students can also choose from a large selection of concentrations from within each major. For example, students majoring in Chemistry can choose to focus on chemical physics, polymers, secondary education, or any other fields related to the topic. "In terms of majors, you have a lot of options," said one student. Furthermore, a great number of students at LSU are also pre-professional, focusing their studies to prepare for graduate school in medicine, engineering, and a variety of academic fields. "A lot of people know exactly what to study. That is why we have so many pre-somethings at LSU," said one student. "It is also a good thing to know your major before you come here because then you don't spend too much time on unrelated classes."

The class size at LSU can be slightly overwhelming for some incoming freshmen. Some lectures can have several hundred people, and students are often sitting in places where they can barely spot the instructor. Of course, those are mostly introductory classes. Smaller seminars that encourage student participation are also available, especially for upperclassmen. Some majors, like those in humanities, can sometimes have much smaller classes earlier in the students' academic years. People in majors that require a long list of introductory classes, such as biology, can expect to have many large lectures before finding smaller classes.

Registration for classes can also be difficult, especially for smaller classes. "It can be really frustrating," said one student. "Sometimes, you just get unlucky and cannot be in the classes you like." For all those wishing to have an easier time with registration and better access to smaller classes, the University does have an honors program, which allows students to enroll in relatively small classes that focus on discussions. Furthermore, honors students at LSU must complete more extensive independent projects and theses.

According to most students, the classes are manageable at LSU. "You just have to make sure that you are not taking five really hard classes all at once," said one student. Professors are generally helpful and open to students' suggestions. However, it is certainly much easier to know professors for all those in smaller classes. It is more difficult for students in large lectures to approach their instructor. Of course, the teaching assistants from those lectures can be valuable resources, at least for the most part. "Some of the teaching assistants really try to help us," said one student. "You should definitely take advantage of this opportunity. Sometimes, they can be much more helpful than professors." Different tutoring and counseling facilities are also widely available to those needing help in topics such as mathematics and writing.

Most students are certainly satisfied with their academic experience and believe that not only do they learn a great deal in classrooms, but they can also acquire a lot of knowledge from one another. "You will find a lot of intelligent people who are going to blow you away with their knowledge," said one student. "We have people of diverse interests, and you can learn so much from them just by having a conversation with them."

Baton Rouge

As the second largest city of Louisiana, Baton Rouge is home to more than 200,000 people. It is also one of the most important ports on the Mississippi River. The city has also been one of the fastest-growing metropolitan areas of the United States. In addition, southern Louisiana is well known for its culture. After all, there is still a strong French influence in that part of the country, which is certainly reflected by Baton Rouge and its celebration of Mardi Gras. "Baton Rouge is the capital of Louisiana and probably the most important city after New Orleans," said one student. "So we have a lot of things to do here. But many people just don't take the time to explore the city." Indeed, a number of students have indicated that they spend much of their time within the University's campus and rarely venture outside, thus missing out on many of the activities provided by Baton Rouge.

The majority of students live off campus. "You can find a lot of housing at a pretty decent price around campus. Also, you will probably have rooms bigger than what you find in dorms," said one student. However, most people agree that freshmen should live on campus. "Dorm life is part of a college experience," said one student. It is much easier to meet new people and adjust to college life without worrying about finding, paying for, and maintaining off-campus housing. According to students, the dorm rooms are well kept, but very small.

The University operates two residential dining locations, as well as a large number of retail eateries. The meal plans consist of meals, served at one of the two dining halls, and paw points, which are dining dollars that can be used at any of the retail locations, which range from McDonald's to small coffee shops. "The food here is fine," said one student. "And if you don't like dining halls, there are a lot of really good eateries around campus."

Greek life is a major part of the social scene at LSU. The fraternities and sororities host some of the biggest parties on weekends. For those not interested in Greek life, there are many bars and clubs around LSU. At the same time, the city of Baton Rouge certainly presents many nightlife activities for students. The school maintains a relatively strict alcohol policy, but, as long as the parties are approved beforehand, students generally encounter no problem with the campus authorities.

Geaux Tigers

It is almost impossible to talk about LSU without mentioning football. The team has the 12th most victories in NCAA history, three national championships, and 13 conference titles. Playing in a stadium that seats more than 90,000 people, the Tigers provide one of the most important weekend activi-

ties for LSU students. Starting with tailgates early in the morning, almost the entirety of Saturdays is reserved for football games. As a result, the University has a very strong school spirit with cheers of "Geaux Tigers" instead of "Go Tigers" to emphasize the Cajun history of Louisiana.

> **"LSU is great. We have a little bit of everything."**

"LSU is great. We have a little bit of everything," said one student. That pretty much sums up student experience at LSU. There are plenty of academic and social opportunities. Although some parts of college life, such as big lectures and on-campus housing, are not as great, most students are happy with their college choice and the education that they receive.—*Xiaohang Liu and Paul Treadgold*

FYI
What is the typical weekend schedule? "Football."
If I could change one thing about LSU, I'd "build more parking spaces."
Three things every student at LSU should do before graduating are "explore Baton Rouge, attend a football game, and go to a Mardi Gras parade."

Loyola University of New Orleans

Address: 6363 St. Charles Avenue, Campus Box 18 New Orleans, LA 70118-6195

Phone: 504-865-3240

E-mail address: admit@loyno.edu

Web site URL: www.loyno.edu

Year Founded: 1912

Private or Public: Private

Religious Affiliation: Roman Catholic

Location: Urban

Number of Applicants: 5,399

Percent Accepted: 57%

Percent Accepted who enroll: 25%

Number Entering: 773

Number of Transfers Accepted each Year: 231

Middle 50% SAT range: M: 540–650, CR: 570–670, Wr: 550–660

Middle 50% ACT range: 24–29

Early admission program EA/ED/None: None

Percentage accepted through EA or ED: NA

EA and ED deadline: NA

Regular Deadline: None/ Priority Application deadline: 12/1

Application Fee: $20

Full time Undergraduate enrollment: 2,859

Total enrollment: 4,772

Percent Male: 41%

Percent Female: 59%

Total Percent Minority or Unreported: 45%

Percent African-American: 17%

Percent Asian/Pacific Islander: 4%

Percent Hispanic: 13%

Percent Native-American: 1%

Percent International: 2%

Percent in-state/out of state: 42%/58%

Percent from Public HS: Unreported

Retention Rate: 82%

Graduation Rate 4-year: Unreported

Graduation Rate 6-year: Unreported

Percent Undergraduates in On-campus housing: 49%

Number of official organized extracurricular organizations: 90

3 Most popular majors: Marketing, Communication Studies, Psychology

Student/Faculty ratio: 10:1

Average Class Size: Unreported

Percent of students going to grad school: 64%

Tuition and Fees: $33,302

In-State Tuition and Fees if different: No difference

Cost for Room and Board: $10,900

Percent receiving financial aid out of those who apply, first year: 85%

Percent receiving financial aid among all students: 99%

I magine the quintessential college experience: arriving for the first day of freshman year with suitcases in hand, feeling lightweight as your body fills with anticipation as you face the school you will spend the next four years attending. At Loyola University of New Orleans, a sprawling luxurious green front lawn in front of the century old Marquette Hall, which faces New Orleans' stunning Audubon Park, makes the first-impression experience truly memorable.

Small University in the Big Easy

Loyola is a Jesuit university situated in uptown New Orleans, directly in front of the historic St. Charles Avenue streetcar line. The Loyola campus is very centralized with most buildings and student dormitories within half a mile of each other. "It is easy to get to class on time," one student said. "You can just roll out of bed and get to class in three to five minutes. It is great to have such a small campus." Although Loyola is religiously affiliated, students do not feel the weight of the school's

Catholic ties on a day-to-day basis. "Professors will sometimes mention the Jesuit ideals that the university is built upon, but there is not a feeling of Catholicism everywhere you go," said one student. Another student noted that the only time he is reminded of the university's religious ties is when he walks by the Holy Name of Jesus Church to the left of Marquette Hall and witnesses newlywed couples emerge. "This happens a lot," he said, especially during the spring.

Many students noted that they enjoyed the year-round subtropical climate in New Orleans, which although may be sweltering in the summer never becomes too chilly in the winter. New Orleans' Audubon Park, a block off campus, is especially vibrant with floral colors in the spring.

New Orleans itself is an exciting city that students love to become involved in: through community service, culinary touring or nightlife. New Orleans boasts many cultural festivals, ranging from Po-Boy fest, which celebrates the traditional French bread sandwich, to the Jazz and Heritage Festival, which draws artists such as Simon and Garfunkle and Pearl Jam. One student said the most popular festival with Loyola students is the Voodoo Experience, a festival, held in October. "Voodoo Fest," as students call it, features popular music like Eminem and Ozzy Osbourne.

The city may be so enticing that people who grow up in New Orleans never want to leave. One student said, "I feel that Loyola is maybe 66 percent local (New Orleanian), and 33 percent out-of-city. Or maybe 75 percent to 25 percent."

Loyola's website reports that 58 percent of students come from out of state, with 48 states represented. However, some students feel that classmates originally from New Orleans may be more prominent on campus.

And All that Jazz

Students say that Mass Communications and Music are the two strong and popular areas of study for undergraduates. In fact, Loyola offers four derivations on the Mass Communications major: Advertising, Journalism, Media Studies and Public Relations. Loyola offers fourteen different majors involving music, ranging from Music Composition to Vocal Performance to Music Industry Studies to Music Therapy, and it boasts successful music graduates including New Orleans-natives Harry Connick Jr. and Ellis Marsalis. Although the plethora of music classes may seem a haven for a music enthusiast, one student said, "I have heard that music industries and music are pretty hard." Music students are faced with "a lot of work," the student said, "but they enjoy it as far as I can tell." And all students enjoy the benefits of having a strong music program. "The free student jazz performances are wonderful," one student said.

> **"It is easy to get to class on time. You can just roll out of bed."**

For other majors, like the sciences and social studies, one student commented that the workload for these courses was not too bad, but not too easy. The student said, "For every lecture period, maybe about 1.5 or 2 hours is put into studying and reviewing material covered that day." Students have a lot of help though in covering and understanding their coursework. A student said, "Faculty members are indeed very accessible and very friendly. The fact that Loyola is so small means that the teachers develop a closer relationship with their students than perhaps a bigger university would."

Southern Comfortable

In terms of social life on campus, many students noted that everyone at Loyola was reasonably friendly. "Everybody's relatively nice," one student said. "It's pretty easy to make friends." The student added, "New Orleans is just a friendly city." The student population is very diverse. One student commented that there is not one dominant social scene, that there is a generally even mix of different kinds of people. "It seems to be an even mixture of your typical preps and hipsters," a student said.

Many students drink, one student said, but binge drinking "is not a big problem." Loyola's policy on alcohol, the student explained is, "If you have alcohol in your room and you're not 21 and they [the Loyola police] catch you, you get a fine. If they catch you with drugs in your room you get arrested, not necessarily expelled." New Orleans' drinking laws are fairly lenient; people over 21 can publicly carry open plastic containers containing alcohol. The open container law is very rare in other cities.

Greek life is not big at Loyola, although the university does have sororities and fraternities. One student compared Greek life at Loyola to other universities in the state: "It's nothing like Louisiana State University or Tulane University. It's just not super important to be in a frat or sorority here."

Another student mentioned how close the ties are between Loyola and Tulane University, situated directly next to Loyola and often overlapping in student life. One student said, "I have a whole lot more friends at Tulane than here at Loyola, and I hang out with those Tulane friends in most of my free time."

Student life within Loyola usually stays on campus, save for local festivals or concerts. The most popular social venues include the just off-campus Friar Tucks and Club Ampersand and the Howling Wolf in downtown New Orleans.

Sweet Home Louisiana

Loyola's beautiful campus and happy student body would make anyone feel at home. Although Loyola has a large proportion of students from Louisiana, non-locals revel in local festivities and southern culture. Loyola students like the tight-knit nature of a small school on a small campus within a large, vibrant city.—*Susannah Albert-Chandhok*

FYI
If you come to Loyola, you'd better bring "a friendly attitude."
It you come to Loyola, you'd better leave "a heavy coat."
Every student should, before graduating, attend the Voodoo Experience, a festival that is "life changing."

T u l a n e   U n i v e r s i t y

Address: 6823 St. Charles Avenue, New Orleans, LA 70118
Phone: 504-865-5731
E-mail address: undergrad.admission@tulane.edu
Web site URL: www.tulane.edu
Year Founded: 1834
Private or Public: Private
Religious Affiliation: None
Location: Urban
Number of Applicants: 34,125
Percent Accepted: 27%
Percent Accepted who enroll: 17%
Number Entering: 1,560
Number of Transfers Accepted each Year: 425
Middle 50% SAT range: M: 620–700, CR: 630–720, Wr: 640–720
Middle 50% ACT range: 29–32
Early admission program EA/ED/None: EA

Percentage accepted through EA or ED: Unreported
EA and ED deadline: 1-Nov
Regular Deadline: 15-Jan
Application Fee: $0
Full time Undergraduate enrollment: 6,749
Total enrollment: 9,328
Percent Male: 46%
Percent Female: 54%
Total Percent Minority or Unreported: 42%
Percent African-American: 7%
Percent Asian/Pacific Islander: 4%
Percent Hispanic: 4%
Percent Native-American: 1.3%
Percent International: 3%
Percent in-state/out of state: 16%/84%
Percent from Public HS: Unreported
Retention Rate: 87%
Graduation Rate 4-year: 74%

Graduation Rate 6-year: Unreported
Percent Undergraduates in On-campus housing: 51%
Number of official organized extracurricular organizations: 250
3 Most popular majors: Business, Health Services, Psychology
Student/Faculty ratio: Unreported
Average Class Size: 19
Percent of students going to grad school: Unreported
Tuition and Fees: $38,664
In-State Tuition and Fees if different: No difference
Cost for Room and Board: $9,296
Percent receiving financial aid out of those who apply, first year: 73%
Percent receiving financial aid among all students: Unreported

G oing to jazz concerts, eating authentic Southern foods, experiencing Mardi Gras—all typical occurrences in the life of a Tulane student. Located in New Orleans, Louisiana, Tulane University is the home of the Green Waves. With undergraduates from all 50 states and over 35 different countries, Tulane is "one of the most diverse schools in the South," according to a current student.

Intimate Intellectualism

Students describe the academic life at Tulane as challenging and rewarding. The workload is on the heavier side and, as one Tulane junior stated, "It's a pretty big course load, but it trains you to be an adult and to learn to balance leisure and scholarship." Class sizes are relatively small, but this does not mean it is difficult to get into the courses you want to take. All students interviewed said they had never had a problem securing a spot in a class.

Business, Latin American studies, and political science are popular majors for Tulane students, with many students also choosing to identify themselves as pre-med in addition to their declared major. Tulane also offers an intensive architecture program in which students graduate in five years with a masters degree.

If you plan on pursuing Latin American or

Caribbean studies, Tulane has one of the premier departments in the country. The Latin American Studies Department also gives students ample opportunity to go out into the community and experience Latin American culture. One freshman said she taught an ESL class to Spanish-speaking residents of New Orleans in conjunction with her LAS class.

Students are generally emphatic about how easy it is to speak with professors and other faculty members at Tulane. A Tulane senior said, "I can't even emphasize how easy it is to develop a relationship with our teachers. Every teacher I've had has known my name, and they are willing to go to great lengths to help you out in any way they can." There are no classes at Tulane taught exclusively by teaching assistants, which increases face-to-face interaction with the professors.

Mardi Gras Merriment

According to students, Tulane is not the place to go if you are looking for an overly competitive academic atmosphere. Students describe the environment as "not too intensive," though there is a considerable amount of work assigned. In other words, academics are important to Tulane students, but they do find time to relax and socialize.

The social scene at Tulane does not revolve around Greek life—most students say the partying goes on off campus, in the city of New Orleans. Weekends are generally eventful at Tulane, with the large majority of students staying on campus during the weekend. Students say they are never at a loss for things to do: "There are always new bars and clubs to explore," said a Tulane senior. Tuesdays and Thursdays are the most popular nights to go out, and The Boot, a local bar, is often the premier destination. The Boot's claim to fame is 50-cent-drink night on Tuesdays, with other specials throughout the week.

"It's a pretty big course load, but it trains you to be an adult and to learn to balance leisure and scholarship."

Typically, classes do not meet on Monday and Fat Tuesday in February, so that students can enjoy Mardi Gras, a yearly festival featuring parades, food, and entertainment. The Tulane student council also sponsors a yearly Craw Fest, where local jazz bands perform on campus throughout the day. In 2007, over 14,000 lbs. of crawfish were consumed by the Tulane students who attended the event. Voodoo Fest is also held every year in New Orleans (though it is not affiliated with Tulane) and features popular rock, pop, and hip-hop acts.

Alcohol and drug policies on campus are strictly enforced, and the places and circumstances under which alcohol can be consumed on campus are very limited. Counselors closely monitor freshmen dorms to ensure that students are not violating Tulane's strict 21-and-over alcohol policy, but regardless of the grade level students interviewed said that the majority of their classmates drink. They also said they had never felt pressured to drink and the social environment was very friendly and inviting.

Still Going Strong

Tulane students insist that the effects of Hurricane Katrina are essentially nonexistent on campus. The school's location is elevated, so even in the immediate aftermath of the hurricane damage was limited. There was flooding on the ground floor of some buildings, but all of these have been redone. The only structure currently under construction from hurricane-related damage is the library, which sustained slight water damage in the basement. In terms of Katrina's effects on the area surrounding campus, students once again said that it is limited. Damage is especially minimal in areas like uptown, where students hang out on the weekends. "The visible damage is in the residential areas where you can see abandoned houses and stuff, but Tulane students don't normally go there," said one sophomore.

Tulane is geographically diverse, with 80 percent of students coming from homes 500 miles away or further, but according to students, racial diversity is not as robust. One Tulane student said the school was "mostly white" and another said that "preppy" is a popular style on campus.

Many students on campus are employed part-time in addition to their studies. Some work on campus and are involved in work-study programs. The most common campus jobs are related to housing, such as working at the front desk or being a residential assistant. Other students have retail jobs and work in the shops on Magazine Street, a popular shopping area.

There are an endless number of housing options at Tulane, including same-sex dorms, honor student dorms, and the newly opened Wall residential college, in which students live with a University fellow. Students say there are a good number of people who live on campus all four years, but there is an abundance of reasonably priced off-campus housing available. Sharp and Monroe are considered the more social freshman dorms, mostly because "they have community bathrooms, which help you make friends," said one Tulane junior.

In terms of safety, Tulane students responded that they don't feel unsafe on campus, but that New Orleans is just like any other metropolitan area and has its dangers. A junior said, "You're in a city, so you have to use common sense, but the French Quarter and Bourbon Street are generally pretty safe." The campus is also equipped with a blue light system, which allows students to call Tulane police officers at emergency stations located all over campus.

But that is not to say relations between Tulane and the surrounding community are strained. On the contrary, a freshman student was surprised by how the city and the University were interconnected. "People in New Orleans like Tulane and they are incredibly welcoming to students," she said.

Sports are not a very high priority on campus, but Tulane's baseball team is nationally ranked, and Green Wave football games take place in the famed New Orleans Superdome. Tickets to most sporting events are free to students.—*Samantha Broussard-Wilson*

FYI

If you come to Tulane, you'd better bring "rain boots."

What's the typical weekend schedule? "Take a riverboat ride down the Mississippi and finish the day off with a snack at Café du Monde."

If I could change one thing about Tulane, I'd "make the meal plan more flexible."

Three things every Tulane student should do before graduating are "experience Mardi Gras, go to the French Quarter, and eat at Giacomo's Restaurant."

Maine

B ates College, a small liberal arts
school generally grouped with other
Maine colleges such as Bowdoin and
Colby, is located in Lewiston, Maine, a town
whose claim to fame, as one student pointed
out, is that "Mohammed Ali fought here."
However, this middle-of-nowhere school
proudly boasts such a fun-loving, tight-knit
college community that students overwhelmingly proclaim that they could not
imagine themselves elsewhere.

More Professors Than Students?

Students at Bates know they are getting a
first-class education; national surveys consistently rank Bates among the top liberal
arts colleges in the nation. Though small liberal arts colleges often do not have the resources to offer the wide array of subject areas and depth of study that universities can
provide, students at Bates almost universally cite the small class size as something
that sets Bates apart from other colleges. A
large number of classes have 19 students
or less, and even larger lecture classes usually don't have many more than 75 students.
The Bates Web site cites the student-to-
professor ratio as 10 to 1 and stresses the
college's focus on small group learning in
settings such as seminars and laboratories.
According to one freshman, "The great thing
about Bates is that the classes are pretty
small. You are not merely considered a number in the classroom, but instead you become an active participant whom the
professor really gets to know." Professors
are also easily approachable outside the

classroom and are extremely receptive to student interest; another student commented, "In my experience, professors are very happy to talk outside of class about their research, any problems you may be having in the class, concerns, or just life in general. I've also realized that professors are happy to talk to students who aren't in their classes if they show an interest in the professor's field." Though a small college, Bates offers the diversity of a liberal arts education and does have distributional requirements, including a three-science-class requirement that "for nonscience people is just too much!"

> "The great thing about Bates is that the classes are pretty small. You are not merely considered a number in the classroom, but instead you become an active participant whom the professor really gets to know."

Bates is a very good school, and in terms of workload there is "a LOT of reading." According to a freshman, "the workload can be intense when midterms and finals come around, but normally it is manageable if you learn how to organize your time." Despite the workload, students observe very little competition both in and out of the classroom.

Small School, Big Parties
Bates, located in tiny Lewiston, Maine, does not boast a thriving metropolis as one of its attractions. However, students don't seem to mind; there are enough parties, events and activities on campus to keep most students from having to leave at all. According to one student, "Because there's not a lot to do in Lewiston, people stay on campus and party in the dorms and houses." Students cite dorm parties, concerts, comedy shows, dances, and off-campus parties as just some of the wide array of activities offered within the confines of Bates. The small nature of the school is conducive to creating a cohesive community, and students are generally extremely happy with their on-campus social life; as one girl commented, "Students generally don't want to leave campus because there's too much going on and they don't want to miss it. I can't imagine missing a weekend here!"

There are no fraternities or sororities at Bates; however, this is generally considered an advantage rather than a disadvantage. One freshman commented, "There is no Greek life

at Bates, which I think most of the students appreciate. The social scene is much more open because of the lack of a Greek system." The students make up for this with huge annual parties, such as the '80s dance, Halloween dance, and foam dance, which are "well-attended, and everyone goes all-out and gets really into them."

In terms of drinking, the school has a relatively strict hard-liquor policy: students are subject to a three-strike rule applying to hard liquor that lasts all four years. The three-strike rule requires anyone seen in a room with hard liquor to be given a strike; students with three strikes must meet with the dean. However, this rule applies only to hard liquor and drugs; the school is much more lenient in regards to wine and beer. According to students, "A lot of students do drink, but it is definitely not something you need to do to have fun here, and I know a lot of people who go out each weekend and never drink." Bates also offers a wide array of extracurricular activities, unrelated to partying, that are enjoyed by many. Athletics are popular, and students can participate on the varsity, club, or intramural level. In addition, there are four competitive a cappella groups that are extremely popular. One student exclaimed, "The Deansmen and the Manic Optimists are all-male groups, the Merimanders are all women, and the Crosstones are coed. They are all amazing! They have concerts every once in a while and they are always packed!"

For those few students who have cars and want to get off campus, Lewiston is located relatively close to Freeport, a shopping hub, and Portland, which boasts great restaurants, a bustling city life, and a wide array of ski slopes. However, the center of Bates is clearly the campus itself, and students see this is as one of Bates's major attractions. Another student commented, "Every once in a while people will drive out to dinner on the weekends, or those who have cars will drive to ski resorts, but most of the time students stay on campus." As campus parties span three- or four-day weekends, starting on Thursday and continuing to Sunday, students don't want to miss out on anything that goes on!

Close Quarters=Close Friends
Students overwhelmingly describe the Bates population as extremely friendly, welcoming, and accepting. One student proclaimed, "If there's one reason to come to Bates, it's the people." Several students explained that, possibly due to the fact that there are two all-freshman dorms to foster a sense of

family among the members of the class, their best friends have generally been people they lived with freshman year. In addition, pre-orientation programs are offered to give freshmen additional chances to make friends and become comfortable in an environment away from home. Students describe the Bates campus as extremely welcoming, in part due to its small size. One student commented, "It is very easy to meet people because on the weekends you go out with friends from your floor and you end up meeting people from different dorms and classes. The students at Bates are so friendly!" Another student agreed: "It's incredibly easy to meet people because the campus is so small, and everyone's looking for new friends."

Generally, students who go to Bates are perceived as well-off, and, though the school has been making efforts to diversify the campus, it is primarily white, with a majority of students coming from the New England area. However, the environment at Bates is relatively laid-back; as one student commented, "When walking around campus, you wouldn't necessarily know that the students come from families with money—students really don't flaunt it. The 'dress-code' is very laid-back, which is great. People wear sweatpants everywhere, and that's completely accepted. While some people do get more dressed up on the weekends, it's certainly not fancy at all; I wore heels one night and felt completely out of place."

Family Away from Home

At Bates, the relatively small campus is designed to foster a sense of community among the students. Most freshmen are placed in one of three freshman dorms: Smith, Clason, and Milliken. Upperclassmen often move off campus to nearby houses or, according to one student, "an area called the village, which is made up of apartment-like buildings with suites inside."

One unique thing about Bates is that there is only one dining hall, which was created in response to a request from the students to create an even more close-knit community. Commons, the dining hall, is "the hot spot on campus." The students describe the food as "surprisingly good" and describe Commons as the perfect place to hang out, chat, and people-watch. It's a lucky thing that the food in Commons is good; students explain that there are not many restaurants near campus, and other dining options are somewhat limited.

In terms of favorite hangouts, there is also Pgill (full name: Pettengill Hall), a building open 24 hours a day that contains classrooms, lounges, professors' offices, and "really comfortable couches." Pgill is described by one freshman as "a much more relaxed study space than the library, and it's nice to have another place to go to work. It also has a wall of windows that overlooks the pond, so it's absolutely gorgeous."

Bates is known for being in the middle of nowhere, and it does not shy away from this reputation. However, its tightly-knit community provides a second family for many—an aspect praised as almost everyone's favorite thing about Bates. In the midst of impressive academics and a beautiful landscape, this home away from home hosts some of the happiest students around.
—*Michelle Katz*

FYI

If you come to Bates, you'd better bring "a big winter coat and slippers from L.L.Bean."

What's the typical weekend schedule? "Go out on Friday night, sports or homework on Saturdays and then out, work on Sundays. Weekend mornings are usually dedicated to long brunches at Commons."

If I could change one thing about Bates, "I'd create an underground tunnel for students to get to Commons and other buildings without having to freeze!"

Three things every student at Bates should do before graduating are "do the puddle jump (jump in the pond in the middle of January as part of Winter Carnival), go to Commons drunk, and spend a full night in Pgill."

B o w d o i n   C o l l e g e

Address: 5000 College Station, Brunswick, ME 04011-8441
Phone: 207-725-3100
E-mail address: admissions@bowdoin.edu
Web site URL: www.bowdoin.edu/admissions
Year Founded: 1794
Private or Public: Private
Religious Affiliation: None
Location: Suburban
Number of Applicants: 6,033
Percent Accepted: 19%
Percent Accepted who enroll: 44%
Number Entering: 491
Number of Transfers Accepted each Year: 6
Middle 50% SAT range: M: 650–750, **CR:** 650–760, **Wr:** 660–750
Middle 50% ACT range: 29–33

Early admission program EA/ED/None: ED
Percentage accepted through EA or ED: 18%
EA and ED deadline: 1-Nov
Regular Deadline: 1-Jan
Application Fee: $60
Full time Undergraduate enrollment: 1,751
Total enrollment: 1,762
Percent Male: 49%
Percent Female: 51%
Total Percent Minority or Unreported: 27%
Percent African-American: 6%
Percent Asian/Pacific Islander: 11%
Percent Hispanic: 9%
Percent Native-American: 1%
Percent International: Unreported
Percent in-state/out of state: 12%/88%
Percent from Public HS: 55%

Retention Rate: 98%
Graduation Rate 4-year: 86%
Graduation Rate 6-year: 91%
Percent Undergraduates in On-campus housing: 94%
Number of official organized extracurricular organizations: 109
3 Most popular majors: Government, Economics, English
Student/Faculty ratio: 10:1
Average Class Size: 16
Percent of students going to grad school: 80%
Tuition and Fees: $38,190
In-State Tuition and Fees if different: No difference
Cost for Room and Board: $10,380
Percent receiving financial aid out of those who apply, first year: 74%
Percent receiving financial aid among all students: 41%

B owdoin is one of those unique colleges that appears genuinely loved by all its students, and the intensity of this ardor expands well beyond the unmatched quality of the dining scene and cuisine—though the focus on time spent eating together, in a way, does exemplify values held by this highly-selective, extremely intimate liberal arts college tucked up in Brunswick, Maine, where all members of the campus seem to share a particular drive for a broader perspective beyond what they're studying, devoting a lot of their time to activities and pursuits outside of the classroom.

Professors in the Know
Bowdoin fosters an incredibly supportive learning environment, and students seldom talk about their grades. The biggest lecture very rarely spills over 50 students, while the rest of the courses range from 15 to 30, depending on the department. "Though Bowdoin has a lot fewer options than some other schools, generally you can take what you want. At bigger schools people are talking about some great class with some great professor but it's impossible to get into—here, there aren't as many class offerings but you can actually do the things that are advertised," said a senior.

Top majors are Government, Biology, English, and Economics, and while students all have something they know they want to take, they are eager to apply their knowledge more broadly. The workload is difficult to generalize and dependent on a person's schedule, but according to a student, "I feel like if you want to get an A, it's totally achievable." For anyone having trouble in a course, he or she can talk to the professor and connect with a tutor at the Center for Learning and Teaching, free of charge.

The classroom exudes an academic vitality, where "everyone sort of carves their own path," said a student. With a ten-to-one faculty to student ratio, professors are unbelievably accessible, almost universally responsive, and understanding about deadlines and extensions. "My Constitutional law professor has been at Bowdoin for 50 years, went to Bowdoin, and has no phone or email but is constantly having office hours. I've never had a professor not know who I am," said a senior. What is exceptional about Bowdoin professors is that they don't limit their advice to what they teach in the classroom, but often push students towards people or clubs they think they will do well in. "They have a grasp of the social scene and will help you bond with other students," said a junior.

A Foodie's Paradise: Fine Dining and Good Living

The two dining halls are a crux of campus life, and for good reason. "It's the number one reason I decided to go here—no one will ever shut up about how great the food is. The size of the school facilitates this feeling you want to be in the dining hall because that's where you see everyone. I'll sit there for two hours at dinner while people come and go. I feel like that's what college is all about," said a senior. There's even a challenge known as "kill the night," the object being to linger the longest in the dining hall at every meal for one day. In terms of the two dining halls, one is bigger and more open and the second a little cozier, but there is no kind of social split between the two as might be found at another college; rather, there is a strong sense of social cohesion. There are a lot of specialty dishes and locally-sourced food, customizable meals, plus themed nights multiple times a month. For a taste: lobster on the first day of school, and sometimes blow-torched crème brûlée.

The freshmen are on a weekly 19-meal plan while upperclassmen have more choice, and if hungry outside of mealtimes there is the café in the student union and "Super Snack" on Thursday, Friday and Saturday nights from 11 p.m. to 1:30 a.m. The student union is also a central hang-out spot where people can play pool, collect mail, or study.

The campus is mostly red brick buildings with white trim around the windows, but there is also some variation in the architecture. "All the buildings built before the 1960s are absolutely beautiful, especially in the winter," said a student, who also praised the Walker Art Building by the prominent architects McKim, Meade and White. The science

buildings are more modern while the Chapel lends a touch of Gothic feel.

Most people live on campus the first three years, though housing is said to get worse after freshman year. There are nine freshman dorms, two of which are filled with doubles and the rest consisting of quads or quints with rooms connected by a common room and sharing hall bathrooms. Each dorm has an RA and each hall a proctor, who are focused on safety rather than getting kids in trouble. These dorms have all been recently redone and are located in the center of campus with 60 students in each. Proctors are on duty during weekends with food and movies, and serve as a friend and ally for their freshmen. "You get the talk but it's just to scare you—they're just looking out for your best interests. They see how important it is to have that support," said a freshman.

After freshman year, students can move into upperclassman dorms or one of the eight social houses, converted frats which now organize school social events. Each freshman dorm is affiliated with a social house to give new students an even more inclusive social environment, and members of the houses are matched with freshman buddies. The social houses have nice accommodation but generally come with party-planning responsibilities, and though the administration is trying to change this, they are currently occupied with mostly sophomores. "It's a little sad because each social house has no institutional history and it's so regulated by the school who gets to live in each one of them, so there's no thread between years. They're so PC about it with even ratios and the right kind of people who are going to program events," complained a senior. For sophomores not inclined to live in a social house, there are apartments a quarter mile away from campus which count as on-campus housing. After freshman year, the dorms are bigger, each with a few hundred students.

The Tower, where a lot of seniors live, has divided reviews; one student described it as "a visual eyesore inside and out." Luckily, there are tons of houses (less so apartments) off-campus that you can split with friends for relatively cheap. A large number of students have jobs as part of work-study or are just looking to make some extra money, and there are plenty of opportunities, whether in the café, dining halls, bookstore, art museum, or elsewhere.

With such a prominent number of athletes, Bowdoin has a heavy sports culture, but besides that, there's no dominating sort of vibe. "It's pretty well-rounded in terms of the kind of people who go here, from the Outing Club to the art department. It's a very balanced place," said one student. Over the past ten years, the school has tried hard to diversify in terms of both racial make-up and geographic distribution—as one student phrased it, "to transform Bowdoin from a bastion of rich, white male students to a place where you can be surrounded by diversity." There are lots of New Englanders moseying around in sweatpants who will work in finance after graduation, plenty of students from the South very involved in religious activities, and a number of people from scattered parts of the country. "Everyone is pretty laid-back but at the same time motivated and interesting," said a student. There is a paucity of international students, and internationals don't receive financial aid. However, for all others, Bowdoin continues to be need-blind with a no loans policy, meaning that it meets the full calculated financial need of all enrolled and entering first-year students—one of the few schools to stay so through the financial crisis.

Pursuits and Places Outside the Classroom
There are a slew of clubs and organizations on campus, and people are constantly motivated to start their own. The Outing Club, a cappella groups, and the weekly newspaper, *The Orient*, all have large memberships, and clubs involved with gender and sexual violence have recently received a lot of attention. "Everyone at Bowdoin is passionate about at least one or two extracurricular activities. They're heavily involved, not just pre-professional; it's one thing that binds us all together," remarked a student.

For a change of pace, students can also meander around town. Compared to almost all small towns in which elite small colleges are located, "Brunswick is by far the best," according to a senior. The town doesn't revolve around the college but is proud to have it there, and relations between the school and residents are very smooth. "There's a misconception about Maine that it's the middle of nowhere and there's nothing. But you have everything you need within five or ten minutes," said a student. Downtown has small, family-owned shops and restaurants, while a five-minute drive

away (either by Zipcar or taxi) is a shopping complex with anything you're missing: Wal-Mart, Best Buy, and the usual. There's a farmer's market on the town green on Fridays and a converted mill at the end of town overlooking the river that now holds a café and gallery. Outside of Brunswick there's also Portland, a great city within half an hour's drive and soon to be accessible by a new train line.

Party Hard or Lay Low
Frats were scrapped twelve years ago and turned into the social houses which Bowdoin has today. Social houses put together campus-wide parties, with usually two every weekend. As can be the case, "if you don't drink alcohol, it can be very difficult at first to adjust," a student admitted. The houses are the dominant social scene for first and second-years, while juniors and seniors tend to have more private parties in their own off-campus houses. "I've heard there is a party every night of the week but most people only go out weekends. It depends on your schedule," said a student. Everything is usually over by one or two, but not because of security; campus security is best represented by one of the security staff who is loved to death by students. Similar to proctors, "he makes it extremely apparent his mission is our safety and not getting us in trouble," said a student.

> "I've never had a professor not know who I am."

For a freshman partied out after a crazy few months or someone who prefers low-key weekend activities, there are movies, dance showcases, music recitals and singing concerts to see as well. Sometimes bands or other performers are brought in from outside campus. "Ivies" is a huge and eagerly-anticipated event in the spring hosting a bunch of bands, concerts, and parties.

Though drinking is big, drugs are not at all prevalent, and there is also the chemical-free social house and freshman dorm for those who don't want to be involved in either.

Bowdoin has an incredibly active student body—both physically and intellectually. Students don't have a single-minded academic focus, but realize the importance of outside pursuits. There will always be a sports game to watch, a discussion to take part in, or a group of students engaged in conversation late into the evening in one of the dining halls, a delicious meal sitting pleasantly in their stomachs.—*TaoTao Holmes*

FYI

If you come to Bowdoin, you'd better bring "your favorite recipes, because the dining hall will cook them."

If I could change one thing about Bowdoin, "I wish we had more international students, and sports weren't such a centerpiece."

"What surprised me the most about Bowdoin when I arrived was that all the staff are incredibly kind people who are really committed to making the experience for students as good as it can be. There's a really strong bond between students and staff."

Colby College

Address: 4000 Mayflower Hill Waterville, ME 04901-8848
Phone: 207-859-4828
E-mail address: admissions@colby.edu
Web site URL: www.colby.edu
Year Founded: 1813
Private or Public: Private
Religious Affiliation: None
Location: Rural
Number of Applicants: 4,835
Percent Accepted: 31%
Percent Accepted who enroll: 32%
Number Entering: 482
Number of Transfers Accepted each Year: 9
Middle 50% SAT range: M: 640–710, CR: 640–720, Wr: 630–710
Middle 50% ACT range: 28–31
Early admission program EA/ED/None: ED
Percentage accepted through EA or ED: 43%

EA and ED deadline: 1-Jan
Regular Deadline: 1-Jan
Application Fee: $65
Full time Undergraduate enrollment: 1,846
Total enrollment: 1,846
Percent Male: 46%
Percent Female: 54%
Total Percent Minority or Unreported: 14%
Percent African-American: 2%
Percent Asian/Pacific Islander: 8%
Percent Hispanic: 3%
Percent Native-American: <1%
Percent International: 5%
Percent in-state/out of state: 10%/90%
Percent from Public HS: Unreported
Retention Rate: 96%
Graduation Rate 4-year: 83%

Graduation Rate 6-year: 88%
Percent Undergraduates in On-campus housing: 94%
Number of official organized extracurricular organizations: 98
3 Most popular majors: Biology, Economics, Political Science
Student/Faculty ratio: 10:1
Average Class Size: 12
Percent of students going to grad school: Unreported
Tuition and Fees: $48,520
In-State Tuition and Fees if different: No difference
Cost for Room and Board: Included
Percent receiving financial aid out of those who apply, first year: 73%
Percent receiving financial aid among all students: 43%

Tucked away on Mayflower Hill in the tiny town of Waterville, Maine, Colby College offers top-notch academic programs, a friendly student community, and some of the best dining hall food in the country. The campus itself plays a huge role in Colby's student life, even though downtown Waterville is just around the corner. With lots of volunteer and study-abroad op-

tions and a wide spectrum of political and social opportunities, Colby students may be right in believing they have it all.

Campus on a Hill

Colby's setting atop Mayflower Hill, though perfectly picturesque in any season of the year, isolates the school from the town. The fact that "a lot of people are from New England and are white," as one student put it, probably doesn't help. "They call it the Colby bubble," said a sophomore of the school's insularity. "If you get involved with the community," she added, "[people on campus] call it 'bursting the bubble.' "

The steps of Miller Library have served as a popular site for drunken revelry for decades, according to a 1970 graduate and current students. The long-time tradition known as Champagne Steps, when seniors celebrated their last day of classes by drinking on the library's steps, was abolished after 20 students were hospitalized for alcohol poisoning during the 2008 event. But Mules continue to occupy the steps every year for Dog Head, the weekend closest to St. Patrick's Day. "People start drinking themselves into oblivion on Friday and don't stop until Sunday. Everybody is on the steps to watch the sunrise," said one student.

This school's drinking culture has some serious history: Colby is widely credited with having invented the drinking game Beer Die in the 1970s. The game, which is similar to beer pong but uses a die, was allegedly invented by some brothers in Colby's chapter of the frat Lambda Chi Alpha. Today, players of Beer Die can be found on college campuses nationwide. Though the game is still played, Colby frats and sororities were banned in 1984.

Cracking the Books

Colby prides itself on "project-based learning" and learning by doing, and students are generally pretty satisfied with the school's academic offerings. There are some standard requirements (a freshman English course and credits in science, lab science, literature, social science, and language through the 127 level), but Colby has a "diversity requirement" for graduation as well. This means taking two courses that deal with diversity issues in the U.S. and in other countries.

Colby has another unique offering: "Jan Plan," the month-long winter term when students have the opportunity to take on intensive projects outside of their major. "If you're a physics major, you can explore your interest in photography," said one student.

People cited biology, economics, languages, English, government, and international relations as popular majors. "Generally when you tell someone you are a humanities major they will almost inevitably roll their eyes," wrote one student. "Economics/Government majors think they are God's gift to the earth and will undoubtedly tell

you that their major is the hardest major," she added.

As for Colby's easiest majors, geology came to many people's lips. "It's known as rocks for jocks," said a sophomore. Another student wrote that if you're a geology major at Colby, "you probably smoke a lot of weed." And Colby students say they don't have to devote too much energy to getting into classes, with possible exceptions being Jan Plan courses and certain special programs like the dual-degree engineering program with Dartmouth College.

Relatively small classes (students estimate the biggest lectures to be around 40 students), approachable professors, and a hefty but manageable workload are a few of the things students appreciate about Colby. However, it's safe to say that students find time in their week to unwind as well.

Mule Pride

From sports to student government to community service, Colby offers a lot to do outside of the classroom. "People at Colby are generally very involved, usually in many diverse extracurricular activities," wrote one student. Colby's Student Government Association is a popular campus activity. It sets campus policies and handles student funding proposals.

> **"[Colby is] surprisingly vibrant for such a small school."**

Sports are huge on campus: one sophomore called the annual Colby-Bowdoin hockey game the single biggest campus event of the year. The school has a "disproportionate number of athletes" for its small size, the same student remarked. Less than fifty miles from Sugarloaf Mountain and with an average annual snowfall of 60 inches, Colby has a strong ski team and an active Outing Club. The Outing Club owns its own cabin and organizes hiking trips on the weekend. Varsity games are well-attended, students say, but intramurals are popular too.

Social Scene

While a sheltered environment sometimes goes hand in hand with a monotonous social scene, Colby proves quite the contrary—it is "surprisingly vibrant for such a small school," intimates a freshman. Waterville truly is the ideal balance of city life and calm. The beautifully cozy ambiance provides small-town tranquility, a limitless array of outdoor activities, both on land and in water, a college bar, and campus-wide events like Loudness Weekends, fun festivals that allow students a breather. Meanwhile, the campus' accessibility to the city of Freeport and the bigger city of Boston by school transportation caters to students' more material needs—shopping galore. A car can come in very handy. The absence of Greek life on campus only ups the standard of dorm-life liveliness—there is no shortage of fun. It only makes sense that Colby claims the game of Beer Die as its own. As with many colleges, drinking is an inevitable part of the culture. Colby, however, has taken the initiative to prohibit hard liquor, though one sophomore says—unless you are caught red-handed, in which case you must face the consequences—a simple: "Security Guard: Were you drinking hard alcohol? Student: No. Security Guard: Ok" will do. While drinking is especially predominant here, perhaps due to the lack of big-city attractions, students can always opt out. In fact, substance-free housing encourages just this, giving those who wish to stay sober a safe haven. While marijuana and cocaine are used in certain crowds, drugs are not a dominant recreational activity. A portrait of the typical student? That of a well-to-do Caucasian jock from somewhere on the East Coast (a generalization, of course, but not all false). But don't get the wrong idea—Colby has recently pushed to greatly diversify its admits, implementing recruiting programs and the like.

Campus Life

While dorms are said to improve with seniority, where you live depends mainly on your luck in the draw—once you have completed your first year, the lottery system kicks in. The mixing of freshmen, sophomores, juniors, and seniors allows everyone to get to know each other, regardless of year. Some residences deliberately appeal to certain kinds of people, such as the artistically inclined. Others do so less intentionally, such as the famed Dana—characteristically wild—and its substance-free opposite, Foss. Senior year some choose to leave the dorms for places in the city. Campus Advisors living alongside students can help with any qualms or questions that may arise. Students can always switch things up meal-wise. Where to eat is a choice between dining halls—Roberts, Dana, and Foss—among which cooking styles vary greatly. Students are open to meeting new people—the campus's friendly air creates an inherent sense of safety.

Colby College really does have a little bit, or should I say a lot, of everything. With the "Jan Plan," you can get creative; with the wide-offering of sports, you can be athletic; you can also challenge yourself with the small-class curriculum, get to know teachers, and just enjoy the East Coast landscape minus the city smog.—*Charlotte McDonald and Liliana Cousins*

FYI
If you come to Colby, "you'd better bring a sweater. And a coat. And a scarf, and gloves, and a hat."
If you come to Colby, you'd better leave behind "Bowdoin paraphernalia."
Three things every student at Colby should do before graduating are "climb up to the top of the Clock Tower," and go to ". . . Big G's (sandwich shop) and Dog Head . . . the party weekend closest to St. Patrick's Day."

College of the Atlantic

Address: 105 Eden Street, Bar Harbor, ME 04609
Phone: 207-288-5015
E-mail address: inquiry@coa.edu
Web site URL: www.coa.edu
Year Founded: 1969
Private or Public: Private
Religious Affiliation: None
Location: Rural
Number of Applicants: 314
Percent Accepted: 69%
Percent Accepted who enroll: 32%
Number Entering: 70
Number of Transfers Accepted each Year: 18
Middle 50% SAT range: M: 500–650, CR: 600–690, Wr: 550–680
Middle 50% ACT range: 25–29
Early admission program EA/ED/None: ED

Percentage accepted through EA or ED: 44%
EA and ED deadline: 1-Dec
Regular Deadline: 15-Feb
Application Fee: $45
Full time Undergraduate enrollment: 353
Total enrollment: 370
Percent Male: 36%
Percent Female: 64%
Total Percent Minority or Unreported: 2%
Percent African-American: 0%
Percent Asian/Pacific Islander: 1%
Percent Hispanic: 1%
Percent Native-American: 0%
Percent International: 14%
Percent in-state/out of state: 20%/80%
Percent from Public HS: Unreported
Retention Rate: 82%

Graduation Rate 4-year: 45%
Graduation Rate 6-year: 61%
Percent Undergraduates in On-campus housing: 43%
Number of official organized extracurricular organizations: Unreported
3 Most popular majors: Biology, Ecology, Education
Student/Faculty ratio: 11:1
Average Class Size: 12
Percent of students going to grad school: 55.0%
Tuition and Fees: $31,470
In-State Tuition and Fees if different: No difference
Cost for Room and Board: $8,490
Percent receiving financial aid out of those who apply, first year: 95%
Percent receiving financial aid among all students: 82%

I n 1969 a bunch of Harvard grads got together and decided that people would benefit by learning to understand the importance of how humans interact with their social and natural environments. The interdisciplinary approach they drew up boiled everything down to what they called Human Ecology. They chose the picturesque little seaside town of Bar Harbor, Maine, as the site for their project. Soon enough, they had created a small school of extraordinary opportunities that challenged students to rethink their roles in the world.

And the Meaning of Life Is . . .

Before graduation, every College of the Atlantic (COA) student is required to produce a thesis that answers the question "What is human ecology?" Human Ecology, the sole major at COA, introduces students to an interdisciplinary approach to defining the relationship between humans and the natural environment. Yes, it's a big topic to tackle, but when you are taking classes like "Landscapes of Power," "The Aesthetics of Violence," and "Use and Abuse of our Public Lands," somehow the answer tends to work itself out.

The degree requirements are extensive, but reveal COA's unique learning philosophy. To graduate, students must engage in community service, pursue an internship of at least one term, create a final project, and write a Human Ecology essay discussing their development as a human ecologist.

Although some struggle to find their area of focus, most say that COA "doesn't box you in with a major." Students can switch their focuses within the Human Ecology major. One senior reported that she had switched her focus from environmental law to Latin American studies to a preveterinary school track. However, with a student body of approximately 360 and faculty of approximately 40, COA is a "hard place to specialize when there are two professors who are the math department and another two who are the philosophy department," according to one third-year student. The 80 classes offered per trimester also quickly fill up to their average limit of 18. Some students find it frustrating that the small school may not offer classes within their particular interest.

In turn, COA encourages students to pursue independent studies. One student explained, "If you're motivated, good, if not, you might have a hard time here. For example, most of my work in the last year and a half has been independent, outside of class. I did an internship, then a group study, followed by a residency (the equivalent of three interconnected independent studies), and when I get back from Yucatan I'm going to do my senior project." Graduation requirements also call for students to take time off from campus to do an internship.

On average, students take three classes per trimester—"four can be a lot." The work-load focuses on class presentations and "intense" papers, as opposed to exams. An 11:1 student-faculty ratio means that students get individual attention and know their professors well—everyone is on a first-name basis!

Classes also make use of research resources that include Mt. Desert Rock and Great Duck Island Lighthouse, Mt. Desert Island Biological Laboratory, Jackson Laboratory, a weather station, and a Global Monitoring System. "We may, for example, dissect whales or seals found on the coast and determine the cause of death," explains one student.

Housing: Converted Mansions, but Limited Space

COA guarantees housing, usually singles, for first-years only. The three-level horseshoe-shaped Blair-Tyson dorm houses about 40 students. Around six to eight students share a kitchen and a bathroom, which features recycled toilet paper and no stalls! Seafox, a converted mansion, is "supposedly" substance-free, but really just a more quiet dorm of 12 students with spectacular views of the ocean. RAs are pretty easygoing about marijuana and alcohol and even bring their first-years to off-campus parties to bond with upperclassmen. One RA admitted, "I'm pretty loose about it. Although if someone is having a problem, I'd certainly confront him about it."

Most upperclassmen envy the first-years who get to stay on campus. "I had a blast!" claimed a former Blair-Tyson dweller. "But there's not enough room for us, which is a bummer." Upperclassmen find apartments in town about five minutes away or in more remote locations reached by bike or car.

The Grub: A Vegan's Paradise

The environmentally conscious student body enjoys top-ranked cooking at its sole dining hall Take-a-Break, or TAB in local lingo. PETA (People for the Ethical Treatment of Animals) has consistently ranked TAB one of the best college dining halls for its vegetarian and vegan fare and once gave it the privileged title of "Veggie Valedictorian" in 2002. "The worst thing about the dining hall is its dining hours: dinner between 5:30 and 6:30 is kind of ridiculous," complained one student. Also, no meals are served on the weekends, so students make use of the many on-campus kitchens.

The food is all organic and mostly from local farms, including the COA's own Beech Hill Farm where students can participate in the work-study program or volunteer. All waste is disposed of in the school's compost garden. Being on the ocean, TAB features a lot of fresh seafood. "Basically, it's not McDonald's, so don't come looking for it," affirmed one senior.

The Weekend Chill

The illegal substance of choice is reportedly marijuana, "unsurprising" for the "chill" school that enrolls many "hippied-out" students. As opposed to hard liquor, beer is the choice beverage. "My buddies and I might throw back a couple of beers, but we don't often get rip-roaring drunk," reported a third-year student. Another student warned, "There are no crazy discos or mad party places, so if that's what you're looking for you might have a hard time here. It is Maine, after all." Students claim that hard drugs are pretty rare.

Because there are no Wednesday classes (due to Student Government meetings), "there are two weekends, Tuesday nights and Friday and Saturday nights." The scene starts, according to one student, "ridiculously early! Things get started around 8:00 and end by 11:30 or 12:00." Parties are held mainly at upperclassmen residences. The Thirsty Whale, Little Anthony's, and Nakorn Thai are popular town bars. "Only really good IDs work," complained one student about the strict drinking policy.

As for the dating scene, news travels fast. One senior lamented her days as a first-year, when she "may have made one too many 'mistakes' that I couldn't escape. I saw them around nearly every day." Some students admit COA is a hard place to date because there are not a lot of new people to meet around. But the small size "makes random hookups a lot less random." COA is also very tolerant and accepting of homosexual relationships. Reportedly, "lesbians are usually more open than gay males."

Students Take Charge

The Student Government at COA is a remarkably powerful body. It has significant say in all major decisions of the school. Students even attend Trustee meetings. Classes do not meet on Wednesdays to accommodate Student Government committee meetings in which most students participate. Additionally, at 1 p.m. every Wednesday an All College Meeting to which all student organizations and committees report takes place. One student complains, however, "It's always the same people that show up and, for the most part, say the same things, so reaching common decisions has less to do with compromise and more with tiring your opponent."

The Student Activities Committee, a branch of the Student Government, brings about two or three bands per term to perform in TAB. The committee also sponsors coffeehouses, weekly Open Mike nights, the Winter Carnival and Earth Day.

For the Outdoorsman in You

COA sports teams are completely nonexistent. But students are serious about outdoor activities, rain or shine. First-years pile all the essentials—boots, bikes, backpacks, cross-country skis, you name it—into the family car when they first arrive. With Acadia National Park in COA's backyard, students can be found scaling the island's mountains (at least ten!) on weekends and have often tackled them all by graduation. Students have free passes to the local YMCA, can explore the miles of bike trails, catch a free whale-watching ride with the Allied Whale (a program for sea-mammal study and saving), or sit on the dock with their toes in the water and watch the sailboats float by.

Winter term is known as the trimester for hard work because sub-zero temperatures supposedly keep people inside. This hibernation is overstated, claimed one student. Even when Bar Harbor shuts down at the end of tourist season, COA students are still recreating outdoors with cross-country ski-ing, snowshoeing, broomball and even midnight dips in the ocean. With all these activities, TV is reportedly "*not* a big pastime." At COA, something like the campus tree swing is a big attraction.

Who You'll Meet

Students at COA report that Earth Day is "the only day that we actually get off." Naturally a place like this is going to attract a certain kind of student. One student described the typical student as "someone who smells like tea-tree oil, has dreadlocks, wears Birkenstocks and is environmentally aware, politically conscious, outdoorsy, pretty athletic and earthy." Oh, and liberal. "There are maybe three Republicans here," warned one student. "I would not come here if I were a Republican." Although the school is often stereotyped, many students admit surprise at the diversity of opinion. One third-year student remarks, "I wasn't expecting anyone to challenge me." Another student determined the "dirty hippie" population to be less than a quarter of the school.

> "I would not come here if I were a Republican."

Students are generally from an upper-middle class socioeconomic background, and though a portion of the student body hails from Maine, students come from all over the United States. For such a small school, COA boasts a significant number of international students who are attracted by the special full-scholarship package as well as the uniqueness of the school. In one student's words, "COA students usually have really strong beliefs about a lot of things, and like to voice them. I guess another way to look at it is that if you took the staple 'weird kids' from any high school, most of them would fit in just fine at COA."

—*Baily Blair*

FYI
If you come to COA you'd better bring "a Nalgene, a backpack and long johns."
What is a typical weekend schedule? "Go for a hike, do some reading, chill with friends and lay low."
If I could change one thing about COA, I'd "move it to the tropics or a big city."
Three things every student should do before graduating are "join the Yucatan Program, go for a swim at Sand Beach on a night in January and summit all the mountains on the island."

University of Maine / Orono

Address: 5713 Chadbourne Hall, Orono, ME 04469-5713
Phone: 207-581-1561
E-mail address: um-admit@maine.edu
Web site URL: www.umaine.edu
Year Founded: 1865
Private or Public: Public
Religious Affiliation: None
Location: Rural
Number of Applicants: 6,958
Percent Accepted: 77%
Percent Accepted who enroll: 34%
Number Entering: 1,839
Number of Transfers Accepted each Year: 716
Middle 50% SAT range: M: 480–600, CR: 480–580, Wr: 470–570
Middle 50% ACT range: 19–25
Early admission program EA/ED/None: EA

Percentage accepted through EA or ED: Unreported
EA and ED deadline: 15-Dec
Regular Deadline: Rolling
Application Fee: $40
Full time Undergraduate enrollment: 9,596
Total enrollment: 11,912
Percent Male: 50%
Percent Female: 50%
Total Percent Minority or Unreported: 6%
Percent African-American: 1%
Percent Asian/Pacific Islander: 1%
Percent Hispanic: 1%
Percent Native-American: 2%
Percent International: 2%
Percent in-state/out of state: 84%/16%
Percent from Public HS: Unreported
Retention Rate: 78%

Graduation Rate 4-year: 33%
Graduation Rate 6-year: 58%
Percent Undergraduates in On-campus housing: 42%
Number of official organized extracurricular organizations: 224
3 Most popular majors: Business/Commerce, Education, Engineering
Student/Faculty ratio: 16:1
Average Class Size: 15
Percent of students going to grad school: 25%
Tuition and Fees: $22,510
In-State Tuition and Fees if different: $9,100
Cost for Room and Board: $8,008
Percent receiving financial aid out of those who apply, first year: Unreported
Percent receiving financial aid among all students: Unreported

A big state school in the middle of the woods, with a cold climate to boot, might seem daunting at first. But as students at the University of Maine will tell you, there are many reasons to brave the freezing temperatures and take advantage of this vibrant community. The University that once had a live black bear as its official mascot and was known for being a legendary party school has since evolved into a respected national research university, but the students are still just as supportive of their UMaine Black Bears. From the cheering crowds at the Alfond Arena to the picnickers taking advantage of the first day of spring, it's clear that the University of Maine provides a unique opportunity for both in- and out-of-staters to make the most of the Pine Tree State.

Bear-ing All with Bananas
Founded in 1865, the UMaine campus in Orono is the largest in the University of Maine system. As a public state school, it's not surprising that 84 percent of its student body hails from Maine itself. But the 16 percent remaining call 47 states and numerous countries home, making for a campus that is surprisingly diverse for a state that one student called "one of the whitest states, if not the whitest." She continued, "The University of Maine is probably the place to go if you're looking for some ethnic and religious diversity because there is a lot of it on this campus, all things considered being in Maine." The minority students, who make up six percent of undergraduates, have the opportunity to participate in a number of ethnic and cultural organizations, including the Asian Student Association and the Black Student Union.

Most of the student population, generally either "Mainers" or New Englanders, sport a preppy style, usually American Eagle or Abercrombie, students said. Others said the campus has its fair share of rebels, both in terms of fashion and lifestyle. One girl confessed, "We're all kind of hicks." But she was quick to point out that "There are those guys who wear flannel, but they're not roaming around hunting things."

There are a few things that do unite just about all UMaine students, and one of them is supporting their Black Bears. Legend has it that the University's original mascot was a live black bear cub that lived in one of the fraternity's basements when not appearing at sporting events. Today's incarnation, Bananas the Bear, may do a better job of pumping up the crowds; the original cub was fired after attacking the University of Connecticut husky at a basketball game.

"We're all kind of hicks."

The hockey team is universally cited as the biggest draw for sports spectators. The school pep band always makes an appearance, and the roaring crowds of both UMaine students and Maine locals are a constant fixture at the Alfond Arena, usually lining up outside for tickets far in advance. The men's ice hockey team, two-time NCAA Division I national champions, in 1993 and 1999, is a great source of pride for the entire state. "People go crazy and wear jerseys and paint their faces," a junior described.

The other athletics teams, which also engage in Division I competition, may not have as much star power, but their games also attract many fans. Football is also very popular, and the basketball team's rivalry with the New Hampshire Wildcats, at 105 seasons in a row, is the longest continuous basketball rivalry between any two non–Ivy League schools.

Making a Large University Small

Black Bears can carry their determination into the classroom, too, with plenty of opportunities available at UMaine for academic excellence. The general education requirements, or "Gen Eds," are designed to produce "broadly educated persons who can appreciate the achievements of civilization, understand the tensions within it, and contribute to resolving them." Each student must take a certain number of credits in the following areas: science, human values and social context, mathematics, writing, and ethics. Every student, regardless of major, must also complete a "capstone experience," usually during the senior year, which is the culmination of his or her specific course of study. All Gen Eds must be taken for a letter grade in order to satisfy the requirement. "I'm on a one-track [course of study]," a music education major said. "The

Gen Eds require me to get out of that box for a minute and open my mind to other subject areas. There's probably a little bit of groaning, but it's one of those things that gets done, often freshman year."

The most popular majors are business, education and engineering, with the latter generally cited as one of the most challenging offered at the University, as well as one of the most famous departments. The sciences in general, especially the nursing and biology programs, are well known for their rigor and progressiveness. The marine biology department is also lauded.

When students are accepted into the University of Maine, they gain entrance to specific programs based on the strength of their applications. If they do not meet the requirements for a program or are unsure of what they want to concentrate in, first-years enroll in the Exploration Program, which allows them to transition to college life and settle on an academic area, even to bolster their qualifications for a certain program. Some of the benefits of this option include an academic advisor with whom they meet on a regular basis and the opportunity to take a first-year seminar. Students looking for a more personalized education throughout their four years at the University can opt to enroll in the Honors College if they make the cut. Honors students enjoy smaller classes and close working relationships with faculty members. They also have the option of designated honors housing.

As can be expected of a large state school, students often encounter difficulties in gaining entrance to certain high-demand classes, but "teachers sometimes make exceptions." Class sizes range from around 25 in the smaller lectures to 200 to 300 in the largest survey courses, but one girl said she has a class with only three people. Classes are usually offered once a year, if not each semester, so the most common reason that students enroll for a fifth year is that they were undecided about their major, not that they could not get into core classes.

A junior cited the school's size as one of the biggest academic attractions: "I think there's something for everyone. Because we are a university, the biggest university in the state, and we have a lot of students, there's pretty much going to be a major for you."

Raising the Steins

"A lot of people have the perception that UMaine is a huge party school because at one point it was, and I don't think it necessarily is anymore," a sophomore said. Indeed, the University has recently been taking steps to curb out-of-control partying, with both reputation and students' safety in mind. "The University's known as being a party school, so it's really important to [the administration] that we crack down, and that we don't allow freshmen to be drunk all the time," a junior explained. The RAs in each dorm, where drinking is prohibited, are known for being fairly strict. The repercussions for breaking the rules include attending alcohol education meetings, and repeat offenders can be kicked out of the dorms. "Does that mean [drinking] never happens?" one student asked rhetorically. "No, but it is punishable."

Since it's fairly difficult to party in on-campus housing, much of the party scene takes place in the frats and the off-campus apartments. While one girl said she was surprised that Greek life was so present on campus, she said the presence of the frats and sororities has not been a negative part of her experience. The frats hold many of the parties, and Friday and Saturday nights are known as the big nights to go out. Pot is pretty commonplace, as it is on most college campuses, and binge drinking is not a major problem, perhaps in part because of the 2001 founding of Maine's Higher Education Alcohol Prevention Project. The initiative aimed to address the problem of binge drinking as it worsened on college campuses. However, the celebrated college fight song, the Maine Stein Song, is still proudly shouted at athletic events. As undergraduates sing "Fill the steins to dear old Maine," they had better have their IDs on them.

The off-campus bar scene in Orono is not too exciting; there are a couple in town, along with a dance club that a good number of people frequent. There isn't much to do overall in Orono. Besides the legendary Pat's Pizza and a number of other coffee shops and restaurants, it is a quiet town with residents that generally have good relations with the University. In fact, many of them are affiliated with UMaine. For more bars and restaurants, as well as a grocery store, some students take the 10-minute drive to nearby Bangor, the third-largest city in the state.

Indoors and Outdoors

There's a lot to occupy students' time on campus, though. They can even get fed reasonably well. York, Hilltop, and Wells Commons offer all-you-care-to-eat dining. The latter two were recently renovated and offer a variety of standard and multi-ethnic cuisines. Students cited the Maine Marketplace in the Memorial Union as the most popular dining option, though. Here, students can use their meal plans to purchase a wide range of a la carte meals, including pizza, sandwiches, burgers, sushi, Chinese and Mexican food. They can either use one meal swipe and receive an entrée and snacks, or they can pay by the item. A number of meal plans are available, comprising both meal swipes and dining funds.

The 19 residence halls are generally considered to be acceptable, students say. Freshmen participate in the First Year Residence Experience (FYRE) and are assigned to one of the following dorms: Androscoggin, Cumberland, Gannett, Knox, Oxford, Somerset, Balentine, Penobscot, and Colvin. The latter three are designated for honors students. These are traditional undergraduate residence halls, usually with two students to a room, while upperclassmen have this option as well as the choice of living in suites. "Some of the dorms are on the older side, but I think overall they're not too awful," a sophomore concluded. As part of the FYRE, freshmen are grouped together in one part of campus and have the opportunity to make friends with many of their classmates through this close-knit community.

Theme housing includes a substance-free dorm and an "outdoorsy" dorm, the latter of which organizes trips to the mountains and the surrounding area to ski, bike, hike, and participate in all manner of recreational activities. A junior pointed out that none of the dorms, and indeed none of the buildings on the UMaine campus, are taller than four stories. She said she thinks it is because the University is built on an island in a marsh, and that buildings cannot be taller than they are because the campus will sink into the water, but she admitted that it could be just a rumor.

Many students have cars, even freshmen, and parking can be a difficult issue. The significant number of commuter students contributes to the congestion. Permits cost $50 for the year, with decals designating cars as faculty, resident or commuter, with corresponding lots. Those who trespass into other lots "are lucky if they aren't ticketed." But students point out that cars are useful for going home or just into town. While campus is considered to be "pretty safe," students interviewed did say they wish it were better lit, both because it would make them feel more secure at night and because it is difficult for drivers to see pedestrians.

The architecture on campus is mostly

brick, with many trees and green spaces adding life. In the winter, snow coats everything, but it is "still aesthetically pleasing." One student said her favorite thing to do is to sit on the Mall, an open space in the middle of campus, at the beginning of spring when "the campus is buzzing and everyone is happy." With a number of construction projects recently completed and others in progress, the UMaine campus seems to always be an exciting place. The Collins Center for the Arts was recently renovated, as was the gym.

Most UMaine students do their best to take advantage of their surroundings, often going on trips to Acadia National Park or other natural areas. But whether you're a flannel-wearing mountain man or someone who prefers to stay indoors during inclement weather, there are plenty of opportunities to do both at the University of Maine. One student said she had gotten used to the school's size, saying, "It's kind of nice having a lot more students—more things get contributed to the campus, and there are more ideas floating around." Another added, "I have plenty of time in my life to move away and see the world, but I'm glad I stayed in Maine for college."—*Kimberly Chow*

FYI
If you come to the University of Maine, you'd better bring "a pair of winter boots: it was negative 20 degrees at one point."
What's the typical weekend schedule? "On Friday, go to a hockey game, then hang out with your friends at Pat's Pizza; sleep in on Saturday, maybe go to another athletic event, then hit up the frats; Sunday, catch up on work."
If I could change one thing about the University of Maine, "I would make the weather warmer!"
Three things every student at the University of Maine should do before graduating are "go to a hockey game, sit on the Mall in the spring, and eat at Pat's Pizza."

Maryland

Address: 1021 Dulaney Valley Road, Towson, MD 21204-2753

Phone: 410-337-6100

E-mail address: admissions@goucher.edu

Web site URL: www.goucher.edu

Year Founded: 1885

Private or Public: Private

Religious Affiliation: None

Location: Suburban

Number of Applicants: 3,563

Percent Accepted: 66%

Percent Accepted who enroll: 17%

Number Entering: 399

Number of Transfers Accepted each Year: 118

Middle 50% SAT range: M: 510–620, CR: 540–670, Wr: 540–650

Middle 50% ACT range: Unreported

Early admission program EA/ED/None: EA

Percentage accepted through EA or ED: 43%

EA and ED deadline: 1-Dec

Regular Deadline: 1-Feb

Application Fee: $40

Full time Undergraduate enrollment: 1,472

Total enrollment: 2,362

Percent Male: 31%

Percent Female: 69%

Total Percent Minority or Unreported: 25%

Percent African-American: 6%

Percent Asian/Pacific Islander: 3%

Percent Hispanic: 4%

Percent Native-American: <1%

Percent International: 1%

Percent in-state/out of state: 23%/77%

Percent from Public HS: 67%

Retention Rate: 78%

Graduation Rate 4-year: 57%

Graduation Rate 6-year: 62%

Percent Undergraduates in On-campus housing: 80%

Number of official organized extracurricular organizations: 60

3 Most popular majors: English, Communications, Psychology

Student/Faculty ratio: 9:1

Average Class Size: 15

Percent of students going to grad school: Unreported

Tuition and Fees: $32,636

In-State Tuition and Fees if different: No difference

Cost for Room and Board: $10,104

Percent receiving financial aid out of those who apply, first year: 81%

Percent receiving financial aid among all students: 59%

Goucher College, located just eight miles outside of Baltimore in the town of Towson, is a small liberal arts college that focuses on big issues. Although the school enrolls nearly 1,500 undergraduates, their resources for students go far beyond the 287 acres of Goucher property. With new study-abroad requirements, for which students are granted at least $1,200 to cover travel costs, inter-institutional programs with Johns Hopkins University and with Baltimore Hebrew University, and many opportunities for work and study in Baltimore and Washington D.C., Goucher's small community has become a college recognized for expanding knowledge outside of the small liberal arts college bubble.

Education Without Boundaries

With a motto like "Education without Boundaries," Goucher offers students plenty of opportunities in and out of the classroom. With thirty-one majors and six interdisciplinary areas, a five-year BA/BS program in Science and Engineering with Johns Hopkins, and numerous study-abroad programs available during the optional January term, Goucher makes it easy for students to pursue any interest they may have. Many students agree that although there are relatively few of them, their academic interests vary widely. Psychology is the most popular major on campus, and the visual and performing arts have become more popular over the years, especially with Goucher's renowned dance major. But if students still feel confined by the majors, Goucher allows them to create their own.

Goucher's general education requirements (also known as Gen Ed) include proficiency in a language, English composition, and computer technology along with a distribution of courses in the arts, natural sciences, humanities, social sciences, and mathematics. Most nonscience majors who are looking to fill their natural sciences "Gen Ed" requirement take the largest course—up to around one hundred students—at Goucher, "Introduction to Psychology," taught by the beloved Dr. Ann McKim. Dr. McKim is a "very memorable and very enthusiastic" professor who is known for keeping her students—all one hundred of them—interested and entertained.

Freshmen are also required to take two classes. One is a freshman seminar and the other is a Connections class, where freshmen meet with their upperclassmen peer mediators and talk about important issues regarding college life. However, some freshmen say the class is only effective if the peer mediator is actually dedicated to the class, which is not always the case. Overall, many freshman agree that assimilating into Goucher is easy from the beginning, and the required freshman classes can be a "great way" to meet new people and learn about a topic they would "not usually be interested in." Still, students say that freshman year can lead to some serious culture shock, as new students adjust—and even conform—to the very liberal atmosphere of the small campus.

In terms of academic difficulty, Goucher gets mixed reviews, but one senior said "that is only because some majors are more difficult than others." The English and Natural Science majors get reviews of being more difficult, while Psychology and Communications are known for being more "lenient with grading." Overall, most students agree that "you only get out of classes what you put into them" and "if you really want an A, and if you work hard enough, it is attainable." One of the reasons many students can succeed in their classes is because of the accessibility of professors. Goucher has a 9:1 student to teacher ratio and an average class size of 15, which translates into having professors "almost always able to meet when you want to schedule a meeting." Some students even said they have become friendly with professors who they've never even had "because Goucher tries to make professors and students on a more equal level; we call most teachers by their first names."

A Unique Social Experience

Even before freshman year, each class of Goucher students has the opportunity to meet people with all different interests through preorientation programs. Students agree that while the diversity—cultural, geographic, and socioeconomic—at Goucher is not very great, it improves each year. For a small liberal arts school, some students were "surprised by how many lacrosse 'bros' and athletes there are." But overall the "stereotypical" Goucher student is "very hippy-ish and free, from a middle class family on the East Coast." Overall, students are "really friendly" and "people will always be waving to you on the Van Meter Highway" (Goucher's walkway between the academic and residential quads).

"Right now, my main group of friends are the people on my floor and the people I do [activities] with," says one freshman. Seniors and freshmen both agree that the friends they have are the ones they live with and the ones with whom they participate in extracurricular activities. Usually "the athletes hang out together," but athletes agree that they "don't feel limited, even by age. Most parties have people of every age." While there is not a strong divide between students, "there are definitely different groups." One student on the women's lacrosse team said that "parties are mostly small groups of friends . . . our school is too small and parties would be broken up if they were over thirty people." With no Greek system at Goucher, parties are generally confined to students' rooms.

> **"We're a very liberal school . . . it kind of comes with the territory."**

While parties are small, that does not stop Goucher students from partying as hard as at any other college. Many students agree that alcohol is very common on campus, and marijuana is as well because "we're a very liberal school . . . it kind of comes with the territory." Students who are less interested in partying say that it can be "difficult to find alternatives—you have to try." While alcohol and marijuana can be found, the rules are "definitely enforced," especially by Community Assistants (CAs)—upperclassmen who oversee dorm life—who get reviews between being "really relaxed" and "pretty strict." The CAs are not just in charge of making sure parties don't get out of control, but they also deal with issues between roommates and with technical problems, and they can advise students on anything from classes to clubs.

Goucher social life at night does not consist only of small parties in dorm rooms. Students also hang out in the Gopher Hole, a coffeehouse on campus that's open late, often has live music on weekends, and serves food like quesadillas and "really good" smoothies. In the middle of the fall semester, students gear up for "Humans vs. Zombies," a weekend-long game that involves many pumped-up members of the student body, Nerf guns, and mild "implications of violence." Another big social event is Get into Goucher Day (GIG), when all classes are canceled on a surprise day and the campus is converted into an amusement park. Many students call it "the best day of the year." The "formal" event of the year is Gala, a night of dancing and good food. However, not every student can go to Gala, as the limited number of tickets is distributed based on seniority, starting with the seniors and "trickling down" to a few lucky freshmen.

Outside of the usual weekend events, many Gophers, as Goucher students are commonly called, are involved in volunteering, jobs, and internships. By senior year, about seventy percent of Goucher students will have had an internship. Many students find job opportunities on campus, but with Baltimore nearby and a mall in the neighborhood, many students work off campus. The Goucher student body is also involved in helping the community, through on- and off-campus organizations. Goucher also features some "unique" clubs such as the Goucher Pirate Alliance, which is known for having bake sales where the members dress up in pirate garb. Otherwise, there are over sixty other options for students, ranging from student government to the campus radio station to student publications, such as the newspaper *The Quindecim* (*The Q*).

With seventeen NCAA Division III teams at Goucher, athletes have a big presence on campus. However, many students admit that sports at Goucher are "mostly athletes going to athletes' games." Despite the fact that sports do not get too much nonathlete spirit, students agree "we have a lot of school spirit, just not in the traditional way of going to sports games." The athletic program at Goucher is ever expanding, with brand-new fields and a new cardio center and weight room. All facilities are open for nonathletic use, and Gophers are excited about the renovations.

Going Green at Goucher

Goucher's new initiative to "go green" has been extremely effective and gets high marks from students. Over recent years, Goucher has expanded its "green" program by building environmentally friendly buildings, selecting a "green supplier" to cater the dining halls, selling "eco-friendly" items at the bookstore, and holding many events for students to learn about sustainability. Ground broke in 2007 for the Athenaeum, Goucher's new "green building," which now holds the library, performance space, an art gallery, a computer lab, a restaurant, and many more facilities. Students can enjoy the quadlike outdoor terrace, which is on the roof of the building and carpeted with grass. While Goucher is calling the Athenaeum its "Crowning Jewel," students say that the campus "is [already] really beautiful" and is laid out "really well."

For students who live in dorms, there are a few buildings that students can pick based on a lottery system. Most dorms have students of all ages, but some are more "luxurious" than others.

Sophomores, juniors, and seniors can also live off campus in apartments, many of which are owned by Goucher. When students want to go into Baltimore or Washington, D.C. (an hour away from campus), "about half of students have cars," but there is also a shuttle that goes between Goucher and the other universities in Baltimore, ending at the Harbor in Baltimore. "Zipcars are also an option for students who don't have cars but want to rent one."

When Goucher students get hungry, they have a lot of different options both on and around campus. Ranging from Stimson, the largest dining hall, to the Cheesecake Factory that recently opened, Goucher students have a myriad of options when it comes to eating. Students are "pretty satisfied" with the food on campus. In Heubeck Dining Hall, students have different stations to choose from, including a deli station and the sustainable Global Green Exhibition station.

Overall, Goucher students are proud of their campus and of what Goucher has to offer them. Goucher students are quick to point out the interesting facts that make their school unique. Gophers tell legends about the twenty-four mile-per-hour speed limit sign, the nuclear fallout shelter, the mummy that Johns Hopkins allegedly "stole" from their school, and the beautiful trails located right off campus. Students agree that in the end, it's the school's "quirky self- expression that is inherent in most students" that makes Goucher different from any other school.—*Willi Rechler*

FYI

If you come to Goucher you better bring "plenty of warm layers for the winter," "a Nerf gun for Humans vs. Zombies," "a blanket for outside lounging," and "lots of Expo markers for your white board."

A typical weekend at Goucher is "everyone goes out Friday to the harbor or an off-campus party, then to the Gopher Hole or game room," and Saturdays consist of "brunch in the morning, then repeat Friday night" with Sunday "a full day in the library."

If I could change one thing about Goucher I'd "make us have more school spirit."

Three things every student at Goucher should do before graduating are "Go to the Gopher Hole events, get their own radio show, and attend a Goucher party."

Johns Hopkins University

Address: 3400 North Charles Street, Mason Hall, Baltimore, MD 21218
Phone: 410-516-8171
E-mail address: apphelp@jhu.edu
Web site URL: www.jhu.edu
Year Founded: 1876
Private or Public: Private
Religious Affiliation: None
Location: Urban
Number of Applicants: 14,848
Percent Accepted: 24%
Percent Accepted who enroll: 33%
Number Entering: 1,206
Number of Transfers Accepted each Year: 26
Middle 50% SAT range: M: 660–770, CR: 630–730, Wr: 630–730
Middle 50% ACT range: 28–33
Early admission program EA/ED/None: ED

Percentage accepted through EA or ED: Unreported
EA and ED deadline: 1-Nov
Regular Deadline: 1-Jan
Application Fee: $70
Full time Undergraduate enrollment: 4,591
Total enrollment: 6,437
Percent Male: 53%
Percent Female: 47%
Total Percent Minority or Unreported: 44%
Percent African-American: 4%
Percent Asian/Pacific Islander: 19%
Percent Hispanic: 8%
Percent Native-American: <1%
Percent International: 8%
Percent in-state/out of state: 13%/87%
Percent from Public HS: 69%
Retention Rate: 97%
Graduation Rate 4-year: 81%

Graduation Rate 6-year: 89%
Percent Undergraduates in On-campus housing: 60%
Number of official organized extracurricular organizations: 250
3 Most popular majors: Biomedical/Medical Engineering, Economics, International Relations and Affairs
Student/Faculty ratio: Unreported
Average Class Size: 14
Percent of students going to grad school: 38%
Tuition and Fees: $37,700
In-State Tuition and Fees if different: No difference
Cost for Room and Board: $11,578
Percent receiving financial aid out of those who apply, first year: 47%
Percent receiving financial aid among all students: 46%

There are two things bound to bother most students at Johns Hopkins University. The first is leaving the "s" off of Johns when speaking the name of this prestigious Baltimore institution. Founded in 1876 as the nation's first research university, Johns Hopkins was named for its first benefactor whose given name was actually Johns, his mother's maiden name. The second "no-no" is the assumption that all Hopkins students are either premeds or hard-core science majors. Although celebrated for its medical school and for providing an unsurpassed premedical education, Johns Hopkins is also extremely strong in the humanities, social sciences, and engineering. Its International Relations program is considered perhaps the finest in the nation, and its writing and art history majors are top ranked. In fact, only about 30 percent of entering freshmen at Hopkins profess an interest in medicine, a number that diminishes over time.

Homewood Bound

Although the Johns Hopkins Medical Institutions are world-renowned, the heart of the university can be found at its Homewood campus, a beautifully manicured 140-acre parklike setting adorned with redbrick Georgian Federalist-style buildings. Brick, granite, and marble walkways wend their way through lush green lawns, sculpture gardens, and beds of blue and white flowers. "The beach," an expanse of lawn that extends out from the Milton S. Eisenhower Library, is a magnet for students who want to relax, sunbathe, or socialize. All freshmen and sophomores live in or adjacent to Homewood. Freshmen live in the Alumni Memorial Residences (AMRs), or enjoy the air-conditioning in Buildings A and B. While air-conditioning in Baltimore has its advantages, many freshmen prefer the AMR setup. "I made so many friends in AMR I," one sophomore said. "It was a great place to live and a great way to meet a lot of people." Some freshmen and many sophomores live in Wolman and McCoy, which have kitchenettes and large common areas. In the past, upperclassmen have had to live off campus in apartments that abut Homewood. With the completion of Charles Commons in 2006, more students have opted to remain in university-operated facilities. Charles Commons, an extremely attractive and functional new building, houses more than 600 undergraduates as well as the 29,000-square-foot Barnes and Noble campus bookstore. Situated across Charles Street, a main thoroughfare that borders the main campus, it is a convenient and desirable residence. "Charles Commons is impressive," said one junior. "The suites are really well appointed and the opportunities for socializing in the dining facility and the common spaces really make this a fantastic place to live. It is a major addition to campus life." In addition, the University has taken over several existing apartment buildings adjacent to the new facility, performing some renovations and instituting better security.

The level of security and the degree of safety on campus in view of Baltimore's urban problems and crime rate (which is falling) are important concerns voiced by prospective students. The university has invested a great deal of time and money in assuring that there are plenty of "Hop Cops" to patrol the campus at all times, security guards at the entrances to all of the dormitories and affiliated apartments, and 24/7 walking escorts and vans available to students. "The campus is safe as long as you are aware of your surroundings," said a junior. "It's like any urban school."

Several other building projects are being pursued concurrently to both expand the campus and substantially renovate existing classroom facilities. The Decker Quadrangle venture, completed in November 2007, created a new public entrance to the campus, a new visitors and admissions center, a building to house the computational sciences departments, and a substantial underground parking facility. In addition, Gilman Hall, the heart of the Homewood, is in the process of undergoing a complete renovation, the plans of which call for the creation of a movie theater and glass-enclosed atrium.

Dining options have expanded greatly on campus and many of the dining areas and food courts have been renovated. Vegetarian and kosher foods are available at all times in certain of the venues. Freshmen are required to participate in the meal plan, while upperclassmen generally choose to prepare their own meals.

Academics: Hold the Stereotypes, Please

The student body at Johns Hopkins is ethnically diverse and a significant international population is represented on campus. The academic curriculum is rigorous, and students quickly come to realize that the "grade inflation" found at most other top colleges and universities is not characteristic of classes here. Many courses are graded on a curve. Contrary to the common stereotype that Hopkins undergraduates, particularly premeds, are intensely competitive and will work to the detriment of their fellow classmates, stealing reading materials and sabotaging lab projects, most students find their peers to be helpful and more internally motivated than externally driven by grades. "The Hopkins stereotype is ridiculous," said one senior premed. "I have never heard of a single instance of such nonsense. In fact, sophomore year my chemistry lab partner once stayed up with me all night to try to help me figure out why my data did not work out."

Perhaps to diminish the stress of grades and to promote an easier transition to the academic rigor of the Hopkins's curriculum, first-semester grades are "covered," which means they are never seen by graduate schools and are not factored into calculations of a student's GPA. First-semester grades are simply designated on the transcript as Satisfactory or Unsatisfactory. This policy has been uniformly applauded by Hopkins students, who consider covered first-semester grades to be a factor encouraging them to be more eclectic in their choice of courses and less concerned about not doing well during the period of their first exposure to the demands of academic, social, and extracurricular life at Hopkins.

Students are affiliated with one of two undergraduate divisions of Johns Hopkins, the Zanvyl Krieger School of Arts and Sciences, and the G. W. C. Whiting School of Engineering. The former is the core institution at Hopkins and enrolls approximately 63 percent of the student body, the remainder being part of the Whiting School. Most students find the professors to be extremely approachable and committed, especially in the upper-level classes, which are small. "I very quickly learned that the best person to answer a question that I might have had was the professor herself," one student said. Teachers generally do not just go through the motions at review sessions. "One evening, my biochemistry professor ran a study group until midnight and did not leave until every question was answered!" Students in Arts and Sciences choose from over 60 established undergraduate majors and minors. Many of these programs are ranked among the best in the country. In addition, students may design an interdisciplinary major with the assistance of a faculty adviser.

> **"I very quickly learned that the best person to answer a question that I might have had was the professor herself."**

Distribution requirements for Arts and Science undergraduates are far from onerous and there is a loose core curriculum. A minimum of 30 credits out of the 120 required for the B.A. degree must be obtained in areas outside of the major. For majors in the humanities or social sciences, 12 of the 30 are required to fall within the disciplines of science or mathematics. Natural or quan-

titative science majors must earn at least 18–21 credits in the humanities or social sciences. In addition, Arts and Science students must take at least 4 courses that are designated writing-intensive.

Students in the G. W. C. Whiting School of Engineering pursue majors in nine distinct areas of study, including Mathematics and Statistics, Biomedical Engineering, Chemical Engineering, and Computer Science. The Department of Biomedical Engineering was ranked the best in the country by *U.S. News and World Report* and the Department of Geography and Environmental Engineering in the top five nationally. Generally between 120 and 130 credits are required for a B.S. or B.A. degree from the Whiting school.

Between semesters, Hopkins undergraduates are given a unique, voluntary opportunity to receive up to two Pass/Fail "enrichment" credits in one of four areas, including Academic Enrichment, Personal Enrichment, Experiential Learning, and Study Abroad. Academic Enrichment courses are free. Every January during Intersession, many students avail themselves of the chance to take an interesting class while enjoying part of their winter break on campus.

Taking Learning Beyond the Classroom

Research at Johns Hopkins is particularly encouraged, and there are enormous opportunities for students to become involved in projects with renowned faculty members, especially in the natural, social, and behavioral sciences. It is estimated that nearly 80 percent of Hopkins undergraduates engage in some sort of research outside of the classroom. The dedication of Johns Hopkins to research is reflected in the fact that the university ranks number one in the receipt of federal funds for research and development in science, medicine, and engineering. One female junior commented that she has "been involved in three different research projects since coming to Hopkins, both in my major (Psychology) and at the Medical School. The experience has been amazing and my advisor is always available to talk about our work."

Up to 70 percent of Hopkins students get involved in volunteer work in the community and frequently tutor inner-city elementary school students in a variety of subjects. In addition, there are 250 undergraduate clubs to attract students including a variety of publications and singing groups. "There is something for everybody's interest," said one male freshman. "I am still deciding about which of the many different school publications I want to join." The *Johns Hopkins News-Letter*, founded in 1896, is the oldest continuously published newspaper in the country and one of the most popular extracurricular venues.

Work Hard, Play Hard

No one would deny that Johns Hopkins students take their academic responsibilities very seriously. During finals period, the main library's doors are open all night, and the facility is generally full to the rafters at that time. Nevertheless, Hopkins students take their socializing seriously as well. Most students feel that the social life on campus has been steadily improving. During freshman year, the main party venues are the fraternity houses, which are situated off campus. About 1,000 undergraduates belong to one of eleven fraternities and seven sororities. Freshmen especially find frat parties an excellent way to meet classmates, albeit hot and noisy. Upperclassmen, however, generally choose "house parties" in student apartments instead of the frat scene. "Underclassmen are easy to please because they don't know any better," chuckled one male senior. "By junior year, you just don't want to chug frat Jell-O shots." Near campus, in the surrounding Charles Village, PJs and Charles Village Pub (CVP) are popular watering holes. Off campus, a short cab ride away, the Inner Harbor is a draw for students on the weekends, especially in the area called Power Plant. In addition, many undergraduates go to Fells Point, where there are several clubs. Excellent shopping and restaurants can be found in neighboring Towson.

Lacrosse! Lacrosse! Lacrosse!

Hopkins fields teams in all major collegiate sports, but lacrosse is unquestionably the preeminent Blue Jay sport on campus, and the source of a great deal of school spirit. In fact, Johns Hopkins lacrosse is Division I, while all other sports teams compete in Division III. Lacrosse players are actively recruited at Hopkins, and such efforts have resulted in 44 national titles for the men's team, including nine NCAA Division I titles, the most recent being awarded in 2007. Women's lacrosse too has become extremely competitive.

Hopkins has fielded top Division III teams in baseball, basketball, fencing, swimming, and water polo. For students who prefer just keeping in shape, Hopkins opened a 60,000-square-foot recreation center in 2001 that includes a climbing wall in addition to the usual cardiovascular conditioning machines.

No one would argue that Johns Hopkins is a party school. Its curriculum is intense but rewarding and the opportunities for research unsurpassed. If you are a serious student who is looking for an ethnically diverse and academically superlative school in an urban setting, and you appreciate opportunities for research, then Hopkins may just be the place for you. Loving lacrosse wouldn't hurt either!—*Jonathan Berken*

FYI

If you come to Johns Hopkins, you'd better bring "an 'I love Lacrosse' T-shirt."

What is a typical weekend schedule? "Go out Friday night, study Saturday morning, go to a lacrosse match or other sporting event in the afternoon, go to a frat or house party Saturday night, wake up late and study all day Sunday."

If I could change one thing about Johns Hopkins, I'd "get rid of bell-curve grading in classes."

Three things that every student at Johns Hopkins should do before graduating are "go to Pete's Grill, go to Fell's Point for Halloween, and cheer on the Blue Jays."

St. John's College

Address: PO Box 2800
Annapolis, MD 21404
Phone: 410-626-2522
E-mail address:
admissions@sjca.edu
Web site URL:
www.stjohnscollege.edu
Year Founded: 1696
Private or Public:
Private
Religious Affiliation: None
Location: Suburban
Number of Applicants:
390
Percent Accepted: 82%
**Percent Accepted who
enroll:** 43%
Number Entering: 137
**Number of Transfers
Accepted each Year:**
20
Middle 50% SAT range: M:
570–670, CR: 630–730,
Wr: Unreported
Middle 50% ACT range:
Unreported
**Early admission program
EA/ED/None:** None

**Percentage accepted
through EA or ED:**
NA
EA and ED deadline: NA
Regular Deadline: None/
Priority Application deadline:
March 1
Application Fee: $0
**Full time Undergraduate
enrollment:** 463
Total enrollment: 541
Percent Male: 51%
Percent Female: 49%
**Total Percent Minority or
Unreported:** 15%
Percent African-American:
1%
**Percent Asian/Pacific
Islander:** 1%
Percent Hispanic: 4%
Percent Native-American:
1%
Percent International: 4%
**Percent in-state/out of
state:** 12%/88%
Percent from Public HS:
65%
Retention Rate: 82%

Graduation Rate 4-year:
55%
Graduation Rate 6-year:
70%
**Percent Undergraduates in
On-campus housing:** 80%
**Number of official organized
extracurricular
organizations:** 30
3 Most popular majors:
Unreported
Student/Faculty ratio:
Unreported
Average Class Size: 15
**Percent of students going to
grad school:** 10%
Tuition and Fees:
$39,992
**In-State Tuition and Fees if
different:** No difference
Cost for Room and Board:
$9,600
**Percent receiving financial
aid out of those who apply,
first year:** 91%
**Percent receiving financial
aid among all students:**
20%

For anyone who has dreamed of sitting around a beautiful campus in one of America's oldest towns, reading the great works of the Western Canon like Aristotle, Ptolemy, and Kant, and discussing them with a tight-knit community of thoughtful students, St. John's College is a dream.

A True Liberal Arts School

Perhaps the truest liberal arts college in the United States, the St. John's education, or "The Program" as they call it, is unique. Students spend four years learning math (calculus, astronomy, and geometry) and seminar (literature, philosophy, and classics), three years of science (biology, chemistry, physics), one year of music, and four years of language (French and Greek), using only primary source materials; students never use textbooks, instead, Euclid guides students through geometry, Plato through philosophy, and Newton through physics.

The college believes that there is no greater teacher than the books themselves. Thus, pro-fessors at St. John's are called "tutors" and their job is not to lecture but to guide a discussion that will lead students, or "Johnnies" to the heart of the books. "Everyone is interested in reading and discussing, and it always amazes me how willing people are to talk about anything and everything," one student notes. Students agree that the academic experience is extraordinary and the best part of St. John's. "If academics are not the reason why you want to go to St. John's then you should not apply," a student commented.

Grades Don't Matter

St. John's encourages students to learn for themselves, not for the sake of a grade. According to one student, "We're encouraged to learn for the sake of learning, not for the sake of a little number on a piece of paper." There are no exams or formal grading given during the semester, and although grades are given at the end of each course (primarily so students can apply to graduate school) students can choose not to look at them. Although most students appreciate the independence the school gives them by deemphasizing grades, some students complain that because of the lack of formal assessments, the grades given can seem arbitrary because the grading standards are left entirely up to each tutor. "While in one class, you might get an A with a certain type of performance, in another class you might get a B or a C with the same type of performance, and you never know which one it is until the semester is over," a senior described.

A Quaint and Historic Town

Annapolis is a quaint colonial town set on the Chesapeake Bay that for a few years served as the capital of the United States under George Washington's presidency. Today, the town is host to both St. John's and the US Naval Academy. Despite its quaint historic charm and the presence of several colleges, the town gets mixed reviews from students. While one student describes its history and architecture as "an absolute gem" she also notes that it lacks in entertainment options. The one-of-a-kind shops and sailing culture tend to appeal to an older crowd, and although there are a few good restaurants, only a small number of pubs are open late. Students also find that though the campus is well situated close to the historic district of Annapolis, the public transportation system is unreliable and can make going to the mall or the movies or anywhere that is not within walking distance quite difficult. Nevertheless, students note that with the rigors of the academic program, they have limited time to leave campus anyway.

When Not Reading or Sleeping . . .

Outside of attending classes and lots of studying, on-campus life revolves around extracurricular activities and "hanging out." Popular extracurricular activities include the King William Players which puts on a play each semester, *The Gadfly*, the student newspaper, and an active intramural sports scene. One student notes that though there are a number of experienced athletes, "The environment is surprisingly open to people who have never played sports before." Less popular clubs tend to have a high turnover rate; "There are a lot of clubs on campus, but around half of them disappear by the end of the semester or the year."

The campus coffee shop, located right at the heart of campus, serves as a central social center because of its quaint, comfortable atmosphere and "the best food on-campus, al-

though that isn't saying much." Other Johnnies, referred to as "room-Johnnies," tend to stay in their rooms occasionally socializing with their neighbors but rarely leaving the building except to go to class and the dining hall. "Quad-Johnnies," a subset mostly composed of social freshmen, tend to hang out on the quad socializing and drinking. Be warned, however, that the administration can be particularly strict about underage drinking. Although everyone agrees that underage drinking is prevalent, every once in a while the college cracks down. "My year, they kicked out four sophomores for underage drinking," a student notes.

A Tight-Knit Community

With only 400 to 500 students, St. John's is a very small community; by the end of freshman year everyone at least recognizes everybody. While some students like the tight community others are bothered by the fact that "everyone on the campus knows your business."

"Everyone is interested in reading and discussing, and it always amazes me how willing people are to talk about anything and everything."

Additionally, many students complain about the lack of diversity on campus although in some ways this is improving. "Most people come from upper-class well-educated families while there are a minority of students from middle-class backgrounds." Ethnic and racial diversity is also limited. "The school has tried to recruit more ethnic and racial minorities but they've been very unsuccessful." According to one student, the biggest problem is economics. "The school is really expensive, and does not offer a traditional education which would provide the graduating students with a specific field or career." Furthermore, while the school offers need-based financial aid, it can still be very expensive for students from disadvantaged backgrounds. "The first year, the college offered me a fairly generous aid package, but after that it decreased significantly; I'm graduating with $65,000 in loans," a senior says. He also notes that some of the most interesting students have had to leave because of financial difficulties. Yet despite the lack of ethnic and socioeconomic diversity, in recent years, the international student body has increased and the college is making a noticeable recruiting effort in non-traditional locations. At the very least, students say that there is tons of "intellectual diversity" and for a school that is all about ideas, that is the most important thing.

Leaving the Cave

A given week at St. John's includes reading the great works of western literature and discussing them with classmates hours into the night. On Mondays and Thursdays the whole campus attends their seminars at the same time. On Wednesdays, quad-Johnnies gather in the quad to celebrate the weekly New Year, because "Johnnies learn more in a week than most college students do in a year," and on Fridays, many students attend the campus lecture which occasionally brings in notable speakers such as Elie Wiesel and Andrew Young. On weekends, students hang out at Annapolis bars, talk at the coffee shop or go to campus parties ranging from the occasional waltz party, a St. John's tradition, to more standard college parties at off-campus houses. Between all of this, they are reading constantly. More than anything else, St. John's College is the ultimate college of the mind and "everything else is secondary."—*Sage Snider*

FYI

If you come to St. John's, you'd better bring: a thick skin because it can be difficult academically and socially.

What's the typical weekend schedule? Friday night lecture, the movie club shows a classic movie on Saturday nights, off-campus parties (usually one or two), and lots of lots of philosophical conversations.

Three things every student at St. John's should do before graduating are: Get a Hodson Trust Internship, take out all your tutors to lunch, and go to Croquet Weekend where St. John's beats the Naval Academy at Croquet!

St. Mary's College

Address: 18952 East Fisher Road, St. Mary's City, MD 20686-3001

Phone: 240-895-5000

E-mail address: admissions@smcm.edu

Web site URL: www.smcm.edu

Year Founded: 1840

Private or Public: Public

Religious Affiliation: None

Location: Rural

Number of Applicants: 2,723

Percent Accepted: 55%

Percent Accepted who enroll: 32%

Number Entering: 454

Number of Transfers Accepted each Year: 99

Middle 50% SAT range: M: 570–660, CR: 580–680, Wr: 570–680

Middle 50% ACT range: 24–29

Early admission program EA/ED/None: ED

Percentage accepted through EA or ED: 47%

EA and ED deadline: 1-Nov

Regular Deadline: 1-Jan

Application Fee: $40

Full time Undergraduate enrollment: 2,035

Total enrollment: 2,065

Percent Male: 43%

Percent Female: 57%

Total Percent Minority or Unreported: 24%

Percent African-American: 8%

Percent Asian/Pacific Islander: 4%

Percent Hispanic: 5%

Percent Native-American: 1%

Percent International: 2%

Percent in-state/out of state: 83%/17%

Percent from Public HS: 70%

Retention Rate: 90%

Graduation Rate 4-year: 67%

Graduation Rate 6-year: 74%

Percent Undergraduates in On-campus housing: 81%

Number of official organized extracurricular organizations: 116

3 Most popular majors: Economics, English, Psychology

Student/Faculty ratio: 12:1

Average Class Size: 13

Percent of students going to grad school: 34%

Tuition and Fees: $23,454

In-State Tuition and Fees if different: $12,604

Cost for Room and Board: $9,225

Percent receiving financial aid out of those who apply, first year: 64%

Percent receiving financial aid among all students: 61%

A public university that traces its origin to the 1840s, St. Mary's College is the public honors college of Maryland. Located about 40 miles from Washington D.C. on the western shore of the Chesapeake Bay, St. Mary's College is a highly regarded liberal arts institution. Although it does offer a Master's program in teaching, the college's primary focus is definitely undergraduate education. As most people who attend state schools crowd into large lecture halls of universities that enroll tens of thousands of both undergraduate and graduate students, St. Mary's College provides schooling with individual attention at the cost of a public university.

State, Yet not State

In accordance with most state governments, Maryland has its own charter system that incorporates all public institutions of higher learning. For years, St. Mary's College was part of the system but opted out in 1992 during a fiscal crisis and was subsequently named the public honors college of Maryland. The concept is that everyone at St. Mary's College is an honor student. At the outset, it may seem strange. After all, what difference does it make to bestow the title honors college when everyone at the school is at the same level? Compared to the rest of the University System of Maryland, however, St. Mary's College is supposed to represent the top institution that offers the best intellectual environment. In fact, according to *U.S. News & World Report*, the college is ranked number one among all public liberal arts colleges.

St. Mary's College is a small school. With approximately 2,000 students, it is smaller than many high schools around the country. The advantage of the small size is that it ensures personal attention by the faculty to the students. "Because the school is so small, it is much easier to get to know professors," said one student. "By graduation, I feel that I know most people who are on campus, both professors and students." To enhance the intimacy of St. Mary's learning environment, the classes are mostly seminars where students learn through discussions and debates. "I sat through a couple of classes that have fewer than 10 people," said one student. "It is great because then you have more time to present about your own views."

One disadvantage of St. Mary's College is the number of academic programs. In fact, the school only has 22 majors, and one of them is the student-designed program of study, in which one can come up with his or her own curriculum based on the courses offered by the college. Of course, any program made by a student is subject to approval by the school administration. The 21 other majors are the more traditional liberal arts programs, such as biology, history, and economics. "It is true that we don't have many choices," said one student. "But we are a liberal arts college, so you need to understand that people who come here are looking for a general type of education, not something specific like electrical engineering." Although most students do consider the number of majors a downside of St. Mary's College, most of them do not feel affected because they enjoy having a liberal arts education. "Studying at St Mary's is not about knowing all the facts about a field. It is all about developing the skills you need to succeed," said one student.

Since everyone is an honors student, the workload is certainly heavy, and students are relatively competitive. "There are a lot of smart people who really want to do well in school," said one student. "And sometimes, it is hard to keep up with them." According to students, it is important to remain well organized. After all, students who are poor planners tend to be easily overwhelmed by schoolwork. "You have to make sure that you do not fall behind," said one student. "It can be really difficult to keep up with classes afterwards." Despite the intensity of some of the classes, it is important to point out that the majority of students are able to manage their schedules with relative ease and have plenty of time to participate in different extracurricular activities. "You have to work hard, but since we are an honors college, most people who came here are definitely ready for this type of pressure," said one student.

> **"By graduation, I feel that I know most people who are on campus, both professors and students."**

As one of the top 100 liberal arts colleges in the country, the admissions process is very competitive. Only approximately half of the applicants are accepted. "Students at St. Mary's are very smart," said one student. "But don't be intimidated by other people. If you get in, that means you are smart too."

The Beginning of America

One of the most important facets of the college advertised by promotional materials of

St. Mary's College is its location. At the out-set, for a college student, perhaps there is nothing special about St. Mary's City, where the college is located. In fact, many people may think that the location is a disadvan-tage. After all, the so-called city is more sim-ilar to a village. What is special about St. Mary's City, however, is that it is the fourth-oldest British settlement in the United States. Large portions of the city are now consid-ered National Historic Landmarks. 'The his-torical importance of St. Mary's City cannot be overlooked," said one student. "There is not much to do here, but at least we live in a historic place with a beautiful campus of nice, old buildings."

The great majority of students live on campus. After all, it is a small school in a rather removed part of Maryland, thus the sense of community provided by college residences can be very helpful to many students. Freshman housing is generally closely monitored by staff members and has many more features that provide advice and support to students. "Getting to know peo-ple who live around you is the first step to making friends in college," said one student. "That is why living on campus during fresh-man year is so important." After the first-year, upperclassmen can enjoy greater freedom and independence in one of the town houses or apartment-style residences. The quality of the dorms is generally consid-ered adequate by the students. "I definitely would love to have big rooms, but, having been to other schools' dorms, I think we are actually pretty decent," said one student.

The main dining hall is called the Great Room, which can seat about 400 students and serves as an all-you-can-eat facility. Be-yond the Great Room, there are also a few sandwich and coffee places around campus. Students can choose from eight different meal plans, though there are limitations based on the year. For example, freshmen only have access to three different plans, all of which focus on eating at the dining hall instead of using flex dollars at different restaurants around campus. For upperclass-men, obviously there are more options, since some students are by then living off campus.

Many parties happen on campus because that is where the majority of students are lo-cated. However, most people do feel that St. Mary's City is not very interesting with very few activities for students, especially during weekends, a time when people finally find some time to relax. Many do choose to go to Washington D.C. or even Baltimore during weekends to enjoy a more vibrant city at-mosphere.

An Honors Experience

St. Mary's College may not be very different from any other small liberal arts schools. Af-ter all, it is located in a rather removed part of the state. It has only 2,000 students and offers few majors. However, what distin-guishes St. Mary's College is that it is a public college providing a great education. Whenever a school offers strong academics at a discounted price, it certainly becomes a college choice worthy of consideration. —*Xiaohang Liu*

FYI
If you come to St. Mary's College, you'd better bring "a car."
What is the typical weekend schedule? "Work during the day, party at night."
If I could change one thing about St. Mary's College, "I'd add more majors."
Three things every student at St. Mary's College should do before graduating are "take a trip to
   Washington, D.C., tour the history of St. Mary's City, and remember to have fun."

United States Naval Academy

Address: 117 Decatur Road, Annapolis, MD 21402
Phone: 410-293-1914
E-mail address: webmail@usna.edu
Web site URL: www.usna.edu
Year Founded: 1845
Private or Public: Public
Religious Affiliation: None
Location: Suburban
Number of Applicants: 10,960
Percent Accepted: 14%
Percent Accepted who enroll: 82%
Number Entering: 1,261
Number of Transfers Accepted each Year: Unreported
Middle 50% SAT range: M: 600–700, **CR:** 560–670, **Wr:** Unreported
Middle 50% ACT range: Unreported
Early admission program EA/ED/None: None

Percentage accepted through EA or ED: NA
EA and ED deadline: NA
Regular Deadline: 31-Jan
Application Fee: $0
Full time Undergraduate enrollment: 4,489
Total enrollment: 4,489
Percent Male: 80%
Percent Female: 20%
Total Percent Minority or Unreported: 25%
Percent African-American: 4%
Percent Asian/Pacific Islander: 3%
Percent Hispanic: 11%
Percent Native-American: <1%
Percent International: 1%
Percent in-state/out of state: 5%/95%
Percent from Public HS: 60%
Retention Rate: 96%

Graduation Rate 4-year: 84%
Graduation Rate 6-year: NA
Percent Undergraduates in On-campus housing: 100%
Number of official organized extracurricular organizations: 70
3 Most popular majors: Economics, Political Science, Systems Engineering
Student/Faculty ratio: 8:1
Average Class Size: 16
Percent of students going to grad school: 2%
Tuition and Fees: $0
In-State Tuition and Fees if different: No difference
Cost for Room and Board: $0
Percent receiving financial aid out of those who apply, first year: NA
Percent receiving financial aid among all students: NA

The United States Naval Academy is situated in Annapolis, MD. Founded in 1845 by the Secretary of the Navy, George Bancroft, the historic academy is responsible for the training of future officers of the Navy or Marine Corps. Despite its strict regimen and array of rules and hazing rites of passage that range from the silly to the unbearable, the camaraderie that develops among the midshipmen is incomparable. Students praise the institution not only for its training, but for the faculty's dedication in doing everything in their power to see their students succeed.

Fit Mind and Body

The Naval Academy stresses academia, resulting in what some students consider a "much heavier course load than that of other schools." Students are not allowed to take fewer than 15 credits a semester. As one student explained, "You don't have the option to take longer than four years. If you are on that path then you get kicked out before graduation time." Of course, the fac-

ulty's dedication to its students undoubtedly pays off in USNA's small classes, which have "between 15 and 25 students, and no graduate students" teaching. All professors have PhDs and "they're really available," one student said. Aside from its emphasis on a class hierarchy, the Naval Academy at times tends to resemble high school in other ways—"a strict high school," that is. "It's hard to do bad here because the professors are always on you." Engineering is the most popular major at USNA, perhaps due in part to the Academy's recent quota that enables "only 30 percent of the students" to be humanities majors. Balancing a heavy course load is only encumbered by fulfillment of one's military requirements. "Your final GPA is a combination of your academic grades, military grades, and physical fitness grades."

Love Hurts

"The upperclassmen run the school and they can punish you." Unfortunately, unlike high school, there's no running to the administration to escape initiation traditions or seniors with paddles, à la *Fast Times at Ridgemont High*. "The first year is basically being initiated into a superfraternity." The Academy is particularly rough with its freshmen, as that first year is key for weeding out the dedicated from the not-so-much. One student exclaimed that, "only 84 percent of the initial class size graduates." Those 25 percent might have failed following the simplest of rules, such as the one that prohibits freshmen from touching their beds from 6:30 a.m. to 10:30 p.m. Frosh regulations are severe. Plebes, first-year students, "only get to leave campus from 10 to 10 on Saturday" and, in a fraternity pledge mentality, must "run in the hallway." And newcomers ought to remember to put all DVDs away. Freshmen are prohibited from listening to music or watching movies. Of course, in addition to the strict restraints on daily activities, plebes lament that "there's a lot of bullshit knowledge you have to know" upon an upperclassman's request, such as three current newspaper articles in advance or how many days until Thanksgiving break. Although "it's a hard system," many of the rules are relinquished in one's sophomore year. In addition to a few overnights, students agree, "the biggest thing you get as a sophomore is that you get to sleep during the day."

> "The party scene here is in the weight room."

The Crisco of Camaraderie
One of the Academy's most memorable traditions occurs upon completion of freshman year, when the students climb Herndon, a 21-foot structure shaped like the Washington Monument. "There's a freshman cover [hat] that's replaced with a midshipman cover," a student explained. "Before you climb it, they put grease, Crisco, all around it." The inch-thick fat coating results in tedious hours during which thousands of students attempt to climb the slippery monument. Other traditions include painting the statue in the center of campus before every football game. And the easiest way Naval Academy students can guarantee a goodnight peck? It's USNA tradition that if a girl puts on a guy's cover, she owes him a kiss. "A regular girl," one student clarified, "not a Naval Academy girl."

Party in the Weight Room
"The party scene here is in the weight room." Although the Annapolis scene is "great if you're 21," since drinking is not allowed on campus and students are only allowed out during certain hours on the weekends, students find that "most people honestly do work, run, workout, and go out to eat on the weekends." Plebes are not allowed to drink, even if they are 21. Most people abide by the rigorously enforced rules, especially since "underage drinking is punished severely" and there are random weekend Breathalyzers for the underage. On the other hand, seniors are allowed to buy beer at the school restaurant or drink at the officer's club, as long as they don't come back belligerent. Perhaps the slew of rules and punishments account for why intramural sports, although mandatory, provide the social aspect that is sometimes hindered by USNA's strict policies. Football is huge at the Naval Academy, with pep rallies and mandatory attendance at the games greatly promoting school spirit. While such camaraderie is prevalent throughout the school, it is stronger within each company—the 140 people or so with whom a student lives and interacts. There are 30 companies in total.

No Kissing, No Asking, No Telling
You're not allowed to show affection in any form at the Academy. There is no kissing and while PDAs are often in poor etiquette anyway, USNA makes sure to enforce Emily Post's seduction guidelines. "Girls are allowed in guys' rooms, although the door must remain open and there must be no physical contact." Students agreed that such seriousness is understandable. "Although females are only 20 percent of the school, I feel that the administration has done an excellent job making everything equal and not tolerating any discriminative practices—no matter how mild," praised one student. Despite the female-friendly environment, one male student claimed that, "Most females here tend to have a chip on their shoulder due to the male environment." Of course, despite the rule-infused school, the Naval Academy isn't a completely hands-off boys club. "We have dances and you're allowed to bring dates to those." The dances are "a pretty big deal." One of the biggest events is the Ring Dance at the end of the year. "It's kind of like prom, that type of big, and you get your ring, and you get it in the water from the seven seas and your date is supposed to put it on you." Of course, dancing or lifting weights, "homosexuality is definitely very taboo." Students said it is "not

accepted at all, but then again, nobody expects it to be in the military." Most cite the "very conservative student body" as one of the main reasons for the "don't ask, don't tell" mentality that is prevalent on campus. —*Dana Schuster*

University of Maryland, College Park

Address: Mitchell Building
College Park, MD
20742-5235
Phone: 301-314-8385
E-mail address:
um-admit@uga.umd.edu
Web site URL: www.umd.edu
Year Founded: 1856
Private or Public: Public
Religious Affiliation: None
Location: Suburban
Number of Applicants:
24,176
Percent Accepted: 47%
Percent Accepted who
enroll: 37%
Number Entering: 4,204
Number of Transfers
Accepted each Year: 3,672
Middle 50% SAT range: M:
600–700, CR: 570–680,
Wr: Unreported
Middle 50% ACT range:
Unreported
Early admission program
EA/ED/None: EA

Percentage accepted
through EA or ED:
Unreported
EA and ED deadline: 1-Dec
Regular Deadline: 01/20
Application Fee: $55
Full time Undergraduate
enrollment: 25,813
Total enrollment: 35,853
Percent Male: 52%
Percent Female: 48%
Total Percent Minority or
Unreported: 43%
Percent African-American:
13%
Percent Asian/Pacific
Islander: 15%
Percent Hispanic: 6%
Percent Native-American:
0%
Percent International: 2%
Percent in-state/out of
state: 76%/24%
Percent from Public HS:
Unreported
Retention Rate: 94%

Graduation Rate 4-year: 63%
Graduation Rate 6-year: 81%
Percent Undergraduates in
On-campus housing: 41%
Number of official organized
extracurricular
organizations: 527
3 Most popular majors:
Criminology, Economics,
Political Science and
Government
Student/Faculty ratio: 18:1
Average Class Size: 25
Percent of students going to
grad school: Unreported
Tuition and Fees: $23,076
In-State Tuition and Fees if
different: $8,005
Cost for Room and Board:
$9,109
Percent receiving financial
aid out of those who apply,
first year: 58%
Percent receiving financial
aid among all students:
39%

Less then fifteen miles from the nation's capital, the University of Maryland sits on more than a thousand acres of green, suburban grass. Home of the Terrapins, Maryland is well known as a prestigious research university with Division I athletics and a strong sense of school pride. The school's numerous academic, extracurricular, and athletic options provide plenty of opportunities for its 25,000 students, so it's no surprise that wherever one goes on campus, shouts of "Go Terps!" are sure to be heard.

Options for Everyone

With over a hundred academic majors and eleven colleges and schools, the University of Maryland offers every student the chance to study what they love. Applicants select one of the eleven schools on their UMD application, and while many students choose the more traditional College of Arts and Humanities, a great deal apply to the Robert H. Smith School of Business, the Philip Merrill College of Journalism, the College of Education, and other schools.

All Maryland students need to complete 120 course credits in order to graduate, with a minimum of 12 credits per semester to be considered a "full-time student." The school has a CORE program, which consists of nine course credits in the humanities, ten in math and science, nine in social sciences and history, and three in emerging issues. There are a few more specific English and math requirements. Maryland also requires each student to get six credits at the advanced level in one or more fields outside their major, but many students chose to take a few more classes and use those six credits towards a certificate. Most Maryland students don't feel too daunted by the requirements, and note that "it's pretty easy to fulfill them without really trying," because there are so many interesting classes to take.

The university also has a variety of special academic programs, including the College Park Scholars program and the Honors College. The College Park Scholars program, which is divided into a variety of academic fields ranging from Media, Self, and Society to Global Public Health, allows students the opportunity to live in a unique residential community, take exclusive courses, and interact with professors in smaller class settings. The prestigious Honors College offers students access to many interdisciplinary courses and multi-year programs, such as the Gemstone research program. Overall, students are very impressed with Maryland's academic program, and some even argue that the school "doesn't get all the credit it deserves."

The one down side to Maryland's academics, according to some students, is the grading system. At UMD, there's no difference between an A– and an A+; with both grades, students are awarded a 4.0 grade point average. However, the same holds true for grades in the B range—and anything in the B range earns the student a 3.0. While this can be seen as "an advantage for A– students," some students feel discouraged knowing that their B+ is worth the same amount as their classmate's B–.

The "Horseshoe" and the "Graham Cracker," Just Minutes from the White House

One way that many students make Maryland's large campus feel smaller is by getting involved with the popular Greek system. With dozens of fraternities and sororities to choose from, any student who wants to "go Greek" can easily find his or her niche. Fraternity housing can be found on "Frat Row," also known as the "Horseshoe" because of the shape the fraternity houses make. Right next to the Horseshoe is the "Graham Cracker," another complex of fraternity and sorority houses. Frat parties are a common occurrence, with multiple parties happening each weekend. Other perks of being involved in the Frat system include special events during Homecoming and Greek Week.

However, the frat party scene does not completely dominate social life at Maryland. Frat Row sits on one side of Route 1, the main street in College Park, which is also home to a variety of restaurants and bars popular with UMD undergrads. Because Route 1 is so close to campus, it's a popular location for any Maryland student looking for a night out. Many students also chose to take the Metro (a four-dollar ticket and thirty-minute ride) to Washington, D.C., where they can enjoy the restaurants, bars, and clubs. Maryland students love having a "movie-esque" campus so close to a big city, because "there's always something to do," and whenever they "don't feel like spending money to go out in D.C., there's always a frat party or a bar close to campus where you'll have a good time."

Although drugs and alcohol are prohibited by the school, most students don't feel threatened by the administration. RAs are pretty lenient, and students say that it's unlikely someone will be punished unless they're "being ridiculous." Although some students smoke pot, most agree that alcohol is much more prevalent on campus.

Overall, Maryland students feel as if there is a good balance between studying and partying. "Maryland studies very hard and parties very hard," one student said, while another pointed out that there were never weeks devoted solely to studying or solely to partying. One student described Maryland as "a more down-to-earth version of lots of bigger state schools." Then again, UMD has gotten billed as one of the Top 20 Party Schools for the last few years.

Learning, Laughing, and Laying Out on the "Mall"

With 36 residence halls and a variety of off-campus housing options, every student can find something comfortable at Maryland. Students can apply for housing and request specific dorms, such as Cecil, an all-girls hall, or Elkton, the notorious party dorm. With such a huge campus, many students have to walk pretty far to get to class, but most students ignore distance when choosing their residence halls. One of the best ways to make friends at Maryland is by getting to know the people on your floor, and most students credit their housing arrangements with making them feel at home.

About 76% of UMD students are Maryland natives, and many others are from the nearby New Jersey, Pennsylvania, and New York areas. However, the student body still feels very diverse. "Any type of person can go [to Maryland]," and "there's always somewhere to fit in." One of the most popular campus locations is the "Mall," a large, shallow reflecting pool modeled after the pool in front of the Lincoln Memorial in Washington, D.C. When weather permits, Maryland students love to lie out, study, or play games of football—and, on occasion, Quidditch—on the beautiful green grass surrounding the Mall. Students also frequent the Stamp Student Union, the student activities center that's home to the University Book Center, the Hoff Theater, and numerous dining options.

Although Terps love their campus, most agree that the city of College Park is pretty "sketchy." Students are advised not to walk alone at night, and some cautious girls even carry pepper spray when they go out. Another common complaint is the quality of the dining hall food. However, the dining halls "always have chicken fingers and fries," and are also vegan-friendly, with salad bars and vegan options readily available. For freshmen who want to avoid the dining halls, the meal plan also includes "TerpBucks," meal dollars that can be used at the Union Shop and popular chain restaurants like Starbucks.

A Toast to Testudo

When Maryland students aren't studying or partying, chances are they're involved with one or more of the school's numerous extracurricular programs. Freshmen get to know all of the university's extracurricular opportunities by attending the First Look Fair, during which all of the organizations line up on the Mall and try to recruit new members. "Everyone reads the *Diamondback*," Maryland's main college paper, and other on-campus publications are also popular. With numerous a cappella, comedy, and service groups, there's something for everyone.

Maryland is well known for its Division I athletics teams, and many students flock to the football and basketball games every year. Student attendance is high even when the teams have losing seasons, partly because students can get free tickets to the games. Their mascot, Testudo—a diamondback terrapin always clad in UMD red—is one of the most famous mascots in college sports.

> **"Maryland is like a more down-to-earth version of some other big state schools."**

However, Testudo is more than just a mascot—he's also the center of one of the most famous campus superstitions. Maryland students say that "rubbing Testudo's nose"—that is, the nose of a statue of the beloved tortoise—will bring good luck. The legend goes on to say that the one year the main statue of Testudo was under renovation, the overall campus GPA dropped significantly.

One thing that stands out about UMD is the amount of school spirit and the unity among the student body. Although the students are "very diverse" and come from all socioeconomic, ethnic, and religious backgrounds, they all have one thing in common: Terrapin pride. Walking along the lush, green grass towards many of the freshman dorms, it's impossible to miss the welcoming sign painted on the football stadium: Home of the Maryland Terrapins. For UMD students, home is where Testudo is.—*Iva Velickovic*

FYI
If I could change one thing about Maryland, it would be the neighborhood. It's pretty sketchy, and I feel unsafe walking around at night.
One thing I wish I knew before I came to Maryland was that freshmen are allowed to bring cars. You do have to pay a fee, but it's totally worth it because it gives you the opportunity to explore Bethesda, DC, and other places nearby.

Massachusetts

Amherst College

Address: PO Box 5000
Amherst, MA 01002
Phone: 413-542-2328
E-mail address:
admissions@amherst.edu
Web site URL:
www.amherst.edu
Year Founded: 1821
Private or Public: Private
Religious Affiliation: None
Location: Rural
Number of Applicants: 7,745
Percent Accepted: 15%
**Percent Accepted who
enroll:** 38%
Number Entering: 452
**Number of Transfers
Accepted each Year:** 14
Middle 50% SAT range:
M:660–760, CR: 670–770,
Wr: 670–760
Middle 50% ACT range: 31
**Early admission program
EA/ED/None:** ED
**Percentage accepted
through EA or ED:** 34%

EA and ED deadline:
15-Nov
Regular Deadline: 1-Jan
Application Fee: $60
**Full time Undergraduate
enrollment:** 1,683
Total enrollment: 1,683
Percent Male: 50%
Percent Female: 50%
**Total Percent Minority or
Unreported:** 38%
Percent African-American:
11%
**Percent Asian/Pacific
Islander:** 11%
Percent Hispanic: 11%
Percent Native-American:
<1%
Percent International: 7%
**Percent in-state/out of
state:** 10%/90%
Percent from Public HS:
58%
Retention Rate: 97%
Graduation Rate 4-year:
96%

Graduation Rate 6-year:
98%
**Percent Undergraduates
in On-campus housing:**
98%
**Number of official organized
extracurricular
organizations:** 100
3 Most popular majors:
Political Science,
Psychology, Economics
Student/Faculty ratio: 8:1
Average Class Size: 17
**Percent of students going to
grad school:** 75%
Tuition and Fees: $36,970
**In-State Tuition and Fees if
different:** No difference
Cost for Room and Board:
$9,790
**Percent receiving financial
aid out of those who apply,
first year:** 80%
**Percent receiving financial
aid among all students:**
52%

G iven their many, varied interests, you might be surprised to find that the overwhelming majority of students at Amherst College at least agree about one thing: "the 'h' in the name is not pronounced." Yet, regardless of this phonetic unity, Amherstians pride themselves on their school's diversity, be it academic, social or extracurricular. With 36 available majors and 100 student organizations to choose from, it's no wonder that Amherst's 1,700 undergraduates feel that they can do almost anything at a place which—despite its intimate size—offers some of the most wide-ranging options anywhere.

Open Curriculum, Open Minds

Multiple students note that the first thing that comes to mind when thinking about academics at Amherst is the school's distinctive lack of a core curriculum. With the exception of a required seminar in freshman year, Amherst allows its students the freedom to design their own course of study, which gives them full responsibility over their educational choices.

On the whole, Amherstians are content with these First-Year Seminars, which focus on subjects ranging from happiness to history to physics to philosophy. "The seminars are there just to ensure that you can think, write and analyze a text cogently before you settle on a particular major," said one freshman at the end of his first semester. "Besides, the fact that there are around 30 of them means that there's something available for everyone, whatever their interests." Students praise the discussion-based nature of these seminars, which lets them bounce their ideas off of one another and their professors in a collaborative setting.

Nor do Amherstians object to having to declare a major by the end of their second year and having to complete 32 credits in order to graduate. Majors typically span from eight to ten courses, but can be tailored to any given student's personal preferences. The great thing about having no distributional requirements, students say, is that the curriculum's structure lies at the individual's discretion. "Since there are no core requirements," one senior double-majoring in English and Russian noted, "I've been able to take classes in 11 or 12 different departments already, no problem." During his junior year, the same student also tried his hand at jazz guitar, in lessons which were wholly funded by the school, and took a cognitive spirituality class with the head of the physics department, Arthur Zajonc, who was the personal physics tutor to the Dalai Lama for a year. Hence, as a sophomore majoring in psychology pointed out, one of Amherst's biggest selling points is that "the incentive for students to take a certain class is entirely their own desire to be in that class; unlike at other colleges, it's not about climbing the distributional ladder."

> "Great professors in small departments with lots of money means that you can do almost anything you want."

Some students, however, are frustrated by the difficulties of registering for courses taught by Amherst's "celebrity professors"— such as Arthur Zajonc in physics, Hadley Arkes in philosophy and Austin Sarat in political science—because class sizes are limited. "Upperclassmen and people who have settled on a major typically get preference," said one sophomore. "But, the trade-off is that if you get into one of these classes, the experience is that much more intimate." Indeed, Amherstians praise the small size of both seminars and lectures, which, according to one junior, typically average about 17 and 40 people respectively. This allows for students to develop more personal relationships with their peers and their teachers within and outside of the classroom. Dinners at professors' houses are not unheard of. Meanwhile, students at Amherst praise the wide availability of educational resources, whatever their own individual pursuits entail. As one senior put it, "great professors in

small departments with lots of money means that you can do almost anything you want."

Small classes at the college incentivize students to come prepared and ready to participate. "Silence from one side of the discussion table is much more noticeable in a tiny classroom setting," one freshman said. Yet, Amherst students of all years find that the intimacy of their academic experience creates an atmosphere of friendly cooperation rather than fierce competition. Cliché though it may be, students are convinced that they work hard—and play hard—together. "Amherst is by far the most relaxed place I've been," one sophomore claimed. "People here just want to pursue their interests and breathe; it's totally chill."

But if they happen to get tired of its small classrooms and need a change of pace, Amherst also offers it students the opportunity to take courses at four other nearby institutions through its membership in the Five College Consortium. The consortium is an unusual cooperative arrangement among Amherst, Smith, Mount Holyoke, and Hampshire Colleges and the University of Massachusetts-Amherst, where all five campuses are linked by a free bus system. "By their fourth year here," one senior noted, "I'd say about 75% of people have taken at least one course somewhere else, since some courses just aren't available at Amherst," such as certain language classes, or those that relate more specifically to job skills.

Amherst: Where Only the "h" is Silent

Passion for learning aside, students at Amherst are convinced that they know how to have a good time. Amherstians, they report, orchestrate a careful balancing act between their studies and their social lives every week. Though one sophomore noted that some students can seem like "academic zombies from Sunday through Wednesday," he went on to say that "everybody seems to forget their work from Thursday night until Sunday morning."

So what do students at Amherst do to keep themselves busy during weekends? Well, as with so many other aspects of their school, Amherstians have options. Even though there are no official fraternities on campus, students can "almost always find typical college beer-fest parties in 'the Socials,'" a quad surrounded by dorms with suites. "The Social Quad has wonderful dorms," one junior stated, "but on weekends, they smell like alcohol and are pretty much on a non-stop

Massachusetts

rave." Luckily for those who choose not to party, the Social Quad is all the way at the bottom of a hill, "so you can't really hear the music," and substance-free housing is available to freshmen upon request. "But there's absolutely no pressure to drink if you don't want to," one freshman noted.

Given this, students still seem to agree that Amherst's administration has a somewhat lax policy when it comes to dealing with drinking on campus. In line with the school's mission to respect its members' diversity of lifestyle, Amherst rarely invades upon its students' personal lives, unless their behavior becomes disruptive or dangerous. "They basically spend the first three months telling us how to drink safely, since we're not supposed to be doing it in the first place," one freshman said. "But they're only going to bust a party if things really get out of hand." Amherst also hosts a special TAP ("The Amherst Party") once a month, which, according to one student, are "really safe, really fun, and really big . . . and not just in the drinking or bump-and-grind sense." Traditional themes include an '80s dance party, a Halloween costume party, and a tropical Luau.

In addition to extra courses, the Five College Consortium offers Amherst students the opportunity to go off campus and meet other people if they ever feel caught in "the Amherst bubble." In the words of one senior who gives tours at Amherst, "it actually does make a difference having 35,000 people your age within a 10 mile radius. It means that you can pretty much always find a new crowd if you want, but also that there's just generally lots of fun stuff going on in the area." He pointed out the fact that Amherst is located in the Pioneer Valley, the second largest booking venue in all of New England, which means that there are "concerts, clubs, bars, all kinds of ridiculous festivals, readings by traveling writers, academic symposia every month."

Besides standard partying, students say that there are always on-campus events like movie showings in the campus center, comedy club performances, and free concerts in the recital hall. One student, for example, mentioned the fact that "theatre majors are actually required to write or direct a play, so there are about three or four plays here every two weeks or so." At Amherst, students claim, "there will never be a night where you don't have something to do."

Purple Pride and Decent Dorms

Other than how they pronounce the name of their college, Amherst students also agree

that athletes have a noticeable presence on campus. By one junior football player's estimates, for instance, about a third of the school plays a varsity sport. The integration of athletes and their non-athletic counterparts in the same dorms, moreover, appears to lead to a lot of school spirit, since "basically everybody knows someone on one sports team or another." "We support our athletes a lot," one sophomore said. "They're basically our heroes." This is especially true in games against Amherst's longtime rivals—such as Williams, Middlebury, and Wesleyan—for which almost everybody comes out wearing purple and white. And though athletes at Amherst get all the glory when they triumph on weekends, students concur that there is not a 'jock or not' divide at their college. "Most athletes here are pretty nice," another sophomore noted. "They're not your stereotypical jocks. A lot of them actually have the impulse to be socially active and do community service work."

Dorms, as one senior put it, "are sort of a mixed bag." While most Amherstians praise the spacious living arrangements in buildings like Appleton, Valentine, James, and Sterns, some lament having to live in "trailer-like arrangements," which one freshman attributed to "Amherst over-accepting students this year." On the other hand, the majority of students are content with regular dorms that consist of "one bathroom, one RC per floor, and anywhere from 15 to 20 people per floor." And though living arrangements for first semester freshmen are about the same—singles or doubles, but no personal bathrooms—upperclassmen get the choice of having suites or multiple bathrooms. One junior also mentioned special subsidy- and language-housing on campus, which centers around a common language, culture or sometimes a religious belief.

Regardless of the housing situation, Amherstians agree that their campus is very safe with very few problems. "Whenever there's a police incident in the Five College area, we get a police notification via email," one freshman said. "Security presence is noticeable, but by no means overbearing." So, students at Amherst are largely free to enjoy their college's idyllic setting and the beautiful New England feel of the entire place without any safety concerns.

Ultimately, students at Amherst say that they can pursue their interests because they live amid conditions which are conducive to their drive and enthusiasm across a wide range of academic, social and extracurricular lifestyles. With a student body the size of most American public high schools, it's no wonder that Amherstians left and right praise the "intimate atmosphere" that their school fosters. "Everyone here is looking out for one another," one senior said proudly. "It's as simple as that."—*Andrew Giambrone and Danielle Trubow*

FYI

If you come to Amherst, make sure to bring "the preppiest winter clothes you can find in a 10 mile radius; we have a reputation to uphold with the other colleges in the consortium, you know?"

Three things you have to do before you graduate are: "take a class with Austin Sarat, attend Hampshire Halloween, and sled down Memorial Hill."

What surprised me most about Amherst when I arrived was "the prevalence of athletes and their influence on social life."

Babson College

Address: 231 Forest Street Babson Park, MA 02457

Phone: 800-488-3696

E-mail address: ugradadmission@babson.edu

Web site URL: www.babson.edu

Year Founded: 1919

Private or Public: Private

Religious Affiliation: None

Location: Suburban

Number of Applicants: 3,530

Percent Accepted: 35%

Percent Accepted who enroll: 34%

Number Entering: 453

Number of Transfers Accepted each Year: 83

Middle 50% SAT range: M: 590–680, CR: 560–640, Wr: 570–650

Middle 50% ACT range: 25–29

Early admission program EA/ED/None: EA and ED

Percentage accepted through EA or ED: Unreported

EA and ED deadline: 1-Nov

Regular Deadline: 15-Jan

Application Fee: $65

Full time Undergraduate enrollment: 1,851

Total enrollment: 3,439

Percent Male: 60%

Percent Female: 40%

Total Percent Minority or Unreported: 44%

Percent African-American: 6%

Percent Asian/Pacific Islander: 14%

Percent Hispanic: 10%

Percent Native-American: <1%

Percent International: 22%

Percent in-state/out of state: 54%/46%

Percent from Public HS: 50%

Retention Rate: 93%

Graduation Rate 4-year: 84%

Graduation Rate 6-year: 87%

Percent Undergraduates in On-campus housing: 86%

Number of official organized extracurricular organizations: 60

3 Most popular majors: Accounting, Business Operations, Finance

Student/Faculty ratio: 16:1

Average Class Size: 35

Percent of students going to grad school: Unreported

Tuition and Fees: $36,096

In-State Tuition and Fees if different: No difference

Cost for Room and Board: $12,020

Percent receiving financial aid out of those who apply, first year: Unreported

Percent receiving financial aid among all students: 42%

Babson College, located in the Babson Park section of Wellesley, Massachusetts, is a school that strives to create the next business leaders of the world. This undergraduate program combines liberal arts and business in order to teach its students the values of a "practical business education." From the beginning of freshman year, students create their own business, immediately reinforcing the concept of experi- ence instead of only in-class learning. Although Babson features a relatively wealthy student body, Babsonians are still ambitious to learn how to succeed in the business world.

Hands-on Preparation for the Real World

Babson students are required to start their own business—the first of many—in a freshman-year class called Foundations of Management and Entrepreneurship (FME). In this program, a team of students learns how to create and run a business, which at the end of the course is liquidated and the profits donated to charity. The course teaches students that becoming a CEO requires teamwork, plenty of effort, and true dedication.

But it is not all business at Babson. Freshmen take three additional classes that are mostly chosen for them. Two of the classes are in the liberal arts, and students say that the majority of liberal arts classes try to connect to business "every once in a while," although that does not mean that the teachers work together to distribute workloads. One sophomore said although he didn't expect professors from different departments to work together, "There have been plenty of times when I have 60 pages of reading and a test to study for on the same day. It can be overbearing at times." When students reach their junior and senior years, there is much more flexibility in their schedules.

Although Babson students are not required to pick a concentration outside of business, most do. Babson's concentrations provide ways for students to focus on the part of business that they love. Concentrations range from American studies to statistics to the literary and visual arts. The most common concentrations are Entrepreneurship and Finance. Whether a student chooses a concentration or not, everyone graduates with a BA in Business.

Babson has about 1,800 enrolled undergraduates, which translates to small classes. According to one senior, "The biggest class at Babson is FME, which has about sixty students. After that, you'll never have more than forty in a class." Most liberal arts classes are even smaller, including a few ten-person classes. The size of all classes at Babson gives students an opportunity to be in contact with some of the most influential business leaders of today. Rather than just hiring teachers who have studied business and have followed business trends, Babson also hires CEOs, CFOs, and other executives of major businesses, such as the popular professor Leonard Green, CEO of the Green Group. Although the teachers have high-powered jobs and often busy lives, Babson students give rave reviews to teacher-student relations. Professors at Babson have a reputation for helping outside of the classroom with not only class work, but in the workforce. Some teachers help students find

jobs, and that provides opportunities that are "huge when you hit senior year".

Grading at Babson is notoriously difficult, but students say an "A" is attainable when enough effort is put in. One senior said that participation is a component in grading, so interaction with other students and professors "is important, and can make a little bit of a difference in your grade." Some students are convinced that there is grade "deflation" for many classes, although teachers and many students insist that it does not exist. The real difficulty, one student said, is that "teachers have very high expectations for Babson students."

The Business Mentality

Babson's focus on business means that students are generally very driven toward their specific interests. Due to the nature of this attitude, some students say that the social environment is an even mix between collaborative and competitive. Babson fosters the idea of group work, which means that there are always people to help you. However, many point out that when they leave Babson, everyone is going into the same industry, which can create "some tension between students, because you know that you'll eventually be competing with your best friends for the same job." Many students agree that the balance between working together and working against each other is another way that Babson mimics the business world.

> "Upperclassmen pay attention and look out for underclassmen with similar interests. Everyone wants to help freshmen because they are always looking for new people to start a business with."

The business mentality of Babson really helps the freshmen assimilate into the student body. "Upperclassmen pay attention and look out for underclassmen with similar interests. Everyone wants to help freshmen because they are always looking for new people to start a business with," one freshman remarked. The freshmen do not only get support from upperclassmen, but First Year Seminar (FYS) also provides busy freshmen with weekly information on time management along with help with classes through a peer mentor, their FYS professor, and a faculty advisor. One freshman said that it could even get "overwhelming at how many people are checking up on you."

Babson Doesn't Just Work Hard . . .

As hard as students work at Babson, a combination of three-day weekends (there are rarely classes on Fridays), monthly "Knight" dance parties in the Knight auditorium, and the on-campus Pub create an environment where students can balance work and play. Students generally agree that a vast majority of students drink. Other "hard drugs" are not too common, except many students admit to using Adderall on school nights to focus. The policy on alcohol is not completely loose, but partygoers are given several warnings by RAs before the Babson Police (affectionately called Babo) are called in to break up the party. The jobs of the RAs are to look out for the students, not get them in trouble. The new honor code states that students have an obligation to help, not to report students who get sick from alcohol.

Outside of the dorm room parties, one sophomore club athlete said "you will always find a party on campus." The pub on campus, Roger's Pub, is open to all students, and those over 21 wear wristbands so they can purchase drinks. Once the pub closes at midnight, everyone disperses from the pub to either frat parties or parties in suites where a bunch of friends—often varsity athletes—live together. With all of the events on campus, commuting to Boston is not too common among students. The students who usually travel to Boston at night are often international students who have apartments there. On campus, there are many events not based around alcohol that are widely attended by students. The Campus Activities Board plans around 50 events a year, including "Knight parties." Many campus-sponsored events attract all kinds of people, and often incorporate international culture. For example, the South Asian club throws a Bhangra dance on campus that attracts many students, especially because of the "intrigue of free food." Any time a student wants to plan a campus-wide event, Babson can subsidize the party or gathering.

Who Are The Future Business Leaders of the World?

The "stereotypical" Babson student is a "white, wealthy, preppy workaholic who is very self-involved." However, diversity on campus is growing, and with every year, the numbers of international students and women increase. According to a senior girl, "The difference in numbers between men and women is not obvious at all. The only times we think about it is when people are making jokes about it." In the case of international students, who make up about 20 percent of the population, the stereotype is that they are "rich" and often "royalty from some country." Most of the people who live off campus are international students, students say, and the perception is that many international students are known for having "multiple expensive cars." Overall, students agree that many Babsonians can be a "little flashy." "There are some kids who have more than one car with them," one freshman noted. But despite the stereotypes, the truth is that there are students from all socioeconomic backgrounds, and there are many students on financial aid and scholarship, with students receiving a total of about $24 million in financial aid, in addition to Babson grants, each year. Babson offers many scholarships to students that are based on all different criteria to accommodate people from all backgrounds.

When living on campus, the dorm situation "gets better with seniority," and varies depending on where you live. Few people complain about housing, as most dorms are described as being "better than those at the other colleges I've visited." Babson also gets high marks when it comes to roommate pairing. Freshmen agree that Babson "really takes your rooming form into consideration." Overall, the care that Babson puts into its social life allows students to enjoy their experience as a businessperson and a scholar.—*Willi Rechler*

FYI

If I could change one thing about Babson, "I'd move it out of the middle of dry-town Wellesley and put the same campus in the middle of Boston!"

If you come to Babson, you'd better bring: "your Blackberry, a suit, a Northface . . . and a whole bunch of business ideas before FME starts."

Three things every student at Babson should do before graduating are: 1) "Get a 100 on an exam," 2) "Take a class with Len Green," and 3) "Stay at a Knight Party until 2 a.m."

What is the typical weekend schedule? "Weekends start on Thursday night and everyone's at pub. Friday night is a lighter night, but people go out or go to Boston, and Saturday is a big campus party night. On Sunday, everything shuts down and everyone does work."

Boston College

Address: 140 Commonwealth Avenue, Chestnut Hill, MA 02467
Phone: 800-360-2522
E-mail address: NA
Web site URL: www.bc.edu
Year Founded: 1863
Private or Public: Private
Religious Affiliation: Roman Catholic
Location: Suburban
Number of Applicants: 30,845
Percent Accepted: 26%
Percent Accepted who enroll: 27%
Number Entering: 2,167
Number of Transfers Accepted each Year: 166
Middle 50% SAT range: M: 640–730, CR: 610–700, Wr: 620–710
Middle 50% ACT range: 28–32
Early admission program EA/ED/None: EA

Percentage accepted through EA or ED: 36%
EA and ED deadline: 1-Nov
Regular Deadline: 1-Jan
Application Fee: $70
Full time Undergraduate enrollment: 9,060
Total enrollment: 13,087
Percent Male: 49%
Percent Female: 51%
Total Percent Minority or Unreported: 29%
Percent African-American: 6%
Percent Asian/Pacific Islander: 9%
Percent Hispanic: 8%
Percent Native-American: <1%
Percent International: 3%
Percent in-state/out of state: 29%/71%
Percent from Public HS: 53%
Retention Rate: 96%
Graduation Rate 4-year: Unreported

Graduation Rate 6-year: Unreported
Percent Undergraduates in On-campus housing: 82%
Number of official organized extracurricular organizations: 223
3 Most popular majors: Communication, English, Finance
Student/Faculty ratio: 13:1
Average Class Size: 15
Percent of students going to grad school: 25%
Tuition and Fees: $37,950
In-State Tuition and Fees if different: No difference
Cost for Room and Board: $11,610
Percent receiving financial aid out of those who apply, first year: 77%
Percent receiving financial aid among all students: 70%

The location is superb: the village of Chestnut Hill is just a short train ride away from the exciting city of Boston. The academics are excellent; the high standards and diverse curriculum ensure quality education. To top it off, whether you prefer parties or tailgates or a cappella shows, you don't have to choose because you can attend all three in just one day. BC boasts impressive credentials on many fronts.

Attention: Get to Work!

Being a liberal arts school, BC ensures that each of its students receives a broad education encompassing many disciplines. The college is made up of four schools: the College of Arts and Sciences, Lynch School of Education, Carroll School of Management, and the Connell School of Nursing. Each school has its own set of specific requirements. However, classes in literature, modern history, philosophy, theology, the natural sciences, the social sciences, the arts, cultural diversity, and writing are common to all. But the requirements are rarely a point of complaint since they are fairly easy to fulfill. As one junior pointed out, "While you have the required math class you dread, and a language requirement, I appreciate the core for letting me explore my options."

With options, each student can make what he or she wants out of his college experience. To make their schedules more interesting, students can take classes such as sign language, dance, or the anticonsumerist "Shop till you drop." Students recommend taking a class with Professor Seth Jacobs, who teaches history and is an expert on the Vietnam War. Class sizes vary from 12-person seminars where personal attention abounds to 200-person lectures for those who like the anonymity. Moreover, the workload, while generally manageable, can certainly be adjusted. The communication major is known for its lighter workload and higher GPAs, while the sciences are collectively acknowledged to be difficult. As one student put it, "If you want an A, you have to work for it." The professors are known to be accessible and hold regular office hours for those willing to make the effort to talk to them.

Change on the Horizon

The students are guaranteed housing for three years at BC. This means that about half of the junior class moves off campus each year. For those who do remain on campus, the choices vary by year. Dorms are assigned through a lottery. The freshmen are divided between Upper and Newton campuses, the latter being more secluded from the general population of the college while providing a close-knit sense of community. Since housing improves with seniority, the seniors get to choose from among four-to-six-person suites in apartment-style housing, featuring private bathrooms and kitchens. For the more outgoing, there is also the option of living in the senior-only mods, which are known for their spacious backyards and party-friendly atmosphere.

There are six dining halls on campus, and the food gets thumbs up from the students, although the meal plans are considered overpriced. A popular option is Lyons dining hall, affectionately named "The Rat," which features plenty of fried options. McElroy and Corcoran Commons are praised for their long hours; some days they stay open till two a.m. As an alternative, students often venture out to Cleveland Circle, where there are a large variety of restaurants ranging from sushi places to an Applebee's. Of course, there is always the option of checking out the multitude of restaurants in Boston: "Take the train in and you have the world at your fingertips," one junior points out.

There are no central hanging-out areas on campus, but the cafeterias serve as worthy substitutes. The green areas around campus also provide good spots to relax in the afternoons, and the students enjoy the beautiful flowers planted throughout. As one senior said, while the overall look of BC is very pretty, "The campus is confused." The architecture ranges from gothic to modern, and there are some in-between. Currently, BC is working on a 10-year plan to renovate the campus by updating outdated dorms and academic buildings. As one student said, "Change is on the horizon."

Party Like It's Your Job

When the weekend comes around, BC students take the opportunity to exercise their right to play hard. For seniors, the definition of a weekend is rather flexible, and the fun starts as early as Wednesday. As one student claimed, "The school is a lot more social than I'd expected." Bars such as Mary Ann's and Roggie's Brew & Grille on Cleveland Circle (a center of shopping and social activity) are cited as local favorites for hanging out. Those of legal drinking age (read: with good fake IDs) take the opportunity to travel into the nearby Boston area, with its vibrant bar and club scene.

Most of the students, however, simply seek fun locally; while there are no frats, students take advantage of the plentiful parties at the senior mods or at the apartments of students who live off campus. The mods are also a regular tailgating site before sporting events. Another popular event on campus is the exclusive Middlemarch dance, which requires participation in a scavenger hunt to obtain tickets.

Drinking is a regular activity on campus in spite of the official dry campus rules. RAs are present in every dorm and, while most are pretty lenient, they are known to be stricter on the underclassmen. Students advise "be smart," as there are ways to get around the watchful eyes of administration.

The atmosphere is generally friendly, and people meet friends through classes or dorms. Unfortunately, students often complain that the school lacks diversity in terms of ethnicity and economic background. The stereotypical BC student looks like he or she "stepped out of a J. Crew catalog with a hangover." To battle the stereotypes, groups like AHANA (African-American, Hispanic, Asian, and Native American) work on campus to increase diversity.

Super Involved

An important part of BC is its abundant school spirit. Each class has its own motto printed on the iconic gold "Superfan" T-shirt which is adorned by an eagle, the school mascot. Students proudly wear it during all sporting events. Football, basketball, and hockey have the highest attendance rates. Those who don't want the strenuous commitment of a varsity sport get involved in the popular intramural teams around campus, soccer and basketball being the most widespread.

Outside of sports, regular extracurricular involvement is at a high level. Among the most popular organizations are student government, College Republicans and Democrats, and dance teams of all sorts. *The Heights* is the student-run newspaper. The Jesuit background of the college is most felt in the level of student involvement on campus. The tradition emphasizes volunteer work on campus, and the Appalachia Volunteers program, which does work in the Appalachian region for organizations such as Habitat for Humanity, boasts a membership of over 600 students. Many students also hold jobs as part of the work-study program; the dining hall employs the most students.

"You get here and even though it might not have been your first choice, you see all the upperclassmen say they love it," one senior said. "You learn to love it as much as they do." At BC you work hard, play often, and explore plenty. A great college experience is guaranteed.—*Dorota Poplawska*

FYI

If you come to BC, you'd better bring "money and a popped collar."

What is the typical weekend schedule? "Sleep till noon, go to a football game on Saturday, and party at night."

If I could change one thing about BC, I'd "make it more diverse."

Three things every student should do before graduating from BC are "spend the night at Bapst Library, participate in Marathon Monday [the Boston Marathon], and attend a football game at Alumni Stadium."

Boston University

Address: 121 Bay State Road Boston, MA 02215	**Percentage accepted through EA or ED:** 37%	**Graduation Rate 4-year:** 75%
Phone: 617-353-2300	**EA and ED deadline:** 1-Nov	**Graduation Rate 6-year:** 80%
E-mail address: admissions@bu.edu	**Regular Deadline:** 1-Jan	**Percent Undergraduates in On-campus housing:** 65%
Web site URL: www.bu.edu	**Application Fee:** $75	**Number of official organized extracurricular organizations:** 400
Year Founded: 1839	**Full time Undergraduate enrollment:** 18,733	
Private or Public: Private	**Total enrollment:** 19,951	**3 Most popular majors:** Business, International Relations, Psychology
Religious Affiliation: None	**Percent Male:** 41%	
Location: Urban	**Percent Female:** 59%	
Number of Applicants: 33,390	**Total Percent Minority or Unreported:** 48%	**Student/Faculty ratio:** 14:1
Percent Accepted: 59%	**Percent African-American:** 3%	**Average Class Size:** 15
Percent Accepted who enroll: 22%		**Percent of students going to grad school:** 29%
Number Entering: 4,163	**Percent Asian/Pacific Islander:** 12%	**Tuition and Fees:** $37,050
Number of Transfers Accepted each Year: 752	**Percent Hispanic:** 6%	**In-State Tuition and Fees if different:** No difference
Middle 50% SAT range: M: 590–690, **CR:** 580–680, **Wr:** 590–670	**Percent Native-American:** <1%	**Cost for Room and Board:** $11,418
	Percent International: 9%	**Percent receiving financial aid out of those who apply, first year:** 80%
Middle 50% ACT range: 25–30	**Percent in-state/out of state:** 23%/77%	
Early admission program EA/ED/None: ED	**Percent from Public HS:** 74%	**Percent receiving financial aid among all students:** 44%
	Retention Rate: 91%	

L ocated conveniently in the heart of Boston, Boston University presents its students with solid academics, friendly people, and a famous hockey team. And, if you're looking for off-campus adventures, the Boston T will take you anywhere

you like in one of the most exciting and historic cities in the country.

What Do You Make of It?

Among BU's 17 graduate and undergraduate schools and 250 degree programs, there is plenty of room to maneuver. Still, as one sophomore commented, "it seems like everyone is either a premed or pre-law." Other popular majors include international relations, psychology, and management. The university curriculum also offers a challenging honors program for ambitious freshmen and sophomores. Like most universities, BU holds large lectures for most introductory courses with smaller discussion sections attached. Upper-level classes shrink significantly to as low as 10 or even five students. Surprisingly, competition for those classes is not really a problem, and an undergrad's chances only improve with seniority. And if lady luck is not on your side, "there are so many options, you can always find something else you will enjoy," like a class taught by Elie Wiesel, Nobel Peace Prize–winner and one of the most popular professors at BU.

Rumors about grade deflation at BU are universally acknowledged to be based on "a misconception," according to one sophomore, "no one has ever been able to prove its existence." At BU, students praise their professors for being accessible; as one student stated, the experience is "what you make of it."

No ID, No Way
Despite the strictly enforced policies against drinking, alcohol still finds its way into the lives of most BU students. Student social life is diverse in terms of locale; many undergraduates center their weekends around parties at off-campus apartments or the few off-campus frats (not funded or recognized by the university). The nearby colleges such as MIT and Harvard also offer viable party options. One student said that the Boston scene "opens up many social lives for those over 21 (or those with a really good fake ID)," and upperclassmen flock to the numerous bars and clubs in the area, such as Jillian's and The Dugout. Without an ID, students are out of luck, as Boston recently passed a law prohibiting any underage clubs, causing many undergrads to simply take their chances in the RA–monitored dorms (although some say that that is a riskier option). BU weekends typically start on Thursday for those resourceful enough to avoid the Friday classes. If you prefer your weekends dry, never fear—there are still vibrant options for a social life outside of drinking activities, many of which take place in Boston, a city that provides endless restaurants, theaters, and shopping along Newbury Street.

From Jail to Hotel
The dorms at BU vary from great apartment-style dorms to small closetlike rooms. Competition is stiff for the recently built student village apartments, as well as two other residences that were former hotels on Commonwealth Avenue. Yet getting a good dorm is a matter of luck of the draw. One student warned that some of the dorms "have been designed by an architect who used to design jails." Warren Towers, the freshman dorm, has some of the least desirable rooms; however it makes up for it by having its own vibrant and close-knit social community. Students describe the campus, which is divided into East and West, as "long and skinny." The West campus is the more lively side, since it tends to house more athletes and parties. Moreover, many students move off campus after their sophomore years. The primary complaints from all students concerned BU's old-fashioned guest policy: coed sleepovers were prohibited. And although students realize that the policy is meant to ensure safety on campus, it is commonly referred to as "outdated." Recently the student governing body at Boston University, the Student Union, worked with the administration to change the guest policy to give students more freedom as well as more responsibility.

Fortunately, food rates pretty well at BU. There are five dining halls on campus and endless restaurants, some favorites of which include T. Anthony's pizza restaurant or anything in the North End. For those on the run, there are fallback options such as the George Sherman Union and numerous small convenience stores along the campus.

BU students generally do not bring cars to campus, and as anyone who has ever driven in Boston will tell you, it is not a good idea to have a car. Besides the nightmarish parking, students agree that Boston's one-way streets will significantly impede even the most experienced of navigators. The extensive subway system known as the T, however, more than makes up for the lack of personal transportation.

East Coast Style
This ultimate East Coast university has a generally friendly atmosphere. Students say that it is easiest to meet people through dorms and extracurriculars, although sometimes smaller classes foster friendships too. Students claim that BU could be more diverse, but there are actually students from all 50 states and over 100 countries. Every

race and ethnicity is represented, usually to a far greater degree than is the case at state universities.

> "There are so many options, you can always find something else you will enjoy."

Some of the most popular clubs at Boston University are student governments and the programming council. The campus is also home to many cultural clubs like the Indian Club, which is one of the biggest organizations on campus. Students report that many, if not most, of their peers have jobs. Many work on campus in dining halls through work-study programs. Others find that Boston has plentiful job opportunities, including waiting tables or working as cashiers.

Skates Are Required

Yearly balls and dances as well as weekly parties bring tradition to BU. "We also have an up-and-coming basketball program and a very popular, very involved new student spirit group nicknamed 'the Dog Pound,'" said a student representative. And, since the school does not have a football team, what spirit exists is entirely poured into the hockey team; hockey games are some of the most crowded and energetic events at BU, with the pep rallies against BU rival, Boston College, widely attended. In fact, the BU versus BC hockey game is one of the most entertaining and well-attended events on campus.

For those who have no interest in hockey, Boston provides more than enough sports teams for which to root, including the Celtics, the Red Sox, and the New England Patriots. For those hoping for an active life of their own, the university has many popular intramural teams, as well as a three-floor fitness and recreation center.

Boston University may not have the packed football stadiums of other schools, but BU students have pride in their school. And with Boston as the students' backyard playground, who could say no to that?
—*Dorota Poplawska*

FYI
If you come to BU, you'd better bring "money."
What is the typical weekend schedule? "Wake up late, gym, dinner and desserts at North End, party."
If I could change one thing about BU, I'd "improve the guest policy to something less strict."
Three things every student at BU should do before graduating are "Go to a baseball game at Fenway Park, attend a BU versus BC hockey game, and attend an Elie Wiesel lecture."

Brandeis University

Address: 415 South St., MS003, Waltham, MA 02454-9110

Phone: 781-736-3500

E-mail address: admissions@brandeis.edu

Web site URL: www.brandeis.edu

Year Founded: 1948

Private or Public: Private

Religious Affiliation: None

Location: Suburban

Number of Applicants: 7,724

Percent Accepted: 33%

Percent Accepted who enroll: 30%

Number Entering: 759

Number of Transfers Accepted each Year: 102

Middle 50% SAT range: M: 650–730, CR: 640–720, Wr: 540–730

Middle 50% ACT range: 29–32

Early admission program EA/ED/None: ED

Percentage accepted through EA or ED: 32%

EA and ED deadline: 15-Nov

Regular Deadline: 15-Jan

Application Fee: $55

Full time Undergraduate enrollment: 3,216

Total enrollment: 5,327

Percent Male: 44%

Percent Female: 56%

Total Percent Minority or Unreported: 19%

Percent African-American: 4%

Percent Asian/Pacific Islander: 10%

Percent Hispanic: 5%

Percent Native-American: <1%

Percent International: 8%

Percent in-state/out of state: 26%/74%

Percent from Public HS: Unreported

Retention Rate: 93%

Graduation Rate 4-year: 86%

Graduation Rate 6-year: 88%

Percent Undergraduates in On-campus housing: 77%

Number of official organized extracurricular organizations: 253

3 Most popular majors: Biology, Economics, Psychology

Student/Faculty ratio: 8:1

Average Class Size: 15

Percent of students going to grad school: Unreported

Tuition and Fees: $37,294

In-State Tuition and Fees if different: No difference

Cost for Room and Board: $10,354

Percent receiving financial aid out of those who apply, first year: 53%

Percent receiving financial aid among all students: 48%

What do an Olympic fencer, the author of *Tuesdays With Morrie* and *The Five People You Meet in Heaven*, and Bill Schneider have in common? The answer's a no-brainer: they're all alumni of Brandeis University, one of the youngest and most renowned private research universities in America.

Located in Waltham, Massachusetts, Brandeis is just nine miles west from Boston, simultaneously offering students easy access to the exciting city life and the comforts of a suburban campus. Besides its academic prowess (*U.S. News and World Report* has ranked it among the top 35 national universities every year since its inception), Brandeis is famous for its emphasis on community service and its extraordinarily high percentage of Jewish students, for which the reason can be traced back to its unusual founding as the nation's only nonsectarian Jewish-sponsored college.

Academics: Intense but Intimate

Brandeis boasts a rigorous liberal arts education that "combines the faculty and resources of a world-class research institution with the intimacy and personal attention of a small liberal arts college"—and they're perfectly entitled to their bragging rights. Not only does Brandeis count among its faculty "six members of the National Academies, four Howard Hughes Medical Institute investigators, three Pulitzer Prize winners and two MacArthur Foundation 'genius grant' recipients," but it's also not uncommon for a freshman to be learning from these academic giants in an intimate setting. According to one freshman, "Last term I was one of about three freshmen in a 30-person writing Intensive journalism class with Professor Eileen McNamara, the Pulitzer Prize winner. I was intimidated at first since the professor was so well known and I was obviously young (it was an entirely discussion based class), but I spoke with her on the first day and she said it was fine for me to be in that class—she was very open to her students' ideas, although she made her opinions known too, and I soon became comfortable."

The existence of University Seminars also makes distinguished faculty easily accessible to students. A hallmark of the Brandeis curriculum, University Seminars are designed specifically for freshmen and emphasize the importance of interdisciplinary studies. It is a course requirement for freshmen, along with the other requirements of Science, Social Science, Humanities, Creative Art, Quantitative Reasoning, Writing, Foreign Language, Oral Communication, Non-Western and Comparative Studies, and Physical Education. Students can fulfill the last requirement with anything from intense self-designed workout classes in the gym to Dance Dance Revolution and yoga.

The wide range of distributional requirements and the diversity of Brandeis itself have made Ethnic Studies and International and Global Studies two popular majors, along with Psychology and Biology (a common major for premed students). Other popular yet not-so-commonplace majors and minors include Peace, Conflict, and Co-existence, the Near-Eastern Judaic Studies, HSSP (Health: Science, Society and Policy Program), and Social Justice and Social Policy.

> "A lot of classes can count for many different things, so it's really easy to double major and pick up a minor on top of that."

This may seem like a lot to ask, but Brandeis students are up on the game. "A lot of classes can count for many different things, so it's really easy to double major and pick up a minor on top of that," noted one Anthropology/Social Science major. "And they leave you room for fun classes, too." Of course, students don't mean "fun" in the sense of an easy class—the typical Brandeis student is eager to get as much as they can out of any class. And it's easy to find your niche in the wide range of classes they offer at the school. You might be interested in the English class "Witchcraft and Magic in the Renaissance," or a section of an introductory Global Studies class that teaches you everything you

would ever want to know about Bollywood movies, or something totally unrelated.

"I love that there are very few set tracks or prerequisites for the humanities classes," said one International and Global Studies major. "A lot of people come here thinking they'll be premed and end up changing their minds because of a really cool seminar they initially took just to fulfill a requirement."

Because Brandeis is fairly small (a little over 3,000 undergrads), almost all classes are taught by teachers, with TAs only grading papers or leading discussions. And although some professors are more popular than others, "they do a really good job having us sign up for classes—they arrange it in time blocks, and popular classes are often changed to earlier time slots. Upperclassmen do get higher priority, but if you're dedicated enough to wake up for an 8AM class, you'll almost always get in. It's really fair."

"Party school" Recognition by Playboy?

"Brandeis isn't a party school," the interviewed students of Brandeis said unanimously. There is a fair amount of people who are very much into the party scene, but they are definitely not the majority; as one freshman described, "If you walk around campus on a Friday night, you're not going to see a lot of parties."

This is in part due to the proximity of Boston, for many students use the campus shuttles (coined Bran Vans) to gain access to the bars and restaurants of Harvard Square or Newbury Street in downtown Boston. "The Bran Vans are really convenient. They go everywhere and most come every 15 minutes and run till 2AM," said one student. "With them and the city buses, you really don't need cars unless you want to go to the mall or something. And parking's such a hassle."

Alcohol and pot are easy to come by at Brandeis, where people are more open to drugs than most nearby colleges—"You smell it everywhere, so you eventually get used to it," quipped one freshman. It's very rare that a student will feel pressured to do something he or she is not inclined to do. Normally, Brandeis students see themselves as members of a "geeky but extremely friendly campus": "Most people are pretty geeky about wanting A's," noted one girl.

But when Brandeis students go out, they go *out*: in *Playboy*'s 2010 list of top party schools of the nation, the school's Liquid Latex Body Art Show was listed as Best

College-Supported Art Project. "Apparently the performers wear thongs and body paint, and that's it," said one freshman about the notorious performance. "It's supposed to be amazing, though Pachanga (a school-sponsored dance) was pretty wild too—there was a line of ambulances waiting at the door because so many people go to the hospital for alcohol poisoning every time the party's hosted. It really didn't seem like Brandeis at all."

Castle on a Hill

At 235 acres, the Brandeis campus is fairly small, making it very convenient for the students to walk from class to class. One student boasted that although she had two successive classes on opposite sides of the campus, she was able to cross campus in a record 10 minutes. "But it's close to impossible to bike in most places because this is the hilliest school I have ever seen. It's great for sledding, though; when you're studying in the library during the winter, you can hear people screaming as they sled downhill."

Although there are no theme dorms at Brandeis, there are special community service-intensive areas within residential halls to which interested students apply. There is also a picturesque castle, complete with staircases and hallways that lead nowhere, random sinks, and a rumor of secret passages—it's no surprise that it's the most popular residential hall of all.

With outstanding academics, tons of interaction between faculty and students, and a cozy campus close to a big city without being in it, it's not hard to see why the majority of students said they would choose Brandeis again if they had the choice.—*Lahn Matsumoto*

FYI

If you come to Brandeis, you'd better bring "snow boots, a cheery disposition, and a sled for the library hill."

If you come to Brandeis, you'd better leave "your bathing suit (there isn't an on-campus pool—yet) and Kosher food (it's taken care of!)" behind.

What is the typical weekend schedule? "Fridays we go to a few classes, 'comprehend' the weekend's homework, watch a free showing of a newly released movie, hang out with friends until late, and maybe go to a party. Saturdays we brunch at Usdan, go sledding, hang out, or go to some student events shindig, begin homework, and stay up late. Sundays we sleep in, brunch at Usdan again, and do homework at the library with friends."

If I could change one thing about Brandeis, "I'd make dining hall hours more regular (weekends are really annoying and things close by 7 pm) and/or have more flexible meal plans that are less expensive."

The biggest college-wide tradition/event at Brandeis is "the Liquid Latex Dance Show and the Pachanga dance."

Clark University

Address: 950 Main Street, Worcester, MA 01610-1477
Phone: 508-793-7431
E-mail address: admissions@clarku.edu
Web site URL: www.clarku.edu/admissions
Year Founded: 1887
Private or Public: Private
Religious Affiliation: None
Location: Urban
Number of Applicants: 5,299
Percent Accepted: 56%
Percent Accepted who enroll: 20%
Number Entering: 650
Number of Transfers Accepted each Year: 166
Middle 50% SAT range: M: 540–650, CR: 550–660, Wr: 550–660
Middle 50% ACT range: 24–28
Early admission program EA/ED/None: ED
Percentage accepted through EA or ED: 76%

EA and ED deadline: NA
Regular Deadline: 15-Jan
Application Fee: $55
Full time Undergraduate enrollment: 2,222
Total enrollment: 3,330
Percent Male: 40%
Percent Female: 60%
Total Percent Minority or Unreported: 12%
Percent African-American: 2%
Percent Asian/Pacific Islander: 6%
Percent Hispanic: 4%
Percent Native-American: 1%
Percent International: Unreported
Percent in-state/out of state: 34%/66%
Percent from Public HS: 74%
Retention Rate: 91%
Graduation Rate 4-year: 73%

Graduation Rate 6-year: 76%
Percent Undergraduates in On-campus housing: 74%
Number of official organized extracurricular organizations: 94
3 Most popular majors: Psychology, Government, Biology/Biochemistry
Student/Faculty ratio: 10:1
Average Class Size: 21
Percent of students going to grad school: 36%
Tuition and Fees: $34,220
In-State Tuition and Fees if different: No difference
Cost for Room and Board: $6,650
Percent receiving financial aid out of those who apply, first year: 74%
Percent receiving financial aid among all students: 52%

Founded in 1887, Clark University is a college with a rich history. Originally founded as an all-graduate university, it is one of three institutions that helped establish the Association of American Universities. Quietly existing in the city of Worcester, Massachusetts, Clark still retains its prestige not only as a graduate institution, but also as a place where undergraduates can grow in a learning environment. Fittingly, their motto is, "Challenge convention, Change our world."

Not Just Psych

Clark is widely known for its psychology department. As one student said, "Almost everyone here is a psych major." Clark's prominent connection with psychology dates back to its first president, G. Stanley Hall, founder of the American Psychological Association and the first person to earn a PhD in psychology from Harvard. Psychoanalysis was first brought to the United States through Sigmund Freud's "Clark Lectures" at the university. Two statues commemorate Freud's visits and one student commented that "Freud is our unofficial mascot."

Although psychology is the most popular major at Clark, Government and International Relations, Biology, Business Management, and Communication and Culture are close behind. In general, Clarkies find their classes "laid-back" and "uncompetitive." One student commented that Clark has "a lot of active and outspoken people who are passionate about what they believe in but I don't feel like people are stepping all over each other to outdo one another." The average class size at Clark is 21, and students tend to enjoy the intimate environment and the close relationships that fosters. It is in this intimate classroom setting where students take unique and thought-provoking classes such as "Political Science Fiction."

The Price is Right: Five for Four

Clark has 31 majors and 30 minors for students to choose from, and it is the only institution that offers Holocaust and Genocide Studies as an undergraduate concentration.

If those options aren't good enough for you, you can create your own major through the self-designed major program. This multi-discipline major allows students to combine over three departments to pursue research and knowledge in the field of their dreams. For more ambitious students, Clark recommends the Accelerated B.A./Master's Program, also known as the "Fifth-Year-Free" Program. Every year, 20 percent of the graduating class stays behind at Clark for a fifth year, free of charge, to pursue a Master's Degree in one of 12 areas including management, history, chemistry, geographic information sciences, and education. Established in 1994, this program has received national attention for its admirable aim to have students "deepen their knowledge of a particular field and enhance their credentials for the job market."

Home is Where Themes, RAs, and Cheese Steaks Are

During their four years at Clark, 74 percent of students live on campus. Due to the plethora of on-campus housing options, many students have no regrets about staying there. Freshmen live in one of three first-year halls: Bullock, Wright, and Sanford. Although most of these rooms are singles, doubles, or triples, some lucky denizens of Sanford Hall enjoy spacious suites with a common living space and a private bathroom.

> "We have a lot of active and outspoken people who are passionate about what they believe in, but I don't feel like people are stepping all over each other to outdo one another."

In order to address the needs of gay, lesbian, and transgender students, Clark has adopted a gender-blind/neutral housing policy where students can opt to share a room with other students regardless of sex. For those concerned with awkward 3 a.m. bathroom encounters, Dodd Hall offers single-sex housing for women. Juniors and seniors mainly live in Maywood Street Hall where four-, five-, or six-person suites provide students with apartment-like comfort and privacy.

In addition, the Theme House Program at Clark creates an opportunity for students to merge their personal and academic interests. A member of Clark's faculty is assigned to each house and, along with the Group Leader, organizes social events and educational programs to foster a sense of community on campus. Some of these Theme Houses include the Body and Soul House, the Just Yell Fire self-defense house, the Sexual Wellness and Awareness House, and Everyday is a Holiday House, a humble abode dedicated to celebrating lesser-known holidays around the world.

Unlike some schools, the presence of Residential Advisors significantly impacts the residential experience of each hall. Each year there are typically 35 RAs, of which 20 are First Year Experience RAs who specialize in the needs of freshmen. One student notes, "If you get a cool RA, you get cool activities!" RAs shape students' daily lives by throwing social functions, as well as by writing up rambunctious partiers for violating campus alcohol policies. Although RAs come in all shapes, sizes, and degrees of leniency, most agree that RAs, in general, are "chill" and "super-friendly."

Food at Clark brings a less enthusiastic response. "Boring and not really edible," commented one sophomore. After a new food distributor was brought into Clark, reactions were not favorable. "The best thing they have is probably the Philly cheese steak," said one student. No wonder vegans and vegetarians often find the food in "The Caf" unsuitable for their needs. However, there are alternatives for the ravenous Clarkie—the Bistro is an on-campus café that offers students savory sandwiches and eggs cooked every way possible. Also, the city of Worcester offers restaurants within walking distance of central campus for students looking to satiate their culinary cravings.

Out on the "Woo-town"

The city of Worcester (pronounced by locals as "WOO-stah") is 40 miles from Boston and the second largest city in Massachusetts. One student finds Woo-town "not a particularly busy city—but there are plenty of grocery stores and huge theaters where we get some great bands like Marilyn Manson and Gym Class Heroes." Although most activities off campus are hard to get to without a car, there is a Student Council Van that conveniently transports students to the mall on the weekends and the "Woo Bus" makes various parts of Worcester accessible.

Some students are concerned about the safety of Worcester, particular in Main South, the neighborhood where Clark is located. "Never walk alone," says one student. Dorm rooms are generally safe, but off-campus students should make sure to lock up properly. However, one veteran Clarkie says, "There are cop checkposts everywhere and, if you are responsible, you'll be fine. Nowhere in the world is it safe to walk around with a laptop at 3 a.m."

Hookahs and Drinking Sprees

On the weekends, some Clarkies take the train into Boston to barhop while most stay on campus for the partying. "Clark is not a dry campus," but students say it is "essential" to have an ID for the occasional "State Liquor run." Smoking culture, especially hookah smoking, is very popular at Clark. The University recently loosened their smok-ing policy and now students can be found puffing away on the green without being bothered.

Several times a year, campus-wide events take center stage in the social scene at Clark. One of the most beloved is "Spree Day," during the spring semester. Tradition holds that the date be kept secret, but students always seem to know when it will take place. On this most-anticipated day, classes are canceled, a carnival and concert are held on the green, livers are destroyed by 10 a.m., and hangovers nursed by 4 p.m. Though Spree Day only comes once a year, students agree that Clark is a great place to spend four wonderful years of their lives.—*Lee Komeda*

FYI

If you come to Clark, you'd better bring "a hookah."
What is the typical weekend schedule? "Friday, take the free buses during the day to go to malls and Boston. Saturday, attend a few parties and smoke a hookah. Sundays are reserved for studying."
If I could change one thing about Clark, I'd "change its size. Sometimes it's too small and gossipy."
Three things every student at Clark should do before graduating are "get involved with a student group, get to know President Bassett, and go to a foam party."

Emerson College

Address: 10 Boylston Street Boston, MA 02116
Phone: 617-824-8600
E-mail address: admission@emerson.edu
Web site URL: www.emerson.edu
Year Founded: 1880
Private or Public: Private
Religious Affiliation: None
Location: Urban
Number of Applicants: 6,944
Percent Accepted: 37%
Percent Accepted who enroll: 30%
Number Entering: 774
Number of Transfers Accepted each Year: 423
Middle 50% SAT range: M: 550–640, Cr: 580–670, Wr: 640–700
Middle 50% ACT range: 24–29
Early admission program EA/ED/None: EA

Percentage accepted through EA or ED: 59%
EA and ED deadline: 1-Nov
Regular Deadline: 5-Jan
Application Fee: $60
Full time Undergraduate enrollment: 3,293
Total enrollment: 4,197
Percent Male: 44%
Percent Female: 56%
Total Percent Minority or Unreported: 24%
Percent African-American: 3%
Percent Asian/Pacific Islander: 4%
Percent Hispanic: 6%
Percent Native-American: 1%
Percent International: 10%
Percent in-state/out of state: 20%/80%
Percent from Public HS: 72%
Retention Rate: 88%

Graduation Rate 4-year: 72%
Graduation Rate 6-year: 72%
Percent Undergraduates in On-campus housing: 42%
Number of official organized extracurricular organizations: 60
3 Most popular majors: Cinematography, Writing, Arts
Student/Faculty ratio: 14:1
Average Class Size: 14
Percent of students going to grad school: 13%
Tuition and Fees: $26,880
In-State Tuition and Fees if different: No difference
Cost for Room and Board: $11,376
Percent receiving financial aid out of those who apply, first year: Unreported
Percent receiving financial aid among all students: 54%

For those looking for a creative and unique learning experience in the heart of Boston, Emerson is the school for you. As one of the premier colleges dedicated to communications and the arts, Emerson makes sure to ground its specialized focus in a liberal arts context. Budding creators and performers are sure to flourish on Emerson's supportive campus.

More Than Just Arts

Emerson is far from your typical college. It uniquely combines a preprofessional art curriculum with a more traditional liberal arts experience and prides itself on striking a balance between the two. Emerson students are encouraged to cultivate their creativity and passion, while building upon a traditional foundation.

Emerson students have a variety of requirements to fulfill throughout the course of four years—some of which must be completed by the end of the freshman year. Freshmen are required to take two writing courses, which draw some complaints for being substandard. In keeping with Emerson's liberal arts base, students must take courses in history, non-western civilization, psychology or philosophy, and research and expository writing. The required curriculum also includes aesthetics, fine arts, and performing arts. One student commented that at times "the school definitely focuses more on its job-specific courses, and many of the liberal arts courses tend to go by the wayside as far as strong teachers go," but students generally seem to find the requirements more helpful than not. One senior reflected that, "All students appreciate the exposure to other disciplines."

Emerson students choose between two schools, the School of the Arts and the School of Communications, when declaring their major. The School of the Arts includes the performing arts, visual and media arts, and writing, while the School of Communications encompasses communication sciences, journalism, and marketing. Many students declare their major, and in effect their school, after their freshman year, but as one freshman noted, "When students are unsure of their major, they often declare it as media studies," presumably with the option of changing at a later date. Although students are technically divided by their choice of school, many students laud the benefits of having both schools under one roof. There is a great deal of involvement between the two because students are re-quired to take classes from both, as well because of the interdisciplinary nature inherent in many of Emerson's courses. One student remarked that the existence of both schools encourages both professors and students to look at their subject in the context of other disciplines. For example, within a writing course, a professor may reference a film or television show, giving students a broader prospective.

Study abroad is a very popular option among Emerson students. Most students participate in one, if not more, of the three programs run by the University. Kasteel Well in the Netherlands is one popular destination that opens up all of Europe to students. The Los Angeles program sends students to California for a semester to take advantage of internship opportunities and networking in the entertainment industry. The Prague Summer Film Festival is another very popular opportunity to study abroad.

Emerson students show creativity even when picking their majors. It is extremely popular to double major, minor, or even create your own major. Some have been known to both double-major and double-minor. Students often pick unrelated subjects to study, reflecting their varied interests. Some of the popular majors include marketing and film. Theater is known as a difficult major, as is communication disorders. Writing is another particularly rigorous major. Emerson boasts some very interesting courses, including History of Burlesque. One common complaint centers on the length of classes. Emerson classes last from between an hour and fifteen minutes to almost two hours. On the upside, classes are generally small, with the largest classes rarely topping 100 students. TAs are rare and one senior claimed, "I have never had a TA or even heard of one at Emerson." The consensus among students is that the workload is what you make it. And, on top of the normal paper writing and reading, Emerson students "come to act, produce films, write poetry, and create art."

Student Body

Emerson prides itself on representing a diverse range of opinions and people. Students are practically required to arrive on campus with an open mind and according to one student, "I found kids I could get along with and relate to, and I think even if something isn't your style, you can still fit in." This attitude aside, there are some stereotypes for the student body, including "white, rich, gay" and crazy liberal. Many are very politically active on campus. Students laughingly joke that all incoming guys will be "gay by May," but this is offset by an extremely accepting atmosphere on campus. This does mean dating can be tough for girls on campus. Students often look to other colleges in Boston for dating opportunities. One large complaint heard among students is that Emerson is not racially or economically diverse. But the overwhelming atmosphere is one of creativity, diversity, and enthusiasm.

> "I found kids I could get along with and relate to, and I think even if something isn't your style, you can still fit in."

This creativity is directly channeled into the variety of activities Emerson students take on. Many of these directly relate to majors, especially with fields such as film studies. Emerson provides the means and equipment to support creative endeavors. There are student publications, theater groups, one of the most popular college radio stations, as well as opportunities all over Boston. Emerson recently renovated the Cutler Majestic Theatre, a former opera house, as a venue for student productions, as well as visiting artists.

Not Your Average Campus

For students, "Emerson IS Boston." The school and the city are well integrated and inseparable as an experience. Weekends are jam packed because of all the bars, theaters, and events Boston offers, but that does not mean there is a lack of things to do on campus. From shows to parties, there is something to satisfy everyone. Upperclassmen often gather on campus for parties. According to one senior, "Emerson students really like to dress up for each other and spend money. It wouldn't be strange to go to a semiformal cocktail mixer." Greek life exists, but is far from a defining social force.

Emerson students are guaranteed housing for their first two years and these are not two years of suffering. Descriptions of housing have included "awesome" and "like hotels." Some students live in standard doubles off a hall in the Little Building, while Piano Row boasts newer suite-type rooms. Upperclassmen tend to move off campus into apartments. On campus, there are RAs and strict alcohol regulations in the dorms, but those over 21 are allowed to drink. Food on campus is described as "fine, but can get old." There are cafés and convenience stores in the dorm, but there are also thousands of cheap food options all around Boston. On-campus facilities also boast a library that caters to communication majors, a new gym and soccer field, and a new performing arts theater that was featured in the Martin Scorsese film, *The Departed*.

Emerson boasts a world-class location in the heart of the theater district of Boston. Emerson's students are just as familiar with the city around them as they are with the campus. Combined with the diversity and interdisciplinary academic and art focus, Emerson is a truly unique and exciting experience for students looking to make the most of their four years at college.—*Janet Yang*

FYI
If you come to Emerson you better bring "a Mac, knowledge of art and film, and big sunglasses."
The typical weekend schedule is "dinner at a trendy restaurant in Boston, seeing an Emerson show, going to a cast party, film shoot wrap party or cocktail party."
If I could change one thing it would be "the scarcity of straight men."
Three things every student should do before graduation are "see a show in the Majestic, study abroad, and go to the EVVY awards."

College of the Holy Cross

Address: 1 College Street
Worcester, MA 01610-2395
Phone: 508-793-2443
E-mail address:
admissions@holycross.edu
Web site URL:
www.holycross.edu
Year Founded: 1843
Private or Public: Private
Religious Affiliation: Roman
Catholic
Location: Urban
Number of Applicants:
7,227
Percent Accepted: 34%
**Percent Accepted who
enroll:** 30%
Number Entering: 738
**Number of Transfers
Accepted each Year:**
49
Middle 50% SAT range: M:
600–680, CR: 580–720,
Wr: Unreported
Middle 50% ACT range:
Unreported
**Early admission program
EA/ED/None:** ED

**Percentage accepted
through EA or ED:**
Unreported
EA and ED deadline: 15-Dec
Regular Deadline: 15-Jan
Application Fee: $60
**Full time Undergraduate
enrollment:** 2,898
Total enrollment: 2,898
Percent Male: 43%
Percent Female: 57%
**Total Percent Minority or
Unreported:** 39%
Percent African-American:
5%
**Percent Asian/Pacific
Islander:** 6%
Percent Hispanic: 9%
Percent Native-American:
<1%
Percent International: 2%
**Percent in-state/out of
state:** 38%/62%
Percent from Public HS:
44%
Retention Rate: 95%
Graduation Rate 4-year:
92%

Graduation Rate 6-year:
92%
**Percent Undergraduates in
On-campus housing:** 89%
**Number of official organized
extracurricular
organizations:** 104
3 Most popular majors:
Economics, English
Language and Literature,
Political Science and
Government
Student/Faculty ratio:
10:1
Average Class Size: 14
**Percent of students going to
grad school:** 23%
Tuition and Fees: $38,180
**In-State Tuition and Fees if
different:** No difference
Cost for Room and Board:
$10,620
**Percent receiving financial
aid out of those who apply,
first year:** 77%
**Percent receiving financial
aid among all students:**
54%

Nestled in the city of Worcester, Massachusetts, is the College of the Holy Cross, America's oldest Roman Catholic College. Initially founded in 1843 as a Jesuit school for boys, today the school prides itself in the diversity of experiences that students have, the rigor of the academic programs, and the tight-knit community formed around the city.

Optional: SATs

Holy Cross is exclusively an undergraduate institution; therefore students receive the undivided attention of faculty and administration. When asked why she chose Holy Cross over other colleges, a senior replied, "Because I knew that I would be in an environment that prioritized academics above everything." In choosing its students, Holy Cross prioritizes a candidate's interests, activities, recommendations, and high school transcript over standardized tests scores. In fact, while they are suggested, the SAT and ACT are not required for applying to Holy Cross.

A Bachelor of Arts degree is awarded to all that complete 32 semester-long courses, with requirements in arts, literature, religion, philosophy, history, and cross-cultural studies. Twenty-eight majors are offered and students can also select concentrations as well. Like many liberal arts colleges, pre-professional track programs such as pre-business, pre-medicine, and pre-dental are offered as well. Holy Cross is particularly noted for its economics, chemistry, political science, and English departments. Also worthy of mention is its classics department, which is one of the largest in America. Uniquely, the department integrates Greek and Latin Studies with advanced information technology and archaeology.

Academic learning outside of the classroom is also highly valued at Holy Cross, which is why they encourage students to participate in "Experiential Learning" programs. Student can take a semester or a year abroad or participate in the Semester Away Program which allows students to pursue academic interests that are not available at Holy Cross at other institutions, but many complained that the semester-long options were limited. The summer internship programs are offered to certain sophomores and juniors as an opportunity to gain professional experiences related to a student's career related goals. These internships, developed through a network of parents, alumni, and friends of Holy Cross, have been extremely popular.

Holy Cross boasts a faculty to student ratio of ten to one. However, don't expect classes to be easy because they are small. "Classes were very challenging and the professors definitely expected a lot," one recent alumna stated. But have no fear, you'll have plenty of support. "The professors always knew who you were and were great about being there for you, whether it be holding review sessions or extending office hours."

Easy Street and the "Woorats"
Residential life at Holy Cross is divided into three different areas of campus comprising 10 residence halls. As freshmen, you will be placed in one of the residence halls located at the northern end of campus known as Easy Street. While the option of moving off campus is available for second, third, and fourth year students, most Holy Cross students stay in campus housing for their entire four years. Upperclassmen mainly live in the lower part of campus, in the halls of Alumni, Carlin, Loyola, and Williams. The most coveted of them all are the apartments in Williams Hall. After construction was completed in 2003, upperclassmen fought at the annual lottery for these apartments equipped with separate showers, kitchens, living rooms, and individual bedrooms.

For food, Holy Cross students have a wide variety of options. In addition to the main dining room, there is the food court, the lunch-through-late-night Crossroads, or Cool Beans and CB2, both coffee shops. Most students have no complaints about the dining services at Holy Cross. "I really like the food at Holy Cross!" gushed one student. "They have specialty nights in the dining hall like Thanksgiving dinner and Birthday Cake night!" For those with special dietary needs, the dining services have Weight Watcher meals, heart-healthy selections, and vegetarian entrees.

While campus is generally a good place to live, Worcester (pronounced Wooster) has its ups and downs. "Town-gown" relationships have gotten better in the past few years, but there is a divide between the "Woorats" and the Holy Cross Crusaders. "The locals are usually pretty nice to students as long as you don't go out of your way to offend them," said one student. Holy Cross shares Worcester with Worcester Polytechnic Institute and Clark University and is in a "consortium" with them, encouraging interaction between the students.

Bleeding Purple
Holy Cross's athletic teams are known as the Crusaders, and the official school color is the royal purple used by Emperor Constantine the Great. Holy Cross is one of the founding members of the Patriot League, which also includes American University, United States Military Academy, Bucknell University, Colgate University, Lafayette College, Lehigh University, and the United States Naval Academy. Athletic support and school spirit are very high at Holy Cross. "Holy Cross has a ton of school pride. We bleed purple! When the basketball championships were held here, everyone was painted in purple and you had to stand diagonally to fit into the gym!" gushed one track and field runner.

> **"Holy Cross has a ton of school pride. We bleed purple!"**

School pride is also sustained by the large number of campus-wide events and traditions held annually. Some of these events are organized by the Purple Key Society, a service honor society dedicated to increasing school spirit and community building. One of them is the 100 Days Dance, held when 100 days are left for the graduating class. This includes a dinner followed by a dance where each attendee makes a list of seniors that they try to kiss before the night is over. PKS also organizes the Purple Pride Day, when the entire school is covered in royal purple, and purple T-shirts, cookies, balloons, and stickers are given out to foster enthusiasm for the school. Another tradition is Skirt Day, which is considered the first day of spring and girls (who make up 57 percent of the student population) wear skirts for the first time in the year.

The social scene at Holy Cross is regarded with much enthusiasm as well. While there are no fraternities or sororities on campus, residence halls serve their function as smaller social communities within the campus. In particular, Wheeler Hall is known as the rowdiest hall. "It was great, everyone knew your name, and we were the only dorm [for underclassmen] not off Easy Street," says one ex-Wheeler resident. Wheeler Hall is also the birthplace of the popular campus sport, Stickball, which started in the 1940s. You can have a great time even if you aren't in Wheeler too. On Tuesdays, upperclassmen, mainly seniors, congregate at the Pub in the Hogan Campus Center. For those underage, Tuesdays mean going to the "10 spot," an open mic night for

bands and performances held at Crossroads, one of the food courts. Worcester also has plenty to offer for social activities. Students often frequent the malls at Solomon Pond and the restaurants on Shrewsbury Street.

Achieving a good balance of academics, athletics, and socializing seems to be the modus operandi of these students. All three aspects of college life are met with enthusiasm and open-mindedness at Holy Cross. If this sounds like your cup of tea, "going purple" may be a good idea for next year.—*Lee Komeda*

FYI

If you come to Holy Cross, you'd better bring "purple face paint!"

What's the typical weekend schedule? "Go to a sports game, study, go to the movies or a restaurant on Shrewsbury Street, hang out in friends' rooms, and study, study, study on Sunday!"

If I could change one thing about Holy Cross, it would offer "more semester-long abroad programs. It is tough to go away for a whole year."

Three things students should do before graduating: "Participate in the Appalachia Service Project, go on the Silent Retreat, and enjoy Cape Week."

Hampshire College

Address: 893 West Street Amherst, MA 01002

Phone: 877-937-4267

E-mail address: admissions@hampshire.edu

Web site URL: www.hampshire.edu

Year Founded: 1970

Private or Public: Private

Religious Affiliation: None

Location: Suburban

Number of Applicants: 2,842

Percent Accepted: 61%

Percent Accepted who enroll: 27%

Number Entering: 437

Number of Transfers Accepted each Year: 33

Middle 50% SAT range: M: 540–660, CR: 610–700, Wr: 590–700

Middle 50% ACT range: 26–29

Early admission program EA/ED/None: EA and ED

Percentage accepted through EA or ED: 25%

EA and ED deadline: 15-Nov

Regular Deadline: 15-Jan

Application Fee: $55

Full time Undergraduate enrollment: 1,428

Total enrollment: 1,428

Percent Male: 42%

Percent Female: 58%

Total Percent Minority or Unreported: 15%

Percent African-American: 5%

Percent Asian/Pacific Islander: 4%

Percent Hispanic: 6%

Percent Native-American: 1%

Percent International: Unreported

Percent in-state/out of state: 18%/82%

Percent from Public HS: 48%

Retention Rate: 79%

Graduation Rate 4-year: 52%

Graduation Rate 6-year: 65%

Percent Undergraduates in On-campus housing: 90%

Number of official organized extracurricular organizations: 94

3 Most popular majors: Film/Video and Photography, English, Fine arts

Student/Faculty ratio: 11:1

Average Class Size: 16

Percent of students going to grad school: 50%

Tuition and Fees: $37,789

In-State Tuition and Fees if different: No difference

Cost for Room and Board: $10,080

Percent receiving financial aid out of those who apply, first year: 88%

Percent receiving financial aid among all students: 55%

A small, liberal arts college in Western Massachusetts, Hampshire may sound like it would provide the traditional New England undergraduate experience. Hampshire, though, provides an anything but traditional eight semesters for its 1,500 students. There are no grades. There are no "majors." There are, however, students devoted to learning, and faculty members committed to guiding their otherwise self-directed pupils along their intellectual journeys. Hampshire is also a member of the Five College Consortium, along with Amherst College, Mount Holyoke College, Smith College, and University of Massachusetts Amherst, which gives more breadth and depth to its resources. A student sums up Hampshire by saying, "Hampshire is a sanctuary where you come to find and hone the craft you choose."

Hampshire's Roots
The idea for Hampshire germinated in 1958, when the presidents of the other four Consortium colleges decided to re-evaluate the idea of a liberal arts education. They outlined their conclusions in a document called "The New College Plan," and many of these same ideas echo in Hampshire's founding curriculum. Hampshire then physically sprouted from purchased orchards and farmland, admitted its first students in 1970, and grew into the "experimental" college it is known as today.

The Individual Experience: Academics
Instead of "majors," Hampshire students craft an interdisciplinary course of study made up of three Divisions over the course of their time at Hampshire. In Division I: Basic Studies, students choose one class offered by each of the five schools of Cognitive Science; Humanities, Arts, and Cultural Studies; Interdisciplinary Arts; Natural Science; and Social Science, in addition to three more classes of their own choosing. In Division II: The Concentration, students narrow their academic focus and might choose to pursue an internship, international exchange program, or delve into a different kind of field study. Division III: Advanced Study, serves as the culminating project for Hampshire students. With the freedom of the academic curriculum, though, comes the responsibility of constructing it. One student said, "The Div System allows you to build exactly the kind of academic experience you're interested in and is a big reason

why I wanted to come to Hampshire. I didn't want to be checking off boxes for requirements. It's a lot more responsibility because classes are your choice so you have to make those classes worthwhile." The written evaluations students receive from professors at the end of a class, though, (instead of grades) help guide this unique learning process. A student said that the written evaluations "are an amazing sign of respect because the teacher has to know who you are. They help create a really special, productive student-teacher relationship and I feel better giving a graduate school a written evaluation from my teachers instead of just letter grades because I feel like they say so much more." Once a student's academic requirements have been filled, he or she is declared, "Div-free" and loudly rings the bell by the library in celebration.

The Div III projects year to year not only showcase the uniqueness of the academic interests of the Hampshire student body, but also the uniqueness of its student personalities in general. There is no "cookie cutter" Hampshire student, despite the "earthy" or "hippie" stereotype. The typical student, though, is "somebody who's passionate about something and has decided to live their life by practicing that something. A Hampshire student is someone who's interested in looking at themselves and what they want to do through as many lenses as possible." If you walked into SAGA (which appears to be a capitalized acronym but is not, just another amusing example of Hampshire bending the boundaries), the main dining hall, a student says you would most likely hear a conversation about, "anything from gender to Israel v. Palestine to a new yo-yo trick to *Anna Karenina* and everybody talks about quality of food, but especially talks about classes. We don't switch off when we get to the dining hall. I see lots of kids eating with books and I think that's wonderful. Discussions are opened by classes, not closed when they end."

The Green Experience: Eco-friendly Environment
Hampshire is incredibly and undeniably "green"—and not just because of its eight-hundred acres of woods or nearby mountain range. Students, faculty, and staff at Hampshire remain dedicated to reducing their carbon footprint. Most recently, the college has installed an innovative Solar Canopy at the Chuck and Polly Longsworth Arts Center, made up of 2,880 square feet of photovoltaic

modules. Hampshire has also recently acquired environmentally friendly self-service cars with ZipCar, Inc., that are available across campus to any member of the Hampshire community. The college also boasts a free, private bus system that runs between the Five Colleges; the Hampshire College Farm, a working farm that promotes sustainable agricultural practices; a campus-wide composting program, and many more "green" initiatives.

Besides conserving the environment, Hampshire students love to play in it. ORPA, the Outdoors Program/Recreational Athletics group, gives students the opportunity to backpack, hike, even rock climb, and students can rent cross-country skis, sleeping bags, tents, and other outdoor equipment whenever the spirit moves them. Mixed Nuts, a student run food market started in the 1970s, serves as another example of Hampshire's verdant streaks. The dining hall also offers numerous vegetarian and vegan options, for the "green" at heart (or stomach).

The Living and Social Environment

Most first year Hampshire students live in single dorms, but second, third and fourth year students live in "mods," a defining feature of the college. "Mods" are apartment-style dorms that can house between four and ten students and are equipped with a kitchen, a common room area, and at least one or two (sometimes three) bathrooms. It is within this living environment that the Hampshire social scene flourishes. A Hampshire student described dorm life like this: "My hall is like a really tight-knit family. We're all cool with each other. I practice music with an amazing violinist who lives next to me and usually go to the lounge a lot to hang out with people. My new favorite thing is just to eat goat cheese on bread in my room with my friends and talk about interesting things. There's a different smell on every floor, though. The bottom floor might smell like weed, the second floor like incense, the third like throw-up, and the fourth like fruit. Dorm life is also interesting because it's all these different personalities stuck in one space and nobody wants to go outside because it's so cold so just because of our geography are made to love each other."

Though the college does have a reputation for drug use, many students resent this claim and say that overall, the social scene is much more diverse because the people are so multi-faceted and multi-dimensional. One student says, "Hampshire kids have really weird talents. Kids ride around on unicycles and are professional yo-yo-ers and hypnotists. We're a very eclectic crowd and we're really weird. We make everything into a question which can be obnoxious but is always really interesting." Special speakers, local bands, and the social life at the other Consortium schools are available to students, which broadens the variety of available activities.

Even if Hampshire is not "traditional" in the traditional sense, there are still long-standing customs that define Hampshire's social year. One is Hampshire Halloween, which used to be called "Trip or Treat" in its early heyday. Now, the campus-wide party has scaled back a bit and is "invite only," meaning Hampshire students receive a limited number of tickets to dole out to non-Hampshire students. Despite these efforts to contain the party, Hampshire students still say proudly that, "it's a lot of fun. Mostly people just get really drunk and really super out of it but the best part is checking out all the amazing costumes. It's a wild time. There are huge fireworks and people are going wild and it feels totally surreal." Another treasured Hampshire holiday is the Keg Hunt, which takes place on Easter. What replaces the eggs goes without saying, and students, Solo cups in hand, enjoy the search and usually frolic in the grass with a Frisbee after the kegs have been found and enjoyed. The annual Drag Ball also occurs in the spring. Students attend this dance dressed as members of the opposite gender.

An Individual's Overall Experience

Hampshire has been called the "graduate school for undergraduates" because of its strong emphasis on independent course study. A student at Hampshire can explore, focus, and come to define his or her academic passions in a way not many other colleges can offer, but only if the student expends the effort to do so. A student explains, "Here you're put in the driver's seat and I really love that about Hampshire but it's also very scary."—*Madeline Duff*

FYI
A Hampshire student needs "a cause, self-discipline, the will to exercise, and a pencil to write down all the interesting things that happen in a given day."
Hampshire's greatest weakness is "that since it's so individual it can sometimes be isolating and hard to connect with a large group of people. Sometimes we get so caught up in individualizing our projects that we lose sight of the collective group around us."

Harvard University

Address: 86 Brattle Street Cambridge, MA 02138	**Percentage accepted through EA or ED:** NA	**Graduation Rate 6-year:** 98%
Phone: 617-495-1551	**EA and ED deadline:** NA	**Percent Undergraduates in On-campus housing:**
E-mail address: college@fas.harvard.edu	**Regular Deadline:** 1-Jan	Unreported
Web site URL: www.harvard.edu	**Application Fee:** $65	**Number of official organized extracurricular**
Year Founded: 1636	**Full time Undergraduate enrollment:** 6,651	**organizations:** 400
Private or Public: Private	**Total enrollment:** 20,263	**3 Most popular majors:**
Religious Affiliation: None	**Percent Male:** 50%	Economics, Government,
Location: Urban	**Percent Female:** 50%	Psychology
Number of Applicants: 27,642	**Total Percent Minority or Unreported:** 33%	**Student/Faculty ratio:** Unreported
Percent Accepted: 8%	**Percent African-American:** 8%	**Average Class Size:** <20
Percent Accepted who enroll: 76%	**Percent Asian/Pacific Islander:** 17%	**Percent of students going to grad school:** Unreported
Number Entering: 1,658	**Percent Hispanic:** 7%	**Tuition and Fees:** $36,173
Number of Transfers Accepted each Year: Unreported	**Percent Native-American:** 1%	**In-State Tuition and Fees if different:** No difference
Middle 50% SAT range: M: 700–780, **CR:** 690–800, **Wr:** 690–790	**Percent International:** 10% **Percent in-state/out of state:** 16%/84%	**Cost for Room and Board:** $11,042 **Percent receiving financial aid out of those who apply, first year:** 88%
Middle 50% ACT range: 31–35	**Percent from Public HS:** 66%	
Early admission program EA/ED/None: None	**Retention Rate:** 97% **Graduation Rate 4-year:** 97%	**Percent receiving financial aid among all students:** 60%

Founded in 1636, Harvard University is the oldest college in the United States and often considered one of the top universities in the world. Students, known affectionately as "Cantabs," enjoy easy access to world-renowned professors, high-achieving classmates, and city life in Boston. With 44 Nobel Laureates as former and current faculty, there is little doubt that Harvard has a wealth of resources and opportunities to offer both its students as well as graduates.

Aiming for A's

Harvard undoubtedly commands international recognition for its outstanding academics and highly intelligent student population. Although students generally graduate in four years, some choose to undergo Advanced Standing, a program which allows students to graduate in three years before obtaining a Master's degree. At Harvard, majors are known as concentrations, and some of the most popular ones include Economics, Mathematics, Government and Pre-Med.

Core classes tend to have up to 400 to 500 students, although seminars, which are non-core classes, are typically much smaller. According to one freshman, "the classes are competitive in the sense that everyone strives to do well, but people don't think of other students as competition. We enjoy having other help." While engineering, math, or science classes are known for their extra difficulty, Cantabs do not mind the added challenge. One student remarked, "You gotta take what you gotta take." Despite the reputed difficulty of science classes, however, Harvard students looking for a hands-on learning experience can take "Cooking for Science," cooking in class while learning the scientific principles behind each delicious meal.

In general, grading at Harvard is relatively laid-back. According to one freshman, "grading tends to be very forgiving at Harvard. There is definitely a sense of grade inflation on campus, as most classes are typically curved to a B+, although professors do have full control over their own grading styles." Another student added, "Getting a B+ or A– is very doable, although getting an A will take a bit of work." Yet, it isn't the inflated grading policy that characterizes Harvard's academic atmosphere. "I like the flexibility that we have in choosing classes, and I like that there are lots of introductory classes in very different subjects, which makes exploring possible," said one student. "I really appreciate the caliber of our professors and how it can really contribute to the quality of classes." If students do feel stressed out, they can participate in Primal Scream, a campus tradition in which students collectively scream as loudly as they can the night before finals, before resuming their studies.

While most appreciate Harvard's academic excellence, some criticize the lack of academic advising available to students. According to one sophomore, "students are given three advisers during their freshman year, but these advisers usually have little impact on a freshman's academic life because organized contact is typically rare." Others cite inconsistencies among different course sections for a particular class; nonetheless, Harvard students are overall content with their academic experience and appreciate everything that their university has to offer.

Partyin' It Up, Crimson Style

Social life at Harvard surrounds its prestigious Final Clubs, who host parties and social events over the weekends for stressed out students. Those interested in partying elsewhere can also find parties hosted by student groups in dining halls or student dorms. Alcohol is prevalent, although students are not generally pressured to drink. According to one student, "there is a distinct drinking culture at Harvard, but there are enough students that do not drink so that they are not particularly disadvantaged socially if they choose not to drink." Harvard also has its fair share of substance abuse, although neither drugs nor binge drinking is a major problem on campus. According to one freshman, "you can pretty much get away with alcohol and drugs as long as you don't do it so excessively that you to go to the hospital or start to disturb the public."

Alcohol and partying aside, students interested in a different social experience are definitely not left out in the cold, thanks largely to Boston's various shops and restaurants, including a nearby Chipotle franchise that remains a favorite among students. Others choose to spend their weekends on campus, enjoying free time with their friends or catching up on homework in Lamonte Library.

Not Your Typical House

Before arriving on campus as freshmen, Harvard students fill out a housing application form in order to find a compatible roommate. Freshmen are randomly assigned to one of the 17 freshman dormitories and live in the same room for one year. In March of freshmen year, however, Harvard students receive their "House" affiliations through a randomized process known as "sorting," which designates their intra-Harvard identity. Each House contains dorm rooms for undergraduates, resident tutors, its own dining hall, library, administrative officials, as well as other student facilities. Students are assigned to one of 12 Harvard houses with up to seven of their friends, creating a "blocking group."

Students typically live on campus for all four years and, for the most part, dorm life has remained fairly consistent. Students entering the Harvard Class of 2015, however, should be aware of recent renovations that are slated to begin in 2012. According to one student, "Harvard has voted in recent weeks to allocated nearly $1 billion in funds to renovating the Upperclass Houses, meaning that current high school students entering Harvard in the coming years should be able to experience a more enhanced House experience."

Unsurprisingly, campus architecture is "old . . . really old" and campus scenery is characterized by red brick and grassy lawns. Tourists at the Crimson Ivy often visit the Science Center, which houses five lecture halls and numerous academic departments, and Annenberg Hall, the centrally located freshman dining hall that still remains a favorite among tourists.

The Whole Package

Harvard students are as serious about their academics as they are about their extracurricular activities. Some prominent organizations on campus include the International Relations Council, *The Lampoon*, *The Crimson*, and Women in Business (which has over 400 members). Not everything about Harvard is always serious, though. Students in Hasty Pudding Theatricals come together every year to award the Hasty Pudding Man and Woman of the Year, reflecting a fun side of Harvard students that doesn't take away from their passion. According to one freshman, "something unique about Harvard is really the commitment people have to their extracurriculars. People do a million things—and stay active in all of them."

> "People from the outside describe us as being cocky, but I don't really see much of that inside Harvard."

Outside of campus clubs and organizations, Crimson students are also extremely active in the job market. One of the biggest employers is Harvard Student Agencies, Inc., an organization comprised of many subsidiary agencies that employ students all over campus. While some student employees work at HAS cleaners offering laundry plans, others sell Harvard apparel at The Harvard Shop; some even take advantage of alcohol on campus, working as bartenders for HSA Bartending. Others take more traditional roles as student workers in campus libraries or research assistants for Harvard professors.

Unlike club activities, however, sports are not a major presence on campus. As one student aptly said, "games are free for a reason." Another student added that "while there is a bit of pride associated with Harvard athletics, attending athletic events is usually not the thing to do." This doesn't mean, however, that Harvard students are completely sports illiterate. During the annual Harvard-Yale football game, Cantabs eagerly don Crimson scarves and sweaters, proudly showing their collegiate loyalty and support for the Harvard football team. According to one sophomore, "there is a big athletic presence on campus, and student athletes are definitely a big part of the Harvard community, so it's very common for students to go to athletic events to see their friends in action."

Overall, Harvard is an excellent school for students seeking a first-class academic experience and the company of some of the world's brightest minds. Unlike contemporary portrayals of the University, Cantabs are generally down-to-earth and can successfully strike a balance between studying hard and playing hard.—*Caroline Tan*

FYI
If you come to Harvard, you'd better bring "tourist repellant, a lot of warm clothes, and your own toilet paper."
Three things every student at Harvard should do are "hook up with someone in the stacks of Widener Library, run Primal Scream, and pee on the John Harvard statue."
What surprised me the most about Harvard is that "it's better than you could ever imagine. Seriously."

Massachusetts Institute of Technology

Address: 77 Massachusetts Avenue, Cambridge, MA 02139-4307
Phone: 617-253-1000
E-mail address: admissions@mit.edu
Web site URL: www.mit.edu
Year Founded: 1861
Private or Public: Private
Religious Affiliation: None
Location: Urban
Number of Applicants: 12,445
Percent Accepted: 12%
Percent Accepted who enroll: 69%
Number Entering: 1,067
Number of Transfers Accepted each Year: 17
Middle 50% SAT range: M: 720–800, CR: 660–760, Wr: 660–750
Middle 50% ACT range: 31–34
Early admission program EA/ED/None: EA

Percentage accepted through EA or ED: 30%
EA and ED deadline: 1-Nov
Regular Deadline: 1-Jan
Application Fee: $65
Full time Undergraduate enrollment: 4,172
Total enrollment: 10,220
Percent Male: 54%
Percent Female: 46%
Total Percent Minority or Unreported: 60%
Percent African-American: 9%
Percent Asian/Pacific Islander: 26%
Percent Hispanic: 12%
Percent Native-American: 1%
Percent International: 8%
Percent in-state/out of state: 10%/90%
Percent from Public HS: 70%
Retention Rate: 98%

Graduation Rate 4-year: 83%
Graduation Rate 6-year: 91%
Percent Undergraduates in On-campus housing: 90%
Number of official organized extracurricular organizations: 415
3 Most popular majors: Engineering, Computer Science, Physical Science
Student/Faculty ratio: 6:1
Average Class Size: 9
Percent of students going to grad school: 50%
Tuition and Fees: $36,390
In-State Tuition and Fees if different: No difference
Cost for Room and Board: $10,860
Percent receiving financial aid out of those who apply, first year: 82%
Percent receiving financial aid among all students: 64%

Nestled in the quintessential college town of Cambridge is one of the nation's most prestigious and intellectually demanding universities, the Massachusetts Institute of Technology. Famous world-round for producing brilliant engineers and scientists, MIT nevertheless offers a richly diverse community of scholars all united by a passion for learning. Distinguished equally for its undergraduate research opportunities, its humanities program, and its legendary hacking tradition, MIT promises an unforgettably rewarding experience for those students ready to meet the challenge.

Not for Everyone

MIT students will admit that the school's ponderous, often overwhelming workload and academic rigor is not for everyone, yet the students who feed off and thrive in the intense environment never stop savoring its fruits. "MIT opens up an entire world of possibilities," gushed one student. "It's a lot of work," another student admitted, "but it's so, so worth it by the time you're done." Students state that with their first class, their entire thinking process is transformed, for professors don't seek simply to recite and impart facts and formulas: they try to change how students' assimilate and apply information by teaching them how to think, rather than what to think. It is that principle of organic problem-solving that sets MIT apart as an extraordinary institution of undergraduate learning.

MIT requires every student to take 17 General Institute Requirements before graduation: nine in math, science, and technology, and eight in the humanities, arts, and social sciences. Those students who desire a more intimate learning environment to support them in satisfying these requirements can join one of four Freshman Learning Communities, small and cohesive groups that foster close interaction between faculty and students. And to ease all freshmen into the system, MIT offers a pass/no record grading scale the first semester, in which an A, B, or C appears uniformly as a pass grade while a D or F is completely erased from the student's permanent transcript. The second semester, freshmen are graded on an A/B/C/no record basis. "The pass/no record grading has really given me a chance to explore my interests outside of academics and discover all the opportunities MIT has to offer," shared one freshman. And students definitely need that transition period. Yet, ultimately, one student reflected, "People here tend to be pretty apathetic with regards to GPA. There's no such thing as Latin honors here, and people do tend to be pretty idealistic (sadistic?) with regards to classes, taking tons and tons at a time, putting learning before grades."

> **"It's a lot of work, but it's so, so worth it by the time you're done."**

The typical MIT workload is four to five classes requiring a total time commitment of 50 to 60 hours each week: "You're pretty much working all the time—it's like community bonding happens over working nonstop." And although classes often contract to as few as 10 students for higher-level courses, freshman year can congest up to 400 students into a lecture hall, especially in introductory classes. Yet professors are accessible if you take the initiative to talk to them—that means being persistent at packed office hours—and students study collaboratively rather than competitively: "The professors write the problem sets in such a way that it is absolutely indispensable that you work in groups in order to finish."

From A Cappella to Video Games: Giving the Brain a Break

As heavy as is the workload, however, MIT students still find the time to invest in sundry extracurricular activities. Featuring everything from the Underwater Hockey Group and the Laboratory of Chocolate Science to Engineers Without Borders and the Black Students Association, MIT's 415 student organizations offer an outlet for all students. And if you have a passion that has not yet been provided for, you can easily create a club of your own, no matter how outlandish the purpose. "The cool thing about MIT is that everybody is really passionate about something, usually random things, so you can voice crazy ideas and people won't

look at you strangely," explained one student.

Noted for its large number of a cappella and choral groups, as well as for its tremendous Undergraduate Research Opportunities Program (UROP), in which 80 percent of students participate, MIT offers students several ways to get involved. One of the best times to explore nascent interests is Independent Activities Period (IAP), a month-long session in January, after Winter Break, during which students can stay on campus or go abroad to pursue personal projects or take different types of classes.

MIT is also one of the few top-ten research universities characterized by an incredibly vibrant Greek life. Fifty percent of undergraduate men, and 27 percent of undergraduate women, belong to one of the 27 fraternities or 6 sororities on campus, but these are not the students who would normally join the Greek system. Rather than the bacchanalian party scene dominant at other colleges, Greek life at MIT is an "academic support system" of students all motivating and encouraging one another to persist in a fiercely challenging intellectual environment. Thus, although Greek life does figure prominently in the MIT social scene, it is not the center of attention: hundreds of students take advantage of the weekend frat parties, sometimes even inviting their friends from other Boston universities, but many more—particularly upperclassmen—choose to patronize one of the several local bars for their taste of nightlife. Avalon, Embassy, and Crossroads Irish Pub are all favorites.

Those students desiring some fun without alcohol can partake in Cambridge's many theater, arts, and shopping options. Popular are CambridgeSide Galleria, a mall that offers a free shuttle service to MIT's Kendall Square, and Central Square, the center of the music scene. Students also occasionally frequent the Museum of Science and the Museum of Fine Arts, to both of which they are given free daily admission. Or, if students have too much work and just need a short brain break, especially on weeknights, dorms are always prime locations for spontaneous fun. At any one time, a visitor can observe students relaxing by playing with foam weapons, competing in video games, or participating in hypothetical scenarios involving spaceships or engineering technologies. "These seemingly silly activities can be a huge stress relief when you've spent the last several hours doing problem sets in your room," shared one student.

They also reflect students' willingness and eagerness to explore new things, regardless of the consequences. "There's a lot of eccentric expression here—for example, the dorms are laced with murals of internet memes and other generally humorous images, which form a part of student expression. Also, there is a lot of secretive stuff going on around campus—for example, an explosion can go off at all random hours of the night and produce a mushroom cloud several hundred feet high—and those sorts of random things become pretty commonplace."

Perhaps the best description of the MIT experience is the school motto the students have created for themselves: I.H.T.F.P., which represents both "I hate this f-ing place" and "I have truly found paradise." These constantly busy, perpetually sleep-deprived students have still learned how to uncover and savor the fun in every activity, whether it's an onerous problem set or the latest scandalous prank. Therefore, despite the challenges and the expressed duality of the MIT experience, "it's a relationship still full more of love than of hate: a lot of love, and a few hard nights."—*Sejal Hathi*

FYI

If you come to MIT, you'd better bring: energy drinks, a bike, cooking utensils, a nerf gun, and an oscilloscope.

What's the typical weekend schedule? Sleep in, work nonstop until you can let loose at a party.

If I could change one thing about MIT, I'd: make the advising more standardized.

Three things every student at MIT should do before graduating are: participate in Mystery Hunt, go on an Orange Tour, and take linguistics with Norvin Richards.

Mount Holyoke College

Address: 50 College Street South Hadley, MA 01075
Phone: 413-538-2023
E-mail address: admission@mtholyoke.edu
Web site URL: www.mtholyoke.edu
Year Founded: 1837
Private or Public: Private
Religious Affiliation: None
Location: Suburban
Number of Applicants: 3,194
Percent Accepted: 52%
Percent Accepted who enroll: 31%
Number Entering: 522
Number of Transfers Accepted each Year: 102
Middle 50% SAT range: M: 590–690, CR: 640–730, Wr: 630–710
Middle 50% ACT range: 26–30
Early admission program EA/ED/None: ED

Percentage accepted through EA or ED: Unreported
EA and ED deadline: 15-Nov
Regular Deadline: 15-Jan
Application Fee: $60; online application is free
Full time Undergraduate enrollment: 2,201
Total enrollment: 2,201
Percent Male: 0%
Percent Female: 100%
Total Percent Minority or Unreported: 34%
Percent African-American: 5%
Percent Asian/Pacific Islander: 13%
Percent Hispanic: 6%
Percent Native-American: <1%
Percent International: 13%
Percent in-state/out of state: 20%/80%
Percent from Public HS: 61%
Retention Rate: 94%

Graduation Rate 4-year: 78%
Graduation Rate 6-year: 81%
Percent Undergraduates in On-campus housing: 93%
Number of official organized extracurricular organizations: 150
3 Most popular majors: Biology, English, International Relations
Student/Faculty ratio: 10:1
Average Class Size: 16
Percent of students going to grad school: 20%
Tuition and Fees: $37,646
In-State Tuition and Fees if different: No difference
Cost for Room and Board: $11,020
Percent receiving financial aid out of those who apply, first year: 85%
Percent receiving financial aid among all students: 60%

Located in the calm hamlet of South Hadley, Massachusetts, Mount Holyoke College is a women's college known for both its homey feel and high-powered academics. The campus is known as one of the most beautiful in the country, and helps to foster close bonds among the tight-knit community. As a member of the Five College Consortium, Mount Holyoke students are able to take classes and interact with students at Smith College, University of Massachusetts at Amherst, Amherst College, and Hampshire College. Caring professors and individualized support help students take advantage of a myriad of academic and social opportunities.

Vigorous Academics

Academics at Mount Holyoke can be described as "very rigorous." Students are required to fulfill a variety of distributional requirements that include three courses in the humanities, two courses in science and math, and two courses in the social sciences. They must also fulfill a foreign language requirement, a multicultural perspectives course, and six units of physical education. Although such requirements may seem daunting, most describe them as "not hard to meet at all" and note that "you can fit your interests within the requirements." Students are also required to choose a minor, second major, or a certificate program through one of the Five Colleges. In addition, Mount Holyoke offers dual-degree engineering programs through MIT, California Institute of Technology, and the Thayer School of Engineering at Dartmouth. Some of the more popular majors include biology, English, and international relations. Smaller but very well-regarded departments include astronomy and gender studies. The popular first-year seminar program, which includes such courses as "Gods and Monsters" and "African Cinema," allows freshmen to get to know their professors and fellow students during their first semester on campus. Although professors are known for assigning a demanding workload—"every professor thinks that his class is your top priority," noted one student—they are universally praised for being accessible, engaging, and genuinely interested in their students. Courses such as dance, scuba diving, and horseback riding provide a break from academic life and take advantage of the college's beautiful natural surroundings.

Mount Holyoke is also unique in that it offers an optional January term, or J-term, a month when students can take advantage of workshops or study abroad. Students are able to cross-register at any of the members of the Five College Consortium, which are all serviced by a free busing system among the different campuses. The system allows students to take courses in subjects not offered at Mount Holyoke and meet students at nearby schools.

Lakes and Waterfalls

With a campus designed by Olmstead and Sons, the developers of Central Park, it's not hard to see why Mount Holyoke's surroundings are unequivocally described as "beautiful." Featuring two lakes and seven waterfalls, the campus is dotted with benches for studying and talking. Although the closest town, South Hadley, is considered small and sleepy, students can easily travel to Amherst or Northampton using the college's busing system when they feel the need to get away.

The dorms, which house approximately 93 percent of students, are praised for fostering close relations among the student body. Most dorms house students from all four classes, allowing students the chance to get to know upperclassmen. Freshmen are assigned housing based on extensive surveys and usually live in doubles or triples. By their senior year, most students live in singles. Dorms vary in size and age, ranging from modern brick buildings to ivy-covered halls with a view of one of the college's lakes. All dorms are governed by a Hall President, or HP, and three to six Student Advisors, or SAs. These students host study breaks, help with acclimation to college life, and ensure enforcement of rules. Although Public Safety maintains a presence on campus and open alcohol isn't technically allowed in hallways, students say they find few problems with the school's regulations. "They just want to make sure that we're safe," said a junior.

The quality of the food is widely praised, with one student even describing it as "delicious!" Every dorm features a dining hall, and cafés in the campus center and the library relieve hunger pangs between meals or at night. Vegetarian, vegan, kosher, and halal options are offered at every meal. Students can also load money onto their meal cards to use off campus.

Activities for All

Extracurricular life at Mount Holyoke is characterized by variety and passion. Sports, which consist of 14 varsity teams and various club sports, are very popular among students, particularly crew, rugby, hockey, and Ultimate Frisbee. Even if they don't join a team, many girls enthusiastically cheer on their classmates on the field. The newly refurbished athletic center, which features TV-equipped cardio machines and is open to all students, garners glowing reviews. Music and dance also play an important part of life on campus, with the college boasting many a cappella groups, performing ensembles, and outside concerts. SGA, the Student Government Association, is another popular way for students to get involved. Other student groups discussing issues of diversity and sexual identity feature prominently in campus life.

Socially, students remark that although people with similar interests tend to stick together, Mount Holyoke is an overwhelmingly friendly place. "This is not a party school," a sophomore asserted. Although many students drink, options abound for those who choose not to imbibe. On-campus social activities include dorm parties, movies, and a cappella jams. Las Vegas Night, Mount Holyoke's biggest party of the year, features dancing and gambling. Other popular on-campus events include the "Drag Ball" in early February and Spring Carnival Weekend, which attracts dance and musical performers to the college. During the weekends,

many students use the bus system to meet members of the opposite sex at Amherst or UMass. "Although Mount Holyoke is a women's college, you are not abandoned to a corner of the earth were there are no men," joked one senior.

Atypical Experience
While Mount Holyoke, as a women's college, may not offer the typical college experience, students are overwhelmingly happy with the school. "Although I never saw myself at a women's college, I wouldn't trade a minute of my time here for anything," declared one senior. Students believe that the benefits of an all-female environment more than make up for the extra trouble they have to go to to meet members of the opposite sex. Openness and acceptance characterize the campus, and Mount Holyokers are known for being open-minded, down-to-earth, and intelligent. The student body is incredibly diverse, with an exceptionally high number of international students. The school is also accepting of students of all sexual orientations and relationships.

Although Mount Holyoke is not for everyone, the majority of students who attend the college are extremely happy with it. "Mount Holyoke provides such a great balance of academics with a well-rounded life," says one senior. "I couldn't imagine myself anywhere else."—*Elizabeth Chrystal*

FYI

If you come to Mount Holyoke, you'd better bring "a box full of costumes—you've never seen so many theme parties in your life!"

What's the typical weekend schedule? "Hang out on Friday with friends; relax, shop, or go to a sports game on Saturday, go out to a party on-campus or by taking a bus off-campus; have brunch and do homework on Sunday."

If I could change one thing about Mount Holyoke, I'd "make South Hadley a little more exciting. It's very quaint, but it seems a bit isolated after four years."

Three things every student at Mount Holyoke should do before graduating are "climb Mount Holyoke on Mountain Day, go to an a cappella jam, and enjoy crepes at Sunday brunch."

Northeastern University

Address: 360 Huntington Avenue, Boston, MA 02115
Phone: 617-373-2200
E-mail address: admissions@neu.edu
Web site URL: www.northeastern.edu
Year Founded: 1898
Private or Public: Private
Religious Affiliation: None
Location: Urban
Number of Applicants: 34,005
Percent Accepted: 41%
Percent Accepted who enroll: 20%
Number Entering: 2,833
Number of Transfers Accepted each Year: 1,287
Middle 50% SAT range: M: 620–700, CR: 580–670, Wr: 580–670
Middle 50% ACT range: 27–31
Early admission program EA/ED/None: EA

Percentage accepted through EA or ED: Unreported
EA and ED deadline: 1-Nov
Regular Deadline: 15-Jan
Application Fee: $70
Full time Undergraduate enrollment: 15,699
Total enrollment: 22,091
Percent Male: 49%
Percent Female: 51%
Total Percent Minority or Unreported: Unreported
Percent African-American: 4%
Percent Asian/Pacific Islander: 9%
Percent Hispanic: 5%
Percent Native-American: 1%
Percent International: 8%
Percent in-state/out of state: 39%/61%
Percent from Public HS: Unreported
Retention Rate: 91%
Graduation Rate 4-year: Unreported

Graduation Rate 6-year: 75%
Percent Undergraduates in On-campus housing: 50%
Number of official organized extracurricular organizations: 225
3 Most popular majors: Business/Marketing, Engineering, Health Professions and related sciences
Student/Faculty ratio: 15:1
Average Class Size: 26
Percent of students going to grad school: 18%
Tuition and Fees: $34,950
In-State Tuition and Fees if different: No difference
Cost for Room and Board: $12,350
Percent receiving financial aid out of those who apply, first year: Unreported
Percent receiving financial aid among all students: Unreported

I nterested in gaining the advantage of real-life work experience during your college years? If so, Northeastern and its unique Cooperative Education program might be for you. Northeastern University (NU) places a distinct emphasis on prepro-fessional training as well as education and offers its students a co-op internship pro-gram that places them with various compa-nies during the academic year.

One Step Ahead: the Co-op Program

At Northeastern, students alternate be-tween classroom study and periods of paid, professional experience. Each period is six months, which means, as one student put it, "You don't really have summers that much." It also means that the majority of students go to school for five years, rather than the typical four at other schools.

At the same time, though, students who participate in the co-op program gain a dis-tinct advantage in the "real world." "You come out of college with a stacked resume; you know how to interview, and you know how to be professional. You just have an edge on everybody." The real-life experience also allows a student to "get a good sense of whether you're in the right field." This means, of course, that even though you don't officially select a major until sophomore year, many students applying to NU have a clear idea of what career they wish to pur-sue. For those who do know where they would like to end up after college, this pro-gram not only gives them a lot of resume-building experience, but it also connects them with potential employers and business opportunities. Upon graduating, many stu-dents are offered jobs at the companies they worked at in the co-op program. As one stu-dent working for an inventing company in New Hampshire declared, "I'm learning more by working than [I am] in classes."

Approximately 90 percent of NU's student

body participates in the co-op program. In fact, it seems that "most kids that come to NU come for the co-op program." Students who choose to start the co-op freshman year take an orientation class and begin work sophomore year. Co-op classes are required and can focus on job-relevant skills such as interviewing or writing résumés. Students are also assigned co-op faculty coordinators who help them find opportunities that match their goals and interests. However, while these resources are available, it is up to the student to schedule and prepare for interviews, as well as perform well on the job. Even then, NU cannot guarantee that each student will have a job during the co-op term. Also, if students accept positions outside the Boston area, they are responsible for finding their own housing and transportation in the area they choose. But if a student plans to accept a local position, he or she may continue living in the NU residence hall.

> "You come out of college with a stacked resume; you know how to interview, and you know how to be professional. You just have an edge on everybody."

The hard work seems to be well worth it: students graduate from college and can move straight into the workforce. Another appealing incentive is the pay: students who opt to enroll in the co-op program can earn a lot of money during their six-month work periods.

The Penthouse Suite

Most students feel that the on-campus freshman housing at Northeastern is "basically like any other school"—neither exceptional nor terrible. Quality does vary, since some buildings have been renovated in recent years while others have not, but overall the freshman housing is generally described as "decent." Upperclassmen housing, on the other hand, is "*so* nice." "From sophomore year on, the housing is either relatively new or has been renovated within the last decade." Many residential halls, such as the West Village halls or Davenport Commons, have units that can include two to three bedrooms, two bathrooms, a "huge" living room, and a kitchen. Other amenities include cable TV, air-conditioning, and high-speed Inter-

net. West Village E is particularly-famous; made completely of glass, it is what's known as the penthouse suite, with two glass walls that overlook a stunning view of downtown Boston. Such luxury, though, comes with a price. "It's really expensive," one student complained, so much so that "it's actually much cheaper to live off campus"—a bold statement when weighed against the difficulty of finding affordable housing in Boston.

For those who do choose to live on campus, buildings are divided into single-sex wings, and NU offers special-interest housing, such as a "wellness" dorm (the alcohol, drug, and smoke-free Coe Hall), an honors dorm, and an international dorm. Each residential section is assigned a Resident Assistant (RA). Some students claim that their RAs have been lax about alcohol policies, provided that students respect the rules and property. One admitted, though, that this was the exception more than the rule. "I had an RA who was really relaxed about alcohol, but a lot of the RAs in other dorms were very strict and kids were always getting into trouble."

Students seem to be impressed with the campus facilities because "everything on campus is really well-maintained." This may be because the administration is "very responsive to student suggestions, and if there is a complaint, "everything gets fixed pretty quickly." Some of the facilities available to students are the Marino Recreation Center, where students, athlete and nonathlete alike, can work out, and the Matthews Arena, the oldest indoor arena in the world. This is where the hockey teams play, and games attract an enthusiastic following, outside the University as well as within. Every year, for example, the city holds the Beanpot, a tournament in which Northeastern, Boston University, Boston College, and Harvard compete for bragging rights as the best hockey team in the city. It's held at the TD Banknorth Garden arena and attracts quite a crowd. The University also maintains common areas stocked with pool tables and lounge chairs. Some of the most popular hang-out areas are the Curry Student Center and the Cyber Café in Snell Library.

Students have several options when it comes to dining. Along with its three dining halls, there are several restaurants on campus, including Taco Bell, Starbucks, Pizza Hut, Wendy's, and Qdoba. The University offers several meal-plan options, one of which includes putting money on a Husky Card, which can also be used at local, off-campus eateries. This option conveniently allows students to take advantage of NU's advantageous location in the hustle and bustle of Boston. There are several good eateries near campus, and one particular favorite is Chicken Lou's, a "little shack" at which you'll have "probably the best food you will ever eat—you would stand in line in the Massachusetts cold for that food."

So Much to Do, So Much to See
As for extracurricular activities, students at NU have a variety of choices. "The administration is very lenient with on-campus organizations," and the student government, in charge of approving clubs, distributes a hefty allocation of money to these student groups. One of the most popular clubs—and also the largest with over 600 members—is NUCALLS. Members of this organization are students fluent in other languages, and they offer peers interested in learning that language tutoring sessions for free. Intramural sports are also a popular pastime, one of the most popular sports being broomball. "Broomball is huge around campus," and students sign up for teams in the spring and fall to play a carefully organized series of games that culminate in that semester's playoffs. Other organizations are more typical, like the Student Government Association and daily newspapers, while other are more unique, like *The Northeastern University Times New Roman*, a humor newspaper. Greek life is present on campus, but it is not a driving force. Only about 8 percent of the total student body joins fraternities or sororities, and although they throw occasional parties, no one seems to be in any hurry to rush them.

Party City: Boston, the College Town
The social scene at Northeastern comes alive each weekend. Drinking is prevalent, but there is also a significant percentage of the student population that opts not to drink. And for those who do, alcohol is relatively easy to come by, as are parties. Some of the most popular events on campus are SpringFest, Midnight Madness, and International Carnevale. Partying on campus has its downside, though, because the University has strict rules about drinking. "The school is looking to get you into trouble," cautioned one student.

However, being in a city like Boston, NU's social scene is not limited to on-campus events. It lies in the midst of several other universities—"It's a five-minute walk to Boston University, a 15-minute train ride to Boston College, and a 20-minute train ride to MIT or Harvard"—which means students at NU have several opportunities to meet students from other schools. It also gives students a wide variety of parties to choose from on weekends. "There are just so many options; I know there are always hundreds of things going on in the city." Another student said, "I can party anywhere—at a house, apartment, fraternity, or bars, clubs, concerts, and other schools."

Clubbing used to be a popular weekend activity for many NU students, but in light of new legislation, clubs are no longer 18 and up. What's more, fakes are not a good idea when partying in the city because "all the cops are out to get you." While many students enjoy spending time at bars or clubs on the weekend, these establishments tend to be extremely strict when it comes to IDs. "Every liquor store scans IDs, and several bars black light them." If a student is 21 or older, popular clubs include Avalon, Roxy, and Matrix; the most popular bar is Punter's.

The Sum Total
Overall, Northeastern students take advantage of the opportunities the school provides. The urban campus provides an endless stream of events and activities, and students actively participate in campus life, joining groups and enjoying their college years to the fullest. While enjoying the NU social scene, students simultaneously gain work experience in the co-op program, which distinguishes Northeastern from other universities. The expertise gained in real job experience gives graduating students a considerable edge post-college and is perfect for motivated, career-oriented students. All of this, combined with a respectable faculty, diverse student body, and fast-paced Boston environment, offers Northeastern students a unique and fruitful experience.—*Caroline Garner*

FYI

If you come to Northeastern, you'd better bring "skis or snowboards, to take advantage of all the ski trips the school organizes."

What's the typical weekend schedule? "Drink when and where you can, or go clubbing. Fit in a little work."

If I could change one thing about Northeastern, it would be "the proportion of students from certain regions; most are from the New England area."

Three things every student at Northeastern should do before graduating are "do the co-op program, go to a Red Sox or Patriot game, and explore what the city has to offer."

Simmons College

Address: 300 The Fenway Boston, MA 02115
Phone: 617-521-2051
E-mail address: ugadm@simmons.edu
Web site URL: www.simmons.edu
Year Founded: 1899
Private or Public: Private
Religious Affiliation: None
Location: Urban
Number of Applicants: 3,222
Percent Accepted: 54%
Percent Accepted who enroll: 22%
Number Entering: 391
Number of Transfers Accepted each Year: 158
Middle 50% SAT range: M: 500–590, CR: 510–600, Wr: 520–620
Middle 50% ACT range: 22–26
Early admission program EA/ED/None: EA

Percentage accepted through EA or ED: 57%
EA and ED deadline: 1-Dec
Regular Deadline: 1-Feb
Application Fee: $55
Full time Undergraduate enrollment: 1,850
Total enrollment: 2,060
Percent Male: 1%
Percent Female: 99%
Total Percent Minority or Unreported: 27%
Percent African-American: 6%
Percent Asian/Pacific Islander: 7%
Percent Hispanic: 4%
Percent Native-American: <1%
Percent International: 3%
Percent in-state/out of state: 64%/36%
Percent from Public HS: Unreported
Retention Rate: 83%

Graduation Rate 4-year: 62%
Graduation Rate 6-year: 72%
Percent Undergraduates in On-campus housing: 55%
Number of official organized extracurricular organizations: 80
3 Most popular majors: Nursing, Psychology, Biology
Student/Faculty ratio: 13:1
Average Class Size: 16
Percent of students going to grad school: Unreported
Tuition and Fees: $27,468
In-State Tuition and Fees if different: No difference
Cost for Room and Board: $11,138
Percent receiving financial aid out of those who apply, first year: 72%
Percent receiving financial aid among all students: 70%

Nestled in the bustling city of Boston rests the tranquil oasis of Simmons College. Roughly 2,000 young women attend Simmons for its liberal arts with a special focus on science. Students rave about the close-knit student body and excellent, approachable professors, which combine to form a welcoming and laid-back atmosphere.

Science Anyone?

Simmons College offers a liberal arts education with special career preparation opportunities. The nursing program feeds student internships in the city, while the physical therapy major has a six-year doctorate pro-

gram. Science at Simmons is especially strong. Nursing, biology, and chemistry are considered the most difficult majors, while communications and psychology are "not as demanding, but still difficult," according to one student. Class size is small, making it easy to enroll in most classes and enabling students to take a more active role in the classroom. Students rave about their professors. One student explained, "[The professors] give you their e-mail, cell phone number, home number, office number, and office hours. They want you to come and talk to them. They are interested in helping their students."

Students must fulfill academic distributional requirements in six "modes of inquiry": Creative and Performing Arts; Language, Literature and Culture; Quantitative Analysis and Reasoning; Scientific Inquiry; Social and Historical Perspectives; and Psychological and Ethical Development. In the process, students become more well-rounded and prepared for life after college. The requirements are surprisingly unrestrictive, though, and one student commented, "I found that I was able to experiment more during my freshman year than my friends at other schools."

An Escape from Beantown

The Simmons campus receives high marks from its students. Its peaceful green quadrangle in the middle of a busy Boston neighborhood serves as a quiet haven. One student exclaimed, "Our campus is beautiful. Most people come onto campus and forget they are in a city. When you walk through the gates, it feels very much unlike a city and a lot more like home." The campus is divided into an academic portion and a residential portion separated by one city block. The residential campus consists of a picturesque quadrangle bounded by the College's residence halls and Bartol Dining Hall. Also located on the residential campus is the Holmes Sports Center, boasting an eight-lane swimming pool, suspended track, weight room, sauna, basketball court, dance studio, and squash courts. Next door is the Simmons Health Center, which offers its comprehensive services to students.

> "[The professors] give you their e-mail, cell phone number, home number, office number, and office hours. They want you to come and talk to them. They are interested in helping their students."

Approximately a five-minute walk from the residential campus is the main campus. Here the College's main classrooms are located in the Main College Building (affectionately referred to as the "MCB") and the Park Science Building, where all science courses are taught. The main campus also hosts the Beatley Library and the newly constructed and unusually named One Palace Road Building. One Palace Road provides a number of student resources such as career services and counseling, as well as two graduate school departments.

Standard of Living at Simmons

The quality of dorm rooms differs at Simmons depending on renovations and specific buildings. Most freshmen live in doubles in Mesick, Morse, or Simmons Hall, but there are a few triples. There is an RA on every floor, and one student said, "They're just there to help out, and are not too strict." Students are very pleased with their living situation. Recently renovated Evans Hall and Arnold Hall are "really nice and the only ones with elevators on campus," one student reported. Praise is not as free-flowing, though, when students are asked about the food at Simmons. Bartol Dining Hall is Simmons' main dining hall and students label the food as "fair." Luckily for hungry Simmons students, the best of Boston's restaurants, with its first-class seafood and ethnic fare, lie just outside the College's gates. Other dining options available to students on campus include the Quadside Café, serving as a snack bar and grocery, The Fens, with a deli and grill, and Java City (Simmons' Coffee Kiosk), which doles out coffee and snacks.

Livin' It Up in Beantown

One student put it best by saying, "Basically, Boston becomes your campus." For this group of young women, the possibilities of the city are boundless. Students are able to take advantage of the city's many fabulous restaurants, go shopping on Newbury Street, attend a Boston Red Sox game, and go to a concert at the Orpheum Theater. Boston offers anything and everything under the sun . . . and under the moon as well, as Simmons girls take advantage of the city's exciting nightlife.

Simmons is a dry campus, and because of alcohol and noise restrictions students often go out to Boston clubs or to frat parties at BU and MIT for a more festive atmosphere. One student comments that because of this situation, "Simmons girls have a lot of random hookups because they really don't know when the next chance will be." These meetings often develop into something more substantial, however, and students note that many of their peers are involved in serious relationships—both heterosexual and homosexual.

From Tea to Tennis

Students describe the student body as "intelligent" and "friendly." The small class size promotes unity and school spirit. According to one student, a tradition that has been going on for a few years now is the Friday Hall Teas, where all the girls from each hall come together to "have tea or snack on goodies and just hang out and have fun."

Many Simmons students take part in sports and other extracurricular activities. The campus is described by one "as very active and involved." Simmons is home to eight Division III varsity sports, and one student described Simmons sports as "not awful"—basketball and soccer seemed to be the most popular sports among students. Other student organizations such as Simmons College Outreach, a student-run community service organization, and the Student Government Organization are just two of the many student activities and clubs in which students take part.

When John Simmons founded this college in 1899, his mission was to allow women to earn the "livelihood" they deserved and to create a new generation of well-educated women. Today his mission continues to be realized, as Simmons produces well-prepared, independent women ready to enter the world.—*Kieran Locke*

FYI
If you come to Simmons College, you'd better bring a "Boston Red Sox hat."
What's the typical weekend schedule? "Hanging out, shopping, and eating in Harvard Square or on Newbury Street and going to an occasional party at a fraternity from a neighboring college."
If I could change one thing about Simmons, "I would change the dining-hall food."
Three things every student at Simmons should do before graduating are "visit the Isabella Stuart Gardner Museum, eat Ankara Frozen Yogurt, and go on the Swan Boats in Boston Commons."

Smith College

Address: 7 College Lane Northampton, MA 01063
Phone: 413-585-2500
E-mail address: admission@smith.edu
Web site URL: www.smith.edu
Year Founded: 1871
Private or Public: Private
Religious Affiliation: None
Location: Suburban
Number of Applicants: 4,015
Percent Accepted: 47%
Percent Accepted who enroll: 34%
Number Entering: 631
Number of Transfers Accepted each Year: 119
Middle 50% SAT range: M: 570–680, CR: 600–710, Wr: 590–700
Middle 50% ACT range: 25–31
Early admission program EA/ED/None: ED

Percentage accepted through EA or ED: 9%
EA and ED deadline: 15-Nov
Regular Deadline: 15-Jan
Application Fee: $60
Full time Undergraduate enrollment: 2,588
Total enrollment: 3,101
Percent Male: 0%
Percent Female: 100%
Total Percent Minority or Unreported: 27%
Percent African-American: 7%
Percent Asian/Pacific Islander: 13%
Percent Hispanic: 7%
Percent Native-American: <1%
Percent International: Unreported
Percent in-state/out of state: 23%/77%
Percent from Public HS: Unreported

Retention Rate: 90%
Graduation Rate 4-year: 83%
Graduation Rate 6-year: 88%
Percent Undergraduates in On-campus housing: 90%
Number of official organized extracurricular organizations: 134
3 Most popular majors: Government, Psychology, Art
Student/Faculty ratio: 9:1
Average Class Size: 12
Percent of students going to grad school: Unreported
Tuition and Fees: $36,058
In-State Tuition and Fees if different: No difference
Cost for Room and Board: $12,050
Percent receiving financial aid out of those who apply, first year: 87%
Percent receiving financial aid among all students: 53%

Nestled in the bright, still beauty of New England, Smith College is a women's liberal arts college full of tradition and brimming with life. Founded in 1871, it is one of the Seven Sister colleges, and a member of the Five Colleges consortium. It is among the largest women's colleges in the United States with around 2600 undergraduates enrolled at any given time. With a strong academic standing and a vibrant residential life, Smith is a good choice for any intelligent and highly-motivated woman seeking a college education.

Academics

Smith's academic rigor is well-documented, both in liberal arts and in the sciences. Among other things, it is the only women's college in the United States with its own accredited undergraduate engineering degree, and boasts a formidable list of 37 departmental majors, 10 interdepartmental majors, and various minors, as well as the possibility for a student to design her own major. These majors range from the commonplace such as Chemistry and Sociology down to the unique and downright weird, such as Landscape Studies. However, according to Smith official tallies, their most popular majors remain Government, Psychology, Art, English, Economics and Biology.

In keeping with this wide range of disciplines offered, Smith's curriculum is decidedly open-ended, with no particular mandatory classes, and indeed no requirements to take classes in any particular field. The exception to this almost complete freedom in course selection is if the student wishes to be eligible for Latin Honors or a Liberal Arts Commendation. In that case, she must have had at least one course in the seven fields of literature, history, social science, natural science, mathematics/philosophy, arts, and foreign language.

Despite being a large liberal arts college, Smith is still small in comparison with most universities. One freshman was impressed with the intimacy of classes, saying that all her small classes—generally around fifteen people—were taught by professors. "TAs are for drop-in questions," she says. However, she acknowledges that "some classes are challenging," especially those involving a great deal of reading and essay-writing. Another student concurs that "overall academics are tough, though it does vary per class."

Smith Traditions

Imagine: you wake up in the morning, groggy and grumpy, remembering you have a class in fifteen minutes. Then, you hear the bells ringing out all across campus. You throw open the curtains, and look out at a beautiful autumn day. It's Mountain Day at Smith, where all classes are cancelled in favor of enjoying the fall, and the surrounding farms are open for apple and pumpkin picking. Students appreciate the tradition and the breath of fresh air: a freshman observes that "it is a great chance to get to know your friends and housemates in a completely stress-free environment. It is just so much fun."

Mountain day isn't the only tradition at Smith. Other events occur throughout the school year, such as the Convocation party, which is a celebration of the beginning of the fall semester and a welcoming-home party rolled all in one, where students walk around in bizarre and creative themed attire.

Other annual traditions include Illumination night, held the weekend before commencement, where the campus is lit by candles and lanterns, and seniors are serenaded on the steps of the library before being ceremoniously pushed off the stairs, symbolizing their sudden, flailing entry into the "real world." There is very much a sense in which Smith's time-honored traditions, carried on year by year, bring living and breathing history into the course of the year.

Life Long Friends

When asked about life at Smith, one student commented, "Social life here is pretty diverse. There are people partying and people who study all the time." Another student adds that "The typical weekly schedule is school during the homework and homework at night," while "the typical weekend schedule is parties at night and homework, especially on Sundays, during the day." If anything, social life at Smith seems to be centered around the "houses," which are renovated mansions serving as self-contained dormitories. Freshmen are assigned randomly to a house, though there is the possibility to move to another house. There are various housing options, including substance-free housing, a French house, and an in-house dining co-op house.

Indeed, Smith's housing is exceptionally nice. Although the average single measures around 9' x 10', while the average double is 12' x 14', individual rooms vary, and there are many more singles than doubles in most houses, meaning that students will have singles for at least two years out of their four at Smith. Most houses have their own dining halls, parlors, kitchens and laundry rooms. In addition, many of the houses overlook the scenic Paradise Pond, which sports a waterfall and is hemmed with trees and spacious green lawns.

While room draws, house transfer requests and sometimes roommate assignment are handled through school administration, administration does not usually have a direct presence in the houses. Instead, two senior students, the head resident and the house coordinator, are responsible for the day-to-day running of the house, giving it an intimacy that is not usually found in large dormitories. "Every house is like a family," enthuses one student. "The house system enables us to be very close and be life-long friends."

Feminism and awareness

Smith is a women's college, and it shows. A quick glance through Smith's largest publication, *The Sophian*, reveals a sharp awareness of gender issues, as well as a rare and refreshing openness of discourse about issues such as lesbianism and transsexuality. "Public Safety's new self-defense course aims to empower women," says an article,

while another opines that "transgender tolerance [. . .] can be explained just as carefully now as civil unions were back then." One current freshman feels that Smith being a women's college shapes life at Smith. When asked what Smith offers that another college couldn't, she replied, "It makes me more confident about myself being a woman."

> "[Smith] makes me more confident about myself being a woman."

Indeed, the same confidence lies in Smith itself, which brims with all the beloved traditions of a venerable old institution, while at the same time possessing a bold modernity in its ideas. I have roots in the past, it seems to proclaim, but my eyes are very much on the future. For the similarly bold, motivated and intelligent, Smith may well be the perfect choice.—*Sijia Song*

FYI
If you come to Smith, what should you definitely bring? "An open mind."
What is the typical weekend schedule? "Parties at night and homework, especially on Sundays, during the day."
If there's one thing you could change about Smith, what would it be? "I would not change anything. It would not be Smith if something changed."

Tufts University

Address: Bendetson Hall 2
The Green, Medford, MA
02155
Phone: 617-627-3170
E-mail address:
undergraduate.admissions@
tufts.edu
Web site URL: www.tufts.edu
Year Founded: 1852
Private or Public: Private
Religious Affiliation:
None
Location: Suburban
Number of Applicants:
15,042
Percent Accepted: 27%
**Percent Accepted who
enroll:** 33%
Number Entering: 1,314
**Number of Transfers
Accepted each Year:** 148
Middle 50% SAT range: M:
680–750, CR: 680–750,
Wr: 680–760
Middle 50% ACT range:
30–33
**Early admission program
EA/ED/None:** ED

**Percentage accepted
through EA or ED:**
Unreported
EA and ED deadline:
1-Nov
Regular Deadline: 1-Jan
Application Fee: $70
**Full time Undergraduate
enrollment:** 5,164
Total enrollment: 10,252
Percent Male: 49%
Percent Female: 51%
**Total Percent Minority or
Unreported:** 30%
Percent African-American:
5%
**Percent Asian/Pacific
Islander:** 13%
Percent Hispanic: 6%
Percent Native-American:
<1%
Percent International:
14%
**Percent in-state/out of
state:** 33%/67%
Percent from Public HS:
77%
Retention Rate: 96%

Graduation Rate 4-year:
92%
Graduation Rate 6-year:
92%
**Percent Undergraduates
in On-campus housing:**
64%
**Number of official organized
extracurricular
organizations:** 250
3 Most popular majors:
International Relations,
Biology, Political Science
Student/Faculty ratio: 7:1
Average Class Size: 20
**Percent of students going to
grad school:** Unreported
Tuition and Fees: $39,432
**In-State Tuition and Fees if
different:** No difference
Cost for Room and Board:
$10,746
**Percent receiving financial
aid out of those who apply,
first year:** 39%
**Percent receiving financial
aid among all students:**
40%

The geographical region between the cities of Somerville and Cambridge boasts some of the brightest and most talented young students in the world. Called the "Brainpower Triangle," its borders are delineated by the location of three of the top institutions in America—Harvard University, Massachusetts Institute of Technology, and Tufts University. Tufts, a private institution, is renowned for its internationalism, study abroad programs, and of course, its giant elephant mascot. Tufts is located on Walnut Hill in Medford, where diligent Jumbos trek up every morning, rain or shine (or sleet, snow, hail).

An Experimental College

Tufts is divided into 10 schools, two of which are devoted to undergraduate studies: the School of Arts and Sciences and the School of Engineering. Tufts boasts a rigorous undergraduate program focusing on interdisciplinary studies. It's no surprise then, that International Relations, which combines

history, politics, humanities, and economics, is the most popular major. "I loved being an IR major—I got to learn everything I was interested in," one recent graduate said. The IR program is a department on its own, but it also "borrows" faculty from 16 other departments. But don't be fooled by the breadth of the major, because it's definitely not lacking in depth. While most majors only require six semesters of foreign languages, IR requires eight semesters.

IR is not the only area in which Tufts undergraduates excel. In addition to other programs that are typical of other liberal arts colleges, Tufts has a unique program called The Experimental College. "The oldest organization of its kind in the United States," the Ex College offers over 100 courses that explore issues of current importance and interdisciplinary courses that are not offered in the more orthodox departments. This includes the peer-taught first-year seminar programs called Explorations and Perspectives. Seniors and juniors teach these classes and are awarded graduation credit for their leadership. Some past favorites include "Beyond BeBop: Miles and Coltrane," and "Adolescent Fiction."

This involvement of the students in teaching is indicative of the Tufts academic experience as a whole. Tufts has a student-faculty ratio of seven to one, and classes rarely exceed 100 students. Most of the classes are discussion style and teaching assistants are rarely needed. "During my junior year I got to know my professors really well. They're very approachable and I've gone out to drink with one of them once!" exclaimed one senior. The caliber of professors that work at Tufts is top-notch and something that the students consider themselves lucky to have access to. Notable faculty include a former American Psychological Association president and many Nobel Prize recipients.

The Pen Is Mightier than the Jumbo

Tufts claims the honor of the first American football game between two American colleges. Although Tufts was victorious against Harvard in 1875, athletics have been somewhat lacking in recent years. Tufts is a member of the NCAA Division III in sports and is also a member of the New England Small College Athletic Conference. While the mighty Jumbos excel in particular games such as squash and sailing, athletics is not their forte. This might be attributed either to the fact that Tufts does not offer scholarships for athletes, or "because our mascot is a gigantic elephant," one student speculated. While varsity athletics may lack in school spirit, have no fear if you are a sports buff. Tufts has a 70,000 square-foot indoor sports center which includes four tennis courts, a state-of-the-art fitness center, and a six-lane indoor pool and a sauna—everything you need to stay in shape.

> "[A cappella] is everywhere. You can't escape it."

If you think that trekking up the hill every morning is enough exercise for you, there are plenty of other organizations to be involved in at Tufts. If you're a singer, you can join one of Tuft's six a cappella groups. "It's everywhere," said one nonsinger. "You can't escape it." Many of these groups are award-winning and go on national tours over breaks. For in-

stance, the Beelzebubs, or Bubs, as they are commonly called, had the esteemed a cappella honor of opening for the renowned Rockapella group this winter at their concert in downtown Boston.

If singing's not your thing, perhaps you can find your niche in one of the numerous on-campus publications. The *Tufts Daily* is where most Jumbos get their news from, and writers for the *Daily* have gone on after Tufts to be writers for the *New York Times* and the *Boston Herald*. Those looking to do journalism on the side can opt to write for the *Tufts Observer*, a weekly magazine. "The amount of work and commitment I have for the *Observer* is great—it doesn't take over my life, but it's enough for me to take it seriously," one writer said. One of the most anticipated publications on campus is *The Zamboni*, "Tufts' only intentionally funny magazine." This 16-page tabloid is issued six times during the year, and while reviews of it are mixed among the student population ("THEY seem to think it's funny"), it is your survival guide to the ins and outs of the Tufts social scene.

Fakes, Frats, and Forests

While many students may cite the school's proximity to Boston as one of the reasons why they chose to go to Tufts, in reality, most of the partying takes place on campus. Boston "sucks for underage kids" due to its strict ID-ing policy and underclassmen do not enjoy the same level of leniency with underage drinking that one may find in other big cities like New York. "Having a good fake is essential," one sophomore said. Once they are 21, Tufts kids often frequent the bars in the Medford area—the Somerville Theater is good for musical groups, and there are a few 19+ clubs that are good for a night of dancing. If you do make it to Boston for a night of fun, most of the places to go are on Lansdowne Street, where many clubs and bars are lined up for convenient "hopping around." "Avalon is the best one," said one Lansdowne Street enthusiast. "On Thursday and Friday it is 19 plus and they play really good music!"

There's plenty of partying to do on campus as well. Most of them are "keggers" thrown by frats. Tufts is very Greek-friendly, housing 11 fraternities and five sororities. While the sororities seldom throw wild, crazy parties, the frat scene is very prominent on campus as they organize large theme parties throughout the year. The Tufts administration has been "chill" about the underage drinking and partying that goes on at these frats and sees Greek life as an opportunity for Tufts students to form a community of their own and to exemplify leadership. However, students have noted that recently they have been stricter about alcohol violations than in the past.

Unfortunately, doing kegstands and going to clubs can get a little old after four years. So Tufts students take the opportunity to use the Loj, a retreat destination that is owned by Tufts and open to all of the Tufts community. Located in Woodstock,

New Hampshire, the Loj offers opportunities to go skiing, hiking, apple picking, rock climbing, and swimming. To get involved in maintaining and running trips to the Loj, one can join the Tufts Mountain Club, an outdoor club dedicated to "exploring the great outdoors, physically exerting yourself," says a recent alum. So whether you have the study hard, party harder mentality of a frat brother or if you like to muse about philosophy over a fire and a glass of wine, Tufts has a little bit of something for everyone.—*Lee Komeda*

FYI

If you come to Tufts, you better bring "about 10 foldable umbrellas because chances are, you'll lose half of them and your roommate will steal the other half."

If I could change one thing about Tufts, I would change "the school color and mascot: Jumbo is just weird."

What's the typical weekend schedule? "On any given weekend you can probably find people going out to the local pubs on Thursday and Fridays. Saturday you might hit up a concert or a play and then head over to a frat house for a themed party. Sunday, if you can manage to get yourself out of bed, STUDY!"

Three things every student should do before graduating from Tufts are "take a special someone to the Library roof, have Sunday lunch at Dewick, and go to Spring Fling."

University of Massachusetts / Amherst

Address: 37 Mather Drive Amherst, MA 01003-9291
Phone: 413-545-0222
E-mail address: mail@admission.umass.edu
Web site URL: www.umass.edu
Year Founded: 1863
Private or Public: Public
Religious Affiliation: None
Location: Suburban
Number of Applicants: 27,138
Percent Accepted: 66%
Percent Accepted who enroll: 24%
Number Entering: 4,272
Number of Transfers Accepted each Year: 1,989
Middle 50% SAT range: M: 520–630, CR: 510–610, Wr: Unreported
Middle 50% ACT range: Unreported
Early admission program EA/ED/None: EA

Percentage accepted through EA or ED: 25%
EA and ED deadline: 1-Nov
Regular Deadline: 15-Jan
Application Fee: $40
Full time Undergraduate enrollment: 20,114
Total enrollment: 25,873
Percent Male: 51%
Percent Female: 49%
Total Percent Minority or Unreported: 29%
Percent African-American: 5%
Percent Asian/Pacific Islander: 8%
Percent Hispanic: 4%
Percent Native-American: 0%
Percent International: 1%
Percent in-state/out of state: 81%/19%
Percent from Public HS: Unreported
Retention Rate: 86%
Graduation Rate 4-year: 51%

Graduation Rate 6-year: 68%
Percent Undergraduates in On-campus housing: 63%
Number of official organized extracurricular organizations: 280
3 Most popular majors: Biological and Physical Sciences, English Language and Literature, Psychology
Student/Faculty ratio: 18:1
Average Class Size: 25
Percent of students going to grad school: Unreported
Tuition and Fees: $21,729
In-State Tuition and Fees if different: $10,232
Cost for Room and Board: $8,114
Percent receiving financial aid out of those who apply, first year: 63%
Percent receiving financial aid among all students: 53%

Located in the largest community of the Hampshire County, UMass Amherst welcomes every year more than 4000 freshmen. The campus is located in the small town of Amherst, MA, which rests 90 miles from Boston and 175 miles from New York City. UMass Amherst is part of the five public university system of the Commonwealth of Massachusetts, which includes UMass Boston, UMass Dartmouth, and UMass Lowell. While being a large research university with more than 20,000 undergraduates, students seem to agree that there is a place for everyone at UMass.

Party School! Or Party school?

Although for a long time UMass Amherst has maintained the reputation of a large "party school," students say it is a matter of choice and relativity. Students note that while there are parties every night in different dorms, at off-campus houses, and especially at fraternities, and some people start their weekend early, there is no pressure to do so. People party as much as they want and as much as they can afford. "Social life in college is all up to the individual. There are plenty of opportunities to be social but people don't have to be," comments a freshman. One student points out that UMass Amherst might seem like a party school because it is bigger in size, and therefore able to host more parties, but that in comparison to smaller schools, the ratio is the same.

Speaking of parties and weekend fun, the Greek scene is very popular at UMass Amherst. Parties organized at fraternities and sororities often have long waiting lines and there is an admission fee for most of them, a student noted. A considerable amount of the student population participates, since there are ten fraternities and sororities on campus. And if you are worried about the hazing to mark your initiation in the Greek life, don't be. There is no hazing allowed for fraternities or sororities at UMass Amherst. That's right, it is against school policy to make freshmen haze for acceptance; it is also against state law.

Yet, while fraternities and athletics cover a large part of the social scene, students report enjoying the size of the school, as it does not allow for a dominant group, or specific cliques to be formed, since there are so many different people. Also, the number of students makes it easy to meet new people, and feel like you are in a new place every day, a freshman commented.

If you are worried of walking around the campus at night while coming back from a party, students said that there is no need. Apart from intoxicated students coming back, students report feeling safe and able to walk at night. One student commented, "It is a safe place, you just need to look out for drunk kids doing stupid stuff."

If parties on campus are not of your liking, you can always leave the campus and explore Amherst. While students noted that Amherst's scenery is certainly not urban, many love it! Students agreed that there are a lot of good pizza places to eat around town, and great coffee shops. However, students complain that there aren't enough shops close to their residences. One freshman noted, "It is a hassle to take the bus everywhere to go shopping." And while some upperclassmen have cars, students said that it is uncommon for freshmen.

Five at The Price of One

One unique aspect of the academics experience at UMass Amherst is the ability to attend five schools at the same time, students comment. Through the Five College Consortium, which is a partnership between five schools which include Smith, Mount Holyoke, Amherst, and Hampshire Colleges, UMass Amherst students, upon the completion of their first semester, can take classes for credit at the other four colleges. Students comment that in doing so they have the chance to broaden the range of people they know and friends they meet. What's more, students can have their meals, and use resources such as libraries, and borrowing books at all colleges.

"The only way to get a desired result in class is to go to every class, pay attention, do homework, and study hard," one freshman says. Students report that studying and homework take up most of their time. They agree that the party scene is present, but mostly on weekends. Most students have class every day, from Monday to Friday, and they study during the day on weekends, and party later.

Almost 90 majors are offered to students, as well as the possibility to minor in distinct fields of study. If students feel that none of the majors fully encompasses all their interests and future career paths, they can construct their own program of study, through the Bachelor's Degree with Individual Concentration, which allows students to designed their own major.

Most people though report finding something they love at UMass Amherst and even enjoying the general requirements they have to fulfill in order to get their degree. These requirements include one class in writing, basic math skills, analytical reasoning, biological and physical world, social world, interdisciplinary courses, social and cultural diversity. However, students report finding it easy to fulfill these requirements, even though only one of the courses taken in their major department counts towards their requirements, and they add that they can even take many classes that interest them. They do however express unhappiness at finding that there is a great focus on the research aspect of the school, and not as much undergraduate focus as they expected. One freshman comments, "I was surprised that Teacher's Assistants teach my discussion sections."

Minutemen Cribs

UMass Amherst students are diverse in their personalities and interests, and so are their places of residence. A freshman commented that there are distinct personalities and characteristics associated with each dorm, such as "the athletes'" dorm, "the blonde-girl" dorm, the "party" dorm, the "geek" dorm. Many students are assigned to specific dorms on the basis of interest and major for students who declare their major upon matriculation through the Talent Advancement Programs. TAP is designed to group students with similar interests, so that it is easier for the RAs to organize activities and trips specifically oriented towards the students' interests. Many students reported this to be something they would change about their school, because it disables them from befriending people of different interests. For freshmen that matriculate with an undeclared major, residences are assigned through a lottery system, where students rank where they want to live on campus by building during orientation. There are five living areas at UMass Amherst from which students can choose to live in, Southwest, Central, Orchard Hill, North East, and Sylvan. They all vary in architecture and organization. Each of them has its pros and cons, a student commented. While freshmen don't complain about their residences, they agreed that most of the upperclassmen do not live on campus, since the area around offers an accessible residential situation.

In the midst of these five residential areas, UMass students can choose between a variety of housing options ranging from gender free and same-sex housing, co-ed suites, alcohol-free twenty-four hour quiet floors, as well as the Thatcher Language program, which is targeted towards students seeking to achieve proficiency in a foreign language. And for students who don't want to live in a dorm anymore but still want to remain on campus, the university offers the North Apartment program which enables students to rent an apartment right on campus. Groups of students, co-ed or same-sex can get together and apply for housing in these apartments.

> **"Everyone can fit in somewhere at UMass. Go Minutemen!"**

Most students are content with the food served in the dining halls. There are four dining halls on the campus, and all students can have their meals at either of them, or at any of other colleges' dining halls. Students have the choice of having an unlimited meal plan or a more restricted one. Students highly recommended the unlimited one. One freshman noted, "The dining hall has incredible food and a lot of diversity among the meals. There is sushi, stir fry, a sandwich line, a grill station, a salad bar, a vegetarian section and a main meal line that changes throughout the day. Something for everyone." And if you get tired of cafeteria food, you can always use your flex swipe at the on-campus stores and restaurants, though the swipes don't work in the local businesses.

The University has implemented many reconstructions of residences and academic buildings, in their dedication to emphasize the academic aspect of the university, and subdue the rumors of its party-oriented nature, a student suggested. Southwest, one of the residences, is in the process of being renovated and should be finished by next year, a student commented.

As far as substance abuse goes, drugs and alcohol are strictly prohibited by school rules in all the dormitories, but students say that it depends on their RA's policies; some are more lenient than others. And while laws and restrictions apply, a lot of people drink but certainly not everyone. Students commented that while most parties are thrown by upperclassmen that have an easier access to alcohol, it is fairly easy for freshmen and sophomores to have access to alcohol as well.

If you are used to warm and predictable whether, you might want to reconsider your wardrobe. New England weather can be harsh, so bring your jacket, scarf and gloves! As one freshman comments, "If I could change one thing about UMass Amherst I'd

put it in a warm climate, it is damn cold and windy." Yet, while the weather might be challenging, many students love their experience. As a freshman stated, "The atmosphere in Amherst is great. Everyone is very friendly and happy to be at UMass. There is a lot of diversity and clubs. Everyone can fit in somewhere at UMass. Go Minutemen!"—*Iva Popa*

FYI
If you come to UMass Amherst you better bring "snacks, laptop, and an alarm clock."
One thing I would change about my school is "adding more stores on campus."
Three things every student should do before graduating from UMass Amherst: "Meet with a professor, go to athletic events, and meet as many people as possible."

Wellesley College

Address: 106 Central Street Wellesley, MA 02481-8203
Phone: 781-283-2270
E-mail address: admission@wellesley.edu
Web site URL: www.wellesley.edu
Year Founded: 1870
Private or Public: Private
Religious Affiliation: None
Location: Suburban
Number of Applicants: 4,001
Percent Accepted: 36%
Percent Accepted who enroll: 41%
Number Entering: 596
Number of Transfers Accepted each Year: 29
Middle 50% SAT range: M: 630–725, CR: 640–740, Wr: 650–740
Middle 50% ACT range: 28–32
Early admission program EA/ED/None: ED

Percentage accepted through EA or ED: 20%
EA and ED deadline: 1-Nov
Regular Deadline: 15-Jan
Application Fee: $50/free online
Full time Undergraduate enrollment: 2,190
Total enrollment: 2,344
Percent Male: 0%
Percent Female: 100%
Total Percent Minority or Unreported: 39%
Percent African-American: 6%
Percent Asian/Pacific Islander: 26%
Percent Hispanic: 7%
Percent Native-American: <1%
Percent International: 8%
Percent in-state/out of state: 12%/88%
Percent from Public HS: 64%
Retention Rate: 96%

Graduation Rate 4-year: 85%
Graduation Rate 6-year: 91%
Percent Undergraduates in On-campus housing: 97%
Number of official organized extracurricular organizations: 160
3 Most popular majors: Economics, Political Science, English
Student/Faculty ratio: 9:1
Average Class Size: 15
Percent of students going to grad school: 80%
Tuition and Fees: $36,640
In-State Tuition and Fees if different: No difference
Cost for Room and Board: $11,336
Percent receiving financial aid out of those who apply, first year: 55%
Percent receiving financial aid among all students: 59%

In 1870, Henry and Pauline Durant founded Wellesley to give young women a college education as rigorous as that of their male peers. Since then, Wellesley has graduated a large number of famous alumnae, including former Secretary of State

Madeleine Albright and Secretary of State Hillary Clinton. Although the college's cachet may have diminished a little after the spread of coeducation, the passion, drive, and college pride of Wellesley students is as strong as ever.

Bankers and Bluestockings

At Wellesley, schoolwork is king—or should we say, queen. Its liberal arts curriculum expects students to fulfill writing, quantitative reasoning, and foreign language requirements, and take classes in eight of nine distribution areas. In addition, they need to meet the multicultural requirement, studying one unit's worth of non-Western culture. Despite the breadth of the curriculum, students say that the variety of classes makes fulfilling requirements both easy and enjoyable. As one first-year said, "Even if you're not interested in a certain field, you can find something you enjoy." A junior who had completed her requirements sophomore year concurred: "It's really not difficult to fulfill anything."

With 30 departmental and 21 interdepartmental majors, Wellesley offers over 1,000 courses in a diverse selection of academic fields—and Wellesley women love the intellectual buffet. Students were enthusiastic about a wide variety of classes, including seminars on environmentalism, the History of Western Music, and "1968," a course devoted entirely to—you guessed it—the year 1968. One first-year student said she had met people doubling majors like "biology and political science [or] Latin American studies and music." Students agree, however, that the economics department is a big presence on campus. According to data released by the Wellesley College Office for Public Affairs, 15 percent of the Wellesley class of 2009 majored in economics and nearly 30 percent went to work in business after graduation. "A lot of Econ people are trying to go into banking and finance," a junior explained. Other popular majors include political science and psychology. Although students may not declare majors in math and hard sciences in droves, one science major praised the all-female environment for cultivating interest in physics, chemistry, and math, fields that are traditionally underrepresented among women.

Students also praised the professors, who "really want students to talk to them and come to them with any problems," as one junior said. With a 9:1 student-faculty ratio, classes tend toward the intimate. This same junior named the small class sizes as her favorite thing about Wellesley's academics: "I think it makes you a lot more into your work, wanting to participate and be a part of the class." In addition, Wellesley professors tend to be both highly knowledgeable and able to transmit their knowledge to their students. Some have even written the textbooks for the classes they teach. This marriage of availability and fluency in their subject matter makes the professors one of the college's greatest assets.

> "I've met nerdy music people and nerdy politics people . . . Everyone here is nerdy about something."

The Wellesley workload is no joke. Academics take priority over socializing and extracurricular activities, and it shows. "During the week it's just silent, because everyone here is studying," a first-year said. Still, challenging classes don't translate into C's across the board. In 100- and 200-level classes with ten or more students, professors are required to create a curve with a B+ average. (In 300-level classes or higher, or in classes with fewer than ten students, no curve exists.) This works to students' advantage in math and science classes, while the humanities and social science departments tend to · "scale down" the averages because their students usually receive higher grades. As one psychology major described, straight-A students are "either incredibly energetic and brilliant—or they study constantly, don't really socialize, and are otherwise psychotic."

Better get crazy!

Suburban Riches, Boston Fun

Wellesley is a small, affluent town outside of Boston. Students say there's not too much interaction between students and residents; and as one student put it, "I think the extent of our relationship with the town is walking into town to CVS and to the bank." Two problems keep the college from embracing its town. First, the average college student doesn't have the money for the expensive restaurants and boutiques that the town of Wellesley offers. Second, the town is, in the words of a junior, "not a real town." Simply put, Wellesley's just not big enough to support the pizza places, concert halls, and dance clubs that would draw student interest.

But while students may consider the rich suburban-family demographics of Wellesley a drawback, the town does have some perks. Students are able to find well-paying jobs easily. Babysitting is especially popular— "The people in town are so rich, they pay really well," a junior said.

But despite living in the suburbs, students still have the city just a short ride away. Wellesley's proximity to Boston keeps students connected to urban living. The city is "very accessible" from Wellesley, and it offers good entertainment to young women about town. As one student said, "Boston always has concerts, shopping, whatever you want to do." Trips to Boston aren't exclusive to upperclasswomen. All students flock to Boston for weekend entertainment.

Wellesley Women, Cutting Loose

While an all-female student body may sound like a drag to some, Wellesley women know that single-sex education doesn't lack fun. The Wellesley Senate bus runs a route from Wellesley to the Boston-Cambridge area and back every hour. While MIT frat parties are the most popular destination, a number of colleges in the Boston area host good parties, and students choose which to attend based on the people they know at a given school. The bus goes both ways as well: "We have parties here, and guys will come from Harvard, MIT, Babson, BU, BC, Tufts . . ."

While some Wellesley students celebrate the wealth of parties in the Boston area as an opportunity to meet new people, form a larger community, and meet guys, others dislike the artificiality such party-based interactions promote. One sophomore said, "Personally, only seeing men in a frat-party atmosphere tends to reinforce negative stereotypes about them—that is, they're usually trying to hook up with girls" rather than anything more. Because of the lack of male-female interaction in a more day-to-day casual environment, "it takes a very determined individual to go out and make male friends" as opposed to just hooking up. A first-year commented that her good male friends were the boyfriends of girls on campus.

Of course, one doesn't need men to have friends, or even to date. The lesbian and bisexual community is visible and active on campus. The largest annual party at Wellesley is the Dyke Ball, which began as a prom for students who were unable to attend their high school proms due to their sexual orientation. The Ball is now a campus-wide bash to which all Wellesley students can come and cut loose.

Wellesley students definitely don't need to make the trek to find close friends. Wellesley students will sometimes say that they don't need sororities "because we're all one big sorority." One first-year said she decided to matriculate at Wellesley because of how nice the students were: "Everyone is friendly. Upperclassmen will give you directions, help you with your homework." In addition, the sisterly atmosphere creates a level of freedom in intellectual and social self-expression that many students did not have in high school: "I've met nerdy music people and nerdy politics people . . . Everyone here is nerdy about something. That might be our defining feature. Even the cool kids—there's something like, 'Oh my God, I love physics!' or 'Astronomy is the coolest thing ever!'"

Diversity at Wellesley is more than intellectual. In race, socioeconomic status, political affiliation, and sexual orientation, Wellesley students represent a wide range of experiences. One student remarked, "There've been a ton of times, in a party or in a room, where I've realized I'm the only white person there." Another mentioned, "I have friends who are really rich and really poor." And while the political climate does tend toward the liberal, there is a conservative presence on campus. One first-year student said, "One of my roommates is a Ron Paul supporter, so that was interesting, what with the four pictures of Hillary Clinton on my wall."

Four Flavors at Every Meal

In a Wellesley student's first year, she is assigned a dorm. Each floor has a Resident Assistant, who is a student, and a Resident Director, an adult who usually lives in the dorm with her family. The strictness of dorm policy varies, depending on the RA and RD. After the first year, a lottery system determines what order students get to choose their rooms. Seniors get the first group of random numbers, then juniors, and then sophomores. Students said juniors and seniors are pretty much guaranteed singles. Dorms don't have official themes, but each have their own characteristics. Some dorms are considered party dorms, while another is known for being more reclusive, and still another is the "lesbian social scene" dorm. Students said the new dorms by the science center have larger rooms and quieter surroundings, but not as much character as the older buildings.

While students at many other colleges complain of monotonous meals and poorly cooked food, Wellesley women are positive about their dining halls. Wellesley students are on one of the most flexible meal plans possible—they can eat at any dining hall, at any time, as many times a day as they want. And nearly every dorm, as well as the student center, features a dining hall. Although each hall is supposed to have a theme, some are "hard to decipher." As one first-year student explained, "One of them is supposed to be comfort food, but they serve basically the same food my dorm serves, which is supposed to be eclectic cuisine." Despite the sameness, a student said, "I think that in comparison to other schools, the food is quite good, and the management does a good job of listening to student suggestions."

Apparently, one alumna thought that the dining halls lacked something, so she donated money so that every hall would have four different flavors of ice cream every day, at every meal. Do you need another reason to apply to Wellesley?—*Finola Prendergast*

FYI

If you come to Wellesley, you'd better bring "a nice dress, because there are a lot of times where you need to wear a dress."

What's the typical weekend schedule? "If you're one of those people who's into partying, you'd probably go off campus to Harvard or MIT Friday or Saturday night, and study Sunday. Or go to Boston and shop and eat out."

If I could change one thing about Wellesley, I'd have "more on-campus social life instead of stuff in Boston."

Three things every student at Wellesley should do before graduating are "see the campus from the top of Galen-Stone Tower, skinny dip in Lake Waban, and swing next to the Chapel."

Wheaton College

Address: 26 East Main Street Norton, MA 02766
Phone: 508-286-8251
E-mail address: admission@wheatoncollege.edu
Web site URL: www.wheatoncollege.edu
Year Founded: 1834
Private or Public: Private
Religious Affiliation: None
Location: Rural
Number of Applicants: 3,833
Percent Accepted: 37%
Percent Accepted who enroll: 30%
Number Entering: 418
Number of Transfers Accepted each Year: 28
Middle 50% SAT range: M: 560–650, CR: 580–670, Wr: Unreported
Middle 50% ACT range: 25–29
Early admission program EA/ED/None: ED

Percentage accepted through EA or ED: 66%
EA and ED deadline: 1-Nov
Regular Deadline: 15-Jan
Application Fee: $55
Full time Undergraduate enrollment: 1,552
Total enrollment: 1,552
Percent Male: 40%
Percent Female: 60%
Total Percent Minority or Unreported: 11%
Percent African-American: 5%
Percent Asian/Pacific Islander: 3%
Percent Hispanic: 3%
Percent Native-American: 0%
Percent International: 3%
Percent in-state/out of state: 35%/65%
Percent from Public HS: 63%
Retention Rate: 88%

Graduation Rate 4-year: 79%
Graduation Rate 6-year: 79%
Percent Undergraduates in On-campus housing: 93%
Number of official organized extracurricular organizations: 60
3 Most popular majors: Economics, English, Psychology
Student/Faculty ratio: 10:1
Average Class Size: 15
Percent of students going to grad school: 48%
Tuition and Fees: $36,430
In-State Tuition and Fees if different: No difference
Cost for Room and Board: $8,640
Percent receiving financial aid out of those who apply, first year: 70%
Percent receiving financial aid among all students: 64%

Wheaton is a small liberal arts school located in the sleepy town of Norton, Massachusetts. It boasts a challenging and varied academic program where students can take classes in everything from dreams to globalization. The

Wheaton community is a close-knit group where even the RAs just want to be your friend. Wheaton students have a thriving extracurricular and social scene that is greatly benefited by the campus's location between Providence and Boston, two cities just begging to be explored by car-owning and train-hopping Wheaties.

The Right Balance

Most Wheaton students are very happy with the academic environment of their campus. "The academics are just right," said one freshman. "I'm not overstressed, but I'm being challenged. And here we have the ability to do well in school and be involved in other activities, too." Popular majors include English and education. Education, along with the natural sciences, is said to be one of the hardest majors because the program involves student teaching and requires that students double major. Wheaton is thought of as more of a humanities school, but the administration is beginning an increased focus on science. They have implemented a plan to rebuild all the science buildings on campus by 2014 and are seen as being very encouraging of students pursuing science majors.

Classes are small, usually 10 to 19 students, except in some introductory lectures. Students say that professors are very committed to getting to know them and being a part of their intellectual growth. "One of my professors gave us extra credit just for coming to her office hours so she could get to know us," said one Wheatie. There are no TAs at Wheaton, further enhancing the personalized touch. Though the professors are friendly and helpful, they are tough. Students don't think there is much grade inflation at all at Wheaton and also report relatively few curves. They stress that one must work hard to do well.

Wheaton students say their distribution requirements, called "foundation courses," are reasonable and they have an interesting array of classes in which to fill them. Foundation courses include a first-year seminar, English 101, a math course, two semesters of a foreign language, and one semester of "Beyond the West," i.e., a class that deals with a culture outside of Western society. In first-year seminars, groups of 20 freshmen become acclimated to Wheaton academic life in a laid-back atmosphere while studying topics that vary from "Surgeons and Shamans" to "The Rituals of Dinner." Wheaton also has a program called Connections, where students are able to choose a set of related courses that interest them. Examples of Connections include "Human Biology and Movement," "Modern Italy," and "Music: the Medium and the Message." Students say the Connections courses are an interesting way to fulfill requirements. Wheaties also take advantage of the fact that their college is a part of the 12-college consortium that includes, among others, Amherst, Bowdoin, Wellesley, and Dartmouth. Wheaton students can attend a college in the consortium for a semester or a year. Wheaton also offers numerous and very popular opportunities for study abroad.

A Perfect New England Family

Nearly every student has high praises for the sense of community at Wheaton. "One of the things I noticed at accepted students' day that I didn't notice at others schools was how friendly everyone was," one freshman said. Wheaton upperclassmen are especially enthusiastic about making sure new students feel welcome and are aware of the importance of not making novice Wheatie mistakes. During freshman orientation, upperclassmen herd confused freshmen into the chapel where they begin to chant the incoming class's graduation year. After the chanting, an upperclassman runs through the chapel and squirts water on an unsuspecting frosh who automatically inherits this illustrious job. Besides being simply funny, this tradition emphasizes Wheaton's fun and family-like atmosphere. The fact that Wheaton's student body numbers fewer than 1,600 seems to be an important reason for this. "I like that it is a small school because I can get to know a lot of people well, but still see a few new faces every day," reported one girl. Additionally, "the importance of acceptance and friendship are stressed at Wheaton," says one Wheatie.

In a testament to their widespread acceptance of difference, students are quick to say that there is no "typical" Wheaton student. When pressed, they will admit that most students are middle- or upper-class and from Massachusetts, Maine, Connecticut, and surprisingly, California. "For some reason, lots of people in California know about Wheaton. I guess they like small liberal arts schools," explained one Wheatie. Another trait that bonds Wheaton students together is being physically fit. A large segment of students is involved in athletic endeavors that vary from varsity sports to the equestrian team to intramurals. There are no sororities and fraternities at Wheaton, and many say that the *a cappella* groups function as a more positive version of the Greek system. *A cappella* is very popular at Wheaton, as are a wide range of other extracurricular activities, especially community service groups. "Wheaton has a lot to offer—there's always something to join," explains one Wheatie.

Though they don't like to be typecast, Wheaton students as a whole can be summed up as both studious and typical preppy New England kids. They seem particularly fond of The North Face fleeces, colorful rain boots, and for the female students, designer purses. Wheaton students admit that their campus is not incredibly diverse, though the administration is working hard to change that. Wheaton boasts a thriving cultural center, the Marshall Center for Intercultural Learning, and is involved in a scholarship program called the Posse Foundation. New York City minority students receive scholarships to Wheaton in groups called posses, which helps them feel less isolated while increasing Wheaton's racial diversity.

Road Trippers

On any given weekend, a large contingent of the Wheaton student body can be found in Boston, which is 40 minutes away, or Providence, about 20. Transportation couldn't be easier since many students have cars and the school offers a shuttle that runs every 30 minutes to a nearby train station. Wheaties love hitting the restaurants, theaters, and club scenes of these two New England cities. The administration encourages their students to take advantage of what their excellent location has to offer. Through the Boston and Providence Connections programs, students pay just five dollars for dinner and a concert or play on select nights. A premium outlet mall is very close to campus, giving Wheaton fashionistas yet another attractive weekend option.

Wheaton students' obvious devotion to Boston and Providence trips shouldn't be seen as a sign that there is nothing to do at Wheaton. Some students admitted that some weekends on campus are a little slow, but there are usually a wide variety of on-campus activities to choose from. The Balfour-Hood Campus Center hosts well-attended theme parties in its large lobby, called the Atrium. Wheaton often hosts concerts as well. Recently, students were surprised when a subsidized concert by a Persian pop star, which they wrote off as random and amusing, was

packed with outsiders who happily shelled out $40 a ticket.

> "I know that this might seem pretty lame, but Wheaton really would not function in the same way without the common bond and sense of belonging that the students and professors share."

Wheaton has a campus bar, the Loft, where students can get burgers, pizza, and alcohol "if you're over 21 or have an ID that says you are." Wheaton's 11 theme houses also throw popular parties. The Lyon's Den is the campus coffee shop, and serves as a popular hangout and a more laid-back alternative to the Loft. Though many social events seem to revolve around alcohol, students report not feeling much pressure either way. The administration is fairly lax on students who do drink, and Wheaties are very accepting of students who don't.

Endless Food, and Not Just Wheaties

Most students have good things to say about Wheaton's dining system. They have unlimited access to the two dining halls, one of which stays open until midnight. Pizza and ice cream seem to be available at all times, though there are more nutritious family style options available as well. Unlimited access makes some students grow weary of the selection. "I like the food, but sometimes I get tired of it," said one girl. When this happens, students head to the nearby town of Mansfield to eat at chains like Subway.

The campus is pretty, secluded, and very Ivy League-esque with ivy-covered brick and a quaint pond that surrounds the Chase Dining Hall. The campus is not very big, which adds to the community atmosphere and also helps Wheaties easily get where they need to go. Students like their dorms when there are a proper number of people living in them. Some freshmen find themselves in forced triples on Lower Campus. Upperclassmen, on the other hand, often live on Upper Campus in newly renovated dorms that "are like hotels," said one envious freshman.

Wheaton students are overwhelmingly very pleased with their college. "I know that this might seem pretty lame, but Wheaton really would not function in the same way without the common bond and sense of belonging that the students and professors share," said one Wheatie. The combination of Wheaton's strong sense of community, challenging but manageable academics, and prime location make it a great place to spend four years.—*Keneisha Sinclair*

FYI

If you come to Wheaton, you'd better bring "rain boots and a DVD player because there's no cable."

What is the typical weekend schedule? "Napping after last class on Friday, trips to Boston and Providence, dances at the theme houses and concerts at the Loft, playing in or going to see a game, and lots of homework on Sunday."

If I could change one thing about Wheaton, I'd "make Norton more exciting."

Three things every student at Wheaton should do before graduating are "jump in the pond, study abroad or do a college exchange, and get really involved in a Wheaton extracurricular activity."

Williams College

Address: 33 Stetson Court Williamstown, MA 01267
Phone: 413-597-2211
E-mail address: admission@williams.edu
Web site URL: www.williams.edu
Year Founded: 1793
Private or Public: Private
Religious Affiliation: None
Location: Rural
Number of Applicants: 6,478
Percent Accepted: 18%
Percent Accepted who enroll: 45%
Number Entering: 540
Number of Transfers Accepted each Year: 13
Middle 50% SAT range: M: 670–760, CR: 670–760, Wr: Unreported
Middle 50% ACT range: 29–33
Early admission program EA/ED/None: ED

Percentage accepted through EA or ED: 40%
EA and ED deadline: 10-Nov
Regular Deadline: 15-Dec
Application Fee: $60
Full time Undergraduate enrollment: 1,997
Total enrollment: 2,046
Percent Male: 50%
Percent Female: 50%
Total Percent Minority or Unreported: 29%
Percent African-American: 10%
Percent Asian/Pacific Islander: 11%
Percent Hispanic: 9%
Percent Native-American: 0%
Percent International: 7%
Percent in-state/out of state: 14%/86%
Percent from Public HS: 58%
Retention Rate: 97%

Graduation Rate 4-year: 91%
Graduation Rate 6-year: 91%
Percent Undergraduates in On-campus housing: 93%
Number of official organized extracurricular organizations: 110
3 Most popular majors: Economics, English, Art
Student/Faculty ratio: 7:1
Average Class Size: 9
Percent of students going to grad school: Unreported
Tuition and Fees: $35,438
In-State Tuition and Fees if different: No difference
Cost for Room and Board: $9,470
Percent receiving financial aid out of those who apply, first year: 51%
Percent receiving financial aid among all students: 47%

Founded in 1793 thanks to funds bequeathed by Colonel Ephraim Williams, Williams is a small liberal arts school known for its rigorous academics and picturesque setting. The college is nestled among the Berkshire Mountains in the northwest corner of Massachusetts, a peaceful location about 135 miles from Boston and 165 miles from New York City. Williams boasts an extremely close-knit community that abounds with extracurricular and athletic opportunities.

No Rest for the Weary

One sophomore summed up academics at Williams by stating that "it's very hard to get an A." Academics are known for their rigor, and students generally spend a large part of their days reading and studying. According to another student, "everyone agrees that we work a lot more here than our friends at other schools," and another added that many people "get up early or stay up late to finish their work."

However, students are quick to add that

the academic environment is not competitive, but instead "all about collaboration." The school offers several centers where students can seek help on homework, have a tutor edit a paper, or improve their study skills. Students often work together on problem sets or help friends study for tests. One student declared, "I've been astounded by how willing people are to help."

Students are also pleased with the small class sizes and "personal" feel of academic life. With a student-faculty ratio of seven to one, many classes tend to be around 25 students or fewer. Professors are almost always willing to meet with students outside of class, and occasionally join students for coffee or invite them to dinner. One student proclaimed, "You're not a number. The professors know your name. That's one of the things that first drew me to Williams, and it's definitely true!"

> **"You're not a number. The professors know your name."**

This intimate classroom environment is epitomized by the school's unique tutorial system. Modeled after the tutorial systems of Oxford and Cambridge, the tutorial system spans many disciplines, including the math and science departments. Topics range from a physics tutorial about electromagnetic theory to an economics department course on higher education. Every week, two students meet with one professor to discuss a topic and debate their weekly papers (or, in math and science tutorials, problem sets). Students praise the tutorials for "the opportunity to really learn about a topic in depth," despite the heavy workload. More than half of Williams students graduate having taken one, and some even take two or three.

Williams requires students to take three courses in each of three divisions: Languages and the Arts, Social Studies, and Science and Mathematics. In addition, students must take one course that fulfills the "Exploring Diversity Initiative" requirement, a course that involves quantitative reasoning, and two writing-intensive courses. Finally, students must complete four quarters of physical education, which can be fulfilled by playing a team sport or by taking classes ranging from rock climbing to golf. Most students say that they don't have a problem completing the requirements, since such a broad range of courses are offered that fulfill each distribution. In fact, one sophomore even proclaimed, "I like the requirements!" because it encourages students to dabble in subjects they might otherwise never have tried.

Students also love the freedom offered by Williams' 4-1-4 schedule: four-month fall and spring semesters, with a one-month Winter Study term in January. During Winter Study, students study a variety of unusual topics outside the normal curriculum. Past courses have included "Inside Jury Deliberations" and "Contemporary American Songwriting." Students can also submit their own proposal for a Winter Study project. Many students take advantage of the break to study abroad and take travel classes in locations as varied as Egypt, Vietnam, and Nicaragua. Those who choose to stay on campus take advantage of the lighter academic load—most classes only meet for about 10 hours a week—to meet new people, go skiing, or party.

Popular majors include psychology, economics, biology, history, English, and political science. The art history department is also "world-renowned," with several art museums a short walk away from campus. One student insisted that "everyone should take an art history course while they're here. You can read about an artist for class and then go see one of his paintings a block away!" Study abroad options abound, including the unique Williams-Exeter at Oxford University, in which Williams students become full members of Oxford and gain access to all of its resources. Other opportunities include the Williams-Mystic Program for maritime studies in Mystic, Connecticut, and the new Williams in Africa program.

Williams offers a wide range of academic opportunities, and students are eager to rise to the occasion. As one student put it, "The intelligence of everyone here just blows my mind! Not every conversation here revolves around intellectual ideas, but when you talk to people, it's clear they're really smart."

Purple Mountains and Purple Cows

"Although Williams is a small school, you'd be surprised by how diverse the student body is," one student asserted. "We're not a J. Crew commercial." The campus is "increasingly diverse" geographically and economically, with growing numbers of international students. A sophomore said, "People always surprise me here. Although there are preppy kids, lacrosse guys, and hippie types, no one is one-dimensional." In general, students were characterized as being friendly, outgoing, and athletic. Another student added, "People here do a good job of meeting people outside of their usual 'groups.' Athletes participate in theater. You end up making friends with people from all over."

The vast majority of Williams students, or "Ephs," are involved in one or more extracurricular activities. As one sophomore commented, "Sleep is a very precious commodity. Everyone here is so busy!" Popular activities include a capella groups, dance, and theater, including Cap and Bells—the oldest continuously running student-run college theater group in the country. The Williams Outing Club, which organizes trips and rents equipment for hiking, rock climbing, and winter sports, is also big. Other activities include the student newspaper, the student radio station, and a wide variety of religious organizations. Many students also hold jobs, whether working as tour guides, tutors, or at the library.

About half of all students participate in intercollegiate sports, whether on one of the varsity level or JV teams, or through the club and intramural programs. Williams is consistently ranked as the top Division III school. Popular sports include football, basketball, and crew. In the winter, many people take advantage of Williams' proximity to the mountains to go skiing and snowboarding. The school's athletic complex boasts a pool, squash courts, an ice rink, and a golf course. One sophomore said, "I would have never considered myself an athlete before coming to Williams, but I've really enjoyed participating in sports since I got here."

Even non-athletes enjoy attending games, especially those against rival Amherst. As one junior emphasized, "even if sports aren't your thing, Williams has a ton of things to do. One of the things I love about Williams is how supportive everyone is of each other— people will cheer on their friends whether they're on the field, on the stage, or just taking a test. School spirit is really strong. Our school color, purple, and the purple cow mascot are everywhere!"

From Entryways to JAs

The freshman housing system was unanimously praised. Incoming freshmen are divided into groups of around 20 students, or "entries," who live in the same vertical or horizontal section of a freshman dorm. Each

entry has two Junior Advisors (JAs), who host study breaks during exams, organize trips to see plays or concerts, and occasionally throw parties. JAs are there to make sure that freshmen stay safe and have fun, and do not police students' behavior. Applying to become a JA is an extremely competitive process.

"I became really good friends with the people in my entryway," said one student. "We went to dinner together, we played sports together, and I ended up really getting to know people that I probably wouldn't have met if we hadn't been living in the same entryway." Many freshmen have singles, and while upperclassmen have the option of a double, they are "pretty much guaranteed a single," according to several students.

Upperclassmen live in four clusters, or "neighborhoods," as part of a recent effort by the college to help foster a sense of community similar to that provided by residential houses at other universities. One senior quipped, "It's supposed to be like Harry Potter." Neighborhoods get money to host events, such as barbeques, movies, and dance parties, which students say helps add to the number and variety of events available. The vast majority of students live on-campus all four years, although some seniors choose to live off campus or in Williams-owned "co-ops."

With three dining halls and several snack shops to choose from, students enjoy a wide variety of food, which they describe as "pretty good." That's important, because Williamstown (although very charming) is tiny. One student summed it up: "It's pretty. It's also in the middle of nowhere." Spring Street, the town's main thoroughfare, consists of a few shops, a bar, a bank, and a smattering of ethnic restaurants. Although some students say that the town's small size can feel stifling, one student proclaimed, "Actually, my favorite thing about Williams is that it's rural. The lack of nightlife means that everything people do happens on campus, and promotes more passion for extracurriculars." The college helps compensate for the town's remoteness by funding lots of student activities, and bringing plays, speakers, and DJs to campus. Since there are no fraternities or sororities, parties typically take place in dorm rooms or off-campus houses. All-Campus Entertainment (ACE) also hosts several well-attended theme parties, such as Winter Carnival and Spring Fling. Although a good proportion of students drink, there are plenty of options for those who choose not to imbibe. The student center even hosts a weekly "Stressbusters" event, where students can get free massages and hot drinks.

Students appreciate the college's effort to bring the outside world to campus, raving, "there's always something going on. There is so much more to do than we have time for!"

That said, most students say that they appreciate their friends and fellow students most of all. "Some of my best days at Williams have been spent just hanging out with my friends and talking late into the night," one junior said. "This a great place. There's a real sense that we're all in this together." —*Elizabeth Chrystal*

FYI

If you come to Williams, you'd better bring "a sense of humor for outrageous jokes, including but not limited to people streaking!"

What's the typical weekend schedule? "Go to a sporting event, take advantage of DJs, plays, and dance shows on campus, party in a friend's dorm. Sunday—work!"

If I could change one thing about Williams, I'd "cut down on the workload a bit to be able to take advantage of more of the extracurricular opportunities."

Worcester Polytechnic Institute

Address: 100 Institute Road Worcester, MA 01609

Phone: 5-8-831-5286

E-mail address: admissions@wpi.edu

Web site URL: www.wpi.edu

Year Founded: 1865

Private or Public: Private

Religious Affiliation: None

Location: Urban

Number of Applicants: 5,698

Percent Accepted: 66%

Percent Accepted who enroll: 22%

Number Entering: 805

Number of Transfers Accepted each Year: 79

Middle 50% SAT range: M: 630–710, CR 560–670, Wr: 560–660

Middle 50% ACT range: 25–31

Early admission program EA/ED/None: EA

Percentage accepted through EA or ED: 82%

EA and ED deadline: 1-Nov

Regular Deadline: 1-Feb

Application Fee: $60

Full time Undergraduate enrollment: 3,016

Total enrollment: 4,157

Percent Male: 74%

Percent Female: 26%

Total Percent Minority or Unreported: 12%

Percent African-American: 2%

Percent Asian/Pacific Islander: 6%

Percent Hispanic: 4%

Percent Native-American: 0%

Percent International: 7%

Percent in-state/out of state: 50%/50%

Percent from Public HS: 66%

Retention Rate: 94%

Graduation Rate 4-year: 63%

Graduation Rate 6-year: 64%

Percent Undergraduates in On-campus housing: 59%

Number of official organized extracurricular organizations: 200

3 Most popular majors: Computer Science, Electrical Engineering, Mechanical Engineering

Student/Faculty ratio: 13:1

Average Class Size: 9

Percent of students going to grad school: 29%

Tuition and Fees: $34,300

In-State Tuition and Fees if different: No difference

Cost for Room and Board: $10,410

Percent receiving financial aid out of those who apply, first year: 96%

Percent receiving financial aid among all students: 94%

W PI is a small polytechnic institute located in Worcester, the heart of Massachusetts. This engineering haven follows a mission of educating its students on practical and theoretical levels and providing a well-rounded academic program that is sure to make future employers take notice.

Study, Study, Study!

The school operates on a system that is different from most. Instead of semesters, there are four seven-week terms, two in the fall and two in the spring. Each term students take three courses. In addition to their major requirements, every student is expected to complete nine credits or units worth of projects: a sufficiency project requiring five related courses and a project or seminar in the humanities area; a social entrepreneurship project requiring a project relating to solving a need in society via technology and science; and finally a major-qualifying project, which is a team-based project in your own major field of study. While students claim that the projects are not difficult to finish and are enjoyable hands-on experiences, they also say that it is a good idea to get the projects not in your major out of the way early on. Electrical and computer engineering, computer science, and mechanical engineering are the most popular majors on campus. The students also mentioned Interactive Media and Games Development as one of the unique majors—one student explained, "it's basically majoring in video games." As fun as that sounds, students warn that when you come to WPI, you'd better be prepared to put in the work, no matter what you major in. The terms go by quickly and it's important to keep up with each of your classes so as not to get overwhelmed. Also be prepared to spend many hours at the lab. The Chemical Engineering major has a reputation for an overwhelming workload, and "Chemistry of Thermodynamics" and "Calculus 3" also have reputations for being difficult classes. But don't let the difficulty scare you. WPI has a student-friendly grading system with grades being A, B, C, and NR (No Record). This means if you get below a C, the class does not count toward your overall GPA and it's as if you never took it.

> "The unique thing [about WPI] is that the professors are extremely, extremely helpful; they will know you by your first name."

Classes are generally small with two to nine being the most frequent class size, exceptions being of course the survey courses, which can have over 50 people in a lecture. Despite their small size, the competition for a spot in a class is not a problem, and if you want to get into a class you can always turn to the professor who is likely to sign a permission sheet letting you into the class. The professors get equal praise with the classes; one senior enthused, "The unique thing [about WPI] is that the professors are extremely, extremely helpful; they will know you by your first name."

Students generally praise the academics at WPI, citing the hands-on experiences involved in projects as the best sources of learning. Classes can also be fun and hands-on, such as the Food Engineering class which teaches you all about food structure and preparation. The final project is to make something and bring it in, and students get pretty creative—some make their own chocolate from scratch or even brew their own beer. The school's focus is on technology and science, which is great for those who are sure that they want to pursue those fields. However, one student who decided that he was into humanities late in his college career complained that it was impossible for him to pursue it at WPI since the departments are small and not up to par.

Party: Calculators Optional

Students unanimously proclaim that Greek life is the hub of social life on campus. About 28 percent of males and 30 percent of females join either a fraternity or a sorority, but students commented that it can feel like much more of the student body is involved in the Greek community. While most people drink on campus there is no pressure to do so. One student explained that "there are a lot of people who are not involved in the whole party scene at all and they have their own social views," citing the game developers club and science fiction society as examples of groups that prefer to have their own gatherings. The school itself also provides entertainment options with venues such as the on-campus pub The Goat's Head and Gompei's Gutters, an on-campus bowling alley. Those few who wish to wander off campus and explore the Worcester party scene have the option of clubs and bars near Main Street such as Irish Times and Club Red. Students warn, however, that there is very little to do in Worcester.

There is a stereotype that is associated with technical schools. As one student explained, "People tend to associate the students with the geeky look, with the thick glasses and a part on the side, but [at WPI] it's not a majority at all." But another confessed, "We're a little bit geeky," citing frequent math and science jokes that one hears on campus. Still, there are a diverse variety of students on campus, including a relatively generous community of international students that makes up a little over 7 percent of the student body. It is important to note that women are a minority at the school, making up only 26 percent of the student body. A senior girl, however, described it as not a major problem. "When you're a freshman it's a little bit awkward," she said, and while it takes some getting used to, in the end she reported, "It's not a big deal at all. We're all engineers." Another unifying characteristic is that all students are very friendly and in the freshman year the residence halls and classes offer plenty of opportunities to make good friends.

Is There Room for Me?

For the 59 percent of the student body who lives on campus the options are pretty standard. There are seven dorms in addition to an apartment complex and four smaller houses of 10 to 20 residents. Among these, East Hall is the newest dorm on campus and it's also the most coveted residence for upperclassmen. Due to space restrictions it can be pretty difficult to get into a dorm via the school's lottery system, which is based on seniority.

While the campus is considered safe, the general area outside of campus can be quite sketchy, even dangerous. This can lead to a college bubble feel on campus. At the same time, students don't mind much as they proudly proclaim that WPI is the most beautiful campus among Worcester's numerous colleges. Many like to hang out at the student center, the central hangout spot featuring pool tables, foosball tables, and a food court. When hunger strikes, Morgan Commons serves as the main dining hall. It is rated above average but has a tendency to get monotonous. Other options include a Dunkin' Donuts on campus, a convenience store, and Goat's Head, which doubles as a restaurant. For off-campus options, students recommend Highland Street, which offers many restaurants such as Sahara and Sole Proprietor and several coffee shops such as the Bean Counter.

WPI Spirit

Outside of class there is no lack of activities for the students of WPI. Among the 200 registered student organizations, there is a wide range of options including drama, a robotic team, and *The Towers*, the school newspaper that is beginning to grow in popularity. Athletics also have a great following on campus. One senior explained that there is "wicked lots of school spirit" and "almost fanatical support" for the sports teams, basketball and football being the most popular. For the less athletically gifted there is the option of joining intramural sport teams, which are not as popular but still claim a presence on campus.

With small classes, great professors, and a pretty campus, students generally report being happy with their choice of WPI. The projects focusing on hands-on work further the school's goal of preparing its students for real world jobs. One student assured, "It's an engineer's dream."—*Dorota Poplawska*

FYI
If you come to WPI, you'd better bring "a calculator."
What is the typical weekend schedule? "Homework, homework and more homework, going out to party and hanging out with friends."
If I could change one thing about WPI, I'd "improve the male-to-female ratio."
Three things every student at WPI should do before graduating are "see the gold head trophy which makes rare appearances, jump through the fountain, and go abroad or away for a project."

Michigan

Albion College

Address: 611 East Porter Street, Albion, MI 49224
Phone: 517-629-0321
E-mail address: admissions@albion.edu
Web site URL: www.albion.edu
Year Founded: 1835
Private or Public: Private
Religious Affiliation: Methodist
Location: Suburban
Number of Applicants: 1,958
Percent Accepted: 81%
Percent Accepted who enroll: 30%
Number Entering: 484
Number of Transfers Accepted each Year: 63
Middle 50% SAT range: M: 500–650, CR: 560–630, Wr: 500–630
Middle 50% ACT range: 23–27
Early admission program EA/ED/None: EA

Percentage accepted through EA or ED: Unreported
EA and ED deadline: 1-Dec
Regular Deadline: 1-May
Application Fee: $20
Full time Undergraduate enrollment: 1,860
Total enrollment: 1,860
Percent Male: 48%
Percent Female: 52%
Total Percent Minority or Unreported: 13%
Percent African-American: 3%
Percent Asian/Pacific Islander: 2%
Percent Hispanic: 1%
Percent Native-American: <1%
Percent International: 1%
Percent in-state/out of state: 91%/9%
Percent from Public HS: 75%
Retention Rate: 86%

Graduation Rate 4-year: 63%
Graduation Rate 6-year: 71%
Percent Undergraduates in On-campus housing: 88%
Number of official organized extracurricular organizations: 110
3 Most popular majors: Biology, Economics, Psychology
Student/Faculty ratio: 14:1
Average Class Size: 15
Percent of students going to grad school: 38%
Tuition and Fees: $28,880
In-State Tuition and Fees if different: No difference
Cost for Room and Board: $8,190
Percent receiving financial aid out of those who apply, first year: 85%
Percent receiving financial aid among all students: 94%

E nvision approximately 1,800 students crammed into beautiful, but overpopulated, gothic buildings. Everything is surrounded by large trees. This is Albion College, set within the small city of Albion, Michigan. With its newly renovated science complex, a comprehensive First-Year Experience Program, and a place on *Forbes* magazine's list of the "America's Best College Buys," this midwestern school provides students a strong liberal arts education with all the benefits of a small college.

No-Nonsense Academics

One student boldly remarked, "Albion is a no-nonsense school." Most students stick to standard majors such as economics, psychology, pre-med, and chemistry. The majority of the atypical classes are religious,

one of the more popular of which is called "Death and Dying." The classes are also competitive, in particular the math and science classes; to do well in physical or organic chemistry, you should expect at least 25 hours of studying a week.

In the Albion system, you need 32 credits to graduate, including major and more general liberal arts requirements. Instead of simply creating distributional requirements, each class at Albion is assigned a "mode" and a "category." "Modes"—or the approach to the subject—include Artistic Creation and Analysis, Historical and Cultural Analysis, and Textual Analysis. "Categories"—or the actual subject the class falls under—include Environmental Studies, Gender Studies, and Global Studies. In addition, all freshmen participate in the First-Year Experience, designed to ease students' academic and social transition into college. The program includes Orientation, Common Reading Experience, as well as a set of seminars on topics ranging from "Art in the Environment" to "Vietnam: Then and Now."

Albion also has a few more specific academic programs. One of the best known programs at Albion, the Carl A. Gerstacker Institute for Professional Management, is an honors business program which involves 10 semesters in four years—seven semesters of on-campus study, one summer term after sophomore year, and two internships during the fall term of junior year and the summer after junior year. Many choices for these internships are located in Europe. For students interested in political science, education, law, or community service, Albion also offers the Gerald R. Ford Institute for Public Policy and Service. Founded by the former president, the Institute allows students to pursue a major of their choice while taking classes in fields such as ethics, public policy, and government.

Fight for Your Right to Party

Historically, Albion has been known for a large party scene. But Albion officials have cracked down on the party scene in the College, doling out $500 fines to underage drinkers. There have been problems of over-drinking in the past mainly because a small group of students overdo it and, as one Albion student said, "screwed it up for the rest of us." With its isolated location, life at Albion can get monotonous, leading to occasional problems with drug use. Sometimes, though, the isolation can pay off: during the annual "Senior Week" event at the end of the year, Albion students compete in a drinking Olympics in a barn out of town—not your typical end-of-year venue.

> **"Albion is a no-nonsense school."**

Other than the occasional novel event, one of the drawbacks of the remote campus is that many students have a difficult time finding interesting activities. But with the city of Jackson nearby and Ann Arbor less than an hour away, there are plenty of options for the many students who decide to keep cars on campus.

Fraternity parties epitomize the social scene at Albion. Since the student population is generally friendly and outgoing, the frat scene is more open than at other schools, in-

cluding allowing everyone at the parties. However, the Greek life at Albion has felt the impact of the crackdown on parties, with some students and officials citing the fraternities and sororities as a major source of drinking. But other students are reluctant to call for the elimination of fraternities because many age-old traditions unique to Albion are connected to the Greek system. At least one student expressed a fear about the effect on social life in general, saying that the party scene revolves around the fraternity houses.

Living in Style

Living arrangements are standard for all four years at Albion, with most students living in the dormitories the whole time. The dorm rooms are assigned by seniority, though juniors and seniors sometimes move off campus into neighboring apartments. Freshmen are housed in either Wesley Hall or Seaton Hall; RAs live in all dormitories, and alcohol is prohibited to those who are underage. It depends, however, on how strict the RA is—some supervisors have been known to be lax about the rules.

The dorms are definitely not the only buildings that will catch your eye at Albion. The multimillion-dollar science complex, finished in 2006, is an impressive addition to the campus. Another more noticeable feature of Albion is the quad; located between all the class buildings, the quad is a great place to hang around during the warmer months. The Nature Center is also worth noting for its beautiful landscape. Thought to be the most beautiful spot on campus by many of the students, it is an "unspoiled habitat."

The dining halls are famed for their relatively good cuisine and easily managed meal plans allowing students to pick how many meals they want per week. But be warned that you will have to maintain regular eating patterns, with limited hours. Since the school is relatively small, the only times the dining halls stay open late is during finals. Also, one unique rule is that off-campus residents are not allowed in the dining halls, but with many good restaurants in the town, students have other options when they want to eat out. However when students do venture off campus, they usually try to be back before dark since the surrounding area is not particularly safe.

Extra Awesome Extracurricular

Albion College hosts extracurricular fun for everyone in many forms. Although it is a Division III school, sports are very popular—one student estimated that "half of the campus plays a sport." Basketball and football are the most popular spectator events, but students are known for being fickle fans: at times, they rally in full force for Albion, while other times they skip homecoming games entirely to watch other local rivalries such as the University of Michigan versus Michigan State football game. Intramural sports, including soccer, basketball, volleyball, dodgeball, hockey, and tennis, are a must at this school. The IM fields are given great care and the games are known to get very competitive.

There are also some nonathletic clubs that are very popular. The most recognized are "Break the Silence" (the Gay and Lesbian Awareness Group) and the Medieval Club, which puts on mock sword fights and archery competitions.

Overall, Albion is a small school filled with friendly students. Despite the school's isolation, the campus is a beautiful and safe place where students easily become very personal with their professors and are well-prepared for life outside of college. Ultimately, Albion is a great place for students who want to have fun, but at the same time are willing to work hard.—*Benjamin Dzialo*

FYI

If you come to Albion, you'd better bring "a friendly, outgoing attitude."

What's the typical weekend schedule? "Friday: No class, or class finishes early. Workout, nap, or do nothing with your friends until you start drinking, which will last all night (or you study). Saturday: Maybe get some work done, typically don't do anything; partying at night. Sunday: Cram day. Wake up late, study all day if need be."

If I could change one thing about Albion, I'd "fix the town: people wouldn't drink so much if the town wasn't falling apart, and there was more to do."

Three things every student at Albion should do before graduating are "attend a talk by at least one of the great speakers Albion brings in, walk in the Whitehouse Nature Center in the winter, and talk with a professor outside of class."

Alma College

Address: 614 West Superior Street, Alma, MI 48801-1599
Phone: 989-463-7139
E-mail address: admissions@alma.edu
Web site URL: www.alma.edu
Year Founded: 1886
Private or Public: Private
Religious Affiliation: Presbyterian
Location: Suburban
Number of Applicants: 2,044
Percent Accepted: 73%
Percent Accepted who enroll: 26%
Number Entering: 423
Number of Transfers Accepted each Year: 59
Middle 50% SAT range: M: 520–668, CR: 498–665, Wr: 503–623
Middle 50% ACT range: 21–27
Early admission program EA/ED/None: None

Percentage accepted through EA or ED: NA
EA and ED deadline: NA
Regular Deadline: Rolling
Application Fee: $25
Full time Undergraduate enrollment: 1,384
Total enrollment: 1,384
Percent Male: 45%
Percent Female: 55%
Total Percent Minority or Unreported: 8%
Percent African-American: 2%
Percent Asian/Pacific Islander: 1%
Percent Hispanic: 2%
Percent Native-American: <1%
Percent International: 1%
Percent in-state/out of state: 96%/4%
Percent from Public HS: 91%
Retention Rate: 76%

Graduation Rate 4-year: 60%
Graduation Rate 6-year: 68%
Percent Undergraduates in On-campus housing: 88%
Number of official organized extracurricular organizations: 75
3 Most popular majors: Biology, Business, Kinesiology
Student/Faculty ratio: 13:1
Average Class Size: 15
Percent of students going to grad school: Unreported
Tuition and Fees: $34,586
In-State Tuition and Fees if different: No difference
Cost for Room and Board: $8,120.00
Percent receiving financial aid out of those who apply, first year: 83%
Percent receiving financial aid among all students: 99%

A college smaller than many high schools, Alma College is located almost exactly in the center of Michigan, away from large cities. The removed location can be considered a drawback; however, Alma provides an excellent liberal arts education, while creating a small community of close-knit students. Therefore, for all those looking to receive a good education in a quiet, small town, Alma can be a very good college choice.

Liberal Arts with a Touch

At the majority of liberal arts colleges, the majors are along the lines of political science, biology, history, and economics. These fields include a wide selection of course content and generally do not indicate a specific professional path. Alma, however, despite being known as a liberal arts institution, offers a number of programs not often found in similar schools. For example, Alma offers majors in business administration and athletic training, two topics that are more pre-professional preparations than liberal arts. Nevertheless, in general, the school remains very much a liberal arts institution, providing only about 40 majors and minors. For all those looking for a challenge, students can design their own multidisciplinary concentration with the help of a faculty member in a process called Program of Emphasis. By carefully choosing and linking different sets of classes, students can create their own major. "I think we have a lot of independence in what we can study here," said one student. "It is a liberal arts school, but we also have classes in more practical areas."

Despite the small size of the college, Alma does have an honors program, which includes special seminars, as well as a senior capstone project. The idea is to help the more ambitious students to create their own portfolio of different independent projects. "Being able to complete something outside of class without too much guidance is an important part of academics here at Alma. It teaches you to be independent," said one student.

As a liberal arts college, it is important for students to be well rounded. Therefore, Alma has a relatively lengthy list of required courses. Like most universities, Alma's requirements start with composition and computation, the two most important skills to college success. In addition, students must take classes in foreign awareness, social sciences, humanities, and natural sciences. "I think it is really important to take a variety of classes," said one student. "At the end of the day, that is what you should be expected to do because you go to a liberal arts college."

Classes are small at Alma, and they encourage discussions. Interactions with professors are plentiful and highly encouraged. "I think what surprised me the most is how closely involved professors are in the education of each student," said one junior. "Some of them really put a lot of energy into each student." In addition, it is very easy to see professors outside of the class setting. "Alma is a small town with a small college, so you are bound to see your professors all the time around campus. Most of them are always happy to chat with you about anything," said one student.

Students have no complaint about the workload. "No one is trying to overwhelm you with work," said one student. "But you also have to realize that you go to college, which means more than just showing up to classes." In fact, weekdays are very busy times for Alma students to finish academic work. "If you don't plan ahead, you will be in trouble," said one student.

The college also aims to create a better sense of global perspectives among students. Alma is home to the Posey Global Leadership Program, which offers scholarships to students to travel anywhere in the world to accomplish a self-designed project. The projects over the years have ranged from attending conferences to research projects to international internships. The goal is to expose students to the realities of other countries instead of confining students to simply reading books about foreign lands.

In a Place Far Away

Alma is granted the title of city, but it has fewer than 10,000 people and certainly does not give the college much of an urban atmosphere. "We live in a small town," said one student. "And there really is nothing to do here. All we have in Alma is Alma College." To make the matter worse, no major city is close to Alma. In fact, Grand Rapids is more than 50 miles away, and Detroit is even farther. Therefore, most students remain restricted to the confines of Alma even during weekends. Occasionally, however, some students do choose to venture to Mt. Pleasant, home of the Central Michigan State University, which means a few more restaurants, activities, and many more students. Since many students have cars, it is relatively easy to access Mt. Pleasant, which is about 15 miles away.

The upside of a small college in a small city is that everyone gets to know each other very well. "You just have three hundred people in your class," said one student. "After four years, you become really familiar with them." Greek life exists at Alma, and it provide venues for weekend parties. Besides a few parties around campus, however, weekends tend to be very quiet at Alma. "You have to be satisfied with a little bit of repetitiveness in terms of weekend activities," joked one student.

The great majority of students live on campus. After all, Alma prides itself as a residential liberal arts college. There are six main residences provided by the college. The students are generally satisfied with their living arrangements. "The dorms are definitely better for upperclassmen," said one student. "Overall, I think Alma has pretty good dorms compared to other schools. The rooms are large enough and well maintained."

Unlike larger universities with dozens of dining locations, Alma has only three eateries. In fact, only one can be considered a dining hall. Then again, for a school of fewer than 1,500 students, that is more than enough. The main location is Hamilton Commons, serving breakfast, lunch, and dinner. There is also a quick lunch alternative and a coffee shop that also offers sandwiches and burgers late into the night. "Meals are not bad," said one student. "And I think the hours are flexible enough to meet our needs."

You Must Be From Michigan

The great majority of students at Alma are from Michigan. Therefore, someone who is not from the state may feel slightly out of place, at least during the first couple of months. However, as students point out, Alma is a very friendly college, open to people of all backgrounds. "We don't have much diversity," said one student. "But that is because we are in the middle of nowhere. We have a very accepting environment. In fact, I would love to see more people from outside of Michigan."

> "We have a very accepting environment."

The remote location can also be a great benefit to people who do not enjoy the bright lights of a metropolis. "I love it here because it is so small and intimate," said one student. After all, Alma creates a friendly community of students while providing a great education. For all those willing to sacrifice a few conveniences of big cities for a quiet residential college life, Alma may be the right choice for you.—*Xiaohang Liu*

FYI
If you come to Alma, you'd better bring "a car."
What is the typical weekend schedule? "Party at night and work during the day."
If I could change one thing about Alma, I'd "move it a few miles closer to Grand Rapids."

Hope College

Address: 69 East 10th
Holland, MI 49422 to 9000
Phone: 616-395-7850
E-mail address:
admissions@hope.edu
Web site URL: www.hope.edu
Year Founded: 1862
Private or Public: Private
Religious Affiliation:
Reformed Church
Location: Suburban
Number of Applicants:
2,748
Percent Accepted: 83%
**Percent Accepted who
enroll:** 35%
Number Entering: 799
**Number of Transfers
Accepted each Year:** 57
Middle 50% SAT range: M:
540–660, CR: 530–660,
Wr: Unreported
Middle 50% ACT range:
23–29
**Early admission program
EA/ED/None:** None

**Percentage accepted
through EA or ED:** NA
EA and ED deadline: NA
Regular Deadline: Rolling
Application Fee: $35
**Full time Undergraduate
enrollment:** 3,226
Total enrollment: 6,391
Percent Male: 41%
Percent Female: 59%
**Total Percent Minority or
Unreported:** 2%
Percent African-American:
2%
**Percent Asian/Pacific
Islander:** 2%
Percent Hispanic: 3%
Percent Native-American:
<1%
Percent International: 1%
**Percent in-state/out of
state:** 70%/30%
Percent from Public HS: 88%
Retention Rate: 88%
Graduation Rate 4-year:
62%

Graduation Rate 6-year: 71%
**Percent Undergraduates in
On-campus housing:** 78%
**Number of official organized
extracurricular
organizations:** 67
3 Most popular majors:
Business/Commerce,
General English and
Literature, General
Psychology
Student/Faculty ratio: 12:1
Average Class Size: 18
**Percent of students going to
grad school:** 29%
Tuition and Fees: $24,780
**In-State Tuition and Fees if
different:** No difference
Cost for Room and Board:
$7,650
**Percent receiving financial
aid out of those who apply,
first year:** 97%
**Percent receiving financial
aid among all students:**
88%

S tudents at Hope College come together
for many reasons. In the bleachers and
on the sidelines, they all cheer on their
remarkably successful athletic teams. Walking across their pine tree-lined campus, they
live up to their reputation of Midwestern
friendliness by saying "hi" to everyone they
meet. And in chapel on Sundays, many students at this Christian Reformed college
come together to celebrate their common
religious values. Located near the shores of
Lake Michigan in the heart of pretty downtown Holland, Hope College provides its
students with solid academic programs, the
personal attention only possible at a small
school, and a warm social atmosphere, all
structured around a core of Christian values.

Common Values
Spirituality is important to students at Hope,
and religion influences nearly every aspect
of campus life to some degree. Still, students maintain that nonreligious students
are not pressured to participate in religious
activities, which are all optional. As one ju-

nior said, "At Hope you can be as strong or as
loose in your faith as you want." One of the
most popular religious events on campus is
the Sunday night "singing-and-celebration"
service called the "Gathering." Such a great
number of students pack the chapel for the
Gathering that all the seats fill up, and late
arrivers are left to sit in the aisles or stand in
the back of the building. The Gathering is
just one of the times when religion unites
the student body. Groups of Hope students
travel all over the world every spring break
on mission trips; one junior who spent last
spring break building homes for a deaf community in Jamaica described it as one of the
best experiences of his life. A soccer player
said his coach sometimes uses faith in his
coaching style. Religion even makes its way
into the classroom; according to one senior,
"Some professors do incorporate [religion]
in their classes." While nonreligious students are definitely in the minority at Hope,
they are not excluded from campus life. A
nonreligious student commented that most
students come from a Christian background
and are "open and not afraid to profess their

opinions. However, they are usually not that overbearing."

Students say that the typical Hope student is Christian, usually conservative, and often from Michigan or the greater Midwest. One student said she liked that Hope students are "generally well-rounded and geared toward future goals." The student body is predominantly white. However, Hope, in addition to its Dutch population, also has a substantial Hispanic segment. Attempts have been made to increase the school's diversity, and a senior said she was "surprised at how many students are from out of the state and even the country." However, a sophomore expressed frustration that because so many students have similar, religiously conservative backgrounds, they tend to "generate the same old boring views and stances on subjects." Despite this, he said that there is still a substantial number of "more open-minded" people on campus.

Hitting the Books

Students at Hope universally agree that the best parts of their academic experience are the close relationships they build with the professors, who teach all their classes. One sophomore praised how "available and flexible" they are to student needs. Professors at Hope frequently go to sporting events to cheer on their students and often invite their classes to their homes at the end of the semester for dinner parties. Many students become so close with their professors that they keep in contact even after their classes are over.

Part of the reason students and teachers are able to form such close bonds centers on the small size of classes at Hope. The average class has 10 to 19 students in it. Many upper-level classes are even smaller, allowing students to get personal attention and sometimes even giving them the opportunity to get involved with their professor's research. One junior said he liked Hope's small classes because they gave him the confidence to "be more bold to ask questions" of the professor in front of the group. The small class size does cause some problems, however, since it often becomes difficult for students to get into popular classes that quickly fill up. Students in popular majors sometimes have difficulty getting into courses necessary for graduation and end up needing to either plead to the dean for class admission, or to stay on campus for a summer term in order to graduate on time.

Popular majors at Hope include biology and education, and both of these departments have excellent programs. Students majoring in education get to start doing fieldwork in local classrooms as early as their freshman year. One sophomore said that Hope "prides itself on its sciences," and the humanities majors are often less intense. Hope recently renovated its science buildings, and the premed program has a reputation for getting its students into selective medical schools. Biology is considered one of Hope's most challenging majors, as is religion. Students interested in studying religion benefit from the Western Theological Seminary—right next to Hope—and in fact, every year several students enroll in this seminary after graduation. A junior estimated that Hope students study about three hours a day; students in difficult majors put in a few more hours. Students who want a less-intense academic experience typically major in communications, although there is also substantial interest in broadcast journalism, public relations, and advertising. Academic requirements at Hope include taking several credits of religion and completing at least a 200-level foreign-language class, a class on cultural diversity and a class called "Health Dynamics," which one athlete said "is a joke. It's basically gym class, and even if you play a varsity sport, you still have to take it." Still, most students agree that the annoyance created by some of their distributional requirements and unsuccessful class registration is a small price to pay for the excellent education they receive at Hope.

Kicking Back

When they're not studying, students at Hope enjoy a wide range of social activities. Only a third to a half of the campus drinks, so while a more traditional "party scene" exists for those students who want it, nondrinkers have plenty of social options. The Student Activity Committee (SAC) sponsors movie nights and brings in comedians, magicians, and bands to give performances open to the student body. The campus itself is dry, so technically no alcohol is allowed in the dorms. One junior said that while RAs can be "pretty strict" about this rule at times, people can generally get away with drinking in their dorms as long as everything stays quiet and hidden. A significant proportion of the student body is Greek, although there are few national frats or sororities on campus. Most of the Greek organizations are branches of smaller, local fraternities. They often hold theme parties, but not all of these are open to the whole student body—many are open only to other Greeks. Parties are often also held in some of the off-campus houses, especially those where members of the soccer and football teams live. Upperclassmen who want to enjoy a beer in a slightly classier atmosphere favor the New Holland Brewery, especially on Wednesday "Stein Nights," when students who bring their own beer stein can get it filled up at a discounted price.

> **"The legend goes that you'll find your soul mate at Hope."**

Walking around campus on the average Saturday night, you'll probably see a lot of good-looking people. Hope students are an attractive bunch on the whole. As one student said, "Whenever my friends come to visit from other schools, they always say how hot the girls here are." Since Hope students are almost two-thirds female, this seems like pretty good odds for the guys. But Hope isn't a school for someone looking for a lot of random hookups; many students are involved in serious relationships. "The legend goes that you'll find your soul mate at Hope," said one junior in a committed relationship, and reportedly a lot of Hope students end up marrying others from their school. Students say that Hope is a friendly place. "You could go up to anyone and say hello," according to one student. Partly because of the school's small size, there aren't many cliques, and people tend to have a lot of friends of different ages.

Housing in Holland
Hope students typically live in dorms for their freshman and sophomore years. Students live in double rooms on single-sex hallways and share common bathrooms. "The dorms are overall well-kept and comfortable," said one sophomore, although all the buildings have different reputations. In addition to the coed buildings, there is one all-male dorm and three all-female dorms, including Dykstra, "where all the guys go to scope for women," according to one male student. Kollen Hall is the most social dorm; "It's the party dorm, the loudest and craziest," said one former resident. Voorhees Hall houses "a lot of artsy types," while international students tend to cluster in Scott. By junior year, most Hope students move into the "cottages." These are small houses on the perimeter of campus where groups of about six students live; they are still considered "on-campus housing" and have RAs, but they have their own kitchens and living rooms. The cottages are "a fun alternative to big-school living," according to one upperclassman. Seniors often move off campus, either to houses or to apartments in downtown Holland. In total, there are 11 residence halls, 15 apartment buildings, and 63 cottages.

Hope's campus is small. "You can walk all the way around it in 15 minutes," a junior said. Most academic buildings are in the center of the campus, while the dorms and the cottages are around the perimeter. Many of the historic buildings are red brick, while some of the newer buildings, like the recently constructed science center, are more modern. One senior raved that the campus is "so cute! Hope is big on preserving the old buildings it does have, but also on adding new buildings as the college expands."

Dining hall food is "pretty good" according to most students. Freshmen often eat in Phelps Hall, which supposedly has the worst food on campus; but upperclassmen enjoy eating the much tastier food in Cook Hall, which typically serves a choice of several entrees every night, including vegetarian options. When students get bored of the dining halls, downtown Holland has a variety of unique restaurants less than a five-minute walk from campus. The Windmill is a favorite for breakfast, and students also enjoy relaxing and studying in coffee shops such as Java Joe's (which has a stage where bands perform) and Lemonjello's (pronounced le-MON-jel-lo's by those in the know).

Sports and Spirit
Students leave campus and go into Holland for more than food and coffee, however. Faith-based community service is extremely popular at the school. One junior said there are "a ton of opportunities to work in church soup kitchens or tutor kids or anything like that." Many students also spend their free time playing intramural sports ranging from inner-tube water polo to Ultimate Frisbee. When the weather is warm, students make the short trip down to the shores of beautiful Lake Michigan to hang out on the beach. Hope's Division III varsity athletic teams have had excellent records in the past few years. Both men's and women's basketball and soccer teams are extremely competitive

and draw massive support from both students and members of the community who come out to watch.

The crowds are in large part due to the high level of school spirit at Hope. A combination of factors, including the small size of the student body and the shared core of Christian values, bind students closely to their school. "If I could do it all over again I would definitely, definitely choose Hope," one junior said. "It's been a place where I can get a great education while strengthening my faith. I've gotten to meet some really great people and made friendships I think are going to last for a long time." —*Katherine Kirby Smith*

FYI

If you come to Hope College, you'd better bring "a Nalgene bottle—everybody has one here."
What's a typical weekend schedule? "Friday, hang out with friends or go to a house party at night; Saturday, sleep until noon, study, go see a sporting event, then do something social or go to another party; Sunday, get up early and go to church, eat downtown at the Windmill, study, and go to the Gathering at night."
If I could change one thing about Hope College, I'd "loosen up the housing policy and make it easier to register for classes."
Three things every student at Hope College should do before they graduate are "attend Gathering, go on a mission trip for spring break, and go streaking on a Chapel Run."

Kalamazoo College

Address: 1200 Academy Street, Kalamazoo, MI 49006
Phone: 269-337-7166
E-mail address: admiss@kzoo.edu
Web site URL: www.kzoo.edu
Year Founded: 1833
Private or Public: Private
Religious Affiliation: None
Location: Urban
Number of Applicants: 2,092
Percent Accepted: 63%
Percent Accepted who enroll: 27%
Number Entering: 363
Number of Transfers Accepted each Year: 6
Middle 50% SAT range: M: 570–680, CR: 580–690, Wr: Unreported
Middle 50% ACT range: 26–30
Early admission program EA/ED/None: ED

Percentage accepted through EA or ED: Unreported
EA and ED deadline: 10-Nov
Regular Deadline: 1-Feb
Application Fee: $35
Full time Undergraduate enrollment: 1,340
Total enrollment: 2,748
Percent Male: 42%
Percent Female: 58%
Total Percent Minority or Unreported: 9%
Percent African-American: 4%
Percent Asian/Pacific Islander: 6%
Percent Hispanic: 4%
Percent Native-American: <1%
Percent International: 1%
Percent in-state/out of state: 69%/31%
Percent from Public HS: 85%
Retention Rate: 91%

Graduation Rate 4-year: 70%
Graduation Rate 6-year: 74%
Percent Undergraduates in On-campus housing: 77%
Number of official organized extracurricular organizations: 50
3 Most popular majors: Economics, English Language and Literature, Psychology
Student/Faculty ratio: 13:1
Average Class Size: 16
Percent of students going to grad school: Unreported
Tuition and Fees: $30,723
In-State Tuition and Fees if different: No difference
Cost for Room and Board: $7,443
Percent receiving financial aid out of those who apply, first year: 98%
Percent receiving financial aid among all students: 98%

You go *where*? Students at Kalamazoo College are used to hearing this when they tell people where they go to school. First, there is the hurdle of realizing that Kalamazoo is in fact a real place, not an exotic landscape imagined by Dr. Seuss. Next, people add, "Oh, you mean you go to Western." Kalamazoo College, right in the heart of the bustling and very real city of Kalamazoo, Michigan, is not in fact connected to Western Michigan University, a large state school. K-Zoo, as students affectionately refer to it, is actually a small haven in the midst of a busy city, a community of only 1,340 scholars committed to knowing every face and every name. Despite, or perhaps because of, Kalamazoo's relative obscurity and small size, the school creates an environment where students are encouraged to try everything and stretch beyond the limits of what they think they can do.

The K-Zoo K-Plan

Catchy name aside, this academic program is renowned for its broad spectrum of classes and its emphasis on experimentation. The K-Plan encompasses, but is not limited to, classes chosen from such disparate fields as physical education, foreign language, math, world religion, and a first-quarter freshman literature seminar. Although the task of completing these requirements may seem Herculean, one freshman reassured prospective students that "the K-Plan is not strenuous to fulfill." In fact, she said, "I feel like I'm getting a broad education—I know they don't want me to limit myself." Along with the importance placed on taking a wide variety of classes, comes the out-of-the ordinary schedule. "Kalamazoo is on the quarter system. We start later, in mid-September, and we end in early June," one student explained. The fact that classes only last for 10 weeks as opposed to the typical college schedule of 15, makes the experience "really intense," said one student. However, students appreciate the fact that they can "really dive into a subject" since they take a· course load of about three classes rather than the four or five one might find at a college with the standard schedule. Because of the shorter, more compressed plan, students find that they get to know their classmates and professors very well. Students reported no classes larger than around 25–30 people, which significantly contributes to the sense of having "personal relationships with professors." One student specifically commended the foreign language department on a French class of only nine people. She remarked that the small class size made it easy to "converse and not get lost in the crowd."

The foreign language department goes beyond small class sizes at Kalamazoo. It is such a large and well-established department that more than 80 percent of students study abroad during their time at K-Zoo.

This staggering number is a nod not only to foreign languages themselves, but also to other very popular majors such as economics and international business and relations. Students say that the Center for International Programs is a widely used resource on campus and note that the staff is very helpful with transferring financial aid. The experimentation inherent in the classes students are required to take is mirrored in the popularity of studying abroad, and students appreciate the "balance" between the familiar and the new to which they are exposed at K-Zoo.

Going to the Zoo . . .

. . . Really requires a car. The so-called "K-bubble" of the college is comforting in its very small spread, but when students want to get out into town, they say it can be difficult to find transportation. While The Rave, a theater that sells $5 movie tickets, is within walking distance, students recommend the Hot Spot Shuttle to get to the mall. The school itself is "pretty self-contained, which is kind of a drag," lamented one student. Still, students appreciate the school's attempts to reach out into the urban community with programs such as "Farms to K" and tutoring at local inner city elementary schools. The "Farms to K" program encourages everyone in the city to eat locally and practice conservation. One student said that despite the somewhat isolated campus, the students "reach out to greater Kalamazoo—K-Zoo is a very community-oriented place."

Animal House . . . or Not

It may be hard to get into the city, but the campus itself is conveniently small and compact. The hilly campus has two dorms at the top of the mound and classroom buildings and the rest of the dorms are scattered right at the bottom. Although the hillside dorms are a bit farther away, one student said, "When I say out of the way I mean about a minute out of the way. The walk across campus is five minutes tops." The two freshman dorms are very different, but students say that each has its good qualities. The largest dorm on campus houses 200 students and has movable furniture, whereas the other has two rooms connected by a bathroom. Upperclassmen have the option of living in suites in their dorms, and the housing process is one that relies on seniority for first picks. All the dorms are coed, although students note that they have single-sex halls. The fact that "most people live on campus until senior year" really contributes to a sense of community on the K-Zoo campus. One student remarked, "I was surprised by how much I mixed. There's not a big difference between classes—friends come from all years."

The lack of fraternities and sororities on campus does not mean that there are no other living options. Off-campus housing is just minutes away on foot and students call it very convenient. There are also four theme houses chosen every year. Sophomores fill out applications for a theme in a group and must agree to sponsor one event per quarter. Students are allowed to rush fraternities and sororities at Western Michigan University, but "hardly anyone does," according to one student. That's also where students go for the big parties—"it's pretty low-key on our campus."

> "It's nice to walk around campus and see people you know. It feels like a community."

As far as the campus itself goes, one student said, "It looks very East Coast." With its brick buildings, red brick road, and grassy quad, K-Zoo offers very much the archetypal college setting. The Capital, a big building in the middle of the quad, serves as the center for everything. While Kalamazoo is currently redoing its student center, the new glass-paned expansion of the library overlooking the campus makes up for it in spaces for students. K-Zoo students are proud of the library, redone in 2006. One student boasted, "We've increased the space by 30 percent but increased energy use by only 10 percent. We're very ecologically aware." In addition, the brand-new cafeteria boasts a wooden pizza oven. However, one student said, "I've had worse . . . but they do serve a lot of tofu."

What to Do in the Zoo

Despite the small size of the community, students assure prospective students, or "prospies" as they're known at K-Zoo, that "clubs are filled in." One student said, "I go to a school with a bunch of overachievers, and they want to do everything." As such, students describe a campus with flyers everywhere and event centerpieces on the lunch tables. "Kalamazoo is good about bringing speakers in and providing activities," and the students get "really into what they do." Although students say that the campus "is not sports-oriented whatsoever," they agree that "a lot of people are athletes." The football team may be terrible, but students proudly express their prowess in tennis: "It's what we're known for." Other activities, such as the Frelon Dance Company and the LGBT drag show, Kaleidoscope, provide a wide range of things to do on campus. One student said that "the school allows for you to try more than one thing—you can sing in five different choirs or be as overactive as you want."

The K-Zoo Experience

"People who know about Kalamazoo only have wonderful things to say about it," said one student as she admitted in the same breath that few people fall into this category. But the hidden gem with the "weird name" lives up to its reputation as a school that is challenging while being community-oriented. One student explained, "They want you to try new things and experiment. They expect you'll do great sometimes, and other times you won't do so well." That attitude of exploration and desire to grow beyond the student that arrived on campus permeates every aspect of life. One student summed up the K-Zoo experience when she said, "It's nice to walk around campus and see people you know. It feels like a community."
—*Hannah Jacobson*

FYI

If you come to Kalamazoo, you'd better bring "a warm coat!"

What is the typical weekend schedule? "40-minute Fridays make all Friday classes only 40 minutes, and then we party on Friday and Saturday night, followed by everyone going to brunch on Sunday."

If I could change one thing about Kalamazoo, I'd "make it not snow so much: we get all the lake effect!"

Three things every student at Kalamazoo should do before graduating are "study abroad, do an externship, and mudslide on the hill."

Michigan State University

Address: 250 Hannah Administration Bldg, East Lansing, MI 48824-0590	**Percentage accepted through EA or ED:** NA	**Graduation Rate 4-year:** 73%
Phone: 517-355-8332	**EA and ED deadline:** NA	**Graduation Rate 6-year:** 74%
E-mail address: admis@msu.edu	**Regular Deadline:** Rolling	**Percent Undergraduates in On-campus housing:** 43%
Web site URL: www.msu.edu	**Application Fee:** $35 domestic; $50 international	**Number of official organized**
Year Founded: 1855	**Full time Undergraduate enrollment:** 36,337	**extracurricular organizations:** 600
Private or Public: Public	**Total enrollment:** 46,648	**3 Most popular majors:**
Religious Affiliation: None	**Percent Male:** 46%	Advertising, Finance,
Location: Small city	**Percent Female:** 54%	Education
Number of Applicants: 25,500	**Total Percent Minority or Unreported:** 16%	**Student/Faculty ratio:** 17:1
Percent Accepted: 68%	**Percent African-American:** 7%	**Average Class Size:** 29
Percent Accepted who enroll: 41%	**Percent Asian/Pacific Islander:** 5%	**Percent of students going to grad school:** Unreported
Number Entering: 7,378	**Percent Hispanic:** 3%	**Tuition and Fees:** $25,722
Number of Transfers Accepted each Year: 2,500	**Percent Native-American:** 1%	**In-State Tuition and Fees if different:** $10,264
Middle 50% SAT range: M: 540–660, CR:480–620, Wr: 480–610	**Percent International:** 8%	**Cost for Room and Board:** $7,076
Middle 50% ACT range: 23–27	**Percent in-state/out of state:** 79%/21%	**Percent receiving financial aid out of those who apply, first year:** 64%
Early admission program EA/ED/None: None	**Percent from Public HS:** Unreported	**Percent receiving financial aid among all students:** 45%
	Retention Rate: 91%	

The best test of how long a student has been at Michigan State University is to ask him or her where in Michigan he or she goes to school. The freshest of the freshmen will just say, "East Lansing." The ones who are true MSU Spartans, though, will point to a little spot on their palms near the thumb and say, "right here!" In the Mitten State, you'll find that this is how the real Michiganders show off their home allegiance, and students at Michigan State are happy to become part of it—despite the many feet of snow they're likely to brave during the winter. And there will be lots of them around to ask: with over 36,000 undergrads and 10,000 more in the grad school, MSU has a broad population of students who are joined by an atmosphere of Midwestern friendliness, a curriculum as wide as the student body itself, and a deep love of Spartan football.

Not (Just) Another Big State School

Although it can be daunting to try to pick classes at a school that offers over 200 programs of study, students say that it is precisely that broad spectrum of educational opportunities that they appreciate about MSU. Although many choose to navigate this sea of classes in the main college, MSU offers an honors program for those who want the experience of a smaller community within the school as a whole, and three specialized residential colleges with their own unique programs of study. These residential colleges offer focused curricula ranging from the sciences in Lyman Briggs RC to politics and international relations in James Madison to liberal arts and humanities in the newest residential college, the Arts and Humanities RC. Students used many words to describe these colleges, among them "prestigious," "pompous," "reputable," "great" and "worthwhile," and they note that each college attracts students who are "really interested in the subject matter covered." All three of these colleges offer regular as well as honors programs, and require an application process. Although students say classes in the RCs are known for being "amazingly hard," they all agreed that the smaller class sizes—capped at 25—and access to the "incredible professors" make the experience well worth the extra work.

But special programs are not just for RC students. MSU offers "one of the best study abroad programs in the country—just pick a place, and you can go there," one sophomore explained. A freshman added that the study abroad program offers opportunities "on all seven continents—yes, seven!" Students say that MSU makes it very easy to go abroad, and in fact, James Madison programs have a mandatory internship or semester abroad built in. Students really like the fact that MSU fosters an expectation of going abroad, because "at other schools, it seems like students are afraid to leave campus. Here, it's the norm." In addition, over half the students who study abroad receive some form of financial aid, which "makes a huge difference."

> "It is really easy to find small groups to hang out with and the largeness of the school enables students to have the maximum number of opportunities to pursue whatever they might be into."

This is not to say that students who stay on campus have a chance to get bored—far from it! When asked about popular majors, students came up with everything from Kinesiology to Business to Education to Veterinary Prep to the renowned Agriculture program that was part of Michigan State's original land grant. One graduating senior offered, "With such a big school, the classes offered are endless—I wish I had more time to take all the ones I've been interested in."

Spartans Gone Wild
Warriors inside the classroom, these Spartans also know how to leave the books behind and have fun. Students agree that there is "a large drinking scene" at MSU, but they are quick to say that there are plenty of ways to cut loose without breaking out the alcohol. "The Union and the Student Activities Board also have a lot of events and programs that occur on those nights for those that don't want to have the typical drunken party experience," one student pointed out. Activities ranging from bowling to free movies to student talent shows such as Spartan Idol (singing) and Last Spartan Standing (stand-up comedy) provide great

weekend entertainment that does not revolve around frats. That said, the "beer pong tournaments and special theme nights at clubs" are the more dominant social scenes at MSU, both of which make for an extremely lively campus on the weekends.

But weekends won't be the only time off, and the "Sparticipation" extravaganza at the beginning of the year will help funnel new freshmen into extracurriculars and clubs. This activities bazaar places freshmen in the middle of representatives from all the extracurricular groups, which "can be overwhelming," said one, who quickly added that it "ended up being the best way to just dive in and figure out what I wanted to do." A seasoned sophomore coming at it from the other side also noted, "You get a lot of free stuff and it is the best way to figure out what you might want to be involved in because everyone is in the same place at the same time." Popular extracurriculars include the clearly dominant frat scene, but beyond that, the "huge athletics program" provides a draw, in addition to language clubs, Student Activities Board, poetry and creative writing organizations, and even martial arts. A sophomore said, "there is a lot of pride for the sports teams, and the students are very into supporting the school through sports." This takes the form of cheering on the basketball team from the student section, called the "Izzone," gearing up for football Saturdays, or playing sports on any level from casual dorm wars to more intense club athletics. Students say that the great thing about going to such a large school is that "there is pretty much any and every extracurricular you could ever want—there is something for everyone!"

This is Sparta!
It may be a little less ancient, but the ivy-covered brick of the older buildings on the northern campus of MSU show off the school's picturesque environment. One student raved, "The Red Cedar River runs right through the center of campus and has some really awesome walking paths around it. The botanical gardens are also a must-see." While the dorms themselves are fairly standard, students say they enjoy their time living on campus. "A lot of juniors and seniors move off campus, but dorm locations do get better as you get older, so there's something to be said for that, too," one junior noted. A sophomore added that living in a dorm "has been a great way to meet people and get to know the campus."

As far as going off-campus is concerned, students say that upperclassmen are much more likely to do so if only because freshmen are not allowed to have cars on campus. Still, they say the campus is easy to get around on foot or by bus, and that East Lansing itself is "very pleasant."

Scream 4: Spartan Style

Instead of masked killers, this "scream" is an MSU tradition that takes place every finals week. One student explained that "At exactly midnight, everyone sticks their heads outside whatever room they might be studying in and screams at the top of their lungs." This de-stressing ritual serves as a good reminder that even a big school like MSU allows students to form strong bonds both to each other and to the institution. The fear of large universities is not lost on students, and one shared, "I was really worried that the campus would be too big and that I might get 'lost' with so many people. The great thing is, it is really easy to find small groups to hang out with and the largeness of the school enables students to have the maximum number of opportunities to pursue whatever they might be into." While one student noted a current lack of diversity on campus, she was quick to say that it seems that "the school is doing its best to change that." Other students mentioned the fact that "MSU draws so many different kinds of people" also helps everyone find a place to fit in despite the size. The traditions and incredible school spirit that pervade the campus of MSU give this fiery student body a lot of common ground and a huge number of opportunities to express it, both inside the classroom and out.—*Hannah Jacobson*

FYI

If you come to MSU, you'd better bring "something green for school spirit!"

What's the typical weekend schedule? "Wake up, grab lunch/breakfast, go to work/practice, hang out in the dorm, chill out with the floor mates (usually playing RockBand), go for early dinner, study, party, go to bed."

If I could change one thing about MSU, I'd "make the campus smaller."

Three things every student at MSU should do before graduating are, "have a picture with Sparty the Statue, paint the rock with a group of friends or an organization you are involved in, and take advantage of the study abroad program!"

Michigan Technological University

Address: 1400 Townsend Drive, Houghton, MI 49931
Phone: 888-688-1885
E-mail address: mtu4u@mtu.edu
Web site URL: www.admissions.mtu.edu
Year Founded: 1885
Private or Public: Public
Religious Affiliation: None
Location: Suburban
Number of Applicants: 5,415
Percent Accepted: 77%
Percent Accepted who enroll: 37%
Number Entering: 1,580
Number of Transfers Accepted each Year: 524
Middle 50% SAT range: M: 590–690, CR: 530–650, Wr: 500–620
Middle 50% ACT range: 23–28
Early admission program EA/ED/None: None
Percentage accepted through EA or ED: NA

EA and ED deadline: NA
Regular Deadline: Rolling with priority consideration by Jan. 15
Application Fee: $0
Full time Undergraduate enrollment: 5,591
Total enrollment: 7,014
Percent Male: 77%
Percent Female: 23%
Total Percent Minority or Unreported: 10%
Percent African-American: 2%
Percent Asian/Pacific Islander: 1%
Percent Hispanic: 1%
Percent Native-American: 1%
Percent International: 5%
Percent in-state/out of state: 72% /28%
Percent from Public HS: Unreported
Retention Rate: 82%
Graduation Rate 4-year: 24%

Graduation Rate 6-year: 64%
Percent Undergraduates in On-campus housing: 46%
Number of official organized extracurricular organizations: 180
3 Most popular majors: Engineering, Computing, Natural & Physical Sciences
Student/Faculty ratio: 11:1
Average Class Size: 30
Percent of students going to grad school: Immediately: 14%, Within one year: 20%, within 5 years: 75%, within 10 years: 85%
Tuition and Fees: $22,522
In-State Tuition and Fees if different: $10,762
Cost for Room and Board: $7,738
Percent receiving financial aid out of those who apply, first year: 72%
Percent receiving financial aid among all students: 58%

Originally established in 1885 to train mining engineers, Michigan Tech has evolved into a widely renowned institution with a vast array of opportunities for engineers and nonengineers alike. Located in the upper region of Michigan in the town of Houghton, this midsized college boasts a beautiful campus surrounded by snow-covered mountains, woods, and trails. But don't be fooled by the calm and quiet surroundings—Michigan Tech is one of the busiest places to spend one's college years.

Not Just For Engineers

Michigan Tech prides itself on its abundant research opportunities, especially its prized Enterprise Program. The program provides hands-on work with outfits like NASA, DaimlerChrysler, SBC Ameritech, and the EPA. Teams of 20 to 30 students solve real-world engineering and manufacturing problems submitted by Michigan Tech's industry, business and corporate partners. The field of re-

search for each group varies, including, but not limited to, aerospace, alternative fuels, robotic systems, and wireless communication.

Whether you're doing engineering research or not, chances are you'll be working hard at Michigan Tech. As one student said, "Most people here are very into their schooling, so I am able to keep on track as well." The school's atmosphere is intensely preprofessional; undergraduates are often taking career goals into account as they work. One student explained, "Classes are very tough, but our job placement is very high. For premed majors, there is an 80 percent for med school, while the national average is 40 percent." This type of education guarantees that Michigan Tech students are prepared for the real world.

Small Town Snow Sports

Houghton, Michigan, is a very cold place, so you better bring some snow boots. The campus is covered with snow, water, woods, and trails, and the University even owns its own ski and snowboarding mountains with discounted season passes for students. The powder-covered mountains and serene hills create a calm, safe campus environment—so safe, in fact, that many people claim Houghton to be the safest town in Michigan.

> **"The people here are very laid-back . . . I like the whole 'small town' feel."**

But safe definitely doesn't mean boring. With about 180 student groups on campus, there is certainly no shortage of things to do. "[There is] almost too much to do, there are many things I want to do that I just don't have time for . . . and most people think there is nothing to do up here because we're in the middle of nowhere," one student noted. With about 5,300 undergraduates, Michigan Tech is large enough that each activity attracts a substantial group of students. Yet, it is small enough that students can hold leadership positions without feeling too stressed out about their extracurriculars. As one student explained "The people here are very laid-back . . . I like the whole 'small town' feel."

Life in the Winter Wonderland
In terms of housing, all freshmen are required to live in one of three fully equipped residential halls, encouraging class bonding and facilitating the integration of the "frosh" into the campus scene. After that, students can choose whether or not to stay on campus for their next three years. To keep themselves entertained, Michigan Tech students take advantage of the many concerts and performances staged around campus; performers have included Mary Chapin Carpenter and Tap Dogs Rebooted. Greek life, in spite of its small numbers, has a substantial influence on the campus's social scene. Greeks coordinate several parties every semester for everyone's enjoyment. One of the biggest events of the year is the annual Winter Carnival held in February. Human dogsled races, ice bowling, snow volleyball, and fireworks are all part of the extravaganza that is Winter Carnival. Groups on campus spend weeks preparing and creating statues and snow sculptures and teams to compete in the various races. The event is so popular that it attracts tourists from all over Michigan.

Diversity is a bit lacking at Michigan Tech: the school is about 85–90 percent Caucasian. Yet, students said that there is a growing international and minority presence, and all undergraduates have the option of participating in exchange programs or study abroad. The gender ratio is also unbalanced. Like most tech schools, the male majority leaves the lucky ladies with ample choices. "The dating scene is more competitive here . . . and the women tend to use that to their advantage," one student explained. Overall, students agreed that Michigan Tech "is very accepting" of all types and is working to improve its reputation and racial and gender diversity.

Hockey, Skiing, and . . . Broomball?
With a Division I Men's Hockey team, a dozen DII teams and many intramural teams, it is no surprise that many students choose to stay active. In fact, nearly 90 percent of students partake in intramurals. "A lot of people like to get involved with sports up here . . . it is a great way to stay in shape and meet a lot of people," one intramural athlete noted. The cold weather encourages sports unique to snow and ice. Aside from the usual skiing and ice hockey, students use the icy conditions to play a school favorite: broomball. One student explained the glories of their prized sport: "Broomball is huge up here. It is like hockey played on ice but you wear street shoes and use brooms as hockey sticks . . . you have to wear kneepads though or else you will get very bruised . . . Everybody gets really into it, everybody!" Students can be found playing broomball whenever possible—during intramural games, pickup games, and, of course, during Winter Carnival.

It is this mix of academic seriousness and fun-loving athletic spirit that continues to draw students to Michigan Tech year after year. And if you are excited by its combination of intellectual and athletic rigor, it just might be the place for you. Just don't forget your kneepads.—*Suzanne Salgado*

FYI

If you come to MTU, you'd better bring "snow shoes and a shovel."

What's the typical weekend schedule? "Days are spent at meetings or in the library, nights are for going out with friends, and Sundays especially are for homework."

If I could change one thing about MTU it would be "to have more parking: I have to get up early to get a good parking spot."

Three things every student at MTU should do before graduating are: "Go cliff jumping, explore the copper country, and learn to ski/snowboard (and if you know how to ski or snowboard, go to Mt. Bohemia)."

University of Michigan

Address: 1220 Student Activities Building, Ann Arbor, MI 48109-1316

Phone: 734-764-7433

E-mail address: ugadmiss@umich.edu

Web site URL: www.umich.edu

Year Founded: 1817

Private or Public: Public

Religious Affiliation: None

Location: Urban

Number of Applicants: 27,474

Percent Accepted: 50%

Percent Accepted who enroll: 43%

Number Entering: 5,955

Number of Transfers Accepted each Year: 1,154

Middle 50% SAT range: M: 630–730, CR: 590–690, **Wr:** Unreported

Middle 50% ACT range: 27–31

Early admission program EA/ED/None: EA

Percentage accepted through EA or ED: Unreported

EA and ED deadline: 31-Oct

Regular Deadline: 1-Feb

Application Fee: $40

Full time Undergraduate enrollment: 26,083

Total enrollment: 38,426

Percent Male: 50%

Percent Female: 50%

Total Percent Minority or Unreported: 34%

Percent African-American: 6%

Percent Asian/Pacific Islander: 12%

Percent Hispanic: 5%

Percent Native-American: 1%

Percent International: 5%

Percent in-state/out of state: 68%/32%

Percent from Public HS: Unreported

Retention Rate: 96%

Graduation Rate 4-year: 88%

Graduation Rate 6-year: Unreported

Percent Undergraduates in On-campus housing: 63%

Number of official organized extracurricular organizations: 1000

3 Most popular majors: Business Administration and Management, English Language and Literature, Psychology

Student/Faculty ratio: 15:1

Average Class Size: 25

Percent of students going to grad school: 36%

Tuition and Fees: $33,069

In-State Tuition and Fees if different: $11,037

Cost for Room and Board: $8,590

Percent receiving financial aid out of those who apply, first year: 71%

Percent receiving financial aid among all students: 48%

Home to one of the nation's most celebrated college football teams and the lab where Jonas Salk's team first invented the cure for polio, the University of Michigan is every bit as diverse as its rich history. Located in Ann Arbor, UMich has a student body of over 25,000 and academic and extracurricular opportunities for all of its students. Although the university is recognized nationally for its prestigious academic programs, Michigan is best known for students' enormous pride—after all, students say, it's absolutely true that "It's Great! To Be! A Michigan Wolverine!"

Academics in Ann Arbor

To accommodate the large student body, UM is divided into 11 undergraduate schools and colleges, between which there are over 200 academic departments. Applicants apply directly to one of the eleven, and while most chose the interdisciplinary College of Literature, Arts, and Sciences, other popular choices include the College of Engineering and the School of Art and Design. Within the College of Literature, Arts, and Sciences (LSA), Michigan also offers a Residential College (RC) program. As part of this four-year interdisciplinary liberal arts program,

900 students are given the opportunity to live with over fifty professors in a "living-learning community" in East Quadrangle Residence Hall. Students hail the program as a "great way to get to know your peers, especially in a school so big."

Another great academic option is the University's Honors College. Select students are offered admission into the program, which features unique advising and research programs, special courses that are often unavailable to the general undergraduate population, and its own housing option. There are also specific residential programs based on disciplines such as art, engineering, writing, and more. For those interested in performing research, Michigan's Undergraduate Research Opportunity Program (UROP) provides many opportunities to get involved in professors' research, even as a freshman or sophomore. One common complaint is that although the opportunities are available, it can often be daunting to seek them out as a freshman in a university quite as large as Michigan—but "if you're proactive about it, you can do anything."

Requirements at UMich are diverse, but not too daunting. All students have to take classes in the natural sciences, humanities, social sciences, and language over their four years at the university. Most students complete the majority of their requirements freshman year, before declaring their majors. This leaves them with plenty of time to explore the various courses offered by the university, which stretch from typical science and humanities courses to unique lectures and seminars crafted by well-known professors, such as the Law and Public Policy course taught by U of M's general counsel, who once argued in front of the Supreme Court.

The engineering program is certainly the most competitive of Michigan's many undergraduate programs, although premed, architecture, and business students are competitive to a certain extent. Overall, however, the students praise the university's academic environment as one of cooperation—at a school as big as Michigan, it's very easy to find friends to study with and helpful TAs.

Wild Wild Wolverines

There's always something to do at UMich, and most students say that weekends truly stretch over four or five nights every week. And by no means is the social scene limited to nightlife—Saturdays in the fall are full of tailgates throughout the day. Greek life plays a large role on campus, with over three dozen fraternities and sororities on campus. Many freshmen rush "as a way to make friends," with 16% of guys and about 20% of girls choosing to join a fraternity or sorority. Frat parties make up a considerable amount of the nightlife on Friday and Saturday nights, and are particularly popular with freshmen.

However, the Greek system is by no means the only option for going out at U of M—Ann Arbor has dozens of bars and nightclubs that are extremely popular with the student body. The bar scene doesn't really pick up until junior year, but plays an active role for many upperclassmen. Upperclassmen also have the luxury of having larger parties at off-campus apartments or on-campus Co-Ops.

Alcohol is the "poison of choice" on campus, and most Michigan students say that social events often center on drinking. Although the administration has made attempts to strengthen drinking codes, students say it's easy to avoid trouble. "There's beer everywhere you go," students say, insisting that it's difficult to graduate from U of M without an appreciation for Keystone. There are rumors of an increase in cocaine use on campus in recent years, largely among wealthy students from the east and west coasts. Yet, drugs other than alcohol and, on occasion, marijuana, are far and few.

Great to be an Ann Arbor Wolverine

The University of Michigan and Ann Arbor have a very close relationship—students say that they live in "the perfect college town" and brag that oftentimes, it's hard to tell where UMich ends and Ann Arbor begins. The town also offers many interesting things to do, including art museums, jazz clubs, and plenty of nice restaurants. Most of all, students praise Ann Arbor's Midwestern hospitality, which makes the midsized suburban town very welcoming.

UMich freshmen live on campus, and although some dorms can be far from classes, find their living situations very comfortable. One of the most popular areas for freshmen to live is the Hill, a complex of five dorms—Stockwell, Lloyd Hall, Couzens, Mosher-Jordan (MoJo), and Mary Markley—that each have their own distinct personality. Most students move off campus after their first or second year, although because the campus is so large, their off-campus apartments sometimes end up being closer to academic buildings than the dorms. It also often keeps them far from one of the University of Michigan's biggest campus superstitions—students say that if you walk on the large brass M in the Diag (a large open space in the middle of Central Campus) before your first blue book-exam, you're sure to fail it.

If there's one thing all students at Michigan can agree upon, it's that the university has immense amounts of school pride. Part of the Big Ten conference, U of M has many nationally recognized sports teams that always draw huge crowds, even if it isn't a winning season. Football in particular dominates campus life during fall semester—students spend every Saturday at "The Big House," Michigan's famous stadium which seats over 100,000. Tailgating is also extremely popular among students, who routinely get up earlier on Saturdays than some weekdays to "start the day right." Students, alums, Ann Arbor residents, and fans

from all over flock to the stadium dressed in blue and maize, as if "the whole community had football fever."

> "I've never felt more at home than when I'm sitting in the Big House."

That's really what the University of Michigan is all about—even with such a large student body, sports and school pride truly bring the students at the university together in one giant Wolverine family. And with such a big family, it's certain that students can find exactly what they're looking for, be it academic, extracurricular, or social opportunities. The University's academic offerings are widely respected and certainly can't be overlooked, but it's school pride that really stands out at Michigan—from dorms to classrooms to the Big House, Michigan students are always eager to show off their maize and blue.—*Iva Velickovic*

FYI

If you come to Michigan, you'd better bring "a parka—we get tons of snow every winter!"

The number one thing that surprised me most when I came to Michigan was "how easy it was to find a community in such a big school, especially within the Greek system."

A typical weekend at Michigan includes going out Thursday and Friday, spending most of Saturday tailgating, going out hard on Saturday night, and then finally catching up on work on Sunday.

Minnesota

While students searching for the ideal liberal arts college may turn their sights toward New England or the West Coast, they would be remiss if they did not consider Carleton College, a small college located in the quaint town of Northfield, Minnesota, widely hailed as one of the top liberal arts colleges in the country. Students interested in Carleton should prepare for a highly rigorous academic curriculum, not to mention one of the coldest winters found in the continental United States. But any Carleton student will cheerfully declare that he or she is happy to overlook the subzero temperatures because of the college's friendly student body, approachable professors, and beautiful campus.

A Workload Heavier than the Snowfall

Known for its academic rigor, Carleton prides itself on providing its students with a well-rounded education. While students pronounced the math and the physical science majors to be especially arduous, many agreed that there is no way to get through Carleton without doing one's fair share of work. Students praised Carleton's trimester system for allowing them to dedicate more time to fewer classes, since they are only required to take three at a time. But students also said the fast pace of classes can make each trimester seem like a blur. "If I think about what I learned in the last couple weeks, it feels like it all happened yesterday," said one freshman. Students added that the trimester system has other drawbacks, pointing to a short reading period and the early onset of midterms.

Still, midterms may seem like a small concern in comparison to the myriad distribution requirements each Carleton student must fulfill. Before graduating, each Carleton student must take two arts and literature classes, two humanities classes, three social science classes, and three math or natural science classes. Among Carleton's most distinctive requirements is the writing portfolio students must submit after their sophomore year. Said one English major: "I had a positive experience putting together my portfolio, but if you don't look at the writing portfolio as a way to reflect on yourself, then it's mostly just a hassle and waste of time." Students also have a language requirement, physical education requirement, and one final requirement known as RAD: Recognition and Affirmation of Difference. One senior said of RAD: "It was created as a requirement to improve diversity education, but it's become a little lackluster. It's kind of a useless requirement that no one really thinks about." Still, other students said they appreciated the function of the distribution requirements—including RAD—arguing that the requirements bring variety to the curriculum and provide exposure to a number of interesting topics.

But regardless of the varied opinions on campus toward Carleton's distribution requirements, students voiced unanimous approval of the school's professors and their involvement on campus. Given Carleton's small size, students work closely with their professors and form close relationships over time. "You can talk to professors about everything," one senior said. "People interact closely at Carleton. If I ever write an article for a publication, I can bank on a professor e-mailing me about it and telling me they liked it." Fortunately, small classes abound at Carleton, offering more opportunities for students to get to know their professors. Students said they found little difficulty getting into the courses they desired, noting that in the unlikely event of getting wait-listed, a student can often squeeze his or her way into the class.

But Enough about School . . .
While Carleton's coursework is tough, it is far from the only thing on students' minds. Although Minnesota's harsh winters may seem like a deterrent from social events, students said it only emboldens them to be more outgoing. "We're in the tundra, so we have to find something to do," one student said. On weekends, that "something" usually includes parties in dorms, as well as on-campus and off-campus houses. Students described Carleton's stance on alcohol to be relatively relaxed, noting that the school's main concern is that students remain safe. Beyond alcohol, students said there is very little substance use, with the exception of marijuana, which students said is used no more or less than at other colleges. Still, students said there is no pressure to use alcohol or drugs, and there are many substance-free events on campus, including dance parties occurring about every week.

Yet Carleton students know how to have fun all the time—not just during late weekend nights. Extracurricular opportunities abound on campus, from the newspaper to community service to dance groups. Among the most popular student groups is a dance group called Ebony, which has upward of 100 members. The group requires no previous training to join and has one dance each term, which is usually very well attended. Beyond dance, students find ways to stay in shape. A large majority of Carleton students participate in intramural sports. Still, trumping intramurals and varsity athletics is one sport that permeates every facet of Carleton life: Frisbee. "I've been hit by a Frisbee four times at Carleton," said one upperclassman. "Everyone plays it. It's one of the biggest things about spring." But while students are waiting for spring to arrive, they can be found playing broomball on a flooded rink in the large, open expanse called the Bald Spot.

Living by the Bald Spot
The Bald Spot marks the center of Carleton's picturesque—albeit architecturally eclectic—campus, which is flanked on all sides by Carleton's many academic, recreational, and dormitory buildings. Freshmen are assigned to various dorms with multiple upperclassmen Resident Advisors per floor. RAs at Carleton get to know their freshmen well, as one freshman noted, saying: "I was shocked that these RAs actually cared. They organize weekly study breaks and meet with us regularly." When students become upperclassmen, they have their pick of a variety of housing, including dorms or on-campus houses. Two new dorms opened during the 2009–2010 school year. Since the college restricts the number of upperclassmen living

off-campus, only one in ten Carleton students currently live off-campus.

Not only do students at Carleton praise the housing, but they also give positive reviews to the food. There are two dining halls on campus, one on the west side of campus, the other on the east side of campus. Still, students wishing to get away from dining hall food can always venture into Northfield, where a variety of cafés and eateries abound. Northfield garnered praise from students for its safe environment and quaint shops, and as one sophomore noted, "Northfield is a good college town. It's always crawling with Carleton students, and restaurants are always open late to suit your needs." But after four years spent at Carleton, Northfield can start to feel a bit confining, said one senior. "There are a million little antique stores that are way overpriced, and that's pretty much it," he said. Students needing a break from Northfield can always take a 40-minute drive up to the nearby Twin Cities, although students said almost everyone stays on campus during the weekends.

Uniquely Carleton

When asked what makes Carleton different from other colleges, students quickly point to their peers. Carleton places a high priority on diversity in its student body, and students said they are constantly impressed with the seemingly boundless knowledge and affability of their classmates. Still, students said the majority of their classmates come from upper-middle-class backgrounds, although all agreed that everyone comes to Carleton with an open mind and unique perspective. Car-

leton's LGBT community is small, said one gay student, but the campus is very accepting, and straight students at Carleton seek to be good allies to their queer peers.

But beyond the friendly student body and top-quality education, there are many other facets of Carleton that make it unique. Consider, for example, "Rotblatt," a campus-wide softball game played annually with as many innings as the age of the College (which has climbed above 100). Another famous facet of Carleton life is the Dacie Moses House, a residence left to the school by alumna Dacie Moses, who stipulated in her donation that the house must always have supplies inside for students to bake cookies. Yet Carleton students could not boast about surviving Minnesota without a few winter traditions. One favorite among students is to go sledding down a mammoth hill behind Evans dorm on dining hall trays.

> "I've been hit by a Frisbee four times at Carleton . . . It's one of the biggest things about spring."

While any Carleton student will name a different tradition as their favorite, many look on their time at the college with affection, noting how difficult they know it will be to leave after graduation. From late night hangouts on the top floor of the library to lively discussions in small classes, Carleton students have myriad opportunities to learn from "the best people you'll ever meet," as one student described her classmates.
—*Raymond Carlson*

FYI
If you come to Carleton, you'd better bring "long underwear and a real Frisbee."
What is the typical weekend schedule? "Friday is usually just party hopping, Saturday there's always a dance, Sunday go to brunch and start working on your paper."
If I could change one thing about Carleton, I'd "move Carleton to Minneapolis. The town is a little isolated sometimes."
Three things every student at Carleton should do before graduating are "explore the underground tunnels, even though they're off limits, participate in an intercultural retreat, and go to the Carleton football game against our major rival, St. Olaf."

Gustavus Adolphus College

Address: 800 West College Avenue, St. Peter, MN 56082

Phone: 507-933-7676

E-mail address: admission@gustavus.edu

Web site URL: www.gustavus.edu

Year Founded: 1862

Private or Public: Private

Religious Affiliation: Lutheran

Location: Rural

Number of Applicants: 3,279

Percent Accepted: 71%

Percent Accepted who enroll: 29%

Number Entering: 675

Number of Transfers Accepted each Year: 79

Middle 50% SAT range: Unreported

Middle 50% ACT range: 24–29

Early admission program EA/ED/None: EA

Percentage accepted through EA or ED: 28%

EA and ED deadline: 1-Nov

Regular Deadline: 1-Apr

Application Fee: $0

Full time Undergraduate enrollment: 2,628

Total enrollment: 2,628

Percent Male: 43%

Percent Female: 57%

Total Percent Minority or Unreported: 12%

Percent African-American: 2%

Percent Asian/Pacific Islander: 5%

Percent Hispanic: 2%

Percent Native-American: <1%

Percent International: 2%

Percent in-state/out of state: 80%/20%

Percent from Public HS: 92%

Retention Rate: Unreported

Graduation Rate 4-year: 83%

Graduation Rate 6-year: Unreported

Percent Undergraduates in On-campus housing: 77%

Number of official organized extracurricular organizations: 120

3 Most popular majors: Biology, Psychology, Business

Student/Faculty ratio: 13:1

Average Class Size: 16

Percent of students going to grad school: 34%

Tuition and Fees: $30,420

In-State Tuition and Fees if different: No difference

Cost for Room and Board: $7,460

Percent receiving financial aid out of those who apply, first year: 81%

Percent receiving financial aid among all students: 66%

The Gustavus Adolphus campus, which is seated upon 350 hilltop acres, is the center of the small town of St. Peter. The College is completely self-contained, abutted by a delightful arboretum dense with trees from Minnesota and Sweden. The modern face of the "Gustie" campus owes a lot to the 1998 tornado that nearly shut down the school and after which the College "invested quite a bit in remodeling." According to students, there are "several very new buildings on campus, mixed in with older ones." These newer buildings—constructed around 2003—include a new 200-resident dormitory that offers a mix of regular dorm rooms available to students of all years and apartment-style living for upperclassmen. Also renovated in the past six years are the fitness facilities at the Lund Center, and Old Main, the oldest building on campus.

Living on the Hill

With such a high percentage of Gusties residing on campus—including all first- and second-year students—housing options are very important. Norelius Hall, known to stu-dents as "Coed," houses 400 freshmen and is located at the northern end of the campus. The building set-up includes "sections" of 11 rooms with a common area at the center. The arrangement facilitates interactions and friendships among first-years; one junior reported that even after two years, all of her best friends lived in her "section" in Coed. The remaining freshmen, as well as the rest of the on-campus students, reside in various other mixed-years dormitories. Students of all classes may apply to live in the International Center, where both American and international students reside and participate in programs that foster cultural awareness. The Collegiate Fellow (CF) on every floor is responsible for enforcing dormitory regulations, and while "it totally depends on the CF," many will be strict only "when they have to be," such as issuing citations for underage possession of alcohol in the dorm or excessive noise in the hallways. Those with junior or senior standing may apply for permission to reside off-campus in St. Peter.

On-campus residents take meals at the highly acclaimed cafeteria, The Caf, which has "great food" and a good selection. In addition to a "grill, rotisserie, and sandwich counter," students may select from "fire-oven-baked pizza, pasta, vegetarian selections, ethnic cuisine, a salad bar, and desserts." Meals are offered on a declining balance system; students opt for one of several-sized plans and are charged for the exact amount of food they take by a swipe of their Three Crowns Card. The cafeteria is open daily from 7 a.m. until 11 p.m., although the best selection of food is available at the "usual" eating times. While students may also use meal-plan dollars at the campus center coffee bar, there are no off-campus meal options available.

Not Just a Number

Gustavus Adolphus runs on the semester system, with four-month fall and spring terms sandwiched around a January "J-term" that offers an opportunity for intensive exploration. Each course counts for one credit, and students must complete 34 credits—including three J-term courses—over their four years. Despite the "pretty extensive list of general education requirements" that forms the basis of the college's liberal arts philosophy, many students find space in their schedules to double-major; one student even reported two majors and a minor. Two semesters of foreign language study are included in the general education requirements.

> "It's a nice feeling not to be just a number in the crowd of students. No one really falls into the masses here."

Biology is reportedly a popular major, with psychology quickly gaining sway. Many students also choose to study management. Biology and physics classes are known to be difficult, and one senior called Bio 101 "the true weeding-out class for premed students." While introductory lecture courses may enroll many dozens of students, higher-level classes taken for the major often have fewer than ten people. Registration for classes is online, and students with more credits register first. While getting excluded from capped classes is sometimes a problem for underclassmen, nobody reported trouble enrolling in a class for their major.

In addition to attending some larger lecture classes, every freshman enrolls in a First Term Seminar (FTS), chosen from a wide variety of disciplines. The FTS serves both as an introduction to college writing (a much appreciated writing credit for the general education requirements) and an opportunity to develop a relationship with a faculty member who will serve as the student's adviser until the declaration of a major.

In addition to the formal relationship with their FTS instructors and major advisers, students report the high availability of all of their professors as a great strength of the college. "I've never had a problem catching a professor," said one sophomore, who added that in addition to posting and holding regular office hours, most instructors are available by appointment or for meals. "Even the president of the college eats in The Caf!" According to another student, "when you start to get into your major, the classes get really small, and your professors will see you on campus and know your name. It's a nice feeling not to be just a number in the crowd of students. No one really falls into the masses here."

The Gustie Life

"Gusties" involve themselves in a wide variety of activities, including the *Gustavian Weekly* (the student newspaper), the student senate, College Democrats and Republicans, choir, theater, Queers and Allies, and even the "Gaming Group," which spends its early mornings fencing with foam swords while wearing capes. Because Gustavus Adolphus is a Lutheran college, "there is a huge focus on faith on campus," and there are several Christian student groups. One popular group, Proclaim, is particularly notable for its Tuesday evening contemporary worship service. The high level of participation in extracurricular organizations, religious or otherwise, makes such activities popular ways for Gusties to meet each other.

Fraternities and sororities are moderately popular, with about a quarter of the campus involved in Greek life. The two-week pledge period takes place at the beginning of sophomore year, with prerush events held at the end of the first year. Greek organizations are not allowed to have houses, but many have "unofficial houses," which are best known for their weekend parties. Even so, one sister reports that Greeks are "required to be proactive on campus and do educationals and activities for the rest of campus and for the St. Peter community."

In addition to attending parties at off-campus houses, many freshmen pass their Friday nights at "The Dive," Gustavus Adolphus's campus dance club. One sophomore describes the scene at The Dive as "drunk, sweaty freshmen dancing close together." Having exhausted the limited social options of St. Peter, upperclassmen tend to take their cars to Mankato, about ten minutes away from campus and the home of Minnesota State-Mankato, or to the Twin Cities of St. Paul and Minneapolis, about an hour's drive. The availability of on-campus parking for less than $100 per year makes it possible for the majority of upperclassmen to bring their cars. Gusties usually take trips to Mankato "to shop, go to the bars, or eat out." In addition to the traditional party nights of Friday and Saturday, many students spend Wednesday nights out because few have Thursday classes.

Gustie athletic events are another social outlet for many students, especially when the highly ranked Division III program is enjoying success on the field, court, or rink. Soccer, football, basketball, and hockey ("It's Minnesota!" one student reminds us) are all favorites. At the game, in the classroom, or on campus, there will always be people wearing Gustavus apparel. As one student notes, "If you're a Gustie, you're proud of it."

Despite the variety of activities in which Gustavus Adolphus students involve themselves, many cite the same complaint about the college: a lack of diversity. Gusties acknowledge that the recruitment of minority students is a "genuine" institutional priority but that the school has difficulty drawing students from outside of "Minnesota, Wisconsin, Iowa, and the Dakotas," as one student put it. The College has increased its recruitment of international students, but according to one student, the campus is still "more of a 'tossed salad' than a 'melting pot,'" with minority students befriending other minority students or spending time at the Diversity Center.

A Community of Scholars

Despite Gusties' brief lamentation over the things that their campus lacks, most describe the Gustavus Adolphus experience as an overwhelmingly positive one. Many look forward to the annual Nobel conference in October, when the campus hosts Nobel laureates and other renowned scholars. Previous conference topics have included "Genetics in the New Millennium," "Unveiling the Solar System: 30 Years of Exploration," and "Nature out of Balance: Unlocking the New Ecology." Other major events include the May Day Conference, held every May 1 on topics of peace, and Christmas in Christ Chapel, an annual Christmas program involving "the entire choir and dance departments."

Most of all, Gustavus Adolphus students appreciate the sense of community that the College fosters. One junior said, "I love the idea that I am able to walk around on campus and pretty much have a general sense of who people are, but still be able to meet new people. Because the campus has enough students to do that, I meet someone new practically every day!" Gusties enjoy themselves while taking advantage of the college's myriad opportunities, and many echo this simple sentiment of one senior: "I love this little campus on the hill."—*Douglas London*

FYI

If you come to Gustavus Adolphus, you'd better bring "a snowsuit, mittens, a hat, a facemask, a HUGE jacket, and a strong will to be outside in these subzero temperatures!"

What's the typical weekend schedule? "Depends on who you are. Some drink, some do homework, but it is a guaranteed good time at Gustavus!"

If I could change one thing about Gustavus Adolphus, "I would increase diversity and cultural awareness."

Three things that every student at Gustavus Adolphus should do before graduating are "go 'traying' down Old Main Hill after the first snow, spend a starry night in the Arboretum, and have a 4 a.m. breakfast at Oodles after pulling an all-nighter."

M a c a l e s t e r　　C o l l e g e

Address: 1600 Grand Avenue
St. Paul, MN 55105
Phone: 651-696-6357
E-mail address:
admissions@macalester.edu
Web site URL:
www.macalester.edu
Year Founded: 1874
Private or Public: Private
Religious Affiliation: None
Location: Urban
Number of Applicants:
4,565
Percent Accepted: 46%
**Percent Accepted who
enroll:** 27%
Number Entering: 565
**Number of Transfers
Accepted each Year:**
Unreported
Middle 50% SAT range: M:
640–730, CR: 670–760,
Wr: 660–750
Middle 50% ACT range:
27–32
**Early admission program
EA/ED/None:** ED I, ED II

**Percentage accepted
through EA or ED:**
53%
EA and ED deadline: 15-Nov,
2-Jan
Regular Deadline: 15-Jan
Application Fee: $40
**Full time Undergraduate
enrollment:** 1,958
Total enrollment: 1,996
Percent Male: 42%
Percent Female: 58%
**Total Percent Minority or
Unreported:** 19%
Percent African-American:
4%
**Percent Asian/Pacific
Islander:** 9%
Percent Hispanic: 4%
Percent Native-American:
1%
Percent International: 12%
**Percent in-state/out of
state:** 19%/81%
Percent from Public HS:
59%
Retention Rate: 94%

Graduation Rate 4-year:
87%
Graduation Rate 6-year:
94%
**Percent Undergraduates in
On-campus housing:** 66%
**Number of official organized
extracurricular
organizations:** 80
3 Most popular majors:
Economics, Political Science,
Psychology
Student/Faculty ratio: 11:1
Average Class Size: 18
**Percent of students going to
grad school:** Unreported
Tuition and Fees: $39,974
**In-State Tuition and Fees if
different:** No difference
Cost for Room and Board:
$8,768
**Percent receiving financial
aid out of those who apply,
first year:** 88%
**Percent receiving financial
aid among all students:**
70%

Macalester is a top-notch liberal arts college. Such a description may immediately create an image of a tiny, perhaps elitist, school covered in ivy and far removed from civilization, but it could not be further from the truth. Surely, Macalester does share some features of a stereotypical liberal arts institution. It has a small enrollment of slightly less than 2,000 students and is located in a quiet residential neighborhood. Yet beyond the school's enclave is also one of the largest urban centers in the United States, the Twin Cities, which offers Macalester the unique sense of both bustling city atmosphere and serene small-town tranquility. Furthermore, despite its location in the Midwest, Macalester has a highly diverse population, with more than 10 percent of its student body coming from overseas.

A Friendly Faculty

With a highly selective admissions process that only accepts 40 percent of applicants, Macalester brings together talented students from around the world. The school ranks 26th on the *U.S. News & World Report*, and *The Princeton Review* grades its quality of life at number seven in the nation, showing that it offers a vigorous academic experience coupled with an enjoyable social environment. "The coursework is hard and competitive, as it should be," said one junior. "But I am enjoying every minute of life here."

Macalester offers more than 40 majors, and the most popular ones are Political Science, Biology, Economics, English, and Psychology. For graduation, students must complete a relatively lengthy set of requirements, designed to ensure their breadth of knowledge. These requirements are similar to those of comparable institutions and include courses on social science, natural science, humanities, writing, foreign language, and quantitative reasoning, which is a euphemism for mathematics-related classes. Unique to Macalester and true to its aspiration to become a truly global university, courses on internationalism and multiculturalism are also listed as requirements.

Another important part of the academic experience is the first-year seminar, taken by every freshman in the fall semester. These classes are small, allow close interactions between professors and students, and place a strong emphasis on writing, an essential skill for anyone who would like to succeed in college. The strong point of this program is that the students can choose from a variety of 30 different seminars, ranging from theater to cellular biology. The professor also serves as faculty advisor for students in the class.

Although the requirements sometimes help students in discovering subjects that they would not have touched otherwise, a few students are ambivalent about taking classes in which they have no interest. "I understand that we need to know different subjects, but it is really hard to find a class that interests me and fulfills the requirements at the same time," commented one student.

As a relatively small college focused solely on undergraduate education, Macalester certainly offers an engaging faculty that gives a high level of attention to the students, unlike many larger research universities, where professors are rarely seen outside of the bi-weekly lectures. "If you try, you can get to know some professors really well and be really good friends with them," remarked one senior.

> "St. Paul is great. It is not New York, but it is still an important city with all kinds of cultural activities and work opportunities."

The tradeoff of receiving such personal attention, however, is that the school lacks the scale and infrastructure of larger institutions. Opportunities can be limited for students seeking laboratory or in-depth research experiences. Nevertheless, the college does have state-of-the-art facilities and tries to remedy some of its disadvantages by offering summer research grants. Studying abroad at a major university can also be helpful. However, as one student said, "if you come here, understand that there are limitations to small colleges."

The Twin Cities

Macalester occupies 53 acres of a historic residential quarter. The campus is approximately a mile away from the gorgeous Mis-

sissippi River that separates St. Paul and Minneapolis. Such location allows students to take advantage of city living while enjoying the tranquility of a quiet neighborhood. "St. Paul is great," said one student. "It is not New York, but it is still an important city with all kinds of cultural activities and work opportunities."

On the downside, Minnesota doesn't exactly have San Diego weather. The winters can be very cold. In fact, it has one of the lowest average temperatures of any major metropolitan area in the United States. As one student mentioned, "the winters here are brutal, especially for those from warm places who are not used to this weather." For snow and ice aficionados, however, the Twin Cities certainly receive plenty of precipitation, both during winter—in the form of snow, hail, and sleet—and summer—in the form of thunderstorms.

The Time of Our Lives

Students are required to live on campus for the first two years. Freshmen live in one of the three residential halls specifically reserved for first-year students. Most of them are assigned to doubles, which, as noted by one freshman, "are reasonably well-kept." Lounges are also available for students to meet and socialize. Those interested in gastronomy can take advantage of the kitchens in each residential hall. The upperclassmen generally have rooms that are more spacious and apartment-like. Since Macalester is in a major city, a significant portion of juniors and seniors—about half of them—prefer living off campus. The process of finding a nice home at a low price can be burdensome, but the college does provide rental listings to help its students. In addition to these options, there are also theme houses, including six language houses, the Hebrew House, EcoHouse, the Cultural House, and the Veggie Co-op, available to all after one semester of study.

Despite its small size, a large number of activities can be found on campus during weekends. While some students are drawn by the attractions of the Twin Cities and drift away from the campus during weekends, the majority of students do stay within Macalester, attending different parties or simply hanging out with friends. Given the size of its student body, Macalester has neither fraternities nor sororities. Therefore, most parties happen in dorm rooms. Alcohol, as in most colleges, abounds. Those who wish to remain dry are occasionally pressured to drink, but most of them do not feel out of place by staying sober during parties. "Drinking is widespread," said one student. "But people won't look down on you if you don't drink."

The sports teams compete in Minnesota Intercollegiate Athletic Conference, which belongs to NCAA Division III. "We are a small school," said one junior. "We are not USC or Michigan State, and that shows with our football team." On the other hand, the soccer teams at Macalester are both popular and relatively successful, having achieved consecutive winning seasons. At the same time, a number of students participate in intramural and club sports. "A lot of people enjoy playing sports even though Mac is not a big sports school," said one student.

Good Old Liberals

Macalester has been long considered one of the most liberal colleges in the United States. Therefore, Republicans can feel slightly out of place if they participate in the political scene on campus. "It is rare to find a Republican on campus these days," said one student. "I don't think people would hate someone who is an activist Republican, but I think that person would feel really uncomfortable in political discussions be-

cause he or she will be against everyone else." Nevertheless, most students agree that Macalester is generally tolerant of other people's ideas and serves as a good forum for discussions and debates.

Another unique aspect of Macalester is its large population of foreign students for a relatively small liberal arts college. The school has strongly advocated an internationalization of the campus, and the students are particularly proud of this ethnic and cultural diversity. "I think this is one of the most important parts of Mac," mentioned one student. "Seeing people from everywhere around the world is just wonderful and really helps you learn more about the world."

"I think Macalester deserves more recognition and should be a highly sought-after college," said one student. Indeed, given its academic excellence, Macalester is perhaps not as well known as a few other liberal arts institutions. The location in Minnesota and the harsh winter certainly contribute to it. There are also complaints about the small size and thus the lack of different opportunities. Nonetheless, the students are generally happy and glad that they chose to attend Macalester. Ultimately, that is what is important.
—*Xiaohang Liu*

FYI
If you come to Macalester, you'd better bring "something warm to keep you warm."
What is the typical weekend schedule? "It depends. It is different every weekend. There is so much to offer in the Twin Cities during day and night. But sadly, not everyone takes advantage of it."
If I could change one thing about Macalester, I'd "move this whole place to a lower latitude."
Three things every student at Macalester should do before graduating are "visit the city during the night, live in a theme house, and start a snowball fight."

St. John's University / College of St. Benedict

Address: PO Box 7155
  Collegeville, MN
  56321-7155
Phone: 320-363-2196
E-mail address:
  admissions@csbsju.edu
Web site URL:
  www.csbsju.edu
Year Founded: 1857
Private or Public: Private
Religious Affiliation: Roman
  Catholic
Location: Rural
Number of Applicants:
  3,204
Percent Accepted: 74%
**Percent Accepted who
  enroll:** 44%
Number Entering: 1,052
**Number of Transfers
  Accepted each Year:**
  51
Middle 50% SAT range: M:
  540–660 CR: 500–633,
  Wr: Unreported
Middle 50% ACT range:
  22–28
**Early admission program
  EA/ED/None:** EA

**Percentage accepted
  through EA or ED:**
  Unreported
EA and ED deadline: 15-Dec
Regular Deadline: None/
  Priority Application deadline:
  Nov 15
Application Fee: $0
**Full time Undergraduate
  enrollment:** 3964
Total enrollment: 4039
Percent Male: 48%
Percent Female: 52%
**Total Percent Minority or
  Unreported:** 10%
Percent African-American:
  1%
**Percent Asian/Pacific
  Islander:** 3%
Percent Hispanic: 1%
Percent Native-American:
  <1%
Percent International: 5%
**Percent in-state/out of
  state:** 85%/15%
Percent from Public HS:
  70%
Retention Rate: 90%
Graduation Rate 4-year: 73%

Graduation Rate 6-year:
  Unreported
**Percent Undergraduates in
  On-campus housing:** 80%
**Number of official organized
  extracurricular
  organizations:** 85
3 Most popular majors:
  Biology/Biological Sciences,
  General Business
  Administration and
  Management, General
  Speech and Rhetorical
  Studies
Student/Faculty ratio: 13:1
Average Class Size: 25
**Percent of students going to
  grad school:** 14%
Tuition and Fees: $28,668
**In-State Tuition and Fees if
  different:** No difference
Cost for Room and Board:
  $7,248
**Percent receiving financial
  aid out of those who apply,
  first year:** 94%
**Percent receiving financial
  aid among all students:**
  97%

The "Bennies" and "Johnnies" of College of St. Benedict/St. John's University know they attend a unique institution. Forget for a moment the on-campus abbey and monastery, which house some of the schools' professors. CSB/SJU, one of the top Catholic liberal arts schools in the country, is actually two schools in one: College of St. Benedict, an all-women's school, and St. John's University, an all-men's school. Each boasts its own administration, athletic program, library, bookstore, and dining halls. Yet at the same time, students from both schools interact with each other on a daily basis, both in and out of the classroom. Only late at night, when everyone is (theoretically) asleep, are the two campuses single-sex.

Not only do CSB/SJU students know their campus is unique, they also know it is gorgeous. The campus is surrounded by woods and filled with trails that offer tons of opportunities for exploration and recreation. Some students, for example, enjoy the "chapel walk," a trail which leads to the Stella Maris Chapel on the SJU campus. Legend has it that if two people walk it together, they will get married.

Two of Everything

Because the institution is really two different schools, students benefit from access to facilities on both the St. Ben's and St. John's campuses. When it comes time to study, they may head to either one of two libraries. According to students, the CSB library often turns into "a social gathering" but also features a café where students can grab some caffeine to fuel late-night studying. Meanwhile, the SJU library offers a quieter atmosphere. While its basement, nicknamed "The Dungeon," is "creepy" for some students, it offers others the silence they need. One junior summed up the difference by stating that he studies "in St. John's library when I want to get things done and St. Ben's library when I don't."

Classrooms are also split between the two campuses. But the half hour between classes gives students plenty of time to commute from one side to the other by taking "The Link," a free shuttle bus service. The Link operates day and night to allow students to travel between St. John's and St. Ben's not only for academic purposes but also to visit friends and participate in extracurricular activities.

Throughout their four years on campus, CSB/SJU students have the opportunity to develop strong relationships with their professors. Even at the introductory level, students may work closely with their professors because class sizes are so small. Additionally, all first-year students participate in a symposium, a seminar capped at 18 students. The professor of the symposium class serves as the academic advisor for his or her students, and students say everyone gets to know each other extremely well. And while they do take academics seriously, students say they still maintain a deep sense of community on campus. "People get really competitive, but in a good way," one freshman observed. "It is not like they are ready to kill each other, but they really give their best to be on top."

Bennies and Johnnies have many opportunities to explore their academic options. "I switched majors more times than I can count," admitted a current double major in communications and Spanish, "and I was even able to study abroad for seven months." The sheer diversity of classes offered and opportunities extended to students is also impressive. In particular, study abroad is a very popular option for students on both campuses. One Bennie pointed out, "You ask your friends 'where are you going to study abroad,' not 'are you going to study abroad.'" CSB/SJU offers 17 different semester-long programs in several countries. In many of these programs, students participate with other Bennies and Johnnies and are taught by local professors. Academic advisers are "very helpful" in working with students to include study abroad credits in their academic schedule while still completing required classes and the requirements of their major(s).

Eating and Sleeping
Students are more than satisfied with the housing at both St. Ben's and St. John's, es-

pecially with the apartment-style residences available for juniors and seniors. Luetmer, an on-campus apartment complex for CSB seniors, offers each resident his or her own bedroom and includes a washer and dryer within every apartment. Either a community advisor (CA) in upperclassmen apartments or a resident adviser (RA) in the residence halls will act "as a program planner, conflict solver, therapist, rule enforcer, etc." Furthermore, in accordance with the Benedictine Values, students at SJU adhere to a tradition of keeping the doors to their rooms open when they are in the room. "This allows other students the opportunity to stop in, say hi, and meet new people," pointed out a current sophomore.

Students give campus food mixed reviews. While one student asserted that "it's not that good and it's overpriced," another felt "the food is really good on both campuses." Regardless of how they feel about the food itself, however, students do appreciate the variety of options offered. A popular eating destination is the Refectory, or "the Reef," the dining hall at St. John's.

St. John's and St. Ben's prohibit underage students from drinking on campus, a policy which is strictly enforced. However, on weekends, one freshman observed, "everybody or almost everybody is drinking." A junior added, "If people choose not to drink, they are questioned as to why they made that decision—it seems abnormal." But another student countered, "I get [pressured to drink] more at home with my friends there. I like to have a good time and am pretty crazy without the alcohol, so I seem to fit in just fine." Students over 21 can obtain permits to have parties in their rooms on campus, and St. John's University has its own on-campus pub. Otherwise, students may head to St. Joseph, the town in which College of St. Benedict is located. The small town boasts numerous "party houses" with names such as "Chubbie," "Dingleberry," and "The Chicken Shack."

But weekends at CSB/SJU are about more than just partying. There are frequent opportunities to see movies on campus, attend cultural events such as the Festival of Cultures and the Asian New Year, or even venture into nearby St. Cloud for shopping, dining, or just hanging out. Of course, students also have the option of participating in one of the many extracurricular activities at CSB/SJU. Community service is "a huge thing on campus," and additional opportunities range from writing for the school newspaper to participating in Companions on a

Journey, a faith group, or campus ministry. And of course, there are the football games.

Alumni Gone Wild
Football games are some of the most important student events of the year. "People go crazy!" exclaimed one Bennie. Alumni turn out for the home games with "their spouses, kids, grandkids . . . you name it, they are there." One CSB senior bragged that "there is a lot of pride in being a 'Bennie' or a 'Johnnie.'" As a social event and as a display of school spirit, football games are "definitely a big deal," boasting the "highest attendance for football games among Division III sports." And with a 2007 NCAA Division III national championship under their belts as well as consistently successful seasons in subsequent years, the football games' popularity is well deserved. Students also pointed to hockey and Bennie basketball as other popular sports to attend.

Of course, students have ample opportunities to participate in sports as well. A former varsity swimmer cited his athletic experience on campus as a positive one, stressing that "my coaches were really understanding that my academics come first." Student athletes, who also enjoy a large banquet and dance at the end of the year, note that sports are a great opportunity to meet others. But if the time commitment of a varsity sport is too demanding, participation in intramural sports is always an option. "There is simply no question that the best intramural sport on campus is softball," asserted one Johnnie, who added that large numbers of Bennies and Johnnies turn out every year for the sport.

Feeling Comfortable on Campus
Campus traditions are numerous. Many rave, for example, about the CSB/SJU Thanksgiving dinner. "Students are dressed formal and served as a table. Somebody from the table has to get up and carve the turkey, and then all the food is served family style," one current senior said, adding, "It's really fun." Other traditions range from a large snowball fight on the first snowfall of every year to Pinestock, an annual event in which a "big name band" comes to campus to put on a day-long music festival. "So many students look forward to April!" one Johnnie explained.

> "Both campuses are very welcoming, and the students are very friendly."

Time and again, Bennies and Johnnies point out the feeling of community that truly defines their college experience. "Both campuses are very welcoming, and the students are very friendly," noted one junior. Another pointed to the role of Benedictine Values, a set of 12 Christian guidelines practiced in everyday campus life. Although students may not know them by heart, they nevertheless "play a pretty big role here . . . Students are helpful and very respectful of one another." Remarked one Johnnie, "I wouldn't change my college for all the money in the world."—*Stephanie Brockman*

FYI
If you come to CSB/SJU, you'd better bring "a smile . . . fitting in means being friendly!"
What is the typical weekend schedule? "Finish classes, have some fun, do a little homework, have some fun, finish the homework you didn't do yet, go to church (time permitting)."
If I could change one thing about CSB/SJU, I'd "have more diversity on campus."
Three things that every student at CSB/SJU should do before graduating are "take the Chapel Walk, study abroad, and go to the annual Thanksgiving dinner."

St. Olaf College

Address: 1520 St. Olaf Avenue, Northfield, MN 55057
Phone: 507-786-3025
E-mail address: admissions@stolaf.edu
Web site URL: www.stolaf.edu
Year Founded: 1874
Private or Public: Private
Religious Affiliation: Lutheran
Location: Rural
Number of Applicants: 4,058
Percent Accepted: 59%
Percent Accepted who enroll: 35%
Number Entering: 751
Number of Transfers Accepted each Year: 48
Middle 50% SAT range: M: 600–700, CR: 600–720, Wr: Unreported
Middle 50% ACT range: 24–31
Early admission program EA/ED/None: EA and ED

Percentage accepted through EA or ED: Unreported
EA and ED deadline: ED:1-Nov, EA: 1-Dec
Regular Deadline: 15-Jan
Application Fee: $0
Full time Undergraduate enrollment: 3,073
Total enrollment: 3,073
Percent Male: 45%
Percent Female: 55%
Total Percent Minority or Unreported: 8%
Percent African-American: 1%
Percent Asian/Pacific Islander: 5%
Percent Hispanic: 2%
Percent Native-American: <1%
Percent International: 2%
Percent in-state/out of state: 55%/45%
Percent from Public HS: 84%
Retention Rate: 93%

Graduation Rate 4-year: 82%
Graduation Rate 6-year: 84%
Percent Undergraduates in On-campus housing: 80%
Number of official organized extracurricular organizations: 137
3 Most popular majors: Biology/Biological Sciences, General English Language and Literature, General Mathematics
Student/Faculty ratio: 12:1
Average Class Size: 19
Percent of students going to grad school: 22%
Tuition and Fees: $34,300
In-State Tuition and Fees if different: No difference
Cost for Room and Board: $7,900
Percent receiving financial aid out of those who apply, first year: 82%
Percent receiving financial aid among all students: 83%

St. Olaf College, located in the small but picturesque town of Northfield, Minnesota, is known for building a solid sense of community. With close to the entire student body living on campus and on its gourmet meal plan, the entire collegiate experience is designed to foster a tight-knit and welcoming community. This Lutheran-affiliated college has almost everything a student could want, from a rock climbing wall to a movie theater.

A Solid Liberal Arts Education

St. Olaf is at its core a liberal arts institution and it has general education requirements which every student must complete in order to graduate. These requirements include several writing courses, two religion courses, a science, a science lab, and even an ethics requirement. Students find the requirements relatively easy to fit into the 35 classes that are required to graduate, although it can be harder for some majors such as music for which the general education requirements and the major require-

ments do not really overlap. There are a few classes that are considered "laid-back" that can help a student complete his core requirements. One example is a class that combines physical education with the teaching of ethics.

Perhaps due to the rigorous general education requirements, the requirements for the majors are thought to be less demanding and it is not uncommon for a student to double or even triple major. The most popular option is to have one major as well as a concentration in that major. St. Olaf has 39 graduating majors including 15 teaching certification courses, 20 concentrations, and 17 pre-professional fields. The most popular majors in order are English, biology, mathematics, economics, and psychology.

St. Olaf operates on a 4-1-4 academic schedule. This means that students have two full semesters of four classes or more and an Interim Period, also called J-Term, during the month of January immediately following winter vacation. Students must register for their J-Term class the preceding spring and have a wide variety of classes to choose from. The compact schedule allows for "a truly unique class format," as one student said. These classes are entirely designed by the professor and can include a study abroad component.

At a school with a self-proclaimed "global perspective," students are encouraged to study abroad. One student said that, out of his house of 10, all 10 had studied abroad, and he estimated that nearly 90 percent of the student population will study abroad at some point during their career at St. Olaf. The J-Term is different than the semester options in that it is much more affordable and it is directly under the supervision of St. Olaf professors. One class recently went to Peru to investigate the Peruvian medical experience and to learn about medicine. Another class, studying the evolution of Christianity, visited Martin Luther's hometown in Germany and the Vatican.

"When I walk around campus and say hello to my professors, they know my name, even if I only took one class with them three years ago."

Due to the small class size the students and professors really get to know each other and professors are happy to help students outside of class, take meals with students, and generally be available. One student said, "When I walk around campus and say hello to my professors, they know my name, even if I only took one class with them three years ago." Another student commented on how her professors offered to help her work on her interviewing skills when they knew she was applying for grants. The faculty goes above and beyond its academic calling to help students develop and hone their intellectual curiosity.

An Environmentalist's Haven
At St. Olaf, the environment is a part of everyday life. Surrounded by nature, the student body has an appreciation for conservation not experienced at many other schools. Students regularly talk about things the school is doing to reduce its energy usage and, despite the fact that the school recently acquired a windmill to provide a significant amount of the campus's electricity, students still feel there is more the administration could be doing.

Environmentalism and conservation are a part of the fabric of life at St. Olaf. In the month of February the entire school gets caught up in "Campus Energy Wars." As one student observed, "people get really into it in the dorms. They'll even turn off the hallway lights at night, which caused some tension because people kept on knocking into things." Another student remarked on the willingness of students to call each other out on environmental issues, exclaiming "you get reamed if you throw a can in the trash!" This spirit of environmentalism extends to the classroom. One of the most popular classes at St. Olaf is "Campus Ecology," a class with a big environmental focus that teaches students to apply environmental analyses to the St. Olaf campus and is co-taught by a senior or junior student.

Students' appreciation of the great outdoors is expressed in more leisure-oriented ways as well. The campus abounds with hiking and running trails that students take full advantage of. One student observed, "Most of the school year at St. Olaf is pretty chilly and the winter is downright frigid but you will often see people out cross-country skiing or sledding or playing a pick-up game of broomball on frozen ponds close to campus." Students even sometimes illegally camp in the nearby "natural lands," the better to appreciate the beautiful landscape that surrounds them.

A Campus of Values
St. Olaf College was founded in 1874 by a group of Norwegian-American immigrant pastors and farmers—which, incidentally, explains the prominence of St. Olaf's Norwegian-language department. The College began and continues as a Lutheran institution. There is a chapel located on campus at which many students attend the Sunday service. St. Olaf students are self-described as "homey, family- and value-oriented." While religion is not pressed upon any student and there is an active Muslim community, Protestant Christians and Lutherans in particular are the dominant religious group. There are a number of extracurricular activities that are centered on religion including Bible studies and Christian fellowships, the largest being the Fellowship of Christian Athletes. Most teams say a prayer before starting their game and it is not uncommon to see heads bowed in brief prayer before a meal in the dining hall.

However, students who are not particularly religious are not uncomfortable on campus, nor do they feel judged. One student, when asked about the presence of religion on campus, said that "it can be a little surprising," but went on to explain that people only really talk about religion in religion class as part of the core requirement. Students can find a religion class on almost all major world religions and teachers are careful to allow students to form their own opinions. Some students express their religion by abstaining from sex until marriage or not drinking. One student remarked, "Students have religious views and they follow them."

Social Life

As one student said, "you make it what you want it to be." In general students are satisfied with the social life at St. Olaf. One student describes it as "good, although it can be a little slow." In line with its Lutheran values, the campus is dry, meaning that alcohol is not allowed anywhere on campus. All students are in agreement that this does not inhibit the consumption of alcohol. One student even commented that the prohibition of alcohol leads to binge drinking behavior: "People drink stupidly because they need to pregame faster so they don't get caught." Another student, however, felt that the dry campus "was not really enforced. Usually resident life is semilenient so students drink as much or as little as other college students." This student praised the school for the number of non-alcoholic activities that it organizes in order to support its dry status. Such activities include showings of recent movies every weekend night, dances, different bands and musical groups, and dance performers. Buntrock Commons, the student center, is the home of the Pause, a completely student-run hangout that features pool tables, movies, concerts, and dances.

Due to the dry campus rule, keggers are a nonentity at St. Olaf; closed-door room parties are more the norm. Students also take advantage of the few bars in the town of Northfield. The Rueb 'N' Stein is a campus favorite and has a big Wednesday showing. Froggy Bottom's is another popular bar with a big Thursday night following. For a more chill vibe with live music and imported beers, students go to The Contented Cow, which has more of a pub feel and is a good place for conversation. The dry campus rule also forces students to be somewhat enterprising if they want to throw a big party. Students will sometimes rent a space in the town of Northfield, usually at the Legion, and will host a party there. Such parties are announced via Facebook and generally charge $5 at the door.

Minneapolis and St. Paul are only 45 minutes from the St. Olaf campus, but trips to the Twin Cities are rare, according to students. Seniors are more likely to make the trek to the cities to watch a play or go to a jazz club. In order to get there students need a car, something the school allows but which few students take advantage of. One student remarked that "having a car gives you more freedom." It can be hard to get out of Northfield and sometimes students said they felt a bit isolated. Other students valued the atmosphere that the campus fosters and believe it helps to foster the sense of community that is so strong at St. Olaf.

When asked about the dating scene at St. Olaf, one student replied with some sarcasm, "I wouldn't say it's huge." Another student when asked responded with laughter and went on to explain that the gender gap at St. Olaf, which is 55 percent women and 45 percent men, seems even bigger. St. Olaf students are more likely to still be in a relationship with a high school boyfriend or girlfriend than to casually date in college. Of course, the usual casual college hook-ups do occur here although less frequently than at other schools due to the religious beliefs and values of many students. The tight-knit community feel of the campus also impedes casual dating as most students know each other and news travels fast.

St. Olaf is a beautiful college where students smile and greet each other whether they know each other or not. Students are friendly, welcoming, and open-minded despite the homogeneity of the student body. The rural setting of the campus encourages the tight-knit sense of community that pervades the campus and makes students feel they are taken care of and part of a larger St. Olaf family. St. Olaf seeks to create whole people who are intellectually curious with solid values. "You're not just getting together for class; you're in the same buildings, living together, learning together, and growing together."—*Tara Singh*

FYI
If you come to St. Olaf, you'd better bring "winter sports gear."
What is the typical weekend schedule? "Friday everyone relaxes during the day then goes to a house party or something on campus. Saturday people nap then at night they go to a sporting event or into town. Sundays are a relaxed day to do homework or watch movies."
If I could change one thing about St. Olaf, I'd "not make it a dry campus, more for safety reasons."
Three things every student at St. Olaf should do before graduating are "go to Christmas fest, climb the rock-climbing wall, and spend one night out in the natural lands."

University of Minnesota

Address: 231 Pillsbury Drive, SE, Minneapolis, MN 55455-0213
Phone: 612-625-2008
E-mail address: admissions@umn.edu
Web site URL: www.umn.edu
Year Founded: 1851
Private or Public: Public
Religious Affiliation: None
Location: Urban
Number of Applicants: 26,097
Percent Accepted: 57%
Percent Accepted who enroll: 36%
Number Entering: 5,266
Number of Transfers Accepted each Year: 2,981
Middle 50% SAT range: M: 580–700, CR: 540–680, Wr: 530–660
Middle 50% ACT range: 24–29
Early admission program EA/ED/None: None

Percentage accepted through EA or ED: NA
EA and ED deadline: NA
Regular Deadline: Rolling
Application Fee: $45
Full time Undergraduate enrollment: 32,294
Total enrollment: 47,240
Percent Male: 47%
Percent Female: 53%
Total Percent Minority or Unreported: 25%
Percent African-American: 5%
Percent Asian/Pacific Islander: 9%
Percent Hispanic: 2%
Percent Native-American: 1%
Percent International: 2%
Percent in-state/out of state: 73%/27%
Percent from Public HS: Unreported
Retention Rate: 88%
Graduation Rate 4-year: 66%

Graduation Rate 6-year: Unreported
Percent Undergraduates in On-campus housing: 22%
Number of official organized extracurricular organizations: 600
3 Most popular majors: Biology/Biological Sciences, Journalism, Mechanical Engineering
Student/Faculty ratio: Unreported
Average Class Size: 15
Percent of students going to grad school: Unreported
Tuition and Fees: $14,634
In-State Tuition and Fees if different: $10,634
Cost for Room and Board: $7,280
Percent receiving financial aid out of those who apply, first year: 67%
Percent receiving financial aid among all students: 51%

Nestled at the heart of a metropolis dubbed "the Twin Cities," the University of Minnesota's largest campus has twin sections as well. The Twin Cities campus acts as the center of the University of Minnesota's four-campus system, but branches of the large state university extend to Duluth, Crookston, and Morris.

"A Common Bond for All"

The University's motto says it all. The University of Minnesota, affectionately known as the "U," embraces four locations in five cities and has something to offer all its students. The Twin Cities campus boasts an enrollment of about 50,000 students, both undergraduate and graduate, far more than the remaining three in the system.

But the flagship embraces its twin city roots and is divided into a St. Paul location, which focuses on agriculture, and the Minneapolis campus. The Minneapolis half of the U is further split into the East Campus and West Campus by the Mississippi River and connected by the iconic Washington Avenue Bridge. Adding to the U's sprawling identity, the campus has a few notable "neighborhoods"— Knoll area, Mall area, Health area, Athletic area, and Gateway area. Getting around the large campus can be tricky, especially with the Mighty Mississippi in the way, so signs that make up "the Gopher Way" help students find their way.

The most notable buildings are the Weisman Art Gallery, designed by Frank Gehry, and the historic Greek row located centrally on campus on the Northrup Mall. The U offers eight residence halls and three apartment buildings and guarantees housing to all freshmen. "Living on campus is convenient," but many students commute from their homes near campus, making parking a challenge. Most students live in the "superblock" complex—a four-block area across from the athletics center. Freshmen can live in any of the University's seven dormitories, only two of which are explicitly designated for freshmen. Freshmen are assigned their own Community Advisors, of which there are usually two per floor in each dorm. As one student noted, much of a freshman's social life is centered around their dorm, while upperclassman life is concentrated beyond the campus.

Any students concerned about living in the heart of Minneapolis should be unduly worried; the U's president has put a significant focus on safety, and students praised the array of different resources designed to keep them safe, including security guards who walk pathways at night, security staff in all the dorms, emergency phone hubs located throughout campus, and driving services.

The campus also boasts an impressive student center called Coffman Memorial Union. Not only does the building feature a bowling alley, video games, and billiards, but it also screens movies every weekend that are free to students, faculty, and their relatives. Said one student: "Coffman is a huge component in fostering community."

Go-pher the Gopher

The U boasts a storied athletics tradition centered around the basketball, football, and ice hockey teams. The Golden Gophers participate in a long-standing rivalry game with the University of Wisconsin. "A lot of people go to games and watch them on campus," one student said. Another added, "There is a lot of school pride for sports teams." Dating back to legendary hockey coach Herb Brooks, who later coached the 1980 U.S. men's hockey team to an Olympic gold medal in the "Miracle on Ice," the U's men's ice hockey team has five national championships under its belt. Out-of-staters beware: most hockey recruits hail from Minnesota—all but two

members of the current 26-man team are from the Land of 10,000 Lakes.

Athletics, though, are just one piece of the thriving campus atmosphere. Students cited Greek life, the Black Student Association, and other student organizations as prevalent on campus. "People are usually very committed to extracurricular activities," a student said. "I think they are a good way to meet people and relieve yourself from schoolwork." Still, while Greek life is popular on campus, it does not dominate social life for students at the U. The University's more than 600 student groups offer a wide array of opportunities to get involved in campus life—from the student newspaper to religious organizations. "Whatever you're into, you'll find it at the U, and probably there'll be quite a lot of people with you," one student said.

Choices, Choices, Choices

On such a large campus, academic options are hugely varied—from the agricultural programs offered in St. Paul to the College of Design. "The U of M offers very challenging courses but it also offers many fun courses such as dance, sports, and horseback riding classes," a student said. Some popular majors are political science, psychology, business, and the sciences. "U of M has so many majors to choose from," a student marveled.

> "The U of M offers very challenging courses but it also offers many fun courses such as dance, sports, and horseback riding classes."

Academic advising at the U tends to work well, one student explained, given that there is full-time staff with the specific role of advising students on their academic work. Students are advised by someone within their field of study, and while one student said getting a good adviser can be "pretty hit or miss," it helps to have a full time staff member available to help when needed.

Like any large university, class sizes reach about 100 students for introductory courses, slimming down to about 50 for specialized classes, making it relatively easy for students to get a place in a course.

The workload can get pretty heavy, with an average of two to three papers and exams per class in addition to reading. But a very descriptive course catalog helps narrow down the options. Teachers try to embrace the diversity and variety offered at the U. "I like how teachers are very open minded and teach from many perspectives," a student said. Discussions on the diverse campus are a high point for some students: "What I like most is the different people you meet and the ranges in their experience in what is being taught. The discussion that goes is on in class is really exciting."

One student mentioned the ease with which many people at the University of Minnesota make friends: "Many people meet through classes and become friends as well. People often work and study in groups. People also hang out at the U just for fun." Ultimately, the U is a place where not only hockey-playing Minnesotans but Gophers from over 130 countries around the world can live, learn, and make the most of their college years.—*Brittany Golob and Raymond Carlson*

FYI
If you come to the University of Minnesota, you'd better bring "a planner."
What's the typical weekend schedule? "Friday afternoon you're either going to be out running or be at the Rec before the weekend starts, in the evening you'll most likely be at some social event in the dorms or frat row. Saturday you'll go to a sporting event or concert, Saturday night is a mirror image of Friday, and on Sunday you sleep in, maybe watch football, and then get to work."
If I could change one thing about the University of Minnesota, "I'd make the class sizes smaller."
Three things every student at the University of Minnesota should do before graduating are "study abroad, participate in an extracurricular activity, and go have a burger in the Shake & 80s malt shop."

Mississippi

Millsaps College

Address: 1701 North State Street, Jackson, MS 39210
Phone: 601-974-1050
E-mail address: admissions@millsaps.edu
Web site URL: www.millsaps.edu
Year Founded: 1890
Private or Public: Private
Religious Affiliation: Methodist
Location: Suburban
Number of Applicants: 1,266
Percent Accepted: 77%
Percent Accepted who enroll: 28%
Number Entering: 271
Number of Transfers Accepted each Year: 64
Middle 50% SAT range: M: 538–650, CR: 538–673, Wr: Unreported
Middle 50% ACT range: 23–29
Early admission program EA/ED/None: EA

Percentage accepted through EA or ED: Unreported
EA and ED deadline: 8-Jan
Regular Deadline: 1-Oct
Application Fee: $0
Full time Undergraduate enrollment: 1,013
Total enrollment: 1,118
Percent Male: 48%
Percent Female: 52%
Total Percent Minority or Unreported: 17%
Percent African-American: 9%
Percent Asian/Pacific Islander: 4%
Percent Hispanic: 2%
Percent Native-American: <1%
Percent International: 1%
Percent in-state/out of state: 43%/ 57%
Percent from Public HS: 61%
Retention Rate: 79%

Graduation Rate 4-year: 62%
Graduation Rate 6-year: 66%
Percent Undergraduates in On-campus housing: 81%
Number of official organized extracurricular organizations: 75
3 Most popular majors: Biology, Business, Psychology
Student/Faculty ratio: 11:1
Average Class Size: 8
Percent of students going to grad school: 48%
Tuition and Fees: $24,754
In-State Tuition and Fees if different: No difference
Cost for Room and Board: $8,800
Percent receiving financial aid out of those who apply, first year: 71%
Percent receiving financial aid among all students: 55%

Though largely unknown outside of Mississippi, Millsaps College is highly respected throughout the area as a school that offers a well-rounded liberal arts education at a competitive price. Though Millsaps Majors may seem to have lackluster school spirit when it comes to supporting their athletic teams, most students enjoy life at Millsaps.

Work Hard

Millsaps was the first school in Mississippi to have a chapter of the academic honor society Phi Beta Kappa, and the school generally ranks high both for its academics and for its relatively low tuition. Millsaps offers 35 majors, and though the requirements vary by major, each student must complete 10 core courses, offered in topics ranging from history to science to mathematics.

A major selling point for many students is the small size of the classes at Millsaps. The average class size is 15 people, and the student/faculty ratio is 11:1. This class size fosters open discussion as well as closes relationships between professors and students. According to one student, "The classes are very engaging, very discussion-oriented." Students say that their professors "really do care about their students," and several admitted that they considered the relationships formed with their professors the most valuable part of their college experiences. "I consider some of these professors my friends." While students definitely note that the academic life is very "strenuous," most say they were fulfilled in their academic lives. "I feel like I learn so much."

Party Hard

The social life at Millsaps seems to revolve pretty much exclusively around the Greek system. There are six fraternities and six sororities governed by the Panhellenic Council and the Interfraternity Council. While students say that it is not essential to be in a fraternity or sorority—"It's not like if you aren't Greek you're going to have an awful time"—it seems pretty hard to escape the fact that the Greek scene is *the* scene at Millsaps. This is highlighted in particular by the fact that non-Greeks are referred to as "independents." Though it is perfectly acceptable to be an independent, an independent who won't set foot in a fraternity house might have a hard time finding a party, particularly during freshman and sophomore years. As students get older, however, "they tend to drift off campus more." Many upperclassmen enjoy local spots Hal & Mal's or Schimmels for drinks, music, or just hanging out with their friends. According to one student, "A lot of times you can find your professors at Fenian's."

> **"I consider some of these professors my friends."**

Drinking rules on campus seem to be pretty sensible. Though rowdy behavior in the dormitories is prohibited, students appreciated the fact that "the RAs treat us like adults." The two large campus-wide events every year are the homecoming football game in the fall and Major Madness in the spring. At Major Madness, students gather on "The Bowl"—the large, grassy area in the middle of campus—and play games, eat, drink, and listen to music. Though the musicians are rarely big-name stars—bands have included Better Than Ezra, Stroke Nine, and the North Mississippi All Stars—"It's definitely stuff you can dance to, sing to, and drink to."

With the exception of the homecoming game, Millsaps students in general don't get extremely excited about sports. "It's definitely not like an SEC school, so if people come to Millsaps expecting that, then they're not going to get it." Instead, supporting athletic teams is more of a matter of supporting your friends who happen to be on those teams than a statement of school pride.

On Campus: Where It's At

Approximately 81 percent of Millsaps students live on campus. Most choose to live in the dormitories for all four years, though some upperclassmen move off campus. The housing is divided up by the North Side and the South Side. Freshman year, everyone lives on the North Side. After freshman year, students pick their rooms based on a room draw, which functions on a point system. Each student entering the room draw receives points based on his or her class year and GPA. Students then combine with their roommates and vie for the best dorms. The residence hall rooms are all double-occupancy, and the halls feature traditional double rooms, apartment-style and suite-style rooms. Though the students admit that the dormitories aren't by any means luxurious, "they do their best to make it pleasant." "My friends who are from other colleges always talk about how nice our dorms are here."

For most students, more important than the dorms themselves is the fact that the dorms provide a social outlet as well. "It's really cool when all your friends live on campus." This social atmosphere is also extended to the main cafeteria, also known as "The Caf." The Caf is one of two dining options on campus, the other being the Kava House, which provides quick meals to go. At The Caf, students select from a menu of salads, soups, sandwiches, and daily hot meals. Students generally seem to be quite pleased with the quality of the food, though opinions differ about the variety of food choices. While one senior said that she was "really going to miss [the food] next year," another complained that the food choices were repetitive.

The Center of the State

Students seem to have mixed feelings about being in the city of Jackson itself. In one 2008 ranking, Jackson was ranked the nation's 11th most dangerous city. For this reason, students say they must exercise caution while out on campus, but they don't feel that the crime level in Jackson is detrimental to their college experience. Students are very well aware that "Jackson isn't the safest of cities." While one student said that she generally feels "safe on campus," she was sure to note that she "wouldn't walk around alone in the dark."

One advantage of being in the city of Jackson—which has a population of just under 180,000 people—is the city's position as the capital of the state, and thus the center of state politics. Particularly for students with an interest in politics or governments, Millsaps is a good place to get a taste of the political arena. Students say it is very easy to get internships in the state or local government, and that state officials will sometimes teach classes at Millsaps as adjunct professors.

Though the city of Jackson is very much a political city, students say that campus life is "not too hardcore politically" and that the student body as a whole does not lean very heavily left or right politically. Both "the Millsaps Young Democrats and the Republicans are very well-represented and well-spoken-for." Students say that Millsaps is a place for political expression but that there are also many students who abstain from political discussion altogether.

Diversity?

Students new to Millsaps may be surprised by the lack of geographic and racial diversity. Slightly less than 50 percent of the students are from the state of Mississippi, and the freshman class at Millsaps is generally comprised of approximately 15 to 20 percent minority students. While some students lamented that fact—"I'd like it to be more diverse than it is"—students across the board were impressed by the openness of students to new ideas and to different types of people. "Millsaps is very diverse if you look at the big picture, not just at race." Another noted, "What makes up for [the lack of racial diversity] is the diversity of ideas and of opinions." Though there is little racial diversity on campus, student organizations like the Black Student Association provide minority students with a sense of community.

For many students, the mere size of Millsaps contributes to this openness for different types of students. With just over a thousand undergraduates, "I feel like I've met everyone on campus one way or another," one senior said. Another student chalked up the open-minded atmosphere at Millsaps to the philosophy of education at the school. "They really teach you to be warm-hearted and open to everything and not close-minded at all."—*Susanna Moore*

FYI

If you come to Millsaps, you'd better bring "a willingness to work hard and party hard."
What is the typical weekend schedule? "Friday: go to dinner and to the fraternity houses; Saturday: watch football all day or go to the football game, eat dinner, preparty, and go to the fraternity houses; Sunday: wake up late and do your homework."
If I could change one thing about Millsaps, I'd "make it farther from home."
Three things every student at Millsaps should do before graduating are "swim in the fountains, Bowl-sit, really get to know a professor."

Mississippi State University

Address: P.O. Box 6334
Mississippi State, MS 39762
Phone: 662-325-2224
E-mail address:
admit@msstate.edu
Web site URL:
www.msstate.edu
Year Founded: 1878
Private or Public: Public
Religious Affiliation: None
Location: Rural
Number of Applicants: 7,429
Percent Accepted: 66%
**Percent Accepted who
enroll:** 51%
Number Entering: 2,478
**Number of Transfers
Accepted each Year:** 1,806
Middle 50% SAT range: M:
538–650, CR: 490–630,
Wr: Unreported
Middle 50% ACT range:
20–27
**Early admission program
EA/ED/None:** None
**Percentage accepted
through EA or ED:** NA

EA and ED deadline: NA
Regular Deadline: Rolling
Application Fee: $35
**Full time Undergraduate
enrollment:** 13,049
Total enrollment: 16,785
Percent Male: 51%
Percent Female: 49%
**Total Percent Minority or
Unreported:** 25%
Percent African-American:
21%
**Percent Asian/Pacific
Islander:** 1%
Percent Hispanic: 1%
Percent Native-American:
1%
Percent International: 1%
**Percent in-state/out of
state:** 76% / 24%
Percent from Public HS:
Unreported
Retention Rate: 84%
Graduation Rate 4-year:
60%
Graduation Rate 6-year:
Unreported

**Percent Undergraduates
in On-campus housing:**
26%
**Number of official organized
extracurricular
organizations:** 326
3 Most popular majors:
Business Administration,
Elementary Education,
Physical Education Teaching
& Coaching
Student/Faculty ratio:
15:1
Average Class Size: 25
**Percent of students going to
grad school:** Unreported
Tuition and Fees: $12,503
**In-State Tuition and Fees if
different:** $5,151
Cost for Room and Board:
$7,333
**Percent receiving financial
aid out of those who apply,
first year:** 76%
**Percent receiving financial
aid among all students:**
54%

Located far away from the noises of big cities, Mississippi State University is a large state university. With an enrollment of more than 18,000 students, both graduate and undergraduate, the public university represents one of the most important institutions in the State of Mississippi. Furthermore, although most students come from within the state, nearly a quarter of undergraduates hail from places outside of Mississippi. Not to be confused with the big rival University of Mississippi—better known as Ole Miss—Mississippi State offers a large selection of opportunities to students while allowing them to enjoy college education far away from bustling metropolitan areas in the quiet and beautiful town of Starkville.

Eight Schools

Despite being the largest public university in Mississippi, the college admissions process remains vigorous. In fact, the school accepts only about two-thirds of all applicants.

There are generally a large number of applications in part due to the reputation of the university as a top bargain institution, which provides good education and strong prospects for graduates while being relatively affordable. "I really think that the education I get here is useful," said one student. "For in-state students, it is especially worth it."

What is remarkable for Mississippi State is the wide range of academic opportunities that are available to the students. There are eleven schools on campus, ranging from the traditional College of Arts and Sciences to the School of Veterinarian Medicine. It is certainly possible for students to find the program that will satisfy their academic pursuits. "It is a big school, so we have more than one hundred majors and certifications," said one student. "As long as you put in the energy to find the right school and major for you, I think you will really enjoy the school in terms of academics," added another.

An important characteristic of the academic

program is the availability of professional training, such as Poultry Science, Wildlife, Fisheries and Aquaculture, and Real Estate. All types of curriculum allows students with a clear vision of what they want to do as a professional to directly pursue their future career. "There are a couple of problems with the curriculum here and there," said one student. "But I think the professional preparation is pretty good here."

The number of students per class varies greatly depending on the major and the specific type of course. "There are big lectures, and you may have to try not to fall asleep," said one student. On the other hand, some do like the larger classes because "you can meet more people and really feel like a college student sitting in a big lecture hall."

> "As long as you put in the energy to find the right school and major for you, I think you will really enjoy the school in terms of academics."

Given the large selection of classes, it is very difficult to list all the academic requirements. Nevertheless, all students from Mississippi State must complete the General Education Requirements, which include English, Mathematics, Natural Sciences, Humanities, and Social Sciences. Like in most institutions of higher learning, these requirements are very important in ensuring that all students, regardless of major or future aspirations, will be exposed to a variety of subjects, thus assuring the breadth of education that is considered an important part of the college experience.

As to the most difficult majors, students seem to believe that the College of Architecture, which is an important part of the university's academic program, can provide some late-night assignments. Furthermore, just like in many other schools, engineering is also a difficult program. "I guess college is about what you put into it," said one student. "If you try, you can have a lot of challenges even in those easy majors." In the end, however, the student does believe that "engineering is a lot harder than other programs."

The closeness between instructors and students also varies greatly. "It is a big place, so it is not like a tiny school of a couple hundred people where everyone knows each other," said one senior. However, he does confirm that some professors "do try to get to know students." More importantly and unsurprisingly, students who take the initiative to talk to and engage their professors tend to get more out of their classes and have better academic experiences.

Starkville

Anyone who looks to live in a big metropolis should probably look elsewhere for college. In fact, Jackson, the capital of Mississippi and the largest city in the state, is more than 100 miles away. The city of Columbus is only about 20 miles east of the campus, and with less than 30,000 inhabitants, it hardly represents a major metropolitan area. This, however, does not mean that all those who enjoy city life will be disappointed by Starkville, where the university is located. "I thought I wanted to go to school in a big city, but it turns out that I really like it here," confided one student.

Starkville has its own charms. It is truly a university town. The majority of the activities in Starkville are invariably linked to Mississippi State. "It feels like home," said one student. A number of festivals on visual arts are conducted every year, and the student body generally plays a big role in attending and supporting those events.

The campus is very large, and many students believe that cars are essential. "You will obviously find ways to get around campus without a car. The school will help, but it is so much easier just to have a car," said one student.

The dorms are generally fine. A few newer buildings have been added in recent years, and they have received much better reviews than the older ones. As in many large state universities, the majority of upperclassmen live off-campus. "I think you should try both on-campus and off-campus housing," said one student. "Living in dorms is part of the college experience, but you should also try to do everything on your own once you get older. That's why you live off-campus when you are junior or senior."

The Bulldogs

It goes without saying that football is important at Mississippi State. The biggest day of the year is probably the Egg Bowl, when the two in-state rivals, University of Mississippi and Mississippi State take on each other as part of a regular season game. "This is what the football season is all about," said one student. "As long as we beat Ole Miss, then we are happy with our football team," said another. One tradition is for students to ring cowbells at the game, which supposedly brings good luck. After more than 100 head-to-head games, Ole Miss holds a better record, but it has not stopped the fervent fans of the Mississippi State Bulldogs from showing their support en masse during the games.

In addition to sports, Greek life is also important. The sororities and fraternities are the main venues for parties. And while drinking is part of the night life at Mississippi State, students generally agree that people tend to be careful and do not put too much pressure on others to consume alcohol. "We don't have much of a town around

here, but at least we have lots of people in the university, so the weekends can be fun."

A Southern Environment

Students at Mississippi State are generally satisfied with their college experience. It has a distinct southern character, being situated in the middle of rural Mississippi. The university really stands out as a solid academic institution that prepares students for their future endeavors. At the same time, the rural environment creates a strong sense of community in Starkville. Combining all these factors, Mississippi State is certainly a top destination for those interested in a good, affordable education.—*Xiaohang Liu*

FYI

If you come to Mississippi State, you'd better bring "a car."

What is the typical weekend schedule? "Go to a football game. What else?"

If I could change one thing about Mississippi State, I'd "add a few more thousand people and stores to Starkville."

Three things every student at Mississippi State should do before graduating are "Egg Bowl, travel around the state, and take an architecture class."

University of Mississippi

Address: 145 Martindale University, MS 38677

Phone: 662-915-7226

E-mail address: admissions@olemiss.edu

Web site URL: www.olemiss.edu

Year Founded: 1844

Private or Public: Public

Religious Affiliation: None

Location: Rural

Number of Applicants: 7,946

Percent Accepted: 83%

Percent Accepted who enroll: 37%

Number Entering: 2,437

Number of Transfers Accepted each Year: 1,543

Middle 50% SAT range: M: 460–590, CR: 460–600, Wr: Unreported

Middle 50% ACT range: 20–28

Early admission program EA/ED/None: None

Percentage accepted through EA or ED: NA

EA and ED deadline: NA

Regular Deadline: rolling

Application Fee: $25

Full time Undergraduate enrollment: 12,682

Total enrollment: 14,459

Percent Male: 48%

Percent Female: 52%

Total Percent Minority or Unreported: 18%

Percent African-American: 13%

Percent Asian/Pacific Islander: 1%

Percent Hispanic: 1%

Percent Native-American: 0%

Percent International: 1%

Percent in-state/out of state: 66%/34%

Percent from Public HS: 70%

Retention Rate: 80%

Graduation Rate 4-year: 56%

Graduation Rate 6-year: Unreported

Percent Undergraduates in On-campus housing: 26%

Number of official organized extracurricular organizations: 250

3 Most popular majors: Accounting, Elementary Education and Teaching, Marketing/Marketing Management

Student/Faculty ratio: 19:1

Average Class Size: 15

Percent of students going to grad school: Unreported

Tuition and Fees: $12,468

In-State Tuition and Fees if different: $5,107

Cost for Room and Board: $5,914

Percent receiving financial aid out of those who apply, first year: 61%

Percent receiving financial aid among all students: 36%

The historic institution nestled in the town of Oxford, just 70 miles south of Memphis, is formally known as the University of Mississippi—but to those in the know, it's Ole Miss. First coined in 1897 as the title of the University's yearbook, Ole Miss is more than a mere nickname. It reflects the institution's deeply-rooted traditions, Southern heritage, and welcoming atmosphere. Above all, the name reflects the affection students and alumni feel for their university, with its scenic campus, close-knit feel, and growing international prestige.

An Intimate Public University

Among public universities, Ole Miss has a strong academic reputation—one that has steadily improved in recent years. With seven undergraduate schools—the College of Liberal Arts and the Schools of Accountancy, Applied Sciences, Business Administration, Education, Engineering, and Pharmacy—the University has a program to offer every student, no matter where their academic interests lie. Among the various schools, the College of Liberal Arts and the School of Business Administration boast the highest undergraduate enrollments.

Over the past few years, Ole Miss has garnered a high national rank among public colleges. Students think the University's growing prestige is deserved. "Academic life at Ole Miss is great," said one student. "Most classes aren't too big, and all the professors I have come across are more than willing to help their students in any way possible."

Ole Miss's relatively small undergraduate population gives students easy access to professors and administrators. The administration has an open-door policy, encouraging students to bring concerns or suggestions straight to the top. Professors, likewise, are eager to meet with students. "Because we're not that big, the student-faculty ratio is pretty good," remarked one senior. Most students agree that class size is not overwhelming, especially compared to other public universities. Upper-level courses generally range from 20–30 students, and one upperclassman noted that many professors require participation. Introductory "core" courses, however, can hold over 150 students.

To give underclassmen the opportunity to take smaller, more specialized classes, the University offers several unique programs. Each year, the McDonnell Barksdale Honors College admits around 120 freshmen with exemplary academic records. "A lot of money has been invested in the honors college, and it offers students great resources," said one student. The Croft Institute, Ole Miss's renowned international studies program, is even more selective, accepting only 40 students a year. But these specialized programs are not for the faint of heart. As one senior noted, "Honors College and Croft classes are more difficult than most."

For the first few months of their college careers, all Ole Miss freshmen must take an hour-a-week course called University Studies. Designed to ease the transition into college life, University Studies gives freshmen a chance to learn more about Ole Miss and to meet classmates.

Southern-Style Living

Students give the University's dorms mixed reviews. "They're pretty nice," said one student. Another called them "outdated." Still another insisted that "the ladies' dorms are nicer than the men's." Whatever their opinion, freshmen are required to live on campus. All university housing is gender-segregated by building. The two main freshman dorms are Martin for women and Stockard for men. Visitation hours are relatively strict; guests must leave by 11 p.m. on weeknights and 1 a.m. on weekends, unless a dormitory's students vote in the first week of the semester to extend these hours. Men's and women's dorms are close together, and most students claim not to mind single-sex housing.

Responding to students' complaints about university housing, the administration has begun extensive renovations. Currently under construction is a massive residential college, where students can live all four years. "The residential college will have a computer lab, a gym, a cafeteria, an auditorium, and more," explained one senior. "If I could go back to my freshman year, I would definitely want to live there!"

Although many students think mandatory on-campus housing for freshmen is a good idea—as one student said, "it forces you to get to know campus and your classmates"— almost all upperclassmen live in Greek houses or off campus. Nearby apartments, while slightly less convenient than dorms, give students more freedom and flexibility. Plus, most Ole Miss students own cars, which facilitate trips to class, the grocery store, and even to Memphis (just over an hour away) to shop or go out on weekends.

Rebel Revelry

When it comes to social life, students agree: Ole Miss knows how to party. "We're not ranked the number two party school for nothing," laughed one senior.

The social scene at Ole Miss is extensive and varied. Greek life is popular on campus— 35 percent of undergraduates belong to a fraternity or sorority—and rarely does a weekend go by without a fraternity party taking place. In the spring, each fraternity hosts a no-holds-barred blowout, such as SAE's "Patty Murphy" or ATO's "Gator Bash." Often these parties last an entire weekend, culminating in crawfish cookouts or barbeques with live bands. Fraternity parties are often open to non-Greeks, although students note that women have an easier time getting in than men.

While fraternity and sorority events are a big part of campus life, students agree that non-Greeks won't want for things to do on weekends. "Greek life is a great way to get to know people early on, and fraternity parties are big for freshmen," explained one student. "But as you get older, you find the social scene gears away from fraternity parties—people are over that scene."

The Oxford town square, which students described as "one of a kind," offers plenty of alternatives to the Greek party scene, particularly for the 21-plus crowd. Popular weekend hangouts include: Rooster's, a blues and barbeque joint owned by actor Morgan Freeman; Proud Larry's, a more laid-back bar with live music; and the Library, where students 18 and up can come to dance and watch sports games. Rebel Ride, a free transportation service, drives students home when the bars close at 1 a.m. Said one junior: "Oxford is a small town, but there never seems to be a shortage of things going on."

Grooving at the Grove

In the fall, no Ole Miss weekend would be complete without a Saturday afternoon trip to the Grove. Most days of the year, the 10-acre grassy knoll known as the Grove looks like a simple lawn with the occasional magnolia tree. But on game days, it transforms into what one junior calls a "huge party"—an elaborate tailgating event that is rivaled nowhere. In fact, tailgating is somewhat of a misnomer for Ole Miss's version, which doesn't involve cars, trucks, or parking lots. Rather, tailgaters at the Grove reserve open-air tents of red, white, or blue. Students and families bring grills, nice food, silverware, candles, and occasionally even chandeliers into their tents, and spend the day eating, drinking, and socializing. "Adults and students are chatting, kids are running around—

it's very family-oriented," explained one student. Ever the Southern ladies and gentlemen, many students dress up to tailgate at the Grove; girls wear sundresses and guys wear collared shirts with khakis.

School spirit abounds at Ole Miss, and football games are an integral part of the campus experience. After the Grove, students move to the stadium in their semiformal attire to cheer on the Rebels. One student notes that "tailgating used to be bigger than the football game itself," but in recent years, as the team has improved, games have become increasingly popular. In fact, many students center dates around football games, attending the game and its pre- and postparties with their date. Reflecting on the game day experience, one junior said: "There honestly isn't anything like football season at Ole Miss."

Rebelling Against Racism

The shadow of slavery, segregation, and racism has long lingered over Ole Miss, much as its administration and students have attempted to distance the University from the darker aspects of its past. Founded in 1848, the University closed briefly during the Civil War after its students left to fight as "University Grays" in the Confederate army. After the war, the University remained segregated until 1962, when James Meredith became the first black student to walk the halls of Ole Miss, flanked by federal marshals. Race riots and other violence plagued the campus throughout the Civil Rights Movement.

> **"There honestly isn't anything like football season at Ole Miss."**

While most students agree that racism is a problem of the past, controversy has erupted within the past decade over the University mascot, Colonel Rebel. In 2003, Colonel Rebel—who, according to some, looks like an antebellum plantation owner—was banned from the sidelines of football games, but he remains the University's official mascot. While some students would prefer a less controversial mascot, many students, according to one senior, "just don't think about it."

The mascot controversy aside, Ole Miss has made great strides toward diversity and tolerance in the past decades. Today, 19 percent of its undergraduates are minorities, and most students feel that the University's atmosphere is inclusive. Diversity-oriented undergraduate organizations, such as the group One Mississippi, have been created to address racial issues on campus. "We've had such issues with discrimination in the past that we've really had to face these issues head on," explained one senior. Another student agreed, claiming: "We deal with this issue every day; we talk about it in every single class. We've come a really long way."

Ole Miss is an institution steeped in tradition, from its controversial mascot, to its game days at the Grove, to its beautiful and historic grounds. Throughout the past decades, the University has been filtering the good traditions from the bad, enhancing its academics, its facilities, and its diversity. Yet when asked what sets Ole Miss apart, most students didn't cite its academic excellence or picturesque campus. Rather, students believe that Ole Miss's close-knit, community atmosphere—rare among public universities—is what puts the University in a league of its own. As one student stated simply, "At Ole Miss, you just feel at home."—*Elizabeth Bewley*

FYI

If you come to Ole Miss, you better bring "your tent for the Grove. If you don't, you will miss out on one of the best experiences of your life."

What is the typical weekend schedule? "Head to the bars Library or Rooster's on Thursday night, hit up a fraternity party on Friday, tailgate at the Grove and go to the football game on Saturday."

If I could change one thing about Ole Miss, I'd change "the stereotype of Ole Miss being stuck in Civil War times and still being racist."

The three things that every student at Ole Miss should do before graduating are "go to a football game and tailgate at the Grove, get to know Oxford, and eat catfish at Taylor Grocery just outside of town."

Missouri

University of Missouri / Columbia

Address: 230 Jesse Hall
Columbia, MO 65211
Phone: 573-882-7786
E-mail address:
MU4U@missouri.edu
Web site URL:
admissions.missouri.edu
Year Founded: 1839
Private or Public: Public
Religious Affiliation: None
Location: Suburban
Number of Applicants:
13,102
Percent Accepted: 78%
**Percent Accepted who
enroll:** 47%
Number Entering: 5,027
**Number of Transfers
Accepted each Year:**
Unreported
Middle 50% SAT range:
M: 540–650, CR:
530–650, Wr: Unreported
Middle 50% ACT range:
23–28
**Early admission program
EA/ED/None:** None

**Percentage accepted
through EA or ED:** NA
EA and ED deadline: NA
Regular Deadline: 1-May
Application Fee: $45
**Full time Undergraduate
enrollment:** 22,000
Total enrollment: 28,253
Percent Male: 49%
Percent Female: 51%
**Total Percent Minority or
Unreported:** 12%
Percent African-American:
6%
**Percent Asian/Pacific
Islander:** 3%
Percent Hispanic: 2%
Percent Native-American: 1%
Percent International:
Unreported
**Percent in-state/out of
state:** 86%/14%
Percent from Public HS:
Unreported
Retention Rate: 85%
Graduation Rate 4-year:
69%

Graduation Rate 6-year:
Unreported
**Percent Undergraduates
in On-campus housing:**
37%
**Number of official organized
extracurricular
organizations:** 500
3 Most popular majors:
Business Administration,
Journalism, Psychology
Student/Faculty ratio: 18:1
Average Class Size: 23
**Percent of students
going to grad school:**
Unreported
Tuition and Fees: $19,514
**In-State Tuition and Fees if
different:** $8,450
Cost for Room and Board:
$8,100
**Percent receiving financial
aid out of those who apply,
first year:** 64%
**Percent receiving financial
aid among all students:**
45%

Walking around the Quad, the most striking features are the Columns, monuments from Mizzou's earliest days. Tradition has each year's freshmen walk through the Columns toward Jesse Hall to show their entrance into Mizzou. Graduating seniors walk through the Columns away from Jesse, signifying their exit from college into the real world. In between are four years at the University of Missouri at Columbia, the largest school in the University of Missouri system and, as its Tigers will tell you, the best. It is home to a striking array of students. Greek life predominates on campus, with rambunctious students holding parties regularly and there is a wide spectrum of non-Greeks, ranging from artsy people, Goths, anti-stereotypes, engineering students, and many others. Just about everybody, however, comes together on weekends for football and basketball games, and Mizzou pride is never as strong as when the fans scream from the stands, "MIZ-ZOU!!!"

Hard at Work

As Missouri's flagship state school, Mizzou caters to a large number of students, and so class sizes vary from 15 to 200. The largest and most popular lecture courses, such as Biology 1010 or Psychology 1010 can be daunting, so smaller classes such as "History of the 1960s" or "American Film History, 1945–Present" offer a more intimate atmosphere for students. Most students consider the workload manageable, although perennial: "I always had something to read or there'd be an online quiz or two that I had to take every day," commented a theater major.

Some students say that the most difficult courses at Mizzou are premed and engineering courses, including biochemistry, chemical engineering, and electrical engineering, but a band member pointed out that "all majors have intensely difficult aspects to them. Business students have to struggle through Accounting 1 and 2 and macro- and microeconomics." Another student added that "a lot of majors require intensive writing courses, which are never easy, and the workload increases as you advance into your major." A few special programs help to make sense of Mizzou's large range of academic offerings—there are Freshman Interest Groups for first-year students, Sponsored Learning Communities, and academically oriented organizations on campus.

The standard distributional requirements for a Mizzou degree include college algebra and another math course, English Exposition and Argumentation, a writing-intensive course, American history or government, and a certain number of credits each from sciences, social sciences, and humanities. Many courses can be fulfilled through high school coursework. One student remarked, "I often complained that it was unnecessary for me to take math and science classes . . . but now I understand why. The administration at Mizzou wanted us to be well-rounded. I'm very glad I took biology and algebra and geology, because it really opened my eyes to the world, and helped me understand current events."

Greektown or Not?

Greek life is rampant on campus, with nearly a quarter of the students participating in 52 fraternities and sororities. Opinion on this lifestyle among the remaining students is divided: a large number are very supportive of the community, from Greektown (where most of the houses are located) to the parties they provide from Wednesday through Saturday nights. The remainder complain that "if you don't belong to a Greek group, you might want to avoid living in a dorm that's located so close to Greektown, or it will drive you crazy." For them, there are many other dorms, which all tend to be fairly comfortable. Certain dorms have

become more well known for housing large populations of math and science students or artsy types; the FARC (Fine Arts Residential Community), for example, houses many music students. After freshman or sophomore year, many students will move off campus into apartments or even houses; Columbia, being a small city, offers many inexpensive housing options that are within walking distance of the rest of campus.

With so many students from so many parts of the country, Mizzou has a niche for nearly every student. The school is in the Midwest, so the stereotypical student is a "white, male, Christian Republican who belongs to a frat. Fortunately, that's usually not the case . . . the student body is very racially, ethnically, socially, and politically diverse." Campus security is present, but safety is never a concern. Multiple students said they felt very safe on campus at all hours. One student living in an all-girls dorm said that "We actually are informed of any alerts through e-mail as soon as possible," which is a useful system for such a large state school.

Food is a big deal: all entering freshmen get the famous Tiger-striped ice cream, and all the dining halls have been rated as "tasty." One junior did note, though, that "you have to pay attention to dining hall hours when picking your meal plan." For late-night cravings, the most popular destination is Gumby's. Shakespeare's is also a favorite destination, claiming to have the best pizza in the Midwest.

> "Painted tiger-ears headbands, tiger tails, and black and gold just shower the campus."

Most students are involved with multiple extracurricular groups. The ones with the largest memberships include College Democrats and College Republicans, the Asian American Student Assocation, Black Student Organization, Hillel, and the Muslim Student Organization. Many students remain involved with faith-based organizations. "There are many churches, synagogues, and mosques within walking distance of the campus where students can attend a service," said a business major. The biggest extracurricular is sports, though. "A LOT of students tend to wear Mizzou jerseys on days of competition," said a fan. "MU sports are pretty big in central, rural, and southern Missouri. I can tell ya that, 'cause a lot of people from small towns from all over Missouri would drive up to Columbia to go to football or basketball games—it is something fun for them to do." A clarinet player for the band noted the crazy colors on game days: "Painted tiger-ears headbands (I have one), tiger tails (have one of those too), and black and gold just shower the campus from tots to alums, students to parents." Another student said it straight out: "The one thing that sets us aside from other schools is the spirit; everyone is proud to be a Tiger. MIZ-ZOU!"

The Quad and Beyond

The campus itself stands out as one of the most beautiful areas in Columbia. One upperclassman gushed that "there is an Ivy League feel to the place. And the Quad is just amazing in the spring—people will be playing Frisbee and hanging out by the Columns even at five in the morning!" A fencer said she loves the inner architecture of Ellis, the largest of Mizzou's libraries, as well as the Art Museum. A sophomore pointed out that Mizzou has an amazing athletics center, including a "huge work-out center, many basketball courts, lazy river, saunas, pools, the list keeps going!" With so many varsity sports, the athletic center is almost a given.

When students were asked, they said that they would definitely choose to go to Mizzou again. "I had fun, I learned a lot of good stuff, I met so many cool people from all over who made me open my eyes, I made some lasting wonderful friends, and I didn't expect that I'd have such a great time here!" And the Mizzou Pride lasts the rest of your life!—*Jeffrey Zuckerman*

FYI

If you come to Mizzou, you'd better bring "a cell phone, so that you can always catch up with your pals between classes."

What is the typical weekend schedule? "Friday, go out to a party or club, hang out with your friends and go to Shakespeare's Pizza or order from Gumby's. Saturday, relax in the afternoon, take a walk in the park or go to a football game. In the evening, let loose. Sunday, study and do homework."

If I could change one thing about Mizzou, I'd "complete all the construction so our campus can be its most beautiful."

Three things that every student at Mizzou should do before graduating are "jump in the Brady Fountain, ride the Mizzou Tiger, and take a class about a subject you have no clue about."

University of Missouri / Kansas City

Address: 5100 Rockhill Road 101AC, Kansas City, MO 64114
Phone: 816-235-1111
E-mail address: admit@umkc.edu
Web site URL: www.umkc.edu
Year Founded: 1929
Private or Public: Public
Religious Affiliation: None
Location: Urban
Number of Applicants: 3,458
Percent Accepted: 60%
Percent Accepted who enroll: 44%
Number Entering: 912
Number of Transfers Accepted each Year: 1,858
Middle 50% SAT range: M: 560–690, CR: 560–660, Wr: Unreported
Middle 50% ACT range: 21–28
Early admission program EA/ED/None: None

Percentage accepted through EA or ED: NA
EA and ED deadline: NA
Regular Deadline: Rolling
Application Fee: $35
Full time Undergraduate enrollment: 9,274
Total enrollment: 12,930
Percent Male: 42%
Percent Female: 58%
Total Percent Minority or Unreported: 39%
Percent African-American: 12%
Percent Asian/Pacific Islander: 6%
Percent Hispanic: 4%
Percent Native-American: 1%
Percent International: 2%
Percent in-state/out of state: 74%/26%
Percent from Public HS: Unreported
Retention Rate: 71%
Graduation Rate 4-year: 44%

Graduation Rate 6-year: Unreported
Percent Undergraduates in On-campus housing: 12%
Number of official organized extracurricular organizations: 200
3 Most popular majors: Business/Commerce, Health Services/Allied Health/Health Sciences, Liberal Arts and Sciences/Liberal Studies
Student/Faculty ratio: 10:1
Average Class Size: 15
Percent of students going to grad school: Unreported
Tuition and Fees: $19,363
In-State Tuition and Fees if different: $8,272
Cost for Room and Board: $8,096
Percent receiving financial aid out of those who apply, first year: 79%
Percent receiving financial aid among all students: 63%

O ver 85 percent of University of Missouri Kansas City students live off campus, but that doesn't prevent them from having a full college experience. Those UMKC students with a little bit of initiative enjoy rich academic, extracurricular, and social lives throughout their years at school. With a quickly increasing enrollment and strong focus on research, the University offers a vast range of experiences on an exciting campus.

Small Classes, Big Pride

UMKC students are required to complete 120 credit hours to graduate. If they are pursuing a B.A., they must also take three semesters of the same foreign language. One popular track of study is a six-year medical program, after which graduates receive an M.D. Students may earn a bachelor's degree in over 50 concentrations in the arts, sciences, humanities, social sciences, music, and nursing; UMKC's mission calls for a fo-

cus on "visual and performing arts, health sciences, and urban affairs." In addition, one sophomore communications major reported an extracurricular club for almost every area of study.

Students are proud of UMKC's standing relative to its peer institutions, saying "its research is excellent and so are its teachers." While there can be "a lot of competition for classes," a first-year student reported that "most of my classes have 25 people" or fewer, and upper-level courses tend to be smaller than the required general education classes. Undergraduates commonly interact with the faculty "online through discussion boards." Though one junior mentioned eating meals with her professors "all the time," another student observed that such close interaction occurs even more often in graduate programs or the Conservatory of Music, ranked one of the top in the nation. Other unique programs include the six-year medical program, as well as the reputable Bloch

Missouri

School of Business and Public Affairs and the School of Law. The school boasts the only pharmacy and dental schools in the state. The University has completed a major building project for Health Science 1, to provide more research space and classrooms for the health and life science departments.

Students noted the sizable population of older students and graduate students, making for a less-traditional college setting. As a result, said one undergrad, "UMKC is a great place for self-sufficient scholarly students who are interested in hitting the books."

Double Your Dorms

Oak Street Hall receives praise for the quality of housing it offers. The University is planning to construct a residence with town-style apartments but has not yet taken action. Nevertheless, both campus culture and economics often push students to the houses around campus, with one student noting after one year that it was "much cheaper . . . to rent a house near campus." Dorms, then, are a popular option for students arriving from outside of Kansas City only until they form a group of friends with whom they can move off-campus.

One student described the University's location in the heart of Kansas City as "fantastic." Students spend much of their free time in the Country Club Plaza area of Kansas City, which offers "luxury shopping" and food options to break up the day. One freshman described this spot, along with the Westport area, as the "dominant social scene," since most students do not spend much time on campus while they aren't in class. For those on campus at meal times, the University of Missouri Kansas City offers food at its dining hall on a debit system, with students loading their cards at the beginning of the semester and spending down until the balance is zero. One student critical of the dining hall compared the food to that of her high school cafeteria. Another agreed, saying that the dining hall is "widely criticized." Students not invested in a semester-long meal plan tend not to spend much time in the dining hall because "food is expensive to purchase with cash."

Outside the Classroom and Off the Campus

Since most UMKC students live off-campus, they do much of their socializing there. There are, however, many opportunities for students to get involved with university-sponsored activities as well. In addition to

academically oriented groups and the Student Government Association, there are plenty of opportunities for community service in the Kansas City metro area. Ethnic organizations and academic-focused groups were noted as particularly active. Also, the University boasts seven fraternities and seven sororities. Many students, including those from outside the Kansas City area, make friends "by joining organizations," though one senior found that because so many students leave campus after class, some "organizations are begging for members."

> **"Everyone drinks, except for the really religious types."**

The campus is dry, but that is no stumbling block to the off-campus consumption of alcohol. According to a senior, "Everyone drinks, except for the really religious types." Even so, a female junior reported no pressure as the only non-drinker in her group of friends. Fridays and Saturdays are the most popular nights out, with venues ranging from small gatherings in houses to Westport, "the largest collection of bars in the Great Plains." Most students have "at least one job," at "Starbucks, in retail, work-study," and a variety of other part-time placements. Those who are employed tend to work off-campus, or have an off-campus job to augment their work-study.

Typical Kangaroo?

One freshman recommended dressing up as the UMKC mascot, Kasey the Kangaroo, at least once during college. Given the makeup of the student body, though, the odds are that you will find a different type of student wearing the costume at every game! "You can't really say that we have one particular stereotypical student," said one junior. "Young and old, different cultures, and different attitudes" are all represented at UMKC, even though many students are from small towns in-state. The strongest representation may be of "middle-class white" backgrounds, but students do note the diversity on campus.

To further expose students to a variety of worldviews, UMKC runs an International Academic Programs office, offering students guidance in applying for fellowships and study abroad programs. The University of Missouri Kansas City currently has programs with schools in 21 countries in Europe and Asia, as well as ones in Mexico,

Australia, and New Zealand. The office also works with students to transfer financial aid packages to study abroad programs. On campus, the school boasts an international population of around two percent.

UMKC competes athletically in the Mid-Continent Conference of the NCAA's Division I. The University sponsors a variety of sports, ranging from basketball and volleyball to golf, tennis, softball, and rifle, but for most of the student body, the UMKC-Valparaiso basketball game is the biggest athletic event of the year. For those not inclined to commit to Division I athletics, the

Swinney Recreation Center offers fitness facilities and a swimming pool to the university community.

The University of Missouri Kansas City is a school with many opportunities for academic, extracurricular, and social growth, but it requires some initiative from its somewhat scattered student body. According to those who have taken that extra step, seeking out a professor for lunch or joining a campus political organization can make for a fulfilling college experience, taking advantage of the "good education" that UMKC can provide.—*Douglas London*

FYI

If you come to UMKC, you'd better bring "a sense of humor."

The best places to hang out on the weekend are "Friday and Saturday, go to bars or go out to eat, and sleep in on Sunday."

If I could change one thing about UMKC, "I would make parking free and plentiful."

Three things that every UMKC student should do before graduating are "go on an internship out of state or country, join a club, and live in a dorm."

Washington University in St. Louis

Address: One Brookings Drive
St. Louis, MO 63139-4988
Phone: 314-935-6000
E-mail address:
admissions@wustl.edu
Web site URL:
www.wustl.edu
Year Founded: 1853
Private or Public: Private
Religious Affiliation: None
Location: Urban
Number of Applicants:
22,428
Percent Accepted: 17%
**Percent Accepted who
enroll:** 34%
Number Entering: 1,328
**Number of Transfers
Accepted each Year:** 221
Middle 50% SAT range:
M: 690–780, CR:
680–750, Wr: Unreported
Middle 50% ACT range:
28–34
**Early admission program
EA/ED/None:** ED

**Percentage accepted
through EA or ED:**
Unreported
EA and ED deadline: 15-Nov
Regular Deadline: 15-Jan
Application Fee: $55
**Full time Undergraduate
enrollment:** 6,985
Total enrollment: 12,036
Percent Male: 49%
Percent Female: 51%
**Total Percent Minority or
Unreported:** 16%
Percent African-American:
10%
**Percent Asian/Pacific
Islander:** 12%
Percent Hispanic: 3%
Percent Native-American:
0%
Percent International: 5%
**Percent in-state/out of
state:** 10%/90%
Percent from Public HS:
63%
Retention Rate: 97%

Graduation Rate 4-year:
94%
Graduation Rate 6-year:
Unreported
**Percent Undergraduates in
On-campus housing:** 73%
**Number of official organized
extracurricular
organizations:** 200
3 Most popular majors:
Biology, Finance, Psychology
Student/Faculty ratio: 7:1
Average Class Size: 18
**Percent of students going to
grad school:** 33%
Tuition and Fees: $36,200
**In-State Tuition and Fees if
different:** No difference
Cost for Room and Board:
$11,636
**Percent receiving financial
aid out of those who apply,
first year:** 39%
**Percent receiving financial
aid among all students:**
41%

Walking into the front quad through Brookings Hall, the surrounding green lawns and the collegiate twist on Gothic architecture leap out at you. They are small markers of Washington University's formidable reputation as the "truly quintessential university." Easily in the top 15 colleges nationwide, Wash U (as it is popularly nicknamed) rivals the Ivy League and the best of small liberal-arts schools for scholarship and attention to individual students. Its location in downtown St. Louis, near the green spaces of Forest Park and the trendy stores of the Loop, is suggestive of the vivacity of its student population—vibrant, friendly, and intellectually driven. The school's increasing popularity has been signified recently by unexpectedly large freshman classes, and the atmosphere is full of newfound wonder for the beauty of life in the Midwest.

Intellectualism 101: Going in Premed, Going Out with a Triple Major

The on-campus joke is that "A TON of the freshmen each year come in planning to be premed because the program here is so good, [which] makes the sciences notoriously rigorous and hardcore," as one senior shared. But "by the time people are required to declare a major sophomore year, the distributions across majors are much more even," so Wash U's claim to fame as a liberal arts school has always been an advantage.

The requirements are fairly clear-cut: every student must take Writing I and another writing-intensive course, a quantitative analysis class, and one course each in Cultural Diversity and Social Differentiation. Additionally, two to three classes have to be taken in each of four academic areas: natural science and mathematics, social sciences, textual and historical studies, and language and the arts. Still, this set of general-education requirements is considered to be fairly flexible, and the academic areas offer many options. "Instead of having to suffer through something like chemistry, non-science people can take classes like 'Dinosaurs: Facts and Fiction.' Requirements are really flexible, which is what enables people to do things like triple major," said a female student who is triple-majoring in Political Science, Spanish, and History—hardly impossible at Washington University since requirements for a major tend to be uncomplicated, and the academic guidelines actively encourage multiple majors.

The University prides itself on its freshman programs, which range from the FOCUS program to the Text and Tradition program. There is also a wide variety of freshman seminars within academic departments, which often include international travel. A sophomore who took a class on Michelangelo as a freshman raved, "We got to go to Italy after the semester was over and see some of the sculptures we'd been studying for months!" Some programs have options for a sophomore-year extension, and others lead freshman into exploring different areas of study after their freshman year.

Many introductory classes within Wash U, particularly within the sciences and psychology, enroll "over 100 [students]. Most other classes are small, between five and 20 people," said a premed student, who pointed out that "some very popular classes such as the Human Evolution class taught by the most eloquent speaker on campus have waitlists longer than the amount of seats in the class." An older student explained that "class size depends a lot on what you're taking. [Non-science] majors have much smaller classes. My smallest class ever was one person. Just me, alone with the professor." The professors are touted as being "super-approachable and accessible" by many students on campus, and with good reason—Washington University is primarily a liberal arts school, with scholarship as its first priority.

The workload is intense, no matter what the major. Sciences in particular are difficult due to the large number of potential premeds, and most people feel that "General Chemistry is the 'make it or break it' class . . . finishing it is definitely a milestone in one's academic career." The humanities tend to be easier, particularly the Classics and English, but the workload is intense, no matter what the discipline. Grade inflation is "nonexistent" and not a concern. The stereotypical Wash U student "is a really smart procrastinator, who does it because he or she is smart enough to. They know how to space out their work so they have free time. Everyone pretty much lives in the library right before finals, but generally they know how to balance their time," said a Gregg dorm resident.

Bright Colors, Tight Parties

Social life at Washington University is excellent. The events include First Friday, a campus celebration gearing up to WILD (Walk In, Lay Down), where major bands come to perform, and Thurtene, a carnival. The fraternities, while not a dominant presence, provide entertainment for most freshmen in their first weeks of college (which is why, one member jokes, "for the first month or so all the upperclassmen avoid frat row"), and alcohol is not an issue for those who choose to seek it out. The rule, as reiterated by every student, is that they can't be "flagrant or dangerous." The University tends to stay out of alcohol-related incidents, treating them as health issues rather than disciplinary issues. Also, "one of the best things at Wash U is that there are almost as many different 'scenes' here as there are people. If you don't drink, your closest friends can become the people who also don't. If you're more into other types of activities, you can still have plenty of fun on weekends."

Many events are advertised on one of the most unusual parts of campus: the South 40 underpass. The sides of the underpass as well as underneath are regularly coated with paint, and three geometric sculptures (a square, a pyramid, and a sphere), are available for similar advertising space. Groups often ask art majors to paint these areas, and they work in the evenings, making the walk around the underpass vivid and colorful. One student recalled, "The Jewish Student Union likes to paint [the sphere] to resemble a giant Matzo ball to advertise for their Passover events."

There are a wide range of activities and events at Washington University—people won't really be divided between "school-sponsored events" and "crazy in-suite parties." Frequently, people will go to lectures one evening and frat parties or bars or other suites another. The fact that the campus is very intellectual leads to some interesting twists: a chemistry major recalled one party where people played a game based on a professor's taped lectures. Sometimes the whole school will show up for more famous speakers: an Art History major said that famous people such as "Bill Nye and Paul Rusesabagina (hero of the Rwandan genocide), amongst various other political and academic names, lecture on Wednesdays" as part of the Assembly Series.

Floormate Loving

Relationships at Washington University run the gamut from casual hookups to traditional daters to engaged couples. Most people tend to end up in committed relationships by senior year, but the dating scene is still fresh as an underclassman. A female rated the general student population as "eight out of ten

for attractiveness—altogether we're a good-looking group. There's a false stereotype that girls are ugly at WUSTL; it's actually the engineering guys and they're awkward, not ugly." There are a number of gay and interracial couples, and the population is supportive of both, even though neither are a large presence on campus. STDs tend not to be an issue; an Alpha Phi Omega member said that "these smart students understand all risks they are taking and try to prevent contraction as best they can."

One upperclassman said, "One of my favorite things about Wash U is that you're always meeting new people. It's my senior year and I'm *still* making new friends every weekend." Most students have multiple groups of friends, with different activities providing new friends: classes, extracurriculars, Greek groups, even floormates. A sophomore said "the people on your freshman floor get really close and you stay really close. They're the people you're most likely to stay in contact with after college; in fact, more than half my floor moved together to the floor I'm on now." Another student said there didn't seem to be any social stereotype for Wash U students, only the academic stereotype of laid-back while intellectually intense. There's a mix of all types of students, "including some plain-and-out nerds, who are usually funnier than expected." Certainly there are wealthy students: "It's hard to say because people really don't discuss their financial situations very often, but judging by the cars in the parking lot, there's plenty of money on campus." Still, the University offers many loans and scholarships, the largest being the Compton, Mylonas, Moog, Lien, and Fossett full-tuition scholarships.

A Chancellor and a Rabbit . . .

The administration is constantly responsive to student needs; after a Facebook group called "Wash U really needs to get a fountain up in here" was created, they actually did install one—even though the campus, which includes beautiful pink granite buildings, hardly needed it. Similar responsiveness has been apparent with such issues as the decision to charge for wireless connections on campus; a succession of reactions over two weeks (in the summer, moreover) caused the administration to reevaluate their decision. The chancellor is a large presence on campus, and he is well known for inviting students to his house to go bowling or have a snack with him. Because he is a "very accomplished chemist, and he worked on creating some of the chemicals that are found in the glow stick," as a Student Admissions Committee assistant explained, hundreds of glow sticks are handed out to freshmen to carry during Convocation at the beginning of each year.

> "As part of a class, we got to go to Italy and see Michelangelo's sculptures!"

The campus as a whole is quite unique: it has had the honor of hosting Presidential debates consistently since 1992, and it often sets up its students with political internships. Activism is present on campus, but most students are just happy to be on the South 40, relaxing. Each student polled said that the most interesting thing about campus was The Bunny, a sculpture officially called "Thinker on the Rock." It is usually cited as the ugliest thing on campus, but also the best meeting spot. Stories abound: many students have dressed up the rabbit in clothes, although one girl stated, "Be warned: you will not get your clothes back once you donate them to the bunny."

Every student polled said that, if they had a choice, they would definitely choose Wash U again, and that they wouldn't give up all the options the school affords—study abroad, internships, classes, and social events—— for any other college. One sophomore said, "Academically, this is a very rigorous university. It teaches students how to think critically and to ask questions about the world. Though we put a lot of effort into our work, the reward of completion and knowledge is great." But the student triple majoring in Political Science, Spanish, and History said that what made Washington University truly unique in comparison with Ivy League schools was the opportunity for individual choice: "The Wash U experience is what you make of it, and you're never limited by the preexisting system. I think that's really embodied in something that Dean McLeod, the Dean of Students, says about Wash U. As diverse as Wash U is, he says, the one thing that unites everyone on campus is that 'they want to be active participants in their own education.'"—*Jeffrey Zuckerman*

FYI
If you come to Wash U, you better bring "a laptop with wireless. You'll want the mobility."
What is a typical weekend schedule? "Thursday night: go out on the town. Friday: tie-dye shirts then watch movies on the Swamp. Saturday: homework, pre-party, club circuits. Sunday: homework, socialize in hallway circles, sleep."
If I could change one thing about Wash U, "I'd change the name so that people don't get it mixed up with other schools."
Three things every student at Wash U should do before graduating are "take Intro to Sexuality (a huge lecture class with an absolutely amazing lecturer and fantastic subject material), go bowling at the chancellor's house (at his awesome in-home private bowling alley), and attend WILD."

Montana

Address: Lommasson Center 103, Missoula, MT 59812
Phone: 406-243-6266
E-mail address: admiss@umontana.edu
Web site URL: www.umontana.edu
Year Founded: 1893
Private or Public: Public
Religious Affiliation: None
Location: Urban
Number of Applicants: 4,756
Percent Accepted: 95%
Percent Accepted who enroll: 44%
Number Entering: 1,981
Number of Transfers Accepted each Year: Unreported
Middle 50% SAT range: M: 470–600, CR: 460–600, Wr: 460–580
Middle 50% ACT range: 20–25
Early admission program EA/ED/None: None

Percentage accepted through EA or ED: NA
EA and ED deadline: NA
Regular Deadline: Rolling
Application Fee: $30
Full time Undergraduate enrollment: 11,799
Total enrollment: Unreported
Percent Male: 47%
Percent Female: 53%
Total Percent Minority or Unreported: 18%
Percent African-American: 1%
Percent Asian/Pacific Islander: 1%
Percent Hispanic: 2%
Percent Native-American: 4%
Percent International: 2%
Percent in-state/out of state: 73%/27%
Percent from Public HS: 44%
Retention Rate: 72%
Graduation Rate 4-year: 41%
Graduation Rate 6-year: Unreported

Percent Undergraduates in On-campus housing: 24%
Number of official organized extracurricular organizations: 150
3 Most popular majors: Business Administration and Management, Education, Psychology
Student/Faculty ratio: 19:1
Average Class Size: 14
Percent of students going to grad school: 33%
Tuition and Fees: $16,425
In-State Tuition and Fees if different: $5,150
Cost for Room and Board: $6,258
Percent receiving financial aid out of those who apply, first year: Unreported
Percent receiving financial aid among all students: Unreported

Surrounded by mountains and adjacent to the Clark Fork River, it's no wonder University of Montana students call themselves Grizzlies. "You can literally walk off campus into a wilderness area," raved one freshman. "It's definitely the most beautiful campus I've seen—and I was all over the West Coast looking at schools." Add to that a wide variety of academic options and the thriving small-city nightlife of Missoula, and you get a "really neat place to go to school."

Hitting the Books

UM has programs in the arts and sciences, forestry and conservation, technology, business, education, pharmacy, journalism, and fine arts, offering students a wide variety of majors, from anthropology to zoology and everything in between. Entering freshmen apply to the University of Montana at large; students apply to a specific major before the end of junior year. The popular majors include psychology, forestry, and marketing, which is known for being relatively easy.

Regardless of major, all Grizzlies must take 120 course credits to graduate (an average course load is 15–18 credits, or 4–5 classes, per semester), at least 39 of which must be in upper-division courses. In addition, students must fulfill an English requirement, a mathematics requirement, and a foreign language or symbolic systems requirement. Also, each student must take a total of 27 credits in the following six "perspectives," with at least two credits from each: expressive arts, literary and artistic studies, historical and cultural studies, social sciences, ethical and human values, and natural sciences. To some students, the number of requirements seems like "overkill," though they are "good for someone who doesn't have a major in mind because you can figure out what you want to do." In any case, said one junior, "There's usually enough of a selection that you can find something you'll like—there's so many different choices that if you can't find something you can at least deal with, you're not trying very hard." Indeed, at least some requirements can be met with "easy and interesting" classes like "History of Rock and Roll," "Use and Abuse of Drugs," "Human Sexuality," and "Intro to Anthropology."

> "It's definitely the most beautiful campus I've seen—and I was all over the West Coast looking at schools."

Unfortunately, with over 12,000 undergrads, getting the classes you want can be "pretty hard." "Classes go really fast" in online registration, said one freshman. This leaves some students "stuck with classes at really weird times," but teachers will often sign an override slip if you talk to them in person. Students can also sign up for the Four Bear program, where they plan out a tentative four-year schedule ahead of time with an adviser and get to pick classes before everyone else.

While competition to get into classes is tough, competition within classes is almost nonexistent. "I really would not call UM cutthroat," said one junior. "While it attracts all types, people are generally pretty laid-back here." Class sizes range from 10–25 person upper-division seminars to intro lecture classes with over 400 students. Professors teach the majority of classes, though TAs (who are generally "pretty good") teach basic introductory English and math classes, in addition to leading lab sections. Even in large lecture classes, "there's a lot of access to your professor," said a junior biology major. "If you can't make it to their office hours, they'll go out of their way to meet with you," echoed a freshman. Most students are "pretty happy" with their professors, who, in addition to being "really approachable," are also "extremely knowledgeable" and "enjoy teaching."

Students seeking a more intense education can apply to the Davidson Honors College at the same time they apply to UM. Honors classes are similar in subject matter to non-honors courses, but average 22 students per class. That means "more work—because it's a smaller class, it's not as easy to

sit back and tune out," but also "a lot more discussion, a much better learning environment." Non-honors students can also take honors classes, but honors students get priority and must take at least seven honors courses, including a senior project, to graduate. UM also has a "really strong" study abroad program, which offers the opportunity to study in 38 different countries, including Australia, Canada, Chile, China, France, Morocco, and Thailand.

A Grizzly's Den

Dorms at UM get mixed reviews. All are located "close to the core of campus," no more than a 10-minute walk from classes, and have laundry facilities, game rooms, and lounges. However, they vary in style and quality. Jesse and Aber, the high-rise dorms, are "housing projects designed to pack in as many people as possible," while Craig and Duniway have bigger rooms, and Miller offers singles. Knowles houses honors and international students, Elrod is male-only, and Turner houses only women. Students can also choose substance-free or quiet floors if they so desire.

All students who live in the dorms must purchase a meal plan, which allows students to eat at the Food Zoo (the main cafeteria), as well as at an on-campus food court or coffee shops. The Zoo offers "pretty good variety," and the food is "good for mass production," especially with its new Farm to College program, which brings in fresh meat and vegetables from local farms.

Freshmen, who are required to live on campus, are distributed throughout the various dorms. Events like the weekly "Floor Snack" and monthly trips to a bowling alley or pizza place make it easy to meet new people. These events are organized by upperclassmen RAs, who live on each floor and range from "real well-trained" to "horrible. [They'll] write you up if you're overly loud, drinking, doing anything that's slightly weird." "Overall," said one freshman, "they're good at what they do—they keep the place running really smoothly—but they definitely stick to the rules." Even though the newest dorm, Pantzer, is reserved for upperclassmen, most students move off campus by junior year; however, many claim that "finding something that's affordable close to campus gets difficult."

Unfortunately, "parking on campus is absolutely insane—it's impossible to get a spot," and "public transportation isn't real great," so many students are forced to leave their cars in Park and Ride lots. Luckily, "it's really easy to get around" with a bike, said one Grizzly. Bike lanes are ubiquitous in Missoula, and "everything is really close—I can ride my bike to the mall, Target, and back to campus in like half an hour."

Here Come the MIP's

UM certainly lives up to its reputation as "a really big party school." Every spring, Grizzlies "dress up country style" to attend the Foresters' Ball, in which the forestry department turns the gym into a logging camp, complete with a saloon and "hitching post" where students can get "married." Other popular annual parties include Maggotfest, when rugby teams come from across the nation to compete in the spring tournament, and then have a "giant party with an absurd number of kegs and people pouring beer all over each other."

Although frats throw "their fair share of parties," Greek life is "not very big," which makes the Greek scene a "really tight-knit community" but "not a large part of the social network." Alcohol is generally "pretty easy to get," but drinking is "definitely more of an off-campus thing," since RAs zealously report underage drinking in the dorms. Even off-campus, however, police "are more than eager" to cite students for "a DUI, BUI (biking under the influence), or MIP (minor in possession)."

On most weekends, students frequent house parties or head into the "very active downtown," which includes a variety of restaurants, pool halls, and "a ton of bars that are always packed." Students report that "bars are pretty easy to get into if you know people that know people," even if you're not 21. Non-drinkers enjoy a variety of options as well. Popular with both students and locals is the Elks Lodge, an 18-and-up club in Missoula that invites musical performers every night. On campus, there are "Nite Kourt" events, where university organizations bring in "hypnotists, comedians, all kinds of stuff."

Grizzlies at Play

When they're not partying or studying, UM students are involved in a plethora of extracurricular activities. As one junior put it, "There's pretty much a club for anything you want." The diversity of clubs reflects a diversity of students. Although racial diversity is limited (the student body is "very, very white"), students hail from all over the country, and even as far away as Japan, Korea, Hong Kong, Australia, Germany, and Tajikistan. Organizations include the popular ASUM (student government), which organizes many events on campus, and *Kaimin*, the student newspaper, as well as unusual clubs like the "Footbag Alliance," devoted to hacky sack. As Missoula is the most liberal part of Montana (though not as liberal as some universities in other parts of the country), activism is also big. "There are a lot of causes to rally around," said a junior. "There is always something for people who want to get involved socially or politically."

But the biggest draw is the great outdoors. Students enjoy fly-fishing in the Clark Fork River right off campus, as well as hiking up to the concrete "M" on Mt. Sentinel. There are also many outdoor clubs, which organize weekend camping and backpacking trips to nearby Glacier National Park (2½ hours away), Yellowstone (three hours), or Hot Springs (less than half an hour). Moreover, the Recreation Center, an on-campus facility, rents whitewater rafts, ski equipment, backpacking gear, and kayaks at reduced prices.

The rec center is also "absolutely awesome" during the winter, containing an indoor track, weight machines, exercise rooms, a swimming pool, and a climbing wall. Students looking for more competitive activities can play intramural sports, the most popular of which are Ultimate Frisbee, soccer, softball, and basketball; and for those students who are particularly athletically-inclined, UM also offers 14 Division I varsity sports.

According to most students, there is a lot of school spirit. Students and Missoula residents regularly sell out the 23,000-seat stadium for football games, which feature skydivers jumping onto the field at halftime. Before games, "people go nuts about tailgates—they pull up in motor homes painted with the Montana colors." Whether they come for the exciting party scene, academic choices, or "gorgeous" location, students agree: "UM is a cool place to be."—*Sameer Jain*

FYI

If you come to UM, you'd better bring "Chaco sandals, a warm jacket, and a sense of adventure."

What's the typical weekend schedule? "Thursday: head out to a party. Friday: go to a pool hall or bar downtown, maybe a party. Saturday: tailgate, football game, nap in the afternoon, party at night. Sunday: homework, laundry, recovery. Or head to Glacier National Park or the Hot Springs for the whole weekend."

If I could change one thing about UM, I'd "increase racial diversity: I've seen literally four black people the three months I've been here."

Three things every student should do before graduating are "go to a football game, go to the Foresters' Ball, and hike to the M (a huge white concrete M about 1000 feet up Mt. Sentinel which people hike to all the time)."

Nebraska

Creighton University

Address: 2500 California Plaza, Omaha, NE 68178
Phone: 402-280-2703
E-mail address: admissions@creighton.edu
Web site URL: www.creighton.edu
Year Founded: 1878
Private or Public: Private
Religious Affiliation: Roman Catholic
Location: Urban
Number of Applicants: 3,336
Percent Accepted: 89%
Percent Accepted who enroll: 32%
Number Entering: 950
Number of Transfers Accepted each Year: 165
Middle 50% SAT range: M: 540–650, Cr: 520–630, Wr: 590–690
Middle 50% ACT range: 24–29

Early admission program EA/ED/None: None
Percentage accepted through EA or ED: NA
EA and ED deadline: NA
Regular Deadline: 15-Feb
Application Fee: $40
Full time Undergraduate enrollment: 4,104
Total enrollment: 4,647
Percent Male: 40%
Percent Female: 60%
Total Percent Minority or Unreported: 21%
Percent African-American: 3%
Percent Asian/Pacific Islander: 8%
Percent Hispanic: 3%
Percent Native-American: 1%
Percent International: 1%
Percent in-state/out of state: 37%/63%
Percent from Public HS: 55%

Retention Rate: 86%
Graduation Rate 4-year: 61%
Graduation Rate 6-year: 74%
Percent Undergraduates in On-campus housing: 62%
Number of official organized extracurricular organizations: 182
3 Most popular majors: Business, Health, Psychology
Student/Faculty ratio: 12:1
Average Class Size: 22
Percent of students going to grad school: 70%
Tuition and Fees: $25,262
In-State Tuition and Fees if different: No difference
Cost for Room and Board: $8,180
Percent receiving financial aid out of those who apply, first year: 78%
Percent receiving financial aid among all students: 60%

Founded in 1878 as a private Jesuit university in Omaha, Nebraska, Creighton University has become one of the best institutions of higher learning in the United States. The university's location in Nebraska may turn away many students outside of the Midwest region; however, Creighton provides students with a very good education, notable for the close interactions between students and professors.

The Curriculum

Creighton is a relatively small university. Nevertheless, the school is still divided into nine colleges and twelve research centers.

In fact, the school has the components of major research institutions with the presence of medical, law, and business schools. "We really are a comprehensive university," said one student. "I met people who think that Creighton is just a small college, but we have all the graduate schools."

The small number of undergraduate students and the large scale of the university indicate that students can have close interactions with professors. In fact, classes tend to be relatively small, often under 30 students. As a result, students can have easier access to their instructors who also have more time for individual students. "I got to know a lot of professors really well at Creighton," said one student. "I think that is something that sets Creighton apart." The accessibility of professors can be highly beneficial for the students in both having a better understanding of the course materials and obtaining help for future endeavors.

The undergraduate program offers about 50 majors in three of the colleges, Arts and Sciences, Business Administration, and Nursing. While the majority of majors are the traditional liberal arts programs of study, such as biology, history, and economics, Creighton also lists a number of more specialized curriculums for students who are more interested in professional preparation. Some of these majors include Photo Journalism, Applied Meteorology, and Studio Art. At the same time, the school also provides strong preparatory classes for graduate schools, since a large number of students are pre-medical, pre-dental, and pre-law. The presence of the professional schools on campus certainly helps those students a great deal in experiencing graduate-level classes and even engaging in more sophisticated research projects. "Creighton is proud of its academics," said one student. The different research centers that are spread across campus also allow the more ambitious undergraduates to have more in-depth investigations of topics that interest them.

Creighton also provides a number of honors and leadership programs for students who wish to go beyond the basic required curriculums. In the Arts and Sciences' Honors Program, students will be able to attend more discussion-based classes where people can learn from each other by exchanging ideas. Those in the program will also live together in the same freshman dorm. The College of Business Administration offers a leadership program for students to learn through extracurricular activities.

> "There are a lot of really smart people here. You get to learn a lot from them."

Students believe that the workload is mostly manageable. Although some science classes can be surprisingly difficult for inexperienced freshmen, most people believe that, after one semester at Creighton, students are generally used to the pace and demands of academics. Of course, it is important for prospective students to be ready to work once they arrive and expect to find many people of great talent on campus. "There are a lot of really smart people here," said one student. "You get to learn a lot from them."

According to *U.S. News & World Report*, the university is ranked first among all Midwestern universities where the highest degree offered is the master's degree. It is certainly a very prestigious distinction for the school. The admissions rate is over 80%, but prospective students should definitely expect a competitive selection process, given the relatively high academic standards of the school as well as the quality of applicants.

Gateway to the West

Omaha is the metropolis of Nebraska. It is the county seat and the largest city of the state. For a city known as the Gateway to the West, Omaha's atmosphere falls somewhere between the prairie Midwest and the more fast-paced West Coast. Nevertheless, the city is not exactly a major urban center, and many students believe that it does not offer much to the students. There are a few restaurants, bars, and clubs, features that are expected around a major university. Therefore, most students stay close to campus during much of the school year and do not venture far into the rest of the city. Of course, for students who are interested in outdoor activities, Nebraska certainly provides plenty of opportunities for hiking and boating in the surrounding parks.

Freshmen and sophomores stay on campus at Creighton, and the reviews for housing demonstrate that students are generally fine with their dorms. "The rooms are pretty nice, but they are small," said one student. "As long as you and your roommate get along with the small space, you will like your room." Some of the dorms look like apartment buildings where individual rooms open into one long hallway. Others are arranged in suites, where two bedrooms are connected to a small living room. The majority of juniors and seniors, however, prefer to find housing off-campus of the school.

The dining services provide two main dinning halls, as well as a number of small shops and stores where students use their meal plans. The plans can be as much as 19 meals per week to 60 meals for an entire semester. As to the quality of food, it generally receives reasonably good reviews, at least for college dinning halls. "I go to restaurants once in a while when I am tired of the dinning halls," said one student. "But overall, I would say that they do a pretty good job with the food."

Creighton is home to five fraternities and seven sororities, which represent an important part of the social scene. Greek life is certainly critical in organizing large parties during the weekends. "A lot of people join frats, but you don't have to," said one student. "The school is big enough to find your unique group of friends." Another venue for weekend festivities is in the off-campus housing of students.

Undiscovered Gem

One important part of Creighton University is its Jesuit heritage. While 60% of the students are Roman Catholic, the school welcomes a diverse student body and is happy to embrace people of all faiths, and approximately 20% of the students are considered minorities.

Creighton is considered one of the top universities in the western part of the country and it certainly has the features of an impressive educational institution. The students receive personal attention from the professors, and it has been widely recognized by a number of college reviews as one of the top universities in the nation, thus making it a very good choice for prospective students.—*Xiaohang Liu*

FYI
If you come to Creighton, you'd better bring "warm clothing."
What is the typical weekend schedule? "Parties on Friday and Saturday. Sunday is for work."
If I could change one thing about Creighton, I'd "build more dining halls."
Three things every student at Creighton should do before graduating are "find a good extracurricular organization, go hiking, and make sure you enjoy your four years."

University of Nebraska / Lincoln

Address: 1410 Q Street
Lincoln, NE 68588-0256
Phone: 402-472-2023
E-mail address:
admissions@unl.edu
Web site URL: www.unl.edu
Year Founded: 1869
Private or Public: Public
Religious Affiliation: None
Location: Urban
Number of Applicants: 9,598
Percent Accepted: 62%
**Percent Accepted who
enroll:** 71%
Number Entering: 4,215
**Number of Transfers
Accepted each Year:** 1,246
Middle 50% SAT range:
M: 530–670, **CR:**
500–650, **Wr:** Unreported
Middle 50% ACT range:
22–28
**Early admission program
EA/ED/None:** None
**Percentage accepted
through EA or ED:** NA

EA and ED deadline: NA
Regular Deadline: 1-May
Application Fee: $45
**Full time Undergraduate
enrollment:** 18,053
Total enrollment: 22,550
Percent Male: 54%
Percent Female: 46%
**Total Percent Minority or
Unreported:** 17%
Percent African-American:
2%
**Percent Asian/Pacific
Islander:** 3%
Percent Hispanic: 3%
Percent Native-American:
1%
Percent International: 3%
**Percent in-state/out of
state:** 83%/17%
Percent from Public HS:
Unreported
Retention Rate: 83%
Graduation Rate 4-year:
22%
Graduation Rate 6-year: 42%

**Percent Undergraduates
in On-campus housing:**
41%
**Number of official organized
extracurricular
organizations:** 335
3 Most popular majors:
Business Administration and
Management, Finance,
Psychology
Student/Faculty ratio: 19:1
Average Class Size: 23
**Percent of students
going to grad school:**
Unreported
Tuition and Fees: $17,205
**In-State Tuition and Fees if
different:** $6,585
Cost for Room and Board:
$6,882
**Percent receiving financial
aid out of those who apply,
first year:** 65%
**Percent receiving financial
aid among all students:**
41%

The Big Red. Almost without fail, people across the nation know the Big Red for one thing: their football. With five National Championships under the University of Nebraska's belt, Cornhusker spirit runs deep, especially since Memorial Stadium ranks as the third-largest-populated area of Nebraska after Omaha and Lincoln on game day. To all native Nebraskans and students at the University, there is no messing around when it comes to football.

Making the Grade

Although students may not be as obsessed with academia as they are with UNL football, the University does a lot to accommodate a wide range of interests. By offering over 150 majors and 9 academic colleges intended for those looking to specialize in their given field, students can find what's necessary for a thorough education. For those seeking an accelerated education, the Honors program at Nebraska offers an avenue. Requiring a cumulative 3.5 GPA to participate, those in the Honors program are

provided with special housing, smaller class sizes, and close interaction opportunities with faculty and fellow high-achieving students. Students say that the most academically grueling majors include philosophy, any type of engineering, and organic chemistry. Not all classes are so demanding; UNL provides unique courses such as Introduction to Wine Tasting, Personal Defense, and Ballroom Dancing. One student emphasizes that the "liberal arts environment really encourages students to think freely and pursue individual interests, because it's all offered."

The size of most classes at the University of Nebraska echo the usual class size found at state universities, ranging from 10 to 500 students depending on the type of course with some classes averaging about 150. The general perception about the undergraduate professors is positive. "Professors are friendly and willing to work with individual students' schedules for out-of-class meetings" one sophomore noted. The TAs are a different story, however. Depending on the major, TAs can either be really helpful or hard to understand, as they may not be able to speak English very well.

Lincoln Living

During their freshman year at the University of Nebraska, students are required to live on campus. Most upperclassmen either move into on-campus apartment-style housing or move off campus entirely. Cather and Pound are two upperclassmen dorms, offering laundry facilities and computer clusters on every floor. Although many end up off campus, the majority of students seem to appreciate their freshman living experience. "You meet a lot of people that you might otherwise never get to know, some of whom become your best friends." All of the housing options offered by the University are fully air-conditioned, although those buildings not recently renovated are of noticeably lower quality.

Almost all the freshman dorms are doubles, with two beds, desks, closets, and high-speed wireless internet. RAs (Residential Advisors) are upperclassmen whose job it is to keep the freshman dorms free of alcohol and running smoothly. Those who choose to live off campus are able to take advantage of relatively low Midwestern housing prices. If a student at UNL does not reside on campus or in an apartment outside of the University's provided housing, he/she most likely lives in a fraternity or sorority. There are a total of 37 Greek houses at Nebraska-Lincoln: 14 sororities and 23 fraternities. Those involved in Greek life seem to "hold more leadership positions on campus" according to one senior. Furthermore, those brothers and sisters in Greek houses on campus have statistically higher GPAs than the overall average GPA of students at the University.

As far as food goes, the dining hall situation leaves everyone with a different taste in their mouths. Always noted as clean and not too crowded, the food's quality is recognized as anywhere from "decent but bland" to "everything one would look for in a college dining hall." However, the Training Table, a dining hall where only UNL athletes are allowed to eat, provides the best food. "They offer prime rib, a more diversified menu, and a nutritionist is on staff in order to make sure athletes are getting the nutritional requirements they need" one junior explained.

The Union

When asked what the central hangout on campus is, students emphatically answer, "the Union!" Known to non-Cornhuskers as the Nebraska Union, the Union is unquestionably the most popular campus social center. Home to the University Bookstore, a convenience store, auditorium, copy shop, game room, food court, and big-screen television lounge, the Union has it all. "If anyone ever needs to study with a group or catch up with some friends, the Union is the place to meet," declared one sophomore. Other than the Union, many Cornhuskers cite Memorial Stadium as the most prized location on campus. Renovated in 1999, the Stadium is now equipped with $40 million worth of new skyboxes.

It's All in Lincoln

If students aren't attending individual parties, team parties, or frat parties, "Haymarket is definitely the place to go" a junior explained. Located in downtown Lincoln, the Haymarket is full of restaurants and shops and is most commonly cited as the place to go for a date or to check out the bar scene on a Saturday night. Because Lincoln caters to college life and is the only real city for miles, many students will stay on campus for the better part of the year. "You really have to stay in the city because there really isn't anywhere else to go" a student said.

Aside from holding the highest grades on campus, the Greek houses are infamous for throwing some of the best parties annually. Hosting parties with themes anywhere from "Doctors and Nurses" to "Hollywood," "The frats are definitely where it's at," one student declared. Partying usually starts on Thursday nights and lasts until Saturday night. However, most Saturday nights in the fall are spent recovering from a full day at the Cornhusker tailgate rooting on the Big Red.

> "There is a pride in being a Cornhusker that blows me away."

Outside of academics and athletics, there are a wide range of other possibilities offered through the university and separate student organizations. Students are heavily involved in everything from community outreach volunteer programs to on-campus publications like the *Daily Nebraskan*. Cornhuskers are very satisfied overall with the extracurricular life on campus.

It's All About Football

While football most definitely pulls the biggest crowds, all athletic teams really bring a lot to Cornhusker spirit. Even when teams aren't as successful, they are still able to bring out a crowd. There are a great number of successful teams, including the men's gymnastics team, who have eight national titles under their belts, the women's indoor track and field team with three, and the women's volleyball team with three. For those athletes who aren't quite at the D-1 level, Nebraska offers a very competitive intramural sports program. Being the most popular extracurricular activity, intramural sports serve as a great way to "meet new people." For those students just looking to get a workout in, there's the Lee Sapp Recreational Center, which boasts two indoor tracks, a climbing wall, a weight room, and basketball and racquetball courts. With facilities that nice, there's no excuse not to hit the gym.

For most state universities it's tricky to pinpoint one unifying factor that really seems to bring the campus together. But for Nebraska-Lincoln, it's quite obvious and goes beyond the football field. When asked what the one factor is that differentiates UNL from any other university, one sophomore noted it was "the school spirit absolutely without question. There is a pride in being a Cornhusker that blows me away." UNL is the pride of all of Nebraska and regular Nebraskans, students, and faculty aren't afraid to show it. For Nebraskans far and wide, including those who live and study on UNL's campus or are just there for the game, it really is all about football.—*Taylor Ritzel*

FYI

If you come to the U of Nebraska, you better bring "a warm winter coat. You usually have to walk a little ways to class and it can get very cold."

What's the typical weekend schedule? "Go to a frat party on Thursday and Friday nights, prime before the football game on Saturday, get pizza in Haymarket after, wake up late on Sunday and do homework in the afternoon."

If I could change one thing about the U of Nebraska, "I'd get rid of the train tracks that run through campus. You have to wait on your way to class while trains pass."

Three things every student should do at the U of Nebraska before graduating are "swim in the fountain in front of the Union, pass library class, and go to a football game."

Nevada

University of Nevada, Reno

Address: Mail Stop 120
Reno, NV 89557
Phone: 775-784-4700
E-mail address:
asknevada@unr.edu
Web site URL: www.unr.edu
Year Founded: 1864
Private or Public: Public
Religious Affiliation: None
Location: Urban
Number of Applicants: 4,024
Percent Accepted: 88%
**Percent Accepted who
enroll:** 58%
Number Entering: 2,047
**Number of Transfers
Accepted each Year:**
1,516
Middle 50% SAT range:
M: 480–600, **CR:**
470–590, **Wr:** Unreported
Middle 50% ACT range:
20–25
**Early admission program
EA/ED/None:** None

**Percentage accepted
through EA or ED:** NA
EA and ED deadline: NA
Regular Deadline: Rolling
Application Fee: $60
**Full time Undergraduate
enrollment:** 13,205
Total enrollment: 16,458
Percent Male: 46%
Percent Female: 54%
**Total Percent Minority or
Unreported:** 27%
Percent African-American:
2%
**Percent Asian/Pacific
Islander:** 7%
Percent Hispanic: 7%
Percent Native-American:
1%
Percent International: 3%
**Percent in-state/out of
state:** 82%/18%
Percent from Public HS:
Unreported
Retention Rate: 76%

Graduation Rate 4-year: 14%
Graduation Rate 6-year: 46%
**Percent Undergraduates in
On-campus housing:** 14%
**Number of official organized
extracurricular
organizations:** Unreported
3 Most popular majors:
Business/Marketing, Biology,
Health Professions
Student/Faculty ratio: 15:1
Average Class Size: 26
**Percent of students going to
grad school:** Unreported
Tuition and Fees: $15,656
**In-State Tuition and Fees if
different:** $4,561
Cost for Room and Board:
$9,989
**Percent receiving financial
aid out of those who apply,
first year:** 60%
**Percent receiving financial
aid among all students:**
Unreported

In the "Biggest Little City in the World," University of Nevada, Reno is the state's flagship public university. More than 10,000 undergraduates attend the institution, along with nearly 5,000 graduate students. Therefore, UNR certainly offers a wide array of academic opportunities for students. As one-half of the University of Nevada system, which also has a location in Las Vegas, UNR has a long tradition of providing good academic programs to students from around the country and even the world. Sure, it is a state-run public university, drawing most of the student body from Nevada, but many people from out-of-state do come to UNR to enjoy a relatively affordable education of good quality.

A School of Pulitzers

The history of UNR traces back to the 1800s, but its transformation into today's modern university began in the 1960s when it opened its first medical school. From that point, the school continued to expand in the breadth of academic programs, resulting in a dozen schools and colleges that would satisfy any type of academic pursuit. There are the traditional liberal arts, business, and engineering programs. In addition, UNR also offers degrees in community health sciences, social work, and, of course, journalism. In fact, the Reynolds School of Journalism has produced seven Pulitzer Prize winners. It is therefore not surprising that it has an enrollment of over 500 undergraduates pursuing either majors or minors in journalism.

"Reynolds is really prestigious in journalism," said one student. "I think that is why it is a pretty popular major."

One other point of interest is the Mackay School of Earth Sciences and Engineering, which teaches topics such as geology, hydrogeology, and mining. "I don't think you will find too many earth science schools like Mackay," said one student. The combination of engineering and geology makes students' experience particularly rewarding. The university is also home to a major seismology laboratory that operates a series of measuring stations across Nevada to evaluate earthquake risks in the region. Therefore, UNR certainly offers academic opportunities that go beyond the traditional form of classroom teaching.

For those interested in the more traditional fields, UNR presents students with over 80 undergraduate programs, not to mention the presence of graduate classes and students, which means even more opportunities for students. For those who would like to leave Nevada and experience the world, the foreign exchange program, University Studies Abroad Consortium, largely led by UNR, allows students to study in one of 25 countries for the summer, the semester, or even the whole school year. UNR prides itself in its involvement with the program as well as the great abroad experience it provides for students. "I really like our study abroad program," said one student. "It's good to be able to see the world for a semester, and the school makes the application process pretty easy."

Although UNR does have a selective admissions process, nearly 90% of applicants are accepted to enter the freshman class every year. "We are not going to pride ourselves as a selective school, but I think we still have a fairly high academic standard," said one student. "The graduation rate is not that high, but it all depends on the individual," added another. At the end of the day, a large selection of academic opportunities certainly exists and is widely available at UNR, and whether a student succeeds is certainly contingent on the efforts put forth by the person. It must also be pointed out that the education is relatively affordable, especially given today's prices of private college tuition. Therefore, even for out-of-state students, a degree at UNR can be much cheaper and provide much greater value than at other institutions.

Consistent with the mission to educate not only for a career but to broaden each student's worldview, a program called Core Curriculum must be completed by all undergraduates. It means that some students will have to take classes that they do not particularly enjoy. However, depending on the students, these courses can be extremely valuable, especially in making students aware of fields in which they have very little knowledge. "I did not like sciences," said a student. "But the classes I took to fulfill the requirements are actually pretty good and taught me a lot of useful knowledge." Students must receive a minimum of 33 credits in the Core Curriculum, which includes the traditional requirements of mathematics, natural sciences, English, art, social sciences, and humanities. In addition, students must also complete the Capstone Courses, which take on an interdisciplinary approach to education, as well as Diversity Courses, which aim to teach students about cultures outside of the Western tradition.

> "We are not Vegas, but we can have pretty good nightlife here, too."

Students generally agree that they are not overworked and do have the time to enjoy pursuits other than academics, such as engaging in academic activities or having a good time during the weekends. "It all depends on the classes you take," said one student. "Overall, the work is not that bad."

The Biggest Little City
Reno is not Las Vegas, but the differences are smaller than one would expect. Just like its much more famous gambling counterpart, Reno is known to be home to a number of casinos and resorts. Fifty years ago, the city was the heart of the gambling world. However, with the rise of Las Vegas, some of the larger casinos have disappeared, replaced by smaller ones. In recent years, different revitalization projects have restored some of the city's former glory. Despite stiff competition from Las Vegas, Reno remains a popular spot for tourists, thus creating a vibrant nightlife. Even though the city is not particularly large, it certainly provides students at UNR plenty of options for the weekends.

Located at the foot of the Sierra Nevada Mountains, Reno is also close to a number of state parks and national forests, thus a great place for students interested in outdoor activities. "It is a city with lots of tourists," said one student. "We are not in Las Vegas, but we can have pretty good nightlife here, too. Plus, I am not sure that I want to go to college in Vegas. It is too big and noisy for me."

As in most parts of Nevada, the best form of transportation is by car, especially given the large number of students living off campus. The residence halls, however, are not terrible. "I don't know why there are so few people living on campus. It is not that bad here and more convenient because you don't have to take care of everything yourself." Argenta Hall, the newest addition to the dorms, is especially desirable because of the availability of bathrooms in every room, as well as newer furniture. There are also a number of dining options ranging from 1 meal per week to lunch-only options for commuters.

The Wolf Packs

UNR does have a strong football tradition, exemplified by a stadium that can accommodate 30,000 spectators and being a highly competitive team in Division I. The most important rivalry is obviously in-state foe, University of Nevada, Las Vegas. The winner of the annual contest receives the Fremont Cannon, a trophy replicating an actual Howitzer cannon and representing the heaviest and the most expensive award in college football.

Students generally agree that UNR is a very good college choice. It combines affordability, academic opportunities, and a great supporting staff. For those who would like to take advantage of a large and resourceful state university, UNR is certainly a good destination for prospective students.
—*Xiaohang Liu*

FYI
If you come to UNR, you'd better bring "some gambling skills if you want to frequent the casinos."
What is the typical weekend schedule? "Lots of parties and a little bit of work"
If I could change one thing about UNR, I'd "make public transportation better."
Three things every student at UNR should do before graduating are "see UNR beat UNLV, go to casinos, and take advantage of nightlife at Reno."

New Hampshire

Dartmouth College

Address: 6016 McNutt Hall
  Hanover, NH 03755
Phone: 603-646-2875
E-mail address:
  admissions.office@dartmouth
  .edu
Web site URL:
  www.dartmouth.edu
Year Founded: 1769
Private or Public: Private
Religious Affiliation: None
Location: Suburban
Number of Applicants:
  13,712
Percent Accepted: 16%
**Percent Accepted who
  enroll:** 49%
Number Entering: 1,075
**Number of Transfers
  Accepted each Year:** 43
Middle 50% SAT range:
  **M: 680–780, Cr: 670–770,
  Wr: 700–770**
Middle 50% ACT range: 28–34
**Early admission program
  EA/ED/None:** ED

**Percentage accepted
  through EA or ED:** 37%
EA and ED deadline: 1-Nov
Regular Deadline: 1-Jan
Application Fee: $70
**Full time Undergraduate
  enrollment:** 4,085
Total enrollment: 5,437
Percent Male: 49%
Percent Female: 51%
**Total Percent Minority or
  Unreported:** 42%
Percent African-American:
  7%
**Percent Asian/Pacific
  Islander:** 14%
Percent Hispanic: 6%
Percent Native-American:
  4%
Percent International: 5%
**Percent in-state/out of
  state:** 4%/96%
Percent from Public HS:
  61%
Retention Rate: 98%
Graduation Rate 4-year: 86%

Graduation Rate 6-year:
  94%
**Percent Undergraduates
  in On-campus housing:**
  85%
**Number of official organized
  extracurricular
  organizations:** 330
3 Most popular majors:
  Economics, Psychology,
  Sociology
Student/Faculty ratio: 8:1
Average Class Size: 13
**Percent of students going to
  grad school:** Unreported
Tuition and Fees: $33,297
**In-State Tuition and Fees if
  different:** No difference
Cost for Room and Board:
  $9,840
**Percent receiving financial
  aid out of those who apply,
  first year:** 81%
**Percent receiving financial
  aid among all students:**
  49%

Located in the pristine wilderness of western New Hampshire, Dartmouth College is the smallest Ivy League college. Its roughly 4,000 students enjoy a rewarding Ivy League education filled with academic opportunities. Dartmouth students also enjoy the benefit of a secluded northern New England campus, as well as an active student community that boasts a diverse array of activities. Indeed, Dartmouth students are very much satisfied with their college experience, exemplified by the university's strong academic programs, exciting campus environment, and numerous extracurricular opportunities.

Seduced by Seclusion

Located in Hanover, New Hampshire, Dartmouth boasts a beautiful natural environment that, according to one freshman, includes "hiking and biking trails amidst beautiful nature scenes, and .the bliss of not having any major cities nearby." During the fall and spring months, this environment allows students to enjoy a variety of outdoor activities. One of them is the Dartmouth Outing Club's (or DOC's) freshman trip, in which students take a camping trip throughout northern New England before their fall term. Taking this trip and seeing New England's beautiful streams, rivers, forests, hills, and valleys gives these students a great way to bond and explore. During the winter, according to one sophomore, "when Dartmouth gets a thousand inches of snow and the temperature rarely climbs above freezing, students have frequent midnight snowball fights, take skiing trips, and even sled together on the nearby golf course. The experience is unfathomably fun." To some students, the winter can be a bit much, however. One freshman complained, "By the time December came I had to wear three layers of clothing just to go outside." However, most find that Dartmouth's natural environment and cooler climate shapes the college experience in a positive way.

Dartmouth students enjoy the benefits of small-town life as residents of Hanover, which has a population of about 11,000. As one freshman explained, "Hanover is that quaint little town that everyone sees as part of the American Dream: it has one small street called Main Street lined with mom-and-pop stores, and everyone is really friendly." Students frequently go to Main Street to eat at small restaurants such as Mali's or shop at the Gap, the town's only major clothing store. Nevertheless, to many Dartmouth students, Hanover can at times be very dull. As one junior complained, "Hanover has almost nothing to do. It has one street with a couple of shops and restaurants and nothing else." However, most Dartmouth students generally do enjoy living in Hanover.

A New and Unique Spin on Ivy League Academics

Dartmouth's academic year is split up into quarterly terms, allowing students to take more classes and to schedule an "off" term during which they have no classes and can use their time for other pursuits, such as internships. Students also have a set of distributional requirements including, among others, a first-year seminar, a quantitative reasoning class, a literature class, and three physical education classes. Though some students find this program too regimented, most appreciate it. As one freshman said, "The best part about Dartmouth's academics is that you have to try new things. For example, at a different college, I might not have been able to take a class on Slavic folklore to meet a college requirement. Having these requirements lets me get the best of all academic areas. That's what makes Dartmouth stand out."

An important component of Dartmouth academic life is the accessibility of its professors. As one sophomore said, "Professors have a strong presence, and at times even seem more like older students than faculty members." To ensure that students can have personal interactions with their professors, Dartmouth even has a "Take a Professor to

Lunch" program, in which Dartmouth students schedule a lunch meeting with their professors that Dartmouth pays for. As one junior said, "This program is great because it lets me establish a personal relationship with my professors, who really seem to care." Dartmouth's uniquely amiable and accessible faculty is truly one of the best parts of its academic life. In addition, the overall scholastic program is very strong. "No matter what your major is," said one junior, "you will be able to find plenty of excellent classes and a top-notch faculty here."

> "Even during the winter months when Dartmouth gets a thousand inches of snow, students make the most of their environment. The experience is unfathomably fun."

Despite Dartmouth's great academic reputation, however, it still has a few shortcomings. Many students think that Dartmouth is not the humanities school it should be. "There aren't many history majors, language majors, or women's studies majors," said one freshman. "Also, planning to take certain classes can get complicated, since students generally need to take one term off each year to pursue internship opportunities or to relax."

Simplicity with Sophistication: Campus Life at Dartmouth

The vast majority of students at Dartmouth live on campus, and most are quite satisfied with campus life. Due to Dartmouth's relatively small campus, most dorms are not very far from class. Such a setting allows students to bond quickly and have a positive experience. "The average dorm floor has 16 people, give or take," one freshman said. "Each floor has several bathrooms, and each building has its own kitchen and hangout areas, so crowding is not really an issue." Undergraduate Advisors, who supervise the dorms, are also quite friendly and helpful. As one freshman put it, UGAs "are great with helping freshman and getting them acclimated to life at Dartmouth through advice and hosting dorm parties and events."

Most of the dorms have ample accommodations. By far the most coveted dorm, however, is the Wheelock building, to which the students apply separately for housing. One freshman said that his dorm "had three rooms for two people, and was huge." Wheelock students also enjoy a variety of interesting discussion groups. "Living in Wheelock feels like living in an intellectual community within an intellectual community," one student said. Though other dorms are decent, students caution prospective freshmen to be wary of the River, which is considered the worst building. One freshman complained that her room was so small that she "could only fit furniture in by squeezing it in at awkward angles," while another student complained that the kitchen at the River "is really old, and has a pipe sticking out of the wall." However, on balance, dorm life at Dartmouth is a fun experience.

Though students think that Hanover can be dull, they also believe that Dartmouth's campus life can be both entertaining and enriching. Most students cite their quad area, known as "the Green," as one of their favorite hangouts. Events at the Green include a campus-wide snowball fight and a massive student bonfire. Dining service is also great. The 11 different eateries provide plenty of options for students. The Hopkins Center for the Performing Arts is also a student hub. The Hopkins Center hosts plays, classical and rock concerts, and movie nights. As one student put it, "The Hopkins Center is Dartmouth's house of entertainment." Overall, Dartmouth students have an enjoyable campus life and are rarely without something fun to do.

The Three Ps: Partying, Politics, and Philanthropy

Best known by many as a premier party school from the movie *Animal House*, Dartmouth has a reputation for a particularly vibrant Greek scene. As one freshman noted, "Greek life on campus is prevalent with a capital P. Socially speaking, you might almost feel restricted in your weekend options if you don't join." However, though *Animal House* does speak truth to the prevalence of Greek life on campus, most students feel it is not completely accurate. As one student noted, "Greek life here is not that intense. People party, sure, but they do so responsibly. Dartmouth also has a lot of other on-campus activities." As one sophomore put it, "Greek life is a big part of the Dartmouth social scene, but it is not coercive, and the parties are not that extreme. Even if you don't drink, Greek events can be

a blast, and they really create a strong sense of community here. Sometimes movies like *Animal House* only tell part of the truth."

Students also see community service as an integral part of Dartmouth's extracurricular offerings. The Tucker Foundation, Dartmouth's umbrella service organization, encourages student involvement with organizations such as Big Brothers Big Sisters of America, the American Cancer Society, and with projects such as AIDS Global Health Day. The Tucker Foundation also sponsors student service trips, including recovery work trips to New Orleans and service trips to Latin America. Studying abroad is also an activity in which almost all Dartmouth students participate. As one student put it, "Dartmouth has a great study abroad program with opportunities almost anywhere."

Another salient part of Dartmouth life is politics, especially during the start of every presidential election. Since Dartmouth is located in New Hampshire, which has the earliest presidential primary election in the nation, political life at Dartmouth can be quite intense. This past year, Dartmouth hosted a nationally televised debate for the Democratic Party's presidential candidates. One freshman vividly recalls the experience: "There was so much excitement on campus. Watch parties were thrown, and the auditorium was packed. I got to meet all the candidates, and the discussions with friends afterwards were incredible. One friend even told me that President Barack Obama went to one of his watch parties after the debate." In addition to presidential elections, many students find that politics affects them in other ways: students join advocacy groups, become involved in state politics, and enjoy political discussions. Overall, one of Dartmouth's best-kept secrets is its political atmosphere. Though many of its own students do not see Dartmouth as a political college, the environment is great for all those who are interested in politics.

Dartmouth is a prestigious Ivy League college that provides students with a strong academic program, an entertaining campus, and a lively social scene. As one student best put it, "Dartmouth is a place of incredible opportunity and intellectualism, where ambitious students go to challenge others, be challenged, and continue the lifelong process of enriching themselves through learning." —*Andrew Pearlmutter*

FYI

If you come to Dartmouth, you'd better bring "a warm winter coat."

What is the typical weekend schedule? "Friday nights are spent hanging out at a friend's dorm or going to a show or movie at the Hopkins Center. On Saturdays, do something athletic or do some other extracurricular activity and then go to a frat party at night. On Sundays, most students sleep in, and then study all day."

If I could change one thing about Dartmouth, I'd "renovate the River dorm building and make its rooms bigger."

Three things every student at Dartmouth should do before graduating are "go on a Dartmouth Outing Club trip, participate in the annual bonfires and snowball fights on the Green, and go to a frat party."

University of New Hampshire

Address: 4 Garrison Avenue Durham, NH 03824
Phone: 603-862-1360
E-mail address: admissions@unh.edu
Web site URL: www.unh.edu
Year Founded: 1866
Private or Public: Public
Religious Affiliation: None
Location: Rural
Number of Applicants: 14,382
Percent Accepted: 59%
Percent Accepted who enroll: 31%
Number Entering: 2,643
Number of Transfers Accepted each Year: 939
Middle 50% SAT range: M: 510–620, CR: 500–610, Wr: Unreported
Middle 50% ACT range: Unreported
Early admission program EA/ED/None: EA

Percentage accepted through EA or ED: Unreported
EA and ED deadline: 1-Nov
Regular Deadline: 1-Feb
Application Fee: $45
Full time Undergraduate enrollment: 12,067
Total enrollment: 15,053
Percent Male: 44%
Percent Female: 56%
Total Percent Minority or Unreported: 19%
Percent African-American: 1%
Percent Asian/Pacific Islander: 2%
Percent Hispanic: 2%
Percent Native-American: 0%
Percent International: 1%
Percent in-state/out of state: 55%/45%
Percent from Public HS: 84%
Retention Rate: 87%
Graduation Rate 4-year: 51%
Graduation Rate 6-year: 71%

Percent Undergraduates in On-campus housing: 55%
Number of official organized extracurricular organizations: 200
3 Most popular majors: Business Administration and Management; Communication, Journalism, and Related Programs; Psychology
Student/Faculty ratio: 18:1
Average Class Size: 15
Percent of students going to grad school: Unreported
Tuition and Fees: $25,236
In-State Tuition and Fees if different: $11,756
Cost for Room and Board: $8,596
Percent receiving financial aid out of those who apply, first year: 72%
Percent receiving financial aid among all students: 59%

Situated in rural Durham, yet only an hour from Boston, the University of New Hampshire is a model of contrasts. A land-grant, sea-grant, and space-grant institution, UNH cultivates cutting-edge research on par with that of most large universities. At the same time, its idyllic location and relatively small size allow students to foster close relationships with professors and a feeling of community often lacking at many of those same large institutions. Opportunities abound for the UNH student, and an ex-cellent system of support ensures that those students who want to gain a lot from their experience will certainly do so.

Making the Grade

With seven schools and colleges, and over 100 majors, UNH's academic scene is as lively as its social one. While popular majors include Psychology, Mechanical Engineering, Business Administration, Nursing, and Hospitality Management, students can also choose to concentrate in fields like Entrepreneurial Venture Creation or Soil Science.

Graduation requirements are heavy, including 10 general education requirements and 4 writing intensive courses, and although there are dozens of options to choose from to satisfy each requirement, the most popular Gen Ed courses, such as "Making Babies," "Elements of Weather," and "Germs," are often difficult to get into. "Still," added one student, "professors often try to help students who really want to take a particular class by making room where they can." Another explained that, "The professors are amazing. They are really approachable, which I don't think often happens in academia."

While class sizes can be as large as 500 students in a lecture, most students get more personal attention with average class sizes much smaller for beginner level and upper level courses.

The effort it takes to earn a UNH degree depends on the major and courses that you choose. Engineering, medical sciences, nursing, and social work majors are all considered difficult, and "Business Statistics" and "Organic Chemistry" rank at the top of students' "Most Difficult Classes" lists.

While most professors claim that two hours a night dedicated to a course can earn students their desired grade, students add the qualification that that number really depends on the course. But no matter what courses you are taking, "Mid-semester can be super-crazy, when papers, presentations, and exams creep up on you."

While some students claim that the university's status as a public school has its disadvantages, others appreciate that its large size allow it greater funding and resources in the sciences. UNH offers its students Undergraduate Research Awards (URA) worth up to $1600, Summer Undergraduate Research Funding (SURF) worth $3500, and International Summer Research Opportunities Program (IROP) funding, which averaged $6300 per person in 2007. One student, who studied the socio-cultural effects of architectural change in Sri Lanka with an award, claimed that through UNH she received "an opportunity that not many undergrads get."

Another, whose project involved solar neutron detection in Scotland, described the IROP as "the single best program that any university can hope to offer." UNH is also one of only nine universities in the nation that has been distinguished as a land-grant, sea-grant, and space-grant institution.

Tonight's Gonna Be a Good, Good Night . . .

. . . If you can avoid being busted. Though one student explains that "UNH provides a lot of alternative programming on weekends to discourage students' need to drink," drug and alcohol violations are the most commonly punished student offenses on the campus. A 2007 study examining land-grant colleges in New England showed that UNH had the highest number of on-campus arrests for violations of liquor laws, with a total of 264 arrests in 2007.

Nevertheless, students claim that, despite their wild reputation, drinking is not the only way to have fun on campus and that many students drink little, if at all. "It is just as easy to find students who don't drink on weekends as it is to find those who do," said one student. Another added, "I'm not into the drinking scene at all, so I was wondering if I would feel a lot of pressure to drink here, but there is a niche for everyone. Drinking is certainly there, and I'm aware of it, but they do a good job of enforcing the rules."

To help keep students amused *sans* alcohol, the university hosts frequent events, ranging from Casino Nights to Stress-Relief Nights to twice-weekly movie nights. And beyond the typical weekend parties, UNH hosts several larger events throughout the year. Its most popular, Spring Climax, is a music festival that has featured acts like Snoop Dogg, Ludacris, Lupe Fiasco, Demetri Martin, and Bob Saget.

For students who want to go off-campus, the university offers a free weekend shuttle to the coastal town of Portsmouth, seven miles from the UNH campus. In addition, Residential Assistants (RAs) keep their residents amused with tie-dye socials, game nights, and dance (or Dance Dance Revolution) parties.

Of course, social life doesn't just happen on the weekends; with over 180 student organizations, UNH offers something to fulfill every interest. If you've thought of it, UNH likely has it. From the Dairy Club ("increasing student awareness of career opportunities in dairy and related agricultural industries"), to Greek Intervarsity ("A movement of Greeks to experience God and change the world"), UNH offers a host of bizarrely themed clubs, alongside numerous more typical college organizations, such as Habitat For Humanity and French Club.

Fraternities and sororities are frequented by about 10% of the undergraduate population. With approximately 15,000 students, one senior explains, "Joining campus sports and organizations is the best way to make this campus seem smaller." Another said, "The social life at UNH is very active. There is something for everyone. In fact, you often have to ensure that you are not overextending yourself, as it is very easy to let your social life overtake your academic work."

The Double Hockey Sticks
Ask most any UNH student and you'll find that one of the most important parts of the UNH social life, whether you're a player or a spectator, is hockey. The Wildcats lay claim to having trained several future NHL players, including Ty Conklin of the St. Louis Blues, Dan Winnik of the Phoenix Coyotes, and James Van Riemsdyk of the Philadephia Flyers. "The men's hockey games are some of the biggest events on campus," said one student.

But playing UNH sports is not just for future professional athletes. UNH offers varsity, club, and intramural teams designed to accommodate every skill level. Varsity athletes are either recruited or endure an intense try-out process, club sports are less rigorous but still compete against other schools, and intramurals are played only between teams of UNH students.

She's a Brick House
UNH's housing, a mishmash of old and new buildings, has something to offer for all students. According to one student, "There are traditional dorms (singles, doubles, triples, forced-triples . . .), suites, and on-campus apartments. They range from as old as the early 1900's to as new as 2008. Some buildings are newly renovated, while others need renovation badly."

Two freshman dorms are located next to what is widely considered one of the best dining halls on campus and are "a great place to be," explained one senior. Students are generally divided by academic major during their freshman year, and a third building, Alexander Hall, has been designated for those freshmen who enter as undeclared liberal arts majors. Students are particularly impressed by the activities organized for freshman dorm members, including trips to Boston and the beach.

For upperclassmen, housing is more varied: Athletes tend to fill Congreve, Lord, or McLaughlin Halls, while honors students cluster in Hubbard. For many juniors and seniors, the lure of adult life leads them to live off-campus in apartments in Durham, Dover, Newmarket, or Portsmouth.

The Freshman 15
"While it's not your mother's home cooking, it's still one of the best college dining halls I've ever visited," said one student of UNH's food offerings. Students at the university can choose between three different dining halls, each with its own atmosphere and flavors. In addition to unlimited meals (except on the commuter meal plan), students on any of the UNH meal plans receive either Dining Dollars or "Cat's Cache," which can be spent around campus or at many locations in Durham, and are often accompanied by useful discounts. Students claim that the pricing is reasonable, but that sometimes the food gets boring as, "It's served on a loop," said one student. "You have to get creative."

Saving the Rainforest
Students who spent large chunks of their childhood watching "Captain Planet," may want to attend a college where they can help save the earth just by going. If that's the case, UNH is a good place to start. In 2009, the university was awarded the National Campus Sustainability Leadership Award. In 2010, it was given the highest grade of any school by the Sustainable Endowments Initiative.

> **"I really think your college experience is what you make of it, but also that UNH had exceptional opportunities."**

Students are constantly reminded of their commitment to the environment through energy saving competitions, clotheslines in some of the dorms, and an annual music festival dedicated to sustainable living called Solarfest. UNH has also recently sought to increase the sustainability of its dining practices by purchasing more organic food and buying more food from local farmers.

Most students feel that both the university and its students do a good job maintaining their commitment to sustainability. According to one Environmental Science major, "Environmental clubs have a strong presence on campus, and many of those clubs are activist groups."

Famous Last Words
"I really think your college experience is what you make of it, but also that UNH had exceptional opportunities," explained a member of the class of 2005 who is now attending

Harvard Divinity School. A current UNH student added that, "Being involved on campus is really important . . . there are so many things to try here that can really make a big difference to your undergraduate experience." UNH, with its large student body, ample resources, and beautiful campus, offers students the chance at a full undergraduate experience, but that experience only comes to those who are willing to take the responsibility for their own happiness.—*Heather Robinson*

FYI

If you come to UNH, you'd better bring "rain boots. I didn't expect it to be so wet here!"

What's the typical weekend schedule? "Meals are crucial on weekends. That's when you meet up with your friends and decide what you're doing for the night. A lot of times there will be parties and sports events on the weekend, which are a blast. The nightlife usually starts around seven or eight."

If I could change one thing about UNH, I'd "definitely look into finding ways to lower tuition. If you're an in-state student, it is pretty expensive to go here, even though it is supposed to be more affordable."

Three things every student at UNH should do before graduating are "go to a UNH Hockey Game, play broomball, and obviously, take the class 'Making Babies.' "

New Jersey

As one of New Jersey's premier institutions of higher education, TCNJ embodies both the academic experience of a top-notch institution and the price tag of a state school. Therefore, each year, students from every corner of the United States flock to this highly regarded university to learn with each other and from each other.

An Academic Smorgasbord
Students at TCNJ are ready to work. With seven schools spanning fifty disciplines in liberal arts, it has something for everyone. The newly adopted four-credit system, along with a revamped core curriculum, challenges students to engage in rigorous academic training without wearing out. All entering freshmen participate in the "First Year Experience," a wide array of freshman-specific

seminars that include anything from "Forensic Science" to "Harry Potter Literature."

The chemistry major offered at TCNJ is one of the most intensive in the nation. According to students, it is in fact more intensive than the engineering program. The chemistry major requires sixteen courses—more than the usual twelve courses per major—in a tight-knit environment where students receive direct individual attention from faculty advisors. The one drawback, as a current chemistry major noted, is that the "course schedule is pretty much fixed for all four years" due to the strenuous nature of the program.

For the medically inclined, TCNJ offers a combined seven-year B.S./M.D. program with the University of Medicine and Dentistry of New Jersey. Admission to this medical-scholar program is highly selective, but it offers a fast track to those who are set on a career in medicine.

Education is one of the most popular majors, stemming from TCNJ's original establishment as a teacher's training school. Communications, biology, accounting, and nursing/exercise science are also popular. Whatever the course of study, students can expect to get very individualized care. Introductory courses, however, can be a little tougher with large lectures of upwards of one hundred students. Faculty advisors generally work hard to find resources for students, said one freshman. If there are still any lingering academic yearnings that have not been satisfied, the global study abroad program offers students the opportunities to experience the world.

The Lion's Den
Housing on campus can be a bit confusing for some students. TCNJ guarantees housing for all freshmen and sophomores. The proportion of freshmen who live on campus is ninety-five percent, which decreases to fifty percent for juniors and seniors. The overall on-campus housing rate is about 48 percent. Freshmen are housed in Traverse, Cromwell, or Wolfe Halls, while upperclassmen are scattered in the other dorms and the many townhouses rented by TCNJ. Upperclassmen also have the options of private apartments in the city of Ewing specifically priced for college students as well as fraternity or sorority houses on and off campus.

TCNJ is in the midst of expanding its housing availability to include juniors and seniors with construction of new apartment suites, located a little farther from central campus, which opened in 2009. The rooms may be small, but many say they offer a feel of coziness. Campus living also contributes to the "tight bonds and camaraderie" among floor mates, noted one freshman. Most residences are centrally located with all buildings and facilities accessible within a ten-minute walk.

Campus safety is an important issue for TCNJ. The College has its very own campus police force that patrols at night in addition to the seventy safety posts located around campus that the students can access in case of emergency. They can also use the safety posts to ask for police escorts during the night. Resident Advisors in the dorms are also in place to ensure a safe learning environment, but they are more focused on fostering a sense of family. "You can walk into

their rooms just to chat or get advice" and they will often "throw floor-wide birthday parties" to bring people together, said one junior. RAs are looked on less as authority figures and more as friends.

> "From martial arts to campus religion to community service, there's always something to do. I'm never bored."

Dining options at TCNJ receive mixed reviews. One trend is that students definitely need to be selective about what they do or do not eat. The food is served buffet-style in the main dining hall. There is a good selection of dishes, but they must be chosen wisely, according to a senior. Options for vegans and vegetarians are scarce. They will have the salad bar as their main staple in addition to a very limited menu of vegetarian dishes. Current students would also like to see the dining halls open a little later since the main dining hall, Eicke, closes promptly at 8 p.m, but there are also other campus-run cafés and eateries. Off-campus dining, on the other hand, might prove more satiating to the gourmet connoisseurs. The city of Ewing is very well aware of TCNJ's presence, and the students have a selection of restaurants that are moderately priced and of exceptional quality.

The Life of a Lion
Prospective students should not be fooled by the small college atmosphere of TCNJ. The party scene thrives there. Thanks to the four-credit schedule system, most students do not have classes on Wednesday, which makes Tuesday a prime time for parties. Friday, of course, is the other main party night. Options include fraternity/sorority parties, private dorms, clubs, bars, and private off-campus parties. There are also many school-sponsored events, parties, and dances, beginning with Homecoming. One complaint is that students should not expect any hot clubs or anchored social spots in Ewing. Those dissatisfied with entertainment options choose to venture into nearby metropolitan areas such as New York or Philadelphia. Downtown Trenton is also a bus ride away with popular student hangouts, eateries, bars, and clubs. Overall, however, the off-campus social scene is a bit lacking as much of the action takes place within the TCNJ bubble.

Aside from the party scene, there are also

a number of activities on campus so that it is almost impossible to be bored. "From martial arts to campus religion to community service, there's always something to do. I'm never bored," said one student. Indeed anyone can find his or her niche at TCNJ, which boasts over 180 student organizations to suit every taste. It even has a Medieval Knight Club, which is one of the more interesting favorites of students.

The Bottom Line

Many students are very happy to be a part of the TCNJ family and often show their school pride by wearing their TCNJ apparel. Sports are also major contributors to school spirit. People at TCNJ are prone to be the "athletic type," noted one freshman. People "love to exercise" and make great use of the jogging and biking trails that surround campus.

Students are generally happy with their TCNJ experience and point to the astounding homimess that they feel once arriving on campus. They are part of a community rather than a face in the crowd. This feature of TCNJ makes the freshman experience particularly enjoyable and helps their transition to college life. "No one feels alone or segregated," explained one sophomore. Although the consensus seems to point toward a general contentedness, there are also some things students would like to see improve. For one, the location of TCNJ limits nightlife off campus. Students who wish to be closer to metropolitan areas can find New York and Philadelphia to be quite a commute. However, location is the only big complaint students have about TCNJ. The mix of academics, sports, extracurricular activities, and the sense of community makes TCNJ a fulfilling place to embark on the journey of higher education.—*Hai Pham*

FYI

If you come to TCNJ, you better bring "a fan."
What is the typical weekend schedule? "Sleep in late, hang out with friends, hit up downtown Trenton, party with friends, and recuperate for the next week."
If you could change one thing about TCNJ, what would it be? "I'd like to change the location to a more urban, metropolitan area where more entertainment options are available on the weekends."
Three things every student should do before graduating are "swim in the water fountain of the science department, eat in downtown Trenton, and go to a Lion football game."

Drew University

Address: 36 Madison Avenue
Madison, NJ 07940
Phone: 973-408-3739
E-mail address:
cadm@drew.edu
Web site URL: www.drew.edu
Year Founded: 1868
Private or Public: Private
Religious Affiliation:
Methodist
Location: Surburban
Number of Applicants: 4,191
Percent Accepted: 64%
**Percent Accepted who
enroll:** 17%
Number Entering: 456
**Number of Transfers
Accepted each Year:** 108
Middle 50% SAT range: M:
530–630, **CR:** 530–650,
Wr: 610–690
Middle 50% ACT range:
24–28
**Early admission program
EA/ED/None:** ED

**Percentage accepted
through EA or ED:** 77%
EA and ED deadline: 1-Dec
Regular Deadline: 15-Feb
Application Fee: $50
**Full time Undergraduate
enrollment:** 1,608
Total enrollment: 2,411
Percent Male: 40%
Percent Female: 60%
**Total Percent Minority or
Unreported:** 34%
Percent African-American:
5%
**Percent Asian/Pacific
Islander:** 6%
Percent Hispanic: 6%
Percent Native-American:
1%
Percent International: 1%
**Percent in-state/out of
state:** 57%/43%
Percent from Public HS:
61%
Retention Rate: 83%

Graduation Rate 4-year: 69%
Graduation Rate 6-year: 76%
**Percent Undergraduates in
On-campus housing:** 87%
**Number of official organized
extracurricular
organizations:** 80
3 Most popular majors:
Economics, Political Science,
Psychology
Student/Faculty ratio: 11:1
Average Class Size: 19
**Percent of students going to
grad school:** 33%
Tuition and Fees: $34,230
**In-State Tuition and Fees if
different:** No difference
Cost for Room and Board:
$9,476
**Percent receiving financial
aid out of those who apply,
first year:** Unreported
**Percent receiving financial
aid among all students:**
51%

D rew University, founded in 1868 on a beautiful green wood in northern New Jersey, forms a very close community with a student body of fewer than 1800 undergraduates. Despite the urban and suburban surroundings, the campus maintains its loveliness. From recent technological updates in classrooms to the construction of an environmentally-friendly dormitory, Drew looks to the future and focuses on the well-being and education of its students by providing the smaller community with the resources of a much larger university.

A Close Family

Drew University is a liberal arts school that ensures its students have a breadth of studies by requiring that they complete a major and a minor. Drew offers over 50 programs of study for students these majors and minors, and also allows students to propose their own chosen topics for a major. Subjects like English and political science are incredibly popular. However, one student said, "while political science is huge, there is a pretty even split between the arts and humanities and some of the sciences,

like biology. Drew is arguably stronger in the sciences than the humanities."

Many students at Drew also complete premedical and pre-law programs, and some enroll in the special dual-degree programs in medicine and in engineering and applied science.

The small size of the school is a huge point of pride for the students and professors at Drew. The small classes at Drew let professors really get to know their students, and students have plenty of access to their professors. One student said the largest class he ever took was "less than 30 people. It is smaller than high school, and everyone is way closer with each other and their teachers." One of his classmates agreed, and was excited to say that when students approach professors for help outside of class, "they are more than willing to help."

Almost all classes are taught by professors, except for required freshman writing classes, which are taught by teaching assistants but are still as small as seven people per class. This writing course is required, as well as "Common Hour, a discussion-based symposium for freshmen." After completing these courses, students must also meet credit requirements for arts and literature, humanities, social sciences, science, and math.

Students have the option of graduating with honors in their disciplines by writing an Honors Thesis. Also, Drew very recently introduced the Baldwin Honors program which identifies incoming freshmen, places them in honors courses, and focuses them on a community initiative in their junior year—a service learning project dealing with citizenship, social change, or community education—which culminates in a final capstone project in senior year.

Life in the Suites

Madison, New Jersey, is the rather wealthy town that surrounds Drew and housing there is very expensive and scarce. Most students spend their four years on Drew's campus with their classmates. This leads to a very tight-knit community. One student said, "It's incredible how quickly you can make friends here."

On campus, freshmen are sorted into one of four freshman dorms, and upperclassmen are housed by lottery. The dorms run from singles to doubles and to suites, and residents can opt for coed floors. Each floor is divided between two residential advisers, who are overseen by each dorm building's residential director. According to one freshman, "RAs are generally nice people and aren't out to get you, but they are there to uphold the rules, so don't cross them." Another student said that "you just need to be smart about things, and you won't get into trouble."

Drew University has only one central dining hall, Commons, which is located near most of the living spaces. According to one student, "the food is good, and with the meal plan you can choose points for the café and snack bar in the main classroom buildings." A snack bar in the University Center is "more expensive, but has better food."

Fun in the Suites

Most students stay at Drew during the weekends. Madison, New Jersey, "is not a town that offers a whole lot to college students," according to one Drew student, "but New York City is just an hour away." Parties are a popular weekend activity in student dorms. "Upperclassmen athletes usually have large parties," one student said. These take place in The Suites, which is a dorm for upperclassmen. Special annual events include the

Holiday Ball, a winter formal open to everyone, and Junior-Senior, a dance specifically for upperclassmen.

> "It is smaller than high school, and everyone is way closer with each other and their teachers."

Drinking is very common on campus, but students who chose not to partake are still welcome at parties and can find things to do on the weekends, including many social events with various clubs and student groups, and plenty of student performances throughout the year. One senior said, "Most people drink, but some don't. There are nights where it is fun and nights when nothing really goes on. I'm not a huge drinker and I still have fun, so it works for me."

Always Something Going On

Drew students are active in very many extracurricular activities on campus, including writing for the campus newspaper *The Acorn*, community service organizations, and year-round performances with the consistently nationally-ranked theatre department. "Student productions in the theatre usually have bigger audiences than the sports team," said one student, and according to one senior, most people "are very passionate about their work and their fun in their activities. There is always something going on."

Drew doesn't have a football team, so "varsity soccer and team rugby are probably the biggest sports here." Drew is a member of Division III and has fifteen varsity teams, and also has club teams and intramurals for those looking for fun and socializing without much commitment. Still, intramurals participants "have lots of fun, but tend to be cutthroat at times actually." Students also have the opportunity to keep in shape when they visit Simon Forum and Athletic Center which houses state-of the art gym facilities and an indoor track.

Even though the small school attracts most of its students from New Jersey and the surrounding area, there still exists a "good amount of diversity in the student body" at Drew. One freshman shared, "The people here are pretty friendly in general, and I love the school for its open-mindedness." This love also extends to the wonderful faculty and facilities that the university provides for its students.—*Connor Moseley*

FYI
If you come to Drew, you'd better bring "a bike to get from the dorms to class."
What is the typical weekend schedule? "Crazy parties in the Suites, free movies, and catching up
   on homework,"
Three things every student at Drew should do before graduating are "go to the Shakespeare
   Theatre, attend Holiday Ball, and go mud-sliding and take a swim in Tipple Pond in the rain."
What surprised me most about Drew when I arrived was "how many squirrels and deer can live on
   one campus."

Princeton University

Address: PO Box 430
   Princeton, NJ 08544-0430
Phone: 609-258-3060
E-mail address:
   uaoffice@princeton.edu
Web site URL:
   www.princeton.edu
Year Founded: 1746
Private or Public: Private
Religious Affiliation: None
Location: Suburban
Number of Applicants:
   21,370
Percent Accepted: 10%
**Percent Accepted who
   enroll:** 59%
Number Entering: 1,243
**Number of Transfers
   Accepted each Year:**
   Unreported
Middle 50% SAT range:
   M: 700–790, CR:
   690–790, Wr: 690–780
Middle 50% ACT range:
   31–34
**Early admission program
   EA/ED/None:** None

**Percentage accepted
   through EA or ED:** NA
EA and ED deadline: NA
Regular Deadline: 1-Jan
Application Fee: $65
**Full time Undergraduate
   enrollment:** 4,981
Total enrollment: 6,785
Percent Male: 53%
Percent Female: 47%
**Total Percent Minority or
   Unreported:** 50%
Percent African-American:
   8%
**Percent Asian/Pacific
   Islander:** 15%
Percent Hispanic: 7%
Percent Native-American:
   1%
Percent International: 10%
**Percent in-state/out of
   state:** 16%/84%
Percent from Public HS:
   58%
Retention Rate: 98%
Graduation Rate 4-year:
   90%

Graduation Rate 6-year:
   Unreported
**Percent Undergraduates
   in On-campus housing:**
   98%
**Number of official organized
   extracurricular
   organizations:** 250
3 Most popular majors:
   Economics, History, Political
   Science
Student/Faculty ratio: 5:1
Average Class Size: 16
**Percent of students
   going to grad school:**
   Unreported
Tuition and Fees: $34,290
**In-State Tuition and Fees if
   different:** No difference
Cost for Room and Board:
   $11,405
**Percent receiving financial
   aid out of those who apply,
   first year:** 85%
**Percent receiving financial
   aid among all students:**
   54%

There's no doubt about it—Princeton is a hard school. It's one that's hard to get into, and maybe even harder to do well in. But to be fair most students at Princeton enjoy their experience, despite the incredible effort they put into their studies, because of the tremendous rewards that await them upon graduation. Consistently ranked first or second every year from 2001 to 2010 by *U.S. News and World Report*, it's no coincidence that Princeton offers its students an unparalleled experience in undergraduate education, something that's sure to be widely respected after graduation. Al-

though students spend a lot of time on work, they also have a good time partaking in Princeton's many traditions, which makes their undergraduate experience particularly unique and enriching.

Work Hard and Play Hard. Really, Really Hard.
One student said, "Most people would probably agree with the following description: Princeton is a great place to be from, but not particularly great to be at." Students said that the value and prestige of receiving a Princeton diploma makes the hard work

worth it, but in between the hard work, there is also a lot that can be gained through Princeton's unparalleled undergraduate experience. "The attention that we get as undergraduates from most professors is unique. Princeton focuses much more heavily on its undergraduates than its graduate students," one sophomore explained. He also added that Princeton's senior thesis, a comprehensive research project in one's major required of nearly all seniors to graduate, is something else that makes the Princeton experience especially valuable.

> "If you strike the right balance between studying and partying, it doesn't feel like school is taking over your life. I came in expecting to work with no rest whatsoever and that hasn't been the case."

But prospective students need not fear *too* much about the hard work. One freshman said, "I guess the most important thing has been to work hard and play hard. If you strike the right balance between studying and partying, it doesn't feel like school is taking over your life. I came in expecting to work with no rest whatsoever and that hasn't been the case." Students say that there is definitely a spectrum of students, ranging from those who take very easy classes and go out four to five days a week, to those who spend a large majority of their time on their studies. But students warn pre-frosh to mentally prepare themselves for the curriculum ahead of them. One sophomore said, "I definitely did not expect to be so unprepared for the difficult coursework and in general I didn't expect the workload to be so heavy." But students can find solace in the fact that they're not facing this alone. "The best thing about Princeton is the academic environment. You might be working your butt off but it's nice knowing other people are doing the same thing," one freshman said.

Deflated Spirits

While Princeton offers an unparalleled experience in an excellent undergraduate instruction, the university also has a policy of "grade deflation," which is a real and genuine concern for students on campus. Students said that Princeton began a grade deflation policy a few years ago by which approximately only 35 percent of students in a department are allowed to receive A's. Stu-

dents say that the official reason is that Princeton wants to hold its students to the highest standard by fighting grade inflation and only giving A's to work that deserves the highest grades. This hasn't been happily received by the student population, and some say that it negatively affects the learning atmosphere. "The existence of a hard quota makes it seem like students not only have to do well in classes, but they have to do it better than the other 65 percent of students to get an A, so this fosters competition instead of cooperation," one student said.

In addition, students feel that institutions of similar caliber, notably Harvard and Yale, have grade inflation, which disadvantages Princeton students upon graduation as they try to apply for graduate school and professional programs, or enter the workforce. One freshman noted, "Apparently, Princeton sends out a letter explaining grade deflation to grad schools and companies, but no one knows if they actually bother reading those letters, so I, among many others, worry about that."

It's Not About the Food, It's About the Name

While Princeton does have a residential college system, there isn't intense rivalry between the colleges as is usually the case at similar schools. For the first two years, students can't transfer to be with their friends at other colleges, but by junior year students move to upperclassmen dorms and living arrangements become more flexible. There are three four-year and three two-year residential colleges, so as upperclassmen students can live in university housing on campus with college affiliation, but do not need to live in the college itself. While there are organized activities within colleges such as study breaks, trips, and intramurals, Princeton's social life entirely revolves around the eating clubs, a culture that is unique to Princeton.

In a sense, eating clubs are exactly what they sound like—places to eat. Upperclassmen have the option to either go independent or to join an eating club as their "meal plan" of sorts. There are two types of eating clubs: bicker and sign in. For bicker clubs students must go through an application process—or bickering, as Princetonians call it—and be selected by the committees of each of these clubs. These clubs are large mansions all located along Prospect Avenue, which is conveniently called the Street by Princeton students.

Ironically, the prestige of each eating club is not about the food at all, but about its name. Bicker clubs are obviously more exclusive than sign-in clubs, but some bicker clubs have such a high reputation that membership is incredibly competitive. For example, students say that Ivy consists of the wealthy, the connected, and the athletic, while Tower has mostly students from the selective Woodrow Wilson School of Public Affairs. In addition, members of certain fraternities and certain sport teams are unofficially "set" for certain eating clubs, so getting into extremely selective eating clubs is very hard, although students say that knowing "the right people" definitely helps with the process. Regarding the selectivity and prestige of the eating clubs, one student said, "The bickering process is definitely stressful and it can be very frustrating when you know there's just nothing you can do to get in because of your background. For example, Ivy costs something like $15,000 a year, so that automatically excludes the poor."

Eating Clubs or Drinking Clubs?

While eating clubs obviously serve their purpose of providing food for students, they also provide something else: drinks, drinks, drinks. Eating clubs double as party places, and although only club members can eat at the eating clubs, the clubs usually allow everyone to party, so students frequently hit up the Street on weekends. "Everyone goes to the Street, period. It's the center of Princeton's party life in the truest sense of 'party' since there aren't really any other options," one student said. He explained that free beer and music draw people to the Street on Thursday and, while most people go to dorm parties on Friday, the Street picks up again on Saturday.

Students say that the parties are usually pretty good. "There are 10 eating clubs, so you're bound to find a good one." Although it's technically illegal, it's an accepted fact that all the eating clubs serve alcohol to minors. Three eating clubs were recently closed for serving alcohol to minors, and students say that when things like that happen, eating clubs usually tighten alcohol policy, but that it usually doesn't last very long. "Princeton doesn't directly own the eating clubs so they can't really do anything about it," one student explained. Students say that administrators are in discussions about having public safety officers patrolling halls to bust parties, but before this the alcohol policy was pretty loose. Students said that they

can only get in trouble for serving alcohol to minors or drinking outside, and that officers only check if students are serving alcohol to minors when parties get really loud and are reported to public safety. "Very few people get into trouble and they're usually only put on probation, but one of the few things Princeton is very anal about is that there are absolutely no drinking games."

Outside the Classroom, Inside the Bubble

Princeton is not much of a college town. Students describe it as a "rich suburb" that doesn't offer much for its college students. "Princeton feels like a tight-knit community because it's kind of isolated and everything is within walking distance. You barely ever step foot outside of campus." Students admit that this creates a "bubble culture," but one said that most people don't seem to mind, and may even really like it. "It's like a castle in the middle of nowhere, as we usually say. I like the relative isolation and peace, and having everything I need close by." However, many students still complain that the town doesn't really have things for college students to do, like bars, clubs, or shopping areas.

But the lack of opportunities in the town may be good in at least one aspect—it makes Princeton students look to their own campus for activities outside the classroom. Students say that extracurricular involvement varies from person to person. Some people are heavily involved, while others might have other time commitments such as sports that prevent them from devoting lots of time to other activities. Some of the more prominent clubs include the Black Men's Awareness Group (BMAG), Student Volunteer Council (SVC), and the Asian American Student Association (AASA), while a cappella and dance groups are also very popular on campus. "Most people are committed to one thing, and I get the feeling that the majority of the students are involved in some sort of activity. There are so many things here that you're bound to find something you like, whether that's music, intramurals, or theater stuff."

Out on the fields, Princeton boasts one of the strongest athletic programs in the Ivy League. Princeton has consistently been ranked at the top of *Time* magazine's "Strongest College Sports Teams" lists, and *Sports Illustrated* has ranked Princeton as a top 10 school for athletics. Princeton is particularly well known for its men's and women's crews, which have won several NCAA and Eastern Sprints titles in recent years. In addition, Princeton's men's lacrosse team is widely recognized as a perennial powerhouse in the Division I ranks. Other successful Princeton athletic programs include women's soccer and field hockey, which has won every field hockey conference title since 1994. Princeton athletics is a powerhouse in the Ivy League, which is a definite plus for those who are looking for a prestigious academic experience in addition to a strong athletic experience.

Keeping It Old School

While students agree that Princeton has moved away from its stereotyped image as an elitist school for stuck-up, old-money prep-school kids, the school still has strong roots and values in traditions, as the eating clubs suggest. One of Princeton's traditions is the bonfire held on Cannon Green behind Nassau Hall, which happens when Princeton beats both its rivals—Harvard and Yale—at football in the same season. "It's pretty special, since it doesn't happen that often. Everyone congregates and screams," one sophomore said. Like many other Ivy League universities, Princeton has a myth regarding exiting particular gates as an undergraduate. At the end of Princeton's graduation ceremony, the new graduates proceed out through FitzRandolph Gate as a symbol of leaving college and entering the real world. But according to tradition, anyone who leaves campus through this gate before their own graduation date will not graduate, so students use side exits instead.

Students warn that the old-school tradition of Princeton may also attract a certain type of student, namely those from "old money." While most students are generally pleasant, students warn that those who have not been thoroughly exposed to the East Coast prep school culture may be in for an initial shock. One student who came from a city public school said he was surprised by the "jock-ish" and "elitist" atmosphere at Princeton. "There are a lot more affluent and wealthy kids here—some really do flaunt it and most don't hide it. I don't have a problem with rich people, and I've certainly met people who are rich and nice, but it's just that they sometimes come across as being obnoxious in the way they act." But another student said that this attitude is not necessarily entirely related to social class, and may have a lot to do with the competitive nature of Princeton's atmosphere. "Of course, there are many rich and snobby people who dress very preppy-ish, but other people are just jerks when it comes to schoolwork, being unhelpful and arrogant. Unless you're lucky, you really have to look around for nice and helpful students."

All in all, Princeton students tend to be happy with their educational experience, even if it means that they're working incredibly hard for the four years they're at school. But between the hard work to get those coveted A's, Princeton students still find the time to pursue passions and party hard, and many keep going by keeping their eyes on the end goal: the prestige that comes with their diploma. The quality of education that Princeton students get is arguably the best on an undergraduate level, and the Princeton name will undoubtedly help students as they leave the bubble and venture off into the world. As one alumni noted, "People know that Princeton graduates will know how to solve anything if you give them enough time to figure out a way."—*Della Fok*

FYI

If you come to Princeton, you'd better bring "obnoxiously preppy clothes for lawn parties, which is when the eating clubs invite bands to come play. It starts Sunday afternoon so everyone's hungover by nine. It happens once each semester, but it's huge."

What is the typical weekend schedule? "If you're a slacker, jock, or something of that nature, you start partying on Thursday nights. If you're a nerd, you probably have 98,234 problem sets due on Friday, so you stay inside to do those. On Friday nights usually only one eating club is open, basically for the sake of the nerds, but for the rest of campus, Friday is usually pretty relaxed: the evenings are often filled with events like dance shows and concerts. Saturday is pretty dead until nighttime, which is hardcore partying, of course, and then Sunday is homework day for everyone."

If I could change one thing about Princeton, I'd "change the grading policy. Enough said."

Three things every student at Princeton should do before graduating are "go sledding with cafeteria trays at the golf course behind Forbes, one of the six residential colleges, sneak into the underground steam pipe tunnel system and make it out unscathed, and see the Triangle Show, which is this really famous theater group from Princeton that tours nationally every year."

Rutgers / The State University of New Jersey

Address: 65 Davidson Road
Piscataway, NJ 08854-8097
Phone: 732-932-4636
E-mail address:
admissions@ugadm.rutgers.
edu
Web site URL:
www.rutgers.edu
Year Founded: 1766
Private or Public: Public
Religious Affiliation: None
Location: Suburban
Number of Applicants: 28,208
Percent Accepted: 56%
**Percent Accepted who
enroll:** 35%
Number Entering: 5,508
**Number of Transfers
Accepted each Year:** 2,906
Middle 50% SAT range: M:
560–670, CR: 530–630,
Wr: Unreported
Middle 50% ACT range:
Unreported
**Early admission program
EA/ED/None:** None

**Percentage accepted
through EA or ED:** NA
EA and ED deadline: NA
Regular Deadline: Rolling
Application Fee: $60
**Full time Undergraduate
enrollment:** 3,694
Total enrollment: 26,829
Percent Male: 51%
Percent Female: 49%
**Total Percent Minority or
Unreported:** 48%
Percent African-American:
9%
**Percent Asian/Pacific
Islander:** 24%
Percent Hispanic: 8%
Percent Native-American:
<1%
Percent International: 2%
**Percent in-state/out of
state:** 93%/7%
Percent from Public HS:
Unreported
Retention Rate: Unreported
Graduation Rate 4-year: 58%

Graduation Rate 6-year:
Unreported
**Percent Undergraduates
in On-campus housing:**
49%
**Number of official organized
extracurricular
organizations:** 400
3 Most popular majors:
Biology, Engineering,
Business
Student/Faculty ratio: 14:1
Average Class Size: 27
**Percent of students going to
grad school:** Unreported
Tuition and Fees: $21,306
**In-State Tuition and Fees if
different:** $11,358
Cost for Room and Board:
$9,378
**Percent receiving financial
aid out of those who apply,
first year:** 67%
**Percent receiving financial
aid among all students:**
69%

Named most diverse national university for the 13th consecutive year in *U.S. News & World Report,* Rutgers University is a public research university that boasts a wealth of academic programs, resources, and opportunities both in and out of the classroom. With campuses in three distinct Garden State locales, Rutgers, the only university to reject an invitation to the Ivy League, is a serious academic institution rooted in a deep commitment to public education.

A Three-for-One Deal

Rutgers comprises three campuses, the largest and oldest of which is located in the central New Jersey cities of New Brunswick and Piscataway. The smaller southern campus at Camden and northern location at Newark flank the center, forming a university that literally spans the state. Each of the three campuses is distinct in its academic offerings, extracurricular activities and so-

cial life. One thing's for sure—the Rutgers experience is diverse.

New Brunswick students estimate that the ratio of students who live on campus versus those who live off campus is about even, while Newark students said that far more students live off campus. "Most people are dying to get off campus after their second year," revealed one New Brunswick junior resident. Because Rutgers is a public university, it is known to adhere to stringent underage drinking restrictions; students cited this fact as motivation for the move off campus. Douglass Residential College of the New Brunswick campus is an all-female housing option, though in any given year the building may include coed dorms.

All of the campuses boast a wealth of extracurricular activities and clubs, with intramural sports the most popular. Rutgers students point to the variety of options open to those looking for fun: movie theaters, the mall, restaurants, and parties. The consensus among students is that their weekend parties are top-notch. "Come Friday and Saturday night, Rutgers is the place to be," bragged one sophomore. However, since many students have jobs, the weekend is not all about partying. Greek life is not very expansive, with active life primarily at its College Avenue and Livingston locations on the New Brunswick campus. The Livingston locations feature minority and ethnic fraternities and sororities.

In terms of the population's diversity, Rutgers students agree that the University hits the mark and makes continual efforts to maintain its inclusiveness. But they do criticize the disjointed nature of campus life and fault the inefficiency of the transportation system. "Even though nextbus.com reduces the wait, Route 18 construction makes traffic a constant issue," one junior said. Beyond the system of buses that attempts to connect the Rutgers experience on a practical level, the University attempts to create social spaces that foster diversity. The formation of new residential colleges (the first of which is the aforementioned Douglass) represents such an administrative attempt to foster exchange in living communities.

Rutgersfest, the annual campus-wide blowout before final exams, brings three performing artists or groups to the stage to celebrate the closing of the academic year. Even in this endeavor, students cite the diversity of acts as reflecting the diversity of those in the crowd. "Some people come to Rutgers and have an utter culture shock," said one New Yorker. However, students are quick to explain that the diversity of Rutgers is healthy and productive, and when asked about resultant tensions, dispelled the idea. "I have never encountered a problem with it," said one junior. "The people who come here with no experience with difference don't react with prejudice; they tend to be happy to get a taste of the real world."

An End to the "Rutgers Screw"

With the freshman class of 2007, the previous staples of the New Brunswick campus— Douglas, Livingston, Rutgers, and University Colleges—were combined into one undergraduate liberal arts college: The School of Arts and Sciences. This advanced conglomerate offers an expanded set of over 100 majors spanning the humanities, biological sciences, mathematics, and more.

The change was simply one component of the "undergraduate transformation" recently undergone by Rutgers's largest campus. And while most students have praised the effort

for making their educational experience much less complicated, others have criticized it for doing the exact opposite. "It was a good idea in theory, but we weren't ready for it," remarked one junior resident advisor. She lamented that her residents "had no idea what they were doing" and that the academic advising that accompanied the new system needs work. "Academically and residence-wise, things are still in transition," she said.

Despite these administrative hassles, students generally praised the changes. A major benefit of this system is its ability to bring an end to the notorious "Rutgers Screw." Defined by students as a buzzword for the popular notion that, by the time you reach senior status, some unknown requirement or misinformation will keep you from graduating, the "Rutgers Screw" now faces extinction under the transformation's streamlined requirements and staff. Rather than being restricted by college, students can now seek advisers under the unified college to avoid the common pitfall.

Students also hailed the changes for bringing them together. Previously, each campus had its own traditions, but now Rutgers students are working to forge a single community. "Cap and Skull," a Rutgers College secret society based on leadership and academics prowess, now extends membership invitations to the entire university. According to one exercise and sports science major, "Whatever people have to say about the transformation, it has increased campus unity."

A Warm Welcome

Freshman classes have the advantage of walking into this heightened spirit of cohesion. Upperclassmen characterized their freshman orientations as mediocre, but lauded the newest orientation efforts and the improvement of the football team as ways of bringing the class together. "This year's orientation was amazing, with all these events. We even had a throw-down where we could win prizes," a freshman New Jersey native said. One sophomore commented that the orientation "built them more into a community than [his] first year." Yet even before these changes students remembered the Rutgers freshman experience fondly. One junior exclaimed, "My freshman year at Rutgers was the most amazing experience I've ever had; I love Rutgers and I wouldn't pick another school."

Incoming classes will also be welcomed by various new, albeit uniform, academic requirements. In place of the previous "non-Western" requirement are the more expansive categories of "Diversity" and "Global Awareness." Those new to Rutgers will still have to pass "Expository Writing," a Rutgers staple known to students as "Expos," to graduate. This infamous RU requirement brought a series of groans from students across the spectrum in terms of major, interests, and origin. The sole comfort students offered regarding the course was that those taking it are by no means alone. "Everyone goes through it; the beauty of it is that you have four years to knock it out," advised one senior. For those weary of getting lost in a sea of numbers, but valuing the resources of a research university, the transformation also ensures that freshmen have the opportunity to engage in new first-year seminars—classes capped at 20 and taught by distinguished Rutgers faculty, aimed at engaging students in serious, speculative dialogue.

Spectacle Sports

Rutgers played Princeton University in the first ever game of intercollegiate football in 1869 (where the present-day Rutgers gymnasium now stands) and won. So it comes as no surprise that a strong tradition of university athletics continues to this day.

The Scarlet Knights have a dedicated and spirited fan base, drawing huge crowds from across the lecture hall aisle. At Rutgers, football dominates the athletic scene. Students cite the team's improvement in recent years for a surge in school spirit. "All I wear is Rutgers clothing," one senior said. Last year, the Scarlet Knights performed well enough to reach the International Bowl in Toronto, Canada, with their star player, Brian Leonard. Leonard was recently drafted into the NFL to play for the St. Louis Rams. According to students, the team has continued to improve as new stars have risen in his wake. Knights say that RU Football has become a huge campus event and school spirit has risen alongside the stats. "I have never seen so many Rutgers sweatshirts," commented one senior.

> "My freshman year at Rutgers was the most amazing experience I've ever had; I love Rutgers and I wouldn't pick another school."

Football is not the only sport that draws crowds at Rutgers. The women's basketball team is renowned for its prowess on the court and has become the media darling of college sports. The team and the school have not let the recent Don Imus controversy derail their efforts. "It really affected us when it happened, but now everything's been smoothed over," said one junior. She went on to explain how the proliferation of Facebook groups and spread of support further unified the school in the face of the media flurry. "School spirit translated into solidarity."—*Nicholle Manners*

FYI

If you come to Rutgers, you'd better bring "a Rutgers T-shirt because you'd better not be wearing another college's shirt."

What is the typical weekend schedule? "Friday: go to the dining hall, go to work, do your homework, go out; Saturday: sleep in late, go to a football game and go out; Sunday: sleep in late and do your homework."

If I could change one thing about Rutgers, I'd "change the bus system and make morning classes later."

Three things every student at Rutgers should do before graduating are "go to a football game, eat a fat sandwich at the Grease Trucks, and go to the Zimmerlie Art Museum."

Seton Hall University

Address: Seton Hall University
　South Orange, NJ 07079
Phone: 973-761-9332
E-mail address:
　thehall@shu.edu
Web site URL: www.shu.edu
Year Founded: 1856
Private or Public: Private
Religious Affiliation:
　Roman Catholic
Location: Suburban
Number of Applicants: 6,626
Percent Accepted: 79%
Percent Accepted who
　enroll: 26%
Number Entering: 1,322
Number of Transfers
　Accepted each Year: 444
Middle 50% SAT range: M:
　480–590, CR: 470–580,
　Wr: 470–580
Middle 50% ACT range:
　Unreported
Early admission program
　EA/ED/None: None

Percentage accepted
　through EA or ED: NA
EA and ED deadline: NA
Regular Deadline: Rolling
Application Fee: $55
Full time Undergraduate
　enrollment: 4,594
Total enrollment: 5,187
Percent Male: 44%
Percent Female: 56%
Total Percent Minority or
　Unreported: 50%
Percent African-American:
　11%
Percent Asian/Pacific
　Islander: 6%
Percent Hispanic: 10%
Percent Native-American:
　<1%
Percent International: 3%
Percent in-state/out of
　state: 75%/25%
Percent from Public HS:
　70%
Retention Rate: 83%

Graduation Rate 4-year: 41%
Graduation Rate 6-year: 56%
Percent Undergraduates in
　On-campus housing: 46%
Number of official organized
　extracurricular
　organizations: 100
3 Most popular majors:
　Business, Health
　Professions, Social Sciences
Student/Faculty ratio: 13:1
Average Class Size: 14
Percent of students going to
　grad school: 30%
Tuition and Fees: $27,420
In-State Tuition and Fees if
　different: No difference
Cost for Room and Board:
　$11,360
Percent receiving financial
　aid out of those who apply,
　first year: 91%
Percent receiving financial
　aid among all students:
　86%

S
eton Hall University is a private Roman Catholic university tucked away in suburban South Orange, New Jersey yet surrounded by one of the largest metropolitan areas in the world. The school is steeped in its long-standing Catholic tradition, as the most prominent Catholic university in New Jersey, while being surrounded by the immense diversity and culture in nearby Newark and New York City. The school is most known for its business and diplomacy programs as well as nursing and education. With a mix of old school traditions, new school cosmopolitanism, and focused academics, Seton Hall University offers a place for those who wish to pursue a worldly education in the safety of a tucked away suburb.

Getting Down to Business
Business seems to be the focus of the undergraduate academic atmosphere at Seton Hall University. "The Stillman School of Business is our most visible and well-known program," remarks a sophomore. Indeed, the undergraduate business program is highly regarded across the Northeast and currently holds the top spot in the state of New Jersey. The Diplomacy program comes in second with regards to presence and prestige. All incoming freshman are enrolled in one of the six undergraduate schools of the university: Business, Education and Human Services, Nursing, Theology, Diplomacy and International Relations, and the College of Arts and Sciences—Seton Hall's largest undergraduate school. The Nursing and Education programs round out the most popular majors for undergraduates.

The breadth and depth of study at Seton Hall, a liberal arts focused university, depends mainly on the program of study. Math, science, engineering, and nursing programs are markedly more challenging and rigorous than humanities majors, as students point out. The Nursing program is one of the hardest majors at Seton Hall owing to the intensive field and clinic work on which students are graded. Business writing is another notoriously difficult class that all Seton Hall business majors must take. Notoriously easy classes include University Life and Journey of Transformation. These are courses required by the school taken generally in the first year. University Life is simply a course that teaches students how to survive college in regards to study habits, dorm life, etc. Journey of Transformation is a religion course in which students read different religious pieces and then discuss them openly in class. This course is basically an opinion course and ". . . as long as you do the readings you'll get a good grade," says a sophomore.

Regardless of major and class choices, all students at Seton Hall must complete a set of core courses in the Seton Hall curriculum in order to be eligible for the bachelor's degree. The hallmark of the 16-credit core is anchored by classes such as Journey of Transformation, Christianity and Culture in Dialogue, and Engaging the World. These classes in addition to University Life and Core English courses provide students with a uniquely Seton education steeped in the Catholic tradition. In addition to the hallmark courses, students must complete proficiency-infused courses in reading and writing, oral communication, information fluency, numeracy, and critical thinking. "It can be a pain sometimes," reminisced a senior. "Having to fulfill all those requirements in addition to a major; it kind of limits you to the amount of 'just for fun' classes you can take." Still, others praise the core curriculum for opening up their education to courses they would have never taken otherwise.

Perhaps one of Seton's biggest assets is the faculty on hand to help students learn and grow as individuals. Professors tend to be very accessible and "down to earth," remarked a junior. In fact, many classes are taught by professors with very little being taught by TAs. This creates an intimate, small-group learning environment where many students study. It's also a reason for capped classes that may be an annoyance. Some well-known and well-liked professors include Professor Kwame of the Political Science department, Professor Madrazo of the English and Business departments, Professor Athens of the Criminal Justice department, and Professor Rubino in the School of Nursing. However, some students do complain that some professors let their personal beliefs and biases permeate through their teaching. All in all though, professors are generally accessible and well-liked.

Dorm Life
Incoming freshman are all randomly assigned to one of two dorms: Aquinas Hall and Boland Hall. Roommates are matched according to an online profile created on the housing website. Both buildings are far from central campus with rooms being "not that nice, but tolerable," according to a freshman. Suites of four to five share a common space with a suite bathroom. However, dorm picks do get better with seniority. After freshman year, students get to choose where and with whom they'd like to live. The rooming draw operates on a priority points system where points are earned by attending campus events and activities. Those with the most points get priority pick in the room draw. Upperclassmen dorm rooms come carpeted and often with a sink and mirror in each room. Resident Assistants, or RAs, live in student dorms. Their job is basically just to monitor noise levels, swipe students in at the front desk, and regulate guest policies. They are somewhat strict when it comes to noise levels during quiet hours, but aside from that you "hardly notice them," says a sophomore.

"Seton Hall harbors a variety of different people, with some of the nicest yet some of the rudest people."

The architecture at Seton Hall is very institutional-looking. "It's not that exciting to look at honestly," remarked a freshman. Popular hangout spots include the Green where students congregate and play sports. Aside from that, other popular hangouts include the Walsh Library and other buildings. Campus eateries are also a place of congregation and socialization with the main dining hall, "inner-caf," serving buffet style meals and other fast-grab "outer-caf" eateries catering to students on-the-go. Students on meal plans have a certain number of meal swipes per semester and a certain amount of "pirate bucks" that are redeemable at the outer-caf eateries. These include a pizzeria, Nathan's sandwich shop, and the Express which has snacks and drinks.

Seton Hall Social Club
Seton Hall tends to be a cliquey school with different groups mostly keeping to themselves. Since the school does have a lot of commuter students, the campus tends to empty out on the weekends; that and the close proximity to NYC. Students do generally go out on the weekends, but the options are a little limited in South Orange. However, the excitement of New York City is just a train ride away. Just as the student population is

very diverse, the personalities you'll find here tend to encompass a very wide scope. "Seton Hall harbors a variety of different people, with some of the nicest yet some of the rudest people," warns a sophomore. The different mix of student backgrounds, commuters, and personality types make for a mishmash of experiences and social scenes.

Although Seton Hall is a dry campus, drinking seems to be a dominant force in the social life of students. Alcohol is only allowed in upperclassmen dorms contingent upon checking in an amount suitable for "personal consumption." But everyone "seems to drink here," says a senior. Still, those who choose not to drink find their own group and their own scene.

Aside from partying, Seton Hall students are very committed to extracurricular and service activities. The most prominent clubs on campus are the Student Activities Board, WSOU student-run radio station, Black Student Union, and the campus publications The Setonian and The Stillman Exchange. The Setonian is the general campus newspaper while the rival Stillman Exchange is written specifically by Stillman Business School students. Extracurriculars aside, sports and athletic pride play a huge role in organizing undergraduate life. Though Seton Hall does not have a football team, the basketball team is wildly popular with basketball season almost always selling out. The track team was also very popular until it was cut from the budget in the spring of 2010. Overall, "While there are a number of great programs at Seton Hall, there could always be more. For the ones we do offer, I feel they are great. I still wish there were more though," says a sophomore.

The Seton Hall Experience

In general, life at Seton Hall tends to be good. Students are happy to be immersed in such cultural and academic diversity on a manageable campus. The Catholic tradition of education may be new for some, but no one doubts that it permeates through all facets of life at Seton Hall. "You can't walk down the street without seeing a priest or minister waving to students somewhere," noted a sophomore. Seton Hall takes great pride in its Catholic community and has become very well-known for it. Some students who come here love it while others don't. It comes down to a matter of preference and taste for what kind of education experience one is looking to have for the next four years.—*Hai Pham*

FYI

If you come to Seton Hall, you should you bring "a train pass to go out on the weekends, go home, or visit college friends."

What's the typical weekend schedule like? "Party Friday and Saturday nights. Attend a sporting event Saturday or hop a bus to New York City or the mall and study on Sunday."

If you could change one thing about Seton Hall, what would it be? "I'd make the buildings a little more exciting to look at and have students a little less cliquey and more social all around."

Stevens Institute of Technology

Address: One Castle Point on Hudson, Hoboken, NJ 07030

Phone: 201-216-5194

E-mail address: admissions@stevens.edu

Web site URL: www.stevens.edu

Year Founded: 1870

Private or Public: Private

Religious Affiliation: None

Location: Suburban

Number of Applicants: 3,058

Percent Accepted: 51%

Percent Accepted who enroll: 38%

Number Entering: 569

Number of Transfers Accepted each Year: 83

Middle 50% SAT range: M: 620–710, CR: 550–650, Wr: Unreported

Middle 50% ACT range: 24–30

Early admission program EA/ED/None: ED

Percentage accepted through EA or ED: 78%

EA and ED deadline: 15-Nov

Regular Deadline: 1-Feb

Application Fee: $55

Full time Undergraduate enrollment: 2,044

Total enrollment: 2,044

Percent Male: 72%

Percent Female: 28%

Total Percent Minority or Unreported: 39%

Percent African-American: 2%

Percent Asian/Pacific Islander: 12%

Percent Hispanic: 8%

Percent Native-American: <1%

Percent International: 6%

Percent in-state/out of state: 62% /38%

Percent from Public HS: 80%

Retention Rate: 89%

Graduation Rate 4-year: 38%

Graduation Rate 6-year: 74%

Percent Undergraduates in On-campus housing: 85%

Number of official organized extracurricular organizations: 120

3 Most popular majors: Engineering, Business Administration and Management, General Computer/Information Technology Services, Administration and Management

Student/Faculty ratio: 8:1

Average Class Size: 26

Percent of students going to grad school: 18%

Tuition and Fees: $36,800

In-State Tuition and Fees if different: No difference

Cost for Room and Board: $11,100

Percent receiving financial aid out of those who apply, first year: 82%

Percent receiving financial aid among all students: 75%

As the name of the school implies, Stevens focuses on the sciences. Though students are hard workers and want to do well, they also try to have fun and take advantage of Hoboken, New Jersey, where the school is located, and New York, which is just across the river. The juxtaposition of the small school and the two larger cities, in addition to the concentration on the sciences, makes for what students term an "atypical" college experience.

No Room for Slackers

At the start of freshman year, students choose their major and take the specific set of courses their chosen track dictates. This system means that the same group of students often has the same classes together for the entire day. "It feels a little bit like middle school," remarked a sophomore. Students praise the fact that incoming freshmen get their own laptops for free and say that they put their computers to good use during class time. Students must take 19 to 21 credit hours a semester, which is "a pretty obscene number." The large number of classes and the substantial amount of work given in each course mean that students work very hard much of the time. "You have to be self-motivated to get the work done here," said one junior. "Nobody is holding your hand. Nobody is checking up on you. It is a good thing to have that sort of academic freedom, but you have to make sure you are cut out for this kind of system."

Those looking for guidance from professors or teaching assistants (TAs) can run into trouble. "Professors can be a little hard to connect to sometimes. They are brilliant, but sometimes this doesn't translate into being able to teach." The quality of TAs varies. Some can be helpful, whereas others can be limited by their poor command of the English language.

Engineering, the most popular major, is also cited as one of the most difficult. Though "there are no easy majors here," business technology has the least amount of work, with a relatively easy core. Students can opt to lighten their academic load by spreading it over five years instead of four through the Reduced Load program. The fifth year is tuition-free.

Several other special academic programs exist at Stevens. There are seven-year doctorate, medical, and dentistry programs, as well as a co-op program in which students attend Stevens for five years but work for three semesters at a company instead of going to class. Recruiting companies in the past have included Merck and Johnson & Johnson. Co-op experiences vary. Though some students report that they worked as "personal gofers," others say they have a rewarding educational experience that can only come from "being out in the real world and seeing what it is like, without the pressure of actually having to earn your living because you are still in school."

Greeks and Athletes

Greek organizations are an important part of student life. Besides holding their own events, it often feels like "frats and sororities run everything on campus." The presence of a Greek system makes the student body segment into cliques. "It ends up that the Greeks stay with the Greeks, the athletes with the athletes, the nerds with the nerds," explained one student. However, these cliques do not stop all types of students from participating in extracurricular activities. Most people are involved with at least one group. Many students are also part of the campus work-study program.

Students tend to care little about athletics unless they are in them. Though Stevens has good lacrosse and soccer teams, the fans cheering on the sidelines at games are often exclusively composed of other athletes. Athletes seem not to mind, though, saying that the tightly-knit athletic community lends a lot of support, something that is desperately needed in order to balance athletics and a demanding academic schedule.

Students who are not involved in varsity sports can use the recently renovated Charles V. Schaefer Jr. Athletic Center, which offers squash, tennis, and basketball courts as well as a gym and pool. Intramural sports are also popular.

Weekends at Stevens

There has been a recent crackdown on underage drinking on campus, which particularly affected fraternities. Any Greek organiza-tion found serving alcohol to students under 21 was forced to shut down. Much of the drinking culture was driven off campus into Hoboken and New York City. Fraternities do remain popular, sponsoring Halloween and Christmas parties, among others. The male-female ratio on campus—approximately three to one—means that girls are "rare and really have their choice of guys."

Students who look to imbibe in Hoboken are not short of places to go. Rumor says that Hoboken has more bars per square mile than any other city in the world. Being underage is sometimes a problem, but a freshman explained, "We know how to get around the age restriction." Students also frequent New York City, which offers a wealth of opportunities and nightlife right across the Hudson River.

> **"People think that we spend all our time in front of our computer monitors, but we really do go out."**

There are also weekend activities on campus. A lecture hall in the Buchard Building moonlights as a movie theater. Jacobus Hall has a student lounge with a climbing wall, large television, and pool table.

During the weekends, it often feels like the student population thins. Many students at Stevens are from other areas of New Jersey, and a good portion of the student body goes home on the weekends. Though many dislike the feeling of going to a "suitcase school," one freshman said that being able to go home on the weekends made his transition to college life less stressful.

The Stevens Stereotype

Campus housing is generally considered adequate. Freshmen are guaranteed housing. After the first year, upperclassmen fight for rooms in one of the five dorms. Students like that their rooms are close to their classes, especially during the winter, when the campus turns into a "wind tunnel." Despite the windiness, students like their campus, which has sweeping lawns and views of the New York City skyline.

One student explained that dining at Stevens simply, "is not good." However, the dining service is working to improve the quality of the food, and there is now more variety as well as tastier offerings. There are also many eateries in Hoboken, and, of course, there is always New York City.

Students enjoy going into both Hoboken and New York City and insist that, contrary to the "Stevens stereotype," they do go there to party. "People think that we spend all our time in front of our computer monitors, but we really do go out. Stevens in many ways is an atypical college experience, but we do do normal college things." If you have the motivation and the focus to handle the academics and the independence to handle the social scene, Stevens Institute of Technology can provide an educational and enjoyable, though "atypical," college experience.
—*Erica Rothman*

FYI
If you come to Stevens, you'd better bring "your calculator."
What is the typical weekend schedule? "Hang out on campus Friday, head into the city on Saturday, and spend all of Sunday into Monday doing schoolwork."
If I could change one thing about Stevens, I would "make it less of a suitcase school."
Three things every student at Stevens should do before graduating are "hang out at a Hoboken bar, throw a Frisbee on the lawn looking out on the city skyline, and spend lots of time complaining about all the work you have to do."

New Mexico

Address: Box 30001, MSC 3A
Las Cruces, NM
88003-8001
Phone: 575-646-3121
E-mail address:
admissions@nmsu.edu
Web site URL: www.nmsu.edu
Year Founded: 1888
Private or Public: Public
Religious Affiliation: None
Location: Urban
Number of Applicants: 5,960
Percent Accepted: 82%
**Percent Accepted who
enroll:** 51%
Number Entering: 2,518
**Number of Transfers
Accepted each Year:** 887
Middle 50% SAT range:
M: 430–550, CR:
420–540, Wr: 410–530
Middle 50% ACT range: 18–24
**Early admission program
EA/ED/None:** None
**Percentage accepted
through EA or ED:** NA

EA and ED deadline: NA
Regular Deadline: Rolling
Application Fee: $20
**Full time Undergraduate
enrollment:** 13,677
Total enrollment: 17,200
Percent Male: 46%
Percent Female: 54%
**Total Percent Minority or
Unreported:** 62%
Percent African-American:
4%
**Percent Asian/Pacific
Islander:** 1%
Percent Hispanic: 45%
Percent Native-American:
4%
Percent International: 4%
**Percent in-state/out of
state:** 79%/21%
Percent from Public HS:
Unreported
Retention Rate: Unreported
Graduation Rate 4-year: 12%
Graduation Rate 6-year:
42%

**Percent Undergraduates in
On-campus housing:**
Unreported
**Number of official organized
extracurricular
organizations:** 263
3 Most popular majors:
Business/Commerce,
Curriculum and Instruction,
Electronics
Student/Faculty ratio: 18:1
Average Class Size: 16
**Percent of students
going to grad school:**
Unreported
Tuition and Fees: $14,180
**In-State Tuition and Fees if
different:** $4,758
Cost for Room and Board:
$5,766
**Percent receiving financial
aid out of those who apply,
first year:** 76%
**Percent receiving financial
aid among all students:**
56%

S urrounded by desert, New Mexico
State University is home to more than
13,000 undergraduates and more
than 3,000 graduate students. The college
town of Las Cruces serves as the main campus for the university, but several of its
many institutes, research centers, and academic programs are spread throughout the
rest of New Mexico. A highly diverse campus, the university is known to provide a
wide range of academic programs at an affordable price. In fact, NMSU awards degrees ranging from associate to doctorates
and has extensive research facilities for
those interested in going beyond classes
and obtaining opportunities to become involved in the more sophisticated academic
projects.

A Research Institution

The university is divided into nine different
colleges, including the College of Honors,
providing more in-depth education in
smaller classes, and the Graduate School.
The other parts of NMSU are the Colleges of
Agricultural, Consumer, and Environmental
Sciences, Arts and Sciences, Business, Education, Engineering, Health and Social Services, and Extended Learning. "You can find
all the majors you want here," said one student. "I have friends going to small schools,
and I heard that they just have a small number of majors and minors. Here, we have
everything."

The undergraduate program boasts more
than 80 majors, including rather ingenious
programs such as Turfgrass Science and

Management, Rangeland Resources, and Horticulture. The large number of specialized majors in agriculture is due to the institution's original purpose. After all, first opened in New Mexico during the late 1800s, the university originally aimed to educate people about farming and pasturing. Today, of course, NMSU has expanded into a prominent research institution. Nevertheless, it maintained significant resources into programs related to agriculture and environmental sciences. "It should not be a surprise that there is so much emphasis on agriculture," said one student. "It is a really important field in New Mexico."

NMSU is very proud that it is among the 100 top institutions in federal research expenditures. The government spends millions every year on the university to conduct experiments and carry out projects. Among the most impressive federal expenditure is the NASA Space Grant, used to ensure the continuation of aerospace research in the United States. The position of the university as a Hispanic-serving institution—awarded for its large student population of Hispanics, which is just below one-half of the entire student body—also ensures that the school remains considerate of the importance of diversity and provides opportunities to all students.

> "You should come here and expect to work."

Given the university's mission of being accessible to students from all backgrounds, the admissions process is not particularly selective. In fact, more than 80% of applicants are accepted every year. At the same time, there are more than 3,000 part-time students, since the school aims to offer as much flexibility as possible to everyone who wishes to receive a good education. However, it does not mean that the school is not strong academically. "You should come here and expect to work," said one student. "Going to NMSU is not an easy walk in the park."

As in most universities, undergraduates are required to take a series of general education courses in addition to those in their majors. The goal is to ensure that everyone receives at least a broad overview of the topics that are present in academia. This should broaden the students' horizon and perhaps interest them in subjects that they never heard of previously. The core requirements are classified in five categories: communications, mathematics, laboratory sciences, social sciences, and humanities. Furthermore, NMSU has a special program entitled "Viewing a Wider World." They are two upper level courses outside students' own departments so that they can have an in-depth academic experience in a new subject. "It is a fun program," said one student. "You get to experience new things in 'Viewing a Wider World.'"

It must also be pointed out that students at NMSU tend to be happy with the interactions with professors. Of course, much of the accessibility of instructors depends on the personalities of the professors as well as the initiatives taken by students. Nevertheless, overall, students are happy with their instructors' willingness to talk to them about classes or even issues outside of academia, such as careers and student life.

Not Just Las Cruces

Although the university is mostly located in Las Cruces, the second largest city in New Mexico, it also has 33 extensions and 10 research centers spread across the state. Therefore, students can be spread out, especially if they would like to take advantage of one of the research facilities in another part of the state. Nevertheless, the majority of students enjoy their stay in Las Cruces. The weather, of course, can he slightly difficult for people from out-of-state to acclimate to, given the desert environment. It can be very dry during large portions of the year, combined with large fluctuations in temperature. However, as pointed out by one student, "you don't really think too much about the weather when you are a student. Having a good quality of life on campus is much more important than better weather."

Given its status as a college town, Las Cruces does offer a number of local nightclubs and weekend activities that are catered for students. "It is not New York City," said one student. "But I have no complaints about the nightlife here." Greek life does exist and provides on-campus parties, but it remains only a small part of the college community.

Because of the large number of in-state students and commuters, many students do choose to live off campus. Nevertheless, students are generally fine with the housing options offered by the university. "The rooms are small, but that is how it works with college housing anywhere," said one student. The school also offers an array of dining options to accommodate both those who eat in dining halls every day and those who simply pick up lunch near classes before heading back to their off-campus housing.

Diverse Campus

One of the strengths of NMSU is the diversity of its student body. The school boasts students from all 50 states and 71 countries. "We have people from everywhere," said one student. "I know that people think this is a mostly Hispanic school, but it is actually very diverse and you get to meet people from all over the world."

The NMSU sports teams are called the Aggies, in honor of the school's agricultural heritage. As with most state universities, the biggest rival is the other part of New Mexico's public institution of higher learning, University of New Mexico. The rivalry is so intense that it has been transformed into a formal point system based on head-to-head competition of all sports teams. At the end of the year, a trophy is presented to the winning school. Unfortunately for the Aggies, in the brief history of the competition, University of New Mexico has so far dominated the contest.

Ultimately, students come to NMSU for academic opportunities. Given the affordability of the school, especially for those from New Mexico, it provides an excellent education, as long as the students do their best to enjoy all the facilities and programs that are widely available on campus. —*Xiaohang Liu*

FYI
If you come to NMSU, you'd better bring "sunscreen."
What is the typical weekend schedule? "Get on a trip to El Paso."
If I could change one thing about NMSU, I'd "make the campus smaller and tighter."
Three things every student at NMSU should do before graduating are "go to El Paso, visit other parts of the university besides Las Cruces, and join a club."

University of New Mexico

Address: PO Box 4895 Albuquerque, NM 87131-00001
Phone: 505-277-2466
E-mail address: apply@unm.edu
Web site URL: www.unm.edu
Year Founded: 1889
Private or Public: Public
Religious Affiliation: None
Location: Urban
Number of Applicants: 7,134
Percent Accepted: 74%
Percent Accepted who enroll: 58%
Number Entering: 3,021
Number of Transfers Accepted each Year: Unreported
Middle 50% SAT range: M: 470–590, CR: 470–600, Wr: Unreported
Middle 50% ACT range: 19–25
Early admission program EA/ED/None: None

Percentage accepted through EA or ED: NA
EA and ED deadline: NA
Regular Deadline: 15-Jun
Application Fee: $20
Full time Undergraduate enrollment: 18,743
Total enrollment: 24,814
Percent Male: 41%
Percent Female: 59%
Total Percent Minority or Unreported: 49%
Percent African-American: 3%
Percent Asian/Pacific Islander: 4%
Percent Hispanic: 42%
Percent Native-American: 7%
Percent International: 1%
Percent in-state/out of state: 79%/21%
Percent from Public HS: Unreported
Retention Rate: Unreported
Graduation Rate 4-year: 44%

Graduation Rate 6-year: Unreported
Percent Undergraduates in On-campus housing: 8%
Number of official organized extracurricular organizations: 315
3 Most popular majors: Biology/Biological Sciences, Business Administration and Management, Psychology
Student/Faculty ratio: 20:1
Average Class Size: 24
Percent of students going to grad school: Unreported
Tuition and Fees: $15,708
In-State Tuition and Fees if different: $4,834
Cost for Room and Board: $7,336
Percent receiving financial aid out of those who apply, first year: Unreported
Percent receiving financial aid among all students: Unreported

In Albuquerque—one of the fastest growing cities in the United States—is found the University of New Mexico, a large institution of higher learning well known for its Pueblo Revival architecture and large campus. More than 27,000 students, including nearly 20,000 undergraduates study in one of UNM's four campuses. Although it looks like a standard state institution of higher learning, many features of the university, such as the large array of opportunities and the diversity of the student body can certainly make college experience at UNM particularly enjoyable.

Going Professional

There are twelve different schools and colleges within UNM, demonstrating the scope of the university and the wide range of academic programs. Every school within the university offers undergraduate degrees, except the Schools of Law, Medicine, Public Administration, and Pharmacy, which only provide training to those seeking master's or higher degrees. Even the School of Management has an undergraduate business degree for undergraduates, making students interested in business particularly grateful. "It is really great to have a business program for college students, especially in the School of Management itself," said one student. "You get to learn more and even mingle with people studying Masters of Business Administration, so it is a wonderful program here."

The university offers more than 200 programs, including more than 90 majors for undergraduates. In addition, there are also a number of certificate curriculums, which can enrich students' academic experience and provide them with solid training for future employment. At the same time, it is important to point out that the school also has very good liberal arts degrees in the College of Arts and Sciences, which give students both the depth and breadth of skills and knowledge that they need to succeed in careers.

A large percentage of students at UNM, on the other hand, do consider their education mostly as preparation for specific professions. In this aspect, given the large number of programs in engineering, health, and education, the university certainly offers the curriculums that can satisfy almost anyone. "I think a lot of people have a job in mind when they come here," said one student. "And we have tons of weird majors so I think everyone will end up finding a suitable major."

The difficulties of the classes depend on the professor and the major. The science and engineering courses, as in most universities around the country, can pose headaches for students. "There are always a lot of freshmen who want to do engineering, but then they realize how hard it is because of the introductory classes and choose something else," said one student. This does not mean that those majors are too difficult for most people. It just implies that some curriculums demand slightly more effort and dedication. "You have to come here and expect to work. The classes are not that difficult if you actually plan ahead and stick to your schedule," said one student.

> "You have to come here and expect to work. The classes are not that difficult if you actually plan ahead and stick to your schedule."

The College of Fine Arts is outstanding, and it includes one of the better-known programs in photography in the country. Furthermore, the Schools of Nursing and Medicine also boast a number of nationally recognized specialties that have placed UNM as a major institution of both teaching and research.

The classes at NMU tend to be relatively large, with lectures that can go up to several hundred people. The experience with the accessibility of professors, on the other hand, can vary from student to student. Some people do stumble upon classes where instructors are very open to interact with students. Others meet professors that are simply unavailable outside of class. The consensus, however, is that the students should make the effort to reach out to faculty members. This can greatly enrich the academic experience.

NMU is a state university dedicated to provide opportunities to the public at large. Therefore, the admissions process is not particularly selective, though only about 70% of the applicants are accepted. "You will find very intelligent people here," said one student. "And a lot of them have very different experiences than you, so you can learn a lot from them."

As in most universities and despite the preprofessional tracks of many NMU students, all undergraduates must complete a series of core requirements before graduation. These courses are classified under seven different categories, notably writing, mathematics, natural sciences, social sciences, humanities, foreign languages, and fine arts. While the completion of some requirements can appear cumbersome, they are not designed to overwhelm students. Instead, they attempt to expand everyone's horizon and knowledge in different areas.

Pueblo Revival

The 600-acre Albuquerque campus is well known for its architecture, under the name of Pueblo Revival. It is characterized by adobe constructions, highly prevalent throughout New Mexico. "I really enjoy the southwestern architecture here," said one student. In addition, the university has spent a great deal of resources in renovations and constructions, resulting in a number of large, state-of-the-art facilities, notably the Schools of Architecture and Engineering.

Although Albuquerque is also home to several other institutions of higher learning, UNM certainly stands as its most important university and one of the vital parts of the city's economy. At the same time, Albuquerque is also rapidly growing, as the population of the United States shifts toward the Southwest. "The city will be very big in a few more years," said one student. "There will be a lot of job opportunities just here in Albuquerque."

The urban location of UNM means that students will be able to enjoy the benefits of city living. Restaurants, bars, and other hangout places abound in the city. Furthermore, the students will be able to enjoy not only the numerous activities organized on campus by the university and the student body, but they will also have the opportunities to attend different shows and events that are held around Albuquerque.

Given the diversity of students—undergraduate, graduate, and people pursuing continuing education, the sense of college community can be somewhat lost on such a large campus. "It is not hard to meet people," said one student. "But it is not like we are a tight-knit community like those small colleges in rural places." Indeed, there are a large number of commuters attending the university, and that can certainly have some adverse effects on the social scene. Nevertheless, the social life on campus certainly exists, with parties and different festivities. In addition, as one student pointed out, "there are so many people here, so you will definitely find plenty of friends."

Life on Campus

In 2009, UNM decided to renovate a number of residential facilities to make them more appealing to the students. The enhancement of the dorms may increase the satisfaction of dorm life and thus bring more people to live on campus.

Given the university's size and scope, academic opportunities abound at UNM. At the same time, life at Albuquerque can certainly be very enjoyable. That is why UNM attracts thousands of students every year from not only New Mexico but also around the world.—*Xiaohang Liu*

FYI
If you come to UNM, you'd better bring a "readiness for dryness."
If I could change one thing about UNM, I'd "make some classes smaller."
Three things every student at UNM should do before graduating are "visit other places of New Mexico, join a club, and take a class at the School of Fine Arts."

New York

Adelphi University

Address: 1 South Avenue
Garden City, NY 11530
Phone: 516-877-3050
E-mail address:
admissions@adelphi.edu
Web site URL:
www.adelphi.edu
Year Founded: 1896
Private or Public: Private
Religious Affiliation: None
Location: Suburban
Number of Applicants:
6,865
Percent Accepted: 69%
**Percent Accepted who
enroll:** 21%
Number Entering: 944
**Number of Transfers
Accepted each Year:** 956
Middle 50% SAT range: M:
500–590, CR: 470–580,
Wr: 470–580
Middle 50% ACT range:
20–26
**Early admission program
EA/ED/None:** EA

**Percentage accepted
through EA or ED:** 84%
EA and ED deadline:
1-Dec
Regular Deadline: Rolling
Application Fee: $35
**Full time Undergraduate
enrollment:** 5,137
Total enrollment: 8,354
Percent Male: 30%
Percent Female: 70%
**Total Percent Minority or
Unreported:** 49%
Percent African-American:
13%
**Percent Asian/Pacific
Islander:** 7%
Percent Hispanic: 6%
Percent Native-American:
<1%
Percent International: 3%
**Percent in-state/out of
state:** 92%/8%
Percent from Public HS:
Unreported
Retention Rate: 81%

Graduation Rate 4-year:
56%
Graduation Rate 6-year:
63%
**Percent Undergraduates in
On-campus housing:** 23%
**Number of official organized
extracurricular
organizations:** 80
3 Most popular majors:
Business, Education, Nursing
Student/Faculty ratio: 9:1
Average Class Size: 25
**Percent of students going to
grad school:** 38%
Tuition and Fees: $25,240
**In-State Tuition and Fees if
different:** No difference
Cost for Room and Board:
$10,000
**Percent receiving financial
aid out of those who apply,
first year:** 93%
**Percent receiving financial
aid among all students:**
88%

Tucked away in the middle of an afflu-ent Long Island residential district, the Adelphi campus setting attracts students who reside in nearby communities. If you live on Long Island and are consider-ing commuting to college, you'll find your-self among friends at Adelphi. Although the student body may be comprised of a large commuter population, the university suc-cessfully creates an intimate college ex-perience both socially and academically. Adelphi not only provides students with a solid base in academics, it also offers students pre-professional tracks so they may immediately pursue their passions. If you are a student looking to branch out of your home community without really leaving it, Adelphi can offer the best of both worlds. While one student cautions "Adelphi isn't for everyone—the commuter-school aspect sets it apart," its tradition of strong programs and commitment to developing career opportu-nities make it worth a closer look.

A Variety of Options

Students interested in Adelphi have the op-tion of applying to the College of Arts and Sciences, the Derner Institute of Advanced Psychological Studies, the Honors College, the School of Business, the School of Educa-tion, the School of Nursing or the School of Social Work. The schools each have differ-ent requirements, but students in the popu-lar College of Arts and Sciences must take General Education courses that, while "fairly numerous," are "pretty easy as long as you show up." These courses include a freshman orientation experience, an English composition seminar, a freshman seminar, and at least six credits in each of four areas: arts, humanities and languages, natural sciences and math, and the social sciences. One student complained that of those courses there were "a handful I haven't liked." Freshmen also say the required seminar and orientation course are "a necessary annoyance."

Students cite the nursing and business programs as particularly strong. One student raved, "My experiences working in a hospital a few times a week really prepared me for a career in nursing." However, the quality of the experience is very dependent on the teacher you get, a problem that students in various programs and majors mentioned. A communications major said that his professors' personalities had ranged from very enthusiastic about the subject to simply uninspired and "big assigners of busy work."

Many qualified students choose to enroll in the Honors Program, especially because of the generous scholarships Adelphi offers. Honors students live, attend classes, and study together in this exclusive academic and living arrangement, which is "almost its own separate community." However, "you should visit the campus before you just accept the scholarship," warns one student, "because it is a pretty different college experience." For the rest of the population, one of the most common grievances is the difficulty in enrolling in classes. One student complains, "I've been trying to get into this one class for two years and haven't been able to." But once you get into courses, the atmosphere is "very tight-knit, with a close student-faculty relationship," because of the school's small size. Students even mention going into the city for performances and then to bars with their professors.

Adelphi's humanities courses are "much better and more popular" than its math and science offerings, and students "wouldn't recommend the school for pre-med." But many professors "make you think outside the box." Overall, students classified their schoolwork at Adelphi as "definitely not too hard" and found that "grading is fair and lenient."

Seeking Out the Scene

Adelphi's status as largely a commuter school situated in a wealthy Long Island suburb is one of the main obstacles to a really active social life. So many students go home on the weekends that "the campus can be pretty dead by Thursday night," and surrounding Garden City is such a sheltered community that there isn't much night life nearby. In fact, when the campus hosted a Roots concert, it was shut down early because neighbors complained of the noise. The school hosts many other events in the University Center.

Those students who live on or near campus find a reasonable social scene at a few local bars and clubs, where Adelphi's ten fraternities and sororities often host gatherings for the student body. There are "quite a few" students in Greek organizations, and some "really make themselves known through advertising and recruiting," but because of the Garden City rule that "classifies more than six unrelated girls in a house as a brothel," the sororities don't have their own housing.

Students called Adelphi "more of a drinking school," saying that most people drink in their rooms before heading out to bars and clubs, but since the dorms are dry, "it's hard to tell how many people drink because they have to keep it pretty quiet." Overall, it's very self-controlled, and drugs "can be hard to find," although "pot is available if you want it" and "a lot of people smoke."

One student said that if you want to get socially involved at Adelphi, "you have to actively seek out the scene," whether by attending weekly comedy shows, sampling the popular theater program or heading out to New York City. The train station is on the edge of campus, just a few blocks away, and the trip takes about 45 minutes. Students really feel that the city is the redeeming factor in the otherwise quiet environment of Garden City—there are just so many opportunities for entertainment, from plays and museums to well-attended bars and clubs.

Most people meet their friends based on their living situations, whether in the dorms or off campus, but the small class sizes make it easy to meet people who share your academic interests. Students characterize the stereotypical Adelphi students as "very Long Islandish: girls get really dressed up to go to class, and boys can be very fashionable and wealthy too." However, others say that there is a lot of diversity at Adelphi, particularly because it attracts many international students. One senior explained, "There is more diversity of culture than of race, because within the largely white population, many nations are represented."

One student said that one of the most surprising aspects of Adelphi is that its student population is predominantly female. "There are a lot of hookups because guys who are hot and straight are usually taken, and you have to be quick," she admitted. The school does have an overall accepting attitude toward the gay population, which is sizable—in fact, a senior estimated that "half the males are probably gay." In the spring, the Lesbian-Gay-Bisexual-Transsexual-Queer (LGBTQ) organization puts on mock "weddings" just to show the community's support for gay couples.

People Do Live Here

Adelphi's campus is described as "truly beautiful," and students estimate that the university spends a sizable amount of money just on landscaping. The effect is a picturesque campus with spacious lawns and well-kept foliage. While many Adelphi students choose to live at home and commute to school, there is a lot of competition for housing on or near campus. Students who live in the dorms have the choice of air conditioning, which is more expensive, but students say that "it's pretty cool in Garden City, so the lack of A/C isn't a big deal." If you want housing and are new to the school, you are entered in a lottery to try to get a room in the full dorms, but if you have already been living there a semester, you have "squatter's rights" and can keep your room. One student explained, "You'll most likely get housing if you want it, but you have to be on top of the deadlines." All of the rooms are doubles and triples, and some doubles used to be triples, so "they're pretty big." The honors dorms have suites, which include a living room and two doubles.

There is an RA on each floor and a residential health director in each building, and while they do enforce the strict no-alcohol policy of the dorms, they are usually "nice and will work with you in other areas." However, "you will get in trouble and your alcohol will be confiscated if you're going to be dumb about it." New Hall is the newest dorm and is thought to be the nicest, while Earle Hall is known for housing a lot of theater majors.

Off-campus housing is apparently more difficult to find, since there are "few apartments for college students" due to the rich residential neighborhood around the campus. When they do find housing, it is usually pretty expensive as well. Students say that pricey off-campus housing is the reason why so many choose to live at home.

Downtown Garden City, a mile away, offers some shopping, including a popular mall, movies, and the nearest grocery store. A shuttle bus takes students to and from the downtown district, but "it can be unreliable or not frequent enough." It's a good idea to bring a car so you can get out of the area, but "the traffic gets pretty bad" and "one of the biggest problems on campus right now is the lack of parking available." However, the university is working to construct a new parking facility.

Students who live on campus are required to purchase a meal plan. However, many do so unwillingly. The food is reportedly "absolutely terrible," but there are other on-campus options, like at Post Hall, which houses a Sbarro, the Panther Grill and a convenience store, where students can use their meal cards like credit cards. Overall, though, there "isn't much variety and the food is of dubious quality" in the two dining halls. Students say they order takeout from local restaurants a couple times a week and sometimes go out to eat on the weekends. The nearby Chinese and Italian restaurants are "especially good," but "if you drive you can find a lot more options."

Getting Involved

One problem that many students pointed out about student involvement on campus is that it seems very low and apathetic. A senior said that she feels like "people just want to sit around and complain about how there's nothing to do instead of taking advantage of campus events." However, Adelphi does boast a number of organizations that attract loyal followings, such as the Theater Club, the NAACP, Circle K and its student newspaper, *The Delphian*. Many students also get involved in the Student Government Association, which allows them to voice their opinions about the Adelphi community and lobby for change.

> **"You won't get lost in the crowd at Adelphi."**

Adelphi is the home of a men's Division I soccer team, and all its other teams are Division II. Students say that "it's not a big athletic school, but a lot of people are interested in going to the games and supporting the Panthers." In fact, one of Adelphi's most fun annual traditions is Midnight Madness, when the men and women's basketball teams are announced at midnight at the beginning of the season, and the school's hip-hop team performs. One guy said, "It's one of the few events that almost everyone goes to and shows their school pride." For those who want to get more involved, intramural sports "always have flyers up" and can even get "intensely competitive."

Many students have jobs, whether working for the school on-campus or in the surrounding community. One popular off-campus option is working in the downtown mall. However, a particularly exciting aspect of attending Adelphi is the opportunity to participate in internships in New York City. Many students take advantage of this unique privilege and spend time learning more about their fields of interests.

While Adelphi may not be the typical college experience, it offers a variety of opportunities, from the excitement and internationalism of nearby New York City to renowned professional programs truly dedicated to preparing students for careers. While the school is ideal for many who are looking for a good school close to home, others may want to consider the additional advantages it holds. Even with the lack of an on-campus community, life at Adelphi is close-knit and friendly. As one student put it, "You won't get lost in the crowd at Adelphi."—*Kimberly Chow*

FYI

If you come to Adelphi, you'd better bring "a willingness to involve yourself in campus activities, because the school needs more participation."

What's the typical weekend schedule? "Hanging out with friends and having dinner on Friday, going to the City on Saturday, going to bars and clubs at night, or just going home for the weekend."

If I could change one thing about Adelphi, "I would increase communication between the administration and students, because sometimes I feel like I'm on my own when planning my studies."

Three things every student at Adelphi should do before graduating are "attend the Erotic Student Film Festival, participate in the Student Government Association, and sneak onto the roof of the science building for the great view."

Alfred University

Address: One Saxon Drive Alfred, NY 14802-1205
Phone: 607-871-2115
E-mail address: admissions@alfred.edu
Web site URL: www.alfred.edu
Year Founded: 1836
Private or Public: Private
Religious Affiliation: None
Location: Rural
Number of Applicants: 2,355
Percent Accepted: 74%
Percent Accepted who enroll: 28%
Number Entering: 487
Number of Transfers Accepted each Year: 131
Middle 50% SAT range: M: 500–620, CR: 440–610, Wr: Unreported
Middle 50% ACT range: 22–27
Early admission program EA/ED/None: ED

Percentage accepted through EA or ED: Unreported
EA and ED deadline: 1-Dec
Regular Deadline: Rolling
Application Fee: $40
Full time Undergraduate enrollment: 2,030
Total enrollment: 2,030
Percent Male: 47%
Percent Female: 53%
Total Percent Minority or Unreported: 37%
Percent African-American: 4%
Percent Asian/Pacific Islander: 2%
Percent Hispanic: 3%
Percent Native-American: <1%
Percent International: 3%
Percent in-state/out of state: 65%/35%
Percent from Public HS: Unreported
Retention Rate: 82%

Graduation Rate 4-year: 49%
Graduation Rate 6-year: 67%
Percent Undergraduates in On-campus housing: 67%
Number of official organized extracurricular organizations: 90
3 Most popular majors: Business, Ceramics, Fine/Studio Arts
Student/Faculty ratio: 12:1
Average Class Size: 15
Percent of students going to grad school: 29%
Tuition and Fees: $24,278
In-State Tuition and Fees if different: No difference
Cost for Room and Board: $10,796
Percent receiving financial aid out of those who apply, first year: 85%
Percent receiving financial aid among all students: 90%

Set in a quaint and historic village in upstate New York, Alfred University is far from the frenetic pulse of Manhattan. But what the campus lacks in big-city glamour, it makes up for in small-town charm and rustic beauty. Alfred is described as a "welcoming" and "very liberal" school, with a "gorgeous campus" to boot. And don't let the university's small size fool you—with four separate schools, students can be sure to find a course of study that interests them. Home to a world-renowned ceramic engineering program, Alfred offers a plethora of academic opportunities for everyone from painters to engineers to aspiring CEOs.

An Academic Buffet

Incoming freshmen can apply to one of four schools: the College of Business, the School of Engineering, the School of Art and Design, or the College of Liberal Arts and Sciences. For those interested in entering the College of Business, Alfred offers degrees in accounting, business administration, finance and marketing. While all the schools are considered challenging, the School of Engineering is particularly work-intensive. Students also point out the internationally known School of Art and Design as offering a challenging but well-respected program. In the academic realm, Alfred is perhaps best known for its School of Ceramic Engineering. Boasting an international reputation, this "super-selective" school is the only center in the United States that offers a Ph.D. program in the field. As one student said, "Ceramics is definitely a big thing at Alfred." However, Ceramic Engineering's eminence also comes with a heavy workload—according to one student, "those people . . . never sleep."

Those seeking a more generalized course of study can enroll in the College of Liberal Arts and Sciences, which includes a First-Year Experience (FYE) Program. FYE aims to expand students' horizons by exploring issues of race, ethnicity, and gender. The general education requirements also ensure that liberal arts students are exposed to a variety of topics. The requirements are divided into three "basic competencies": writing, foreign language, and quantitative reasoning, as well as six "areas of knowledge": literature, philosophy or religion, the arts, historical studies, natural sciences, and social sciences. Students in all schools must take a course in physical education—"I guess they want us all to be fit," one student said.

Students who want to study the arts while still enjoying the breadth of a liberal arts education can participate in BAFA, a unique program which allows fine arts scholars to gain a Bachelor of Arts degree. Unlike those seeking entrance to the School of Art and Design, BAFA applicants do not need to submit a portfolio. However, the program does require that students meet all general education requirements. Students say these differences prompt a light-hearted rivalry between Art School and BAFA students: "They just kind of rag on each other," said one student.

Alfred also has an honors program, which currently enrolls about 120 students. The program is known for offering seminars on unusual and intriguing topics. Recent course titles include "T'ai Chi," "Theory/Practice of Time Travel," and "Nip, Tuck, Perm, Pierce, and Tattoo: Adventures with Embodied Culture." In addition to enjoying classes on offbeat topics, program participants benefit from mentorship and thesis funding.

One benefit of attending a small university such as Alfred is small class size—most courses enroll fewer than 20 students, and even large lectures remain below 100. Intimate class settings are a key attribute of the Alfred academic experience: "You're not just a number," one junior said. Not surprisingly, Alfred students form close bonds with their instructors that extend outside the classroom: "We see them all over town." As a whole, professors at this liberal university are described as "accepting," "very accessible," and "easy to talk to."

The Daily Grind

Incoming students are housed in one of the many all-freshmen dorms, which are corridor-style and coed. Among these halls, the recently renovated Barresi receives high marks, while the other freshmen dorms are "not so nice." Openhym, one of the largest halls, includes large lounges on each floor and a late-night study area. Resident Advisors live with the freshmen. Students say RAs vary in strictness—some write up students frequently, while others are more laid-back. Upperclassmen dorms include Kruson, Bartlett, and the Brick. The Brick, used as an infirmary during World War II, houses mostly juniors and seniors. As the building is a coveted residence among upperclassmen, students say one must get lucky in the housing lottery to claim a room there.

Alfred recently switched to a new dining service and now features stations for stir fry, pizza, and grilled food. Students are generally pleased with the results. While the dining halls are still "working out the kinks," there are now a plethora of vegetarian options from which to choose. However, one student noted that the meal plan, required for those living on campus, is "ridiculously expensive." Students who tire of the dining hall can use their "dining dollars" as a debit card at two cafés on campus. Popular off-campus spots include the Terra Cotta Coffee House; Old West; Nana's Japanese Café; and Café Za, a restaurant and bar.

Set in the foothills of the Allegheny Mountains, the university boasts a "gorgeous" and "very safe" campus. Historical brick architecture blends with the work of Alfred art students to create a "beautiful setting." One student noted that her favorite place on campus was the Bandstand, a huge gazebo beside the campus creek where students can be found playing drums on the weekends. The Powell Campus Center, which houses a radio station and most club meetings, is another popular hangout.

> "The campus has gotten really liberal since they've gotten rid of the frats and sororities."

While the campus may be idyllic, town-gown relations aren't always as peaceful. "Our campus is super liberal, but as soon as you go across the street, it's super conservative," one student said. Tensions can arise with the local authorities. "The police hate us!" one sophomore said. In support of this claim, a student cited the $50 "disorderly conduct" fine she received from local police for skateboarding across campus at night. That said, students feel extremely safe on campus. The school provides security phones and an escort service for those walking home at night.

Sports fanatics be warned: At Alfred, arts easily trump athletics. As one student said, "If you want to be into sports, don't go to Alfred." Despite the more artistic vibe on campus, football and lacrosse games do attract fans. Intramural sports are popular, and the newly renovated gym boasts a complete fitness center and nightly open swim. Popular extracurricular groups on campus include Pirate Theater, Spectrum (the gay, lesbian, bisexual, and transgendered alliance) and the radio stations.

Seeking a Scene

When asked to describe her peers, one junior expressed her appreciation for the variety of "types" on campus. Indeed, the broad range of academic programs available at Alfred helps to ensure a diverse student body. Business students sporting "preppy collared shirts" intermingle with "artists wearing hippie clothes" and "normal liberal arts students wearing jeans and a sweater." However, another student noted the prevalence of students from upstate New York who have "face-piercings and crazy hair" and "wear thrift store clothes, or sew their own clothes out of thrift store clothes." One student also noted the well-known clique of undergrads known as "Art Stars." "They make really weird art and then say you aren't as intellectually in tune with art as they are if you don't understand it."

Given Alfred's diverse student body and unique academic programs, it's no surprise that nightlife options aren't your typical university fare. Alfred abolished Greek organizations in 2002, following the fraternity-related death of a student. While those still yearning for the traditional frat party can head to nearby Alfred State, most students remain on campus. Instead of frequenting frat row, they gravitate toward off-campus get-togethers and art house parties featuring rock bands. The Student Activities Board also brings musicians and comedians to campus on a regular basis. Popular annual events include the Winter Blues Bash, Glam Slam and Hot Dog Day, a weekend of activities held in conjunction with Alfred State to raise money for charities. The weekend is marked by performances, a parade through town, street vendors selling hand-made pottery, and the mud Olympics. During the spring event, "alcohol runs freely through the streets," and students get a welcome break from their studies.

An Eye-Opening Education

Not only has the lack of Greek activity not hindered Alfred's night life, but it also may contribute to the freethinking atmosphere that characterizes the school. "The campus has gotten really liberal since they've gotten rid of the frats and sororities," one student said. "Tolerance has definitely gone up a lot." Another cited the support among students and administration alike for Spectrum's "Gay? Fine by Me" T-shirt campaign as testament of the open-minded atmosphere that pervades campus.

For those looking to study art, ceramic engineering, business, or the liberal arts, Alfred University offers stellar academic programs in a quaint, picturesque village. The small-town surroundings and tight-knit campus make it easy for students to form fast friendships. But what students emphasize most about Alfred is its liberal, open-minded atmosphere. One previously "sheltered" student described her experience at Alfred as a "real eye-opener."—*Chrissy Levine*

FYI

If you come to Alfred, you'd better bring "an open mind—if not, people won't even talk to you. And a really heavy coat."

What's the typical weekend schedule? "Friday: go to Nevan's theater on campus to watch a movie; Saturday: sleep in, brunch, basketball game, go dancing with your friends; Sunday: sleep in, wake up at noon, study all day."

If I could change one thing about Alfred, I'd "change the hills. It's beautiful, but it's a pain in the butt to walk everywhere."

Three things every student at Alfred should do before graduating are "participate in Mud Olympics, go Dumpster diving, and get a radio station."

Bard College

Address: PO Box 5000 Annandale-on-Hudson, NY 12504
Phone: 845-758-7472
E-mail address: admissions@bard.edu
Web site URL: www.bard.edu
Year Founded: 1860
Private or Public: Private
Religious Affiliation: None
Location: Rural
Number of Applicants: 5,459
Percent Accepted: 25%
Percent Accepted who enroll: 38%
Number Entering: 517
Number of Transfers Accepted each Year: 79
Middle 50% SAT range: M: 650–690, CR: 680–740, Wr: Unreported
Middle 50% ACT range: Unreported
Early admission program EA/ED/None: EA

Percentage accepted through EA or ED: 65%
EA and ED deadline: 1-Nov
Regular Deadline: 15-Jan
Application Fee: $50
Full time Undergraduate enrollment: 1,873
Total enrollment: 2,148
Percent Male: 43%
Percent Female: 57%
Total Percent Minority or Unreported: 30%
Percent African-American: 2%
Percent Asian/Pacific Islander: 3%
Percent Hispanic: 3%
Percent Native-American: <1%
Percent International: 10%
Percent in-state/out of state: 24%/76%
Percent from Public HS: 64%
Retention Rate: 83%

Graduation Rate 4-year: 68%
Graduation Rate 6-year: 75%
Percent Undergraduates in On-campus housing: 75%
Number of official organized extracurricular organizations: 120
3 Most popular majors: English, Social Sciences, Visual and Performing Arts
Student/Faculty ratio: 9:1
Average Class Size: 15
Percent of students going to grad school: Unreported
Tuition and Fees: $38,374
In-State Tuition and Fees if different: No difference
Cost for Room and Board: $10,866
Percent receiving financial aid out of those who apply, first year: 100%
Percent receiving financial aid among all students: 62%

Small classes, no core curriculum, and clubs like the "Surrealist Circus"—all of these are typical of Bard College. Located in upstate New York, Bard provides interested students with a unique type of liberal arts education and the opportunity to explore all kinds of enjoyable activities during their four years—even if they involve juggling.

Academics of Choice

At Bard, students are required to design their own course of study based on what admissions materials term a "series of active choices." This decidedly active role in shaping one's own curriculum allows students to focus in on the area they most want to explore. But this doesn't mean there are no distributional requirements. Although the requirements include, for example, a laboratory science course, such classes can thankfully be fulfilled by the likes of "Acoustics"—though one junior claimed he had to remain on a "wait list for two or three semesters before getting a chance to take it." Despite the fact that at first glance, the requirements seem to be easy, they can often be neglected by students in favor of a more major-intensive curriculum. "My advisors are brilliant professors, but maybe not as helpful as they could have been," explained one student who realized in the middle of his junior year that he was missing five distributional requirements. He also emphasized, however, that professors are "very accessible . . . and give a lot of individualized attention," even personal comments on student transcripts.

One of the features that sets Bard apart is that there are no actual "majors"; instead, students go through an intensive process known as "moderation" in which they present papers and sit before a board of professors in the department they want to study in. "You can either be accepted into your major or deferred in which case you have to re-moderate. In very few of the majors you can be rejected, such as photography or film, which are the more competitive departments," explained a member of the radio group. Bard has also started a five-year business program.

That said, the most popular "majors" at Bard include film and music, which are also extremely competitive. "There is a cold-calloused filtering system . . . professors in the film department won't take you seriously until you actually declare that you're a film major," one student warned. Other difficult majors include economics and political science. Students claim that the least popular major at Bard is "probably Business Skills . . . considering the strong distaste for capitalism here."

A Change of Party Scenery

Bard was once known as one of the biggest party schools in the U.S. In recent years, however, there has been a "massive fragmentation" of the traditional party scene at Bard, forcing students to find other options for the building known as the "Old Gym," which once housed famous events such as "drag races." At present, several years after the Old Gym's closure to social events, no good candidates for a new location have been found. "There's some controversy over the newer options," one student explained.

And although many mourn the drastic change in the party scene at Bard, others say it is still "not as bad as other schools . . . we still live up to [our reputation], though it's much tamer than we used to be."

Political Un-Diversity

Bard is notorious for being one of the most liberal schools in America. "Politically, Bard is not diverse at all," one student explained. "Ethnically there's some diversity, but mostly the student body is composed of wealthy, white Americans." The students, however, are known to be extremely friendly and open-minded and, as one student put it, there is "no place where it's cooler to be gay than Bard." Putnam County, where Bard is located, is a well-known right-wing stronghold, but students claim there is no tension between the community and the college.

Tranquil, Beautiful, Isolated

Bard is located next to the Hudson River and has some remarkable views of the Catskill Mountains. The natural surroundings, however, aren't all that Bard has to offer. Its architecture is greatly varied and noteworthy, too. The Blithewood Manor, home to the Levy Economics Institute, is frequented by students in warmer weather to hang out in the gardens. "We'll go and watch the sunset . . . the views are really beautiful." Also, the Richard B. Fisher Center for the Performing Arts, designed by Frank Gehry, is extremely popular with both tourists and students.

> **"I fell in love with this place and have no desire to leave."**

As for dorms, there exists a fair amount of variety. Students can choose from a vegan co-op, the hotel-like Robbins house, or the ecologically sound Village Dorms (among many others). The Upper College Village Dorms, designed in conjunction with Bard students, are constructed from non-virgin timber sources, and are heated through a geothermal heat exchange system. About half of the dorms have singles, and most of them are coed. Students who live on campus are required to have a meal plan, which caters to vegans, vegetarians, and non-vegetarians. The food is in general pretty good, but one student warned, "The fish and pork should definitely be avoided."

Clubs and Circuses

There are approximately 90 student organizations at Bard. One of the most well-known clubs on campus is the Surrealist Circus made up of some of the "most creative and boldest people here, in a place where there are many creative and bold people." Bard also boasts several model student civic groups, such as the Bard New Orleans Project, which sent 150 student-volunteers to help repair some of the flood damage incurred by Hurricane Katrina. There is a general lack of enthusiasm for sports at Bard, but that doesn't mean that there aren't any.

Soccer is probably the most popular sport on campus, due in part to the lavish facilities donated by an heir to the Ferrari fortune. There are several varsity and club sports for those who wish to get their athleticism on.

Although the Bard College experience requires dedication and foresight on behalf of the students, studying at Bard is incredibly rewarding. As one student put it, "On my first visit to Bard I thought it was a wondrous institution, and so far I have not been proven wrong. I fell in love with this place and have no desire to leave."—*Melissa-Victoria King*

FYI

If you come to Bard, you'd better bring "a bike."

What's a typical weekend schedule? "There is no typical anything here. There are many exceptions to week rules."

If I could change one thing about Bard, I'd "give athletes the ability to pre-register for morning classes, so they don't interfere with practice and games."

Three things every student at Bard should do before graduating Bard are "attend an American Symphony Orchestra performance or theatrical production at the Fisher Center, see the Surrealist Circus perform in the spring, and attend one of the infamous *Moderator* magazine release parties."

Barnard College

Address: 3009 Broadway New York, NY 10027

Phone: 212-854-2014

E-mail address: admissions@barnard.edu

Web site URL: www.barnard.edu

Year Founded: 1889

Private or Public: Private

Religious Affiliation: None

Location: Urban

Number of Applicants: 4,274

Percent Accepted: 28%

Percent Accepted who enroll: 47%

Number Entering: 574

Number of Transfers Accepted each Year: 135

Middle 50% SAT range: M: 610–700, CR: 640–740, Wr: 650–750

Middle 50% ACT range: 28–31

Early admission program EA/ED/None: ED

Percentage accepted through EA or ED: 48%

EA and ED deadline: 15-Nov

Regular Deadline: 1-Jan

Application Fee: $55

Full time Undergraduate enrollment: 2,356

Total enrollment: 2,356

Percent Male: 0%

Percent Female: 100%

Total Percent Minority or Unreported: 33%

Percent African-American: 5%

Percent Asian/Pacific Islander: 16%

Percent Hispanic: 9%

Percent Native-American: 1%

Percent International: Unreported

Percent in-state/out of state: 31%/69%

Percent from Public HS: 53%

Retention Rate: 95%

Graduation Rate 4-year: 82%

Graduation Rate 6-year: 89%

Percent Undergraduates in On-campus housing: 91%

Number of official organized extracurricular organizations: 100

3 Most popular majors: English, Psychology, Economics

Student/Faculty ratio: 10:1

Average Class Size: 20

Percent of students going to grad school: 22%

Tuition and Fees: $37,528

In-State Tuition and Fees if different: No difference

Cost for Room and Board: $11,926

Percent receiving financial aid out of those who apply, first year: Unreported

Percent receiving financial aid among all students: 42%

Barnard is an all-women liberal arts college. This fact might turn away many female high school students searching for colleges, but a closer look at Barnard shows that it is very different from the stereotype often assigned to single-sex schools. Indeed, this top-notch university located in the middle of Manhattan offers its students not only a great education but also an exciting social life outside the classroom.

A Unique Partnership

Although it is an independent entity with its own faculty, budget, and administration, Barnard is actually an all-women undergraduate institution within Columbia University, meaning that the students have access to all the facilities, classes, and resources that characterize large research institutions. Barnard students can take classes at both their own college and Columbia. As one student noted, "The level of education at Barnard is not very different from that of Columbia because we are in the same classes." One of the interesting results of this rather special partnership is that students are selected by Barnard's own admissions office but receive Columbia degrees. But this is not to say that applying to Barnard is a much easier way of becoming a Columbia student. In fact, only 26.5% of applicants were accepted by Barnard in 2010.

Following the Way of Reason

As a top-ranked liberal arts college, Barnard certainly offers a very strong academic program. True to its motto, "Following the Way of Reason," Barnard insists on providing its students with extensive training in analytical skills, both in depth and in breadth. In order to graduate, each student must have completed 122 points' worth of coursework, including two points' worth of physical education. The number of points assigned to each class varies, but it is generally around three to five.

All freshmen have to take an English class, given the importance of writing at Barnard, and a seminar offering students a chance to challenge themselves intellectually with small group discussions. In addition, all students have to fulfill the General Education Requirements in nine different subject areas, also known as the Nine Ways of Knowing, ranging from laboratory science to visual and performing arts. The student reactions to these rather extensive requirements are mixed. Some believe that "the requirements are cumbersome and unproductive." Others, however, claim that "these classes can broaden the students' horizons."

Barnard is also a highly competitive school. According to one junior, "The classes here are no joke. Most people work very hard to get good grades." At the same time, classes offered by Barnard are generally small and free of teaching assistants. One student noted, "We interact with professors, not TAs, unlike my friends at other, bigger colleges." This certainly demonstrates one of the major benefits of studying at Barnard: the combination of a small college atmosphere with the colossal resources of an Ivy League university.

Location, Location, Location

Barnard is situated in the Morningside Heights neighborhood of Manhattan. It is only two blocks away from the Hudson River and a short walk from Central Park. Its convenient location in the middle of New York City is one of the main reasons people decide to come to Barnard. In the words of one student, "I wanted to go to a liberal arts school in a big city, and Barnard fit perfectly." Despite being in the Big Apple, Barnard is actually surrounded by several other academic institutions such as the Manhattan School of Music, Jewish Theological Seminary, and most importantly Columbia University, which is right across the street.

> **"The classes here are no joke. Most people work very hard to get good grades."**

These surroundings not only contribute to an educational atmosphere but also offer a much more exciting social life. One student remarked, "Barnard is an all-women school, but we get to meet with guys all the time around campus and in the City." Given the cross-registration of classes, as well as an exchange program with The Juilliard School, it is not at all difficult to meet people from other colleges, both male and female, by simply staying on campus. In addition, New York City itself presents a great social environment. During the weekends, bars and clubs across the city are top choices for Barnard students, who can then meet people from practically everywhere. This lively city life, however, also has downsides. As one student pointed out, "People like to go off-campus on weekends, so the campus is depleted of people. If you like to stay on campus and do things with people from your own college, then it is sometimes difficult."

Living on Campus

First-year students must live in the Quad and can only choose between a double and a triple. This has led to many complaints from students about the lack of space. Nevertheless, one student mentioned that colleges in metropolitan areas "all have cramped dorms. We live in New York City, so people can't expect to have huge singles." Residential advisors help first-year students make the transition to college life. They are trained to help in a variety of issues and generally try to be friends and not supervisors. As one student commented, "RAs are friendly, and they can be very helpful if you take the initiative to ask them for advice."

After freshman year, students can choose to live in Barnard dorms, Columbia dorms, or one of the eight off-campus buildings. They can also find off-campus apartments themselves. Despite this opportunity of living independently in one of the busiest cities in the world, however, the cost of renting off-campus is quite prohibitive, and a great majority of Barnard students stays on-campus. In addition, Barnard and Columbia offer an educational atmosphere with quads and greens, quite different from the city high-rises, which, as admitted by many students, "can be intimidating at times."

Dining in the City

First-year students must choose Barnard's "Unlimited meals per term" meal plan, although there are three other meal plans available after freshman year. Food at Barnard can be summarized, in the opinion of one student, as "acceptable." The college offers a great variety of food options, but there are only two dining locations on campus. Many residences are equipped with kitchens, allowing students to cook their own meals. Cooking, however, can be time-consuming. According to one student, "The kitchens can be very convenient, but don't count on having the time to cook meals everyday." With countless restaurants and cafés nearby, dining out is thus a very popular, though expensive, option for the students.

Barnard Bear or Columbia Lions

Although Barnard has the Bear as its mascot, athletes can compete in varsity sports only through Columbia teams—the Lions, which do not incite much interest among Barnard students. "We really don't have that much school spirit," explained one student. "We don't know how much we should identify ourselves with Columbia." Nevertheless, the association with a prominent Ivy League school, which can be overshadowing at times, also offers many benefits that outweigh its disadvantages. Given the quality of education it provides, Barnard stands as a top choice for female students searching for first-class education in an exciting urban environment.—*Xiaohang Liu*

FYI
If you come to Barnard, you'd better bring "clothes suitable for clubs."
What is the typical weekend schedule? "Friday tends to be comparatively quiet. Saturday is when you go downtown and have lots of fun. Sunday is for homework."
If I could change one thing about Barnard, I'd "build better dorms."
Three things every student at Barnard should do before graduating are "go to Midnight Breakfast, travel to every corner of New York City, and have fun on Barnard Spirit Day."

New York City is unique. Known for its skyscrapers and disorderly traffic, the Big Apple is also home to over half a million students. It even has its own university system. In fact, the City University of New York, most often abbreviated as CUNY, is the largest urban public university and the third largest university system in the country, ranked after the public universities of New York State and California. It encompasses 23 schools, including 11 four-year colleges, six community colleges, and six graduate and professional schools. The number of students is also stunning. CUNY enrolls approximately 260,000 university-level students, not to mention a similar number of individuals in adult, continuing, and professional education. A unique arrangement, CUNY is independent of New York State's own public university system, although it does receive funding from both the state and city governments.

Anything for Anyone

The sheer number of institutions and academic programs means a variety of options available to students. There are in fact more than 200 majors for undergraduates, thus providing the opportunity to receive training in either the traditional liberal arts or in career-oriented programs, such as Legal Assistant Studies, available at New York City College of Technology, or Television and Radio, offered by Brooklyn College. "There are all kinds of options for students, and the degrees are very practical and will help us immensely in finding jobs and doing well in them," one student said.

Given the number of options for students, CUNY has divided specialties among its schools. For example, City College is best known for its engineering program. Hunter College, on the other hand, has a large number of students enrolled in its highly acclaimed nursing school. Baruch College offers an undergraduate program within its Zicklin School, known as the largest collegiate business school in the country.

At the same time, the size of CUNY also implies a highly bureaucratic methodology of dealing with students. Surely, studying in New York City is very different from attending a small, rural college, where the school by itself represents a distinct community. The students attending any of the CUNY institutions find that they have to be independent and discover their own options rather than relying on advising from the school faculty and administrators, from whom it is sometimes difficult to obtain valuable guidance. Registering for classes can be frustrating, especially for freshmen and sophomores who are looking for relatively small classes. Nevertheless, this lack of personal attention is not unique at CUNY. In fact, students in most large universities have difficulties in navigating through the complex institutional bureaucracy. "I would like to have more individual attention. Everybody does," said one student. "But my friends in other state schools are also experiencing the same thing. And at least CUNY is now working on new programs to give us a little more personal attention."

Diverse Environment

New York City often boasts its diversity as a major strength, and the same can be said about CUNY. The location invariably means that the student body hails from all imaginable backgrounds. Indeed, more than 30 percent of undergraduates were born outside of the United States, and nearly 40 percent have a native language other than English. More than 150 countries are represented within the CUNY system. "It is a very international school. If you try, you will learn a lot about other cultures," one student explained.

Life in the Big Apple

As its name indicates, CUNY mostly serves students from New York City. Approximately 70 percent of undergraduates have attended public high schools within the City. This means that most people know about the Big Apple fairly well even before enrollment. Financially, it also makes sense for New York students to attend the school. After all, they do not have to pay the hefty charges of room and board. Many live with their families and have part-time jobs off campus.

One major drawback of CUNY is the lack of a collegiate atmosphere. Most students live off campus, and many schools do not even offer dormitories. This is because

CUNY is a commuter school. Students go to classes during the day and often have jobs at nights and during weekends. Therefore, many people take more than the traditional four years to graduate, and nearly 30 percent of undergraduates are at least 25 years old. "This is not your normal liberal arts experience," one student said. "People here are practical and have many other things going on besides school."

CUNY makes people independent. The students have to learn to take initiative and find their own opportunities. CUNY does not provide the highly protective and perhaps even insular environment of a traditional four-year college. Instead, it provides a good—and often very practical—education, and the students are on their own for other aspects of collegiate life, such as finding their own social circles and living arrangements. In the end, CUNY is for those who are looking for a good education in a diverse environment without placing too much emphasis on a traditional campus life.—*Xlaohang Liu*

City University of New York / City College

Address: 160 Convent Avenue, New York, NY 10031
Phone: 212-650-6977
E-mail address: admissions@ccny.cuny.edu
Web site URL: www.ccny.cuny.edu
Year Founded: 1847
Private or Public: Public
Religious Affiliation: None
Location: Urban
Number of Applicants: 17,816
Percent Accepted: 45%
Percent Accepted who enroll: 25%
Number Entering: 1,768
Number of Transfers Accepted each Year: 1,578
Middle 50% SAT range: M: 460–590, CR: 430–550, Wr: Unreported
Middle 50% ACT range: Unreported
Early admission program EA/ED/None: None

Percentage accepted through EA or ED: NA
EA and ED deadline: NA
Regular Deadline: None/ Priority Applicaton deadline: 15-Mar
Application Fee: $65
Full time Undergraduate enrollment: 8,145
Total enrollment: 11,310
Percent Male: 47%
Percent Female: 53%
Total Percent Minority or Unreported: 71%
Percent African-American: 21%
Percent Asian/Pacific Islander: 25%
Percent Hispanic: 34%
Percent Native-American: <1%
Percent International: 12%
Percent in-state/out of state: 98%/2%
Percent from Public HS: 85%
Retention Rate: Unreported

Graduation Rate 4-year: 50%
Graduation Rate 6-year: 65%
Percent Undergraduates in On-campus housing: 0%
Number of official organized extracurricular organizations: 145
3 Most popular majors: Engineering, Architecture, Psychology
Student/Faculty ratio: 13:1
Average Class Size: 25
Percent of students going to grad school: Unreported
Tuition and Fees: $11,129
In-State Tuition and Fees if different: $4,329
Cost for Room and Board: $9,900 Room Only
Percent receiving financial aid out of those who apply, first year: 96%
Percent receiving financial aid among all students: 85%

Located in the heart of Harlem, City College is one of the quiet academic gems of New York, producing alumni such as Colin Powell and former New York Mayor Ed Koch, and with faculty such as the co-founder of the String Theory of physics, Michio Kaku. While students at CCNY come from all sorts of backgrounds and living situations, most are from New York City itself. At CCNY, students must balance the rigorous amount of studying required to truly learn and very full personal lives.

An Immovable Foundation

Students at City College are required to maintain a 2.0 GPA or higher throughout the course of their college careers in order to graduate. At the same time, students in the

Macaulay Honors College must graduate in four years, and are required to take six liberal arts courses, four of them focusing on New York City—its art, peoples, science and technology, and its future. For students in the Sophie Davis Biomedical program, which provides students with a bachelor's degree as well as the first two years of medical school in the course of five years, every student must get a B or better in every class. Each major has its own requirements. When it comes to grading, there isn't much of a curve, but each professor makes up his or her own rubric, and so it can be kind of surprising. Stated one sophomore, "Don't come in assuming just because City's a CUNY it will be easy. I started with that notion, but my classes have changed my opinion pretty quickly."

Students all agree that the work required at CCNY is more demanding than expected, but is also quite rewarding. "For a lot of students, it's been quite some time since they were last in school, but now they are back, and are willing to work really hard to understand the material," one biology major said. In order to address the needs of a wide variety of students, the school is divided into the social sciences, the humanities, the "hard" sciences, a school of education, a school of engineering, and a school of architecture. Students major in every aspect of these programs, but everyone agrees that Engineering, the first public engineering program of its kind, and Architecture, the only public architecture program in the city, are the most popular.

As far as faculty goes, students feel that City College professors are among the most quirky and unique around. One student recalled, "I had one Earth Science professor who was also a poet. For a lecture on tornadoes, he explained it in a sort of sexual poem. I won't go into explicit detail, but I now know that tornadoes form from the friction between little tiny air molecules, that there's a building-up phase and then once all the liquid is gone . . . you know." Other students agree that the professors make the material more interesting, and insert a lot of their own personality. Furthermore, they are all very accessible to students who are willing to visit them during office hours, and are usually happy to have students assist them in research. Also, students in the honors program and at Sophie Davis are assigned advisors who help them with everything from finding scholarships to making sure the students are on top of their classes.

Classes run a wide range of sizes from introductory psychology lectures of about 400 people to labs with just around 15. Students feel that even though the work is very rigorous, everyone is really supportive of one another: "At Sophie, you'd expect us all to be kind of cut-throat about grades and stuff, but since we all have a seat guaranteed at med school, it's actually designed for everyone to help one another out. It's like that at the rest of the college as well."

Overall, students feel that the education they get at CCNY offers them opportunities that would otherwise not be there. "There's an openness to atypical students here, students who have kids or jobs, that I haven't heard of anywhere else," one student said. "There's a lot of support for everyone, and I think much of that comes from our diverse backgrounds and areas of study." At the same time, there is little communication between those areas of study, and students sometimes are frustrated by taking classes outside of their major.

A Commuter School Where People Know Your Name

CCNY's location at the top of a very windy hill makes it somewhat of a unique site, one that its students must trek to everyday. "The 1 Train, the A Train, the D Train, the C, the B, they all come here, but then *you* have to climb up the hill!" one student summed up. "To tell you the truth though, taking the train is a good time to do work, to catch up with friends, and to make new ones." Unfortunately, since it is a commuter school, it can be hard for the average student to meet new people, unless they share a common class or club, or are in the same program. "Most people come to campus, go to class, and then go home, unless they have a club or something," one student said.

At the same time, students tend to be very friendly, and very, very diverse: "It's a good atmosphere. A lot of people are here to get a college degree after not having the chance to for a while, so there's camaraderie between everyone, because everyone is focused on learning and graduating." Upperclassmen tend to help out underclassmen, and there are several programs through which students can get tutoring from one another.

Students do come together for events every couple of months, such as for Relay for Life, Go Green Carnivale, a joint event between the Green Society and the Caribbean Students Club, and the "Fifth Year Blow-out," an event at Sophie Davis where the graduating class puts on a massive talent show. Fraternities are present, and do occasionally throw parties, perform community service, and have events on-campus, although some students feel that they aren't a major scene.

Every Thursday, students have "club hours," where the organizations meet, discuss plans, and do whatever they are designed to do. Ranging from Intramural Volleyball to the Baskerville Chemical Society, clubs are designed to fulfill every student interest. "There are about a million clubs," exaggerated one student, "and if there isn't one for something you're interested in, you can start a club really easily." CCNY competes against other CUNY schools in a variety of varsity sports, but support is somewhat lacking: "Most people aren't very involved. They don't even know our mascot (it's the beaver)!" one freshman lamented.

On the weekends, students tend to do their own thing. "Most kids go home, study, and chill with their friends and family," reported one student who lives on campus. "Some of the upperclassmen go out to bars because they're legal, but underclassmen tend not to drink." Some drinking does go on in the dormitories, but the school has a zero-tolerance policy toward alcohol and drugs on campus.

Study, Eat, Breathe, Sleep: In Harlem

Most students live off campus, either at home or in apartments near the campus, in order to cut down on travel time. The school does offer housing for students a few blocks away from campus, in a building known as "The Towers," but rent is very high, with some rooms going for $1000 a month. The rooms themselves are functional and new, but many feel that the Towers are not worth the price. Also, the dorms are open to students from all over the city.

As for location, many students are big fans of the surrounding area. "There are a lot of great places to eat around here," one student said. There is some controversy amongst the students regarding safety in the area. "There's a lot of hype about, you know, 'Ohhh it's Harlem, it's not safe,'" complained a female student, "but my last lab ends at 7:50, and I feel perfectly safe." "After it gets dark, you should travel in groups," countered another. Still, there is consensus that around the campus itself, there are no major problems.

> "There's a lot of support for everyone, and I think much of that comes from our diverse backgrounds and areas of study."

Many students like to avoid the cafeteria, which tends to be expensive and doesn't offer many choices. "It's fuel, but it's not great," an engineer said. Instead, many buy food in the delis and restaurants in the neighborhood, while others bring food from home and eat it on the Quad. "The Quad is a great place in the spring and summer when the weather's nice. Otherwise, it's too cold and windy," explained a student from Brooklyn. Students also like to eat in the stairways in the North Academic Center, and to hang out in the castle-like Shepherd Hall.

At CCNY, you can find a diverse group of students coming together with one common goal and interest: learning. Students are often surprised by the challenging curriculum they deal with, but are supported by a caring and dense network of professors and friends. "When I went through the college admissions process, it wasn't until the very end that I decided to come to City," explained an Honors College student, "but it really surprised me. The tuition is lower than almost anywhere else, but what really got me was how generous the people were. There are things that you can go through, but still bounce back. City College has taught me that. I would definitely pick it again."—*Simon Warren*

FYI

If you come to CCNY, you'd better bring "a MetroCard."

What is the typical weekend schedule? "It depends on the weekend. If you have a test coming up, it could be study eat, sleep, repeat, or if it's a more relaxed week, it could be go home, relax, maybe go to a party, and study on Sunday."

If I could change one thing about CCNY, I'd "make the dorms cheaper. A lot cheaper."

Three things every student at City College should do before graduating are "go to a concert at the Apollo, rub Lincoln's nose, and play pool in the Student Lounge."

City University of New York / Hunter College

Address: 695 Park Ave, Room N203, New York, NY 10065
Phone: 212-772-4490
E-mail address: admissions@hunter.cuny.edu
Web site URL: www.hunter.cuny.edu
Year Founded: 1950
Private or Public: Public
Religious Affiliation: None
Location: Urban
Number of Applicants: 24,701
Percent Accepted: 30%
Percent Accepted who enroll: 25%
Number Entering: 1,854
Number of Transfers Accepted each Year: Unreported
Middle 50% SAT range: M: 500–600, **CR:** 480–580, **Wr:** Unreported
Middle 50% ACT range: Unreported

Early admission program EA/ED/None: None
Percentage accepted through EA or ED: NA
EA and ED deadline: NA
Regular Deadline: 15-Mar
Application Fee: $65
Full time Undergraduate enrollment: 15,718
Total enrollment: 21,278
Percent Male: 32%
Percent Female: 68%
Total Percent Minority or Unreported: 59%
Percent African-American: 12%
Percent Asian/Pacific Islander: 18%
Percent Hispanic: 19%
Percent Native-American: <1%
Percent International: 10%
Percent in-state/out of state: 96%/4%
Percent from Public HS: 70%

Retention Rate: 82%
Graduation Rate 4-year: 17%
Graduation Rate 6-year: 40%
Percent Undergraduates in On-campus housing: 4%
Number of official organized extracurricular organizations: 150
3 Most popular majors: Social Sciences, English, Psychology
Student/Faculty ratio: 15:1
Average Class Size: 25
Percent of students going to grad school: Unreported
Tuition and Fees: $10,800
In-State Tuition and Fees if different: $4,000
Cost for Room and Board: $7,958
Percent receiving financial aid out of those who apply, first year: 55%
Percent receiving financial aid among all students: Unreported

W ith its well-rounded core requirements, CUNY Hunter provides students with a solid education in the middle of New York City, even if the living arrangements sometimes leave a little to be desired. Hunter draws some of the most independent students in New York City and is able to give them a good training in almost every discipline. At Hunter, students are motivated to study and maintain separate lives outside the classroom.

Well-Rounded in the Big Apple

Hunter puts a heavy emphasis on a well-rounded curriculum. All students must take classes in math, U.S. history, English, foreign language, writing, natural science, arts, social sciences, and pluralism and diversity, which deal with, for instance, non-European history and women's studies. For students at Hunter's Honors Program, they also have to take four seminars about New York City over the course of their four years in the school.

Many students are pre-med, which is known for being very challenging. Other popular majors are literature, psychology and social science. Hunter's education and nursing programs are also outstanding. For those on the pre-med track, many of the classes, such as freshman biology, are designed to "weed out" people who are not committed to becoming doctors. Still, students find that the level of difficulty allows them to appreciate the curriculum. According to one student, "Organic Chemistry tries to teach you the psychology of the carbon atom by making it personal. Don't go in expecting an easy A or B. Expect to learn."

Other classes are more varied in terms of difficulty, as well as class size. While science and honors classes fill up quickly, humanities tends to have small classes, with a maximum of 20 students. Despite the extensive general requirements, the school tries to offer very specific classes, such as "Dante's *Divine Comedy*," "Understanding the Sixties," and "the Psychology of Human Sexuality." These courses are very popular.

Students also greatly enjoy the classes in the Honors Program. "I try to take at least one Honors class a semester," said one sophomore. "The classes are smaller, and the professors are more interested in what they are teaching and whom they are teaching." In addition to these classes, Honors students also get priority when picking classes, not to mention free laptop, free tuition, and guaranteed free housing. There is also a program called the Opportunity Fund, which provides $75,000 for study abroad, internship, projects, or other activities for each Honors student. "It's a pretty good deal. The Honors Program is the only reason I'm going to Hunter," said one student.

Every student has an advisor over the course of four years who offers guidance when needed. Professors are generally reachable and helpful. While "some professors don't expect much out of students and are boring and not challenging," many are "easy to get along with and very helpful if you are serious about getting help." Students feel that advisors are excellent resources and that it is a very good idea to take the time to get their advice.

As for grading, it is varied. "In general, it is not too tough," said one student. "Depending on the class and the professor, it can be harder. Frosh bio and literature are tough, but usually classes are not too harsh, just about right."

Hunter offers its students a well-rounded education with specific classes that excite and engage students, even though the required curriculum is sometimes cumbersome. One student summed up the attitude toward the requirements: "What I like most about studying at Hunter is that as hard as it is to complete the general education requirements, you see why they exist and appreciate them. Hunter exposes you to everything. But the general education requirements are also my least favorite part. People don't like them because they are required and feel that there is no time to fulfill everything."

Close to Home

Most students at Hunter do not live on campus. Hunter is unique among the CUNYs in that it guarantees housing to all of its Honors students. Students not in the Honors Program can also apply to live on campus through a very competitive online process. Every room is a single, and students get to keep the same room all four years, if they wish.

According to campus legend, Hunter's one dorm, Brookdale, was at one point an asylum for the insane. Now, instead of rooms for electroshock therapy on the first floor and a morgue in the basement, it houses a very popular game room and a swimming pool. Students love the fact that they have private rooms and that all the rooms are identical, although half of them face a courtyard and are slightly more coveted. Living at Hunter is arranged by floor, with an RA and a CA (Community Assistant), both undergraduates, on every floor. There are monthly floor meetings, where students can find out what is happening on their floor and settle issues. Floors can also be all-female or 24-hour quiet.

Students find that the school buildings are quite impressive. "There is a subway stop that gets off right into the school, so it is really convenient," said one student. Everyone takes public transportation to get to and from the school. In addition, the architecture makes it stand out. One of four buildings that make up the school's campus, the Thomas Hunter Building, looks like a castle but has bridges on the third floor, which cross over Lexington Avenue. There is also a recently renovated swimming pool, a new chemistry laboratory, and an athletic facility for all students.

As for food, the cafeteria is not well used. It closes before dinner so that students have to go out, order food, make something, or heat up leftovers. Luckily, the options around the neighborhood are plentiful. Each floor in the dorm has a kitchen, and many students are able to go home during the weekend for home-cooked meals.

The neighborhood surrounding Hunter is mostly safe, and the school is well incorporated into the community. Since the campus is open at night, people come and go freely, but to get into the buildings, particularly Brookdale, they are required to have several ID checks.

Hunting for Friends

When it comes to social life, Hunter is unlike many others. Since most students live elsewhere in the City, many people go home or work after class and don't stay on campus. One student explained, "We're a commuter school, so there isn't much of a sense of community here. There is not an area where students can come together and relax." On the other hand, students living in Brookdale do have the opportunity to get to know their neighbors, and students can hang out between classes at an Honors lounge.

On the weekends, many students go home,

although there are house parties. Many students also go out to eat or hang out with friends. Since the school is located on Manhattan's Upper East Side, there are many excellent choices when it comes to restaurants, and some students go to bars as well. However, there is no tolerance for underage drinking. "The security guards at the dorm are very strict," explained one student. "If you come back drunk, they will call an ambulance to take you one block, and you have to pay the fee." There are harsher penalties for those caught drinking in the dorm itself. However, most students reported that binge drinking is not much of a problem at all, and that almost everything happens behind closed doors.

Most friendships are made in classes, clubs, and dorms. Those in the Honors Program have an easier time of meeting new people because "you are kind of forced to, or at least you have a greater chance of meeting people. Most students come in, then go home, and don't really have a chance to sit down and get to know their classmates." Still, the consensus is that almost everyone is friendly and that the student body is one of the most diverse. "I wouldn't be surprised if every single country and nationality were represented," said one student. "You see every type of dress. You have rich people and less fortunate people. On a gradient, I would say it is completely diverse." Other students point out that people of all ages attend the school.

Hunter students also take advantage of the school's location, and get to spend time in some of New York's coolest locations. One sophomore recounted, "I once went to celebrate my friend's birthday on the Brooklyn Bridge." Every year, a big event is the Relay for Life, when Hunter and Baruch combine to form the CUNY Manhattan team. The Undergraduate Student Government also organizes events occasionally.

Big-Hearted Hawks
Hunter offers many extracurricular activities, particularly community service groups

and cultural organizations. Many people have jobs or internships, and most people are highly committed to their chosen activities. Fraternities and sororities exist on Hunter's campus, but rather than being communities of people who live and drink together, Hunter's Greek life is focused almost entirely on community service. Campus publications are popular, including the newspaper, called the *Hunter Envoy*, and the literary publication, the *Olive Branch*. Groups like the Socialist Club also put out newsletters.

> "What I like most about studying at Hunter is that hard as it is to complete the general education requirements, you see why they exist and appreciate them. Hunter exposes you to everything."

When it comes to sports, the athletes themselves take their sports very seriously. However, most students feel that there is little school pride. "We may not have a football team," said one, "but I am not sure." The athletic facilities are more widely used for relaxation and fun. There are basketball courts, a gym, a pool, and a small bowling alley.

Hunter students come from everywhere. It is a fantastic place to get a solid—and for Honors students, free—education from one of the top public universities in the United States. While it is easy to feel somewhat disconnected and without a community, students do find friendships and social lives. Academically, Hunter gives students a firm background, although some students would prefer to have more freedom when it comes to choosing classes. As one student put it, "if I had to pick schools again, I think I would choose the Honors College at Hunter again. You get to be independent and don't have to rely on your parents for tuition. There are great professors and advisors who help you find internships. Overall, it is a good deal."
—*Simon Warren*

FYI
If you come to Hunter, you'd better bring "sneakers."
What is the typical weekend schedule? "Go home or stay in the dorm, study or hang out. Some people volunteer or work."
If I could change one thing about Hunter, I'd "change the food plan. There is none."
Three things every student at Hunter should do before graduating are "walk from Hunter to Central Park, see the swimming pool, and get used to crowded hallways."

City University of New York / Queens College

Address: 65-30 Kissena Boulevard, Flushing, NY 11367
Phone: 718-997-5600
E-mail address: vincent.angrisani@qc.cuny.edu
Web site URL: www.qc.cuny.edu
Year Founded: 1937
Private or Public: Public
Religious Affiliation: None
Location: Urban
Number of Applicants: 14,436
Percent Accepted: 38%
Percent Accepted who enroll: 10%
Number Entering: 1,642
Number of Transfers Accepted each Year: 2,977
Middle 50% SAT range: M: 480–580, CR: 450–550, Wr: 490–550
Middle 50% ACT range: Unreported

Early admission program EA/ED/None: None
Percentage accepted through EA or ED: NA
EA and ED deadline: NA
Regular Deadline: Rolling
Application Fee: $65
Full time Undergraduate enrollment: 14,618
Total enrollment: 18,928
Percent Male: 39%
Percent Female: 61%
Total Percent Minority or Unreported: 56%
Percent African-American: 7%
Percent Asian/Pacific Islander: 25%
Percent Hispanic: 17%
Percent Native-American: <1%
Percent International: 6%
Percent in-state/out of state: 99%/1%
Percent from Public HS: Unreported

Retention Rate: 84%
Graduation Rate 4-year: 26%
Graduation Rate 6-year: 31%
Percent Undergraduates in On-campus housing: 0%
Number of official organized extracurricular organizations: 114
3 Most popular majors: Accounting, Psychology, General Sociology
Student/Faculty ratio: 17:1
Average Class Size: 25
Percent of students going to grad school: 17%
Tuition and Fees: $9,017
In-State Tuition and Fees if different: $4,377
Cost for Room and Board: $11,125
Percent receiving financial aid out of those who apply, first year: 55%
Percent receiving financial aid among all students: 58%

Sprawled over 77 acres in the residential neighborhood of Flushing, NY, just a 30-minute drive from midtown Manhattan, Queens College offers "an incredibly beautiful view of the city skyline" and a convenient location for thousands of New York City students. Less apparent, but just as spectacular, are the vast array of academic, social, and extracurricular opportunities this commuter college provides.

An Amazing Academic Assortment

Queens College offers a variety of academic options to meet the needs of a diverse group of students. The college offers 70 majors, of which the most popular are accounting, sociology, business administration and psychology (known as a "joke major" for its relative ease). There is also "a good load of people in the sciences," which are reportedly "incredibly tough"—"much harder" than other majors.

Whatever their major, all students are required to take at least 120 credits (each class is worth three to five credits, depending on difficulty), a Freshman English course and three additional writing intensive courses. They also must demonstrate competency in English, mathematics, physical education and a foreign language and must complete Liberal Arts and Science Area Requirements (LASAR) in seven areas. Students must also take three writing intensive units. The requirements are "somewhat inconvenient if you have a major that has lots of requirements in itself," but "it's actually not too bad to fulfill them—you just happen to end up taking them," and students averse to math and science can take "fake math and science classes" like statistics or psychology instead, while Urban Studies 101 is known as an easy way to fulfill the social science requirement. Freshmen get help planning their schedule during a mandatory advising session, and all students can consult the Advising Center on a drop-in basis, through e-mail, or by appointment.

Unfortunately, with an undergraduate population of over 14,000 (there are also more than 4,000 graduate students), many students find that registering for classes (online or in person) can be "really frustrating," especially for smaller, upper-level seminars. Students taking classes for their major get first choice, followed by seniors, juniors, sophomores and freshmen. As a result, "class registration can sometimes take a very long time, and in that time you can get closed out of classes." However, according to one senior, "if you go directly to the department or appeal to the professor, you can almost always get in."

Given its large student body, Queens College offers a surprising level of personal attention. While large introductory lectures have up to 200 students, upper level seminars, recitation sections and labs rarely exceed 20 students. Although sections and labs are often led by graduate student TA's, all seminars and lectures are taught by professors, who are, in the words of one senior, "the normal mix—some good, some not so great." Other students noted that "professors are very available and very enthusiastic, even in large lecture classes," so that "even if you're sitting in a class with 100 other people, you can get to know the professor if you want to."

While some professors are tougher than others, the workload is generally "not too much, but definitely not a walk in the park." As one sophomore put it, "You can get by taking the easiest classes, and there are definitely classes where if you're half awake you'll do fine, but you can also have an academically challenging college experience."

Students looking to take their education to a higher level can take advantage of plentiful undergraduate research opportunities or study abroad in 30 countries (popular destinations include Israel, England, Australia, the Galapagos Islands, and Florence, Italy). They can also take honors track classes, which are small, rigorous classes taught by top professors.

While honors track classes are open to all students, Queens College admits only a handful of exceptionally talented and motivated students per year to the Macaulay Honors College, a program where students take classes on the Queens College campus, but receive fully paid tuition, funding for internships and study abroad, an academic stipend, a free laptop and free access to museums across New York City. Honors College students must take four Honors College seminars in addition to taking regular

Queens College classes. According to one enthusiastic sophomore who had considered several Ivy League schools, these seminars offer "academically challenging, small classes" and "really amazing" professors, making for an experience comparable to that of a top small liberal-arts institution.

Queens College also features the SEEK program—which provides low-income, first-generation college students free tuition and additional guidance—as well as weekend classes, night classes, a program for adults 25 years and older and even the Center for Unlimited Enrichment, which lets senior citizens take classes at reduced cost. The college is also home to the renowned Aaron Copland School of Music, to which students apply separately.

This vast array of academic choices attracts students of all ages, races and income levels. "You have an enormous variety," raved one sophomore. "People who are 45, and people who are 18. People who are interested in politics, and people who are interested in music. The people in my medical anthropology class last semester had such varied life experiences, and the conversation took such interesting turns. It makes the education so much more enriching."

Campus Life for Commuters

Like most of the other CUNY colleges, Queens College is a commuter school. There are no dorms, and most students live at home with their parents, though a few rent apartments near campus. Students either take a public bus or drive to school, though the amount of on-campus parking, assigned by a lottery system, is "not necessarily adequate."

Because they live off campus, many students spend little time on campus outside of class. "You go to class and go home," said one sophomore. "You don't really chill there for the heck of it." Some students say this makes it difficult to get to know their classmates. Still, students report that their peers are "friendly," and for those who want to get involved on campus, plenty of opportunities are available.

Freshmen can enroll in the Freshman Year Initiative program, where students take three of their classes with the same 40 students, giving them a chance to build strong relationships. Another common way to meet people is through extracurricular clubs and organizations. The most popular clubs are cultural groups such as Hillel and Latin

American Club, the weekly *Knight News*, and student government; but with over 100 organizations to choose from, "if you can think of it, it's there." Most clubs have offices in the Student Union, which also has game rooms and big-screen TVs, making it a popular hangout during lunch.

On-campus dining includes a main cafeteria (which ranges from "not very appetizing" to "repetitive but pretty good"), a kosher cafeteria, a Chinese restaurant and several cafés. There are also several small restaurants right across from campus on Main St., including the popular Gino's pizzeria.

In addition to lunchtime, students have "free hours" twice a week during which no classes are held, providing a convenient time for students to hang out, hold club meetings, or "during the not-so-freezing days of summer and spring," play pickup football or Frisbee on the quad.

Although Queens is the only CUNY college to have Division II sports, there is no football team, and sports play a small role in the lives of most students. Most teams "aren't bad," but attending games is "hardly popular," though tennis and volleyball matches do draw some spectators. The on-campus gym, pool, weight room and tennis courts are free of charge to all students, but "no one really takes advantage of them" unless they are taking classes in sports or physical education. There is also a small intramural program for students who are interested.

> "It's a little bit more difficult because it's a commuter campus, but it's really what you make of it. There are definitely opportunities to have a campus life."

Because so many students live far from campus, few stick around for nighttime activities. As a result, "there is little to no drug/alcohol presence on campus. People who want to indulge in either tend to hang out off campus." There are a handful of fraternities and sororities, but since none of them have houses, they are a minor presence. However, clubs and associations will often sponsor on-campus parties, which are usually on the weekends, and "fairly well-attended." Throughout the week, students can also attend frequent lectures, concerts, and plays on campus, often held at the Kupferberg Center for the Arts.

A sophomore summed up life at Queens College with the following words: "It's a little bit more difficult because it's a commuter campus, but it's really what you make of it. There are definitely opportunities to have a campus life."—*Sameer Jain*

FYI

If you come to Queens College, you'd better bring "passion for something: anything," "an apartment," and "a laptop."

What's the typical weekend schedule? "Go to a part-time job, internship, or use the time to study." "At night, go into the city."

If I could change one thing about Queens College, I'd change "being part of a city bureaucracy. It's really awful: getting things done means many, many forms in triplicate and many meetings and many hurdles in terms of protocol."

Three things every student at Queens College should do before graduating are "play a game of pick-up Frisbee on the main quad; visit the on-campus museums: the art gallery in the library, all three of the galleries in Klapper Hall, the Louis Armstrong archives in Rosenthal Library and the geology exhibits; and study abroad (huge selection, and the cost is equivalent to CUNY credit tuition)."

Clarkson University

Address: Holcroft House, PO Box 5605, Potsdam, NY 13699
Phone: 315-268-6480
E-mail address: admission@clarkson.edu
Web site URL: www.clarkson.edu
Year Founded: 1896
Private or Public: Private
Religious Affiliation: None
Location: Rural
Number of Applicants: 3,204
Percent Accepted: 79%
Percent Accepted who enroll: 29%
Number Entering: 735
Number of Transfers Accepted each Year: 151
Middle 50% SAT range: M: 610–660, CR: 500–560, Wr: 480–590
Middle 50% ACT range: 24–28
Early admission program EA/ED/None: ED

Percentage accepted through EA or ED: 14%
EA and ED deadline: 1-Dec
Regular Deadline: 15-Jan
Application Fee: $50
Full time Undergraduate enrollment: 2,593
Total enrollment: 2,994
Percent Male: 73%
Percent Female: 27%
Total Percent Minority or Unreported: 9%
Percent African-American: 3%
Percent Asian/Pacific Islander: 3%
Percent Hispanic: 3%
Percent Native-American: <1%
Percent International: 4%
Percent in-state/out of state: 73%/27%
Percent from Public HS: Unreported
Retention Rate: 83%

Graduation Rate 4-year: 58%
Graduation Rate 6-year: 71%
Percent Undergraduates in On-campus housing: 82%
Number of official organized extracurricular organizations: 56
3 Most popular majors: Biology, Business, Engineering
Student/Faculty ratio: 15:1
Average Class Size: 18
Percent of students going to grad school: Unreported
Tuition and Fees: $32,220
In-State Tuition and Fees if different: No difference
Cost for Room and Board: $11,118
Percent receiving financial aid out of those who apply, first year: 100%
Percent receiving financial aid among all students: 98%

L ocated far away from the bustling noises of cities, Clarkson University is a small community of mostly undergraduates in the northern Adirondack Mountains. Nevertheless, despite its relatively small enrollment of 3,000 students, Clarkson is certainly not a small, liberal college. Not only does it have graduate programs, it is also a prominent research institution. Therefore, Clarkson is one of the rare schools that offer not only the closeness of a small village, but also the facilities of a well-recognized research university.

Small Classes, Big Dreams

Most universities similar to the scale of Clarkson generally only offer one single school, such as the College of Arts and Sciences. Clarkson, on the other hand, is divided into three different institutions: the Wallace H. Coulter School of Engineering, the School of Business, and the School of Arts and Sciences. "We are not a big school," said one student. "But we have all the components that you find at really large schools."

Indeed, despite being in the village of Potsdam, which has a population of only 10,000 people, Clarkson certainly offers the types of programs that are only available at major research institutions.

The school offers more than 50 academic programs, and a large portion of them are in science and engineering. Therefore, it is without surprise that a significant number of students at Clarkson are engineering majors. The academic programs in the field include the traditional curriculums of chemical, mechanical, and electrical engineering. At the same time, Clarkson also provides a number of unique and highly specialized programs of study, such as biomedical and rehabilitation engineering and aeronautical engineering. "If you are interested in becoming an engineer, you should definitely consider Clarkson," said one student.

The business program at Clarkson is also considered top-notch. "There are a lot of kids in business too," said one student. "Maybe that's because we have some unique programs in business." Given the university's reputation as a very technical institution, the School of Business also offers very specific coursework to ensure that the students will have a set of practical skills once they leave college. Unlike the generalized business administration programs at most universities, Clarkson has majors such as Financial Information and Analysis and Global Supply Chain Management so that students will acquire knowledge that can be directly transferred to their future professions.

> **"If you are interested in becoming an engineer, you should definitely consider Clarkson."**

Furthermore, there is also an interdisciplinary engineering and management program, which combines the two strengths of the university. It is especially valuable for students who would like to be business managers in fields related to technology, because then they would have knowledge and skills in both areas. Of course, in addition to the engineering and business programs, the School of Arts and Sciences also offers curriculums in liberal arts for all those who do not wish to have such specialized education in college.

Of course, it is also important to point out that given the emphasis on technical skills, students are given a relatively heavy workload. "You have to work hard," said one student. "This is not a place where you can slack off and expect to get by," said one student. Although the coursework is not overwhelming, · it is certainly important for prospective students to realize that expectations are high at Clarkson. "We are not the most famous college out there, but the professors expect you to do all the work and be really well prepared for classes," said one student. The *U.S. News & World Report* ranks Clarkson among the 120 top national universities in the United States. Therefore, the entrance to the college can be selective, though more than 70 percent of applicants are accepted every year.

The advantage of being at a small college with emphasis on research is that the professors are quite knowledgeable in their fields and provide access to students. "I was a little surprised at how some professors really want to get to know us," said one student. "I used to be under the impression that

professors just lecture and do not care, but I was wrong. They actually want to know about what ideas we have."

Those interested in more in-depth study can also stay on campus, given the presence of a number of research centers, including the Center for Advanced Materials Processing and the Center for Rehabilitation Engineering, Science, and Technology, which demonstrate how Clarkson is a prominent leader in both materials science and biomedical engineering.

Potsdam and Upstate New York

Clarkson is located on several hundred wooden acres of one of the most rural areas of New York State. Despite being a very small town, Potsdam is also an educational center. Besides Clarkson, the State University of New York, Potsdam, is also located in the area, not to mention SUNY Canton and Saint Lawrence University. Therefore, the small town does provide the different amenities that are well suited for college students, such as a number of bars, restaurants, and other hangout places. "It is not as bad as it sounds," said one student. "Sure, Potsdam is a little boring because it is so small. Yet if you go out and see it for yourself, you will find things to do. Also, the school does organize activities on campus."

The weather, of course, can be cold and uninviting, particularly during the winter, but students certainly do not think that is unbearable. "A lot of people here are used to it, because they are from the state," said one student. "Even if they are not from the region, you will get used to it."

Since Potsdam is small, most students live on campus. Freshmen live in doubles, and upperclassmen have more options, which include apartments and suites. College residences have residential advisors, who act both as enforcers of rules and as counselors to students. The school also offers themed housing in which people of similar interests enjoy their stay on campus together. Some of the themes include entrepreneurs, art, and outdoor activities. The idea is to ensure that students can learn from one another and perhaps organize events together. Of course, a small number of students—roughly 15 percent—choose to live off campus or in one of the Greek houses.

Clarkson offers six dining locations. There are also a variety of dining plans, ranging from 75 meals per semester to 21 meals per week. As in most universities, the reviews for college food are mixed. Most people point out that they do grow tired of the dining halls eventually and often seek different restaurants and eateries to satiate their hunger. "The food is not that bad," said one student. "But after eating all those meals here, you just get tired of them."

Hockey and Party

There are a number of fraternities and sororities at Clarkson, and they offer a good deal of parties during the weekends as well as some community service work for Potsdam. One particular drawback at Clarkson is the small population of female students. Nearly three-quarters of students are male. However, as pointed out by one student,

"there are enough people here. Even though there are a lot more male students than female students, I don't think it has that large an impact on anyone's social life."

Despite the small size of Clarkson, it is also a Division I hockey powerhouse. The Golden Knights, which have been very successful, generally draw major crowds.

Clarkson is certainly special. Most universities similar to Clarkson in size and location tend to emphasize liberal arts. Clarkson, on the other hand, provides top-notch technical training to students. Therefore, if you can brave the cold of Upstate New York to enjoy education at a quality institution, you should definitely take a good look at Clarkson.—*Xiaohang Liu*

FYI

If you come to Clarkson, you'd better bring "clothes to keep you warm."
What is the typical weekend schedule? "Do some work, go to hockey games if you can, and make up for all the lost sleep during the week."
If I could change one thing about Clarkson, I'd "move it to some place just a little warmer."
Three things every student at Clarkson should do before graduating are "go to a Golden Knights' game, make sure you get to know Potsdam, and go to Canada if just because it is so close."

Colgate University

Address: 13 Oak Drive Hamilton, NY 13346
Phone: 315-228-7401
E-mail address: admission@mail.colgate.edu
Web site URL: www.colgate.edu
Year Founded: 1819
Private or Public: Private
Religious Affiliation: None
Location: Rural
Number of Applicants: 9,416
Percent Accepted: 24%
Percent Accepted who enroll: 33%
Number Entering: 738
Number of Transfers Accepted each Year: 20
Middle 50% SAT range: M: 640–730, CR: 630–730, Wr: Unreported
Middle 50% ACT range: 29–32
Early admission program EA/ED/None: ED

Percentage accepted through EA or ED: Unreported
EA and ED deadline: 15-Nov
Regular Deadline: 15-Jan
Application Fee: $55
Full time Undergraduate enrollment: 2,868
Total enrollment: 2,903
Percent Male: 49%
Percent Female: 51%
Total Percent Minority or Unreported: 19%
Percent African-American: 6%
Percent Asian/Pacific Islander: 6%
Percent Hispanic: 6%
Percent Native-American: <1%
Percent International: 5%
Percent in-state/out of state: 28%/72%
Percent from Public HS: Unreported
Retention Rate: 93%

Graduation Rate 4-year: 91%
Graduation Rate 6-year: 91%
Percent Undergraduates in On-campus housing: 92%
Number of official organized extracurricular organizations: 186
3 Most popular majors: Biology, English, Psychology
Student/Faculty ratio: 10:1
Average Class Size: 18
Percent of students going to grad school: 20%
Tuition and Fees: $39,545
In-State Tuition and Fees if different: No difference
Cost for Room and Board: $9,625
Percent receiving financial aid out of those who apply, first year: 81%
Percent receiving financial aid among all students: 32%

Thirteen dollars, 13 prayers, and 13 articles. That was the beginning of Colgate University. In 1817, 13 men met in Hamilton, New York, and founded the Baptist Education Society. Almost two centuries later, Colgate University is considered one of the country's top liberal arts universities. With a student population of about 2,800, Colgate seemingly combines the best of both worlds—the intimacy of a liberal arts college and the strong athletics program of a big university.

Nuts for Nature!

Like many of its peers in the world of liberal arts universities, Colgate is located in a small, serene location. Hamilton, a village of around 3,500 people, is nestled right in the middle of New York State, about an hour's drive from Syracuse. It is also two hours away from Cornell University, Colgate's biggest rival in sports.

Quaint Hamilton Village is almost the same size of Colgate, which leads to good town-gown relationships. Even though it celebrated its bicentennial in 1995, the village, originally called "Payne's Settlement," has changed very little. Some students do feel that Colgate's location is a significant shortcoming of the university, given the fact that "there is really not much to do outside of the campus." "Everything in Hamilton revolves around Colgate," added another student, "There is really nothing for entertainment around here."

Nevertheless, students agree that the campus is beautiful. Gorgeous architecture is an important aspect of the university, especially Memorial Chapel's golden steeple, the most recognizable feature on campus. Its pristine location in Upstate New York is also a prime attraction for nature lovers. "Colgate is perfect for people who enjoy the beauty of nature," one student said. Taylor Lake and Payne Creek both sit inside Colgate's campus and provide a relaxing backdrop to an otherwise hectic campus. To make use of all of its surroundings, Colgate's outdoor education program provides a fully equipped Base Camp right on campus, so students can take out rentals for snowshoeing, skiing, backpacking, and even camping. Colgate even maintains a camp in Upper Saranac Lake in the Adirondacks for the exclusive use of its faculty and students.

Despite any perceived shortcomings of the town, Colgate maintains a good relationship with Hamilton, where most of the Colgate faculty and staff live. In fact, about 85 percent of the faculty lives within 10 minutes of the university. Another contributor to the goodwill between Hamilton and Colgate? As one student pointed out, "most locals go on vacation over Spring Party Weekend."

The Colgate Core

Colgate's admission process might not be as competitive as the Ivies, but it remains a highly selective school with an admissions rate of about 30 percent. The average combined math and critical reading score on the SAT was 1397, and nearly 80 percent of its students are in the top 10 percent of their high schools. The average GPA for the class of 2013 was 3.73. "Given the admission standards," said a student, "the people here are generally smart and willing to work hard."

Colgate is a challenging school. Students need to work hard to get good grades, and several introductory classes are particularly difficult. As one student pointed out, "The intro classes are designed to cull the weak." Nevertheless, most students are happy with their classes, which are generally very small, giving students the opportunity to closely interact with their professors.

Undergrads can choose between 51 different majors. There is a core requirement that expects students to take four special classes by the end of their sophomore year. Two of these courses teach students about Western civilization and their contemporary challenges. The other courses are designed to give students a better understanding of a specific culture in the non-Western world and the effects of science and technology.

Colgaters have to take a minimum of 32 classes to graduate, including six classes for distributional requirements in humanities, social sciences, mathematics, and natural sciences and two physical education credits, a specialty of Colgate. Most students are fine with the requirements. According to a student, "the required Core classes are easy but usually involve a lot of reading." The gym classes, however, have mixed reviews. While some love the idea of going outdoors to learn about hiking and survival skills, many others do not think that they should be part of the college curriculum. "I appreciate the goals of the gym classes, but I just don't think that they should still be here at the college level," said a student. "We have so many intramural sports anyway, and half of the students participate in them."

Weekends That Never End

People work hard at Colgate because of the vigorous academic standards, but they also party hard. Undergrads agree that most Colgate students have a solid sense of self-discipline that allows them to do well academically, while enjoying the nightlife.

Since a great majority of Colgate students stay on campus, there is no shortage of things to do. There are always parties going on throughout the week, not just during the weekends. Fraternity parties are probably the most prominent social scene on campus, although the sports teams are also frequent fiesta hosts. Teams often have townhouses or apartments where students go for partying and dancing. For those who grow tired of the Greek system, the Jug is the most frequented bar for Colgate students, who generally agree that everyone should go there before graduating.

> **"As one student pointed out, 'most locals go on vacation over Spring Party Weekend.'"**

With all the partying, most students drink significant amounts of alcohol. But, as many students point out, drinking is not a particular problem on campus. Nevertheless, although there are also social opportunities for those who stay away from the parties, students agree that these are generally limited. Given the number of parties available, it becomes hard for students not to take advantage of them. Plus, since dating is "not the norm" at Colgate, parties seem to facilitate the more prominent random hook-up scene.

Dorms and Diversity

Students at Colgate are generally happy with their freshmen housing, which is fortunate because 92 percent of all Colgate students live in residence halls and university-owned houses. Freshmen are required to live in residence halls, but as they move up, they are free to choose between a wide array of options, including townhouses, apartments, and suites. Another way in which Colgate differs from most colleges is that fraternities and sororities must live in university-owned houses. But most students see no problems with on-campus living. "The residences are great," said a student. "There are nice theme houses for upperclassmen."

Colgate is often seen as a relatively rich, upper-class school, but 29 percent of admitted students are from multicultural backgrounds. Nonetheless, the school tries to attract a more diverse student body, both ethnically and financially. "Colgate is filled with rich, upper-class kids," one student admitted. "But it definitely isn't as preppy as it is made out to be. People are generally laid-back and looking for a good time."

And who wouldn't be laid-back with the serene backdrop of upstate New York and a motivated and fun-loving student body? As one student said, "Colgate is one of those schools that find the right balance between partying and studying. That's why it is so great." When the men of the Baptist Education Society met in 1819, who knew that they would make 13 such a lucky number for 2,800 undergraduates?—*Xiaohang Liu*

FYI
If you come to Colgate, you'd better bring "a worn-in hoodie."
What is the typical weekend schedule? "Friday: happy that it's Friday. Saturday: party time. Sunday: freak out at the amount of work and spend the whole day in library."
If I could change one thing about Colgate, I'd "move campus to a warmer climate."
Three things every student at Colgate should do before graduating are "go to the Jug, sled around the campus, and hit some balls at the driving range overlooking campus."

Columbia University

Address: 1130 Amsterdam Avenue, New York, NY 10027
Phone: 212-854-2522
E-mail address: ugrad-ask@columbia.edu
Web site URL: www.studentaffairs.columbia.edu/admissions
Year Founded: 1754
Private or Public: Private
Religious Affiliation: None
Location: Urban
Number of Applicants: 22,584
Percent Accepted: 10%
Percent Accepted who enroll: 58%
Number Entering: 1,431
Number of Transfers Accepted each Year: 109
Middle 50% SAT range: M: 670–780, Cr 660–760, Wr: 650–760
Middle 50% ACT range: 29–34
Early admission program EA/ED/None: ED

Percentage accepted through EA or ED: 25%
EA and ED deadline: 1-Nov
Regular Deadline: 2-Jan
Application Fee: $70
Full time Undergraduate enrollment: 5,678
Total enrollment: 28,518
Percent Male: 53%
Percent Female: 47%
Total Percent Minority or Unreported: 51%
Percent African-American: 11%
Percent Asian/Pacific Islander: 23%
Percent Hispanic: 12%
Percent Native-American: 1%
Percent International: 10%
Percent in-state/out of state: 25%/75%
Percent from Public HS: 57%
Retention Rate: 98%
Graduation Rate 4-year: 85%

Graduation Rate 6-year: 94%
Percent Undergraduates in On-campus housing: 95%
Number of official organized extracurricular organizations: 450
3 Most popular majors: History, Political Science, Engineering
Student/Faculty ratio: 6:1
Average Class Size: 15
Percent of students going to grad school: Unreported
Tuition and Fees: $39,806
In-State Tuition and Fees if different: No difference
Cost for Room and Board: $9,980
Percent receiving financial aid out of those who apply, first year: 79%
Percent receiving financial aid among all students: 50%

E stablished in lower Manhattan in 1754 as King's College by King George II of England, Columbia University has lived up to its original charge of providing an education that would "enlarge the mind, improve the understanding, and polish the whole man." First housed in a schoolhouse adjacent to Trinity Church on lower Broadway, the school moved to its present 36-acre site at the turn of the twentieth century. This relocation from a relatively uniform upper-class neighborhood to a far more diverse community, Morningside Heights between the Upper West Side and Harlem, is symbolic of Columbia's metamorphosis from an Anglican colonial college to a vibrant and diverse Ivy League university where free speech, student activism, and community involvement are among its most outstanding attributes.

E Pluribus Unum
Although Columbia College has always been the heart and soul of the university, it was not until the end of the 19th century that the various schools that make up the undergraduate and graduate parts of the school were incorporated under a central administration. It was at this time that the "mining school" established in 1864—that would later evolve into the Fu Foundation School of Engineering and Applied Science—and Barnard College for women came formally under the aegis of the university. At the same time, Columbia Teachers College, the Columbia University School of Law, and the Columbia University School of Medicine were officially integrated into the university system. Finally, in 1897, the newly reorganized entity moved to a new campus at 116th Street and Broadway designed by the celebrated architectural firm of McKim, Mead & White. Today, these magnificent examples of turn-of-the-century urban design, crowned by the Low Memorial Library and the huge plaza that it looks out upon, have been complemented by some rather inharmonious modern buildings, the most

controversial of which is the Lerner Hall Student Center. Completed in 1999, the design of the 225,000-square-foot edifice, with its glass walls and escalating ramps, has been nearly universally panned by critics and students alike. "It looks like a huge ant farm," complained one student. "And it is rather hard to socialize on an incline."

Cutting to the Core and Going Swimming

It is impossible to talk about Columbia's academics without immediately referring to what is known as the Core Curriculum, a series of seminar-sized required courses in literature, philosophy, history, music, art, and science that are considered to provide the essentials of a liberal education. While some latitude is afforded in the choice of science classes, courses entitled Contemporary Civilization, Literature Humanities, Art Humanities, Music Humanities, and Frontiers in Science are compulsory. While the Core Curriculum is not for everyone, most agree that it provides an excellent foundation for a liberal arts education. Literature Humanities, a year-long course in Western literature that spans Homer to Virginia Woolf, is a particularly popular class, as is Contemporary Civilization, a course that exposes students to many of the seminal texts dealing with Western philosophy.

"The Core curriculum is one of the reasons I came to Columbia," states a freshman. "The Core exposes you to so many different things you otherwise wouldn't have the chance to study. Every college student should learn from these writers and thinkers." Students find that, to some degree, the Core experience depends on the professors that you get for a particular subject. Opined one coed, "There is some luck involved in fulfilling the Core requirements, since you can't choose your profs for most courses."

In addition to the required courses in literature, philosophy, art, and music, the Core also demands the equivalent of two years of language at the college level and two courses in the Global Core, classes that deal with issues of multiculturalism, race, and gender. This requirement, in fact, is a relatively recent addition to the Core Curriculum, added by the college's Committee on the Core, in reaction to student criticism about the paucity of works by women and non-white, non-Western writers.

A rarity among colleges today, the Core Curriculum mandates that students take a minimum of two courses in physical education. "There are so many offerings," says one sophomore, "that it is always possible to find classes that suit even the most dedicated 'couch potato.'" In addition to the required gym classes, students must be able to swim seventy-five yards in the Uris Pool without resting. Although a seemingly unusual graduation prerequisite, Columbia College is not the only Ivy concerned with whether its undergraduates sink or swim. Cornell and Dartmouth also demand competence in the water.

Students must declare a "major" or a "concentration" (a less extensive version of the major that requires fewer courses) by the end of their sophomore year. Undergraduates may also "double major" or may fulfill the requirements of a major and concentration at the same time. Beyond the Core and the major or concentration, students choose from a wide variety of electives in any department in order to complete the minimum of 124 "points" necessary to graduate.

Location! Location! Location!

Columbia's location in New York, one of the world's greatest cities, is truly one of its most appealing calling cards, and it is not an overstatement to say that New York City can be viewed as an extension of the classroom. Opportunities abound to explore Manhattan's renowned museums (which are free for Columbia students) and to attend the finest theatrical and musical productions. "There are very few classes that meet on Fridays, so weekends start early," states one senior. "Many of us spend Saturday and Sunday afternoons exploring the city." In addition, the culinary diversity of New York lies at the doorstep of the university, as well as nightlife and shopping.

The Living Is Easy

The vast majority of Columbia undergraduates (99 percent of freshmen and 94 percent of upperclassmen) live on campus in university residence halls, and housing is guaranteed to all students throughout their four years. Freshmen choose to live in singles, doubles, or suites in one of five buildings located on the perimeter of South Field, the university's main quadrangle. The suite dorm is considered the most "social," while students looking for a "quieter dorm life" prefer the two mixed-suite dorms. One freshman said, "The dorms are pretty nice and having freshmen housing located in one portion of the campus is really conducive to making a lot of friends right away. My floor is very close and my floor mates are my best friends. The all-freshmen dorms are very social." Upperclassmen are housed by lottery. Single students share apartments or live in dormitory-style accommodations or studios, while couples generally live in studios and one-bedroom units. Families with dependent children live in "family units."

The area around Columbia University is considered very safe. "The campus is fairly small and very secure," notes a senior. "There is a security guard 24/7 at the entrance to all dorms."

Mealtime

Dining options vary from "meals" served in the John Jay dining hall Monday through Saturday, to "Columbia points" which are redeemable for à la carte selections at twelve locations on campus. While all freshmen are required to enroll in the meal plan, it is optional for upperclassmen. After the first year, students may enroll in "dining dollars" or "flex accounts," both of which have dollar balance accounts accessed through the Columbia Card, the university's ID. Kosher food can be found at the John Jay dining hall and at Barnard College for women, the Columbia affiliate located just across the street from the main campus.

Women at Columbia: the College and Barnard

Columbia College first admitted women in 1983 after merger negotiations with Barnard, an all-female college located across Broadway from Columbia, fell apart. While the university has remained closely affiliated with Barnard and students from Columbia's "sister" school can cross-register with Columbia students and freely participate in extracurricular activities, including athletics, some Columbia women do not always look at their Barnard counterparts as full equals. "Since the admissions criteria are more competitive for women at the College than they are for Barnard women, some classmates of mine consider Barnard students as being not as smart or diverse as Columbia women," said one junior. "Personally, I disagree. I have made many friends at Barnard and they are intelligent and interesting."

Outside of the Classroom

Like all outstanding colleges, the extracurricular life at Columbia is extremely diverse. There are a wide variety of publications including the *Columbia Daily Spectator*, the nation's second-oldest college newspaper, and the *Columbia Review*, the oldest student literary magazine. The Philolexian Society is one of the oldest collegiate literary societies in America. Columbia also fields teams in Mock Trial, Model United Nations, and debate.

There are a dozen a cappella groups and numerous musical groups, including the Columbia University Orchestra, the oldest continually performing university orchestra in the nation. Opportunities for theater performance and comedy abound, including Fruit Paunch, Columbia's improv comedy group.

Where the Lions Roar

There are 31 men's and women's sports teams representing the Lions of Columbia. Barnard students participate on the Columbia women's squads. Although the football teams have not fared well in recent years, many other sports teams have. In 2007, the Men's Track Team won the 4x800 Penn Relay, the first time that an Ivy League track team was victorious in this event in over three decades. Many of Columbia's athletic facilities can be found at the Baker Athletics Complex, located north of the main campus. This campus includes the football field as well as facilities for baseball, soccer, field hockey, crew, tennis, and track. "Having the football field distant from the main campus is a negative," argues one freshman. "I think that is a big reason why a lot of students do not attend the games. My friends and I would rather hang around campus or go downtown on Saturdays rather than going all the way uptown to see our team lose."

The Social Scene

With the Big Apple at their doorstep, most Columbia students avail themselves of the tremendous cultural and culinary opportunities on the weekends, although social life is usually a blend of on- and off-campus activities. "Most people go out on Thursday nights to relax, because there are only a few classes that meet on Fridays," reports one junior. "We usually sleep in on Fridays and get a head start on work and spend Saturday and Sunday afternoons exploring the city. Most people go off campus to one of the many neighborhood restaurants and bars." Students generally divide their weekend time between the Columbia neighborhood, which is full of nightlife, and downtown Manhattan. "Columbia doesn't have a big party atmosphere," notes a senior. "But students love hanging out together. On the weekends, if the weather is nice, we like relaxing in the floor lounge, hanging out on the steps of Low Library, and having lunch at one of the many on-campus dining locations."

While there are over 20 fraternities and sororities at Columbia, only about 10 percent of undergrads participate in Greek life. "Frat life is definitely present on campus, but it is far from dominant," reports one sophomore. "You can choose to be very involved in it, or you can get through four years without ever going to a frat party."

A Tradition of Activism

Student activism has long characterized the student body. In 1968, students occupied several campus buildings in protest over the university's participation in the Institute for Defense Analyses, a weapons research agency tied to the Pentagon, and what was perceived as a lack of sensitivity toward the African-American population in neighboring Harlem. In the 1970s and 1980s, there were protests and strikes over the university's investments in companies supporting apartheid in South Africa. In 1996, student protests resulted in the addition of Ethnic Studies to the Core Curriculum. In late 2007, some students went on a hunger strike in protest over Columbia's planned large-scale expansion into Manhattanville, a neighborhood north of the main campus.

Free speech is alive and well at Columbia, regardless of the degree to which such speech goes against the grain. This was evidenced in late 2007 by the visit of Iranian President Mahmoud Ahmadinejad to the campus, a demagogic leader whose anti-American policies are well known. In fall of 2008 alone Columbia University hosted visits from Barack Obama, John McCain, and Hillary Clinton.

Columbia University is, overall, a superb academic institution that prides itself on its emphasis on the well-rounded education of its students. Its Core Curriculum is prime evidence of this, and it is essentially impossible to graduate from Columbia without having developed a broad appreciation for classical academic values. If you love learning, crave the excitement of the Big Apple, and know how to swim, Columbia may be just the school for you.—*Jonathan Berken*

FYI
If you come to Columbia, you'd better bring "a subway map."
What is a typical weekend schedule? "Sleep in on Fridays and get some work done. Explore the city Saturday and Sunday afternoons and hang out with friends on Saturday night."
If I could change one thing about Columbia, I'd "improve the advising system."
Three things that every student at Columbia should do before graduating are "get lost in the city with friends at two in the morning, eat a gigantic slice of Koronet's pizza, and hang out on the steps of Low Library."

The Cooper Union for the Advancement of Science and Art

Address: 30 Cooper Square New York, NY 10003
Phone: 212-353-4120
E-mail address: admissions@cooper.edu
Web site URL: www.cooper.edu
Year Founded: 1859
Private or Public: Private
Religious Affiliation: None
Location: Urban
Number of Applicants: 3,055
Percent Accepted: 9%
Percent Accepted who enroll: 73%
Number Entering: 206
Number of Transfers Accepted each Year: 40
Middle 50% SAT range: M: 640–780, CR: 620–710, Wr: Unreported
Middle 50% ACT range: 29–33
Early admission program EA/ED/None: ED
Percentage accepted through EA or ED: 16%

EA and ED deadline: 1-Dec
Regular Deadline: 1-Jan
Application Fee: $65
Full time Undergraduate enrollment: 917
Total enrollment: 969
Percent Male: 64%
Percent Female: 36%
Total Percent Minority or Unreported: 58%
Percent African-American: 5%
Percent Asian/Pacific Islander: 17%
Percent Hispanic: 7%
Percent Native-American: <1%
Percent International: 16%
Percent in-state/out of state: 60%/40%
Percent from Public HS: 65%
Retention Rate: 92%
Graduation Rate 4-year: 67%
Graduation Rate 6-year: 70%

Percent Undergraduates in On-campus housing: 20%
Number of official organized extracurricular organizations: 90
3 Most popular majors: Electrical, Electronics, and Communications Engineering; Fine Arts and Art Studies; Mechanical Engineering
Student/Faculty ratio: 8:1
Average Class Size: 14
Percent of students going to grad school: 60%
Tuition and Fees: $35,000
In-State Tuition and Fees if different: No difference
Cost for Room and Board: $13,700
Percent receiving financial aid out of those who apply, first year: 50%
Percent receiving financial aid among all students: 30%

Also known as The Cooper Union, or "Cooper," this small university of about 900 undergraduate students occupies five buildings in the East Village neighborhood of Manhattan. Cooper is prominent for its high selectivity, rigorous programs, and especially motivated and focused student body. Over 200 new undergraduates matriculate each year as students of engineering, architecture, or fine arts. Since its founding, Cooper has granted every student free tuition upon acceptance, in line with its mission of making quality education "free as air and water." Because of the school's urban location and specialized approach to learning, many students believe that studying at Cooper is "not a typical college experience," but one that will prepare them for successful careers in the real world.

Three Schools in One

Prospective Cooper students apply and gain acceptance to three different schools: the Irwin S. Chanin School of Architecture, the School of Art and the Albert Nerken School of Engineering. With about 550 students, the engineering school is the largest, and it offers majors in mechanical, chemical, civil, and electrical engineering. The art and architecture programs are smaller, with about 200 students each. All of Cooper's programs are highly ranked and selective. Aside from submitting test scores and transcripts, applicants to the art and architecture schools must complete "home tests" meant to gauge their talent through conceptual problems and art projects. In addition, they prepare extensive portfolios of their work, which may be presented to members of the selection committee at several portfolio review days and open houses that take place throughout the year. One artist believes that this long, multi-part process is designed to find people who are truly passionate about their work. "Stay true to yourself, and Cooper is such a great institution, they will be able to recognize your own talent," she said.

For underclassmen at Cooper, core requirements and major-specific prerequisites fill up much of the course schedule. Four semesters of general humanities seminars must be taken by students of all majors. Engineers generally find that these classes are a good way to balance their otherwise heavily quantitative course loads. An engineering student commented that the humanities courses are designed to be less arduous than courses within the majors. Students who enjoy the topics presented to them in these courses may choose to take electives in psychology, sociology, creative writing, economics, international relations, and other fields when they have more free scheduling space in their junior and senior years. Should a student find Cooper's moderate selection of humanities and social science courses insufficient, he or she is permitted to take classes at NYU or The New School.

No One Holds your Hand
The consensus among students is that Cooper is tough. Engineers should be prepared to do a substantial amount of self-studying. "For me, the hardest part in adjusting to academics [during my freshman year] was having to deal with not having teachers so much as professors," said a chemical engineering student. "A lot of these professors are so smart so they explain it straight out of the book like how you'd explain it to a Ph.D., but they don't know that we don't necessarily think like that yet." Grading is described as "harsh but fair." A civil engineer still remembers the despair he felt throughout his freshman year when he would spend hours on an assignment only to receive a C or low B grade.

Artists and architects are said to "always be in the studio." Studio work is taken very seriously. One artist stated that the major is mostly self-driven and that students independently design and execute projects with the light-handed guidance of instructors. "It's not really about the grade. Most of the students here don't really care about the grading process," she said.

When it comes to academic and career advising, students also have to be especially proactive. "It's really hard to be here if no one is holding your hand," said one student. "It's up to you to network." An architecture major said that she has found professors to offer extremely helpful advice on difficult assignments and general concerns if you seek them out. "But they won't give you the answers," she added. "You learn the process of learning from your own work."

Meanwhile, several students emphasized that Cooper's students are generally supportive of one another. "We all know it's hard. It's not that we're stupid, it's just hard," said an engineering student. "I haven't really felt like anyone's cutthroat. Everyone works really hard, and we're all around to help each other out. No one's out there to do better than anyone else."

Most students at Cooper are driven by a strong sense of purpose, and the student body has been described as overall "down to earth and practical." "I don't think you would go to Cooper if you weren't at least somewhat certain of what you wanted to do," said a sophomore engineer. It is rare for students to change disciplines during their time at Cooper, and most strive to establish themselves career-wise by joining professional societies of engineers or securing internships and jobs both on- and off-campus. Alumni connections are strong and the counseling office helps students to secure valuable opportunities in the city. Even with such strong backgrounds in their particular disciplines, however, a significant number of students graduate to pursue medical school, law school, or business school after their time at Cooper.

Freedom is a Two-Edged Sword
Cooper students are not guaranteed housing after their freshman year. The dorms are "apartment-style" and include a bathroom, kitchen, common room, and one or two bedrooms. There is no dining hall, so students frequently eat out. In some cases, even freshmen will be denied housing due to lack of space in the dormitories. Upperclassmen and those denied housing will need to search for and rent apartments either near school or in the other boroughs of New York City. A significant number of students commute to school daily, which some say detracts from Cooper's social scene.

While some students find the process of searching for an apartment to be a major obstacle, others enjoy the independence of living off campus. "It's kind of nice being on your own because it's the taste of real life," said one student. "East village is in the middle of everything, so there is a lot of really good food."

Indeed, students have a range of options within walking distance, from cheap falafel, one dollar pizza, and baked snacks to Thai food, fresh groceries, and high end restaurants.

> "Stay true to yourself, and Cooper is such a great institution, they will be able to recognize your own talent."

Many students cite off-campus housing along with packed schedules to be the primary hindrances to social interaction between students. There are virtually no common "hang out spots," and because most people meet friends through taking the same classes, it is rare for students to make friends in disciplines other than their own. Nevertheless, core requirement classes, sports teams, clubs, and mixed freshman dormitories enable students to bridge the gap between disciplines to some extent.

Partying is rare on any night of the week, especially when the workload is heavy. Late at night during finals week for instance, it will be normal to see that groups of students have taken over classrooms to study, talk, eat, and perhaps watch movies—"just chilling" in each other's company. Rarely able to find free time, artists also relax while working in the studio by snacking, chatting, and sometimes playing movies on their computers. Cooper students are not ashamed to acknowledge that this might seem "very nerdy." In fact, many recognize it and take pride in it as part of their school culture. "Everyone is busy all the time," said a sophomore artist. "I basically live in my studio, but I live there with the 30 other kids in my class." A senior civil engineer echoed that statement. "[Your classmates] are the people you essentially go to war with— war against the classes," he said. "What we have is like a brotherhood."—*Justine Yan*

FYI
If you come to Cooper, you'd better bring "something to keep you going, give you inspiration, [or] something you take solace in, like a teddy bear."
If I could change one thing about Cooper, "The schools would interact more. [Currently] the artists and engineers are complete opposite and barely socialize ever."
Three things every student at Cooper should do before graduating are "explore New York City, try to go to art openings every Tuesday, where students in school get to display their own work, and go on a ski trip in January."

Cornell University

Address: 410 Thurston Avenue, Ithaca, NY 14850
Phone: 607-255-5241
E-mail address: admissions@cornell.edu
Web site URL: www.cornell.edu
Year Founded: 1865
Private or Public: Private
Religious Affiliation: None
Location: Suburban
Number of Applicants: 25,617
Percent Accepted: 25%
Percent Accepted who enroll: 47%
Number Entering: 3,010
Number of Transfers Accepted each Year: 768
Middle 50% SAT range: M: 660–760, Cr: 620–730, Wr: 670–740
Middle 50% ACT range: 28–32
Early admission program EA/ED/None: ED

Percentage accepted through EA or ED: 37%
EA and ED deadline: 1-Nov
Regular Deadline: 1-Jan
Application Fee: $65
Full time Undergraduate enrollment: 13,523
Total enrollment: 18,885
Percent Male: 51%
Percent Female: 49%
Total Percent Minority or Unreported: 58%
Percent African-American: 5%
Percent Asian/Pacific Islander: 16%
Percent Hispanic: 6%
Percent Native-American: 1%
Percent International: 8%
Percent in-state/out of state: 38%/62%
Percent from Public HS: Unreported
Retention Rate: 96%

Graduation Rate 4-year: 84%
Graduation Rate 6-year: 92%
Percent Undergraduates in On-campus housing: 46%
Number of official organized extracurricular organizations: 823
3 Most popular majors: Business, Engineering, Biology
Student/Faculty ratio: 9:1
Average Class Size: 26
Percent of students going to grad school: 71%
Tuition and Fees: $34,600
In-State Tuition and Fees if different: No difference
Cost for Room and Board: $11,190
Percent receiving financial aid out of those who apply, first year: 88%
Percent receiving financial aid among all students: 40%

The youngest of the eight Ivy League institutions, Cornell University is well known both domestically and internationally as one of the premier educational establishments in the world. It boasts an immense array of resources and opportunities for its nearly 14,000 undergraduates. In addition, its location at the southern tip of the beautiful Finger Lakes gives the prestigious university a lovely learning environment—to the delight of all who enjoy the quiet, intimate atmosphere of small college towns and the chagrin of those who prefer the lively ambiance of big cities. If you would like to study in a large, top-notch institution and do not mind a rather removed location, Cornell ought to be among your top college choices.

Enjoyment of Nature

"The beautiful campus is the reason I came to Cornell," said one student. Indeed, for all those who enjoy nature, Cornell is certainly the place to be. It is located at the southern end of Cayuga Lake in the Finger Lakes region of upstate New York. The university takes pride in its two beautiful gorges, which offer the students small areas of wildlife right in the middle of campus. Many students take the gorge trails on their way to classes to enjoy sight of the numerous waterfalls that dot the creeks. The school's location in the valley of Cayuga Lake also means that there are a lot of hills. In fact, Cornell is situated on the East Hill, which overlooks the city of Ithaca. This poses considerable inconveniences to the students. As one sophomore pointed out, "The hilly roads sometimes just make you not want to go to classes, especially during the winter."

Ithaca is a stereotypical college town, and Cornell is certainly its dominant institution. In fact, there are only about 30,000 people living in the city, a small figure considering that over 20,000 students are enrolled at Cornell. Ithaca Commons is the most important downtown business hub. However, Collegetown, the southern part of the campus, also has some commercial areas and is much more accessible to students.

Despite the natural beauty, Cornell is certainly remote and hardly accessible to any major cities. "We don't even have a highway around," said one student. "You have to drive around hill after hill to get to Cornell."

The location issue is certainly one of the major complaints and an important factor to consider for prospective students. "Cornell is in the middle of nowhere," remarked one student. "So if you like to leave campus for the weekend once in a while, it might not be a good idea to come here."

Private and Public

Cornell is unique among Ivy League schools for its distinct status as both a private and a public institution. The schools of Agriculture and Life Sciences, Human Ecology, and Industrial and Labor Relations are public schools. New York residents can pay about $15,000 less tuition when attending those three colleges. Other than that, "there is really no difference between the public and private parts of Cornell," said one student. "The quality of teaching is the same for all of them."

The seven colleges at Cornell include some highly specialized ones, such as Industrial and Labor Relations and Hotel Management, and broader ones, such as the College of Arts and Sciences, which is also the largest with more than 4,000 students. Also popular are the College of Agriculture and the College of Engineering, which attract most of those who are interested in science and engineering. High school students apply to one of the specific schools during the admission process, which is highly competitive for every school, as the admission rate is about 20%.

The rural environment of Cornell might turn away some students, but the academics for such a large and resourceful university can be tailored to satisfy almost any kind of learner. "In terms of academics, we have something for everyone," said one student. The school offers about 80 majors, including several unusual ones such as Fiber Science and Apparel Design. Since the Finger Lakes region is also the second largest producer of wine in the United States, Cornell is well known for offering several classes in wine tasting, which are very popular.

The class size at Cornell varies widely. For freshmen, the introductory lectures are quite large, many with hundreds of students. "Some big lecture classes can have 500 people, and the personal attention that students often get at smaller schools is almost nonexistent here," said one student. Indeed, for those classes, the students almost exclusively deal with teaching assistants, not professors. For upperclassmen, the choices of classes broaden, and students can enjoy a huge selection of both large lectures and small seminars. "We have so many different opportunities," said one student. "So it is very important for the students to take advantage of them."

The coursework at Cornell is very challenging. "All incoming students should expect a lot of work," said one sophomore. The different colleges at Cornell have separate guidelines for graduation requirements, which tend to be extensive. One student said, "The required courses are sometimes good, but most of them are simply not useful." In addition, Cornell University mandates that all students take two semesters of physical education or an equivalent such as joining a sports team or even the marching band. In addition, everyone is required to pass a swim test.

Best Food

Cornell offers a variety of housing options. Most freshmen choose the traditional dorm buildings, but they also have the opportunity of living in Balch Hall, which is for first-year women only, the Townhouse Community, or one of the nine Program Houses, which are themed buildings that gather students of similar interests. Freshmen live in North Campus so that they get to know each other during their first year. The students are generally satisfied with their housing assignments, and there are generally plenty of singles available. One student pointed out, "compared to dorms in most other colleges, Cornell offers more choices, which is generally a good thing." Upperclassmen have even more options, and many of them live off-campus.

> "In terms of academics, we have something for everyone."

Cornell is known to have one of the nation's best dining services. There are 31 dining locations on campus, ranging from all-you-can-eat dining halls to à la carte cafés. In addition, there are three convenience stores to serve all those looking for snacks or daily necessities. Nevertheless, despite these excellent campus services, some upperclassmen do point out that "because of Cornell's reputation, many students' expectations of dining halls are too high when they first come here."

Fraternities

There are more than 60 fraternities and sororities at Cornell, and they boast 30% of the student population. These numbers mean that Greek life is an important part of Cornell's social scene. Freshmen especially tend to frequent the numerous frat parties during weekends. Drinking is, of course, one of the main activities there, but those who do not drink are not left out of the social scene. "If you don't drink, there are certainly a lot of activities that you are missing out on, but it's a big school. You can find many people who don't drink and still have fun," said one student.

The life of a student at Cornell can be summarized in one word: choices. Whether it is dining, classes, housing, or weekend parties, the university offers its students a great number of options and a tremendous array of opportunities to explore. Despite its removed location and the lack of personal attention often associated with large institutions, Cornell, with the resources and reputation of a world-class university, is still a top choice for those looking for an exciting and challenging college experience.—*Xiaohang Liu*

FYI

If you come to Cornell, you'd better bring "a bicycle to ride around campus."
What is the typical weekend schedule? "Just like most universities: parties Friday and Saturday nights, and recovering from the parties the rest of the time."
If I could change one thing about Cornell, I'd "move it next to New York City."
Three things every student at Cornell should do before graduating are "travel to every part of the campus—there is always something to discover, go to every single dining hall, and go swimming in the gorge, if you dare."

Eastman School of Music

Address: 26 Gibbs Street Rochester, NY 14604
Phone: 716-274-1060
E-mail address: admissions@esm.rochester.edu
Web site URL: www.rochester.edu/eastman
Year Founded: 1921
Private or Public: Private
Religious Affiliation: None
Location: Urban
Number of Applicants: 917
Percent Accepted: 29%
Percent Accepted who enroll: 47%
Number Entering: 125
Number of Transfers Accepted each Year: 20
Middle 50% SAT range: Unreported
Middle 50% ACT range: 22–28
Early admission program EA/ED/None: None

Percentage accepted through EA or ED: NA
EA and ED deadline: NA
Regular Deadline: Rolling
Application Fee: $100
Full time Undergraduate enrollment: 500
Total enrollment: 900
Percent Male: 45%
Percent Female: 55%
Total Percent Minority or Unreported: 11%
Percent African-American: 3%
Percent Asian/Pacific Islander: 6%
Percent Hispanic: 2%
Percent Native-American: 1%
Percent International: Unreported
Percent in-state/out of state: 17%/83%
Percent from Public HS: 80%
Retention Rate: 89%

Graduation Rate 4-year: 72%
Graduation Rate 6-year: 86%
Percent Undergraduates in On-campus housing: 73%
Number of official organized extracurricular organizations: 8
3 Most popular majors: Music
Student/Faculty ratio: 4:1
Average Class Size: 5
Percent of students going to grad school: 79%
Tuition and Fees: $20,320
In-State Tuition and Fees if different: No difference
Cost for Room and Board: $7,152
Percent receiving financial aid out of those who apply, first year: Unreported
Percent receiving financial aid among all students: 70%

D o you love music? Not just as a hobby, but as your life? Do you love music enough to practice until you get calluses from playing your instrument for so long? Enough to sing not just in the shower, but for hours at a time? If you do, you probably already know about this world-renowned music school. At the Eastman School of Music, serious musicians can immerse themselves in an environment where everyone thinks about, listens to, or plays music 24 hours a day.

Learning About Music

Eastman provides its students with a rigorous and thorough musical education as well as a solid humanities background. Most students are performance majors (the technical name is "applied music"). The next most popular majors are music education, composition and theory. The performance major requires three years of theory, two years of music history—covering everything from Gregorian chants to contemporary music—and, of course, weekly lessons. Performance majors must be competent piano players regardless of their chosen instrument. All performance majors must take Piano 101 and 102, or test out of this requirement. Eastman also has a humanities requirement, which can be filled with a one-semester Freshman Writing Seminar; courses in literature, history, languages, and philosophy; or a combination of these. Eastman students are serious about their humanities classes as well as their music, and classes are not easy. As one undergrad explained, "It seems like either you do really well or you completely fail." By senior year, most of Eastman's requirements are out of the way and students have more flexible schedules that allow them to audition for jobs or graduate school.

> ### "It's not like a big old party school."

Students interested in a more balanced course load between their liberal arts or science studies and their music concentration can pursue a B.A. or B.S. program at Eastman. Following this track, students take 40–60 percent of their courses in their music concentration of choice, compared to 80–90 percent for those pursuing a Bachelor of Music.

Because Eastman is part of the University of Rochester, students have access to the university's libraries and other facilities. Some of the humanities classes are held on the U of R campus, although as one student said, "You can make it all four years without leaving this campus." The reason many like to stay on the Eastman campus is the 15- to 20-minute bus ride to the U of R.

Students who apply to Eastman can ask to work with a particular professor, and many choose the school primarily to do just that. One student, for example, said he met his cello teacher at a summer music camp and decided to go to Eastman so he could continue to study with her. Some popular professors include clarinetist Kenneth Grant, pianist Barry Snyder, and flautist Bonita Boyd. The members of the Cleveland String Quartet also teach at Eastman and attract many to their classes and concerts. Students have substantial contact with faculty members, both in lessons and in other contexts such as chamber groups.

Living and Breathing Music

Everything at Eastman revolves around music. The musical motif on campus is inescapable; the snack bar is called the Orchestra Pit and the newspaper is called *Clef Notes*. Students rave about their "access to music on hand anytime." They can go to concerts every night if they want to; Eastman's calendar is filled with student and faculty performances by soloists and groups in the Eastman Theater, concerts every other week by the Rochester Philharmonic Orchestra (Eastman students get free tickets), and limitless other performances. Eastman's Sibley Library also has an enormous music collection (the second-largest in the nation), including books, manuscripts and recordings of "just about everything," one student said. Whenever undergrads want to listen to music but just can't find a concert to go to, they can always listen to their favorite symphony or opera at the library. Students who want to participate in athletics, student government, and other nonmusical extracurricular activities can journey over to the University of Rochester campus.

For those with the energy to play for more than the three to six hours they're expected to practice each day, there are plenty of opportunities to perform. Some students give several recitals a year, while others only do one in their four years at school. Many undergrads participate in chamber orchestras, quartets, or other small ensembles, either for credit or for fun. Jazz bands and string quartets are in constant demand at local restaurants and bars. Traveling Broadway shows that come to Rochester sometimes need a player to fill in and look to Eastman students for help. Students also have many chances to play at church services, weddings, and other special events.

Few Distractions

The Eastman campus is small, with just three buildings located in the heart of downtown Rochester: Eastman Commons, Sibley Library, and a classroom building. The food at the cafeteria is "pretty normal," according to one student. "It's got a salad and pasta bar, burgers and fries, and a frozen yogurt machine." In the dorm, freshmen live in doubles, and all upperclassmen have singles. Moving off campus is a popular option for juniors and seniors, but freshmen and sophomores are required to live on campus. Many students prefer the dorm because the surrounding neighborhood reportedly "isn't the greatest." Dorm life exposes students to an environment where everyone knows everyone else and has the same interests, so life can get a little boring. For those who need to get away, popular options include the Rochester Club, which features jazz every Friday night, and the Spaghetti Warehouse. Students also like to hang out and "go crazy" at nearby dance clubs in downtown Rochester.

Campus social life is somewhat limited. As one student explained, "It's not like a big old party school." For those who favor the Greek scene, there is one all-male fraternity, one sorority and one coed fraternity. The all-male and all-female groups each have a floor of the 14-story Eastman Commons to themselves. The all-male fraternity sponsors most of the parties, while the other Greek groups focus on community service work. Eastman has two annual formals, one in the fall and one in the spring. Small parties in the dorm are common; one student remarked that the delivery truck from a local liquor store is frequently spotted outside the dorm. Students don't seem to mind the low-key social scene; as one sophomore pointed out, "The fewer distractions, the easier it is to concentrate on practicing—which is good, I guess."

Freshmen typically arrive at Eastman from all corners of the world with visions of their names in lights. Each dreams of being the next great viola player, soprano soloist, or jazz pianist. These dreams become transformed over the next few years into more realistic aspirations. One junior explained that it doesn't matter to her whether she ends up as the soloist with a major symphony or a player in a community orchestra: "As long as I'm playing, that's cool with me."—*Susanna Chu*

FYI

If you come to Eastman, you'd better bring, "a lamp, because the dorms don't have overhead lighting."
What is the typical weekend schedule? "Practice and go to concerts."
If I could change one thing about Eastman, I would "change the weather!"
Three things every student at Eastman should do before graduating are "attend a seminar by a world-famous musician, play every instrument once, and go see Niagara Falls."

Eugene Lang College

Address: 65 W 11th Street Rm. 353, New York, NY 10011
Phone: 212-229-5665
E-mail address: langadmission@newschool.edu
Web site URL: www.newschool.edu/lang
Year Founded: 1978
Private or Public: Private
Religious Affiliation: None
Location: Urban
Number of Applicants: 1,670
Percent Accepted: 63%
Percent Accepted who enroll: 30%
Number Entering: 321
Number of Transfers Accepted each Year: 239
Middle 50% SAT range: M: 490–610, CR: 555–665, Wr: 560–660
Middle 50% ACT range: 23–28
Early admission program EA/ED/None: ED

Percentage accepted through EA or ED: Unreported
EA and ED deadline: 15-Nov
Regular Deadline: 1-Feb
Application Fee: $50
Full time Undergraduate enrollment: 1,294
Total enrollment: 1,294
Percent Male: 31%
Percent Female: 69%
Total Percent Minority or Unreported: 39%
Percent African-American: 4%
Percent Asian/Pacific Islander: 5%
Percent Hispanic: 6%
Percent Native-American: <1%
Percent International: 4%
Percent in-state/out of state: 32%/68%
Percent from Public HS: Unreported
Retention Rate: 73%

Graduation Rate 4-year: 35%
Graduation Rate 6-year: 47%
Percent Undergraduates in On-campus housing: 27%
Number of official organized extracurricular organizations: 34
3 Most popular majors: Unreported
Student/Faculty ratio: 15:1
Average Class Size: 16
Percent of students going to grad school: Unreported
Tuition and Fees: $33,060
In-State Tuition and Fees if different: No difference
Cost for Room and Board: $12,390
Percent receiving financial aid out of those who apply, first year: 71%
Percent receiving financial aid among all students: 51%

Students at Eugene Lang College know that theirs is not the typical college experience. They wouldn't have it any other way. "There was nowhere else I could see myself going," said one student. "I had to come to Eugene Lang." Eugene Lang College, also known as The New School for Liberal Arts, is one of eight colleges that comprise The New School, located in New York City's Greenwich Village. Founded in 1919 by a small group of intellectuals, The New School began as a forum for discussion, inviting the public to its lectures and encouraging dissent. Over the next 70 years, The New School founded seven other divisions, or colleges, including a design school and a program in jazz and contemporary music. Students apply to one of The New School's eight branches, but they reap the benefits of the close partnership of the divisions. Depending on their program of study, students are allowed to take a certain number of classes at other divisions of The New School. Students also report a great deal of "non-academic interac-

tion" between students in different divisions, as residence halls are not divided by college, and school-sponsored events bring New School students together.

An Engaging Environment

Students agree that the school's philosophy of learning distinguishes it from other colleges. Classes at Eugene Lang are virtually all seminars, though recently a two-lecture requirement was instituted for all students. Still, at Eugene Lang, the focus is on small classes and intense discussion. Students praised the richness of the classroom environment: "Students bring so many different arenas of thought into the classes, which make the classes deep and meaningful." The curriculum at Lang is highly interdisciplinary, with such programs as Arts in Context—the study of fine or performing arts in the context of the liberal arts—and Cultural Studies and Media. Furthermore, Eugene Lang is committed to developing exceptional writers. Writing is one of the most popular concentrations at Lang (which does not have "majors"), and one student pointed out that "even if you're not in the writing program, classes at Lang are writing-intensive." All freshmen are required to take a year-long writing class, about which students have mixed opinions. One student found the first semester of the class, on essay-writing, to be unhelpful, but she raved about the class's second semester, which surveyed methods of research. In general, however, students had nothing but praise for the academic experience at Eugene Lang. The small seminars allow for a high level of engagement with the material, students claim, and Lang's interdisciplinary approach fosters an uncommon academic experience. "People think hard about what they are reading and how it applies to their lives," one student said.

To Dorm or Not to Dorm?

Lang freshmen are guaranteed housing, and most choose to live on campus. Students reflected positively on their experience in dorms, pointing out that dorm life introduced them to the Lang community and often helped establish lasting relationships. Students from different divisions of The New School live together in the dorms, and one student praised this integration as a means of "bringing different people together to share their experiences, which is what The New School is all about." Loeb Hall is particularly coveted, since University Health Services are located there. The New School's dorms include many rooms with in-suite kitchens, making on-campus living an attractive alternative to finding an apartment in the city. What's more, with the exception of two, all dorms are located close to campus, while off-campus students must pay more to live close by or, more often, live in Brooklyn and endure the hassle of commuting to school.

Regardless, most students choose to live off campus after their freshman year. One upperclassman claimed that choosing to live on campus as an upperclassman was "a bad decision, because you're over the freshman thing—yelling in the dorms and going out a lot—but you're living with freshmen."

Because of the popularity of off-campus living, most Lang students have moderate or minimal interaction with the school's food service. Students who live on campus must purchase a meal plan, though depending on the dorm in which they live, students may be able to choose a less inclusive plan. One student maintained, "You can get better food around the city for the same price," though

he did point out that the cafeterias are conveniently located.

Student Politics and Bizarre Bars

Students at Eugene Lang are involved in both the campus community and the city community. Students claim that there is "a lot of programming for people looking for a college community," including frequent, sponsored events such as conferences, lectures and readings. But students also point out that many Lang students are more interested in exploring New York City than becoming involved in the Lang community. One student admitted that Lang is "infamous for not having much community" but added that this is "a superficial judgment." Indeed, many students enjoy off-campus parties that are "packed with Lang students." In conclusion, most students enjoy the opportunity to immerse oneself in the culture of New York and "make friends all over the city" while having the chance to "make of the Lang community what you want to make of it." Students point out that the interaction between Eugene Lang and the city is essential to the college's mission to integrate the arts and ideas of the city into the learning process. For example, many classes send students out into the city to study its religious culture or art.

> "Students bring so many different arenas of thought into the classes, which make the classes deep and meaningful."

One group of students, however, is committed to building community at Lang. The Lang Student Union, which is a consensus-based rather than representative body, meets regularly and is open to all Lang students. Student Union facilitators present proposals, which a single student has the power to block. Students speak highly of the consensus system, claiming that "it's rare that a compromise can't be reached" through negotiation. One Student Union facilitator highlighted a difficulty of the consensus system, however, pointing out that at a school as diverse as Lang, it's often difficult for students to agree on what they want.

Lang students are busy off campus as well. Many students work in the city, often as event promoters or party planners. As a result, many Lang students have ins at exclusive New York clubs. Otherwise, the weekend finds Lang students at apartment parties or nearby bars and clubs such as French Roast (a combination restaurant, bar and café) and the Bulgarian Culture Club. One student described Lang haunts as "weird places, with cheap drinks, that are on the verge of being incredibly bizarre."

One thing Lang students don't experience on the weekend is the college football game. There are no varsity sports teams at Lang, and there are a few IMs coordinated through the local YMCA, but students say that they are not popular. Lang does offer less traditional physical activities, such as Capoeira, yoga, salsa dancing, and meditation. One student recalled an epic dodgeball game, organized by a cultural studies professor, with particular fondness. But those looking for a traditional sports scene should look elsewhere.

To be sure, Eugene Lang is not your typical college. As students point out, taking the road less traveled is in Lang's nature: "The courses at Lang encourage you to think about things in different ways," said one student. "You piece together your own history."—*Kathleen Reeves*

FYI

If you come to Eugene Lang, you'd better bring "Said's *On Orientalism* and Foucault's *Discipline and Punish*, which are central to Eugene Lang's canon."

What's the typical weekend schedule? "The weekend starts on Thursday night. Friday is free for jobs, sleeping in or museum visits, and Friday and Saturday nights, we head to bars, coffee shops or apartment parties or visit friends at other schools around the city."

If you could change one thing about Eugene Lang, it'd be "the bureaucracy. Communication between the administration and the student body is often mediocre, and it's hard to get things changed or implement new programs."

Three things every student at Eugene Lang should do before graduating are "attend a reading by professors in the Writing Concentration, or read your own at an open mic event; read *The Weekly Observer*, an online publication, to find out about the many school-sponsored events, such as Air America tapings or a social justice conference; and attend a Student Union meeting."

Fordham University

Address: 441 East Fordham Road, New York, NY 100458
Phone: 718-817-4000
E-mail address: enroll@fordham.edu
Web site URL: www.fordham.edu
Year Founded: 1841
Private or Public: Private
Religious Affiliation: Roman Catholic-Jesuit
Location: Urban
Number of Applicants: 18,161
Percent Accepted: 47%
Percent Accepted who enroll: 20%
Number Entering: 1,702
Number of Transfers Accepted each Year: 683
Middle 50% SAT range: M: 560–660, CR: 570–670, Wr: 560–660
Middle 50% ACT range: 25–29

Early admission program EA/ED/None: EA
Percentage accepted through EA or ED: Unreported
EA and ED deadline: 1-Nov
Regular Deadline: 15-Jan
Application Fee: $50
Full time Undergraduate enrollment: 7,994
Total enrollment: 13,181
Percent Male: 37%
Percent Female: 63%
Total Percent Minority or Unreported: 37%
Percent African-American: 6%
Percent Asian/Pacific Islander: 6%
Percent Hispanic: 12%
Percent Native-American: <1%
Percent International: 2%
Percent in-state/out of state: 54%/46%
Percent from Public HS: 47%

Retention Rate: 90%
Graduation Rate 4-year: 71%
Graduation Rate 6-year: 76%
Percent Undergraduates in On-campus housing: 56%
Number of official organized extracurricular organizations: 133
3 Most popular majors: Business, Communication, Social Sciences
Student/Faculty ratio: 12:1
Average Class Size: 16
Percent of students going to grad school: 25%
Tuition and Fees: $35,257
In-State Tuition and Fees if different: No difference
Cost for Room and Board: Included
Percent receiving financial aid out of those who apply, first year: 74%
Percent receiving financial aid among all students: 63%

Combining the best of both worlds, Fordham is a small school in a big city. Featuring main campuses in Manhattan (Lincoln Center) the Bronx (Rose Hill), and most recently, Westchester, the school fosters an intimate environment while offering all the opportunities of New York City. One sophomore said, "The school is small enough that I always know at least two people who I am going out with, but it's also big enough so that I am meeting new people every day."

Up Close and Personal

The small school environment is something that Fordham students cannot praise enough. One junior gushed about how pleasant it was "to be more than just a name on the roster." The average class size is 22 and lectures hold about 40 students. The very few large lectures that the college offers hold about 100 people and are broken up into smaller discussion sections. There is also an atmosphere of intimacy with the professors, all of whom carry the reputation of being very accessible and keen to form long-term academic relationships with students.

The Fordham curriculum features an extensive list of requirements that dominate freshman and sophomore schedules. In the spirit of a true liberal arts education, the core strives to expose students to everything from math and English to theology, fine arts, and foreign languages. One junior complained that because of the core, "it's frustrating when the time comes to pick a major because you don't get into those classes until junior year." The wide variety of programs offered at Fordham does not make it easier to choose—the school's College of Business Administration, honors program, dance program, and the superb theater program are just a few of the many programs that stand out.

When it comes to academics, Fordham prides itself on rejecting grade inflation; students bemoan the grading curve as rather harsh and are used to working hard both inside and outside the classroom to earn their good grades. The introductory Accounting class is especially notorious for its level of difficulty. However, to compensate there are Music History and Life on Planet Earth, which are both known to be gut courses.

Work Hard, Play in New York City

The absence of Greek life on campus escapes the notice of most Fordham students. This is no surprise, however, as the students have New York City as their playground. The freshmen are known to frequent The Jolly Tinker, also known as Tinkers, a local bar. One sophomore explained, "As an upperclassman, you become more independent and Tinkers gets old." The students from Rose Hill campus center their social life mainly around what is known as the tri-bar area: Ziggy's, Mugzy's, and Howl at the Moon Inc (or Howl for short). Meanwhile, the more centrally located students of Lincoln Center go out to various Manhattan hotspots. The technically dry campus and presence of RAs discourages dorm parties; however, it is not unusual to hear of a house party at the apartment of one of the many upperclassmen who live off campus.

One junior described the social scene as revolving around the "work hard, play hard" mentality. People are very social and go out every weekend, and since the majority of students are able to avoid Wednesday classes, Tuesday night is also a popular choice for a fun night out. Fordham is a dry campus, meaning that students cannot have alcohol unless everyone in the room is 21. Despite the restrictions, drinking is a prominent feature on campus, and drugs, while more subdued, are not uncommon. The school, however, does make an effort to provide fun events such as Homecoming, President's Ball, and Spring Weekend. The Lincoln Center campus also features endless theater and other fine arts performances, which are popular among the students.

While the school is "definitely a clique school" as one junior described it, people are generally friendly and easy to meet. Friends are made mostly through classes, but also through dorms and extracurricular activities. A typical student of Rose Hill campus is described as "well-outfitted with designer labels and likely to be from New Jersey, Connecticut, or Long Island." The more colorful and diverse Lincoln Center campus is composed of mostly international and artsy crowds. Lack of diversity is a common complaint about the university, although the various cultural groups such as the Philippine-American Club and the Hispanic club El Grito de Lares are prominent on campus and organize a variety of cultural events.

The Fordham Bubble

Despite the urban location, the picturesque campus is a bubble into which students can escape. Gothic architecture, well-kept grassy areas, and the occasional good ghost story (the campus has been featured as one of the most haunted places in the U.S.) are welcoming to students. On warm days walking past Edward's Parade which students simply refer to as "Eddie's," "the field is covered with people—students lying in the sun, playing soccer, Frisbee."

Fordham may be considered a commuter school. Most students move off campus after their sophomore year or even earlier. The scarce housing is not guaranteed for everyone, and the dorms are nothing out of the ordinary. The coveted Walsh and O'Hare apartment-style residence halls are usually reserved for upperclassmen. Housing is assigned by lottery, so students rely on accumulated "credit hours" and strokes of luck for better housing options. The administration does get a lot of credit though for its above-average efforts to honor roommate requests. Freshman housing options include Alumni Court North and South, and Hughes Hall. Queen's Court is also a popular choice for freshmen, but they must first write a letter to the nun who is the head of the house to convince her why they belong there.

> **"Coming to New York City, I expected it to be less personal, but Fordham really surprised me in its friendly atmosphere."**

The Bronx location of Rose Hill, while not ideal, is not much of a problem. The campus is unanimously hailed as very safe, complete with tall gates separating it from the neighborhood and guards who scrutinize the ID of everyone who passes through. Students are always traveling into and around the city and visiting spots such as Fordham Road, which features great alternative shopping, or Arthur Avenue, which offers excellent dining and entertainment venues. The NYC public transportation system precludes the need for a car so parking is also not a problem.

"Food, I'd give it 60 out of 100," a sophomore assessed. While the Marketplace is a pretty dining hall, it tends to disappoint in both quality and variety. The alternative options, however, offer a welcome counterbalance. Flex dollars work at the more popular spots such as the Grill, the student deli, and Dagger John's University Restaurant. One thing students cannot complain about is lack of options for dining out—restaurants are plentiful and diverse, and the Bronx version of Little Italy offers excellent choices right in Fordham's backyard.

Get Active!
Students described school pride as "up and coming." This means that currently, while there is enough support for the sports teams (basketball games sell out, so get your tickets early!), the teams don't have the most successful records. But sports on campus do have a large presence in the form of intramurals, where teams such as the Flying Jesuits Ultimate Frisbee team are quite popular. The student newspaper, *The Ram*, is a weekly publication and many students also enjoy the controversial quips of *The Paper*, an alternative news source akin to *The Onion*.

Fordham students are active and committed to their extracurricular activities. Performance groups such as Mimes and Mummers and Experimental Theatre are very popular. Fashion for Philanthropy is a well-liked option, and many also take advantage of the volunteer opportunities in the shelters and other social justice organizations of the Bronx. Many students also choose to take advantage of New York City, and many work in internships in various businesses around the city.

Opportunities are definitely not lacking at Fordham. "Coming to New York City, I expected it to be less personal, but Fordham really surprised me in its friendly atmosphere," one junior said. Whether you want a sense of close community or a big city to seek adventure, Fordham has it all.—*Dorota Poplawska*

FYI
If you come to Fordham, you'd better bring "your designer shades."
What is the typical weekend schedule? "Hit the tri-bar area on Friday, Saturday sleep in, enjoy a day in the city shopping and at night it's bars again."
If I could change one thing about Fordham, I'd "make it more diverse."
Three things every student at Fordham should do before graduating are "eat out on Arthur Ave., go streaking across Eddie's Parade, and ride the Ram statue."

Hamilton College

Address: 198 College Hill
   Road, Clinton, NY 13323
Phone: 315-859-4421
E-mail address:
   admission@hamilton.edu
Web site URL:
   www.hamilton.edu
Year Founded: 1812
Private or Public: Private
Religious Affiliation: None
Location: Rural
Number of Applicants:
   4,962
Percent Accepted: 28%
**Percent Accepted who
   enroll:** 34%
Number Entering: 472
**Number of Transfers
   Accepted each Year:** 37
Middle 50% SAT range: M:
   640–720, CR: 640–740,
   Wr: Unreported
Middle 50% ACT range:
   Unreported
**Early admission program
   EA/ED/None:** ED

**Percentage accepted
   through EA or ED:** 47%
EA and ED deadline:
   15-Nov
Regular Deadline: 1-Jan
Application Fee: $75
**Full time Undergraduate
   enrollment:** 1,842
Total enrollment: 1,842
Percent Male: 48%
Percent Female: 52%
**Total Percent Minority or
   Unreported:** 34%
Percent African-American:
   4%
**Percent Asian/Pacific
   Islander:** 8%
Percent Hispanic: 6%
Percent Native-American:
   1%
Percent International: 5%
**Percent in-state/out of
   state:** 30%/70%
Percent from Public HS:
   60%
Retention Rate: 96%

Graduation Rate 4-year: 85%
Graduation Rate 6-year: 90%
**Percent Undergraduates
   in On-campus housing:**
   98%
**Number of official organized
   extracurricular
   organizations:** 80
3 Most popular majors:
   Economics, Mathematics,
   Politics and Government
Student/Faculty ratio: 10:1
Average Class Size: 14
**Percent of students going to
   grad school:** 40%
Tuition and Fees: $38,600
**In-State Tuition and Fees if
   different:** No difference
Cost for Room and Board:
   $9,810
**Percent receiving financial
   aid out of those who apply,
   first year:** 78%
**Percent receiving financial
   aid among all students:**
   41%

For a small school, it's a big deal. A reputation as a writer's college, an idyllic location in upstate New York and constant inclusion on "Little Ivies" lists have made Hamilton College a well-known destination for students across the USA. Add into the mix quirks like no distributional requirements and a campus that melds the new and the old, and you have a reputable, unique liberal arts college.

Build-an-Education

With the "open" curriculum, students are able to achieve the 32 credits they need to graduate in any number of ways. One freshman noted that she "never feel[s] forced into a class [she doesn't] want to take" while an upperclassman raved about the option to create one's own major. The only restriction is the writing requirement: each student must take 3 writing-intensive courses. Yet these too are "offered in almost all . . . subjects," a pre-med student explained, which means that even the science-minded

can easily attain the credits they need. This is possibly one of the reasons why strong majors range from Mathematics (though this department's popularity must be helped by its sushi-themed information sessions) to Creative Writing, Neuroscience to History. The same student may thus be taking classes with both a visiting neuroscience expert and a women's studies professor publishing her third book.

Yet academic life is not all fun and games. "Registering for classes is hell," one international student bluntly stated. With most classes comprising 15-20 people and few having more than 35, this is believable. A Hamilton education is not for the fainthearted: even a 200-level class might have homework due every 2 days. Balance, therefore, is key—most students interviewed emphasized this, mentioning that they purposely take classes with varying testing schedules. As they state that grading is difficult and A's are rare, this is probably a good strategic choice. "Weekdays means sitting and studying," a freshman clarified with a sigh. This can pay off: those with GPAs above 90% are placed on the Dean's List. For those who need external help, the world-class writing center and friendly math tutors supplement class time.

Amidst all this, professors and peers seem to play a crucial, calming role. The former are easy to get in touch with, often build close relationships with students and are popular among those they teach, with some, like Professors Nancy and Peter Rebinowitz, becoming almost campus celebrities. Even better: they are honest. One freshman said she was very glad her teachers told her "about the workload upfront—no bad surprises." And then there's the latter. Some variant of "every student is just as passionate as I am" was one of the first things out of interviewees' mouths. Fortunately, Hamilton seems to escape an issue that plagues many top colleges: over-competitiveness. This is just one manifestation of the sense of community permeating the school.

A Divided Campus, Social Spaces and Occasional Hay

You might want to sit down for this one: Hamilton College actually used to be two colleges, Hamilton for men and Kirkland for women. Today, the two are known as the "Light Side" and the "Dark Side," with a feigned rivalry and moaning about the 7-minute walk between them defining their playful relationship. It is the former, with its classic architecture, that students see as a haven for lax-bros and the prep-school brigade, while the modern, "funky concrete" Dark Side is viewed as housing "the hipsters and hippies, who are always sitting in the coffee shop listening to Phoenix on the big couches," said a student athlete. Freshmen are randomly assigned to dorms, and are placed via housing draw come sophomore year. Options abound for the selective, though, with some buildings designated as substance-free, for instance.

Off-campus living, on the other hand, is highly uncommon. Yet many argue that cars are integral to get anywhere. The town of Clinton seems to not satisfy Hamilton students—some visit regularly but many share the attitude of one freshman, who isn't sure if going into what her peers call "the village" is "worth the walk back up the Hill." It does however offer varied dining options for those tired of Hamilton Dining, featuring In-

dian, Mexican and Chinese cuisine alongside fast food staples.

But being sick of the food seems to be less likely these days. "The dining halls have stepped up their game," an international student explained. The three halls are also flexible with repeat meal swipes—"you can always go and get a snack."

Going out to party is a big part of life at Hamilton, as at any other college. Options vary: the majority of students drink, but the college helps sponsor non-alcoholic events as well. While one freshman said she was "unsure about how much fun [teetotalers] have," there does not seem to be any stigma attached to their decision.

College-sanctioned parties are hosted in the 4 "social spaces" that various organizations, from the eclectic a capella groups to cultural ones, can book. While large and raucous, such parties have a strict code that one student shared with us: "if the campus police arrive, put your drink down . . . just don't be drunk at the party." The administration is very strict about hard liquor, though its policies about beer are lax.

> "Strong majors range from Mathematics (though this department's popularity must be helped by its sushi-themed information sessions) to Creative Writing, Neuroscience to History"

Frat parties are another option. Greek events are open to all, and though many students do end up rushing, this is not seen as essential. Students flock to these events, as well as dorm parties and the occasional annual affair, such as the Farm Party, a bonanza of flannel and hay.

"A Nice Mix"

One aspect of Hamilton that every student commented on was its mix. Home to what a freshman called "liberal arts college hipsters, preppy lax bros and athletes, and outdoorsy granola eaters," it seems this college has no dearth of subcultures for one to slot into. Respondents spoke of making friends via the cozy classes, chance library encounters, or drunken nights out. Classic college behavior is clearly alive and well here.

Close-knit athletic teams, from women's rugby to football, and popular organizations like the Outdoors Club and service organization HAVOC also play key roles in bringing students together. Shared interests make for relationships that last and mean something to the individuals in them.

Adding to this sense of community is an institutional commitment to diversity. Hamilton participates in the national POSSE program, which brings student leaders from oft-neglected public high schools to top colleges across the States, while also running its own Hamilton Educational Opportunity Program for economically disadvantaged students in New York state. Together, these two keep the College on the Hill grounded, accessible and far from snooty.

A liberal arts college with the money to garner university-style resources, Hamilton is a popular and well-liked destination. "Hell yeah" was one girl's sentiment when asked about whether she'd enroll there again, and no respondents were unhappy with their experience. Offering an education in diverse subjects, and very generous financial aid packages, it breaks out of the "remote, humanities-obsessed" LAC stereotype. Few other schools are home to such a reputable, accessible milieu.—*Akbar S. Ahmed*

FYI

If you come to Hamilton, you'd better bring "a good hangover remedy."

Three things every Hamilton student has to do before graduating are "Hug the statue of Alexander Hamilton naked, hook up in the Kirner-Johnson building, and eat a panini at Opus, the campus coffee-shop."

What differentiates Hamilton: the open curriculum, student-faculty closeness and the streaking team.

H o b a r t   a n d   W i l l i a m   S m i t h   C o l l e g e s

Address: 629 South Main Street, Geneva, NY 14456
Phone: 315-781-3622
E-mail address: admissions@hws.edu
Web site URL: www.hws.edu
Year Founded: 1822
Private or Public: Private
Religious Affiliation: None
Location: Rural
Number of Applicants: 3,410
Percent Accepted: 65%
Percent Accepted who enroll: 25%
Number Entering: 545
Number of Transfers Accepted each Year: 27
Middle 50% SAT range: M: 540–630, CR: 530–640, Wr: Unreported
Middle 50% ACT range: 24–27
Early admission program EA/ED/None: ED

Percentage accepted through EA or ED: Unreported
EA and ED deadline: 15-Nov
Regular Deadline: 1-Feb
Application Fee: $45
Full time Undergraduate enrollment: 1,868
Total enrollment: 2,069
Percent Male: 46%
Percent Female: 54%
Total Percent Minority or Unreported: 4%
Percent African-American: 3%
Percent Asian/Pacific Islander: 2%
Percent Hispanic: 4%
Percent Native-American: <1%
Percent International: 2%
Percent in-state/out of state: 45%/55%
Percent from Public HS: 65%
Retention Rate: 85%
Graduation Rate 4-year: Unreported

Graduation Rate 6-year: Unreported
Percent Undergraduates in On-campus housing: 90%
Number of official organized extracurricular organizations: 77
3 Most popular majors: Economics, General English Language and Literature, General History
Student/Faculty ratio: 11:1
Average Class Size: 18
Percent of students going to grad school: 30%
Tuition and Fees: $31,850
In-State Tuition and Fees if different: No difference
Cost for Room and Board: $8,386
Percent receiving financial aid out of those who apply, first year: 74%
Percent receiving financial aid among all students: 64%

Set atop a hill, adjacent to the majestic Seneca Lake, sits the campus of Hobart and William Smith Colleges. HWS is actually two schools with separate deans, admissions officers, student governments, and athletic departments. Women apply to William Smith and men apply to Hobart, but all students attend the same classes and share the same beautiful campus. Due largely to its small student body of around 2,000 undergraduates, HWS is the perfect school for college applicants looking for an intimate community and a chance to build strong relationships with professors.

A Liberal Arts Education

Hobart's academics are in very much the typical liberal arts style. Following a semester schedule, students are expected to take four classes each term. It's required for students to take classes in each of the basic disciplinary areas including art and civic engagement. The art credit can be satisfied by a semester of music lessons and a credit for civic engagement, for example, can be earned by volunteering for America Reads. Depending on the subject and professor, class sizes can vary but on average are about 20 students. With 49 majors ranging from English to Studio Art and 20 minors from Child Advocacy to Peace Studies, students are also still given the choice to design their own majors. "It's a liberal arts education: strong across the board," one student affirmed. The worst academic characteristic at HWS, according to one student, is that "some of the students in the classes don't appreciate where they are. You can find peers who challenge you, but sometimes they can be entirely uninspiring." Similarly uninspiring are gut classes like "Rocks for Jocks" also known as Geology 101, and "Shakespeare for Non-majors." Pat McGuire, an economics professor characterized by his sweater vests, and Craig Rimmerman, a political science and public policy professor, are both passionate and invested educators to look out for when searching for an extra class. Despite the inevitable hard professor, students consistently praise the teaching staff for their passion, accessibility and personal investment in their students.

"Because class size and the HWS community are small, you can get a lot of one-on-one time with the professors who are passionate about their subject and about teaching," a student explained. "If you stand out, you can benefit enormously from them."

With an intimate academic setting and thoroughly invested faculty, it is easy to get individual help and to form strong connections with professors, but there are always international opportunities if HWS gets too small. Taking advantage of the well-developed opportunities abroad for students, many take a break from HWS and venture off to other countries for a semester or year abroad.

Luck of the Draw

Housing, much like other college campuses, is often the luck of the draw. Freshmen are placed in a dorm before arriving on campus. Some are placed in "Dirty Durfee," though according to one student, it may not be all that dirty anymore, or in the new dorms recently constructed on the hill. As for upperclassmen, they enter a lottery with their future roommates. Choices for living range from an all-girls dorm, an all-guys dorm, coed housing, fraternities, or theme housing. Students are allowed to create their own theme house by petitioning the dean and getting a group of people together. Some recent theme houses have been the Political Activism House, the Honors House, and the Outdoor Recreation House. Senior year students can live in O'Dell's Village, a group of condominiums on the far side of campus equipped with a bathroom and kitchen. Seniors can also live off campus if they choose. "Housing is where you meet most of your friends," a student said.

Saga is the main dining hall on campus. With its three-tiered construction, Saga has the feel of a gymnasium, and the all-you-can-eat menu can be a physical challenge for your digestive system. Saga is part of the newly renovated campus center, and students enjoy hanging out there and socializing. If Saga doesn't hit the spot, there is a café that is à la carte and a pub that serves food and beer if you are of age. Oftentimes during the warmer months, students will take lunch out on the quad and lie out in the sun or walk up the hill to the lake.

Around the World . . . or Not

Campus social life seems to be characterized by hanging out on the quad during warmer months, dormitory socializing, hitting up Parker's or whichever bar hasn't been shut down by the local police, and the occasional frat party (no sororities, sorry, girls!). Students typically stagger into the Water Street Café or Bagels and Cakes the "morning after" for a rejuvenating breakfast. With only six fraternities, Greek life isn't a big presence on campus and there is no pressure to join. One campus party to look forward to is the spontaneous "Around the World" party, which happens a few times a year in O'Dell's Village. Typically, a resident of one unit will decide on a whim that it's time for a night of "Around the World." Each unit chooses a different drink from some place in the world and students walk around the village trying each drink.

> "Because class size and the HWS community are small, you can get a lot of one-on-one time with the professors who are passionate about their subject and about teaching."

Although they have parties with diverse drinks, the attendees, for the most part, are not. The majority of the student body at HWS are white middle-class Americans, many of whom are from upstate New York or Massachusetts. The cultural clubs are strong, close-knit organizations as a result of their small numbers and provide a welcoming community within HWS for its minority students. What HWS lacks in student diversity, it makes up for in diversity of opportunities. HWS has everything from an NCAA Division I national championship-winning sailing team to a coed "drinking team with a softball problem," and students have the freedom to start their own clubs. Students are deeply dedicated to their extracurricular activities and find it easy to be "a big fish in a little pond." On Seneca Lake in beautiful Geneva, New York, with a plethora of academic and extracurricular opportunities, many students have found that they are happy where they are. One recent graduate said that HWS was the best place for him because "it gave me the opportunity to pursue any extracurricular or academic goal I wanted. The small community really offers the opportunity for leadership." —*Hayden Mulligan*

FYI

If you come to HWS, you'd better bring "a windbreaker because campus gets cold from the breeze off the lake."

What's the typical weekend schedule? "Saturdays are brunch at Saga, studying, head to Parker's, back to the frats for late night fun and Sundays are devoted to studying."

If I could change one thing about HWS, "I'd enhance the theater and fine arts departments."

Three things every student should do before graduating are "swim in Seneca Lake, go on a Finger Lakes wine tour, and eat a meal with their favorite professor."

Hofstra University

Address: 100 Hofstra University Bernon Hall Hempstead, NY 11549
Phone: 516-463-6700
E-mail address: admissions@hofstra.edu
Web site URL: www.hofstra.edu
Year Founded: 1932
Private or Public: Private
Religious Affiliation: None
Location: Suburban
Number of Applicants: 18,471
Percent Accepted: 54%
Percent Accepted who enroll: 17%
Number Entering: 1,730
Number of Transfers Accepted each Year: 641
Middle 50% SAT range: M: 550–630, CR: 540–630, Wr: Unreported
Middle 50% ACT range: 23–26
Early admission program EA/ED/None: EA

Percentage accepted through EA or ED: 36%
EA and ED deadline: 15-Dec
Regular Deadline: Rolling
Application Fee: $50
Full time Undergraduate enrollment: 8,444
Total enrollment: 11,187
Percent Male: 46%
Percent Female: 54%
Total Percent Minority or Unreported: 17%
Percent African-American: 9%
Percent Asian/Pacific Islander: 5%
Percent Hispanic: 7%
Percent Native-American: <1%
Percent International: 1%
Percent in-state/out of state: 50%/50%
Percent from Public HS: Unreported
Retention Rate: 79%
Graduation Rate 4-year: 34%

Graduation Rate 6-year: 53%
Percent Undergraduates in On-campus housing: 80%
Number of official organized extracurricular organizations: 124
3 Most popular majors: Accounting, Marketing/Marketing Management, General Psychology
Student/Faculty ratio: 14:1
Average Class Size: 16
Percent of students going to grad school: 29%
Tuition and Fees: $25,700
In-State Tuition and Fees if different: No difference
Cost for Room and Board: $10,300
Percent receiving financial aid out of those who apply, first year: 90%
Percent receiving financial aid among all students: 84%

Formerly an extension of New York University, Hofstra University is now an independent institution of higher learning to more than 12,000 undergraduates and postgraduates. Located on Long Island away from the noises of New York, yet close enough for students to have easy access to all the amenities of the Big Apple, Hofstra offers a large number of opportunities in academics and research, allowing students to have a meaningful and fulfilling college education. Furthermore, the university is well known for its dedication to education in public service, including serving as the host of one of the 2008 presidential debates. With its great location and strong academics, Hofstra is an intriguing college choice for prospective students.

Nine Schools

The university is divided into nine different units, offering close to 150 undergraduate majors. "We have a big selection of majors.

As long as you know what interests you, Hofstra has something for you," said one student. In fact, the majors range from the usual liberal arts degrees to some unique ones rarely found in other universities, such as Exercise Specialist and Urban Ecology. "I think what is great here is that you can have broad majors like Economics or more specific majors like Business Economics," said one student. "That type of flexibility makes sure that you can receive the kind of education that you want."

The one shortcoming, however, is the lack of options in engineering and science. "I think we are so much more focused on social sciences than things like physics and mechanical engineering," said one student. Nevertheless, the university is certainly attempting to strengthen its science departments, starting with the establishment of a medical school in 2011. The idea is that it will raise the profile of the university in the scientific community and enlarge the number of opportunities in the field for both undergraduate and graduate students. It also means greater research opportunities for the more entrepreneurial students.

The university also offers an honors program, available through first-year application. Students who achieve high scores during their time at Hofstra are also invited to join the Honors College. During the first year, honors students enroll in a program called Culture and Expression, which consists of two courses per semester that are often used to introduce students to the art of small class discussions. The idea is that students learn from professors and from each other through debate and discussions, not just through lectures. In addition, students can also enroll in Honors Housing, creating an intellectually stimulating community both inside and outside of the classrooms.

Similar to most universities, Hofstra has a lengthy list of distributional requirements, which are courses that students must take before graduation. They are designed to expose students to a variety of academic fields. These courses include humanities, natural science, social science, and cross-culture, very similar to the undergraduate requirements in other colleges. What is unique about Hofstra is the need to complete classes in interdisciplinary studies, meaning courses that combine contents from different fields of study. "I know some people think it is a pain to complete all the required classes," said one student. "I think they can be tedious, but you still have some flexibility; you are likely to find a few classes that you enjoy."

The classes at Hofstra are relatively small, compared to other universities of similar size. As to the difficulties of classes, they tend to vary. "If you do not want to have too much work, talk to people who have taken the classes with the same professor before to learn about the work load before you take the class," said one student. "It is all about researching about your classes before enrolling in them." Many professors can be very helpful, as long as the student reaches out to them. "Professors are friendly, but it is not like they are going to approach you if you don't understand anything. You need to be proactive," said one student. Overall, students believe that they have access to a very good undergraduate education.

Hofstra does have a competitive admissions process. In fact, less than 60 percent of students are accepted every

year. According to students, the university boasts people of great talent and abilities. "You'll find some really intelligent people here," said one student. "And a lot of people have unique talents in music or art. It is really amazing."

Hempstead and New York

Hempstead, where Hofstra is situated, is on Long Island. For students, activities around the immediate area are limited. Of course, given the large student population, there are plenty of parties happening around campus. However, overall, the village does not offer much beyond a small collection of bars and restaurants. The good news is that New York City is only half-an-hour away by train. "I go to the city all the time," said one student. "Even if you are on Long Island, the public transportation is very convenient in getting you to the city." Once students are in Manhattan, of course, there are plenty of things to do from concerts to shopping to the great nightlife of New York City.

> **"You'll find some really intelligent people here."**

Over 4,000 students live in Hofstra's residential halls, which range from the traditional dorms to apartments. The university offers residences in six different locations, all of which are conveniently located with easy access to classrooms. Despite the large number of options, the quality of living arrangement is very similar, and students are mostly satisfied, though not overly enthusiastic. "The dorms are what you would expect for college: small but adequate," said one student. While university residences are highly recommended for freshmen so that they can meet more people and become used to the college environment, many upperclassmen move off campus into the surrounding apartments and houses. "I think it is important that people learn to live completely independently. I think you are still sheltered when you live in dorms," said one student.

There are more than 20 dining halls, cafés, and restaurants on the campus of Hofstra. The school runs more than a dozen of those facilities, thus offering a large number of choices. However, as students point out, the variety of options does not mean that the food is great. "I have to go off campus for dining a few times a week," said one student. "The food is fine, but it gets boring and repetitive after a while."

Greek life is an important part of social life at Hofstra as there are a large number of fraternities and sororities on campus. Nevertheless, students who are not interested in them can find plenty of other social opportunities with different clubs, organizations, or simply people they meet in classes or around campus.

Urban and Suburban

The fact that Hofstra falls between an urban and a suburban university is a great selling point. Students are able to enjoy the relative quietness of a Long Island village while being less than an hour away from one of the busiest cities in the world. As a major university with a large number of research centers, academic opportunities abound for students, making Hofstra an excellent choice to spend four years of your life. —*Xiaohang Liu*

FYI
If you come to Hofstra, you'd better bring "school spirit."
What is the typical weekend schedule? "Go to NYC."
If I could change one thing about Hofstra, I'd "change the distributional requirements."
Three things every student at Hofstra should do before graduating are "go to Dutch Festival, go to NYC often, and visit the rest of Long Island, too."

Ithaca College

Address: 100 Job Hall, Ithaca, NY 14850-7020
Phone: 607-274-3124
E-mail address: admission@ithaca.edu
Web site URL: www.ithaca.edu
Year Founded: 1892
Private or Public: Private
Religious Affiliation: None
Location: Suburban
Number of Applicants: 11,235
Percent Accepted: 74%
Percent Accepted who enroll: 22%
Number Entering: 1,797
Number of Transfers Accepted each Year: 143
Middle 50% SAT range: M: 540–630, CR: 530–630, Wr: Unreported
Middle 50% ACT range: Unreported
Early admission program EA/ED/None: None

Percentage accepted through EA or ED: NA
EA and ED deadline: NA
Regular Deadline: 1-Feb
Application Fee: $60
Full time Undergraduate enrollment: 6,260
Total enrollment: 11,999
Percent Male: 45%
Percent Female: 55%
Total Percent Minority or Unreported: 10%
Percent African-American: 3%
Percent Asian/Pacific Islander: 4%
Percent Hispanic: 4%
Percent Native-American: <1%
Percent International: 2%
Percent in-state/out of state: 46%/54%
Percent from Public HS: 75%
Retention Rate: 84%
Graduation Rate 4-year: 71%

Graduation Rate 6-year: 76%
Percent Undergraduates in On-campus housing: 70%
Number of official organized extracurricular organizations: 172
3 Most popular majors: Communication Studies, Visual and Performing Arts, Business/Marketing
Student/Faculty ratio: 12:1
Average Class Size: 16
Percent of students going to grad school: 40%
Tuition and Fees: $30,606
In-State Tuition and Fees if different: No difference
Cost for Room and Board: $11,162
Percent receiving financial aid out of those who apply, first year: 90%
Percent receiving financial aid among all students: 85%

Ithaca College may have started out as a conservatory of music in downtown Ithaca, but it now offers strong academics in addition to a world-class music program. Though many students may look at Ithaca and see only Cornell, Ithaca College offers students a smaller, tightly-knit community combined with a great education.

"We're Equipped with the Biggest . . . Radio Tower"

Out of Ithaca College's six undergraduate schools—including Communications, Health Sciences, Humanities and Science, the Music School, Interdisciplinary and International Studies and the Business School—Communications, along with Health Sciences and the Music School, are the three most popular.

Most of the Roy H. Park School of Communications students (or "Parkies" as they're called) end up winning national honors from the top professional organizations and are often offered great opportunities both on campus and off campus. IC also has two radio stations. IC's radio tower is the biggest thing on Ithaca's skyline. The Music School is considered to be the hardest school, both in terms of admittance and academic rigor. The students at this school are also the ones who "do their own thing," effectively separated from the rest of the college. As one senior music student said, "Music majors don't have a lot of free time, with recital attendances, ensemble requirements, practices, etc."

The Health Science and Human Performance School have mainly two types of majors, the Physical Therapy majors (PTs) and the Physical Education majors (PEs). Due to the physical component of the two majors, it is not surprising, said one student, that the "PTs are a bunch of jocks." The program offers several combined bachelor's and master's five year programs, many of which also provide professional certification.

While there is a General Education requirement and most departments push for students to take courses outside their school, students end up really "staying within their schools." A very popular course, however, that many students across the schools end up taking is "Anatomy and Physiology," mainly because it is a requirement for many majors, and it fulfills a common science requirement.

The academics at IC "aren't necessarily hard," but they do give "a substantial amount of homework, about four-five hours' worth a night," said one student, though students at all the schools seemed to agree. Teachers are "really open and willing to talk, especially outside of class" and they're "genuinely interested in helping you in the class."

IC isn't considered to be of the same academic caliber as its neighbor Cornell University, but that doesn't mean the teaching quality suffers. "I was surprised," one student noted, "that almost all the professors here are well-known in their fields." Due to the college's relatively small size, only intro classes are large, and most classes have only 20–30 students. "Make a good impression early," one student recommended. "IC is small enough that by the time junior and senior year comes around, you'll have a rep, and you'll want it to be a good one." Another student agreed that the smaller campus required student interaction. "Ithaca College is definitely not the place to go if you want to stay in the background."

Division III Contenders and Other Extracurriculars

The large amount of jocks from the Health Science School translates into a great athletic program and great athletic teams. Ithaca College has one of the strongest athletic programs in the NCAA's Division III. School spirit is fierce at Ithaca College, which generates not only great games but also great attendance. The IC Bombers are well known for their football team and women's crew team, and "everyone and their mom[s] attend the football games." The big football game of the year is the Cortaca Jug, against the SUNY Cortland Red Dragons, "which you must go to" to cheer on the team, though admittedly it's also "an excuse to get drunk." Other particularly popular sports include baseball, softball, and women's lacrosse. If you don't have the time for varsity sports, there are also club sports and recreational (intramural) sports. Students can be competitive and aggressive on the field, but they are all there "just to have fun." Despite the heavy athletic programs, the athletic facilities are still "pretty accessible."

Of course, if sports aren't your thing, there are numerous extracurricular clubs and community service opportunities. Specifically, there are a large number of performing opportunities and performances to attend. But be forewarned: "If you're not a music major, it's really hard to get lessons because they're in great demand." A lot of clubs on campus "fall in with the Ithaca atmosphere and end up being about human rights, animal rights or union rights." Everyone can get a job on campus, but finding a job off campus is a lot harder because, as one student said, "we have to compete with all those people at Cornell."

White Bread

The stereotype of the students is that they are "white bread, mainly white, upper middle class students from the Northeast" who can afford the hefty tag attached to an IC education. When asked whether there is a lot of ethnic diversity on campus, students commented "not really, unless you're in the music school." However, "the gay and lesbian population is well-sized."

> "Ithaca College is definitely not the place to go if you want to stay in the background."

The common stereotype is that IC students are either artsy, due to the strong Music School and Theatre departments, or jocks, because of the Health Science School. "Parkies are a mix—half jocks (marketing, television and radio) and half artists (visual arts and cinematography)." Most students agree that the stereotype is mainly true, but "there are enough exceptions to make life interesting."

Staying on (or off) Campus

Residential housing, one freshman said, is "nice but not that great." According to several upperclassmen, "The buildings aren't ugly, and the rooms are small but adequate." While IC offers a large variety of halls to live in (some coed, others single-sex), the majority of students cite residential life as "not a strength of IC." Most students move off campus senior year but are required to live on campus the first three years. The Towers (two large towers that are dorms) are the most prominent features of Ithaca College. Visible from almost anywhere in Ithaca, they are famous for both the fact that they sometimes have parties (one of two places to party on campus) and that on New Year's eve, the lights in the building change year numbers (i.e., from 08 to 09). The Terraces are the only dorms that offer suites, and most seniors either live in the Garden apartments, the recently built Circle apartments or move off campus to live on Prospect Street. Almost all of the halls (except the apartments) house freshmen, but the Upper and Lower quads have a larger concentration of underclassmen.

"Ithaca College really makes an effort to help freshmen transition," said one student. In addition to the three residential halls the school offers to freshmen only (with twice as many RAs), the college also hosts events, technically open to all undergraduates but specifically targeting freshmen, as an alternative to drinking. With concerts, comedians and dances, IC makes an effort to help students feel comfortable on campus. "The school really tries to limit the amount of underage drinking on campus." Drinking still occurs, just not on campus. Most parties are held off campus, specifically on Prospect Street, known as "the college town of IC." On Friday and Saturday nights, people can expect parties on Prospect Street and in the Circle apartments. However, most of the partying by Ithaca College students doesn't occur there either. In fact, most partying doesn't even happen on the Ithaca College side of Ithaca. "If you want to party, go to a Cornell frat party." That's right, IC students go to Cornell frat parties, mainly because "alcohol is a lot less controlled there. And as it turns out, they aren't nerds after all."

In terms of the drug scene, IC is becoming more and more a non-smoking campus (at least in the Residence Halls), but most people at IC who smoke, smoke pot. Greek life isn't all that big on the IC campus except for a few small music fraternities and sororities. Finally, students are not thrilled with the food options on campus. "The food here isn't all that great either, unless you go to Terrace, which is pretty good." Rated between the three dining halls, Terrace is the best, Campus Center the worst, and Towers is somewhere in-between. Terrace is described as "beautiful, because it has fountains in the dining hall, and offers a great variety of food." Meal plans are required for those who live on-campus, and they all cost the same, although different combination plans are offered with the possibility of "Bonus Bucks" that can be used for food elsewhere. "Bonus bucks make life so much simpler since I'm freed from having to eat on campus and can eat at random times."

"Ithaca is Gorges"

Ithaca is a great, "but small," community to live in, which is "very open." "Most people take enough advantage of Ithaca" but in order to do so "you *need* a car." In fact, most upperclassmen have cars, though freshmen find it harder to have a car on campus because they have to pay more for student parking. "People feel the need to get off campus sometimes, and cars are the way to do it." The other source of transportation is Ithaca's bus service TCAT, a "wonderful resource, especially if you don't want to drive during Ithaca's winters." Two of the most popular clubs among Ithaca College students are the Haunt and the Octopus downtown, known for their live (and most of the time, local) music. Popular bars are Micawbers, Moonshadow Tavern, and Blue Stone, but like most bars in Ithaca, "don't expect the bars to fill up until after 11."

If partying is not your thing, the town of Ithaca offers an assortment of other things to do. The many waterfalls and state parks near Ithaca make it one of the most beautiful places to live. Right near the campus is Six Mile Creek, a "wonderful place to go skinny dipping." Another popular activity is gorge jumping (a word of caution, clear the rocks!). If it's "Ithacating—any form of pre-

cipitation with a cloudy sky"—you can always go to one of the two independent movie theaters in town, or hang around the Ithaca Commons.

A Word on the Weather

If there is one thing upon which all students agree it is this: Ithaca is cold. Yet IC students understand that they live in Ithaca, and thus must live with Ithaca's weather. Ithaca is known for not only its freezing winters, cloudy and rainy springs and falls, but also for the erratic changes from one to another. "Only in Ithaca could you experience all the seasons in one day." It starts to snow in late October and early November, and despite the spring thaws, it's possible for it to snow in May.— *Jesse Dong*

FYI
If you come to Ithaca College, you'd better bring "good winter boots and an appreciation for sports and music."
What is the typical weekend schedule? "Party at a Cornell frat party Friday night, cheer on the IC Bombers, attend a performance, party some more at Cornell and hit up a few bars, spend all of Sunday doing homework."
If I could change one thing about Ithaca College, I'd "make it more handicapped accessible."
Three things every student should do before graduating from Ithaca College are "jump in the fountain, go to a Cornell frat party, and attend the Cortaca Jug."

The Juilliard School

Address: 60 Lincoln Center Plaza, New York, NY 10023-6588
Phone: 212-799-2000 ext.223
E-mail address: admissions@julliard.edu
Web site URL: www.juilliard.edu
Year Founded: 1905
Private or Public: Private
Religious Affiliation: None
Location: Urban
Number of Applicants: 2,138
Percent Accepted: 8%
Percent Accepted who enroll: 75%
Number Entering: 122
Number of Transfers Accepted each Year: Unreported
Middle 50% SAT range: Not Considered
Middle 50% ACT range: Not Considered
Early admission program EA/ED/None: None

Percentage accepted through EA or ED: NA
EA and ED deadline: NA
Regular Deadline: 15-Nov or 1-Dec, depending on major
Application Fee: $50 or $100, depending on major
Full time Undergraduate enrollment: 500
Total enrollment: 842
Percent Male: 53%
Percent Female: 47%
Total Percent Minority or Unreported: 51%
Percent African-American: 9%
Percent Asian/Pacific Islander: 17%
Percent Hispanic: 5%
Percent Native-American: <1%
Percent International: 17%
Percent in-state/out of state: 82%/18%
Percent from Public HS: Unreported
Retention Rate: 94%

Graduation Rate 4-year: 80%
Graduation Rate 6-year: 83%
Percent Undergraduates in On-campus housing: 50%
Number of official organized extracurricular organizations: Unreported
3 Most popular majors: Piano and organ, Stringed instruments, Voice and opera
Student/Faculty ratio: 3:1
Average Class Size: 6
Percent of students going to grad school: Unreported
Tuition and Fees: $28,640
In-State Tuition and Fees if different: No difference
Cost for Room and Board: $11,250
Percent receiving financial aid out of those who apply, first year: 85%
Percent receiving financial aid among all students: Unreported

The Juilliard School, currently located at Lincoln Center in New York City, is a conservatory style post-secondary institution founded in 1905 that trains undergraduate and graduate students in dance, music, and drama. Juilliard has an 8% acceptance rate of students who apply and undergo a rigorous audition process to ensure that Juilliard hones the best talent in the performing arts. It is not a surprise, therefore, that Juilliard is one of the top performing arts conservatories in the world.

Huge Talent in a Tiny Campus

Located in the performing arts capital of the world, the Juilliard School has produced hundreds of top-notch artists from its two-building campus in New York City. Distinguished alumni include world-class violinist Itzhak Perlman, groundbreaking choreographer Paul Taylor, and award-winning actor Robin Williams. Juilliard, a conservatory school of about 1000 students, is located in Manhattan's Upper West Side at Lincoln Center, home to New York Philharmonic, the Metropolitan Opera, and New York City Ballet. The conservatory's close proximity to renown performance companies provides Juilliard students valuable connections and work-study opportunities. While Juilliard's music division is the largest program, the dance and drama programs are much smaller yet equally reputable.

Preparing for the Professional Path . . . and Also Going to College

Entering Juilliard is extremely competitive as auditions are the determining factor and the school has only an 8% acceptance rate. Upon entering the school, the students are immersed in their art, spending up to 14 hours in class and rehearsals before starting their academic work. Juilliard's academic program differs substantially from that of liberal-arts colleges because most classes Juilliard students take are related to their artistic division and rarely if ever do they take math or sciences courses. All Juilliard students complete a core Humanities class, which most students describe as an English class. Students are subsequently required to take one academic course a year that is not related to their division, courses that are considered electives. There are a few opportunities to take classes at Columbia or Barnard, but most students do not have the time. A music student said, "Humanities courses are very intense and I think some of the teachers forget we're there for music. Finally [you] finish your work and you have to go practice." Finding a balance among academic coursework with technique classes, rehearsals, private lessons, and individual practice is extremely hard according to students. Juilliard academic courses are small, around 15 students. Several students noted that the academic coursework is very rigorous. One student said, "[The] top notch professors, most of them went to ivy league schools and expect ivy league work."

As a result of the rigorous workloads, Juilliard's social life varies among the divisions. Music majors have to spend their weekend days practicing according to one student: "It's usually practicing during the day . . . not everyone does or can go out at night." Some students said that while some students do opt to go out on the weekends, others spend their Saturday nights practicing and rehearsing. The dance and drama majors are perceived to have a more flexible weekend schedule. A dance student said, "The dancers are kind of the crazy ones, going out, dressing up and having fun. A lot of musicians don't really go out on the weekends." She added that many students go to upperclassmen off-campus apartments for house parties or see performances downtown, for which they can get free or discounted tickets. A drama student said that "It's hard to be at Juilliard and not be social—at least for the drama students." Yet he also said that students are very balanced when it comes to drinking because there is no time to recover from a couple of nights out in a row and this would take a toll on one's schoolwork. A music student stated that students have fun but, "[they] never let partying get in the way of their goals."

Juilliard's campus consists of two connected buildings, the main building where classes meet and the dormitory building. All freshmen are required to live in the dormitories and each is paired with a roommate of a different division to promote social interactions among the different divisions that can end up polarized. Some upperclassmen remain in the dorms but most usually move off-campus to Upper West Side apartments. Students generally feel safe on campus, and they feel safe to practice until late at night because they can enter the dorm building without having to go outside.

The Music Men (and Women)
The Music division is the largest division in the school, consisting of about 600 students and incorporating vocal/opera and jazz studies in addition to traditional orchestral instrumental study. At the audition final round students perform in front of the faculty, and each student is chosen by a faculty member to pursue private instruction. The music student's relationship with his private instructor is very important as it helps foster individual improvement and collaboration with the teacher. The relationship provides the student with opportunities for further music study outside of school. As one student described, "[Students] go where the teacher teaches in the summer to continue studying all year," although another option is participating in summer music festivals. During the school year, however, many students form extracurricular small chamber music ensembles and can obtain work experience through job opportunities offered through Juilliard's career office to play at weddings or other events. Another popular work-study job available at Juilliard is ushering at local theaters.

One student said that the general perception of music study at Juilliard is that students "hop around the hallway and play instruments" yet she also emphasizes the difficulty of her field of study. Required classes include private lessons, piano class, music theory (which also involves musical composition), ear training, and music history. Students participate in an orchestra which allows students of different grades to collaborate and interact. A first-year student remarked, "Upperclassmen were very welcoming; since this school is so small there is more socializing among all the classes." Apart from the orchestral and music ensembles, however, the music division does not have a division-wide community as the division is relatively large and comprised of many sub-divisions based on instrument type. Nevertheless, most of the students interviewed agreed that Juilliard students display a lot of pride in their school.

Home is Where the Barre is

The dance division is the most physically-demanding discipline offered at Juilliard, and the exertion only complicates the balance between academic work and dance classes with only 15-minute breaks between classes. Entering the Juilliard dance department is physically trying—right from the three to four hour audition, where students take a ballet and modern dance class before the first cut, and those who qualify perform a choreographed solo. Students who pass the second cut then experience a rehearsal-setting class where they display their skills in partnering and learning new choreography before the final round, which is an interview. The extremely selective dance department admits about 25 students a year. One student said that the auditions were "nerve-wracking in that they make cuts."

As a result, class sizes are very small, with an entire grade participating in the same modern class for example. Dance students have to take a number of required courses apart from ballet and modern technique classes, including anatomy, dance history, and literature in music (a music theory course taught by a composer rather than a musician). Rehearsals, which can last late into the night, and performances also factor into students grades. Students at the end of the day are exhausted; on weekends many students sleep-in and try to go out on weekends, although they find it difficult.

As is common in the performing arts world, many of the dance students in a class already know each other from prior dance schools and summer dance intensives. Nevertheless the small group of dancers creates an intimate community which allows freshmen to interact with sophomore and seniors alike. Freshmen start to interact with seniors through Freshmen Initiation in which freshmen are paired with a senior and find out who the senior is only after completing a series of (usually embarrassing) tasks. Another tradition is that seniors celebrate the last Wednesday of their college career of their school years by running around the dance studios naked.

All Their World is a Stage

The drama division is the smallest division in the school, and it also includes a playwright subdivision that accepts only three students a year. A short personal statement determines if a student is granted an audition that includes a recitation of two Shakespearean and two contemporary monologues; the total audition lasted the entire day for some students between callbacks and waiting periods. Once accepted, drama students enter a close-knit group where drama traditions and stories are kept secret although a dance student mentioned that drama first-year students visit Times Square and "do some ridiculous acts."

While a drama class consists of under 20 students, the class is divided into four groups and different groups of four to five students take classes together. Drama students take a wide variety of classes including improvisation, miming, clowning with masks, stage combat, diction. A surprising requirement is three 90-minute sessions of strenuous physical workout, which include tai chi and yoga. Concerning the workouts a drama student said "[It] makes a massive difference when you're in classes 14 hours a day. You can endure longer." Not only do drama students endure long weekdays, they also have Saturday rehearsals which last up to six hours. There may be less pressure for rehearsals when there are no performances taking place, but the professors increase the workload such as more poems to learn or vocal skills to practice. "We're never taking it easy," says one drama student.

> **"Once you're in . . . you don't have to outdo each other. We already know you're one of the best"**

Students may have endured a grueling audition, but they do not audition for shows while in college. Instead, drama professors select students for specific roles in performances based on a student's fit in a role or a student's need to be challenged. The teachers' close relationship has provided students with surprise benefits. One student said, "[I was surprised at] how successfully the teachers have brought out qualities and useful tools that I already have. They drag things out that anybody could have expected I have."

Attributes Across the Artistic Arenas

Contrary to popular belief, students from all divisions agree that there is little competition among students. One student said that if there is any competition present is mostly internal competition to improve one's skills. Another student added that "Once you're in [Juilliard] . . . you don't have to outdo each other. We already know you're one of the best."Juilliard also has a collaborate attitude among the divisions. The school hosts a ChoreoComp where third-year composers create music that dance majors use for choreography.

The school holds auditions across the country, but there are many international students at Juilliard as well, showing the school's commitment to recruiting the best artists to go on toward bright futures in the arts. Juilliard students are focused on their career from the start, cognizant of the heavy work involved. Students recommend others to see as many in-school performances as possible because of the high calibre of talent. Yet they also make sure to take advantage of New York City to reap the benefits of living at the heart of a vibrating arts culture that is even more accessible through Juilliard's resources.

Encore Remarks

The Juilliard School is extremely selective because they are creating the next generation of top-notch artists. Juilliard students undergo an intense liberal-arts program in addition to their artistic specialties. The students' coursework is integral to professional development as they hone their skills and artistry. As rising professional artists, Juilliard students are extraordinarily dedicated to their crafts. Some students succeed in balancing work and play, but for many students their work is also their play because their desire to reach their potential is the ultimate game to win.—*Clarissa Marzán*

FYI
If you come to Juilliard you'd better bring "ear plugs (the musicians practice all the time)."
If you come to Juilliard you'd better leave behind "your math and science textbooks"
If there was one thing I could change about Julliard would be to "make the music division smaller."

Manhattanville College

Address: 2900 Purchase Street, Purchase, NY 10577
Phone: 914-323-5464
E-mail address: admissions@mville.edu
Web site URL: www.manhattanville.edu
Year Founded: 1841
Private or Public: Private
Religious Affiliation: None
Location: Urban
Number of Applicants: 3,927
Percent Accepted: 50%
Percent Accepted who enroll: 27%
Number Entering: 535
Number of Transfers Accepted each Year: Unreported
Middle 50% SAT range: M: 500–610, CR: 500–620, Wr: Unreported
Middle 50% ACT range: 20–25
Early admission program EA/ED/None: ED

Percentage accepted through EA or ED: Unreported
EA and ED deadline: 1-Dec
Regular Deadline: 1-Mar
Application Fee: $65
Full time Undergraduate enrollment: 1,845
Total enrollment: 3,022
Percent Male: 33%
Percent Female: 67%
Total Percent Minority or Unreported: 47%
Percent African-American: 7%
Percent Asian/Pacific Islander: 2%
Percent Hispanic: 15%
Percent Native-American: <1%
Percent International: 8%
Percent in-state/out of state: 64% /36%
Percent from Public HS: Unreported
Retention Rate: 74%

Graduation Rate 4-year: 51%
Graduation Rate 6-year: 57%
Percent Undergraduates in On-campus housing: 76%
Number of official organized extracurricular organizations: 48
3 Most popular majors: Business, Psychology, Visual & Performing Arts
Student/Faculty ratio: 11:1
Average Class Size: 14
Percent of students going to grad school: Unreported
Tuition and Fees: $31,620
In-State Tuition and Fees if different: No difference
Cost for Room and Board: $13,040
Percent receiving financial aid out of those who apply, first year: 94%
Percent receiving financial aid among all students: 68%

With its 100-acre campus located in Purchase, New York, a small town thirty minutes from New York City, Manhattanville College offers its students the intimate academic environment of a small college while encouraging them to explore the diversity, resources, and opportunities of the nearby city. Manhattanville students receive a distinctively personal and well-rounded liberal-arts education and do not need to worry about a lack of activities to keep them busy—even if they have to travel the thirty minutes to find them.

All Planned Out: Preceptorial and Portfolio

Although Manhattanville is a small school with only 1,700 full-time undergrads, it offers over fifty majors and minors, as well as the option to design your own. As one student studying dance and business noted, "I looked at all the schools in the tri-state area. Manhattanville was the only one that said I could major in Irish Step Dancing." All students are required to have a minor in addition to a major. Some students said the choice gained in the number of majors is lost in the limitations imposed by many distributional requirements. Students must take six credits from four of five areas: mathematics and science, social sciences, humanities, languages, and fine arts. But an upperclassman offered advice, saying that these involved requirements can actually make a course load "less intimidating when your semester is not entirely consumed by classes specific to your major."

Apart from the distributional requirements, all freshmen take the Preceptorial, a year-long seminar that functions to help students develop college-level thinking, reading, and writing skills, introduce them to important topics in various fields, and guide them in their studies at Manhattanville. Students may choose among Preceptorials covering a diverse array of issues in current events. The instructor of a Preceptorial is also the students' freshman-year academic advisor who will be one of the many faculty members who "really care about the education of each individual student" throughout college. Manhattanville students really do gush about the degree of personal attention given to them: "I have gotten to know all of my professors personally, and I can go to them whenever I need help or mentoring."

> "I looked at all the schools in the tri-state area. Manhattanville was the only one that said I could major in Irish Step Dancing."

Another distinctive feature of the Manhattanville education is the Portfolio System. Each student meets with a faculty advisor to plot his or her academic path at the beginning of freshman year. In the spring of each following year, students meet again with their advisors to assess their progress, adjust their plans, and put their best work into a portfolio. At the end of senior year, faculty members evaluate the students' portfolios before allowing them to graduate. Students find that the portfolio actually helps them greatly during their studies because it forces them to plan ahead, as well as after graduation, because they have already gathered and reflected upon their best work and are therefore prepared for graduate school or a job search.

Outside the Classroom

While Manhattanville's academic program and small size create a great sense of academic closeness, the campus, in terms of social life, is not very close-knit. This is due in part to the proximity and appeal of the city, but also because many of the students at Manhattanville are from the tri-state area and either commute daily or go home often on the weekends. As a result, the campus is not as lively as many other colleges on the weekends.

There are, however, a number of major activities throughout each year that attract most of the student body, including Fall Fest, a carnival-like music festival, and its spring counterpart, Quad Jam. Reid Hall—better known as "the Castle"—is the site of the "Castle parties," formals in the winter and spring. The Castle parties bring students together, as an upperclassman reflected: "Most students go to the formals, and they all have different themes, which makes each one special." In addition, there are over thirty clubs and organizations rang-

ing across broad interests, from the Latin Dance Club to the History Club to the Punk Rock Appreciation Club. Students said one of the most popular activities is writing for *The Touchstone*, the Manhattanville newspaper. The student government acts as a liaison between the students and the administration, often planning activities to try to keep the campus lively on the weekends for the students who remain on campus.

But the outward migration of students on the weekends is not to say that the facilities and dorms are lacking. Students have a number of housing options, as there are four dorms, all of which are coed and said to be comfortable. Spellman, a "dry hall," is the freshmen dormitory. Upperclassmen can choose from Founders, Damman, and Tenney, the latter two of which offer various suite-style living options. Students can choose between different-sized suites, with the option of both singles and doubles that share a bathroom and common room. Students have a choice between meal plans that vary in the number of meals taken in Benziger Dining Hall and "meal points" redeemable at local cafés and a pub. Dorms also have communal kitchens that students can use if they get tired of dining hall fare.

Manhattanville to Manhattan

Manhattanville is unique in the extent to which it encourages its students to drift from the quiet serenity of Purchase once in a while. The college sponsors trips to New York City that are often integrated into academic coursework. These trips also give students a chance to decide if they truly want to experience life in the city, in which case Manhattanville offers a Semester in New York City program. Participants who are fortunate enough to make the cut live in the city, taking classes taught by Manhattanville professors and gaining work experience in internship positions at major companies located in the Big Apple.

There are also trips whose sole purpose is simply to give students a chance to explore the fun side of New York City, through events like a cruise around Manhattan, visits to the Metropolitan Museum of Art, and ice-skating in Central Park. The Office of Student Activities subsidizes some of the trips, allowing students to see shows like *The Lion King* on Broadway and the Radio City Christmas Spectacular for affordable prices. Students often also visit New York City on their own, taking in the sights and just enjoying themselves on the weekends, a possibility thanks to the Metro-North train connecting Purchase to the city.

Manhattanville is ideal for students who seek personal attention, opportunities in a nearby dynamic city, and a serene campus to return to after an exciting weekend. As one student put it, "The best thing to do is just walk around [New York City]. It's so exciting. Then I get to come back up to Manhattanville where I feel so safe."—*Michelle Yu*

FYI

If you come to Manhattanville, you'd better bring "a lot of Tupperware, Mac 'n' Cheese, and ramen noodles."

What is the typical weekend schedule? "Going out to the city, staying in the dorm drifting from room to room with friends, or going to the pub to eat and watch TV."

If I could change one thing about Manhattanville, I'd "[improve] the lack of events on campus."

Three things every student at Manhattanville should do before graduating are "go to all the Castle parties and sports events, go to the White Plains Diner at 3 a.m., and camp out on the quad."

New York University

Address: 22 Washington Square North, New York, NY 10011	**Early admission program EA/ED/None:** ED	**Graduation Rate 4-year:** 77%
Phone: 212-998-4500	**Percentage accepted through EA or ED:** 33%	**Graduation Rate 6-year:** Unreported
E-mail address: admission@nyu.edu	**EA and ED deadline:** 1-Nov	**Percent Undergraduates in On-campus housing:** 52%
Web site URL: www.nyu.edu	**Regular Deadline:** 13-Jul	**Number of official organized extracurricular organizations:** 350
Year Founded: 1831	**Application Fee:** $65	
Private or Public: Private	**Full time Undergraduate enrollment:** 19,482	**3 Most popular majors:** Drama, Finance, Liberal Arts
Religious Affiliation: None	**Total enrollment:** 20,965	**Student/Faculty ratio:** 12:1
Location: Urban	**Percent Male:** 40%	**Average Class Size:** 15
Number of Applicants: 37,245	**Percent Female:** 60%	**Percent of students going to grad school:** 24%
Percent Accepted: 32%	**Total Percent Minority or Unreported:** 53%	**Tuition and Fees:** $37,372
Percent Accepted who enroll: 39%	**Percent African-American:** 4%	**In-State Tuition and Fees if different:** No difference
Number Entering: 4,648	**Percent Asian/Pacific Islander:** 19%	**Cost for Room and Board:** $12,810
Number of Transfers Accepted each Year: Unreported	**Percent Hispanic:** 8%	**Percent receiving financial aid out of those who apply, first year:** 80%
	Percent Native-American: 0%	
Middle 50% SAT range: M: 630–720, **CR:** 620–720, **Wr:** 620–720	**Percent International:** 6%	**Percent receiving financial aid among all students:** 53%
	Percent in-state/out of state: 64%/36%	
Middle 50% ACT range: 28–31	**Percent from Public HS:** 65%	
	Retention Rate: 92%	

New York University was founded in 1831 by Albert Gallatin with a goal to establish "in this immense and fast-growing city . . . a system of rational and practical education fitting for all and graciously open to all." Today's NYU students agree that this goal has been met. "NYU has a variety of different schools that provide different types of education and skills," said one freshman. "It truly has something for everyone."

Fourteen Schools, Fourteen Stereotypes

The university comprises 18 different schools, colleges, and divisions that specialize in everything from the arts to business to nothing in particular. "Tisch kids work on film and production; the College kids are into liberal arts; Gallatin kids don't know what they want to do and are pretty much free to make it up as they go along," summarized one junior. The university's roughly 19,000 undergraduates are distributed amongst the schools—but not evenly. The majority of undergraduates enroll in the College of Arts and Sciences (CAS).

When asked to explain the typical NYU student, one Tisch student said the task was impossible. "I can't define a typical NYU student without splitting the stereotype into schools," he explained.

Despite the clear breakdown of these conceptions, students praised the university for fostering interaction between students, regardless of school. "We live together. We don't get separated. The lack of separation spreads into our social lives" said one sophomore. Others agreed. "There are a lot of misconceptions, but NYU is really just one school."

Size Isn't Everything

At a university this large, you might assume students are necessarily disjointed and separated. But at NYU, even without a central campus, there is something about these "Violets" that keeps everyone together.

"NYU is not too big," concluded one Stern student. "It's very possible to know a lot of people and be very involved, and by being involved, to get to know a lot more people. It's definitely what you make of it." Other students agreed, stressing that students have to be proactive to take full advantage of all that the university has to offer. "As long as you stand up and get involved it's very possible to know people high up and get your face recognized," said one senior.

Despite the size of its population, students say NYU never fails to cater to its students' diverse and eclectic appetites. "We're one of the top schools in the country for providing vegan and vegetarian options at all our dining halls, and kosher options as well," said one junior. "They observe Shabbat in one of the dining halls every week." In addition to more traditional dining hall experiences, students can eat at places like Chick Fil-A, Quiznos, Dunkin' Donuts, and Starbucks. Overall, students praised the university for providing, if not gourmet food, at least a wealth of options. "You can't complain for the most part."

The City That Never Sleeps . . . and the Students That Don't Either

To say that NYU doesn't offer your typical college experience is an understatement.

With the heart of the university located in hip, bustling Greenwich Village, students have the luxury of spending four years with New York City as their workplace and playground. And since the university has seriously improved its transportation system in recent years, students at NYU freely engage in the wealth of opportunities in and around their sprawling campus.

"The social life is great, though it's not your normal college scene," explained one senior. Although NYU features some Greek life, there is not much of a formalized network of fraternal organizations on campus. Students described its members as the "few and the proud," saying that they are often indistinguishable from the general population. The university nightlife is primarily focused on the city's various offerings. "There aren't any house parties or frat parties, but you go bar and club hopping."

Some students complained that the social life is overly centered on the city itself. "You go to clubs and a lot of them are big student spots, but unless it's a 'college night,' a lot of times, I'm not even sure who my peers are," said one freshman. "It's really strange that way. The nightlife culture almost forces you to arrive with a fake ID in hand." However, she was quick to add—"Of course, it's fun. Unlike my friends at other colleges, I'm guaranteed a party come Friday or Saturday night . . . or even Tuesday night."

Sports fans might not be as fond of the fun offered up by NYU. Without a football team, the university lacks what some might consider an intrinsic element of any college experience. Though host to spectacle-drawing varsity sports teams like volleyball, basketball, fencing, and soccer, NYU students consistently fail to flock to the stands. "Attendance at sports events is, well, there really isn't attendance at sports events," said one junior. Yet despite lackluster athletic support, NYU students are by no means lacking in school spirit or university pride. "There's not really a sport that brings us together, but NYU kids love NYU. There's a lot of school spirit here."

But We Work Too!

NYU maintains much of its popular academic reputation courtesy of the Leonard N. Stern School of Business and Tisch School of the Arts. But students say the university's excellence reaches far beyond the likely targets. Many cited the economics department as an undiscovered NYU jewel. "We've been the Number One Dream School for a few years now," said one sophomore. "You don't get that way by focusing only on a small group of specialized students," she continued. "Obviously, the university is offering something for us all."

> "There's not really a sport that brings us together, but NYU kids love NYU. There's a lot of school spirit here."

Other students were quick to explain deficiencies in the overall system. "I wish I had smaller classes," said one freshman. "As much as NYU tells you you're not just another number, with some professors it just seems that way." Many courses include lectures and smaller, weekly sessions led by teaching assistants (TAs). One CAS junior succinctly declared, "TAs are pretty much a regular thing here."

Gallatin is often cited as offering more opportunities for small seminars than CAS, but as students advance in their majors, they are given preference to enter seminars in CAS, each generally including roughly 20 stu-

dents. "It's a university. Lectures are part of the definition of that term. It's just part of the deal, but as you get older, you have more opportunities to take intimate classes," explained one sophomore.

Shanghai? Ghana? Don't You Wanna?

Whether or not NYU offers the most opportunities for small classes, it is certainly the ideal school for a student looking to study abroad. The university offers study abroad programs in over 25 countries—if you can bear to separate yourself from the bright city lights. Students from other colleges and universities are routinely offered opportunities to study abroad as part of NYU's expansive program. "Where else could you spend the semester in Shanghai or Ghana?" asked an enthusiastic junior. "It's just the best place to be for people who want to learn firsthand about other cultures."

NYU is famous (and infamous) for both its nightlife and its internships. Those looking to capitalize on a variety of resources, work on their dance moves, and master the Big Apple during their college years will find such a choice quite appealing.—*Nicholle Manners*

FYI

If you come to NYU, you'd better bring "a sense of openness because it's a very diverse school."

What's the typical weekend schedule? "Work during the day, party at night all through the weekend starting Thursday night."

If I could change one thing about NYU, I'd "improve financial aid and alumni support: excluding Stern."

Three things every student at NYU should do before graduating are "explore the city, study abroad, and meet lots of new people."

Parsons School of Design

Address: 65 Fifth Avenue, New York, NY 10011
Phone: 212-229-8910
E-mail address: parsadm@newschool.edu
Web site URL: www.parsons.edu
Year Founded: 1896
Private or Public: Private
Religious Affiliation: None
Location: Urban
Number of Applicants: 2,921
Percent Accepted: 50%
Percent Accepted who enroll: 44%
Number Entering: 653
Number of Transfers Accepted each Year: Unreported
Middle 50% SAT range: M: 490–610, CR: 480–590, Wr: 490–600
Middle 50% ACT range: 22–26
Early admission program EA/ED/None: None

Percentage accepted through EA or ED: NA
EA and ED deadline: NA
Regular Deadline: 1-Mar
Application Fee: $50
Full time Undergraduate enrollment: 3,180
Total enrollment: 3,815
Percent Male: 22%
Percent Female: 78%
Total Percent Minority or Unreported: Unreported
Percent African-American: 4%
Percent Asian/Pacific Islander: 17%
Percent Hispanic: 7%
Percent Native-American: 0%
Percent International: 33%
Percent in-state/out of state: 27%/73%
Percent from Public HS: Unreported
Retention Rate: 87%
Graduation Rate 4-year: 53%

Graduation Rate 6-year: Unreported
Percent Undergraduates in On-campus housing: 23%
Number of official organized extracurricular organizations: 25
3 Most popular majors: Design, Fashion, Illustration
Student/Faculty ratio: 9:1
Average Class Size: Unreported
Percent of students going to grad school: Unreported
Tuition and Fees: $34,460
In-State Tuition and Fees if different: No difference
Cost for Room and Board: $12,390
Percent receiving financial aid out of those who apply, first year: 88%
Percent receiving financial aid among all students: 44%

D o you ever dream about your name featured on white tents in Bryant Park during Fashion Week? Do you know you want to spend a life creating and designing but don't quite know how to do it? Do you watch *Project Runway* religiously? If you answered "YES!" to any of these questions, perhaps Parsons School of Design is the right place for you. Founded in 1896 as an art school, Parsons has a rich history of having the first undergraduate programs in disciplines like graphics design, interior design, and advertising. It is now part of The New School, a university network in New York City known for its avant-garde teaching style and unique philosophy. Parsons students enjoy the energy of New York City, the mentorship of notable faculty, and learn the necessary skills to enter the art world after graduation.

The Foundations and Beyond

Undergraduates at Parsons can graduate in four years and obtain either a Bachelor of Fine Arts or a Bachelor of Business Admin-

istration. Those who are particularly ambitious and desire a more varied education experience can opt for the five-year joint BFA and BA program, called the BAFA program. This program is hosted in conjunction with Eugene Lang College. Students are often overwhelmed by the changes that college brings and by the stimuli that a new environment provides. Parsons tackles this problem by having every freshman take "Foundation" courses. "They're mandatory for the BFA program . . . some of the stuff seems repetitive and dull, but it just made the classes that I took my sophomore year so much more rewarding and interesting," one junior said. The program ensures that students have the necessary technical and methodological understanding of art to succeed in future classes. These classes are broad enough to be applicable to whatever majors the students choose in the end, along with being designed to enhance visual thinking.

Some of the more popular majors at Parsons are Illustration, Design and Visual

Communications, and Fashion Apparel Design. The Fashion Design department at Parsons is perhaps the most renowned—its graduates include fashion designers Donna Karan and Tom Ford, plus Tim Gunn, mentor to the designers on *Project Runaway* and the former dean of this department. Students in this major are known to be "very cutthroat" and a sense of intense competition is omnipresent in these classrooms. "People are not only very secretive about what they're designing but are constantly trying to outdo each other," one Fashion Design major said. However, she added, "But some people are genuinely helpful and will give you ideas. I guess you just have to find the right crowd."

> **"You become a pro at finding free things to do. But otherwise you will be spending a lot of money on the weekends."**

Another program for students who are particularly driven and motivated is the Chase Scholars Program. Named for William Merritt Chase, the Impressionist painter who founded the art school that eventually became Parsons, Chase Scholars have a "strong interest in design, high academic achievement, and well-developed critical thinking skills but limited studio experience." Special scholarships are also given to those who get into the program.

Jet-Setting

If you start to feel a little overwhelmed by the competition at Parsons, you may want to consider going abroad. "Many juniors take a semester or the whole year to go abroad. I was in Paris the first semester this year. It was wonderful to be studying in a different culture!" one junior raved. Paris is a popular destination for juniors not only because "it's the only city that holds a candle to New York in terms of it being a fashion and art mecca," but because Parsons has a campus in Paris. Some areas of study in which Parsons Paris excels are Communication Design, Fashion Design, and Photography and Fine Arts. Other exchange programs that are available include the Chelsea College of Art and Design in London, Sydney College of the Arts in Australia, and Bezalel Academy of Art and Design in Jerusalem, Israel.

If you can't bear to leave New York for a semester but still want to go abroad, Parsons has an excellent international summer program. These Summer Intensive Studies are open to both Parsons students and non-Parsons students, and are typically five weeks long. Classes try to mesh the subject matter with the culture and history of the host country. For instance, the Summer Intensive Studies in Paris offered "Architecture and Interiors of Paris: A Drawing Investigation and Photography in Paris."

"A Mini-Version of New York"

Even if you don't go abroad, you will be exposed to different ways of thinking, different cultures and backgrounds due to the diversity of people at Parsons. While there will be many resident New Yorkers in your classes, many students are from out of state and abroad. Parsons recognizes the importance of having a diverse learning environment and is particularly international-student-friendly. The summer before freshman year, international students attend the Summer Orientation Program for International Students (SOPIS). This is an opportunity for international students to get settled in a little early but also for a chance to take English as a Foreign Language (ESL) classes and to learn about the city and how the American university system works. "Parsons is like a mini version of the city itself. There are so many people here from other places in the world—we're all learning and inspiring each other everyday," one New York native said.

The Big Apple

Not uncommon of schools in large metropolises, Parsons lacks a central campus with greens and dorms. The main campus is in Greenwich Village and the other campus is in the Garment District—fittingly, the David M. Schwartz Fashion Education Center is located there. Parsons has a few residence halls for its students. The Marlton House is most famous for housing Beat poets in the 1960s. The most popular dorm is the Union Square Residence, where students have Union Square Park and its concerts, farmers markets and shopping right at their doorstep. Freshmen primarily live in Loeb Hall and the 13th Street Residence. Meal plans are available and there are many options in terms of eating venues that Parsons students share with students from The New School.

While the residence halls save students the hassle of finding an apartment in Manhattan, many students choose to live off campus. "Moving off was the best thing for me; I live with someone who goes to NYU and it's been awesome. I'm more independent and I've learned how to cook!" one senior said. Because so many students move off campus, the social scene at Parsons is very fragmented and school spirit is a little weak. However, most students don't seem to mind this, for "there's always something to do in New York."

On or off campus, all students agree that New York is an expensive city to live in: "You become a pro at finding free things to do. But otherwise you will be spending a lot of money on the weekends." But New York serves as an inspiration and playground for all Parsons students. Endless galleries and museums, concerts and music, good places to eat, and the eclectic bar and clubbing scene are all taken advantage of. The fact that there are very few social opportunities on campus does not hinder these students from finding their own niche in the city. The power and the liveliness of New York City is integral to the Parsons experience—so if you think you can thrive in a bustling city life and manage the workload, Parsons may be the school for you!—*Lee Komeda*

FYI

If you come to Parsons, you'd better bring "a good winter jacket, a fake ID, and a need for creative outlet!"

What's the typical weekend schedule? "Drink and smoke at a friend's apartment and go out to hit up a few bars. Or, alternatively, I could be in the studio working non-stop."

If I could change one thing about Parsons: "a central hangout spot would be great . . . also if the two campuses were closer together."

Three things you should do before graduating are "meet as many people and network for the future, participate in the fashion show, go to as many museums as possible."

Rensselaer Polytechnic Insititute of Technology

Address: 110 Eighth Street Troy, NY 12180-3590
Phone: 518-276-6216
E-mail address: admissions@rpi.edu
Web site URL: www.rpi.edu
Year Founded: 1824
Private or Public: Private
Religious Affiliation: None
Location: Suburban
Number of Applicants: 11,249
Percent Accepted: 44%
Percent Accepted who enroll: 27%
Number Entering: 1,356
Number of Transfers Accepted each Year: 199
Middle 50% SAT range: M: 650–730, CR: 600–690, Wr: 580–680
Middle 50% ACT range: 24–29
Early admission program EA/ED/None: EA
Percentage accepted through EA or ED: 47%

EA and ED deadline: 1-Nov
Regular Deadline: 15-Jan
Application Fee: $70
Full time Undergraduate enrollment: 5,394
Total enrollment: 7,521
Percent Male: 73%
Percent Female: 27%
Total Percent Minority or Unreported: 26%
Percent African-American: 4%
Percent Asian/Pacific Islander: 11%
Percent Hispanic: 6%
Percent Native-American: <1%
Percent International: 2%
Percent in-state/out of state: 41%/59%
Percent from Public HS: 72%
Retention Rate: 95%
Graduation Rate 4-year: 64%
Graduation Rate 6-year: 82%

Percent Undergraduates in On-campus housing: 53%
Number of official organized extracurricular organizations: 164
3 Most popular majors: Business, Computer Engineering, Electrical Electronics and Communications Engineering
Student/Faculty ratio: 14:1
Average Class Size: 17
Percent of students going to grad school: 24%
Tuition and Fees: $36,950
In-State Tuition and Fees if different: No difference
Cost for Room and Board: $10,730
Percent receiving financial aid out of those who apply, first year: 98%
Percent receiving financial aid among all students: 94%

Located in upstate New York, Rensselaer Polytechnic Institute is known for churning out Noble Prize–bound engineers and NHL-bound hockey pros. Though the heavy workload and brutal winter weather can be intimidating, RPI's strong programs and cutting-edge facilities make it a mecca for engineers, architects and hockey fans alike.

A (Metric) Ton of Work

When asked why he chose RPI, one student simply said: "It sets you apart in the engineering world." RPI's stellar reputation and top-notch academic programs make it an appealing option for students interested in engineering and a host of other fields. Students can apply to one of five schools within the university: Science, Architecture, Engineering, Humanities and Social Sciences or Management and Technology. The architecture program is praised for its professors and its small size—while the university enrolls over 5,000 undergraduates, the prestigious architecture school enrolls 60–70 freshmen per year. Those who make the cut gain access to RPI's lighting research center, one of the best in the country. While RPI is predominantly known as an engineering school, the school is working to further develop its programs in other areas. The new EMPAC (Experimental Media Performing Arts Center) will mix cutting-edge technology with the arts, a reflection of the growing diversification of academic options.

Slackers beware: RPI academics are intense. As one engineering student said: "It's definitely a lot harder than I thought it'd be. They say it's hard, but it really is. They're not lying." It's common knowledge that students must spend at least 30 hours a week outside of class "to even have a chance in hell of getting by." Most people devote much more time than that, setting aside an entire day (9 a.m. to midnight) each week to catch up on work. At least the professors believe in curving. Though students' final grades are determined by how well they perform in comparison to their peers, competition is not cutthroat. While it does exist, some say "It's us against the teacher more than us against ourselves." Furthermore, the combination of a rigorous program and RPI's good name means that graduates are well-prepared for the working world. Students praise the career center and the university as a whole for its focus on landing students enviable jobs after graduation.

All students in the engineering program must take a set of core classes, usually during their first three or four semesters. While students say that the relevance between these core classes and their specific major can seem doubtful at first, professors aim to make the courses applicable to all programs. "You might not know what it relates to when you take it, but longer down the road you get it," said one junior.

With rigorous programs and a large student body, RPI undergrads are encouraged to take a proactive stance in their education. "If you don't put out the effort, you're a number," said one student. Extensive class preparation is required, and students must learn a number of things on their own from the textbook. Students say it "goes both ways" in terms of professor accessibility—some are always available while others are constantly traveling the world. The university is known for offering undergraduates an abundance of research opportunities.

Bricks & Bread

Campus buildings boast the best of both worlds: on the outside, the gothic structures have a "traditional, collegiate look," while on the inside they offer cutting-edge technology. Most of the campus is wireless, and every classroom is set up so that students can plug in their laptops. The university even provides incoming freshmen with a personal laptop and wireless card.

> "The standard-issue RPI kid is probably a big computer nerd."

The Quad, RPI's largest residence area, sits on the main campus. It houses upperclassmen in single, double, or triple rooms. There are also 10 residence halls, including five freshmen dorms, surrounding the Commons Dining Hall. Upperclassmen looking to escape traditional dorm life can live in the recently renovated apartments, which are complete with a kitchen and dining area. While only first-year students are promised on-campus housing, upper-class students say they don't have any difficulty finding residences to their liking.

The dining hall receives lukewarm ratings in terms of quality—it's "hit or miss." At least "[it] doesn't cause any problems internally and tastes decent," as one content diner reported. There are six styles of food to choose from each night, so "you can always find something that you like." And for those fearing the Freshman 15—"there are lots of healthy options." Students are generally pleased with the flexible meal plans. "In theory you can go to the dining hall 15 times a day."

Most upperclassmen don't have meal plans, so they cook their own food or purchase meals at the student union. The student-run Rensselaer Union, which incorporates campus-wide technology, is a popular student hang-out. It features two floors of food courts, including a Starbucks and café. The U-shaped quad is another destination for those seeking a place to chill. But the academic rigors don't leave many stretches of time for ambitious RPI students to just lie low. "Honestly, you're going to find most people in the student union center or on their computers," said one student.

A Social Scavenger Hunt

Students agree that the low-key nightlife at RPI demands a "proactive attitude" from those seeking a quality party. "There's stuff to do," said one student, "but it's not the University of Miami." Fraternities and sororities have a big presence on campus, with more than a quarter of the university involved, and current students encourage incoming freshmen to consider rushing. However, the RPI administration has been tightening the reins on underage drinking in recent years, making fraternities hesitant to throw full-scale parties, and leaving the nightlife-starved student body even hungrier for a full social calendar. "Our school is trying to deal with underage drinking. They feel they should be changing policies for the entire United States," said one frustrated Greek member. Outside of the Greek system, popular annual parties include the Big Red Freak-Out, to support the hockey team, and Grand Marshal week, when the elections for student representatives take place. GM week is full of games, and students enjoy time off from classes. In general, students point to the academic intensity as the reason behind the tame party scene. "People are so busy— you don't have time to party until the weekend."

While some students complain that the surrounding town of Troy is, to put it bluntly, "pretty crappy," as well as a bit unsafe, others indicate the recent renewal effort that the city has been experiencing. Its art community in particular has made Troy more attractive. For those so inclined, students of drinking age point out worthwhile destinations like Club Lime, a rugby bar

called The Ruck, and O'Learys for food. Troy and Albany also host occasional concerts. While most upperclassmen have a car on campus, few venture outside of the Troy area on a regular basis. Many students choose to hang out with friends made through activities, rather than just those from within the major.

"The Odds Are Good but the Goods Are Odd"

RPI students are known for their book smarts, but some confess that their peers' social skills could use a little fine-tuning. "The standard-issue RPI kid is probably a big computer nerd," admitted one junior, echoing a common view on campus. One student painted the caricature of an RPI student as someone who "walks around in a black trench coat, doesn't speak any English, and stays in his room to play videogames or download porn." Indeed, the high-tech atmosphere can have a downside: it's not uncommon for some students to stay glued to their laptops through the weekend. "They're very computer-oriented students," explained one undergrad; "[they] make my college look bad!" However, many RPI students are witty, outgoing, and have a great sense of humor; they assure others that the caricature is not the norm and that "there is plenty of social interaction on campus." Overall, undergrads are described as friendly, laid-back, and into outdoor activities. One junior summed up the situation by saying that there are two kinds of smarts—book smarts and wit—and every RPI student has at least one in the bag.

There are few complaints about ethnic diversity at RPI—the strong academic programs draw students from across the world. But students tend to be less enthusiastic about the gender ratio and dating prospects. The skewed male-female ratio of 3:1 can definitely put a kink in a guy's game. As one Greek brother said: "There are 32 fraternities and 5 sororities—just by that fact you can kind of figure it out." Not surprisingly, long-term relationships tend to prevail over random hook-ups: "If a guy finds a girl, he usually hangs on to her." Guys sometimes complain of RIBS ("ratio-induced bitch syndrome") among the minority sex, as "very pretty girls get hit on all the time, so they think they're the greatest thing in the world." Female students have their own set of troubles, though. "The guys always complain about the fact that there are no girls, but a lot of the guys are the ones who sit in the rooms and play videogames," one female explained. "Girls also have difficulty."

Puck Pros

Hockey is huge at RPI. "Going to a hockey game is like going to a professional game," explained one student. In fact, some players do head straight from RPI to the NHL, including such notable alumni as Joe Juneau and Adam Oates. Men's and women's hockey are the only Division I sports at the university, but football also attracts large crowds. RPI is planning to construct the new East Campus Athletic Village, which will include a new football field, gym, 50-meter pool and tennis courts. Whether it's on the varsity, club or recreational level, many students participate in some sort of athletic activity off campus. Undergrads can often be found skateboard-

ing, riding bikes, or in the midst of a snowball fight.

Making the Most of It

While the stereotype of the RPI computer nerd seems to have some truth behind it, students have a sense of humor about it and prove that social interaction doesn't have to be limited to study sessions and videogame marathons. Facing a massive workload and large introductory classes, students are urged to shape their own paths at RPI, and to make time for fun. "You're going to go crazy if you don't take control of what you're doing," said one student. Another RPI undergrad offered this piece of advice to incoming freshmen: "Bring a willingness to do everything you can. The work is going to be really hard, but you're not going to be able to make it without friends."—*Christen Martosella*

FYI

If you come to RPI, you'd better bring "a work ethic."

What's the typical weekend schedule? "Friday: go to O'Leary's for chicken wings, pizza, beer; after that, go to a frat house or wherever to party; Saturday morning: lounge around for brunch, maybe go to an RPI football game or Greek event; Saturday night: bar or house party; Sunday: do work."

If I could change one thing about RPI, I'd "make people more socially involved."

Three things every student should do before graduating are "look into joining Greek life; go to a hockey game: preferably the big game against Clarkson in February; and plan your own schedule: make sure that your senior year you can take one semester that's not crazy."

Rochester Institute of Technology

Address: 60 Lomb Memorial Drive, Rochester, NY 14623-5604
Phone: 585-475-6631
E-mail address: admissions@rit.edu
Web site URL: www.rit.edu
Year Founded: 1829
Private or Public: Private
Religious Affiliation: None
Location: Suburban
Number of Applicants: 12,725
Percent Accepted: 60%
Percent Accepted who enroll: 30%
Number Entering: 2,616
Number of Transfers Accepted each Year: 1,203
Middle 50% SAT range: M: 560–670, CR: 540–630, Wr: 520–610
Middle 50% ACT range: 24–29
Early admission program EA/ED/None: ED

Percentage accepted through EA or ED: 66%
EA and ED deadline: 1-Dec
Regular Deadline: 1-Feb
Application Fee: $50
Full time Undergraduate enrollment: 3,861
Total enrollment: 6,494
Percent Male: 67%
Percent Female: 33%
Total Percent Minority or Unreported: 32%
Percent African-American: 5%
Percent Asian/Pacific Islander: 5%
Percent Hispanic: 4%
Percent Native-American: <1%
Percent International: 11%
Percent in-state/out of state: 55%/45%
Percent from Public HS: 85%
Retention Rate: 88%
Graduation Rate 4-year: 62%

Graduation Rate 6-year: Unreported
Percent Undergraduates in On-campus housing: 68%
Number of official organized extracurricular organizations: 175
3 Most popular majors: Business, Information Technology, Photography
Student/Faculty ratio: 14:1
Average Class Size: 15
Percent of students going to grad school: 15%
Tuition and Fees: $28,035
In-State Tuition and Fees if different: No difference
Cost for Room and Board: $9,381
Percent receiving financial aid out of those who apply, first year: 86%
Percent receiving financial aid among all students: 77%

Located in the industrial city of Rochester in upstate New York, Rochester Institute of Technology has been providing career-oriented education for more than 125 years. With a driven student body of more than 17,000 students, eight colleges across different academic disciplines and a hallmark co-op program, RIT offers an enriching academic experience while students are at the college in order to prepare the students for the abundance of opportunities at their disposal for life after college.

A Kaleidoscopic Assortment of Courses

RIT has something for every one. Within its network of eight colleges, which covers academic disciplines in the liberal arts to computer sciences in B. Thomas Golisano College of Computing and Information Sciences to E. Philip Saunders College of Business and everything in between, RIT offers 90 programs of study. There is also an honor's program that grants students access to special courses as well as extra research or study abroad advising. Beyond the wide array of academic options, RIT also provides specificity so that students can delve into field as particular as New Media Development, Bioinformatics, and Photojournalism. "I like the specialization that RIT provides," said one student, "it lets me study exactly what I want."

In terms of classes, RIT operates on a quarter system. This means that four 10-week terms make up an academic year. However, the school year is also divided up into fall and spring semesters, each ranging from 15-17 weeks. As a result, there are semester courses as well as quarter courses.

Despite the emphasis on a career-oriented education in a technology related field, there is no shortage of unique courses that spice up the academic inventory. Classes such as "Big Bang and Black Holes," or

New York

"Busting Myth" are interesting but usually not too hard to get into. On the other hand, students fight for extremely popular courses such as "Foods of the World."

Beyond the Classroom
Lucky for RIT students, the enriching assortment of academic courses is only the beginning of what RIT has to offer. The university takes much pride in its Cooperative Education program, which has become increasingly popular among students. Affectionately called Co-op, the program allows students to start accumulating professional work experience related to their specific field of study after completing the first two years of coursework in their academic program. The co-op program allows students to gain first-hand experience in the professional world and earn a reasonable salary while learning. "The co-op program was the biggest draw for me," said an undergraduate student, "in a newly-recovered and highly competitive economy, "co-oping" means that you study for your first and second years, then spend four quarters working in the real workplace. This guarantees you contacts in at least at one company, and you'll have a better idea of what you want to focus on. RIT also has really good placement at large tech companies such as Apple, Microsoft, and Google," said one student. According to another student, the co-op program is just one way in which "RIT treats its students like students and not like numbers."

Behind the Bricks
RIT is known for having over 15 million bricks among the walls of buildings and pathways on campus. These bricks house a myriad of dorms of all shapes and formations along with the accompaniment of state of the art facilities. All the freshmen live in dorms with two resident assistants on each floor. After the first year, most students move into on-campus apartments, which vary in sizes and conditions. To cater to its students' diverse interests, there is also specialized housing. According to one student, "there are standard residential dorms with special interest hours for art, photography, engineering, computer science, foreign language, etc." With such an assortment of housing options, RIT is continuously expanding, with the recent completion of "Global Village." In order to improve the quality of students' lives, RIT also has excellent gyms in locations such as the Student Life Center. The pools not only offer plenty of space for lap swimming but also a hot tub for relaxation.

> "RIT treats its students like students and not like numbers."

Besides dormitories, academic buildings and student centers, there are five main dining halls along with smaller eateries and food stores sprinkled all across the campus. "Gracie's" or as one student nicknamed it "Greasie's" is frequented by freshmen as their required meal plan provides for a certain number of meals at Gracie's every week and a certain dollar amount of "Food Debit" that allows them to buy food at other dining halls or stores. Upperclassmen often opt for a plan of only Food Debit, which grants them more freedom. Consequently, they frequent other dining halls such as Commons, which is not only close to student dorms but like Gracie's can also be reached without going outside during the brutal winters. Brick City is another popular dining hall that not only offers great food but also plenty of space to relax. Other student favorites include Salsarita's at Global Village for its Mexican food and Java Wally's for a good cup of joe.

A Unique Melting Pot
While RIT has students from all of the fifty states and ninety-five countries, its demographic is unlike any other college. To start off, its male to female ratio is 2:1. Moreover, the National Technical Institute of the Deaf also contributes to the uniqueness of RIT's student demographic. In general, student body is perceived to be predominately Caucasian with a significant percentage of the population consisting of students from New York.

Campus Festivities
Don't let all the pre-professional talk fool you. Outside the classroom, RIT students are a spirited bunch. Here, hockey dominates the sport scene, even more so than football. Last year, RIT Men's hockey went to the NCAA Frozen Four championship and this year RIT Women's hockey is ranked #1 in the nation. As a result, hockey games often bring out students' school pride and the ice rink is packed with cheering students.

On a less conventional side of things, two annual traditions bring together the student body. In the beginning of the school year, there is "Mud Tug." As part of a classic autumn tradition, students spray down a field to make it muddy, and have a tug of war tournament while raising money for a charity. In the winter, there is a seasonal festival known as Freezefest. Then, in the spring, students gear up for a massive game of Humans versus Zombies, played with Nerf guns, socks, and green bandanas. "If you're okay devoting three-plus weeks to constant paranoia and looking like a bit of a fool, it's lots of fun and really well-run. Otherwise, it can be just as fun watching others play," said an undergraduate

Overall, RIT's diverse array of courses and spectrum of themed housing offers an exciting collegiate environment. Moreover, for students who have a clear sense of their future careers and want to develop themselves in a classroom as well as a workplace setting, RIT's famed "co-op" offers a slew of opportunities to bridge the gap between school and the real world.— *Jenny Dai & Sharon Yin*

FYI

If you come to RIT, leave your football at home. Bring a hockey stick or a Frisbee instead.

What differentiates RIT from other colleges is "between all the buildings, pathways, and so on, there are over 15 million bricks on campus."

The biggest rivalry on campus is the rivalry between the computer science majors and the software engineering majors.

S a r a h   L a w r e n c e   C o l l e g e

Address: 1 Mead Way Bronxville, NY 10708-5999

Phone: 914-395-2510

E-mail address: slcadmit@sarahlawrence.edu

Web site URL: www.sarahlawrence.edu

Year Founded: 1926

Private or Public: Private

Religious Affiliation: None

Location: Urban

Number of Applicants: 2,785

Percent Accepted: 46%

Percent Accepted who enroll: 27%

Number Entering: 347

Number of Transfers Accepted each Year: 97

Middle 50% SAT range: Does Not Require

Middle 50% ACT range: Does Not Require

Early admission program EA/ED/None: ED

Percentage accepted through EA or ED: 24%

EA and ED deadline: 15-Nov

Regular Deadline: 1-Jan

Application Fee: $60

Full time Undergraduate enrollment: 1,389

Total enrollment: 1,791

Percent Male: 27%

Percent Female: 73%

Total Percent Minority or Unreported: 35%

Percent African-American: 4%

Percent Asian/Pacific Islander: 5%

Percent Hispanic: 5%

Percent Native-American: <1%

Percent International: 3%

Percent in-state/out of state: 25%/75%

Percent from Public HS: Unreported

Retention Rate: 80%

Graduation Rate 4-year: 67%

Graduation Rate 6-year: 72%

Percent Undergraduates in On-campus housing: 85%

Number of official organized extracurricular organizations: 70

3 Most popular majors: Unreported

Student/Faculty ratio: 9:1

Average Class Size: 19

Percent of students going to grad school: Unreported

Tuition and Fees: $40,350

In-State Tuition and Fees if different: No difference

Cost for Room and Board: $13,716

Percent receiving financial aid out of those who apply, first year: 50%

Percent receiving financial aid among all students: 53%

T wenty minutes outside of Manhattan by bus, in the hills of suburban New York, lies one of the nation's most highly respected liberal arts institutions, Sarah Lawrence College. Initially founded as a women's college in 1926, the college opened its doors to men in 1968 and continues to maintain a small size and stellar student-to-faculty ratio. With unique academic offerings and a plethora of on-campus activities, Sarah Lawrence effortlessly blends all of the perks of a small school with the resources of a much larger artistic community.

Making the Grade, where None are Given

Sarah Lawrence doesn't have "arbitrary" academic requirements; instead, students follow guidelines that call for one course in three out of four academic disciplines: social sciences and history, creative and performing arts, humanities, and natural sciences and math. Every class at Sarah Lawrence "is full of people who want to be there," and most are discussion-based seminars that are capped at fifteen students. There are no TAs at Sarah Lawrence, and the students benefit from the "extremely accessible faculty." The college gives students the opportunity to explore various fields and enhance their creativity, even if it takes them in unexpected directions—a perfect example famous fashion designer and Sarah Lawrence alum Vera Wang, who came to the college as a pre-med and ended up focusing on theater and art history.

SLC also gives students a unique opportunity to get to know their professors through the conference system. Instead of cramming for finals, the conference system allows students to meet with professors outside of class to develop a long-term project—anything from a long-term paper to performance art—that will incorporate what they've learned in the course. Registration at Sarah Lawrence involves interviewing professors to see if the coursework is compatible with a student's interests and how the student thinks the course and final project will factor in to his or her academic career. Sarah Lawrence students agree that independence and determination are key to success at the college, but also praise the academic advising system as a way to help students figure out what they want from their academic experience. Each student at Sarah Lawrence is assigned a "don," an academic advisor in their field who will help them select classes and provide support for any and all scholastic issues.

Rather than focus on grading, professors at Sarah Lawrence write detailed, candid evaluations of a student's work at the end of the semester. Students are aware that professors can—and will—come down hard on them if they aren't prepared for class, and most praise the evaluation system as "much more valuable than a letter grade."

Because of the college's small class sizes and close-knit campus, many Sarah Lawrence juniors decide to expand their horizons beyond their college bubble and study abroad for a semester or two. Sarah Lawrence students agree that "going abroad spring semester junior year is a must," and the college offers numerous exciting programs in Florence, Paris, and even Cuba. For actors, there's also the prestigious London Theater Program, which gives students the opportunity to work with leading British directors and actors.

Yet, no matter where Sarah Lawrence students roam, be it to Italy or nearby New York for class trips to museums, they all agree that the academic environment is one of the college's greatest assets. Students talk about academics "even on weekends" and find that the discussion format they're so used to in classes often finds it way to dining hall dinner tables or the school's beautiful quads. A Sarah Lawrence education is "really about pushing boundaries and learning for the sake of learning."

Small School, Big City

Students' creativity permeates throughout life at Sarah Lawrence, and makes itself particularly noticeable on weekends. There's "always a lot to do on campus," including numerous plays, dance recitals, concerts, poetry readings, and art exhibits. The theater department organizes more than thirty performances each year, ensuring that students always have numerous opportunities to support their theatrically-inclined friends. Students also say that there's "every type of drinker" at Sarah Lawrence, from those who chose to stay sober to "the heavyweight drunks who stumble home every Thursday, Friday, and Saturday."

One thing that Sarah Lawrence doesn't have is Greek life—there are no fraternities or sororities at the college, but most students say that they aren't missed. Instead of "crowded parties with kegs," Sarah Lawrence students prefer to go to off-campus parties or take a 20-minute bus ride into New York City on Saturday nights. Trips into New York are certainly one of the most popular options for going out at Sarah Lawrence, "which can be pretty disappointing for freshmen who aren't used to having to travel to have fun." Although most weekends at SLC can be low-key, students do try to organize the occasional large-scale party, such as Bacchanalia and the well-known Coming Out Dance, which has been prevented in recent years because of problems with drinking.

Liberal, Artsy Living

With an undergraduate population of just over 1,300, Sarah Lawrence is the epitome of a small liberal arts institution. Students love the "tight-knit" community the college's small size creates, and praise the fact that "you see people you know everywhere, so you always feel at home." Most students are creative and passionate about the arts, but support for athletic teams is lacking. However, that's not to say that Sarah Lawrence doesn't have plenty of school pride—as one of the most prestigious liberal arts institutions, Sarah Lawrence has a very strong sense of tradition and students are proud of their rich history.

> **"Fun at Sarah Lawrence is artsy or in New York."**

One of the biggest complaints about the college is its overall lack of diversity, in numerous aspects. Although students come from all over the country and numerous international countries, only 40% are on financial aid, a testament to the college's lack of socio-economic diversity. Most Sarah Lawrence students are "flaming liberals,"

and "the far-and-few conservatives have a pretty quiet voice on campus." However, despite the lack of diversity, SLC boasts a very accepting environment, where "everything, from sexuality to religion to whatever, is accepted." Initially founded as a women's college, Sarah Lawrence does have its fair share of "die-hard feminists" and "plenty of gay men," but students do say that everyone on campus has diverse interests and goals.

The campus is fairly self-contained, particularly for freshmen and sophomores. Freshmen say that dorms can be comfortable depending on where you live, with Andrews Court and Gilbert being two of the more popular dorms. In addition to dorms, the college has on-campus houses, which come with kitchens, single bedrooms, and spacious common rooms. Housing is decided by lottery, but it's "fairly easy to get a single after sophomore year, if you want one." Some seniors chose to live in off-campus apartments in nearby Yonkers because of their affordability, and cars are popular among upperclassmen.

For numerous reasons, the students at Sarah Lawrence are enamored with their small college's liberal-arts focus and distinct community. Dedicated to both intellectual discovery and artistic ventures, Sarah Lawrence offers a unique academic environment and a living community sure to make students find their niche and feel at home.—*Iva Velickovic*

FYI
Sarah Lawrence is different from most other colleges because of "its unlimited commitment to its students, evidenced by the unique conference system."
What surprised me most about Sarah Lawrence was "how hard it was to put anyone in a box. Sure, we're all pretty artsy, but SLC students have interests that range from astrophysics to sports, too."
If I could change one thing about Sarah Lawrence, "it'd be that most upperclassmen leave campus on weekends."

Skidmore College

Address: 815 North Broadway
Saratoga Springs, NY
12866-1632
Phone: 518-580-5570
E-mail address:
admissions@skidmore.edu
Web site URL:
www.skidmore.edu
Year Founded: 1903
Private or Public: Private
Religious Affiliation: None
Location: Suburban
Number of Applicants: 6,768
Percent Accepted: 37%
**Percent Accepted who
enroll:** 28%
Number Entering: 682
**Number of Transfers
Accepted each Year:** 86
**Middle 50% SAT range: M:
580–670, CR:580–680,
Wr: 590–690**
Middle 50% ACT range:
26–30
**Early admission program
EA/ED/None:** ED

**Percentage accepted
through EA or ED:** 43%
EA and ED deadline: 15-Nov
Regular Deadline: 15-Jan
Application Fee: $60
**Full time Undergraduate
enrollment:** 2,717
Total enrollment: 2,809
Percent Male: 40%
Percent Female: 60%
**Total Percent Minority or
Unreported:** 34%
Percent African-American:
3%
**Percent Asian/Pacific
Islander:** 7%
Percent Hispanic: 5%
Percent Native-American:
<1%
Percent International: 3%
**Percent in-state/out of
state:** 68%/32%
Percent from Public HS: 63%
Retention Rate: 94%
Graduation Rate 4-year:
78%

Graduation Rate 6-year:
80%
**Percent Undergraduates in
On-campus housing:** 85%
**Number of official organized
extracurricular
organizations:** 80
3 Most popular majors:
Business, English,
Psychology
Student/Faculty ratio:
9:1
Average Class Size: 15
**Percent of students going to
grad school:** 19%
Tuition and Fees: $36,126
**In-State Tuition and Fees if
different:** No difference
Cost for Room and Board:
$9,836
**Percent receiving financial
aid out of those who apply,
first year:** 49%
**Percent receiving financial
aid among all students:**
50%

Tucked away in the affluent horse racing town of Saratoga Springs, NY, Skidmore College's close-knit student body offers a welcoming social atmosphere, both during the week and on the weekends. The relatively young liberal arts college boasts small class sizes, accessible faculty, and plenty to keep students busy, though look elsewhere for spirited crowds at riotous athletic events. For those unfazed by the winter cold and seeking a comfortable balance between studies and parties, the Skidmore Thoroughbreds make a solid bet.

Intimate Academia, in and out of the Classroom

Freshman are eagerly welcomed into the Skidmore community with a supportive system intertwining the classroom and dorm. All freshmen take a freshman seminar which doubles as their adviser group, the teacher filling the role of adviser and the seminars often focusing on less traditional topics such as food and cooking. Skidmore also

tries to house students of these seminars together to further strengthen friendships among peers.

Don't let Skidmore's small size, with classes on average 16 students and sometimes as few as eight, give the impression that its academics are limited. It offers degrees in over 60 areas of study, the popular majors tending to be business, English and psychology. An attractive aspect for many is the ready-made interdepartmental double majors, such as Sociology and Anthropology, and Business and Spanish. There are also strong studio art, dance, and music programs.

"I couldn't ask for more opportunities to study what I love with no boundaries. I am a double major with a minor, and no one ever told me I couldn't do it. I was only encouraged by the faculty who worked with me to make it all possible," said a senior. An exercise science major also praised her experience, lauding the excellent resources and facilities available to her.

The biggest intro class is a tidy 30 or so

people. Getting into the smaller, more sought-after classes can be tough as an underclassman due a lottery system favoring the upperclassmen. There are a set of general requirements that cover the academic spectrum as at other liberal arts institutions. "I think a lot of them are necessary and give good breadth, but they can sometimes be a little too strict for what classes they count toward," said senior. Another complaint about the administrative side of academics was that "it's not always clear exactly what your requirements are or what you should do to fulfill them—what's the best course of action before you get in your major."

Teachers are always around and have plenty of office hours, and there are no TAs in sight. If you make the effort to connect, then teachers will too. "The teachers are great—they're always open to making time outside of class to talk," said a sophomore. Well-known profs include Stephen Millhouser, who has written for the New Yorker, and Sheldon Solloman, professor of the challenging but popular Intro to Psych course.

Students agree that the workload is moderate if time is managed well. "There are no infinitely or notoriously hard classes. If you work hard you'll get an A. It's not like I'm struggling to pass," said a student. For those who want a challenge, there is the Honors Forum track which involves a selection process. Grading varies between teachers but is very fair. Some classes will curve so you have the chance to do better. Some have an optional final, and others have several tests throughout with the lowest grade dropped. In addition, department heads are available to discuss any problems that may arise with certain courses or teachers.

Divided but Inclusive

The social scene at Skidmore is slightly divided, a fact apparent upon walking into the dining hall. "On the blue side, the athletes, on the red side, the more artsy kids," said a student. Despite this general trend, which, of course, does not include everyone, meeting new people and mixing among social groups is common and easy to do. "There's a strong sense of community. The school is small enough that you feel like you know everyone, but I'm somehow still meeting new, awesome people every weekend," remarked a senior. According to another, "No one is really discriminating towards who they hang out with. People have, usu-ally, various friend groups. I never felt awkward in a group just because I didn't have a lot of the same interests or wasn't a member of a certain club or whatever." The student body isn't terribly diverse, and among minorities there can be some self-segregation. Most students fall under the umbrella of white, middle- and upper-middle class, fairly liberal kids from the northeast and some from the west coast.

Since students living in dorms have a mandatory meal plan, a lot of hanging out goes on in the dining hall, known fondly as the D-Hall. The one dining hall, which was redone in the past five years, is open from 7 a.m. to 11 p.m. and meal plans are quite flexible; while all freshmen have unlimited meals, upperclassmen can put money on their cards and refill when it runs out. The food is generally good, and even "awesome," according to one student, who also liked being able to see the staff prepare and cook the food.

The dorms are not bad, and the apartments off campus are well-praised. Freshmen have one roommate, possibly two (increasingly likely with growing class sizes) and space is generous as college rooms go. Most of the dorms are suites, so several rooms will all share a bathroom, a relief for those fearing big, grungy hall bathrooms. Juniors either move off campus or live in Scribner Village, an apartment complex on the edge of the main campus. Seniors generally live in Northwoods, a complex built five years ago with three or four students to a suite with a kitchen and bathroom, though Scribner and Northwoods are not grade-exclusive. Other new buildings on campus include the Zankel Music Center featuring a beautiful concert hall and the Tang Teaching Museum and Art Gallery.

Freshman dorms all have RAs who vary in strictness. "You have to enforce rules, but you're left a lot of personal discretion. If it's not out of control, I just ask students to stop. Some RAs write people up, but there's leeway," said one RA, a senior.

One complaint of Skidmore students is the lack of school spirit for sports teams. At a small, D3 school, varsity sports aren't the main focus. People sometimes come out and support when teams are doing well—basketball and field hockey recently earned high attendance—but in general there isn't a huge sports following. The hockey team is trying to increase fans by providing buses to games, since the rink isn't on campus, but it still tends to draw the same small crowd.

Fun Day and Other Fun

There's plenty stirring up outside the classroom to keep students at Skidmore from growing bored. A number of clubs and organizations have a solid membership and are fairly active, though not students' first priority. While the *Skidmore News*, the weekly newspaper, is "not that great," the school's radio station is popular and there is a TV station, SkidTV, for anyone interested. The Equestrian program and Outdoors Club draw in a large group, while those less active may opt for art or even knitting clubs. Intramurals are offered in all the standard sports and pull a decent crowd.

Students can look forward to a number of annual, school-wide events. Fun Day, at the end of April or early May, is the most highly anticipated; there are bounce castles and bands on the green, and everyone tends to get pretty tipsy. There is also Moorbid, the big Halloween dance, Beatlemania, a fall concert showcasing lots of different performances of Beatles songs, Junior Ring, a semiformal, and the Hunt, a huge, underground scavenger hunt requiring participants to complete ridiculous tasks. Every year, two concerts featuring bands brought in from outside also offer entertainment.

A lot of students keep busy with jobs, either on campus in the dining hall, library, gym, or academic services, or in Saratoga. Students with cars can take the occasional road trip to places like Montreal or Lake George, but for the most part people stay on campus.

Let the (Weekend) Races Begin!

Saratoga is a great town "if you do your research and utilize what's there," according to a local student. Besides the famous horse track, there are cross country running and skiing races, a state park down the road and a mall nearby. Saratoga's tourist-driven downtown and Broadway Street offer a range of restaurants and bars, all within walking distance of campus; if not inclined to walk, there are buses running from all over town, including one to and from Skidmore every half-hour. Relations with the town are neither great or terrible; Saratoga leans to the right while Skidmore tends towards the left.

"Weekends at Skidmore are kind of touch and go. Some weekend are awesome with tons of parties and places to go, and others are better spent with a few friends," said a senior. There's a good bar scene in Saratoga for upperclassmen or underclassmen with fakes, and school-funded activities on campus for those underage. There's almost always something to do, but it does sometimes quiet down, especially during exam time.

As for Greek life, "there are no frats, which is great. Sometimes athlete houses sort of take the form of mini-frats, but not really, and they certainly don't dominate the social life at all," said a senior. Athletic teams and other groups, such as the Outing Club, host parties at their off-campus houses, and "depending on the house you sort of know what to expect from the parties. The sports teams' houses are sometimes exclusive but other parties not really. It really depends on the size," said a student. All of the biggest parties are at off-campus houses and are a bread and butter destination for freshmen, who also tend to spend a lot of time hanging out in large groups in the dorm. The weekend is Thursday through Saturday night, with Friday the most low-key. Upperclassmen often leave parties and delve into the Saratoga nightlife after midnight.

> "The school is small enough that you feel like you know everyone, but I'm somehow still meeting new, awesome people every weekend."

Skidmore is technically a dry campus, but security is generally pretty tolerant. "It's inevitable that drinking will be going on, so what they do is make sure it's as safe as possible. They're realistic about it," said a student. The policies are not too strict; "If you get caught drinking when you're underage there is a fine and you have to call your parents (it's 50 dollars or something, depending). It's not a zero tolerance policy, but it could be worse. People get in minor trouble a lot—get caught drinking in their dorm room. There are very few instances of serious trouble," said another. Drinking certainly isn't a requisite, and some students refrain, though the vast majority does drink, and drugs are also quite prevalent.

Overall, Skidmore students find little fault with their school. Despite some separation among social groups, everyone still gets along. Though the horse racing season dies away in September, the start of Skidmore's school year is when Saratoga Springs truly comes alive.—*TaoTao Holmes*

If you come to Skidmore, you'd better bring "really good snow boots (Uggs won't cut it), a desire to drink huge amounts of coffee, and a corkscrew."

If I could change one thing about Skidmore, I'd "have a little more school spirit."

Three things every student at Skidmore should do before graduating are "Lie out on the green all day on the first nice day of spring (50 degrees out constitutes a nice day), go to Compton's Diner when it opens at 3 a.m., because you were downtown anyway so why not?, and have one doughboy (a hot cheese and chicken hot pocket) delivered to campus from Esporanto's, they are SO worth it."

St. Lawrence University

Address: 23 Romoda Drive Canton, NY 13617

Phone: 800-285-1856

E-mail address: admissions@stlawu.edu

Web site URL: www.stlawu.edu

Year Founded: 1856

Private or Public: Private

Religious Affiliation: None

Location: Rural

Number of Applicants: 5,419

Percent Accepted: 34%

Percent Accepted who enroll: 34%

Number Entering: 616

Number of Transfers Accepted each Year: 40

Middle 50% SAT range: M: 570–640, CR: 570–640, Wr: 560–650

Middle 50% ACT range: 25–29

Early admission program EA/ED/None: ED I, ED II

Percentage accepted through EA or ED: Unreported

EA and ED deadline: 15-Nov, 15-Jan

Regular Deadline: 1-Feb

Application Fee: $60

Full time Undergraduate enrollment: 2,193

Total enrollment: 2,325

Percent Male: 45%

Percent Female: 55%

Total Percent Minority or Unreported: 10%

Percent African-American: 3%

Percent Asian/Pacific Islander: 2%

Percent Hispanic: 3%

Percent Native-American: <1%

Percent International: Unreported

Percent in-state/out of state: 42%/58%

Percent from Public HS: 69%

Retention Rate: 88%

Graduation Rate 4-year: 78%

Graduation Rate 6-year: 80%

Percent Undergraduates in On-campus housing: 98%

Number of official organized extracurricular organizations: 129

3 Most popular majors: Psychology, Economics, English

Student/Faculty ratio: 11:1

Average Class Size: 16

Percent of students going to grad school: 20%

Tuition and Fees: $37,915

In-State Tuition and Fees if different: No difference

Cost for Room and Board: $9,645

Percent receiving financial aid out of those who apply, first year: 62%

Percent receiving financial aid among all students: Unreported

Tucked into a corner of the Adirondacks, in a small town in New York near the Canadian border, sits St. Lawrence University—just small enough to fit into the little town but big enough for its students to call it home. The relatively small size of SLU allows the formation of a close-knit community, both within the student body and between the students and faculty. The rural location affords opportunities for outdoor activities and gives the campus its beautiful backdrop, the pride of many an SLU student. Even though many students complain about the huge piles of snow in the cold winter months, most agree that the warmth of the friendly people around them more than makes up for the weather.

Studying at SLU

Academics at St. Lawrence are described as difficult at times, but, as one student said, "you don't have to be doing work ALL the time." Some of the popular departments include economics, psychology and biology. Because of the small size of SLU, students benefit from small class sizes and they enjoy close contact with professors right from the start of their freshman year. Many professors provide students with their home phone numbers and encourage students to contact them with questions or problems.

Students reported that essentially all classes enroll no more than 25 students (the average is 16), are taught exclusively by professors, and have a TA or two to give extra help to students who need it. Small class size rarely results in students being shut out of classes they want to take, though. Registration now takes place online and involves meeting with an advisor to gain a PIN that is then used to select classes.

St. Lawrence's academic program includes a fair number of requirements. Undergraduates must take a class in each of the following areas: "Arts or Expression," humanities, math, and social science. They also must fulfill a natural science requirement, which must include one course with a lab. Opinions of these requirements vary from "a hassle" to "a good way to get us to start exploring different departments." In addition, freshmen participate in the First Year Program, a semester-long course devoted to developing oral and written communication skills, taken with other students from the same dorm. While many students acknowledge the benefits of FYP, others complain about how the course often conflicts with other desired courses.

> **"You don't have to be doing work ALL the time."**

When students at St. Lawrence want to study, they often head for Owen D. Young library, the main library on campus. ODY is a fairly modern building; although its aesthetic merits are often debated, most agree that the recent renovation has made the atmosphere on the inside cheerful and stimulating. However, the lively atmosphere also frequently inspires conversation, and many students describe ODY as more of a social place than a studious one. For hard-core studying, Madill, the science library, is your best bet.

Living and Eating

Housing at SLU is mainly in dorms, although there are also off-campus options such as Greek and theme housing and athletic suites. The dorms are mostly set up in traditional singles and doubles, and are coed, but some dorms also offer the option of suites with kitchens, mostly for upperclassmen. Students cite Sykes as one of the best dorms, with Whitman as the best dorm for freshmen. On the other hand, Lee and Rebert halls are said to be the worst, although

even in those less desirable dorms, rooms are reportedly spacious and nicely furnished. Almost universally, students praise their dorms, whether they live in the best or worst location, for the sense of community fostered there.

As upperclassmen, students at St. Lawrence have more housing options, although finding an apartment in Canton isn't one of them; the university requires that undergraduates reside on campus. However, many upperclassmen choose to live in Greek houses, which lie just at the edge of campus; one student living in her sorority house described her experience by saying it is "very home-like, and there is always something to do." Theme housing is another alternative to dorms available after freshman year, and such houses include a house for environmentalists, for people who enjoy outdoor activities, and for cultural groups and international students. Seniors can also apply to live in on-campus townhouses.

SLU students tend to give their meal plan and dining options high ratings. There are three on-campus eating establishments: Dana Dining Hall (a traditional cafeteria), the Time Out Café and the Northstar Café in the New Student Center. The cafés have more of a relaxed atmosphere where students go to hang out and relax, and the food there is considered the best of the options on campus, particularly the chicken wrap sandwiches. There are two meal plans available to students, the 21-meal plan, which is only accepted at Dana, and a declining-balance plan which is accepted at all three on-campus locations. While students favor the declining-balance plan because of its flexibility, most agree that it is impossible not to run out of money before the end of the semester, and so that plan is better for students who are not eating all of their meals on campus.

When students get tired of the places to eat on campus or just want to treat themselves, they look to the restaurants in the town of Canton. For quick meals, there are the standard chains: McDonald's, Burger King and Pizza Hut, and also A-1 Oriental Kitchen, which is a popular delivery choice. Other restaurants in Canton include Sergi's Pizza, which has pizza and Italian food, Jerek Subs, Josie's and Phoebe's; the Cactus Grill, a Mexican restaurant located in nearby Potsdam, is also frequented by many St. Lawrence students. During Family Weekend, students often take their parents to McCarthy's.

Life After Studying

Students at St. Lawrence spend a lot of time on extracurricular activities, and there is "always something to get involved in." One of the most active groups on campus seems to be the Outing Club, which goes on lots of trips and does other activities together. A recently founded karate club, which is student-run and student-taught, is growing rapidly, an example of the ample opportunity to start new organizations if you are interested. Many students also spend their time working for *The Hill News*, the main weekly publication of St. Lawrence.

Sports are also an option at St. Lawrence, both for fans and athletes. Varsity soccer and hockey are the most popular, with rugby and lacrosse games also drawing crowds. School spirit peaks at the time of the Clarkson-SLU hockey game, and the long-time rivalry draws huge crowds. Students say that you have to get tickets at least a week in advance if you don't want to stand up to watch the game, but that it is one of the highlights of the year that cannot be missed. Sports are not limited only to varsity athletes, though, as St. Lawrence has a wide variety of intramural teams, which allow people of all levels the opportunity to play. In addition, the athletic facilities are described as "great, and always available to everybody." All of the sports facilities have been recently renovated, and according to one student athlete, "facilities at SLU are in tip-top shape." In 2007, SLU carried out a drastic multimillion-dollar expansion of its arts facilities and its Science Center to im-prove student life. Unfortunately, the social life and weekend plans are definitely limited by the small student body and the school's rural locale. Some things that students do when they are hanging out or partying include shooting pool, going to see a movie (free on campus), going to see a band playing at Java House or going to a frat party. However, students complain that campus security and Canton police strongly frown upon student alcohol use. On top of that, on-campus and off-campus parties alike tend to get shut down soon after they begin. Thus, most students say that they spend a lot of time hanging out in bars in Canton with their friends or taking trips on the weekend to Ottawa, the capital of Canada, or to Syracuse, both of which are within a few hours' driving distance.

Even though there may be downsides to living in a remote, rural town, students at St. Lawrence agree that the beauty of their campus and the surrounding area is worth it. The architecture of the university, a mixture of old and modern buildings, the quaintness of the town of Canton, and the beauty of the mountains and forests make St. Lawrence a scenic and pleasant place. If you are looking for a school with a fast-paced, urban environment and a restaurant and club for every night of the week, SLU may not be for you; however, if you want a school with a tight-knit community of professors and students, set in a beautiful landscape offering a place to hike or just sit and contemplate, St. Lawrence University could be the one.—*Lisa Smith*

FYI

If you come to St. Lawrence, you'd better bring "a jacket. It's really cold out."

What is the typical weekend schedule? "There are two groups on campus. For one group, the weekend starts on Thursday nights ['Thirsty Thursday'], and they go to bars. The other group is the outdoorsy group. They go to the Adirondack Mountains to go hiking, backpacking, skiing, and kayaking."

If I could change one thing about St. Lawrence, I would "make it so that the clubs could be completely student-run."

Three things every student at St. Lawrence should do before graduating are "streak the Candlelight Freshman Experience, ring the bells in the chapel, and attend a Laurentian Singers Concert."

State University of New York System

As one of the largest university systems in the nation, The State University of New York covers immense geographic and academic areas. With 64 campuses comprising large research universities, smaller colleges, and community colleges, the SUNY system is the most comprehensive and far-reaching state higher education system in the nation. Students may take advantage of the wide array of educational offerings such as vocational, technical, Associate, Baccalaureate, Graduate, and Post-Graduate programs.

Well-known campuses include Albany, Binghamton, Buffalo, New Paltz, Potsdam, and Stony Brook among many others. With over 423,000 undergraduates and roughly 465,000 in total, the State University of New York system has one of the most diverse student populations in any state system. With so many campuses and options, the application process for the SUNY system is streamlined using the Common Application for the majority of the campuses.

As with many state university systems, the majority of students hail from the state of New York. Although there are some out-of-state students, they only make up less than one-sixth of the population. That is because in-state students are offered tremendous reductions in tuition and fees. In fact, average SUNY costs for in-state residents are often one-third of tuition and fees of other state university systems. This combination of value and opportunities attracts a very large number of students to the SUNY system each year.

However, with large numbers also come some downfalls. The immense student populations of SUNY campuses and the SUNY system itself make it hard for students to receive individualized attention if they do not seek it. It is easy to get lost in a huge lecture hall of students unless a concerted effort is made to reach out to faculty members. However, once students learn to become self-sufficient and be proactive in their education, the opportunities abound. The sheer size of SUNY system allows for amazing intrasystem and intersystem networking for research, academics, and social life.

Still, with all pros and cons presented, the affordability, value, and opportunities that the SUNY system offers continue to attract many bright students each year. With so many options from which to choose, students are free to make a place for themselves in the many campuses, specialties, and academic choices. Such is only made available by the large yet encompassing nature of the SUNY system.—*Hai Pham*

State University of New York / Albany

Address: 1400 Washington Avenue, Albany, NY 12222
Phone: 518-442-5435
E-mail address: ugadmissions@albany.edu
Web site URL: www.albany.edu
Year Founded: 1844
Private or Public: Public
Religious Affiliation: None
Location: Suburban
Number of Applicants: 20,249
Percent Accepted: 52%
Percent Accepted who enroll: 24%
Number Entering: 2,519
Number of Transfers Accepted each Year: 2,351
Middle 50% SAT range: M: 510–610, CR: 500–590, Wr: Unreported
Middle 50% ACT range: 22–26
Early admission program EA/ED/None: EA

Percentage accepted through EA or ED: Unreported
EA and ED deadline: 15-Nov
Regular Deadline: 1-Mar
Application Fee: $40
Full time Undergraduate enrollment: 11,959
Total enrollment: 12,748
Percent Male: 49%
Percent Female: 51%
Total Percent Minority or Unreported: 43%
Percent African-American: 9%
Percent Asian/Pacific Islander: 7%
Percent Hispanic: 8%
Percent Native-American: <1%
Percent International: 2%
Percent in-state/out of state: 92%/8%
Percent from Public HS: Unreported
Retention Rate: 84%
Graduation Rate 4-year: 61%

Graduation Rate 6-year: Unreported
Percent Undergraduates in On-campus housing: 57%
Number of official organized extracurricular organizations: 160
3 Most popular majors: Business/Commerce, General English Language and Literature, General Psychology
Student/Faculty ratio: 19:1
Average Class Size: 25
Percent of students going to grad school: 50%
Tuition and Fees: $12,347
In-State Tuition and Fees if different: $6,087
Cost for Room and Board: $9,778
Percent receiving financial aid out of those who apply, first year: 61%
Percent receiving financial aid among all students: 60%

The State University of New York (SUNY) system is one of the best public college networks in the nation. Founded in 1844, Albany is one of the more highly regarded SUNY schools. Though it has a bit of a party school reputation, Albany offers impressive academic resources—and less impressive guidance systems—to its body of undergrads and grad students, a diverse bunch who range from nerdy bookworms to seven-days-a-week booze-hounds.

A Feast of Academic Options

As one of the more prominent SUNY campuses, Albany is known for its plethora of academic resources. But as is the case in many state-run institutions, help is hard to come by. Undergraduate advisors are notoriously unhelpful. As a result, much of a student's experience at Albany depends on his or her major and ability to figure things out alone. "The thing about Albany's academics is that it can really vary from student to student as to what their experience will be," one student commented. "Some people breeze right through doing practically nothing, while other students work ridiculously hard all the time."

Albany has particularly strong programs in political science, psychology, sociology, business and physics, to name a few. Lately, the university has gained attention for its writing program after the founding of The Writers' Institute in 1983 by novelist William Kennedy. The institute has boosted Albany's curriculum by beefing up the writing-related offerings and bringing famous authors to speak on campus. Biology is another strong department at Albany. Students interested in messing around with lab rats can check out the Mutant Mouse Regional Resource Center, a bank of specimens with "unique phenotypes" on campus. Students in the public service sector often take advantage of the internship opportunities afforded by Albany's location. Albany also offers 40 different BA/MA combination degree tracks.

Albany has a comprehensive core curriculum called the General Education Program. According to the school's Web site, the program "proposes a set of knowledge areas, perspectives, and competencies considered by the University to be central to the intellectual development of every undergraduate." Students must demonstrate proficiency in disciplinary perspectives, cultural and historical perspectives, mathematics and statistics, communication and reasoning, and foreign language. Although these classes are not very difficult, some students complain that it is very hard to fulfill Gen Ed requirements. "It is almost impossible to get into Gen Ed course classes," one junior said. "[Albany] seems to be accepting more and more students, but not really opening up more classes."

A New York State of Mind

Located in upstate New York in the state capital, Albany's picturesque autumns quickly turn into brutal winters, though this is par for the course in the Northeast. Still, trekking across the frozen tundra between Albany's three campus centers is often a trying affair. While walking, students can admire the architecture of Edward Durell Stone, designer of Lincoln Center, though they may tire of this pastime when they realize that many buildings are reproduced almost identically throughout the campus.

About 93 percent of Albany's students hail from the Empire State. The freshman facebook reads like the Long Island-Westchester Yellow Pages—and with good reason. New Yorkers pay about $12,000 tuition per semester, or half what out-of-state students pay, plus roughly $9,000 for room and board.

The campus is divided into two main locations—uptown and downtown. On Uptown Campus, students live in four symmetrical quads named Indian, Dutch, Colonial, and State—after New York's four historical periods. Students also live in the apartment-style Freedom and Empire Commons dorms, as well as the Alumni quad downtown. The dorms are generally described as average. Most are low-rise buildings surrounding a central tower, and consist of suites with two to three rooms with a common area.

Getting good housing can be competitive, especially when it comes to Empire, one of the nicest dorms on campus. An Empire suite consists of four singles and two bath-

rooms, and comes pre-furnished with couches and dressers, a full kitchen, plus a washing machine and a dryer. "It definitely beats collecting quarters and lugging your laundry to a basement," said one junior. "[Empire] is more expensive, but it's worth it." Dorms such as Wellness Co-op, Bleecker Women's Leadership Project House, and Student Leadership and Healthy Lifestyle House offer themed housing for those with special interests. Recently, the university announced three new Living/Learning Communities for upperclassmen: Anime House, China House and Francophone House.

The number one complaint of Albany students is the weather, but food is a close second. The university's dining system is about as popular as MC Hammer—and Albany food didn't even experience a brief burst of popularity in the early 1990s. Students often chose to eat downtown instead of testing the mush dished out by university cooks.

Perhaps the dining situation has an impact on school spirit—Albany students are lukewarm when it comes to representing their university. According to one student, "Sports at Albany are horrible . . . there is very little school spirit and events are not well-attended. The school has tried to change that recently, but it has not been very successful yet."

> "The freshman-sophomore party experience is nuts, but so much fun."

Albany offers standard extracurricular fare, including intramurals, student government, performance organizations, frats and sororities. Earth Tones (all-male) and Serendipity (all-female), two a cappella groups, are big attractions on campus. The Albany Student Press publishes a newspaper one day a week, and the Student Association governs student affairs and plans campus events.

Party Time

Though Albany no longer shows up on Top 10 Party School lists as it did throughout much of the 1990s, it is hardly a dry campus. Fraternities and sororities are not recognized by the school, but they do exist. However, it is the bar scene that dominates campus party life. "Bring enough money to drink," one student said. "That's the main source of entertainment here at Albany . . . if you wanna make it a relaxing night, you know exactly what to buy from your local provider." Famous festivities include Fountain Day, a celebration of the return of water to the campus fountain at the end of winter; Kegs and Eggs, a springtime drunkfest; and Party in the Park, a year-end party featuring live music and plenty of eats.

Despite its reputation, Albany has fairly strict rules on underage drinking: two strikes and you're kicked out of housing. But the regulations are rarely enforced. "It really depends on your RAs," one student said. "I always drank in my dorm room and never got in trouble for it . . . As long as you're not really loud it'll be fine."

Albany students report that partying is more frequent for underclassmen, and some freshmen and sophomores go out almost every night of the week. Upperclassmen don't go out as much as they start to buckle down and focus on their studies. "The freshman-sophomore party experience is nuts, but so much fun," one junior remarked. "I wouldn't trade those years for anything."

SUNY Albany is a big school with big resources, but it's not too big a drain on the pocketbook. For most, Albany is what you make of it. Students just have to make sure they don't get lost in the shuffle, and most seem to make it a productive and enjoyable time in the capital of the Empire State. —*Zack O'Malley Greenburg*

FYI

If you come to SUNY Albany, you'd better bring "an umbrella, a warm jacket, beer money, and food to keep in your room."

What is the typical weekend schedule? "Starts on Thursday, which is mainly a bar night: you won't really find parties around. Friday: hit up happy hour around four o'clock (Paulie's is the cheapest), then maybe go to some parties. Saturday morning: recover, enjoy the fine cuisine that is Chartwell's brunch omelettes made to order. Saturday night: go out to the bars, unless a good friend is throwing a party. Older crowd is farther downtown. Sunday: sleep in and watch movies on HBO."

If I could change one thing about SUNY Albany, I'd "change the food. It really is just bad, except the cookies . . . they're good."

Three things every student at SUNY Albany should do before graduating are "experience a warm Fountain Day, attend Kegs and Eggs, and go to class drunk."

State University of New York / Binghamton

Address: PO Box 6000
Binghamton, NY
13902-6000
Phone: 607-777-2171
E-mail address:
admit@binghamton.edu
Web site URL:
www.binghamton.edu
Year Founded: 1946
Private or Public: Public
Religious Affiliation: None
Location: Suburban
Number of Applicants:
25,242
Percent Accepted: 39%
**Percent Accepted who
enroll:** 24%
Number Entering: 2,304
**Number of Transfers
Accepted each Year:** 1,787
**Middle 50% SAT range: M:
610–690, CR: 570–660,
Wr:** Unreported
Middle 50% ACT range:
25–29
**Early admission program
EA/ED/None:** EA
**Percentage accepted
through EA or ED:** 53%

EA and ED deadline: 15-Nov
Regular Deadline: None/
Priority Applicaton deadline:
1-Dec
Application Fee: $40
**Full time Undergraduate
enrollment:** 11,042
Total enrollment: 11,515
Percent Male: 54%
Percent Female: 46%
**Total Percent Minority or
Unreported:** 44%
Percent African-American:
7%
**Percent Asian/Pacific
Islander:** 12%
Percent Hispanic: 8%
Percent Native-American:
<1%
Percent International: 8%
**Percent in-state/out of
state:** 90%/10%
Percent from Public HS:
87%
Retention Rate: 90%
Graduation Rate 4-year:
66%
Graduation Rate 6-year:
Unreported

**Percent Undergraduates
in On-campus housing:**
56%
**Number of official organized
extracurricular
organizations:** 200
3 Most popular majors:
Business Administration and
Management, General
English Language and
Literature, General
Psychology
Student/Faculty ratio:
20:1
Average Class Size: 29
**Percent of students
going to grad school:**
45%
Tuition and Fees: $12,332
**In-State Tuition and Fees if
different:** $6,072
Cost for Room and Board:
$9,774
**Percent receiving financial
aid out of those who apply,
first year:** 78%
**Percent receiving financial
aid among all students:**
68%

One of the best, if not the best, school in the State University of New York system, Binghamton offers its diverse student body a wide variety of courses, majors, and living arrangements. The student body comes from around the country and the world, though mostly from the metro New York City area. As part of a fast-growing university, Binghamton is full of challenges and excitements.

Ivy of the SUNYs

At Binghamton, students can enroll and take classes in any of the five colleges: the Harpur College of Arts and Sciences, the Decker School of Nursing, the College of Community and Public Affairs, the School of Management (SOM), and the Thomas J. Watson School of Engineering and Applied Sciences. They can also take classes in the College of Education. All students are required to fulfill general education require-

ments through Harpur. The required courses include writing, pluralism and language. After that, majors and schools have their own requirements.

The options for majors are "literally endless." At the School of Management, now one of the top fifteen public business schools in the country, Marketing, Accounting, and Finance are the top majors, but the school provides students with a solid balance of humanities and math for a future in the business world. At Harpur, English, Psychology, and Economics are very popular, while at Watson, Mechanical and Chemical Engineering are the top majors. At Decker, all students major in Nursing, making up a class of around 115 students.

Another popular option is for students to create their own majors. "A lot of the majors are quite broad, but by creating your own major, you can focus it," said one senior.

The classes at Binghamton range from

large lectures to small discussion sections and seminars. For the most part, students feel that the general education requirements limit what they are able to take, but many find the classes surprisingly engaging and enjoyable. "The great thing about the critical literature class is that you spend the whole class arguing," said one sophomore.

Most students find the workload bearable, but a hundred plus pages of reading a week for one history class led one SOM student to say, "Nothing in college comes easy." At Decker, Watson, and SOM, students all have large amounts of work, but they manage to cope. As one nursing student put it, "it gets very, very tiring, but overall, it is worth it."

Students at the management school value the opportunity to address all aspects of the business world—be it from the accounting side or from the humanities side—as they are required to take classes that give them a well-rounded view. Students at Harpur enjoy the unique classes their college has to offer, such as American Sign Language, History of Pop Music, and the combined major of "Philosophy, Politics, and Law."

> "Binghamton has a lot to offer. It's a growing school . . . Everyone's very active in making the school work."

When it comes to interacting with professors, most students say that, like everything else at Binghamton, the experience depends on the individual. Most professors are willing to meet with students and are approachable on all topics, but it is up to the students to reach out first.

Living it up in the Parlor City
Much of the partying at Binghamton takes place off-campus. Many students head into town to visit the bars or house parties in the city. Since the town relies on students for a fair amount of income, and students rely on the town for places to go, the relationship between the university and the city is relatively friendly. Students mostly go to town on the weekends, but every weeknight sees some students.

The major obstacle for students is the distance between campus and downtown Binghamton. "We're technically on the outskirts of Binghamton, so you have to take a bus or a cab to get downtown," said one student. A great number of students have cars, but parking is difficult, and freshmen are not allowed to have cars in their first year. Nonetheless, as one student pointed out, "if you don't have a car, one of your friends will." Binghamton also offers great restaurants. Places like the Lost Dog Café, Number 5, Grande's, CyberCafe West, and J Michael's are rated highly by students. "It is really important to know these places, because it is food that you actually want to eat," said one senior. "It is a rare find, it is delicious, and it is a way to escape university life." And not only do students go downtown to visit bars and restaurants but also the fraternities. Many students feel that while the fraternities are a noticeable presence on campus, Greek life is not the entire party scene. Still, one student said, "If you're not in a sorority or a frat, you kind of miss out on a social life. I'm not affiliated with any of those clubs. I have fun, but it is not the same."

Binge drinking is not a serious problem, but the university has a zero-tolerance policy on alcohol and does everything it can to help students avoid troubles. For those who prefer to stay sober and on-campus, Binghamton offers its students an alcohol-free option called "Late Nite Binghamton," which has activities including laser tag, video game tournaments, and performances by student groups. Every year, the school organizes Spring Fling, featuring a performance by a live band, as well as carnival rides. Events like Midnight Madness, an event to kick off the men's basketball season, also garner a lot of attendees.

The student body of Binghamton reflects the multi-faceted nature of the school itself. "We're not a party school and not a very expensive school, so there's a good mix of kids from a lot of different backgrounds. It seems everyone just respects each other. I'd have to characterize them as very down to earth," said one student. Others agree that the population of Binghamton is diverse. There are a great number of international students, coming mostly from Korea, China, and Turkey.

Most students are friendly, outgoing, and willing to make friends with most of their classmates. Many people are still close friends with the people they met in their first year, through either living in the same dormitories, taking the same classes, or participating in the same extracurricular activities. Everyone reports that the friendships are strong. "The people I met, I wouldn't trade them for the world," said one senior.

We Are Community

An interesting aspect of life at Binghamton is the community assignment. In freshman year, students choose to live in one of the five communities that make up Binghamton. Each community has its own unique character in architecture, layout, and, of course, the students. Dickinson, the oldest community built with corridor-style dorms is known as a diverse, social dorm, while Hinman is considered a quieter, more studious community. College in the Woods has the reputation of housing a large number of "hipsters and hippies," and Newing is seen as a more Greek-oriented community. Mountainview, the newest of the communities, has air conditioning and apartment-style suites. It is home to a large number of athletes and international students. With the campus broken into communities, students get an intimate community life similar to what they would find at a smaller college while still having the resources and variety of a larger state university.

After their sophomore year, students have the choice of living off campus, either in the two upper-classmen-only housing complexes or off campus entirely. Upperclassmen feel that living off campus gives them more independence, and it's cheaper than living in student housing. Living off campus also gives students the option of making their own food. Consensus is that the food at each of the five community dining halls is decent, but, after a while, it gets tiring. Students are mixed about the pay-as-you-go plan, in which they pay for individual dishes.

In terms of aesthetics, the university has been remodeling for the past few years, and now the campus is becoming greener than ever. Two new dormitories are being built, and the natural preserve, one of Binghamton's standout assets, is becoming increasingly popular. The biggest draw for students is the size of the school. While it's a large, public university, the scale of it is rather small, with everything within ten to fifteen minutes of walking distance. Students also love that the campus, when seen from above, is in the shape of a brain. "If I'm meeting someone somewhere, it's really convenient to decide whether we should meet on the inside or the outside of the brain," said one student.

Bearcats and Other Wild Things

Even though Binghamton doesn't have a football team, there is a great deal of school pride in sports, particularly when it comes to men's basketball and soccer. The school plays NCAA Division I athletics and has a newly remodeled event center as well as two fitness centers, tennis courts, an indoor track, and space for numerous club teams. Club teams and intramurals are similarly big at Binghamton, with very competitive club teams and a wide range of intramural sports. Some students complain that the facilities are on the expensive side and hard to get to, while others feel the options available are worth the extra cost.

Students also have the opportunity to participate in extracurricular activities outside of athletics like the a cappella groups on campus or the radio station. "We have one of the last free-format radio stations in the country," said one student who currently works as a DJ. Students also get involved in the governing of their community and individual buildings, and a great number of jobs are available on campus through the school. Interested students are able to work at a wide variety of jobs, from setting up the dining halls, where the hours are considered rather inflexible, to internships at the events center. Publications like the *Pipe Dream* report on campus issues and events happening around the school.

Binghamton students are a very mixed crowd, living in a multi-faceted school. They feel that their lives and the lives of their friends are balanced between studying, work, and fun. As a senior summed up, "Binghamton has a lot to offer. It's a growing school. There's a weird stigma people have when applying to SUNYs. Binghamton breaks out of that. Everyone's very active in making the school work."—*Simon Warren*

FYI

If you come to Binghamton, you'd better bring "an umbrella, a blanket, and a willingness to work."

What is the typical weekend schedule? "Friday, go out to the bars or a party. Saturday, do your work, or whatever extracurricular you're involved in, and go out at night. Sunday, do whatever work you haven't done yet, and get ready for the week."

If I could change one thing about Binghamton, I'd "make the transportation system in Binghamton run more efficiently and directly."

Three things every student at Binghamton should do before graduating are "hike to the top of the nature preserve, go to a basketball or soccer game, and eat at the Lost Dog Café."

State University of New York / Buffalo

Address: 17 Capen Hall
Buffalo, NY 14260-1660
Phone: 716-645-6900
E-mail address:
ub-admissions@buffalo.edu
Web site URL:
www.admissions.buffalo.edu
Year Founded: 1846
Private or Public: Public
Religious Affiliation: None
Location: Urban
Number of Applicants:
19,784
Percent Accepted: 52%
**Percent Accepted who
enroll:** 31%
Number Entering:
3,154
**Number of Transfers
Accepted each Year:**
3,442
Middle 50% SAT range:
M: 550–650, CR: 500–600,
Wr: Unreported
Middle 50% ACT range:
23–27
**Early admission program
EA/ED/None:** ED

**Percentage accepted
through EA or ED:** 70%
EA and ED deadline: 1-Nov
Regular Deadline: None/
Priority Application Deadline:
1-Nov
Application Fee: $40
**Full time Undergraduate
enrollment:** 17,780
Total enrollment:
28,192
Percent Male: 54%
Percent Female: 46%
**Total Percent Minority or
Unreported:** 30%
Percent African-American:
7%
**Percent Asian/Pacific
Islander:** 9%
Percent Hispanic: 4%
Percent Native-American:
<1%
Percent International: 12%
**Percent in-state/out of
state:** 84%/16%
Percent from Public HS:
Unreported
Retention Rate: 87%

Graduation Rate 4-year:
40%
Graduation Rate 6-year:
65%
**Percent Undergraduates in
On-campus housing:** 35%
**Number of official organized
extracurricular
organizations:** >200
3 Most popular majors:
Business, Psychology,
Communication
Student/Faculty ratio: 16:1
Average Class Size: 24
**Percent of students going to
grad school:** 36%
Tuition and Fees:
$14,914
**In-State Tuition and Fees if
different:** $7,014
Cost for Room and Board:
$10,092
**Percent receiving financial
aid out of those who apply,
first year:** 67%
**Percent receiving financial
aid among all students:**
75%

SUNY Buffalo, known as UB to students, is the largest of the 64 State Universities of New York. Established in 1846, UB is one of the most versatile public schools on the East Coast. Most students at UB are from the state of New York, but there are also quite a few students from all around the nation. Since UB is one of the larger public schools on the East Coast, UB students may find themselves getting lost in the crowd, but those who find their niche at the school can take full advantage of the many options available to them.

Diversity in Study

Students at UB are a diverse bunch and have academic options to match up. UB offers 84 undergraduate majors which students can combine in double majors and minors. A junior, who has taken advantage of the many subjects available, remarked, "I am major-

ing in Social Science and doing a minor in Sociology." In addition, there are special major programs in which individuals can devise their own programs of study. For those who are creative in designing their own majors, UB offers this option. For the ambitious, UB also offers combined-degree programs for some majors where driven students can obtain both their bachelor's and master's degrees in five years. "You can basically study anything you want at UB. A lot of students double-major or -minor or design their own majors," one student said.

UB encourages high achievement from its students. Every year, UB picks 250 incoming freshmen who have demonstrated academic prowess to join the University Honors College, which allows students to receive merit-based scholarships for their four years at UB. In addition, UB has the Distinguished Honors Program, which provides a free, all-expenses-paid undergraduate education. This opportunity is given to as many as 20 lucky students a year.

While many students are pre-pharmacy, pre-business, pre-med, or pre-law at UB, architecture is surprisingly one of the most popular majors at UB. Students agree that UB is a big science and engineering school and these classes are usually harder and heavier in workload. One UB student remarked, "My workload usually depends on what classes I choose to take even if they're not science classes." To graduate, students must have completed 120 credits as well as taken all the required classes for their respective majors or minors. Freshmen also have to take a combination of core classes that usually are outside of their major. Although many students dislike these classes of 300 to 400, some freshmen find what they want to study through their core courses.

> "You can basically study anything you want at UB. A lot of students double-major or -minor or design their own majors."

Students agree that being at a public school means that it is harder to get into classes. "People that have more credits get to register for classes first, so if you are a junior or senior you would get the classes that you need while the rest of the students who have fewer credits might not be able to get in," said a junior at UB. But a freshman noted, "If I really need a class for my major, I can speak to my academic counselor and have him 'force register' me into a class, which they usually will do." UB students study hard and they have the largest library system of all the State Universities of New York, with one of the biggest collections. Libraries are usually crowded before finals and midterms.

Dorms Become Like Second Homes

Dorm life is big on campus and students and RAs alike try to make dorms and living spaces as homey as possible. A student said, "My RA is pretty cool; she's nice and comes up with events for our floor to do every month and she decorates all our halls." Students at UB participate in dorm activities sponsored by their RAs and often build great fellowships with those they live with.

One UB student who lived on campus said, "Dorms in UB are pretty okay compared to some that I've seen from other schools. The rooms are an okay size, not too small, but not too big either." For a public school, UB dorms seem to satisfy its students. Dorm life at UB is fairly typical: students learn to live with floor mates and roommates in harmony. A junior remarked, "Dorm life can get very noisy. People sometimes come back from parties at four in the morning."

UB has three different campuses. North campus is the busy, lively part of the university which is located in suburban Amherst. It has more than 100 buildings and is currently under construction for new student housing. The dorms share a public bathroom and kitchen on every floor so students tend to mingle and know those who live on the same floor. South campus is located in Buffalo. The architecture is classified as more historic, with a bell tower completing the look. South campus dorms are suite-style; students share a bathroom with their suite rather than their floor. Downtown Campus, the newest addition to the UB campus, is located in downtown Buffalo. It is known for its new buildings and state-of-the-art life sciences buildings.

Victor E. and Victoria S.

The Bulls, Victor E. and Victoria S., are UB's official mascots, and they have certainly brought a lot of victory to the school. The football, baseball, softball, volleyball, basketball, wrestling, swimming, tennis, cross country, soccer, rowing, and track and field teams are all represented in the NCAA Division I. UB athletes have their school to thank in pushing them on to victory; football is a big deal at UB and students will often go to their school's football teams to cheer for their school. A junior at UB said that of all her experiences so far at UB, "sports are a big thing at UB and football is the most popular." The UB Stadium seats 29,013 people, which adds to the exhilarating athletic experience for students and athletes alike. In addition, UB basketball players receive a lot of school pride from students; the Alumni Arena is the second-largest on-campus basketball complex in the state. UB students also participate in intramural sports with other students on campus, where they can hang out with friends and catch a game of Frisbee or just jog around campus before the heavy snows set in for the winter.

The Proof Is In the Numbers

Because UB is such a large school, there are tons of things to do and people to meet. Looking back on his years at UB, a senior said, "I ended up finding the right group of people at UB who have become my best friends . . . there are so many different people at UB that you're bound to find the right group." The diverse group of students are offered seemingly endless opportunities to get involved in clubs and activities outside the classroom, and students are very active in their extracurricular activities. One student was thankful for her work-study job at the architecture and planning library, where she can contribute to her tuition. UB offers work-study to many students on campus and quite a few students work during their undergraduate years.

The biggest social events of the year at UB are Fall Fest and Spring Fest, which are held on UB's North Campus. In 2007, Spring Fest was held on Earth Day and musicians such as Jason Mraz and the band Juxtaposse performed for enthusiastic UB students. Other social events at UB usually happen within dorms, where suite mates or roommates may throw a party for their floor and invite friends.

Although only around 10 percent of the UB student body is involved in Greek life at UB, fraternities and sororities play a big part in the school's social scene. A student in an Asian-interest sorority at UB said, "Greek life is not as popular as it was in the past, but it's still pretty big at UB. It's pretty competitive to rush and it definitely has a dominant presence." Although Greek organizations are competitive in looking for potentials, they also support each other when throwing social or community-wide events on campus.

SUNY Buffalo offers a wide range of academic and extracurricular options to its many students. Students come to accept and even enjoy the city of Buffalo and learn to find their true niche.—*Emily Chen*

FYI

If you come to UB, you better bring "snow clothes because it snows A LOT!"

What is the typical weekend schedule like? "Friday classes and parties at night, sleep in on Saturday, go off campus with some friends to the mall and eat out and spend the night watching a movie with friends, Sunday sleep in and finish up homework for the rest of the week."

If I could change one thing about UB, I'd "add more social places near the school for students to go when they just want to have fun."

Three things every student at UB should do before graduating are "take advantage of internships and international opportunities, go to the annual Welcome Back Party hosted by the Lambdas, and go to a football game."

State University of New York / Stony Brook

Address: 118 Administration Building, Stony Brook, NY 11794-1901
Phone: 631-632-6868
E-mail address: enroll@stonybrook.edu
Web site URL: www.stonybrook.edu
Year Founded: 1957
Private or Public: Public
Religious Affiliation: None
Location: Suburban
Number of Applicants: 27,822
Percent Accepted: 41%
Percent Accepted who enroll: 24%
Number Entering: 2,734
Number of Transfers Accepted each Year: 3,200
Middle 50% SAT range: M: 570–660, CR: 520–610, Wr: 510–610
Middle 50% ACT range: 24–28
Early admission program EA/ED/None: EA

Percentage accepted through EA or ED: 44%
EA and ED deadline: 15-Nov
Regular Deadline: Rolling 1-Dec recommended
Application Fee: $40
Full time Undergraduate enrollment: 14,735
Total enrollment: 23,994
Percent Male: 51%
Percent Female: 49%
Total Percent Minority or Unreported: 38%
Percent African-American: 7%
Percent Asian/Pacific Islander: 22%
Percent Hispanic: 8%
Percent Native-American: <1%
Percent International: Unreported
Percent in-state/out of state: 87%/13%
Percent from Public HS: Unreported
Retention Rate: 89%

Graduation Rate 4-year: 44%
Graduation Rate 6-year: 59%
Percent Undergraduates in On-campus housing: 52%
Number of official organized extracurricular organizations: 286
3 Most popular majors: Biology, Psychology, Business Management
Student/Faculty ratio: 18:1
Average Class Size: 26
Percent of students going to grad school: 34%
Tuition and Fees: $12,070
In-State Tuition and Fees if different: $5,810
Cost for Room and Board: $9,132
Percent receiving financial aid out of those who apply, first year: 72%
Percent receiving financial aid among all students: 57%

When it opened doors in 1957, what was the first version of SUNY Stony Brook had only 100 students. Today, the university enrolls more than 14,000 undergraduates and possesses a campus of more than 1,300 acres. It is a major research institution of New York's public university system and operates some of the nation's premier science laboratories. Although the location of Stony Brook on Long Island seems to suggest proximity to New York City, it actually takes a long ride by train to Manhattan, given the size of Long Island. Nevertheless, the suburban university certainly has its own appeal and presents an interesting experience for all students.

The Best of Both Worlds

Stony Brook has a great reputation as a school that combines research with education. It is considered one of the top 100 national universities by the *U.S. News & World Report* for its undergraduate education. At the same time, it is a member of the Associa-

tion of American Universities, a group of top 62 research institutions. "I know that we have a lot of Nobel Prize winners over the years," said one student. "So it is really cool to know that you go to a school with some really respected professors."

The university is divided into eleven schools. Most students are enrolled in the College of Arts and Sciences. The College of Engineering and Applied Sciences is often considered one of the prominent institutions within the university because of the significant presence of research activities in the field. The C. N. Yang Institute for Theoretical Physics, named for a former Nobel Prize winner, is one of the most important research centers in the field and has had successes in many areas since its creation in the 1960s. Furthermore, Stony Brook is also one of the operators of Brookhaven National Laboratory, originally dedicated to nuclear technology research during the Cold War and now expanded into other areas of physics, chemistry, and biology. Despite the research being conducted at Stony Brook, some people do not believe that it adds much to the student experience. "I think the research centers are the high points of the university," said one student. "It shows how many great things the school has accomplished. On the flip side, they don't really help the college students that much because they are so far apart from the undergraduate programs."

For a college as large as Stony Brook, the number of majors is relatively small. In fact, the school offers 65 majors and 77 minors, certainly not a small number, but many schools of comparable size have close to 200 programs. Nevertheless, the students think that the academic options are sufficient. "I know that other schools have really specialized majors," said one student. "But you want to learn a little bit of everything as an undergraduate, so I would prefer a more general program like what we have here." The most popular majors include the usual suspects, such as psychology and political science. However, significant portion of the student body is also engaged in applied mathematics and statistics, demonstrating the school's commitment to science and engineering.

The series of required classes at Stony Brook has a big name: Diversified Education Curriculum, which is essentially the same as the core requirements of other universities. Students are expected to refine the basic skills in writing, mathematics, and logic. In addition, they must take classes in different academic fields, such as science and humanities, and acquire some global understanding by enrolling in courses about non-Western cultures. "I like the idea of the requirements, but when they are put into practice, they can be really annoying because I am not into what some of the classes teach," said one student.

In general, students find the course load manageable. One drawback is the number of large lectures and the lack of accessibility to smaller classes that encourage discussions. Of course, there are plenty of small seminars. Nevertheless, most classes revolve around the professors spitting out information about a topic, and students scramble to take down what is being said and try to remember and apply that information. "It is a big school, so there is not that much individual attention," said one student. On the other hand, other students think that individual attention can be had. It just requires a little extra effort. "You have to take the initiative to talk to professors after class or at their offices," said one student. "Most people just never bother to do it."

Central Long Island

Stony Brook is a nice, residential hamlet of slightly over 10,000 people. There are not many commercial activities, thus offering the university a relatively quiet atmosphere. Many students come from Long Island and thus are very familiar with the area. Nevertheless, given that it is located in a residential area, Stony Brook is not particularly interesting. To find better nightlife and more diverse weekend activities, students can go to Manhattan, which is about 50 miles away, most easily accessible by local railways. Some people not familiar with the area may mistakenly believe that Long Island is very close to New York City, but it is certainly not the case for much of the island, which stretches nearly 100 miles away from the Big Apple. "Manhattan is close, but you have to plan ahead if you want to go there, or you may end up getting back here really late at night," said one student.

> "You have to take the initiative to talk to professors after class or at their offices."

No one is required to live on campus, though over 80 percent of the freshman class does. After all, it is convenient and a good way to meet people. Those who do not live on campus during first year often live within the area and can easily commute from home. More than 8,000 undergraduates total live in residences provided by the university, which consist of 28 residence halls and 23 apartment buildings. The dorms are arranged into six different quads, each of which contains three to five dorm buildings. The idea is to create smaller, more intimate communities within a large university. "The rooms are not that bad, and they provide most of the services you need, like wireless Internet," said one student. "That is why I think it is a better option to live in the school dorms than off campus, where the rent can be actually pretty expensive, and you don't have all the amenities you get in the school."

Dining at Stony Brook may not be healthy, as many of the better options consist of fast food, but the university certainly provides a great variety of choices. The food is a combination of dining-hall style buffet, sit-down restaurants, and fast food chains, thus a large number of eateries and convenience stores.

Greek life is an important part of the social life. There are 31 fraternities and sororities recognized by the university. Since it is a large campus, people can always find parties on campus during weekends, though it is important to know that many people do choose to go to New York City for a more exciting nightlife or simply go home, if their home is close to campus.

An Experience to Remember

Students at Stony Brook come from all types of background, creating a diverse campus. Although the great majority of students are New Yorkers who take advantage of the low tuition, there are plenty of out-of-state students, not to mention people coming from overseas. "It is fun to know people of all interests," said one student. "I think that, when you graduate, you will definitely leave here with a great education and some great memories."—*Xiaohang Liu, Paul Treadgold*

FYI

What is the typical weekend schedule? "You should spend one of the days in NYC, and there are some clubs you can go to here."

If I could change one thing about Stony Brook, I'd "make classes smaller."

Three things every student at Stony Brook should do before graduating are "go to a sporting event, go to NYC, and live off campus for a year."

Syracuse University

Address: 900 South Crouse Avenue, Syracuse, NY 13244-2130
Phone: 315-443-3611
E-mail address: orange@syr.edu
Web site URL: www.syr.edu
Year Founded: 1870
Private or Public: Private
Religious Affiliation: None
Location: Urban
Number of Applicants: 22,058
Percent Accepted: 52%
Percent Accepted who enroll: 27%
Number Entering: 3,473
Number of Transfers Accepted each Year: 305
Middle 50% SAT range: M: 550–650, CR: 520–620, Wr: 530–630
Middle 50% ACT range: 23–28
Early admission program EA/ED/None: ED

Percentage accepted through EA or ED: 77%
EA and ED deadline: 15-Nov
Regular Deadline: 1-Jan
Application Fee: $70
Full time Undergraduate enrollment: 12,981
Total enrollment: 19,366
Percent Male: 43%
Percent Female: 57%
Total Percent Minority or Unreported: 28%
Percent African-American: 7%
Percent Asian/Pacific Islander: 10%
Percent Hispanic: 7%
Percent Native-American: <1%
Percent International: 6%
Percent in-state/out of state: 40%/60%
Percent from Public HS: 72%
Retention Rate: 91%
Graduation Rate 4-year: 71%

Graduation Rate 6-year: 82%
Percent Undergraduates in On-campus housing: 75%
Number of official organized extracurricular organizations: 377
3 Most popular majors: Psychology, Architecture, Information Management & Technology
Student/Faculty ratio: 15:1
Average Class Size: 24
Percent of students going to grad school: 16%
Tuition and Fees: $32,180
In-State Tuition and Fees if different: No difference
Cost for Room and Board: $11,656
Percent receiving financial aid out of those who apply, first year: 75%
Percent receiving financial aid among all students: 79%

Perhaps best known to outsiders as the home of the Orange, a successful athletic program of the Big East Confer- ence, Syracuse University is an outstanding institution of higher learning for nearly 20,000 undergraduate and graduate students. Located on a hill southeast of downtown Syracuse, the university is also a leading research institution in upstate New York. Although the bitter, snowy winters are a concern for many prospective students, Syracuse presents a large array of academic opportunities and a very fulfilling social life, thus making it a great college choice for students from around the world.

Having a Plan

The undergraduate program at Syracuse can be pursued in one of the nine colleges: Architecture, Arts and Sciences, Education, Engineering and Computer Sciences, Human Ecology, Information Studies, Management, Public Communications, and Visual and Performing Arts. When a high school senior applies to Syracuse, he or she must make a choice among these colleges. There is also the option of dual enrollment, if the applicant has an interest in two different fields. However, it is clear that the university wants students to make a choice before they enter the university. Of course, it does not mean that the student's academic options are limited once they arrive on campus. After all, the College of Arts and Sciences has a large selection of different majors.

> "Newhouse is definitely the best-known school at Syracuse. A lot of the events held there get a lot of attention from the press."

Although each college has its own strengths and weaknesses, most students agree that the most prestigious one is the S.I. Newhouse School of Public Communications, which is considered one of the best journalism schools in the United States. It has produced a large number of well-known journalists and broadcasters, such as Bob Costas and Steve Kroft. "Newhouse is definitely the best known school at Syracuse," said one student. "A lot of the events held there get a lot of attention from the press."

The School of Architecture is also recognized as one of the best in the country. It is the fourth oldest in the country, tracing its origin to the 1870s. "If you want to go into architecture, you might want to take a close look at Syracuse. It has a strong faculty and a lot of bright students," said one senior.

A large university, Syracuse offers more than 200 undergraduate majors, including several that are rarely found in other colleges,

such as Printmaking and Ceramics. "We definitely have a lot of majors and minors as well," said one student. "You are a little constrained because they are in a specific college and can only choose majors in that college, but it is always possible to take classes in other disciplines, which is fun."

Classes at Syracuse vary in difficulty, depending on the professors. Careful research at the beginning of the semester will go a long way in helping students obtain the optimal workload. "You should look into the course content before you take a class so that you are not surprised at how much you have to work or how your grade ends up," said one student. The class size, on the other hand, is reasonable. Although popular introductory classes can have more than 200 students, upperclassmen have the opportunity to enroll in seminars of 10 to 20 people, thus having more time for class discussions and debates.

Syracuse also has an Honors Program available to students in any of the colleges. It is designed to enrich curriculums in whatever fields of study the students chose. There are a number of required courses for Honors students so that everyone has a breadth of experiences as well as strong global awareness and civic engagement. Another special program is Syracuse University in Florence, often considered as one of the best study abroad initiatives in the country. In this program established in 1959, students live with host families and study in a small Syracuse campus only ten minutes away from the city of Florence. In addition, the university also offers Discovery Florence, available only to first-semester freshmen entering the College of Arts and Sciences. Unlike most study abroad programs that are mostly available to juniors and seniors, Syracuse freshmen receive the opportunity to go overseas and experience life in a historic European city.

As one of the top 60 national universities ranked by the *U.S. News & World Report*, Syracuse has a selective admissions process. At the same time, it also means a student body that is both talented and focused on academics.

Central New York

Syracuse is the heart of Central New York. Its metropolitan area is comprised of more than 600,000 people. All the usual amenities of a big city are present in Syracuse, ranging from sports complexes to convention centers to a number of colleges and universities. Nevertheless, it is important to point out that Syracuse, despite being the fifth most populous city in New York, is not a booming metropolis. The relative decline of the region over the last few decades resulted in a lackluster appeal of the city to students. "We don't go to downtown often," said one student. "I don't feel that there is much to do here outside of the campus." Indeed, much of the recent development in the city has centered on the university, which plays an important role in Syracuse's economy.

Areas immediately north of the main campus area are good hangout places, especially the few blocks around Marshall Street, which feature a number of bars and restaurants mostly catering to students. Of course, given its proximity to the campus, it is generally filled with students, especially during weekends. Furthermore, Greek life is an important part of social life. With over 40 fraternities and sororities, parties are not hard to find, starting on Thursdays. It is also useful to note that many Greek houses are located very close to the center of the campus. "Restaurants, bars, clubs, and frats are all conveniently located," said one student. "That is one of the best parts of being at Syracuse."

The majority of students at Syracuse live on campus. It is a convenient way to meet people, not to mention easier access to classrooms and different university facilities. The drawback, however, is the freedom from more intense monitoring of student behavior and alcohol use by the university. The quality of the rooms is considered average for most universities, and there are options of learning communities and interest houses, where people of similar lifestyles or interests live together. Starting from junior year, many students do choose to leave dorm rooms and settle in one of the many houses or apartment buildings in nearby areas.

The dining services operate five main dining centers with all-you-can-eat meals, and all of them have options that accommodate vegetarians and vegans. In addition, there are eateries within campus buildings, including a food court that features different fast food chains.

Syracuse Orange

One of the best-known parts of Syracuse is the men's basketball team, which has appeared three times in the national title game. However, the most successful team must be men's lacrosse, which won the 2009 national championship. Playing in a dome that accommodates up to 49,000 people, the Syracuse Orange is an important force in NCAA Division I sports.

Ultimately, Syracuse, though located in the blustery cold of upstate New York, provides a good education, fun social life, and ardent school spirit. What is there not to like?—*Xiaohang Liu*

FYI
If you come to Syracuse, you'd better bring "something orange."
What is the typical weekend schedule? "Sometimes I feel like I spend the entire weekend on Marshall Street."
If I could change one thing about Syracuse, I'd "make the city a little more fun."
Three things every student at Syracuse should do before graduating are "go to a lacrosse game, snow fight, and take a class at Newhouse."

Union College

Address: 807 Union Street
  Schenectady, NY 12308
Phone: 518-388-6112
E-mail address:
  admissions@union.edu
Web site URL: www.union.edu
Year Founded: 1795
Private or Public: Private
Religious Affiliation: None
Location: Urban
Number of Applicants:
  5,271
Percent Accepted: 39%
Percent Accepted who
  enroll: 28%
Number Entering: 580
Number of Transfers
  Accepted each Year: 43
Middle 50% SAT range: M:
  600–680, CR: 570–660,
  Wr: 560–670
Middle 50% ACT range:
  26–30
Early admission program
  EA/ED/None: ED

Percentage accepted
  through EA or ED: 77%
EA and ED deadline: 15-Nov
Regular Deadline: 15-Jan
Application Fee: $50
Full time Undergraduate
  enrollment: 2,240
Total enrollment: 2,240
Percent Male: 52%
Percent Female: 48%
Total Percent Minority or
  Unreported: 19%
Percent African-American:
  4%
Percent Asian/Pacific
  Islander: 6%
Percent Hispanic: 5%
Percent Native-American:
  <1%
Percent International: 3%
Percent in-state/out of
  state: 41%/59%
Percent from Public HS:
  70%
Retention Rate: 93%

Graduation Rate 4-year: 76%
Graduation Rate 6-year: 83%
Percent Undergraduates in
  On-campus housing: 88%
Number of official organized
  extracurricular
  organizations: 100
3 Most popular majors:
  History, Political Science,
  Psychology
Student/Faculty ratio: 10:1
Average Class Size: 16
Percent of students going to
  grad school: 35%
Tuition and Fees: $48,552
In-State Tuition and Fees if
  different: No difference
Cost for Room and Board:
  Included
Percent receiving financial
  aid out of those who apply,
  first year: 86%
Percent receiving financial
  aid among all students:
  60%

The name "Union College" reflects the founders' belief in creating one of the country's first nondenominational colleges where there is "a sense of community devoted to unity rather than sectarianism." Located in downtown Schenectady, New York, Union College is a small liberal arts school dedicated to "broadly educating future citizens of the world." With its unique architecture, such as the 16-sided Nott Memorial built in 1813, and its long history, Union College provides its students with an experience different from any other liberal arts college.

An Education for the "life of the mind."

Union College is what one student calls an "engineering liberal arts college." Although engineering majors are required to take 40 courses over their four years as opposed to the liberal art majors' 36 courses, all students are required to fulfill the General Education curriculum requirements. The General Education requirements include a distribution of courses in the humanities, social sciences, natural sciences, and math-

ematics. Freshmen are required to take a First-year Preceptorial class, which hones writing skills; sophomores are required to take a Sophomore Research Seminar; and seniors must complete a thesis. The requirements may sound demanding, but many students agree that they are "rather easy to accomplish" because there are "so many options for classes." In addition to the majors and minors, Union offers several accelerated programs that provide students with the chance to earn two degrees. For example, the Leadership in Medicine eight-year program offers a combination of a bachelor's, master's and doctoral degree for students in consortium with Albany Medical College. In the Law and Public Policy program, Union and Albany Law School select up to 10 incoming Union students to complete BA and JD degrees in six years.

For students on the Union bachelor's degree track, Bioengineering and Economics are two of the more popular majors. No matter what the major, class sizes are almost always below 25 and get smaller as the level of the class increases. "Even the lectures are small compared to most colleges," one junior said. Small class sizes also allow student-teacher relationships to be "great." One senior noted, "I never had a professor I couldn't go to for help." Some professors even take students out to dinner if the class is small enough. A first-year Union student laughed and said, "You know that the teachers are dedicated once your teacher asks you why you missed class the next time they see you." One of the most renowned professors on campus is Professor Stephen Berk, whose Holocaust class is extremely popular with students.

Union follows the trimester system, as opposed to the semester calendar of most other colleges. Union begins two weeks later than most schools in the fall and has a winter break of six weeks, which some students say is "too long." During that break, a student can take a three-week Mini Term abroad to one of ten possible country options. While most schools end in May, the end of the third trimester is in the middle of June. With the trimester system, students have the advantage of taking only three to four classes per trimester. But classes that would be 15 weeks at another school are condensed to 10 weeks at Union.

A focus of the Union experience is studying abroad, which is recommended to every student, and which about 50 percent of students actually do. The Terms Abroad Programs are offered on nearly every continent. Each academic department has its own programs, which are offered for trimester periods, sometimes even for non-majors. In the Marine Studies program in the spring, students travel to conduct research from Cape Cod to Bermuda to Canada. For those who want to study abroad, conduct research or find an interesting job, Union offers many fellowships and scholarships for students of every year.

The First Greeks

Known as the Mother of Fraternities, Union College was where the first three Greek societies were created. Greek life on campus is "pretty big," with about 50 percent of sophomores, juniors and seniors in one of the twelve fraternities and five sororities on campus. But for those not interested in joining, "you will not be ostracized," and almost all parties are open to the entire student body. In response to the social focus on Greek life, in 2004 the college created the Minerva Houses, a residential program made of seven houses to which incoming students are randomly assigned. Each house has its own council and holds its own events, ranging from lunches with professors to all-night dance parties. The houses provide another social outlet for students if Greek life is too much. But some students resent the houses for "trying to define our social lives."

Party nights at Union are usually on Wednesdays, Fridays, and Saturdays because most classes meet on Mondays, Wednesdays and Fridays. Many parties, especially the frat parties, feature an abundance of alcohol, and many students agree that "binge drinking is a problem, but other drugs are not too visible on campus although they are there." But students also deal with a strongly enforced alcohol and drug policy on campus. If a student acquires five points—for being found drinking or doing drugs on campus several times—they are required to talk to the dean, and with eight points, a student is kicked out.

> "It looks like a North Face factory exploded just off campus and showered everyone with fleeces and jackets."

Students at Union have the opportunity to get to know many of their fellow students because of the small community that Union creates. Many students agree that because Union is so small, everyone is very friendly. Although the interests of students are diverse, most students are from the "Northeast and white," and are from "upper-middle class families." "Most people here are pretty well-off," one student said. The "stereotypical Union kid" is often "preppy" and come winter, it "looks like a North Face factory exploded just off campus and showered everyone with fleeces and jackets."

Life in Schenectady

Union is notorious for its poor relations with the surrounding city. Most students agree that Schenectady is not the best city for a college campus, and while not too many students go into Schenectady, Union takes precautionary steps to make sure every student is safe. Almost all students live on campus, which helps foster Union's community sense. Freshmen have the choice between four different dorms, and by sophomore year, students live in suites that have two bedrooms and a common room. Upperclassmen have the option of living in the Minerva

House—an option not available to freshmen— or some apartments on or off campus, as housing is guaranteed until junior year. Some of the dorms include College Park Hall, once a Ramada Inn, which includes air conditioning and individual bathrooms. Union also has theme houses where students can live, such as the Iris House, which raises LGBTQ awareness, and the Ozone House, which promotes environmental awareness.

One thing many students agree on is the beauty of Union. In addition to the majestic Nott Memorial building at the center of the campus, other architectural features include the "modern" Olin Center, a sciences building, and the "Greek-like architecture" of Old Chapel. Union makes it very clear that its architecture is unique as is its campus plan, which was the first unified college campus plan in the United States. Another distinctive part of campus is the Reamer Campus Center, which is "always bustling with activity" and there are always "at least a dozen people you know in there at a given time." The first floor of the Campus Center is the central hangout place for students, and at the Campus Center, students can get "better" food than offered in the dining halls.

Most students on campus have meal plans, including upperclassmen, because of the limited dining options off-campus. The West Dining Hall and the Upper Dining Hall are the main dining halls for students. Around campus, there are other options such as Starbucks, a convenience store and the sit-down Café Ozone, where students can use their student card to get lunch on Fridays. Off-campus food options are five to ten minutes away and require a car. Getting to one of the off-campus food destinations is not a problem for the many upperclassmen who keep a car on campus. Although Schenectady does not have a good reputation among most students, some would say that during the day, Schenectady is a "quaint"

and "pleasant town" to go to for a crepe, to see a movie or to go rock-climbing.

Where Hockey Rules

With student clubs abundant and ranging from politics to cultural activities to social action to sports, every Union student has the opportunity to take part in a group that they are interested in. If they can't find one, all it takes is an online form and 20 signatures to make a new student group. Some of the more prominent clubs are Colleges Against Cancer, which hosts the annual Relay for Life to raise cancer awareness, *Concordiensis*, the weekly school newspaper, men and women's club rugby, and Springfest, the club that organizes the annual Springfest Concert. Recent performers include Pat McGee and Rahzel.

The sport with the largest presence on campus is the Men's hockey team, Union's only NCAA Division I sport. Hockey games are known for having a "full student section" with "screaming fans that heckle the other team." Other sports that have big turnouts include football and many games where Union is playing rival Rennselaer Polytechnic Institute. For non-athletes, the fitness center at the Alumni Gymnasium has been updated over the past five years and provides students with new equipment to stay in shape. Another option for non-varsity athletes is intramural sports, which are "very competitive" on campus. Intramurals include soccer, basketball, and the ever-popular broomball.

Between its "seven traditions" that students insist everyone must take part in before graduating (such as a "naked Nott run" around the Memorial) to its unique academic opportunities, Union provides its students with a community that cannot be replicated anywhere else. One freshman noted that the campus is "very united and everyone learns everyone else's face. It's like a big high school, but better."—*Willi Rechler*

FYI
If you come to Union, you'd better bring "a HUGE winter jacket."
What is the typical weekend schedule? "Go out on Wednesday for a mostly bar night, house or frat party on Friday and Saturday" and "wake up late Sunday, have brunch at West dining hall, and go back to sleep."
If I could change one thing about Union, I'd "get in better touch with Schenectady. The Union bubble needs to pop."
Three things every student at Union should do before graduating are "paint the Idol, do a naked Nott run, and complete the other five traditions that you will learn when you're here!"

United States Military Academy

Address: 646 Swift Road West Point, NY 10996-1905
Phone: 845-938-4041
E-mail address: admissions@usma.edu
Web site URL: www.usma.edu
Year Founded: 1802
Private or Public: Public
Religious Affiliation: None
Location: Rural
Number of Applicants: 10,778
Percent Accepted: 14%
Percent Accepted who enroll: 78%
Number Entering: 1,199
Number of Transfers Accepted each Year: Unreported
Middle 50% SAT range: M: 590–680, CR: 560–670, Wr: Unreported
Middle 50% ACT range: 25–30
Early admission program EA/ED/None: None

Percentage accepted through EA or ED: NA
EA and ED deadline: NA
Regular Deadline: 28-Feb
Application Fee: $0
Full time Undergraduate enrollment: 4,553
Total enrollment: 4,553
Percent Male: 86%
Percent Female: 14%
Total Percent Minority or Unreported: 25%
Percent African-American: 6%
Percent Asian/Pacific Islander: 7%
Percent Hispanic: 8%
Percent Native-American: 1%
Percent International: 1%
Percent in-state/out of state: 7%/93%
Percent from Public HS: 86%
Retention Rate: 91%

Graduation Rate 4-year: 76%
Graduation Rate 6-year: 78%
Percent Undergraduates in On-campus housing: 100%
Number of official organized extracurricular organizations: 105
3 Most popular majors: Business, Economics, Engineering
Student/Faculty ratio: 7:1
Average Class Size: 14
Percent of students going to grad school: 100%
Tuition and Fees: $0
In-State Tuition and Fees if different: No difference
Cost for Room and Board: $0
Percent receiving financial aid out of those who apply, first year: NA
Percent receiving financial aid among all students: NA

Located along the scenic Hudson River in upstate New York, the United States Military Academy, or West Point, has provided officer training to the United States Army since 1801. Founded by Thomas Jefferson, the academy endeavors to produce soldiers, scholars, and leaders.

Before the official start of the academic year, cadets must complete a "basic training" curriculum during the summer. During this intensive training, a large part consists of physical exercises such as "ruck marching"—or "marching with a load on your back" in addition to such basic skills like shooting a rifle, properly wearing the uniform, and field-based first aid, including inserting an IV into a fellow cadet. But the cadets tend to learn quickly—or they face "learning from mistakes with corrective PT (physical training)."

Military Academics

During their first two years at West Point, cadets are required to fill a "core curriculum," completing basic requirements in Military History, Chemistry, Leadership, Computer Science, Economics, English, History, International Relations, Law, Literature, Mathematics, Philosophy, Physical Geography, Physics, Political Science, and Terrain Analysis. After completing the requirements, cadets choose one of greater than forty majors, including Nuclear Engineering. Popular majors include "anything engineering," with systems engineering being one of the most coveted. Current cadets report that pure sciences, such as Chemistry and Physics, have the reputation of being the most demanding, while systems management is one of the easiest majors. Students also laud the faculty of the engineering departments, claiming that the "Army" experience of the vast majority of instructors (over ninety percent) allows them to show students the real-world applicability of their studies.

With all classes capped at 18 students and a student-teacher ratio of six to one, students enjoy the attention given by the faculty. Though academics are a critical part of the overall GPA, a cadet's grading average also comprises the military and physical portions of their education. While the physical portion derives from the cadet's performances in sports and the Army Physical Fitness test, composed of pushups, sit-ups and a two mile run, the military portion is dependent on "how well you take care of those under you" and performance in basic and summer training.

However, academics still retains the central focus—since 1923, more than 80 students at the Academy have been named Rhodes Scholars.

The "Lowest of the Low"
Students are required to live on campus for their four years at the Academy, with a daily 11:30 p.m. curfew. The dorms, called "barracks," vary widely in form and quality—with some having four rooms per floor and sharing one communal bathroom to others with twenty to thirty rooms and two communal baths—but virtually all rooms house two to three cadets. Students are assigned to their particular barracks on the basis of their platoon, a subdivision in the military structure present at West Point. The entire student body divides into a grouping of four regiments, which are then subdivided into two battalions, both of which are comprised of eight companies with four platoons each.

Instead of a traditional RA system, cadets are subjected to a rigorous hierarchy with freshmen, nicknamed plebes, required to obey virtually any command given by an upperclassman. However, platoon leaders, who are upperclassmen, reside with the freshmen, providing them with leaders to give guidance. "We're the lowest of the low," one current plebe said.

As plebes rise through the ranks, the quality of the rooms typically improves, making the chances of having only one roommate, instead of two, the norm for "plebe" year, decrease.

Recent construction projects on campus include Jefferson Hall–USMA Library and Learning Center, a multimillion dollar, 141,000-square-foot new facility . . . and a science center.

Diversity in the Army
Cadets claim that diversity is present throughout the Academy, though males make up the vast majority of the class. Females comprise only fourteen percent of the academy, with a relatively high drop-out rate. While the initial ratio of females to males is

five to one, by senior year, the ratio drops to ten to one. One female cadet claims that she commonly is "the only girl" or "one of three" girls in her classes. Students cite the struggle of being a student-athlete, with virtually all students involved in some form of athletics, and the increasing amount of responsibility as one moves up the ranks, for the high departure rate for females. In addition, one cadet claims that, due to the relatively higher proportion of females being recruited athletes, and experiencing the associated stresses, they tend to be "the first to go"—part of the relatively large amount of students: twenty-two percent—who fail to graduate.

In sophomore year, students are responsible for one "plebe," and, in junior or senior year, this sense of ownership expands to a squad or company, and then a battalion or regiment—"so it doesn't get any easier," creating higher drop-out rates.

Though West Point can boast of "international cadets," and students from every state are represented at the Academy, cadets from both California and Florida can seem over-represented, claim the students. However, every demographic category seems well-represented, they said.

A "Relaxed" Weekend
Though freshmen say most weekends "you can hang out here and do homework," cadets receive one pass per semester, which they typically use to travel to New York, a trip of a bit more than an hour. In addition, unless a cadet is on "restriction"—a form of probation—they are allowed "walking privileges" around the town, where activities traditionally consist of going into the town of West Point to eat or just hang out.

> "Everywhere we go we are constantly reminded that we represent not only West Point but the US Army."

Alcohol is strictly forbidden in the barracks and cadets attest that "it is not as prevalent as it is at most colleges," but "we have it here." If a cadet is caught with alcohol, they are served an "alcohol board" which consists of an inquisition by the "brigade chain of command" and typically results in "walking hours" where a cadet must walk with a rifle for a period of five hours in a central area of campus.

Cadets enjoy the vibrant extracurricular environment, with some noting the language clubs as being particularly popular for their "trip sections" in which the Portuguese club travels to Brazil over spring break, while the French club travels to Paris, or other French-speaking African countries. Other activities include *Pointer View*, the official newspaper of the school, and even a Close Combat (Paintball) club.

And this extracurricular vitality translates into a drive to succeed characteristic of the Academy. "Everywhere we go we are constantly reminded that we represent not only West Point but the US Army," a cadet said.— *John Klement*

FYI

If you come to West Point, you'd better bring: "You don't necessarily need anything because they issue you everything when you get here"

If I could change one thing about West Point, it would be "nearly impossible to answer because a lot of what we do is based on tradition."

What's the typical weekend schedule? "If it's a football game weekend and if your regiment is doing the parade you get up a little earlier on Saturday to form up for that or guard and usher detail; Sunday: Recall formation at seven o'clock, then evening study period until taps at eleven-thirty."

University of Rochester

Address: 300 Wilson Boulevard, Rochester, NY 14627
Phone: 888-822-2256
E-mail address: admit@admissions.rochester.edu
Web site URL: www.enrollment.rochester.edu/admissions
Year Founded: 1850
Private or Public: Public
Religious Affiliation: None
Location: Suburban
Number of Applicants: 12,111
Percent Accepted: 38%
Percent Accepted who enroll: 23%
Number Entering: 1,087
Number of Transfers Accepted each Year: 198
Middle 50% SAT range: M: 650–750, CR: 610–720, Wr: 620–720
Middle 50% ACT range: 28–33

Early admission program EA/ED/None: ED
Percentage accepted through EA or ED: 27%
EA and ED deadline: 1-Nov
Regular Deadline: 1-Jan
Application Fee: $60, $30 online
Full time Undergraduate enrollment: 5,447
Total enrollment: 9,976
Percent Male: 50%
Percent Female: 50%
Total Percent Minority or Unreported: 28%
Percent African-American: 4%
Percent Asian/Pacific Islander: 10%
Percent Hispanic: 4%
Percent Native-American: <1%
Percent International: 8%
Percent in-state/out of state: 50%/50%
Percent from Public HS: 75%
Retention Rate: 96%

Graduation Rate 4-year: 74%
Graduation Rate 6-year: 85%
Percent Undergraduates in On-campus housing: 86%
Number of official organized extracurricular organizations: 220
3 Most popular majors: Biological Sciences, Engineering, Psychology
Student/Faculty ratio: 9:1
Average Class Size: 29
Percent of students going to grad school: 88%
Tuition and Fees: $38,690
In-State Tuition and Fees if different: No difference
Cost for Room and Board: $11,200
Percent receiving financial aid out of those who apply, first year: Unreported
Percent receiving financial aid among all students: Unreported

Nationally recognized for its focus on the sciences, the University of Rochester is one New York's most popular research universities. Home to some five thousand undergrads with interests ranging from optics to Indian dance,

Rochester has world-class facilities, comfortable housing options, and an open curriculum that encourages its students to explore their interests. Rochester students are not only "independent and capable, but also extremely friendly," and are always eager to expand their horizons, be it by studying abroad or making friends by sledding on dining hall trays.

A Scientific Focus

Founded in 1850, Rochester has been known as one of the nation's top research institutions for decades. Hailed as one of the 25 "New Ivies," Rochester boasts particularly strong science programs, including the nation's oldest optics program. "Science and social science seem more dominant" than humanities majors, but the university also offers "super popular" economics and political science majors that are also nationally recognized. Other offerings for non-science types include a respected film program and degrees offered through the prestigious Eastman School of Music. In addition, the school offers numerous scholar programs, including REBS (Rochester Early Business Scholars) and REMS (Rochester Early Medical Scholars), which give students guaranteed admission to the business or medical school upon matriculation as a freshman.

Rochester students praise their academic environment as "stimulating," noting that although classes can be difficult, the quality of the professors makes them worth the effort. Although some classes are graded on a curve, students would say that "there's basically no grade inflation." "The general attitude at Rochester is that if you put in the effort, you'll do well." Rochester students are also quick to praise their graduation requirements—or rather, the lack thereof. There's only one class that all Rochester students are required to take: a freshman writing seminar. Rochester students across the board list the lax requirements as one of their favorite things about the school; they know they can "take whatever [they] want, without having to worry about getting math or foreign language credits." However, many Rochester students do take numerous classes outside of their major. There's a "general consensus" among science majors that one can't leave Rochester without taking popular International Relations or humanities courses; "you'd have to search pretty hard to find a science major at Rochester who didn't have some intellectual interest outside of his field." These interests are nourished by the school's cluster system, by which students have to take a cluster of courses from two fields other than their major. The "clusters" consist of three related courses that can be completed over a student's four years, and "are really easy to do."

Although "intro classes can be pretty big," with around one hundred students per class, students say that the student-faculty ratio improves as one gets older. Seniors in advanced seminars sometimes have as few as five people in their classes, and even freshmen and sophomores note that there are numerous opportunities to take small seminars.

> **"If you put in the effort, you'll do well."**

For those looking for a break from New York winters, study abroad is a popular option. Although the school is eager to help students "go basically wherever they want to," a particularly popular destination is Arezzo, Italy, where UR has its own specific program to cater to students' needs. The school encourages students to "learn outside of their comfort zone," and even offers a special Take Five Program, which allows students to study a field different from their major for a fifth year after graduation tuition-free.

Social

"At any school that studies as hard as Rochester, you're definitely going to find kids partying hard, too." For students who want to go out, on-campus frat parties and off-campus bars are popular options, although upperclassmen tend to "stick to parties at off-campus apartments and the like." This is partly due to the dorm's "strict" alcohol policy, which students say can be a pain to avoid even though "the penalties aren't too bad." Frat parties are more typical "freshman fare," and Greek life doesn't play a central role on campus—in fact, "it's easy to go all four year at Rochester without ever setting foot in a frat house." For those who want quiet weekends, it's easy to find relaxing ways to spend a Friday and Saturday night.

Music, dance, and a capella groups are big on campus, and most offer a wide range of options on weekends, ranging from shows to parties. "Every girl at Roch is obsessed with the Midnight Ramblers," campus's most famous a capella group. The Midnight Ramblers are known for their talent and their extremely popular social events, and most

Rochester students are quick to tell outsiders that "they were picked by Ben Folds to be on his CD, so you know they're pretty awesome."

One famous Rochester event is Meliora Weekend, "a combination of homecoming, parents' weekend, and a giant class reunion" that brings thousands of Rochester students, parents, and alums together for a weekend of "awesome parties" and an "overall great time." The weekend's festivities also include a keynote speaker, and the university has drawn some pretty notable ones in the past, including Colin Powell, Anderson Cooper, and Stephen Colbert. Rochester also celebrates "Dandelion Day" each spring with a vast array of outdoor activities, including campus-wide games and a "fairly famous" band.

"Sports? What Sports?"

Located on the banks of the Genessee River, Rochester's campus is known for its scenic views and sled-worthy hills. Freshman dorms tend to be small, but "everyone's a little too focused on their classes to complain about housing." Sophomores and juniors have a wider variety of housing options, including larger singles and comfortable suites. Seniors often chose to live in university housing off campus, such as spacious apartments "perfect for lower-key parties."

School pride at athletic events "could use work," but is never listed as a complaint among the Rochester student body. All Rochester students "like what they're doing, they just don't show it in an in-your-face sports kind of way." Although there are plenty of athletes on campus, the school's sports teams aren't particularly popular. Students do participate in a wide variety of extracurriculars however, from nationally ranked Indian dance groups such as Raas to numerous volunteer organizations.

School pride is manifested in the "general feeling of community" one gets from the small class sizes and close-knit living quarters, as well as during campus traditions such as Meliora Weekend or Nick Tahoe's run, a competition organized by frats that involves a mad dash and the quick consumption of a "garbage plate." (The dish is another Rochester tradition, a "huge and delicious" plate at a local restaurant that "you'll enjoy, but only want to eat once.")

Although Rochester is most widely known for its stellar science programs, students say there's "an art to being a Rochester student." Students need a particular combination of academic interest, determination, and independence to succeed at UR—"if you know what you want to do, whether it's something extracurricular or related to going out on a weekend, Rochester has all the opportunities you'll ever need. If you don't . . . figure it out."—*Iva Velickovic*

FYI
The number one thing I wish I knew before I came to Rochester was "how cold it is—bring your snow boots!"
I chose Rochester because "the only thing that impressed me more than the academic programs was the school's comprehensive financial aid offerings."
Three things every Rochester student has to do before graduation are "climb to the top of Rush Rhees (the library), sled down the back of Sue B (the Susan B. Anthony residence hall for freshman) on dining hall trays, and eat a garbage plate."

Vassar College

Address: 124 Raymond Avenue, Poughkeepsie, NY 12604
Phone: 845-437-7000
E-mail address: admissons@vassar.edu
Web site URL: www.vassar.edu
Year Founded: 1861
Private or Public: Private
Religious Affiliation: None
Location: Suburban
Number of Applicants: 7,361
Percent Accepted: 25%
Percent Accepted who enroll: 35%
Number Entering: 640
Number of Transfers Accepted each Year: 29
Middle 50% SAT range: M: 650–720, CR: 670–750, Wr: 660–750
Middle 50% ACT range: 29–33
Early admission program EA/ED/None: ED

Percentage accepted through EA or ED: 38%
EA and ED deadline: 15-Nov
Regular Deadline: 1-Jan
Application Fee: $60
Full time Undergraduate enrollment: 2,389
Total enrollment: 2,389
Percent Male: 43%
Percent Female: 57%
Total Percent Minority or Unreported: Unreported
Percent African-American: 6%
Percent Asian/Pacific Islander: 11%
Percent Hispanic: 6%
Percent Native-American: <1%
Percent International: 7%
Percent in-state/out of state: 26%/74%
Percent from Public HS: 65%
Retention Rate: 96%
Graduation Rate 4-year: 87%

Graduation Rate 6-year: Unreported
Percent Undergraduates in On-campus housing: 95%
Number of official organized extracurricular organizations: 105
3 Most popular majors: Social Sciences, Visual and Performing Arts, Foreign Language and Literature
Student/Faculty ratio: 8:1
Average Class Size: 15
Percent of students going to grad school: 20%
Tuition and Fees: $40,210
In-State Tuition and Fees if different: No difference
Cost for Room and Board: $9,040
Percent receiving financial aid out of those who apply, first year: 84%
Percent receiving financial aid among all students: 57%

A small liberal arts college in upstate New York, Vassar is many a student's dream. It is home to top-notch academics and one of the most scenic campuses in the country. Even if the weather is not always pleasant, Vassar's friendly atmosphere and students' smiling faces ensure a warm welcome.

We Put the Liberal in Liberal Arts

Vassar is committed to letting their students have a variety of options that they can explore. For this reason the graduation requirements outside of one's major are minimal. Students must take a freshman writing class, a foreign language class which one can place out of with a test, and finally a quantitative analysis class which can be fulfilled with classes in a variety of fields. Moreover, Vassar offers an independent major option which allows the students to create their own major which, as one student exclaimed, can be "anything under the sun." Within the structured majors, English, political science and psychology are the most popular majors. Even in these popular majors, however, one does not have to worry about overwhelming class sizes. The intro classes at Vassar, which are considered big, number between 25 and 35 people while most classes have only 10 people, and one student even reported being one of three students in one of her classes. Students warned that "you can't hide" in these classes.

The workload in general, as one student described it, is "very manageable and professors are very understanding." One student asserted that "people will work with you to accommodate your needs. It can be difficult but there is a lot of support built into the system." The professors are in general praised as very accessible. Among them the students recommended Joe Nevins, who teaches "Geography of Mass Violence," and English professor Peter Antelyes. As for other classes, organic chemistry and most intro science classes are cited as difficult, while "Nutrition and Exercise" is a gut class. Among the more interesting classes, students recommended the psychology department's "Sex on the Brain" class and cited cross-departmental classes such as "Psychology of Art" and "Psychological Perspectives on the Holocaust" as worth checking out.

A School That Parties Together . . .

Vassar does not have a Greek system, but no one seems to miss it. Off campus, the town of Poughkeepsie is not considered to be very safe, and the bar scene is pretty dismal. Exceptions are Babycakes and The Dutch, which both offer cheap beer on Thursday nights. For these reasons the campus itself is the center of social life. Students say that parties happen all around campus—there is a lot of camaraderie and "everyone hangs out with everyone else." The only ones that are separated are the seniors, who live separately in all-senior housing and hold their own parties there too. Students also come together at The Mug, an on-campus club/bar that features concerts on Tuesdays. In springtime the biggest event on campus is Founder's Day, which involves carnivals and various other activities on Sunset Hill. The Halloween party is another big event on campus. Most students drink on campus but there is no pressure to do so. While the campus security patrols the campus, the rules seem to be enforced rather arbitrarily and you never know if you'll get written up.

The atmosphere on campus is pretty warm as the students are described as very friendly and constantly wearing a smile. While ethnic diversity is rather limited, there is a large gay community at the college, and sexual diversity, according to one student, "adds another dimension" to the campus: "[Vassar] is very open about race, class, and sexuality. There are always dialogues going on and [diversity] is celebrated."

How Many Gardeners Does It Take . . .

There are nine dorms on campus, and freshmen, sophomores and juniors all live together, thus creating "a great sense of community." This is evidenced by the fact that only about two percent of the student body chooses to live off campus. Once you get assigned to a dorm you stay there for your first three years and it is rare to transfer out. Community building begins freshman year as there are no RAs in the dorms, only Student Fellows, who are sophomores who provide advising and guidance for the freshmen. Their role is more like that of an older sibling than a policy enforcer, and they have no power to get their advisees in trouble or written up. The communities within colleges contribute to the personalities of the dorms. Davidson is a family-oriented dorm, Lathrope is the party dorm, and Cushing is the antisocial crowd since it's out of the way from the other dorms. Strong House is the all-female dorm. In addition, each year 20 students live in the Ferry House, which is the co-op house on campus where students live, work, and cook together. Seniors live in apartment complexes with four to five students to each apartment.

The campus is described as having the "classic academia feel," with brick buildings and lovely landscaping. The campus is an arboretum, so as one student described it "there are lots of pretty trees and sometimes they go overboard on landscaping." She also said that "walking around on campus is definitely a pleasant experience." The quad, which is surrounded by dorms, is the central hangout spot, and when the good weather arrives it is home to many students taking in the sunrays. Across the street from the campus there is more opportunity for outdoor activity as it is the location of the college-owned farm, cited as a great place for jogging. Otherwise, students do not venture off campus much as the town-gown relations are rather strained and one student even reported having trash thrown at her when she was running on the streets of Poughkeepsie. In an effort to bridge the gap between the school and community, the college decided to move the school bookstore off campus, and students are hoping that it will be the first step toward improving relations.

The main dining hall on campus is ACDC (All Campus Dining Center) and The Retreat is its smaller, to-go counterpart. The students praise the dining halls for having very good vegetarian and vegan options and generally describe the options as tasty and varied. For those wishing to venture outside of the meal plan, there are nearby Thai Spice, Tokyo Express and Babycakes which are all favorites with students. For late-night options students heartily recommend The Acropolis and its cheese fries.

A Traditional School

Among the 105 registered on-campus student organizations there are plenty of options. Some of the more prominent options are The Vassar Greens, an environmental club; the Barefoot Monkeys, a circus group; and also the various a cappella and drama options. The school's newspaper, *The Miscellany News*, is also pretty popular. Sports, on the other hand, often suffer from a lack of support. While intramurals have high participation, students complain that school spirit is rather low and not many people attend games or sporting events.

To make up for the lack of school spirit, Vassar is very rich in traditions. Primal Scream occurs each semester before finals, when all the students gather on the quad to scream in unison and let out their frustration. During this time in the spring semester, seniors also streak naked through the library. Another senior tradition is ringing the bell on top of the Main building, and throughout the designated day there are very long lines leading to the top as everyone awaits their turn to ring the bell and write their names on the wall of the room. Scantily Clad is an annual dance party involving Jell-O wrestling, but it's not the only one that involves food. In the beginning of the year, as an initiation process for the freshmen, the seniors go around campus visiting freshmen dorms where freshmen greet them with songs they have written for them and then proceed to enter into a food fight against the seniors.

> **"Vassar is very open about race, class, and sexuality. There are always dialogues going on."**

The community bonds at Vassar create an uncompetitive atmosphere where, according to one student, "everyone is low-key, nice and friendly, and smart but low-key." For this reason students find it easy to fall in love with the school, and when asked if they would choose it all over again, they proclaim without hesitation a definite "Yes, 100 percent."—*Dorota Poplawska*

FYI
If you come to Vassar, you'd better bring "the craziest clothes you own and a smile."
What is the typical weekend schedule? "Go out Thursday, Friday, and Saturday to a play or performance after dinner and later to campus parties or the Mug; during the day relax, do laundry and read."
If I could change one thing about Vassar, I'd "improve the town-gown relations."
Three things every student at Vassar should do before graduating are "ring the bell on top of Main building, visit the Vassar farm, and try the sweet potato fries at The Retreat."

Wells College

Address: 170 Main Street
Aurora, NY 13026
Phone: 315-364-3264
E-mail address:
admissions@wells.edu
Web site URL: www.wells.edu
Year Founded: 1868
Private or Public: Private
Religious Affiliation: None
Location: Rural
Number of Applicants: 1,148
Percent Accepted: 65%
**Percent Accepted who
enroll:** 24%
Number Entering: 174
**Number of Transfers
Accepted each Year:**
113
**Middle 50% SAT range: M:
490–590, CR: 510–640,
Wr:** Unrepoted
Middle 50% ACT range:
21–27
**Early admission program
EA/ED/None:** ED

**Percentage accepted
through EA or ED:** 80%
EA and ED deadline: 15-Dec
Regular Deadline: 1-Feb
Application Fee: $40
**Full time Undergraduate
enrollment:** 557
Total enrollment: 557
Percent Male: 23%
Percent Female: 77%
**Total Percent Minority or
Unreported:** 13%
Percent African-American:
6%
**Percent Asian/Pacific
Islander:** 2%
Percent Hispanic: 4%
Percent Native-American:
1%
Percent International: 2%
**Percent in-state/out of
state:** 69%/31%
Percent from Public HS:
88%
Retention Rate: 76%

Graduation Rate 4-year: 47%
Graduation Rate 6-year: 48%
**Percent Undergraduates in
On-campus housing:** 86%
**Number of official organized
extracurricular
organizations:** 35
3 Most popular majors:
English, History, Psychology
Student/Faculty ratio: 9:1
Average Class Size: 15
**Percent of students going to
grad school:** 44%
Tuition and Fees:
$29,680
**In-State Tuition and Fees if
different:** No difference
Cost for Room and Board:
$8,420
**Percent receiving financial
aid out of those who apply,
first year:** 71%
**Percent receiving financial
aid among all students:**
76%

Pick a tradition, any tradition. Wells has more than enough to go around. Yet despite their overwhelming popularity amongst students, one of the school's most significant traditions has recently been broken. Wells, formerly an all-girls school, admitted its first coed class in the fall of 2005. The close community spirit engendered by such a small campus, however, ensured a smooth change. "For the most part I have had no problems at all," remarked one male freshman. "I feel very at home and the people here are very nice." Indeed, at Wells, community and tradition blend to create the "relaxed and laid-back campus" students value.

One-on-One

Within the framework of a small student body, students have considerable access to their professors. "The one-on-one time that students at Wells get is priceless," remarked one Public Affairs major. The quality of Wells professors makes this accessibility especially appealing. "Many of my professors are literally brilliant," one freshman exclaimed. And while the grading may be tough, "you learn quite a bit."

One of the more interesting courses offered at Wells is Book Arts, in which students study the processes of book binding and book restoration, and even learn how to use a printing press. "It's really neat," one junior remarked. He also commented on the uniqueness of the college's Book Arts center. Wells also has much to offer to those interested in education. An elementary school, Peachtown, is located on campus and Wells students are greatly involved in its activities.

Science and math majors are a minority. One math major did complain about the lack of incentive to enter her field. "To give copious awards for sports or writing doesn't really encourage others to major in math," she noted. Still, she praised the department itself. "I enjoy it and find it challenging, especially the upper level courses, which is what I wanted when I came here."

Breathtaking Beauty

Most students are content living on campus. "The campus is absolutely breathtaking. I mean it is really, really beautiful," one freshman explained. However, the process of determining where to live on campus can be slightly more involved. Weld "has the best kitchen and individual bathrooms" while Glenn Park, the former home of Wells's founder, boasts spiral staircases and numerous lounges. Main, the biggest residence hall, also hosts the dining hall and is effectively the center of campus. In addition, the fourth floor serves as the Healthy Lifestyles floor, which offers a living environment in which "people don't come up drunk or create havoc." While Leach "is crazy," students tend to avoid Dodge because "the style is a bit . . . retro" and it is farther than the other dorms from academic buildings.

No matter where students end up, the natural beauty of Wells's campus is available for everyone to enjoy. Students have access to the nearby lake for everything from science classes to skinny dipping, and many enjoy spending time on the docks. "There are trees everywhere—I came here because of the trees," one student asserted, adding that "the town of Aurora is also incredibly picturesque."

Just as students agree on the beauty of campus, they also agree on the quality of the food. Unfortunately, the consensus is not a positive one. "The dining hall is awful," complained one junior. "It's so bad," explained a sophomore, "that I *lost* 15 pounds freshman year." Still, there are a few who have good things to say about the food served on campus, so not all is lost. One senior praised "Dean Green's macaroni and cheese at soul food/home cooking night," explaining that "the administration actually comes and serves food sometimes." Furthermore, each residence hall has its own kitchen, so students always have the option of cooking for themselves.

On and Off Campus

The close relationship between the administration and students is not limited simply to the dining hall. "Wells has a ton of committees where students go right to the administration," said one Performing Arts major. "We have committees for everything from the dining hall to student diversity that meet with the senior staff on a regular basis." Aside from such committees, students have a wide range of opportunities for involvement on campus. Since Wells is strictly an undergraduate institution, Wells women and men have the opportunity to work as TAs in different subjects. Others spend their time in activities ranging from choirs, to the Japanese Culture Club, to groups such as Q&A (Queers and Allies).

Despite the abundance of extracurricular activities on campus, Wells students usually head to nearby Cornell or Ithaca College for parties. And while drinking on campus does exist, "it is usually pretty discreet in dorms. People are fairly mellow." As one junior explained, "people come to Wells to study . . . not party." Still, many students enjoy the social activities centered at Wells. One senior pointed to Sex Collective and the Women's Resource Center as one of her favorites, crediting them with "The Erotic Ball" and "The BDP" (Big Dyke Party).

Whether or not they choose to party in Ithaca, Wells women and men tend to agree that having a car on campus is very convenient. Though Wells offers shuttle van services to a variety of locations, one sophomore points out that they "don't go to too many places and the times at which you're allowed to take the van are set by the Transportation Department." Cars offer students the freedom of movement that shuttles simply cannot provide.

Above All, Tradition

Students love the great variety of traditions on campus, citing them as a large part of what makes Wells unique. The role of traditions is deeply ingrained in campus life, and begins every year with the Senior Champagne Breakfast and Opening Convocations. "We [the entire school] all make a huge circle in front of Macmillian and . . . light candles," a current freshman reported. After convocation, seniors jump into the lake wearing their lingerie.

> **"People come to Wells to study . . . not party."**

"Moving Up Day" is also a monumental event at Wells, officially marking the transition as students move from one year to the next or from student to alum. "The fire alarms are pulled around 6 or 7 a.m. and everyone gathers in front of Main building," one student recounted. "We 'circle up' and do the classes song . . . After singing, the seniors race to get in line to kiss the feet of the statue of Minerva." Traditions marking the end of the school year include dancing around the sycamore tree on the last day of classes.

No matter which tradition they chose as their favorite, students are enthusiastic about the atmosphere such customs create. "I think it's special; I've never heard of these traditions anywhere else," noted one sophomore.

Wells has much to offer its undergraduates, and students find that their experiences more than exceed expectations. As one senior reflected, "the minute I stepped on campus I fell in love with it. It's exactly the place I knew I had to be and there has never been a moment . . . that I second guessed my decision." She added, "It has helped me grow as a person and challenged me in ways that I'm not sure I would have been at other schools. I love Wells and everything it has done for me."—*Stephanie Brockman*

FYI

If you come to Wells, you'd better bring "a car."

What is the typical weekend schedule? "Sleep, study, then head to Cornell."

If I could change one thing about Wells, I'd "move it closer to a city."

Three things that every student at Wells should do before graduating are "participate in all the traditions they can, skinny dip in the lake, be in a theater or dance production."

Yeshiva University

Address: 500 West 185th Street New York, NY 10033	**EA and ED deadline:** NA	**Percent Undergraduates in On-campus housing:**
Phone: 212-960-5277	**Regular Deadline:** 15-Feb	Unreported
E-mail address: yuadmit@yu.edu	**Application Fee:** $65	**Number of official organized extracurricular**
Web site URL: www.yu.edu	**Full time Undergraduate enrollment:** 3,076	**organizations:** Unreported
Year Founded: 1886	**Total enrollment:** 3,076	**3 Most popular majors:**
Private or Public: Private	**Percent Male:** 52%	Judaic Studies, Political
Religious Affiliation: Jewish	**Percent Female:** 48%	Science, Psychology
Location: Urban	**Total Percent Minority or**	**Student/Faculty ratio:**
Number of Applicants: Unreported	**Unreported:** 7%	Unreported
Percent Accepted: 69%	**Percent African-American:** 2%	**Average Class Size:** Unreported
Percent Accepted who enroll: Unreported	**Percent Asian/Pacific Islander:** 3%	**Percent of students going to grad school:**
Number Entering: 769	**Percent Hispanic:** 2%	Unreported
Number of Transfers Accepted each Year: Unreported	**Percent Native-American:** 0%	**Tuition and Fees:** $31,594
	Percent International: Unreported	**In-State Tuition and Fees if different:** No difference
Middle 50% SAT range: M: 570–680, CR: 550–670, Wr: Unreported	**Percent in-state/out of state:** Unreported	**Cost for Room and Board:** $9,880
Middle 50% ACT range: Unreported	**Percent from Public HS:** Unreported	**Percent receiving financial aid out of those**
Early admission program EA/ED/None: None	**Retention Rate:** 88%	**who apply, first year:** Unreported
	Graduation Rate 4-year: Unreported	**Percent receiving financial aid among all students:**
Percentage accepted through EA or ED: NA	**Graduation Rate 6-year:** Unreported	Unreported

Yeshiva University, a prominent Jewish university, offers its students the unique opportunity to spend their freshman year on the other side of the Atlantic. With 45 yeshivas and institutions located throughout Israel to choose from, YU students can earn a year's worth of credits and enter YU with sophomore standing. All credits earned are transferable from Israel to YU in New York.

Two in One Curriculum

Yeshiva University emphasizes both secular and religious studies. Undergraduates' double curriculum encompasses the Judaic areas such as Halacha (Jewish law), the Bible and the Talmud, as well as the liberal arts and sciences. YU is made up of Yeshiva College for men and Stern College for women. The two gender-segregated campuses are located in Upper Manhattan and Midtown Manhattan, respectively. Students may also enroll in special schools such as the Belz School of Music and the Sy Syms School of Business. In order to fulfill the Judaic studies requirement, Yeshiva College students choose from a variety of classes offered at James Striar School of General Jewish Study, the Isaac Breuer College of Hebraic Studies, the Irving I. Stone Beit Midrash program, and the Yeshiva Program/Mazer School of Talmudic Studies. Students generally take Judaic courses in the morning, while reserving their afternoons for secular studies. One student described the graduation requirements as "doable" and "not burdensome." Many undergrads also take advantage of the opportunity to spend their freshman year in Israel through the S. Daniel Abraham Program.

Rewarding Academics

With over 30 majors to choose from, YU also offers a plethora of joint degree programs in engineering, dentistry, optometry, podiatry, Jewish studies, social work, nursing, and psychology. The S. Daniel Abraham Honors Program at Stern College and the Jay and Jeanie Schottenstein Honors Program at Yeshiva College allow students with high SAT scores to enhance the rigor of their studies.

Students seem to find their classes "rewarding." One commented that "the teachers are of a sound quality" while another said that "the professors are reachable, making it not intimidating to ask a question." Some of the more popular majors are business and sociology. One sociology major said, "it is a pretty easy major" compared to the "harder majors" in the sciences. YU will also help in the job search after college. One student felt strongly that "they will hook you up with a pretty good job right after you get out." Despite the greater number of hours YU students spend in the classroom, students enjoy their dual curriculum.

Competitive Out of the Classroom

Although Yeshiva University is "sometimes lacking school spirit," the men's basketball team is the big draw of the school's varsity sports program. For the less athletically gifted, there is a wide range of ways to compete at YU in a non-varsity setting. YU has developed a strong, completely student-run intramural sports program that offers everything from bumper pool to an Iron Man competition. But do not be fooled by the intramural sports label, IMs "tend to be very competitive." Other popular ways to stay in shape are at the well-liked Furst Gymnasium and the Gottesman Swimming Pool.

The Western Capital of the Jewish World

Like many New York City schools, one of YU's greatest assets is its location. A Jewish university situated in the "Western Capital of the Jewish World," boasting the greatest Jewish population outside of Israel, provides religious students easy access to kosher dining and synagogues. Yeshiva college students love that they can get on the subway from their Upper Manhattan campus and take advantage of the Big Apple's many diversions. Stern girls find themselves in Midtown with convenient access to Times Square. Very few students have cars, so the average YU student relies on New York's public transportation system.

There are not many bars located around Yeshiva College. Thursday nights and Saturday nights are the big going out nights. One junior remarked that while "the more religious crowd tends to hang out at restaurants downtown . . . some YU kids actually experience the real NYC nightlife." This can vary from bars and restaurants to trendy clubs. The on-campus party scene is limited. There are currently no fraternities, but there is an effort being made to establish a chapter of AEPi, a national Jewish fraternity.

Basic Accommodations

The majority of those attending YU live within a three-block radius of campus. Underclassmen generally live in school-operated dorms while upperclassmen usually move into apartments. Some students who live in the New York–New Jersey area commute to school. There are three main dorms. The Rubin Dorm is located on top of a cafeteria and athletic center. The MUSS Dorm, considered to be the least nice of the three, is situated above the main Beit Midrash. Morge is the largest dorm and is found in the center of campus. One freshman said his dorm room "is depressing, but it gets the job done." Every floor has its own RA, who usually is "friendly and not strict." The Wilf campus, where the Yeshiva College for men is set, spans three blocks and all the housing options lie within easy walking distance. The Stern College for women, located at the Beren campus in Mid-town Manhattan, offers independent housing in addition to three residence halls: 36th Street, Brookdale, and Schottenstein. All of these options are just a few blocks away from the Stern Campus Main Building at 34th and Lexington.

> "There are no real traditions at YU, except for the Torah."

Students must sign up for the school-run meal program. All the food is kosher and "it is not terrible." However, one sophomore complained, "I feel like I am paying 15 dollars for a tuna sandwich." Along with the perks of being in NYC, including great restaurants, there are drawbacks. In the past, there have been reported muggings on or near campus. The school takes security very seriously and places 24-hour security guards on campus street corners to protect students.

The Last Word

Yeshiva University is a religious Jewish institution and as such there is little religious diversity on campus. One sophomore stressed that the typical YU student is upper-middle-class, Jewish, and white. But YU is filled with Jewish students from outside of the United States. The university draws students from Canada, France, Israel, and South America, among other places. Since a large portion of students spend their freshman year studying in Israel, many arrive on campus with already established friendships. The general vibe on campus is "real friendly." There is a lot of camaraderie between students of all years. Underclassmen are often in the same classes as upperclassmen, and "they tend to know each other from the same neighborhoods, high schools, or yeshivas in Israel." A religious university without much of a party scene, YU is in many ways a unique school. As one student put it, "There are no real traditions at YU, except for the Torah."—*Harry Etra*

FYI

If you come to Yeshiva University, you'd better bring "a yarmulke."

What is the typical weekend schedule? "Hang out with friends on Thursday (no class on Friday), go away for Shabbat, and back to chilling on Saturday night."

If I could change one thing about Yeshiva, I'd "make it more competitive to get in."

Three things every student at Yeshiva should do before graduating are "go to a Yankees game, spend a Shabbat on campus, and play in the dirty snow."

North Carolina

A long with a reputation for conservatism, Davidson College boasts a reputation for excellence. Since its founding by Presbyterians in 1837, the 1,700-student residential haven has made itself known by leaving its mark on several noteworthy individuals who have passed through its grassy courtyards and majestic colonial halls. As one student noted, "Woodrow Wilson went to school here for a year, then left and went to Princeton because it was too hard."

A Core that's No Bore

The crux of the Davidson education is undoubtedly its adherence to the liberal arts philosophy of expanding the mind through exposure to multiple disciplines. The core curriculum demands ten courses in six general categories: literature, fine arts, history, religion and philosophy, natural sciences/math and social sciences. If that isn't enough structure, Davidson also requires its students to take three semesters or the equivalent of a foreign language, four physical education courses, one composition credit in the first year to establish skills in college-level writing, and a cultural diversity course focusing on a non-Western region. Academically claustrophobic individuals can rest assured that Davidson's rigid core program is broadened by a unique set of in-class opportunities. One student explained, "For a composition course, 'Trial of Jesus,' my group created a newspaper meant to depict the way Jesus' execution might have been reported in the ancient Roman Empire."

Students reported that although fulfilling requirements may seem a daunting task at first, doing so is actually rather easy. Four AP credits are accepted and may be used to eliminate introductory requirements and accelerate within a discipline. What shocks incoming freshmen is the general academic rigor from which President Wilson reportedly shied away. Grade inflation is a distant myth. According to one student, "People lament that if they had gone elsewhere they would have had higher GPAs." Another student noted that, "A papers are now B or B- papers." The tougher majors are generally agreed to be those in the sciences, including chemistry, biology and the notorious pre-med track—the Medical Humanities concentration, while majors such as Psychology, English and Anthropology are in most cases a bit easier to digest.

> "People lament that if they had gone elsewhere they would have had higher GPAs."

While there's certainly no dearth of challenges, Davidson offers an impressive set of resources in all areas of academic life. Compassionate student-professor relationship stories are commonplace—and it's no surprise in a place with a student-faculty ratio of 10 to 1. The largest classes are capped at 35 in the humanities and 32 in the sciences, but "as soon as you move into upper level courses the cap drops drastically to 20, 15, 10, 8, even 5 students," says one student. Classes are not difficult to get into, but if there are problems, many a solution has been reached by e-mailing the reputedly accommodating professors. TAs are better known as ATs and are primarily available for hour-long language sessions during which students meet in a group and speak a particular language. The CIS, or Center for Interdisciplinary Studies, is the undecided, jack-of-all-trades student's academic haven. Faculty in CIS is available to work with students who wish to construct a major Davidson does not offer. One student reported that "recent majors have ranged from neuroscience to choral conducting to

international politics to medical ethics." Apparently, the sky is the limit.

Charming or Claustrophobic?

Davidson College's campus is composed of regal Georgian architecture, miles of grassy hills, a set of cross country trails that "snake through the woods next to campus," consistently temperate weather that "never seems to be overcast," the idyllic scenery of Lake Norman, and a famously charming wishing well. A responsible, active police force contributes to the general feeling of safety that students experience while on campus. However, the sense of intimacy that for some enhances the beauty of their "small but charming" home is a bit oppressive for others. According to one student, "Campus can get very claustrophobic after a while, [so] it is great to have your own car."

Though a convenient asset and a means for getting to a mall (one feature that Davidson lacks), a car isn't necessary for experiencing the various charms and treats that the quaint town of Davidson has to offer. Most students report that they go off campus a few times a week, and although Davidson is only about 20 miles north of Charlotte, most tend to stick to their small-town surroundings. However, one student stated that "if you want to go shopping, you go somewhere else." The town does have a CVS and a few small, rather expensive boutiques, but its strengths are undoubtedly its culinary highlights, which include a restaurant that is famous for its sumptuous chocolate milkshakes and Summit, an excellent coffee shop that is frequented by many Davidson Wildcats.

The majority of students live on campus and have few complaints in terms of housing and dining. Freshmen can self-select a roommate or fill out a short questionnaire that the staff uses to pair them to their roommates. Two Hall Counselors, upperclassmen in charge of enforcing rules and serving as role models and sources of advice for their corresponding freshmen, are assigned to each freshman floor. Doubles and singles are available after the first year, and most seniors live in an apartment with four or five roommates. Floors are single-sex with the exception of Belk. Freshmen start with the largest meal plan, known as "the 19," which can be reduced or eliminated as desired. The student ID can be used at multiple locations on campus and even at a few local restaurants. The dining hall, along with being aesthetically pleasing and offering a plethora of options, is not segmented by cliques and is "great for people-watching," one student noted.

Tradition Meets Innovation

The focal points of Davidson's diverse social life illustrate the clash between convention and ingenuity, habit and experiment. The Union, the group responsible for organizing campus-wide events, works to provide students with a number of stimulating pursuits, whether through lectures and talks, or more leisurely movie nights and free pottery painting sessions. The student center, which was dubbed by one student the "hub of all campus activity," houses the campus P.O. boxes, as well as a café, and is open at all hours for casual socializing, group projects, or those notorious late-night cramming sessions.

The Union also strives to offer "social alternatives to the Patterson Court Scene." Patterson Court is the formal name for the eight international fraternities, four female eating houses and one coed eating house that compose Davidson's active Greek scene. The eating houses came about when Davidson began enrolling women. Female students rush for spots in the eating houses and about 70 percent of Davidson's female students hold membership. Forty percent of men participate in a fraternity. Though the Greek scene is rather dominant on campus, parties are open to all and generally adopt themes ranging from toga to boy-band or tacky parties.

Students admit that although the school's policy is strict when it comes to alcohol, it is definitely available to those who want it. In fact, each incoming freshman is assigned an upperclassman "sibling" of the opposite sex who is officially supposed to help the student meet upperclassmen, but who unofficially is there to "mainly just buy you alcohol."

Students generally agree that random hook-ups are significantly more common than official dates, for as one student noted, the campus is almost too "secluded" for a romantic night out on the town. But despite all this arbitrary "messing around," students report that STDs are not rampant. In regard to alcohol, the administration makes efforts to involve itself through Davidson's 101 courses, which basically teach students how to act responsibly when engaging in potentially dangerous activities, such as sex and drinking. "Davidson 101 courses present sexual activity as a normal activity for college students. However, I know of many who disagree and feel targeted for not being sexually active," one student revealed.

Pearls and Polos

Davidson certainly manages to attract to its campus a "quiet, hard-working, respectful" student body, but this convention is accepted a bit more easily than the one that involves, as one student termed it, the "stereotype of the rich, snobby white kids who wear sundresses and polos to class every day." Many students emphasize the above as simply an exaggerated generalization. But according to one student, "Most people dress VERY preppy. Collared polos, khaki shorts, loafers, and pearl earrings are the standards. Most are fairly wealthy, as can be seen by their clothes, cell phones, vacations, houses, cars, and dorm rooms." Students also express dissatisfaction with the lack of international diversity. On the other hand, while, as one student noted, "most people are similar and come from similar backgrounds," another commented that "the school is really working on diversifying the student body." Additionally, groups do not tend to self-segregate, so the level of diversity that does exist is enhanced by a willingness to interact with various types of people.

Surely there is a general mold for the typical Davidson student's background. But this cast tends to disintegrate in the face of the manifold extracurricular opportunities that are available to every student. Sports range from the more popular football and Division I basketball to the less widely acclaimed flickerball. Students report that community service and activism groups are the most popular on campus. And there always exists the opportunity to translate a novel idea into a new club for those to whom the more conventional organizations do not appeal. According to one student on the possibility for redefinition in such a diverse extracurricular community, "I feel free to participate in what I want to here without feeling like I will get dissolved irrecoverably into a certain group or clique."—*Juliann Rowe*

FYI
If you come to Davidson, you'd better bring "a futon, flip-flops, and plenty of suits/dresses."
What's the typical weekend schedule? "Wake up around 11 or 12, have brunch, study for a while, go out to eat, and head down to the Court/Union/watch a movie."
If I could change one thing about Davidson, I'd "give less work and put up more swings."
Three things every student at Davidson should do before graduating are "go to Lake Campus, order food from Bonsai, and attend Thursday night worship."

Duke University

Address: 2138 Campus Drive Durham, NC 27708	**Percentage accepted through EA or ED:** 31%	**Graduation Rate 6-year:** 92%
Phone: 919-684-3214	**EA and ED deadline:** 1-Nov	**Percent Undergraduates in On-campus housing:** 82%
E-mail address: admissions@duke.edu	**Regular Deadline:** 2-Jan	**Number of official organized extracurricular**
Web site URL: www.duke.edu	**Application Fee:** $75	**organizations:** 200
Year Founded: 1838	**Full time Undergraduate enrollment:** 6,259	**3 Most popular majors:**
Private or Public: Private	**Total enrollment:** 11,680	Economics, Psychology,
Religious Affiliation: Methodist	**Percent Male:** 52%	Public Policy
Location: Urban	**Percent Female:** 48%	**Student/Faculty ratio:** 11:1
Number of Applicants: 18,638	**Total Percent Minority or Unreported:** 32%	**Average Class Size:** 14
Percent Accepted: 21%	**Percent African-American:** 11%	**Percent of students going to grad school:** 62%
Percent Accepted who enroll: 43%	**Percent Asian/Pacific Islander:** 14%	**Tuition and Fees:** $31,420
Number Entering: 1,683	**Percent Hispanic:** 7%	**In-State Tuition and Fees if different:** No difference
Number of Transfers Accepted each Year: 41	**Percent Native-American:** 1%	**Cost for Room and Board:** $8,950
Middle 50% SAT range: M: 680–790, **Cr:** 660–750, **Wr:** 680–780	**Percent International:** 7%	**Percent receiving financial aid out of those who apply, first year:**
Middle 50% ACT range: 29–34	**Percent in-state/out of state:** 15%/85%	Unreported
	Percent from Public HS: 65%	**Percent receiving financial aid among all students:**
Early admission program EA/ED/None: ED	**Retention Rate:** 96%	39%
	Graduation Rate 4-year: 86%	

Perhaps best known among sports fans for its successful basketball team, Duke University is also recognized as one of the most prestigious establishments of higher learning in the United States. An urban school in Durham, North Carolina, Duke has a distinct Southern atmosphere as well as an intellectually stimulating environment. Given the university's athletic excellence, school spirit is, by no doubt, very strong and an important part of campus life. This unique combination of sports powerhouse and outstanding research institution offers a unique college experience, much cherished by Duke's students.

Three Schools

Duke is composed of ten schools, two of which—Trinity College of Arts and Sciences, and the Pratt School of Engineering—offer degrees to undergraduate students. There are more than 40 majors available, as well as about 20 certificate programs, which are the equivalent of minors. Duke also has a distinct option at Trinity College called Program II, which allows students to design

their own interdisciplinary curriculum. According to one student, "Program II is definitely something worth exploring because it can be made to accommodate personal interests."

To graduate, students must complete 34 semester courses. Trinity College has a lengthy set of general requirements so that each student is exposed to a broad range of subjects. Everyone must take classes in what are called Five Areas of Knowledge and Six Modes of Inquiry, which range from arts and literature to science and technology. These requirements attract mixed reviews. Some students are glad they are learning a variety of topics; others are frustrated by the fact that they have to take classes they are not interested in. The Pratt School requires, in addition to classes in math, science, and engineering, one credit in writing and five credits in the humanities and social sciences.

The coursework at Duke is certainly challenging, although it always depends on the specific classes and majors. As one student pointed out, "if you choose your classes wisely, you can make it as easy or as hard as you want." In addition, the difficulty also depends on majors. The economics department is quite strict with grading, while some students find some humanities departments prone to grade inflation. This is not always the case, however, as most students agree that grading varies greatly from class to class.

Gothic and Georgian

Duke's campus is an interesting combination of Georgian architecture in the East Campus and Gothic revivalism in the West. This results in a beautiful campus as well as a great intellectual atmosphere. "The Gothic buildings here are a joy to walk by every day," said one student.

Duke owns more than 8,000 acres of land, including a 7,000-acre forest just west of the campus, a stunning botanical garden, a golf course, and a marine lab on the Atlantic Coast, more than 150 miles from the main campus. "Duke has lots of resources," said one student. "You can find a lot of great facilities here that you would not find anywhere else."

> "Duke has lots of resources. You can find a lot of great facilities here that you would not find anywhere else."

Freshmen reside in the East Campus, the oldest section of the university, where are located 14 residential halls. Nine of them are conveniently built around a central quad, which also includes a science building, the Lilly Library, Baldwin Auditorium, which is one of Duke's major landmarks, and East Union, where are found two dining halls, a convenient store and other services. The other five residences for freshmen are not part of the quad but have the benefits of close proximity to Brodie Gym and air conditioning in several buildings, which is very important considering that North Carolina can be very hot during the first and last months of the school year. For upperclassmen, there are other housing options available in both the West and Central Campuses. Only seniors are allowed to live off campus, and the university has a community housing program that helps students find rentals in the Durham area.

All freshmen must enroll in a full meal plan. Upperclassmen, however, have a variety of options available. In addition, meal plans include dining points, which can be used for pizza deliveries, groceries, and restaurants. According to one student, this point system "is really flexible and allows students to explore different dining places around the area." As to the school's own dining service, most students agree that it is "good but nothing to rave about."

Weekends

Fraternities are the most important element of party scene at Duke. About 32 percent of the student population is associated with one of Duke's 37 Greek organizations. Drinking, of course, is a dominant, though not essential, part of social life. The school is also trying to find ways to engage students in campus weekend activities, given several incidents at off-campus fraternities during recent years and complaints from Durham residents. Nevertheless, Greek life remains an indispensable part of the party nights, which are scattered throughout the week, including on some weekdays.

Although Duke has the reputation of being a "preppy" college, many students there believe that it is a misconception. "Everyone here is very friendly," said one student. "Surely there are some preppy kids just like everywhere else, but overall I think we have a great social environment."

The interactions between Durham and Duke, however, are rather limited. Durham is the fourth largest city in North Carolina and has many points of interest outside of Duke University, including bars and restaurants. Nevertheless, safety is always a concern, and most students do not venture far beyond the boundaries of the campus. "Students generally think of themselves as part of the Duke community," said one student. "There is not much feeling of being a member of the Durham community."

Blue Devils

Duke has a long history of athletic excellence. The varsity sports teams are known as Blue Devils and are part of the Atlantic Coast Conference. The men's basketball team headed by Coach Mike Krzyzewski is known as one of the most successful teams in the history of college sports. According to one student, "basketball is by far the most important sport, and everyone cares about how the team is doing." Both men's and women's lacrosse teams have also been immensely successful in the last few years, despite the recent issues surrounding the men's team that grabbed national headlines. The best team on campus, however, is probably the women's golf team, which won five national championships, including three consecutively from 2005 to 2007.

All the sports trophies result in the importance of athletics in the social scene at Duke and a fervent school spirit that some students describe as almost "maniacal," especially when Duke is playing against its most notable rival, University of North Carolina, Chapel Hill, which is only about 10 miles away. Out of the rivalry was created the fa-

mous tradition of Krzyzewskiville, where students live outdoors next to the Cameron Stadium in tents for weeks prior to the UNC-Duke game. "It is a great experience," said one student. "It shows how dedicated we are to school spirit."

Clearly, Duke can claim a spot among the colleges with the most ardent sports fans. In addition to this strong school spirit, however, Duke also offers top-notch facility and faculty. With its commitment to both athletics and academics, Duke stands as one of the top college choices for students around the world.—*Xiaohang Liu*

FYI

If you come to Duke, you'd better bring "a tent to camp outside Cameron."
What is the typical weekend schedule? "School work during the day, and fun time during the night."
If I could change one thing about Duke, I'd "reduce the so-called General Education Requirements."
Three things every student at Duke should do before graduating are "tent outside Cameron, go to as many basketball games as possible, and go to the Marine Lab."

Elon University

Address: 700 Campus Box Elon, NC 27244
Phone: 336-278-3566
E-mail address: admissions@elon.edu
Web site URL: www.elon.edu
Year Founded: 1889
Private or Public: Private
Religious Affiliation: United Church of Christ
Location: Suburban
Number of Applicants: 9,505
Percent Accepted: 41%
Percent Accepted who enroll: 33%
Number Entering: 1,286
Number of Transfers Accepted each Year: 190
Middle 50% SAT range: M: 570–660, CR: 560–650, Wr: 570–660
Middle 50% ACT range: 23–28
Early admission program EA/ED/None: EA and ED
Percentage accepted through EA or ED: 60%

EA and ED deadline: 1-Nov
Regular Deadline: 10-Jan
Application Fee: $50
Full time Undergraduate enrollment: 4,950
Total enrollment: 5,300
Percent Male: 40%
Percent Female: 60%
Total Percent Minority or Unreported: 13%
Percent African-American: 5%
Percent Asian/Pacific Islander: 2%
Percent Hispanic: 1%
Percent Native-American: 0%
Percent International: Unreported
Percent in-state/out of state: 30%/70%
Percent from Public HS: Unreported
Retention Rate: 90%
Graduation Rate 4-year: 74%

Graduation Rate 6-year: Unreported
Percent Undergraduates in On-campus housing: 60%
Number of official organized extracurricular organizations: 150
3 Most popular majors: Business, Communications, Education
Student/Faculty ratio: 14:1
Average Class Size: Unreported
Percent of students going to grad school: Unreported
Tuition and Fees: $22,166
In-State Tuition and Fees if different: No difference
Cost for Room and Board: $7,296
Percent receiving financial aid out of those who apply, first year: 58%
Percent receiving financial aid among all students: 31%

Elon University, founded in 1889, is located in sunny Elon, North Carolina, halfway between Greensboro and the Research Triangle of Raleigh, Durham, and Chapel Hill. It is a friendly, intimate Southern campus, one of the most beautiful in the country, and it aims to provide students with a well-rounded education as well as opportunities to explore their interests outside the classroom. The friendliness of students and faculty, the beauty of the campus, and many important annual traditions bring everyone together to make Elon a unified and lively college community.

Learning In and Out of the Classroom

Whether Elon students are studying abroad for a summer, taking classes in the spring and fall terms, or learning about a unique subject during winter term, the University prides itself on offering students the chance to have close relationships with their professors and plenty of academic support. Most students agree that one of Elon's strengths is this accessibility of the faculty. "It's so obvious they want to help you . . . They want to make sure you do well," one freshman said. All professors are required to have office hours each week, and some even give out home phone numbers to students. "I like the teachers and the fact that I am able to get to know them on a more personal level because the class sizes are so small," a junior said. In fact, large lecture halls filled with 500 students or more simply do not exist at Elon. The largest class size is 33 students, but the average class size is just 21. Students agree that this gives Elon, a school with 5,032 undergraduates, a small and intimate feel.

Elon University is comprised of five colleges: Elon College of Arts and Sciences, the Love School of Business, the School of Communications, the School of Education, and the School of Law. These five colleges offer more than 50 majors and employ 358 full-time faculty. Perhaps one of Elon's most distinctive academic features is its 4-1-4 calendar. Elon students have two four-month semesters in the fall and spring, buffeted by a four-week winter term in between. It is during winter term that students have the opportunity to participate in a diverse array of activities and classes. Each student takes one class that meets for three hours a day, and the classes offered range from yoga and quilting to the Business of NASCAR and Local Government Simulation. Some of these classes even take trips to sites that are relevant to the material they are covering. For instance, this year's Business of NASCAR class took a trip to the Daytona International Speedway.

Although Elon does offer a wide variety of unique classes during its winter term, one freshman said that she wished the regular terms offered "more weird, obscure, cool classes. I feel like we have a lot of the basics but not as many of those cool classes." The winter term is also a good time for students to study abroad, and many do take advantage of Elon's study abroad opportunities. Seventy percent of Elon students choose to study abroad at some point during their college careers.

Elon also offers seven Fellows programs, which allow students who have directed interests coming into college, such as business, education, or teaching, to take classes that suit their career goals early on and to make connections that may help them with their pursuits later in life. The Fellows in each program take classes together and some even go on trips together during the winter term. For instance, one freshman in the Business Fellows program this year took a class called Business and Sustainability for her winter term and traveled to Mexico for a week. She visited family-owned companies and small businesses to learn how isolated villages sustain themselves. Experiences such as this one are not uncommon at Elon, especially since business and communications are generally considered Elon's two strongest and most popular fields of study.

Just as Elon students are committed to excellence in their academic endeavors, so too are they committed to involvement in their extracurricular activities. From Phoenix 14, the television broadcasting club, to *The Pendulum*, Elon's student newspaper and its most popular campus publication, the University offers students a wide variety of ways to pursue their interests outside the classroom. There are clubs for almost everything—even a Hide-and-Go-Seek Club. No matter what the activity, one freshman noted that "everyone is involved in a lot of different things and it's really easy to get involved in a lot of things." Jobs are also fairly easy to come by if students take the initiative to look around. Shops in the city employ many students and there are also plenty of available jobs on campus.

Elon boasts 16 men's and women's varsity NCAA Division I sports teams and offers 18 intramural and 21 club sports. Although most students would not say that athletics form a dominant presence on campus, one senior said, "People go to the games frequently, but there is not a huge expectation for excellence or winning championships. It is more of a school spirit thing." Intramurals, on the other hand, spark fierce competition amongst Elon students. Flag football, soccer, and basketball are particularly competitive, according to one junior.

Living the Greek Life

From frat parties to movies in nearby Burlington to nights out at one of the three bars on campus, Elon offers just about all types of social life. Although most students would agree that Greek life is a dominant force on campus (about 40 percent of girls join sororities and about 20 percent of boys join fraternities), it is not the only option. "Even if you're not involved in Greek life, you're still included," one freshman said. Another freshman agreed that "Greek life can be as big a part of Elon as you make it. Either you can become super involved, or not so involved. It is up to the individual student." In general, Elon can be a party school for those students who are looking for that atmosphere, but it can also be a very calm place for students who are not.

In this respect, alcohol can play a large role in students' social lives or it can play a very minimal role. "There is alcohol if you want to find it, but not everyone drinks," said one freshman. In fact, some organizations are completely sober and will not serve any alcohol at their events. Elon's alcohol policy is fairly strict. If students are caught with alcohol, they must write an essay and take an online health course. The University is most concerned with students' health and safety, but it also views alcohol possession and drinking as a disciplinary issue. If students are caught with alcohol three times, they run the risk of suspension, and since drinking games are illegal in the state of North Carolina, students caught playing these games may face harsher punishments.

Most weekends, the typical Elon student will go out starting on Thursday night, usually to a bar on campus. Friday and Saturday nights are comprised of frat parties or bars again. Other students with cars may visit Burlington or Raleigh nearby to get dinner or see a movie. The town of Elon itself is small, but it does have some good restaurants, a mall, a Target, and a movie theater

that students visit on the weekends. However, for the most part, students enjoy staying on campus. "I like staying on campus and having that community feeling," one freshman said.

One way that Elon creates this community feeling is through several annual parties and events that bring all students together. There is an 80s party, Festivus (a day-long mud party), a Glow-in-the-Dark Dance, the Elon-a-Thon (a 24-hour dance marathon put on for charity in April that the entire school participates in) and the Polar Bear Plunge (a fundraiser in which students jump into Elon's frigid lake). These traditions keep Elon students feeling connected to the university and help them to develop friendships that will last a lifetime.

Elon students say that everyone on campus is pretty friendly. "Everyone is just smiling and happy all the time and says hi to everyone even if they don't know them," one freshman said. It is easy to meet people in classes, Fellows programs, sororities and fraternities, clubs, and especially through living residences. One of the reasons it's fairly easy to make friends, according to one senior, is that "everyone's really, really outgoing. It's kind of amazing actually."

Although Elon students hail from all across the United States as well as from 50 countries, it is lacking slightly in diversity. There are plenty of people from the Northern and Western United States who are surprised to be referred to as "sir" and "ma'am" when they get to Elon, but 25 percent of the student body does come from North Carolina. The University is working on increasing its diversity, but for the most part, students classify Elon as a preppy school with a hint of Southern flavor.

What it Means to be a Phoenix

Although Elon provides students with a multitude of on-campus housing options, most students choose to move off-campus by junior year. Freshmen are required to live on campus in dorms comprised of suites or halls, some of which are coed. Dorms are assigned on a first come, first served basis beginning when a student accepts his or her offer of admission to Elon. Many sophomores, juniors and seniors try to move into The Oaks or Danieley Apartments, two on-campus apartment-style housing options that are very popular.

However, it is hard for many students to give up living on a campus that is so gorgeous. Elon's campus is considered to be one of the most beautiful in the country, complete with all the amenities necessary for comfortable student life in traditional red-brick, white-column Southern architecture. The campus itself is a botanical garden and is filled with beautiful walkways, fountains, and even a lake.

A central gathering place on campus is the Moseley Center, which contains the admissions office, the campus store, the information desk, a coffee shop, a few large rooms used for receptions, hangout places, the mail room, Octagon (a student grocery store), and much more. When the weather is nice, "you can always see students playing Frisbee in the grass, sun tanning, or just doing homework" outside of Moseley, according to one freshman.

> "Everyone's really, really outgoing. It's kind of amazing actually."

In terms of campus security, most students would agree that Elon, North Carolina, provides a fairly safe environment for the University. The town is very supportive of the University and its inhabitants are similar socioeconomically to the students. One senior said that "Elon is really safe and small and tucked-away. It's pretty quiet." The University even offers "Safe Rides," a service that can be called to deliver students wherever they need to go on campus at night if they do not feel safe walking alone.

Students at Elon have mixed feelings about their dining options. They can be on a 10-, 15-, or 19-meal plan that also includes meal dollars available for use at some local restaurants or for snacks in between meals. Dining halls are open all day and there are many to choose from, so it is hard to get bored with the options on campus. Most students agree that dining hall food is fairly good, but it can get old after a while. One senior rated the food around an A– or a B+. But if the dining halls don't live up to students' expectations, the city of Elon has numerous restaurants that students can go to and use "Phoenix cash" to buy food.

Although Elon is a comparatively young school, it is grounded in strong traditions that unite the entire community. For instance, every Tuesday, Elon students gather outside for College Coffee, a chance to talk with professors and fellow students in an informal setting over bagels, donuts, muffins, and coffee. Another tradition important to Elon students centers around Convocation and Graduation. During Convocation in the fall, new students are welcomed with an acorn to symbolize their potential for growth in their four years of college to come. At Graduation, they are each awarded a sapling to show how they have developed as a result of their time at Elon.

And at the end of those four years, Elon students generally feel that their time in college was a rewarding, fulfilling experience and that they would choose Elon over again if they had the opportunity. One freshman said, "We have such a strong community and everyone is so welcoming and supportive of everyone . . . I thought I'd be really homesick, but I instantly felt warm and comforted and like I'd been here forever. Elon is just such a happy place." So for students who want an education both in and out of the classroom in a welcoming, intimate setting, Elon is the perfect college option.—*Arielle Stambler*

FYI

Three things every student at Elon should do before graduating are "jump in the fountain (even though you get fined), do the Polar Bear Plunge, and go to a homecoming game."

What surprised me the most about Elon when I arrived was "how friendly Elon's staff was. The woman that always checks me out when I get my morning coffee always strikes up a conversation with me and gets me cheerful and excited for my day."

If you come to Elon, you'd better bring "summer dresses, pearls, and gym clothes."

If I could change one thing about Elon, "I'd make it more diverse."

North Carolina School of the Arts

Address: 1533 South Main Street, Winston-Salem, NC 27127
Phone: 336-770-3290
E-mail address: admissions@ncarts.edu
Web site URL: www.ncarts.edu
Year Founded: 1963
Private or Public: Public
Religious Affiliation: None
Location: Urban
Number of Applicants: 679
Percent Accepted: 51%
Percent Accepted who enroll: 54%
Number Entering: 186
Number of Transfers Accepted each Year: Unreported
Middle 50% SAT range: M: 500–620, CR: 540–640, Wr: 600–700
Middle 50% ACT range: 20–25
Early admission program EA/ED/None: None

Percentage accepted through EA or ED: NA
EA and ED deadline: NA
Regular Deadline: 29-Jan
Application Fee: $50
Full time Undergraduate enrollment: 743
Total enrollment: 857
Percent Male: 60%
Percent Female: 40%
Total Percent Minority or Unreported: 18%
Percent African-American: 10%
Percent Asian/Pacific Islander: 2%
Percent Hispanic: 5%
Percent Native-American: 1%
Percent International: 1%
Percent in-state/out of state: 48%/52%
Percent from Public HS: Unreported
Retention Rate: 75%
Graduation Rate 4-year: 40%

Graduation Rate 6-year: 48%
Percent Undergraduates in On-campus housing: 55%
Number of official organized extracurricular organizations: Unreported
3 Most popular majors: Unreported
Student/Faculty ratio: 8:1
Average Class Size: 14
Percent of students going to grad school: Unreported
Tuition and Fees: $15,104
In-State Tuition and Fees if different: $3,224
Cost for Room and Board: $6,831
Percent receiving financial aid out of those who apply, first year: 77%
Percent receiving financial aid among all students: 49%

With some of the most talented students around—actors, dancers, musicians, filmmakers and production designers—uniting behind their beloved mascot the "fighting pickle," the North Carolina School of the Arts (NCSA) defies categorization. This small, competitive arts conservatory is neither an ordinary college nor an ordinary arts school: quirky, intimate and friendly, NCSA attracts applicants from all over the world and commands a respect among professional artists that rivals its more well-known competitors. For students truly passionate about their arts, NCSA provides intensive training with top-notch faculty for a fraction of the price of private conservatories.

Let's Go, Pickles!

The "School of the Arts," as locals sometimes call NCSA, is comprised of five arts schools: Dance, including modern and ballet; Drama; Filmmaking; Music; and Design

and Production, which trains students in set design, costuming, wigs and makeup, sound and lighting and is referred to as "D&P." Each school has its own culture and its own stereotypes—"you can usually tell what school someone is from by the way they're dressed," said a fourth-year Drama major—but the schools are united in the large quantity of work they demand. Some students chafe at the intense classes and rehearsals, which can run from 8 a.m. to midnight at peak times of year, but "the heavy workload tends to weed out those who are not up to standards."

While students from different schools may not see each other in their arts classes, General Studies classes are a different story. As NCSA's academic component, General Studies offers classes in the liberal arts and sciences, specially geared to students who care more about perfecting their plié than learning about Copernicus. That's not to say the classes are dumbed down. Students describe their academic professors as "better than you would expect for an arts school," but say it's hard to find time to do General Studies work when the arts classes are so demanding. For the most part, the faculty understands that students "are artists and don't want to major in math."

A Chance to Show Your Stuff

For a school whose goal is to teach students to create art, students say NCSA "realizes that the reason we attend is to actually do the work we are majoring in, not just to learn," and performance opportunities abound. In addition to participating in major performances, students have the option to perform chamber music, do outreach in the community and participate in the annual summer production of *The Lost Colony* on Roanoke Island, ensuring that graduates of NCSA have had plenty of chances to practice their art in "exceptional" facilities.

Most students come to NCSA because of particular programs or faculty members. In general, students say the arts faculty at NCSA is "stellar" and the standards that they expect of their students are high. Each member of the faculty is an expert—ballet students are taught by former principal dancers of the New York City Ballet, and music students learn from teachers that have played with the world's major orchestras. Despite their prestige in the art world, in general teachers "make themselves ridiculously accessible." In addition to the level of know-how on staff, well-known artists are often brought in for classes or concerts. But no matter how good the faculty is, "at NCSA, hands-on experience is usually considered the best teacher."

Within departments, competition can sometimes be fierce; students must be invited by the faculty to return the following year. In some departments, students speak of an unofficial cut system in which a few students are not invited back after sophomore year. This practice seems to have recently subsided—facing state budget cuts, the school "needs the money"—but some students still worry that their spot "may be in jeopardy." For the most part, though, students tend to think positively and most say that they get along very well. After all, "a little competition can be healthy."

You Want Grits with That?

Set in the laid-back, small Southern city of Winston-Salem (often known to locals as "Winston"), NCSA provides its students with a very different experience from other arts schools, which are typically located in major urban centers. While the city may not be exciting, as one student said "it has its own charm." Students say they rarely interact with the locals, but Winston-Salem residents often make up a large percentage of the audiences at student shows. The NCSA production of *The Nutcracker* is a holiday favorite in the city, selling out over a week of performances before going on tour and being shown on public television.

What, then, is there to do in Winston? Students in search of a drink often head to the Black Bear and other bars on Burke Street, while shoppers find that Hanes Mall is "good-sized but nothing special." People looking to strut their stuff on the dance floor might not be so lucky, though: "There are no real dance clubs in Winston; you have to go to Greensboro for that," and students stress that having a car is necessary. "A car is important if you want to do *anything* off campus . . . like go out to eat, buy groceries, or go to a bar. Nothing is within walking distance and there is no ubiquitous college town shopping-eating-walking main street area," said one student.

Campus, for the most part, is "fairly safe" despite its location near some "creepy" areas. Nevertheless, "nothing really bad ever seems to happen, no matter how much people like to talk," and students say the area is improving. Straddling two neighborhoods, the campus connects the "beautiful, historic Washington Park area" with "what used to be the projects. Though they are no longer there, that neighborhood is still kind of sketchy."

Dorms like Prison Cells

All freshmen and sophomores are required to live on campus, either in the residence halls, which go by the letters A through F, or in apartment-style buildings. The residence halls get uniformly negative reviews, despite fostering a "nice feeling of camaraderie." One senior who has been an RA called the A-F buildings "gross" and mentioned the traditional rumor that they were built following the plans of a women's prison. "Though not disgusting or dirty, the rooms and halls are less than aesthetically pleasing. The walls are cinderblock and the floors are linoleum. My suggestion: get your mom/girlfriend/sister to help you decorate." Students looking to escape to the newer apartment-style buildings have to pay a bit more, but most juniors and seniors decide to live off campus. Competition is fierce for nearby houses, but students say apartments around the city are generally easy to get.

While some students complain that the dining hall food is lackluster, it has been improving since the recent renovation of the Hanes Student Commons. "I personally have seen the food go from bland to exotic," one student said. "They have a huge selection and really good vegetarian dishes." When venturing off campus for a change of taste, most students cite the nearby Acadia Grill as a popular choice, along with inexpensive Mexican restaurants.

> "An NCSA degree could get you the job. Along with your talent, of course."

NCSA operates a high school program on the same campus as the college, which garners mixed reactions from college students. While there is generally "no reason to interact with the high schoolers," it can be weird seeing them in the cafeteria. It's "more amusing than annoying, although on-campus life would be cooler if they weren't around," said one student.

Practice Hard, Party Harder

With the hectic schedule of classes and rehearsals which frequently spill over into the weekend, it can be difficult to find a moment to unwind. When students do get a moment, going to friends' performances is a popular choice. Generally free, the performances are "a great opportunity to see the nation's best up-and-coming artists." The Filmmaking school offers free screenings on the weekends and many students use the "well-equipped gym" to work out or play impromptu games. As for parties, most of them are off campus and students say they can get pretty wild: "there's a lot of rehearsal—we try to balance it with a lot of letting loose." Alcohol and drugs are fairly common—"it's

an arts school"—but NCSA is now a dry campus, even for students over 21, so on-campus libations have to be fairly discreet.

The school organizes a few social events during the year, like skiing and hiking trips and Fall Fest, but most students agree that a lot of the on-campus events are "a joke." The ever-popular exception is the annual Beaux Arts costume ball. Turning one of the film soundstages into a dance floor—lighting and sound are designed by D&P students and generally top-notch—the costume ball is an excuse to wear something completely outlandish or close to nothing at all. An NCSA degree serves as a lifelong Beaux Arts invitation, so the party is often a meeting place for young alumni that still live in the area.

Students describe NCSA as very accepting: "most students are progressive, open-minded and busy . . . all sorts of things that would be considered weird or even bizarre are accepted as normal." Despite a state quota requirement that about half the students must be from North Carolina, NCSA manages to attract a fairly diverse student body with students from almost every state and several foreign countries. LGBT students feel welcome as well, as the school is "sexually diverse and prides itself on being an open-minded environment."

"If your goals for college are to let loose, have fun, casually meet hundreds of people and be the stud of your favorite fraternity, you're shit out of luck," said one senior. "Though the social life is not what you'd find at a larger school, the friendships made here are formed by a love of art and are deep and real. There is a huge amount of respect among students for each other as artists . . . and a strong sense of community." With its intimate size and friendly, anything-goes culture, NCSA belies a performing arts powerhouse. With well-known alumni appearing on stages and movie screens around the world and the reputation of the school steadily growing, "an NCSA degree could get you the job. Along with your talent, of course."—*Charles Cardinaux*

FYI

If you come to NCSA, you'd better bring "something with caffeine."

What's the typical weekend schedule? "Sleep in if you can, rehearse all day, and check out the parties or a film screening at night."

If I could change one thing about NCSA, I'd "allow more unexcused absences in General Studies classes!"

Three things every student at NCSA should do before graduating are "see the work of all the various programs at least once, watch a sunrise from the library or Performance Place rooftops (officially illegal: use the trellis), and choose having fun over work from time to time."

North Carolina State University

Address: 203 Peele Hall, Box 7103, Raleigh, NC 27695
Phone: 919-515-2434
E-mail address: undergrad-admissions@ncsu.edu
Web site URL: www.ncsu.edu
Year Founded: 1887
Private or Public: Public
Religious Affiliation: None
Location: Urban
Number of Applicants: 17,652
Percent Accepted: 59%
Percent Accepted who enroll: 45%
Number Entering: 4,660
Number of Transfers Accepted each Year: Unreported
Middle 50% SAT range: M: 560–660, CR: 520–620, Wr: 510–610
Middle 50% ACT range: 22–27
Early admission program EA/ED/None: EA

Percentage accepted through EA or ED: Unreported
EA and ED deadline: 1-Nov
Regular Deadline: 1-Feb
Application Fee: $70
Full time Undergraduate enrollment: 24,145
Total enrollment: 24,741
Percent Male: 56%
Percent Female: 44%
Total Percent Minority or Unreported: 22%
Percent African-American: 9%
Percent Asian/Pacific Islander: 5%
Percent Hispanic: 3%
Percent Native-American: 1%
Percent International: 2%
Percent in-state/out of state: 93%/7%
Percent from Public HS: 90%
Retention Rate: 89%

Graduation Rate 4-year: 36%
Graduation Rate 6-year: Unreported
Percent Undergraduates in On-campus housing: 35%
Number of official organized extracurricular organizations: 365
3 Most popular majors: Biology, Management, Mechanical Engineering
Student/Faculty ratio: 16:1
Average Class Size: 29
Percent of students going to grad school: 31%
Tuition and Fees: $17,572
In-State Tuition and Fees if different: $5,274
Cost for Room and Board: $7,982
Percent receiving financial aid out of those who apply, first year: 60%
Percent receiving financial aid among all students: 42%

A land-grant college founded in 1887 primarily as an agricultural school, North Carolina State University is now one of the most important research institutions in the nation. With more than 25,000 undergraduates and over 8,500 graduates, it is the largest school within the University of North Carolina system. With its urban location in the fast-growing city of Raleigh, a strong school spirit in large part due to the Wolfpack, and a strong international reputation as a major research university, North Carolina State is a top destination for those looking for a fulfilling experience—both academic and social—at a large, resourceful university.

Technology and Research

As in all major public institutions of higher learning, North Carolina State is divided into twelve different schools, ten of which are available to undergraduates, including First-Year College, which provides basic educational training to first-year students so that they can be well prepared for more spe-

cific programs of study in the future. Another interesting school within North Carolina State is the College of Textiles. It has not only majors in the manufacturing of textiles but also training in related business management topics. Although it does have the traditional liberal arts curriculums, the university is certainly focused on specialized fields in engineering, business, and agriculture. "We are big on technology, so we have a lot of engineers," said one student.

North Carolina Sate offers more than 100 majors, not to mention a number of associate degrees in the School of Agriculture and Life Sciences. These include the traditional fields of Biology and Economics, as well as the highly specialized curriculums of Watershed Hydrology and Biological Oceanography. "Academically, we have everything," said one student. "One of the reasons that I came here is because we have so many different, really specialized majors that are useful for jobs in the future."

The classes at North Carolina State can be very large, especially the introductory classes, which are popular not necessarily because they are particularly good but because everyone has to take them for their majors. "The professors can be really impersonal for the big lectures," said one student. "I really recommend small classes if you want to get to know the professors." Of course, it can be relatively difficult for students to enroll in the smaller classes, where students are able to talk more and interact with both their peers and their instructors. This is because there are stricter limits in the number of people per class, thus preventing many interested students, particularly freshmen, from getting into their favorite courses.

> "One of the reasons that I came here is because we have so many different, really specialized majors that are useful for jobs in the future."

One important aspect of North Carolina State is that it is a well-known research university. Surely, the large number of students on campus can be intimidating for some people who are more used to small schools, but the benefits of attending a school with research centers and top-notch facilities certainly cannot be ignored. The university is particularly proud of its Centennial Campus, more than 1,000 acres dedicated to house different research facilities, classrooms, and offices. The idea was to build partnerships between North Carolina State and other entities that are interested in education and research, such as government, corporations, and non-profit organizations. Students can find many opportunities for work, internship, and academic research on the Centennial Campus, which is still in the process of constructing new buildings and facilities. Of course, the downside of the university's focus on research is that the Centennial Campus, as well as other university facilities, is generally used for engineering and biomedical sciences, which, at the outset, reduces the relative importance of humanities and social sciences departments at North Carolina State.

In the *U.S. News & World Report*, North Carolina State is ranked among the top 90 national universities in the United States. The admissions process can be very selective, as nearly half of the applicants are rejected every year. "Just because we are a big state school, it doesn't mean that we are not really selective," said one student. "I feel the people here are very smart and skilled."

Capital of North Carolina

North Carolina State occupies more than 2,100 acres of Raleigh, the state capital and one of the fastest growing cities in the United States. In recent years, the city has become a top destination for businesses, particularly in technology-related industries. It is also considered one of the best places for young professionals. Furthermore, along with Chapel Hill and Durham, home to University of North Carolina and Duke, respectively, Raleigh also forms the famous Research Triangle Park, which is the largest research park in the United States. Therefore, the location of the North Carolina State is already very conducive to students' professional development. "I really like Raleigh," said one student. "It is a lively city."

Given the location, students can find plenty of activities in the city. The array of restaurants, bars, and clubs throughout Raleigh certainly enrich the weekend experiences of students. "I decided to live off campus because the city has so much that I don't have to be limited to the campus," said one student.

Although the majority of upperclassmen live off campus, freshmen generally stay in dorms. After all, living with fellow students in university-provided facilities is often considered one of the most important elements of the college experience. Given the scope of North Carolina State, the dorms vary greatly, ranging from apartment complexes to traditional residential halls. "One of the best things of living in dorms is that you get to meet more people of your year," said one student. "If you are off campus, your neighbor could be anybody, but here in dorms, you have more of a sense of community, which is great." Unlike most colleges that operate a large number of dining facilities, North Carolina State only has three main dining halls. Of course, there are also food courts and a number of stores and eateries easily accessible from the campus. Only freshmen living in dorms are required to have meal plans, and off-campus students generally find meals on their own without going to the university's dining halls.

Wolfpack

For a university that has the size and scope of North Carolina State, sports teams represent an important part of the college experience. The Wolfpack, as the teams are called,

630 North Carolina

play in 24 varsity sports. Since football is played in a stadium of 50,000 spectators, and the basketball games have a capacity of nearly 20,000 fans, these games are quite popular with students, particularly for those with fervent school spirit. As with most teams with long histories, the Wolfpack has a fiery rival in University of North Carolina at Chapel Hill. The basketball teams have played each other more than 200 times and the football teams nearly 100 times, with University of North Carolina having the clear advantage. Fortunately, North Carolina State has found success in the last three football encounters to close the gap.

The party scene is certainly lively at North Carolina State. There are plenty of parties during the weekends, both in students' apartments and in fraternities and sororities. "Weekends are really fun," said one student. "You get to go to the city or just have fun on campus because there are always parties going on."

North Carolina State is certainly one of the top research institutions in the United States. It provides strong technical training to students academically as well as a lively social life during the weekends. For students from North Carolina, the price tag is also relatively low, making the university certainly a good destination for college-bound students.—*Xiaohang Liu*

FYI

If you come to North Carolina State, you'd better bring "a readiness to work."

What is the typical weekend schedule? "Party on Friday and Saturday nights. But make sure you wake up early on Sunday so that you won't be overwhelmed during the week."

Three things every student at North Carolina State should do before graduating are "take classes outside of your major just for fun, go to a football game, and get to know Raleigh."

University of North Carolina / Chapel Hill

Address: Jackson Hall CB #2200, Chapel Hill, NC 27599-2200
Phone: 919-966-3621
E-mail address: unchelp@admissions.unc.edu
Web site URL: www.unc.edu
Year Founded: 1789
Private or Public: Public
Religious Affiliation: None
Location: Suburban
Number of Applicants: 20,090
Percent Accepted: 35%
Percent Accepted who enroll: 55%
Number Entering: 3,880
Number of Transfers Accepted each Year: 1,115
Middle 50% SAT range: M: 610–700, CR: 600–700, Wr: 590–690
Middle 50% ACT range: 26–31
Early admission program EA/ED/None: EA

Percentage accepted through EA or ED: Unreported
EA and ED deadline: 1-Nov
Regular Deadline: 15-Jan
Application Fee: $70
Full time Undergraduate enrollment: 17,628
Total enrollment: 25,805
Percent Male: 42%
Percent Female: 58%
Total Percent Minority or Unreported: 28%
Percent African-American: 11%
Percent Asian/Pacific Islander: 7%
Percent Hispanic: 4%
Percent Native-American: 1%
Percent International: 1%
Percent in-state/out of state: 83%/17%
Percent from Public HS: 83%
Retention Rate: Unreported
Graduation Rate 4-year: 86%

Graduation Rate 6-year: Unreported
Percent Undergraduates in On-campus housing: 46%
Number of official organized extracurricular organizations: 557
3 Most popular majors: Biology/biological Sciences, Mass Communication/Media Studies, Psychology
Student/Faculty ratio: Unreported
Average Class Size: 15
Percent of students going to grad school: 28%
Tuition and Fees: $22,295
In-State Tuition and Fees if different: $5,397
Cost for Room and Board: $7,334
Percent receiving financial aid out of those who apply, first year: 43%
Percent receiving financial aid among all students: 32%

With strong academics, great athletics and a pretty campus to boot, the University of North Carolina at Chapel Hill is a great choice for just about any student. This large Southern university does everything big, including its Southern hospitality. So put on your Carolina Blue shirt and come on down!

Is Bigger Better?
Starting with the class of 2010, the university introduced new graduation requirements that are quite extensive. While some students praise the system, saying that it "more fully encapsulates the purpose of a liberal arts education," others point out that changing your major is a difficult feat with all the new requirements and that you might have to stay for an additional semester to complete course work unless you enter with plenty of AP credits. Survey courses are pretty much guaranteed to be 400-person classes. A good way to get a taste of a small class early on is to participate in one of the First Year Seminars. In addition to being small, which is a rare find at UNC, they are generally interesting, tackling subjects such as "U.S.-Cuban Relations." Large sizes of classes aside, students praised the feel of community, as most said they don't view their peers as competition.

The school prides itself on having very strong journalism and business programs, both of which are pretty difficult to get into. With UNC's strong academic reputation also come challenging classes. Grading varies from department to department with some, such as the communications department, being more notorious for grade inflation. Students generally agree that each A requires hard work and is unlikely to be handed out easily. Students warn that the most failed course at UNC is "Calculus 231" (Calculus of One Variable I). In addition, be wary as intro classes such as intro biology, intro statistics and intro international relations are designed to weed out the people who are not serious about the major. On the other end of the spectrum, for an easy A, students recommend "Race and Ethnic Relations" and most communications classes. As at most schools, it is still the professor that makes the class, and UNC students give high marks to their professors. The professors are generally pretty accessible and open to meeting students. One senior remarked that the professors were always "as helpful as I needed them to be." Professor Ralph Byrns in the economics department is a favorite,

drawing crowds even as early as 9:30 in the morning. Additionally UNC is home to several other famous professors, including Professor Christopher Browning, a prominent Holocaust historian, and Professor Andrew Reynolds, who helped write the Afghani and Iraqi constitutions. The academic options are broadened via the very selective Robertson Scholars program, which allows UNC students to take classes not offered at UNC at neighboring Duke University.

Party in the South [Campus]
As a state school, UNC operates under the North Carolina requirement that at least 82 percent of students must be from in-state. For this reason, the rare out-of-state students complain that when they initially arrived on campus, everyone else already knew at least a few people from their high school who also attended. Don't worry about being lonely in this large school, though, as freshman dorms, freshman seminars and other classes facilitate friendships. And as one student from the Northeast emphasized, the people are very friendly; in fact, he quipped, "It took me a while to get used to."

The social scene as described by one senior can be split into three categories: the Greek life, the bars and clubs on Franklin Street, and the dorm parties in the suites of South Campus. The underage underclassmen tend to gravitate toward the freshmen-dominated South Campus where the crazy parties are concentrated. Upperclassmen and those with fake IDs can usually be found on Franklin Street, an area that offers a plethora of options. Some of the more popular choices include La Rez, East End, and Top of the Hill. Frats are conspicuous during rush week when a lot of students take advantage of their parties; however, for the remaining part of the year the 16 percent of Greeks on campus are not a very big deal to the rest of the student body. While most people drink, there is no pressure to join in drinking. The practical reality, according to one student, is that the university's priority is to make sure you are safe. For this reason, unless you are being obnoxious or disruptive, the RAs will leave you alone. "RAs are not secret police or anything," one senior explained. For after-party options, students cite the Cosmic Cantina, a Mexican hole in the wall, as a great late-night destination.

See You in the Pit!
The campus is unofficially divided into three areas: North, South and Middle. Most of the

freshmen are housed on South Campus, where suites and large dorms encourage socializing, although there is an integration effort going on that has the administration encouraging first years to move to other parts and mingle with the upperclassmen. While the rest of the campus is characterized by run-of-the-mill dorms, upperclassmen also have the option of living in apartment-style houses in Ram Village. Avery in Middle Campus is cited as the athlete dorm. Students get assigned to dorms via a lottery system based on seniority, although there is always an option of not taking any chances and remaining in the room you currently have. The most popular option of all, however, is living off campus, and 53 percent of students do just that.

The campus draws many compliments from its students, who describe it as "scenic" and full of brick walkways. The only complaint is the never-ending and sometimes disruptive construction due to an ambitious long-term remodeling plan that the university is currently undergoing. The most popular place on campus is the Pit. A central meeting point between the student union, dining hall and a library, the Pit is home to many student organization meetings, people on their way to other destinations and "even occasionally preachers." It is said that all students pass by the Pit at least once a day.

When asked about food, the consensus, as one student summed up, is that the two dining halls on campus are "mediocre at best." However, whenever sick of the dining halls, the students can always turn to the endless stream of restaurants on Franklin Street that are bound to satisfy the choosiest of taste buds.

Duke Sucks!

If you are a basketball fan, UNC is the place to be. The Tar Heels bleed Carolina blue and the atmosphere, according to one student, can be described as "mania and fervor" and another added, "There is crazy school spirit. People here can be a little insane about sports." The basketball, baseball and foot-

ball teams are successful and draw full crowds to the games. Tickets are in such high demand that the university has a lottery system in place for those who wish to attend. The most anticipated game of the year is, of course, the one against the perennial archrival Duke. A win against Duke is lavishly celebrated by the student body on Franklin Street, where crowds gather to build fires and jump over them in joy. But sports are not confined to only varsity-level talent. The intramural program at the school is also a very popular option. To get the coveted IM champion T-shirt, students compete in a plethora of sports. "There are sports I've never even heard of," claimed one student, perhaps referring to the popular IM underwater hockey. Outside of the sports scene, other extracurriculars also abound, with the Campus Y, a social advocacy umbrella group, and *The Daily Tar Heel* being some of the more popular options. There are also many a cappella groups, and proud students reported that one member participated in the 2009 American Idol competition and advanced to the final 36.

> "There is crazy school spirit. People here can be a little insane about sports."

UNC is a great deal on many fronts and a small bill for the North Carolina students. Lucky North Carolina residents take up at least 82 percent of the student population, but the coveted 18 percent left for out-of-state students is well worth the competition. The relaxed Southern atmosphere makes it a pleasant environment even though students warn that it is more conservative and bigger than one might expect. Overall, however, once you get there you are bound to catch at least some of the school spirit. In no time you'll also be chanting: Go, Heels!—*Dorota Poplawska*

FYI
If you come to UNC, you'd better bring "a lot of school spirit."
What is the typical weekend schedule? "Go to the South Point mall on Saturday, at night go to bars and restaurants on Franklin Street and do homework on Sunday."
If I could change one thing about UNC, I'd "have more small classes."
Three things every student at UNC should do before graduating are "attend a Carolina-Duke basketball game, rush Franklin Street after beating Duke, and have fro-yo (frozen yogurt) at Yogurt Pump."

Wake Forest University

Address: PO Box 7305 Reynolda Station, Winston-Salem, NC 27109	**Percentage accepted through EA or ED:** Unreported	**Graduation Rate 4-year:** 78% **Graduation Rate 6-year:** 78%
Phone: 336-758-5201	**EA and ED deadline:** 15-Nov	**Percent Undergraduates in On-campus housing:** 69%
E-mail address: admissions@wfu.edu	**Regular Deadline:** 15-Jan **Application Fee:** $50	**Number of official organized extracurricular organizations:** 168
Web site URL: www.wfu.edu **Year Founded:** 1834	**Full time Undergraduate enrollment:** 4,412	**3 Most popular majors:** Business, Political Science, Psychology
Private or Public: Private **Religious Affiliation:** None	**Total enrollment:** 5,759 **Percent Male:** 49%	
Location: Urban	**Percent Female:** 51%	
Number of Applicants: 7,177	**Total Percent Minority or Unreported:** 14%	**Student/Faculty ratio:** 10:1 **Average Class Size:** 14
Percent Accepted: 42%	**Percent African-American:** 7%	**Percent of students going to grad school:** 59%
Percent Accepted who enroll: 37%	**Percent Asian/Pacific Islander:** 5%	**Tuition and Fees:** $36,560 **In-State Tuition and Fees if**
Number Entering: 1,124	**Percent Hispanic:** 2%	**different:** No difference
Number of Transfers Accepted each Year: 88	**Percent Native-American:** 1%	**Cost for Room and Board:** $9,867
Middle 50% SAT range: M: 610–700, CR: 630–710, Wr: Unreported	**Percent International:** 1% **Percent in-state/out of**	**Percent receiving financial aid out of those who apply,**
Middle 50% ACT range: 27–31	**state:** 25%/75% **Percent from Public HS:**	**first year:** 39% **Percent receiving financial**
Early admission program EA/ED/None: ED	65% **Retention Rate:** 94%	**aid among all students:** 34%

Just outside of the Raleigh-Durham research triangle, in the green hills of Winston-Salem, North Carolina, lies one of America's premier small colleges, Wake Forest University. The campus is frequently described as "preppy" and has an active Greek life, but the university is extremely committed to both athletics and academics as well, boasting active Division I sports teams and top-notch research facilities. The small class sizes and well-known faculty members—including Maya Angelou—only add to Wake Forest's prestige and Southern charm.

Life at Work Forest

With less than five thousand students, Wake Forest ensures personalized, one-on-one experiences with professors and comfortable class discussions. Students say they "love knowing all of [their] professors on a personal level" and say that the faculty members are "so, so helpful" and "always available." One freshman said that her biggest class had sixty students, and juniors and seniors confirmed that large lecture classes were far and few. The university also offers a First-Year Seminar program, which gives freshmen the opportunity to discuss interesting topics with sixteen of their peers and professors who are distinguished in their fields. Applicants interested in research will not be disappointed by Wake's resources, as many current students say the university "has all the resources that are normally found at larger schools."

In addition to the small class sizes, Wake Forest is known for its academic intensity. Students at the school agree that there is truth to the common nickname "Work Forest," and say that while the grading scale can differ from class to class, one does have to put in effort to do well. Attendance and participation factor into one's grade in many classes, and one student noted that "even the less-devoted students have their noses buried in books for at least a couple hours each day." Part of that studying is devoted to fulfilling distribution requirements; before graduation, students are required to take one or two courses in each of five divisions: social sciences, math and natural sciences, fine arts, humanities, and literature. Wake students also have to complete two courses in health and exercise science. Popular majors include Communications and Political Science, and the university's Calloway School of Business and Accountancy has a particularly strong reputation in the field.

WFU also has numerous study-abroad opportunities, with particularly popular programs in England and Venice. Students would say that "about half" of the undergraduate population chooses to study abroad during their four years, and "the administration encourages students to seek out new experiences." Wake Forest also has a prestigious Scholars Program, which awards exceptional students with full-ride scholarships to the university.

Frat Forest?

Although the academics can be challenging, Wake Forest students know the importance of balancing their schedules with fun. "There's a lot of truth to the saying 'work hard, play hard' around here," one student said, explaining that most WFU students go out at least once a weekend and "the campus is lively until four in the morning on Saturdays." Wake Wednesdays are a popular night to go out, followed by "slightly lower-key" Thursdays and "loud and busy" Fridays and Saturdays.

Wake's social scene tends to center on Greek life. Although the more than two dozen fraternities and sororities aren't housed on a traditional Greek Row—instead, they have specific sections of dorms set aside for them, and "lounges" in those areas are designated for parties open to the entire campus. "There's pressure to go Greek," students say, and a typical Saturday night is never complete without a trip to one of the many fraternities for beer and socializing. Although "the lack of diversity of Wake's social scene can get old," one student said, "there's always one thing that redeems it: everyone at Wake seems so spirited and energetic!"

Wake Forest isn't a dry campus, and "most students definitely stick to drinking over heavy drugs." Drinking is common at numerous social events, be it a low-key lounge party or large campus-wide event. The RAs are fairly lenient, and are just there to make sure students are "happy and safe." Although it's much less common, "there are still those who use drugs, with pot being the most common," one student said. There are a few rumors about cocaine use on campus, but drinking clearly remains the most popular social activity.

A Comfortable Community

Wake Forest students take pride in their beautiful North Carolina campus, praising the large magnolia quad in the center of campus and the region's relatively mild weather. Housing options vary and improve as students get older, and are randomly assigned to freshmen or done by lottery for upperclassmen. Upperclassmen housing options include on-campus apartments, many of which feature in-suite bathrooms and kitchenettes and are "the high point of on-campus housing." WFU is constantly adding to its housing options, and one of the newer dorms "is almost like a luxury hotel, featuring everything from solar-powered generators to monitors on every floor that keep students informed on daily news."

The small campus fosters "a sense of community that you don't see at bigger schools," and students often praise the university's small size as the source of many campus traditions. During exam week, for example, it's traditional for students and the library staff to "set up pranks and social activities to relieve stress." 2010's festivities included a breakfast buffet and a waterfall of condoms, and "the whole campus spent weeks talking" about the events.

> "Know professors on a personal level."

Students agree that to a large extent, the university's close-knit atmosphere stems from its commitment to athletics. One of the first things the freshman class learns during orientation week is the fight song, which can often be heard at the Division I football and basketball games. "It can be competitive to get good seats" at sporting events, and despite the recent disappointing football season, "students still flocked to the games." One of the most well-known Wake Forest traditions arose out of the student body's "tremendous" passion for football; after a big win, students cover the trees on campus in toilet paper in an activity known as "rolling the Quad." It's no surprise that sports are so popular at Wake—the university claims famous athletes like the NBA's Tim Duncan, Chris Paul, and Josh Howard as alums!

One common complaint about the university is that it's not as diverse, ethnically or socio-economically, as the admissions officers would like applicants to believe. "The stereotypes are true," one student said. "Most Wake students are popped-collar preps" from comfortable backgrounds. However, "cultural groups on campus have become more active recently," and students are open and accepting of all of their peers.

"When you go to a small school, it's all about having a strong sense of community," one student said. From rolling the quad to pulling pranks in the library, it's clear that Wake Forest students are proud to show that sense of community off. Although the university is small in size, its plethora of resources—academic, extracurricular, and social—ensures that any student will be able to find his or her niche in Winston-Salem. Whether it be in the small seminars the school is known for or in the crowd at football and basketball games, Wake's Demon Deacons aren't afraid to show off their school pride.
—*Iva Velickovic*

FYI

If I could change one thing about Wake Forest, "I'd mix up the social scene a little bit. If you're into frat parties, Wake is the place for you, but if you're looking for a different way to spend your Saturday nights, you might have to look around a little."

The number one thing that surprised me most when I came to Wake Forest was "how many opportunities it has for the arts, like a student-hosted film festival."

If you come to Wake Forest, you'd better bring "rain boots (the drainage system is awful), but leave your heaviest jacket at home."

North Dakota

University of North Dakota

Address: 205 Twamley Hall, 264 Centennial Drive, Grand Forks, ND 58202-8357

Phone: 800-225-5863

E-mail address: enrollmentservices @mail.und.nodak.edu

Web site URL: www.und.edu

Year Founded: 1883

Private or Public: Public

Religious Affiliation: None

Location: Suburban

Number of Applicants: 4,069

Percent Accepted: 75%

Percent Accepted who enroll: 63%

Number Entering: 1,926

Number of Transfers Accepted each Year: 1,048

Middle 50% SAT range: Unreported

Middle 50% ACT range: 20–25

Early admission program EA/ED/None: None

Percentage accepted through EA or ED: NA

EA and ED deadline: NA

Regular Deadline: Rolling

Application Fee: $35

Full time Undergraduate enrollment: 10,085

Total enrollment: 12,070

Percent Male: 56%

Percent Female: 44%

Total Percent Minority or Unreported: 13%

Percent African-American: 1%

Percent Asian/Pacific Islander: 1%

Percent Hispanic: 1%

Percent Native-American: 3%

Percent International: 4%

Percent in-state/out of state: 52%/48%

Percent from Public HS: 92%

Retention Rate: 78%

Graduation Rate 4-year: 54%

Graduation Rate 6-year: Unreported

Percent Undergraduates in On-campus housing: 31%

Number of official organized extracurricular organizations: 230

3 Most popular majors: Airline/Commercial/Professional Pilot and Flight Crew, Nursing/Registered Nurse RN, ASN, BSN, MSN, Psychology

Student/Faculty ratio: 18:1

Average Class Size: 15

Percent of students going to grad school: 24%

Tuition and Fees: $15,325

In-State Tuition and Fees if different: $6,513

Cost for Room and Board: $5,735

Percent receiving financial aid out of those who apply, first year: 70%

Percent receiving financial aid among all students: 59%

Founded in 1883, the University of North Dakota (UND) is the flagship institution of higher learning funded by the state government. Despite being located in a rather unpopulated region of the country, UND is a popular destination for not only students from the state of North Dakota but also students from the rest of the United States, as well as a number of foreign countries. In fact, unlike many other state schools, more than half of the students at UND hail from outside of North Dakota. The second largest employer in the state, UND is also a vital player in the state economy. By providing students with a balanced college experience of exciting social life and good academics, the university is certainly a very good choice for all those who are willing to make the tradeoff of staying in a remote part of the country.

Not Just About Flying

More than 10,000 undergraduates are enrolled at UND, along with over 2,500 postgraduates. The university offers a complete set of graduate, professional, and continuing education colleges that cover the educational needs of many types of students. There are ten academic divisions at UND, including the schools of law and medicine. Within these schools, the university offers more than 200 fields of study. The most famous division of UND is the John D. Odegard School of Aerospace Sciences. More than 1,500 students are enrolled in the school, which also has the largest fleet of aircraft dedicated for civilian training. The Grand Forks International Airport serves as the training site for approximately 120 planes. In North Dakota, the United States Air Force has a significant presence. Therefore, it is not surprising the state's main public university is intensely focused on the topic and counts among one of the premier outer-space research institutions in the country. "The School of Aerospace Sciences is definitely the most prestigious part of UND," said one student. "It is really good for pilot training and space research."

Although the departments in aerospace are considered the most widely recognized divisions of UND, the rest of the academic programs are also very strong. The university has nearly 90 majors. In addition, a large selection of minors is available for entrepreneurial students who would like to enrich their academic experience. The certificate programs can also be useful for students who are looking for pre-professional training in a particular field, and students are generally satisfied with the scope of academia at UND. "I don't feel like the school is missing any important majors," said the student. "Whether you are pre-med or majoring in liberal arts, you will find the programs that suit you."

For a relatively large public school, the degree of interaction between students and professors at UND is strong. Introductory classes can be very large, with more than one hundred people filling lecture halls. However, these courses generally have a number of teaching assistants assigned to help students with their work. These graduate students can be invaluable in helping those who are falling behind as well as teaching more materials to students who would like to study a particular topic in detail. For upper-level classes, the size can be significantly reduced, often with fewer than 20 students per class. In those courses, discussions between students and professors are vital, since much of the teaching is done through conversations and debates rather than lectures.

Prior to graduation, students are required to choose from a list of general education courses. These classes are designed to improve the basic skills of students and offer some background in all major academic fields. The four core groups of courses are communication, social sciences, arts and humanities, and mathematics, science, and technology. While some students think the requirements are not very useful, others believe that these courses have introduced them to interesting new topics. "I think the general education requirements are great," said one student. "I never knew I would be so interested in geography after taking a class in it."

> "I never felt overwhelmed here. I think the academics here are pretty relaxed."

Most students are very happy with the workload at UND. The classes tend to be manageable, allowing students to undertake jobs or extracurricular activities during the week, as well as having fun during the weekends. "I never felt overwhelmed here," said one student. "I think the academics here are pretty relaxed."

The Flatland

One of the most important drawbacks for prospective students in choosing UND is the location of the university, particularly for those from outside the state. The winters can be harsh. Those who have little experience with the cold weather may be not too pleasantly surprised during the winter, when the entire campus can be covered with snow. Furthermore, UND is in Grand Forks, more than 70 miles from Fargo, the most important metropolitan area in North Dakota. For those looking to go to major cities several times during the school year, the closest is Winnipeg in Manitoba, Canada or Minneapolis, both at much more than 150 miles away. "Grand Forks is a small city," said one student. "But that should be what you expect when you come to North Dakota for college."

Despite the issue with the scope of the city, some students do enjoy the remoteness of Grand Forks. "I wanted to go to someplace quiet where you can actually study," said one student. In addition, the small college community creates a sense of safety and closeness, not to mention the fact that there are a number of restaurants and bars around campus where students can socialize outside of the school setting.

The majority of students live off campus, and the freshmen are not required to live in dorms. However, many do choose to live there to get used to the college environment, meet new people, and, of course, have convenient access to the different university facilities. Students are generally satisfied with the school's housing arrangement. There are single-sex residential halls available to students, but most of them are coeducational and arranged in suites. Three main dining centers serve the campus. A number of coffee shops, convenience stores, and food courts are also spread out across the campus to ensure that all students have easy access to dining services.

UND has twelve fraternities and six sororities, and they certainly represent an important part of weekend festivities. For those not interested in the Greek system, students can also find parties around campus in student apartments and houses. However, it must be pointed out that the alcohol policy is relatively strict in on-campus housing.

The National Champions

The university has dedicated significant resources to the men's hockey team, particularly in the construction of the Ralph Engelstad Arena, which seats more than 10,000 spectators. This is in large part due to the popularity of the sport on campus and the immense success of the team over the years, with seven national championships. After a series of reforms in the collegiate sports programs, all teams of UND compete at the NCAA Division I level.

UND students tend to show up in huge numbers to support their hockey team, and it represents an important social venue for students. With a large selection of academic programs and the large number of out-of-state students, UND is certainly a very attractive college choice. Of course, the diversity of the student body and the remoteness of the university are clear disadvantages, but, overall, students are very satisfied with their experience at UND.—*Xiaohang Liu*

FYI
If you come to UND, you'd better bring "many winter coats."
What is the typical weekend schedule? "Go to hockey games. The football games are pretty cool too."
If I could change one thing about UND, I'd "move it south."
Three things every student at UND should do before graduating are "go to a hockey game against University of Minnesota, have a trip to Canada, and join an extracurricular organization."

Ohio

Bowling Green State University

Address: 110 McFall Center
Bowling Green, OH 43403
Phone: 419-372-2478
E-mail address:
admissions@bgsu.edu
Web site URL: www.bgsu.edu
Year Founded: 1910
Private or Public: Public
Religious Affiliation: None
Location: Suburban
Number of Applicants:
11,111
Percent Accepted: 87%
Percent Accepted who
enroll: 32%
Number Entering: 3,079
Number of Transfers
Accepted each Year: 886
Middle 50% SAT range: M:
450–550, CR: 440–600,
Wr: 435–535
Middle 50% ACT range:
19–24
Early admission program
EA/ED/None: None

Percentage accepted
through EA or ED: NA
EA and ED deadline: NA
Regular Deadline: Rolling
Application Fee: $40
Full time Undergraduate
enrollment: 14,862
Total enrollment: 17,874
Percent Male: 47%
Percent Female: 53%
Total Percent Minority or
Unreported: 21%
Percent African-American:
10%
Percent Asian/Pacific
Islander: 1%
Percent Hispanic: 3%
Percent Native-American:
<1%
Percent International: 2%
Percent in-state/out of
state: 90%/10%
Percent from Public HS:
Unreported
Retention Rate: 73%

Graduation Rate 4-year: 33%
Graduation Rate 6-year: 57%
Percent Undergraduates in
On-campus housing: 41%
Number of official organized
extracurricular
organizations: 280
3 Most popular majors:
Biology, Psychology,
Management
Student/Faculty ratio: 18:1
Average Class Size: 25
Percent of students going to
grad school: Unreported
Tuition and Fees: $16,368
In-State Tuition and Fees if
different: $9,060
Cost for Room and Board:
$7,220
Percent receiving financial
aid out of those who apply,
first year: 74%
Percent receiving financial
aid among all students:
65%

If you're looking for a college town atmosphere, die-hard school spirit, and a relaxed intellectual environment, then Bowling Green State University may be the place for you. With almost 20,000 students, BGSU is filled with tons of different people, opinions, interests, and opportunities. Students are eager to point out that in spite of the relatively small population of the town (around 29,600), Bowling Green doesn't feel that small. Located only 20 miles south of Toledo, the campus is within easy driving distance to larger cities, offering a wide variety of restaurants, events, and clubs, although most students said they usually stay close to campus to participate in the vibrant social scene.

Better than "Normal"

When classes first started in 1914, BGSU was actually called Bowling Green State Normal College, tuition was free, and the only courses offered were education classes for women. The school dropped the "Normal" from its name in 1929, and students today agree that the school is far more interesting than its founding name implies. With over 200 majors and programs offered, a competitive honors curriculum, and a very active study abroad program, BGSU has expanded to offer just about any type of academic environment for its students. And while tuition is no longer free and the campus has long been coed, students say the focus on teacher preparation and the desire to make education affordable are still at the core of BG's academic philosophy. Students agreed that education is still the most popular major, adding that "it seems like everywhere you turn, you meet another future teacher." Indeed, BGSU ranks as a top producer of teachers in the country. With such a high number in one major, it might seem that enrollment in education classes would be competitive. But students said that registering for classes in general is fairly easy. The most frustrating part is getting put on waiting lists, but "with a little determination, it all works out in the end."

No matter what major you decide to pursue, students said BGSU does a good job of offering lots of opportunities to make your education entertaining and affordable with easily accessible resources for fellowships, internships, foreign exchange programs, and scholarships or financial aid. The university can accommodate almost any of your wildest travel plans, with foreign exchange programs in over 30 different countries as well as domestic opportunities for study or work experience. The same generosity with which BG approaches study abroad also translates to their financial aid packages. Nearly 70 percent of students receive financial aid, and the university also offers over $20 million in scholarship money and an extensive work-study program.

Students generally don't talk about their grades or feel a lot of pressure to compete with their classmates. This laid-back atmosphere is to the advantage of self-motivated students, and those in the honors program will find themselves with a demanding schedule no matter what. But others said the relaxed environment makes it almost too easy to forget about classes and only focus on the weekend.

Bleacher Creatures and Dancing Queens

Without a doubt, school pride is an important part of any student's time at BGSU. In the 1970s, a student group of die-hard BGSU Falcons fans dressed up in different Halloween costumes for every hockey game, eventually earning a spot in *Sports Illustrated* as the famous masked "Bleacher Creatures." Today, students channel this school spirit mainly during the annual football game against their archrival, the University of Toledo Rockets, for which fans show up in unusually large numbers. "I never watch football ever, but I've never missed a BG/UT game," one student added. BG has 17 NCAA Division I varsity sports teams to cheer on, and a ton of club sports for anyone to join, including ice hockey, ultimate Frisbee and lacrosse. At games, students don their school colors, overlooking in the heat of the moment the unsightly combination of murky brown and bright orange.

In addition to sports events, there are a ton of school-sponsored activities to partici-

pate in if athletics doesn't get you going. There are over 300 student-run organizations on campus, and the administration makes it relatively easy to start your own group if your interests aren't already represented. BG students seem more than up for the challenge of spearheading campus events, with student-run social and cultural activities going on "pretty much all the time." Among students' favorites are homecoming, family weekend, sibs-kids weekend, and the dance marathon—student-run events that bring the large campus together and often raise funds for charities and minorities. "I've helped work on the dance marathon for two years now and it's my favorite part of the year," one student said. "It's a really unique experience that the whole student body can come together on." Students can also enjoy theatrical and musical productions at the two large performance halls in the Moore Musical Arts Center, or take a trip to the spacious Fine Arts galleries to see exhibitions from BG student artists.

Another fundamental part of the BGSU lifestyle is the Greek system. Fraternities and sororities abound on campus, with over 43 different houses for students to choose from. About 12% of students opt for the Greek life, while others often attend the parties without choosing to rush.

Each month, BG offers its students close to 300 events and activities, ensuring that there is never a dull moment if you take advantage of the opportunities. Some students said they worried at first about the small-town setting, but the diversity of activities on campus really makes BG come alive so it can feel a lot bigger than the somewhat rural campus seems at first.

Home Sweet Home

BGSU has seven residence halls, some limited to upper- or underclassmen, and all with unique personalities and generally similar accommodations. As a rule, all underclassmen, except those who live at home, must live on campus, but students said they didn't really mind the restriction. Generally, they neither love nor hate the dorms. "The dorms are actually decent," one student said. "They can be pretty small and cramped, though, especially if you're not best buds with your roommate." Generally, the quality and size of the rooms increases as you get older. For example, Founders and Offenhauer (predominately upperclassmen dorms) have air conditioning, while the all-freshman dorm MacDonald is known for its closet-like bedrooms and sardine lifestyle.

All rooms are equipped with computer connections and cable television access. Each residential hall has its own laundry room, as well as a study area, TV lounge and computer lab for its students. All the dorms are centrally located on campus, so that you can easily get to all classes by bike or on foot. Shuttle services also are available to take students to main buildings, which they said are especially useful in the winter when it gets "really freakin' cold." Although students are allowed to have cars on campus and many do, the student parking lots are so inconvenient that "you end up walking just about as far as you would have if you hadn't driven in the first place."

> "It's nice being able to walk everywhere, and I like that I always run into somebody I know."

Even though Bowling Green is a small town, students said they are never hard-pressed for a place to eat. During the week, students often hang out at the student union, enjoying fast food or the popular Zza's pizza from the food court, a latte from the Starbucks, or a home-cooked meal at the Bowling Greenery. Commons also offers all-you-can-eat-meals, although students warned that the options can often get pretty repetitive, especially at the MacDonald's dining center.

In general, students said living at BG was comfortable and relaxing. "It's safe, friendly, and laid-back," a student said. "It's nice being able to walk everywhere, and I like that I always run into somebody I know."

Close to 20,000 students attend BGSU, making it one of the larger public universities in the country. Only 10 percent of the students are non-residents, with about 500 international undergraduates from 90 countries. At about 21 percent minority, students said diversity is, of course, present on campus but is not a major part of campus life. "I hear a lot of stuff about the preppy frat boy from BG," one student said, "but it's not really like that. That's just the stereotype we get." And with multicultural organizations, hundreds of different student groups, and so many different academic majors, students said diversity of interests is really the main point.

Campus Culture

On the weekends, BGSU's diverse student body really spreads out, with some sticking to the campus events, others partying it up with a few friends, and still others driving out of town, either for a trip home or to livelier club scenes in neighboring cities. Although Bowling Green is a dry campus, with strict enforcement in the residence halls, undergraduate students said underage drinking can thrive at BG as much as at any other college, with the aid of a fake ID, an older friend, or simply a keg at an off-campus party. "If you're underage and you want to drink, it's not hard. You can go to a frat, a bar or club, or just stay in your room and keep it down," one student said. But if drinking's not for you, many students enjoy quieter nights at the movies, the theater, or hanging out in one of the local eateries.

A large number of students do drive out of town on the weekends, either going home if they live close by or visiting friends in Toledo or other nearby towns. Some students said commuting on the weekends can detract from the vibrant social scene BGSU tries hard to create, and that if you stick around, you'll find it can really be an exciting place to be on a Friday night.—*Maggie Reid*

FYI
If you come to BGSU, you'd better bring "a warm coat for the frigid winters."
What is the typical weekend schedule? "Friday: pre-game with your friends, go out to a frat or house party, bar hopping, some late night food. Saturday: sleep till noon, do it all again. Sunday: sleep all day and do your homework that's been piling up."
If I could change one thing about BGSU, "it would be the long months of cold, wind, and snow."
Three things every student should do before graduating from BGSU are "make it to every UT football game, go to at least one frat party, and take advantage of the small, personal environment to really get to know your fellow classmates and your professors. You can make great lifelong connections at a place like BG."

Case Western Reserve University

Address: 10900 Euclid Avenue, Cleveland, OH 44106
Phone: 216-368-4450
E-mail address: admission@case.edu
Web site URL: www.case.edu
Year Founded: 1826
Private or Public: Private
Religious Affiliation: None
Location: Urban
Number of Applicants: 7,351
Percent Accepted: 73%
Percent Accepted who enroll: 19%
Number Entering: 1,026
Number of Transfers Accepted each Year: 107
Middle 50% SAT range: M: 620–720, CR: 590–690, Wr: 580–680
Middle 50% ACT range: 26–32
Early admission program EA/ED/None: ED
Percentage accepted through EA or ED: 38%

EA and ED deadline: 1-Nov
Regular Deadline: 15-Jan
Application Fee: $0
Full time Undergraduate enrollment: 4,207
Total enrollment: 8,166
Percent Male: 57%
Percent Female: 43%
Total Percent Minority or Unreported: 25%
Percent African-American: 6%
Percent Asian/Pacific Islander: 17%
Percent Hispanic: 2%
Percent Native-American: <1%
Percent International: 4%
Percent in-state/out of state: 54%/46%
Percent from Public HS: Unreported
Retention Rate: 91%
Graduation Rate 4-year: 57%
Graduation Rate 6-year: 78%

Percent Undergraduates in On-campus housing: 78%
Number of official organized extracurricular organizations: 150
3 Most popular majors: Biology, Biomedical Engineering, Business Administration and Management
Student/Faculty ratio: 10:1
Average Class Size: 20
Percent of students going to grad school: Unreported
Tuition and Fees: $35,572
In-State Tuition and Fees if different: No difference
Cost for Room and Board: $10,450
Percent receiving financial aid out of those who apply, first year: 90%
Percent receiving financial aid among all students: 84%

As the product of a merger of two established institutes of science—Case Institute of Technology and Western Reserve University—Case exemplifies the ideal of a technical university where superior academics coupled with a diverse student body provide an enlightening experience.

Academics at Case

Case is famous for its top-ranking science and engineering programs, and ranks perennially in the top 10 undergraduate biomedical engineering programs in the country. Consequently, the majority of students you'll meet at Case will be studying engineering, pre-medicine, and the "hard sciences." However, as one student commented, "Case has been working hard to increase the number of humanities majors."

Case also offers a variety of special programs aimed at students wishing to accelerate through their education, one of the most popular and selective of which is the Pre-Professional Scholars Program. Through PPSP, students are offered conditional placement in Case's graduate schools for law, social work, and dentistry. Competition for a space in the PPSP medicine program is especially intense—only around 20 to 25 students out of an applicant pool of 700 are accepted into the program annually. As a result, a coveted position in the PPSP medicine program becomes one of the most attractive aspects of Case; one pre-med student confessed, "I came to Case because I was accepted into PPSP."

Despite the heavy concentration of students in the sciences and engineering, Case is dedicated to educating their students in all areas, enabling them to become more well-rounded people with diverse interests. Case students are required to explore different areas, such as the arts, the humanities, and the social sciences, as well as courses in "global and cultural diversity."

The number of credits required for majors at Case differ according to department. While the arts and humanities programs require fewer credits and thus allow students more freedom to survey other fields, science and engineering programs require more credits. Though the requirements for science majors seem stringent, students say they leave feeling well prepared. A biomedical engineering major asserted, "The curriculum definitely takes care of every aspect of BME that's necessary, including polymers, imaging and electrics, and biomechanics."

Introductory classes are often lecture-based, with 100 to 300 students in each class. However, Case supplies "Supplemental Instructors" (SIs), who hold review sessions and are known to be "very helpful." As students progress to courses more specific to certain majors, however, typical class size decreases to a cozy 20–30, ensuring more personal attention for each student. Case also requires 16 credits in seminar classes, beginning with the freshman seminar program, SAGES (Seminar Approach to General Education and Scholarship), which is designed to encourage students to "discover . . . the endless opportunities and resources here at Case [as well as] . . . perspectives, passions, and creativity."

Social Scene

There's no question that Case students study hard, but beyond their grueling Sunday through Thursday nights, they also enjoy a vibrant and diverse social scene centered around Case's popular fraternities and sororities. Nearly a quarter of the student body is involved in the Greek scene, and as a result students report that "either you or many of your friends" are fraternity boys or sorority girls. Campus-wide Greek events are commonplace, and one of the most famous is Greek Week, when fraternities and sororities compete in numerous events. Interested students are given the opportunity to get to know their potential brotherhoods or sisterhoods through a series of events, get-togethers, and longer parties before receiving a bid to join.

Although Greek life does compose a large part of Case's social scene, students report that "the Greek community is normally very open." Although some girls complain that it is slightly more difficult to "make a ton of friends as a non-Greek," the majority of students feel that "Greeks are integrated into the campus, and are very inclusive."

While a decent percentage of students at Case come from Ohio, the student body at Case still "embodies diversity in geography, ethnicity, and particularly interests." Consequently, students at Case expect to meet and make friends from varied backgrounds. One student comments, "Sure, we are a nerdy school . . . but most people are socially inclined. I think that [Case] provides opportunities to meet all of the different sorts of people you'd like."

On-campus entertainment consists of performances and events run by a large variety of student groups such as IMPROVment on Friday nights and Spot Night on Wednesday nights, when local bands play. Alcohol is technically banned from campus, but one student reported it is nonetheless "easy to find," though "binge drinking and drugs are not problems on campus."

Case athletics have been increasing in popularity and rank in recent years. The Case football team ended the 2007 season with the school's first University Athletic Association Championship in football. The team was undefeated in 2008 but didn't get far in the NCAA Division III playoffs. Intramural sports, including less traditional events such as dodgeball, are "intense as heck." Three-quarters of the undergraduate body participate in intramurals during their four years at Case.

> "Sure, we are a nerdy school . . . but most people are socially inclined. I think that [Case] provides opportunities to meet all of the different sorts of people you'd like."

Students can also explore the large array of off-campus entertainment. Whether you'd like to go shopping, dining, clubbing, or bowling, there are options accessible on foot or by bus. One of the most popular and unique neighborhoods near Case is Coventry, which can be reached by walking or by "Greenies," the green campus shuttle buses. Coventry is a shopping district with an eclectic mix of stores full of "books, toys, and random cool things" in addition to restaurants offering international cuisine. Sports fans can cheer on the nearby Cleveland Indians and Cavaliers, music aficionados can enjoy their favorite bands at the House of Blues, and window-shoppers can indulge themselves at Beachwood, an upscale mall accessible by bus from campus.

Of course, you can also take advantage of Case's proximity to the University Circle and enjoy masterpieces at the Cleveland Museum of Art, scientific artifacts and displays at Cleveland Museum of Natural History, shows at the Cleveland Play House, and of course the concerts of the world-renowned Cleveland Orchestra at Severance Hall, all within one mile of campus. But when you're traveling to and from locations off-campus at night, be aware that, as with most universities located in urban environments, safety is key. Although Case is currently updating emergency phones and security is "everywhere," "you should [still] definitely be smart about where you go and what you do."

Living at Case

Students are required to live on campus for the first two years of school, unless they live at home and commute. Freshmen dorms are usually doubles located in the "upper three floors of four-storied buildings" and are "fair sized, but without air conditioning." Students are allowed to choose their own rooms and dorms, pending availability, as well as their own roommates.

Many upperclassmen choose to move off

campus, but a significantly larger percentage of them stay on campus due to the recent addition of the "Village at 115." Described as a "swanky hotel" by some, Village at 115 offers the luxury of an apartment with the convenience of living on campus. However, the major complaint about both upperclassmen and underclassmen housing is that "classes are too far away from the dorms."

There are two main dining halls on campus: Fribley (South) and Leutner (North). Students are free to dine at either dining hall, though Fribley is considered better. Flexible meal plans come with "Case cash," which can be used at local restaurants.

The numerous resources and opportunities Case Western Reserve University offers impact its students for a lifetime. Students describe their time at Case as "demanding but rewarding," and with its superior academics and flourishing social scene Case offers its students an ideal environment to enhance their education and social connections.
—*Chaoran Chen*

FYI

If you come to Case, you'd better bring "a computer and a warm winter coat."
What is the typical weekend schedule? "Every weekend is different" and "students can generally do whatever they choose," but Friday and Saturday tend to be nights to find a party or enjoy events off campus, whereas Sunday night is reserved exclusively for studying.
If I could change one thing about Case, I'd "make everyone more positive."
Three things every student at Case should do before graduating are "go to a concert by the Cleveland Orchestra, meet Lebron James, and explore University Circle's museums."

College of Wooster

Address: 847 College
Avenue, Wooster, OH
44691
Phone: 800-877-9905
E-mail address:
admissions@wooster.edu
Web site URL:
www.wooster.edu
Year Founded: 1866
Private or Public: Private
Religious Affiliation: None
Location: Suburban
Number of Applicants:
3,445
Percent Accepted: 81%
**Percent Accepted who
enroll:** 20%
Number Entering: 513
**Number of Transfers
Accepted each Year:** 45
Middle 50% SAT range:
M: 540–660, CR: 540–670,
Wr: Unreported
Middle 50% ACT range:
23–29
**Early admission program
EA/ED/None:** ED, EA

**Percentage accepted
through EA or ED:**
Unreported
EA and ED deadline: 1-Dec,
15-Jan
Regular Deadline: 1-Feb
Application Fee: $40
**Full time Undergraduate
enrollment:** 1,864
Total enrollment: 1,864
Percent Male: 47%
Percent Female: 53%
**Total Percent Minority or
Unreported:** 10%
Percent African-American:
5%
**Percent Asian/Pacific
Islander:** 3%
Percent Hispanic: 2%
Percent Native-American:
<1%
Percent International: 5%
**Percent in-state/out of
state:** 39%/ 61%
Percent from Public HS:
Unreported
Retention Rate: 88%

Graduation Rate 4-year: 64%
Graduation Rate 6-year:
73%
**Percent Undergraduates in
On-campus housing:** 100%
**Number of official organized
extracurricular
organizations:** 130
3 Most popular majors:
Psychology, Political Science,
English
Student/Faculty ratio: 12:1
Average Class Size: 17
**Percent of students going to
grad school:** 40%
Tuition and Fees: $42,420
comprehensive fee
**In-State Tuition and Fees if
different:** No difference
Cost for Room and Board:
Included
**Percent receiving financial
aid out of those who apply,
first year:** 82%
**Percent receiving financial
aid among all students:**
17%

A small liberal arts college with less than 2,000 students, the College of Wooster may not be as well known as many other similar institutions, but it provides an outstanding education and a supportive intellectual environment to all students. Founded in 1866 and following a mission to educate everyone, Wooster's first PhD was granted to a female student during the 1880s. Today, Wooster focuses only on the undergraduate education of students, and the school is known for its unique Independent Study program, a yearlong senior project that culminates in an oral defense of a thesis in front of a committee. While it seems to be a college with a challenging environment, Wooster also provides an intimate atmosphere that closely supports both the academic and social aspects of student life.

Independence

Being in college means a greater degree of freedom as well as learning about becoming independent. That is exactly what Wooster chooses to foster among its students. The idea is that all students should pursue their own interests at their own initiative. Therefore, one portion of the degree requirement is that everyone must complete three courses of independent study. The first class is generally taken in junior year, during which students learn about research skills and methods. The last two courses are part of the senior thesis where students come up with their own projects. This program traces its beginnings to the 1940s and has since then been both lauded and imitated by many different universities. "I think it can seem really challenging at first," said one student. "But with the support we have here from professors, it becomes a very interesting experience."

Another part of Wooster's goal to foster independence is the availability of student-designed majors. Of course, it has to go through approvals by different levels of the college's bureaucracy to ensure academic vigor and coherence; nevertheless, it is a great way for the more ambitious students to create their personal programs of study instead of following academic plans designed by others. For those not interested in an independent program, there are about 40 majors, not a particularly large number, but that is characteristic of liberal arts schools, where students are expected to achieve a broad range of knowledge. Although the university has pre-professional programs in law, medicine, and engineering, the focus of the college is on liberal arts, which can be somewhat disappointing for all those interested in learning about more practical topics. "I always wanted to take a couple of interesting classes in engineering," said one student. "And I have been very much disappointed, but I guess I should have expected that from a liberal arts school."

> "With the support we have here from professors, [the Independent Study Program] becomes a very interesting experience."

Very interestingly, each major only requires seven to nine courses in the specific department. Therefore, students have greater freedom in choosing their classes. It also means a lengthy list of core requirement classes in which everyone must enroll. Similar to many universities, the required courses include writing, mathematics, foreign languages, and cultural perspectives. In order to graduate, all students must also take a class examining the religious dimension of human interactions. "The required classes are some of the best ones that I have had at Wooster," said one student.

Given the focus on independence, the academic life at Wooster is rather vigorous. Students are expected to work hard in their classes. "There are a lot of smart people here," said one student. "During freshman year, I was really shocked at the amount of work, maybe because my high school was not that demanding." At the same time, professors are very easily accessible. "I think the best thing here is that we are really small, and you can get to know some professors well as long as you try to meet them and talk to them," said one student.

Another advantage of Wooster is the lack of big lectures. For the school, an introductory class of 40 people would be considered very large, compared to large universities that have hundreds of people crammed into a single lecture hall. Therefore, Wooster is

able to create an intimate academic atmosphere. Of course, the drawback is that, unlike in large lectures, no one can remain relatively anonymous in a class, and students are expected to participate more in class discussions.

Wooster, the Town

The college is located in Wooster, Ohio, about 50 miles south of Cleveland. It is well known as a college town. Not only is it home to Wooster College, it also includes the Agricultural Technical Institute of the Ohio State University and a major research center on agricultural development. From these institutions, it is clear that the city is highly focused on agriculture, especially in its surrounding areas. Students certainly lament the fact that Wooster lacks the benefits of large cities. "There is not much to do around here, which is exacerbated by the fact that we are in such a small school," said one student. Others, however, believe that Wooster offers a great college town atmosphere that is conducive to learning. "Coming from a big city, I really enjoy the more relaxed life here," said one student.

The great majority of undergraduates live on campus for the entirety of their college education. Only a negligible number of students choose to live elsewhere. The college offers 12 different residential halls. Each floor of the residential hall has a Resident Assistant whose main purpose is to help freshmen settle in and become accustomed to college life. The rooms, like most college dormitories, are very small. "If you have not already, I think you should learn about working outside of your room, because there is not much space," said one student. Most people, however, agree that the residences are adequate, and there is no major complaint about the living arrangement.

The dining services operate two large eateries. In addition, there are two coffee locations and one convenience store. It does not seem to be a large number of options, but considering that the school enrolls fewer than 2,000 students, the dining services certainly provides adequate options for students. "It is not really great food," said one student. "But I have no complaint."

Given the size of the college, students eventually become familiar with a large portion of the undergraduate population. "You get to know not only people of your own year," said one student. "But you are also going to meet plenty of people of other years because we are a very close community." The social life on the weekends, however, can be rather repetitive. Those looking for the nightlife of big cities will be disappointed, especially given the fact that Cleveland is more than an hour away. Surrounding campus, there are a number of bars and clubs, and both the students and the school administration do try to create their own events. However, given the size of the school and the city, it is clear that many students wish they could have access to a greater variety of activities.

An Unknown Gem

The diversity of Wooster is a potential area of improvement for the university. The majority of the student body is white with only a limited number of minorities, though students agree that they have a very tolerant and open-minded campus. In many ways, Wooster is a school that is perhaps not particularly well known, but offers a great intellectual atmosphere that rivals many of the top liberal arts colleges and is certainly a great choice for four years of undergraduate study.—*Xiaohang Liu*

FYI

If you come to Wooster, you'd better bring "a car."

What is the typical weekend schedule? "Doing work and party at night."

If I could change one thing about Wooster, I'd "make it a little warmer during winters."

Three things every student at Wooster should do before graduating are "go to sporting events, hang out at the Underground, and participate in community service."

Denison University

Address: 100 West College PO Box B, Granville, OH 43023
Phone: 740-587-6276
E-mail address: admissions@denison.edu
Web site URL: www.denison.edu
Year Founded: 1831
Private or Public: Private
Religious Affiliation: None
Location: Suburban
Number of Applicants: 5,181
Percent Accepted: 39%
Percent Accepted who enroll: 29%
Number Entering: 586
Number of Transfers Accepted each Year: 30
Middle 50% SAT range: M: 590–680, Cr: 580–690, Wr: 620–690
Middle 50% ACT range: 26–30
Early admission program EA/ED/None: ED

Percentage accepted through EA or ED: 14%
EA and ED deadline: 1-Nov
Regular Deadline: 15-Jan
Application Fee: $40
Full time Undergraduate enrollment: 2,212
Total enrollment: 2,212
Percent Male: 43%
Percent Female: 57%
Total Percent Minority or Unreported: 18%
Percent African-American: 5%
Percent Asian/Pacific Islander: 3%
Percent Hispanic: 2%
Percent Native-American: 1%
Percent International: 5%
Percent in-state/out of state: 43%/57%
Percent from Public HS: 70%
Retention Rate: 93%

Graduation Rate 4-year: 78%
Graduation Rate 6-year: 82%
Percent Undergraduates in On-campus housing: 99%
Number of official organized extracurricular organizations: 156
3 Most popular majors: Communications, Economics, English
Student/Faculty ratio: 11:1
Average Class Size: 19
Percent of students going to grad school: 27%
Tuition and Fees: $32,160
In-State Tuition and Fees if different: No difference
Cost for Room and Board: $8,570
Percent receiving financial aid out of those who apply, first year: 76%
Percent receiving financial aid among all students: 43%

In the middle of Licking County, Ohio, there is a big hill with a tiny town nestled at the bottom. Granville might not be the place you would expect to find a slew of college students, but take a hike up the hill and you will come upon the warm brick buildings and expansive green areas that make up the campus of Denison University. The school may match the small size of the town at its feet, but the 2,100 undergraduates manage to create an environment where they can work—and play—with plenty of variety. While Denison is known for its traditional, preppy vibe, the genuine homeyness of this "Little Utopia" is just as prevalent as a popped collar.

The Learning Curve

"A lot of my friends work pretty constantly," said one freshman, whose sentiments were echoed by other Denison students. There's no denying that the workload is heavy, and the word "slacker" does not seem to be part of the school's vocabulary. Although another student added that "teachers are tough graders and classes are challenging," in the rigorous general curriculum, ambitious students may also elect to be part of Denison's intensive honors program. But the demanding academics should not deter prospective Denisonians—the courses may be tough, but students generally praise the school's extensive academic resources.

One freshman mentioned that it can be difficult to get into the necessary introductory-level classes that are prerequisites for most of the more in-depth classes at Denison, but most students appreciate the small size of these capped classes. Students estimate that the average class ranges from about 15 to 20 people, which creates a comfortable environment for students to take risks in discussions. One student said that class is "like a dialogue between the students and the professors," which means that "students are known for their ideas—not by their ID numbers." In addition, Denison is set apart by its commitment to having only professors teach classes—TA's are around only to help grade. Students say they feel much more engaged in class because the people who really know and care about the subject are directly involved and invested in conveying material. While such a setup might be intimidating elsewhere, the small classes make interactions with the professors very easy, and students say that their teachers are both approachable and eager for students to communicate with them.

It is not only the professors who like to talk about school outside of class—the students, too, are often found debating on their way out of the classroom. One student recounted a day in the dining hall when an entire class convened spontaneously to discuss the topic of the previous day's class—not for credit, not for a grade, but because, as students note, Denisonians are passionate about what they learn. Students say most people are used to getting all As in high school, but that "it's more about actually knowing things than being able to recite details and facts."

City Upon a Hill

Denison clearly takes its role as an educator very seriously, and the campus reflects this goal. At the heart of the school are the academic buildings, which are surrounded by the residential dorms. Although the classrooms are in the middle, the real hub of campus is the Union, which students say "is always full of people." The building, with a food court and a bar for upperclassmen, provides a welcome respite from studying and a convenient meeting spot for students coming from any part of campus. Although the locations are generally divided by age, students say that almost everyone lives on campus. That, and the lack of any fraternity houses, contributes to a great deal of campus unity and a "cohesiveness that brings a lot to the school."

> **"Students are known for their ideas—not by their ID numbers."**

While students say that the housing is uniformly excellent, some people go a more alternative route. While still on campus, South houses many art majors, and "team" houses, such as baseball and rugby, are also popular. For more of an unconventional experience, the Homestead, which lies about a mile away from the campus, provides students with the opportunity to get just a little bit closer to nature. Students say that each dorm has its own personality, but since the housing process is done by lottery, residences hold students with many diverse interests and activities. The freshmen live on West or North quad, all in substance-free dorms. Even so, the ubiquitous college party dorm still exists in the form of Shorney, which has four coed floors and only one that is single-sex. The sophomores and juniors who live on East, meanwhile, tend to host most of the parties in conjunction with seniors in the on-campus Hayes or Sunset apartment complexes. Even better than partying, procrastination is made infinitely easier by the "amazing technology" to be found in every dorm and all across campus—students say that all the dorms and buildings are fully wireless, and one student estimated that "there are more computers on campus than people!"

The Sunset Strip

When the workweek weighs down backpacks, and minds are crammed with all the information they can handle, even the most diligent worker needs some release. "There's lots of partying, I'm not going to lie," said one student. "This is a small school in the middle of nowhere." Although most of the parties center on alcohol, students are quick to assert that people who do not drink are by no means out of luck on the weekends. One student conceded that "people definitely party with a different group if they don't drink, but it's not a big deal." Because alcohol is not allowed in the freshman dorms, most of the partying takes place in the senior Sunset apartments. The big partying days of Wednesday, Friday, and Saturday afford plenty of time to hit the senior apartments, the sophomore and junior housing, and the club and team houses. The school is not particularly harsh with its alcohol policies, but students caution that write-ups are not unheard of, and the school cracks down hard on all illegal drugs. Still, students find the social scene to be "chill and comfortable," but stimulating because "all ages hang out together." In describing the partying at Denison, one student summed it up perfectly: "fun but not too crazy."

The Hills Are Alive

Not only with the sound of music, but also the telltale scuffling of sports, the whirring of the printing press, and every activity in between. For a very small school, Denison "really pushes that students do get involved with something, whether it's a sport, a club of some kind, or a sorority or frat." Because Granville is such a "teeny town," students find what they want right on campus. "The school provides us with lots of things to do—they know how isolated we are." Most people are very involved in activities outside of academics and are very familiar with the other students.

Denison is a Division III school, which means that, while it is "not incredibly selective as to who is capable of playing," many more people have the opportunity to participate. While students are all for playing sports, the games themselves are not particularly well attended: students caution that the football team is so bad that people almost never go to games, but lacrosse and soccer do draw some fans. Club and intramural sports also tend to be popular, especially Frisbee, rugby, soccer, and tennis.

If sports are not particularly intriguing, there are any number of activities that are "easy to get involved in." One freshman remarked, "I don't know one person who isn't involved in at least one thing outside of class." Students are part of a diverse range of extracurriculars, including environmental clubs, singing groups, and fraternities and sororities—which count one-third of the student body among their brothers and sisters. Political groups are not particularly big on campus, but students mention a generally moderate to conservative vibe. One thing everyone can agree on is the popularity of the *Bullsheet*, a daily paper that is comprised entirely of student work—a better alternative to the actual school newspaper, students say. No matter what people decide to become involved in, students say it is easy to jump in immediately and be welcomed to the group.

D-Day

It may not require quite the military force of Normandy, but there is definitely an invasion of Denison's campus once a year. Each year, the school brings in a big-name musical act, which remains a surprise until announced at homecoming. Previous acts have included Third Eye Blind, Juvenile, and the Roots, and students say no one misses this event.

There is another "D" word that is not quite as much a part of the Denison tradition: diversity. "The lack of diversity surprised me," said one student, who also felt that the current homogeneity "causes problems when people of different races do come in." Students appreciate that Denison is working to make the school a more open place by sponsoring forums and dedicating itself to creating a less tense environment, but the problem is not only racial. One student candidly stated, "The tuition is quite expensive, so inevitably you are going to get a wealthier population," although others mentioned that the school gives almost everyone very generous financial aid packages.

The tradition that characterizes Denison above all is that of cohesiveness. Students may seem reserved at first, but in the end the friendliness of the student body and the accessibility of the professors create an atmosphere that allows for growth in many areas. One student encapsulated the essence of a Denison education: "It is a good learning environment that builds you as a person rather than just a student."—*Hannah Jacobson*

FYI

If you come to Denison, you'd better bring "a lot of dress-up clothes and random things you think you'll never wear: we have tons of theme parties!"

What is the typical weekend schedule? "On Friday, take a long nap—then at six, it starts getting loud, at seven, you come out of your room to start socializing and hall bonding before pregaming and heading out to party. On Saturday, the campus is vacant until four because everyone is sleeping and/or hungover, then you do it all again until Sunday, when we do homework. And eat."

If I could change one thing about Denison, I'd "make it more diverse."

Three things every student at Denison should do before graduating are "party in the wigwam built in the woods behind the Sunset parking lot, go onto the fourth floor of Talbot and look out at the amazing view of the rolling hills, and go to Brew's restaurant in Granville and Wit's for the best ice cream ever."

Kent State University

Address: 314 University Library, Kent, OH 44242

Phone: 330-672-3000

E-mail address: admissions@kent.edu

Web site URL: www.kent.edu

Year Founded: 1910

Private or Public: Public

Religious Affiliation: None

Location: Suburban

Number of Applicants: 12,325

Percent Accepted: 89%

Percent Accepted who enroll: 35%

Number Entering: 3,831

Number of Transfers Accepted each Year: 920

Middle 50% SAT range: M: 460–590, CR: 460–580, Wr: Unreported

Middle 50% ACT range: 19–24

Early admission program EA/ED/None: None

Percentage accepted through EA or ED: NA

EA and ED deadline: NA

Regular Deadline: 1-Aug

Application Fee: $55

Full time Undergraduate enrollment: 29,227

Total enrollment: 34,056

Percent Male: 39%

Percent Female: 61%

Total Percent Minority or Unreported: 17%

Percent African-American: 9%

Percent Asian/Pacific Islander: 2%

Percent Hispanic: 2%

Percent Native-American: <1%

Percent International: Unreported

Percent in-state/out of state: 87%/13%

Percent from Public HS: Unreported

Retention Rate: 71%

Graduation Rate 4-year: 26%

Graduation Rate 6-year: Unreported

Percent Undergraduates in On-campus housing: 35%

Number of official organized extracurricular organizations: 400

3 Most popular majors: Business/Marketing, Education, Health Professions

Student/Faculty ratio: 18:1

Average Class Size: Unreported

Percent of students going to grad school: Unreported

Tuition and Fees: $15,862

In-State Tuition and Fees if different: $8,430

Cost for Room and Board: $7,200

Percent receiving financial aid out of those who apply, first year: 81%

Percent receiving financial aid among all students: 63%

K ent State University, despite its place in history as a hotbed of political progressivism, is a quiet, laid-back institution. Kent offers a wide variety of academic opportunities, with a friendly atmosphere for an institution of its size. With over 26,000 undergraduate students at the central campus and 35,000 overall, Kent State is the second-largest university in Ohio. Although the campus is not very diverse—most of its students are in-state, Caucasian and middle-class—it offers its students various opportunities academically and socially. Kent State University also has a network of regional campuses across Ohio, catering to commuter students.

Liberal Education at a Large University

Kent State University gives its students some freedom to choose their own schedules within the constraints of Liberal Education Requirements, or LER. Every undergraduate student must attain credit in composition, mathematics and critical reasoning, logic and foreign language, humanities and fine arts, social sciences, basic sciences and diversity. Most students seem to think that the LER is worthwhile, forcing them to explore classes they otherwise would not take.

"Human Sexuality" is a popular course, which one girl described as "one of the most fun classes I've taken in my life." Another popular class, a science class designed for non-science students, is called "Seven Ideas that Struck the Universe." Although most students seem to enjoy their classes, other students complain that the set of classes that complete the LER is too restricting.

Most introductory classes have 100 to 175 students, but the size can vary. Language classes and labs generally have fewer than 20 students, and class size drops once you start taking classes in the major. Professors teach all of the classes except labs, which are run by teaching assistants under the direction of a professor. Although there are no discussion sections to supplement lectures, professors have office hours set aside for helping students. The professors are for the most part approachable and helpful. Some professors even set time aside to help students on an Internet chat. These chats, as well as syllabi and class notes, are part of the Kent Web server.

Among the most popular majors at Kent, the fashion program is outstanding and is ranked as one of the top fashion programs in the nation. Some of the less popular majors are still high quality and offer excellent experiences. Many majors offer study abroad programs: The fashion and architecture programs offer studies in Venice, the journalism program in London and Paris, and the conservation program in Australia and Mexico.

Suitcasers and Party Animals

The weekend social life at Kent State is, for most of the campus, admittedly lacking. Many students describe Kent State as a "suitcase campus," where half the on-campus students go home for the weekends. The students who remain on campus are left with a variety of things to do, though one must take the initiative to take advantage of the options.

Partying is a big deal for those left on campus for the weekends. Because drinking is strictly prohibited in most of the dorms, most of the partying occurs off campus at

the fraternity houses. The Greek scene is influential on campus, because the frats host most of the parties. Some of the more elite national fraternities are on Frat Row, but those are mostly dry. The party fraternities are located off East Main Street, a main strip that is a center of off-campus life. There are a lot of fast food joints on East Main, where students can often be seen "getting their 3 a.m. Taco Bell."

> Many students describe Kent State as a "suitcase campus," where half the on-campus students go home for the weekends.

For students who do not like the fraternity scene, there are a lot of other options. Upperclassmen usually hang out at their off-campus apartments. Wednesday is notorious for karaoke. On the weekends, those who are old enough go to the bars and clubs of downtown Kent. Many students spend their weekends participating in one of the multitude of extracurricular organizations. There are many different organizations on campus, some of the more popular being community service organizations, the College Democrats, the Dive (a Christian youth group started only a few years ago) and Project Sound (a group that brings local bands to campus). Other students play sports, and for those who do not go home for the weekend, joining a traveling sports team is a great alternative.

Sports are a big deal on campus. Basketball is especially popular, since the men's team enjoyed success in the conference tournament, bringing home the championship in 2008. The football team is not as good but still enjoys the prevalent Kent State pride. Intramural sports are also very competitive; one intramural softball team was even sponsored by a local business. The recent rage has been club dodgeball, which is played in one of the indoor facilities. The new recreation center sports two pools, indoor basketball, volleyball and track, a spa area and an indoor soccer arena.

On-Campus Housing: The "Freshman Experience" and More

Housing on campus is described as scarce. Not too long ago, a fire in one of the dorms caused students to be temporarily removed for cleanup, and the university had trouble finding space for the displaced students. Although there are some space issues, most students seemed satisfied with their experience in the dorms.

Freshmen have the option either to live in normal on-campus housing or to live in the special Freshman (or First Year) Experience dorms. Although the rooms in the Freshman Experience dorms are smaller, there are some benefits to staying in them. For one, only freshmen live in the dorms, so it makes it easy for new students to meet each other. Furthermore, they are smaller than normal dorms—at about 100 students, rather than about 750 students—which leads to a more intimate atmosphere.

Most students move off campus their junior year to apartments in the Kent area. The university requires that non-commuting students live on campus their first two years. The upperclassmen who choose to stay on campus have a pretty good choice of dorms. The standard room is a double, but some students pay more for a single, or buy out a quad with a friend for extra space. The housing has been undergoing renovation, and some "very elaborate" dorms were recently finished, which a senior called "an apartment on campus you don't have to clean." For this reason, there was an increase in upperclassmen living on campus a couple of years ago.

The security inside the dorms is fairly strict. One particularly annoyed student described the security guards as "pompous" and "self-righteous," but there is a general consensus that the policies are invasive. When an offense is committed, such as being caught drinking or partying, a strike is marked against a student. When a student accumulates enough strikes, they go to administrative courts. Although the police are not contacted, the process is still described as "irritating." Though alcohol is strictly prohibited in most dorms, there is "more [on-campus drinking] going on than people realize."

The food at Kent State gets mixed reviews from the students. One girl stated that the food is "OK, not as healthy as it could be," while another claims that "we have a very good variety." Students have a meal plan, which is based on credit that can be spent at a dining hall or at the food court. "The Hub" at the student center offers some fast food, including Quizno's, Einstein's Bagels, A&W and Ambrosia. There is even a restaurant, which offers full-service meals—a popular place to take someone out for a date. A lot of students carry a Flash Cash card, which works with the meal plan and is also accepted at most local businesses.

May 4, 1970, and Kent State Today

The incident on May 4, 1970, when four student protesters were shot and killed at Kent State, is a stunning reminder of the tension between students and the government. Today, there is a memorial to the event, and every year the campus throws a big party on the anniversary. In recent years, the partying has been curbed because of problems in the past with rowdy crowds.

The campus today is surprisingly apolitical. There is still some bad blood between the city of Kent and Kent State University, but political protests are not very common on campus. Political activism is kept at a minimum because of a "general apathy" around campus. One junior girl stated that "everyone has their own opinions, but nobody makes the effort to do anything with it." There has been some activity during recent presidential elections, but it is difficult to get the students interested in school politics. A "big protest" recently drew only 300 students.

Kent State University has a "pretty spread-out campus," with lots of open fields and sidewalks. There is a pretty forested area with a natural creek near the biology building. The architecture of the buildings varies. One can easily tell where they are by looking at the nearby buildings, as each area has a unique architecture. The art center in the center of campus is pretty and decorated with installation projects made by the students. Although a lot of students own cars, because of a parking problem most students walk around campus. The bus system has recently been revamped, and buses stop every seven minutes. Otherwise, it could take 30 minutes to walk across campus. During the "real bad-ass winter," the bus system becomes a serious boon to students, especially since the sidewalks do not always get plowed.

The campus is well-lit at night, and the students feel very safe, even when walking alone. Crime is a rare occurrence. There is an escort service available for those students who feel they need it. Overall, the campus receives high marks for atmosphere. The students are very comfortable, and all have loved their experiences there. One journalism major had misgivings when she came, but she soon changed her mind. She said, "Kent State grabbed me, pulled me in, and I never wanted to leave."—*Ryan Galisewski*

Kenyon College

Address: Ransom Hall Gambier, OH 43022

Phone: 740-427-5776

E-mail address: admissions@kenyon.edu

Web site URL: www.kenyon.edu

Year Founded: 1824

Private or Public: Private

Religious Affiliation: None

Location: Rural

Number of Applicants: 3,992

Percent Accepted: 39%

Percent Accepted who enroll: 31%

Number Entering: 469

Number of Transfers Accepted each Year: 10

Middle 50% SAT range: M: 600–680, CR: 630–720, Wr: 620–730

Middle 50% ACT range: 28–32

Early admission program EA/ED/None: ED I, ED II

Percentage accepted through EA or ED: 45%

EA and ED deadline: 15-Nov and 15-Jan

Regular Deadline: 15-Jan

Application Fee: $45 (waived for online application)

Full time Undergraduate enrollment: 1,618

Total enrollment: 1,633

Percent Male: 48%

Percent Female: 52%

Total Percent Minority or Unreported: 14%

Percent African-American: 4%

Percent Asian/Pacific Islander: 6%

Percent Hispanic: 3%

Percent Native-American: <1%

Percent International: 4%

Percent in-state/out of state: 17%/83%

Percent from Public HS: 54%

Retention Rate: 91%

Graduation Rate 4-year: 85%

Graduation Rate 6-year: 89%

Percent Undergraduates in On-campus housing: 98%

Number of official organized extracurricular organizations: >140

3 Most popular majors: English, Political Science, Economics/International Studies

Student/Faculty ratio: 10:1

Average Class Size: 17

Percent of students going to grad school: 70%

Tuition and Fees: $40,980

In-State Tuition and Fees if different: No difference

Cost for Room and Board: $7,260

Percent receiving financial aid out of those who apply, first year: 84%

Percent receiving financial aid among all students: 75%

A midst the valleys and rolling hills of Gambier, Ohio, lies the rural liberal arts paradise that is Kenyon College. With only about 1,640 students, Kenyon has managed to carve out a reputation for itself as an academically challenging, artistically stimulating, and fun-loving place to spend those four formative years. And you can do it all surrounded by the pristine beauty of Kenyon's own nature preserve.

Comps but no Core

The small, intimate nature of the Kenyon community is definitely intensified when it comes to the academic community. Since the average class size is 15, students report that they definitely get a lot of one-on-one attention from their professors (and it's just professors—no TAs at Kenyon!). This can range from office hours to home visits, but professor accessibility is one of the highlights of academic life at Kenyon. In fact, one student said that, "There used to be a rule that all professors had to live on campus . . . It's not true anymore, but they're all still very close."

Rather than a standard set of core requirements, Kenyon students complete nine "units," or two semesters, of courses outside their own majors, whose requirements are often rigorous enough without the added stress. And instead of a thesis, Kenyon seniors prepare senior "exercises," more popularly known as "comps," in which they execute some kind of culminating project that encapsulates their studies during the last four years. The comps allow for a whole range of creative freedom, but can be stressful. One senior double-major in English and Dance and Drama said that she's excited about the original play she is writing but admitted that she "pretty much lives in the library these days."

Yet all of these requirements do not deter determined Kenyon students from double majoring or from enjoying their classes in popular majors like English, psychology, and political science. And there are popular courses that draw in students from all sorts of specialty areas, including an anthropology seminar on drinking culture and an English course entitled, "Strange Fish and Bearded Women." Overall, while students agree that academics are "challenging, they are also definitely what you make of it—you get out what you put back in."

Frats and "Phling"
Outside of the classroom, Kenyon students are sociable and easy to get along with. As one student asserted, "Compared to other places I've been, this place is incredibly friendly." The small community makes it easy to make friends. "If you sit on the bench on Middle Path, you can see everyone at Kenyon pass by. It's impossible to walk somewhere and not see everyone you know." Yet there is definitely a downside, as one senior admitted. "Everyone definitely knows everyone else's business here . . . we call it the fishbowl." While the Kenyon community is made up of people from all different states and countries, the majority of the students at Kenyon are admittedly white and upper-middle-class. Yet students are quick to say that Kenyon is an accepting and welcoming place, regardless of background.

While Kenyon is a beautiful and safe campus ("we don't even lock our doors here," one student said), it can also get to be "pretty isolated." Luckily, nearby Ohio towns and cities provide a whole host of entertainment options, including movie theaters in Columbus and bands at schools like Ohio State. Students report that while a car is helpful, it is not necessary, since there are shuttles that can take undergrads to nearby towns, and the campus itself is navigable on foot. Of course, for those who choose to stay on campus during the weekends, there is an incredible amount of things to do, from shows and concerts, to film series and frat parties. And students report that while "you can always go to a frat party," Greek life definitely does not dominate the Kenyon social scene.

> **"It's impossible to walk somewhere and not see everyone you know."**

Kenyon is not a dry campus and one student claimed that "most of the campus does drink." However, other students contended that "you definitely don't have to drink here to have a good time." For those who prefer their weekends dry, the Kenyon After Dark sponsors a whole host of activities, including first-run movie premieres and an Iron Chef Dessert contest, for people to enjoy (soberly or not). In fact, campus-wide parties and activities are an especially prominent part of Kenyon social life. One of the most popular is "Philander's Phebruary Phling," an event that takes place the first weekend in February. There's a different theme every year, and students get together to dance, drink, and stay warm during the onset of winter.

Life in the "Fishbowl"
All students at Kenyon must live on campus, which helps to make the housing process easier to settle than at other schools. Housing is determined by lottery, which can often be a hit-or-miss process, yet students report that they usually manage to live with friends and form even tighter bonds with roommates by the time they graduate. While one student said that "The best way to describe our living conditions is 'Spartan,'" others insisted that the school's neo-Gothic architecture is "simple but pretty." The different dorms at Kenyon do have their own distinct characters and features: Old Kenyon, the oldest building on campus, is supposedly haunted, while Caples is the tallest building in Knox County. There are Community Advisors (CAs) who live on both freshman and upperclassman halls, but students say that they aren't too strict.

When it comes to food, students report that the college has made a conscious effort to improve its culinary standing in the last few years. One senior stated that "The food started out awful, but it's gotten a lot better over the last few years—there's a sushi place at the gym, and there's a lot more focus on vegan and vegetarian options." There's not actually a meal plan at Kenyon—students just get all-you-can-eat meals at Pierce, the school's one dining hall that has recently been renovated. For those hoping to find food elsewhere, students say that the Gambier Grill offers yummy and affordable American fare, while the Kenyon Inn is nice but a bit more expensive. And, if you're willing to drive, the Chinese and Mexican restaurants at Mt. Vernon are usually worth the trip.

Students at Kenyon can choose from a plethora of extracurricular activities to occupy their time. There are a cappella and theater groups galore—in fact, many shows traditionally left a seat open during their performances for Paul Newman, one of the school's most famous alumni. Sadly, he recently died after a long-term illness and will be greatly missed. Community service is another outlet—students say that Habitat for Humanity is growing into an increasingly popular way to spend a Saturday morning. From hosting a show on Kenyon's radio station to joining the Mock Trial team, there is no shortage of opportunity to stay busy.

For the more athletically inclined, one of Kenyon's most famous Division III sports teams is the men's diving and swimming team, which has won 30 championships since 1980. The basketball and lacrosse teams are also growing in popularity, as is IM Ultimate Frisbee. In fact, the Kenyon College Ultimate Frisbee Team (KCUF) holds an event called the "Skivies Snow Bowl," in which players strip down to their underwear to play. One student admits that "Student support for the sports teams tends to be a little lacking—we aren't a place with killer school spirit." Yet the school's new athletic center and revamping of the intramural sports system leaves students optimistic about the future of Kenyon athletics.

Tradition!

Kenyon lore is rife with unique stories and enduring traditions. On the final night of freshman orientation, all freshmen stand on the steps of the theater building and sing Kenyon's four college songs as upperclassmen stand and jeer. Four years later, after their baccalaureate service, the seniors do it again, clothed in caps and gowns. It is this sense of community and continuity that binds Kenyon students together during their time together and makes the supportive and intimate atmosphere such a fun place to be; as one senior explained, "I love it here. I can safely say without feeling trite that this is truly a special place."—*Alexandra Bicks*

FYI

If you come to Kenyon, you'd better bring "a pair of boots—no one told me how cold Ohio would be and how much it would rain and snow!"

What's a typical weekend schedule? "Friday afternoon, finish up class, de-stress, dinner; Friday night, an a cappella concert or a play, then a few different apt. parties (maybe the one bar on campus); Saturday, sleep in, work; Saturday night, about the same (although maybe go out to eat one of those nights); Sunday, everyone does homework."

If I could change one thing about Kenyon, I'd "want there to be more diversity."

Three things everyone should do before graduating from Kenyon are "eat pie from Peggy Sue's (about 20 minutes away), go on Tim Shutt's ghost tour, go swimming in the nearby river down the hill."

Miami University

Address: 301 South Campus Avenue, Oxford, OH 45056
Phone: 513-529-2531
E-mail address: admission@muohio.edu
Web site URL: www.muohio.edu
Year Founded: 1809
Private or Public: Public
Religious Affiliation: None
Location: Rural
Number of Applicants: 16,772
Percent Accepted: 79%
Percent Accepted who enroll: 24%
Number Entering: 3,236
Number of Transfers Accepted each Year: 522
Middle 50% SAT range: M: 560–660, CR: 530–630, Wr: Unreported
Middle 50% ACT range: 24–29
Early admission program EA/ED/None: EA and ED

Percentage accepted through EA or ED: Unreported
EA and ED deadline: 1-Nov (ED), 1-Dec (EA)
Regular Deadline: 1-Feb
Application Fee: $50
Full time Undergraduate enrollment: 14,457
Total enrollment: 16,884
Percent Male: 47%
Percent Female: 53%
Total Percent Minority or Unreported: 10%
Percent African-American: 4%
Percent Asian/Pacific Islander: 3%
Percent Hispanic: 2%
Percent Native-American: 1%
Percent International: 3%
Percent in-state/out of state: 70%/30%
Percent from Public HS: Unreported
Retention Rate: 89%

Graduation Rate 4-year: 70%
Graduation Rate 6-year: 82%
Percent Undergraduates in On-campus housing: 50%
Number of official organized extracurricular organizations: 350
3 Most popular majors: Finance, Marketing, Psychology
Student/Faculty ratio: 15:1
Average Class Size: 31
Percent of students going to grad school: Unreported
Tuition and Fees: $16,952
In-State Tuition and Fees if different: $26,202
Cost for Room and Board: $9,458
Percent receiving financial aid out of those who apply, first year: 68%
Percent receiving financial aid among all students: Unreported

The deceptively named Miami University is not located in Miami, Florida. Rather, it is in Oxford, Ohio. The name came from the Miami Indians who used to live in the area. The tenth public college founded in the United States, Miami University offers "truly the quintessential college experience," said one freshman. Indeed, Miami University offers a combination of solid academics and strong party scene that is "just how I imagined college would be."

Hitting the Books

Miami University has a core curriculum of "Foundation Courses" that are usually taken during the freshman and sophomore years. The requirement is met by taking 36 credit hours in English composition, the fine arts, humanities, and social sciences; cultures; natural sciences; and mathematics, formal reasoning, and technology. While introductory courses are large, the majority of classes are small. "You can really get to know your professors, though maybe less in your freshman year than as an upperclassman," said one junior.

The academic advising system is generally considered "solid." All students have a first-year advisor who lives with them in their dorm. Another advisor replaces the first one when a major is declared during sophomore year. A student's studies in his or her major ends with the Senior Capstone, which is a project designed to combine a liberal arts education with the specialty of a major.

Because preference for class choices is given to athletes, graduate students and honor students, it can be nearly impossible for freshmen and sophomores to get into certain classes. However, "persistence pays off. If you hang around a class for long enough and talk to the teacher, you can usually find yourself a place," explained one sophomore.

Though "the schoolwork here can basically be as hard as you want to make it," students unanimously agree that the hardest majors are business and pre-med. The Oxford Scholars honors program is also challenging.

Also, Miami University ranks among the top institutions in the nation for the number of students participating in study abroad programs each year (more than 1,500). Many students opt to leave the country for a semester or a year, though the shorter summer programs are another popular option.

A Beautiful Campus

Robert Frost once said that Miami University was "the most beautiful college there ever was," and students take pride in their picturesque campus. "I'm a senior, and I'm still regularly in awe of how beautiful it is here," said one student. The colonial-style brick buildings divide the five sections of campus: the north, south, east, west, and central quads.

Students rave about how well their facilities are maintained. "Everything is kept very clean and pristine—my friends who visit are always surprised at how nicely our buildings are kept," said a sophomore. Dorm quality does vary, though, from mediocre to hotel-like. First-year residence halls are themed and offer theme-related events throughout the year. Types of hall themes include arts, foreign languages, health and wellness, honors and scholars, and leadership. After sophomore year, about 50 percent of students choose to move off campus and into the town of Oxford.

Dining hall food and services are well reviewed by students. Dining halls are located close to residences, and when the cafeterias close, there is a variety of late-night options available from a convenience store in the student center and other locations around campus. Popular off-campus options include the Alexander House, Kona Bistro, and Bagel and Deli.

Greek Life Dominates

Just less than half of the student body is involved with a fraternity or sorority, but students think that it often feels like many more students go Greek. "Being Greek is pretty much the only thing to do here if you want to have a social life," commented one student. "The school is located in a cornfield, and there's pretty much nothing to do but to drink," explained one freshman. "And you're going to drink with your fraternity or sorority." Indeed, the lack of any sort of off-campus scene is what drives so many students into the Greek system. Rushing is an important and stressful time on campus for the prospective Greek community.

Students enjoy the themed parties, semiformals, and formals thrown by fraternities and sororities, but also insist that the Greek system is useful in other aspects. "Every group does support a cause and benefits the community," said one senior, who then admitted, "It's really all about the parties and socializing." Those few who insist on avoiding Greek life often live on West Campus.

> "Every fraternity and sorority does support a cause and benefits the community . . . but it's really all about the parties and socializing."

Aside from fraternities and sororities, there are many extracurricular activities from which to choose, ranging from career-focused groups to volunteer organizations. Intramural sports are also popular, especially broomball, a sport invented at Miami University that is played on ice without skates. Varsity sports are substantially less popular. Attendance at games is sparse, and only hockey games draw crowds.

Welcome to J. Crew U.

Students at Miami University are generally described as thin, blond, and rich. "Everyone drives huge SUVs and is very conservative," said a junior. The student body dresses mostly in clothes from J. Crew and Abercrombie, leading some to nickname Miami University "J. Crew U." The generally white, upper-middle-class student body led one student to complain, "All Miami students are basically the same. It's very overbearing at times." A male student observed that much of the female population is very concerned with health, fitness, and physical appearance. However, one freshman also said that this means "everyone is very good-looking."

Miami's good academic program, beautiful campus, and lively social scene remain attractive despite the homogeneous student body and focus on physical appearance. Students say that in spite of Miami University's shortcomings, they "would definitely come to Miami if they had to do college all over again."—*Erica Rothman*

Oberlin College

Address: 101 North Professor Street, Oberlin, OH 44074
Phone: 440-775-8411
E-mail address: college.admission@oberlin.edu
Web site URL: www.oberlin.edu
Year Founded: 1833
Private or Public: Private
Religious Affiliation: None
Location: Rural
Number of Applicants: 7,014
Percent Accepted: 31%
Percent Accepted who enroll: 34%
Number Entering: 745
Number of Transfers Accepted each Year: Unreported
Middle 50% SAT range: M: 610–710, **CR:** 640–750, **Wr:** 630–730
Middle 50% ACT range: 26–32
Early admission program EA/ED/None: ED

Percentage accepted through EA or ED: 60%
EA and ED deadline: 15-Nov
Regular Deadline: 15-Jan
Application Fee: $35
Full time Undergraduate enrollment: 2,839
Total enrollment: 2,865
Percent Male: 45%
Percent Female: 55%
Total Percent Minority or Unreported: 25%
Percent African-American: 6%
Percent Asian/Pacific Islander: 8%
Percent Hispanic: 5%
Percent Native-American: 1%
Percent International: 6%
Percent in-state/out of state: 10%/90%
Percent from Public HS: 60%
Retention Rate: 92%

Graduation Rate 4-year: 65%
Graduation Rate 6-year: Unreported
Percent Undergraduates in On-campus housing: 86%
Number of official organized extracurricular organizations: 125
3 Most popular majors: English, History, Biology
Student/Faculty ratio: 9:1
Average Class Size: 12
Percent of students going to grad school: Unreported
Tuition and Fees: $36,282
In-State Tuition and Fees if different: No difference
Cost for Room and Board: $9,280
Percent receiving financial aid out of those who apply, first year: 88%
Percent receiving financial aid among all students: 53%

K nown as a small, freewheeling college with academics among the best and excellent opportunities for music and other arts, Oberlin provides a wealth of academic and extracurricular opportunities. Oberlin is perhaps most distinguished from other schools of its size by its conservatory, which trains musicians and provides students in the College with ample opportunity to play, study, and listen to music, too. Oberlin was founded as a coed school in 1833, and, four years later, it graduated the first women in the country to earn AB degrees. Oberlin was also the first racially integrated college in the nation. Today, Oberlin maintains its welcoming attitude, often drawing students because of its offerings in music and its equal strength in the humanities and sciences.

College and Con

Oberlin students tend to be passionate about academics and care about doing well in classes, but students said the academic atmosphere is mostly relaxed. Students study a lot, but they collaborate rather than compete, except, at times, in the Conservatory, where the nature of performance lends itself to competition. "The Con is pretty damn competitive; the College is really chill," one student said. Students in the Conservatory also take College classes, and College students can study in the Con, though to do so is less common. There are also a fair number of double-degree students who study in both schools.

Students often get to know their professors well. Even in the biggest classes—the most popular introductory science courses can reach up to two hundred students—the professor will always know students' names by the end of the semester. In some smaller classes, individual weekly conferences with the professor are required. Although students often hear stories of others who visit professors' houses or babysit for their kids, one student said relationships with professors "depend on what you make of it."

Oberlin students fulfill distributional requirements known as the 9-9-9 requirement: Nine credits must be completed in each of the social sciences, humanities, and natural sciences. Students complain about the complicated online registration system, which can prevent students from registering in their preferred classes, but getting into classes is easy if students simply go to class on the first day.

Compared to other small liberal arts colleges, Oberlin's science offerings are particularly strong. The school also offers one of the only neuroscience departments among colleges of its size. Biology, politics, neuroscience, and history are among the most popular majors.

Each year, students embark on projects of their choosing during Winter Term. Throughout January, students can work on farms in Costa Rica, tutor students in Oberlin public schools, get an internship, or watch and research movies—pretty much any proposal will be approved, one student said. A small percentage of students stay on campus, while many venture around the world and escape Ohio's cold winter.

Oberlin's Experimental College offers students the opportunity to teach classes. Up to 150 classes, with subjects ranging from steel drums to Korean to the television series *The West Wing*, are offered each term. Each class counts for one credit, and students say ExCo classes are an opportunity not to be missed.

Singing, Soccer, and the 'Sco

Oberlin fields varsity athletic teams, but they are far from being a central part of campus life. The teams are rarely successful, and one sophomore counted "booing our sports teams" on a list of ways to be active at Ober-

lin. While many students love intramurals, varsity athletes "seem like a completely different breed of student," said another sophomore.

Soccer, Frisbee, and Quidditch are among the most popular sports for the casual athlete. According to one Conservatory student, "people like to be active here, surprisingly." To do so, many participate in various kinds of dance; swing dancing and tango are popular activities. Organized dance groups' performances—mostly modern dance—are also very well attended.

Thanks in large part to the Conservatory, music thrives at Oberlin. There are 500 concerts—all free—on campus each year. A capella is very popular and quite competitive. "Everyone plays acoustic guitar and sings and is incredible at those things," one student said. Theatre, too, is very popular, with shows running every weekend.

A majority of students hold jobs on campus, and many work for campus publications or the radio station. The campus newspaper, *The Oberlin Review*, is published weekly. Political activism also draws widespread interest.

> "People here are definitely smart, but I've also noticed a large majority are funny."

Outside of organized extracurricular life, Oberlin students spend a lot of time hanging out with friends in dorm rooms. Oberlin has no fraternities or sororities. Parties are usually held in off-campus houses, but students say they tend to get shut down by campus authorities, sending partygoers back to their rooms later on a Friday or Saturday night. Still, two annual campus-wide parties, the Drag Ball and Safer Sex Night, draw the vast majority of the student population. Safer Sex Night, hosted by the Sexual Information Center, involves scantily clad students and free condoms and works both as an avenue for education about safe sex and an opportunity for a big party. Besides the two big events, it's always easy to find a party because most are publicized on Facebook. The 'Sco, a student-run night club at the Student Union, is another popular weekend destination.

Putting the "Liberal" in Liberal Arts

Oberlin may have a reputation as a hippie school, but students say they were pleasantly surprised to find lots of "normal people." The school has its share of hipsters and vegans, but Obies come in many forms. "It's pretty easy to be yourself here," one student said. "I expected it to be weirder." Oberlin students are not preppy and are generally "artistic, pretty laid back, and intelligent," a student said. "People here are definitely smart, and I've also noticed a large majority are funny," said another student.

The student population is diverse in all respects—except political affiliation. "There are about five people in the Oberlin College Republicans," one student said. Still, students are invested in politics. Students come to Oberlin from around the country and the world. "It's not all white rich kids by any means," one student said, but, according to another, "I wouldn't stress [diversity] as far as Admissions does."

Students say most people on campus drink, though those who don't can still easily find things to do on weekends, especially because of the abundance of performances of every kind Marijuana smoking, though less dominant, is also a fairly common activity once weekend parties have been busted by authorities. Students say other drugs are rarely encountered on campus.

When the weather is nice, students congregate every Friday afternoon on the grassy Wilder Bowl in a tradition known as TGIF. Most of the campus spends the afternoon hanging out, listening to live music, drinking, and eating. Clubs use the opportunity to advertise, soccer balls and Frisbees abound, musicians pull out the guitars, and gymnasts and jugglers perform. Think stereotypical college catalogue picture on steroids, and in real life.

At Home at Oberlin

Students live in dorms consisting mostly of doubles and closed doubles, which consist of two separated rooms, only one of which connects to the hall. "Freshman dorms are pretty crappy," said one sophomore. But a new freshman dorm is vastly nicer and much coveted. Seniors may enter a lottery to win the chance to live off campus. Students can also opt to live in program houses or village housing, which offers houses on campus, mostly for seniors.

Food at Oberlin received mixed reviews, but it's always possible to find something healthy and good to eat at one of the three dining halls. Oberlin dining halls are also home to one of the greatest things ever to grace a college campus: Fourth Meal. Every night, Sunday through Thursday, from 10:00 to 11:30 pm, dining halls serve a meal. "It's awesome. I wish I had it when I was a kid," one student said.

If one finds the dining halls to be unsatisfactory, one can turn to a co-op. Co-ops often define their members' social lives—one student described them as "self-segregating"—and they provide good food. They're especially popular among vegans, who may find the dining halls' offerings limited.

Oberlin is located in Oberlin, Ohio, which is small but offers good restaurants and coffee shops in close proximity to the College. More adventurous students can drive 40 minutes to Cleveland. About half the students have cars, so one will always have a friend who can drive. Although trips to Cleveland are not frequent—"Cleveland is not exactly a hoppin' hot spot," one student said, though the city's museums, including the Rock and Roll Hall of Fame, are well worth the drive.

Students at Oberlin are friendly, especially during the first weeks of the year, when it's common to strike up a conversation with a stranger in the dining hall and—pronto—make a friend. Although school spirit may not be obvious in sports arenas, Obies love their school. As one politics major said, "Students are obsessed with putting the letter O in front of everything."—*Julia Fisher*

FYI
If you come to Oberlin, you'd better bring "a smile, a Frisbee or hackeysack, and an open mind."
What's the typical weekend schedule? "TGIF, dinner, a play or performance, try to go to a party, hang out if that doesn't work. On Saturday, sleep 'til noon, work in Mudd Library, party. On Sunday, homework."
Three things every Oberlin student should do before graduating are "go to a swing dance, go somewhere cool for Winter Term, go to every concert you can."

Ohio State University

Address: 190 N. Oval Mall
Columbus, OH 43210
Phone: 614-292-3980
E-mail address:
askabuckeye@osu.edu
Web site URL: www.osu.edu
Year Founded: 1870
Private or Public: Public
Religious Affiliation: None
Location: Urban
Number of Applicants:
21,508
Percent Accepted: 59%
**Percent Accepted who
enroll:** 49%
Number Entering: 6,168
**Number of Transfers
Accepted each Year:** 2,198
Middle 50% SAT range:
M: 590–680, CR: 540–650,
Wr: 540–650
Middle 50% ACT range:
25–29
**Early admission program
EA/ED/None:** None

**Percentage accepted
through EA or ED:** NA
EA and ED deadline: NA
Regular Deadline: 1-Feb
Application Fee: $40
**Full time Undergraduate
enrollment:** 39,209
Total enrollment: 52,568
Percent Male: 51%
Percent Female: 49%
**Total Percent Minority or
Unreported:** 15%
Percent African-American:
7%
**Percent Asian/Pacific
Islander:** 5%
Percent Hispanic: 3%
Percent Native-American: 1%
Percent International:
Unreported
**Percent in-state/out of
state:** 89%/11%
Percent from Public HS:
Unreported
Retention Rate: 92%

Graduation Rate 4-year: 46%
Graduation Rate 6-year: 71%
**Percent Undergraduates in
On-campus housing:** 24%
**Number of official organized
extracurricular
organizations:** 800
3 Most popular majors:
Biology, Political Science,
Psychology
Student/Faculty ratio: 13:1
Average Class Size: 28
**Percent of students going to
grad school:** Unreported
Tuition and Fees: $21,015
**In-State Tuition and Fees if
different:** $8,298
Cost for Room and Board:
$7,365
**Percent receiving financial
aid out of those who apply,
first year:** 89%
**Percent receiving financial
aid among all students:**
Unreported

The Ohio State University has its own airport. Not every university can boast that, but then again, not every university can say that it is the largest university in the United States. Ohio State stands as the flagship establishment of the state's public system of superior education and is widely regarded as the best public university in Ohio. In this Big Ten School, everything is supersized—from the student body to the academic choices, the football games to the extracurricular activities. As one current sophomore said, "You cannot describe Ohio State without using a superlative."

Size Does Matter!

"When I tell people I meet that I go to OSU, the first thing they say is how big it is," said one undergraduate. Located in Columbus, Ohio State University is surrounded by over a million and a half people. Ohio's government, various professional sports teams, and unique venues all surround the school and provide tons of possibilities for students to explore their environment and act as contributing citizens.

When the school was established in 1870, the founders intended to prepare students for a career in fields related to mechanics and agriculture. School administrators have extended this traditional curriculum to include both liberal arts and technical studies. Inside the walls of the school, students intermingle, intellectualize, and enjoy the giant campus. With over 160 different majors and 20 different undergraduate schools and colleges, students are hardly limited when it comes to class choice and student interest.

"We are literally surrounded by opportunities," one junior said. "If you want to do it, it's there." Another student agreed: "OSU's big size is what makes OSU such a great school."

For such a large university, classes tend to be relatively small. Only 7 percent of classes are over 100 students, and 77 percent of classes are capped at 39 students. Undergrads say that regardless of class size, "professors are accessible and are willing to meet. Many are especially good at responding to e-mails when students have questions regarding the class material."

Living in the Buckeye State

Freshmen are required to live on campus unless they are commuting. Students reside in what OSU refers to as "towers" and "houses." The difference between the two is that towers tend to be high-rise buildings of over 20 stories, whereas houses tend to stand only three floors high. There are 31 different residence halls on campus, and many are devoted to themed housing such as the First Year Collegian Learning Community, which offers math and science tutoring in the dorms, and the Spanish Language and Culture Halls, which feature conversation tables and a close relationship with the Ohio State Department of Spanish. Most students recommend the South Campus dorms for their location and atmosphere. One student said that "the three residential areas attract very different crowds, and all three have different vibes. South Campus definitely attracts the livelier crowd."

Ohio State offers many different dining plans, ranging from the Deluxe Plan (250 "swipes" or meals per quarter) to Commuter Plus (40 swipes per quarter). As for eating locations, students may choose from places such as all-you-can-eat North Commons and Kennedy Commons, the take-out fast-food restaurant Buckeye Express, or even Viewpoint Bistro, which will cost two to three swipes in exchange for waiter service. Ohio State students also relish the opportunity to enjoy the abundance of restaurants on High Street. As one former student said, "You can find anything your mouth desires on High Street. There are four-star restaurants and many small cafés. Food there, overall, is edible."

Greek Life and the Social Scene

Consistently ranked among the top party schools in the nation, Greek life plays a large part of the social scene at Ohio State. The biggest campus parties and events are sponsored and held by fraternities and sororities. The best place to find a good party on campus is on Indianola Avenue, where many of the Greek organizations are. Students tend to party-hop all night long, but the fun doesn't stop when the sun rises. During OSU football games, the streets are filled with people tailgating. Despite their killer keggers, most students agree that Greeks' contributions to the OSU community extend beyond their conspicuous penchant for partying—most notably, their involvement with community service.

> "You cannot describe Ohio State without using a superlative."

If the Greek scene doesn't sound appealing, there is no cause for worry. Ohio State offers more than 800 registered student organizations and the vast array of cultures, ethnicities, and religious groups make exploring new experiences at OSU an endless adventure. It's impossible to pass the Oval, which one student describes as "our huge kinda Central Park–ish thing," without seeing one student group or another promoting a cause. Ohio State students can always be seen playing football, debating, tanning, and maybe even attending an Earth Sciences class or a Tai Chi lesson smack in the middle of the Oval.

O-HI-OOOO!

"Football at OSU is almost a religion," said one junior. "Even if you don't like it coming in, you'll love it coming out." Another student said, "No one cares about hating [Michigan] the state, but definitely the school." Together, these two students are describing "The Game"—the annual Ohio State versus Michigan football game. The bitter rivalry is lived out through an intense week aptly titled "Beat Michigan Week," which is dense with partying and proud displays of the student body's hard-core school spirit, such as jumping into Mirror Lake with fellow Buckeyes while singing and chanting.

While the attachment that Ohio State students hold for their football team may be overwhelming for some, in the end, "what it comes down to is a deep love for our college and everything that endears us to it."— *Daniel Friedman and Christine Grace Lin*

FYI
If you come to OSU, you better bring "a wardrobe that includes a lot of red and buckeye pride!"
What's the typical weekend schedule? "Kegs and eggs for breakfast, and football. Attend a game or watch it on TV. Either way, no exceptions."
If I could change one thing about OSU, I'd "change the police and parking rules . . . the police seem to pull people over a lot because they're bored. And parking is horrible!"
Three things every OSU student should do before graduating are "attend an OSU football game with 100,000 ebullient people in scarlet attire, sit by Mirror Lake at night, and run across the Oval naked at night."

Ohio University

Address: 120 Chubb Hall Athens, OH 45701-2979	**Percentage accepted through EA or ED:** NA	**Graduation Rate 6-year:** 71%
Phone: 740-593-4100	**EA and ED deadline:** NA	**Percent Undergraduates in**
E-mail address: admissions@ohio.edu	**Regular Deadline:** 1-Feb **Application Fee:** $45	**On-campus housing:** 46% **Number of official organized**
Web site URL: www.ohio.edu/admissions	**Full time Undergraduate enrollment:** 16,189	**extracurricular organizations:** 360
Year Founded: 1804	**Total enrollment:** 20,960	**3 Most popular majors:**
Private or Public: Public	**Percent Male:** 49%	Recreation & Sports
Religious Affiliation: None	**Percent Female:** 51%	Sciences, Journalism,
Location: Rural	**Total Percent Minority or**	Psychology
Number of Applicants: 13,366	**Unreported:** 11%	**Student/Faculty ratio:** 19:1
Percent Accepted: 85%	**Percent African-American:** 5%	**Average Class Size:** 24 **Percent of students going to**
Percent Accepted who enroll: 35%	**Percent Asian/Pacific Islander:** 1%	**grad school:** 25% **Tuition and Fees:** $17,871
Number Entering: 3,960	**Percent Hispanic:** 2%	**In-State Tuition and Fees if**
Number of Transfers Accepted each Year: 859	**Percent Native-American:** 0% **Percent International:** 3%	**different:** $8,907 **Cost for Room and Board:**
Middle 50% SAT range: M: 490–600, CR: 480–600, Wr: 470–580	**Percent in-state/out of state:** 89%/11%	$8,946 **Percent receiving financial aid out of those who apply,**
Middle 50% ACT range: 21–26	**Percent from Public HS:** 89%	**first year:** 26% **Percent receiving financial**
Early admission program EA/ED/None: None	**Retention Rate:** 80% **Graduation Rate 4-year:** 48%	**aid among all students:** 23%

The oldest institution of higher learning in the state, Ohio University (OU) is located in Athens, a historic city far removed from major metropolitan areas but certainly reminiscent of the quintessential college town. In 1804, the first year of enrollment at OU, only three students entered the university. Today, more than 20,000 undergraduate and postgraduate students are on the campus of OU, which is now more than 1,800 acres. It is a major university with a large number of academic options and an even greater reputation for being one of the top party schools in the nation. The combination of the two certainly makes OU a captivating option for prospective students.

Books Come First?

Given the fact that OU is known for parties and beer, some people may be slightly concerned about the academic quality of the institution. However, according to most students, OU is certainly not a place to slack off for four years. "We have many programs that are highly regarded," said one student. The university is divided into 11 different colleges and schools. Among them, the Scripps College of Communication is considered the strongest institution at OU with top-notch faculty and students in journalism and broadcasting. Furthermore, the engineering school is also known for research in avionics and electronics. Another distinction at OU is that it awards osteopathic medicine degrees, which are very rare in the United States. In addition, thousands of students study in one of the several satellite locations of OU, such as Chillicothe and Lancaster.

OU offers more than 250 programs of study for undergraduates. Therefore, opportunities abound for students. "We might have a reputation of party school," said one student. "But if you look at the academic programs, they are comprehensive and vigorous." Indeed, the university covers everything from early childhood education to industrial engineering.

There is also an Honors Tutorial College at OU. The idea of this program, which is slightly different from that of other universities, is to provide opportunities to teach students through so-called tutorials, or one-on-one sessions, as well as small seminars. Only 220 students in fewer than 30 programs of study are enrolled in this honors program. Students enter through a special application when they apply for freshman admissions to the university. It is a very competitive process and requires on-campus interviews as part of the evaluation for admission into the honors college.

The general education requirements—or, for the lack of simple terms, classes that you must take—are straightforward. Students must complete three tiers. The first tier consists of the most basic skills: mathematics and English composition. Students are placed in mathematics classes based on their standardized test scores or through a placement test at the beginning of the year. The second tier includes different distributional areas, such as science, arts, and humanities. Finally, the third tier is much more flexible—since it depends on the student's discipline—and is mostly designed for upperclassmen.

> **"We have many [academic] programs that are highly regarded."**

Similar to most universities, the class size diminishes as the course level rises. For most seniors and juniors, classes tend to be fewer than 30 people. Freshmen, on the other hand, are much more likely to experience large lectures of several hundred students. Nevertheless, it is not always a bad thing to be in big lectures, depending on each person's preference. "I enjoy big classes, because I am not really into class discussions," said one student. "Some people like me learn better through listening to what the professors say. Others prefer discussions."

Are the classes difficult? It is certainly dependent on professors and on the students' abilities. For the most part, students believe that their work is manageable. OU has a good academic reputation; therefore, it is not a place to party every hour of the day, but students are generally confident that they can get through most of their schoolwork, while being involved in multiple extracurricular activities or jobs.

OU may not be considered as one of the best colleges in the United States, but it still entered rankings by the *U.S. News & World Report* at number 115 for national universities. Therefore, it belongs to the top tier of all colleges in the country and has a competitive admissions process. "I think we

have a lot of talented kids at OU," said one student.

Athens

As a small college town, Athens is certainly not as exciting as New York City in terms of the number of activities and social opportunities. On the other hand, Athens is the place to be for one interesting endeavor: ghost hunting.

While it may be hard to believe, different books and television shows have pointed out the small city in southern Ohio as one of the most haunted places on earth. Different folklore stories abound on the witches and spirits that are floating around the city and OU in particular. There is, of course, not much hard evidence to scare anyone away from the city, but it is certainly something worth noting about Athens. To make things even more exciting, OU is home to an asylum known for paranormal activities.

The ghost stories, however, do not seem to faze too many of the 20,000 students at OU, since they choose to attend the school regardless of the unknown spirits. The university requires all freshmen and sophomores to remain in on-campus housing and to use the meal plans. There are more than 40 residential halls at the school, and students are generally satisfied with their living arrangements. Most upperclassmen choose to live off campus in surrounding areas. Those who are not in residences, however, are not concerned with being cut off from friends at the university. After all, most apartments and houses are only a few minutes' walk to the campus, and students mostly crowd into the same neighborhood of Athens.

The dining services operate four main locations as well as a number of smaller cafés. The food is not great but acceptable, just like most universities. "I hear from people that schools with the best dining halls also become boring to students after a while," said one student. "So I have no complaint. The food gets boring, but that is what I expected when I came here."

What OU does better than dining is partying. Greek life is very important at OU. Fraternities and sororities host large parties. The large number of local bars also represents great places for people to socialize. Alcohol, of course, is an important part of the party scene, but people who do not drink can also feel part of the social life. "I don't think anyone is being forced to drink," said one student. "Whatever your lifestyle is, I think most people are considerate about it."

Bobcats

When people talk about collegiate sports in Ohio, the dominant football team of Ohio State certainly comes to mind. However, OU is also an important force in Division I sports. It features 16 varsity teams in the top division. Women's cross-country and soccer have won more titles than have any other teams of the Mid-Atlantic Conference. Women's field hockey has also been very dominant in recent years, capturing the title in 2009. The biggest rival for OU is Miami University.

As one student pointed out, "We are good at parties and books, so why not come to OU?" That is certainly a question worth asking for any high school seniors, especially those in Ohio who can get a relatively affordable in-state education.—*Xiaohang Liu*

FYI
What is the typical weekend schedule? "There is always a huge party somewhere."
If I could change one thing about OU, I'd "actually try to find some ghosts."
Three things every student at OU should do before graduating are "enjoy your time here, go to football games, and go see the rest of Ohio if you are not from here."

Ohio Wesleyan University

Address: 61 South Sandusky Street Delaware, OH 43015
Phone: 740-368-3020
E-mail address: owuadmit@owu.edu
Web site URL: www.owu.edu
Year Founded: 1842
Private or Public: Private
Religious Affiliation: Methodist
Location: Suburban
Number of Applicants: 3,814
Percent Accepted: 66%
Percent Accepted who enroll: 23%
Number Entering: 576
Number of Transfers Accepted each Year: Unreported
Middle 50% SAT range: M: 540–650, CR: 530–650, Wr: Unreported
Middle 50% ACT range: 24–29
Early admission program EA/ED/None: EA and ED

Percentage accepted through EA or ED: Unreported
EA and ED deadline: 1-Dec
Regular Deadline: 1-Mar
Application Fee: $35
Full time Undergraduate enrollment: 1,960
Total enrollment: 1,960
Percent Male: 48%
Percent Female: 52%
Total Percent Minority or Unreported: 21%
Percent African-American: 5%
Percent Asian/Pacific Islander: 2%
Percent Hispanic: 1%
Percent Native-American: 0%
Percent International: 9%
Percent in-state/out of state: 54%/46%
Percent from Public HS: 77%
Retention Rate: 84%
Graduation Rate 4-year: 60%

Graduation Rate 6-year: Unreported
Percent Undergraduates in On-campus housing: 82%
Number of official organized extracurricular organizations: 86
3 Most popular majors: Economics, Pre-med, Psychology
Student/Faculty ratio: 12:1
Average Class Size: Unreported
Percent of students going to grad school: 32%
Tuition and Fees: $33,660
In-State Tuition and Fees if different: No difference
Cost for Room and Board: $8,270
Percent receiving financial aid out of those who apply, first year: 88%
Percent receiving financial aid among all students: 60%

I f you didn't know it was there, you might drive past the tiny town of Delaware, Ohio, population 25,000, without a second glance. But at the core of this small community there is a thriving college with students passionate enough to more than compensate for their low numbers. At Ohio Wesleyan University, you will find a campus that celebrates its Midwestern friendliness, with a close-knit undergraduate community of exceptionally warm and down-to-earth students who make the town worth much more than just a passing glimpse.

A Full Spectrum of Knowledge: OWU and the Liberal Arts Education

When it comes to academics, OWU sends a clear message to its students: education requires knowledge and proficiency in a broad range of areas, which leads to the fairly expansive set of Distributional Requirements. In addition to three classes each in the humanities, social sciences, and natural sciences, students are required to take two semesters of writing-intensive classes, a foreign language, and diversity-geared courses as well as one fine art class and a new one-semester quantitative reasoning requirement. Although this may seem overwhelming, students say that a wide range of interesting classes can fulfill the requirements. One student remarked, "I like to be able to choose classes I like within a department." Others, however, take a different course: "Personally, I don't seek out classes that fill requirements; I just look for classes I find interesting and fulfill requirements along the way."

Nor is it a problem if a student wants a more academically challenging schedule within the OWU environment. The Ohio Wesleyan Honors Program is open to freshmen, based on their high school GPA and standardized test scores, but it is also possible to join later as an upperclassman. One honors student said the program "opens up a lot of interdisciplinary courses" that she would not otherwise have been exposed to, and that while "expectations are higher in terms of quality," the quantity of work does not increase significantly. One student described the program in terms of being "faster and more in-depth," but also noted that "all the majors have difficult courses." Because of this, other students are valuable resources as unofficial advisors when choosing a schedule. Some areas are always difficult, and popular majors including Zoology, Psychology, Education, and Politics & Government all have their fair share of challenging coursework.

OWU tends to stress sciences over the humanities, although the less scientifically inclined students feel that their smaller programs give them closer relationships with professors who really care about both the material and their students. One English major said that "professors make themselves really available—they take their jobs as teachers very seriously." Professors can focus their full attention on the undergraduates, as one junior remarked: "You get to know the teachers as well as you know the other students." This extends to class work as well, since professors have a strong hand in shaping the curriculum. Because professors teach what they like, students find them engaging, dynamic, and relevant.

Dorm-Dwellers and SLUTs

OWU has all the housing fixtures one might expect in a college setting, but what sets the college apart is its unique cluster of "SLUs," or Small Living Units. The students who decide to take advantage of these themed houses are affectionately referred to as "SLUTs," or Small Living Unit Tenants. Each SLU holds events and lectures that relate to its focus, and they also offer an alternative to the frat party scene. The interests covered by the SLUs are many and varied, some of which are the Women's House, the International House, and the philosophical House of Thought. With so many areas covered, many students find a niche in SLUs. All freshmen live in the dorms along with most sophomores; it is only in the junior year that people begin to move off campus, although even juniors tend to stay. One sophomore noted that OWU is "a very residential campus."

Geography 101

When students live where they eat and study where they sleep, there will understandably be some feeling of claustrophobia. OWU combats these limitations with its unique dumbbell-shaped campus, which has academic buildings on one side with residential housing on the other, connected by a main "highway" called the JAYwalk. The walkway serves as a common meeting-place for students to see and be seen between classes, and it is also flanked by the James A. Young Memorial Library. One sophomore said, "There is a consistent flow of people at certain hours of the day, and most students eat lunch on the JAYwalk." This central hangout is in the middle of an eclectic and architecturally varied campus—students all agree that the mixed architecture lends OWU a distinctly diverse feel.

The Alpha, Beta, Gammas of OWU Social Life

"Wednesday is the new Thursday," remarked one sophomore, when asked about the campus party scene. Other students concur, mentioning Friday and Saturday in addition to Wednesday as the biggest party days at OWU. As for how students get down on those nights, people mentioned a variety of locales: Delaware bars, off-campus apartment parties, SLU parties, and, most frequently, frat parties. One Delta Gamma sister estimated that 30 percent of students are somehow involved in Greek life on campus, and she said that the fraternity and sorority system has a strong presence, especially in the social life of OWU students. Although one senior mentioned that "people party with their own social groups," dance parties tend to bring people together and mix groups.

> "The professors take their jobs as teachers very seriously, and both the students and the faculty are very invested in providing an enriching experience for everyone."

As for the inevitable problems that arise from college partying, students say that the on-campus public safety officers are often willing to let alcohol charges drop if the student is polite. Students applaud the university's decision to charge students for possession rather than consumption, which allows ill students to go to the hospital for help without getting in trouble. While the off-campus police tend to be much stricter, one sophomore says that on university property, "there is an understanding that drinking occurs, and they're more worried about our safety than the fact that we drink."

Crossing the Delaware

If frat parties aren't so appealing, it might be difficult to find something to do on a weekend night. "There's not a lot to do in Delaware," admitted one sophomore, who also noted that "Columbus is a tease because it's not as close as you think it is." Delaware's small size led one senior to remark that "the town exists because the college is here." However, others point to eclectic boutiques and high-quality restaurants as characteristic of their college's hometown. Students generally feel some connection to the town and don't find relations to be particularly hostile, but all mention that there could be quite a bit of improvement. One student noted, "You could go through four years at OWU without

meeting people in Delaware, but there are a lot of connections if you look for them."

After the Library Closes

OWU students are dedicated to their academic lives, but they are also committed to many activities outside the classroom. From advocacy groups such as STAND (Students Taking Action Now: Darfur) to warm and fuzzy clubs like Pet Pals, which allows students to work at animal shelters, OWU offers a large variety of extracurriculars, especially given its small size. Highlights include the WCSA, the student government, which is very active and plays a large role in decision-making on campus. Students say that it is easy to get involved with groups as early as freshman year. One sophomore noted, "Attendance can be a problem in terms of turnout, but those who are in the clubs are very dedicated."

Sports also have a large presence in the campus community. Students mention that there is a fair amount of school pride, although potentially somewhat less than at other schools. But people turn out for big games such as Homecoming and rivalry match-ups, and the Division III standing attracts some athletes who want to play in more games. In addition to involvement in a varsity sport, many people decide to play at the intramural or club level. The school has recently worked on the athletic fields and the gym, so there is a clear emphasis on sports as an important part of the school environment and many athletes to reap the benefits.

According to students, the undergrads at OWU are always willing to meet new people and work in different settings. That enthusiasm permeates the entire campus, as one student pointed to the "friendly, open atmosphere" as a major reason she decided to attend OWU. At a place where "the students and the faculty are very invested in providing an enriching experience for everyone," it is important to note that a good quality to bring is the desire to know everyone on campus. One student put it perfectly: "Although there are many different small groups on campus, there is a great sense of a larger community—coming in I had a good feeling about it, and that stuck with me."
—*Hannah Jacobson*

FYI

If you come to Ohio Wesleyan, you'd better bring "an umbrella: the weather in Ohio is very unpredictable!"

What is the typical weekend schedule? "Get out of class and take a nap before meeting up with people for dinner and then pre-gaming in a group. Go to at least one party or jump between a few on Friday night. Eat a late lunch on Saturday, go out that night, and worry about homework on Sunday. And sleep a lot: you don't have time to do that during the week!"

If I could change one thing about Ohio Wesleyan, I'd "make it more handicapped accessible."

Three things every student at Ohio Wesleyan should do before graduating are "go to an SLU party, attend a reception at Professor Olmstead's house, and go to the academic side of campus at night to see the stained-glass windows in Slocum Hall!"

University of Cincinnati

Address: P.O. Box 210091 Cincinnati, OH 45221–0091
Phone: 513-556-1100
E-mail address: admissions@uc.edu
Web site URL: www.uc.edu
Year Founded: 1819
Private or Public: Public
Religious Affiliation: None
Location: Urban
Number of Applicants: 11,876
Percent Accepted: 75%
Percent Accepted who enroll: 40%
Number Entering: 3,528
Number of Transfers Accepted each Year: 1,542
Middle 50% SAT range: M: 500–630, CR: 490–610, Wr: 470–590
Middle 50% ACT range: 21–27
Early admission program EA/ED/None: None

Percentage accepted through EA or ED: NA
EA and ED deadline: NA
Regular Deadline: 1-Sep
Application Fee: $40
Full time Undergraduate enrollment: 20,501
Total enrollment: 28,332
Percent Male: 50%
Percent Female: 50%
Total Percent Minority or Unreported: 23%
Percent African-American: 12%
Percent Asian/Pacific Islander: 3%
Percent Hispanic: 2%
Percent Native-American: <1%
Percent International: 1%
Percent in-state/out of state: 90%/10%
Percent from Public HS: Unreported
Retention Rate: 82%

Graduation Rate 4-year: 19%
Graduation Rate 6-year: 54%
Percent Undergraduates in On-campus housing: 71%
Number of official organized extracurricular organizations: 250
3 Most popular majors: Communications, Marketing, Psychology
Student/Faculty ratio: 14:1
Average Class Size: 13
Percent of students going to grad school: Unreported
Tuition and Fees: $23,922
In-State Tuition and Fees if different: $9,399
Cost for Room and Board: $9,240
Percent receiving financial aid out of those who apply, first year: 60%
Percent receiving financial aid among all students: 78%

A prominent public university in Ohio, the University of Cincinnati is home to more than 20,000 undergraduates and 9,000 postgraduates. It also provides important research facilities for the University of Ohio system. Founded in 1819 as an institution focused on medical sciences, the university has now expanded into 14 different schools and is a major player in research, both in technology and in social sciences. With its scope of academic programs and good professional preparation, UC presents an attractive option for students from not only Ohio but also around the world.

A Research Institution

Out of the 20,000 undergraduates, nearly one-third of them are part-time students. This is in part due to the wide range of programs at UC. In fact, the school has a large selection of Associate programs. Furthermore, the university is also home to students in professional schools, doctoral, post-doctoral, and continuing education. "I guess you can say that we meet people of all walks of life at UC," said one student.

The university is divided into 14 different schools, ranging from Applied Health Sciences to Education, Criminal Justice, and

Human Services. In addition, there are two regional campuses. The College-Conservatory of Music in particular is known as one of the best in the country. It has a total enrollment of roughly 1,500 and provides a wide range of arts programs, such as music, dance, and electronic media. "[The Conservatory] is definitely the most prestigious school at UC," said one student. Furthermore, some of the university's programs in criminal justice and architecture are also considered among the best in the United States. The College of Nursing is also recognized as the first one to issue baccalaureate degrees in the field. "You will be surprised at how we have quite a few famous departments," said one student.

The university offers more than 300 undergraduate degree programs, a very high number even for a large institution like UC. Students of all tastes can certainly find the appropriate curriculums that satiate their personal interests, as well as preparing them for future endeavors. The different certificate programs also allow students to enrich their academic experiences. "I think we have plenty of majors, too many even, to choose from," said one student.

"We meet people of all walks of life at UC."

Since many students at UC are using their education directly as a springboard for a specific career path, the university has created the co-op program designed to receive actual professional training and practice as part of their education. In fact, UC has the largest co-op program in the country, and students from many departments, notably engineering, are required to complete different co-op assignments before they can receive their degree. "I really think that it helps you a lot in finding the right career and in actually practicing it," said one student. "The things you learn in classes can be very different from what happens in the real world, so it is nice for you to actually have a hands-on experience."

As in all large universities, the introductory classes can have hundreds of students, and the interactions between students and professors are generally limited in those cases. Nevertheless, particularly for upperclassmen, smaller classes certainly do exist, and the students can have an easier time contacting professors and asking questions. "I found a bunch of accessible professors here," said one student. "I also know that some of my friends really never talk to professors, but I think it is because they never tried." Indeed, building a relationship with one of the many highly knowledgeable professors at UC often depends on initiatives by the students.

Before graduation, students must complete a series of required coursework so that their undergraduate education goes beyond their actual majors. Slightly different from other universities, the requirements at UC are divided into only four categories: critical thinking, effective communications, social responsibility, and knowledge integration. Different courses are classified under those categories. "The requirements are OK," said one student. "I know it is important to learn a little bit of everything."

UC is also one of the most important research institutions in Ohio. Furthermore, unlike many universities that focus research on one specific area, UC has something for everyone. Given its tradition originally as a college of medical education, there are a large array of research centers for cancer, biology, and clinical research. At the same time, it also has the Center for Entrepreneurship Education and Research as well as the Institute for Policy Research, thus providing opportunities for those more interested in business and social sciences.

Cincy

Cincinnati, more fondly known as "Cincy" by some residents, is a major metropolitan area and thus offers the benefits of city living to the students of UC.

Weekend activities are certainly enriched by the location of UC. The city provides its large selection of restaurants, bars, and clubs. Furthermore, for sports enthusiasts, Cincinnati is also home to the National Football League's Bengals and Major League Baseball's Reds. However, it may be difficult sometimes for students to find the time or the energy to go to some of those events in the city. "I am a big Reds fan," said one student. "But when you are in college, you can have so many things to do that you just don't even think of going to a baseball game."

The Greek life is an important part of the party scene at UC. There are over 35 fraternities and sororities, and they contribute a great deal to the parties as well as a number of activities and events on campus. At the same time, those who are not interested in the fraternities and sororities can also find parties in off-campus housing. "It is a big school," said one student. "If you try, you will definitely find a good group of friends."

Since UC is an urban school, the dorms tend to look like big apartment buildings. A significant number of upperclassmen also choose to live off campus, since it is generally easy to find apartments that are not too far from classes, thus allowing students to achieve a great deal of independence without causing much inconvenience. "Based on what I saw from other schools," said one student. "The dorms here are actually pretty good."

The reviews on the dining service, as is the case with most universities, vary greatly. Some people are not impressed at all. Others believe that it is very good. The good news is that UC is in Cincinnati, and plenty of options are available for people who either hate dining hall food or do not participate in the meal plans.

Cheer Cincinnati

The UC Bearcats have a highly successful athletic program. Games by the men's basketball and football teams can often be found on nationally televised broadcasts due to their immense success. The students, of course, are very enthusiastic in their support for the teams, even though the tickets are sometimes hard to find.

UC provides very good programs that combine academic work and practical training. It is also a major research institution, thus giving students the opportunities to make further explorations in their fields. The academics, combined with the urban location, certainly makes UC a college choice worthy of consideration.—*Xiaohang Liu*

FYI

If I could change one thing about UC, I'd "improve the weather somehow."

Three things every student at UC should do before graduating are "go to sports games, have a trip to Kentucky, and join a club."

W i t t e n b e r g U n i v e r s i t y

Address: PO Box 720
  Springfield, OH 45501
Phone: 937-327-6314
E-mail address:
  admission@wittenberg.edu
Web site URL:
  www.wittenberg.edu
Year Founded: 1845
Private or Public: Private
Religious Affiliation: Lutheran
Location: Rural
Number of Applicants:
  2,887
Percent Accepted: 73%
**Percent Accepted who
  enroll:** 26%
Number Entering: 551
**Number of Transfers
  Accepted each Year:** 79
Middle 50% SAT range:
  M: 500–559, CR: 490–610,
  Wr: Unreported
Middle 50% ACT range:
  22–27
**Early admission program
  EA/ED/None:** ED

**Percentage accepted
  through EA or ED:** 89%
EA and ED deadline: 15-Nov
Regular Deadline: 1-Dec
Application Fee: $40
**Full time Undergraduate
  enrollment:** 1,967
Total enrollment: 1,978
Percent Male: 45%
Percent Female: 55%
**Total Percent Minority or
  Unreported:** 7%
Percent African-American:
  5%
**Percent Asian/Pacific
  Islander:** 1%
Percent Hispanic: 1%
Percent Native-American:
  0%
Percent International: 2%
**Percent in-state/out of
  state:** 76%/24%
Percent from Public HS:
  Unreported
Retention Rate: 80%
Graduation Rate 4-year: 56%

Graduation Rate 6-year:
  57%
**Percent Undergraduates
  in On-campus housing:**
  82%
**Number of official organized
  extracurricular
  organizations:** 129
3 Most popular majors:
  Biology, Business, Education
Student/Faculty ratio:
  12:1
Average Class Size: 25
**Percent of students going to
  grad school:** 74%
Tuition and Fees: $32,936
**In-State Tuition and Fees if
  different:** No difference
Cost for Room and Board:
  $8,314
**Percent receiving financial
  aid out of those who apply,
  first year:** 99%
**Percent receiving financial
  aid among all students:**
  99%

Wittenberg is a breath of fresh air for those tired of visiting colleges where the campus is packed with hordes of students grubbed out in last night's pajamas and sweats heading in every direction. If you want to attend a school where the students are well dressed, always remember to accessorize with gleaming smiles, and where everybody knows your name, well then, Wittenberg is definitely the school for you.

We're Talking Quality, not Quantity

When asked about why they chose Wittenberg, most students commented on the small class sizes and the atmosphere. One girl stated that "From my visit and onward, everyone has been very friendly. Having small class sizes has been beneficial as well, because the professors are much more available when you may need one." As far as class sizes go, don't expect to be a nameless face in an auditorium lecture course. "Class sizes are wonderful! I've never been in a class with more than 30!" a student exclaimed. Class sizes generally range from 12 to 35 students, with basic introductory classes having 35. Higher-level courses are "generally in the teens, but sometimes even less."

The small size of Wittenberg presents students with a lot of personal attention. One junior stated that, "Since I have been here, I have had countless meetings with faculty discussing future career plans and paths to take. Because the school is small, focus is more on the individual."

> "Because the school is small, focus is more on the individual."

Grading at Wittenberg is done on a 10-point scale. Classes are challenging, but students love to work together, and the faculty loves to help. "The students are intelligent; the professors are incredible," a campus newspaper boasted in an article, adding that, "We have more Professors of the Year than any other school in Ohio. We have 25 Fulbright Scholars. Our faculty is incredible." Since Wittenberg professors will know students on a first-name basis, it is hard not to work hard. "There is a lot more expected out of the students ... students definitely strive to get good grades. The library is always packed and groups of students working on projects can be found all over campus."

As far as requirements go, there are prerequisites in each of the following seven areas: Integrated Learning; Natural World; Social Institutions; Fine, Performing, and Literary Arts; Religious and Philosophical Inquiry; Western Historical Perspectives; Non-Western Cultures. Further requirements dictate that you must cover areas of writing, research, foreign language, computing, speaking and mathematics. There is also a physical activity requirement, which can be fulfilled by participation in intercollegiate athletics, or by taking various health and fitness courses. Community service is also mandatory. Sophomores must complete 30 hours of community service over the course of one term.

The most popular majors at Witt are Management and Education, but students also rave about Witt's English program. One senior pre-law English Literature major commented that, "the English department here is amazing. I get to work closely with professors; the entire English department knows me well, and is always willing to help." Be on the lookout for East Asian Studies, too, which was named as an increasingly popular major. For those students who aren't too eager to comply with a pre-arranged curriculum, there is also the option of designing your own major. Students can pick classes from a variety of disciplines to cater to their own interests and needs. Communications and Management are generally considered "the easy way out," while the sciences are considered to be the toughest courses at the university. One student commented that "Biology is a pretty difficult major, just because so many classes are required, but it's still totally worth it." And despite not being "remotely near any large body of water," one sophomore said that "we actually have an excellent Marine Biology program."

While students love the small school, they are also encouraged to study abroad. "The program is excellent!" exclaimed one student. Offering more than 40 options in countries all over the world—from Buddhist temples to safaris in Kenya—the school is very supportive of students going abroad for a semester or an entire year.

Dodgeball Anyone?

Despite Wittenberg's small size, there is a huge selection of clubs and organizations to join. A female student explained that "Most everyone is involved in at least one thing. It's just so easy because Witt offers something for everyone. We have everything from Student Senate to an improv comedy group called Pocket Lint. If you're interested in something, chances are we have something for it. And if not, it's so easy to create one." Don't believe her? Wittenberg's array of sports include archery, cricket and even dodgeball!

Despite the university's efforts to branch out by implementing regional recruitment on the East Coast and in the Midwest, "Wittenberg probably isn't as diverse as it would like to be," although students all agree that the school is actively working on rectifying the problem. Currently, the minority population is lower than most other schools, but there are still many campus groups promoting diversity, including the Concerned Black Students, Jewish Culture Club, Hispanic Culture Club and Gay/Straight Alliance. The Polis House, a dorm dedicated to international awareness, promotes cultural awareness by hosting celebrations of holidays for different cultures.

The other six dorms on campus are Tower, Firesetine, Ferncliff, Myers, New Residence and Woodlawn. Dorms are assigned to freshmen based on when their applications and tuition fees are submitted. Post-freshman year, there are housing lotteries that students must attend in order to be placed in a dorm. After a student acquires over 60 hours of credit, off-campus housing options are made available, though this is also done via a lottery process. Students have mixed feelings regarding whether on- or off-campus housing is better. One upperclassman stated that "Most everyone lives on-campus, and it's so much more fun that way. People that live off-campus don't make as many friends as fast as those who live in the dorms. There are a few kids from the Springfield area who only live a few minutes away but still choose to live on-campus anyway." (Wittenberg is located in the middle of Springfield, Ohio, which is described as being "pretty crappy on the south side, but really nice on the north side.") Most students agree that dorms are the easiest place to meet people. But while one student commented that the close proximity promoted by dorm life makes it "hard to not

wanna get to know them," another student added that "you might not always get along."

Greek-ing and Streaking

About one-third of students who live off campus at Wittenberg are in a Greek house. The six sororities and six fraternities on campus are responsible for most of the school's partying. Alcohol is allowed in dorms but only as long as you are 21. (South Hall is the only substance-free residence hall.) The school's enforcement of drugs and alcohol policies are "about middle of the road. Don't be stupid, and you won't get caught." Do not expect to see any frat boys doing keg stands here though—the school has banned beer kegs from all Wittenberg-owned housing, so fraternities do not generally provide alcohol, and parties are mostly BYOB. Despite the keg-ban, fraternities do throw parties "all the time," and "pretty good parties, actually. . . ." Aside from fraternity parties, students also enjoy hangouts such as the school's Student Union, which has yummy late-night food and a bar. The Ringside Bar is also a student favorite; kids go throughout the week to unwind with a few drinks.

A description of Wittenberg is incomplete without mention of the Hollow, a grassy valley that is perfect for sunbathing and playing Frisbee on sunny days, sledding on snowy winter days, and streaking at night, regardless of the weather. The Hollow hosts Witt-Fest, the annual spring music festival sponsored by Union Board. Past WittFest performers have included the Nappy Roots, American Hi-Fi, Hootie and the Blowfish and 10,000 Maniacs. Springfield residents also attend the music festival, and there are carnival activities, such as inflatable obstacle courses, to provide amusement while the bands play.

Ultimately, students describe life at Wittenberg as "the perfect fit." The small-town feel of the school and the surrounding city draws people in. "The only bad thing about it being so small is that everyone knows everyone else's business. We tend to call it Wittenberg High School sometimes," explains one student. Wittenberg is a school where everybody knows your name—and then some.—*Christine Grace Lin*

FYI
If you come to Wittenberg, you'd better bring "your own case of beer or a flask."
What's the typical weekend schedule? "Go to the football game if it's a home game, hang out at the Hollow if it's nice out, catch up on work, and hit a few frat parties."
If I could change one thing about Wittenberg, I'd "make it just a little bit bigger. An extra 500 students would spice up campus life."
The three things every student should do before graduating are "study abroad, study abroad, study abroad!"

Oklahoma

Oklahoma State University

Address: 219 Student Union
  Stillwater, OK 74078
Phone: 405-744-5358
E-mail address:
  admit@okstate.edu
Web site URL:
  osu.okstate.edu
Year Founded: 1890
Private or Public: Public
Religious Affiliation: None
Location: Suburban
Number of Applicants: 6,406
Percent Accepted: 89%
Percent Accepted who
  enroll: 51%
Number Entering: 2,928
Number of Transfers
  Accepted each Year:
  Unreported
Middle 50% SAT range:
  M: 500–620, **CR:** 480–600,
  Wr: Unreported
Middle 50% ACT range: 22–27
Early admission program
  EA/ED/None: None

Percentage accepted
  through EA or ED: NA
EA and ED deadline: NA
Regular Deadline: Rolling
Application Fee: $40
Full time Undergraduate
  enrollment: 18,600
Total enrollment: 22,862
Percent Male: 52%
Percent Female: 48%
Total Percent Minority or
  Unreported: 22%
Percent African-American: 4%
Percent Asian/Pacific
  Islander: 2%
Percent Hispanic: 3%
Percent Native-American:
  10%
Percent International: 2%
Percent in-state/out of
  state: 84%/16%
Percent from Public HS:
  Unreported
Retention Rate: 77%
Graduation Rate 4-year: 29%

Graduation Rate 6-year:
  Unreported
Percent Undergraduates in
  On-campus housing: 38%
Number of official organized
  extracurricular
  organizations: 400
3 Most popular majors:
  Accounting, Aerospace,
  Agriculture
Student/Faculty ratio: 18:1
Average Class Size: 24
Percent of students going to
  grad school: Unreported
Tuition and Fees: $17,241
In-State Tuition and Fees if
  different: $6,887
Cost for Room and Board:
  $6,358
Percent receiving financial
  aid out of those who apply,
  first year: 73%
Percent receiving financial
  aid among all students:
  47%

The most challenging time of the year for most college students is undoubtedly the season when classes have finished, all graded work has been completed, and there is only one hurdle yet to be jumped: finals. And while a typical exam week unfortunately means lots of stress, lots of cramming, and not a lot of sleep, Oklahoma State University has found the perfect cure for the inevitable agony that stands between students and their vacation. Hugs. Lots of unlimited Hugs in the Free Hugs for Finals Week.

And while you might hesitate to judge a school based on hugs, students at OSU believe the hugs during finals week make a broader statement about how the university takes care of its students. Even with a student body exceeding 18,000, all individuals receive the attention and support they need to have a successful college career.

Orange You Going to Study Tonight?

As with any university, Oklahoma State has many different kinds of students. As one junior put it, "There are the thinking people, and the not-quite-as-smart people." Members of both categories spend a fair amount of time studying. A general rule of thumb is to spend two hours studying for every hour of class time. Upperclassmen tend to spend more time studying than freshmen, but "no matter what year you are, or what classes you're taking, you're always going to have time to have fun and chill with your friends, and still make good grades."

So what do OSU students like to study?

Regardless of major, everyone is required to take two courses in each of five general areas—English, math, humanities, social studies and science. The most popular major is definitely the Business major, while the most difficult ones are Engineering and Pre-Med. OSU's Hotel and Restaurant Administration program is unique and well known across the country.

For applicants who tend to shy away from equations, Oklahoma State is also strong in the humanities. While students who choose one of these majors are definitely in the minority, they often go on to earn graduate degrees in their respective areas of study. One senior said, "You might be a business major because you couldn't really decide on anything else, but if you're a humanities major, you know that's what you want to do."

Regardless of what they choose to study, a great tutoring program is available to all OSU undergrads. For any and every subject, the school provides individual tutoring free of charge. One student who took advantage of this option found it to be rewarding: "The tutors were definitely a big help for a couple of my tougher classes."

It Takes a Village

OSU students are generally pleased with their living situations. The school's arrangements can certainly be characterized as diverse—there are on-campus apartments, lots of quads (four people with singles who share a bathroom and living room), and also more traditional housing. Compared to other large state schools, a surprising number of upperclassmen choose to live on-campus. This is partly because of the recently completed dorm complex called The Village, which consists of six "brand-new, beautiful buildings that pretty much make you love your residential life." Each floor in The Village has a common area furnished with comfy couches and also a community kitchen—perfect for cooking up a late-night snack with some friends.

Integral to residential life at OSU are the Residential Advisors and Community Mentors. While one of their duties is to enforce university rules, these upperclassmen are also there to "make freshmen feel welcome, help them get involved, and generally be a friendly helper." New students will likely form a close relationship with their advisor or mentor, since there is one for every 20 or so students. And as long as you don't get caught in your dorm guzzling a beer, you can expect that relationship to be a rewarding one.

That Rustic Feeling

Anyone who has visited the Oklahoma State campus agrees that it's pleasing to the senses. In terms of architecture, most of the buildings are old and made of bricks, with what one junior called "a little bit of a rustic feel." Another student said she was very fond of her surroundings: "Our campus is really gorgeous, especially in the spring when the flowers are blooming."

While OSU out of necessity has a fairly big campus, students have an easy time of getting from place to place by walking or biking. Conveniently located near the center of campus is Edmon Low Library, a favorite place to study or to wander stacks that contain more than 2.5 million volumes. After hitting the books, students might make a trip to the Colvin Recreation Center, which might best be described as "a glorious piece of workout heaven." The Center is very popular and includes 10 basketball courts, indoor and outdoor swimming pools, an indoor track, and racquetball and volleyball courts.

> "There's not just something for everyone, there are three things for everyone."

Another source of pride for OSU students is the Student Union building. Touted as the largest in the country, it offers a place to relax, hang out with friends, and grab some food. The Union also has the main bookstore and a clothing shop, where you'll find plenty of orange-and-black clothes for your wardrobe.

Fitting In

With about 400 undergraduate organizations, students at OSU find that they have many ways to become active. These include political, cultural, preprofessional, and recreational groups. There are also clubs for each major and many club sports teams. One student said, "There's not just something for everyone, there are three things for everyone."

Oklahoma State also has a vibrant Greek scene. One junior estimated that perhaps one in five students are in fraternities or sororities. He said that going Greek "isn't a necessity, but it is cool if that's what you want to do. And if you don't want to do it, that's fine too." Most students agree that the Greek life is somewhat separated from other social scenes on campus—the frat parties are usually invite-only.

The Oklahoma Two-Step

Oklahoma State undergrads certainly know how to have a good time. When the weekends come around, students like to "hit up the bars on The Strip, maybe go to a party some place off campus, or go out to eat with friends." Popular campus restaurants include the West Side Café and the Service Station, both of which have fast, cheap food. Students craving a more classy setting might dine at the Rancher's Club—an upscale on-campus restaurant that attracts visitors from all over the state.

Much of social life occurs off campus. Stillwater's most well-known dance club is called the Tumbleweed. This unique joint consists of two rooms—one that plays hip/hop and modern tunes, and another that features country music favorites for a line-dancing and two-stepping crowd.

Although Oklahoma State is a dry campus, it's no secret that a majority of students like to relax after a week of classes by downing a few drinks. One popular hangout spot is Eskimo Joe's, a bar and restaurant that is considered the heart of Stillwater. Students often go there on "Thirsty Thursdays," where they can enjoy cheese fries and five-dollar unlimited beer. An OSU senior even joked that "one percent of the beer consumed in the United States is probably consumed in Stillwater."

If students want to get away for the weekend, many choose to visit Tulsa or Oklahoma City, both of which are about an hour away by car. Both cities offer opportunities to go shopping, see a movie, go to a concert, or try out a new restaurant.

It'll Be Bedlam

If there is one thing that all Oklahoma State students can agree on, it's that they love beating OU. The rivalry between these two schools, known as the Bedlam series, is a fierce one with a long history. Students clad in Cowboy orange turn out in huge numbers for the football and basketball games, because "even the people who know nothing about sports love to root against OU."

The chance to see exciting games in packed stadiums against a big rival is only one of many fun opportunities available to students at Oklahoma State. A big school that takes care of the individual, OSU is a comfortable home for its students. And don't forget about the free pancakes.—*Henry Agnew*

FYI
If you come to Oklahoma State, you'd better bring "your party hat."
What is the typical weekend schedule? "Definitely go out on Thursday, hopefully go to class on Friday, then chill with friends, go to the game on Saturday, then hit the books Sunday night."
If I could change one thing about Oklahoma State, I'd "increase student involvement in campus activities."
Three things every student at Oklahoma State should do before graduating are "eat at Shortcake's diner, play Frisbee on Library Lawn, and go to a Bedlam game and root against the Sooners."

Oral Roberts University

Address: 7777 S. Lewis
Avenue, Tulsa, OK 74171
Phone: 918-495-6518
E-mail address:
admissions@oru.edu
Web site URL: www.oru.edu
Year Founded: 1963
Private or Public: Private
Religious Affiliation:
None
Location: Urban
Number of Applicants: 1,201
Percent Accepted: 75%
Percent Accepted who
enroll: 67%
Number Entering: 602
Number of Transfers
Accepted each Year:
Unreported
Middle 50% SAT range:
M: 440–580, CR: 480–600,
Wr: Unreported
Middle 50% ACT range:
20–25
Early admission program
EA/ED/None: EA

Percentage accepted
through EA or ED:
Unreported
EA and ED deadline: 15-Nov
Regular Deadline: Roling
Application Fee: $35
Full time Undergraduate
enrollment: 2,790
Total enrollment: 3,303
Percent Male: 40%
Percent Female: 60%
Total Percent Minority or
Unreported: 38%
Percent African-American:
18%
Percent Asian/Pacific
Islander: 3%
Percent Hispanic: 6%
Percent Native-American: 2%
Percent International: 7%
Percent in-state/out of
state: 49%/61%
Percent from Public HS: 75%
Retention Rate: 77%
Graduation Rate 4-year:
54%

Graduation Rate 6-year:
Unreported
Percent Undergraduates in
On-campus housing: 75%
Number of official organized
extracurricular
organizations: Unreported
3 Most popular majors:
Marketing, Mass
Communication, Theology
Student/Faculty ratio:
Unreported
Average Class Size:
Unreported
Percent of students going to
grad school: 50%
Tuition and Fees: $18,386
In-State Tuition and Fees if
different: No difference
Cost for Room and Board:
$7,610
Percent receiving financial
aid out of those who apply,
first year: 87%
Percent receiving financial aid
among all students: 75%

Sixty-foot, thirty-ton bronze Praying Hands grace the main entrance to Oral Roberts University, indicating to all visitors that ORU not only offers its students academic guidance from the Ivory Tower, it also directs students to depend on a lifetime's teachings from God. Due to its religious founding, students at the university are encouraged to continually grow academically, physically *and* spiritually. They are given the unique opportunity to combine a top-notch education with a passionate religious and cultural experience. These aspects of the ORU experience require students to adhere to strict rules such as a dress code as well as to refrain from the partying that is characteristic of your "typical" college experience. Students are also required to participate in mandatory chapel services twice a week so they can continually live out the school founder's vision. Evangelist Oral Roberts claims that God instructed him to found a university based on "God's commission and the holy spirit." Roberts obeyed this mandate and in 1965 opened Oral Roberts University in Tulsa. Few universities can claim that they were built as a result of a message directly from God, but Oral Roberts University is one of the few that can.

Academics

As a Christian school, Oral Roberts University emphasizes students' personal spiritual growth alongside a challenging academic education. Students at Oral Roberts say academics are noticeably "above average" and "top-notch." Students have the option to enroll in one of seven undergraduate schools: the School of Arts & Sciences, the School of Science and Engineering, the School of Theology and Missions, the School of Business, the School of Education, the School of Life-Long Education or the Anna Vaughn School of Nursing.

The seven schools vary in difficulty, but all are known to be academically rigorous. According to one student, "The School of Education is very tough. There is a lot required of education majors, but it is a good thing. We have an exceptional program here and it makes the hard work worth it, because I know I am getting the best, top-of-the-line education." The School of LifeLong Education provides flexible, quality education programs to adult learners and non-traditional students. The business school is considered "exceptional" and also offers a five-year MBA program. The School of Nursing is also "well-known and hard." Not surprisingly, the theology department within the School of Arts and Sciences is "incredible."

Especially attractive is the Honors Program, which admits 16 to 18 top applicants every year as Fellows. These students enroll in one three-credit hour Fellows Seminar each semester, in addition to one or two other Honors credit courses. Other highly qualified applicants are designated as Honors Program Scholars. Honors students are even invited to live in special dormitory wings with respected quiet hours, and a "quality academic atmosphere."

> The religious atmosphere at Oral Roberts emphasizes a non-competitive academic environment where "everybody would rather help you than compete against you." According to one student, competition is found "only in intramurals," an important part of campus life at ORU.

Faculty and staff at ORU devote themselves to building a university for God by actively participating in the lives of their students. ORU students appreciate this devotion and recognize its contribution to the successful academic environment. According to one undergraduate, "All faculty are extremely willing to go the extra mile for their students." Many students even describe faculty-student relationships as their favorite aspect of ORU academics, specifically noting the "personal help [the students] receive."

In Pursuit of Principled Social Life

ORU has been described as a place where students "get their learning and keep their burning." So life at the university goes well beyond academics. One unique feature of the ORU is an honor code which is taken very seriously and forbids the use of alcohol, tobacco and drugs, as well as lying, cheating, cursing and premarital sex. The honor code, which is submitted with the application to the university, also requires students to attend all classes and chapel services and to

participate in a physical fitness program. Unlike most universities around the country, weekend activities are not centered on drinking. This may be a result of the honor code, or it may just be a result of students' adherence to Christian values. Although drinking is not very common, it does occur, but usually off campus. According to one student, "nobody really drinks in the dorms unless they keep it on the down low." Drugs are even less prevalent than alcohol.

Instead of drinking, students who stay on campus spend their free time playing intramurals and attending dorm and sporting events. Most students do not stay on campus during the weekend. Instead, they tend to visit coffee shops, restaurants and clubs, as well as commuter students' homes away from campus. Students usually have cars so they can visit these off-campus sites, as "Tulsa does not have a good public transportation system." According to one student, "Tulsa is very boring without a car."

One student said that stereotypical ORU students may be described "as Bible beaters and Jesus-freaks but also as hard-working, honest, respected people." While the student population at ORU boasts geographic diversity, in that the school attracts students from 49 states and 70 nations, all students are connected by their faith. "For the most part everybody has a relationship with God, which makes the people pretty much all the same. But as far as culture goes, there is a good mix," said one student.

Living as "Brothers" and "Sisters"

Most students will live in dorms unless they are commuters, married or over age twenty-five. Students generally do not mind that they are required to live on campus, because it creates a sense of "community spirit." Dorms are divided into wings, and freshmen are randomly assigned to a wing in a single-sex dorm. Each male wing is paired with a specific female wing, and "brother wings" and "sister wings" allow freshmen to meet members of the opposite sex. Brother and sister wings "plan events together, sit together in chapel, and also have designated seats" together in the cafeteria. Freshmen may request a particular dorm if they have had family in that dorm, or they may be recruited by a particular wing. The wings that "recruit, draft on, and initiate people" are similar to fraternities, except the students live in dormitory halls, instead of separate houses elsewhere on campus. One of the oldest and most respected wings on campus is known as YoungBlood. Dorms are also known for their particular personalities. According to one student, "Claudius is the freshman, fun, social dorm. EMR is the fun, manly man's dorm. Michael and Wesley are for more of the pretty boys. Gabby is for the rich girls."

Freshmen generally find it easy to make friends in their own wings, or in their respective brother or sister wing. Additionally, freshmen do not feel excluded from upperclassmen's activities since "everybody is included in whatever is going on." But according to one senior, the upperclassmen have much less free time for socializing. Every floor has an RA and a chaplain. RAs enforce curfews, notify students of events, and maintain general order on the floor. Chaplains provide students with spiritual support.

One thing ORU students all agree on is the strangeness and originality of campus architecture. One student describes it as "space age" and another describes it as "like the Jetsons." Most find it ugly at first, but all agree that it grows on them. Currently, roofs of buildings are being improved and construction for a new student center is underway.

Students generally hang out in and around the cafeteria and at the restaurants on campus, such as the Eagle's Nest or the Internet café. When the weather is nice, they spend time on the quad as well. Favorite places on campus include the Prayer Gardens, surrounding the base of the 200-foot tall Prayer Tower which serves as the visitor's center and the Kenneth H. Cooper Aerobics Center (AC), a two-story building housing athletic facilities and exercise equipment. Located in a very safe neighborhood, ORU offers an extremely safe campus environment. There are no problems between the students and the residents of the surrounding neighborhoods. As one student put it, "They love us."

There is only one cafeteria on campus, but according to a student, it has "good variety. They try hard. You have to be creative sometimes." Another student agrees it is "better than most cafeterias I have eaten in, but it still gets old and is avoided most of the time." Students are required to be on an unlimited, 17-, 14-, or 10-meal per week meal plan and each comes with a certain number of Eagle Bucks that can be used at different restaurants, as well as the coffee shop or bookstore. Even when the students tire of cafeteria food, it is not a problem since Tulsa boasts "a huge restaurant variety—anything and everything you can imagine."

Sports as a Requirement

Oral Roberts University aims to "educate the whole man: spirit, mind and body. Staying in shape and treating our bodies well is just as important as our mental state." In addition to most students' abstention from alcohol, drugs and tobacco, students are all required to participate in some sort of physical activity. One way to do this is to participate in a varsity sport. The Oral Roberts Golden Eagles compete in eight Division I sports for both men and women. Though the school is fairly young and school pride and traditions are still developing, sporting events are well-attended. Basketball is especially popular at the 10,000-seat Mabee Basketball Stadium. For students who do not want the time commitment of Division I athletics, intramurals are popular as well. Intramural sports such as basketball, soccer, volleyball, flag football, tennis, badminton and Ping-Pong are extremely competitive.

> **"Staying in shape and treating our bodies well is just as important as our mental state."**

Outside of academics and athletics, students have many job opportunities on and off campus. Students are very committed to their extracurricular activities as well. Some students take part in mission trips; others write for the school newspaper, *The Oracle;* and some are involved in community outreach or the Leadership Academy. A unique group called the Student Association allows students to play an active role in the decision-making and programming of the university.

ORU instructs its young people in how to combine morality with worldly endeavors like business and medicine and other professional arenas featured in its academic programs. The university's facilities, high-tech amenities and space-age architecture contrast greatly with the university's embrace of an old-school mentality concerning academic life. Students all agree that devotion to God comes first; they love being in a strict academic environment where they are given the opportunity to "grow as a Christian." In the words of University Chancellor Roberts (who is son of the university's founder) ORU is a "ministry with a University not a University with a ministry." If you are seeking a spiritual, as well as an academic, collegiate experience, you may be one of the growing number of applicants considering Oral Roberts University.—*Jessica Rubin*

FYI

If you come to Oral Roberts, you'd better bring "flip-flops" and "your Bible . . . I guess."

What's the typical weekend schedule? "Friday: Coffee shops, local concerts at Cain's Ballroom, out to eat and a movie. Saturday: maybe a basketball game or a drive-in movie. Sunday: Church, lunch and a nap. Next, the campus worship service."

If I could change one thing about Oral Roberts, I'd "get rid of the curfew and allow coed dorms" and "get more people to come here!"

Three things every student at Oral Roberts should do before graduating are "swim in the fountains, run the Howard Run (streaking around Howard Auditorium) and love our President."

University of Oklahoma

Address: 1000 Asp Avenue Norman, OK 73019-4076

Phone: 405-325-2252

E-mail address: admrec@ou.edu

Web site URL: www.ou.edu

Year Founded: 1890

Private or Public: Public

Religious Affiliation: None

Location: Urban

Number of Applicants: 8,768

Percent Accepted: 89%

Percent Accepted who enroll: 49%

Number Entering: 3,843

Number of Transfers Accepted each Year: 3,500

Middle 50% SAT range: M: 540–660, CR: 510–640, Wr: Unreported

Middle 50% ACT range: 23–28

Early admission program EA/ED/None: None

Percentage accepted through EA or ED: NA

EA and ED deadline: NA

Regular Deadline: 1-Apr

Application Fee: $40

Full time Undergraduate enrollment: 20,714

Total enrollment: 27,448

Percent Male: 50%

Percent Female: 50%

Total Percent Minority or Unreported: 26%

Percent African-American: 6%

Percent Asian/Pacific Islander: 6%

Percent Hispanic: 4%

Percent Native-American: 7%

Percent International: 3%

Percent in-state/out of state: 75%/25%

Percent from Public HS: Unreported

Retention Rate: Unreported

Graduation Rate 4-year: 26%

Graduation Rate 6-year: 59%

Percent Undergraduates in On-campus housing: 28%

Number of official organized extracurricular organizations: 338

3 Most popular majors: Journalism, Management Science, Zoology/Animal Biology

Student/Faculty ratio: 18:1

Average Class Size: 15

Percent of students going to grad school: Unreported

Tuition and Fees: $17,404

In-State Tuition and Fees if different: $7,423

Cost for Room and Board: $7,376

Percent receiving financial aid out of those who apply, first year: 81%

Percent receiving financial aid among all students: 49%

Nestled in America's heartland, in the small town of Norman (just south of Oklahoma City), lies the University of Oklahoma. But OU, as the university is commonly called, is much more than the visible cluster of red brick buildings and bustling students. It is truly its own world, filled with incredible school spirit and rich tradition. Just two minutes at an OU football game (especially the "Red River Rivalry," the face-off between OU and its archrival, the University of Texas) will lead any observer to realize that OU is no typical school. The "Boomer, Sooner" chant that fills the stadium will amaze visitors and excite students, alumni, and fans.

Who are the Boomers and Sooners, you ask? Well, the Boomers were pioneers who helped bring about Oklahoma's opening to settlers in the 1880s. The Sooners, on the other hand, were those unruly settlers who slipped in before President Harrison officially opened the territory. Today, the Sooners are the 20,000 plus students that make up the University of Oklahoma.

Party Like A Greek

In terms of extracurricular activities, Greek life and athletics rule the roost at OU. Fifty percent of Sooners belong to a fraternity or sorority (it's no wonder, since there are 45 of them on campus!). For Greek women, the school year starts a week early with rush in August. To accommodate this, on-campus housing permits freshman girls to move in before rush begins, so they are comfortably settled for the hectic week. Said one member, "Rush is a crazy process, but it's worth it in the end."

One aspect of Greek life that almost every participant appreciates is the exciting party scene. Theme parties, fraternity/sorority mixers, and date parties are just a few of the social events in the Greek world, and "rarely does a weekend go by without some kind of sorority/fraternity event." The Greek system is a major part of OU's social life, but it isn't the only part. "Obviously, there is a large fraternity and sorority life but not so big that it's hard to make friends without being in one," explained one freshman. Many students find friends in other extracurricular activities— sports, theater, political or community service organizations—and others meet people just by "going to dinner, studying, and hanging out in the dorms." For those who are part of a fraternity or sorority, parties often take place in fraternity houses, but plenty of parties are held in non-Greek houses or apartments also.

> OU may have a student body of over 20,000, but that doesn't mean hundreds of students are packed into every class.

The weekend usually starts on Thursday at OU, and Sooners know how to finish off each school week in style. Thursdays are often packed with fraternity parties and house parties. Fridays can be party nights too, but as one student explains, "Fridays are usually a little more low-key." Many students choose to just "hang out and rest up" for Saturday— and if it's a football weekend, that rest is much needed. "Everyone goes to the game at least four hours early to tailgate." School spirit abounds, with face paint, OU T-shirts, and flags everywhere. "There are a lot of die-hard Sooners out there—people who literally bleed crimson." Many alumni also attend each game. "Sooner Born, Sooner Bred" seems to be a motto most OU fans live by.

However, extreme school spirit has its downsides. If the Sooners lose, prepare to mourn. One freshman described the first OU loss she witnessed: "No one talked for about three days." Some students got angry, turning over trash cans and loudly lamenting the loss, but most just "walked around like zombies." But after a win, Norman rejoices. No one

throws a better victory party than a Sooner, and campus is certainly alive on these Saturday nights (and, well, most Saturday nights). Although OU has recently cracked down on underage drinking, implementing an intimidating-but-rarely-enforced Three Strike System, students don't have to look very far to find alcohol. As one student puts it, "OU is a dry campus, but I haven't seen much dryness."

Still, while football and partying are like oxygen to many Sooners, there are many other weekend activities to appeal to every interest. Many students spend their weekends seeing productions at the OU School of Drama, watching free new-release movies in the student union's theater, visiting Oklahoma City, or simply relaxing. And there is certainly no lack of clubs and activities at OU. "There are millions of organizations," commented one student. "Some students seem to do everything, and others do absolutely nothing." Whether you prefer to spend your free time saving the environment, playing Guitar Hero, or partying, you can do it at OU.

A More Academic Image

OU may have a student body of over 20,000, but that doesn't mean hundreds of students are packed into every class. "I had one class of about 100 kids," states one student, "but most of my classes have about 35 students." All classes are taught by professors, and most students claim that professors are remarkably accessible, considering the number of students they teach. "You can e-mail professors anytime, even in a class of 200. They're really good about helping students out." However, getting into first-choice classes can be challenging. "I got into most of the classes I wanted," says one freshman, "but it's hard because freshmen register last."

The work at OU can be challenging, but "once you learn how to handle it, it's definitely manageable." In recent years, the university seems to be shooting for a more "academic image." Among the current Sooner student body are nearly 600 enrolled National Merit Scholars; in fact, OU has the most National Merit Scholars in the nation enrolled per capita at a public university. The university is also among the top five in Rhodes Scholar graduates.

OU makes sure its top scholars are rewarded. Students in the Honors College (who must qualify with higher test scores and high school GPA) benefit from an early registration process, which allows them to enroll in "practically any class they want." Honors College students are the only ones who can graduate with honors, and they can enroll in small sections of about 20 students.

House Rules

On-campus housing is mandatory for all freshman students under age twenty (although there seem to be some exceptions to this rule), but many students choose to remain on campus all four years. OU's dorms are in the middle of a renovation project. Of the dorms, Couch and Walker are the most popular. "Couch is nice because it's been renovated, and all the furniture can be moved around." Couch also has the added bonus of the Couch Express, a small store and grill. Walker has a small convenience store named Xcetera, but it hasn't been renovated yet. Adams, another freshman dorm, is "not quite as nice." It has a Burger King on the ground floor, but "none of the towers connect, and the floor plan is really confusing." Freshman dorms are coed by floor, and upperclass dorms are coed by suite. RAs live on the floors with freshmen and are "pretty helpful," although they do have to enforce the visitor rules, which state that coed visitors must leave freshman rooms by 12 a.m. on weeknights and 2 a.m. on weekends.

OU's on-campus dining facilities get mixed reviews, but most students agree that there is certainly plenty of variety available. Students can use meal points at the cafeteria, any on-campus convenience stores, and at the food court in the Student Union, which is a popular hangout. Many students move off campus after their freshman year, but plenty of students remain. "Some people think it's weird to live on campus after freshman year," explained one student, "but it's so much more convenient."

For students who live off-campus, finding parking on campus can be a real pain. "You have to get to campus pretty early just to find a parking spot." Although there is public transit around campus and Norman, most students have cars. "I don't know what I'd do without my car," one student said. "If you want to go anywhere off campus, you pretty much need to drive."

And where do students go in their cars? One favorite in Norman is the Classic 50s Drive-In, which caters to Sooners with tasty hamburgers, shakes, and other staples. There are several other popular restaurants in Norman, as well as some "cute little shops" and a mall. "Biggest surprise about OU: I looooove Norman!" exclaimed one student. "To me, it is the perfect college town." One thing that is unique about Norman is that it is "all OU, all the time." And, if the small-town scene gets too repetitive, Oklahoma City is just 15 miles down the highway.

Southern Style

At first glance, OU's student body seems pretty homogeneous. "Most of the students are white, but there are a lot of African-American and Hispanic students also." Sooners have a reputation for being an unusually attractive bunch, but they don't necessarily flaunt it. "Most people are pretty casual—you know, T-shirts, jeans, flip-flops." In other words, no one is ostracized for wearing sweats to class. Still, in true Southern fashion, most OU students try to look good and keep fit, often using the university's gym facilities or intramural sports teams to help them along the way. One stereotype most Sooners would like to banish, however, is that "we are *not* rednecks." The majority of students come from Oklahoma, the Midwest, and Texas, but students come to OU from all over the country and even outside the country. And because of OU's theater and arts departments and on-campus museums, Sooners have plenty of cultural outlets. "There are lots of neat, cultured people here."

But, cultured or uncultured, majority or minority, Greek or non-Greek, all OU students have one thing in common: Sooner pride. Many students make up the fourth or fifth generation in their family to attend OU. And when they make the annual 187-mile trek from Norman down to Dallas for the OU/UT game, it doesn't matter where they're from or what they look like—all that matters is the color of their T-shirt and the cheer on their lips: "Boomer Sooner!"—*Elizabeth Bewley*

FYI

If you come to the University of Oklahoma, you'd better bring "your adventurous side, your pride, and sometimes a winter jacket."

What is the typical weekend schedule? "Head to a frat party on Friday night (assuming you can get in), go to a football game Saturday morning after the tailgate, and sleep in Sunday."

If I could change one thing about the University of Oklahoma, I'd "change its proximity to outside life."

Three things every University of Oklahoma student should do before graduating are "go to the UT/Oklahoma football game, take advantage of agriculture in the area, and join a fraternity."

University of Tulsa

Address: 800 South Tucker Drive, Tulsa, OK 74104-3189
Phone: 918 631-2307
E-mail address: admission@utulsa.edu
Web site URL: www.utulsa.edu
Year Founded: 1894
Private or Public: Private
Religious Affiliation: Presbyterian
Location: Suburban
Number of Applicants: 4,714
Percent Accepted: 46%
Percent Accepted who enroll: 32%
Number Entering: 692
Number of Transfers Accepted each Year: 270
Middle 50% SAT range: M: 550–700, CR: 540–700, Wr: Unreported
Middle 50% ACT range: 25–31
Early admission program EA/ED/None: None

Percentage accepted through EA or ED: NA
EA and ED deadline: NA
Regular Deadline: Rolling
Application Fee: $35
Full time Undergraduate enrollment: 3,049
Total enrollment: 3,724
Percent Male: 51%
Percent Female: 49%
Total Percent Minority or Unreported: 36%
Percent African-American: 5%
Percent Asian/Pacific Islander: 4%
Percent Hispanic: 5%
Percent Native-American: 4%
Percent International: 14%
Percent in-state/out of state: 52%/48%
Percent from Public HS: 78%
Retention Rate: 88%
Graduation Rate 4-year: 48%
Graduation Rate 6-year: 62%

Percent Undergraduates in On-campus housing: 70%
Number of official organized extracurricular organizations: 245
3 Most popular majors: Business/Marketing, Engineering, Visual and Performing Arts
Student/Faculty ratio: 10:1
Average Class Size: 14
Percent of students going to grad school: 41%
Tuition and Fees: $23,940
In-State Tuition and Fees if different: No difference
Cost for Room and Board: $7,776
Percent receiving financial aid out of those who apply, first year: 49%
Percent receiving financial aid among all students: 44%

In the alphabet of life, the letter "T" stands for many things: tortoise, telepathy, toiletries, tots. But when "t" stands for tenacity, talent, tradition and togetherness, all in one setting, that is when it also stands for TU, also known as the University of Tulsa. Now, you may be saying to yourself, TU? Did you say TU? Because then should it not be Tulsa University rather than the University of Tulsa? Perhaps yes. Perhaps no. And perhaps this grammatical flip-flop, though perplexing, perfectly demonstrates the small-size/big-time duality which TU actualizes.

Hackedemics
Across the board, TU is habitually known for its challenging academics (especially in the field of engineering). And this can be attractive to strong-minded and/or intelligent young adults (indeed one of every ten students currently enrolled at TU is a National Merit Scholar). But we all know the most attractive attribute about a college to any young adult person is how that education will help him to land an eight-figure salary, become an icon and/or hack into neighboring governments' intelligence computers. Yet TU already knows all of that.

The University of Tulsa is "one of six pioneer institutions selected by the National Science Foundation to participate in the Federal Cyber Service Initiative (aka Cyber Corps) to train students for federal careers as computer security experts." This basically translates to "TU receiving $2.7 million to create a band of information security specialists who know how to defend the free world and defend the Internet from hackers." These students come out of the program not only with a degree in computer science and a couple years of their tuition paid for, but also "multiple federal-level computer security certificates as endorsed by the CNSS." They also get a new pick-up line: "Excuse me, I seemed to have dropped my multiple federal-level computer security certificates around here . . ."

However, if computers are not your "bag," TU also receives funding for the "Tulsa Undergraduate Research Challenge, which lets students get involved in advanced research with faculty members as early as their freshman year." It is no wonder that 46 Tulsa students have received Goldwater scholarships since 1995. But the "level of academic strain or prowess is totally dependent on what you want and your major—communication majors have it relatively easy, whereas students with majors like nursing and engineering can easily take up residency in the library."

Classes for Claustrophobics

Come to the University of Tulsa and never feel the restless constriction of cramming into a 500-seat auditorium with a bunch of pungent, pajama-wearing cohorts for the introductory lecture of Rocks for Jocks 101. Why? Because at TU, the average class-size is 14 students, 62 percent of classes are under 20 students, and only 1 percent of classes holds 50 or more students. This allows for one-on-one instruction in an environment that "feels like home," an environment where "the teachers become easy friends and mentors, who are so approachable, accommodating, and helpful." Sounds like a little slice of heaven, eh? Except in heaven you do not have to factor in "attendance policies that can lower your grade making it so you can't skip class." In a class of 100, it is possible, but in a class of 12, hiding an absence can prove fruitless. Nonetheless, young adults (local, national, or international) continue to flock to TU in droves, thanks to the attentive faculty, the 10:1 student/teacher ratio, and the fact that "the school is small enough to not feel invisible, but also big enough where you are always meeting new people."

You and Me and Greek Makes Three

This constant confluence of new friendships may in a large part be related to how actively involved the students are within campus organizations. Ninety percent of students participate in some sort of club or organization—the "big ones" being: Young Democrats, FCA, Intramurals or SA. SA is the Student Association which organizes most of the "big events" on campus, including Homecoming and Springfest—"a week of activities, free stuff and concerts (Ben Folds, Hanson, 50 Cent, Vertical Horizon, etc.), with amazing tailgating on the 'U' before the football game."

> "The school is small enough to not feel invisible, but also big enough where you are always meeting new people."

Many of the other annual events are held by Greek frats or sororities, most have "phil-

anthropy weeks that are way fun—usually games, competitions and then parties on the weekends—all to raise money for their chosen organization." A favorite is the Lambda Chi Alpha's LUAU which is a "sand volleyball tourney where they cover a parking lot with sand and anyone can play, it's kinda a big deal." At TU, only about a fifth of the students pledge a fraternity or sorority, making Greek life "an option but not a must." If a frat holds a party or philanthropic event, anyone can attend, "so people do not feel like they have to go Greek in order to have a social life."

In fact, if you want an ample social network, intramurals might be a better bet. Eighty percent of the students partake of the intramural program, and "it is a common dream to win an intramural championship of some sort." The program is run through Collins Fitness Center, a brand-new fitness haven that came about during recent renovations (along with "amazing dorms—LaFortune is the best, the Twin dorms are the worst"). Most students describe the new fitness center as "unreal" though a few add "it is something that some huge rapper would own complete with plasma screens everywhere and every kind of workout machine you can imagine."

Running Backs, Recorders, and Robots

We know TU students love to win academic awards and that they love to play intramurals, but what happens when you combine the two? You get student-athletes who love to win and student-athletic-supporters who love to watch them win! TU basketball games have "long been known as a Tulsa tradition" and "for once, the football team is doing well!" In fact, the Golden Hurricane (or so they are known because of 1. their tendency to "roar through opponents" and 2. Georgia Tech was already known as the tornado) has had recent success not only in football bowl games but also in soccer. But in the words of an insightful fan, "winning is not the best part; the best part is that the school is small enough that you know most or a lot of the athletes and this personal connection makes cheering at sporting events or watching them on TV a lot more fun because you are watching your friends."

As touching as that is, what if you do not like watching sports? Not a problem! TU has a large visual and performing arts contingency, and with the city of Tulsa boasting a professional opera company, a national ballet company, and a symphony, the two share an intimate interaction. Often "kids have gotten to fill in with the symphony" and the Tulsa Ballet has adopted a 330-pound "fighting robot" built by TU students for a Battle Bots competition. Fortunately, "the bot had been stripped of its steel spikes and bullet-proof panels, allowing it to give a delicate ride to a full-length mirror and interact with the dancers."

Love and Leisure T-Town Style

If you are a TU student your hangout is either the library or the "Ack-Ack." Funnily enough, at TU "the library is almost a social scene; it's fun," and ACAC is similar to a student union and the only place where you can use meal points outside of the cafeteria. Off campus, many students enjoy spending time at Utica Square, a trendy yet quaint outdoor shopping/eating/walking Mecca that is home to Santa's cottage during the winter months and Queenside's bakery year-round ("It has egg salad to die for."). They also enjoy a trip to Philbrook Museum or the Tulsa Rose Garden, "where you can have a picnic at Woodward Park and watch a movie on your laptop."

But what if you are, perhaps, more nocturnal? Where do the creatures of the night hang out? Well, a typical TU Friday night could consist of "going to a bar, then ending back up at a small apartment/house party." Apparently, there used to be more house parties, but because of recent university mandates, "the parties are now being regulated and have significantly decreased in size and quantity; as a result people frequent the bar scene more." The main watering-holes are Rehab, Hardwood's or The Buccaneer (a dive-bar affectionately called The Buc). All are located across the street from campus, and "are always offering some kind of beer special or TU student discount." Then there are other, more upscale restaurant/bar districts like Brookside, Cherry Street or the Riverwalk (also a divine location to go for a jog). If you are not invited to a private apartment party, there are normally language house/frat parties, though those are known to "get kind of old after sophomore or junior year." Dorms also sometimes sponsor functions, and then "there are always City of Tulsa sponsored events like Mayfest or Oktoberfest (one fest has a lot of watercolors and live music and the other fest has a lot of potato pancakes, polka, and beer)." If those combined with Springfest are not enough fests for you, there is even a Harley Motorcycle Festival "where they close down Brookside every year and have a huge party."

But what is a party if one is alone? The dating scene at the University of Tulsa is like a good male/female relationship—discordant. Boys will tell you "it is good, there is a range of different people around and you can find your athletic or partyer or smart person and dates can be as simple as going to a party together." Girls will tell you "it's not bad, there are dating prospects although not too many of quality." But one thing is sure, "it is a small school so there is a clear understanding of who is dating who."

Max Forman once said: "Education seems to be in America the only commodity of which the customer tries to get as little as he can for his money." Apparently, Max Forman has never seen the University of Tulsa, especially during its current booms of a growing international student population, continuing nationally recognized academic award winners, and improving athletic victors. But the special charm of the University of Tulsa is that "as cliché as this sounds, the school feels like one big family," no matter how it orders its name.—*Jocelyn Ranne*

FYI

If you come to TU, you'd better bring "a variety of clothing (for all seasons) because it could be 70 degrees one day and snowing the next, and some cash. Things are expensive on campus, and campus police only know how to do one thing: and that's give out tickets."

What's the typical weekend schedule? "Friday night can start with dinner on Brookside, then parties start around 11 p.m. (most people check out frat row). Saturday you wake up (late) do some homework, check out a sporting event, and then repeat. You do work when you can, but it is mainly partying and catching up on sleep!"

If I could change one thing about TU, "I would get more quick and good food options on campus."

Three things that every TU student should do before graduating are "camp out on the 'U' (the big U-shaped grassy area in between the dorms, library, and classroom buildings), join an organization, and climb up on the roof of the library to go stargazing."

Oregon

Lewis & Clark College

Address: 10015 SW Terwilliger Boulevard Portland, OR 97219
Phone: 503-768-6613
E-mail address: admissions@lclark.edu
Web site URL: www.lclark.edu
Year Founded: 1867
Private or Public: Private
Religious Affiliation: None
Location: Urban
Number of Applicants: 5,360
Percent Accepted: 56%
Percent Accepted who enroll: 17%
Number Entering: 507
Number of Transfers Accepted each Year: 68
Middle 50% SAT range: M: 590–680, CR: 610–700, Wr: 590–680
Middle 50% ACT range: 26–31
Early admission program EA/ED/None: EA

Percentage accepted through EA or ED: Unreported
EA and ED deadline: 1-Nov
Regular Deadline: 1-Feb
Application Fee: $50
Full time Undergraduate enrollment: 1,964
Total enrollment: 2,836
Percent Male: 36%
Percent Female: 64%
Total Percent Minority or Unreported: 21%
Percent African-American: 1%
Percent Asian/Pacific Islander: 6%
Percent Hispanic: 5%
Percent Native-American: <1%
Percent International: 5%
Percent in-state/out of state: 13%/87%
Percent from Public HS: 76%
Retention Rate: 83%
Graduation Rate 4-year: Unreported

Graduation Rate 6-year: Unreported
Percent Undergraduates in On-campus housing: 67%
Number of official organized extracurricular organizations: 85
3 Most popular majors: Psychology, Visual and Performing arts, English
Student/Faculty ratio: 13:1
Average Class Size: 20
Percent of students going to grad school: 10%
Tuition and Fees: $33,726
In-State Tuition and Fees if different: No difference
Cost for Room and Board: $8,820
Percent receiving financial aid out of those who apply, first year: 73%
Percent receiving financial aid among all students: 86%

L ewis & Clark students love Portland. The passionate and worldly minds that attend the small classes of Lewis & Clark are also frequent visitors to downtown coffee shops and the famous Powell's Books. But it's not all about the city. Lewis & Clark's international focus, commitment to small classes and dedicated professors also draw students to this spectacular wooded estate.

Small Classes, Devoted Professors

Small classes and attentive professors are trademarks of Lewis & Clark's strong academic life. The average class size is 19 students, yet the biggest science class can hold around 70 students. While it varies among majors, most students agree that this small class size fosters discussion and "encourages students to think." Professors are "super passionate" and "want to be there and connect with students." Because of this familiar interaction, and the fact that there are no TAs, students often develop close personal relationships with their professors.

Moreover, students explain that the closely knit nature of the academic community encourages them to be committed to their schoolwork, which they describe as "challenging." Nonetheless, while students generally "do well in school," grades are not widely discussed on campus. The sole academic complaint seems to be that, being a smaller school, Lewis & Clark simply does not offer enough majors or courses from which to choose.

Perhaps to offset this disadvantage, Lewis

& Clark students are encouraged to go abroad, and over 300 students each year take advantage of the school's programs in other countries. Students can choose locations all around the world, including Kenya, Germany, France, India and Australia. Most appreciate the experience of going abroad and the global perspective their comrades bring to discussions. Because of the interest in global affairs, popular majors include International Affairs and Languages.

> "This ebb and flow of upperclassmen as some leave to study and others return from studying abroad creates a 'transient school.'"

In terms of requirements, most students said they were "pretty standard" and not overly burdensome. All freshmen are required to take "Exploration and Discovery," a yearlong course meant as an overview of the most important works and topics of the diverse field of liberal arts. Students are split into small seminars, but each seminar regardless of professor is meant to cover the same material. Professors of every discipline teach the course, so students' experiences in the course vary depending on their professor. When Lewis & Clark students need to hit the books, they use the "totally awesome" Watzek Library. There are study rooms for group study, long tables, and private carrels with computer hookups that allow students to check their e-mail from a laptop.

Hippies and Hipsters

Students at Lewis & Clark form a homogeneously progressive and liberal community. Although there is an "overwhelming number of international students," people drawn to Lewis & Clark are generally interested in a lot of the same issues. Most are liberal and interested in change, taking on issues which range from sustainability to involvement in the community. Students express a tension between a desire for a more diverse campus and the appeal of their "Lewis & Clark bubble." Indeed, in some class discussions there is "little debate," and rarely a conservative or deeply religious belief voiced. Additionally, some pessimistically feel that students may superficially judge their peers: "If you don't buy organic food, you're not making the world a better place."

The social scene at Lewis & Clark is "intensely laid-back." The Greek system was abolished in the 1970s with a donor's amendment, but students don't seem to miss it. Apparently the donor would not give the school her fortune unless the school promised to prohibit Greek houses, install an all-women's dorm, and serve ice cream at every meal.

Since freshmen and sophomores are required to live on campus, many of the underclassmen social events take place on campus. As a technically dry campus, students have to find ways around the prohibition on alcohol on campus to avoid write-ups by the campus police. While Lewis & Clark is not your typical "party school," students do certainly have a good time. Underclassmen manage to drink in small groups in the dorms, and bigger parties are held off campus. Binge drinking, though, is not common. Some students smoke pot, but, much like drinking, drug use is a "private hangout thing."

Finally, Portland is a big part of the social scene at Lewis & Clark. The campus is a 10-minute drive from the city or 30 minutes on the school-run shuttle. Students often make use of the free shuttle that goes into downtown and surrounding areas every hour until 2 a.m. In Portland, the city has one of the most accessible public transport systems including a "great bus system." One of the major draws for many students is being able to explore the different areas of the city. Whether walking along Hawthorne Boulevard to find some new music, going to a film festival or attending "First Thursday," a program where all of the art galleries in Portland have new shows, Lewis & Clark students are drawn to the Portland scene. Coffee shops are a common place to do work or just hang out, and Powell's, the largest independent bookstore in America, is another big attraction.

"Summer Camp at a Park"

Lewis & Clark's campus is a lush, green area that used to be a rich donor's estate. As one would expect from a former estate, the buildings do not resemble typical college administrative buildings but remind one of "Snow White cottages." On the "fairly small" campus there is a reflecting pool, a rose garden, "lots of trees, and grassy space for people to lay out on sunny days." Unfortunately, those sunny days are few and far between. The charm of a lush campus with "spectacular" views of Mt. Hood make up for the wet and misty atmosphere.

LC students live in "typical college dorms" their first two years when they are required to live on campus. Many consider this a burden and would like to have the cheaper option of living off campus. There are, however, some perks to dorm living. As a way to meet people, some of the housing facilities have themed floors, such as an "environmental activism floor" and an "international floor." Room size varies from dorm to dorm, but almost all are coed by floor.

Upperclassmen commonly move off campus either into a house with friends or an apartment. Because the area surrounding Lewis & Clark is suburban and fairly isolated, many live in Portland proper. This move off campus can create a schism between the upper- and underclassmen. Once students move off campus they "don't really see the people on campus" and sometimes become less involved in campus activities because "it's hard to get back to campus for a 7:00 meeting. You are probably only going to go if it's something really important to you." Some upperclassmen do not feel as connected to the college but still prefer living off campus to the isolation they sometimes feel in the dorms.

The one dining hall on campus serves "reasonably good" food. Affectionately called "The Bon" after the college's catering company, Bon Appétit, it provides plenty of vegan and vegetarian options. Bon Appétit is considered one of the best food catering services in the Northwest and offers many types of food at different "stations." The meal plan is fairly flexible; students can choose the number of meals they want per week and also buy "flex points" that they can use as dollars at various à la carte places around campus.

Enjoying the Outdoors

With students living on such a verdant campus, it is no surprise that many of them enjoy outdoor activities. "College of the Outdoors" is a college-funded program that offers trips for everything from skiing to backpacking to canoeing to rock climbing. With the Oregon coast two hours away and Mt. Hood just an hour, there are plenty of spectacular sights to visit. Almost all students take advantage of these trips that can last a weekend or a day. Transportation is provided, and students can borrow any gear that they may need.

Varsity and club sports are "not big" on campus, although the ultimate Frisbee and basketball teams do have a significant following. There are "quite a few athletes" on campus, and those who do not play varsity sports can compete in intramural sports. These are fairly popular activities on campus, especially volleyball, skiing, and soccer.

Beyond athletics, students can also join a variety of clubs on campus or work in the student-run co-op that serves as a popular social hangout. The co-op is a place for students to sell their art, play music or just relax and have a cup of coffee. Social justice and activist clubs are big on campus, and other popular organizations include the women's center and the black student union.

Although students rarely display school spirit, their mascot, a Pioneer, is still a fitting symbol for Lewis & Clark students. Their attitude is reflected in one of the school's mottos, "Do not follow where the path may lead, go instead where there is no path and blaze a trail." Students enjoy the companionship of fellow well-traveled and independent students. Those committed to change and the generating of new ideas thrive at Lewis & Clark—they can get a strong liberal arts education in a small school setting.
—*Rachel Jeffers*

FYI

If you come to Lewis & Clark, you'd better bring "a raincoat, tofu and a pair of Chaco sandals."

The typical weekend schedule? "Brunch in your pajamas, work in a coffee shop downtown and go to a movie or concert."

If I could change one thing about Lewis & Clark, I'd "diversify the student body in terms of background and ideology."

Three things every student at Lewis & Clark should do before graduating are "spend all day in Powell's, go to dinner with your professor, and go camping on the coast."

Oregon State University

Address: 104 Kerr Administration Building Corvallis, OR 97331-2106

Phone: 541-737-4411

E-mail address: osuamit@oregonstate.edu

Web site URL: www.oregonstate.edu

Year Founded: 1858

Private or Public: Public

Religious Affiliation: None

Location: Suburban

Number of Applicants: 8,149

Percent Accepted: 86%

Percent Accepted who enroll: 42%

Number Entering: 2,953

Number of Transfers Accepted each Year: Unreported

Middle 50% SAT range: M: 490–610, CR: 460–580, Wr: Unreported

Middle 50% ACT range: 20–26

Early admission program EA/ED/None: EA

Percentage accepted through EA or ED: Unreported

EA and ED deadline: 1-Nov

Regular Deadline: 1-Sep

Application Fee: $50

Full time Undergraduate enrollment: 16,673

Total enrollment: 19,768

Percent Male: 54%

Percent Female: 46%

Total Percent Minority or Unreported: 30%

Percent African-American: 1%

Percent Asian/Pacific Islander: 8%

Percent Hispanic: 4%

Percent Native-American: 1%

Percent International: 2%

Percent in-state/out of state: 89%/11%

Percent from Public HS: Unreported

Retention Rate: 81%

Graduation Rate 4-year: 30%

Graduation Rate 6-year: Unreported

Percent Undergraduates in On-campus housing: 19%

Number of official organized extracurricular organizations: 350

3 Most popular majors: Business, Health, natural Sciences

Student/Faculty ratio: 18:1

Average Class Size: 26

Percent of students going to grad school: Unreported

Tuition and Fees: $18,823

In-State Tuition and Fees if different: $6,187

Cost for Room and Board: $8,208

Percent receiving financial aid out of those who apply, first year: 62%

Percent receiving financial aid among all students: 48%

The consensus among students at Oregon State University is that the privilege of being a Beaver is worth the constant rain in Corvallis, Oregon, a quintessential college town settled on the banks of the Willamette River in northwestern Oregon. While many students report much satisfaction with their school choice, many also struggle to define what differentiates OSU from other universities. One student echoed the thoughts of his peers when he called OSU "pretty typical for its size." Still, Oregon State offers top-notch engineering, agriculture and business programs, and those prepared to embrace a small town at the expense of cultural diversity will find a strong sense of community and a spirited atmosphere at Oregon State University.

Freshman Year, Stadium Style

Graduating from Oregon State requires a strong foundation in what the university calls the Baccalaureate Core. While some of these courses focus on basic skills such as mathematics and writing, others are designed to prepare students to participate in contemporary dialogue on topics such as "Social Processes and Institutions" and "Western Culture." Most students reflect on the "Bacc Core" with positive feelings and enjoy having common ground with all their classmates. In one senior's words, "I found it pretty enjoyable. If the Core weren't in place, most people would never take classes in, for example, 'Difference, Power and Discrimination.'" That said, another consequence of the Core is that the majority of students' classes in the first two years are part of the Core requirements, and therefore tend to be lecture classes. Students complain that these classes often have as many as 400 students and are not as challenging as they would like. Pair these required classes with introductory-level courses for large, popular majors (like those in the College of Business, which also accommodate hundreds of students in large lecture halls) and the early years at OSU can feel very impersonal. Because of a limited number of choices of lower-level Core classes, registration can be a nightmare. Students who fail to plan carefully or register early are sometimes left with no option except to remain at the university a semester or a year longer than planned to get the credits they need. The problem is exacerbated for students in small or new departments. In the words of one sophomore majoring in New Media Communications, "A lot of classes are only offered once a year, so students like me have to plan their schedules very carefully." Four years can also turn into five when students retake classes in which they weren't satisfied with their grade, or change majors multiple times.

Many students choose to attend Oregon State on the strength of its engineering and forestry programs, which are well-respected and have competitive application processes and high standards for accepted students. The university is also home to an Honors College, which offers an Honors degree and smaller classes, lending students a sense of greater intimacy while still providing the broad range of classes available at a large university. OSU's College of Business, already the umbrella for a number of popular majors, recently reorganized itself in a Professional School model and a career-oriented focus, and has become increasingly popular since then. Programs in fashion design and retail management are also favorites and many students consider them to be challenging. A common thread connecting the most popular departments and courses at Oregon State is immediate applicability—students' favorite classes are the ones in which professors impart real-world experience and design a curriculum with potential for direct application to the job market.

Students say they find professors to be accessible and friendly at office hours, and reliable about responding to e-mails. This proves critical for students who take online classes that rely on electronic communication exclusively. Many students use former professors to plug gaps in the academic advising system, which can be hit-or-miss. Advisors are in short supply and "don't like to meet with you very often," one junior said. "We're a large university, so it's easy to fall through the cracks," said another student. Career Services, however, is a bright spot. The office offers a sizable job fair each semester—and occasionally job fairs dedicated exclusively to the very popular engineering programs—and many companies in the Pacific Northwest recruit on campus. Career advisors can also direct students to a one-time class in which students pay eight dollars for training in dining and networking etiquette, as well as to a for-credit class on professional development where students learn the ins and outs of résumé and cover letter writing and practice interviewing.

Geeked Out For Greeks

The Greek system at Oregon State University is flourishing. Greek parties are major social events on weekends, and various Greek houses throw annual themed parties which students, affiliated or not, say they look forward to. OSU's campus is dry only for underage students, and even the Office of Student Conduct and Affairs acknowledges that alcohol is widely used on campus. Students agree that drinking is an ingrained feature of the social experience at the university. In one sophomore's words, "Sure, you can not drink. People will judge you, but you can make that decision." Both the Greek system and house parties are accessible to students of all ages, but the social scene opens up for undergraduates when they turn twenty-one and can access the bars in Corvallis, which are popular hangouts for upperclassmen. One student added that a fun activity for students who don't enjoy structured parties or the bar scene is simply "getting together with friends to have a drink and watch a basketball game."

Students at Oregon State University appreciate the outdoorsy campus atmosphere. Boating and swimming activities on the Willamette are popular in warm weather, and Corvallis boasts an impressive network of jogging and biking trails. "The ocean's about an hour away, and so are the mountains. You've kind of got it all, and not everyone can say that," one junior said enthusiastically. And of course, with so much rain, the city is perennially green, which makes for "a really pretty campus," another student said. Residents of Corvallis, meanwhile, embrace the university culture and students. "People are friendly when they find out you're a student," one junior noted, and even people not affiliated with the university call themselves Beavers and support the OSU teams.

For all their enjoyment of the area, students make no bones about the size of Corvallis and the attendant dearth of novel things to do. The nearest major retail stores and movie theaters are in Albany, about 15 miles away, which makes a car a necessity. Many students at Oregon State hail from the area and so have an easy time bringing a car to campus, and a less-easy time finding parking. A number of students maintain an even stronger tie to home and choose to live with their parents while attending OSU. These, along with the students who buy houses with friends or lease off-campus apartments, rather than reside in university dorms, make up the majority of the student body. Freshmen are "sort of expected to live in the dorms," one sophomore said; most students plug into social life on campus by way of the friends they make in these early living arrangements. After freshman year, groups of friends move off campus together but stay close to and still spend much time on the campus, which is considered very safe at night. On-campus dining options are more than tolerable, if repetitive, and have flexible hours. Students can use money on their student IDs at a Carl's Jr. on campus, should they really need a culinary escape, and there are numerous fast-food restaurants within walking distance. One senior characterized the Corvallis dining experience as "generally quick, in and out in 10 minutes or less."

Ducks and Beavers, Oh My

As one sophomore put it, "If you're a Duck or a Beaver, you're nothing else." The Ducks, of course, are the OSU rivals at the University of Oregon in Eugene. In preparation for the annual football match between the universities—known fondly as the Civil War game—the state of Oregon divides its allegiances with no looking back. With increasing successes, including a trip to the Rose Bowl, the Oregon State University football team has the whole of Corvallis behind it, and the baseball team enjoys similar successes and support. The Beaver Dam is a club for student supporters of the OSU Beavers and is one of the most popular clubs on campus, since a one-time $15 fee entitles members to priority seating at games. One student recalled that upon visiting campus, he was struck by "the huge number of people wearing the school colors, more than I'd seen anywhere else."

Student government, in the form of the Associated Students of Oregon State University (ASOSU), is also active and effective,

with good access to university administration and much student support. Many students participate in the university's Senate, and students generally appreciate the events the ASOSU brings to campus, including stand-up comedians and a battle of the bands. Recently, a group of professional snowboarders visited the campus and brought their own snow to perform demonstrations. Intramural sports are popular on campus, the most prominent being volleyball and flag football, and many students make frequent use of the athletic facilities in Dixon Recreation Center.

The OSU administration is proud of the number of cultural houses on its campus, but one member of the Hispanic Cultural Center was quick to point out that having many cultural houses does not necessarily equal diversity. He added, "I guess for someone who's never been in a diverse community before, it could be new and diverse-seeming, but if you come from another culture, it can feel like you've never seen so many white people in one spot." But few students complain of attitudes of intolerance on campus, ostensibly in part because of the explicit inclusion of coursework on diversity in the Bacc Core.

> "The ocean's about an hour away, and so are the mountains. You've kind of got it all, and not everyone can say that."

Students at Oregon State University celebrate "a real sense of togetherness," in the words of one student, even if they are unable to identify quite what it is that bonds them or sets them apart. Many students are surprised by "how small the school feels, and how you see people you know everywhere you go," even though the university is home to tens of thousands of students. In short, students who seek what is in many ways the prototypical college experience—a strong football and Greek-oriented culture at a large university—will likely have no regrets about choosing to attend Oregon State University.—*Elizabeth Woods*

FYI

If you come to Oregon State University, you'd better bring "a rain jacket. If you bring an umbrella, the native Oregonians will think you're from California and can't handle the rain."

What's the typical weekend schedule? "Drive to Portland for an afternoon in the city on Saturday, come back for a game Saturday night, stay up late at parties with friends, sleep in and do work on Sunday."

If I could change one thing about Oregon State University, I'd "locate it in a bigger city with more to do."

Three things every student should do at Oregon State University before graduating are "float the Willamette River, go jogging in the rain, and go to the Civil War football game."

Reed College

Address: 3203 SE Woodstock Boulevard, Portland, OR 97202-8199
Phone: 800-547-4750
E-mail address: admission@reed.edu
Web site URL: www.reed.edu
Year Founded: 1909
Private or Public: Private
Religious Affiliation: None
Location: Urban
Number of Applicants: 3,161
Percent Accepted: 41%
Percent Accepted who enroll: 29%
Number Entering: 368
Number of Transfers Accepted each Year: 82
Middle 50% SAT range: M: 610–720, CR: 640–750, Wr: 620–720
Middle 50% ACT range: 30–33
Early admission program EA/ED/None: ED I, ED II

Percentage accepted through EA or ED: 56%
EA and ED deadline: 15-Nov and 20-Dec
Regular Deadline: 15-Jan
Application Fee: $50
Full time Undergraduate enrollment: 1,418
Total enrollment: 1,477
Percent Male: 45%
Percent Female: 55%
Total Percent Minority or Unreported: 27%
Percent African-American: 4%
Percent Asian/Pacific Islander: 12%
Percent Hispanic: 8%
Percent Native-American: <1%
Percent International: 6%
Percent in-state/out of state: 8%/92%
Percent from Public HS: 59%
Retention Rate: 88%

Graduation Rate 4-year: 59%
Graduation Rate 6-year: 78%
Percent Undergraduates in On-campus housing: 70%
Number of official organized extracurricular organizations: 101
3 Most popular majors: English, Biology, Anthropology
Student/Faculty ratio: 10:1
Average Class Size: 15
Percent of students going to grad school: 65%
Tuition and Fees: $39,700
In-State Tuition and Fees if different: No difference
Cost for Room and Board: $10,250
Percent receiving financial aid out of those who apply, first year: Unreported
Percent receiving financial aid among all students: 50%

I f you dream of being either a frat brother or the girl who dates a frat brother, don't expect Reed College to be the place for you. Reed is a small school in Portland, Oregon, with a quirky student body, small class sizes, intense academic programs and a beautiful campus. If you're an open-minded intellectual who doesn't like the prep or jock factor of many other prestigious, academically challenging schools, you will feel at home at Reed.

Academic Masochism

Reedies are quick to admit that the workload at their school is a serious challenge.

One student explained that it's not uncommon to routinely spend seven hours straight working in the library. "I know that when I graduate, I'm going to have to learn how to function in the real world again, because I've been so immersed in academia," one Reedie said. However, students' academic loads are made bearable by their brilliant but approachable professors. There are no TAs at Reed, since all classes are taught by professors. It's easy to get on a first name basis with them because classes are usually no bigger than 30 students. "It's great to be at a table with a few other students, sitting across from a professor who wrote the book for the course," one student noted.

Students say all majors and classes are difficult, and "there isn't anything you can slack off in." Popular majors include English, classics and religion. Psychology is considered the major for the Reedie looking for a less arduous program, but students warn that this fact means it's overwhelming instead of incredibly overwhelming. Though Reed is thought of as more of a humanities-based school, science majors are becoming increasingly popular. "The sciences are strong at Reed as well," one student said, "we even have a nuclear reactor on campus now."

Two of the school's toughest courses, a writing-intensive freshman humanities course and the senior thesis, are required, but students have few complaints about them. The mandatory freshman course is "a common experience that unifies the student body and it's a great foundation for the rest of the Reed education," said one student.

Though free-spirited, Reedies are all focused and genuinely devoted to the pursuit of intellectual growth. "You go to Reed because you want to go to grad school," one student said simply. Whether they're designing their own physics experiments or writing their senior thesis on Shakespeare, Reedies are always passionate about what they do. "It's cool to be in an environment where everyone's interested in what they're studying," said one student. The students get to show off their laid-back side and introduce fellow students to their interests during Paideia, an event that takes place the week after winter break. During Paideia, everyone in the Reed community—except for professors—has the opportunity to teach a class. Reedies have taught everything from bike repair to politics during this week.

Study Hard, Party Hard

"The typical Reed student basically wouldn't fit in anywhere else. They're bookish, liberal hipsters, and also friendly and fun-loving," one Reedie said. Students explain that there is no social hierarchy at their school and everyone is accepting of each other. There are no cliques of popular jocks, since Reed doesn't participate in intercollegiate sports. Reedies instead use their competitive spirit in intracollege Ultimate Frisbee and rugby games.

Students' only complaint about their fellow Reedies is the fact that there isn't enough racial diversity. "Reed is basically white and rich," one sophomore said. Despite the racial homogeneity of the current student population, students report that Reed is working to recruit a more multicultural student body. Others compliment Reed for its financial aid efforts that attract students from a variety of socioeconomic backgrounds.

Most Reed students are heavily involved in extracurricular activities and unique student organizations. Popular groups include the Bike Co-Op and the Reed Kommunal Shit Kollectiv, fondly known as RKSK, which organizes parties and gives out free goodies to students in the spirit of communism. When Reedies aren't studying or involved in student organizations, they are doing their other favorite activity: partying. "I put up with five days of shit for two nights of awesome," one student noted. Most Reedies love a good party as much as they love a good lecture. "There's always something going on: parties, dances or great concerts," one enthusiastic student said. The biggest party of the year is Renaissance Fayre, a three-day party unanimously praised by Reed students that starts after the seniors turn in their theses. Alcohol and drugs are widespread at this and many other events, so much so that the other nickname for Reed students is Weedies. "There's really good pot in Oregon," one student explained. Many students said that a great deal of the smoking of this really good pot takes place at the student union. "Though there is a fair amount of alcohol and drug use, people are responsible and there's no pressure to take part if you don't want to," said one freshman.

> "At Reed we say that you can have only three of the following five: good academic performance, a relationship, a good group of friends, extracurricular activities, or sleep."

For those who don't want to socialize under the influence, there is a substance-free dorm and many substance-free activities sponsored on campus. Many students said that because of Reed's pot-smoking image, the administration is now trying to keep substance use in check. However, students insist that there will continue to be many good times to be had at Reed. Because of the school's liberal Honor Principle, students can't get busted for alcohol or drug use unless they harm or embarrass another student. "The focus of the Honor Principle is student responsibility instead of keeping us from having fun," said one student.

With their heavy workloads, many student organizations, and plentiful parties, most Reedies say that it is difficult to date seriously. "After you've been doing work all day, all you want to do is sleep. The last thing you want is to have to take someone out to dinner," explained one Reedie. Though some report having long-term relationships, most say that there are a lot of random hookups. "At Reed we say that you can have only three of the following five: good academic performance, a relationship, a good group of friends, extracurricular activities, or sleep," concluded one student.

Eating in the Reed Bubble

Most Reedies report that there is so much to do on campus, they don't often venture into Portland. "Sometimes it feels like we're in a Reed bubble and not really in Portland," one student said. There is a good selection of restaurants to visit when students do take the short bike ride to the city, but students don't seem to suffer from a lack of good food on campus either. A private food contractor, otherwise known as a catering company, provides Reedies with their meals. The food is said to be "pretty damn good" with a plethora of vegetarian and vegan options.

The only complaint Reed students do have with their dining services is the way their meal plans are set up. Each student starts off the semester with a certain amount of points, known as Commons Cash. Each food item costs a certain amount of Commons Cash, meaning students must budget the amount of money they spend at each meal. Many students find themselves very close to the end of their Commons Cash before the end of the semester is in sight. This reality forces some to leave the Reed bubble and find their nourishment in Portland, if they would rather not replenish their Commons Cash account.

Pretty Sweet Campus

Reedies have praise for their college's campus. "It's really beautiful. There are tons of trees and the buildings are all brick and pretty. Some of the dorms are sort of strange looking, but they're all fine," one student said. Even if a few of the dorms look weird, no one has any complaints about how they are set up inside. All dorms are coed and not segregated by grade. There are about 20 students per floor and one RA whose job is to offer advice and study breaks, not supervision. "Most rooms are divided doubles, which works well because everyone gets their own space," said one Reedie. Students report that the administration does a great job choosing roommates for freshmen. Old Dorm Block, which is prettier than it sounds, is one of the most popular residences. Students say that though Reed's dorms are popular, many upperclassmen live off campus. Suitable housing abounds, with plenty of apartments right across the street from campus.

Though they say that prospective students should definitely visit Reed before they make a decision, Reedies couldn't be happier with their college. As one freshman concluded, "If you're intelligent, ready to debate about anything, willing to be crazy and not afraid of weird shit, Reed is the place for you."—*Keneisha Sinclair*

FYI

If you come to Reed, you'd better bring "the mental capacity for all the work and costumes for the theme parties."

The typical weekend schedule is "work all Friday afternoon and then party, work all Saturday morning, then go to a concert or play and then party, and work like crazy all Sunday."

If I could change one thing about Reed, "I'd make it more diverse."

Three things every student at Reed should do before graduating are "go to the Rhody Gardens at night, chase the Doyle Owl, and write a great thesis."

University of Oregon

Address: 1217 University of Oregon, Eugene, OR 97403
Phone: 800-232-3825
E-mail address: uoadmit@uoregon.edu
Web site URL: www.uoregon.edu
Year Founded: 1876
Private or Public: Public
Religious Affiliation: None
Location: Urban
Number of Applicants: 10,012
Percent Accepted: 88%
Percent Accepted who enroll: 35%
Number Entering: 3,207
Number of Transfers Accepted each Year: 2,086
Middle 50% SAT range: M: 496–611, CR: 486–606, Wr: Unreported
Middle 50% ACT range: Unreported
Early admission program EA/ED/None: EA

Percentage accepted through EA or ED: Unreported
EA and ED deadline: 1-Nov
Regular Deadline: Jan 15
Application Fee: $50
Full time Undergraduate enrollment: 16,473
Total enrollment: 20,394
Percent Male: 53%
Percent Female: 47%
Total Percent Minority or Unreported: 14%
Percent African-American: 2%
Percent Asian/Pacific Islander: 6%
Percent Hispanic: 4%
Percent Native-American: 1%
Percent International: 1%
Percent in-state/out of state: 68%/32%
Percent from Public HS: Unreported
Retention Rate: 84%
Graduation Rate 4-year: 65%

Graduation Rate 6-year: Unreported
Percent Undergraduates in On-campus housing: 22%
Number of official organized extracurricular organizations: 250
3 Most popular majors: Business Administration/Management, Journalism, Psychology
Student/Faculty ratio: 18:1
Average Class Size: 20
Percent of students going to grad school: Unreported
Tuition and Fees: $19,992
In-State Tuition and Fees if different: $6,435
Cost for Room and Board: $8,478
Percent receiving financial aid out of those who apply, first year: 60%
Percent receiving financial aid among all students: 33%

Located in Eugene, the University of Oregon is a big school by numbers and a liberal arts school by heart. Boasting intelligent and approachable professors alongside a powerhouse football program, Oregon is full of school spirit despite the often dismal weather.

Relaxed Academic Environment

Academically, Oregon offers the best of both a large research university and a liberal arts curriculum. With scores of classes to choose from and accessible faculty, students find themselves in a "relaxed academic environment" where they can explore diverse subjects and create close relationships to professors. It is true that for many introduction level classes, students may find themselves surrounded by hundreds of their classmates—one student reported a class of around 500. However, these classes are often tempered with really small discussion sections and a wide range of seminar-style classes.

To encourage students to explore new subjects, Oregon developed a general education curriculum. To earn a typical bachelor's degree, students must take classes in three "areas of human knowledge"—arts and letters, social science, and science. In addition, students interested in a Bachelor of Arts must fulfill a foreign language requirement, and students pursuing a Bachelor of Science must study math. Students find the requirements somewhat irritating, but one student summed them up perfectly. "You end up getting a broader education," she said. "It's annoying, but it's worth it."

With almost 80 majors, finding an interesting subject matter isn't an issue. Students cited the psychology, business, and political science departments as particularly popular. For ambitious students, there is the opportunity to double major or explore Oregon's scores of minors and several certificates.

In addition, Oregon is home to the Robert D. Clark Honors College, the oldest of its kind. With its separate application and more rigorous admissions process (with an additional essay required), the Clark Honors College is home to 200 or so incoming students each year. They are required to take several different classes and write a thesis to earn a diploma, but they can take advantage of an average class size of 19, student: teacher ratio of 18:1, and a smaller community.

The biggest change from high school academics, students said, was the increased amount of reading and emphasis on tests. However, the professors are there from day one to ease the transition. They encourage students to use them as a resource. One freshman mentioned that "most have quite a few office hours during the week and want to meet with students or help with questions." Some professors offer office hours in cafés. Another offers an even better incentive—students that attend office hours are entered into a drawing whose winners get a dinner with the professor and homemade apple pie. "All the professors I've had are really low-key, laid back and very approachable," said one student. "Don't get me wrong though; there's always those few who aren't any of these things, but I like to believe and I have experienced that most professors are pretty good," another added.

All in all, it is not too difficult to do well, if you "do what you're supposed to do, listen in class" and make use of the incredible resources Oregon presents. One student noted that "some classes are pretty difficult and you need to work hard to do well and others are more laid back. It's really great when you get a schedule with a good mixture."

Outside the Classroom

At the end of the week, Oregon students are pumped to catch up on sleep and have a lot of fun. A typical weekend is very relaxed, with time to hang out with friends and "catch up online with TV shows." Nights often involve partying within the Oregon community. A freshman in a sorority said that sororities and fraternities were "dominant in our life" but didn't have too much of a presence for the rest of campus. That being said, there are many Greek parties over the course of any given weekend.

Oregon is a dry campus, with drinking prohibited within the dorms, fraternities and sororities. With a "Greek police" that goes after those seen holding a beer, students are much more likely to "pre-game" and drink before going to a party. In addition, marijuana is very prevalent on campus, for those who are interested.

Dorms are the center of life for most freshmen, though after a year in the dorms, many upperclassmen move to off-campus apartments. Prior to arriving in Oregon, students fill out surveys indicating their personalities, cleanliness and music choice, among other things, to help Oregon pair up compatible students. One student said that "dorms are a great way of meeting people . . . during the beginning of the year it's really easy to meet people if you're open to it."

Generally, there are 2 RAs per hall, whose jobs are to organize activities, keep the peace, and, if you're lucky, make spaghetti dinners. Students described them as "like camp counselors, but less in your face."

Students love the campus, full of "brick buildings, trees, and grass everywhere." One student is particularly a fan of the Frolf (Frisbee golf) course, which "shows the beauty of what is on campus." Oregon is not too big of a school, and while many students have bikes, one student estimated that "at a really slow, leisurely walk" it would take less than 10 minutes to get from her dorm to her farthest class.

> "Within minutes of being on campus, I could just tell that I would be really happy here and I was right."

Eugene, Oregon, is a small city centered around the university. Students feel very attached to Eugene culture. "The whole town loves the Ducks," one student said. Though homelessness in Eugene is an issue, students describe the campus as pretty safe. "If it's at night, you walk with a friend and make good decisions," said a freshman, who was comforted by the fact that "cops are everywhere, and everything is lit."

There are a couple of dining halls, which have different specialties. Though there is a grocery store nearby, many students see cooking as a "hassle rather than a convenience." Students cited Hamilton's fish tacos, Caron's lamb kabobs, and the New England clam chowder as being particularly good.

Mighty Ducks

Oregon students take pride in the school's stellar athletic program, especially its prowess as a Division I football powerhouse. "Sports are huge here!" one student said, saying that the school is "all about football because we have a good team." Football games are especially amazing—it is likely that at some point in their Oregon career, many students will boast a Facebook profile picture of them screaming at a football game and wearing a duck mouth.

Besides football, the baseball, girls volleyball and lacrosse teams are fan favorites. For those lacking unbelievable athletic skills, many students go running on their own and "everyone does at least one intramural sport."

It's Gray, Not Grey

Located in the Pacific Northwest, Oregon gets plenty of rain. However, don't have too negative an outlook. One student said he

was surprised that it hasn't actually rained as much as he expected.

At the end of the day, Oregon is still a big school with over 20,000 students. The concept of a community is still very tricky. "When it comes to sports," one student said, "our community (students and faculty) all come together and it is quite amazing. When sports are not involved, we could easily just be random strangers to each other."

However, most students don't regret their decision to come to Oregon for a second. One student said that he never expected to go to Oregon. "But within minutes of being on campus, I could just tell that I would be really happy here and I was right."—*Mason Kroll*

FYI

If you come to Oregon, you'd better bring "rain boots and an umbrella"
What surprised me the most about Oregon was "how friendly everyone was."
If I could change one thing about Oregon, I'd "change the rain into sun, because when the sun is out here and the weather is somewhat warm, the campus is so beautiful and it is so great being outside."

Willamette University

Address: 900 State Street Salem, OR 97301
Phone: 503-370-6303
E-mail address: libarts@willamette.edu
Web site URL: www.willamette.edu
Year Founded: 1842
Private or Public: Private
Religious Affiliation: Methodist
Location: Urban
Number of Applicants: 2,983
Percent Accepted: 77%
Percent Accepted who enroll: 19%
Number Entering: 435
Number of Transfers Accepted each Year: 102
Middle 50% SAT range: M: 550–660, CR: 570–690, Wr: 550–660
Middle 50% ACT range: 25–29
Early admission program EA/ED/None: EA

Percentage accepted through EA or ED: 91%
EA and ED deadline: 1-Dec
Regular Deadline: 15-Jan
Application Fee: $50
Full time Undergraduate enrollment: 1,932
Total enrollment: 2,320
Percent Male: 45%
Percent Female: 55%
Total Percent Minority or Unreported: 13%
Percent African-American: 4%
Percent Asian/Pacific Islander: 5%
Percent Hispanic: 3%
Percent Native-American: 0%
Percent International: 5%
Percent in-state/out of state: 31%/69 %
Percent from Public HS: 80%
Retention Rate: 87%

Graduation Rate 4-year: 72%
Graduation Rate 6-year: 73%
Percent Undergraduates in On-campus housing: 68%
Number of official organized extracurricular organizations: 107
3 Most popular majors: Biology, Economics, Psychology
Student/Faculty ratio: 11:1
Average Class Size: 15
Percent of students going to grad school: 41%
Tuition and Fees: $28,416
In-State Tuition and Fees if different: No difference
Cost for Room and Board: $7,000
Percent receiving financial aid out of those who apply, first year: 92%
Percent receiving financial aid among all students: 92%

With majestic brick buildings and a stream running through campus, Willamette University, the first on the West Coast, offers a quintessential liberal arts education in the heart of Salem, Oregon. Willamette students treat college as a time to branch out and discover their passions, from Frisbee to scuba diving. Though the rain-heavy winters can be a bit dreary, close friendships and a glowing community give Willamette students a love of their school and a love of learning.

Emphasis on Inquiry

Students consider the best part of a Willamette education the intimate classroom setting. With an average class size of 14, even popular introductory level classes have no more than 30 students. In such a small class, professors always know their students on a personal basis, encouraging them to ask questions. Professors are "very passionate about what they do," keeping classes interesting and very fluid. "If the conversation takes them elsewhere, they can follow," said one sophomore, who loved the interesting class discussions.

Willamette students also enjoy an extensive class selection, with classes ranging from "Men Looking at Women: a Study of Film" to "Writing Political Humor." Students consider Willamette's music department especially incredible, though they say that music and chemistry majors are notoriously difficult.

Like their counterparts at most liberal arts institutions, Willamette students must complete Gen Ed (general education) requirements, including foreign language, four writing-centered courses, and two Quantitative and Analytical Reasoning courses. In addition, students must take classes in each of six modes of inquiry: Understanding the Natural World; Creating in the Arts; Analyzing Arguments, Reasons, and Values; Thinking Historically; Interpreting Texts; and Understanding Society.

Students are rarely frustrated by these requirements; as many Willamette students initially are undeclared, they use the fulfillment of these requirements as a path to explore their own interests and take classes outside of their comfort zones. In addition, most people go way beyond the requirements, with a large percentage completing either a major and a minor or a double major.

Some students find it difficult for non-majors to get into certain classes, especially arts classes where classes are small and demand is high. However, another student said that with persistence, professors are understanding: "For the most part, if you show up you can get into any class."

Workloads can be light or heavy, depending on class selection. "I didn't get into really hard classes, so I have about 2 hours of work a night," one freshman stated. "But I have friends that don't have lives because they have so much homework." Early risers are in for a shock; one student noted, "You don't really go to bed before 10 o'clock." Students who wish to do well must remember to put the proper effort into their classes. "If you study hard and do your homework it will reflect on your grades," one student said. "It's not difficult to get an A, it just means a lot of work."

A Small Pond

"Everyone kind of knows everyone," one student said. "Walking to and from class, you'll know every third person." "People know how you're doing, what you're up to and who you are much more than other, bigger schools," another added. Students find everyone at the school friendly, open-minded and accepting, and feel comfortable to be themselves in every situation. From the beginning, students form close friendships, whether on pre-orientation trips ("Four years later, everyone on those trips are still super bonded," a student said), through classes, or in the dorms.

> **"Everyone kind of knows everyone. Walking to and from class, you'll know every third person."**

Dorms are a big part of social life, with weekly activities from midnight munchies every Monday to game nights on Thursdays. Separated mainly into east side and west side, dorms often throw parties and, on Halloween, the Willamette International Studies House even redecorates as a Haunted House. Also, there are some themed ones, such as the outdoor adventure house and a substance-free one. While there are RAs on almost every floor, students agree they are pretty relaxed and chill, not out to get you.

Most people stay on campus over the weekends, but some leave to go home or to concerts in nearby Seattle or Portland (the latter around one hour away). Though there's not much to do in downtown Salem, on- and off-campus parties dominate the weekend social scene. Greek life is very prevalent on campus, but definitely doesn't overtake the rest of the social scene.

While there is a lot of drinking and a good deal of marijuana, a large amount of the student body doesn't drink at all—in fact, 2 out of the 5 fraternities are substance-free. School policy on underage drinking is understanding; if students get caught, there is an education system rather than a punishment system. According to a sophomore, students go to a hearing where they think about "how their actions have affected the community, and what they can do to make up for how they've taken from the community."

Sundays are often study days, and students take advantage of the beautiful campus and nearby coffee shops to get their work done. On particularly sunny days, students set up chairs by the Mill Stream (which forms a W in the center of campus) and enjoy the weather. Students especially sing the praises of the Bistro, a student-run coffee shop with a nice vibe that always plays music and sells a bunch of yummy treats. Sunday nights also offer hefty discounts at nearby restaurants, especially at the Ram, an American barbeque "like Outback Steakhouse with less steak and less Australia," said a freshman.

With over 100 clubs and varying levels of commitment, students can find many ways to get involved outside the classroom. Becoming a member of a club is a great way to socialize. One of the biggest on campus is the outdoors club, which offers tons of hiking, camping, and other nature trips. *The Collegian*, Willamette's weekly newspaper, includes staff writers and a slew of contributing writers; anyone can write for it. To get your own show on WU Wire, Willamette's radio station, a sophomore, who hosts shows Wednesday evenings, said that "all you have to do is fill out an application and select your time slot."

If even planning a Hawaiian luau or learning to flame-juggle sounds dull, it is pretty easy to start a club. With a petition signed by at least 10 people, the student body council will fund a new club.

Many students take advantage of Willamette's central location in Salem, across the street from Oregon's capitol building. Internships and community service abound, both in the political arena and in the nearby elementary school and hospital. In fact, students often find local politicians eating in the Willamette dining halls.

Home of the Bearcats

In the early days of the school, Willamette's football coach commented that his team was "as strong as a bear and quick as a cat," thus beginning a long tradition of Bearcat athletics. Though Willamette is no means a sports-dominated school, it boasts 16 Division III teams and lots of school spirit. Especially when playing rival Linfield College, students will show up to the games en masse, often donning red-and-gold shirts given to them in the beginning of the year. One student noted that "your group of friends is from everywhere, and you hang out with pretty much everyone from the school," meaning that it's likely students will be cheering on their friends.

Students not so interested in varsity athletics still have tons of other options, especially in the form of club and intramural sports. Club sports can either be relatively competitive, such as the rugby and ultimate Frisbee teams, or skills building, such as the Juggle/Unicycle club and, for those who wish they were at Hogwarts, the Quidditch club.

Run through an online, Facebook-like system called Athleague, intramurals offer another chance to run around outside. With several traditional leagues and many tournaments (including paper football), students compete for the coveted intramural t-shirt. "If you wear an IM shirt on campus, you're a champion," said one sophomore who already has two under his belt.

Other Cultures Just a Skybridge Away

Nearly 50 years ago, Willamette established a strong connection with a school in Japan, and in 1985, the Tokyo International University in America (TIUA) was created minutes away from campus. Each year, 100–200 foreign exchange students come from Japan to study in America. Though sometimes they may be shy, don't be afraid to branch out; by the end of the year they warm up and some students even request a TIUA roommate. TIUA leads to a huge Japanese presence on campus, whether you're interested in Japanese studies, study abroad in East Asia, or the Japanese cuisine found daily in Kaneko Café (including sushi Tuesdays).

Willamette prides itself on stellar for-credit study abroad opportunities, offering many programs of its own during the school year and breaks and accepting most from other institutions. More than half of the student body engages in some program within their four years at school in countries ranging from Argentina to France to Ghana.

The Willamette Community

Students love living at Willamette. The campus itself is incredibly safe and people often leave their laptops in places for hours at a time and they aren't touched.

Willamette as a community aims to be very socially aware, constantly working hard to be more sustainable and reduce waste, with weekly trayless Tuesdays. In the main cafeteria, students say there is a push for organic and healthy food, and above every entrée lies a list of ingredients. In general, food is surprisingly good, and with a flexible meal plan, students can enjoy the particularly tasty desserts.

The four months of constant rain should not place a deterrent on anyone who wishes to attend Willamette. "As long as you have rain boots and a North Face jacket, you'll be fine," one student advised.

The only time the rain comes into play is on someone's birthday. If you celebrate your birthday at school, make sure to dress appropriately. Your friends will throw you into the nearby stream (the verb that arises is "mill streamed"), which can be fun or very cold, depending on the season. Another campus legend is that if a couple kisses under the star trees (a set of five trees that, when looked at from below, make a star shape), they will get married. "And it's happened a surprising amount of times," one student noted.

Students love the tight knit and really supportive community that surrounds them every day at Willamette. "Anywhere you go on campus, you'll see a friendly face," one student said. Willamette would be nothing without its collection of interested, aware, and friendly students. "The people are what I like most about it," one student said. "The connections that I've made and the things I've learned from the people I've met at Willamette are definitely what I found to be the most valuable takeaway from college."
—*Mason Kroll*

FYI

What surprised me the most about Willamette when I arrived was "the laid back nature of the professors."

If I could change one thing about Willamette, it would be "its location—Salem's not really an ideal place to have a college."

If you come to Willamette, you'd better bring "rainboots; it rains straight for four months in a row."

Three things every student at Willamette should do before graduating are "get mill-streamed, try an intramural sport, and appear in the Collegian."

Pennsylvania

Allegheny College

Address: Box 5, 520 North Main Street, Meadville, PA 16335

Phone: 814-332-4351

E-mail address: admissions@allegheny.edu

Web site URL: www.allegheny.edu

Year Founded: 1815

Private or Public: Private

Religious Affiliation: United Methodist

Location: Rural

Number of Applicants: 4,243

Percent Accepted: 61%

Percent Accepted who enroll: 22%

Number Entering: 591

Number of Transfers Accepted each Year: 57

Middle 50% SAT range: M: 560–650, CR: 550–660, Wr: Unreported

Middle 50% ACT range: 23–28

Early admission program EA/ED/None: ED

Percentage accepted through EA or ED: 71%

EA and ED deadline: 15-Nov

Regular Deadline: 15-Feb

Application Fee: $35

Full time Undergraduate enrollment: 2,082

Total enrollment: 2,125

Percent Male: 44%

Percent Female: 56%

Total Percent Minority or Unreported: 8%

Percent African-American: 3%

Percent Asian/Pacific Islander: 3%

Percent Hispanic: 2%

Percent Native-American: 0%

Percent International: Unreported

Percent in-state/out of state: 60%/40%

Percent from Public HS: 83%

Retention Rate: 88%

Graduation Rate 4-year: 69%

Graduation Rate 6-year: 74%

Percent Undergraduates in On-campus housing: 78%

Number of official organized extracurricular organizations: 78

3 Most popular majors: Biology, Economics, Psychology

Student/Faculty ratio: 13:1

Average Class Size: 19

Percent of students going to grad school: 54%

Tuition and Fees: $32,000

In-State Tuition and Fees if different: No difference

Cost for Room and Board: $8,000

Percent receiving financial aid out of those who apply, first year: 83%

Percent receiving financial aid among all students: 69%

Founded in 1815, Allegheny is one of the oldest colleges in the United States. With a history longer than that of some of the finest and most reputed universities in the country, Allegheny College features a beautiful, pastoral campus with great learning opportunities, for which it earned a place among the top 40 schools in *Colleges that Change Lives*. If you are looking for an excellent liberal arts education and do not mind living in a quiet, small town located hours away from any major cities, consider Allegheny as a potential college choice.

Meadville? Where is That?

Meadville is a small, "post-industrial" town in western Pennsylvania. It is home to a population of only 14,000 people. The closest metropolitan area is Pittsburgh, PA, which is about 90 minutes away. Cleveland, the next nearest city, requires two hours of driving. As a result, although the school offers a quiet learning environment, it certainly has "neither the number nor the quality of activities that can be found in large metropolitan areas." While the Gator Activities Programming invites entertainers to perform on campus, it is obvious that "if you've always wanted to be in a city and have flashing lights and tons of things to do on the weekends, don't bother." Nevertheless, most students agree that "Allegheny has a beautiful campus." The college covers nearly 540 acres, including a natural reserve of 283 acres, as well as 203 acres dedicated to recreation. The campus offers great facilities such as an observatory, an art gallery, and a TV station, all for a small enrollment of about 2,100 students. With the nearby lakes and state parks, Allegheny is a great place for the enjoyment of nature and tranquility. As one student explained, "If you are looking for a small college in a rural and laid-back community, Allegheny is the place for you."

The college's relationship with Meadville, however, remains rather detached. "There tends to be clash between 'townies' and us Alleghenians," said a student. "But we are truthfully working on the relationship." While most students in the college come from middle-class families, the formerly industrial Meadville has been facing economic difficulties since the 1980s. As a result, Allegheny students are sometimes just seen as "a bunch of rich kids." At the same time, one student remarked, "The campus is rather closed off to the town of Meadville, although there are some students that go to bars and go shopping." There are about 30 restaurants in the area and several small stores. Nevertheless, with the nearest mall about 30 minutes away, "the town doesn't really have anything interesting for us to go there," one senior said.

Despite being in an isolated location, however, the students are very content with the safety of both Allegheny College and Meadville. Few dangerous incidents ever occur in the area, and the students agree that Allegheny is "a peaceful residential campus."

Majorly into Minors

A top-100 liberal arts college according to *U.S. News & World Report*, Allegheny provides its students with a well-rounded academic program. It is a relatively selective school: more than 75 percent of its students were in the top 20 percent of their high schools. The acceptance rate is generally around 60 percent, giving Allegheny a body of capable students. "Academics are the reason that everyone comes here," said a student.

Allegheny is well known for its science departments. "We have one of the best placements into med school in the nation," one Alleghenian said. "Our science departments are very hard. We don't curve grades like other colleges." Despite the belief that humanities and social science classes are less interesting and less difficult than science classes, most students agree that Allegheny "boasts excellent faculty in all fields." The construction of a $23 million state-of-the-art communications and theater center was completed in the spring of 2009 to help improve the school's reputation in humanities and arts.

The classes are based on hour credits. Most classes are four credits, and the stu-

dents need 131 credit hours to graduate. People generally take four to five classes per semester. One of the distinctive elements of Allegheny is its requirement of both a major and a minor, or a second major, which helps people to "achieve a more rounded education." The minor cannot be in the same academic division (humanities, natural sciences, and social sciences) as the major, meaning that the students have to take classes in very different fields, thus achieving the goal of a liberal arts education.

The school also has a vigorous set of requirements for its students. In addition to the mandatory classes in humanities, sciences, and social sciences, everyone is required to take three courses on academic planning, starting from second semester of freshman year to the end of sophomore year, to help prepare for the design of their programs of study and their activities. They also need to take three FS seminars during their freshman and sophomore years. These classes focus mostly on improving the students' ability to research and communicate ideas. There are more than 80 different seminars available to the students.

> "I've babysat kids for professors before. We are all equals here and students help professors and professors help students."

By the end of their sophomore year, students choose their majors among the 30 offered by Allegheny. The major requires anywhere from 36 to 48 credit hours and the completion of a junior seminar and a senior project. Students can also make their own major if they can justify the point of having their own course of study. The minor requires 20 credits, 12 of which must be outside the division of the graduation major.

The course load is often agreed to be challenging among Alleghenians. According to one student, "Allegheny College has one of the largest work loads for any class whether it be sciences, social sciences, or humanities. All areas are challenging—and encouraging—which Allegheny College facilitates its students to experience."

2,100 Students, One Tight-Knit Experience

Students at Allegheny maintain close ties with their professors. "Students and professors are all very close," said an Alleghenian.

"Professors often invite students to their house for a meal." Indeed, the small classes give plenty of opportunities for the students to interact with the faculty. When asked about the relationship between the students and the faculty, one interviewee said, "I've babysat kids for professors before. We are all equals here and students help professors and professors help students."

The dorms are similar to most colleges. About 78 percent of the students live on campus, with all students except seniors required to do so. According to an Alleghenian, a typical room would be "double 17 by 15, no AC." "Only the more expensive, new dorms have AC," added another student, who also pointed

out that, "Bathroom and shower space is not an issue. There are plenty of those."

Greek life is an important part of Allegheny. Being part of a fraternity or sorority gives sisters and brothers access to a series of activities. Nevertheless, there are plenty of other activities on campus so that the students do not feel left out if they opt out of Greek life. Alcohol is an important part of parties, and it generally can be found by anyone.

Allegheny is trying hard to improve its diversity. Currently, less than 9 percent of Alleghenians are ethnic minorities. The administration is making it a priority to recruit more minority applicants.—*Xiaohang Liu*

FYI

If you come to Allegheny, you'd better bring "a Nalgene. We are big on those."
If I could change one thing about Allegheny, I'd "lower the cost of tuition."
Three things every student at Allegheny should do before graduating are "go to Eddie's Footlong for hotdogs, play pool in the Game Room, and take yoga classes."

Bryn Mawr College

Address: 101 North Merion Avenue, Bryn Mawr, PA 19010-2859
Phone: 610-526-5152
E-mail address: admissions@brynmawr.edu
Web site URL: www.brynmawr.edu
Year Founded: 1885
Private or Public: Private
Religious Affiliation: None
Location: Urban
Number of Applicants: 2,150
Percent Accepted: 49%
Percent Accepted who enroll: 35%
Number Entering: 366
Number of Transfers Accepted each Year: 25
Middle 50% SAT range: M: 580–680, CR: 620–730, Wr: 620–720
Middle 50% ACT range: 27–31
Early admission program EA/ED/None: ED

Percentage accepted through EA or ED: 19%
EA and ED deadline: 15-Nov
Regular Deadline: 15-Jan
Application Fee: $50
Full time Undergraduate enrollment: 1,287
Total enrollment: 1,745
Percent Male: 0%
Percent Female: 100%
Total Percent Minority or Unreported: 22%
Percent African-American: 6%
Percent Asian/Pacific Islander: 12%
Percent Hispanic: 4%
Percent Native-American: 1%
Percent International: 7%
Percent in-state/out of state: 16%/84%
Percent from Public HS: Unreported
Retention Rate: 90%
Graduation Rate 4-year: 81%

Graduation Rate 6-year: 85%
Percent Undergraduates in On-campus housing: 95%
Number of official organized extracurricular organizations: 94
3 Most popular majors: English, Mathematics, Psychology
Student/Faculty ratio: 8:1
Average Class Size: 16
Percent of students going to grad school: Unreported
Tuition and Fees: $36,540
In-State Tuition and Fees if different: No difference
Cost for Room and Board: $11,520
Percent receiving financial aid out of those who apply, first year: 62%
Percent receiving financial aid among all students: 62%

Located in an ideal location just outside a major metropolis, Bryn Mawr's beautiful campus and motivated student body make it a desirable choice for many young women.

The common trait among all Mawrtyrs, as

they're called, is their overwhelming passion for their school.

Smaller Is Better

Academics receive top priority at Bryn Mawr, where they are described as "challenging but so rewarding." Despite the heavy workload, most students could not be happier. The school attempts to prevent a cutthroat environment with a unique honor code forbidding the discussion of grades between students. The honor code is strictly enforced and applies to class rank as well, which is not disclosed until graduation.

The most popular majors are English, Mathematics and Psychology. All students must take a Freshman Liberal Studies Seminar, known as the College Seminar, intended to prepare freshmen for college writing, especially for classes in which papers are required such as English, History, Anthropology and Sociology. In addition to the College Seminar, students must also fulfill core requirements intended to impart a broad liberal arts foundation. These include two labs, two natural sciences, two humanities and two social sciences. One of the best classes is said to be "Identification in Cinema," a film minor/art history major course taught by perennial favorite Homay King. In addition to King, the most popular professors include Mary Louise Cookson, a mathematics professor, and Gary McDonough, director of the Growth and Structure of Cities Program. In addition to Bryn Mawr's extensive course offerings, students have the option of taking classes at nearby Haverford College, Swarthmore College and the University of Pennsylvania.

The school also allows students to design their own Independent major. One student explained, "Any gap you may find in course offerings, you can often work with professors to fill, if you are truly interested and willing to commit to it." Another student knew of friends who had majored in Feminist Studies, Theater Studies, Film, and American Cultural Studies, all as Independent majors.

Unsurprisingly, classes at Bryn Mawr are small. Intimate classes foster intimate student/professor bonds. In addition to office hours, many professors make themselves accessible to students at all hours. Outside of the academic arena, many students babysit for their professors, walk their dogs, or go to their homes for dinner on a regular basis.

Another aspect of classes at Bryn Mawr is their accessibility to all class years. With a few exceptions, classes have a mix of freshmen through seniors. One student praised

this feature because it "gave me the opportunity to make friends who were older than me and acted as mentors."

Quiet but Lively

Bryn Mawr's location has a significant impact on its social scene. Students do not bewail its all-female student body because of the coed mingling afforded by the proximity of neighboring colleges Swarthmore and Haverford, with which Bryn Mawr has always enjoyed a close relationship. Haverford tends to have keg parties and dances, and the regular shuttle between the schools makes for easy access to parties.

Students at Bryn Mawr say that underage students looking to drink do not encounter many obstacles. Thursdays and Saturdays are the big party nights on campus, while Fridays are more toned down. "Thursday people party hard, and grin and bear it through their Friday classes," one student explained. When it comes to partying, as with most things at Bryn Mawr, tradition prevails. The biggest party of the year occurs at Halloween. There is usually a themed "East/West party" held in the connected Pembroke East and West dorms. Bryn Mawr and Haverford each host a drag ball, at Haverford the fall semester and at Bryn Mawr in the spring. Perry House and Radnor, both dorms, are known for throwing good parties. Radnor is sometimes unofficially used as a venue for small bands. According to one student, many of the best parties are after-parties following events like dance performances, culture shows, debate team meets, or a capella concerts.

Beyond the party scene, students hang out in local coffee shops like Cosi or Starbucks or the new coffee shop in town called Milkboy, where local musicians perform and which holds open mike nights. There is a larger Milkboy in an adjacent town two miles away. Both are affiliated with a local record production company of the same name and a current Bryn Mawr student has two albums out on their label. Another option for those interested in the arts is the renovated Bryn Mawr Film Institute, which shows art-house films and has begun cooperating with the Film Studies Department at Bryn Mawr.

For those looking to get away from campus, the local commuter rail system provides easy access to Philadelphia's Art Museum, restaurants and nightlife. The largest mall on the East Coast is 10 minutes from campus.

Most socializing takes place on campus, however, and is associated in some way with academics. One student explains that "while people are definitely social, it's nice to know you won't be the only one in the library on a Friday night." Most students hang out in their halls with friends, or in Canaday Library, which is "open, well-lit, and has sofas everywhere." The café inside, the Lusty Cup, is on the same floor as the 24-hour computing suite, making it a popular study area. A lot of socializing centers around clubs, sports and other extracurriculars because Mawrtyrs tend to be very involved.

Campus Life

At Bryn Mawr "the living is definitely good." Campus architecture is classic Gothic, with beautiful stained-glass windows and imposing stone. The newest dorm, Erdman, was designed by Louis Kahn as a modern Scottish castle. Students live in one of 14 residence halls. The absence of specially designated freshman dorms means that freshman housing can rival senior housing. Every dorm has women from all four years, and there is almost no difference in quality of rooms from freshman to senior year. Many rooms have bay windows, wood paneling, and fireplaces; some even have walk-in closets. Campus safety is not a concern. Students feel completely secure, even at night. Bryn Mawr's suburban location means that many students rarely lock their doors or their bikes, and lost wallets have been known to come back to their owners before they were noticed to be missing. Students love the dorms and campus in general, which could explain why 95 percent of the students choose to live on campus.

The food on campus is another reason. The dining halls at Bryn Mawr receive high marks all around. They are "very vegetarian and somewhat vegan friendly." The dining halls are completely student staffed as all freshmen who desire a campus job must start in the dining halls. Outside of the dining halls, there are also many excellent restaurants in the area and in nearby Philadelphia. Like the classes, dining halls are open to Haverford students as well, but since breakfast ends up being almost only Bryn Mawr women, you get lots of people in pajamas. In many cases, that's how they stay throughout the day. Designer brands can be spotted on campus, but for the most part dress is casual throughout the week. On the weekends students get dressed up and made up, and head out for fun. Though there may not be guys enrolled at Bryn Mawr, there are generally quite a few on campus. The women decide as a floor at the beginning of the year whether

their bathroom will be coed. Visiting men are simply expected to act responsibly.

Extracurriculars are another aspect which benefits from the small size of the school. According to one student, "If it isn't here already, you can make it happen." The small size of Bryn Mawr also allows freshmen to play an active role in their extracurricular activities. Student government is one of the largest organizations on campus, along with the Bi-College News, the Haverford-Bryn Mawr newspaper. There is also an active political community, with groups that span the political spectrum. Political groups are extremely active, and there are tons of dance groups (everything from Asian fusion to classical ballet) and a cappella. An active Rainbow Alliance helps to promote an open, accepting atmosphere for LGBT students.

> **"If it isn't here already, you can make it happen."**

The diversity of the student body is universally praised. Students come from all around the country and the world. Campus is described as being virtually "clique-free," and students say that there is no segregation whatsoever. "It's very, very diverse economically, socially, politically and religiously," one student said. Diversity is not only evident in the student body, but openly discussed as well. "We talk about it, a lot," a student explained. This often entails bringing up and discussing problems, as well as acknowledging any failures to address diversity issues within the community.

For all their strengths, Mawrtyrs rarely dominate the athletic field. School spirit is definitely not lacking in the least, but unfortunately that doesn't carry over to achieving many victories. There are exceptions, however. In 2007, Bryn Mawr's coed rugby team won the EPRU Division III championship and competed at nationals. Win or lose, students go out to support their teams (and Haverford's) even at away games. For the nonvarsity athletic types, there are good gym facilities, a pool, and plenty of safe places to run around campus. For almost every varsity sport there is a corresponding club team, so anyone can participate.

Tradition Reigns

Bryn Mawr's most distinguishing characteristic may be the Traditions (with a capital T). These are four events held throughout the year, aimed at welcoming the underclassmen into the community. The first Tradition is Parade Night, which welcomes the freshmen to campus with the singing of the school song. Lantern Night follows, each class holding up a lantern of a different color to identify themselves. Third is Hell Week, during which the sophomores get freshmen to do all sorts of crazy things, which the upperclassmen help them evade. Finally, in May the college president rides a horse into campus to begin the May Day celebrations, which focus on the senior class. One unspoken tradition is skinny dipping in the Cloisters, an act inspired by alumna Katharine Hepburn.

There is almost unanimous agreement among Bryn Mawr students that there is no place they would rather be. "So many of my classmates have described their attraction to Bryn Mawr as 'falling in love' or being 'magical,'" one student said. Small classes, a beautiful campus in a great location, and a diverse, passionate student body all make for a nearly ideal college experience. One student described her peers as "amazing." Another remarked that meeting alumnae is like meeting aunts or old family friends because of the shared bond that comes from the Bryn Mawr experience.—*Laura Sullivan*

FYI

If you come to Bryn Mawr, you'd better bring "passion: in studying, partying, rallying and relaxing. We are a pretty devoted-to-our-causes campus."

What's the typical weekend schedule? "Friday: relax if you have no class and go out at night. Saturday: during the day study, play a sport, volunteer, rehearse, work and then party. Sunday: spend far too long at brunch, study for an hour, eat dinner, go to SGA (our student government's open meeting), hang out with friends, stay in the library until midnight."

If I could change one thing about Bryn Mawr, I would "expand the Bryn Mawr bubble to include Philadelphia, get more students involved in off-campus communities."

Three things that every student should do before graduating are "get sunburned on May Day, join the crowd at 4 a.m. in Guild during finals, and sing good-night to the seniors during Step Sing."

Bucknell University

Address: 701 Moore Avenue Lewisburg, PA 17837

Phone: 570-577-1101

E-mail address: admissions@bucknell.edu

Web site URL: www.bucknell.edu

Year Founded: 1864

Private or Public: Private

Religious Affiliation: None

Location: Rural

Number of Applicants: 8,024

Percent Accepted: 30%

Percent Accepted who enroll: 40%

Number Entering: 957

Number of Transfers Accepted each Year: 57

Middle 50% SAT range: M: 630–710, CR: 600–680, Wr: 610–700

Middle 50% ACT range: 27–31

Early admission program EA/ED/None: ED

Percentage accepted through EA or ED: 39%

EA and ED deadline: 15-Nov

Regular Deadline: 15-Jan

Application Fee: $60

Full time Undergraduate enrollment: 3,583

Total enrollment: 3,719

Percent Male: 47%

Percent Female: 53%

Total Percent Minority or Unreported: 13%

Percent African-American: 3%

Percent Asian/Pacific Islander: 6%

Percent Hispanic: 4%

Percent Native-American: <1%

Percent International: 3%

Percent in-state/out of state: 25%/75%

Percent from Public HS: Unreported

Retention Rate: 95%

Graduation Rate 4-year: 85%

Graduation Rate 6-year: 88%

Percent Undergraduates in On-campus housing: 86%

Number of official organized extracurricular organizations: 150

3 Most popular majors: Biology, Business Administration, Economics

Student/Faculty ratio: 11:1

Average Class Size: 26

Percent of students going to grad school: Unreported

Tuition and Fees: $39,434

In-State Tuition and Fees if different: No difference

Cost for Room and Board: $8,728

Percent receiving financial aid out of those who apply, first year: 62%

Percent receiving financial aid among all students: 58%

Bucknell, a liberal arts school situated in rural central Pennsylvania, offers the quintessential small campus feel. Small class sizes, close relationships between teachers and students, flexible and accommodating faculty, and beautiful new facilities are all qualities that create the charming and personable feel of this community.

Accessible Academic Area

Like many small schools, Bucknell can boast an excellent student-teacher ratio that results in personal relationships between students and faculty. Students claim professors are flexible and almost always available: "You can just walk right into their office at almost any time and sit down and talk," says one student. Students' descriptions of professors have really revealed the faculty's involvement and investment in their students. As one student said, "I really feel like the teachers are there to teach us, not just instruct us. It is a subtle but important difference." Only professors teach courses and teaching assistants, sometimes considered a nuisance when left in charge, are employed as a helpful supplement to lecture courses.

Perhaps one of the most impressive features of the academic curricula is the consistently small class sizes. The "large" intro level courses are sparse and usually have about 100 people. For the most part you will find yourself in more personal class settings of 20 to 30 people. As you move into the upper level courses classes are even more intimate, ranging from 13 to 20 people. Some classes are competitive to get into, especially those at the upper levels, but like one student said, "most of the time I haven't had a problem with getting into a class; the biggest problem I have had is fitting a class into my schedule when there are a lot of cool classes I want to take. The one time I had a problem, I just spoke with the teacher and he let me in."

The workload, like at any college, "is what you make it. You can get by taking easy courses or you can challenge yourself. But to get an A you really have to work at it." The prestigious management and engineering schools draw in a lot of majors; however, economics, biology, English and psychology are common majors as well. Though Bucknell may boast a strong science and quantitative course program, its smaller majors like International Relations and Animal Behavior have strong reputations as well. Bucknell operates on a semester system and like any good liberal arts college, is invested in a well-rounded education for its students based in a core curriculum. Core requirements are broad topics, including intellectual skills courses, tools for critical engagement courses, and disciplinary perspectives.

Out Late Livin' the Life

With the majority of the students living on-campus and being fairly isolated, the party scene is the center of campus social life and is hard to miss every Wednesday, Friday, and Saturday. Greek life at Bucknell is big; in fact over 50% of sophomores, juniors, and seniors are in a frat or sorority. But students are not allowed to rush until their sophomore year, so a lot of underclassman partying occurs on campus in the dorms. Though membership in a sorority or fraternity will definitely improve your party options, if that is not your thing you can still make it onto the register list (which is the list of invites for the select campus-wide frat parties) if you have any friends in the house. Specific sports teams will often dominate a frat house. Perhaps this innate segregation within the student body leads to exclusive, tight-knit groups, but as one non-frat student said, "the people are cliquey, but it is a big party scene and once you are out it is easy to meet people."

> "I really feel like the teachers are there to teach us, not just instruct us. It is a subtle but important difference."

About 10 percent of students live in off-campus housing, called "downtown houses," which gives students the freedom to host their own parties on their own property. But not all this wild partying goes unchecked. It has been observed that police enforcement has been increasing over the last year or so, even in the downtown housing area. One needs to be aware that the school has in place a policy that discourages underage and out-of-hand drinking. It is a point system where, for example, one or two points will be given if an underage student is caught with an open drink, and 10 points can earn a suspension.

The school sponsors interesting non–alcohol related evening activities such as concerts and guest speakers: "Just the other day Bill Nye the Science Guy came and the auditorium was completely full, which doesn't happen that often," said one student.

However, concerts and speakers are much more of a rarity than parties and are not always students' number one choice.

There isn't much of a dating scene at Bucknell. Most students would generally agree that random hook-ups are much more common and dating is not the norm. As one freshman said, "Oh yeah, hook-ups are definitely popular. I've hooked up with six people already and it's only been a month and a half!" What a statement, but overzealous freshman status is not something that should be overlooked in this case!

Wait, Who Are You?

When asked to describe the student body with a stereotype, one student said "preppy white people. You look around and all the guys are wearing red shorts, or yellow shorts, or khaki shorts with a polo and popped collar." This view that there is a homogenous student population both racially, socioeconomically, and even ideologically is consistent with student perceptions and diversity statistics. As one west-coaster put it, "There is a feeling of East Coast pretension; the people are a little more self-centered than I am used to on the West Coast." Though there is a fairly balanced pool of political views, that is obviously not enough to be considered truly diverse, and the school administration seems to be aware of this and has invested in long-term plans to improve the diversity of the student population.

The Bucknell Bubble

The campus is an idyllic rural setting with beautiful, mostly historic buildings in the red brick, Georgian revival architectural style with a couple of modern buildings in-between. In fact, a new engineering building was added to the campus and is shared by undergrads and the small graduate population as well. Everything is easy to get to, making "it the epitome of a walking campus." For the most part all the dorms are nice places to live, maybe with the exception of some freshman housing. The freshman housing is fairly spread out, but the central freshman hall, as one can imagine, is the less desirable of the living spaces and is assigned to you ahead of arrival. Starting sophomore year, students enter the room lottery. Bucknell has a unique system called "block booking rooms" which guarantees that you can live next to your friends no matter if you are in different rooms with different lottery numbers or not. It's also easy to do. Though not all dorms are a microcosm of the student body, there are two that have become the designated athlete dorms, one that is reserved for sorority living because there are no sorority houses, a special-interest house that is substance-free, and one dorm that is more or less the quiet dorm, or "geeky dorm."

The meal plans and dining halls are flexible and tasty. There is an assortment of meal plans to choose from catering to different eating habits that range from the unlimited plan to the declining balance where items are charged to your account individually. There are various dining areas, each with a different taste and style, including a "marketplace," and most of which are open from 7 a.m. to midnight (though not always serving hot food), which is convenient for late-night studiers. Most students are satisfied with their on-campus cuisine and don't go out to the "downtown" area (which is misleading because it is really just a main drag) to eat out at the restaurants or bars.

Free Time . . . What?

Students have endless opportunities to get involved in clubs, volunteering, organizations, and sports. There are over 150 clubs and organizations operating through the school and twenty-seven men's and women's varsity athletic teams. Students seem to feel that the sports teams have a large presence on campus. To facilitate such interests, the school has built impressive athletic centers including a new field house, and a new basketball arena for games, and there are complete weight and exercise facilities for athletes and non-athletes alike. The student body has quite a bit of team spirit and pride for their school sports, with men's basketball definitely taking the cake. Almost every game is sold out. When asked what makes Bucknell unique, one varsity athlete answered "the mix of a Division 1 athletic program and a small school environment."—*Shaughnessy Costigan*

Carnegie Mellon University

Address: 5000 Forbes Avenue, Pittsburgh, PA 15213
Phone: 412-268-2082
E-mail address: undergraduate-admissions@andrew.cmu.edu
Web site URL: www.cmu.edu
Year Founded: 1900
Private or Public: Private
Religious Affiliation: None
Location: Suburban
Number of Applicants: 13,527
Percent Accepted: 38%
Percent Accepted who enroll: 29%
Number Entering: 1,465
Number of Transfers Accepted each Year: 59
Middle 50% SAT range: M: 670–780, CR: 620–720, Wr: 620–710
Middle 50% ACT range: Unreported
Early admission program EA/ED/None: ED

Percentage accepted through EA or ED: 17%
EA and ED deadline: 1-Nov
Regular Deadline: 1-Jan
Application Fee: $70
Full time Undergraduate enrollment: 5,998
Total enrollment: 11,064
Percent Male: 59%
Percent Female: 41%
Total Percent Minority or Unreported: 61%
Percent African-American: 5%
Percent Asian/Pacific Islander: 22%
Percent Hispanic: 6%
Percent Native-American: 1%
Percent International: 15%
Percent in-state/out of state: 23%/77%
Percent from Public HS: Unreported
Retention Rate: 95%
Graduation Rate 4-year: 70%

Graduation Rate 6-year: 86%
Percent Undergraduates in On-campus housing: 64%
Number of official organized extracurricular organizations: 225
3 Most popular majors: Computer Engineering, Computer Science, Liberal Arts and Sciences
Student/Faculty ratio: Unreported
Average Class Size: 15
Percent of students going to grad school: Unreported
Tuition and Fees: $39,564
In-State Tuition and Fees if different: No difference
Cost for Room and Board: $10,050
Percent receiving financial aid out of those who apply, first year: 75%
Percent receiving financial aid among all students: 64%

One group of students is painting a fence in the center of campus to advertise an upcoming party. Others are watching a play put on by the drama school. In the computer clusters, some students are playing Starcraft. Many engineering students are in the library working on problem sets. On a typical Saturday night at Carnegie Mellon University, students do all these things and more.

We Make Robots, but We Aren't Robots

Carnegie Mellon University is made up of six separate undergraduate colleges: the Mellon College of Science, the Carnegie Institute of Technology, the College of Fine Arts, the College of Humanities and Social Sciences, the Tepper School of Business, and the School of Computer Science. When applying to Carnegie Mellon, students are accepted into a specific school. Each school and each major has different requirements. Many consider the requirements in engineering to be the most burdensome and the requirements for majors in the College of Humanities and Social Sciences to be the easiest. Some undergraduates complain that it can be difficult to take a class outside your own college. According to one freshman in the College of Humanities and Social Sciences, "It is close to impossible to take a class in the College of Fine Arts (art/drama/music) if you are not enrolled in that school."

Most undergraduates describe the academics as "rigorous" and "intense." The most prestigious and the most difficult majors are generally in the arts, engineering, and computer science. Classes are difficult and fast-paced, but the work often produces tangible results very quickly: "We learned how to build robots within the first three weeks of class, and then built a robot every week after that," said a student. One engineering student commented, "You get a great education because you learn how to think, not just mechanically compute. We make robots, but *we* aren't robots." On the other hand, some students refer to the College of Humanities and Social Sciences as "H & Less Stress." Students consider English, psychology, and modern languages to be the slacker majors. Carnegie Mellon offers a wide variety of majors; in fact, the school is the only college in America to offer a bagpipe major.

An engineering student raved about the quality of her professors: "I have had teachers respond to my emails within five minutes at 12:30 a.m." Some students in the College of Humanities and Social Sciences are less satisfied with the quality of the teaching: "The caliber of the professors [in arts and sciences] is nowhere near that of the other schools." Class sizes range from below 20 for seminars and electives to about 100 people for introductory classes, although the size of some popular lecture classes can be twice that.

What is a Social Life?

Because of the intense academics, some students complain about the lack of social life on campus. According to a freshman, "The social life here is what you make of it. Midnight is the time to go down to clusters, do the insane amount of work given here, or duke it out in Starcraft." One senior said the typical weekend at CMU is 70 percent work, 30 percent fun. One-dollar movies play on campus Thursday through Saturday nights. There are also weekly late-night programs sponsored by different clubs. Many students give high marks to the plays that the drama school produces. Students also go out to restaurants and bars close by in Oakland and Squirrel Hill. One student said, "Some people also take advantage of the free pool tables, Ping-Pong, foosball and shuffleboard

in the UC game room. And there is always studying."

The fraternities and sororities on campus are easy to rush and an integral part of the social scene on campus. Parties are held regularly—especially by Kappa Kappa Gamma, Phi Kappa Theta and Theta Xi. Unfortunately, parties are often little more than crappy beer and bad music, according to students, except for the occasional beach party, jungle party or foam party. "You can avoid Greek life if you just join other activities," said one student. However, freshmen usually only have the option of frat parties because they don't know enough people to go to other parties. Underage drinking is officially not allowed on campus, and those caught imbibing illegally will be punished. However, "it's pretty easy to get alcohol if you want it," said one girl. "As long as no one sees it and you're not being stupid, there haven't been many incidents involving underage drinking busts."

> "You can always find someone to hang out with who's exactly like you, or someone whose mind-set is totally different."

CMU is diverse inside as well as outside the classroom. Students hail from all 50 states and 45 different countries and are self-described as "intellectual, studious, talented, ambitious and competitive." According to one student, "You can always find someone to hang out with who's exactly like you, or someone whose mind-set is totally different." Freshman year is the best, according to a student, because "by sophomore year, a lot of people keep their doors shut." The social groups that form during freshman year often stay together over the four years. One junior said that Carnegie Mellon "is very cliquish—especially among the ethnic groups." "CMU has a varied assortment of personalities, from übergeeky (computer science majors) to the girls that you didn't like in high school (business majors)," said a senior. "Most people are really nice, although sometimes you have to be the outgoing one.... You definitely see a lot of clubs that I doubt exist at other schools, like the robotics club. Just the other day, they had a competition to make robots that can create root beer floats!"

Many females complain about the selection of men on campus. Even though 59 percent of the undergraduate population is male, some complain that a large percentage of the guys lack social skills. According to one female freshman, "The odds are good, but the goods are odd."

Adequate Dorms and Food

Only freshmen are required to live on campus. The quality of the dorms varies greatly from dorm to dorm. Most students feel that the housing is adequate, if a little small. Students rated RAs in the dorms as considerate, helpful and nice. Mudge, a converted mansion, is the students' favorite dorm, with suite-style, spacious rooms and a gorgeous courtyard. Some of the newer dorms, like New House, even have air conditioning, which can be nice on those still, hot days at the beginning of the school year. Donner, on the other hand, is "a dungeon, with small dingy rooms and shared bathrooms." Some students opt after the first year to live in the cheaper apartments off campus, although there aren't many nice places nearby. If you are willing to take a five-minute bus ride (which is free with tuition), many more options open up. Many students like living in the dorms because "you get to meet people, there are fun events (like pancake night, movie night, etc.) and lots of people to help with your homework!"

The food and the dining halls were given negative reviews in general, but many students say the situation is improving. Some students complain that the meal plan is too expensive. One senior female said, "Even the smallest meal plan is too much food for me." Depending on the meal plan, you get a certain number of "blocks," which can be used for all-you-can-eat cafeteria food or to buy a certain amount of food at a number of different campus eateries. The selection includes Skibo Coffeehouse, Asiana (with good BBQ chicken), and Taste of India. There is even a sushi place, a deli, and a completely vegan-friendly eatery. In addition, there is always some place to find food at 11 or 12 at night. One student said, "There aren't a lot of healthy choices, and not enough normal food, like lasagna or meatloaf kind of things. It's also pretty expensive if you just buy a meal with cash." Freshmen have to use their blocks during certain time slots and at certain places in order to avoid losing them. Upperclassmen warn future freshmen to get as small a dining plan as possible. Those in the dining hall are either "in cliques or loners," said one sophomore. Instead, people choose to eat off campus, at the numerous food trucks near campus, or to cook for themselves. For dates,

students often leave campus and head over to Station Square, an area with nice restaurants.

Pittsburgh

CMU is a small campus, with many patches of grass and yellow-brick buildings with copper roofs that have turned green over the years. "This is a beautiful and safe campus," said one freshman. The art building is especially notable. One student said, "Every time I walk in the art building I see some new—usually odd, but amazing—work of art." "It's very pleasant here," one student said of the campus, but added a caveat: "Unless it's a really nice day, you won't see anyone hanging out outside—we're notorious for hanging out in computer clusters."

CMU is located in the suburbs of Pittsburgh, an area considered safe, although "like any big city there are some shady areas." Students give Pittsburgh high ratings, and one student happily commented, "I love the fact that I am in a city but at the same time feel that I have an actual campus." Another student said, "There are many restaurants, bars and museums within a mile of campus." The buses are free with college ID, so it is easy to get into the city. UPitt is also nearby and provides lots to do on weekends.

Filled with Traditions

One tradition at Carnegie Mellon is "painting the fence." In the center of the Cut—the green that runs across campus—is a steel fence covered with hundreds of layers of paint. Students are allowed to paint the fence between midnight and dawn. Most nights a student group will go out under the moonlight and paint the fence to advertise their event. Some students stay behind until the sun rises, guarding the fence to make sure their work does not get painted over.

The campus is also proud of the Scottish ancestry of CMU's founder, Andrew Carnegie. There is a Kiltie band and bagpipers that play at football games. Carnegie Mellon also has an annual spring carnival. Events include a buggy race, officially called Sweepstakes, where CMU students compete in an on-land version of tobogganing around campus; Mobot, where students build robots that race though a course; and Fiesta de Primavera, an end-of-the-year celebration that includes volleyball, jousting, sumo outfits, slides, flypaper and big punching gloves.

In short, if you prefer building robots to football, and if cutting-edge technology is as important to you as a great arts program, then CMU is the place to be.—*Harrison Korn*

FYI

If you come to Carnegie Mellon, you'd better bring "your calculator."

What is the typical weekend schedule? "Read 500+ pages, write papers, do laundry, project meetings, research, eat, sleep . . ."

If I could change one thing about Carnegie Mellon, "I would make the food better."

Three things every student at Carnegie Mellon should do before graduating are "paint the fence, develop a social life, and play capture the flag in Wean."

Dickinson College

Address: P.O. Box 1773 Carlisle, PA 17013
Phone: 717-245-1231
E-mail address: admit@dickinson.edu
Web site URL: www.dickinson.edu
Year Founded: 1783
Private or Public: Private
Religious Affiliation: None
Location: Suburban
Number of Applicants: 5,349
Percent Accepted: 43%
Percent Accepted who enroll: 27%
Number Entering: 621
Number of Transfers Accepted each Year: 27
Middle 50% SAT range: M: 600–680, Cr: 600–690, Wr: 650–720
Middle 50% ACT range: 26–30
Early admission program EA/ED/None: EA and ED

Percentage accepted through EA or ED: 56%
EA and ED deadline: 15-Nov
Regular Deadline: 1-Feb
Application Fee: $60
Full time Undergraduate enrollment: 2,369
Total enrollment: 2,369
Percent Male: 44%
Percent Female: 56%
Total Percent Minority or Unreported: 24%
Percent African-American: 5%
Percent Asian/Pacific Islander: 4%
Percent Hispanic: 4%
Percent Native-American: 5%
Percent International: 6%
Percent in-state/out of state: 27%/73%
Percent from Public HS: 61%
Retention Rate: 91%

Graduation Rate 4-year: 78%
Graduation Rate 6-year: 82%
Percent Undergraduates in On-campus housing: 92%
Number of official organized extracurricular organizations: 140
3 Most popular majors: Businss, Political Science, Psychology
Student/Faculty ratio: 12:1
Average Class Size: 13
Percent of students going to grad school: 36%
Tuition and Fees: $35,450
In-State Tuition and Fees if different: No difference
Cost for Room and Board: $8,980
Percent receiving financial aid out of those who apply, first year: 78%
Percent receiving financial aid among all students: 48%

Located in the tiny town of Carlisle, Pa., Dickinson is a close-knit school with prestigious international business, foreign language, and political science programs. Dickinson is perfect for the student who dreams of traveling the globe, but wants to go to a college where everyone knows his or her name and Greek life abounds. It is also a great place for preps and those who love them.

Go to Class, Go Abroad

One of the first things that Dickinson students proudly mention about their school is its small class sizes. There are virtually no classes with more than 40 students, with many Dickinsonians happily saying that their classes have even fewer students. Stu-

dents also praise their professors for being extremely approachable and helpful. "Our professors care a lot and are truly interested in what the students have to offer," said one freshman.

When your professors care and your classes are small, you better go to class. Dickinson assures that this happens with a strict attendance policy. Up to 20 percent of the grade for a course can be based on attendance, so those who care about their GPAs don't skip. Students say that it's relatively easy to get into classes that you want. Freshmen are encouraged to take 400-level courses with upperclassmen. Students said that you should expect to work at Dickinson, but that "it's the ideal workload. It's not too easy, but it's not too hard either."

Like most colleges, Dickinson has distribution requirements that students need to fulfill outside of their majors. They must take a writing course and a quantitative course, as well as courses in the arts and humanities, the social sciences, the laboratory sciences, U.S. diversity, Comparative Civilizations, physical education and language. Dickinsonians say that the distribution requirements are easy to complete, and just like at the local Wal-Mart, you can often get a "two for the price of one" deal where one class fulfills two requirements. However, many students admit that people put off their distribution requirements and then have to cram them all into senior year. In addition to trying to knock out a few requirements, all freshmen take a Freshman Seminar. In these seminars, students build on the research and writing skills they honed before they got to Dickinson by studying topics that appeal to them.

> "Basically, if you're a guy, you have to join a frat or you'll be a social pariah."

Students are equally enthusiastic about Dickinson's study abroad program. Students can go abroad for a semester or a year to a variety of Dickinson-affiliated programs around the world. Students go to countries in Europe, Africa, Asia and South and Central America simply to take classes in a setting more exciting than small-town Pennsylvania or to totally immerse themselves in a different culture. Most of the programs are not in big cities, but in small towns where students live with host families and can avoid annoying tourists. Dickinson's study abroad program is so popular that one student said, "Every winter it's like a new class of people arrives because so many juniors are coming back from study abroad." International business, foreign language and East Asian studies classes are extremely popular and renowned at Dickinson, further proving the international leanings of its students.

The Greekfest
Social life at Dickinson is dominated by Greek life. Fraternity parties are usually open to everyone and always very well attended. Students could not stress enough the importance of the frat scene. "Basically, if you're a guy, you have to join a frat or you'll be a social pariah," one student explained simply. There are four sororities on campus, including the infamous Kappas,

who are known as "snobby and exclusive," but girls do not have to join them to be a part of the social life, since guys love girls to come to their frat parties.

Just like any other school with a huge Greek life, alcohol is abundant at Dickinson. In fact, Dickinson is sometimes called "Drinkinson." The administration is not at all happy with this nickname and is very tough on alcohol. They forbid kegs on campus and will take away the house of any fraternity that has a keg for fear that they promote binge drinking. The fraternities have found clever ways around the keg restriction by having cocktail parties. Students also say that the strict rules are often unsuccessfully enforced.

Dickinson is not all about drunken debauchery. Frequent dances and concerts are hosted at the Depot and the Quarry, two on-campus hangouts. For such a small school, Dickinson attracts some big names to these events. "I was in the front row at the Death Cab for Cutie concert and there were like only 50 people there. It was amazing," one satisfied student said. These kinds of events offer a fun occasional alternative to getting drunk at the frats.

Happy Little Preppy Family
Dickinsonians are pleased with the close-knit community that makes up their school. While one student complained that she feels like she "knows the entire student body," most students like the communal feel. Dickinson must do a great job of choosing roommates for freshmen, because the friends they make in their dorms their first year are the friends they have for the next three. "Most freshmen roommates stay together," one student explained.

The fact that it's a school where everyone knows your name really has an effect on the Dickinson dating scene. "By the time they're upperclassmen, most students are in relationships here, but many freshmen are still in their high-school relationships or having random hook-ups," said one student. Some Dickinsonians utilize their study-abroad yearnings closer to home by hooking up in the East Asian Studies room. Dickinson students are careful not to hook up too randomly, however, because the fear of running out of attractive partners in such a tiny school is real.

Dickinson students do more than party, hook up and make phone calls to their long-distance loves. They participate in varsity, club or intramural sports with soccer, basketball and volleyball being the most popular.

They are involved with student government, school publications, drama, comedy and foreign language clubs. Some students stressed that Dickinson needs to create community-service organizations to add a giving-back element to student activities.

The typical Dickinsonian, students say, is a white, upper-middle-class, private-school grad from the East Coast. "I really need to get a Polo shirt. I don't have one and everyone has them here," one student responded when asked about Dickinson's prep factor. The administration strives for diversity, but like many things at Dickinson, it ends up having an international flavor. "Our diversity is from international students. Most of the black people you'll see on campus aren't from the United States but from Africa," one freshman explained.

Pretty Campus, Ugly Town
Dickinsonians have little praise for the town of Carlisle. "It's a typical mid-Pennsylvanian town: boring, kind of trashy, and there's nothing to do," complained one student. Another summed up Carlisle by simply explaining that many residents have mullets. To escape the small-town stuff, students can make the 20-minute trip to Harrisburg, Pennsylvania's capital.

Though they are displeased with the town, Dickinson students don't complain too much since their campus is beautiful. "It's just what a college should look like," one student said. Dickinsonians laud their campus's limestone buildings, wide open space and lush hills. The school is not only pleasing to the eye, but also pleasing to the stomach. Its meals are time and again rated among the best of college cafeteria food. Dickinsonians have slightly less praise for their dorms, at least the inside of them. Though most are renovated and some—like Goodyear, an upperclassman dorm—are legendary, some students complain about forced triples and huge differences in the amount of students housed in different dormitories. "My dorm has 40 people and the other freshman one has 400. It's nice, because my dormmates are like my family, but sometimes I wish our dorm was bigger," one girl explained.

Dickinson seems to have it all. It offers its students the chance to be a part of a close-knit community but travel around the world, the chance to live in a small town but visit a big city, and the chance to party hard but challenge oneself academically. With all these options, Dickinsonians graduate feeling as if they made the right choice.—*Keneisha Sinclair*

FYI
If you come to Dickinson, you'd better bring "a Polo or Lacoste shirt."
The typical weekend schedule is "Friday: watch a movie, then get dressed up and pregame before going to the frats; Saturday: sleep, do work, go out to dinner, then go to the frats; Sunday: sleep and do your work."
If I could change one thing about Dickinson, "I'd make it not so focused on Greek life."
Three things every student at Dickinson should do before graduating are "hook up in the East Asian Studies room, study abroad and walk to the Wal-Mart."

Drexel University

Address: 3141 Chestnut Street, Philadelphia, PA 19104
Phone: 215-895-2400
E-mail address: enroll@drexel.edu
Web site URL: www.drexel.edu
Year Founded: 1891
Private or Public: Private
Religious Affiliation: None
Location: Urban
Number of Applicants: 3,823
Percent Accepted: 72%
Percent Accepted who enroll: 45%
Number Entering: 1,238
Number of Transfers Accepted each Year: Unreported
Middle 50% SAT range: M: 560–670, **CR:** 530–630, **Wr:** Unreported
Middle 50% ACT range: 20–27
Early admission program EA/ED/None: None

Percentage accepted through EA or ED: NA
EA and ED deadline: NA
Regular Deadline: 1-Mar
Application Fee: $50
Full time Undergraduate enrollment: 10,318
Total enrollment: 17,001
Percent Male: 57%
Percent Female: 43%
Total Percent Minority or Unreported: 26%
Percent African-American: 10%
Percent Asian/Pacific Islander: 13%
Percent Hispanic: 3%
Percent Native-American: 1%
Percent International: Unreported
Percent in-state/out of state: 52%/48%
Percent from Public HS: 70%
Retention Rate: 84%
Graduation Rate 4-year: 53%

Graduation Rate 6-year: 60%
Percent Undergraduates in On-campus housing: 35%
Number of official organized extracurricular organizations: 136
3 Most popular majors: Information Science, Mechanical Engineering, Business Administration
Student/Faculty ratio: 15:1
Average Class Size: 14
Percent of students going to grad school: 18%
Tuition and Fees: $27,200
In-State Tuition and Fees if different: No difference
Cost for Room and Board: $11,610
Percent receiving financial aid out of those who apply, first year: Unreported
Percent receiving financial aid among all students: Unreported

S ituated in the University City district in the heart of Philadelphia, Drexel University is a private university devoted to intensive education and hands-on training. Although infamous for its not so pleasant architecture, Drexel University is more known for its innovative and famous cooperative educational programs across many disciplines in numerous fields. Famous for its engineering, business, and nursing programs, Drexel aims to educate knowledgeable yet practical students who are ready to enter the workforce immediately after graduation.

Co-op and No-op

Academics at Drexel can be overwhelming at times, especially when it comes to deciding what to study. The undergraduate colleges include the College of Information Sciences and Technology, College of Arts and Sciences, College of Engineering, Goodwin College of Professional Studies, LeBow College of Business, Westphal College of Media Arts and Design, and the College of Nursing and Health Professions. All students at Drexel complete the University/College core requirements by taking classes in computing, writing, math, analysis, economics, history, philosophy, political science, humanities, and the fine arts. The core curriculum is rounded off by an early capstone course in The Drexel Experience where students learn about navigating the college experience and transitioning smoothly from high school to college, especially college life in a city like Philadelphia. Classes combine a variety of classroom based lectures and smaller group sections where students break off into small groups. "The majority of classes can be overwhelmingly large, with a sense of anonymity, but professors are always accessible," says a freshman.

The most popular majors at Drexel include business administration, mechanical engineering, information science, biology, and nursing. The school of engineering is perhaps one of Drexel's most well-known programs with degrees offered in a wide variety of fields and only one of 17 programs nationwide to offer the Bachelor's of Engineering in Architectural Engineering. The engineering curriculum is one of the harder programs on campus, with intensive core studies in engineering sciences and specialization in the many sub-fields of engineering. As one of the country's largest private engineering schools, Drexel students have access to a wide array of resources and help while still having "accessible Professors who all love engineering," as one junior said. What's unique about Drexel's program, however, is the opportunity to work and learn hands-on while still in school. Many Drexel engineering undergraduates chose to co-op, or intern, with an employer while still in school.

Speaking of co-ops, Drexel has one of the largest co-op programs out of all private and public universities in the country that is highly distinguished in education. Students choosing to partake in the co-op spend the year after their sophomore or junior year working full-time, basically interning, for companies, businesses, non-profits, or other organizations, depending on their intended field of study. While the majority of co-ops take place in the greater Philadelphia region, national and international co-op opportunities are available to "cater to every major, every taste, and every person," noted a sophomore. Prominently featured companies that students work for include but are not limited to: GlaxoSmithKline, Unisys Corporation, Microsoft, Lockheed Martin, Comcast, and QVC. Typical salaries for co-op students can range from $400 per week for those in accounting positions to upwards of $800 dollars per week for chemical engineering positions. Students typically earn anywhere from $11K to $17K during a six month period during their co-op experience. "It's great to be able to make some money, network, and get real-world work experience while still in school!" reminisced a senior. Perhaps that is the reason why the majority of students opt for the co-op; earning their degree in five years rather than the typical four years at most other institutions. It is also the reason why many employers tend to hire full-time employees from former co-op interns.

In . . . West Philadelphia

Life at Drexel can be as exciting or tame as one wants it to be. The location in the heart of Philadelphia, with access to major public transportation hubs, allows students to partake in the rich cultural, academic, and entertainment opportunities that The City of Brotherly Love has to offer. Entrenched in University City, Drexel students have the option to, and often do, party at neighboring schools such as the University of Pennsylvania. The party scene often revolves around dorm parties on the weekends with others choosing to hit Center City or surrounding clubs. Of course, as with nearly every college campus, alcohol is a part of the college scene but it's not dominating by any means. In a city rich with arts, entertainment, and restaurants, there are many things to do to suit everyone's tastes.

Philadelphia offers great night life and day life. With its rich history, the city is home to historical landmarks such as the Franklin Court, a Philadelphia tribute to Benjamin Franklin, and the Betsy Ross House. The Liberty Bell is also a popular tourist attraction in addition to Fairmount Park, the largest landscaped urban park in the world with over two hundred statues. Arts and entertainment can be found along the Avenue of the Arts with the Philadelphia Orchestra, Academy of Music, Arden Theater, and the world famous Philadelphia Museum of Art among many others. Shopping ventures at The Gallery at Market East, Chestnut Hill Shops, Liberty Place, Center City, and the Italian Market can be had for a mere subway ride from campus.

> "It's great to be able to make some money, network, and get real-world work experience while still in school!"

Life on campus can feel a little bit claustrophobic. Some students complain of the "institutional" looking buildings that "aren't that great to look at," as a freshman remarked. All freshmen are required to live on campus for their first year. The majority of all students are housed in Calhoun, Caneris, Kelly, Myers, North, Race Street, Towers, and Van Rensselaer Halls. Students in the Pennoni Honors College are singly housed in the brand-new Millennium Hall together as a learning community with their own Honors Lounge. Students may also elect to live with others who have the same academic interests as themselves in learning communities. Each community is housed in a designated area of a residence hall with a common area. Students can choose communities with interests in business, engineering, Honors College, media and design, informational technology, health professions, and a special Sophomore Year Experience community. All residences are in close proximity of the Northside Dining Terrace, Handschumacher Dining Center, and Ross Commons. The two Dining Centers offer typical take-out fare with a variety of choices and Commons offers snacks in addition to full meals. "The food can get a little dull after a while," said a senior. However, most students tend to move off campus and room with their friends in private apartments after freshman year. Still, some stay in university housing.

The Scene

The social scene at Drexel can be a little cliquey, but everyone "seems to be nice," said a junior. Everyone seems to find their group of friends that they stick to for college. The student body can be a little homogenous. "There is a large contingent of international students, but everyone else seems to be white and from the tri-state area," remarked a freshman. However, that's changing as more and more students are attracted to the school and the recruiting effort to attract these students. Still, if one is looking for a multicultural melting pot on campus, look again. Luckily, Philadelphia offers all of that and more. In spite of the lack of diversity, everyone finds their niche within the larger Drexel community in the numerous clubs, activities, and IM sports. "It is what you make of it," said a senior.

Regardless, one thing is for certain: the Drexel experience is quite a unique one that can be very challenging and rewarding. "You get what you put in," reminisced a senior. The combination of strong business, engineering, and health professions programs coupled with real-world practical experience offered by the co-op program delivers an educational experience that is unlike most.—*Hai Pham*

FYI
If you come to Drexel, you should bring "your party clothes, something homey, and a desire to intern."
If I could change one thing, it would be "more diversity."
Three things everyone needs to do before graduating: "Get a cheesesteak from Geno's, frolic in Fairmount Park, and visit the Italian Market."

Franklin & Marshall College

Address: PO Box 3003 Lancaster, MA 17604-3003	**EA and ED deadline:** 15-Nov	**Graduation Rate 6-year:** 84%
Phone: 877-678-9111	**Regular Deadline:** 1-Feb	**Percent Undergraduates**
E-mail address: admission@fandm.edu	**Application Fee:** $50	**in On-campus housing:** 80%
Web site URL: www.fandm.edu	**Full time Undergraduate enrollment:** 2,164	**Number of official organized extracurricular**
Year Founded: 1787	**Total enrollment:** 2,164	**organizations:** 90
Private or Public: Private	**Percent Male:** 48%	**3 Most popular majors:**
Religious Affiliation: None	**Percent Female:** 52%	Business, Government,
Location: Rural	**Total Percent Minority or**	Biology
Number of Applicants: 5,632	**Unreported:** 12%	**Student/Faculty ratio:** 10:1
Percent Accepted: 36%	**Percent African-American:** 4%	**Average Class Size:** 19
Percent Accepted who enroll: 29%	**Percent Asian/Pacific Islander:** 4%	**Percent of students going to grad school:** 25%
Number Entering: 589	**Percent Hispanic:** 4%	
Number of Transfers Accepted each Year: 42	**Percent Native-American:** <1%	**Tuition and Fees:** $38,630
Middle 50% SAT range: M: 610–690, CR: 600–690, Wr: Unreported	**Percent International:** 9%	**In-State Tuition and Fees if different:** No difference
Middle 50% ACT range: Unreported	**Percent in-state/out of state:** 34%/66%	**Cost for Room and Board:** $9,870
Early admission program EA/ED/None: ED	**Percent from Public HS:** 56%	**Percent receiving financial aid out of those who apply, first year:** Unreported
Percentage accepted through EA or ED: 57%	**Retention Rate:** 94% **Graduation Rate 4-year:** 79%	**Percent receiving financial aid among all students:** 40%

Though they call themselves Diplomats, not many Franklin & Marshall students will be heading to Washington to write legislation. Despite its liberal arts reputation and mascot, Franklin & Marshall is a school that caters to the sciences. Double majors and extracurricular leaders thrive in the close community at F&M, where high expectations are found inside and outside the classroom. Students at the College jump headlong into community service, pursue hands-on academics and research opportunities, and take advantage of unmatched faculty interactions. However, their drive doesn't force them underground—Diplomats know how to have fun like students at any other college.

Small Classes, Big Research Opportunities

Though F&M specializes in the sciences, students can experience a diverse set of classes and departments before choosing a major. "In general, it's a liberal arts curriculum," one student said. "They have a core curriculum but they really try to promote freedom in choice of study." Students must take classes from each of the three realms of study in the "Foundations" program: Mind, Self and Spirit; the Natural World; and Community, Culture and Society. This core provides the base on which upperclassmen build their majors.

Many students arrive in Lancaster expecting to major in F&M's impressive pre-med program. The pre-med track often proves to be more difficult than prospective students had imagined, as one biochemistry major pointed out: "There's a huge population of pre-med students here and that population decreases each year, pretty much exponentially." The same student, expressing a sentiment common among F&M science majors, said the only easy majors were "anything not science." Among non-science majors, the most popular concentrations include government, psychology, and business. But one English and neuroscience double major noted that "it's not unusual to see students majoring in two very different areas of study."

In either the sciences or the liberal arts, students agree that faculty interaction sets F&M apart. With a student-to-faculty ratio of 10:1, non-introductory classes are typically small and professors accessible. Even larger lectures often come to less than 50 students. One student doing chemistry research alongside his professor said that research opportunities at this small college "are readily available to the extent that they would be at any research university." Many students stay over the summer in nearby apartments to get involved with F&M faculty. Research, both during the year and over the summer, gives underclassmen the chance to contribute to groundbreaking work. "It's not just those in the sciences who want kids in their majors to take part in their research," one student said. "And I'm always invited over to the professors' houses for dinner afterwards to meet their families."

Lancaster Living

As one of the oldest colleges in the country, F&M is full of open spaces. In the fall and spring, Hartman Green swells with students playing Frisbee, reading, and generally enjoying themselves. Freshmen and sophomores are required to live on campus, all within a block or two of the Green. Most agree that the accommodations are comfortable but not exceptional. Hallways include both first-year and second-year students, with the latter having the option of living in doubles or suites. After sophomore year, most students move into the abundant and affordable housing that the school offers across the street.

Lancaster provides F&M students with more than they usually expect when arriving on campus. Although small and relatively rural, the downtown area is full of fresh farm markets, affordable restaurants, and several clubs for students on the weekends. The restaurants become a tantalizing diversion from the typical college grub, about which one student reasoned, "I don't think college food is ever as good as home, but it won't kill you." And if you just can't resist a real home-cooked meal, many students from the East Coast use cars to escape to Philadelphia and Baltimore, which are both two hours away. "The campus doesn't become a ghost town on the weekend, but it is definitely convenient," one Philadelphian said.

The Weekend Wrap-up

Whether it's the weekend or not, students say that the campus is known to be cliquey. Fraternities and sororities are not officially recognized by the College but do exist in noticeable numbers. Nevertheless, Greek life does not dominate the social scene. "Greek life is an accessory," one student said. "By no means do you have to be in it to meet friends." Among the student body there is a clear divide between those who drink and those who do not. Those who don't drink argue that alcohol is only a small part of life at F&M: "What people say who came here 20 years ago is you have a miserable time here if you don't associate with Greek life, but what I see tells me that isn't the case." In contrast, those who do drink claim they can't imagine the school without it. Recently the administration has been increasingly strict in enforcing alcohol policies, including the prohibition of alcohol in dormitories of students under 21. In addition, local police have increased their watch over college night life—to the extent of breaking up parties and using undercover agents. Some say the police have taken it too far. "They're cracking down on us this year," said one frustrated student.

> "The first thing you notice is it's a pretty homogeneous student body. You'll probably see rich and white, for one thing."

Much like frats, athletics play an accessory role on campus. Sports teams are a popular yet limited outlet for school pride. While the Division III squash, basketball and football programs are perennially solid, few students go crazy for them. Instead, Diplomats find other ways to show their school pride. "A lot of people walk around in F&M clothing," one student said.

The Typical Diplomat

Students insist diversity improves each year, but few have any difficulty in describing the average F&M student. Almost all are academically driven. Almost all are interested in getting involved in activities outside the classroom. And almost all are upper-middleclass, white Northeasterners. "There's a distinct lack of diversity," one sophomore sighed. "The first thing you notice is it's a pretty homogeneous student body. You'll probably see rich and white, for one thing."

In addition to a lack of racial and socioeconomic diversity, several students added that religious and sexual diversity is relatively rare. But religious and social minorities that do exist emerge as a vocal faction of the student body. Hillel, the center for Jewish life, hosts events geared at all students regardless of faith, in part because F&M is "still predominantly WASP." The small gay population is visibly noticeable, but not very important in the social lives of straight students.

Politically, F&M is not particularly vocal despite a fairly diverse collection of political leanings. While one sophomore suggested that there was an even split between conser-

vatives and liberals, she added that most campus conservatives were liberal on social issues. For this reason, most students can be found in greater Lancaster volunteering. Tutoring, mentoring and volunteering with the elderly are popular options.

For most Diplomats, academics still come first. Each student comes to F&M interested in learning for learning's sake, and the drive of the typical F&M student reflects this interest. "There are a lot of competitive people here," one student conceded. "But the people who are competitive are competitive with themselves. I'd say students are definitely in it for the long haul together."—*Andrew Bartholomew*

FYI

If you come to Franklin & Marshall, you'd better bring "the drive to take advantage of all the academic opportunities."

What's the typical weekend schedule? "Thursdays and Fridays: Parties start around 11:00. Saturdays: Quiet during the day. Parties start earlier. Sunday: Homework day."

If I could change one thing about Franklin & Marshall, it'd be "the police cracking down on us."

Three things every student should do before graduating are "pee on the Ben Franklin statue while drunk," "go to the Farmers' Market downtown," and "eat dinner with your professor."

Gettysburg College

Address: 300 North Washington Street Gettysburg, PA 17325
Phone: 717-337-6100
E-mail address: admiss@gettysburg.edu
Web site URL: www.gettysburg.edu
Year Founded: 1832
Private or Public: Private
Religious Affiliation: Lutheran
Location: Suburban
Number of Applicants: 5,794
Percent Accepted: 37%
Percent Accepted who enroll: 33%
Number Entering: 714
Number of Transfers Accepted each Year: 15
Middle 50% SAT range: M: 610–670, CR: 610–690, Wr: Unreported
Middle 50% ACT range: 27–29
Early admission program EA/ED/None: ED I, ED II

Percentage accepted through EA or ED: 40%
EA and ED deadline: 15-Nov, 15-Jan
Regular Deadline: 1-Feb
Application Fee: $55
Full time Undergraduate enrollment: 2,497
Total enrollment: 2,497
Percent Male: 49%
Percent Female: 51%
Total Percent Minority or Unreported: 10%
Percent African-American: 3%
Percent Asian/Pacific Islander: 1%
Percent Hispanic: 2%
Percent Native-American: 1%
Percent International: 4%
Percent in-state/out of state: 22%/78%
Percent from Public HS: 66%
Retention Rate: 92%
Graduation Rate 4-year: 80%

Graduation Rate 6-year: 84%
Percent Undergraduates in On-campus housing: 90%
Number of official organized extracurricular organizations: 140
3 Most popular majors: Management, Political Science, English
Student/Faculty ratio: 11:1
Average Class Size: 18
Percent of students going to grad school: 35%
Tuition and Fees: $37,600
In-State Tuition and Fees if different: No difference
Cost for Room and Board: $9,100
Percent receiving financial aid out of those who apply, first year: 70%
Percent receiving financial aid among all students: 70%

A mention of Gettysburg College most often brings to mind the picturesque fields that served as major battlefields during the Civil War and the location of Abraham Lincoln's famous Gettysburg Address. Come to Gettysburg, though, and you will find more than just a campus steeped in history. On this site of enormous historical importance, Gettysburg students live and learn in the most thoroughly modern of facilities. At this small liberal arts college, students are accomplishing more than war reenactments and historical tours. They thrive in both the intimate academic atmosphere and the extensive social scene.

Integrated Learning

Classes at Gettysburg tend to be very small, and with a student-to-faculty ratio of 11:1, it's no wonder classes rarely reach twenty students. Professors teach all classes, and students agree that the professors are very accessible. According to one senior, "The professors here teach what they are passionate about. They really respect us and are interested in our minds." This type of enthusiasm appears to be uniformly present throughout the student body. Students start out freshman year with a unique Gettysburg experience, the First Year Seminars. Freshmen pick from a variety of courses like "The Makings of the Great American Musical." The learning experience does not stop at the end of the sixteen-person seminar, however. Residential Hall assignments for freshmen are directly linked to their freshman seminar and college writing courses; that way informal discussion is facilitated outside the classroom setting. Students come to Gettysburg fairly aware of the requirements of the college, from the freshman seminar to the requirements mandating that students take courses in fields outside their major. Gettysburg students seem to agree that the requirements provide a broad liberal arts base without restricting their ability to explore. The part that draws the most complaints is the natural science requirement. But, as one student pointed out, "The science departments seem to understand and create a few courses designed for seniors to meet their graduation requirements as painlessly as possible." These include courses such as "Chesapeake Bay" and "Natural Catastrophes and Geologic Hazards," which fill up within minutes of the beginning of senior course registration.

Gettysburg students cite the most popular majors as political science, history, psychology, English and management, which is also named one of the easiest majors. The sciences are generally regarded as the hardest majors. Some of the more popular classes include "Philosophy of Food," "The Bible and Modern Moral Issues" and "Economics of Sports." Students here fall within a range of attitudes toward academics, ranging from the super-motivated to the apathetic. Most students, though, "take academics pretty seriously and take an active stance in their education." According to one student, "The perfect description of Gettysburg College is that you work for a B, but you work your butt off for an A." In the words of another senior, "Gettysburg provides a great library and an amazing faculty. Anyone who claims he isn't get anything out of his academic endeavors isn't trying hard enough."

Immaculate Grounds

Students universally agree that Gettysburg provides world-class facilities. Musselman Library remains open twenty-four hours Sunday through Thursday and provides tables for group studying, as well as quiet zones with a variety of seating and lighting options and even private rooms for studying. One student professes his love for the library's availability and says, "I don't think anyone can every truly appreciate how valuable the library hours are until your computer breaks at 2 a.m. when you have a paper due or when your roommate throws a party the night before an exam." The Breidenbaugh, where most English classes are held, is cited as a particularly beautiful building on campus.

There are currently two gyms: Bream, the main gym with an indoor track and weightlifting room, and Plank, the smaller gym with a cardio and aerobics focus. There are complaints that both gyms fill up quickly because of the popularity of working out among students, so Bream gym has been recently renovated to address this issue. There are also swimming pools and numerous sports fields on campus.

The town of Gettysburg itself is somewhat sleepy and isolated and caters mostly to tourism. Students often get involved in the town via tutoring or other forms of volunteer work. Students also benefit from some of the bars and restaurants, the local movie theatre, the outlet mall nearby and the proximity to Baltimore and Washington, D.C.

Trapped On-Campus

Students regard residential life as above average. According to one student, "After visiting other schools, it seems Gettysburg has some of the nicest dorms." Housing gets better as you rise through the ranks. Freshmen live in standard doubles off a hallway, but upperclassmen dorms can be described as downright luxurious. Dorms have common rooms, often with big-screen TVs. Many options are apartment-style with a full kitchen, living room, and private bathroom. Seniors generally get suite-style housing with all singles in the Quarry Suites. There are also theme houses owned by the college that are often closer to campus than dorms are. Many male students opt to live in their fraternity houses. Juniors and seniors are allowed to live off campus, but ninety percent of students choose to stay on campus. On-campus housing provides many parking options and there are even opportunities for coed living. There are Residential Assistants, but most understand the realities of college life and enforce rules reasonably. No alcohol is allowed in freshmen dorms, though.

Gettysburg food is often ranked in the top twenty nationally. One student goes as far as to call it "incredibly good for a college dining hall." One dining option, Servo, boasts a sauté line, grill and sandwich area, eggs made to order, and a vegan corner. In the College Union Building is a coffee shop, bookstore, and the Bullet Hole, another dining option that serves quick meals and is open later than any of the other options. Ike's serves made-to-order subs, soup and wraps. As satisfied as students are, though, it is not uncommon to head off campus to eat on weekends at places such as Pizza House or nearby chain restaurants.

Popped Collars and Pearls

The Vineyard Vines and Vera Bradley sold in the school bookstore sum up the stereotype of the average Gettysburg student. Drawing its student population mostly from the tri-state area and New England, students seem to feel that one thing Gettysburg does lack is diversity on campus, both racially and economically. Many are white and preppy and come from a privileged, private-school background that is reflected by the BMWs, Jaguars and Range Rovers littering the student parking lots. While students laud the administration for working to increase diversity on campus, there is still little intermixing between various groups. On the upside, one student remarks, "That is not to say there is an 'I'm better than you' attitude on campus and most students, regardless of income

level, would feel comfortable at this school." Students are also universally described as friendly and approachable. The small, tightly knit campus means that people are welcoming and willing to lend a hand.

> "It's a safe bet that if you're not out at a frat sometime between Wednesday and Saturday, then you're probably not doing anything entertaining."

Students are also involved in a variety of extracurricular activities that draw people together. Division III sports are popular, although by junior year, many nonstarters tend to drop out. Football is the most vocal and visible team because of its size, but lacrosse has also been nationally ranked for the past four years. Men's and women's soccer have also been recently nationally ranked and were in the playoffs. Games often attract sports fans cheering their Bullets on. Intramurals, service organizations and various clubs also draw a large crowd.

To Be Greek or Not to Be

Gentlemen, you better set foot on campus ready to make friends with some girls! Greek life is the single largest affiliation on campus and accounts for almost half of the campus population. Frat parties tend to dominate weekend activities, especially for underclassmen, and it is always advisable for guys to show up with a few extra girls in tow to ensure admittance. According to one student, "It's a safe bet that if you're not out at a frat sometime between Wednesday and Saturday, then you're probably not doing anything entertaining." On weekends, students frat-hop with ease between houses located within feet of each other. Some popular fraternities include Phi Delt and Phi Sig. Sororities are also popular, but because they are not allowed to live in sorority houses together, they do not play the same role that fraternities do. Gettysburg students seem to agree that many groups of friends who may have split somewhat because of their choices to go Greek or not often reunite as upperclassmen when both Greeks and independents tend to seek out non-Greek activities.

Sports teams also play a prominent role on campus. Many students enter their freshman year affiliated with one of Gettysburg's Division III teams and that is often reflected in the social scenes. Tuesdays are a popular night to attend "Pitchers," the weekly event at a local bar involving two-dollar pitchers of beer. Some of the other social options include campus-wide activities and trips put on by the Campus Activities Board. Springfest is a yearly event that kicks off with a spring concert drawing students, alumni and faculty. Crab Fest is another popular event where the dining hall sets out a picnic of all-you-can-eat crabs set to music. Thanksgiving Dinner is eagerly anticipated during the fall semester because the dining hall organizes a family-style Thanksgiving dinner for the entire student body. Snow Ball is the annual winter dance that provides free food and drink, as well as an opportunity to dress up.

Gettysburg College is a campus rich with historical buildings, significant Civil War sites, and even rumors of hauntings. These traditions provide a background for the talented students who are drawn to both Gettysburg's history and its state-of-the-art facilities and inspiring faculty. This beautiful school full of beautiful people boasts an intimate learning environment and social scene with something for everyone.—*Janet Yang*

FYI

If you come to Gettysburg you better bring "a bike in order to enjoy all the battlefields."
What's the typical weekend schedule? "Go to an outlet mall, go out for a nice meal with your friends off campus, drink at a frat party or somewhere else, and maybe watch a movie with friends."
If I could change one thing about Gettysburg, I'd "make it more diverse."
Three things every student at Gettysburg should do before graduating are "go on a GRAB (Gettysburg Recreational Activities Board) trip, swim in the fountain in the center of campus, and walk through the battlefields."

Haverford College

Address: 370 Lancaster Avenue, Haverford, PA 19041
Phone: 610-896-1350
E-mail address: admissions@haverford.edu
Web site URL: www.haverford.edu
Year Founded: 1833
Private or Public: Private
Religious Affiliation: None
Location: Suburban
Number of Applicants: 3,492
Percent Accepted: 25%
Percent Accepted who enroll: 35%
Number Entering: 315
Number of Transfers Accepted each Year: 89
Middle 50% SAT range: M: 640–740, CR: 650–750, Wr: 650–750
Middle 50% ACT range: Unreported
Early admission program EA/ED/None: ED
Percentage accepted through EA or ED: 35%

EA and ED deadline: 15-Nov
Regular Deadline: 15-Jan
Application Fee: $60
Full time Undergraduate enrollment: 1,169
Total enrollment: 1,169
Percent Male: 46%
Percent Female: 54%
Total Percent Minority or Unreported: 4%
Percent African-American: 8%
Percent Asian/Pacific Islander: 11%
Percent Hispanic: 8%
Percent Native-American: <1%
Percent International: 4%
Percent in-state/out of state: 13%/87%
Percent from Public HS: 55%
Retention Rate: 96%
Graduation Rate 4-year: 91%
Graduation Rate 6-year: 93%

Percent Undergraduates in On-campus housing: 99%
Number of official organized extracurricular organizations: 93
3 Most popular majors: Biology/Biological Sciences, General Economics, General English Language and Literature
Student/Faculty ratio: 8:1
Average Class Size: 9
Percent of students going to grad school: 18%
Tuition and Fees: $37,175
In-State Tuition and Fees if different: No difference
Cost for Room and Board: $11,450
Percent receiving financial aid out of those who apply, first year: 41%
Percent receiving financial aid among all students: 42%

Founded in 1833 by members of the Religious Society of Friends, this small liberal arts college—with a student body of just under 1200—has never lost sight of its Quaker roots. A deep concern for social justice and a unique emphasis on an honor code that students say "fosters an environment of tolerance and acceptance" combine with rigorous academics, unusual traditions and a tight-knit community to give the quirky, driven students at Haverford College a truly one-of-a-kind educational experience.

On My Honor

Probably the most important single factor that shapes the Haverford experience, and one repeatedly cited by students as "what differentiates Haverford from other schools," is the Honor Code, a philosophy of integrity that is affirmed by the student body each year. The Honor Code governs all aspects of students' conduct, from academics to residential life, and all those interviewed stressed its important role in making the school "a very warm and welcoming place with an undeniable sense of community." Because it is maintained and enforced by the students (four members of each class are elected each year to serve on the Honor Council), Haverfordians have "tremendous self-governance" over the conduct of the student body: "We all have a common understanding of how we all want to be treated, and for the most part, we follow through with it." The power of the Honor Code at Haverford may seem unusual to an outsider, but students say over and over again how the Honor Code affects every facet of their lives: "The Honor Code is a huge part of the school. Sure, it may create the HaverBubble, but most of the time when it comes down to it, trust, concern, and respect really flourish here."

Tough Love (It's Academic)

Most students say they came to Haverford primarily for the rigorous academics, and it certainly lives up to its reputation. Descriptions of schoolwork range from "demanding" to "very challenging" to "incredibly heavy." As one student put it, "The workload is such that it isn't too hard to just get by, but if you want to do really well it takes a lot of hard work, much more than what you expect from a college workload." Another noted that "around midterm time, a lot of people don't sleep."

But students agree that Haverford provides an excellent academic support system; its small size and accessible faculty enable students to receive much more personal attention and guidance than they would in a large research university. Furthermore, Haverford academics are unusual in that there is almost no feeling of competition between students, resulting from a tacit don't-ask-don't-tell policy regarding grades. Said one student, "Here at Haverford, we have a sort-of rule where you don't talk about grades with people, because what we really want to avoid is one of these hyper-competitive academic scenarios."

> "The Honor Code is a huge part of the school. Sure, it may create the HaverBubble, but most of the time when it comes down to it, trust, concern, and respect really flourish here."

Like many aspects of college life, Haverford's academic requirements hearken back to its Quaker heritage. In addition to a standard set of distributional requirements—three courses each in the humanities, natural sciences and social sciences, at least one of which must be quantitative, a year of a foreign language, a freshman writing seminar and a physical education requirement—all students are also required to take a course in social justice, which "ties into our Quaker roots and an awareness of community issues." Students can satisfy these requirements with a wide range of courses. Though Haverford cannot in itself offer the broad course possibilities of a research university, it compensates by participating in a tri-college consortium with nearby Swarthmore and Bryn Mawr colleges, enabling Haverfordians to take courses at the other two institutions and receive credit through their own. Haverford's size also means that classes are much smaller and more intimate: only one percent of classes have more than 50 students, and the average class size is 9. One senior reports that "even as a frosh, I was taking classes with 12 students in them. Now, as a senior, I regularly have four- to 10-person classes."

Haverford professors garner high praise from students, both for their general knowledge and for their friendliness and accessibility to students. All classes are taught by full professors, and small class sizes enable professors to pay a great deal of individual attention to each person, both in class and out of it. According to one student, "Most of my friends have babysat, house-sat, or pet-sat for a prof at some point, and it's not unusual to see professors playing with their kids or dogs around the duck pond. Because profs live on campus, they're just as much a part of the community as we are . . . They really consider us their academic colleagues, and some of my favorite friends are professors." Some particularly outstanding professors cited by students include Ashok Gangadean in the philosophy department and Bill Hohenstein, associate professor emeritus of sociology.

Furthermore, Haverford's three Academic Centers—the Center for Peace and Global Citizenship, the Hurford Humanities Center, and the Integrated Natural Sciences Center—help expand the academic experience by bringing speakers to campus and providing opportunities for research and internships.

Overall, Haverford's small size proves to be a great advantage in providing students with an exceptional undergraduate education. Students consistently praise the small class sizes and emphasis on individual student-teacher relations, which provide a support system that helps students bear the workload with aplomb. Said one student, "Haverford is a highly rigorous but incredibly nurturing academic environment. It's impossible to get lost in the shuffle here, even if you try. If you come to Haverford, you will succeed."

A Sense of Community

With Haverford's size and location—a well-to-do, wooded suburban area 20 minutes from the center of Philadelphia—it is no surprise that the vast majority of students (estimated at 99 percent) live on campus for all four years, either in a residence hall or in college-owned apartments. Housing is assigned through a lottery system with preference given by seniority, but students say that "freshman dorms are often nicer than upperclassman dorms; they're more centrally located and are very cohesive." Some upperclassmen residences have themes or personalities; "Drinker House," home to a large number of athletes, lives up to its name by throwing regular parties.

And speaking of parties, Haverford does in fact throw them—though a student adds that "95 percent of the partying is done by 40 percent of the campus." Haverford's alcohol policy is fairly relaxed, and students say the college doesn't really stop people from partying in their rooms if they so desire. With no fraternities or sororities, Haverford's parties mostly go on in dorms or apartments, especially the so-called "party houses" like Drinker. If partying is your thing, it's only a matter of knowing where to look. One student called Haverford the "kind of place where you can either do nothing or be doing everything, depending on how much effort you put into your social life. . . . There's always something going on, but the onus is on you to figure out what's happening." Thus, students say that some people end up spending four years holed up in their rooms, while others throw themselves into extracurricular activities or parties. Socialization at Haverford, like many things in the college, is purely a matter of effort.

If you're more inclined to head off campus looking for fun, there are plenty of options in that realm as well. The local area features restaurants like Fellini's, Bertucci's and Khajuraho, as well as Roach & O'Brien Bar, and though students must take a short train ride to get to the bustling city life available at urban schools, Haverford does enjoy the advantage of being completely safe by day and night. Students also like to visit nearby colleges like Bryn Mawr—incidentally, dining at Bryn Mawr is an option for students on the Haverford meal plan—head into Philly for a night on the town, or shop at the King of Prussia Mall.

In terms of diversity, ethnic and otherwise, Haverford is rather limited by its size: "It is getting much more diverse ethnically in recent years. But it is still perceived to be a school dominated by rich white kids . . . but this perception is slowly changing." In fact, 4 percent of students self-identify as minorities, and 45 states and nearly 40 countries are represented in the student body. Socially speaking, Bryn Mawr students are fond of saying that the stereotypical Haverfordian is "short, Jewish, and named Dan," and while that characterization is far from universally true, 'Fordians cheerfully acknowledge that "the typical Haverford student is nerdier than average [and] fairly awkward." Nevertheless, Haverfordians also tend to be friendly, tolerant and accepting, "pretty humble and down to earth. Students are chill and take life as it comes." And most agree that "making friends at Haverford is VERY easy," in large part because of the community spirit and camaraderie the small-college atmosphere fosters. "Once you meet people you know you're going to see them again at some point . . . you never go from one place to another without seeing someone you know."

School Spirit?

Perhaps not surprisingly, "rah-rah" school spirit and athletic pride aren't really Haverford's cup of tea. While over 40 percent of the student body plays varsity sports, with standouts being cross-country and track, students admit that athletics "aren't terribly large here in terms of school pride" and that "most people don't know when a game's going on." For those who are interested in sports, however, Haverford boasts a newly opened gym facility with state-of-the-art equipment.

Haverford also provides plenty of opportunities for extracurriculars, though on a rather small scale. While there are a number of organizations on campus—service groups and projects are particularly popular—they tend to attract a relatively small number of people, and students often pursue extracurricular involvement on an independent, individual basis. The partnership with Bryn Mawr does help to expand these options, however.

As with partying, students report, Haverford extracurriculars are what you make of them; some people focus exclusively on academics, while some throw themselves into outside activities. The campus also provides plenty of job opportunities for interested students, with a minimum wage of $8.50 for most positions.

On the whole, the main point students stress about life at Haverford is the unique freedom and the opportunities that they enjoy. Education, socializing and—thanks to the Honor Code—even policy enforcement are in the hands of the students, creating a sense of autonomy and responsibility unmatched at most other colleges. And nerdiness aside, Haverfordians really do know how to have fun. As one student admitted, "The only thing that surprised me about Haverford was how much fun everyone was. I expected there to be a lot of nerdy kids, and there are, but they know how to have a good conversation and a great time. I love meeting new people, and the quality and enthusiasm of those people makes the school feel much bigger than it might otherwise."—*Amy Koenig*

FYI

If you come to Haverford, you'd better bring "a dorky sense of humor, a North Face or EMS fleece, and lots of DVDs."

What is the typical weekend schedule? "Friday: have pastabilities in the DC, go to an a cappella or improv show, and make the rounds of the parties. Wake up late Saturday, hang out on campus or at King of Prussia Mall, have dinner out, and go to some parties. Sunday? Brunch at the DC, and then study all day!"

If I could change one thing about Haverford, I'd "have students relax a little more."

Three things every student at Haverford should do before graduating are "swim in the duck pond, go tunneling and sleep over in Magill (library)."

Lafayette College

Address: 118 Markle Hall
Easton, PA 18042
Phone: 610-330-5355
E-mail address:
admissions@lafayette.edu
Web site URL:
www.lafayette.edu
Year Founded: 1826
Private or Public: Private
Religious Affiliation:
Presbyterian
Location: Suburban
Number of Applicants: 5,635
Percent Accepted: 42%
Percent Accepted who
enroll: 26%
Number Entering: 616
Number of Transfers
Accepted each Year: 43
Middle 50% SAT range:
M: 600–710, CR:570–670,
Wr: 580–680
Middle 50% ACT range: 26–30
Early admission program
EA/ED/None: ED I, ED II

Percentage accepted
through EA or ED: 44%
EA and ED deadline:
15-Nov–1-Jan
Regular Deadline: 1-Jan
Application Fee: $60
Full time Undergraduate
enrollment: 2,365
Total enrollment: 2,406
Percent Male: 54%
Percent Female: 46%
Total Percent Minority or
Unreported: 15%
Percent African-American:
5%
Percent Asian/Pacific
Islander: 4%
Percent Hispanic: 6%
Percent Native-American:
<1%
Percent International: 7%
Percent in-state/out of
state: 20%/80%
Percent from Public HS: 72%
Retention Rate: 95%

Graduation Rate 4-year: 86%
Graduation Rate 6-year: 90%
Percent Undergraduates in
On-campus housing: 94%
Number of official organized
extracurricular
organizations: 250
3 Most popular majors:
Social Science, Engineering,
Psychology
Student/Faculty ratio: 11:1
Average Class Size: 19
Percent of students going to
grad school: 18%
Tuition and Fees: $37,520
In-State Tuition and Fees if
different: No difference
Cost for Room and Board:
$11,799
Percent receiving financial
aid out of those who apply,
first year: 64%
Percent receiving financial
aid among all students:
56%

Lafayette College is a relatively unknown jewel hidden in the woods of Easton, Pennsylvania. A small liberal arts college that emphasizes a focused curriculum of core classes, Lafayette offers 47 different majors across four overarching disciplines: the natural sciences, social sciences, engineering, and humanities, all with a focus on the philosophy of a truly liberal arts education. This unique school with a student body consisting only of undergraduates provides a very focused education with students receiving more individualized attention than those at larger, public universities. Students at Lafayette receive an equitable amount of resources without having to compete with graduate students for attention, money, and advising. The sprawling 110-acre campus provides ample room to live, learn, and grow in a small, yet academically challenging environment.

Academically Speaking

Lafayette College boasts a wide array of classes in 25 fields with hundreds of classes to choose from. Even with this large selections, students are still required to complete 32 credits for a bachelor's degree or 38 credits in engineering in addition to the general "core" requirements. Students must maintain at least a 2.00 GPA in order to graduate. Some courses to expect are the First Year Seminars, English 110, Values and Science/Technology Seminars, and two writing courses in order to fulfill the writing requirement of the bachelor's degree; however, they are left up to the discretion of the faculty depending on students' abilities and entering qualifications. The requirement may seem stiffer than most other schools' but a sophomore noted that "It forces you to really sharpen your ability to communicate an idea intelligently." Indeed, the core curriculum at Lafayette exposes students to many different fields in academia, forcing students out of their comfort zones to explore a truly liberal education. Students may combine two fields in interdisciplinary study, double major, or design their own major in two coordinating departments to fit their educational needs. The new program in policy studies that was created in 2006 allows students to cross traditional majors to combine the fields of management, design, and evaluation of policies and institutions. These and other programs aim to keep Lafayette students "interested and engaged in their education," as one Senior remarked.

> **"[The academic requirement] forces you to really sharpen your ability to communicate an idea intelligently."**

Engagement doesn't stop with just interesting classes, but also interesting professors. The relatively small size and low student-to-faculty ratio of the school allows for superb undergraduate focus and attention. Professors take a vested interest in their students' success since they have so few and the student body itself is small. Students generally find professors easy to approach in and out of class for help, guidance, or advice. Although many find this to be a point of comfort, others find it hard to avoid professors or other students on Lafayette's campus. Others complain that the size at times, although homey, feels a little stifling. "You tend to see the same types of people around here," says a Freshman.

Leopard Life
In Freshman year, all students are required to live on campus. Freshmen are assigned roommates and dorms according to a survey each student fills out before coming to campus. Freshmen are assigned preferences on a first come, first serve basis with South College taking the cake as the most desirable freshman dorm. Rooms are usually adequately spacious with nice amenities owing to recent renovations by the college. Upperclassmen housing is determined by an annual lottery draw where Seniors have top pick and the rest picking in subsequent order. Students may choose to live in traditional dorm set-ups or opt to live in special interest housing catering to cultural, language, and academic interests. High honor students, called "McKelvy Scholars," are invited to live in special housing in McKelvy House, and this is a mark of distinction that is bestowed upon only twenty students each year.

Aside from on campus housing, some upperclassmen choose to live off campus in private apartments or Greek-affiliated fraternity and sorority houses. However, in recent years Lafayette has altered housing policies to lure students back on campus by mandating that students live in college-owned properties. The housing draws for

this "off campus" housing are often inundated past capacity with Seniors once again getting first pick. These students may be lucky enough to escape the overbearing RAs that some students complain about at Lafayette. "It's like someone is always watching your every move," says a Junior. Some feel that the RAs are too strict, too power hungry, or just doing their job. Whichever the case, it seems unanimous that the student body would like to see less overbearing RAs.

Dining at Lafayette complements the housing very well: with variety. There are larger dining halls that accommodate buffet style dining for those on meal plans. Other "student restaurants" like Farinon and Marquis restaurant serve a select variety of retail-style dishes. Food choices range from Italian to Mediterranean, Southern, and many more types of cuisines. Most students seem to be approving of the food quality here due to the many offerings that the college has put together. In Freshman year, all students are required to be on the standard full meal plan with twenty-one meals per week. In subsequent years, students may choose from other meal plans according to their choice.

The campus itself is situated on a beautiful suburban landscape in Easton. The actual campus is very well patrolled by campus police and is very safe according to students. However, surrounding neighborhoods are not so friendly so students "have to be smart," says a Senior. The Town-Gown relationship between Lafayette and Easton seems to have had some tension in recent years as college parties spill over into adjacent communities, often resulting in unhappy residents. The administration has responded by increasingly cracking down on parties, especially those that serve alcohol.

The Life, The Rivalry
Lafayette and its arch-rival neighbor, Lehigh University, have a long on-going feud in both academics and sports. Lafayette is not to be taken lightly because despite its small size, all 23 intercollegiate sports are NCAA Division I. Football and basketball seem to dominate the scene here as most other sports' facilities are not on the main grounds of campus. Students gather for the Lafayette-Lehigh game that is played annually in a tradition dating back to almost a century ago. The rivalry between Lehigh and Lafayette is comparable to that between Harvard and Yale, steeped in tradition and time. Students are mostly proud of their school and have some school spirit to show. Aside from

athletics, the social scene is split between the frat scene and extracurriculars with the more "jockey" type being drawn to frats. However, with stricter party/alcohol enforcement efforts by the administration, the once thriving Greek scene has dwindled down to about 12 fraternities and sororities. Still, they dominate a sizable chunk of the social scene at Lafayette with 30% of the student population participating. Extracurricular organizations are the other pedestal of Lafayette social life, with many students choosing to do community service with well-known groups such as Engineers Without Borders, pursue academic interests in Academic Club, or explore career-oriented groups such as the Investment Club. Whatever the taste, Lafayette has something for everyone.

Off campus, there aren't too many options open for students. As a result of on-campus party policing, many underclassmen seek out off-campus parties while upperclassmen prefer the town bars. For those seeking big city adventures, Philadelphia is about an hour away by bus or car. Whatever the case, students find ways to keep themselves busy and entertained.—*Hai Pham*

FYI

If you come to Lafayette, you'd better bring a rug and other home amenities.

What's the typical schedule like? Classes and homework during the weekdays, party during the weekend (sometimes starting on Wednesday), and relaxing/preparing for class on Sunday.

If you could change one thing what would it be? "The administration here need to chill out a little more and not take everything so seriously."

Lehigh University

Address: 27 Memorial Drive West, Bethlehem, PA 18015
Phone: 610-758-3100
E-mail address: admissions@lehigh.edu
Web site URL: www.lehigh.edu/admissions
Year Founded: 1865
Private or Public: Private
Religious Affiliation: None
Location: Suburban
Number of Applicants: 12,955
Percent Accepted: 28%
Percent Accepted who enroll: 33%
Number Entering: 1,270
Number of Transfers Accepted each Year: 65
Middle 50% SAT range: M: 640–720, CR: 590–680, Wr: Unreported
Middle 50% ACT range: 28–32
Early admission program EA/ED/None: ED I, ED II

Percentage accepted through EA or ED: 40%
EA and ED deadline: 15-Nov, 1-Jan
Regular Deadline: 1-Jan
Application Fee: $70
Full time Undergraduate enrollment: 4,732
Total enrollment: 6,800
Percent Male: 57%
Percent Female: 43%
Total Percent Minority or Unreported: 27%
Percent African-American: 5%
Percent Asian/Pacific Islander: 8%
Percent Hispanic: 5%
Percent Native-American: 0%
Percent International: 6%
Percent in-state/out of state: 25%/75%
Percent from Public HS: 66%
Retention Rate: 94%
Graduation Rate 4-year: 72%

Graduation Rate 6-year: 83%
Percent Undergraduates in On-campus housing: 70%
Number of official organized extracurricular organizations: 150
3 Most popular majors: Finance, International Relations, Mechanical Engineering
Student/Faculty ratio: 9:1
Average Class Size: 26
Percent of students going to grad school: 30%
Tuition and Fees: $37,250
In-State Tuition and Fees if different: No difference
Cost for Room and Board: $9,770
Percent receiving financial aid out of those who apply, first year: 42%
Percent receiving financial aid among all students: 50%

In the little town of Bethlehem, Pennsylvania, a bright and shining star lights the way for students as they climb the central campus hillside in search of a place where they can stop to rest for the evening. The star is a large statue built on the peak of this "Christmas city," and the site of repose is a collection of Greek houses at the top of the hill. Known for its unique balance between a challenging academic curriculum and a hardcore party scene, Lehigh University offers what one student called "a dynamic learning environment customized to individual interest" and a close-knit community where students are determined to learn as much as they can while still finding plenty of time to kick back and enjoy themselves.

What Kind of Engineer Are You?

The University is composed of four different colleges: the College of Arts and Sciences, the College of Business and Economics, the College of Education (which is more focused on graduate work) and the College of Engineering and Applied Science. While Lehigh is home to students with a wide variety of academic interests, the school is particularly renowned for its engineering and its business programs. About 30 percent of the student body majors in one of the 15 types of engineering, while another 30 percent chooses to study finance, accounting, or other aspects of economics. According to one student, "When people ask you what your major is, they generally just skip right to, 'What kind of engineer are you?'" It is common for students to take on a second major or a minor, and several people commented on the interesting propensity of engineers to minor in music. One psychology major confirmed the high majority of business and engineering students, but was also quick to point out that the College of Arts and Sciences actually has the highest enrollment. About 40 percent of the student body is in arts and sciences, but because a good portion of those are only pursuing a minor in the arts, only about 20 percent have a true liberal arts major. Another student pointed out, "They're trying to tweak admissions to get more academic diversity, but right now it's heavily geared toward business and hard sciences." The newly introduced Global Citizenship program lets students give their majors an international perspective.

Most students say that they have never had trouble registering for or getting into a course, except for some of the base, extremely popular, and easy classes (there aren't many of them) such as Intro Psych or Religion 101. Lehigh prides itself on its small class sizes; apart from a few large freshman lectures, most classes have between 15 and 30 students, with language classes being even smaller. Although the University is known for its academic rigor, most students say that competition among classmates is uncommon. "People are friendly here," one sophomore said. "Classes are small enough that you can really get to know people. We study in groups a lot, especially for projects in the business school that require us to work in teams." Said another student, "You really have to be able to work as a team and help each other out." In addition to great interaction between the students, everyone has the opportunity to take advantage of an incredibly dedicated and knowledgeable faculty. "We have great student-professor relations," commented one freshman. "No matter what time I walk into a professor's office, they've never not had time to talk to me." Added another student, "I like the professor enthusiasm. You can really tell that they love what they're doing, which makes something dull more bearable. I love that they're crazy about what they're teaching."

Students call the workload "decent, as long as you go to class and keep up with the work—otherwise you have to learn everything on your own!" Grading is strict and curving is rare, so "it's very difficult to get an A." Professors do expect a lot, but students are willing to work hard in order to learn the material and get the grade.

Bottoms Up!

The competition at Lehigh, according to one student, seems to have more to do with the social scene than it does with the classroom. "It's a competition to see who can do the best while also drinking the most," she declared. Social life is dominated by the fraternities and sororities, with about 30 percent of the student body deciding to pledge at one of the 27 Greek houses. "If you're not in a fraternity or a sorority, you're usually on an athletic team," said one varsity runner. "Or you're just weird." Another student, when asked about Greek life, laughed and said, "It's a big part of Lehigh! It's a big deal and if that's your scene, then definitely take advantage of it; but if you don't join, you can easily find your own friends, your own group, and plenty of things to do on campus." Most parties take place Thursday through Saturday on top of the hill where all the houses are, although there are a few special occasions during the year when students party all week (usually for the annual Lehigh-Lafayette football game in the fall and Greek Week in the spring). Seniors often go with friends to bars in the surrounding area.

Drinking policies are not strongly enforced. According to one student, "The administration doesn't do much because they know we balance partying with academics. As long as we care about school as well, they're willing to let some things slide." Another noted, "The people who are most highly respected are those who are at the top of their classes but who also drink; students take pride in being able to keep studies up, but also party all the time."

> **"You could hit copy and paste and 4,500 kids later you'd have Lehigh!"**

Although parties are definitely enjoyable, they are not usually the best places to meet people. Most students say that they met their friends through classes or clubs, or because they lived near each other. "Classes are small and people are friendly, so it's easy to make friends," said one freshman. One major complaint about the Lehigh population is that it lacks ethnic and cultural diversity; though there are a fair number of international students, and the last three classes have been the most diverse in school history, even geographic diversity is still low. Most students hail from the East Coast. "We're a pretty homogeneous place," said one student. "You could hit copy and paste and 4,500 kids later you'd have Lehigh!" Several students described themselves and their classmates as "preppy," with many in the upper-middle class and several with "UGG boots, messy ponytails and popped collars." Still, even though the minority population is small, everyone is inclusive and "people mix well together."

Life on the Hill

Freshmen and sophomores are required to live in dormitories on campus, while most upperclassmen move to Greek, athletic, or other residential houses in the surrounding area. Freshman dorms are randomly assigned, and several of the nicer ones are described as "palaces." There is no real separation between the campus and the town, so many "off-campus" houses are actually closer to University buildings than the dormitories are. Although underclassmen dorms are assigned randomly, they still have slight personality distinctions. Usually, the quieter dorms are at

the bottom of the hill and the rowdier dorms are towards the top. In general, students enjoy living on campus in the "big, beautiful buildings," and many stay on campus as upperclassmen even though doing so is not a requirement. "I like the fact that campus is a small community where you see a lot of same people every day," said one freshman. Several people described campus architecture as "gothic, ivy-covered, with that classic college look." Another student added, "It IS built on a hill, though—that's the one drawback!" An additional disadvantage, according to some, is the drabness of the surrounding town. "I won't call it a dump," said one student, "but it isn't great." The huge difference between the economic status of the campus and the town does lead to a "bad relationship" between the students and the surrounding community, which is unfortunate but hopefully improvable through outreach programs and extracurricular community service.

When it comes to extracurricular activities, most students participate in community service programs through their Greek house or athletic team. Almost all student organizations, such as the newspaper or drama productions, are completely student-run. There are several musical organizations on campus, including the Philharmonic Orchestra, the marching band, the jazz band and a variety of smaller ensembles. Varsity sports enjoy a popular following on campus, especially the football and basketball teams. According to one student, "Football games are the place to be on the weekends and people also get crazy at basketball games, but wrestling is the most revered sport on campus. Some of the wrestlers have gone to the Olympics!" Intramurals also constitute a big part of the sporting scene on campus. "Soccer and rugby especially are pretty big and pretty competitive, but everyone can play and lots of people really get into it," said one student.

When asked what differentiates their school from others, students again remarked on the apparently equal value conferred upon both drinking and academics. "It's a little unique in its magnitude," noted one student. "People go nuts for both! You study like a maniac, and then you drink like a maniac." Most people agree that the beautiful campus, the stimulating classes and the friendly community all make them glad they chose Lehigh. Said one sophomore, "Freshman year is definitely an adjustment, as it would be anywhere. Definitely as you move up, you find more and more things you enjoy. It's a great place to spend four years!"—*Lindsay Starck*

FYI

If you come to Lehigh, you'd better bring "hiking boots, because you have to climb up that huge hill every day!"

What's the typical weekend schedule? "Thursday, drink; Friday, drink; Saturday, drink; Sunday, study."

If I could change one thing about Lehigh, I'd "do something about the homogenous student population."

Three things every student at Lehigh should do before graduating are "watch a football game on the grassy knoll, hike up to see the Bethlehem star, eat at Johnny's Bagels."

Muhlenberg College

Address: 2400 Chew Street Allentown, PA 18104

Phone: 484-664-3200

E-mail address: admissions@muhlenberg.edu

Web site URL: www.muhlenberg.edu

Year Founded: 1848

Private or Public: Private

Religious Affiliation: Lutheran

Location: Urban

Number of Applicants: 4,703

Percent Accepted: 37%

Percent Accepted who enroll: 32%

Number Entering: 551

Number of Transfers Accepted each Year: 25

Middle 50% SAT range: M: 560–660, **CR:** 560–660, **Wr:** 560–660

Middle 50% ACT range: 24–29

Early admission program EA/ED/None: ED

Percentage accepted through EA or ED: Unreported

EA and ED deadline: 1-Feb

Regular Deadline: 15-Feb

Application Fee: $50

Full time Undergraduate enrollment: 2,492

Total enrollment: 2,492

Percent Male: 42%

Percent Female: 58%

Total Percent Minority or Unreported: 9%

Percent African-American: 2%

Percent Asian/Pacific Islander: 3%

Percent Hispanic: 4%

Percent Native-American: <1%

Percent International: <1%

Percent in-state/out of state: 23%/77%

Percent from Public HS: 70%

Retention Rate: 93%

Graduation Rate 4-year: 79%

Graduation Rate 6-year: 84%

Percent Undergraduates in On-campus housing: 92%

Number of official organized extracurricular organizations: 100

3 Most popular majors: Business/Commerce, Drama/Theatre, Psychology

Student/Faculty ratio: 11:1

Average Class Size: 19

Percent of students going to grad school: Unreported

Tuition and Fees: 35,375

In-State Tuition and Fees if different: No difference

Cost for Room and Board: $8,060

Percent receiving financial aid out of those who apply, first year: 70%

Percent receiving financial aid among all students: 46%

A small liberal arts college tucked away in suburban Allentown, Pennsylvania, Muhlenberg College truly offers an intimate college experience. From the quaint 81-acre campus to the modest student population, Muhlenberg is sure to make one feel like part of a small, close-knit community. However, small size doesn't mean small offerings. With over 60 majors and 100 campus organizations to choose from, Muhlenberg offers a sizable array of options for a small school. Students emerge from Muhlenberg with an excellent education, preparation for their career goals, and a stronger sense of self.

Strong Academics, Strong Students

Muhlenberg prides itself on preparing students for whatever challenge they will face, be it graduate school admissions, working towards a career, or simply being better equipped for life. Owing to the College's commitment to a liberal arts education, all students fulfill general education requirements, including two semesters of foreign language study, science, mathematics, physical education, and the fine arts. Fear not, however, as these requirements are aimed at giving a student a well-rounded education. "No one graduates from Muhlenberg with a one-dimensional education," a senior said. "General education requirements are easily fulfilled and allow everyone to actually have a real sense of liberal arts and engage with the liberal arts in their education," a freshman remarked. Students are grounded from the very beginning in the physical sciences, social sciences and the humanities in order to expose them to academia in both breadth and depth.

The workload at Muhlenberg is also about as diverse as the number of majors the school offers. General introductory classes tend to be fairly easy while more advanced science classes can wrack any genius's brain. "It really depends on the class and the professor. Classes like fitness and wellness are jokes," a freshman said. But do not be misled. Muhlenberg is renowned for its pre-medicine program due to its highly respected science departments. They also have a praised, innovative program in neuroscience that is popular among students and gaining a reputation among academic circles. Pre-med students have a pretty challenging course load that is typical of the pre-med track at any school. Most students can expect to study at least two hours per day for each class; multiplying that by the usual four-class schedule results in about eight hours of study time per day. Some majors allow for less work in the typical homework sense, but more time devoted in the art studio, theater or dance studio. Even though dance majors are not spending as much time hitting the books as pre-meds, all students at Muhlenberg devote time to their education.

Devoted study doesn't mean there is no room for academic fun. Unusual classes such as "To Hell and Back" and "Bugs and Us" allow students to integrate non-traditional learning into their education with hands-on experiences in interesting subjects of study. Whatever the preference, students are sure to find something that interests them at Muhlenberg. The individualized attention that a small college affords is also an important part of the College experience. Class sizes are usually less than 20, excluding the large introductory science courses, and professors are very accessible. "Most of the professors are really nice and truly want you to succeed," a sophomore said. They can be one of the most valuable resources to students in terms of mastering course material or just building relationships.

What Muhlenberg does lack doesn't come in terms of quality but more so size. Academic departments are generally good, but some departments are undersized due to Muhlenberg's small size as a liberal arts college. Some students complain that although there are many programs offered, there's just not enough of the financial pie to go around for everyone. "Some departments could use expansion," a senior opined. It is apparent that the tradeoff cost for highly individualized attention would be a smaller, less extensive program.

Ride the Mule

For a small college, Muhlenberg does have a vibrant social scene on campus. No scene dominates another here; everyone pretty much finds his or her place. Options are plentiful and students usually find what it is they're looking for. Weekends at the 'Berg are filled with variety—there's the frat scene, the usual dorm parties, and many non-partying alternatives. The Muhlenberg Activities Council works hard to put on events during the weekends for those for whom partying isn't their cup of tea. Movies, bowling, concerts, comedians, sports and other events are regularly held for those looking to have good, clean old-fashioned fun.

> "The best part of campus is that it is small, and it is almost impossible to be late getting to classes or appointments."

Of course, alcohol is part of the party scene like at any other school, but at Muhlenberg, it doesn't dominate. Some people drink, and they find it easy to acquire alcohol. Others choose not to drink and find it equally easy to hang out with people who also choose not to drink. Just like alcohol, the Greek life at Muhlenberg is also a selective choice. Only about 20 percent of the student body is involved with Greek life. The school is large enough for people to make many new acquaintances, but small enough so that it doesn't become stifling or overpowering.

A highlight of a small college social scene is the fact that mostly everyone knows each other. People become close with most of their dorm-mates quite quickly due to the sheer amount of time spent interacting with each other. Classmates also quickly become good friends as many within the same major spend much academic time with each other as well. Classes, labs, performances and more begin to pile up once the semester gets rolling, so it helps to have a core group of study buddies as well as friends. If that's not enough, "everyone on campus seems to be friendly," a freshman observed. There are no social divides between majors, ages or clubs. The social scene is not cliquey, but at times it can seem very homogenous. "Some people might think that Muhlenberg is a bunch of rich white kids," a senior said, but there are still plenty of opportunities for people to find their place.

Life at the 'Berg
Situated on a hilltop in the West End neighborhood of Allentown, Pennsylvania, Muhlenberg's campus offers old-school, small-town charm alongside the modernity of world-class facilities. Campus grounds are kept pristine throughout the school year. Students praise the gorgeous campus and the relative ease of walking from place to place around campus. "The best part of campus is that it is small, and it is almost impossible to be late getting to classes or appointments," a freshman remarked.

Housing at Muhlenberg can be pretty sweet as well. Even though the college and campus themselves are small, there are still lots of options for housing. Freshmen usually live on campus in one of the three designated freshman dorms with quiet dorms available for those who prefer their dorms to be a quiet study space. Then there are the party dorms for the more socially inclined. Housing is set up in a hall system where students share communal bathrooms in a hall with singles, doubles and sometimes triples that they share with roommates. Most dorms are equipped with air conditioning while Brown, the all-female dorm, is equipped with 15-foot ceilings and hardwood floors. Others might not get so lucky. But seniors have the additional option to live off campus in suite-style arrangements through the Muhlenberg Independent Living Experience (M.I.L.E.) program. M.I.L.E. houses are owned and operated by the college. They include a kitchen, living room and multiple bedroom arrangements.

Dining at Muhlenberg is also very diversified. The main dining hall, affectionately known as the Garden Room, serves up traditional cuisine in a buffet-style setting. Choices are usually varied with vegetarian and vegan options consistently available. Aside from the daily hustle and bustle of the dining hall, students may also choose from Sandella's, Cyclone Salads, Freshens Smoothies, Java Joe, and the GQ (General's Quarters), the latter of which serves up late night munchies. With so much variety, students rarely get bored with the selection at Muhlenberg— but beware, choose wisely as some establishments are better than others depending on taste preferences.

If college food doesn't satiate satisfactorily, there are many restaurants around campus in Allentown. The area around Chew Street is full of businesses catering to the College community. However, town-gown relations aren't the best. Tough neighborhoods located near campus contribute to a divide between "rich" students and their counterparts who actually live in Allentown. Allentown is also just that: a town. Don't expect to find cosmopolitan entertainment options in the immediate area, but Philadelphia is only an hour away while New York City is about two hours away. Students always manage to keep themselves occupied.

Friendly Fro-Yo Fanatics
In all, Muhlenberg students claim they are some of the happiest students to be found in the Tri-State area. From the opening convocation in the chapel to the candlelight ceremony at orientation, students truly feel like an essential part of an academic community. Termed the "caring college" by its denizens, Muhlenberg is home to students known to be diverse in their interests, friends and goals. Many of them welcome "newbies" with open arms, oftentimes over frozen yogurt, a campus-wide obsession. As much as frozen yogurt is a part of the Muhlenberg culture, so are friendliness and acceptance. If a small, close campus doesn't feel stifling, then Muhlenberg College might be the one for some prospective students. The lack of entertainment options is mostly offset by the proliferation of activities on campus and students are generally happy in spite of the occasional feeling of living in a Muhlenberg bubble.—*Hai Pham*

FYI
Four things everyone should do before graduation are "eat fro-yo, play in the snow, see a speaker, and go to Hillel's Bagel Brunch."
What's the typical weekend schedule? "People go to parties, hang out in the dorms with their friends, participate in campus events, see a performance, go to the mall, and Sundays are mostly spent studying."
If you come to Muhlenberg you'd better bring "your work ethic, UGGs and a smile."
If I could change one thing about Muhlenberg, "I wish it weren't located in Allentown but somewhere more urban."

Penn State University

Address: 201 Shields Building, Box 3000 University Park, PA 16802-1294
Phone: 814-865-5471
E-mail address: admissions@psu.edu
Web site URL: www.psu.edu
Year Founded: 1855
Private or Public: Public
Religious Affiliation: None
Location: Urban
Number of Applicants: 48,093
Percent Accepted: 42%
Percent Accepted who enroll: 36%
Number Entering: 7,234
Number of Transfers Accepted each Year: 108
Middle 50% SAT range: M: 570–670, **CR:** 530–630, **Wr:** Unreported
Middle 50% ACT range: 27–32
Early admission program EA/ED/None: ED

Percentage accepted through EA or ED: 57%
EA and ED deadline: 15-Nov
Regular Deadline: 15-Jan
Application Fee: $50
Full time Undergraduate enrollment: 37,988
Total enrollment: 44,118
Percent Male: 55%
Percent Female: 45%
Total Percent Minority or Unreported: 13%
Percent African-American: 4%
Percent Asian/Pacific Islander: 6%
Percent Hispanic: 4%
Percent Native-American: 0%
Percent International: 3%
Percent in-state/out of state: 75%/25%
Percent from Public HS: Unreported
Retention Rate: 96%
Graduation Rate 4-year: 84%

Graduation Rate 6-year: 88%
Percent Undergraduates in On-campus housing: 82%
Number of official organized extracurricular organizations: 246
3 Most popular majors: Economics, Psychology, Biology
Student/Faculty ratio: 8:1
Average Class Size: 28
Percent of students going to grad school: Unreported
Tuition and Fees: $24,940
In-State Tuition and Fees if different: $13,706
Cost for Room and Board: $8,270
Percent receiving financial aid out of those who apply, first year: 65%
Percent receiving financial aid among all students: 48%

For students looking for a fun and stimulating college experience, this school may be the ticket. With around 40,000 students, Penn State can be the perfect college experience for those seeking a big student body and strong technical programs. Penn State is a land-grant public research university offering undergraduate, graduate, and professional programs. The University features over 160 majors and a wealth of extracurricular activities, which, coupled with a legendary school spirit, can make for a fantastic four years.

University Park, the Place to Be

Penn State actually has 24 campuses spread across the state, with the largest, the University Park campus, located geographically in the middle of Pennsylvania. The University Park campus is the most prestigious and selective of the Penn State locations, having an undergraduate acceptance rate of approximately 51 percent. University Park is comprised of 13 distinct "colleges," including the Colleges of Agricultural Sciences,

Arts and Architecture, Business, Communications, and Earth and Mineral Sciences for example. The University also recently approved a School of International Affairs to be a part of the Dickson School of Law.

Penn State's scientific and research programs are considered the strongest at the university. The meteorology program is particularly well known, as is the College of Agricultural Sciences, having fantastic facilities and a number of livestock. And for the non-technical oriented, The University boasts a breadth of offerings satisfying almost any program you could be looking for. "Pretty much any interest can be pursued given the opportunities here," said one senior. "The wide variety of programs and courses available to students is one of the most appealing aspects of Penn State."

To graduate, students are required to complete Penn State's general education requirements, which consist of 45 credits distributed across disciplines. Undergraduates take classes in the humanities, arts, natural and social sciences, health, communications and quantifications, and physical education. Every year, 1800 students are admitted to the University's Schreyer Honors College, established in 1980. With a mission to "achieve academic excellence with integrity, build a global perspective, and create opportunities for civic engagement and leadership," the Schreyer program offers a curriculum which one student described as "rigorous, and sometimes quite competitive, but manageable." Students in the Schreyer Honors College take classes in both the honors program and the regular college. Key features of the program are generous study abroad funding and a wealth of internships and co-ops for the ambitious.

Social Scene and Student Life

Asked what some of the most fun activities going on outside of class are, nearly every Penn State student will mention football. The Nittany Lions, as they are called, compete in the NCAA Division I league and are a member of the Big Ten Conference, the United States' oldest Division I college athletic conference. With one of the most tradition-rich football programs in the U.S., PSU games attract huge crowds. "Almost everyone goes to the football games," notes one sophomore. "The tailgates are super popular, especially among underclassman, and are a fantastic way to spend your Saturday."

For students under 21, frat and apartment parties are often the social event of choice in the evenings on the weekends. While local bars aren't known to be strict, they don't have much popularity among underclassmen. "Frats are a big part of the social scene; they're a lot of fun too for guys that are looking to get involved," said a Penn State freshman. While many students say their weekly workload can be challenging, "people definitely party hard on the weekends." By the numbers, slightly over 20 percent of Penn State students are affiliated with Greek organizations.

Penn State students over 21 can be found enjoying the nightlife on College Avenue, a great college town environment with plenty of restaurants and bars for people to choose from. And for those that aren't heavy partiers, PSU offers plenty of activities and organizations that are known to have fun, substance-free entertainment on weekends. "Movies and concerts are always popular choices," notes one senior.

Beyond football games and nighttime partying, outdoor activities are widespread among University Park students. The beautiful surrounding countryside is ideal for hiking. When cold weather sets in, nearby mountains are prime destinations for PSU skiers and snowboarders. Nearly 250 student clubs and organizations ensure that there are always activities going on and there is always something for everyone. Plenty of community service opportunities exist as well and involve a large portion of the PSU student body.

Freshmen are required to live on campus, and students find that the on-campus housing is generally pretty good. "I have no complaints with the Penn dorms, they are more or less what I expected," said one freshman. Nonetheless, a majority of students choose to live off-campus in nearby apartments. The meal plan runs on a "pay as you go" point system.

Student Body and Diversity

The vast majority of Penn State students, roughly 75 percent, are residents of Pennsylvania while about 25 percent hail from out of state. While the university's 40,000 strong population certainly has a bit of everything as far as diversity goes, many students note that student body is relatively more homogenous than other comparable institutions. Asian Americans, Hispanics, and African Americans combined account for roughly 14 percent of the school.

Nonetheless, Penn State students say that there are niches for everyone, from "jocks to international students, nerds, the frat scene, we represent basically the whole spectrum," said one sophomore.

> "The tailgates are super popular, especially among underclassman, and are a fantastic way to spend your Saturday."

For a small town state, Penn State does it big—from a huge student body, to major football games, to a wide range of program offerings encompassing agriculture, law, information science and everything in between. If you are looking for a strong honors program, fantastic technical majors, a cheaper alternative to private colleges, or just an awesome time, Penn State may be the place for you; there truly is something for everyone.—*Benjamin Prawdzik*

FYI

If you come to Penn State, you'd better bring "a ton of energy and a great attitude."
What's the typical weekend schedule? "Fratting and football!"
What differentiates Penn State most from other colleges is "how many offerings we have here."

Susquehanna University

Address: 514 University Avenue Selinsgrove, PA 17870
Phone: 570-372-4260
E-mail address: suadmiss@susqu.edu
Web site URL: www.susqu.edu
Year Founded: 1858
Private or Public: Private
Religious Affiliation: Lutheran
Location: Suburban
Number of Applicants: 2,777
Percent Accepted: 73%
Percent Accepted who enroll: 31%
Number Entering: 616
Number of Transfers Accepted each Year: 69
Middle 50% SAT range: M: 520–600, **CR:** 500–610, **Wr:** 500–610
Middle 50% ACT range: 21–26
Early admission program EA/ED/None: ED
Percentage accepted through EA or ED: 83%

EA and ED deadline: 15-Nov
Regular Deadline: 1-Mar
Application Fee: $35
Full time Undergraduate enrollment: 2,137
Total enrollment: 2,137
Percent Male: 47%
Percent Female: 53%
Total Percent Minority or Unreported: 9%
Percent African-American: 2%
Percent Asian/Pacific Islander: 1%
Percent Hispanic: 3%
Percent Native-American: <1%
Percent International: 1%
Percent in-state/out of state: 49%/51%
Percent from Public HS: 85%
Retention Rate: 85%
Graduation Rate 4-year: 79%
Graduation Rate 6-year: 80%
Percent Undergraduates in On-campus housing: 74%

Number of official organized extracurricular organizations: 120
3 Most popular majors: Business Administration and Management, General, Communication Studies/Speech Communication and Rhetoric, Creative Writing
Student/Faculty ratio: 13:1
Average Class Size: 16
Percent of students going to grad school: 23%
Tuition and Fees: $31,080
In-State Tuition and Fees if different: No difference
Cost for Room and Board: $8,800
Percent receiving financial aid out of those who apply, first year: 92%
Percent receiving financial aid among all students: 92%

Located in the quiet town of Selinsgrove, Pennsylvania, Susquehanna is home to a truly unique student body. Susquehanna boasts all the advantages of a small school; students form tight bonds with each other and cultivate close relationships with their professors. But Susquehanna's breadth of academic options, the faculty's willingness to allow students to create their own major, the new Central Curriculum, and its renowned business and creative writing programs give students at Susquehanna opportunities on par with many larger colleges and universities.

Students at Susquehanna are enthusiastic about everything from their classes to their beautiful surroundings. As one student said, "I love the views. You can see mountains and in the fall everything looks so pretty. It's a beautiful campus." Rumors of haunted buildings and yearly Christmas-time readings of "The Night Before Christmas" add to the rich personality of Susquehanna University.

Small and Personalized Classes

When asked about academics at Susquehanna, students praise their small class sizes and friendly professors. At Susquehanna students say that classes have "no more than thirty" students and on average class sizes don't exceed fifteen or twenty. Another student adds that they get even smaller and more personalized "as you get farther into your college education and major."

Although students note that some of the popular classes such as Psych 101, Intro to Film, and certain core science classes, such as geology, fill up very quickly, students do not generally have a problem getting into the classes they want to take. Some "fun classes, like the class about rock music, get filled mostly by seniors, who get first priority in scheduling," but even freshmen and sophomores say that class selection is "not particularly" competitive.

Students note that both the difficulty and quality of a class depends largely on a teacher. One student notes that in some classes, "lack of planning on the professors' part" causes class discussions to go off-topic. But as another student notes, these cases are "exceptions, not the norm." Professors can be tough graders, but one student makes clear that "it isn't all that hard to get an A in most classes if you work hard and put forth the effort."

Susquehanna's nationally ranked Sigmund Weis School of Business is an attractive choice for students aspiring to enter the business world. The program boasts highly qualified faculty and a strong internship program, which gives students real-world experience in their fields.

Students in the Sigmund Weis School have the opportunity to study for a semester in the London Program, where they gain experience in international business environments. One student notes, "Global Business Perspectives is known to be the hardest course. Senior business majors say that if you can make it past that course, you can make it through any business course." Students are teamed up and must complete projects together. At the end of the semester, they make a presentation with analysis and recommendations to real business executives. One student who completed the course said, "It really is a great experience and is a course that is put on your resume after completion."

Not to be outdone is Susquehanna's equally well-regarded creative writing program. One sophomore, creative writing major, notes that it is "one of the most well-developed and renowned undergraduate programs for creative writing." Students in the writing program enjoy personal attention from a large group of excellent professors, including the campus favorite Tom Bailey, who is "renowned for being likable and very inspiring for freshman writers."

Students in the creative writing program bond and form close friendships over their common interest, and sometimes "make jokes about business majors." However, students from all disciplines tend to get along very well, and as one student enthusiastically said, "I am friends with students in many different majors!" Other strong majors include communications, music, and math. Students regard the science, math, and accounting majors as the most difficult, but it is accepted that "all majors really have their setbacks."

Students in all fields of study regard their professors as "accessible and helpful." Concerning her professors, one student said, "I've felt comfortable and welcome going to office hours or contacting them in emails." Another student said, "I like the fact that my professors are there for me." She added enthusiastically, "They want you to just come in for a quick chat even!"

A recent change in Susquehanna's educational philosophy includes the addition of the Susquehanna Central Curriculum. Intended to provide students with "the skills necessary to succeed in graduate studies and in an increasingly diverse marketplace," the Central Curriculum made its debut in the 2009–2010 academic year. The six main areas of focus in the Central Curriculum are Richness of Thought, Natural World, Human Interaction, Intellectual Skills, Connections, and Capstone. Unique to Susquehanna's Central Curriculum is the requirement that students spend a semester or a shorter amount of time outside of Susquehanna, on a Global Opportunities study abroad program.

In addition, students are required to take a course following their time abroad, which encourages them to reflect on their experiences studying abroad. South America, Europe, Southeast Asia and Australia are the most popular destinations, and students receive a lot of funding to either pursue academic goals or volunteer abroad. The Central Curriculum also emphasizes a focus on multiculturalism, ethics, and skill intensives. Unlike the old Core Curriculum, which one student saw as a set of "requirements which could be completed in two years," the Central Curriculum aims to "help you arrange all four of your years" at Susquehanna without limiting academic freedom and flexibility.

Fun but Far

"I sum up our social life like this: We create a lot of fun stuff to do right here on campus because there's not much to do elsewhere besides go to the movies or something."

When asked if Susquehanna students were friendly and outgoing, one student replied "abso-freakin-lutely." Although a fair number of students, including freshmen, have cars, most students like to stay on campus and go out to restaurants, frat parties, or just chill in their dorms and "make their own fun." The most popular pubs to hit up on weekends are Bots and BJ's, "a local place with great chicken wings."

Restaurants on or near campus include Applebee's, T.G.I. Friday's, Tokyo Diner, and plenty of fast food places. Many students like to "just go out for a late dinner" and then watch a movie with friends. Trax is an on-campus nightclub that hosts parties and concerts. When asked what he liked most about Trax, one student enthusiastically responded, "Billiards!" and praised the relaxed atmosphere that surrounds the pool tables.

On Saturday nights, students head down to Orange Street, which is "usually where the parties are at," or University Avenue, which is "sort of like frat row." Greek life at Susquehanna is "insignificant" or "huge" depending on who you ask, but according to one student, "about a quarter" of students are involved, and most students go to the frat parties or have friends in the frats.

At Susquehanna, drinking is what you make of it. "Many people do it, but most are fairly safe about it." Students who choose not to drink say that they can have fun with others who are drinking and not feel pressured to partake. One student, discussing the impact of campus drinking on her decision to attend Susquehanna, said "there are PLENTY of people on campus who don't drink. That was important to me when I came here because I didn't drink in high school." However, Susquehanna is, as one student said, a "wet campus," and alcohol can be obtained by students who seek it. Binge drinking only happens on occasion, and "with the exception of pot," drugs are not common at all.

Unique and cherished events on campus are Fall Weekend and Spring Weekend, "with barbecues on the lawn, and games and activities going on." The foam party in the spring is a "fun and anticipated event" in which the on-campus club "gets turned into a foam-filled pit."

Students are described as being "very well off, but a great portion are very down to earth." One sophomore said "I think that overall people have a great, fun, laid back attitude here; they're rarely competitive." Diversity is generally lacking among the student body, as "most students are white, upper middle class, and live in the tri-state area." However, Susquehanna has "some interesting nationalities represented by our international students," with lots of exchange students from Asian countries and Russia. Susquehanna's small student body makes it "really easy to meet new people," and students generally say that "everyone is very approachable."

Susquehanna has plenty of variety in housing options. Freshman dorms are generally "pretty small," but they are in "nice buildings and very conveniently located." Freshmen are generally placed in doubles and, on occasion, triples. Freshmen say that they get to know the people in their hall very well, and that "most people leave their doors open and there's always people coming and going."

As a freshman, it is possible to express a preference for housing, but there is no guarantee that students will be placed in the buildings they request. Dorms get better with seniority, as Susquehanna's lottery-based housing system gives priority to seniors. Dorms are known to have different personalities. Smith Hall, the largest freshman dorm, is known for being full of, as one student put it, "rowdy party people." One dorm, Seibert Hall, has a 24-hour courtesy policy, allowing students to concentrate on their work at all hours of the day and live noise-free. Hassinger Hall is full of English and creative writing majors, and Aikens Hall is known for being "in between" in terms of noise level. One junior, recalling the time she spent with friends in the three freshmen dorms her first year, said that "All three are nice!"

> "You can see mountains and in the fall everything looks so pretty. It's a beautiful campus."

Students have the option of pledging and living in frats and sororities, and juniors and seniors sometimes live in suites or townhouses off campus, especially along University Avenue, but most students prefer to remain on campus. There is a house specifically for creative writing majors. Alcohol is allowed in most dorms so long as all members of the dorm are 21 or older.

Susquehanna renovates its buildings often, so "everything looks brand new." One student described the architecture as "mostly brick-based and very easy on the eyes." Students are excited about the new science building which is, as one student said, "HUGE," and which opened in the Fall of 2010. Seibert Hall is often cited by students as the most aesthetically appealing building on campus, because "it's got these huge white columns out front." Students like to spend their free time on the Degenstein Lawn playing Frisbee, or in one of the many eateries within the Degenstein

Campus Center. Charlie's Coffeehouse features movie and bingo nights.

Students are generally very pleased with Susquehanna's cafeteria food. The main dining hall features "more homemade type foods," whereas Benny's Bistro, an alternative to the dining hall at which students can pay with their IDs, offers a tasty, if less healthy, alternative. Students can choose from a variety of different meal plans, ranging from ten to twenty-one meals a week. When asked about the dining hall, one student said, "I think the food is really good there and there is a lot to choose from."

Students are looking forward to the opening of a new Panera in Degenstein Hall as yet another eating alternative. The dining hall has "somewhat flexible" meal hours, but students are generally pleased with the ability to use "flex" points, which allow them to purchase food at Clyde's or Benny's outside of normal meal hours. And of course, T.G.I. Friday's and Tokyo Diner are always popular alternatives.

Students feel "very safe" on campus. As one student said, "it's well lit and I've never felt threatened." Another student added, "I've never heard any horror stories," but just in case, "there are blue light boxes being put up in case there is an emergency." Overall, students at Susquehanna feel not only safe, but very happy. Although the campus can "start to feel a little bit small" by senior year, one student said, "I don't really know why you would live off campus, to be honest. Everything is right here." Another student happily added that "in general, on-campus living is great, and I wouldn't trade it for anything."

Sports and Clubs

At Susquehanna, "there's basically a club for any interest you might have." Students are very active, and are involved in everything from the Belly Dance Circle to the Student Activities Committee (SAC), which organizes weekend events. WQSU, Susquehanna's campus radio station, is the third largest college radio station in Pennsylvania. It is a very popular organization, and many new student DJ's are trained every year to broadcast their shows across a radius of 90 miles. Students cite publications, SAC, and Greek organizations as some of their most important commitments.

Plenty of students play sports, and although Susquehanna plays in NCAA Division III, "athletics still have a strong presence, with a lot of school spirit."

Among the popular publications on campus are *The Crusader*, Susquehanna's campus newspaper, *Essay*, an on-campus magazine for creative non-fiction, and *RiverCraft*, Susquehanna's poetry publication. It is very easy for students at Susquehanna to get involved.

Students easily become a big part of a club or group, and one student enthusiastically discussed his involvement as secretary for the Literature Club and DJ at WQSU. At Susquehanna, there are plenty of opportunities for student employment, and most students hold down at least one job. Students can work on campus, taking shifts in the cafeteria or other dining locations, in the library, at Trax, or as tour guides. Some students work at stores and restaurants off campus.—*Eduardo Andino*

FYI

If you come to SU, you'd better bring "a whiteboard for people to leave you notes on, and a very capable laptop computer with all the most recent updates installed; otherwise, you won't be able to get online in your room with the ethernet cables provided by IT."

What's the typical weekend schedule? "Sleep in late, brunch with friends, maybe get laundry and homework done, then a night out or at an on-campus movie or party."

If I could change one thing about SU, "I'd give the freshmen a lot more say in what classes they take in their first semester, because as it is you just take a small survey and then you're assigned to four courses, mostly intended to fulfill curriculum requirements."

Three things every student at SU should do before graduating are "visit the cemetery at the top of the hill on a clear night and stargaze, go to President Lemon's reading of 'The Night Before Christmas' during finals, and take a class with Dr. Randy Robertson."

Swarthmore College

Address: 500 College Avenue
　Swarthmore, PA 19081
Phone: 610-328-8300
E-mail address:
　admissions@swarthmore.edu
Web site URL:
　www.swarthmore.edu
Year Founded: 1864
Private or Public: Private
Religious Affiliation: None
Location: Suburban
Number of Applicants:
　5,242
Percent Accepted: 16%
**Percent Accepted who
　enroll:** 39%
Number Entering: 365
**Number of Transfers
　Accepted each Year:**
　28
**Middle 50% SAT range: M:
　680–760, CR: 680–780,
　Wr:** 680–760
Middle 50% ACT range:
　28–33
**Early admission program
　EA/ED/None:** ED

**Percentage accepted
　through EA or ED:** 34%
EA and ED deadline: 15-Nov
Regular Deadline: 2-Jan
Application Fee: $60
**Full time Undergraduate
　enrollment:** 1,490
Total enrollment: 1,490
Percent Male: 51%
Percent Female: 49%
**Total Percent Minority or
　Unreported:** 48%
Percent African-American:
　10%
**Percent Asian/Pacific
　Islander:** 16%
Percent Hispanic: 12%
Percent Native-American:
　<1%
Percent International: 7%
**Percent in-state/out of
　state:** 12%/88%
Percent from Public HS:
　59%
Retention Rate: 96%
Graduation Rate 4-year:
　90%

Graduation Rate 6-year:
　92%
**Percent Undergraduates in
　On-campus housing:** 95%
**Number of official organized
　extracurricular
　organizations:** 138
3 Most popular majors:
　Biology/Biological Sciences,
　General Economics, General
　Political Science and
　Government
Student/Faculty ratio: 8:1
Average Class Size: 7
**Percent of students going to
　grad school:** 21%
Tuition and Fees: $36,490
**In-State Tuition and Fees if
　different:** No difference
Cost for Room and Board:
　$11,314
**Percent receiving financial
　aid out of those who apply,
　first year:** 48%
**Percent receiving financial
　aid among all students:**
　50%

Tucked away in a quiet Pennsylvania suburb on a campus that is a nationally designated arboretum, Swarthmore boasts a close-knit community of intellectually-driven students. With strong Quaker roots and a renowned Honors program, Swarthmore offers top-notch academics in a low-key environment for its student body of 1500. Swatties are passionate about what they do, both inside and outside the classroom. "Everyone has some obscure interest or talent," one freshman said. "People have more than academic interests."

Know Your Teachers

Students praise Swarthmore's small class sizes and the unique level of access they enjoy to professors. Many classes are seminars, capped at a dozen students, and large classes are those that exceed 30. The largest courses are introductory bio and physics, each about 100 students, but a First-Year Seminar program ensures that freshmen get a taste of small class discussions. The college has no teaching assistants, so all classes are led by professors or visiting specialists in a given field.

Professors, many of whom students call by their first names, often invite students to their houses for dinner and make themselves available well beyond office hours to provide assistance. "It's really easy for them to meet you on a night or a weekend, and they're really open to working with you," said one senior.

Swarthmore is best known for its Honors program, which is modeled on Oxford's tutorial system. Students in the program elect an Honors major and minor, enroll in rigorous small seminars, and conclude their studies with an examination by outside experts in their field of study. While about a third of each class pursues Honors, most students opt to double-major or choose a minor regardless. "It's pretty rare that people only have one major," a senior said. "There's almost a sense that people want to combine really different disciplines together for a major/minor combination, like biology and English or computer science and philosophy."

Complementing traditional academic departments, Swarthmore offers interdisciplinary programs such as Interpretation Theory, Cognitive Science, and Peace and Conflict Studies, which can be chosen as minors or developed into a special major. Swarthmore also attracts students with its engineering program, a rarity among liberal arts colleges. Overall, the most popular majors are biology, economics, and political science. The Education Studies department is also very popular, and students cite Introduction to Education as a course not to be missed. "People go into an Intro Ed course and come out wanting to be either an Ed major or a teacher," one freshman said.

While students come to Swat for its academic rigor, the school can seem overwhelming. "There are times when it's very stressful, and I had a friend who said that other schools' final exams periods are like a regular week here," a senior said. Luckily the school provides plenty of resources, from writing associates who look over essays and lab reports to a tutoring program and counseling services. To ease the transition from high school, the first semester of freshman year is pass/fail, a welcome "safety net" for students as they adjust to the quality of work expected of them. Students emphasize that the academic environment is friendly and uncompetitive. "There's not a whole lot of competition amongst students," a junior said. "People are willing to help each other out."

When Classes Are Done

After hitting the books during the week, Swatties head out on Thursday and Saturday nights. Though the social scene is varied, ranging from dorm-room parties to a capella performances and comedy shows, there are a few weekly staples. Thursdays are Pub Night at Paces, a student-run café that transforms into a "mini-nightclub" on weekends. Olde Club, an intimate concert venue with "stained glass and a Catholic church kind of feel," hosts student bands or alternative music groups from the local area.

Greek life has a minor presence at Swarthmore, but the campus' two fraternities host popular parties on Saturday nights, including a "graffiti party" where "you go in with a white t-shirt and just draw on each other." The annual Halloween party draws students from nearby Haverford and Bryn Mawr colleges, with which Swat forms a tri-college consor-

tium. There is also an annual winter formal, recently staged as a Harry Potter-esque Yule Ball "decked out with ice sculptures, candles, and a couple of wizard rock groups."

Alcohol is "readily available" on campus, and the school's drinking policy is fairly lenient. As one senior explained, "The administration treats us like adults and isn't trying to bust anybody." Though most students drink, those who do not report no pressure to imbibe. "Social life at Swarthmore is really flexible and accepting," said one senior. "Whatever you want to do, there will be people who want to do it with you, whether it's partying or playing Bananagrams on Friday night."

Notable traditions include the Pterodactyl Hunt, a campus-wide role-playing game in which "one team is the Pterodactyls and the other team is the Humans, who try to slay the Pterodactyls," and First and Last Collection, ceremonies held at the beginning and end of a student's college experience in Swat's outdoor amphitheater.

> "Social life at Swarthmore is really flexible and accepting," said one senior. "Whatever you want to do, there will be people who want to do it with you, whether it's partying or playing Bananagrams on Friday night."

For those that wish to break out of the Swarthmore bubble, Philadelphia is a half-hour ride from the on-campus train station. The school also sponsors free shuttles to the city and to nearby movie theaters and shopping centers. However, student life centers on campus. "Some people go into Philly for a day to explore, but most people stick on campus," a freshman said. "I don't know if we're just lazy or if we love our campus so much, but there's enough going on that we can stay on campus and have a good time."

Life in an Arboretum

Swarthmore's architecture is "eclectic," melding nineteenth-century stonework with modern additions like the LEED-certified Science Center. The campus centerpiece is Parrish Hall, part administrative building and part student residence, which overlooks a grassy lawn and popular hangout known as Parrish Beach. The 399-acre campus also contains the Crum Woods, a forested area with trails and a creek. "People build boats out of various materials and race down the creek" in the annual Crum Regatta.

95 percent of students live in campus housing, and students forge lasting bonds with their hallmates. Swarthmore has 17 different dorms, which range from a cozy 8-person home to cottage row houses, condo units, and imposing stone edifices. There is no freshman-only housing; instead, freshmen live on halls alongside sophomores, juniors, and seniors from Day 1. Freshmen all have roommates and typically live in doubles, while juniors and seniors can opt for single rooms.

Students in campus housing are required to be on the meal plan, which provides 14, 17, or 20 meals a week at Sharples, the dining hall. While the food is "pretty solidly mediocre," Sharples serves as an important social area and gathering point. For Screw Your Roommate, in which roommates set each other up on blind dates, couples are told to dress up in matched outfits (Salt and Pepper; Mustard and Ketchup) and meet each other at Sharples. Frat rushing rituals also take place there, such as an applesauce-eating competition. One junior explains: "Every pledge has to challenge a random person in the cafeteria. They'll put a bowl in their face and say 'go!'" The frats "also make the kids crabwalk around the whole cafeteria and race each other."

Other eating options include a few on-campus coffee shops and restaurants in the Ville, as students call the small town bordering Swarthmore. Student favorites in the Ville include pizza parlor Renato's and Vicky's, a breakfast stop.

Swarthmore has one main athletic facility, which "could stand to be repaired," one Varsity athlete said. It includes a fitness center, indoor and outdoor tennis courts, a turf field, a baseball field, a field house, and a pool, all of which are open to Varsity and casual athletes alike. Though "academics are emphasized over everything" at Swat, 40 percent of students play Varsity, club, or intramural sports. The school fields 22 Division III teams, the most popular of which, Men's Soccer, has had a winning streak in recent years. IM soccer is also popular, as are the Ultimate Frisbee and fencing clubs.

Swatties participate in over 100 clubs and organizations, from the Peaslee Debate Society to dance, music, and theater groups. There are five a capella groups, and dance troupe Rhythm and Motion is quite popular. "Either you sing, dance, or you play something," one junior commented. "Everyone does one of those three things." Many students are members of identity-based groups for various religions, ethnicities, and sexual orientations, which are all under the umbrella Intercultural Center. Swatties also engage in service projects through the Lang Center for Civic and Social Responsibility.

Ultimately, what differentiates Swarthmore from other schools is its tough academics and intimate community. "The fact that we're smaller than most schools means we know a lot more people, and we feel connected to more people at the school," one freshman said. "But at the same time, it's not small because we have so many organizations. If you want to do something, you'll be able to find it, or you can start it. And the smallness keeps the class sizes really small, which is a huge bonus." Students characterize their peers as passionate, friendly, and accepting.—*Antonia Woodford*

FYI

If you come to Swarthmore, you'd better bring "a blanket for lying outside on Parrish Beach and looking at the stars, and a hot water kettle (although they're illegal) for late-night tea parties in your dorm."

If you come to Swarthmore, you'd better not bring "a relationship. Most people break up with people they were dating back home."

The biggest college-wide tradition/event at Swarthmore is "watching The Graduate on the very first night before fall classes start. The whole school goes out and sits on the main lawn of the school with a huge projector and watches it."

Temple University

Address: 1801 N. Broad Street, Philadelphia, PA 19122
Phone: 888-340-2222
E-mail address: tudam@temple.edu
Web site URL: www.temple.edu
Year Founded: 1884
Private or Public: Public
Religious Affiliation: None
Location: Urban
Number of Applicants: 17,051
Percent Accepted: 65%
Percent Accepted who enroll: 39%
Number Entering: 4,311
Number of Transfers Accepted each Year: 3,852
Middle 50% SAT range: M: 510–610, CR: 500–600, Wr: 490–590
Middle 50% ACT range: 21–26
Early admission program EA/ED/None: None

Percentage accepted through EA or ED: NA
EA and ED deadline: NA
Regular Deadline: 1-Mar
Application Fee: $50 / $25 for online
Full time Undergraduate enrollment: 23,027
Total enrollment: 35,822
Percent Male: 46%
Percent Female: 54%
Total Percent Minority or Unreported: 31%
Percent African-American: 17%
Percent Asian/Pacific Islander: 10%
Percent Hispanic: 4%
Percent Native-American: <1%
Percent International: 1%
Percent in-state/out of state: 79%/21%
Percent from Public HS: 81%
Retention Rate: 87%

Graduation Rate 4-year: 36%
Graduation Rate 6-year: 63%
Percent Undergraduates in On-campus housing: 19%
Number of official organized extracurricular organizations: 173
3 Most popular majors: Elementary Education, Psychology, Social Work
Student/Faculty ratio: 17:1
Average Class Size: 27
Percent of students going to grad school: Unreported
Tuition and Fees: $20,468
In-State Tuition and Fees if different: $11,448
Cost for Room and Board: $8,884
Percent receiving financial aid out of those who apply, first year: 72%
Percent receiving financial aid among all students: Unreported

Temple University resides within Philadelphia, the largest city in Pennsylvania, and the sixth-most populous city in the nation. As a comprehensive public research university that awards degrees up to a doctoral, Temple largely attracts native Pennsylvanians in order to round out its student body of just under 36,000 students. It's the 26th largest university in America, but students often find that the size does not necessarily become detrimental to their college experience, especially not in historic Philadelphia.

Big Fish in a Bigger Pond

"For the most part I really enjoy my classes. I always feel like I learn at least one new thing in each class," a Temple University freshman informed me. "But they're *so big*." Like most large public-research universities, Temple's introductory classes range upwards of around 300 students at a time. Students say that the class sizes definitely grow smaller as you move further into specialized courses. There are 17 schools within Temple and 4 professional schools. "I think English, Business, and Communications majors are considered easier and Science and Nursing majors are harder, based on what I've heard," one student noted.

"I might have liked a slightly smaller school because making friends my freshman year was pretty hard. My high school wasn't that small either, but I felt just plain lost most of the time," a student told me, disappointed. There is something for everyone to do here, however. With a student radio that has the second largest audience among Philadelphia's radio stations, an independent weekly newspaper, over 200 student organizations, and a fully-staffed, very popular student government, there is no end in sight when it comes to deciding what to do at Temple.

One complaint that was frequently voiced, however, was the lack of communication that occurred between those attending the institution and those running it. "I really can't stand Temple's poor communication skills between students and administration" a freshman stated. "Granted, the University's huge, but it would still be great to have someone who can answer you when you have problems."

Study abroad options are incredibly organized and therefore extremely popular with the student body. "I went to Temple in Japan," a first year law student gushed. "It was amazing! I was allowed to take all of the courses Temple offered and wrap up my language study at the same time. Definitely worth it!" It has become increasingly popular to do a summer internship after spending a year at Temple, a semester abroad in the sophomore year, and taking either junior year or post-senior year abroad.

From Brotherly Love to . . . well, Brotherly Love

While often nicknamed the City of Brotherly Love, Philadelphia has lately been getting much more publicity for the violent crime that often occurs off-campus. Temple University offers a massive alert system that utilizes text, e-mail, and automatic phone calls, as well as a large and well-organized on-campus police force. There are over 600 security cameras mounted throughout the campus and students as well as faculty and staff are taught early on how to utilize emergency numbers and navigate the Philadelphia area. While students agree that living on-campus almost guarantees a safe experience at Temple, one student noted that "Temple is a great school with a lot of opportunity BUT it's in an awful location and you need to be on top of your game to be able to take advantage of the opportunities." Opportunities include trips into New York City, thanks to Philadelphia's 30th Street Station, which offers access to Amtrak, SEPTA, and New Jersey Transit lines.

That said, most people live off campus despite the danger. "I would rather live on campus because walking alone off campus isn't always safe," said a female student, "but my apartment is pretty nice and cheap, and there's a bunch of students living around me, so I'm not too worried." Those living on-campus, number around 10,000, tend to gravitate towards Johnson and Hardwick, which are considered to be freshmen-heavy areas to live in and therefore the best dorms to meet new people in. There are often complaints about delinquency of the juvenile kind – frequent pranks, pulled fire alarms, loud and raucous parties going on late into the night on weekdays – but overall, these two buildings are the place to be. White Hall, as the farthest dorms away from campus, are favored by upperclassmen, while the lavish 1300 and Temple Towers buildings are considered to be the best living arrangements if you're willing to spend a little more.

> "Temple is a great school with a lot of opportunity BUT it's in an awful location and you need to be on top of your game to be able to take advantage of the opportunities."

Living in the city of Philadelphia has its perks. Students rave about the shows they get to see, including "arts festivals, plays, movies, and concerts that I never knew existed, and I lived here for most of my life!" one student exclaimed.

While only 2% of the student body is involved in fraternities or sororities, Greek life at Temple is still large without being in charge. A female junior explained. "I love the frat parties! They're incredibly entertaining and a good way to meet a solid group of guys with pretty much the same values." Most students attend parties thrown at off-campus dormitories or go into clubs around the city. There is definitely something for everyone to do in a city this large.—*Larissa Liburd*

FYI
If you come to Temple University, you'd better leave: your Penn State gear behind.
What's the typical weekend schedule? Partying. There's always a party.
The biggest college-wide tradition/event at Temple University is: Spring Fling.

University of Pennsylvania

Address: 1 College Hall
Philadelphia, PA 19104
Phone: 215-898-7507
E-mail address:
info@admissions.ugao
.upenn.edu
Web site URL:
www.upenn.edu
Year Founded: 1740
Private or Public: Private
Religious Affiliation: None
Location: Urban
Number of Applicants:
22,645
Percent Accepted: 16%
**Percent Accepted who
enroll:** 66%
Number Entering: 2,385
**Number of Transfers
Accepted each Year:** 296
**Middle 50% SAT range: M:
680–770, CR: 650–750,
Wr:** 660–750
Middle 50% ACT range:
29–33
**Early admission program
EA/ED/None:** ED

**Percentage accepted
through EA or ED:**
Unreported
EA and ED deadline: 1-Nov
Regular Deadline: 1-Jan
Application Fee: $75
**Full time Undergraduate
enrollment:** 9,687
Total enrollment: 16,545
Percent Male: 51%
Percent Female: 49%
**Total Percent Minority or
Unreported:** 55%
Percent African-American:
8%
**Percent Asian/Pacific
Islander:** 17%
Percent Hispanic: 6%
Percent Native-American:
0%
Percent International: 10%
**Percent in-state/out of
state:** 19%/81%
Percent from Public HS: 54%
Retention Rate: 98%
Graduation Rate 4-year:
88%

Graduation Rate 6-year:
94%
**Percent Undergraduates in
On-campus housing:** 64%
**Number of official organized
extracurricular
organizations:** 350
3 Most popular majors:
Business Administration and
Management, Finance,
Nursing/Registered Nurse
RN, ASN, BSN, MSN
Student/Faculty ratio: 6:1
Average Class Size: 16
**Percent of students going to
grad school:** 18%
Tuition and Fees: $37,526
**In-State Tuition and Fees if
different:** No difference
Cost for Room and Board:
$10,622
**Percent receiving financial
aid out of those who apply,
first year:** 76%
**Percent receiving financial
aid among all students:**
40%

Bearing the imprint of Benjamin Franklin, arguably America's most celebrated philosopher, the University of Pennsylvania was imbued with a spirit of liberal thinking and scholarship even before it enrolled its first students. Conceived in 1740 and opened in 1751, Penn has lived up to its goal of providing a practical education devoted to liberal arts, business, and public service. Generally acknowledged as the nation's first true university, it is credited with having developed the first modern liberal arts curriculum. Today, Penn's architecturally varied and attractive 269-acre campus located in West Philadelphia is home to an undergraduate student body that has grown to almost 10,000 students, many of whom are international in origin. Despite its growth, the college has remained true to its original mission since its inception.

Four Schools in One

The academic interests of Penn's undergraduates run the gamut, and despite differences in career plans, all students are completely integrated into the fabric of the college. Nevertheless, successful applicants to Penn enter one of the four schools that together create the undergraduate institution. The largest of the schools is the College of Arts and Sciences, to which over six in 10 students belong, followed by the highly competitive Wharton School of Business, which enrolls about 2500 Penn students. Wharton is the only undergraduate business school in the Ivy League and has an unparalleled international reputation. The School of Engineering and Applied Science enrolls just slightly fewer students than does the Wharton undergraduate program, and the relatively small but excellent School of Nursing includes approximately 500 undergrads. Thus, Benjamin Franklin's original goal that Penn teach "everything that is practical, and everything that is ornamental" is certainly well-addressed by the broad range of opportunities available to undergraduates here.

The College of Arts and Sciences allows the most freedom of choice of the four schools at Penn. In this undergraduate school at Penn, students are generally required to take between 12 to 14 courses in their major and around 20 outside of their area of concentration. Included in the latter are courses that fulfill distribution requirements. In 2006, the college has reduced the number of distributional courses necessary to graduate, with the intention of increasing curricular flexibility. Students must now take one course in each of the following areas: Society, History and Tradition, Arts and Letters, Physical World, Living World, Humanities and Social Sciences, Natural Science and Math. Within the framework of these disciplines, undergraduates in the College of Arts and Sciences must also fulfill requirements in quantitative reasoning, foreign language and writing. Noted one sophomore, "Mine was the first class with the new curriculum. My junior and senior friends say that the reduction in distribution requirements makes it much easier to complete your major and still take some great courses that are outside the beaten path." Students preregister for courses, but can change their schedules during a "shopping period." However, noted a junior, "for courses with restricted enrollment, such as seminars, it can be difficult getting in if you have not preregistered, unless someone drops out of the class. Teachers generally try to be accommodating, but they can't always be."

The Wharton School of Business at Penn is world-renowned and the list of its graduates who went on to distinguish themselves in the business world is staggering. It is arguably the best undergraduate business school in the country and, as such, the most competitive of the four schools at Penn in terms of admissions. In contrast to the curriculum of the College of Arts and Sciences, the course of study in this school is much more predetermined. Thirty-seven courses are required to graduate, only two of which must be taken outside of Wharton. There is theoretically a wide variety of possible "concentrations" available within the context of the Bachelor of Science in Economics degree that is awarded to all students, but the vast majority concentrates in the area of finance.

Penn's School of Engineering and Applied Science, or SEAS, like Wharton, has a fairly fixed curriculum. The course of study is traditional, and most students take classes in math, science, engineering, and little else. "I am very happy with my courses," said one senior. "If I wanted to take Old English poetry, I wouldn't be in SEAS."

The School of Nursing prepares its students for a variety of fields related to nursing and the health sciences. A total of 28 classes in nursing and medicine are required, but there is ample room to take other courses in the College of Arts and Sciences. Students concentrate in one of two programs in the school: Family and Community Health and Foundational Sciences and Health Systems.

There are many opportunities for interdisciplinary study at Penn, and the school encourages this type of exploration. Students may pursue dual degrees within, for example, the School of Arts and Sciences, or may enroll in one of the joint degree programs at the school. For example, the Huntsman Program in International Studies and Business awards two simultaneous degrees, a Bachelor of Arts in International Studies from the School of Arts and Sciences and a Bachelor of Science in Economics from the Wharton School. The Lauder Institute of Management and International Studies awards an MBA from Wharton and an MA in International Studies from the School of Arts and Sciences.

Academics are rigorous at Penn, and most students put in a good amount of study time. Students are well aware that exams and course grades are curved, especially in the sciences and math, so there is a fair amount of competition among students. In addition, many undergraduates are premed and prelaw. "That alone leads to competition," said a senior, "but I don't think that Penn students are any more cutthroat than pre-professional students at other schools."

Campus in the City

Penn touts the opportunities of its situation in the city of Philadelphia, a bustling metropolis with a long and interesting history. Undergraduates choose to live in a variety of different types of housing, both on and off campus. Only about 60 percent of undergrads live on campus. Many upperclassmen prefer living off campus in fraternities and sororities or apartments that are generally less expensive than the University housing options.

For those living on campus, there are 11 College Houses, each with its own architectural style, ranging from 24-story high-rise apartment buildings to historic buildings with hardwood floors. Most freshmen live in dorms that surround the Quad. Each facility is home to about 400 students. Dining facilities are in close proximity. Residents of the high-rises have bathrooms and kitchenettes in their suites. In addition to these options are "theme houses" which allow students with similar cultural backgrounds and interests and students with similar academic interests to live together. In addition, fraternities and sororities have been active on campus since the mid-1800s and represent another significant housing option.

Food for Thought

First-year undergraduates are required to enroll in one of four meal plans, all of which include "Dining Dollar$" that can be redeemed at all Penn dining locations, including Starbucks and several on-campus cafés and retail institutions nearby. Upperclassmen who choose to live and eat on campus can choose from among 10 different plans. Dining Dollar$ can be easily added to their accounts. Kosher food is found at Falk Dining Commons and is under Orthodox supervision. In addition, a variety of foods can be purchased at a new "convenience area" in the same facility. The nutritional composition of all meals can be found at kiosks located in each of the dining facilities. Most students do not complain about the food options. "There is always something to fit your dietary needs and preferences," said a sophomore. "And there is an increasing interest in foods that have been grown and prepared with attention to ecological considerations."

An Extracurricular Smorgasbord

Penn boasts a wide array of extracurricular opportunities, including participation on numerous intercollegiate athletic teams. There are 17 men's sports teams and 16 women's teams. In addition, students may participate on intramural teams in 12 sports and on a variety of club sports. Beyond organized sports, huge numbers of students go to the gym on almost a daily basis. The facilities are open Monday through Thursday from 6 a.m. to 1 a.m., so there is little excuse for being a "couch potato." The gyms are also open on the weekends with less extensive hours.

Many students are involved with the numerous publications on campus as well as student government organizations such as the Undergraduate Assembly, the debate team, and the Model UN. In addition, opportunities to sing, dance, and act abound. There are numerous a cappella groups on campus. "Penn is a real extracurricular smorgasbord," said one senior. "I have done a lot of acting and a lot of writing out of class."

Living in and Giving to West Philadelphia

West Philadelphia provides an active and multiethnic neighborhood for Penn students, as well as tremendous opportunities for community service. But many students voice concerns about their safety on campus, especially its immediate environs. They often point to the great "town-gown" discrepancy between the wealth of the University and the majority of its students and the socioeconomic status of the residents of the surrounding neighborhood. Students call this disparity the "Penn Bubble." "I have been here for three years," stated one student, "and I still feel uncomfortable walking around West Philly at night. I don't like going out alone. But many great universities are located in areas where the underprivileged live. You have to be careful, but there are so many opportunities to get involved. On balance, the neighborhood is really a plus." The University has actively focused on security on campus in recent years.

> "Many great universities are located in areas where the underprivileged live. You have to be careful, but there are so many opportunities to get involved."

Penn students actively participate in a wide variety of community service projects. Civic House is the main hub for those interested in such endeavors, providing a liaison between the University and the community. Civic House maintains a community agency database that allows students to locate volunteer organizations that serve the greater West Philadelphia neighborhood.

I'll Drink to That

Like students at the other Ivies, Penn students tend to study hard and play hard. The fraternities and sororities are where a great deal of socializing takes place, especially for the lowerclassmen. Alcohol plays an important role at most weekend parties and it flows more freely in the frats. Most students agree that a significant amount of booze is consumed at Penn. They also note that although there are definite dictates against the availability of alcohol in these venues, the enforcement of such policies is lax. "The RAs and GAs don't allow things to be completely freewheeling," noted one junior, "but they let things go as long as no one gets really out of hand."

As is the case at many other universities, the social scene generally shifts to private parties in students' apartments during the upperclass years. Many Penn students live off campus as juniors and seniors and are less inclined to spend their weekends at the frat parties.

Beyond the Parties

Philadelphia affords virtually unlimited opportunities for social activities beyond the party scene. Every Thursday, Penn's school newspaper, The Daily Pennsylvanian, catalogues the numerous concerts, theatrical performances, and dances that will be taking place that weekend. Most students avail themselves of the city and frequent restaurants, bars, and clubs there. "There are so many things to do in Philly," said a senior. "Sometimes it's nice to get off campus and do some exploring. I am certainly going to miss being in this city after I graduate."

Here's a Toast to Dear Old Penn!

School spirit is alive and well at Penn, and their strong athletic teams reinforce the identification of Penn students with their school. Men's basketball is unquestionably the most popular intercollegiate sport on campus, and Penn's teams have been exceptional in recent years. Games against Princeton, the University's archrival on the court, are packed, and Penn football games have become increasingly popular as well, as a function of the fielding of more competitive teams in recent years.

Penn students traditionally throw toast on the football field after singing a song entitled "Drink a Highball," ever since the drinking age was raised from 18 and most undergraduates could no longer consume the intended cocktail.

. . . As a "Button"

In the center of the Penn campus, there is a huge white button, split asymmetrically, measuring 16 feet in diameter and weighing over 5,000 pounds. Designed by Claes Oldenburg and cast in reinforced aluminum, it faces Benjamin Franklin in front of Penn's Van Pelt Library. According to legend, Benjamin Franklin once popped off a button from his pants after gorging on a huge meal, with the projectile then splitting in two. While the artist himself once remarked that the split in the button divides it into four parts, representing William Penn's original division of Philadelphia into four squares, some argue that it represents the four undergraduate schools at Penn. Others ascribe a variety of other traditions and functions to this sculpture, including as a place to engage in some more risqué public behavior. The Button can, more broadly, be seen as representing a starting point for discussion, inquiry and debate. Students at Penn have never been accused of not thinking.

When polled, the vast majority of students at this exciting Ivy League university, whose national standing in a variety of published surveys has steadily increased in the last decade, love being students there. The diversity of the student body, the quality of the faculty, the opportunities for extracurricular involvement in a large array of activities, the strong sense of school spirit and a commitment to the betterment of the surrounding community are but a few of the elements that have made Penn a truly great place to live and study. If you are willing to work hard and find intellectual challenge up your alley, then you may well find that Benjamin Franklin had the right idea when he popped a few buttons while throwing his weight behind the University of Pennsylvania.
—*Jonathan Berken*

FYI
If you come to Penn, you'd better bring "the ability to throw toast like a discus."
What is a typical weekend schedule? "Party like a rock star all weekend long."
If I could change one thing about Penn, I'd "make West Philly safer."
Three things that every student at Penn should do before graduating are "go see Mask and Wig,
   read Ben Franklin's autobiography and have sex under the Button."

University of Pittsburgh

Address: 4227 Fifth Avenue, First Floor Alumni Hall Pittsburgh, PA 15260
Phone: 412-624-7488
E-mail address: oafa@pitt.edu
Web site URL: www.pitt.edu
Year Founded: 1787
Private or Public: Public
Religious Affiliation: None
Location: Urban
Number of Applicants: 19,056
Percent Accepted: 56%
Percent Accepted who enroll: 32%
Number Entering: 3,419
Number of Transfers Accepted each Year: 1,157
Middle 50% SAT range: M: 580–670, CR: 570–670, **Wr:** Unreported
Middle 50% ACT range: 24–30
Early admission program EA/ED/None: None

Percentage accepted through EA or ED: NA
EA and ED deadline: NA
Regular Deadline: Rolling
Application Fee: $45
Full time Undergraduate enrollment: 17,427
Total enrollment: 25,715
Percent Male: 49%
Percent Female: 51%
Total Percent Minority or Unreported: 19%
Percent African-American: 8%
Percent Asian/Pacific Islander: 5%
Percent Hispanic: 1%
Percent Native-American: 0%
Percent International: 1%
Percent in-state/out of state: 83%/17%
Percent from Public HS: Unreported
Retention Rate: 90%
Graduation Rate 4-year: 56%

Graduation Rate 6-year: 75%
Percent Undergraduates in On-campus housing: 45%
Number of official organized extracurricular organizations: 450
3 Most popular majors: Marketing/Marketing Management, Psychology, Speech and Rhetorical Studies
Student/Faculty ratio: 16:1
Average Class Size: 14
Percent of students going to grad school: 38%
Tuition and Fees: $23,290
In-State Tuition and Fees if different: $13,642
Cost for Room and Board: $8,600
Percent receiving financial aid out of those who apply, first year: 68%
Percent receiving financial aid among all students: 52%

T hough the University of Pittsburgh is definitely a large research institution, it is anything but impersonal. Pitt's wealth of resources allow students the freedom to pursue very individualized academic and extracurricular interests while supplementing their education with the cultural and professional benefits of living in the energetic city of Pittsburgh.

Academics: Every Man for Himself?

Well-known for its medical and nursing schools, Pitt offers difficult pre-med and nursing programs that many incoming students take advantage of—at first. "Tons of freshmen come in pre-med," said one sophomore, "but the science programs are really hard, and not many stick with it." Other popular majors include business, communications, and philosophy, and students say that the creative writing community has a strong support system, as well.

Students praise the University Honors College (UHC) for its flexibility and seem-

ingly limitless opportunities. The UHC has an office in the school's iconic Cathedral of Learning and offers specific classes and a Bachelor of Philosophy degree. However, unlike other universities' honors colleges – which often require membership or enrollment to participate—any student who demonstrates high caliber work and wants to pursue more rigorous, independent study can reap UHC benefits. In addition to offering small courses like "Ethics and Leadership in Organizations" and a philosophy seminar on the apocalypse, UHC also offers many research and summer opportunities, like the Brackenridge summer fellowships. "Through the Brackenridge fellowship, one of my friends did an analysis of Leave it to Beaver as a reflection of social norms," said one senior.

Another special academic option is Pitt's Living Learning Communities. Located on designated floors in Pitt's residence halls, these communities offer students with particular academic or professional interests a way to meet more students like them. In addition, the communities—which range from "Entrepreneurial Experience" to "French Language and Culture"—plan activities to complement each community's focus. Pitt offers learning communities for freshmen without a residential component as well; students in these communities take the same blocks of courses and meet once a week to discuss issues related to their common interest.

Nevertheless, one student said, "The Living Learning Communities are a good idea in theory, but I don't think enough people participate in them for them to be effective." Students agree that most Pitt students are apathetic about the amount of extraordinary opportunities Pitt offers; for example, students say that many people don't take advantage of UHC because they don't seek it out. Students agree that initiative is key to getting what you want from Pitt academics. They praise professors for being very accessible and say that it's fairly easy to take courses outside of one's major. Many students study abroad and emphasize that academic options at Pitt are abundant, though not handed to students on silver platters. "If you initiate independent studies, you can easily work with professors," said one junior politics, philosophy, and economics major. Students say that academics at Pitt tend to be "pretty interdisciplinary" and that professors and departments will work with students' interests, as long as the student takes the initiative. "Not everybody tries to combine departments or propose their own projects, so professors get excited when students do," said one philosophy major.

However, the school's large size means some red tape when it comes to advising and enrolling. While students in the Honors College say they have no problems getting into the courses they want, one junior English major described the online registration process as "very stressful." Another junior complained of the prevalence of night classes, saying, "I've had to take a night class every semester because it's so hard to get into classes." In addition, freshman year courses can be quite large, but by the end of sophomore year, students say that they are happily enrolled in smaller courses.

City Living
Just as Pitt has a wealth of academic opportunities for students to tap into, the University presents students many chances to take advantage of the mid-size city in which it is located. Students rave about PITT ARTS, a

program that facilitates on- and off-campus arts experiences, free admission to Pittsburgh's museums, discounted tickets to arts events, and even free Arts Encounters, weekly opportunities for about 30 students to see a show and enjoy a nice dinner for no cost. While getting tickets can sometimes be competitive, one junior said, "If you've never gone, you get first priority, but I don't think very many people know about it."

Students were apathetic about Pitt's dorm life, saying that by junior year, the vast majority moves to cheaper off-campus housing in the surrounding neighborhood of Oakland. But that doesn't mean they give up Pitt's great on-campus dining options; the school's meal plan is extremely flexible. For foodies, there is no shortage of popular, inexpensive restaurants in the Oakland area to cater to students' late night cravings as well. Most local restaurants—including India Garden, an "amazing" student favorite—offer half-priced food after 10 pm. On Thursday, Friday, and Saturday nights before 3:30 am, students also recommend heading to T-Rav's BBQ Lab for top-notch homemade barbeque staples.

> **"If you go to Pitt, you're part of Pittsburgh."**

Perhaps because of their shared love of Pittsburgh's successful professional sports teams (the city is home to the Penguins, the Pirates, and the Steelers), Pitt students and Pittsburgh residents get along well. "If you go to Pitt, you're part of Pittsburgh," said one senior. Although residents in Oakland sometimes get a little cranky about students' frequent house parties, many students work in the nearby area and say that Pittsburghers love to chat them up. Moreover, while a lot of students participate in work-study programs on-campus, Pitt also allows students to receive academic credit for internships in downtown Pittsburgh, further connecting the University with the community.

Fun and Games
Because of older students' migration to off-campus housing, Pitt's social scene is dominated by house parties. Students say that although there are some good bars in Oakland, most people don't frequent them, and the freshman population dominates attendance at fraternity parties.

But the school's thriving party scene has caused the University some problems. Although students say that the majority drinks, Pitt promotes a zero-tolerance alcohol policy for students under the age of 21, and the policy is strictly enforced (particularly in the dorms near central campus). In fact, some students say that police officers wait at hospitals to cite underage students that show up for alcohol-related medical issues; as a consequence, many students avoid seeking medical attention when they probably should.

Students say that while they value their own extracurricular activities, they often don't interact with students outside of their social groups. In other words, students on the mock trial team hang out with other students on the mock trial team, and students in fraternities and sororities hang out with other students in fraternities and sororities. "I don't think I could tell you who the student-body president is," said one sophomore. Students

are also not big fans of school-sponsored fun, which might contribute to the University's cliquish tendency. "The school's a huge fan of ice cream socials," said one junior. "No one wants to go to that many ice cream socials."

Despite the variety of social groups on campus, students also say the school doesn't boast significant ethnic diversity. "We like to say that Pitt has the most diverse population of white people that you've ever seen," said one junior communications major. "The city is very diverse, but the school just isn't," she added.

Nevertheless, for students who are willing and excited to explore a variety of academic and social options, the University of Pittsburgh is a great choice. Because the school's opportunities run the gamut from cutting-edge undergraduate scientific research at Pitt's renowned medical school to free tickets to theater performances, all kinds of students can find their niche at Pitt if they know where to look.—*Lauren Oyler*

FYI
If you come to Pitt, you'd better bring "initiative and a love of a Pittsburgh sports team."
What's the typical weekend schedule? "Weekends start on Thursday evenings (unless you're a freshman and someone convinced you to take recitations on Friday). On Fridays, go to a house party and then eat at India Garden or T-Rav's for late-night barbecue. Saturdays, attend a theater performance or visit a museum and then party at night. Sundays, get breakfast at Pamela's Diner and study."
If I could change one thing about Pitt, I'd "make it more diverse and get the cliques to mesh a little bit more."

Ursinus College

Address: PO Box 1000, 601 Main Street, Collegeville, PA 19426-1000
Phone: 610-409-3200
E-mail address: admissions@ursinus.edu
Web site URL: www.ursinus.edu
Year Founded: 1869
Private or Public: Private
Religious Affiliation: None
Location: Suburban
Number of Applicants: 6,192
Percent Accepted: 55%
Percent Accepted who enroll: 16%
Number Entering: 545
Number of Transfers Accepted each Year: 11
Middle 50% SAT range: M: 570–670, CR: 570–680, Wr: 560–660
Middle 50% ACT range: 25–29
Early admission program EA/ED/None: EA and ED

Percentage accepted through EA or ED: 62%/62%
EA and ED deadline: 1-Dec, 1-Jan
Regular Deadline: 15-Feb
Application Fee: $50/free online
Full time Undergraduate enrollment: 1,680
Total enrollment: 1,680
Percent Male: 46%
Percent Female: 54%
Total Percent Minority or Unreported: 28%
Percent African-American: 6%
Percent Asian/Pacific Islander: 4%
Percent Hispanic: 3%
Percent Native-American: 0%
Percent International: 1%
Percent in-state/out of state: 58%/42%
Percent from Public HS: 61%
Retention Rate: 88%

Graduation Rate 4-year: 71%
Graduation Rate 6-year: 74%
Percent Undergraduates in On-campus housing: 95%
Number of official organized extracurricular organizations: 88
3 Most popular majors: Biology, Economics, Psychology
Student/Faculty ratio: 12:1
Average Class Size: 9
Percent of students going to grad school: 34%
Tuition and Fees: $36,910
In-State Tuition and Fees if different: No difference
Cost for Room and Board: $8,800
Percent receiving financial aid out of those who apply, first year: Unreported
Percent receiving financial aid among all students: 91%

From day one, students at Ursinus College are placed on an even playing field. All freshmen enter the same rooming lottery, all freshmen are issued Dell laptops, and all freshmen take part in the Common Intellectual Experience (CIE) core curriculum program. But to say that life in Collegeville, Pennsylvania, is ordinary or simple is utterly false. With a lively student body and traditions dating back to the nineteenth century, this small college provides students with the opportunity to work closely with an esteemed faculty and the tools to grow into mature adults who actively explore and question the world around them.

Cooperation and Collaboration

Known for the close relationships between faculty and students, this small college includes a wide range of majors in both the sciences and the humanities. Although Ursinus is known as a popular choice of premed students, the most popular majors for undergraduates are psychology and economics. But UC has majors for everyone—even

dancers—with the addition of dance as a major in recent years.

Part of this collaboration between faculty and students is developed starting from their first days during freshman year, when all Ursinus students participate in the CIE Program—the Common Intellectual Experience. This liberal studies seminar epitomizes the value that the staff at Ursinus puts on the development of conversational skills and well-roundedness of its students. Freshmen are required to take the class for both semesters. Groups of sixteen freshmen address major life questions such as: "What does it mean to be human?", "How should humans live their lives?", and "What is the universe and what should our place be within it?" The course was designed so that each freshman student would be reading the same material at the same time, facilitating discussion amongst the entire entering class. By looking at works of art, classical writing and political theory, professors are leaders but at the same time members of the discussion group. The CIE instructors are from a wide range of disciplines, and this means that there is no expert on the subject; instead, everyone takes part in learning and growth.

Collegeville, PA: Location, Location, Location

Students at Ursinus are not lacking in things to do. With the city of Philadelphia only 30 miles away and free shuttle buses to the city, UC students are not too far away from the Liberty Bell, the Rocky Steps, concerts and urban life. But even with this at their fingertips, many students say they rarely leave their dorms in the quaint town of Collegeville. With 97% of students living on campus, location of dormitories is a big deal. Students living on campus enter the lottery system to determine their living situation. Older students get preference and the prizes tend to be the restored Victorian-era homes that are located right on campus. But no fear, even for freshmen, the living quarters are definitely not like your stereotypical cinderblock high rise, and most freshmen seem to enjoy the dorm atmosphere.

Thanks to its renowned collection of American arts, the Berman Museum brings a great number of art lovers to Collegeville and Ursinus. Besides the beautiful brick walkways and historic buildings, the campus at UC is enhanced by the famous sculptures from the museum. These statues are all over campus and some of them are extremely realistic. One freshman said that everyone "freaks out" when they see the well-known statue of the old lady who is so lifelike it's "creepy." It is pretty common to see tourists and students taking pictures with the old lady.

Mixin' it Up

According to students, there is hardly any difference socially between upperclassmen and "the new kids." Even juniors and seniors involved in frats do not act superior and this is partially due to all the efforts by the administration at Ursinus to raise school unity and keep all the grades mixed. Therefore, for students of many different ages, a typical night out at Ursinus consists of starting out in the Reimert, which is a residence hall made up of large suites that house some local fraternities and sororities. Although there are only a few nationally recognized Greek organizations on campus, some of the favorite social events of the year for many Ursinus students are the "Dated." Joint-hosted by a fraternity and a sorority, these

events are always memorable occasions. Students sign up ahead of time, and they are taken on buses off campus where there are big parties at places like firehouses with dancing, music, etc. Students like the Reimert because it is always open and there are always people ready to have a good time. But if you are not at Reimert, then you'll probably start your night off at one of the houses on Main Street, which tend to be known for their great parties as well.

> "The campus and the people at Ursinus are personable and it is almost impossible to get lost in the shuffle."

With all these parties going on, it makes sense to wonder about the drug policy at Ursinus. Students describe the administration as relatively lenient for everyone except those living in freshman dorms, where rules tend to be stricter. As long as you keep the alcohol within the confines of the buildings, trouble tends to stay away—but things become a little trickier when going outside with alcohol. If caught, a common punishment is said to be community service. But even with the party scene at Ursinus, students appreciate the fact that there is not a big drug scene at the school and that students are not typically pressured into doing things which they do not feel comfortable about.

Activities Galore

Some of the most prominent clubs on campus are *The Grizzly* (the student paper), the Campus Activity Board, Student Government and the Residence Hall Association. According to students, the CAB always has stuff going on in the lounge underneath Wismer Cafeteria such as prerelease movies and casino games. Recently, the Student Council successfully kicked off "Late Night Lower Wismer," where there is popcorn, videogames such as Rockband, a Wii system, a pool table and karaoke. The Wismer Center is considered a major social center on campus that houses dining facilities, social lounges, a snack bar and game room. But even with big clubs such as the CAB and *The Grizzly*, it doesn't mean there aren't any obscure or unique organizations in Collegeville. There is a scuba club and a meditation group that meets once a week to "de-stress."

Athletics are also a big part of extracurricular activities at Ursinus, and about 50% of students compete on varsity sports teams. The Bears are part of the Centennial Conference, founded in 1992 for small mid-Atlantic academic institutions, and compete at the NCAA Division III level against schools such as Dickinson, Bryn Mawr, and Johns Hopkins. In fact, in 2006, the Ursinus field hockey team was the Div. III National Champion. Even though the majority of students participate in either varsity or intramural athletics at school, most still say that sports are not the major focus on campus. But even so, UC students are fortunate to have great facilities. With a marvelous fitness center that boasts new machines and an indoor track, students have little reason not to be active.

History and Tradition

According to lore, the tree under which author J. D. Salinger wrote his book *Catcher in the Rye* while he was a student at Ursinus still stands today near the end zone of the football field. A plaque is now placed outside the room where he lived during his time in Collegeville as a student. Ursinus is a place where tradition and history matter. According to campus tour guides, Ursinus was even at one point in the *Guinness Book of World Records* for having the most marriages among students. From the moment undergraduates go through the typical icebreaker games during their first day as freshmen, a sense of unity is apparent, and this lasts through the years. By the time Ursinus students are seniors and ready to graduate, the majority is even comfortable enough with each other to slide down one of the fountains on campus completely naked. Every year there is also an event called Air Band, which is a lip-synch and dance competition for charity. Ursinus's tradition of equality even extends to the technological realm. Since 2000, Ursinus's laptop initiative has provided every student and faculty member with a laptop. Some of the goals of the project are to improve communications between students and faculty, to bolster the sense of community around campus and to provide equal computer access for all students.

It is this sense of togetherness that brings students to Ursinus. Instead of just being a number, students make real connections that last. There is an appreciation for the small, picturesque campus and the welcoming community where everyone is equally appreciated: students, faculty and staff. According to one sophomore, "The campus and the people at Ursinus are personable and it is almost impossible to get lost in the shuffle."—*Emily St. Jean*

FYI

If you come to Ursinus College, you'd better bring "plenty of snacks because the cafeterias and other eating areas have terrible hours."

What's the typical weekend schedule? "Wake up around 11 or 12, go to brunch until one, study or watch football during the afternoon, dinner, and then out for the rest of the night."

If I could change one thing about Ursinus, I'd change "the school name, because it gets really old hearing people mispronounce the name or make dumb jokes about it."

Three things every student at Ursinus should do before graduating are "slide down a fountain naked before graduation, take a picture with one of the statues on campus (preferably the old lady), and go to a 'Dated.'"

Villanova University

Address: 800 Lancaster Avenue, Villanova, PA 19085-1672
Phone: 610-519-4000
E-mail address: gotovu@villanova.edu
Web site URL: www.villanova.edu
Year Founded: 1842
Private or Public: Private
Religious Affiliation: Roman Catholic
Location: Suburban
Number of Applicants: 13,098
Percent Accepted: 46%
Percent Accepted who enroll: 27%
Number Entering: 1,643
Number of Transfers Accepted each Year: 125
Middle 50% SAT range: M: 620–710, CR: 580–680, Wr: Unreported
Middle 50% ACT range: 28–31
Early admission program EA/ED/None: EA

Percentage accepted through EA or ED: Unreported
EA and ED deadline: 1-Nov
Regular Deadline: 7-Jan
Application Fee: $75
Full time Undergraduate enrollment: 6,390
Total enrollment: 10,152
Percent Male: 49%
Percent Female: 51%
Total Percent Minority or Unreported: 18%
Percent African-American: 4%
Percent Asian/Pacific Islander: 7%
Percent Hispanic: 7%
Percent Native-American: 1%
Percent International: Unreported
Percent in-state/out of state: 25%/75%
Percent from Public HS: 55%
Retention Rate: 95%

Graduation Rate 4-year: 82%
Graduation Rate 6-year: 88%
Percent Undergraduates in On-campus housing: 70%
Number of official organized extracurricular organizations: 250
3 Most popular majors: Nursing, Finance, Communication
Student/Faculty ratio: 11:1
Average Class Size: 22
Percent of students going to grad school: 23%
Tuition and Fees: $36,950
In-State Tuition and Fees if different: No difference
Cost for Room and Board: $10,000
Percent receiving financial aid out of those who apply, first year: 80%
Percent receiving financial aid among all students: 45%

Located 12 miles from Philadelphia in suburban Radnor Township, Villanova's lush 254-acre campus is dominated by the spires of St. Thomas of Villanova Chapel. The school was founded by the Order of Saint Augustine in 1842 and is officially Catholic, though students from all denominations now attend. While St. Augustine looms large in Villanova's core curriculum and institutional memory, current students are more preoccupied with something else: the school's stellar basketball team, which has been ranked top-10 in the nation. "If you go to any basketball game or any sporting event, people paint their bodies in blue and wear Villanova shirts; there's a huge amount of school spirit," one freshman said. What distinguishes the school, the student continued, is "school spirit and a commitment to service."

One Campus, Four Schools

Students apply for admission to one of four undergraduate schools: the College of Liberal Arts and Sciences, the School of Business, the College of Engineering, or the College of Nursing. While the College of Liberal Arts and Sciences is the largest, with about half of each incoming class of 1600, the business and engineering schools are growing more popular, having received competitive national rankings in recent years.

Though each college has its own course requirements, all freshmen take the two-semester core Augustine and Culture Seminar (ACS). "ACS is really just English, but they call it something fancy because we go to a Catholic school," one freshman explained. The course covers literature from Shakespeare to Augustine's "Confessions" and purposely mixes students from different colleges in the same classroom.

Villanova prides itself on its small class sizes, which average about 22 people, students said. While some introductory engineering and nursing lectures can be huge, a first-year business student recalled his surprise at having only 30 students in his largest class, introductory microeconomics. The use of teaching assistants is rare and students find their professors understanding and accessible. "Professors here are very open; they'll invite you to dinner at their house after the last class session," a business student said.

Don't get caught by VEMS

After a week of classes, students go out on Fridays and Saturdays. Many parties are off-campus, leading one freshman to comment that "the party scene doesn't really start until junior year," when students are both allowed to have cars and old enough to frequent bars and clubs in Philadelphia. Other freshmen say that fake IDs are common and that parties closer to campus are not hard to find. Another popular party destination is UPenn, whose alcohol policies are reportedly less stringent than Villanova's.

True to its Catholic roots, Villanova maintains a harsh stance against underage drinking. Resident Assistants (RAs) are required to write up underage students for alcohol possession, and inebriated students who encounter Villanova's Emergency Medical Service team—referred to as "VEMS"—can be put on probation. "They tell you VEMS is student-run and that it won't get you in trouble, but it makes your life shit," one freshman said.

Nightlife aside, students often venture to Philadelphia to shop, eat out, or see a movie. The city is accessible by train (two train lines run through Villanova's campus) or by campus shuttle. The Campus Activities Team organizes everything from trips to Philly for art shows and sports games to on-campus concerts, comedy shows, and karaoke nights. The Connelly Center, a student center and hangout spot, hosts weekly movie screenings and has game tables in its lounges.

Sports, particularly basketball and football games, are a perennial draw for the entire campus community. "Our school has an insane amount of school spirit," one business student said. "People want to go to the basketball game and be surrounded by other Villanova fans. Not just students go; families even bring their small children and come watch the game."

Meet me at the Oreo

On-campus housing is guaranteed for three years, and students live in one of three locations. All freshmen live on South Campus, in residential halls of doubles and triples, and nursing, engineering, business, and arts and sciences students are all intermingled.

While getting to class from South Campus can be somewhat of a trek, South Campus has its own dining hall, known as the Spit (South Pit), and a supermarket, the Sparket (South Campus Market). Sophomores usually live on Main Campus, home to many academic buildings and another dining hall, and juniors move to apartment houses on West Campus. Most seniors are required to find housing off campus.

The cafeteria fare is "pretty good, for people who aren't too picky," a freshman noted. "It's obviously not as good as home-cooked food, but you can still survive on it." For better food on campus, students can head to the Italian Kitchen, the Corner Grill, or the Belle Air Terrace. The Bartley Exchange, in the business building, has "the best food on campus, but for that one you have to use your wallet, not meal points," another student said. Within walking distance, the surrounding area of Radnor also contains some fast food outlets.

> "Our school has an insane amount of school spirit. People want to go to the basketball game and be surrounded by other Villanova fans."

The Connelly Center and the dining halls are popular student hangouts, as is the Pavilion, where the basketball team plays its games. At the center of Main Campus sits the Oreo—"this statue that looks like an oreo"—which serves as both a meeting place and a place for clubs to advertise and recruit new members. Another meeting place is the chapel, whose spires are easily visible from afar. For churchgoing students, Villanova offers frequent masses.

Sports and Service

Among other extracurricular options, many students engage in sports and community service projects. Students who are not Varsity athletes often participate in club or intramural sports, depending on their level of commitment. "Any sports club is really popular; any sport that you can think of, there's probably a club for it," a freshman said, whether your passion be Frisbee or Quidditch.

The St. Thomas of Villanova Day of Service is an annual event that sends groups of students, faculty, staff, and alumni into Philadelphia to perform service projects, which range from cleaning and painting old facilities to preparing and serving food in shelters and soup kitchens. Each year Villanova also hosts the largest student-run Special Olympics in the world, which draws over 1,000 athletes for competitions in six Olympic-type sports.

Greek life is a large, though not dominant, part of campus life, with about 40% of students joining a fraternity or sorority. "You see people wearing Greek letters a lot," one student said. "I think people want to join frats even though the school tries to sway kids away from that." However, as there are no Greek houses on campus, they do not overly impact the social scene, students said.

Villanova has been criticized for its lack of diversity; 75% of the student body is white, lending the school the nickname "Vanilla Nova." As one student said, "While there are people of different races and backgrounds, when people think of Villanova they think of a white preppy student, like girls in UGGs and trench coats." The school is no longer monolithically Catholic, however. The school "isn't pressuring kids to conform or change their beliefs at all," one nonreligious student said. "The school is just offering a new way of thinking."— *Antonia Woodford*

FYI
If I could change one thing about Villanova, I would change "the strict policies."
What differentiates Villanova the most from other colleges is "the amount of school spirit that we have."
Three things every student at Villanova should do before graduating are "go to a basketball game, visit Philadelphia, and do some sort of community service activity, like the Day of Service or the Special Olympics."

Rhode Island

Students considering Brown should not
let its centuries-old Ivy League traditions fool them; Brown's history of
progressive teachings has been a hallmark
of its undergraduate experience since the
school's founding in 1764. Today, you'll find
that Brown has carried this tradition of intellectual and extracurricular curiosity into
the twenty-first century, cementing its place
as a true haven for fine academics and passionate interests in an environment that celebrates free thought.

So Chill and Satisfied
The absence of any general requirements
at Brown is part of its overall atmosphere
of freedom and experimentation. The "New
Curriculum" allows Brown students to shape

their own programs of study, which they said
offers a number of advantages. One senior explained that "when you don't have requirements, it works for both people who don't
know what they want to do and people who
know exactly what they want to do; it helps
you structure your education for whatever fits
you best." He added that, "you get a school
full of people doing what they love." Brown
also offers its famous Satisfactory/No Credit
option, where students can opt to take as
many classes as they like on a pass/fail evaluation basis instead of for a letter grade. While
most students only choose to do this a few
times a year, it lets them experiment in a subject outside their normal area of interest without having to worry about their numerical
performance. One student said that it "goes in

line with Brown's whole philosophy of giving you freedom to explore new fields without feeling that it all has to be related to your future success and your résumé."

Although many students choose to major in International Relations or Biology, they can specialize in more unusual majors or "concentrations" as well. Brown recently expanded its Department of Egyptology to include Ancient Western Asian Studies, and the Neuroscience department is well-known for its professors and cutting-edge research. Professor Emeritus Barrett Hazeltine's popular business management classes attract many students, and Biology professor Ken Miller was recently a leading witness in the Supreme Court case debating the teaching of evolution in schools. Adventurous students interested in the arts may cross-register at the nearby—and equally famed—Rhode Island School of Design.

Students agreed that while introductory courses can have up to a few hundred people in them, upper-level classes shrink in size considerably. Freshmen also have the option to sign up for First Year Seminars capped at 20 students, which offer an opportunity for first-years to get to know each other and a professor in a lively, intimate discussion setting. Professors are described as being very accessible if students need them to be. In addition to being required to host weekly office hours, many Brown professors get to know their students' names, even in large lecture courses. As one student put it, "If you're willing to take a little initiative, you can build really strong relationships."

The pervasive laid-back attitude regarding academics is another strong characteristic of Brown. One senior confided that, "while it's really competitive to get into Brown, it's really not competitive when you get here." Although "the vast majority of people here are still working really hard," students say that it is rare for people to lose their cool about GPAs or class curves—in public, at least. This relaxed philosophy allows people to collaborate on work and generally to "stay away from bragging about how hardworking or stressed you are." Another senior explained that "it's hard to compete because everyone's passionate about their own interests and has their own achievements along different dimensions."

Conservative Commentators Need Not Apply

Every year at Brown, the Queer Alliance hosts "Sex Power God," a wild party at which students are encouraged to wear as little clothing as possible. In 2005, SPG got some surprise attention when it was featured on the TV show "The O'Reilly Factor" as an example of Ivy League–sanctioned debauchery. Although Bill O'Reilly may not approve, students said that one of their favorite aspects of Brown is its liberalism and free-spirited atmosphere. Although they caution against giving in entirely to the conception of Brown students as "pot-smoking, flannel-wearing hippies," in general, students concurred that there's some truth to the image. The campus is "overwhelmingly liberal," although conservatives do have a voice, and students said that "everyone here is interested in making the world a better place."

In terms of encouraging diversity, students said that the admissions office is doing a good job geographically, but social divisions based on income and ethnicity are sometimes apparent. Students agreed that the mostly generous financial aid policy has improved in the past few years and has made attending an elite private school a reality for many low-income students.

Although the actual number of students in fraternities and sororities at Brown may be relatively small, their weekend parties are still very popular, especially among underclassmen. Everyone also finds themselves at parties in the dorms, usually earlier in the night, before they head out to some of the local bars and clubs in the downtown area or on nearby Thayer Street. The club Fish Co. is reportedly the place to be on Wednesday nights. Upperclassmen often attend parties at off-campus houses. Brown's policies on alcohol and drug use are described as "extremely loose," and campus police and Residential Counselors in the dorms "are really there just to make sure that you're being safe and not causing trouble." One girl said that she would often come back to her dorm hall at night and smell pot, but she said that "it's not at all something that people will pressure you to do, although it's definitely there if you want it."

Brown students find it easy to take the bus or train to Boston or New York on the weekends, but many find that just staying on College Hill in Providence is satisfactory. Brown's NCAA Division I teams usually have games, although few students reportedly attend them.

Life on College Hill

Upon setting foot on campus, visitors to Brown immediately notice the striking colonial-style brick buildings and the wide, inviting Main Green. The campus is described as "very New England," complete with ivy and impeccable grounds. However, today's Brown students have adapted their school's austere backdrop to the twenty-first century. On sunny days, students crowd the lawns with lemonade stands, soccer games, back massage stations, and the occasional hookah.

Most freshmen live in Keeney Quadrangle, which houses about 600 students and is known as the "freshman zoo." The rest live in dorms that range from a few blocks to a 10-minute walk away. While Keeney is agreed to be the most social dorm, people said that the other dorms foster long-term relationships as well. Everyone is assigned a roommate in a double, and the traditional long hallways are coed. The bathrooms are supposed to be single-sex, but some students reported having members of the opposite sex invade when their lines were too long. Freshmen are organized into units of 40 to 60 and are assigned undergraduate RCs. Students said they made the majority of their friends in their first-year units, since "it's a large enough group of people that you get a good variety of interests and personalities." After freshman year, students enter the Housing Lottery to draw for several different arrangements, ranging from triples to suites.

The two main all-you-can-eat dining halls, the "V-Dub" and the "Ratty," got mixed reviews, with most students agreeing that the fare quickly grows monotonous, even though the "V-Dub" does have a vegetarian line. The meal plan was recently expanded to allow diners more freedom to use their plans at after-hours eateries on campus, including the Ivy Room and Joe's. Nearby Thayer Street is an ever-popular option for a wide variety of food, from the famous falafels at East Side Pocket to Antonio's Pizza. If you want to venture off the Hill into the downtown area, the Dominican food gets good reviews for its affordability and exotic allure, while Café Paragon is "a good place to go for a good meal with your parents."

While one junior said she did not know why Brown students would need to leave College Hill to entertain themselves, the recently renovated and revitalized downtown Providence is an enticing reason. The city has spruced itself up in the past several years, and its museums, events on the river, and "humongous" mall are attractive study breaks for students.

Campaigns and Cracked Pots

At Brown, students know how to balance ambitious activities with downtime. A sophomore said he thought that "everyone here is involved in at least two or three extracurricular activities, usually very different from each other, and in a very driven way." Politics are a common interest, with the Brown College Democrats widely cited as the most popular organization. One sophomore even said that "a popular joke is that the Brown Green Party is bigger than the campus Republicans." No matter which party you pick, students say that the small size of Rhode Island is conducive in allowing them to get involved in local and statewide politics. "I have a lot of friends who feel like they're making changes in social policy and education reform—they really have an impact on who gets elected." The Queer Alliance draws many members, as do cultural heritage groups and a number of social activism organizations like the Brown Darfur Action Network and Amnesty International. A capella and dance groups also have a strong presence.

Recent years have seen an increase in the involvement of students in community service organizations in downtown Providence, challenging the belief that all Brown students avoid leaving College Hill. Some students also have jobs down the hill, although "Brown provides a lot of opportunities for employment, especially through Dining Services."

> **"It's very Brown to think 'I'm free and naked and helping people by giving them donuts.'"**

Brown students revel in a number of zany traditions that pervade the college's free-spirited atmosphere. Every finals period, a group of students organizes in secret and shows up on campus at a random time to run through the buildings, from the libraries to the dorms, in what is termed the "Naked Donut Run." "It's very Brown to think 'I'm free and naked and helping people by giving them donuts,'" one student remarked. A legend surrounding a mysterious figure from Brown's past has also become tradition. On Friday the 13th, students pay homage to the mythical professor Josiah Carberry, who supposedly studied "psychoceramics," or cracked pots.

"I don't think we conform to non-conformity, but people are not afraid to express themselves," one student said. Indeed, Brown does leave its undergraduates many opportunities for freedom of expression, whether it is by letting students choose their own classes, run a medley of organizations or spearhead campaigns. While it may be famous for its unstructured atmosphere, Brown students find that their self-motivation and passionate interests help them to shape unique college experiences.—*Kimberly Chow*

FYI

If you come to Brown, you'd better bring "liberal political beliefs and a scarf."

What's the typical weekend schedule? "Friday night go to a room party; Saturday sleep in, then do community service in Providence; Saturday night go to a frat or a party thrown by an organization, then do work all Sunday."

If I could change one thing about Brown, "I would want people to venture off College Hill into downtown Providence more."

Three things that every student at Brown should do before graduating: "March against the University, like to protest the bookstore going corporate, take a completely ridiculous class that has nothing to do with your major, and try to get to the tops of as many buildings as you can."

Rhode Island School of Design

Address: 2 College Street Providence, RI 02903

Phone: 401-454-6300

E-mail address: admissions@risd.edu

Web site URL: www.risd.edu

Year Founded: 1877

Private or Public: Private

Religious Affiliation: None

Location: Urban

Number of Applicants: 2,511

Percent Accepted: 34%

Percent Accepted who enroll: 47%

Number Entering: 398

Number of Transfers Accepted each Year: 151

Middle 50% SAT range: M: 550–670, CR: 530–660, Wr: Unreported

Middle 50% ACT range: 22–29

Early admission program EA/ED/None: EA

Percentage accepted through EA or ED: Unreported

EA and ED deadline: 15-Dec

Regular Deadline: 15-Feb

Application Fee: $50

Full time Undergraduate enrollment: 1,882

Total enrollment: 1,882

Percent Male: 35%

Percent Female: 65%

Total Percent Minority or Unreported: 49%

Percent African-American: 2%

Percent Asian/Pacific Islander: 14%

Percent Hispanic: 5%

Percent Native-American: <1%

Percent International: 12%

Percent in-state/out of state: Unreported

Percent from Public HS: 60%

Retention Rate: Unreported

Graduation Rate 4-year: Unreported

Graduation Rate 6-year: Unreported

Percent Undergraduates in On-campus housing: 33%

Number of official organized extracurricular organizations: 35

3 Most popular majors: Graphic Design, Illustration, Industrial Design

Student/Faculty ratio: 11:1

Average Class Size: 13

Percent of students going to grad school: Unreported

Tuition and Fees: $27,510

In-State Tuition and Fees if different: No difference

Cost for Room and Board: $7,709

Percent receiving financial aid out of those who apply, first year: Unreported

Percent receiving financial aid among all students: Unreported

---

The Rhode Island School of Design does not offer your "typical" college experience—there are not many sports teams, social life is secondary to schoolwork, and your English teacher might not care if you don't finish your reading assignment because she knows you spent eight hours doing studio work the day before. RISD (pronounced "RIZ-dee") is a serious school for serious art students. Students at RISD, a small campus in Providence, Rhode Island, that is adjacent to Brown University, can major in apparel design, art education, graphic design, industrial design, illustration, textiles, sculpture, glass, or animation, and there are many other options where those came from.

The campus is home to approximately 1,900 undergraduates. Students say the relatively low number of students allows for very intimate classes, in which the average size is 13 students.

All RISD freshmen are required to take Foundation Studies, a fundamentals program which consists of three classes: Drawing, Two-Dimensional Design, and Three-Dimensional Design. The program is meant to immerse students in the basics of art and visual design, and to help them explore their options in terms of majors. Freshmen are also given second priority (after seniors) in class selection so that they can experiment with classes before making a final decision on their area of concentration.

RISD is organized on a trimester schedule, which has positives and negatives according to students. Students are only given two weeks off for winter break, but they are also able to take more classes in one year. The second semester, which takes place right after winter break, is also unofficially designated as "relaxation time." According to one RISD junior, no one takes more than two classes during this period in January and February. "Most people only take one class during second semester because the first and third semesters are hardcore," she said.

Liberal arts courses are also required of every student, but they are definitely not the concentration of a RISD education. According to a RISD sophomore, History of Art and Visual Culture is the most popular liberal arts department and some students even choose to major in this field rather than in a visual art. Students say the most popular visual art department is Illustration because it offers students a great deal of freedom in their studies and concentration. "It's a very open and free department—you can really take it anywhere you want and there aren't a lot of technical restrictions," one RISD junior said. The consensus among RISD students is that the hardest major is architecture, which some students playfully refer to as "archi-torture."

Getting into the class you want can be a nightmare at RISD, mostly because the class sizes are so small. There is also a precise hierarchy of preference in which seniors get first choice during enrollment, freshmen second choice, juniors third, and sophomores are left to fend for themselves at the bottom. As mentioned earlier, freshmen are given second priority so they can explore different classes before they pick their major. "As a sophomore, it was incredibly difficult to get the classes I wanted. I guess it's

fair in the long run, but it's still pretty frustrating," a current junior said.

According to interviewed students, the workload at RISD is rigorous to say the least. "There's not a lot of time to sleep because you're spending all night cutting paper, making books, and putting together your portfolio," said one RISD senior. Students also emphasize the necessity of attending class and say you are required to get a note from the nurse if you miss class due to illness, "just like high school." RISD students also have the option of taking classes at Brown, so if a RISD student wants to take a math class, there is nothing stopping her. Beginning in the 2008–2009 academic year, Brown and RISD began to collaborate to offer students a dual degree—the completion of a five-year program will allow students to receive a BA from Brown and BFA from RISD. Participating students must live on both campuses for two years each and must complete both degrees.

> **"There's not a lot of time to sleep because you're spending all night cutting paper, making books, and putting together your portfolio."**

Social life has been a point of contention among RISD students, mostly because the school's social scene is somewhat limited. According to one junior, the amount of work assigned to RISD students makes partying difficult, though some students do go to parties at Brown or to bars. All in all, social life is very much contained within the campus and mostly consists of private parties. "This is not a party school; it's a very serious school. If you're someone who wants to go somewhere with lots of parties and things, RISD probably isn't the school for you," one RISD freshman said. But that is not to say students don't make meaningful relationships or have close friends. A junior said everyone has a very good relationship with almost everyone else simply because the school is so small.

RISD freshmen and sophomores are required to live on campus, and many juniors and seniors choose to do so anyway. Freshmen are housed in the Quad, conveniently located right next to the main dining hall, the Met. Construction was recently completed on 15 Westminster, a new dorm building that also happens to be the location of the main library. Students say the new building is "great," "beautiful," and "centrally located," just a quick walk from the graphic design and illustration building. Housing is done by lottery after freshman year.

Despite the statistic that 65 percent of RISD students are female and 35 percent are male, most students said RISD is very diverse, and that you are able to "meet all sorts of people." There is a large population of international students, especially from Korea.

Student Alliance, the student governing body, is the primary student group on the RISD campus. It meets weekly to discuss student issues, which most recently have included concerns regarding social life at RISD. The Alliance is working to get administrative approval for a student center on campus to increase "hang out" space for students. Other student clubs include a cappella groups and cultural clubs. RISD has two varsity sports, basketball and hockey, both of which compete on the Brown campus. "Sports are not that big of a deal on campus," said one sophomore. "But we still support our teams."

Students describe the food at RISD as "decent" and "pretty good," but they do acknowledge that some dining halls have more options than others. A junior student said the best place to grab a quick bite to eat is the Portfolio Café, located right next to the library in Westminster 15.

The bottom line for students at RISD is their artistic education, and most are more than satisfied with the training they have received at the university. "RISD is the perfect school for me because I'm doing what I love," said one senior. "Make sure you really love this kind of work before you decide to come to RISD."—*Samantha Broussard-Wilson*

FYI
If you come to RISD, you'd better bring "your sketchbook."
What is the typical weekend schedule? "Work, work, and maybe a little extra work before bed."
If I could change one thing about RISD, I'd "give the students more time to sleep."
Three things every student at RISD should do before graduating are "go to a hockey game, explore the coffee shops in Providence, and go on any of the excursions offered, like Newport, New York City, or skiing."

Salve Regina University

Address: 100 Ochre Point Avenue, Newport, RI 02840-4192
Phone: 401-341-2908
E-mail address: sruadmis@salve.edu
Web site URL: www.salve.edu
Year Founded: 1947
Private or Public: Private
Religious Affiliation: Roman Catholic
Location: Suburban
Number of Applicants: 5,937
Percent Accepted: 59%
Percent Accepted who enroll: 16%
Number Entering: 560
Number of Transfers Accepted each Year: 121
Middle 50% SAT range: M: 510–590, CR: 510–580, Wr: Unreported
Middle 50% ACT range: 22–26
Early admission program EA/ED/None: EA

Percentage accepted through EA or ED: 26%
EA and ED deadline: 1-Nov
Regular Deadline: 1-Jan
Application Fee: $50
Full time Undergraduate enrollment: 2,127
Total enrollment: 2,700
Percent Male: 31%
Percent Female: 69%
Total Percent Minority or Unreported: 23%
Percent African-American: 1%
Percent Asian/Pacific Islander: 1%
Percent Hispanic: 3%
Percent Native-American: <1%
Percent International: 1%
Percent in-state/out of state: 15%/85%
Percent from Public HS: 62%
Retention Rate: 73%
Graduation Rate 4-year: 63%

Graduation Rate 6-year: 67%
Percent Undergraduates in On-campus housing: 58%
Number of official organized extracurricular organizations: 42
3 Most popular majors: Administration of Justice, Education, Nursing
Student/Faculty ratio: 14:1
Average Class Size: 16
Percent of students going to grad school: 20%
Tuition and Fees: $31,500
In-State Tuition and Fees if different: No difference
Cost for Room and Board: $10,700
Percent receiving financial aid out of those who apply, first year: 68%
Percent receiving financial aid among all students: 71%

Salve Regina College was founded under the tutelage of the Sisters of Mercy and was originally intended to be a liberal arts college in the Catholic tradition. It changed its name to Salve Regina University in 1991, but it still remains a serious liberal arts college with a considerable Catholic bent. Originally started as a nursing program, today's Salve Regina boasts both a popular and competitive nursing component and a wealth of additional programs of study. Students receive a well-rounded, liberal arts education, centered on an intensive core.

Liberal Arts with a Side of Catholicism

Salve Regina's most striking academic feature is the Core Curriculum, which every student must complete in order to graduate. The core is extremely intensive, covering a wide range of subjects and disciplines. The Core Curriculum consists of the Common Core, five courses which every single student takes, and the Core Complement, for which there is a choice between classes that fulfill the requirements. The Common Core includes Philosophy and Religious Studies courses, aimed at helping students understand the widespread influence of Judeo-Christian thought in the world, with a focus on Catholicism. One student described the curriculum as "definitely liberal arts by nature, but with a very religious overtone." Some students do not take kindly to having religion "stuffed down their throats," but others accept it as part of the school's mission. There is also an introductory course taken during freshman year entitled "Portal: Seeking Wisdom," which serves to introduce students to the liberal arts. The Core received mixed reactions from the students. One claimed that it was too restricting and the long list of requirements prevented her from going abroad for a semester. Another found the experience enlightening and instructive, albeit at times overwhelming. Although many of the Core classes deal with very similar subjects, each new subject is somehow refreshing, as one will "get something different out of it looking at it from a different angle than before."

Without a doubt, Salve's greatest academic strength is its commitment to student-professor interaction. One student earnestly said, "I absolutely adore my professors at Salve." When class sizes are so small and such a focus is placed on discussion and student participation, it's no surprise that students and instructors share a strong bond. Most classes have fewer than 20 students, and only the most popular introductory classes have classes larger than 30 students. Such great emphasis on exploration leads to some very lively discussions; students are "always engaged in class." Even in the larger classes, "there's really good discussions that come up," and the professors are still accessible.

> **"Our classes are held in mansions . . . can you say that about another school?"**

Salve students have many choices for their majors. Most liberal arts disciplines are covered, but the most popular majors are reportedly Nursing and Administration of Justice. The nursing program is one of the most difficult tracks at Salve. It has strict requirements: getting a C in *any* nursing course is considered "failing" and results in expulsion from the major. The popularity of the nursing program may explain one of Salve's most interesting facets. The nursing department has "very few male students" and, seeing as it's one of the largest majors, the university as a whole has a high female-to-male ratio.

Salve Girls and Some Salve Guys

One student noted that, "Walking around it's pretty obvious that you run into more girls than guys," but she didn't feel that it was "very noticeable." Unlike many student bodies, Salve seems very comfortable with itself. The school is markedly homogeneous. Naturally, the majority of students are affiliated with the Catholic Church in some way. Although there may be plenty of Catholics, one student warned that "the chapel is small and only a small percentage of students attends mass on Sundays." Furthermore, many of the students are described as white, preppy, and wealthy. One girl noted that, "Many people dress up for classes and carry around their Louis Vuitton and Coach bags." Only one student expressed an odious dislike of the stereotypical Salve kid, bemoaning their New England preppiness, although still admiring the school's quality of teaching. A word for the wise: although it may be difficult to fit into such a crowd, the students are for the most part pretty amiable and social. The typical student also "parties a lot and is very concerned with working out at the gym."

Salve students like to party. The campus is strictly dry, so most students have to go off campus to the apartments of upperclassmen in order to drink on the weekends. Despite being a dry campus, there are a lot of alcohol and drugs; there is a prevalence among the more well-to-do of some "rich man's drugs." It remains difficult and somewhat of a hassle for students to party, especially those that are underage. Many students go to nearby Newport on the weekends to go clubbing and to escape the strict campus rules. For those that do not want to stray far from campus or drink, the University hosts many dry events for the student body. Every spring the campus holds a concert. On top of that, a comedian performs every week, and every once in a while, bands or singers come to the weekly performance.

Newport: Bars, Beaches, and Villas

Salve Regina has "a beautiful campus." Located in historic Newport, Rhode Island, the campus is well-known for the mansions it has acquired for university use; the school was originally founded when the gorgeous Ochre Court was donated to the Sisters of Mercy. Ochre Court is a Newport mansion,

built to be the luxurious residence of a wealthy banker in the Gilded Age of the late nineteenth century. It remains today as the heart of Salve Regina's campus, just as it has always been. When Salve was just a nursing school, it housed the faculty, the students and the classrooms. It is now the location of the admissions office and a small chapel. Today, much of the campus shares the same historic grandeur of the Gilded Age. Classes are held in mansions; some of the main academic buildings, Wakehurst and McAuley, were also donated to the school by wealthy Newport families. The campus lies over the water and is described as "amazingly beautiful" by the students.

Downtown Newport is rather touristy, and the location boasts various places to shop and eat. Some favorite student eateries include the Brick Alley Pub, Sardella's, Puerini's and the Red Parrot. Newport has a lot of unique stores and bars popular among Salve students on the weekends. The most popular beach for students is First Beach, which can be reached from campus on the Cliff Walk. The Cliff Walk stretches over three miles, and goes alongside a precipice overlooking the Atlantic Ocean. It is yet another one of the interesting vistas to be found at this uniquely Catholic liberal arts university founded in the historic city of Newport.—*Ryan Galisewski*

FYI

If you come to Salve Regina, you'd better bring "common sense, money (it would be a shame to put all those awesome stores downtown to waste), and a diverse sense of style."

What is the typical weekend schedule? "Go clubbing in Providence Friday night. Work during the day on Saturday and then go to a friend's party in Newport. Sunday, either go to mass or sleep in and then do work the rest of the day."

If I could change one thing about Salve Regina University, I would "make it a little bit more diverse. It gets boring having to see people who look exactly the same walking around campus."

Three things every Salve Regina University student should do before graduating are "go for a drink at all of the bars on Thames Street and/or Broadway, visit the Breakers mansion before Christmas and go for a drive on Ocean Drive; it's the most beautiful road in the world!"

University of Rhode Island

Address: 14 Upper College Road, Kingston, RI 02881-1322
Phone: 401-874-7000
E-mail address: admission@uri.edu
Web site URL: www.uri.edu
Year Founded: 1892
Private or Public: Public
Religious Affiliation: None
Location: Rural
Number of Applicants: 14,272
Percent Accepted: 79%
Percent Accepted who enroll: 28%
Number Entering: 3,155
Number of Transfers Accepted each Year: 1,068
Middle 50% SAT range: M: 500–590, CR: 480–570, Wr: Unreported
Middle 50% ACT range: Unreported
Early admission program EA/ED/None: EA

Percentage accepted through EA or ED: 64%
EA and ED deadline: 15-Dec
Regular Deadline: 1-Feb
Application Fee: $50
Full time Undergraduate enrollment: 12,516
Total enrollment: 15,080
Percent Male: 42%
Percent Female: 58%
Total Percent Minority or Unreported: 16%
Percent African-American: 4%
Percent Asian/Pacific Islander: 2%
Percent Hispanic: 5%
Percent Native-American: 1%
Percent International: <1%
Percent in-state/out of state: 61%/39%
Percent from Public HS: Unreported
Retention Rate: 81%
Graduation Rate 4-year: 38%

Graduation Rate 6-year: 57%
Percent Undergraduates in On-campus housing: 45%
Number of official organized extracurricular organizations: 100
3 Most popular majors: Business/Marketing, Communications/Journalism, Education
Student/Faculty ratio: 19:1
Average Class Size: 24
Percent of students going to grad school: Unreported
Tuition and Fees: $21,294
In-State Tuition and Fees if different: $6,440
Cost for Room and Board: $8,828
Percent receiving financial aid out of those who apply, first year: 63%
Percent receiving financial aid among all students: 52%

Because the University of Rhode Island is such a populous institution, students' academic adventures really are as fruitful, difficult, or fun as they make them. There is a lot of freedom, which students can either take advantage of or use to their advantage. Says a senior, "You are allowed to create your own minor as long as you obtain a faculty sponsor and the dean of your respective college's permission."

As for the Classroom . . .

As the larger university is separated into individual subject-specific schools, the most popular of which is the more general College of Arts and Sciences, students are able to dive into whatever it is that they are interested in from the start. Already set on becoming a French restaurateur? Enroll in the College of Business Administration. Whatever your forte may be, there is opportunity after opportunity after opportunities; one can pick and choose between schools, take science classes that draw from real-life trips to magnificent Rhode Island waters, and vary class intensity – from the anonymity of

lectures to Honors Program classes. With its broad sampling of students, competition between students varies as well; as with anywhere, some are always going to want to be on top, but the majority work together in a constructive manner. The main academic tension seems to arise between pupils of the hard sciences and those of humanities. There exists an underlying assumption that the former is much more challenging than the latter. If anything, though, comparisons made between the two are done with lightheartedness—not with malice. While there is a selection of smaller discussion-sized classes maxed at 20, they are in high demand; to keep yourself from being one of the many, you should focus on creating some sort of connection with professors, whether during office hours or by talking to Teacher's Assistants. While there definitely is much student support—such as that offered through the Early Alert Program—because the school must cater to the needs of so many students, there is not always a professor on students' backs, making them do their work. How much you prepare for a class really depends on your own self-motivation. Grade-wise, one senior says, "in the physical sciences, it's less about getting an 'A' and more about passing. In the social sciences, it's all about getting an 'A.'"

Social (or Greek) Life?
At the University of Rhode Island, social life flourishes. Students really do come from all different backgrounds; not only racial, but cultural, religious, geographic, and familial. While, as a state school, the majority of students come from around Rhode Island, there is also a good selection from around the country and even world. Some commute; some dorm. All in all, students' search for others with preferences compatible to theirs tends to be rather straightforward. There is some self-segregation; though people tend to be open with one another, cliques are not obsolete. Sororities and fraternities do take up much of the social life, though one student assures that, "Greek life is more about giving back than drinking."

A Student's Paradise
What isn't there to do in a state with such easy access to all we ever desire: oceans, sun, flora, fauna, rousing cities, beaches, charming towns, and—did I mention water? Because Rhode Island itself is the perfect size for an easy commute, not so long as to require extensive driving, students often go off campus for entertainment— exploring the city, the sand, the wilderness, or just connecting with their peers at parties, club get-togethers, and other organized student gatherings. One of the school's perks is that undergraduates need not live in the dorms to have a lively social life; in fact, because the drug and alcohol policy prohibits the on-campus presence of such substances, many events take place at other locations. In fact, because so many commute, there is just as much of a community off campus as there is on. While some students experiment with dorm life in their initial years, many end up later living their own places;

more senior housing, though, is said to be quite the upgrade. Students are not hesitant to give the university's food stellar reviews; one described a typical meal, or shall I say feast, as "omelettes, pancakes, [and] fresh fruit."

Post-Homework
If you're looking for a place to do sports, take a deep breath. Yes, Rhode Island, I will repeat, has pretty much any recreational land formation one could ever want—and students make sure not to miss out on the fun. While many fill their schedules with classic land sports like tennis, hockey, and basketball, there isn't a place more ideal to swim (but where? The choices are many— the pool, the ocean, a pond . . .) or sail. In fact, the University of Rhode Island houses one of the best United States sailing teams. Time commitment varies; if you're really into making sports a huge part of your life, play for a school team; however, don't feel at all pressured—there are a plethora of intramural teams that allow students to de-stress without causing stress. If you're not a sports diehard, there are countless other activities in which you can get involved. Students love their school's theater, close-knit sorority and fraternity groups, fundraising activities, local community service ventures, and research opportunities.

> "Greek Life is more about giving back than drinking."

The University of Rhode Island, as large as it is, has quite the selection of opportunities. There are a lot of students to be met, a lot of clubs to join, a lot of Greek life to become a part of, a lot of activities to pursue, and a lot of things to learn. It is the perfect place for the expansion of one's horizons; make sure you try something new.—*Liliana Cousins*

FYI
If you come to URI, you'd better "leave your parents behind."
Three things every student at URI should do before graduating are "try out the Northwoods Challenge Course [a fun way to exercise alongside friends]; join some of the student organizations; go to Lip Sing ([a] . . . Greek Week event)"
The biggest college-wide tradition/event at URI is "Diversity Week in October."

South Carolina

Address: 105 Sikes Hall
  Clemson, SC 29634-5124
Phone: 864-656-2287
E-mail address:
  cuadmissions@clemson.edu
Web site URL:
  www.clemson.edu
Year Founded: 1889
Private or Public: Public
Religious Affiliation: None
Location: Rural
Number of Applicants:
  16,282
Percent Accepted: 54%
Percent Accepted who
  enroll: 32%
Number Entering: 2,813
Number of Transfers
  Accepted each Year: 816
Middle 50% SAT range: M:
  587–680, CR: 550–640,
  Wr: Unreported
Middle 50% ACT range:
  25–30
Early admission program
  EA/ED/None: None

Percentage accepted
  through EA or ED: NA
EA and ED deadline: NA
Regular Deadline: 1-May
Application Fee: $50
Full time Undergraduate
  enrollment: 14,713
Total enrollment: 18,317
Percent Male: 54%
Percent Female: 46%
Total Percent Minority or
  Unreported: 10%
Percent African-American:
  7%
Percent Asian/Pacific
  Islander: 2%
Percent Hispanic: 1%
Percent Native-American:
  <1%
Percent International: 1%
Percent in-state/out of
  state: 71%/29%
Percent from Public HS:
  Unreported
Retention Rate: 92%
Graduation Rate 4-year: 49%

Graduation Rate 6-year:
  77%
Percent Undergraduates
  in On-campus housing:
  42%
Number of official organized
  extracurricular
  organizations: 292
3 Most popular majors:
  Biology, Business,
  Engineering
Student/Faculty ratio: 14:1
Average Class Size: 31
Percent of students going to
  grad school: Unreported
Tuition and Fees: $24,130
In-State Tuition and Fees if
  different: $11,108
Cost for Room and Board:
  $6,556
Percent receiving financial
  aid out of those who apply,
  first year: 87%
Percent receiving financial
  aid among all students:
  71%

L ocated on the banks of Lake Hartwell in Clemson, South Carolina, a forty minute drive to the mid-sized city of Greenville and over two hours to Columbia, the capital of South Carolina, Clemson boasts a long history of growth from an agricultural institution to South Carolina's flagship institute of engineering. The Tigers, named for their corresponding mascot, were founded by a relation of John C. Calhoun, and still maintain characteristics of the old South.

The Great Divide: Sciences and the Humanities

Students at Clemson can elect to join one of five colleges at their time of application— Agriculture, Forestry and Life Sciences; Architecture, Arts and Humanities; Business

and Behavioral Science; Engineering and Science; and Health, Education and Human Development—though students note that the College of Engineering and Science, in addition to their program in architecture, is most famed. Combined, the colleges offer a range of majors, from packaging science to food science, yet the majority of the majors are science-centric, with students claiming the most popular majors to be those in biology, business, and engineering. While it may be, according to one student, that "anytime I meet a boy, it's a good guess that he is an engineer," health-centric majors, such as nursing or health science, are also very competitive, particularly concerning getting into classes. Students can also opt to enter the Calhoun Honors College, which requires a separate application process and boasts

Freshman Colloquia, small, seminar classes available to freshmen and the option to take "honors" versions of introductory classes. In addition, students within the honors college can enter the "design a course" contest, with recent winners including Graphic Novels.

But, regardless of the college, all students must complete demanding distributional requirements. For example, students in the College of Engineering and Science must complete more than fifteen credits in the humanities and social sciences in order to graduate. Attending a definite "math and science school," students attest that the most difficult majors include engineering and the hard sciences—which make them "work really hard"—in addition to the architecture program. However, students in the parks, recreation and tourism management (PRTM) program's main preoccupation is nicknamed "Party Right Through May," attesting to their relatively light workload. But, when students not in "Party Right Through May" want to opt for an easier workload, they can take "leisure skills" classes, learning about such topics as swing dance, rock climbing and meditation and relaxation. Other interesting and fun courses include First Aid/CPR. Though class size is dependent on major, students agree that after the large prerequisites and general education requirement classes, the average class size becomes closer to twenty.

Even though Clemson is known for its math and science programs, some students still participate in humanities programs and students assert that a wide gap exists between the science and humanities students. While math and science majors absolutely hate humanities classes, and, said one student, "consider humanities harder," humanities majors regard those in the sciences in an analogous way. As such, students think each other absolutely "crazy" for taking classes on the other side of the gap. However, grading is notably difficult in all departments at Clemson, partly due to the lack of grading curves in many departments, so, as students say, "the amount of work that you put in determines the grades that you get." Fittingly, then, students claim that "it's the student's responsibility to put in the work required to get an A"—the student must show drive and initiative to qualify for help from a professor. A plethora of opportunities abounds for students in need of academic aid, which includes free tutors and the academic success center offering academic coaching and counseling sessions.

Faculty members are lauded by the students as being "extremely accessible" with all having set office hours, but, says one student, "are more than willing to set up appointments outside of those hours." Notable faculty members include David Reinking, a famed researcher analyzing the intersection of technology and literacy.

The Tiger Den

After receiving notifications of their admittance, an incoming freshman can submit a housing application, which has "first-come-first-served" priority rankings. Freshmen, for whom living on campus living is required, as it is for all students under the age of twenty-one, typically live in two-person dorms with communal baths. A few lucky freshmen will have the option to live in apartment-style accommodations owned by the University which are lauded for their spaciousness and private kitchens. Honors students can also choose to reside in Holmes Residential Hall, which offers in-suite bathrooms. Students can also choose to participate in a "living-learning community" to bring together persons who share similar interests, be it community service or behavioral science.

> "It's the typical Southern university, with dress ranging from the preppy to straight off the farm kind of redneck."

Though alcohol is strictly prohibited in all of the Freshmen Residence halls, students of age may store alcohol in the University-owned apartments. Smoking, however, is banned in all student housing.

Recent construction at Clemson includes a nearly 100 million dollar wind turbine testing facility, located in the suburbs of Charleston, South Carolina (a four hour trip by car from the campus), and a 31 million dollar renovation to the university's Rudolph E. Lee Hall, which houses the design, build and visual arts program. Emphasizing the university's commitment to the environment, the renovation will include a geothermal heating system and solar panels. Campus largely divides into two sections: central campus and west campus, a gap that can be bridged by a thirty minute walk. West campus, where most apartment-style residential housing is located, hosts the football stadium, "downtown" Clemson, and most other sports training facilities.

Extracurricular activities are frequently cited by students as a main avenue to making friends at the "very friendly" campus of Clemson. Whether it's a religious organization such as the Baptist Collegiate Ministry or the primary student publication, *The Tiger*, students use the organizations to build their own niches.

Tigers on the Prowl

Students claim that Greek Life is dominant in the social life of the University, but students say that "there are plenty of non-Greek individuals on campus." Nonetheless, few parties take place at Clemson which are not directly related to a Fraternity or Sorority. However, the majority of the social activity on campus revolves around Thursday to Saturday night, say current students, when students frequent the fraternity houses and bars in the neighboring city of Clemson, in which the university is integrated. And, though, in the past, Clemson was a "suitcase college," most students now stay on campus during the weekends with many students still possessing a car.

Students report that hard drug use on campus is minimal, with only a prevalence of marijuana among some social groups, but that alcohol binge drinking is a problem on campus. And, although alcohol is strictly prohibited on campus—a policy according to students that the administration "does a good job of keeping things under control"—students say that "things can get a little crazy on home games though."

A common complaint of Clemson University centers on the school's relative lack of diversity. Located in the mountains of South Carolina, the university, the students claim, is "predominately white, upper-middle class and 'Protestant.'" Because the university lies along a lake and is only a short thirty minute drive from the mountains, students say that "the outdoors is a pretty big deal to Clemson." As such, "it's the typical Southern university, with dress ranging from the preppy to straight off the farm kind of redneck," says one current student.

If you are looking for a school with a strong engineering and sciences program in a "small-town" environment with a decidedly southern charm, Clemson is the right school for you. Though the school may suffer from a lack of diversity, the school does have a strong Sorority and Fraternity scene, offering a bevy of social and extracurricular activities.— *John Klement*

FYI
If I could change one thing about Clemson, "I'd change parking . . . They say that no one makes it through four years here without getting a citation."
What differentiates Clemson the most from other colleges "is the excellent location; we're 20 minutes from the lake, 30 minutes from the mountains, 2 hours from Atlanta, 2 hours from Charlotte, . . . 3 hours from the beach. This provides for an unlimited number of fun day trips. Anything you might want to do is totally possible."

Furman University

Address: 3300 Poinsett Highway, Greenville, SC 29613

Phone: 864-294-2034

E-mail address: admissions@furman.edu

Web site URL: www.furman.edu

Year Founded: 1826

Private or Public: Private

Religious Affiliation: None

Location: Urban

Number of Applicants: 4,414

Percent Accepted: 57%

Percent Accepted who enroll: 30%

Number Entering: 754

Number of Transfers Accepted each Year: 45

Middle 50% SAT range: M: 590–690, **CR:** 590–690, **Wr:** 580–680

Middle 50% ACT range: 26–30

Early admission program EA/ED/None: ED

Percentage accepted through EA or ED: 56%

EA and ED deadline: 15-Nov

Regular Deadline: 15-Jan

Application Fee: $50

Full time Undergraduate enrollment: 2,801

Total enrollment: 2,970

Percent Male: 43%

Percent Female: 57%

Total Percent Minority or Unreported: 20%

Percent African-American: 7%

Percent Asian/Pacific Islander: 3%

Percent Hispanic: 2%

Percent Native-American: <1%

Percent International: 2%

Percent in-state/out of state: 30%/70%

Percent from Public HS: 63%

Retention Rate: 92%

Graduation Rate 4-year: 80%

Graduation Rate 6-year: 84%

Percent Undergraduates in On-campus housing: 91%

Number of official organized extracurricular organizations: 143

3 Most popular majors: Communications, History, Political Science and Government

Student/Faculty ratio: 11:1

Average Class Size: 18

Percent of students going to grad school: 40%

Tuition and Fees: $34,568

In-State Tuition and Fees if different: No difference

Cost for Room and Board: $8,966

Percent receiving financial aid out of those who apply, first year: 69%

Percent receiving financial aid among all students: 42%

U pon entering the gates of Furman University, many students forget that they're at college as they stand before what looks like the grounds of a country club. Located 15 minutes away from downtown Greenville, South Carolina, Furman offers its students a strong liberal arts education in a traditional Southern setting. Furman boasts an extraordinarily beautiful and welcoming campus, featuring numerous fountains, a giant lake, a golf course, a spectacular rose garden, and even a black swan (a gift from an alumnus). One student described the appeal of Furman's campus as "so perfect, it's almost unreal."

Spending Time with "James"

While the country club allure and what one student described as the "Fantasy of Furman" are striking, the way students and faculty treat academics is far from a walk in the park. "Academically, students at Furman have a high regard for themselves," a sophomore noted. "There are a lot of people who take their school work very seriously." With the amount of General Education requirements they have, it's no wonder that Furman students have the option to hit the books at all hours of the night, as the library study lounges are open 24/7. However, one student noted that, "While there's a pretty big laundry list of GC's you have to have, they're not extremely difficult courses." One of these requirements is dubbed "Ultimate Questions," an interesting name for a course in religion and ethics that reflects Furman's former religious affiliation. Freshmen are also required to take two seminar-style classes as an introduction to Furman, covering topics such as "Contemporary Issues in Film," "How Science Shapes our Views," and "What is and isn't Language." This is a newly instituted program, and current freshmen expressed mixed feelings about these seminars, saying that they are "either a hit or a miss." At Furman, there's also another unique set of requirements, called Cultural Life Programs or "CLP's," where students must attend 32 events, performances, and talks.

Furman students have a tendency to double major, and one sophomore observed, "What really sets Furman apart, students say, is its excellent faculty." "For some reason, middle of nowhere South Carolina has just brewed incredible teachers," marveled one student. There is also widespread agreement that "the class size really differentiates Furman from other schools." The average class size is 18, and the largest lectures contain a mere 35 people. Teachers strongly urge students to establish a relationship with them. As one student put it, "Everyone cares so much about their education, it's contagious."

It's No New York . . .

Students from farther north than Maryland be warned—you may be in for a culture shock. Despite sharing the liberal arts model of schools in the Northeast, Furman University is culturally very Southern. The majority of its students hail from the Southern states of South Carolina, Tennessee and Georgia, and the sound of "Yes ma'am's" and "Yes sir's" is as central to Furman as the lake located in the middle of its campus. Sundresses, pearls, boat shoes and bow ties dominate tailgates, and smiling and waving to people whom you may have met only once is the norm. "You definitely won't see people wearing hipster, New York-ish stuff," laughed one student. However, some students urge against this stereotype, saying that there is definitely an "outdoorsy," "borderline hippie" subculture if you look for it, and the predominantly Southern demographic "doesn't mean that everyone will fit into that Southern lady, Southern gentleman mold."

Even taking this subculture into account, there seems to be an agreement that "the main student, to be perfectly honest, would be a conservative, preppy, kind of straight-laced person," as one student described. Furman students also tend to be fairly wealthy, as evidenced by the numerous high-end cars on campus and their weekly forays to restaurants in Greenville.

Students also commented on the homogeneity of Furman, which is widely acknowledged as an issue, if not a pressing one. "Race-wise, it's definitely predominantly white and it's not very integrated," said one student. "In general, you tend to see the same kind of person. It's one of the more negative things about Furman."

That Southern Tradition

At Furman, it's not uncommon to see a student squealing and laughing as he or she is unceremoniously dumped into a lake. While someone on a tour of the school might be alarmed, most onlookers at Furman don't cringe at this spectacle; they know that it's an affectionate way for a student's brother hall to offer its birthday wishes. Each dormitory is divided into halls, and each hall has a "brother" or "sister" hall with which it participates in social activities. It's light-hearted traditions like these that make Furman so much fun for its undergraduates. Freshmen begin their life at Furman with the famed "my tie" dance at orientation, or "O-week," knowing that as seniors they will mark the end of their four years with an epic session of "fountain hopping." Some traditions, however, are slightly more serious. For example, if a student kisses someone under the bell tower, word is that they'll probably be getting hitched to that person in the near future. One freshman explained, "A lot of people talk about marriage. It's very much a 'find your one' kind of thing."

> **"For some reason, middle of nowhere South Carolina has just brewed incredible teachers."**

During "O-week," freshmen are introduced to what will initially dictate their social life (at least until spring, when rush takes over): their hall. Over the course of a week, they make cheers, compete with other halls, create silly dances, and get to know their peers in a setting that is "exactly like summer camp." Each hall has a theme like "The Harlem Globetrotters," "Where's Waldo," and "Lilly Pulitzer." Halls plan outings and participate in activities together throughout the school year, providing an immediate and nurturing community. While Greek life is a huge feature at Furman, one sorority girl noted, "The difference is you still maintain close friendships with your hall." However, "Hall is not a make or break kind of situation. If you don't like your hall, stick it out, because spring semester is a ton more fun than fall," she added.

Lakeside Divides

Furman's Southern flavor is mixed with the aftertaste of the school's former Baptist affiliations. The result: a schism on campus between drinkers (typically Greek) and their more religious peers. "Some people who go to church and who are a little more religious do separate themselves. They have their cliques," admitted one student. "It can be hard to find people who both drink and go to church. It's either one or the other," added another student. However, one sophomore stated that if you do party at Furman, you're most likely the "good Southern Christian boy who parties on Saturday night and gets cleaned up to go to church on Sunday morning."

While Furman claims to be a dry campus, it's been revealed to be a "damp campus" in reality. Drinkers generally party off campus at frats or at their favorite bars in Greenville. While alcohol policies certainly aren't lenient, and there can be some "crazy RA's," for the most part, students can get away with their debauchery if they're smart about it.

For those who don't frequent the drinking frats, there is always something to do on campus. Furman Undergraduate Student Activities Board (FUSAB) is constantly putting on events and concerts, bringing in speakers (including all of the presidential candidates—encompassing everyone vying for party nominations—for the 2008 election), and sponsoring screenings of movies such as *Pineapple Express*. However, most students are content with their weekly routine of dinner in Greenville and a movie night in the dorm with friends.

Purple . . . and GREEN

While you may see students clad in purple at a football game, it's probably by accident. Students reported a lack of school spirit at athletic events, and after the Saturday morning football tailgate, most students call it quits after the first quarter. "We're kind of apathetic when it comes to sports," said a former cheerleader.

Fortunately, there are plenty of other arenas that Furman students get passionate about. There are myriad student groups on campus, ranging from those addressing social justice issues to the ever-popular Christian organizations, like the Fellowship of Christian Athletes. The Outdoor Club is incredibly well funded, as is Furman's Student Activities Board, which has worked with budgets of over $250,000. Students also take advantage of the campus itself in their spare time. "Because campus is so beautiful, you can run around the lake or into the woods. You can't do that in big city schools," acknowledged one appreciative student.

Recently, Furman has made a concerted effort to address sustainability. It hosts Cliffs Cottage, *Southern Living*'s first showcase of a sustainable home, right on campus. The public is encouraged to explore the home, and Furman's Office of Sustainability and Environmental Education is soon to be relocated there. Students and faculty alike are the driving force behind the University's exciting green initiatives, and there are plenty of opportunities to get involved.

The Progressive South

Furman is the type of place where students can finish a complex lab report while sitting in rocking chairs on a porch and chatting with friends. It offers a Southern lifestyle with progressive approaches to areas like technology and environment, designating it as a "new age type of university." With its friendly students and nurturing (though somewhat homogenous and conservative) environment, Furman is a wonderful place to be. When asked, more than one student said, "Oh yeah, I'd choose Furman all over again."—*Raphaella Friedman*

FYI
If you come you'd better bring "Pearls and a sundress, and be able to tie a bow tie."
What's the typical weekend schedule? "Finish classes on Friday, might study for a few hours, go out to dinner with friends downtown. You might stay out a little later at a frat on Friday, or go back and watch a movie with some friends. Saturday, put on your pearls, go to the tailgate, go to the football game, maybe study for a few hours, do something low-key at night like walking along the waterfall downtown, come back, go to sleep early because you have church in the morning, after-church study all day."
If I could change one thing about Furman, I'd "make it more diverse in all senses of the word. Geographically, racially, socially, politically."

University of South Carolina

Address: Admissions Office
Columbia, SC 29208
Phone: 803-777-7000
E-mail address:
admissions-ugrad@sc.edu
Web site URL: www.sc.edu
Year Founded: 1801
Private or Public: Public
Religious Affiliation: None
Location: Urban
Number of Applicants:
18,485
Percent Accepted: 70%
**Percent Accepted who
enroll:** 34%
Number Entering: 4,423
**Number of Transfers
Accepted each Year:** 2,055
Middle 50% SAT range: M:
550–650, CR: 540–640,
Wr: Unreported
Middle 50% ACT range: 23–28
**Early admission program
EA/ED/None:** EA
**Percentage accepted
through EA or ED:**
Unreported

EA and ED deadline: 1-Oct
Regular Deadline: 1-Dec
Application Fee: $50
**Full time Undergraduate
enrollment:** 18,827
Total enrollment: 25,823
Percent Male: 43%
Percent Female: 57%
**Total Percent Minority or
Unreported:** 17%
Percent African-American:
7%
**Percent Asian/Pacific
Islander:** 3%
Percent Hispanic: 3%
Percent Native-American:
<1%
Percent International: 1%
**Percent in-state/out of
state:** 62%/38%
Percent from Public HS:
Unreported
Retention Rate: 87%
Graduation Rate 4-year:
67%
Graduation Rate 6-year:
Unreported

**Percent Undergraduates
in On-campus housing:**
40%
**Number of official organized
extracurricular
organizations:** 300
3 Most popular majors:
Business/Marketing, Social
Sciences,
Communications/Journalism
Student/Faculty ratio:
16:1
Average Class Size: Less
than 30
**Percent of students going to
grad school:** Unreported
Tuition and Fees: $22,908
**In-State Tuition and Fees if
different:** $8,838
Cost for Room and Board:
$6,652
**Percent receiving financial
aid out of those who apply,
first year:** 56%
**Percent receiving financial
aid among all students:**
41%

I n spite of initial reservations, "within a week I was obsessed," one senior said of her initial experience at University of South Carolina. This passion seems to extend to most USC students, who sing their school's praises and show their collegiate pride at the drop of a hat or the blow of a whistle. Displays of devotion are especially evident at the popular, and often over the top, football games. But University of South Carolina offers so much more than just grand sporting events. The academic programs, extensive extracurricular choices and an exhausting party scene all contribute to forming a memorable experience that most students, when given the choice, would wish to live all over again.

University 101

Despite USC's large student body, there are few complaints about becoming just a number. The class sizes at the University vary widely from 20 to 300, with intro classes generally on the high end of the spectrum. However, large lectures come equipped with smaller discussion sections to ensure that each student gets personal attention. "I have never taken a class that had more than 50 students," one Honors College student said. Other students praised the numerous options for more intimate academic settings, often citing the professor for "making" the class. One senior raved that "[the professors] have been nothing but awesome," and students have generally described the professorship as being friendly, easily accessible, and diligent to learn the names of all of their students. Among the faculty sit several famous names such as Don Fowler, the former chairman of the Democratic National Committee.

With 14 schools to choose from, the University offers something for everyone. The major unanimously proclaimed as the most sought-after and difficult is the number one, nationally-ranked International Business program. The major accepts only 50 people each year and attracts students from all over the country, as well as many from overseas. South Carolina also offers unique majors such as Sports and Entertainment Management and Hotel and Restaurant Tourism Management. And for the top qualified students of each year, the University features an Honors Program and Capstone Scholars. For freshmen, an atypical class that is offered and sometimes required is University 101, a class that focuses solely on helping students adjust and make the best of university life. Aside from the required English, social science, and history courses (all of which students can place out of), there is a unique assortment of ways students can expand their knowledge, whether by learning how to shag—the dance, that is—or by taking a wine-tasting class or studying Super Bowl commercials (it's actually a class). Overall, the workload itself is deemed manageable. Some students complain about the large amounts of reading they receive, but as one sophomore explained, "People are not missing out on social life."

Where the Beer Is Green and the Beach Is Near

South Carolina offers many great ways to have a good time. Although many students contend that no particular social scene dominates, the Greek parties are the most common ones listed. For the 21+ crowd (or those with really good IDs), there are the Five Points downtown bars. People usually start going out on Thursday night, especially with Thursday being "college night" in the downtown area.

Even though only about 16 percent of students belong to a sorority or a fraternity, students generally agree that Greek life is "really noticeable." During the first week of school, one of the most prominent things on campus is the excess of flyers inviting people to rush. And students estimate that a majority of the population does rush, especially girls. "During my freshman year, half the kids on my floor rushed," one senior remembered. The Greeks, in addition to hosting regular weekend parties, also organize many exclusive theme parties and are the driving force behind Homecoming week festivities.

Nevertheless, as a senior pointed out, "You can have fun even if you're not Greek." Big annual celebrations include St. Patrick's Day at Five Points, when everything is blocked off from the city and the beer is green. Halloween weekend is "always fun." Many alternative entertainment options are provided by the student-run Carolina Productions. The group organizes main events on campus such as concerts, the Wacky Wednesday Booth that plans something new and fun for each Wednesday at the Student Center, and has even been responsible for bringing Bob Saget to campus. For a more low-key night, there are the dorm parties, which are especially popular for underclassmen. But be forewarned. Despite the abundance of partying on campus, the drinking rules are strict—SLED or undercover officers patrol the area and are quick to enforce the rules. All freshman dorms are labeled dry and all rooms in the upperclassmen dorms in which persons under 21 reside are dry, as well. However, as one freshman observed, "You can drink in the dorm—if you can get away with it." The ability to "get away with it" mainly depends on your RA and on how belligerent you become. One junior pointed out that, although "we are not a dry campus," people are understanding of those who do not drink. As an alternative to partying, many students take weekend trips to the plentiful beaches of Charleston.

Our Stereotypes Are Diverse

Many come to South Carolina with the expectation of a crowd of typical Southern girls and frat-guy types. But more often than not, students are pleasantly surprised by the diversity on campus. Although one junior described the day-to-day look as having "a beachy atmosphere—there are shorts and sandals everywhere," there is a greater stylistic range. But it doesn't mean there aren't stereotypes. As one sophomore put it, "You can definitely pick out the Greeks by their clothes, and you can definitely pick out 'emos' by their clothes." Nevertheless, there is a fair amount of geographic and ethnic diversity. Students hail from all 50 states and there is a well-represented international community at South Carolina. Some students acknowledge, however, that the campus often has segregation lines among groups—whites and blacks have their own separate frats and parties. "Walking around campus you [would] think it is segregated," said one student. Students, however, assure that there is no tension on campus, and that the relations among races are by no means "uncivil." Students are making strides to create a more unified collegiate atmosphere, which even in its current state is still generally described as very friendly.

Horseshoes and Pizza Huts

Due to numerous dorm renovation projects, one senior explained that "housing right now is in limbo." Still, all freshmen are required to live on campus, spread out between the freshman-only dorms, many of which are single-sex with strict visitation rules for prospective guests of the opposite sex. All freshman dorms feature suite-style rooms (two double bedrooms, a common room and a bathroom). Due to dorm renovations, the upperclassmen are not guaranteed housing. However, this lack of guarantee is not a major problem; many, if not most, upperclassmen prefer off-campus housing—especially at the nearby university-exclusive apartment complexes. For those who choose to stay on campus, there are several coed options, including Roost, which mainly houses athletes, and the "Green Dorm," a completely environmentally friendly habitat. The University also offers several themed communities such as the French community, the Spanish community (where they speak only the language of affiliation), the International community, and the Music community. Currently, the University is building a multimillion-dollar Research community. The Greeks, especially in their sophomore year, often opt to reside in the multimillion-dollar houses that populate the Greek Village. All students are able to bring cars, and it seems like all do. Parking, or lack thereof, is the most common complaint heard from the students. "To get to class on time, you have to get there 30 minutes before to find a spot to park," one student warned.

> "Everyone here is obsessed with football, even those who are not athletic."

USC students vote the campus food as "most likely to make you gain the Freshman 15." There are five dining halls, including the Russell House, which serves both as the student union and the grand marketplace or main dining hall. Dining options include everything from a salad bar to an overabundance of fast food chains like Burger King, Chick-fil-A, Taco Bell, and Pizza Hut, where students can use their meal plans. Luckily, Columbia houses many privately owned restaurants that, all in all, "give the city more character."

The campus itself is pretty with a smattering of modern industrial buildings, many newly renovated buildings, and—of course—the Horseshoe with "an old, traditional, Southern feel to it." The Horseshoe—you guessed it—is shaped like a horseshoe

and serves as the main, grassy hangout area for students looking to picnic or play Frisbee. Most importantly, the campus is regarded as safe. "Considering the size of this university, they have done a good job of protecting us," one student praised. Call boxes which are located throughout campus (you can't turn around without seeing at least one) serve as emergency call services. A shuttle service also operates on campus.

The Loyal Gamecocks

Many students at South Carolina "rely on organizations to find [their] niche," a senior observed. Some of the more prominent groups include Student Government, the Triple A's (Association of African-Americans), and Carolina Productions. For the politically aspirant, there are the College Republicans and Young Dems; for the journalistically inclined, there is *The Daily Gamecock;* and for the socially focused, there are 15 sororities and 22 frats from which to choose.

If all else fails, the uniting theme of the University seems to be sports. Club and intramural sports serve as competitive, but very fun, alternatives to varsity. But perhaps the most popular way to be involved in the athletic life is actually just attending the varsity games. South Carolina's talented teams are fun to watch and support. The baseball and basketball games are both very well attended, but football remains king. People fight for tickets, which sell out almost immediately. "Everyone here is obsessed with football, even those who are not athletic," one sophomore declared. The annual game against archrival Clemson is among the most exciting and is preceded by the Tiger Burn—a pep rally and ceremonial burning of a papier-mâché Clemson Tiger. The proud Gamecocks attend the games dressed in their best— pearls, cocktail dresses, blazers, and bow ties. The tailgates begin at noon and last for about five or more hours until the game begins. The Gamecocks are known for their loyalty; they cheer loudly until the last minute, win or lose.

It is easy to get swept up in the enthusiasm of the football crowd of the always-filled-to-the-brim Williams-Brice Stadium. Such an exhilarating feeling is a good reflection of the mentality of South Carolina University's students. Any initial reservations incoming students might have are quickly replaced by feelings of school pride and affection. Because whether it be the campus, the vast array of extracurriculars or the friendly people, it is good to be a Gamecock.—*Dorota Poplawska*

FYI
If you come to South Carolina, you'd better bring "Rainbows (sandals that everyone wears) and dressy clothes for those football games."
What is the typical weekend schedule? "Thursday attend college night at Five Points and party on Friday. Saturdays are dominated by tailgates and football games that take up all day. Catch up on work Sunday after sleeping in or going to church."
If I could change one thing about South Carolina, I'd "add more parking spaces."
Three things every student at South Carolina should do before graduating are "go to Five Points, stay till the end of a football game, and get to know a professor on a more personal basis."

Wofford College

Address: 429 North Church Street, Spartanburg, SC 29303-3663

Phone: 864-597-4130

E-mail address: admission@wofford.edu

Web site URL: www.wofford.edu

Year Founded: 1854

Private or Public: Private

Religious Affiliation: United Methodist

Location: Urban

Number of Applicants: 2,442

Percent Accepted: 58%

Percent Accepted who enroll: 28%

Number Entering: 392

Number of Transfers Accepted each Year: 18

Middle 50% SAT range: M: 580–680, CR: 560–670, Wr: 560–660

Middle 50% ACT range: 22–29

Early admission program EA/ED/None: ED

Percentage accepted through EA or ED: 80%

EA and ED deadline: 15-Nov

Regular Deadline: 1-Feb

Application Fee: $35

Full time Undergraduate enrollment: 1,420

Total enrollment: 1,439

Percent Male: 50%

Percent Female: 50%

Total Percent Minority or Unreported: 15%

Percent African-American: 7%

Percent Asian/Pacific Islander: 3%

Percent Hispanic: 2%

Percent Native-American: 0%

Percent International: 1%

Percent in-state/out of state: 60 %/40%

Percent from Public HS: 65%

Retention Rate: 87%

Graduation Rate 4-year: 77%

Graduation Rate 6-year: 82%

Percent Undergraduates in On-campus housing: 94%

Number of official organized extracurricular organizations: 111

3 Most popular majors: Biology, Finance, Foreign languages

Student/Faculty ratio: 11:1

Average Class Size: 18

Percent of students going to grad school: 49%

Tuition and Fees: $30,280

In-State Tuition and Fees if different: No difference

Cost for Room and Board: $8,480

Percent receiving financial aid out of those who apply, first year: 51%

Percent receiving financial aid among all students: 52%

Wofford College offers a tight-knit community and strong teacher-student relationships for a student body that is smaller than that of most high schools. With approximately 1,400 students, Wofford reserves its solid, liberal arts education for a select group of students. Its location in the traditional South impacts student culture; it's no surprise to students that "many of the ladies went to debutante balls." But Wofford stands out primarily for its Division 1 Athletics. With such a small student body, "one in six guys plays football." Pearls, sports, and prep don't diminish the fact that Wofford is widely respected for

its premedicine program and "many students go into politics" after graduation. There's no doubt that Wofford grads impact the lives of South Carolinians since "three of the South Carolina State Supreme Court justices graduated from Wofford."

Is There a Doctor in the Classroom?

Opened in 1854 and still affiliated with the Methodist Church, Wofford has remained small by choice. The administration reportedly has no plans to expand enrollment, but instead plans to concentrate on providing a select group of students with a strong education in the humanities, arts and sciences. Students say that "the small class sizes are really nice." One student warned, however, that due to Wofford's size, "there is not a wide variety of classes." Professors are especially accessible and maintain an "open door policy," according to students. "I didn't expect the professors to be so understanding, but they are like high school teachers in that sense. They want to help you out." Undergraduates are required to take courses in the humanities, English, fine arts, foreign language, science, history, philosophy, math, physical education and religion. These general education requirements are meant to ensure that, by the end of their first two years, students will have taken some classes they normally would not have considered. Students are also required to complete four interim projects. The month of January is designated as Interim, a time between the two regular semesters when students can research, travel, take an internship, or work on an independent project. Interim projects on campus can include courses such as "*The Passion of the Christ* as Film, Sacred Art, Theology, and Cultural Maelstrom" or "Web Design For People Who Do Other Things For a Living." Off-campus travel programs in January 2009 included "Cornbread and Sushi on the Road" and "Intense in Tents: African Culture & Ecology in Namibia." Internship projects and service learning can even take you to Capitol Hill for a month. The Interim permits and encourages teachers and students to explore the new and untried. Even more exciting, most interim projects are graded Pass/Fail.

Among the popular majors at Wofford are biology, business economics, foreign languages, political science, history and English. "Business Economics is seen as a fairly easy program," one student said, "and sociology is picked on for having the easiest major." But "in general everyone respects each other because every major requires a lot of time and effort." The science department is reported to be particularly strong. One student said that, as a physics major, "people tend to hold me in somewhat (unwarranted) high regard because there are so few of us. I have a class this semester where I am the only student in the class." But there is no doubt that the sciences and particularly the biology major are "top-notch" at Wofford and many students go on to medical school.

Tech Savvy

Wofford's efforts to provide cutting-edge technical services to its students are high-

lighted in a January 2006 article on "Coolest Campus Tech" on the *Forbes* Web site (www.forbes.com). The article focuses on the Wofford program called FYI (First Year Interface), which allows freshmen to meet and greet via a MySpace-style Web site. After sharing profiles, photos, bedtimes and partying habits on the site, Wofford lets students who hit it off become roommates. Students may also contact members of the Student Life staff with questions about what to expect when preparing to come to Wofford. The student profiles are searchable for similar interests, geographic areas and other information. Wofford also has begun posting podcasts to its Web site (www.wofford.edu) for downloading and listening to audio recordings of campus programs and events. The College not only uses technology to help its students acclimate to campus: in 2002, Wofford began the Novel Experience—a program that asks incoming students to read an assigned novel over the summer and to write essays prior to arrival in Spartanburg. In early September, a town-gown exercise takes place when student groups and professors are assigned to eat at local restaurants through a lottery, discussing the novel over dinner. About a week later, the author comes to campus for a special address. "Talking with the author and the professors was definitely a highlight," one student said. "Because it happens in the first week of school, you go with your humanities class and you get to know them really well. It helped to make it more comfortable." Rising freshmen also have the option to attend a program called the Summit. This program takes place before the start of school, and new students spend a few days at a summer camp and go whitewater rafting. "It's where you first meet most of the people you come to hang out with."

Dorm Life: A Necessary Experience

An online lottery system sorts all dorm assignments and seniority is prioritized. Halls are coed in four of the dorms; two other dorms have two all-girl halls and all-guy halls per floor. The two freshman dorms accommodate men and women separately. Marsh Hall—the freshman dorm for men—is known as "particularly miserable, crazy, and disgusting all at the same time. But all in all, a necessary experience." Greene Hall is the freshman girls' dorm and "where freshman guys spend most of their time." All students living in dorms have the convenient advantage of a five- or 10-minute walk to classroom buildings. "If I wake up late at 9:20 I can still get to a 9:30 class." On the way, students enjoy the shade of many oak trees or stop to lounge on the benches near the central campus field. There are plans in the works to provide a type of campus "village" to students, comprised of apartment-like facilities in renovated houses Wofford has purchased. Campus is "much safer" than the surrounding areas in Spartanburg. According to students, "it's kind of a rough town in places" and "people tend to stay within the 'Wofford bubble.'"

Frat Row, Football, and More

"Greek life at Wofford is huge" and more than 50 percent of the student body is Greek. The fraternity row (location on campus for fraternity houses and called "the row" by students) is the dominant social scene on campus. It's a popular site for a shaving cream fight and "you can't miss out on slip-and-slide at the row." "The frat row is a typical site of first-time meetings between folks." One of the most talked-about days of the year is Guys' Bid Day, when freshman boys find out which fraternity they're pledging. A popular celebration follows. Spring Weekend has many activities and is a time when "you should party extremely hard." In addition to the popular varsity athletic teams, like men's and women's basketball, "we have an ultimate Frisbee team and a fly fishing organization—which is funded by the school for their equipment and trips." One student called it "a sweet gig."

Wofford and Spartanburg are not interchangeable. With the exception of a few bars and the "gracious discounts" many local businesses offer to students, there is not much interaction. "I don't think that the two are intertwined unless there is an athletic event," one student said. Another student pointed out that "the town's heyday was gone years ago because it was once a big textile city." Wofford is located in "an underprivileged area, so we interact with the community in a variety of ways through service learning and volunteer work," a student said. Wofford reportedly hosts two events during the school year for children in the area to attend. One student said that "Wofford does a great job interacting with the surrounding community." Student groups on campus include Campus Ambassadors, students who volunteer their time to give tours to prospective students, and the Fellowship of Christian Athletes (FCA), which involves many students and "is held in high regard." The Outdoors Club is another option for bikers, hikers and climbers. "Most students are passionate about the clubs they are involved in" and "each group has their fanatics."

Southern Ladies and Gents

There's no getting around it. Most students say that "Wofford is typically viewed as a white, conservative school." Students who attend Wofford are "particularly preppy and from 'old money' families or parents with white-collar careers." One student said, "It seems like everyone's dad is either a doctor or an attorney." While some students admitted there is geographic diversity and students definitely come to Wofford from a variety of states in the Southeast—"there seems like there are as many out-of-state students as there are in-state"—ethnic diversity is not strong. "It's not diverse. Only about 10 percent of the school is made up of minority students." The "frat look" is very popular with "Sperrys, khakis, and sunglasses with Croakies making a dominant appearance all over campus" and "pastel colors are worn by both guys and girls." According to another student, "The attitude is a positive and confident one. Students are proud to be at Wofford." While the Wofford student is stereotypically characterized as rich and preppy, "there are many people who do not fit this stereotype at all. In general, everyone here is friendly and you can always expect a hello when walking down the sidewalks on campus." The same mentality translates to the classroom where "there's always a comfortable setting. You just raise your hand if you have a question and the teacher will answer you."

"Students Are Proud to Be at Wofford."

Any school that takes as much pride in its history as Wofford does is bound to have unique traditions. Old Main was the foundational building of the University and features a misspelled plaque that reads "benificent" rather than "beneficent." For Wofford students, rubbing the mislaid "i" brings them luck on exams. If you're a student who desires personal attention at a small liberal arts college and hopes for the benefits of an incredible network of alumni—"who are always there to offer jobs to the next graduates"—Wofford's luck is just waiting to rub off on you.—*Bess Hinson*

FYI

If you come to Wofford, you'd better bring "sunglasses with Croakies, polo shirts, pearls, and a flask."

What's the typical weekend schedule? "A sports game or workout during the day. Next, dinner or a movie with friends and then to fraternity row all night."

If you could change one thing about Wofford, it'd be "more diversity: a larger variety of students who are also more open-minded."

Three things every student at Wofford should do before graduating are "swim in the fountain after jumping in the mud on Guys' Bid Day, ring the bell in the Old Main building, and date someone."

South Dakota

Address: 414 East Clark Street, Vermillion, SD 57069
Phone: 605-677-5434
E-mail address: admission@usd.edu
Web site URL: www.usd.edu
Year Founded: 1862
Private or Public: Public
Religious Affiliation: None
Location: Rural
Number of Applicants: 3,499
Percent Accepted: 80%
Percent Accepted who enroll: 37%
Number Entering: 1,031
Number of Transfers Accepted each Year: 1,252
Middle 50% SAT range: M: 480–610, **CR:** 470–660, **Wr:** Unreported
Middle 50% ACT range: 20–25
Early admission program EA/ED/None: None

Percentage accepted through EA or ED: NA
EA and ED deadline: NA
Regular Deadline: Rolling
Application Fee: $20
Full time Undergraduate enrollment: 6,844
Total enrollment: 8,721
Percent Male: 38%
Percent Female: 62%
Total Percent Minority or Unreported: 15%
Percent African-American: 2%
Percent Asian/Pacific Islander: 1%
Percent Hispanic: 2%
Percent Native-American: 2%
Percent International: <1%
Percent in-state/out of state: 70%/30%
Percent from Public HS: 94%
Retention Rate: 72%
Graduation Rate 4-year: 20%

Graduation Rate 6-year: 44%
Percent Undergraduates in On-campus housing: 31%
Number of official organized extracurricular organizations: 130
3 Most popular majors: Business/Marketing, Education, Health Professions
Student/Faculty ratio: 14:1
Average Class Size: 24
Percent of students going to grad school: 50%
Tuition and Fees: $7,148
In-State Tuition and Fees if different: $5,828
Cost for Room and Board: $5,442
Percent receiving financial aid out of those who apply, first year: 64%
Percent receiving financial aid among all students: 53%

The University of South Dakota (USD) is the only comprehensive institution of higher learning that offers law, medical, business, and fine arts schools in the state of South Dakota. The state's oldest university, USD is home to over 6,000 undergraduates and 1,800 graduate and professional students. The school offers everything from associate degrees to doctorates. The location of the university in Vermillion, South Dakota, may leave something to be desired, but it remains a very attractive college choice given the number of academic options, especially for in-state students looking for a good education at a relatively affordable price.

College Standardized Tests

USD is divided into seven different schools: the College of Arts and Sciences, Beacom School of Business, School of Education, College of Fine Arts, School of Health Sciences, School of Law, and Sanford School of Medicine. Most undergraduates are in the College of Arts and Sciences, where the majority of majors are found. However, for those who are looking for more specialized programs of study, the other schools certainly offer plenty of options. Moreover, the presence of graduate programs allows the more ambitious undergraduates to take a number of graduate classes, which can be highly rewarding for in-depth study of different topics. "We have a lot of options," said one student. "That is a plus in coming to USD."

The university offers 132 majors and minors, ranging from the traditional tracks in Finance, Business, and Biology to the more specialized ones, such as Alcohol and Drug Studies. The most popular majors are those in business, education, and health care, and many students partake in the pre-professional preparations. After all, a large percentage of students at USD are looking to follow particular professional tracks and make use of their college education for preparing for graduate studies. The pre-professional programs include not only the traditional pre-medicine and pre-law curricula, but also less frequently seen programs, such as pre-occupational therapy and pre-chiropractic. "A lot of people are pre-something," said one student. "And we have a lot of really good programs specifically for those students."

> "Most of the professors that I met have been really nice and actually happy to talk to students."

Although USD is the flagship state university, it is rather small in scale with fewer than 10,000 students. As a result, it creates an intimate academic atmosphere. For the most part, the faculty welcomes interactions with students. The introductory classes are often conducted in large lecture halls, but students have access to a number of small classes where professors and students debate, discuss, and come to conclusions together on a variety of topics. "I have no problem talking to professors," said one student. "Most of the professors that I met have been really nice and actually happy to talk to students." As freshmen tend to have difficulties finding small classes, a program called First Year Experience provides a select number of students with small seminars as well as preferential treatment in enrolling in a number of popular courses. At the same time, the Honors Program is another way to receive more personalized attention in smaller classes and more in-depth investigation of topics.

One feature of USD is the requirement that students take standardized tests during their college years. All undergraduates must take the Collegiate Assessment of Academic Proficiency and achieve a satisfac-

tory grade on the exam. From the outset, it may seem like a nerve-wrecking experience, especially since the test is divided into writing, reading, mathematics, and sciences and must be completed for a student to graduate. However, it is certainly nothing too worrisome for students. It makes sure that students have a minimal grasp of basic skills needed in a college graduate, and most people have no difficulty passing the exam. Even for those who fail the standardized test, they can retake it within a year in order to remain at the university. "It is not a big deal," said one student. "I don't even know why they have it." In addition, prior to the exams, the students would already have completed a number of required courses in mathematics, sciences, composition, and humanities. Therefore, most people are well prepared to be successful at these tests.

Students generally have favorable opinions of the coursework at USD. Students are not overworked. People have time to enjoy a good social life, even during some weekdays. "I think if you manage your courses right, you will definitely have time to do a lot of other things than schoolwork," said one student.

College Town

Vermillion, where USD is located, is a rural, corn-growing city of approximately 10,000 residents. Given the university population of around 10,000 students, it is easy to imagine the importance of the university and the lack of anything particularly exciting within the city limits. Furthermore, Vermillion is also removed from any other metropolitan areas. "It's pretty boring here," said one student. "You can't find anything to do here. We do have a few restaurants and bars around campus, but that's it." The only well-known feature of the city to outsiders is the National Music Museum, which contains some world-renowned collections of musical instruments. "The good part of Vermillion is that it is quiet," said one student.

Students in the first two years must live on campus in one of the residential halls. The rooms are small and not particularly attractive to students, and most of them move off campus after their first two years to the surrounding areas. "The off-campus housing is bigger and easy to find," said one student. Nevertheless, some students think that living in dorms helps them greatly in acclimating to the social and academic environment. "I got to meet a lot of people," said one student. "And when you live in dorms, you don't have to worry about taking care of your housing and food." The dining services offer meal plans for those who eat almost every meal on campus and those who simply eat lunches during weekdays at one of the campus dining locations, and the facilities are located conveniently for students.

The university has a very strict alcohol policy, which is another reason students forgo on-campus living. Most of the weekend festivities occur in off-campus apartments and houses, as well as fraternities and sororities. Finding a hangout or party place during the weekends is certainly difficult, but students should expect to find it within the USD community. "There is not much beside USD at Vermillion," said one student. 'The whole place is pretty boring. Some people go to Sioux Falls for the weekends to find more things to do."

The National Champions

USD's varsity teams have recently been reclassified into NCAA Division I, thus offering top-level athletics for students. A unique aspect of the football team is that the games are played in a dome instead of an open-air stadium, a testament to the cold weather of South Dakota. For football games, the dorms can be very loud and intimidating for opposing teams. More than 120 extracurricular organizations are also available, thus offering even more socializing opportunities.

USD certainly has its drawbacks: small town, cold weather, and strict alcohol policies. The diversity of the student body is certainly another area for potential improvement for the school, as the number of minority students remains small, despite the university's efforts to increase diversity. However, USD also offers a great variety of academic programs and presents students with a balanced social and academic life.—*Xiaohang Liu*

FYI
If you come to USD, you'd better bring "a car."
What is the typical weekend schedule? "Parties start on Thursday and end on Saturday. Sometimes you can even get by not doing too much study on Sunday."
If I could change one thing about USD, I'd "let people hold parties in dorms."
Three things every student at USD should do before graduating are "join a frat, go to the dome for a game, and visit Sioux Falls."

Tennessee

Address: 2000 North Parkway
  Memphis, TN 38112
Phone: 901-843-3700
E-mail address:
  adminfo@rhodes.edu
Web site URL:
  www.rhodes.edu
Year Founded: 1848
Private or Public: Private
Religious Affiliation:
  Presbyterian
Location: Urban
Number of Applicants: 5,167
Percent Accepted: 41%
Percent Accepted who
  enroll: 21%
Number Entering: 431
Number of Transfers
  Accepted each Year: 20
Middle 50% SAT range: M:
  580–700, CR: 570–680,
  Wr: 580–680
Middle 50% ACT range:
  26–30
Early admission program
  EA/ED/None: ED and EA

Percentage accepted
  through EA or ED:
  Unreported
EA and ED deadline: 1-Nov
  (ED), 15-Nov (EA)
Regular Deadline: 15-Jan
Application Fee: $45 (waived
  for online application)
Full time Undergraduate
  enrollment: 1,661
Total enrollment: 1,685
Percent Male: 43%
Percent Female: 57%
Total Percent Minority or
  Unreported: 15%
Percent African-American:
  7%
Percent Asian/Pacific
  Islander: 5%
Percent Hispanic: 2%
Percent Native-American: 1%
Percent International: 4%
Percent in-state/out of
  state: 27%/73%
Percent from Public HS:
  50%

Retention Rate: 88%
Graduation Rate 4-year: 75%
Graduation Rate 6-year:
  82%
Percent Undergraduates in
  On-campus housing: 76%
Number of official organized
  extracurricular
  organizations: 115
3 Most popular majors:
  Biology, Business, History
Student/Faculty ratio: 10:1
Average Class Size: 13
Percent of students going to
  grad school: 33%
Tuition and Fees: $33,710
In-State Tuition and Fees if
  different: No difference
Cost for Room and Board:
  $8,314
Percent receiving financial
  aid out of those who apply,
  first year: Unreported
Percent receiving financial
  aid among all students:
  85%

Nestled in the heart of Memphis, Rhodes College mixes the calm of a small liberal arts college with the hustle of an urban center, enclosed in an oasis of Gothic architecture. For students at Rhodes, having fun is just as important as working hard. Students gain intense academic experiences in a close-knit community, while also enjoying a vibrant social scene.

Professor by Day, Drinking Buddy by Night.

Rhodes holds firmly to the values of a liberal arts school, emphasizing the study of diverse disciplines through a set of core requirements, and is centered around small, discussion-based classes. Students at Rhodes begin their education by fulfilling "founda-

tion requirements," which, as one student described, "represent what the administration deems to be the pillars of the liberal arts ideal." These include the expected writing and history classes as well as a more unique program that divides students into one of two tracks, both of which comprise three classes. "Search" surveys Western thought and philosophy, guiding students through a rigorous examination of the Great Books curriculum, while "Life" focuses on a literary study of religious scripture such as the Torah and the Bible. While devoting so many classes to requirements may seem limiting, the majority of students interviewed felt like the program was a good use of time. One sophomore who had completed the Search track said, "I really enjoyed the comprehensive nature of the foundation requirements. They helped integrate my classes, and it was interesting when something I had learned in history came up the next week in my English class."

The low student-faculty ratio at Rhodes has an immense impact on campus culture. Nearly all classes have fewer than 20 students, and faculty members are known for being readily accessible and willing to help students. One student even claimed that she had the cell phone number of each of her teachers in the event of a last-minute question. Not only had every student interviewed met with professors and attended office hours, but many had even interacted with their teachers outside of the academic setting. A senior described his personal experiences with Rhodes faculty. "I've been to professors' homes for dinner, I've played trivia games with professors, and I've even gone to bars with them." This unusually close relationship between students and faculty reinforces the liberal arts mindset shaping the Rhodes experience.

The Soup Kitchen May Be More Crowded than the Stadium
Rhodes, although a small college with a narrower range of activities than some schools, encourages passion for the extracurricular activities it does sponsor. The school is well known for its Mock trial team, frequently appearing in the national tournament and holding the second most national titles.

> "I've been to professors' homes for dinner, I've played trivia games with professors, and I've even gone to bars with them."

Also prominent are the school's abundant service organizations. Students at Rhodes respond enthusiastically to service challenges. One freshman said, "I've made a lot of my closest friends through working at a soup kitchen once a week. It's really the only time I ever go into Memphis, so it can be an exciting escape from the hustle of campus." The emphasis on service complements the campus' intense Greek life, with fraternities and sororities organizing many service projects.

While "Rhodents" tend to be very committed to their extracurricular activities, Rhodes culture does not embrace the tradition of spectator sports. A senior said, "I've never been to a football game here. Even if I

go to tailgate, no one ever seems to go to the actual game." The small student body makes it extremely easy to play a sport at Rhodes, leading to an unusually large number of student athletes, according to one student, which may contribute to the lack of a football culture. "So many people are involved that it's hard to find time to watch other sports." Students don't seem to regret the lack of enthusiasm for football, though, and are content with the highly successful intramural program.

Go Greek or Go Home
Greek life is a major part of the social scene at Rhodes. About 50% of the students on campus are part of a sorority or a fraternity, and many of the major parties have some affiliation with a house. According to one senior, the rush process for girls is much more intimidating and organized than for boys. However, "a huge number of girls rush every year," she said. For those students not wishing to pursue Greek life, or who wish to be involved socially outside of their fraternities or sororities, there are other options for social interaction. One junior said, "My friends consist of people that I am in similar organizations with, people that share my major, and close friends from freshman year." Because of the small size of the college, however, several students noted that Rhodents tend to form cliques with their close groups of friends.

Even if you don't choose to go Greek, many social activities do involve alcohol. One senior categorized Rhodes' social scene as "get drunk, go crazy." While students said that alcohol use is prevalent on Rhodes' campus, another senior noted that "it's not a big deal if you don't drink at all; people respect that." While a wide range of opinions of alcohol use on campus exist within the student body, the College states that it supports and expects behavior of its students that is "legal, responsible, healthy, and reflective of our community values." An important part of Rhodes' Social and Alcohol Policy is its Good Samaritan Statement, which precludes a student from getting penalized for calling help for an intoxicated person.

Because of Rhodes' location in midtown Memphis, however, students have plenty of off-campus options for entertainment. Many choose to go downtown to Beale Street where they can enjoy live jazz in clubs and bars such as B.B. King's or Silky O'Sullivan's. Most students have cars, as public transportation is not easily available or easy to use.

The Land of the Lynx

When students arrive at Rhodes for their freshman year, they are randomly sorted into a dorm, and unless they specifically request someone, randomly assigned a roommate. For freshman and sophomore years, students are required to live on campus, but can choose to move off campus for junior and senior years. Some of the dorms are themed—there is a biological sciences dorm, as well as a British Studies dorm – but the quality of the Gothic-style dorms is relatively uniform. According to several upperclassmen, housing gets markedly better with seniority. According to one student, "Our dorm life in general is pretty nice . . . juniors and seniors have the option of living in on-campus apartments that are quite coveted." While some students choose to move off-campus, about three-fourths of Rhodents remain on campus all four years.

The food at Rhodes is not, according to many students, one of the highlights of the Rhodes experience. One student complained that "there aren't very many options and what's available often isn't very healthy." When on-campus options are not appealing, students often go into the city of Memphis to find good food options. "Memphis as a city has so much to offer, that it seems odd to eat on campus much," said one student. However, a meal plan is required for all students living on campus.

Between meals and living spaces, there are plenty of places around campus for students to hang out. The Lynx Lair, a student-center type location, has not only food options but also air hockey and Ping-Pong tables. Another busy student hub is the Middle Ground, a coffee shop by the library. The bustling activity in these social hubs reflects on Rhodes' atmosphere as an excellent choice for those who want an active social life. A balanced combination of academic rigor through intense, discussion classes and social vitality through Greek organizations, Rhodes is a "work hard, play hard" school that fulfills any prospective student's liberal arts dream.—*Natasha Thondavadi and Anjali Balakrishna*

FYI

If you come to Rhodes College, you'd better bring "your tie and blazer. Be ready to dress up."
What's the typical weekend schedule at Rhodes? "Party Friday. Party Saturday. Work all Sunday."
Three things every student at Rhodes College should do before graduating are "ride the lynx statue, go to Beale Street, and take a picture in the fountain."

University of Tennessee / Knoxville

Address: 320 Student Service Building, Circle Park Drive Knoxville, TN 37996-0230
Phone: 865-974-1000
E-mail address: admissions@utk.edu
Web site URL: www.tennessee.edu
Year Founded: 1794
Private or Public: Public
Religious Affiliation: None
Location: Urban
Number of Applicants: 12,824
Percent Accepted: 71%
Percent Accepted who enroll: 47%
Number Entering: 4,331
Number of Transfers Accepted each Year: 1,909
Middle 50% SAT range: M: 540–640, CR: 530–630, Wr: Unreported
Middle 50% ACT range: 23–28
Early admission program EA/ED/None: None

Percentage accepted through EA or ED: NA
EA and ED deadline: NA
Regular Deadline: 1-Dec
Application Fee: $30
Full time Undergraduate enrollment: 21,369
Total enrollment: 27,632
Percent Male: 49%
Percent Female: 51%
Total Percent Minority or Unreported: 19%
Percent African-American: 8%
Percent Asian/Pacific Islander: 3%
Percent Hispanic: 3%
Percent Native-American: <1%
Percent International: 1%
Percent in-state/out of state: 86%/14%
Percent from Public HS: Unreported
Retention Rate: 84%
Graduation Rate 4-year: 29%

Graduation Rate 6-year: Unreported
Percent Undergraduates in On-campus housing: 33%
Number of official organized extracurricular organizations: 450
3 Most popular majors: Business/Marketing, Psychology, Social Sciences
Student/Faculty ratio: 16:1
Average Class Size: 25
Percent of students going to grad school: 20%
Tuition and Fees: $18,908
In-State Tuition and Fees if different: $6,250
Cost for Room and Board: $6,676
Percent receiving financial aid out of those who apply, first year: 49%
Percent receiving financial aid among all students: 46%

Knoxville, a small city in the heart of mountainous East Tennessee, is home to the state's major University, the University of Tennessee at Knoxville. At UTK, the scenic surroundings and the urban feel blend for a collegiate environment where students bleed Volunteer orange, party hard, and get their work done.

A Wide Range of Work Loads and Habits

At UTK, academic rigor spans a wide range. Depending on which major you choose, the class difficulty and time commitment to class increases. One freshman said he spends about 5 hours a week on homework, while upperclassmen said it is often the high reading workload that takes up their time. Certain majors, such as nursing, engineering, architecture, and accounting, are considered to be more work intensive majors, while English, psychology, and geography seem to have lighter workloads. "If I didn't study at least a couple hours every day, I would get behind very quickly," said one junior accounting major.

Large lecture classes are often curved, "especially freshman level courses to help newer students transition to college," said one sophomore. It is possible to get straight As in every course, said one junior, but such a feat is not the average goal of UTK students.

Big School, Big Choices

As to be expected at a large university, students say it is difficult to make connections with professors, especially as underclassmen. One freshman cited the lack of intimacy with professors as one of his least favorite aspects of UT academics. Some classes, especially General freshmen lectures like History or Natural Sciences, can have over 200 students in them. But as students begin to take specialized classes in their majors, class size decreases and professor involvement increases. Even as an underclassman, though, it's possible to be enrolled in classes of around 20 students, said one freshman.

Despite the lack of personal attention, students tend to appreciate the opportunities that do come out of being at a large state school. "I really enjoy the wide variety of majors and programs that you can choose at UT," said one senior. Students have the option to take interesting elective classes in areas ranging from Japanese Horror films to the history of Rock 'n' Roll.

Because of its location near the Oak Ridge National Laboratories, science research plays a substantial role in campus life. UT's campus is also home to the "Body Farm," a collection of corpses arranged in various positions used by medical and anthropology students to study forensics.

Good Ole' Rocky Top
Greek life plays a major role on UT's campus, with Frat parties being one of the main weekend activities for students. The fraternities have a row of houses on campus, while sororities do not. The most popular fraternities, Pike, Sigma Chi, Kappa Sigma, and SAE often throw big theme parties like Casino Date party or "Lifestyles of the Rich and Famous," amongst others. The rush process, which occurs during the first few weeks of the fall semester, is notoriously more stressful and structured for sororities than fraternities, said one junior girl. However, some students noted that Greek life is not as big a deal at UT's campus as it is at other SEC schools. Greeks on UT's campus do express pride in their fraternities and sororities, often sporting clothing with their letters on it. In addition to hosting parties, Greek organizations are involved with a lot of philanthropic work on campus.

For most students social life happens off campus—a short walk from school in downtown Knoxville is "The Strip," a row of bars and clubs that are the center of UTK weekend activity. UT's campus itself is supposed to be dry—but as one freshman said, "that's the biggest joke I've ever heard." Campus police are strict when it comes to alcohol and are fairly prominent around the school. The school's zero-tolerance drug policy is very strictly enforced, said one sophomore. Drugs are present on campus, but students said they don't feel pressured to participate.

For students who don't wish to participate in typical "party" activities, UT hosts a number of weekend events to keep students occupied. One freshman noted, "UT always has a lot to do for the weekends." The Campus Entertainment Board brings in performers, from magicians to speakers, and the University Center often screens movies for free for students. Market Square, another social center in downtown Knoxville, has a number of delicious restaurants which students frequent. Additionally, because the majority of students at UT are Tennessee natives, many choose to go home for the weekends. At UT, people are easy to meet, and friendly, said one junior. "Always! It's a Southern thing." While Greek life is a major way to meet people on campus, students find that the majority of their friends come from classes and freshmen dorm life. However, some students do notice the lack of diversity on campus, both racially and politically. And often, this lack of diversity results in discomfort with the unfamiliar. "Our university has had and still has a lot of problems with diversity, whether they admit it or not. People are really hesitant about ANYTHING they're not familiar with," one senior said. But for students who do represent minority populations on campus, this lack of diversity often leads to interesting conversations and friendships. "I'm biracial and Muslim, which at times gets very interesting, in a good way, because we are in the Bible Belt, and a large majority of campus is involved in some form of religious ministry or organization," said one junior boy. Most students seem to be able to find their niche in UT's social scene, and as one sophomore described it, UT is a "great place to live and learn."

Dorm Decisions
All freshmen who live less than 50 miles away from UT are required to live on campus for their first year. Before arriving on campus, students enter their dorm preferences on-line through UT's housing website and are assigned to a dorm. One freshman described the housing for first years as "tight but comfortable." The dorms come in a variety of styles—there are double rooms with a floor bathroom shared with around 20 other students as well as suite-style arrangements with a bathroom for a group of four students. If students have friends that are also going to UT, they can make arrangements to live with them throughout their time at school. The best freshmen dorms, South Carrick, Humes, North Carrick, and Reese, surround the "Presidential," a large quad central to campus. Students in the Honors program live in a separate dorm.

Many upperclassmen, though, choose to live off campus, where apartments can be found for around $400 to $450 per month. One of the major neighborhoods that UT students live in is called "Fort Sanders"—this residential area is also one of the main social hubs on campus. Because housing here is so popular, though, there is often a waitlist.

The Campus Bubble
As one junior said, "UT's campus is not pretty." The buildings, often a mixture of architectural designs, do not seem to have any sort of consistency – but while students sometimes pine for a more aesthetically pleasing campus, the collegiate atmosphere at UT is definitely palpable. "The Hill," the oldest part of campus that houses the school's math and science facilities, is noted for looking the most consistent. There are several central locations around campus where students congregate. Freshmen tend to hang out around the Presidential Courtyard, near their housing and cafeteria, while students in all years frequent the amphitheater, where student groups often organize events. Probably the most popular spot on campus, though, is the University Center, where students can get food, play games, and attend special events. One junior noted a particular bizarre hangout spot—an outdoor vent that emits heat. "People stand over it, even when it's sub-freezing outside, and talk, smoke, and laugh," he said.

Because of UT's heavy emphasis on sports, the exercise facilities are especially popular. "T-Rec," the University's big student gym, has state-of-the-art workout machinery as well as an indoor track, four basketball courts, three racquetball courts, intramural fields, and an indoor and outdoor pool.

Students generally feel safe on UT's campus—however the area around campus is often the target of crime. The Fort is notorious for being the most dangerous spot that students frequent.

Good Eats on and off campus
With five cafeterias and numerous restaurants on campus, students have a wide range of culinary options. Two of the dining halls have recently been renovated, and at the University Center, students can eat at popular chains such as Chik-fil-A and Subway. Students have a choice of five different meal plans, which incorporate "bonus bucks" to be in the restaurants on campus. But it is

the off-campus options that really make the UT culinary experience. One sophomore said "The hardest part isn't finding somewhere good to eat in Knoxville; it's deciding between all the great restaurants!"

> "People are always friendly and easy to meet at UT. It's a Southern thing!"

The restaurants in Knoxville range from "BBQ joints featured on Food Network to modern fusion restaurants and cafes." The Strip—the weekend social hub—is also lined with food options representing many types of cuisine and price ranges. Often, local restaurants like to show their UT pride, giving dishes University-based names.

Bleeding Volunteer Orange
At UT, students have no shortage of extracurricular options—"there are literally hundreds of clubs and organizations to get involved with at UT, all ranging from academic, to student government, to religious and ethnic groups." Because of the school's size, students are able to find organizations that appeal to them. According to one sophomore, "just about everything you want to join or be a part of is available." Apart from student groups, about one half of the student body has a job.

But it is UT Volunteer Athletics that unifies the student body throughout the year. Football and basketball are the most popular sports on campus – a sea of orange packs the 100,000 seat Neyland Stadium on the weekends during football season. "Game days in Knoxville in football season make UT the place to be," said one junior. The athletes are considered "minor celebrities" on campus, and tend to hang out with each other, but athletics are nonetheless a pride of the whole student body. Students belt "Rocky Top" during events, process in the Vol Walk to the games, and tailgate enthusiastically.

Ultimately, UT is a school with an "emphasis on tradition and school spirit." Students are motivated by a number of elements on campus—whether it's sports, Greek life, or academics—and this blend creates a diverse community that allows each Volunteer to find his or her place and college life.—*Anjali Balakrishna*

FYI
If you come to UT, you'd better bring something orange.
What differentiates UTK the most from other colleges is that game day is a holiday and an all-day
event.
Three things every student at UTK should do before graduating are 1. Paint the Rock. 2. Go to the
Vol Walk before a Home Football game. 3. Memorize "Rocky Top" and the "Alma Mater" by heart.

University of the South (Sewanee)

Address: 735 University Avenue, Sewanee, TN 37383-1000
Phone: 931 598-1000
E-mail address: admiss@sewanee.edu
Web site URL: www.sewanee.edu
Year Founded: 1857
Private or Public: Private
Religious Affiliation: Episcopal
Location: Rural
Number of Applicants: 2,481
Percent Accepted: 64%
Percent Accepted who enroll: 25%
Number Entering: 402
Number of Transfers Accepted each Year: Unreported
Middle 50% SAT range: M: 580–680, CR: 568–680, Wr: Unreported
Middle 50% ACT range: 25–30
Early admission program EA/ED/None: ED

Percentage accepted through EA or ED: 50%
EA and ED deadline: 15-Nov
Regular Deadline: 1-Feb
Application Fee: $45
Full time Undergraduate enrollment: 1,431
Total enrollment: 1,536
Percent Male: 41%
Percent Female: 59%
Total Percent Minority or Unreported: 16%
Percent African-American: 4%
Percent Asian/Pacific Islander: 2%
Percent Hispanic: 2%
Percent Native-American: 1%
Percent International: 1%
Percent in-state/out of state: 27%/73%
Percent from Public HS: Unreported
Retention Rate: 88%
Graduation Rate 4-year: 77%

Graduation Rate 6-year: Unreported
Percent Undergraduates in On-campus housing: 93%
Number of official organized extracurricular organizations: Unreported
3 Most popular majors: Social Sciences, English, Visual and Performing Arts
Student/Faculty ratio: 10:1
Average Class Size: Unreported
Percent of students going to grad school: Unreported
Tuition and Fees: $32,760
In-State Tuition and Fees if different: No difference
Cost for Room and Board: $9,360
Percent receiving financial aid out of those who apply, first year: 68%
Percent receiving financial aid among all students: 41%

In the midst of the beautiful rolling hills of East Tennessee lies the small liberal arts paradise of the University of the South at Sewanee. Sewanee, as it is more commonly known, offers a supportive learning environment coupled with a friendly and laid-back social scene. The small and intimate community allows Sewanee kids to spend four years learning from, and partying with, some of the most talented college students in the country.

Class Without TAs
One of Sewanee's biggest draws is its nurturing and accessible academic community.

As one student describes it, "Students are able to get valuable personal instruction from the professors in a very interactive environment where studies are based on discussion, not lecture." The school requires its students to fulfill a set of core requirements, including English, math, history and foreign languages. Some of the more popular majors include forestry and geology, even though they are "extremely challenging." English and history are also favorites, with physics and chemistry universally less popular.

Since Sewanee has no TAs, every single class is taught by professors, a move that elicits only praise from students despite the fact that "grading is fairly strict." Discussions are, as one student puts it, "fun and stimulating" due to the small class size, truly encouraging Sewanee kids to get the most out of their classroom experiences. Professors are described as "friendly and accessible" and "willing to meet with students at any time." One junior even goes so far as to say that "perhaps Sewanee's greatest academic strength is the relationship between students and professors . . . It is very difficult to find a bad teacher here."

Life in the "Bubble"
Outside of the classroom, Sewanee kids are incredibly sociable. As one junior said, "Sewanee people are some of the friendliest people on the planet . . . if there is any true stereotype, it's that all Sewanee students are usually able to get along with everyone." One male student even asserts that "some say we are all Southern hicks . . . but truth be told, I would rather be a Southern gentleman here [than anywhere else]." The stereotype that the population is made up of "privileged white students in a bubble" does admittedly "apply to many people," yet students are quick to defend their school's take on diversity. While the school may be "predominantly white," students insist that "we have a multicultural institute, and we try to promote racial awareness and cultural appreciation," recognizing the University's commitment to strengthening the diversity of the "close, but somewhat isolated, community."

> **"Perhaps Sewanee's greatest academic strength is the relationship between students and professors."**

Regardless of background, sports and extracurricular activities provide a plethora of opportunities for people to get to know their peers. While Sewanee does have a large football team, one junior claims that "sports like basketball and football are not a huge draw for students," while soccer and especially rugby seem to be gaining popularity as the teams score more victories on the field. Intramural sports are also prominent at Sewanee, with women's field hockey and men's basketball described as the most "intense" in which students can participate. If you're just looking to stay in shape, the Fowler Center is a "fairly pleasant" gym

with accessible facilities such as a pool, track, and weight room. For non-athletes, Sewanee offers about 100 clubs, including community service organizations, publications, and theater groups, giving students a variety of different social outlets.

The Sewanee residential community is made up of a variety of dorms and houses, each of which has its own unique character. Freshmen don't have separate housing, but are instead integrated into upperclassmen dorms from the very beginning, with the only difference being that singles are reserved for juniors and seniors. Most students live on campus, since Sewanee seniors are the only group permitted to apply for off-campus housing. Well-known dorms include Cannon Hall, the universally recognized "party dorm," and Humphreys, which "looks like a hotel, inside and out." There are also special language houses, in which students commit to speaking only the particular language of the house, as well as a few single-sex dorms. Student proctors live in the dorms and fulfill the role of RAs, while Assistant Proctors (or APs) "work with freshmen to help them adjust to college life and enforce dorm rules."

Architecturally, students state that "most of the buildings at Sewanee are rather distinctive . . . think Oxford." The gorgeous All Saints' Cathedral, complete with stained glass windows, serves as a prominent campus landmark, while the towers of McClurg Dining Hall have earned it the nickname "Phallus Palace." Inside McClurg, Sewanee's only dining facility, students on a meal plan enjoy the "great number of choices" that the school has to offer. If the campus food starts to get old, Mi Casa Mexican restaurant and Shen Chinese buffet offer quick and easy alternatives.

It's All Greek To Me
The party scene at Sewanee is notorious for being one of the craziest in the country. One student admits, "Sewanee students work hard all week, and yes, we drink hard on the weekends . . . If you're against alcohol, you probably shouldn't go here." The prevalence of alcohol on campus is abetted by the Greek system, which essentially dominates the available social options. However, Sewanee kids are quick to assert that "the fraternity system promotes friendship in the community." The huge number of frats provides interested pledges with a variety of different alternatives, and they all have an open door policy, meaning that "anyone is

allowed to party at any house on any given night."

However, some students warn that "lately the drinking policy has been getting stricter" and that officials have been cracking down on the amount of alcohol the fraternities and sororities are allowed to serve. To get around these regulations, people can also head off-campus for parties in senior residences, where the drinks continue to flow all night long. The University even has its own Tiger Bay Pub, a restaurant that serves beer until 10 p.m. and breakfast for the rest of the night, a sure sign of just how much alcohol serves as a hallmark of the school's social experience.

Despite Sewanee's self-proclaimed status as a wet campus, there are definitely weekend activities that don't necessarily involve alcohol. The Sewanee Union Theater offers sneak previews of upcoming films, while the nearby Lake Cheston club has occasional concerts and shows. Sewanee's proximity to the woods also allows students to enjoy outdoor activities like hiking and camping. The campus is incredibly safe, and town-gown relations are friendly, as many students comment that "[the town of Sewanee] generally tolerates the students, and the beer and liquor stores are especially appreciative of them." In terms of venturing off campus to explore the surrounding areas, Sewanee

kids agree that "most people have cars." Indeed cars are necessary for everything from making Wal-Mart runs in nearby Cowen or Monteagle to making the treks to Nashville or Chattanooga. Popular off-campus clubs include Tubby's in Monteagle, while the coffee house Stirling's and Shenanigans bar and grill draw rave reviews from students. The Four Seasons even offers home cooking, but it is closed during the winter because it serves fresh food directly from nearby farms, a reminder of the advantages of Sewanee's rural location.

A Place Where Angels Dwell

Sewanee lore is rife with unique stories and enduring traditions. Students still "dress for class," meaning that they wear nicer clothes out of a sense of propriety and respect for the professors. Tour guides tell of nearby Civil War bombs and battles, while stories of ghosts and haunted buildings continue to circulate. Legend even has it that angels dwell at the gates of Sewanee, and many students admit to tapping the roof of their car when entering or exiting campus to "summon a 'Sewanee angel'" to protect them. Truly a charmed place, Sewanee offers prospective students a chance for a supportive and rewarding college experience. As one junior states, "Sewanee is just the greatest. Period."—*Alexandra Bicks*

FYI

If you come to Sewanee, you'd better bring "hiking boots, dress attire for class, a smile, and a sense of adventure."

What's a typical weekend schedule? "Friday night, party hard; Saturday morning, sleep; Saturday afternoon, go see some sports events; Saturday night, party hard; Sunday, go to church to make up for Friday and Saturday night, and then study!"

If I could change one thing about Sewanee, I'd "make it closer to a real city: it can get kind of isolated out here."

Three things everyone should do before graduating are "hike the perimeter trail, take interesting classes, and watch a sunset at Morgan's Steep."

Vanderbilt University

Address: 2305 West End Avenue, Nashville, TN 37203
Phone: 615-322-7311
E-mail address: admissions@vanderbilt.edu
Web site URL: www.vanderbilt.edu
Year Founded: 1873
Private or Public: Private
Religious Affiliation: None
Location: Urban
Number of Applicants: 19,353
Percent Accepted: 33%
Percent Accepted who enroll: 26%
Number Entering: 1,673
Number of Transfers Accepted each Year: 193
Middle 50% SAT range: M: 680–760, CR: 650–740, Wr: 650–730
Middle 50% ACT range: 30–33
Early admission program EA/ED/None: ED

Percentage accepted through EA or ED: Unreported
EA and ED deadline: 1-Nov
Regular Deadline: 3-Jan
Application Fee: $50
Full time Undergraduate enrollment: 6,637
Total enrollment: 10,587
Percent Male: 44%
Percent Female: 56%
Total Percent Minority or Unreported: 13%
Percent African-American: 10%
Percent Asian/Pacific Islander: 7%
Percent Hispanic: 6%
Percent Native-American: 1%
Percent International: 4%
Percent in-state/out of state: 16%/84%
Percent from Public HS: Unreported
Retention Rate: 96%
Graduation Rate 4-year: 89%

Graduation Rate 6-year: Unreported
Percent Undergraduates in On-campus housing: 89%
Number of official organized extracurricular organizations: 329
3 Most popular majors: Social Sciences, Engineering, Foreign Languages and Literature
Student/Faculty ratio: 9:1
Average Class Size: 16
Percent of students going to grad school: Unreported
Tuition and Fees: $37,005
In-State Tuition and Fees if different: No difference
Cost for Room and Board: $12,028
Percent receiving financial aid out of those who apply, first year: 86%
Percent receiving financial aid among all students: 46%

S mack-dab in the middle of Music City, USA, Vanderbilt University's idyllic brick buildings and grassy lawns are just blocks away from the good food and quirky culture of Nashville, Tennessee. Competitive both academically and socially, Vandy is a place for those who like to work hard, play hard, and eat great burgers.

Atypical "A's"
On Vanderbilt academics, one freshman concluded: "I am confident that the academics of Vanderbilt are perfectly balanced to allow its students to enjoy the college life, while still being rigorous enough to create respect in the job world and promote learning while on campus." But grade-grubbers be warned: Vanderbilt supports grade *de*flation, an oft-forgotten phenomenon of a pre–SAT tutor America. As one junior elaborated, "B's are easy to get; A's are hard."

Students might have an easier time push- ing 4.0s at the Peabody School of Education. The Human and Organizational Development major is one of the easiest on campus. Engineers, premed students, and economics majors have a tougher time. Some students argued, though, that "each major is challenging . . . but not impossible." According to many students, "curriculum is an integral part of Vanderbilt."

Even in the more difficult majors, most Vanderbilt professors have an open-door policy and boast small class sizes, though large lectures border on 50. Freshmen seeking name-brand profs should enroll in Brian Griffith's "Applied Human Development," John Lachs' "Intro to Philosophy," or Stephen Buckles' introductory economics courses.

Music City Madness
Vanderbilt has "top 20 academics according to *U.S. News* and a top 20 party scene according to *Playboy*." And Hugh Hefner certainly

knows his parties—the entertainment options at Vanderbilt do not disappoint. Between fraternity parties, downtown Music City, movies on Peabody lawn, and on-campus concerts and lectures, Vandy students are never bored. "Being underage is only a problem if you want to go to bars downtown and you don't have a fake ID. Most take anything halfway legit," one junior said. Upperclassmen who are interested, however, can enjoy the Nashville nightlife courtesy of student-friendly cabs that frequent Vanderbilt's campus on the weekends. Underclassmen attend frat parties more often, and enjoy "cool live bands, literally every weekend."

> **"Vanderbilt has top 20 academics according to *U.S. News* and a top 20 party scene according to *Playboy*."**

There are many non-drinkers on campus, but they are well accepted and included in regular goings-on. As one freshman explained, "I know several of my closest friends drink, and I don't drink, but we can still go to the frats and have fun." There is also a Christian fraternity that hosts dry parties. During the daytime, Vanderbilt has hosted many famous lecturers in years past including Maya Angelou and Tennessee native Al Gore. Further, the "Chancellor's Lecture Series" is mandatory for freshmen and open to the public, while the "Sarratt Student Center is a popular hang-out place." Students agreed that the highlight of Vanderbilt social life comes in April with the Rites of Spring. Just before finals, the school hires bands and performers for "a two-day orgy of music" on Alumni Lawn. Past performers include Ludakris, Maroon 5, and Robert Earl Keen.

On-campus dating is, for the most part, limited to formals, but there is a "small scene." It is mostly overwhelmed by "lots of random hook-ups." What does set Vanderbilt apart, according to one student, is that the "student body is unusually attractive," especially the women, he added.

The Vandy Vibe
The Vanderbilt stereotype is what you might expect at a Southern school. One freshman listed the following perceived stereotypes: "Vanderbilt is an all-wealthy white school. Girls are blonde, preppy, fake, and dependent. Guys are party animals and Southern gentlemen. Everyone is from the South, and

everyone dresses to impress." In reality, however, "there are more middle-class students than most people think. About half of the student body receives financial aid." Many students express satisfaction with the student body profile, but a considerable number wish there were more diversity.

Some of the homogeneity around the Vandy campus is attributed to the "huge Greek system." One sophomore wrote that second semester rush is "stressful but fun!" Chi Omega, Delta Delta Delta, Kappa Alpha Theta, Kappa Kappa Gamma, and Kappa Delta are the coveted sororities, while guys elbow to get into Sigma Chi, Sigma Alpha Epsilon, Kappa Alpha, and Pi Kappa Epsilon. The Greek system seems to be a significant forum for making friends at Vandy, and on the homogeneity that it creates, the same student argued that "smart and interesting people are definitely here . . . lots of students who actually care about political and social issues as well as what they look like!"

The Lowdown on Living
All Vanderbilt freshmen live on campus in one of three dorms. Kissam is the least well kept. Composed of single bedrooms, it is viewed as a "bookworm" area. Branscomb, neighbor to Greek row, boasts the best party scene. And Vandy-Barnard is the most popular dorm for freshmen. Most upperclassmen stay on campus, hopefully in Scales or Vaughn, the best upperclass dorms, while others live in fraternity or sorority houses or in other off-campus accommodations. There is an international house called McTyeire "where you have to speak a foreign language and eat dinner there four nights a week," and there is also a philosophy house.

On-campus dining plans are "decent . . . not great but not horrible." Rand, the main dining center, is a nice place to sit and chat with friends for hours on end. When students need a change of pace, however, they can use their meal points at surrounding restaurants: P.F. Chang's, Ken's Sushi, Pancake Pantry, and Bread & Company are all popular. Amerigo's is the hot spot for dates, and Rotier's is the home of the world's best cheeseburger. Vanderbilt also features a significant number of options for those with certain eating requirements, such as the kosher and vegetarian establishments on campus.

Commodores in the Community
Vandy students are avid sports fans. Though the basketball and baseball teams are the most successful, more students frequent

weekly football games in the fall—often with a date and a dress. There is even a "Vanderbilt Fanatics" club that organizes the cheering effort. One nice tradition, according to students, "is for the students to stand and sing the alma mater after each game, win or lose."

For nonvarsity athletes, there are a number of sporting options. One freshman said, "The club and intramural programs are popular and well run." Additionally, there are great facilities for recreational exercise such as swimming, weight lifting, tennis, and basketball. On nice days, many students can be seen running "the loop," a three-mile course around campus.

In terms of nonathletic extracurriculars, Vanderbilt students are very community service oriented. Alternative Spring and Winter Break, which "take several hundred students to another state or country," and Habitat for Humanity are very well respected. Students who aren't involved in community service or the Commodore yearbook (another popular pastime) might take jobs on campus, although most students with jobs are part of the work-study program. Sororities and fraternities are the most time-consuming extracurriculars but Vandy students insist that "academics come first."—*Lauren Ezell*

FYI

If you come to Vanderbilt you better bring "a sundress for football games."
What is a typical weekend schedule? "Study hard, play hard."
If I could change one thing about Vanderbilt, I'd "add more diversity to the student body."
Three things every student at Vanderbilt should do before graduating are "take a drunk picture with Chancellor Gee, take an ASB trip, and get painted up for a football game."

Texas

The history of Baylor University began before Texas even entered the Union as a state. In fact, its official establishment in 1845 was chartered by the then-Republic of Texas. Over one and a half centuries later, Baylor has become not only a well-respected academic institution, but also the largest Baptist-affiliated university in the world, with a total of over 14,000 students. Furthermore, due to its dedication to research activities across all disciplines, Baylor has also emerged as a highly regarded global university, attracting students and faculty from around the world.

No-nonsense Academics

The quality of education offered by Baylor is widely recognized as one of the best in the country. *U.S. News & World Report* recently ranked Baylor as the 79th best national university. In 2007, *Relevant* magazine listed the university as the best Christian college in the country. This means competitive students and challenging academics. "Surely, finding easy classes is not that hard, and sometimes it depends on what you want to achieve in college," said one senior. "But overall, the classes are hard and make you work quite a bit."

Baylor students are also keen on boasting about the range and number of academic opportunities. After all, the University provides 151 different areas of study, not to mention the fact that it also offers 50 study-abroad programs, a rarity even among the largest academic institutions in the United States. Given Baylor's status as a leading research university, undergraduate students who seek to enrich themselves even further can easily gain exposure to the numerous in-depth research projects on campus.

In addition, the undergraduate education at Baylor goes far beyond the traditional liberal arts subjects. The University is divided into 11 different schools, and eight of them—ranging from the customary Arts and Sciences to the Hankamer School of Business to the School of Social Work—have degree-granting programs for undergraduates. Several certification programs are also available for those who seek to link their education directly to future employment, like students who are planning for a career in teaching. "The School of Education is great here at Baylor," affirmed one student. "It gives a lot of opportunities to students to have field experiences and do some actual teaching in classrooms. It prepares us well for our careers."

As its Baptist affiliation would suggest, Baylor maintains considerable emphasis on Christianity in the education of students. The core curriculum that everyone must fulfill before graduation reflects this religious commitment by requiring students to attend Chapel regularly during at least two semesters. Furthermore, everyone must take two specific religion classes: Introduction to Christian Scripture and Introduction to Christian Heritage. "I particularly enjoyed my religion classes. I now know so much more about what it means to be a Christian," one student explained.

The rest of the curriculum varies significantly, given the large differences between majors. However, as in most universities of similar academic vigor, students are required to take classes in a variety of fields, such as English, foreign language, and mathematics. These skills are deemed highly valuable regardless of major. "The required classes can be a pain, but I feel I learned a lot of new things from them," said one student.

Life in Waco
Located on the south side of Waco, Texas, Baylor is generally considered an urban school, but its surroundings are certainly more reminiscent of the suburbs, with low-rise apartments and small houses. Although Waco does employ a large number of commuters, it is certainly not a major metropolitan area and has been suffering from urban decay for several decades. Nevertheless, efforts are now underway, with the help of Baylor, to revive the city. On the other hand,

students do not necessarily feel it is necessary to be part of Waco, and prefer staying on campus. "We have a very big university," one student said. "So I don't feel the need to go to the city, which doesn't have much anyway."

Life on Campus
Freshmen are required to live on campus, unless they live with their parents in McLennan County or have extenuating circumstances such as being married or having dependents. In applying for housing, students can ask for a specific roommate and indicate residential hall preferences. Although there is no guarantee that these requests will be honored, students certainly have a degree of control over their living arrangements. "The rooms are reasonable," one student said. "I have been to dorms of my friends at other colleges, and, compared to them, I think Baylor's housing is not bad." Nevertheless, upperclassmen tend to move off campus to the many surrounding apartments. This means that only about 35 percent of the students are currently living in university facilities; however, Baylor has recently indicated that it recognizes the importance of campus living to education and aims to achieve 50 percent of students living on campus by 2012.

As a Baptist university, the way students behave certainly reflects Christian values. Alcohol, for example, is strictly monitored on campus. Therefore, many parties happen off of University property. Baylor has more than 40 fraternities and sororities, making them an important part of the social scene. For those uninterested in Greek life or alcohol, many other options are also available, especially the different artistic and sporting performances where many people gather and socialize. Furthermore, unlike at most universities in the country, another major and well-attended weekend activity is church. "Of course people go to church on Sundays," one student said. "At the end of the day, this is a Christian university, and going to church is essential for many people here."

Baylor Bears
Baylor, like many other large Texan universities, is a major force in collegiate athletics. The Bears, named after the school mascot, participate in the Big 12 Conference, a highly competitive and prestigious conference of NCAA Division I. Although the football team has not been very successful due

to the quality of its adversaries, the games still attract large crowds and are famous for the Baylor Line, made entirely of a large number of freshmen wearing yellow football jerseys cheering for the team and intimidating the opponents.

> **"You will learn a lot about Texas during your time at Baylor."**

The more successful programs include the baseball team, which regularly provides quality players to Major League Baseball; the women's basketball team; and the track and field team, which is known to have produced one of the most celebrated sprinters in recent memory, world-record holder Michael Johnson. The most outstanding team award, however, probably goes to the tennis team, which has been winning consecutive titles since 2005. "Our teams are very good, so it is only natural that sports are big at Baylor," one student concluded. "The teams and the crowd help us to have a strong school spirit," added another.

Diversity in a Baptist Institution

One of the major factors that may turn away many prospective applicants is the image of a heavily religious university that focuses on proclaiming Christian values. Undoubtedly, Baylor does have a strong emphasis on religion. In fact, its mission statement unambiguously affirms that the goal of the institution is to combine Christianity with academic excellence. "My religion is important to me," one student explained. "That is why I chose

to come here." The requirement of Chapel attendance clearly shows that the school is deeply committed to teaching students about not only religion, but also faith.

On the other hand, Baylor's student body does have substantial diversity, at least for a school of such strong religious affiliation. Minority students account for roughly 35 percent of the total enrollment, a considerable number for most universities. At the same time, more than 80 countries are represented on campus, and the school enrolls about 200 international students. Furthermore, despite the preaching of Christian values, there are a small number of non-Christians. "I know people who are atheists here," said one student. "As long as you can stand having plenty of pious people around you, I don't think you will find it really hard to get by." One drawback, however, is that the University is predominantly Texan in nature. In fact, four out of five students come from the Lone Star State. "You will learn a lot about Texas during your time at Baylor," affirmed one student.

Baylor is unique. With its combination of qualities and weaknesses, students choose to attend this school for a particularly large variety of reasons. Sometimes it is because Baylor is academically industrious. Sometimes it is because of Baylor's religious traditions. Sometimes it is the school spirit. Regardless of their reasons, most students are happy about their choice. Surely the strong emphasis on Christian values and the location in Waco may turn away some potential suitors. At the end of the day, however, Baylor remains a top destination for students from around the world.
—*Xiaohang Liu*

FYI
If you come to Baylor, you'd better bring a "work ethic."
What is the typical weekend schedule? "Parties, but you have to make sure that you will get up in the morning on Sunday for church."
If I could change one thing about Baylor, I'd "make more upperclassmen live on campus."
Three things every student at Baylor should do before graduating are "visit Dallas, study abroad, and go to as many sports games as you can."

Rice University

Address: MS 17 PO, Box 1892, Houston, TX 77251-1892	**EA and ED deadline:** ED: 1-Nov, EA 1-Dec	**Graduation Rate 6-year:** 92%
Phone: 713-348-7423	**Regular Deadline:** 10-Jan	**Percent Undergraduates in On-campus housing:** 68%
E-mail address: admission@rice.edu	**Application Fee:** $50	
Web site URL: www.rice.edu	**Full time Undergraduate enrollment:** 3,154	**Number of official organized extracurricular organizations:** 215
Year Founded: 1912	**Total enrollment:** 5,456	
Private or Public: Private	**Percent Male:** 52%	**3 Most popular majors:** Biology, Economics, Psychology
Religious Affiliation: None	**Percent Female:** 48%	
Location: Urban	**Total Percent Minority or Unreported:** 47%	
Number of Applicants: 8,776	**Percent African-American:** 6%	**Student/Faculty ratio:** 5:1
Percent Accepted: 23%		**Average Class Size:** 16
Percent Accepted who enroll: 34%	**Percent Asian/Pacific Islander:** 18%	**Percent of students going to grad school:** 41%
Number Entering: 714	**Percent Hispanic:** 12%	
Number of Transfers Accepted each Year: 106	**Percent Native-American:** <1%	**Tuition and Fees:** $25,606
Middle 50% SAT range: M: 680–780, CR: 650–740, Wr: 640–740	**Percent International:** 4%	**In-State Tuition and Fees if different:** No difference
	Percent in-state/out of state: 53%/47%	**Cost for Room and Board:** $10,250
Middle 50% ACT range: 30–34	**Percent from Public HS:** Unreported	**Percent receiving financial aid out of those who apply, first year:** 65%
Early admission program EA/ED/None: ED and EA	**Retention Rate:** 97%	
Percentage accepted through EA or ED: 32%	**Graduation Rate 4-year:** 79%	**Percent receiving financial aid among all students:** 64%

With its cleanly manicured lawns, lush green vegetation, and park-like atmosphere, one would hardly guess that Rice University is located just a few miles from downtown Houston, Texas. As one of the nation's top universities, it offers students an unmatched education in addition to a beautiful learning environment.

"We Study a Lot"

In describing Rice, one student said, "You will work so hard here. The students I know could not work more if they wanted to." Even those who choose to take the easier route must fulfill Rice's academic requirements, which can vary in intensity depending on the major and the number of AP credits an individual has coming in. There are three areas of distributional requirements—the humanities, the social sciences, and the natural sciences. Students point out that the requirements have their "ups and downs," but one student said it is beneficial, since "taking classes outside of your major really helps to open your mind."

Many students take a lot of science courses regardless, but there are complaints about the "perfectionist premeds." It is common for students to continue their research at Rice over the summer. One of Rice's most well-known programs is the Rice-Baylor program, which guarantees acceptance to Baylor College of Medicine, the largest medical center in the country, located "right across the street." However, the program only accepts approximately 14 undergrads per year. Unfortunately, many premed students do not have the luxury of going abroad—a hefty sacrifice, considering that about half the University's students do so for at least a semester.

In terms of getting into classes, freshmen often have the most difficulty procuring a spot for the more coveted lectures. The upside for freshmen is that general education classes such as introductory humanities tend to be capped, so they range from 20 to 30 people. Other introductory courses, including biology, chemistry, physics, and constitutionalism, are generally quite large, "which for Rice isn't that big—maybe 100 students." One Rice freshman bragged that "my smallest class is an amazing Introduction to Theater class, which only has about 10 students." Upper-level courses are extremely small at Rice; typically less than 20 to 30 people. One upperclassman said, "I had four classes with fewer than 10 students last year."

While most Rice students are committed to their studies, few deny that some majors are harder than others. Mathematics, physics, and computer science top the list of most demanding majors. However, "every discipline at Rice has very serious students, and those are the ones that study the most—it doesn't depend on the major." "You will spend your four years at this school either working or feeling like you should be working." This deep commitment to academics and intensive studying does have its payoff, however. "There's a deeper level of satisfaction here than at most other schools because we know that 'excellence' should be hard to achieve (and that things can only get easier.)"

The workload is more bearable when students have the opportunity to take classes from famous professors like Dennis Huston, a humanities teacher famous for lectures in which "he spits out obscenities left and right." People actually camp out in front of the registrar's office to ensure a spot in Huston's public speaking class. Bombs and Rockets, a class about the "Politics of American National Security," is another hot ticket. And these classes don't disappoint, with enjoyable assignments to hold students' interest. One premed student was assigned the task of creating artificial blood for one of his science courses.

Grade inflation doesn't seem to be a prominent concern at Rice, where students joke about its prevalence at Ivy League schools. Some classes, such as chemistry, do have what are called "redemption points." In this system, if a student's score on a portion of the final exam is better than that on a test from the beginning of the year, the earlier test score replaces final questions pertaining to the earlier test, resulting in the higher grade.

For all their positive attributes, academics at Rice do have some drawbacks. One student noted that some "professors and classes are not as liberal-artsy or teaching-focused as advertised. You get a lot of indifferent professors and big lecture classes, especially in the math and science departments." For more difficult classes, recitation sessions taught by the TAs are offered. Students seem to have mixed feelings about TAs, some complaining that they only muddle the information and that it can be "really hard to understand" those with foreign accents. This is not always the case, however, and one student praised the grad students at Rice, calling one of her TAs "better than the professor." Whatever the case may be, "between the office hours of the TAs and professors, you can always get help if you need it."

Studying Aside

Rice isn't all brains and no beer (despite its Greek-free status). "Even though Rice students are hardworking, you can find a lot of students that like to party a lot." Although most parties serve up alcohol, there are "always other things to do," one student emphatically pointed out, and nondrinkers are not at all ostracized. "I can't imagine a more accepting social scene." The residential colleges throw a lot of the parties. Well-known bashes include the Annual Night of Decadence, "which is basically a nude party;" Disorientation (at the end of orientation week); and the Tower Party. Late-night games of powderpuff football or just "chilling" with card games or a movie are options for those students who just want to veg out. The dating scene (or lack thereof) at Rice is often blamed on the common stereotype that "most of us guys tend to be shy," one male Rice student explained. And the males' shyness only works to their disadvantage, since "there's a good amount of cute girls on campus." The verdict is still out, however, because other Rice students feel that "you're either in a very serious relationship or you're not dating anyone at all."

Instant Family

The social life at Rice is supplemented by the University's "amazing" residential college system. About 400 people (100 from each grade) live in each of nine colleges, providing an instant family atmosphere ingrained in freshmen from the start of "a great orientation week." Freshmen from each college are divided into groups of eight to 10 students during "O-Week." "You're really tight with them from the start and you do all your activities with your group," a student explained. The colleges "make a very concerted effort to put people from very different backgrounds and with very different interests in each group," one student said.

And yes, the residential colleges definitely do have different personalities, students said, which "are all brainwashed into us during our orientation week." Most students are positive about the system and their experience. One student noted that the system is like "the best parts of a fraternity and a dorm all put together." And don't worry about meeting people outside of your residential college. Classes, parties, or common friends are all ways to extend your social circle, although it does "take a little bit more effort."

Each college has its own master and staff of associates. The master is a tenured professor at the University and handles academic and personal matters, in addition to organizing social events. He or she lives and eats with the students in the residential college. The associates are faculty members, most of whom live outside of Rice, except for the two associates who reside in each college. They provide academic advice and help direct students' career choices.

Dorms vary from college to college, but most students would agree that none are terrible. Rooms range from singles to quads, most of which are located on coed floors and share single-sex bathrooms. There are more singles in the newer colleges, but there's no reason to fear being lonely—usually four singles comprise a suite, with its own common room and bathroom. And don't worry about playing your music too loudly: the RA system is fairly lenient and the RAs "tend to be really cool here and enjoy hanging out with us."

"The education you receive outside the classroom at Rice is what makes me feel like I could have never been happy anywhere else."

Each college has its own dining hall, and though the quality varies, overall the food at Rice is "good by college standards." Even seniors opt to eat in the dining halls because "one of the great things about the college system is that students from all classes interact on a daily basis (primarily at lunch)." On Saturday nights, the cafeterias are closed for all students—a mixed blessing because "it forces one to go off campus." And there are more than enough places to choose from, with a great range in price and quality. When the clock strikes two in the morning, Taco Cabana, "a better, cheaper version of

Taco Bell," is the place to be for post-party munchies. House of Pies is another Rice novelty.

A World Away
What's green, flat, and pretty all around? Why, the campus of Rice University, of course. It features beautiful landscaping and sprawling quads that students said "people are actually encouraged to walk on," although some prefer to utilize the plush grass for napping. The main local attraction is Rice Village, an outdoor mall with a mix of franchises and independent retailers that is "packed with restaurants." But who wants to walk when you can hitch a ride with any of the estimated 40 percent of Rice students who have cars on campus? Beyond campus, Houston has so much to offer, including the Theater District, Chinatown and the Galleria, a "really famous, really large mall," but one student did lament the insular nature of the school. The hedges that surround the "spacious campus sometimes make Rice students forget that there's the city of Houston and even an entire world outside Rice." When they do get outside, favorite Rice bar hangouts in Houston include Bar Houston, Brian O'Neil's, Brock's Bar, and Two Rows. Little Woodrow's is another popular bar in the Village (along with Brian O'Neil's). Luckily for students not blessed with the luxury of wheels, a rail system makes getting places a bit easier. Last year, Rice's president implemented "Passport to Houston," so now all undergraduates can ride the light rail for free, "which makes going to bars, baseball games, and restaurants downtown, as well as the museum district and apartment complexes, very easy."

Outside the Classroom
"The education you receive outside the classroom at Rice is what makes me feel like I could have never been happy anywhere else," one student said. "People game, take salsa lessons, play ultimate Frisbee," and do anything to "enrich themselves," another said of the extracurricular scene at Rice. Although some organizations are more "official" than others, "as long as you have a group of people with a common shared idea, it can be made into an official club." The Cabinet, Parliament, and Diet among others are the names of residential college student governments, and these are a popular activity, even more than their counterpart, the official University student government. Future journalists can take a stab at writing for

Rice's widely read newspaper, *The Thresher*. High participation rates show more than just an interest to beef up résumés. "Everybody does their own thing," and they are appreciated for it. One student went so far as to say that "Rice people will change your life."

Although Rice's athletics are not the pinnacle of the University, the school's baseball team won the College World Series in 2003, made the NCAA tournament in 2006, and advanced to the NCAA Super Regionals. Rice students don't just cheer for the champs, though. A surprising number of people at-tend the football games "even though we're quite pathetic," one student said. College sports are another popular option—teams from various residential colleges compete against one another for the President's Cup. Although there are separate workout facilities for varsity athletes, the general public facility "pales in comparison to Duke's," as one student put it. "You're probably going to have to wait for cardio equipment anytime in the afternoon or evening, and most mornings as well. But the Board of Trustees has stated that a new Rec Center is a priority."
—*Laura Sullivan*

FYI

If you come to Rice you'd better bring "water balloons for O-Week, Beer Bike, and general mayhem."

What is the typical weekend schedule? "A lot of studying and a lot of procrastinating with your friends either partying, going out in Houston, or hanging out at your college."

If I could change one thing about Rice, I'd "help the premeds relax."

Three things every student at Rice should do before graduating are "support their powderpuff team, explore Houston without a car, and advise during O-Week (it's more fun for the advisers than for the freshmen, shhh!)."

Southern Methodist University

Address: PO Box 750181 Dallas, TX 75275-0181

Phone: 214-768-3417

E-mail address: enrol_serv@smu.edu

Web site URL: www.smu.edu

Year Founded: 1911

Private or Public: Private

Religious Affiliation: Methodist

Location: Urban

Number of Applicants: 8,270

Percent Accepted: 50%

Percent Accepted who enroll: 34%

Number Entering: 1,397

Number of Transfers Accepted each Year: 558

Middle 50% SAT range: M: 590–680, CR: 560–660, Wr: 560–660

Middle 50% ACT range: 25–30

Early admission program EA/ED/None: EA

Percentage accepted through EA or ED: Unreported

EA and ED deadline: 1-Nov

Regular Deadline: 15-Mar

Application Fee: $60

Full time Undergraduate enrollment: 6,240

Total enrollment: 10,000

Percent Male: 47%

Percent Female: 53%

Total Percent Minority or Unreported: 26%

Percent African-American: 5%

Percent Asian/Pacific Islander: 6%

Percent Hispanic: 8%

Percent Native-American: <1%

Percent International: 6%

Percent in-state/out of state: 55%/45%

Percent from Public HS: 61%

Retention Rate: 89%

Graduation Rate 4-year: 58%

Graduation Rate 6-year: 73%

Percent Undergraduates in On-campus housing: 31%

Number of official organized extracurricular organizations: 180

3 Most popular majors: Business, Public Relations, Social Science

Student/Faculty ratio: 12:1

Average Class Size: 16

Percent of students going to grad school: Unreported

Tuition and Fees: $31,200

In-State Tuition and Fees if different: No difference

Cost for Room and Board: $12,445

Percent receiving financial aid out of those who apply, first year: 82%

Percent receiving financial aid among all students: 65%

Many Southern Methodist University students are frustrated with the stereotypes associated with common perceptions of their beloved school, complaining that "everyone assumes because we go to SMU we must be rich and Southern." But never fear. "SMU is really working to change its image from 'Southern Millionaires' University' to an academically charged, more demanding and well-respected and recognized university," asserted one proud Mustang. And while there are elements of that academic millionaires' club that still linger on campus (one sophomore insisted that every girl should know to bring "a Lily Pulitzer dress and pearls" to school), this is not by any means all that SMU has to offer. "SMU has top-notch academics, opportunities, professors, location, and students," one senior explained.

Life on a Movie Set

SMU offers nationally recognized programs in fields ranging from business to dance. Although the offerings are rigorous, requirements are flexible enough to allow students to double major, to pick up minors, or to participate in one of the many study-abroad programs that SMU offers. But between the wide variety of academic programs and extensive extracurricular involvements, students must quickly learn to balance their time. One Mustang observed, "There is always something to do, but the library is also always packed!"

"First-years" (never call them "freshmen"!) are required to live on campus. There are a number of different housing options, including an Honors dorm. "I enjoy on-campus living because I don't have to drive much unless I'm going out to eat or shopping," a sophomore RA said. "It's nice being close to all of my classes." Another Mustang chimed in that he "loved living in the dorms! It can get a little loud in the freshman dorms at times, but it is essential to the freshman experience." After first year, the housing choices expand immensely. Sophomore males may decide to move into their fraternity houses (girls have to wait until their junior year to live in the sorority houses), but there are also on-campus as well as off-campus apartments ("It's not cheap, but it's very doable"), and of course, various on-campus residence halls and houses.

The on-campus eating options, centered around the offerings of Umphrey Lee Center, are enough to keep most Mustangs happy. Its pasta bar has a loyal following amongst students, as do the omelets at Mac's Place. In general, on-campus dining offers enough variety that at least one item will please every student's palate. And, for at least one first-year, there's more than enough to keep her happy. "It's all pretty delicious," she said.

But even if the beauty of SMU is not in its dining halls, then the breathtaking campus landscape more than makes up for it. "The whole thing is amazing!" one senior raved. Another added, "It's like a movie campus!" Indeed, the school takes full advantage of the sunny Dallas weather. "The groundskeepers change all the flowers in the flower beds once a month so they're always in season and beautiful." All of this is encased in what one Mustang described as the "Highland Park Bubble." Highland Park, one of the wealthiest neighborhoods in Dallas, surrounds the campus. And while this may make things expensive for students, it also provides them with "small-town shops and little diners." Furthermore, it provides an outstanding level of safety on campus. "I literally walked from one end of the campus to the other at midnight and felt extremely safe," one sophomore said. Indeed, thanks to the fact that the campus lies within the jurisdiction of four different police forces (Highland Park, neighboring University Park, SMU Campus Police, and the Dallas Police), students are well protected at all times.

TVs and Tailgating

On the surface, there is a large element of homogeneity within the student body. "SMU is really conservative. It's kind of like a scaled-down version of UGA or Ole Miss," one sophomore noted. However, there is a subtle streak of diversity that quickly becomes apparent upon closer investigation. For example, the campus boasts far more religious diversity than a school with the word "Methodist" in its name would be expected to have, with 28 religious groups, including Hillel, the Hindu Club, the Baha'i Club, and the Muslim Student Association, operating under the office of the campus chaplain. As one junior explained, "I would say the majority of campus often feels predominantly Christian. However, when you really start to meet people and talk to them, you will find out just how diverse we all really are."

There are a number of ways to get involved in athletics on campus, from intramural sports to the varsity level. And although the school is successful in a number of different sports, football is an undeniable favorite at SMU. Some students complained that this favoritism can be to the detriment of other sports. "Our men's soccer team is ranked number one in our conference, and many people do not have any interest."

Still, there's something to be said for the enthusiasm amongst students when it comes to supporting their football team. Aside from the requisite body-painting and jersey-wearing, Mustangs list tailgating amongst their favorite SMU traditions. Sure, this may sound like a relatively common pastime for a college campus, but don't be fooled. As one first year explained, "It's 'SMU tailgating.' People have big-screen TVs, satellite dishes, leather couches, and other ridiculous tailgating items." Indeed, tailgating draws crowds of Mustangs, alumni, and other fans to the "Boulevard," the road that runs north to south through the center of campus. Groups such as fraternities, sororities, and even different colleges rent out the red and blue tents that line the Boulevard to wait for the game to begin, aided by the large, digital countdown clocks that are scattered throughout the crowd. "Seeing friends, the free food, and the whole aspect of body-painting with fraternity brothers right before the game makes the whole experience a great one."

Going Greek

Despite the fact that only about one third of Mustangs are members of a fraternity or sorority, it is also true that Greek life has a disproportionately strong presence on campus. "At SMU Greek life is huge," one sorority sister asserted. "The school, particularly the admissions office, tries to play it down. But in reality, as proven by statistics, it is the students that are in sororities and fraternities that have the highest average GPA and are the most involved in other programs on campus."

But the Greek system's visibility does not end there. The rush process virtually takes over the entire campus during the week before the start of spring semester in January. Rushees return early to SMU in order to participate in a full week of rush activities, described across the board as "intense." Sorority rushees, for example, have to dress for a different theme each day, whether it be business casual or formal. At the end of the

rush process, all accepted sorority rushees participate in a "Pig Run," which requires the girls, dressed identically in white tops and jeans, to run from the center of campus to Sorority Row, all the while cheered on by the new fraternity pledges. And the enthusiasm extends well past rush. "In the spring everything kind of revolves around Greek life because everyone is so excited about it," a sophomore said.

> "It's 'SMU tailgating.' People have big-screen TVs, satellite dishes, leather couches, and other ridiculous tailgating items."

The process is taken extremely seriously, to the point that potential pledges are not even allowed to interact with Greek members in the fall semester, for fear that groups will attempt to unfairly lure hapless first years into their sororities or fraternities. A small percentage of students, however, may take the process a little too seriously. "There's people who talk about girls transferring because they didn't get the house they wanted," one Mustang remarked, but later admitted to not knowing "how true that is."

The prominence of fraternities and sororities on campus often calls into question the issue of drinking on campus. In fact, aside from tailgates (at which those 21 and older wear bands indicating that they can drink), SMU is a dry campus. Campus police are strict in enforcing the rules. Students do have the option of going both to fraternity parties and to the bars surrounding campus, and many actively take advantage of these opportunities. But at the same time, there are more than enough opportunities for those who choose to stay on campus and not to drink. "SMU does a great job of providing many things to do, such as sneak peek previews for upcoming movies." At times, Southern Methodist University may live up to its reputation as "where rich white kids go to become Greek, party, and find their spouses." But that is far from all the school has to offer. From academics to tradition, SMU provides its students with the opportunity to have a world-class education within the "movie campus" that SMU calls home.—*Stephanie Brockman*

FYI
If you come to SMU, you'd better bring "a sundress for tailgating if you're a girl, and a polo shirt if you're a boy."

What is the typical weekend schedule? "Sleep almost all day on Saturday, wake up in time to tailgate, go pregame and then tailgate, and then go to sleep. Sundays, sleep in, shop, and do some studying."

If I could change one thing about SMU, I'd "dispel the negative stereotypes and rumors about SMU. I think many strong and focused students buy into the rumors and therefore believe SMU would not be a good fit for them."

Three things every student at SMU should do before graduating are "go to Plucker's (a local restaurant with GREAT wings) late night, take 'Crime and Delinquency' with Richard Hawkins, and explore, and probably get lost in, downtown Dallas."

Texas A&M University

Address: P.O. Box 30014 College Station, TX 77843-3014
Phone: 979-845-3741
E-mail address: admissions@tamu.edu
Web site URL: www.tamu.edu
Year Founded: 1876
Private or Public: Public
Religious Affiliation: None
Location: Rural
Number of Applicants: 20,887
Percent Accepted: 70%
Percent Accepted who enroll: 55%
Number Entering: 8,093
Number of Transfers Accepted each Year: 2,295
Middle 50% SAT range: M: 560–670, CR: 520–630, Wr: 500–610
Middle 50% ACT range: 23–29
Early admission program EA/ED/None: None

Percentage accepted through EA or ED: NA
EA and ED deadline: NA
Regular Deadline: 15-Jan
Application Fee: $60
Full time Undergraduate enrollment: 35,271
Total enrollment: 38,430
Percent Male: 50%
Percent Female: 50%
Total Percent Minority or Unreported: 27%
Percent African-American: 4%
Percent Asian/Pacific Islander: 5%
Percent Hispanic: 16%
Percent Native-American: 1.0%
Percent International: 2%
Percent in-state/out of state: 97%/3%
Percent from Public HS: Unreported
Retention Rate: 92%

Graduation Rate 4-year: 41%
Graduation Rate 6-year: 77%
Percent Undergraduates in On-campus housing: 24%
Number of official organized extracurricular organizations: 725
3 Most popular majors: Business/Marketing, Agriculture, Engineering
Student/Faculty ratio: 19:1
Average Class Size: 26
Percent of students going to grad school: Unreported
Tuition and Fees: $22,184
In-State Tuition and Fees if different: $7,844
Cost for Room and Board: $8,000
Percent receiving financial aid out of those who apply, first year: 68%
Percent receiving financial aid among all students: 61%

"From the outside looking in, you can't understand it. And from the inside looking out, you can't explain it." This expression is often used to describe life at Texas A&M University, located in College Station, Texas. Aggies, as the students are called, bleed maroon and white, and school spirit is contagious. Texas A&M is "the perfect school for anyone who loves sports, especially loud, rowdy ones." Students become part of the Aggie family the minute they start Fish Camp, an orientation program for fresh-men, and their ties to the school and to their classmates last a lifetime.

Aggie Academics

Texas A&M, the oldest public university in Texas, is comprised of approximately 39,000 undergraduate students enrolled in one of ten colleges. Given the number of students, "freshman core classes, which are about 200–250 students, are always hard to get into." However, as Aggies progress further and further into their academic careers, they are allowed to register early, before classes fill up with students. When students begin narrowing their field of interest, it becomes easier to enroll in classes because "there are less people vying for space." According to one freshman, "I've never really heard of anyone not getting the classes they wanted, other than people wanting to get the small, easy 'core requirement classes.' Eventually everyone gets the classes they want."

Students typically find classes engaging, and it is easy to find courses tailored towards special interests. According to one senior, "The most interesting class I've taken is a seminar called the Academy for Future International Leaders. It focuses on international leadership, the challenges that our world is facing, and some of the skills our generation will need to solve these tough problems." Texas A&M has many highly regarded professors, like Dr. Ben Welsh, who teaches "Management 105, one of the most popular courses in the state of Texas." Professor Amy Austen is internationally famous, and the "College Station, Galveston, and Qatar Texas A&M campuses all have very large fan clubs in her honor."

Texas A&M is known for its Business and Engineering Schools, and admission to these programs is very competitive. A large number of students pursue coursework in health-related majors as well as sports management. Other popular majors include petroleum engineering, business, biomedical sciences, architecture, and kinesiology. Additionally, Aggies are given the opportunity to receive a military-based education during their college years as members of the Corps of Cadets. This student organization has endured ever since the university's founding, a time when all enrolled students were required to partake in military training.

Other programs that have withstood the test of time are those in the school's College of Agriculture and Life Sciences. According to one Aggie, "Our agricultural studies are great here since we started out as a farming school." In fact, the A&M of Texas A&M used to stand for "agricultural and mechanical." Majors in this department range from agribusiness to dairy science to recreation, park, and tourism science. The term "Aggie" is a direct reference to the school's history as an agricultural school.

Aggies who are unsure of what they want to major in can apply for admission to the General Studies program. General Studies students take classes that fulfill their core curriculum requirements while exploring potential degree plans. Students select a major upon the completion of sixty hours (equivalent to about four to five semesters of coursework).

Campus Life in College Station

Texas A&M's campus sprawls over 500 acres. There are numerous points of interest on campus, including the George (H.W.) Bush Presidential Library and Museum, and the Cushing Memorial Library. The Memorial Student Center, the student union, has been dubbed the campus "living room," and many concerts, lectures, and cultural programs are put on in conjunction with the MSC Student Programs Office. At the time of writing, the Memorial Student Center is currently undergoing a $100 million renovation project, and is scheduled to reopen during the summer of 2012. According to one student, "The campus itself is fairly pretty, but most of the buildings here are big concrete boxes. They all look the same."

The majority of housing on campus is divided into two communities, the Northside or the Southside. The Southside is comprised of newer dorms and is home to Commons, a popular complex made up of four connected dorms. There are configurations available for all personal preferences and budgets. Aggies can also choose to live in on-campus university apartments, while students in the Corps of Cadets are required to live in corps housing. However, according to one student, "There is only room for 8,000 students on campus or about one-fourth of the student body. Basically you live on campus as a freshman and move off your sophomore year." Most students do opt to move off-campus after freshman year but "as long as you get your papers in on-time, you should be able to secure housing."

Student meal plans are available for both students living on and off campus. The Sbisa Dining Center is a popular place for students to dine. Aggies can also get food from commercial chains like Chick-fil-A on their meal plans. Off campus, students flock to the Dixie Chicken, a restaurant/bar on Northgate. According to one freshman, "It's known as 'the Chicken,' and it's pretty much an institution in Aggieland. People carve their names in the wooden wall and tables everywhere; it's got a great atmosphere and feel to it."

Gig 'em Ags!

Texas A&M University is a sports lover's paradise. Aggies love football, and the games in the fall are great socializing and unifying events on campus. At Texas A&M, Yell leaders lead the students instead of cheerleaders at the football games. Students participate in Midnight Yell, "a yell practice held (at midnight) the night before a home football game," explains one Aggie. "Students gather at Kyle Field to practice yells, bring a date, and 'mug down' or get a kiss when the lights go off for a few seconds."

> "For us here at A&M, it's not just a spirit, it's how you live; it becomes part of your life."

Students love camping out to pull tickets for the games. Aggies pitch tents outside the football stadium and play football or board games all night long. It's a great way "to meet so many fun people, and it's a miracle if you see the inside of your tent before 4 AM since you have to wake up at 6:15 AM at the latest to start standing in line to get your tickets." As one student exclaimed, "One time my tentmates and I were woken up at 5:30 in the morning by hurricane force winds and about thirty-five degree weather, but it is something I would do again."

Aggies agree that all students should attend at least one "t.u." game. As one Aggie explains it, "The t.u. game is the game against the University of Texas, known as t.u. to Aggies because there are technically many universities of Texas." Students rave about the "amazing energy" and love that the "third deck of the stadium (which is solid concrete and steel) noticeably vibrates under the Aggies' feet from the volume of the students' voices." The cheers of the fans can be heard at Northgate, which is about a mile away from Kyle Field. Students used to light a Bonfire before the big game until 1999 when 12 students were tragically killed during construction. Currently, students organize the Bonfire and hold it off-campus each year.

When Aggies are not cheering on their teams, they can probably be found at one of the many dance halls in College Station. A large number of students go to three main dance halls: Daisy Dukes ("Dukes"), Hurricane Harry's ("Harry's"), or the Hall of Fame ("the Hall"). Aggies also enjoy going out to Northgate at night to hit the TAMU bars.

According to students, "The Greek scene is not really that big here." As one Aggie explains, "'Fraternity Row' is fairly far from campus, and their parties are never really broadcasted." At Texas A&M, "everyone is so active that the Greeks are just another thing that some people are involved in." Girls in sororities "love it but it does not consume their lives."

Students at Texas A&M have a love/hate relationship with a school of TAMU's size. As one Aggie puts it, "You meet so many kinds of people. Truly. Yes, 90+% of the student body is from Texas, but there are so many types of 'Texans' that I never knew." Students enjoy getting to know people they would have never met otherwise. However, some students lament "it's hard to meet and keep a good group of people." Oftentimes, Aggies find they're good friends with people in their major because they take all the same classes. As one freshman explains, "My incoming freshman class numbers 8,200. That means with approximately 200 school days a year, I can meet ten new people in my class every day of the school year and not meet all of them in four years." Most students appreciate that TAMU is so big that there is a niche for everyone. As one Aggie explains, "You meet plenty of people, but you just have to go the extra mile to actually be close with them because there are just so many people here."

Twelfth Man Traditions

Students at Texas A&M are active in over 1000 different student organizations. Freshmen enjoy getting to know one another in Freshman Leadership Organizations or FLOs. Each FLO has a different focus, and they offer students to assume leadership positions and to organize and execute projects. Students agree that it is easy to start a new club. *The Battalion*, the daily newspaper at TAMU, keeps students in the know with what is happening on campus. According to one Aggie, "The Corps of Cadets is perhaps the most prominent organization on campus. It's essentially the heart of the school."

Texas A&M is famous for its traditions that bond students, both past and present alike. "For us here at A&M," elaborates one Aggie, "it's not just a spirit, it's how you live; it becomes part of your life." The Aggie Ring is possibly one of the most famous traditions. "It's arguably the most well-recognized collegiate ring and has started conversations between strangers all over the world," according to an Aggie senior. Students participate in the activity known as ring dunking. As one student explains, "It's a celebration the day one receives his/her ring. He/she drops it in a pitcher (usually of beer, but most other drinks can be substituted), and the recipient drinks the pitcher as fast as possible to get to the bottom."

Tradition is something Aggies are introduced to when they first decide to enroll at Texas A&M. Incoming freshmen go through an orientation program called Fish Camp. At Fish Camp, freshmen bond with other freshmen and learn about where they will call home for the next four years. As one freshman put it, "After I went through Fish Camp (known to outsiders as brainwashing) being an Aggie was just as much a part of me as being Asian or American. I've talked for hours trying to explain, but I know it's something that someone just has to experience."

Students at Texas A&M are proud of the history of their school. Aggies acknowledge,

"We obviously cannot all know each other, but just being Aggies usually creates a mutual understanding or bond, what we call the Aggie Family." When it comes to traditions, Aggies agree, "Honestly, there are too many to count or explain. TAMU is a school built on tradition. So many things here have been in effect for 100 years, and if someone tries to change them, it could cause an uproar." From their beloved mascot, Reveille, also known as the First Lady of Aggieland, to Aggie Muster, a service put on every year in April to honor the Aggies that have fallen that year, students at Texas A&M love and respect their institution. One Aggie explains, "It is a place unlike any other in my opinion. I know some people call it a cult, and honestly, I thought the same thing. What I, and others, didn't realize is that it is just Texas A&M."—*Alexa Sassin*

FYI

If you come to TAMU, you'd better bring: "Your cowboy boots, your Southern hospitality, lots of maroon, a love of A&M football, and nothing that's remotely close to burnt orange."

What's the typical weekend schedule?: "In the fall, Friday nights involve going over to a friend's house for a while and then heading to Midnight Yell Practice. On Saturday, students get ready for the game, go to tailgates, stand and yell throughout the football game, and then disperse all over College Station afterward. Sundays are the day of rest."

If I could change one thing about TAMU: "I'd create a better music scene, outside of country-western music, which is plentiful."

Three things every student should do before graduation are: "Have a burger at the Dixie Chicken, put a penny on the statue of Lawrence Sullivan Ross before an exam for good luck, and 'mug down' at Midnight Yell Practice."

Texas Christian University

Address: 2800 S. University Drive, Fort Worth, TX 76129	**Percentage accepted through EA or ED:** Unreported	**Graduation Rate 4-year:** 54%
Phone: 817-257-7490	**EA and ED deadline:** 1-Nov	**Graduation Rate 6-year:** 69%
E-mail address: admissions@tcu.edu	**Regular Deadline:** 15-Feb	**Percent Undergraduates in On-campus housing:** 46%
Web site URL: www.tcu.edu	**Application Fee:** $40	**Number of official organized extracurricular organizations:** 205
Year Founded: 1873	**Full time Undergraduate enrollment:** 7,143	
Private or Public: Private	**Total enrollment:** 8,696	**3 Most popular majors:** Business Administration, Nursing, Advertising/Public Relations
Religious Affiliation: Christian Church, Disciples of Christ	**Percent Male:** 41%	
Location: Urban	**Percent Female:** 59%	
Number of Applicants: 12,212	**Total Percent Minority or Unreported:** 17%	**Student/Faculty ratio:** 14:1
Percent Accepted: 50%	**Percent African-American:** 5%	**Average Class Size:** 27
Percent Accepted who enroll: 27%	**Percent Asian/Pacific Islander:** 3%	**Percent of students going to grad school:** 22%
Number Entering: 2,039	**Percent Hispanic:** 7%	**Tuition and Fees:** $28,250
Number of Transfers Accepted each Year: 826	**Percent Native-American:** <1%	**In-State Tuition and Fees if different:** No difference
Middle 50% SAT range: M: 540–640, CR: 520–630, Wr: 530–640	**Percent International:** Unreported	**Cost for Room and Board:** $10,000
Middle 50% ACT range: 23–28	**Percent in-state/out of state:** 73%/27%	**Percent receiving financial aid out of those who apply, first year:** 86%
Early admission program EA/ED/None: ED	**Percent from Public HS:** 72%	**Percent receiving financial aid among all students:** 68%
	Retention Rate: 86%	

Texas Christian University lies in the heart of Dallas/Fort Worth, and it embodies the heart of Texas. From the football stands to the classroom, TCU students carry a "go get 'em" attitude and a horned frog football cheer. As one sophomore so eloquently put it, "I will bleed purple until the day I die."

The Perfect Fit

Texas Christian University offers its students a well-rounded liberal arts education that "gives you a broad experience but [doesn't] force you to delve too deeply into subjects you're not interested in," according to one sophomore. His classmate elaborated: "I revel in the academic life here." That life requires an "essential" core curriculum which consists of credits in the humanities, social sciences, natural sciences, fine arts, mathematics, writing, and oral communication. There is also a Heritage, Mission, Vision, and Values requirement with emphases on reli-

gion, culture, and history. In addition, students at TCU must complete their majors' requirements. One sophomore explained that "people in 'technical' majors like nursing or engineering have it much tougher than the liberal arts majors." Students name biology, physics, mathematics, chemistry, accounting/finance, engineering, and nursing as the difficult majors, and advertising/public relations, communications, interior design, and nutrition as the less demanding ones.

The Neeley School of Business houses the most competitive majors, while hard-core studiers are found racing along the pre-med track. TCU also offers a highly praised Honors Program, which awards early class registration to students invited to the program upon acceptance to TCU, as well as those who prove themselves capable by first semester grades. In order to stay in the Honors Program, students must fulfill additional class requirements. Many pursue the Chancellor's Leadership Program and specialized programs in the business school in place of the generalized honors curriculum. Texas Christian University strives to maintain small classes of 30 to 40 students. Therefore, class registration for popular majors like communications can be difficult when many students compete for the same courses. (Athletes and honors students have the privilege of registering early.) According to TCU students, the process, though potentially frustrating, results in "perfect" class sizes and a manageable workload. One sophomore stated "I feel like academics at TCU are challenging but not burdensome for the most part; students are still able to have a social life and keep a good GPA."

Although lacking worldwide fame, the professors at Texas Christian University are praised by their students. One student caringly described his favorite teachers: "Dr. Patrick Nuss is an amazing teacher in the business school. I particularly enjoy Dr. Blake Hestir of the Philosophy Department (the existentialist, he has a delightfully sinister sense of humor) and Dr. Timothy Parrish of the English Department (the classic ponytail, glasses, preoccupied, brilliant, bad-at-spelling English professor)." Other students reiterated the fact that they cherish their close relationships with professors and cited rare, yet positive, experiences with teaching assistants. "The only grievance I have with classes," one sophomore said, "is that sometimes there are not enough of them." However, the same student went on to explain the University's extraordinary focus on accommodating student concerns. For example, the Schieffer School of Journalism recently added several classes in response to student demand.

Living It Up

TCU party life is divided in two ways: underclassmen and upperclassmen, and Greeks and non-Greeks. Underclassmen go to frat parties, house parties, and mixers on the weekends, while upperclassmen prefer bars. However, obtaining alcohol is not much of a problem for anyone at TCU, even for those who are underage.

Since the University is a Christian school, there are many non-drinkers and more alternative social venues for them to enjoy. A number of concert venues are near campus, and the TCU theater has scheduled performances on most weekends. Further, the Bass Performing Arts Hall provides musical performances, and the Programming Council, part of the student government, plans

movies and concerts for students. There is a student center on campus with a ballroom.

Most campus-wide events at TCU are hosted by independent or Greek organizations. Approximately 45 percent of students are in one of the 39 fraternities or sororities on campus. The rush process consumes a large amount of student energy. Though fraternity rush is relatively laid-back at TCU, sorority rush is incredibly stressful, noted one sophomore. However, another added that "cool" frats and sororities just depend on your preference of people. "Everyone has different ideas about which ones are the best," so there is no real hierarchy in the Texas Christian Greek society. The parties are usually fun and girls are rarely charged for admission or drinks. Most often, it's the fraternity members who fund alcohol purchases and theme parties, the best of which come at Halloween, Christmas, and the end of the year—barring any police presence: "Fort Worth has the largest police force in Texas." The TCU administration is also tough on drinking. Kegs are allowed on campus only for tailgates, and Greek organizations are held liable for any out-of-control events. However, the University has recently installed a "medical amnesty" policy that protects students with alcohol-induced sickness from punishment in order to insure their safe treatment.

A Deficit in Dating and Diversity

The dating life at TCU is minimal. "A lot of people joke that at TCU, you either have a boyfriend or you hook up, but there is little 'dating,'" one sophomore said. This phenomenon may make sense considering that the college is smack in the middle of a state famous for its attractive populace. Who wants to settle down when there's so much to go around? One male student elaborated: "The girls are hot. The guys aren't too shabby from what I hear either. Overall the campus is generally pretty gorgeous. It's easy to forget that there are unattractive people in the world." Aside from all of the ogling on campus, sex keeps a pretty low profile at TCU. There have recently been articles in campus publications about the lurking threat of STDs, but none of the interviewed students cited a significant presence.

In particular, homosexual and interracial couples are few and far between. "There are very few gays," one student noted. Further, the school has a very small minority population. And although most students seem pleased with the student population, they do wish it were more diverse. The overwhelming homogeneity has made minority students somewhat exclusive. "The African-American crowd typically associates solely with each other," one senior said. "Many students assume that if a TCU student is black, he or she is an athlete, which is certainly not the case." The TCU stereotype is "white, rich and Greek." One student passionately described the "typical student" as a "sorority girl wearing her silly big sunglasses and carrying her Prada bag while she talks on her cell phone. She's probably driving her Mercedes, too." Since TCU was rated one of the fittest campuses in the country by *Men's Fitness* magazine, and the Rec Center is one of the hottest daytime spots on campus, chances are that girl has probably worked hard enough to deserve her designer jeans.

Living On, Eating Off
The average freshman dorm at TCU provides "the basic necessities and nothing more." Space is tight, and visiting, alcohol and drug restrictions are even tighter, but students still find the overall dorm experience to be "fine." All dorms come with air-conditioning, heat, and RAs. Most students agreed that the best dorms are Moncrief Hall and Foster Hall, which also happen to be coed. The worst dorm is reportedly Milton Daniel: "It has broken water fountains and smells like puke and carrots on a fairly regular basis." Interestingly, binge drinkers and wild parties are mysteriously attracted to Milton's conditions.

> "The campus is generally pretty gorgeous. It's easy to forget that there are unattractive people in the world."

TCU has a separate endowment dedicated to landscaping, so you can be sure that the physical campus is beautiful—and safe. "I absolutely feel safe at TCU," affirmed one student. The police are easily accessible, and TCU has an all-male organization called "Froggie-Five-O" that gives rides to girls when they have to walk at night. Despite the friendly security services, most upperclassmen move off campus to enjoy apartment or house set-ups and lower prices. Added one sophomore, "Underclassmen are allowed to live off campus, but it is strongly discouraged."

Most students, even residents, eat a fair number of meals off campus, because of the dining halls' expensive prices and inconvenient timing (although the University is planning to improve the cafeterias in the near future). "The only thing that stays open past 2:30 in the afternoon is the Main, which is really fattening and heavy food. Edens, Deco Deli, and Sub Connection are all better options if you don't mind eating really early." The Main's main draw is its social appeal. Most campus cliques (fraternities, athletes) are represented there during the day, so groups of friends might appear just to socialize.

As for off-campus eateries, "the most famous restaurant in Fort Worth is undoubtedly Joe T. Garcia's. It's been around forever!" Italian Inn is also a great but undiscovered date restaurant where the waiters serve and entertain. And although there is a local Starbucks, the Panther City Coffee Co. is heralded as the best spot for an espresso shot.

Texas Is for Football
Football is the most popular spectator sport at Texas Christian University. The Horned Frogs won the Poinsettia Bowl in 2008, but lost its most recent trip to the Fiesta Bowl in 2010. Nonetheless, the football team draws much school spirit from students and alumni alike. In fact, TCU's traditional spectator chant, "Riff Ram Bah Zoo," is one of the oldest cheers in college history.

Unique to TCU are the Purple Hearts, a student organization that helps lure high school football players to the University. "We recruit senior football players for the TCU team through visits to the stadium and the athletic complex at home games," a student explained. For more recreational athletes, IM sports are prevalent at TCU, and the Campus Recreation Center offers state-of-the-art athletic equipment. "Every cardio machine has its own flat-screen TV, and there are really nice weights and stuff. There are also aerobic classes and yoga every day, an indoor and outdoor swimming pool, and indoor and outdoor track."

According to one sophomore, "TCU students are very involved, and spend quite a bit of their time on other activities." About half of the student body works a part-time job, and most are identified by their extracurricular activities. Social organizations, performance groups, intramurals, academic organizations, and service organizations are the most popular. The most heralded organization is Frog Camp, an orientation trip for freshmen for which upperclassmen are leaders. Also highly touted are the Student Government Association, Order of Omega Greek honors society, sports appreciation organizations, and the "eleven40seven" journal of written and visual arts.

Texas Tradition

One thing is clear: TCU is a university bathed in tradition. Along with legendary cheers, students are indoctrinated by a wealth of myth when they accept admission to the school. One student cited the following examples: "When the purple light is on in Frog Fountain, the Chancellor is on campus.

If you kiss the nose of the iron Horned Frog statue, you will have good luck. The bodies of Addison and Randolph Clark (TCU's founders) are actually cremated inside their bronze statues. It is tradition to raise your right hand and make the horned frog sign with your fingers when the chapel bell rings the alma mater." Another noted that President Lyndon B. Johnson himself broke the ground for the Sid Richardson Science Building when it was built in the seventies.

TCU is a place that people fall in love with, from its glorious oaks to its cheesy mascot: "People take a lot of pride from being Frogs—we're the only Horned Frogs in the nation!"—*Lauren Ezell*

FYI
If you come to TCU, you better bring "a lot of Polos."
What is a typical weekend schedule? "Study by day, party by night."
If I could change one thing about TCU, I'd "make it more diverse."
Three things every student at TCU should do before graduating are "Study abroad, jump in Frog Fountain, and go to Joe T's and Ol' South."

Texas Tech University

Address: P.O. Box 45005 Lubbock, TX 79409-5005
Phone: 806-742-1480
E-mail address: admissions@ttu.edu
Web site URL: www.ttu.edu
Year Founded: 1923
Private or Public: Public
Religious Affiliation: None
Location: Urban
Number of Applicants: 13,976
Percent Accepted: 77%
Percent Accepted who enroll: 41%
Number Entering: 4,439
Number of Transfers Accepted each Year: 2,818
Middle 50% SAT range: M: 500–610, CR: 480–580, Wr: 460–560
Middle 50% ACT range: 21–26
Early admission program EA/ED/None: None

Percentage accepted through EA or ED: NA
EA and ED deadline: NA
Regular Deadline: 1-May
Application Fee: $50
Full time Undergraduate enrollment: 21,062
Total enrollment: 23,021
Percent Male: 54%
Percent Female: 46%
Total Percent Minority or Unreported: 24%
Percent African-American: 5%
Percent Asian/Pacific Islander: 4%
Percent Hispanic: 13%
Percent Native-American: 1%
Percent International: 1%
Percent in-state/out of state: 96%/4%
Percent from Public HS: Unreported
Retention Rate: 83%
Graduation Rate 4-year: 27%

Graduation Rate 6-year: 54%
Percent Undergraduates in On-campus housing: 26%
Number of official organized extracurricular organizations: 399
3 Most popular majors: Business/Marketing, Family and Consumer Sciences, Engineering
Student/Faculty ratio: 18:1
Average Class Size: 25
Percent of students going to grad school: Unreported
Tuition and Fees: $15,213
In-State Tuition and Fees if different: $6,783
Cost for Room and Board: $7,310
Percent receiving financial aid out of those who apply, first year: 46%
Percent receiving financial aid among all students: 44%

At a school with over 21,000 undergraduates, it's hard to define the "typical student." But students at Texas Tech are united by their commitment to the University and to the community at large. "This is one of the most exciting times to be a part of Texas Tech," explained one student, who sees a renaissance beginning for the school. "We're an emerging research university now," he said, citing several recently-hired faculty members and the acquisition of a new Vice President of Research for the University. "We want to become a top one."

Such ambition is characteristic of Tech students and is exemplified by the school's Student Government Association. Officers spend up to 40 hours per week at the SGA office, working to promote student needs and to develop and execute initiatives of their own. The SGA created programs such as Take a Kid to the Game, which allows local underprivileged kids to watch the Red Raiders play football and spend the day with a Tech student. The SGA has also worked with the University's career center to attract the attention of prominent Texas-based companies. "We want to do a better job of getting Tech's image out there," said a member of the SGA.

Academics on the Upswing

Students say they are generally happy with the courses offered at Tech, but deciding which classes to take can be a bit of a headache. Students criticized the advising program, claiming that counselors "aren't always helpful." One student, who complicated her degree plan by changing her major, said "it's hard for students who don't know what they want to do right away." While one student remarked that his interactions with advisors "left something to be desired," others reported that advisors can actually be helpful.

> **"This is one of the most exciting times to be a part of Texas Tech."**

Small classes tend to give students the most positive academic experiences at Texas Tech. Introductory classes, particularly in popular departments like business, biology, architecture, and English, may have 400 or more students. One student called his experiences in these classes "disappointing," pointing out that he never got to actually meet his professors. Upper-level classes, however, which contain between 20 and 50 students, are "more fulfilling."

Regardless of class size, professors are "very accessible," offering regular, frequent office hours. Students also praised Tech's academic atmosphere. "It doesn't seem like a high-stress, competitive setting," said one student. "The professors and students are really friendly and open."

One student highlighted Tech's recent academic improvement and potential for future growth. He said that while he is "not happy with where we are right now," the school has made a lot of progress in the past five years, as a greater number of small classes are offered and the quality of professors improves.

At Large in Lubbock

Most students at Texas Tech, especially non-freshmen, live off campus. However, a new on-campus option of two- to three-bedroom apartment-style housing is popular among upperclassmen, one student said. Students said high-quality off-campus housing is relatively easy to find. In addition to the three apartment complexes across the street from campus (one of which is newer and more expensive than the other two), students also live in a residential neighborhood south of campus known as "Tech Terrace." Other popular apartment complexes may be found farther away from campus, but travel to and from these locations usually requires a bus trip.

The University requires that freshmen live on campus, and most students claimed that the experience of living in a dorm was valuable. One student noted that even though she moved off campus by sophomore year, she was "grateful" for her on-campus experience because it was "a great way to meet people." Students also have the option of living on specially assigned Intensive Study or Substance-Free floors (although technically, alcohol and other drugs are prohibited in all dorms).

Student attitudes are generally positive, but not extremely enthusiastic, about the town of Lubbock. One student said that she wished she were in a bigger city—"though I love Lubbock," she added. Students say that the town is safe, and there is a separate on-campus police force. One student explained, "You either love Lubbock or you hate it, because there's not a whole lot to do except get involved with things on campus and in the town."

Gregarious Greeks

Getting involved is what Tech students do best. Whether it's involvement in a community outreach program, writing for Tech's newspaper, *The Daily Toreador*, or membership in a service sorority or fraternity, there is no shortage of extracurricular pursuits at Texas Tech.

While Tech's 400 student organizations cater to a variety of interests, Greek organizations are especially popular. "Greek life is really big, whether you're in it or not," said one student. Fraternities and sororities throw most of the parties at Tech, although because so many students live off campus, non-Greek house parties are common as well. Greek students pointed out that by joining a fraternity or sorority, you are not only part of the single organization, but also a member of the greater Greek community at Tech. "It's nice to know that you can go to any local bar on a Thursday night and see all your friends," said one sorority member. Students at Tech are also attracted to Greek life for its service component, and some choose to join service sororities, which place an even greater emphasis on philanthropy. A student who joined both a Greek sorority and a non-Greek service sorority pointed out that while she enjoys Greek life, she has made closer friends through the service sorority because of its smaller size and more personal atmosphere.

The Center for Campus Life, which is the central office for all registered organizations on campus, is located in the Student Union Building. Since its recent renovation, the Student Union, which houses a bookstore, meeting rooms, TVs, and a computing assistance center, has been especially popular among students. Furthermore, students are enthusiastic about the Student Union's food court, which includes a Chick-fil-A and a Starbucks.

The Center for Campus Life also provides a host of entertainment programs and events that range from concerts, interactive games, and movies to more academic-oriented programs like workshops and lecturers. TAB, the Tech Activities Board, also organizes events such as open mike nights, bowling, and foreign film screenings for those looking for an alternative to the Greek life. When football season is in play, countless students participate in RaiderGate, co-hosted by the student government, which is Texas Tech's version of tailgating, complete with live music and barbecue.

A "Dry" Town

Though Lubbock is a "dry" town and liquor stores are prohibited, bars are exempted from this law. In fact, Lubbock has a colorful bar scene—Bleacher's Sports Café, The Library, Rocky's, and Timmy's are student favorites. In order to purchase alcohol, students drive to an area called the Strip (apparently modeled after Las Vegas) outside of town. "It would be easier to go down to the convenience store and pick something up," one student griped.

While one student said that "a lot of partying goes on" at Tech, another pointed out that there is a "growing minority" that doesn't drink. In any case, students agreed that non-drinkers do not feel uncomfortable at Tech.

Red Raiders in a Red State

Students agree that the political climate at Tech and in Lubbock is "very conservative." One student put it this way: "If you don't love George Bush, you're in the minority." However, an officer of the University Democrats pointed out that liberal students are more common than you might expect, adding that liberalism is "an underground thing."

The student body at Tech is not very diverse, although students claim that the school is taking steps to increase racial diversity. While there is a Gay Straight Alliance at Tech, students agree that the gay community is not very visible. Of the 37 religiously affiliated student organizations at Tech, 30 are Christian groups. One student pointed out that Bible studies are common and well-attended at Tech. Another student agreed that Christian groups are plentiful on campus but added that non-Christians "don't feel out of place."

Tech Takes the Field

Texas Tech is known for its high-caliber sports teams and enthusiastic fans. Cheering on the Red Raiders at football and basketball games is a central part of the Tech experience. Coach Bobby Knight, who retired in February of 2008, helped vault the basketball team into the spotlight, and women's basketball is drawing higher attendance than it ever has before—higher, sometimes, than the men's team. Football, though, is the main attraction, according to students. The pregame festivities alone are impressive, with fraternities, sororities, alumni groups, and even local rodeos sponsoring tailgates. On the Thursday before a game day, students decorate a statue of Will Rogers and his horse, Soapsuds, with red crepe paper. Even without the streamers, this Tech landmark is full of Tech pride. The horse's behind points straight in the direction of Tech's biggest rival, Texas A&M.

Non-varsity athletes at Tech are not just devoted fans; they are devoted players. Tech students are passionate about intramural sports, and since the expansion of the Student Recreation Center, IMs are more popular than ever. Student organizations, Greek organizations, and dorms field IM teams, and, as one student explained, "Everybody plays; everybody wants to be the best." The Rec Center offers classes, workshops, and even massage therapy.

In the classroom, on the football field, or in the community, Red Raiders are proud to be part of the growth and improvement that characterizes Texas Tech. With a wide array of academic offerings, facilities that are constantly improving, and a rich extracurricular scene, Texas Tech is gaining popularity with Texans and non-Texans alike.—*Kathleen Reeves*

FYI

If you come to Texas Tech, you better bring "a day planner, because so many activities are offered on campus, and rain boots, because of the ineffective drainage system."

What's the typical weekend schedule? "Wednesday: Hit up a bar called South Beach; Thursday: Go to the Depot District of town; Friday: Hear a country band play at Wild West; Saturday: Football game day! Afterwards, head to a house party or the bars. Sunday: Wake up, spend all day at the library."

If I could change one thing about Tech, I'd "change the restrictive parking system."

Three things every student at Tech should do before graduating are "attend a football game, get involved in an on-campus organization, and go to Carol of Lights, an annual, nationally recognized holiday lighting ceremony."

Trinity University, San Antonio

Address: One Trinity Place
San Antonio, TX
78212-7200
Phone: 210-999-7207
E-mail address:
admissions@trinity.edu
Web site URL: www.trinity.edu
Year Founded: 1869
Private or Public: Private
Religious Affiliation: None
Location: Urban
Number of Applicants:
3,754
Percent Accepted: 58%
Percent Accepted who enroll: 30%
Number Entering: 655
Number of Transfers Accepted each Year: 37
Middle 50% SAT range: M: 610–690, **CR:** 600–690, **Wr:** Unreported
Middle 50% ACT range: 27–31
Early admission program EA/ED/None: EA and ED
Percentage accepted through EA or ED: Unreported

EA and ED deadline: 1-Nov
Regular Deadline: 1-Feb
Application Fee: $40
Full time Undergraduate enrollment: 2,489
Total enrollment: 2,703
Percent Male: 47%
Percent Female: 53%
Total Percent Minority or Unreported: 40%
Percent African-American: 4%
Percent Asian/Pacific Islander: 7%
Percent Hispanic: 11%
Percent Native-American: 1%
Percent International: 6%
Percent in-state/out of state: 73%/27%
Percent from Public HS: 72%
Retention Rate: 90%
Graduation Rate 4-year: 69%
Graduation Rate 6-year: 79%

Percent Undergraduates in On-campus housing: 71%
Number of official organized extracurricular organizations: 130
3 Most popular majors: Business Administration/Management, English, Communications and Media Studies
Student/Faculty ratio: 9:1
Average Class Size: 16
Percent of students going to grad school: 34%
Tuition and Fees: $27,699
In-State Tuition and Fees if different: No difference
Cost for Room and Board: $8,822
Percent receiving financial aid out of those who apply, first year: 67%
Percent receiving financial aid among all students: 83%

T rinity University in San Antonio, Texas has more than just a stunning hilltop campus that offers students a view of the whole of San Antonio, including the downtown area and the hill country. The university offers all the perks of a large, bustling city while still fostering the growth of a tight-knit undergraduate community. With only 2,600 students and a serious undergraduate focus, Trinity is ideal for students looking for a relatively small private university with a strong liberal arts curriculum. The facilities at Trinity cater to every interest from humanities to sciences and everything in between. Trinity has a rich history of community traditions, which are certain to make every student feel like a part of the close community in the heart of Texas.

Hard Work Pays Off

When students graduate from Trinity, they have "had a taste of pretty much everything that is offered." The broad knowledge base possessed by Trinity graduates is due to the Common Curriculum that the university places great emphasis on. According to one student, Trinity just wants "to make sure you're really well-rounded." There are a wide variety of credits that students must get in areas such as Cultural Heritage, Arts and Literature, Human Social Interaction, Natural Science and Technology, Basic Computer Skills, Foreign Language, Lifetime Fitness, Mathematics and Quantitative Reasoning. In addition, freshmen are required to take a First Year Seminar and a Writing Workshop, one each semester, to make sure they have a solid English foundation to carry them through the duration of their college education. Even though some students might consider the task of completing so many general requirements daunting, one freshman said that the Trinity curriculum is nice because "you can get your core classes done whenever."

With 39 majors and 52 minors, Trinity has plenty of options for every student to explore beyond the Common Curriculum. The only problem, as one senior put it is that the general requirements plus the requirements for individual majors "can add up to be a lot." Of all the majors offered at Trinity, Business and Communications are the two most popular ones. In addition, many students choose to major in one of the modern languages, including Spanish, French, German, Chinese and Russian. Even though the Common Curriculum combined with a major is a substantial amount of work, one student noted,

"[Trinity is] regarded very highly . . . because it's so much work."

Students believe that overall Trinity provides quite a solid liberal arts education with a significant amount of work to boot, but some students say that there are definitely certain departments that give out more work than others. One upperclassman said, "It depends a lot on your major how the workload is." Most students say that science majors tend to be the ones that have heavier workloads, especially the Biochemistry major. Similarly, students add that the individual science classes at Trinity also tend to be the most difficult. A freshman said that Integrative Bio I was her most difficult class and was "impossible to do well in."

Of course, for every "impossible" class to avoid at Trinity, there are plenty of classes that students love to take, including Asian Religions and Classical Rhetorical Theory, which students say are two of the most interesting classes on campus. For freshmen who love the humanities, the HUMA 1600 Readings from Western Culture course presents students with the opportunity to immerse themselves in a comprehensive overview of Western literature while simultaneously knocking out both the First Year Seminar and Writing Workshop in the same semester. Students looking for an easy class will want to head straight to Russian Studies and Cultures, which is considered "a blow-off course for seniors." Regardless of what level of class a student is looking for, from "impossible" to "blow-off" courses, Trinity has something to suit every interest.

Students Who Live Together, Stay Together

Trinity is, at its heart, a strong community dedicated to forging relationships between students where 79 percent of undergraduates live on campus. In order to reinforce the community feel, all freshmen, sophomores and juniors are required to live in Trinity's residence halls, and 30 percent of seniors choose to live on campus as well. The freshman housing is assigned randomly "with the exception of people who request to be on certain 'themed' halls." An upperclassman said that these "themed" residences are not very big but allow students to live with others who share similar interests, such as language immersion and substance-free living. Freshmen who take the HUMA course at Trinity are offered housing with their classmates so that they can have peer study sessions and share ideas with one another more easily. At the end of freshman year, the rising sophomores are randomly assigned numbers that allow them to choose housing, with the lowest numbers going first when choosing their rooms. Once students are juniors, the housing system changes, and they are allowed to choose housing based on the number of hours they have, which helps to reinforce the strong academic nature of Trinity.

Right from the outset, Trinity aims to make its freshmen feel as welcome as possible, beginning with a New Student Orientation program that lasts for one week before classes start. The period of orientation allows students to meet their fellow classmates and bond with them before their lives are overcome with the rigorous academic culture of the university. During the rest of the year, the university sponsors other events, such as Hallympics, in which the residence halls go head-to-head to compete in athletic competitions. Events like Hallympics help to cultivate the feelings of friendship and closeness that many Trinity students say is a very important part of their college experience.

Hitching a Ride
The larger city of San Antonio is highly accessible to members of the Trinity community because the majority of students on campus have cars. It is difficult to get around the surrounding area without a car because the public transportation in San Antonio is fairly scant. With all the highways and the long distances between local attractions, students need some method of transportation to allow them to explore the local bars, clubs, restaurants and other venues in the city. If students don't happen to have a car, it's not a huge problem, students say. As one senior put it, "If you don't have [a car], then you'll definitely know someone who does and can give you a ride."

Work Hard, Play Hard
While students at Trinity love their traditions, they have mixed feelings about the Greek scene. One student added that Greek life is not as big of a part of the Trinity social scene because many students would rather participate in groups such as academic frats, Trinity University Volunteer Action Community, a community service group, and Alpha Phi Omega, a community service fraternity, than spend all their time absorbed in the Greek system. One senior noted that interest in Greek life "seems to be more dominant with the girls." So fraternities and sororities are available at Trinity, but they do not dominate the campus completely. One student said that one good aspect of Trinity's Greek scene is that there is plenty of time to "get accustomed to the school before pledging to a group . . . for the rest of your Trinity years." She said that rush happens during the first semester, and pledging does not occur until the spring, leaving a lot of time in between to make sure the Greek system is a good fit for the students who are thinking of entering into it.

"Work hard, play hard (but smart)."

Of course, the fraternities and sororities that are on campus throw lots of parties. One student noted, "Anyone can find a party whenever they want, but they're pretty boring." Another student said that at parties "you'll find first years through seniors from all over campus." She also noted that after students turn 21, they start to frequent local bars instead of frat parties, visiting bars such as Bombay Bicycle Club and Broadway 5050. With parties and bars comes the drinking culture on campus, which students call "very healthy." One student said that Trinity students "work hard, play hard (but smart)." She added that one of the great things about Trinity is that the administration knows the students are going to drink and makes sure they are safe about it. "Trinity teaches us to be smart, but if something goes wrong, to always call for help," she said. Trinity is not a "dry" campus, and students over 21 are allowed to keep beer and wine in their dorm rooms.

Tradition Keeps a Campus Lively
When students need a break from all of their intense studying, they can turn to the traditions that make Trinity so unique and fun. When a student has a birthday at Trinity, there is often the usual birthday fare—parties, friends, and presents—but what makes birthdays at Trinity extra special is Miller Fountain. Students' friends will kidnap them on their birthday and throw them into the fountain, an experience that is rarely forgotten, especially when a student has a winter birthday.

Another Trinity tradition is known as Calvert Ghosts and happens on Halloween. According to one student, the "freshmen who live in Calvert Hall run around naked on campus," creating an unforgettable Halloween memory for everyone who witnesses the streak. Students also identified the annual library rave as an important tradition and a great way to release pent up stress. During finals week, hundreds of students take a study break and spontaneously break out dancing in the middle of the library. For a more tame tradition, students can attend Vespers, which is the most widely attended event at Trinity. Vespers is a hallmark event on Trinity campus when the President of the university and the Vice Presidents allow students to come to their homes and "enjoy food, drink and each other." One senior said that Vespers is "the best way to de-stress a little before finals and a wonderful way to get into the Christmas spirit."—*Christina Hull*

FYI

If I could change one thing about Trinity, I'd "make sure there were campus dogs in addition to our campus cats."

Three things that every student should do before graduating are "go to the library rave, go to Vespers and get thrown in the fountain."

What differentiates Trinity the most from other colleges is "our close relationships with our professors."

University of Dallas

Address: 1845 East Northgate Drive, Irving, TX 75062
Phone: 972-721-5266
E-mail address: ugadmis@udallas.edu
Web site URL: www.udallas.edu
Year Founded: 1956
Private or Public: Private
Religious Affiliation: Roman Catholic
Location: Urban
Number of Applicants: 1,060
Percent Accepted: 91%
Percent Accepted who enroll: 35%
Number Entering: 342
Number of Transfers Accepted each Year: 81
Middle 50% SAT range: M: 550–650, CR: 560–680, Wr: 530–670
Middle 50% ACT range: 24–29

Early admission program EA/ED/None: EA
Percentage accepted through EA or ED: 35%
EA and ED deadline: 1-Dec
Regular Deadline: 1-Aug
Application Fee: $40
Full time Undergraduate enrollment: 1,299
Total enrollment: 2,977
Percent Male: 49%
Percent Female: 51%
Total Percent Minority or Unreported: 32%
Percent African-American: 1%
Percent Asian/Pacific Islander: 5%
Percent Hispanic: 16%
Percent Native-American: <1%
Percent International: 2%
Percent in-state/out of state: 50%/50%
Percent from Public HS: 45%

Retention Rate: 80%
Graduation Rate 4-year: 46%
Graduation Rate 6-year: 56%
Percent Undergraduates in On-campus housing: 92%
Number of official organized extracurricular organizations: 35
3 Most popular majors: Biology, Business, English
Student/Faculty ratio: 13:1
Average Class Size: 15
Percent of students going to grad school: 25%
Tuition and Fees: $24,770
In-State Tuition and Fees if different: No difference
Cost for Room and Board: $7,885
Percent receiving financial aid out of those who apply, first year: 65%
Percent receiving financial aid among all students: 81%

Amidst the wide variety of colleges and universities in the greater Dallas area, the University of Dallas stands out for its combination of academic rigor and traditional Catholic sensibilities. With a strong emphasis on the Western canon, a comprehensive core curriculum, and a wildly popular study-abroad program in Rome, UD offers its students a structured, traditional education that will serve them well both in and out of the classroom.

Nerdy to the Core

UD has a reputation for being, as one student puts it, a "nerdy" school because of its comprehensive set of requirements known as the core curriculum. The UD core is mostly made up of primary sources that allow students to engage directly with the texts that shaped the foundations of Western thought. Of the credits needed to graduate, 15 are the same for everyone, made up of classes in English, history, theology, philosophy, economics, and politics. In addition, there are science lab, math, and language requirements that complete the core. English is one of the most popular majors at UD, despite the large amounts of reading, writing, and memorization it requires. Psychology is also a favorite, even though majors have to complete a thesis over 100 pages long to graduate. Language and math majors are universally less popular.

No matter what you're majoring in, classes at UD seem to be challenging all around. As one student explains, "UD is hard, a lot harder than the other schools my friends go to . . . you can't find an easy class to shrug off." Though the University is generous with academic and athletic scholarships, they are difficult to maintain: "The academic demands for retaining any scholarships . . . are rigorous, so many students aren't able to slack off even if they don't care." Adding to the academic intensity, there is a very strict attendance policy at UD—missing four classes automatically means that you are dropped from the course. Luckily, students have the support of the faculty to guide them through the rough waters of UD academics; most students are happy with their professors, saying that they are "very accessible—they *want* you to contact them when you need them." Some popular ones include English professor Father Robert Maguire and economics teacher William Doyle, who help UD kids achieve their "number one goal" of truly learning and internalizing the material that they grapple with.

TGIT: Thank God It's Thursday

Of course, there is much more to life at UD besides its standout academic program. While sports admittedly "aren't the focus of UD," students enjoy participating in and cheering on the teams that they have, including the men's rugby and basketball teams, whose games draw a huge following. Support for women's teams is a little "less vigorous," but both genders play baseball, soccer, and lacrosse. In fact, the UD lacrosse team is currently the only collegiate varsity lacrosse team in Texas. The newly renovated athletic center also provides lots of resources for students to stay in shape, including trainers and state-of-the-art equipment. Overall, as one student puts it, sports are "compatible" with the typical UD student way of life, even if they don't dominate it.

While there are approximately 35 extracurricular activities and clubs in which UD kids can participate, the consensus is that "club life isn't too popular in general, [since] a lot of students are busy studying." However, the student government and activities committee is large and attracts more and more people to its ranks in hopes of increasing the popularity of its events. Since there are no sororities or fraternities, on-campus social life at UD seems to revolve around parties in upperclassmen apartments either on campus or across the street in a group known as "Old Mill." Though some students say that "Student Apartment kids tend to stick to themselves," the parties they throw attract partygoers from all over the UD community. As one girl explains, "Younger and older students intermingle, making it easy for there to always be a party to go to if you have the right connections."

UD is a wet school, meaning that drinking is tolerated and prevalent throughout campus. While the drinking scene "never really gets out of control," one student admits that "technically, drinking policy is according to the law of the state of Texas, and if you get caught underage, you do get in trouble." Drinkers "tend to stick together" and congregate either at various parties or at a campus bar and grill called the Rathskeller that is actually on the student meal plan. For those who prefer their weekends dry, the student government sponsors a weekly event known as TGIT ("Thank God It's Thursday"), during which students party and dance to live music without the addition of alcohol.

Living in "the Convent"

Socially, UD provides a safe, friendly environment in which students can get to know each other. Despite the small size of the school (nearly 1,300 students), most students claim that its nurturing environment is a help rather than a hindrance. "It's super easy to meet people your first semester, mostly because the school is so small . . . you immediately find your group of friends and settle in for the haul," said one junior. Diversity is a bit lacking at UD, since "most kids are white, hail from a Catholic (or at least Christian) household, and hold the same basic beliefs in common." However, some students claim that "there is a fair amount of diversity in religions and races," emphasizing that the University recognizes the importance of diversifying the student body and is making a conscious effort to do so. Either way, there is no lack of community at UD. As one junior raves, "That's one thing I love about this school . . . absolutely one hundred percent of [students] are genuine. Students are true to what they believe, kind and caring, and the farthest from a fake crowd you will ever find."

> "Students are true to what they believe, kind and caring, and the farthest from a fake crowd you will ever find."

The Dallas residential community is made up of a variety of houses, each of which has its own unique character. Freshmen and sophomores must live on campus in specific dorms, only one of which is coed. The prevalence of same-sex living "though it may seem like a bother, is actually pretty fun . . . dorm spirit is [awesome]." Of the eight dorms, the all-male Gregory and all-girl Jerome are known as the "party dorms," and Catherine, by contrast, is sometimes called "the Convent." All of them, however, have at least two RAs who are "strict" and "are pretty serious about their roles." While some upperclassmen continue to live on campus after sophomore year, most move to the Old Mill apartments across the street or into those in the Student Apartment complex, which are "a lot nicer . . . there's usually a waitlist to get in." The architecture on campus is "not very pretty to look at, but it serves its purpose"—some of UD's architectural standouts include the Braniff Memorial Tower, which is a "landmark for the University" and the newer Art Village, in which a whole group of buildings is "put on stilts, so . . . they pretty much [look like] they're in the trees."

All UD students who live on campus must be on a meal plan, and freshmen can choose between 14- or 19-meal-per-week plans. After freshman year, you can choose between plans of 19, 14, or 10 meals, and the declining balance can be used at the Rathskeller, which is located below the campus's only dining hall in the Haggar University Center. Most upperclassmen tend to get either the lowest amount of meals or no plan at all, since food-wise, "some days are better than others." Others are less diplomatic, saying, "Let's just put it this way—one of the most popular groups on Facebook is 'I starve myself to go to UD.' No one goes here for the dining services." Despite the lack of gourmet options, the dining hall and student center remains one of the central hangout locations on campus.

Dallas to Rome

Since there's "not much to do on campus," many UD students spend their weekends enjoying the restaurants and club scene in the surrounding Texas area. The town of Irving itself is "a little scruffy" and not quite as nice as the school itself, yet town-gown relations are so calm as to be almost nonexistent, as one student describes: "Some people that live 15 minutes from the University have never even heard of it." To really get a taste of college town life, students recommend heading into the bigger city of Dallas itself for the best bar, shopping, and restaurant scenes. They agree, however, that "[since] most places are a few miles away . . . if you want to hang out outside of campus, you need a car." Whether you want to party in downtown clubs, shop in the popular West End or Las Colinas districts, or just grab dinner and a movie with friends, Dallas offers a plethora of opportunities for fun and relaxation off campus.

Perhaps the most well-known component of life at UD and the one that draws in the most students is its Rome program. Most sophomores spend at least one semester studying at UD's campus at Due Santi, just 20 minutes away from Rome itself. For many UD students, Rome is the highlight of their college career, as they take classes in subjects like ancient architecture and travel throughout Italy and Greece on weekends to see the very monuments they study. The Rome program, with its synthesis of Western tradition and Catholic values, and its application of the concepts learned in the classroom to real life, is the epitome of what makes the University of Dallas "a real, true, Catholic, strenuous liberal arts education that will influence all aspects of students' lives."—*Alexandra Bicks*

University of Houston

Address: 4400 University Drive, Houston, TX 77204-2023
Phone: 713-743-1010
E-mail address: admissions@uh.edu
Web site URL: www.uh.edu
Year Founded: 1927
Private or Public: Public
Religious Affiliation: None
Location: Urban
Number of Applicants: 11,393
Percent Accepted: 70%
Percent Accepted who enroll: 41%
Number Entering: 3,295
Number of Transfers Accepted each Year: 5,687
Middle 50% SAT range: M: 500–620, CR: 470–570, Wr: Unreported
Middle 50% ACT range: 20–25
Early admission program EA/ED/None: None

Percentage accepted through EA or ED: NA
EA and ED deadline: NA
Regular Deadline: 1-Apr
Application Fee: $50
Full time Undergraduate enrollment: 28,056
Total enrollment: 37,000
Percent Male: 49%
Percent Female: 51%
Total Percent Minority or Unreported: 65%
Percent African-American: 13%
Percent Asian/Pacific Islander: 20%
Percent Hispanic: 21%
Percent Native-American: <1%
Percent International: 8%
Percent in-state/out of state: 89/%11%
Percent from Public HS: Unreported
Retention Rate: 79%
Graduation Rate 4-year: 15%

Graduation Rate 6-year: 41%
Percent Undergraduates in On-campus housing: 25%
Number of official organized extracurricular organizations: 300
3 Most popular majors: Liberal Arts and Social Sciences, Business, Natural Sciences and Mathematics
Student/Faculty ratio: 20:1
Average Class Size: 25
Percent of students going to grad school: Unreported
Tuition and Fees: $13,569
In-State Tuition and Fees if different: $6,921
Cost for Room and Board: $6,935
Percent receiving financial aid out of those who apply, first year: 56%
Percent receiving financial aid among all students: 85%

Students who choose the University of Houston prepare for the professional world in a number of unique academic colleges, while enjoying the opportunity of living at home yet remaining involved on campus through intramural sports and numerous clubs. UH remains nearly unmatched among state universities in diversity of student background. Students travel from afar seeking Houston's requirement of a broad field of study, either with a liberal arts education offered by the Honors College or pursuing a mandated minor or double-major.

Renowned Academic Colleges

Opportunity for specialization abounds in the University's 12 academic colleges. In addition to the College of Liberal Arts and Social Sciences, numerous specialized colleges receive wide acclaim. The Conrad N. Hilton College of Hotel and Restaurant Management is "intense like the rest of the school," demanding much of its students in courses that include tours of restaurant and hotel facilities, economic theory, language and etiquette development, and food and beverage courses. Practicum courses put students in real-life employment situations to learn career skills.

The C. T. Bauer College of Business, a home to "great minds," ranks third among public Texas universities. The Colleges of Optometry and Pharmacy garner respect across the state as well. The Gerald D. Hines College of Architecture boasts amazing professors who are also known to solicit their students' help on projects and assist their students in finding internships.

The most selective of the colleges is the Honors College, a highly ranked liberal arts program that enrolls 300 students to study literature and philosophy in a discussion environment. These students take a heavier-than-average course load, possibly 15–16 credit hours instead of a typical student's 12–13 credit schedule. Each semester, Honors students must enroll in at least one course specific to the Honors College. They also must complete a Senior Honors Thesis to finish the program. The Honors College is located "in one of the better parts of campus," with classes held in the University's newly renovated main library. Additional perks include priority registration, a private lounge and study space, and more structured advising. Advising within the Honors College does not require that you "hunt down an advisor," as meetings are pre-planned for all Honors students.

For students who desire a less intense experience than the Honors College, the Scholars' Community, a supplementary course for which all students can apply, caters to the part of the student body that wants to be considered "more academic." The Scholars' Community is reportedly "not as intense" as the Honors College, and these students also enjoy priority registration and may take advantage of free tutoring sessions and special advising.

The University of Houston requires that all students take a core curriculum of 42 credit hours. This core curriculum does not limit students' freedom to explore possible majors, as students can and do change their major any number of times before junior year, when they must decide. Another distinctive aspect of the UH curriculum is that students within the College of Liberal Arts and Social Sciences must complete a minor or second major in addition to their first. Such a requirement ensures that all students study a diversity of topics.

Remarkable Courses
UH Colleges feature talented professors. "I've never had a professor I didn't like," reports one student. Even in comparison to

the Honors College, professors are "just as good," but classes are larger. For example, one introductory chemistry course taught by the enthralling professor Dr. Simon Bott is one of the most interesting but one of the largest courses, with an enrollment of approximately 600 students. Another popular course entitled "Principles of Drug Action" attracts a large number of students who ultimately find a seat in the class before graduating: "It seems like 80 percent go through it." "Beverage Appreciation," offered by the School of Hotel and Restaurant Management, is a popular wine-tasting course for juniors and seniors over 21 aspiring to become hospitality professionals. "Human Situation," an element of the Honors College curriculum, stands out from other courses as a "totally different" approach to reading works of literature and philosophy.

Students notice a constant flow of professors in and out of the University, which can enhance variety and opportunity, but can also make building relationships difficult. "I am having trouble finding professors who are still around to write letters of recommendation," laments one graduate school applicant. Although professors are easily reachable during office hours and by e-mail, "you would really have to work at a relationship" to get to know a member of the faculty.

Uncommon Diversity
The University of Houston has also been identified to its students as "one of the most diverse campuses in the nation." Indeed, few public universities can claim such a high number of international students and such a heterogeneous racial breakdown as the University of Houston. International students commonly hail from countries in Africa and Asia, among others. Students say the University's generous financial aid policies contribute to a diverse student body.

The Commuter Lifestyle
Many students cite a close proximity to home and feasibility of living at home as major reasons for coming to the University of Houston. Alternatively, students who choose to live on campus avoid the stress of a morning commute: "Having to drive is a disadvantage because of traffic." In the past, parking space has been limited, but is expected to improve with the completion of a new parking garage.

In general, students feel that the student body is distributed fairly evenly between commuting students and students who choose to live on campus. Commuting students do not feel separated from their on-campus peers: "I practically live there. I stay so late that some of my classmates don't even know that I commute."

Constant Campus Improvement

The UH campus is set three-quarters of a mile away from a major freeway: "It's a great location because the campus is not totally downtown, so there is less traffic." One disadvantage of an urban campus, however, is that the UH campus adjoins economically troubled areas: "The area around it is not one of the nicest." Although students generally avoid the immediate vicinity, downtown Houston is always accessible. Still, the campus itself is peaceful and refreshing, featuring fountains and architecturally impressive structures.

Living Options for Non-Commuters

Dormitories are the most common choice for housing at UH. "The Quads," which include the preferable Honors dorms, are regarded as the nicest dorm rooms. The basement of one building has a game room and kitchen equipment. Some regard Moody Towers as less appealing than the Quads. One student compares the dorms by the music they play in the cafeterias: nice classical music is standard for the Quads, while a visitor may hear "ghetto hip-hop" in the Towers. Each dorm features a lounge, computer lab with Internet access, small convenience stores, and cafeterias for student use. Apartment-style living is also available in either university-owned or third-party buildings.

Dining options at UH are varied and commended. "UC Satellite," a newer dining area located underground, is "the best secret on campus." In addition to a deli with great sandwiches and a popular sushi bar, it features more commercialized restaurants like Smoothie King; Starbucks; Pizza Hut; Taco Bell; and Kim Son, serving Asian food. In addition, the Hilton Hotel on campus contains an upscale restaurant and a student-run café that operates during the night. Two dorm cafeterias serve "typical dorm food."

The Attractive Force of Activities

Clubs give many students a reason to stay on campus after class. Students remark that "there is a club for everything." Phi Theta Kappa, an honors society, is active and popular for résumé-building. Student Governing Board plans parties and fundraisers. Model UN, although not affiliated with UH, operates on the UH campus. Religious organizations have high membership. For example, the large Lakewood Church holds Sunday service and Bible studies in a part of the campus recently bought out by the church. Interest groups and political organizations represent all sides. A unique Student Alumni Organization plans dinners and events to network undergraduates with alums. Guest speakers can also be arranged by department.

Recreational sports connect the student body outside of class. The Rec Center features rock climbing, a competition swimming pool, a hockey area, and racquetball courts, among other activities. Students often take recreational sports classes and play intramural sports, in which they sometimes go on to compete regionally. Flag football is known as one of the largest intramural programs. Respected varsity sports include competitive cheerleading and diving, which has generated Olympians.

School Spirit Sometimes Lacking

Although the effervescent competitive cheerleading squad is highly ranked, their spirit does not always pour out into the rest of the student body: "Most people didn't even know what was going on during Spirit Week." One reason could be that many students leave campus: "It's a commuter school, so many students don't participate." Some students report that there is "hardly any school pride," but pride seems to be more "a matter of who you hang out with." In response to these complaints, the Cougar Club and the Bleacher Creatures, two pep squads, set out during games to amplify audience enthusiasm.

> **"Most people didn't even know what was going on during Spirit Week."**

One popular social event on campus is the Frontier Fiesta that occurs around the time of Homecoming. It involves tailgating, games, fire shows, and food. Most of the social life on campus revolves around the fraternities and sororities near the apartment buildings, which can be expected to host parties most weekend nights.

824 **Texas**

Downtown Action

One benefit of the University's location is that it allows access to the downtown, Richmond, and trendy Montrose, all of which are popular destinations for students seeking diversion. A shopping center near Rice University attracts UH students after school. Amy's Ice Cream and the 59 Diner also deserve a visit from every student. A collection of small, family-collection museums and the theaters of the Theater District in downtown Houston offer student discounts.

In Need of a New Reputation

UH is sometimes overlooked by Houston residents who are "in a hurry to get away from their parents." Because the University of Houston is located near the homes of many prospective students, they misjudge its value: "It's underestimated because it's in town." And so UH surprises many prospective students. To obtain an accurate perception of the University of Houston, one must investigate its numerous strong academic colleges and its diverse and involved student body.
—*Eric Klein*

FYI

If you come to the University of Houston, you'd better bring "workout clothes for the Rec Center and intramural sports."

What's the typical weekend schedule? "Either go to a restaurant or club in downtown Houston, or get a home-cooked meal if you commute."

If I could change one thing about the University of Houston, I'd "increase the level of school spirit."

Three things every student at the University of Houston should do before graduating are "Go to the Frontier Fiesta, see a play in the theater district, and take 'Principles of Drug Action.'"

University of Texas / Austin

Address: 2400 Inner Campus Drive Austin, TX 78713-8058
Phone: 512 471-3434
E-mail address: NA
Web site URL: www.utexas.edu
Year Founded: 1883
Private or Public: Public
Religious Affiliation: None
Location: Suburban
Number of Applicants: 27,237
Percent Accepted: 51%
Percent Accepted who enroll: 54%
Number Entering: 7,419
Number of Transfers Accepted each Year: 2,859
Middle 50% SAT range: M: 570–690, CR: 540–660, Wr: 540–670
Middle 50% ACT range: 23–29
Early admission program EA/ED/None: None

Percentage accepted through EA or ED: NA
EA and ED deadline: NA
Regular Deadline: 15-Jan
Application Fee: $60
Full time Undergraduate enrollment: 37,459
Total enrollment: 48,401
Percent Male: 47%
Percent Female: 53%
Total Percent Minority or Unreported: 52%
Percent African-American: 5%
Percent Asian/Pacific Islander: 17%
Percent Hispanic: 23%
Percent Native-American: <1%
Percent International: 4%
Percent in-state/out of state: 94%/6%
Percent from Public HS: Unreported
Retention Rate: 92%
Graduation Rate 4-year: 48%

Graduation Rate 6-year: 76%
Percent Undergraduates in On-campus housing: 20%
Number of official organized extracurricular organizations: 900
3 Most popular majors: Social Sciences, Communication/Journalism, Business/Marketing
Student/Faculty ratio: 18:1
Average Class Size: 14
Percent of students going to grad school: Unreported
Tuition and Fees: $26,672
In-State Tuition and Fees if different: $8,090
Cost for Room and Board: $9,246
Percent receiving financial aid out of those who apply, first year: 82%
Percent receiving financial aid among all students: 57%

When you step onto the sunny campus of the University of Texas, you will immediately know that you are "deep in the heart of Texas." It has been said that everything is bigger in Texas, and this assessment certainly applies to UT. With a campus sprawling over 400 acres, 16 different colleges and schools, 90 research units, and 2,500 dedicated full-time faculty members, UT has the resources to provide for the 50,000 people that comprise its student body. UT students can pursue 100 majors in more than 170 fields of study, take part in the tradition of Longhorn football, and enjoy the vast array of political opportunities and musical performances that only can only be found in Austin. The university's ability to combine tradition, excellence, and exploration make it the perfect choice for someone who is looking for a big school that provides learning experiences both inside and outside the classroom.

Learning Longhorn Style

Academics at UT have something for everyone. Many freshmen are admitted directly to a major in one of the university's 11 undergraduate colleges or schools and begin taking classes in that school when they arrive in the fall. Additionally, students who are undecided on their major can enter UT through the School of Undergraduate Studies so that they may have more time to pick a major. Freshmen who begin UT during the fall 2010 semester and beyond will be required to enroll in a signature course and earn a certain number of "flags" in different academic areas. Signature Courses are first-year-only classes like "Spies, Espionage, and Treason" and "Offensive Art" that help freshmen with college-level writing, research, speaking, and discussion skills. Flags are distributional requirements that ensure students are exposed to courses in a variety of areas such as leadership and ethics, quantitative reasoning, and ethnic diversity.

Even though hundreds of people often attend Intro level courses, UT students agree that faculty members are very accessible. One freshman's professor "met with students one-on-one after the first test to help the students prepare better on the next test." With office hours multiple times a week, professors are more than willing to talk to students in their "cozy offices." All freshmen have the opportunity to carve out a smaller community at UT, whether it is through the multiple honors programs or through the First Year Interest Groups. Freshman honors programs range from business to engineering to Plan II.

Plan II is one of the most respected and selective honors programs in the country that "gives students the opportunity to take a broad range of classes within the Liberal Arts school such as Philosophy, Tutorial Courses, Plan II Physics, and World Literature." Admission to this program requires a separate application. While explaining Plan II as a degree is "difficult and confusing to others," students rave that Plan II students have "a great group of people overlooking the program that are very involved in students' lives." The First Year Interest Groups or FIGS are ways for "students who are not in an honors program to form tight knit groups with other students," a freshman explained.

UT has nine Nobel Prize winners and two Pulitzer Prize winners on its faculty. Students unanimously consider School of Communication's Professor John Daly's Interpersonal Communications course to be one of the best the university has to offer. Other classes that draw crowds are courses for business and pre-med students, two of UT's most popular majors. While the campus itself has plenty to offer academically, many Longhorns take advantage of one of UT's 650 study abroad programs. One UT student advised, "If you want to study abroad, think about where you want to go early on and plan accordingly." UT's top study abroad destinations include the United Kingdom, Spain, and Italy.

Life Around the Forty Acres

With a school of UT's size, there is not enough room for everyone to live on campus. However, there are housing options to suit everyone's needs, with 14 dorms on campus and multiple off-campus private dorms. The most famous dorm on campus is Jester, which houses 3,200 students alone. It is so big that it even has its own zip code! Students are encouraged to fill out housing applications along with their applications to the university, and many send in deposits before they are accepted to the school. For those who live off-campus, there is a UT-operated shuttle that helps students get around UT's sprawling campus. The shuttle gets high marks, as one freshman explains, because "you rarely have to wait longer than 10 minutes for the bus to arrive."

UT has an extensive array of dining halls and places to eat on campus. Students praise the variety of foods to eat, with vegan and vegetarian options at every meal. For breakfast, students enjoy making waffles with the waffle machine. As one Longhorn summed it up, "I wouldn't say the food is so delicious that I would never get sick of it, but the food tastes much better than I had expected!"

Longhorns–Keeping Austin Weird

UT students rave about all there is to see and do, both on campus and in and around the city of Austin. UT is home to the world's first photograph, some of the artwork of Frieda Kahlo, and the Blanton Museum, the largest college art museum in the country. History-loving students and visitors alike enjoy the Lyndon Baines Johnson Presidential Library, the most visited presidential library in the United States. The university has welcomed speakers like the Dalai Lama, Barack Obama, Bill Gates, and Al Gore, as well as performers like Jerry Seinfeld and Kanye West in recent years. Students agree that a visit to the Harry Ransome Center is a "must before graduation." Some of the items this cultural archives center contains include a Gutenberg Bible, manuscripts of Ernest Hemingway, and the collections of Woody Allen. Longhorns also enjoy the Texas Revue, the university-wide talent show.

As one senior put it, "The best thing about UT is the variety. There is truly something for everyone." There are over 900 student organizations on campus. Students agree that the best way to make the most of your time at UT is to get involved on campus. Warned one junior, "If you don't get involved, you might run the risk of getting lost in the crowd."

The city of Austin is consistently ranked as one of the most livable cities in America. According to one UT junior, "The city is so driven and energized by our university." Students with interests in politics love that they can intern at the Capitol of Texas. Additionally, Longhorns are committed to the environment, and they have made great strides to make their campus more sustainable and eco-friendly. "I have not met anyone, including my conservative mother, who doesn't love Austin," explained one UT senior. With all of its resources, Austin acts as UT's biggest classroom.

Every year, thousands of music lovers descend upon the "Live Music Capital of the World" for the annual Austin City Limits Music Festival. The South by Southwest Conference exposes students to original music, independent films, and emerging technologies every year. The legendary Cactus Café in the Texas Union is one of the most intimate live music venues in the country.

Students do find the lack of green space on campus frustrating. However, "surrounding Austin helps make up for it with venues like Lady Bird Lake and Zilker Metropolitan Park." Longhorns enjoy taking a break from classes and spending time on the lake. Weekend trips often involve visits to the deep Texas Hill Country. Austin boasts an average daily temperature of about 70 degrees and more than 300 days of sunshine each year, so Longhorns take advantage of the more than 50 miles of hike and bike trails just minutes from campus. Students also enjoy visiting the "famous yet infamous 6th street downtown."

Hook 'em, Horns

At UT, football isn't just a game, it's a way of life. Students spend Saturdays in the fall packing into the 90,000-seat Darrell K. Royal-Texas Memorial Stadium to cheer their beloved Longhorns to victory. Students unanimously agree that the Red River Rivalry game against OU in Dallas's Cotton Bowl is an event not to be missed. UT fans have a lot to cheer for, as the Longhorns have claimed 47 total national championships. Students are united by their love of singing "The Eyes of Texas" at athletic events and seeing the Tower lit burnt orange.

> "I have not met anyone, including my conservative mother, who doesn't love Austin."

Another important aspect of UT life is the Greek system. While a large number of students "go Greek," those who decide not to still are invited to attend the parties. Students enjoy going to fraternity parties on Friday and Saturday nights. Much of UT's social life is centered around Greek-hosted social events, but in a community of 50,000 people, there is always something to do that is not Greek-related.

Students at UT are passionate about all aspects of their collegiate life. UT "definitely combines academics, athletics, and a social scene." Despite all the different activities, interests, and goals of the gigantic student body, all Longhorns are united by the fact that they truly bleed burnt orange. Students initially have to work to carve out a community for themselves by taking the initiative to meet their professors and get involved on campus. According to one Longhorn junior, "Things won't just come to you unless you work for them. I've found, though, that there is a great payoff to this initial investment."
—*Alexa Sassin*

FYI

If you come to UT, you'd better bring some "burnt orange clothes, cowboy boots, and a pair of walking shoes because the campus is big."

What's the typical weekend schedule? "Thursday night: go downtown to Sixth Street. Friday: Go to class and get a little homework done. Head to West Campus to partake in whatever is going on that night. Grab some late night Kerby Lane queso or a Big Bite 'phat sandwich' Saturday: Tailgate with friends before the football game and then cheer on the Longhorns to victory. Later that evening, attend parties hosted by the Greek community. Sunday: Grab breakfast at Juan in a Million. Attend extracurricular meetings. Hit the books and get ready for the school week ahead."

If I could change one thing about UT, I'd: "make more parking available to students."

Three things every student at UT should do before graduation are: "1. Attend the OU/Texas football game.

2. Take a tour of the Tower. 3. Go downtown and explore all Austin has to offer, like the Austin City Limits Music Festival, Sixth Street, and Lady Bird Lake."

Utah

Brigham Young University

Address: A-153 ASB, Provo, UT 84602
Phone: 801-422-2507
E-mail address: admissions@byu.edu
Web site URL: www.byu.edu
Year Founded: 1875
Private or Public: Private
Religious Affiliation: Church of Jesus Christ of Latter-Day Saints
Location: Urban
Number of Applicants: 10,182
Percent Accepted: 68%
Percent Accepted who enroll: 77%
Number Entering: 7,000
Number of Transfers Accepted each Year: 1,500
Middle 50% SAT range: M: 570–680, CR: 550–670, Wr: Unreported
Middle 50% ACT range: 25–30
Early admission program EA/ED/None: None

Percentage accepted through EA or ED: NA
EA and ED deadline: NA
Regular Deadline: 1-Feb
Application Fee: $30
Full time Undergraduate enrollment: 30,000
Total enrollment: 32,992
Percent Male: 51%
Percent Female: 49%
Total Percent Minority or Unreported: 11%
Percent African-American: <1%
Percent Asian/Pacific Islander: 3%
Percent Hispanic: 3%
Percent Native-American: <1%
Percent International: 3%
Percent in-state/out of state: 33%/67%
Percent from Public HS: Unreported
Retention Rate: Unreported
Graduation Rate 4-year: 21%
Graduation Rate 6-year: 54%

Percent Undergraduates in On-campus housing: 11%
Number of official organized extracurricular organizations: 390
3 Most popular majors: Business, Education, Social Sciences
Student/Faculty ratio: 23:1
Average Class Size: 25
Percent of students going to grad school: Unreported
Tuition and Fees: Member of The Church of Jesus Christ of Latter-day Saints: $4,080, Non-member of The Church of Jesus Christ of Latter-day Saints: $9,160
In-State Tuition and Fees if different: No difference
Cost for Room and Board: $6,460
Percent receiving financial aid out of those who apply, first year: 54%
Percent receiving financial aid among all students: 20%

S et on 560 pristine acres in Provo, Utah, Brigham Young University offers a strong academic education in a beautiful environment. With its religious affiliation with the Church of Jesus Christ of Latter-Day Saints, BYU is certainly not your typical college. One of the most significant differences that you might notice is the policy against drinking—and the students' willing adherence to it.

Integrated Secular and Spiritual Education

BYU is known for strong academics, and the reputation is well-deserved. Students say there is a pretty heavy workload, but that they always find time to have fun. A student, reflecting on his and his friends' academic schedules, said "it's not extreme unless you make it that way." Students are also very satisfied with the range of classes offered for every interest at every level. They say that some of the strongest and most popular majors are in business and marketing, education, and social sciences.

The most distinctive aspect of BYU lies in the university's religious affiliation with the Church of Jesus Christ of Latter-Day Saints. Academically, the philosophy of BYU is that truth comes from God, so secular learning and spiritual learning are parts of a whole. Often, students defer enrollment, taking a gap year to do missionary work in a foreign country. Other students attend BYU for their freshman year, and then take a year or two off to complete a mission. The missions also act as immersion programs, allowing students to experience a new and foreign culture. Forty-five percent of students go on mission trips, adding to the international cultural awareness of the campus.

> "People are more creative about things to do because there needs to be more to a party than just an open cooler."

As part of its undergraduate degree requirements, BYU has a University Core consisting of 18 requirements that are divided into five categories: Doctrinal Foundations; The Individual and Society; Skills; Arts, Letters, and Sciences; and Electives. The Doctrinal Foundations requirements include studying the Book of Mormon, the New Testament, and Doctrine and Covenants. These contribute to the 14 credit hours of required religion coursework throughout a student's time at BYU. Every Tuesday, BYU holds Devotionals and forums where students can go to listen to and meet prominent figures in the Church, world leaders, and scholars. Professors in other subjects at the University are encouraged to make connections between their material and religion as well.

Housing and Food

Also, because the Church owns the university, operating costs, tuition, and fees are greatly subsidized, and many students receive full merit-based scholarships. As a result, students laugh about how "food is more expensive than tuition." Meal options for BYU students vary greatly. There are a large variety of places on campus where meal cards can be used, from Cannon Commons, the cafeteria, to the fancy Skyroom Restaurant on the top floor of the student center or the Jamba Juice on campus. Students can also use points from their meal plans to buy groceries from the Creamery.

Students have the options of apartment-style living with in-suite kitchens as well as a foreign language residence where students commit to only speak a selected foreign language while in their apartments. The housing policies at BYU reflect the University's emphasis on chastity. The dorms at BYU are separated by gender with restrictions on people of the opposite sex being in housing

buildings after 1:30 a.m. on Fridays and after midnight on all other days. These policies are actually a part of the Honor Code, which dictates specific visiting hours for each individual dorm and even off-campus housing for single students.

Fun without Alcohol

One significant characteristic that distinguishes BYU from other universities is the spirit and atmosphere of the students' social life. BYU has an honor code that students and faculty alike take very seriously. Among the provisions of the Honor Code are the typical "be honest" and "respect others," but there is also a rule that men must be clean-shaven at all times. The one policy that is most prominently evident—and often shocking to students at other universities—is abstinence from alcohol and caffeine, as dictated by Mormon beliefs.

For many schools, students' social activities will often involve drinking, and it can even be hard to imagine a university where alcohol is not present. But at BYU, students embrace the policy, arguing instead that "it's great for social life." One student said, "People are more creative about things to do because there needs to be more to a party than just an open cooler."

Instead, students have fun at events like dances run by the student government, often multiple times a week, that have themes like swing, 80s, and country. Students say there are always people hanging out in the dorms and around campus. At later hours at night, though, students migrate to outside the dorms because of the gender restrictions on housing buildings. In terms of interaction between the sexes, students say that one of the biggest myths about BYU—namely that students go to BYU to get married—is not that far off the mark. One student noted that students do marry earlier than at other colleges.

Sports and Leisure

BYU's symbol is a giant white "Y" on the mountain above the school. Yes, the mountain is above the school. Students are extremely active in sports, especially skiing and snowboarding. BYU's intramural sports program is very popular, and creative adjustments are made to promote participation. One student remarked, "My favorite weird one is inner-tube water polo. The idea is to make the game more accessible to people who aren't amazing swimmers."

Apart from intramural sports, BYU competes in the NCAA's Division I Mountain

West Conference. The University's varsity sports are competitive, with its football and men's basketball teams ranked fairly high. Other sports in which BYU's Cougars are a major force are volleyball, rugby, and soccer.

People of Provo

Perhaps it is the beauty and peacefulness of Provo that causes it, but the people at BYU are very friendly. One freshman explained, "When you walk past someone here that you don't know, they always say hi instead of awkwardly looking away like anywhere else. It's weird for a few days, but after that, it's wonderful." Additionally, BYU's huge expanse of a campus creates a very serene and isolated environment for students. Many students said that BYU is such a safe place and the students are so respectful toward one another that they don't worry about nodding off to sleep on the grass with their laptops next to them: "The crime report section of the paper is a big joke."

As might be expected by the school's religious affiliation, the vast majority of students are Mormon. At the same time, the Mormon population is largely distributed throughout the world, with the majority living outside of the United States. As a result, even though BYU's student body is religiously homogenous, cultural diversity is not completely lacking. BYU also has a focus in international studies, offering courses in over sixty languages. About one third of the student body is enrolled in foreign language courses during any given semester, a proportion that is four times the national average, and BYU's Russian program is one of the largest in the nation.

BYU provides its students with an academic and social environment that is really unlike that of any other university. While restrictions abound, from the dress code to an emphasis on chastity, students love their beautiful school and the unique experience it gives them.—*Michelle Yu*

FYI
If you come to BYU, you'd better bring "a snowboard or skis, and a razor if you're a guy."
What is the typical weekend schedule? "At least one dance and a well-organized group date, normally something silly and free/cheap."
If I could change one thing about BYU, I'd "loosen the dress code and un-restrict dorm visiting hours."
Three things every student at BYU should do before graduating are "hike the Y, take a dance class, and attend all of the devotionals and forums."

University of Utah

Address: 201 South 1460 East Salt Lake City, UT 84112
Phone: 801-581-7281
E-mail address: admissions@sa.utah.edu
Web site URL: www.utah.edu
Year Founded: 1850
Private or Public: Public
Religious Affiliation: None
Location: Urban
Number of Applicants: 8,364
Percent Accepted: 83%
Percent Accepted who enroll: 40%
Number Entering: 2,769
Number of Transfers Accepted each Year: 2,721
Middle 50% SAT range: M: 500–630, CR: 490–630, WR: 480–600
Middle 50% ACT range: 21–27
Early admission program EA/ED/None: None

Percentage accepted through EA or ED: NA
EA and ED deadline: NA
Regular Deadline: 1-Apr
Application Fee: $35
Full time Undergraduate enrollment: 14,504
Total enrollment: 28,211
Percent Male: 55%
Percent Female: 45%
Total Percent Minority or Unreported: 13%
Percent African-American: 1%
Percent Asian/Pacific Islander: 6%
Percent Hispanic: 5%
Percent Native-American: 1%
Percent International: 3%
Percent in-state/out of state: 83%/17%
Percent from Public HS: Unreported
Retention Rate: 83%

Graduation Rate 4-year: 20%
Graduation Rate 6-year: 51%
Percent Undergraduates in On-campus housing: 8%
Number of official organized extracurricular organizations: 154
3 Most popular majors: Economics, Mass Communications, Psychology
Student/Faculty ratio: 13:1
Average Class Size: 30
Percent of students going to grad school: Unreported
Tuition and Fees: $16,600
In-State Tuition and Fees if different: $5,285
Cost for Room and Board: $5,972
Percent receiving financial aid out of those who apply, first year: 68%
Percent receiving financial aid among all students: 30%

At the feet of the Wasatch Mountains and in the heart of Salt Lake City, the University of Utah, in many ways, offers the best of the West. Motivated students will find it offers all the intellectual challenge they are looking for, and it is an unusual example of a large university where student input matters a great deal. Those seeking a friendly, small-town feel in the setting of a large university and who are willing to forego cultural diversity will find a happy home at the University of Utah.

Hidden Opportunities for Challenge

Students of all levels of seniority agree that it can be easy to coast at the University of Utah ("the U," to those in the know), since there is a strong flow of student-to-student information about which are the easiest classes and most lenient professors. Several of the largest majors also require many large lecture classes—which tend to be the easiest—and relatively few small seminar-style classes. Those same large lecture classes are the paths to general education credits for many students, few of whom struggle to fulfill the distributional re-

quirements. Many students take advantage of this opportunity to get outside their discipline for a painless foray into Survey of Jazz or Introduction to Music, for example.

At the same time, students hoping to be challenged will not be disappointed if they are willing to do their own legwork. The University divides its academic disciplines into colleges, including an Honors College, which offers Honors Degree and Honors Certificate options to accepted applicants. The University has expanded the honors program in the last several years, and students who take part sing praises of more engaged professors, more classroom discussion, and assignments that are, in one student's words, "more open-ended, rather than 'Answer 10 questions from the book.'" The U is also very willing to accept credit for advanced high school classes and even "life experience." One senior remarked with candor, "I knew it was going to be an okay education that would qualify me for graduate school, but the opportunities available surprised me, and I've been very impressed."

There can be no doubt that the University of Utah is a research institution where science

832   U t a h

is king. The University's engineering and pre-medical programs are regarded as the most challenging, and the students in them as the "smartest" at the University. Many students at the U come expressly to take advantage of the science faculty and facilities, and Engineering, Biology, and Chemistry are popular majors. Changing majors and double majoring are very common at the U, so many students have experience in both the sciences and the humanities—departments which are located on opposite sides of the very large campus—and have an easy time finding common academic ground. But students do feel a stark disparity in department funding, with the sciences garnering the majority of state grants to the school. The Utah Science Technology and Research (USTAR) program is a special initiative that directs state funding to scientific research initiatives that program directors hope will result in company and job creation in the state of Utah. The University also continues to draw national attention for its cardiology division and such faculty as geneticist Mario Capecchi, who won the 2007 Nobel Prize in Physiology or Medicine and is a source of pride for students in all disciplines.

> "I knew it was going to be an okay education that would qualify me for graduate school, but the opportunities available surprised me, and I've been very impressed."

The U is well connected to Salt Lake City, where the majority of University of Utah alumni remain after graduation. Many students benefit from the Career Services office, which has access to a strong network of internship and job opportunities in the city. Academic advising is markedly less popular. Students complain of advisors recommending classes that are too easy or unnecessary for their major. Some intrepid students supplement their advising needs: "When the advisors aren't helpful, I turn to former professors. Every time I've wanted to meet with a professor, they've made time for me," explained one student. Faculty at the U is broadly regarded as friendly, accessible, and generally interested in the success and satisfaction of their students. Bad professors are weeded out of the undergraduate teaching body through student advisory committees'

input or through dwindling class sizes that speak for themselves.

Alternatives to Mom and Dad's House

The phrase "commuter campus" is deeply entrenched in University of Utah students' vocabulary. An overwhelming majority of students live off campus, and because much of the student body is from the Salt Lake City area, many live with their parents. Similarly, many students come into the U with the same group of friends they had in high school, and socialize primarily with that group. Those who choose not to live with their parents often find off-campus housing—which is generally cheap in the area around campus—with their network of high school friends. Meanwhile, on-campus housing presents opportunities for students who want to look outside their high school crowd. The University, the International Olympic Committee, and Salt Lake City joined to rebuild University housing when the city hosted the 2002 Winter Olympics and used residence halls for athletes' housing. Dorms are now spacious, and located in one of the prettiest parts of campus. "The residence buildings are red brick, and it's really nice when you can be in your dorm room, and then walk five or 10 minutes and be on the trails where you can walk or hike," said one junior.

Freshmen living on campus are required to buy a meal plan, but upperclassmen housing often includes kitchens. Few students at the U have complaints about the quality of the food, but many find its repetition disappointing. As the U undertakes extensive property development—including renovations of many class buildings and the Marriott Library and construction of a new Student Life Building to replace the Field House as the home of student recreation—the administration is increasingly focusing on taking the University in a greener, more renewable direction. On-campus and off-campus students alike enjoy the social benefits of two fraternity and sorority systems at the University of Utah. The first is the traditional Greek system common to many large universities. "Greek row" is as close to the University proper as it could be while remaining nominally off campus, and therefore exempt from the University's well-enforced dry campus policy. Parties on Greek row are a weekend activity that draws even off-campus students. The other system of fraternities and sororities is an outgrowth of the large number of practicing members of the Church of Jesus Christ of Latter-Day Saints at the U, who make up about half the student body. "The LDS Institute, across the street from campus, is a big hangout," said one student. "They have their own activities and their own version of the Greek system."

Students often occupy themselves outside class at the Gateway, an open-air promenade in downtown Salt Lake City with restaurants and a movie theater, and on nearby ski slopes such as Alta, Snowbird, and Park City, the last of which hosted numerous Winter Olympics events and boasts, in one student's opinion, "the best snow in the world." The OneLove Ski and Snowboard Club and the Utah Freeskier Society are two of the largest student groups on campus. While students do need transportation to the slopes, a car is not a real necessity for taking part in most activities around Salt Lake City. The city is home to a well-developed bus system and light rail, both of which run in and around the campus and are free to University of Utah students. But because so many students come from the area and live off campus, many have cars, so parking near the U is competitive.

Social goings-on at the U are accessible to students of all years and ages. Because the University is home to a large "non-traditional" student population, including older-than-average and married students, many undergraduates find that, in the words of one senior, "They have no idea what year people are," so all comers are welcome at social events.

"I Am a Utah Man, Sir, and Will Be Till I Die; Ki! Yi!"

Recent sports seasons have been good to the University of Utah Utes, which is good news for students at the U, and for residents of much of the Salt Lake City valley, which divides its fervent allegiance between the University of Utah and nearby rival Brigham Young University (BYU). Utah fans sign up in droves to be part of the Mighty Utah Student Section (the MUSS, taken from a line in the school song), which has a waiting list. Membership entitles students to prime seating at Utah games, and one member describes it as "the best rush you could ever have. Since we are a dry campus, where else

are you going to get 5,000 students together at a game to cheer and have a good time?"

The MUSS has done much to address worries about lackluster student involvement at the U. Club officers can be hindered, when organizing events, by the volume of students who live off campus, many of whom also work 20–40 hours per week, and so do not endeavor to participate in the hundreds of student groups on campus. Those students who are involved on campus have undertaken efforts to raise student awareness of the extracurricular opportunities at the U. One such effort is the U Book, a brainchild of the Student Alumni Board. The U Book contains information about various student groups, 50 University of Utah traditions, including athletic events like Homecoming and the Utah-BYU football game, places to visit on campus and around Salt Lake City, and annual student events like the Hunger Banquet.

Still, the size and influence of the Associated Students at the University of Utah (ASUU)—the school's student government—are especially noteworthy given the challenges of engaging a geographically spread-out student body with diverse interests. A relatively large number of students take part and most of the remaining student body is well informed about current issues up for debate. ASUU efforts also produce results. A recent example is the Graduation Guarantee, under which the University guarantees that by fulfilling a series of advising requirements, all incoming freshmen and transfer students will graduate in four years, or the University will pay for or waive the remaining requirements for graduation. The University approved and began implementing the Guarantee shortly after the ASUU passed the student initiative.

The University of Utah adheres to and helps define the libertarian spirit that prevails in much of Utah. Students define the course and rigor of their own education, and many find that what they learn is immediately applicable in the work force; they work together to govern themselves as much as possible, and many remain in the Salt Lake City area and continue to engage with the U as donors, board members, and die-hard Ute fans. In the words of a nostalgic second-semester senior, "I didn't expect to feel this way, but I want to come back, and I want to support my school."—*Elizabeth Woods*

FYI

If you come to the University of Utah, you'd better bring "your skis and good walking shoes to get around campus."

What is the typical weekend schedule? "Go to a concert or other student performance Friday night, sleep in Saturday and have a leisurely brunch with friends, head to the MUSS tailgate and then the football game, and spend the rest of the night at after parties."

If I could change one thing about the University of Utah, I'd "have more people live on campus, to create more of a community."

Three things every student should do before graduating are "join the MUSS, spend time in the Wasatch Mountains, and finish the U Book."

Vermont

Bennington College

Address: One College Drive
  Bennington, VT 05201
Phone: 800-833-6845
E-mail address:
  admissions@bennington.edu
Web site URL:
  www.bennington.edu
Year Founded: 1932
Private or Public: Private
Religious Affiliation: None
Location: Rural
Number of Applicants: 1,057
Percent Accepted: 62%
Percent Accepted who
  enroll: 29%
Number Entering: 190
Number of Transfers
  Accepted each Year:
  56
Middle 50% SAT range: M:
  560–660, CR: 620–720,
  Wr: 646–768
Middle 50% ACT range:
  24–28
Early admission program
  EA/ED/None: ED

Percentage accepted
  through EA or ED: 60%
EA and ED deadline: 15-Nov
Regular Deadline: 3-Jan
Application Fee: $60
Full time Undergraduate
  enrollment: 618
Total enrollment: 618
Percent Male: 34%
Percent Female: 66%
Total Percent Minority or
  Unreported: 17%
Percent African-American:
  2%
Percent Asian/Pacific
  Islander: 2%
Percent Hispanic: 3%
Percent Native-American:
  <1%
Percent International: 4%
Percent in-state/out of
  state: 4%/96%
Percent from Public HS: 59%
Retention Rate: 89%
Graduation Rate 4-year:
  45%

Graduation Rate 6-year:
  59%
Percent Undergraduates
  in On-campus housing:
  98%
Number of official organized
  extracurricular
  organizations: 21
3 Most popular majors:
  Drama, English, Visual and
  Performing Arts
Student/Faculty ratio: 9:1
Average Class Size: 15
Percent of students going to
  grad school: Unreported
Tuition and Fees: $38,270
In-State Tuition and Fees if
  different: No difference
Cost for Room and Board:
  $10,680
Percent receiving financial
  aid out of those who apply,
  first year: 87%
Percent receiving financial
  aid among all students:
  77%

L ocated in the Green Mountains of southwestern Vermont, Bennington College boasts 300 wooded acres, five acres of tilled farmland, 15 acres of wetland, 80 species of trees and 121 species of birds. How's that for diversity?

Small and remote, Bennington attracts an equally intellectually diverse range of students, who come for the individualized academics and the intimate campus—not to mention the theme parties.

Flex Your Academic Muscle

Bennington's academic system is unique. There are no majors at Bennington; instead, students develop a "focus" or a "concentration" themselves with large input from a faculty adviser. Focuses can range from the

more traditional, such as mathematics, to the absolutely untraditional, such as storytelling. With the help of a faculty adviser, students plan their course load to best suit their focus, a method called the Plan Process.

Some students relish this academic freedom, saying that it forces you to really "think about your education" and engage in your academic career. For example, one student, who is focusing on "painting and education," said he planned his course load to involve a lot of sciences so he could learn things like the chemistry used to make paint pigment. A junior with a focus in literature said, "The best students are the ones who do take advantage of the flexibility." Indeed, students agreed that the best academic careers are the ones that are cross-disciplinary, to use all of Bennington's resources.

But while many students laud this different take on academics, others say it encourages floundering, and in fact sometimes attracts "terrifically unmotivated" students. "No one is forced to get specific, so everyone is doing everything," one junior said. "Freedom is good for some people, but for most it is just too much." Along with no majors, grades are also optional at Bennington, with narrative evaluations available as an alternative option. Those with grad school plans typically opt for grades, but many other students opt out, helping to contribute to the somewhat misguided perception of Bennington as a "slacker school."

The most popular concentrations at Bennington are the visual arts, dance, writing, and language programs. In fact, much of modern dance was developed at Bennington, whose program was founded by pioneer Martha Graham. The current faculty boasts many literature standouts, and a recent project brought a group of South African leaders to campus to lead classes in the social sciences.

Because of the "planning" system's built-in one-on-one time with faculty members, and because of the small size of the school, students are very close to professors. "I call most professors by their first name," said the student concentrating in painting and education. Other students say they frequently have lunch with their professors, and know their families. But again, this closeness seems to be a double-edged sword; some students complained that professors are almost "too nice," and as a result there is a kind of pressure to befriend all your professors to get ahead. "Something that goes hand in hand with extremely personal relationships is that there is favoritism."

One of the biggest draws to Bennington is the Field Work Term (FWT), a seven-week winter term during which students take internships at various institutions across the country and the world. An annual requirement for graduation, the FWT provides the opportunity to work at places such as the San Francisco Museum of Modern Art, the Pittsburgh Zoo, and Houghton Mifflin Publishing Company. Many students enjoy the FWT as an opportunity not only to apply what they've learned to the real world, but also to take a break from life at Bennington's small and remote campus.

Do-It-Yourself Extracurriculars

Although it is a small campus, Bennington offers any extracurricular group you might want—if you're willing to create it. Because it is such a small school, most clubs come and go, with students forming new ones every year. Long-term groups include the school newspaper; the literary magazine *Silo*; the campus radio station, WHIP; and the perennially popular Outing Club, which sponsors skiing, horseback riding, rock climbing, and hiking trips in the neighboring Green Mountains. There are also community service groups, including the Student Action Network (SAN) and the Community Outreach Leadership Team (COLT). One current club, sure to be a keeper, is Sugar Bush, in which students make maple syrup from nearby trees.

> **"I feel like the main thing you learn at Bennington is how to educate yourself."**

If you're looking for sports at Bennington, though, you're out of luck. As one junior bluntly puts it, "Why would anyone interested in sports come to Bennington?" There are no varsity sports teams, and the only club team is coed soccer, which has been known to play nearby high schools. And forget about intramurals. (Students have recently started a dodgeball team, though.) Instead, Bennington students focus their energy on the great outdoors, the free fitness classes, and the "great" rec center—complete with climbing wall and sauna.

The Birthplace of the Theme Party

What Bennington may lack in athletics, it surely makes up for in theme parties. "Bennington is pretty much the birthplace of the theme party," one arts concentrator said. Another seconded, "You'll pretty much never go to a party at Bennington that isn't a theme party." Popular parties in the past have included pirates versus ninjas, Pigstock (a pig roast with live music), the "office party," and the huge roller-disco party Rollerama. Every year, the college puts on SunFest, a music festival on the central lawn featuring 10 to 15 bands during the day. The recent addition of MoonFest the night before is also popular.

Although theme parties are truly the dominant social scene, there are a few other outlets for those not wanting to get dressed up. The campus brings in two to three live bands each week, most of which are small, indie-rock groups, most famously the White Stripes. There is also the occasional unthemed house party, though those are few and far between.

Drinking and drugs are both prevalent at Bennington, though not out of control. "Drugs are in your face if you look for them, they are not in your face if you do not," one male junior said. "They don't dominate the social scene. Parties are still fun if you aren't into that stuff—no one is going to force them on you, or think you're not cool if you're not into them."

From Colonial to Co-op

Bennington's version of student housing is as unique as its take on academics. Bennington offers five types of housing: a drug-free house on campus, an organic co-op off campus, colonial houses, 1970s modern houses, and 2001 contemporary houses. Each house accommodates 25 to 30 students and is managed by two students selected by their peers. These students run Sunday evening "coffee houses" to discuss community issues or just to chat. Students across the board describe Bennington housing as "amazing." Not only are the houses beautiful, but the system guarantees that you'll end up living with your friends—and guarantees a single for junior and senior years.

Students are less unequivocally enthusiastic about the meal plan. Though the food is good by college standards, with plenty of vegetarian and meat options, all students must be on the same three-meal-a-day meal plan for all four years. So even though most houses come equipped with a kitchen, students rarely eat anywhere but the dining hall.

In fact, for the most part, students rarely venture far off the Bennington campus. Many students have cars, and thanks to a "ride board," rides are easy to find, but most choose to stay on what they consider a "really self-sufficient campus." That campus, while intellectually and increasingly socioeconomically diverse, is noticeably lacking in ethnic or cultural diversity. "It is sad," one student said. "This is one thing Bennington is—and needs to be—working on." The campus also has an overwhelming majority of women, running to around 70 percent of the undergraduate population. Female students say that this ratio is not as much of a problem as you might think, however, especially since they can meet people much more easily during the Field Work Term. "Ultimately people still have boyfriends, people still meet people."

If students are really itching to meet more people, they can go to nearby Hampshire or Williams Colleges. Most, however, stay in the area of North Bennington—the "ridiculously New England" town where Bennington College is actually located—or Bennington, a larger city. One especially nice aspect of such a remote lifestyle is that students never have to worry about their safety: "Vermont feels like the safest place in the world. I never worry."

Overall, a Bennington education is what you choose to make of it. It is unique, to be sure, but it is that unusual character that allows many students to flourish. For those expecting an easy ride, however, Bennington is not the place, nor is it the place for those who need much hand-holding: "I feel like the main thing you learn at Bennington is how to educate yourself."

And how to throw a damn good theme party.—*Claire Stanford*

FYI
If you come to Bennington, you'd better bring "roller skates, costumes, and false eyelashes."
What's the typical weekend schedule? "Some sort of 'thirsty Thursday' celebration, class Friday, Friday night find out who is having a party in their room. Galavant around after, maybe see what band is playing. Saturday night, dress up in whatever you can find that remotely fits the theme of whatever party is going on, and get drunk. Sunday, recover."
If you could change one thing about Bennington I'd "only admit students who would be terribly excited."
Three things every student should do before graduating are "go in the catacombs, take a private tutorial, and run naked across the Commons lawn."

M a r l b o r o   C o l l e g e

Address: P.O. Box A, 2582 South Road, Marlboro, VT 05344-0300
Phone: 802-258-9236
E-mail address: admissions@marlboro.edu
Web site URL: www.marlboro.edu
Year Founded: 1946
Private or Public: Private
Religious Affiliation: None
Location: Rural
Number of Applicants: 459
Percent Accepted: 68%
Percent Accepted who enroll: 30%
Number Entering: 93
Number of Transfers Accepted each Year: 55
Middle 50% SAT range: M: 510–650, CR: 590–690, Wr: 640–720
Middle 50% ACT range: 24–32
Early admission program EA/ED/None: EA and ED

Percentage accepted through EA or ED: Unreported
EA and ED deadline: ED: Dec. 1; EA: Feb. 1
Regular Deadline: 15-Feb
Application Fee: $50
Full time Undergraduate enrollment: 330
Total enrollment: 330
Percent Male: 43%
Percent Female: 57%
Total Percent Minority or Unreported: 13%
Percent African-American: <1%
Percent Asian/Pacific Islander: 6%
Percent Hispanic: 4%
Percent Native-American: 1%
Percent International: 1%
Percent in-state/out of state: 10%/90%
Percent from Public HS: 70%
Retention Rate: 73%

Graduation Rate 4-year: Unreported
Graduation Rate 6-year: Unreported
Percent Undergraduates in On-campus housing: 80%
Number of official organized extracurricular organizations: 22
3 Most popular majors: English, Social Sciences, Visual & Performing Arts
Student/Faculty ratio: 8:1
Average Class Size: 8
Percent of students going to grad school: Unreported
Tuition and Fees: $32,180
In-State Tuition and Fees if different: No difference
Cost for Room and Board: $9,040
Percent receiving financial aid out of those who apply, first year: Unreported
Percent receiving financial aid among all students: Unreported

Located in rustic Vermont, a 20-minute drive from the nearest town, Marlboro College offers its students an academic sanctuary in the midst of the New England mountains and greenery. With a small student body and a focus on the outdoors and schoolwork, Marlboro provides an intimate environment perfect for those looking for a unique and self-driven collegiate experience.

An Intense Learning Environment

Marlboro, with its lack of athletics and scarcity of extracurricular activities, is primarily a learning-driven college. Students unanimously concur that most non-class time is spent on schoolwork. "It's a really rigorous setting," one junior said. "People just do work all the time. It really affects the social scene." Another junior agreed, "Work *is* our extracurricular activity."

The academic program is lauded as extremely strong all around. Classes are small,

with most classes consisting of about 10 students: "Eighteen students in a class is huge." If students are interested in a topic not offered, one-on-one tutorials can be arranged with professors in fields such as Arabic or fiction writing. There are no required classes except for a writing seminar that must be completed during freshman year.

Because of the small classes and intellectual environment, it is easy for students to form strong bonds with the faculty members leading their classes. "It's up to the students to enhance the faculty-student bond," one junior explained. Another student said professors often eat in the dining hall and are for the most part extremely "affable and approachable." But another student pointed out the one downfall of small classes: students who don't do the reading generally stand out. "You can't hide," said one senior. "Professors will call you if you don't show up for class."

Classes are divided into five basic categories: humanities, social sciences, natural sciences, world studies, and arts. In general, the humanities and literature departments are seen as the strongest, though there is also a notable "film culture," and political science is a very popular concentration. The math and science departments are "growing," though most students concede that those programs are slightly weaker. Recent additions to campus include the Serkin Arts Center and a new World Studies building.

Students choose a self-designed Plan of Concentration (known as "the Plan") to complete their studies at Marlboro. The plan can take many different forms: anything from a 120-page paper to an architectural model to writing a musical. Junior year is spent designing the Plan, and the project is executed during senior year. "Everything culminates in the Plan," one junior said.

"Work *is* our extracurricular activity."

Though most find the academic experience "intense" and "wonderful," for others it can be a little overbearing. "It can definitely be too much for some people," a junior said. In general, though, students say they appreciate the unique structure because it creates a noncompetitive atmosphere, with the focus more on the "academic process." Some people transfer out, one sophomore said, because of the heavy workload, as they look for a college experience where the learning is "less individually driven."

An Intimate Community

The extremely small student body—there are only slightly over 300 students enrolled—makes for a unique collegiate social life. There are rarely huge on-campus parties, and there are no frats or sororities to host gatherings. "Most of our parties are pretty mellow," one junior said. "People will dance; there will be a band playing; people will drink and smoke."

For some students, though, living in such isolation can be restricting. "It kind of feels like we're living in a bubble," a senior said. Brattleboro, the nearest town, does offer "cool coffeehouses and a co-op, which everyone loves because we're all hippies." Students also get off campus to participate in numerous outdoor activities in the surrounding Vermont mountains and lakes.

Despite the lack of prominent social activities, one junior said it was easy to find

ways to have fun. "You just have to make things happen," she said. "There's not the consistent night life that you might find at a large university, but there's usually a few big parties every year and things to do."

Students at Marlboro tend to be of a certain mold. Most students hail from the mid-Atlantic states and New England. A senior summed up the typical Marlboro student: "We tend to be white, of a similar socioeconomic category, and—in general—people who didn't fit in during high school." The small community also means that everyone knows everyone's business. "You can't really avoid the gossip," one freshman said.

Dorms, "Cottages," and a Barn-Turned-Building

The dorms that house Marlboro students reflect the intimate feel of the campus. The dorms are "really small," one senior said—each of the nine on-campus residence halls houses roughly 12 to 30 students, with roughly 80 percent of students living on campus. In general, the rooms are large, though some of the rooms are arranged in an unusual fashion—some freshmen complained about having to live in triples.

While housing is guaranteed for freshmen, it is not guaranteed for the next three years. Typically, 50 or so students (usually sophomores) are forced to live off campus each year. The off-campus dormitories—only a quarter-mile away from central campus—offer an appealing option due to their intimate feel (students described them as "little cottages"). Other students choose to live in Brattleboro in an apartment. One senior who lives in Brattleboro said she enjoys the change of pace after living on the close-knit Marlboro campus for three years: "There's a huge art and music scene."

There are residential advisers in every dorm, though they do not often take on the disciplinarian role. "No one is policing you," a sophomore said. Instead, RAs serve as resources for students and are able to offer advice and answers.

In general, the campus itself is "pretty rustic." A junior said, "The landscape is definitely really nice with all the white buildings, though the architecture could use some work." The on-campus dorms—each built in a slightly different era—are marked by a variety of architecture styles. The main classroom building is a converted barn, and the campus center—marked by its huge wooden rafters—was designed by a student for his Plan.

Food Complaints, Pride, and Broomball

One thing that all Marlboro students seem to agree on is the unappealing food on campus. There is one dining hall on campus and one basic meal plan for all students. A "big issue on campus" according to one junior, the food is a constant source of consternation for students. "There is just no selection whatsoever," one junior said. Though some students said the food was passable and not as bad as it was made out to be, many students have taken to creating their own food options. Many students said the lack of vegetarian and vegan options forced even the most devout vegetarians to start eating meat again; vegetarians currently have the option of filling out forms to request chicken or fish.

In general, as one junior put it, "extracurriculars don't really exist" at Marlboro. Unlike at other schools, where there are certain clubs that exist from year to year, students at Marlboro start up new clubs each year based on interests, which may fizzle and change at any given point in the year. "You can make happen pretty much whatever you want here," one senior said.

"Pride"—the campus shorthand for the Gay-Straight Alliance—is considered the most prominent on-campus organization. Music ensembles tend to attract a fair number of students as well. Many students also join committees to help plan events and deal with other Marlboro-related issues.

While there are no official sports teams, the club soccer team is a source of school pride, as the student body often comes out to support the soccer squad. Frisbee and fencing are other popular sports. The Outdoor Program also plans many trips and excursions every year. Every winter, the whole school participates in a "broomball" tournament—a kind of makeshift hockey game—on the frozen pond on campus, at which school spirit and enthusiasm is often at its highest.

Marlboro College certainly stands out from the endless list of colleges because of its small size and intense academic atmosphere. Though some students said it becomes suffocating and small at times, most students appreciate the closeness of the campus and the bonds they are able to form with faculty. As one student put it, "A typical Marlboro student is one who is interested in his or her education and wants to play a role in it."— *Josh Duboff*

FYI

If you come to Marlboro, you'd better bring "a winter coat, motivation, and a stick of deodorant."
What is the typical weekend schedule? "Eat brunch, read a few books, go to the pond/sledding, eat dinner, read more, party, dance, listen to music, have some good conversations, go to bed."
If I could change one thing about Marlboro, I'd "give the school a lot more money."
The three things every student should do before graduating from Marlboro are "play broomball, skinny-dip in South Pond, get to know each other well."

Middlebury College

Address: The Emma Willard House, Middlebury, VA 05753-6002
Phone: 802-443-3000
E-mail address: admissions@middlebury.edu
Web site URL: www.middlebury.edu
Year Founded: 1800
Private or Public: Private
Religious Affiliation: None
Location: Suburban
Number of Applicants: 7,823
Percent Accepted: 17%
Percent Accepted who enroll: 44%
Number Entering: 576
Number of Transfers Accepted each Year: Unreported
Middle 50% SAT range: M: 640–740, CR: 630–740, Wr: 640–740
Middle 50% ACT range: 29–33
Early admission program EA/ED/None: ED

Percentage accepted through EA or ED: 27%
EA and ED deadline: 1-Nov
Regular Deadline: 1-Jan
Application Fee: $65
Full time Undergraduate enrollment: 2,422
Total enrollment: 2,422
Percent Male: 50%
Percent Female: 50%
Total Percent Minority or Unreported: 41%
Percent African-American: 5%
Percent Asian/Pacific Islander: 10%
Percent Hispanic: 7%
Percent Native-American: 1%
Percent International: 12%
Percent in-state/out of state: 5%/95%
Percent from Public HS: 52%
Retention Rate: 95%
Graduation Rate 4-year: 88%

Graduation Rate 6-year: 92%
Percent Undergraduates in On-campus housing: 97%
Number of official organized extracurricular organizations: 100
3 Most popular majors: Economics, English, Psychology
Student/Faculty ratio: 9:1
Average Class Size: 16
Percent of students going to grad school: Unreported
Tuition and Fees: $49,210
In-State Tuition and Fees if different: No difference
Cost for Room and Board: Included
Percent receiving financial aid out of those who apply, first year: 48%
Percent receiving financial aid among all students: 79%

Indoors and outdoors, in and out of class, Middlebury College offers quirky, fun, and meaningful programs for students willing to take advantage of all that is available on this cozy yet exuberant campus. While the natural beauty of the surrounding Green Mountains and the frigid and pretty Vermont environment humbles the self-proclaimed "outdoorsy-type" of student, the focus and rigor of the academic curriculum similarly humbles students who find themselves at home in the classroom – and the zany thing about Middlebury is that these two categories of students are not mutually exclusive.

Parlez-vous Français?

Breadth and depth are the cornerstones of academics at Middlebury. While Middlebury does not stipulate a core curriculum, it nevertheless ensures its students obtain wide academic exposure through its distributional requirements. Students must take courses in seven out of eight academic categories: literature, the arts, philosophical and religious studies, historical studies, physical and life sciences, deductive reasoning and analytical processes, social analysis, and foreign language. Middlebury also emphasizes an international perspective; to that end, it requires students to take courses in four categories as part of a cultures and civilizations requirement: one in Africa, Asian, or Latin American culture, one comparing cultures and civilizations, one in European culture, and one in North American culture. A freshman seminar and a writing course are also required to graduate. "All the requirements seem daunting at first, but by the time you're finishing up you wish you could take more," a senior admitted. Another senior added, however, that she wished at times she hadn't needed to take so many distributional courses, because it prevented her from taking more interesting courses.

As far as majors go, economics, political science and English are most popular on campus, with psychology and environmental studies not far behind. "It's a fairly typical spread of majors," one student reported, "but everyone takes at least a couple of cool courses completely unrelated to their major." And around 15% of students are double majors; "a lot of people come to Middlebury wanting to do everything; some keep it up all four years, but others decide a double major is not for them," one recent double majoring graduate said.

> "All the requirements seem daunting at first, but by the time you're finishing up you wish you could take more."

Middlebury's course offerings are as strong and wide as you would expect, with two particular strengths that students point to. The first are their language classes; the college boasts a world-renowned language program that encourages study abroad and intensive immersion programs. The other are courses available during "J-term," a one month interim period between the fall and spring semesters during which students take one course, which may range from "Chinese Painting" to "Combinatorial Games and Puzzles."

Students enjoy a "love-hate relationship" with their courses; "most are fairly demanding, but nearly all are interesting in one way or another," according to one student. Class sizes vary depending on subject, with large introductory lectures filled with 70 or more students; over 40 percent of courses, however, have between six and 15 students. These small class sizes are ideal for interacting with professors, who, "for the most part, are sage and know how to convey their material in unique ways." Professors understand the demands placed on students, and most set a "reasonable" amount of work. But this does not preclude some students from feeling overwhelmed, particularly in courses where reading can "seriously accumulate, to the point that you can't keep up with it all," reported a junior pursuing an English major. Still, students agreed that "the vast majority of students love their academic experience at Middlebury, despite the rough moments that occasionally pop up."

Something in Common[s]
The core of residential life at Middlebury lies in its "commons" system, which creates communities in and out of the classroom by assigning students enrolled in a particular freshman seminar to live in the same commons, or dorm building. The five commons compete against each other in intramural sports, and many students identify strongly with their smaller community. Others point to the disparity between colleges; "there's a marked difference between the quality of housing in some of the commons," one student reported. All commons have residential buildings, a dining hall, and host various speakers and events throughout the year. Students can, for the most part, readily change commons and their corresponding housing, though many students find their closest friends in their assigned commons and hence have no desire to change. One student said, "I think of my commons as my family unit—it's my home, I wouldn't think of leaving it." Unsurprisingly, the majority of students live on-campus all four years.

While some students characterize Middlebury as a "resort—Club Midd" for its excellent overall accommodations, housing does tend to vary around campus. And the quality of housing increases with seniority, by most reports; freshman tend to get basic singles and suites while seniors live in spacious apartment-like suites, complete with common rooms and kitchens. "If I were to choose between my suite and those of all my friends at other colleges around the country, I'd pick my suite any day of the week, and I'm sure my friends would too," one junior said.

It is not only housing that is described in superlative terms by Middlebury students; the food, often locally produced, is too. Students praise the basic meal plan, which allows them unlimited access to dining halls. Two freshmen credited the plan for the "freshman 15" they have both put on. Another student said the staff was particularly attentive to students' cravings; she cited an example of her best friend pointing out the lack of a certain food in the dining hall to the chef, who cooked it the very next day. Of course, the nature of dining halls situated within commons means that dinner-table conversations can be just as interesting as the food that is actually on the dinner table itself.

Beyond campus, good food is in abundance. Students particularly appreciate the freshness and taste of produce available in rural Vermont. Not so appreciated, however, is the dearth of options to satisfy late night pangs of hunger, with staples like pizza and Chinese not readily available.

If none of the other food options takes your fancy, you can always turn to Vermont's beloved Ben and Jerry's ice cream!

At the extremes

If Middlebury students are studying hard during the day, you can expect many will be hard at work in the myriad extracurricular organizations in the evenings, and drinking hard on the weekends. "Students take things to the extreme, whatever it is they happen to be doing," said one student. And they do things in characteristically quirky style.

Take social life, for instance. Rather than the frats that dominate many other college campuses, Middlebury has social houses, coed groups of students who throw parties, and a number of local bars frequented by upperclassmen. More zany, however, are the themed dance parties that routinely take place; themes range from contra dance parties, in which couples folk dance in two facing lines of indefinite length, to neon dance parties. More routine is the prevalence of alcohol, which students say is big on campus, whether at small dorm parties or larger parties.

Because of the small campus, there are invariably familiar faces that pop up at every party. Students consider this a mixed blessing. "It's awesome that no matter where you go on the weekend, you'll know someone, but on the other hand, it can get a bit awkward depending on the person and situation," one student said.

Of course, there are alcohol-free alternatives aplenty to fill up your free time, with concerts, movies, and other activities organized throughout the term. According to one student, "there's never a free moment; even when you don't have class and aren't doing some extracurricular, there's always stuff going on around campus."

Extracurricular activities are likewise extremely varied. The proactive student can participate in a comprehensive array of organizations, ranging from the Big Sky Society, celebrating the state of Montana, to Bobolinks, a coed a capella group. One student who has founded his own club said, "If there is no club wacky or adventurous enough to satisfy your tastes, you can simply start one up!" Like at any other college, there are varying levels of commitment; some people choose to prioritize studies over other activities, while others spend the majority of their time with extracurricular clubs.

As for the people that make up these organizations, the self-proclaimed "Midd Kids," they are a motley bunch, as would be expected of an unconventional college like Middlebury. "There is no typical student here," one student offered, but went on to describe a good number of students as extroverted and very much suited to the outdoors. Another student added that there was definitely a "hippie streak" among students at Middlebury, with the rural setting and mix of interesting people augmenting the already open-minded class.

Though Middlebury prides itself on its international student body—students can name friends from all over the world—some are less satisfied by the diversity on campus. "It seems outwardly that we're very diverse, but when you get here, you realize students largely conform to several, predominantly middle-to-upper class stereotypes," one junior commented.

A Community Too Cozy?

At the heart of the Middlebury experience is the intimate community, both of scholars and of friends. This is largely due to the rural setting of the college, with little reason to go off campus save skiing or grocery shopping, and a secure, cozy environment almost free from criminal danger and theft. The same sense of security translates into the Honor Code that students hold dear, which manifests itself in professor-free exams. According to one student, "everybody is bound to each other, so we respect each other and keep each other in check." Even in terms of social life, there is a "symbiotic" relationship between people, with everyone invariably going to each other's events.

Shared values permeate other areas of student life too, with most students holding liberal views and caring for the natural environment that surrounds them. "It can seem quite homogenous, but I guess that's what happens when people are so close and converse together all the time," one student said. Still, that sense of community is what so many Middlebury students first call to mind when they think of their college, and will hold dear long after they leave. "It really is an amazing place – I think every time I see the sun rise over the mountains of all those before me and with me who see the same sight, who are lucky to be part of that same beautiful beginning."—*James Lu*

University of Vermont

Address: South Prospect Street, Burlington, VT 05405-0160
Phone: 802-656-3131
E-mail address: admissions@uvm.edu
Web site URL: www.uvm.edu
Year Founded: 1791
Private or Public: Public
Religious Affiliation: None
Location: Suburban
Number of Applicants: 22,365
Percent Accepted: 70%
Percent Accepted who enroll: 15%
Number Entering: 2,450
Number of Transfers Accepted each Year: 741
Middle 50% SAT range: M: 550–650, CR: 540–640, Wr: 540–640
Middle 50% ACT range: 23–28
Early admission program EA/ED/None: EA
Percentage accepted through EA or ED: 70%

EA and ED deadline: 1-Nov
Regular Deadline: 15-Jan
Application Fee: $45
Full time Undergraduate enrollment: 10,504
Total enrollment: 11,824
Percent Male: 45%
Percent Female: 55%
Total Percent Minority or Unreported: 12%
Percent African-American: 1%
Percent Asian/Pacific Islander: 2%
Percent Hispanic: 4%
Percent Native-American: <1%
Percent International: 1%
Percent in-state/out of state: 26%/74%
Percent from Public HS: Unreported
Retention Rate: 86%
Graduation Rate 4-year: 54%
Graduation Rate 6-year: 69%

Percent Undergraduates in On-campus housing: 54%
Number of official organized extracurricular organizations: 200
3 Most popular majors: Social Sciences, Business/Marketing, Education
Student/Faculty ratio: Unreported
Average Class Size: 19
Percent of students going to grad school: Unreported
Tuition and Fees: $29,682
In-State Tuition and Fees if different: $12,844
Cost for Room and Board: $8,534
Percent receiving financial aid out of those who apply, first year: 76%
Percent receiving financial aid among all students: 55%

W hy is University of Vermont abbreviated UVM? It actually comes from its Latin name, *Universitas Viridis Montis*, which means "University of the Green Mountains." Founded in 1791, the same year Vermont became a state, the University of Vermont lives up to its Latin name, boasting both natural beauty and an environmental focus. With construction of modern suite-based residence halls, a new honors college, and the recent switch to dry dorms, UVM is shedding some of its party image in hopes of emphasizing its appealing academics and location.

ABCs the UVM Way

Undergraduate academics at UVM are broken down into seven different colleges. While each major belongs to a specific college, every student is required to fulfill one three-credit Race and Racism in the U.S. and one Human and Societal Diversity requirement, as well as complete various education requirements in the other colleges, including two semesters of physical education. Luckily breaking a sweat isn't hard to do in Vermont. UVM owns a few natural areas like Mount Mansfield, which it uses for teaching, recreation, and physical education classes.

Because of its close proximity to Canada (a one-hour drive to the border), UVM offers a Canadian Studies major. From anthropology to art history, English to business administration, UVM gives students a unique opportunity to learn about the U.S.A.'s neighbor to the north. It even offers the class Due North, which culminates in a weeklong field trip to Canada to watch a hockey game and visit the Parliament.

UVM offers an array of unique classes like the History of Rock and Roll; The Role of Drugs in Society; Films and Novels of Stephen King; Tolkien's Hobbits; and Pirates, Tacks, and Seadogs. The two classes known for being easy are Introduction to English and Personal Health. But be forewarned: With all the varying courses UVM offers, most students wake up at 6 a.m. on registration day to get into the section they want. However, if students really want to get into a particular class or section, they can petition the professor for an override. Following the prevalent Vermont attitude, professors are required to let in students if the class is required for their major, but they let in almost all students who petition regardless of reason.

Classes tend to be on the rather large side in the beginning of freshman year and get smaller as students progress through their undergraduate careers. Introduction to Psychology has about 200 students, while most introductory classes range from 60 to 100. Upperclassman classes hover around 40 to 60 students, although most seniors will take two or three seminars, which are capped at 20. The main exception is with languages. All foreign language classes are kept small, at around 20 people. All classes are taught by professors, though sections and labs are taught by TAs. "I have had great experiences with TAs," one student said. "I have never had trouble communicating or finding times to meet outside of class with mine." Some professors, like Brookes Cowan, who teaches Introduction to Sociology, are known for being laid-back. Professor Cowan lives in the student off-campus area and interacts very comfortably with her students. "Teachers are very professional, but they're not stuffy, they're very down to earth and very understanding. They understand if something is late due to a family function."

For those seeking an academically rigorous course load, the new Honors Program offers about 400 students such an opportunity. Honors Program students still belong to one of the seven academic colleges, but one class every semester is an honors program seminar of no more than 20 people. All freshmen in the program must take the Making Ethical Choices, Personal, Public, and Professional seminar, but after their first year, they are allowed to choose their seminars. Along with the cohesion of living together in a Residency under a Dean in the new University Heights Complex, the Honors Program offers students special cocurricular and extracurricular opportunities, like field trips to Boston and Montreal, as well as small perks like early registration, extended library borrowing privileges, and discounted tickets to performing arts events.

New Campus Living

UVM just recently finished building new residential halls on Athletic Campus. These residential halls are all LEED certified, which is the highest environmentally sustainable construction certification a building can receive. All freshmen and sophomores are required to live on campus, and then are free to move off as juniors and seniors. Even so, housing is now guaranteed for all four years.

Campus dorms cluster in three places— North Campus, Athletic Campus, and Redstone Campus—although there are a few dorm buildings on Central Campus, as well. North Campus is where most of the "shoebox" dorms are. Redstone Campus is the southeast campus, named after the Redstone Residential buildings. Athletic Campus, the east campus, is noted for its close proximity to the Patrick Gymnasium and is home to the recently constructed new University Heights residential halls and the Living and Learning Buildings. Living and Learning (L&L) are theme dorms, either by suite or by floor. Some examples of themes range from the outdoor floor to the live music floor to the community service floor.

Although UVM is trying to make its dorms a new home away from home for students, most students view them as "a place where you live, not your home." Still, most students agree that they have made some of their most lasting friendships through the dorms.

Meal plans at UVM come in many variations, with different amounts of points and blocks. Points are essentially dollars that you can use at à la carte cafés on campus, while blocks are swipes you use at one of the two all-you-can-eat dining halls that serve standard fare. While the points cafés are really well liked, points can also be used to order pizza from Domino's and Pizza Hut any time of the day and late night, though most off-campus places take Cat Scratch, the UVM student debit account, instead. If students get tired of eating on campus, popular restaurants and cafés in Burlington include Three Tomatoes, Mountaintop Brew, American Flatbread, and Red Onion Sandwich. Fitting in with the hippie image of UVM, most eateries are organic with many vegetarian options, but "are absolutely delicious and cheap!"

Residential Advisors (RAs) may be as young as sophomores and as old as graduate students, and how strict your RA may be depends on who your RA is. However, one student reported that "all RAs still adequately enforce the rules." UVM is not exactly a dry campus (the new Davis Student Center will have a pub), but all residence halls are alcohol-free: "With respect to that rule, RAs make almost no exception." Response to the dry dorm rule has been mixed, because most students drink off campus at house parties and bars. However, "strict enforcement of rules by the administration and the police has diminished our reputation as a party school," one student said. There has been some countereffect such that students have been turning to drugs in dorms as opposed to alcohol. While the person who phones in a drunken friend receives amnesty, anyone found drunk and underage will receive medical attention but will also have to attend counseling, perform community service, and pay a fine after recovery.

Skis, Views and Booze

Burlington is a small, quaint city that feels like a town. With a population of about 42,000, and home to three colleges, Burlington is a true college town. "Almost all stores are mom and pop stores, and with UVM on the hill, and Burlington downtown by the shore of Lake Champlain, it's the most beautiful place to live." The center of downtown Burlington is Church Street, a cobblestone-paved, pedestrian-only eight square blocks, at the end of which sits a majestic old church.

Off-campus living in junior/senior years "is sort of an informal agreement . . . it is ten times cheaper and a different scene." While there are a few frats and sororities at UVM, even some that are community service-based, different social groups tend to mingle and mix off campus at house parties or at bars. The five to six blocks between campus and downtown are where almost all upperclassmen live, and with all of it leading downhill to

downtown and Lake Champlain, there is no bad view. Looking across Lake Champlain, students can see the Adirondack Mountains in New York State. Popular sports bars and pubs are RJs, What Ale's You, and Nectars. Auggies on Tuesday nights serves Hurricanes, massive alcohol drinks, for four dollars, making Auggies the most popular place for college students to beat the midweek blues. The main dance club is Rasputin's, but newly opened club Plan B is gaining popularity, though mainly for an older crowd. Burlington's live music scene is always an option, as well as its many performing arts events for those seeking a different night out.

> "We all consciously chose this school. We didn't come here because we thought it was the best thing to do, it was what we were supposed to do next, or because we couldn't go somewhere else."

Of course, if arts are not your definition of a night out, UVM is part of Division I athletics and "everyone attends the [men's] hockey games," one student said. All sporting event tickets are free to students, but since there are no season tickets available, students must wait in line for tickets to each game. Also highly attended are men's and women's basketball games. UVM has not had a football team since 1974, "presumably to fund our other sports instead." Rather, rugby football remains a popular club sport. But for less competitive players, the big intramural sport is broomball. Over 100 teams sign up for broomball every year, and students rave that "it's so much fun!"

Other popular extracurriculars include Outdoor Club, Skiing and Snowboarding Club, and Volunteers in Action, the umbrella organization for most community service and social justice organizations that sponsors the Alternative Spring Break Trip every year, where groups of ten students go on ten different trips, nine domestic and one abroad, to do community service. The Outdoor Club sponsors really cheap weekend trips every year that are publicized to all students via e-mails. And thanks to the proximity of the many great skiing locations and the discount provided by the club, the Skiing and Snowboarding Club is always a popular activity to join.

A Different Diversity

"What we lack in racial and ethnic diversity, we make up for in a different type of diversity," a senior said. Vermont is the second-whitest state, so racial diversity at UVM is not surprisingly lacking. However students come from all different sorts of socioeconomic classes. Even though the University of Vermont is a public university, the majority of its students—74 percent, as a matter of fact—come from out of state. This is in part due to Vermont's small population, but it is also due to UVM's initial status as a private university, which was only changed in 1865. The result is that both UVM's in-state and out-of-state tuitions fall somewhere between private and public universities.

UVM students still have a liberal and environmental bent, living up to some degree to its "tree hugger" stereotype. "Everyone buys local dairy and veggies," one student explained, while another student added that "there are recycling bins everywhere, and if you don't recycle, anyone on the street would stop to correct you." That's just the Vermont attitude toward life and nature. "That's what makes UVM special," one student said. "We all consciously chose this school. We didn't come here because we thought it was the best thing to do, it was what we were supposed to do next, or because we couldn't go somewhere else. It was because this was the University of *Vermont*."—*Jesse Dong*

FYI
If you come to UVM, you'd better bring "environmental conscience."
What is the typical weekend schedule? "Attend a hockey game Friday night, go hiking or skiing Saturday afternoon, party with friends off campus Saturday night, and spend all of Sunday doing homework."
If I could change one thing about UVM, I'd "make the residences more of a home."
Three things every student should do before graduating from UVM are: "Go to the top of Mt. Mansfield, take part in the naked bike ride, and participate in the polar bear jump."

Virginia

College of William and Mary

Address: PO Box 8795
   Williamsburg, VA
   23187-8795
Phone: 757-221-4223
E-mail address:
   admission@wm.edu
Web site URL: www.wm.edu
Year Founded: 1693
Private or Public: Public
Religious Affiliation: None
Location: Suburban
Number of Applicants:
   11,636
Percent Accepted: 34%
Percent Accepted who
   enroll: 35%
Number Entering: 1,386
Number of Transfers
   Accepted each Year: 356
Middle 50% SAT range: M:
   620–710, CR: 630–730,
   Wr: 610–720
Middle 50% ACT range:
   27–32
Early admission program
   EA/ED/None: ED

Percentage accepted
   through EA or ED: 50%
EA and ED deadline: 1-Nov
Regular Deadline: 1-Jan
Application Fee: $60
Full time Undergraduate
   enrollment: 5,850
Total enrollment: 7,300
Percent Male: 45%
Percent Female: 55%
Total Percent Minority or
   Unreported: 23%
Percent African-American:
   7%
Percent Asian/Pacific
   Islander: 8%
Percent Hispanic: 8%
Percent Native-American:
   1%
Percent International: 2%
Percent in-state/out of
   state: 59%/41%
Percent from Public HS:
   Unreported
Retention Rate: 94%
Graduation Rate 4-year: 90%

Graduation Rate 6-year:
   Unreported
Percent Undergraduates in
   On-campus housing: 67%
Number of official organized
   extracurricular
   organizations: 378
3 Most popular majors:
   Business Administration,
   Psychology, Government
Student/Faculty ratio:
   11:1
Average Class Size: 22
Percent of students going to
   grad school: Unreported
Tuition and Fees: $29,116
In-State Tuition and Fees if
   different: $10,246
Cost for Room and Board:
   $8,030
Percent receiving financial
   aid out of those who apply,
   first year: 82%
Percent receiving financial
   aid among all students:
   58%

The College of William and Mary, founded in 1693, is the second-oldest university in the United States. As its tour guides are quick to tell you, it was the college that Thomas Jefferson attended, the college where George Washington was chancellor, and the college that gave birth to the Phi Beta Kappa society in 1776. Yet William and Mary isn't all about tri-corner hats and resting on past laurels, despite its location in touristy Colonial Williamsburg. What distinguishes William and Mary nowadays, aside from having Sandra Day O'Connor as its chancellor, is its reputation for academic excellence. *U.S. News & World Report* ranked it first among public universities for undergraduate teaching. Results like that have many students here

proudly embracing their label of being a "public Ivy." But William and Mary isn't just about staying locked in the library. The school has a beautiful campus, a successful football team, and serious cash flow from recent donations, donations that are funding a number of renovations and new buildings all around campus.

A Public Ivy

Most students agree that academics take precedence. According to one student, "At William and Mary, it's cool to be smart. People here are a different kind of intelligent." Students must complete 120 credits to graduate, and the average course counts for three or four credits. In addition, students must also fulfill the GERs, or General

Education Requirements, which include one course in mathematics and quantitative reasoning; two courses in the natural sciences; two courses in the social sciences; three courses in world cultures and history; one course in literature or art history; two credits in creative or performing arts; and one course in philosophical, religious, or social thought. Classes at W&M vary in size but all generally fall into one of three categories. The largest are introductory lectures with 100 to 250 people, and the smallest are seminars capped at 15, with classes of 25 to 35 people in between. All freshmen are required to take a freshman seminar; these are generally praised. Students register by class year in a relatively painless process.

William and Mary also rewards its incoming overachievers (generally the top 7 percent of each class) with its James Monroe Scholar Program. In addition to having one of the best dorms on campus (Monroe Hall) reserved exclusively for freshman Monroe Scholars, they get first pick in freshman seminars, have a chance to apply for a $1,000 grant for the summer after freshman year, and are guaranteed $3,000 for an independent project the summer after their sophomore or junior years. Of him to whom much is given, however, much is expected. In an already intense academic environment, the Monroes feel the pressure even more than most.

Among the 50 or so concentrations offered at William and Mary, there is the usual mix of easy and difficult majors. Some of the usual suspects like geology, psychology, and anthropology are popular with the less academically motivated crowd, while biology, chemistry, physics, and computer science are some of the hardest, and most well taught, majors. For those interested in economics, W&M offers a business major affiliated with its business school. For all their stellar reputation, one student believes W&M's academics are actually underrated. "I don't think people are quite aware of how good they are," he explained. Perhaps part of what makes the academics so good is that, for the most part, classes are taught by full professors. In four years, one senior could recall having been taught by a TA only once. Students also give the professors rave reviews, calling them approachable, interested, and "brilliant."

Partying at a Deli?

Students bring the same passion to social activities as they do to their classes. "The same people who hide out in Swem all week

and study, party on the weekends (and during the week)." So what do William and Mary students do when they're not in the newly renovated library? Options abound. Student organizations, which number over 400, are popular, and most people belong to at least one or two clubs: "In all honesty I can say that W&M is where the kids who were involved in high school come to be even more involved in college." There are numerous performing arts and a cappella groups; several publications like the *DoG Street Journal* (referencing Duke of Gloucester Street, the main drag for students and locals) and the *Flat Hat*, W&M's weekly student newspaper; a number of Christian groups; and a whole host of others, from the chess club to the Russian club. Many students' social lives revolve around their organizations, as many clubs sponsor a number of parties and formals. Athletics, of course, play a big part in school life, as was especially the case a few years ago, when the Tribe football team made it all the way to the NCAA I-AA semifinals. Stands were more crowded than they had been in years, and Tribe Pride promises to stay inflated for years to come.

Greek organizations play a large role in the campus social scene as well. According to the W&M administration, 25 percent of undergrads are involved in Greek life, but according to one frat brother, the majority of those students belong to exclusive social service frats, evidence of W&M's passion for volunteerism. "Students praise volunteerism and community service as cool things to do." The school boasts the largest chapter in the country of Alpha Phi Omega and the largest collegiate service fraternity, and the governor recently visited campus to commend W&M for its commitment to service.

The percentage of people who live in traditional party-oriented frat houses is much smaller, and continues to shrink as frats lose their charters or housing by violating alcohol or other policies. The school has attempted to crack down on underage drinking in recent years, but students still manage to circumvent the system. Although the school requires that fraternity parties serving alcohol receive advance approval from the administration, "people can and do drink at the frats." Pregaming in dorm rooms is also popular among underclassmen.

For upperclassmen, off-campus parties, held by clubs, sports teams, or even Greek members living off campus, are popular. Because of regulations, there are no bars near

W&M, but several so-called "delis" in the area reportedly serve the same purpose. In recent years, the delis have started to card more strictly, but for the persistent, alcohol is still available. Since "the most popular of the delis tends to rotate throughout the year," the reputations tend to depend on who and when you ask. The "nicest" of these delis is the Green Leafe, which has Mug Night every Sunday, when you can bring in a mug and they'll fill it with beer for a small price. College Delly, now under new ownership, is also popular and, last spring, Paul's was "the place to go." Aside from the delis, however, students report that there really isn't much off-campus nightlife, though there's always plenty to do on campus. In addition to the party scene, more toned-down events include forums with a host of visiting speakers: "In my years at the College I've seen Ralph Nader and Jon Stewart (he's an alum of ours), and even Kofi Annan and Supreme Court Justice Antonin Scalia."

Multinational Neighbors

In terms of housing, many students stay on campus all four years; as one student said, "I think people stay living on campus because it's very convenient and we have a really tight community." The dorms, which, with a few exceptions, are all coed, are generally pretty nice. Yates, Monroe, and Barret may be a little better than average, and Jamestown North and South are so far away that people dread getting placed there, but the halls are actually in decent shape. The housing system revolves around a lottery that most agree "ends up being pretty fair." Freshman housing is generally pretty good, and friends made in freshman halls often end up being friends for all four years. For those into foreign languages, W&M offers the opportunity to live in houses geared toward a specific language, whether it be Russian, Spanish, or French. Each house has a tutor from one of the countries where the language is spoken and hosts various cultural events. The language houses provide a warm, tight-knit community.

Dining services at William and Mary were significantly better before a budget crisis a few years ago led to cutbacks in quality. The university is, however, trying to remedy this: the main dining hall, "the Caf," recently received a facelift, with improvements including "amazing" food and an Internet café. Students can still find other good-quality offerings around, such as the daily-made sushi, which one student describes as "not

sketchy. It's really good." When the options feel limited, though, students can take a walk around town and find plenty of ways to spice up their dining. Local restaurants like the Fat Canary, Aromas, Trellis, and the Cheese Shop receive good ratings, though the ones in the tourist part of colonial Williamsburg are pretty pricey. There are also two convenience stores open 24-7 in Williamsburg, including the Wawa, without which "students would go crazy."

What really sets William and Mary apart from most colleges, in the opinion of several students, is the sheer beauty of its campus. When these students talk about how spectacular their campus looks, they don't just mean the sites that every William and Mary tour guide points out: the colonial architecture of Old Campus, the famous Sunken Gardens, or even the Crim Dell pond with its storied bridge. (Supposedly, any couple who kisses on the bridge has to get married unless one of them throws the other one off.) These students mean places that are far less touristy, like the amphitheater at Lake Matoaka, which a couple of students said was the most beautiful place they had ever been in their lives.

> **"At William and Mary, it's cool to be smart. People here are a different kind of intelligent."**

The students at William and Mary are aware of its history and traditions. As one student said, "We all know that the Wren Building is the oldest academic building in the country still in use, almost all of us can recite the great history of our college, and almost all of us know the chorus to the alma mater. Our big tradition events such as the Yule Log and Convocation Ceremonies are incredibly crowded and bring us together."

One of the most interesting traditions at W&M is the Triathlon: swimming the Crim Dell pond, streaking the length of the Sunken Gardens, and jumping the Governor's Mansion wall to complete the garden maze inside, all in the same night. True triathletes complete the entire thing nude. It is not uncommon to see people streaking the Sunken Gardens on a typical weekend in the wee hours of the morning. "Some students are so gung-ho as to complete the triathlon not once but many times!"

So in the end, what does William and Mary have to offer? It has a beautiful campus, and thanks to a number of donations it is also poised to complete a number of major renovations. People here are generally pretty studious folks, with a grasp on tradition. If you're looking for a gorgeous place to live and an Ivy League–level education for a public school price, the College of William and Mary is the place for you.—*Laura Sullivan*

FYI
If you come to William and Mary, you'd better bring "a camera."
What's the typical weekend schedule? "Friday: UCAB event/party at a frat; Sat.: sleep in, study some, football game, or other athletic event, dance party; Sun.: study day/stay in."
If I could change one thing about William and Mary, it would be "the food; on-campus food leaves much to be desired, but that's why God created Wawa."
Three things that every student at William and Mary should do before graduation are "camp out and sleep under the stars in the Sunken Gardens (beware of streakers, Matoaka Ampitheater may be a safer bet), take a class in the Wren Building, and complete the triathlon."

George Mason University

Address: 4400 University Drive, Fairfax, VA 22030	**Percentage accepted through EA or ED:** 18%	**Graduation Rate 6-year:** 59%
Phone: 703-993-2400	**EA and ED deadline:** 1-Nov	**Percent Undergraduates in On-campus housing:** 25%
E-mail address: admissions@gmu.edu	**Regular Deadline:** 15-Jan	**Number of official organized extracurricular**
Web site URL: www.gmu.edu	**Application Fee:** $70	**organizations:** 250
Year Founded: 1972	**Full time Undergraduate enrollment:** 18,589	**3 Most popular majors:**
Private or Public: Public	**Total enrollment:** 29,803	Accounting, Political
Religious Affiliation: None	**Percent Male:** 47%	Science, Speech and
Location: Urban	**Percent Female:** 53%	Rhetorical Studies
Number of Applicants: 12,943	**Total Percent Minority or Unreported:** 57%	**Student/Faculty ratio:** 15:1
Percent Accepted: 63%	**Percent African-American:** 7%	**Average Class Size:** 23
Percent Accepted who enroll: 31%	**Percent Asian/Pacific Islander:** 16%	**Percent of students going to grad school:** Unreported
Number Entering: 2,497	**Percent Hispanic:** 6%	**Tuition and Fees:** $22,476
Number of Transfers Accepted each Year: 4,068	**Percent Native-American:** <1%	**In-State Tuition and Fees if different:** $7,512
Middle 50% SAT range: M: 520–610, **CR:** 500–600, **Wr:** Unreported	**Percent International:** 4% **Percent in-state/out of state:** 90%/10%	**Cost for Room and Board:** $7,360 **Percent receiving financial aid out of those who apply,**
Middle 50% ACT range: 22–26	**Percent from Public HS:** 85%	**first year:** 59%
Early admission program EA/ED/None: EA	**Retention Rate:** 84% **Graduation Rate 4-year:** 41%	**Percent receiving financial aid among all students:** 34%

Although George Mason University was established less than forty years ago, it offers something for everyone. Not only does GMU offer unique classes such as African Dance, the educational experience is also distinguished by its easily accessible world class professors. Overall, George Mason features a diverse student population, which is reflected in the myriad extracurricular clubs on campus. Last but not least, having the nation's capital less than an hour away opens the door to wide assortments of internship opportunities for students looking to further pursue their interest.

Location, Location, Location

George Mason has always prided itself in its proximity to Washington, D.C. Its convenient location attracts local students as well as students from all over nation and world. Having D.C. just a metro ride away means not only an abundance of internship opportunities unavailable anywhere else but also exciting off-campus excursions. If students are interested in politics, criminal justice or working government agencies, Capitol Hill and FBI Headquarters etc. are all nearby, making internship a lot easier. On weekends, many students from neighboring cities commute home to spend time with friends or family. Unfortunately, since a large portion of students stream into surrounding cities, the campus is not as lively as others where all the students stay on campus. Nevertheless, "If you get the chance to stay on the weekend, there is always something to do whether it's on or off campus," said one freshman.

While D.C. offers city excitement, the campus has its own social scene as well. Greek life is the more dominant social scene on campus with its constant stream of frat parties and sorority events. However, because George Mason is such a diverse campus, there are other prominent student organizations as well. Religious groups such as Catholic Campus Ministry or Campus Crusade for Christ are well known. The anime club is also popular and famous for its Halloween Party. While the variety in social scenes mirrors the diversity of campus, one thing that unites the diverse campus is Mason Madness, George Mason's version of March Madness. The Patriot Center, George Mason's stadium, offers students free tickets and consequently brings everyone together for home basketball games. They even have "fight cheers." According to one alum, when Mason was in the final 4 in 2006, "it was like the entire campus was one big family coming out to support each other."

Campus Life

Although many students choose to live in off campus apartments and even freshmen are not required to live on campus, many students enjoy dorm life. Freshman dorms are divided into three separate locations though the main one is "President's Park." First year students are usually assigned to singles, doubles, triples or quadruples. These dorm rooms are maintained by a janitorial staff who regularly cleans the shared bathrooms. Moreover, there are Residential Advisers (RAs) on every floor. Before rooming assignments are made, students take a quiz in order to be paired with an RA, who serves as a counselor and advisor. They are there not only to answer questions but also to plan bonding activities such as floor dinners. While they are not super strict with regards to rules, according to one student, they do take students' problems and concerns very seriously. After freshman year, students have the option of keeping their room, in which case they would not have to go through the housing lottery. Otherwise, students who decide to live on campus receive a lottery number according to the amount of academic credits they have accumulated to determine the order of choosing. When the student's turn comes, he/she has a slotted time to go online to select his/her room. On campus, sophomores, juniors and seniors usually live in apartment-style dorms that are complete with a kitchen.

But students who do not live in dorms with kitchens need not worry. At George Mason there is plenty of good food, from dining halls to chain restaurants. The newly opened Southside is a popular buffet styled dining hall where students pay a fee to eat all they want. The George W. Johnson Center is a campus hotspot because it has a plethora of food options from Chick-fil-a to a Chinese restaurant. On its other floors, there is also a computer lab, mail service, and a library, fulfilling all of a student's needs. According to one junior, "when I sit in the food court I feel like I'm at the center of college life." George Mason offers three different types of meal plans to cater to different eating habits. Block and Traditional allow for a fixed amount of meals per semester and per week respectively. There is also the Ultimate, which is unlimited. Besides meal swipes, students can also have Mason Money, which is money that is put on the student's Mason ID and can be used in most restaurants and cafes around campus.

Adventure Classes and Dance Time

Students are very satisfied with the selection of classes offered. If you're looking for more fun and adventurous classes like as Rock Climbing, Trap and Skeet Shooting, Snowboarding, Scuba Diving, and Coastal Kayaking, George Mason is the place for you. "Students rarely sign up for these classes because they require lab and equipment fees and don't meet any specific degree requirements," a senior reported. On the upside, he said they are fairly easy to get into, though he hasn't taken any of these classes himself.

Students seem to enjoy the dance classes offered at GMU. "The most fun class I've taken was Intro to Modern Dance," a senior said. She plans to take African Dance next semester. "Dance classes are fun and a way to get in a good workout," a recent grad who took tap dance recounted.

There are also interesting classes like Criminology or Semester at the Smithsonian where students meet at the National Zoo and work behind the scenes with scientists and zookeepers in the labs and exhibits.

Furthermore, Mason also offers classes like University 100, which helps students adjust from high school to university life and is mandatory for students living in the Living Learning Community (LLC).

> "Everyone at Mason was always very friendly and helpful. Whenever I had a problem or a question there was always someone willing to help or knew someone who could."

A senior mentioned that she particularly enjoyed the creative writing courses at Mason. "Most classes aren't hard to get into, as long as you sign up on time," another senior recounted.

Personal Attention

The advisors and professors are great resources for GMU students. Overall, students say that most of the faculty members are accessible through phone or email and respond relatively quickly. "Everyone at Mason was always very friendly and helpful," a recent grad. "Whenever I had a problem or a question there was always someone willing to help or knew someone who could." Sometimes teachers even allow one-on-one time with each student, for extra and more personal meetings with the teacher. "It really helps, especially if you really need extra time outside of class," a junior said. Since classes are usually fairly small, students are able to get some one-on-one time with the professors in class as well.

Some students interviewed praised the teachers as very easy to talk with, saying, "They know the struggles students go through and will work with you through your assign-

ments." However there were some mixed reviews. "A few professors will ignore student emails and avoid office hours," a freshman said. "Some are friendly, some are not, but you can find out before signing up for a class by checking ratemyprofessors.com or the teaching evaluations posted on the GMU website."

Students say they find there are many resources available for their academic needs. "At any time I could go into the math tutoring center or the writing center to get help with homework," a senior said. Students who need more help in other subjects can go to that department, which sends an email to all departmental majors who are interested in private tutoring.

Mason students have no complaints about early classes. They find that the classes are scheduled at nice times. "I've always had the opportunity to have great schedules," a senior said. A freshman reported, "The academics here are challenging, but easy to get through because of the professors always presenting help."

Out of the Classroom

There are also many clubs and organizations on campus. From the Hockey team to the Drama club to rowing there is something for everyone. There is even an underwater polo team! Yet the men's basketball team remains the most famous team on campus.

Mason's proximity to the nation's capital also draws in students who hope to work for the government as its location lends to federal internships. One freshman said, "I want to eventually join the FBI and Mason is close to FBI HQ, CIA HQ, NCIS HQ, and many other government agencies."

GMU would be a great choice for all students looking for a school that is at once academically and socially enriching. More than that, the location of the university guarantees adventures on campus and a whole new world of opportunities just a train ride away in Washington, D.C.—*Sharon Yin and Jenny Dai*

FYI

If you come to George Mason, you'd better bring an open mind. "This school is so diverse that it is difficult to get by if you aren't tolerant of different types of people with different races, ethnicities, cultures, and sexual orientations."

What's the typical weekend schedule? "Weekends could be just as active as the weekdays. I'd either hang out with friends on campus or we could head into D.C. for a hockey game or to visit the monuments. There was always something to do."

If I could change one thing about GMU, I'd change: "I would say the biggest drawback to Mason is that a lot of people leave campus on the weekend. Usually they go home, or to visit friends at nearby schools."

Hampden-Sydney College

Address: P.O. Box 667
Hampden-Sydney,
VA 23943
Phone: 800-755-0733
E-mail address:
admissions@hsc.edu
Web site URL: www.hsc.edu
Year Founded: 1775
Private or Public: Private
Religious Affiliation:
Presbyterian
Location: Rural
Number of Applicants:
1,553
Percent Accepted: 64%
**Percent Accepted who
enroll:** 32%
Number Entering: 333
**Number of Transfers
Accepted each Year:** 18
Middle 50% SAT range: M:
515–610, **CR:** 500–610,
Wr: 480–590
Middle 50% ACT range:
20–26
**Early admission program
EA/ED/None:** EA and ED

**Percentage accepted
through EA or ED:**
Unreported
EA and ED deadline: 15-Nov
Regular Deadline: 1-Mar
Application Fee: $30
**Full time Undergraduate
enrollment:** 1,120
Total enrollment: 1,120
Percent Male: 100%
Percent Female: 0%
**Total Percent Minority or
Unreported:** 13%
Percent African-American:
4%
**Percent Asian/Pacific
Islander:** 1%
Percent Hispanic: 1%
Percent Native-American:
<1%
Percent International: 2%
**Percent in-state/out of
state:** 68%/32%
Percent from Public HS:
58%
Retention Rate: 79%
Graduation Rate 4-year: 61%

Graduation Rate 6-year:
66%
**Percent Undergraduates
in On-campus housing:**
94%
**Number of official organized
extracurricular
organizations:** 50
3 Most popular majors:
Economics, History,
Government and Foreign
Affairs
Student/Faculty ratio: 10:1
Average Class Size: 15
**Percent of students going to
grad school:** 20%
Tuition and Fees: $28,250
**In-State Tuition and Fees if
different:** No difference
Cost for Room and Board:
$9,228
**Percent receiving financial
aid out of those who apply,
first year:** 98%
**Percent receiving financial
aid among all students:**
54%

S ince its 1775 founding, the mission of
Hampden-Sydney College (HSC) has
been to form "good men and good citizens in an atmosphere of sound learning."
This small all-male school maintains its tradition of excellence by holding students to
the highest standards of character, curriculum, and climate. Tucked away in a small
Virginian pocket of tranquility, HSC exudes
a picturesque, old-school charm. Its effective and extensive honor system creates a
sense of both citizenship and brotherhood.

The Core Curriculum, Liberal
Arts at Its Finest

Hampden-Sydney has a broad core curriculum that ensures that each student has taken
"at least two courses in every discipline"
before graduation. Because these requirements are so extensive, it is common to find
seniors still trying to fulfill them. For this
same reason, many people double major. The
curriculum within the majors is very broad,
and each student must have a complete understanding of a subject. Popular majors in-

clude economics, political science, and history, although in the past few years, religion
has become increasingly popular. While science may not be quite as popular, students
rave about the "must-take class" of "Caveman
Chemistry," a hands-on lab class in which students start off by making fire as the cavemen
did, working their way though human history,
and making plastic as their final project.

But when it comes to academics, Hampden-
Sydney College is not all fun and games. Students must complete the Rhetoric Program,
which consists of enrolling in challenging English classes, writing ten papers every semester, testing grammar proficiency, and taking
an overall final exam. The Rhetoric Program
is tough in the sense that "if you don't pass it,
you don't graduate," but as a result, "everyone
who graduates here can be proficient in writing, and write something that is worth reading." Furthermore, teachers are personally
attentive and usually generous with extensions. "It's almost impossible to graduate with
a 4.0 here because being perfect in your class
is viewed as unattainable," one senior said.

There is reportedly no grade inflation, and a C is often considered average.

We Eat Here, We Sleep Here, We . . . Fish Here?

A 1,100-member all-male college, Hampden-Sydney allows for "an atmosphere where you leave your door open and get to know all of the guys in the hall." Before they arrive, freshmen can choose to live in one of three dorms. Most choose Cushing because of its large rooms and the sense of community fostered by its 16-person corridors. Juniors and seniors have more options, and can even apply to live in college-owned off-campus housing. About 50 students per year do so, "but it's more convenient to live on-campus." The college allows about 35 upperclassmen to live outside college-owned housing. Because the nearest town, Farmville, is a 10-mile drive away, hardly anyone chooses to live in apartments not affiliated with the College. The housing draws are done first by seniority and then by GPA.

The architecture is "old Federal; red brick with white trim." And behind the commons area, at the foot of a hill, is a pond where students like to fish. Concerts, cookouts, pig roasts, and barbecue buffets are also hosted in that area. As far as the dining hall is concerned, food is said to be good, especially in comparison to that at other colleges. However, many students complain about "getting sick of the same good food by the end of the semester."

Intramural Life

The dominant extracurricular is most definitely intramural sports, with a 40 percent participation rate. Intramurals run all year round, and essentials such as soccer, softball, flag football, and basketball are all offered.

With about 25 percent of the school participating, varsity athletics also receive much support, particularly the football team, whose homecoming game kicks off a week of partying with students from the competing school. The football team is also the only sports team large enough to be "a group unto themselves."

In light of the fact that forming clubs at Hampden-Sydney involves little more than "filling out a form," the football players have even formed the Tiger Athletic Club, an organization bearing a likeness to its own frat, "especially due to the fact that they own a house." Other popular activities involve the Outsiders Club (which sponsors outdoor trips such as whitewater rafting), student government, the Young Republicans, and the debate society.

In Style and at Leisure

Although Hampden-Sydney is changing rapidly, it is still typecast as attracting "upper-middle-class white guys who drive SUVs." If dress is any indicator of anything, HSC boys are "not afraid to wear pink or Rainbow sandals, year-round." Popped collars, khakis and shaggy hair are also common sights. Students report that if you wear plaid, people will compliment your "cool pants." Dressing up during the day may not be the norm, but it definitely doesn't stand out.

As far as nightlife is concerned, an attendance policy prevents most students who have Friday classes from going out on Thursday nights. However, on Friday and Saturday nights, students will congregate in the off-campus houses or throw room parties. The alcohol policy is fairly lax. RAs do not go out to search and storm rooms, and most students feel comfortable with the degree of independence accorded them. Over 20 percent of students are members of frats. Fraternity Circle, the location of the frat houses, is the dominant (if not the only) social scene. But fraternity parties are not exclusive to the point where frats throw parties only for themselves; they often host parties specifically for the entire student body. During Greek Week, fraternities open their houses to all students and host popular bands; past acts have included Vanilla Ice and Galactic.

> "The honor system sets us apart. It is really strong and plays a large role on campus."

Contrary to popular belief, meeting girls is really not an issue at Hampden-Sydney College. Girls from other colleges, including the neighboring all-girls college Hollins, visit for the weekend just as boys from HSC visit the girls' schools. Also, the fraternities have frequent mixers with sororities from the University of Richmond and the University of Virginia. The College Activities Committee also hosts events, and efforts to increase the female presence at social events is definitely noticeable. When asked about girls, one student replied, "It enhances our situation being that we are all male. We certainly do form friendships with girls, but during the week when you have work to do, it's nice to hang out with the guys."

Southern Culture of Honor

Although some may be turned off by the "rolling hills and grazing cattle" that surround the school, others like the security of being able to leave their car doors unlocked and not having to swipe to access buildings. For the men of Hampden-Sydney, this sense of trust is a foundation for brotherhood. One student noted, "The honor system sets us apart. It is really strong and plays a large role on campus." Often, professors give tests and leave the room or give take-home tests with the instructions not to use books and to return in two hours. This honor code is strictly enforced:

The minimum punishment for lying, cheating, stealing (or tolerating those who do) ranges anywhere from one semester's suspension to expulsion. The Student Court maintains the code and is responsible for assigning any student accused of an infraction to an undergraduate lawyer while also determining the punishment. Albeit strict, "[the honor code's] effects benefit the entire community." According to one senior, the sense of trust and brotherhood "is really strong and plays a huge role on campus. On the whole, you can do what you want, but you have to grow up quick if you want to make it."—*Christine Kim*

FYI

If you come to Hampden-Sydney, you'd better bring "Seersuckers and loafers."

What's the typical weekend schedule? "Get out of classes, drink with the guys, and wait for the ladies to arrive from SBC, Hollins, and other schools. Go to the frats, dance and get obliterated. Wake up Saturday: during football season, throw on the coat, go to the Founders lot and get completely drunk for free: wear off the hangover, start drinking again. Sunday: wake up, say goodbye to the weekend catch, watch football, do homework."

If I could change one thing about Hampden-Sydney, "We'd have girls. Just kidding. It would be slightly smaller. We're on the verge of becoming too big to be doing what we've been doing since we were founded, such as upholding our honor code."

Three things every student at Hampden-Sydney should do before graduating are "a bell run, take 'Caveman Chemistry,' and play rugby."

Hollins University

Address: PO Box 9707 Roanoke, VA 24020-1707

Phone: 540-362-6401

E-mail address: huadm@hollins.edu

Web site URL: www.hollins.edu

Year Founded: 1842

Private or Public: Private

Religious Affiliation: None

Location: Urban

Number of Applicants: 651

Percent Accepted: 84%

Percent Accepted who enroll: 35%

Number Entering: 193

Number of Transfers Accepted each Year: 50

Middle 50% SAT range: M: 490–620, **CR:** 500–670, **Wr:** 490–620

Middle 50% ACT range: 21–28

Early admission program EA/ED/None: ED

Percentage accepted through EA or ED: Unreported

EA and ED deadline: 1-Dec

Regular Deadline: 1-Feb

Application Fee: $35

Full time Undergraduate enrollment: 799

Total enrollment: 1,049

Percent Male: 1%

Percent Female: 100%

Total Percent Minority or Unreported: 9%

Percent African-American: 8%

Percent Asian/Pacific Islander: 2%

Percent Hispanic: 3%

Percent Native-American: <1%

Percent International: 2%

Percent in-state/out of state: 52%/48%

Percent from Public HS: 77%

Retention Rate: 73%

Graduation Rate 4-year: 57%

Graduation Rate 6-year: 59%

Percent Undergraduates in On-campus housing: 80%

Number of official organized extracurricular organizations: 46

3 Most popular majors: Communication and Media Studies, English Language and Literature, General Psychology

Student/Faculty ratio: 10:1

Average Class Size: 13

Percent of students going to grad school: 22%

Tuition and Fees: $25,110

In-State Tuition and Fees if different: No difference

Cost for Room and Board: $9,140

Percent receiving financial aid out of those who apply, first year: 97%

Percent receiving financial aid among all students: 93%

Respect for tradition and a love for tight-knit community are just two of the values held close to the hearts of students at Hollins University. Academics being no exception, the talented women at Hollins effectively utilize the honored ways of the past to explore and live bright futures as graduates of this distinguished institution.

Scales and Perspectives
A four-year women's university, Hollins divides coursework into four different categories including humanities, social sciences, fine arts, and natural sciences. Rather than taking particular required courses, students must take eight credits from each of these divisions. Though some popular majors at Hollins include economics, history, and psychology, English is by far the largest major. In fact, many students were drawn to Hollins by the reputation of its well-rated, well-funded creative writing program. A unique major is the interdisciplinary major, a program in which students work with two faculty members to compile a major from two or more disciplines suited to students' interests. Challenging classes at Hollins include upper-level political science classes, but all senior seminar 400-level classes, according to one senior, "have as much work as should be expected." While most students are humanities majors, the natural science facilities are still fairly up-to-date, and a new visual arts center sparkles on campus. Hollins also offers a dance program that is always popular with students, who must complete two zero-credit physical education courses before graduation. Second-semester freshmen also apply to enroll in the three-year Batten Leadership Institute, a non-curricular program designed for students to "go above and beyond" to focus on their leadership skills.

Germany in January?
Hollins divides its year into three parts—two semesters plus a four-week January short term. During short term, the University offers intense seminars, internships for upperclassmen, and study-abroad opportunities in Greece, Spain, and Germany. Competition at Hollins is not cutthroat, but many students report a sporting competitiveness in classes. Students at Hollins feel this sense of competition enhances the spirit of sisterhood at the college. As one student noted, "You want to strive to be the best in your class or a particular class, but it's a natural,

healthy competitiveness." The "Hollins family" also extends to the faculty. Many professors live on nearby "faculty row," and it is not uncommon for classes to be moved there, sometimes just in time for dinner. It's no wonder that, with a low student-faculty ratio of ten to one and with 75 percent of classes under 20 students, by their fourth year, many students come to appreciate the special relationships forged with their faculty.

Good Living, Bad Food
Freshman dorms are unusually nice and new, often making the transition from home go much more smoothly. Each single or double is air-conditioned, and each hallway of 15 girls shares a bathroom, kitchen, social room, and study room. Upperclassmen reside in apartments and themed houses such as the Spanish house, French house, or fine arts house. Although these residences lack air-conditioning, most rooms are spacious singles, and one senior living in the Spanish house even boasted of her two closets and hardwood floor.

> "We have all kinds of girls here, from extreme liberal girls to true Southern belles who wear pearls, khakis, and Oxfords."

The food situation at Hollins, however, does not receive such positive reviews. The dining hall has dinner hours (4:30–6:30 p.m.) that most find unusually early, and does not provide as much variation as many would hope for. However, Hollins is very sensitive to the needs voiced by various committees on religious and vegetarian sensitivity, and strives to ensure that an array of specific diets are accommodated. For those who need a quick fix (and we're talking of the fried variety), students can also eat at the Rat, a student center specializing in fast foods.

One- to Two-Beer Kind of School
Many freshmen spend Friday to Sunday at nearby Virginia schools to visit friends and boyfriends. And although Hollins is "a little bit on the outskirts of Roanoke," groups of girls sometimes frequent downtown clubs and bars. Students maintain that they "have all kinds of girls here, from extreme liberal girls to true Southern belles who wear pearls, khakis, and Oxfords." Students note

that Hollins is too small to be cliquish, and as students grow older, greater numbers of on-campus parties occur that are hosted in upperclassman apartments. Hollins girls have been known to occasionally get the party started on Thursday, but Friday and Saturday nights usually prove to be the most exciting. Some find it problematic that Hollins "shares its brother school," Hampden-Sydney College, with the four other women's colleges in the area. All boys aside, Hollins' own student body contains a good mix of partiers and "staunch sober girls" who choose not to drink. However, in general, Hollins students "play by the rules" and don't consider their campus to be a wild party school where students are "allowed to have open glasses anywhere, walking down the hallways . . . drinking themselves silly every weekend." As one student summed it up, "It's a one- to two-beer kind of school."

Let's Get Physical

Hollins' activity board is particularly strong, and "from concerts, to cultural events, to poker nights, there is always something to do no matter what your interests are." Many women are active in student government and community service. HOP, Hollins Outdoor Program, offers mountain climbing, white-water rafting, and other outdoor excursions. It being a Division III school, the sports teams at Hollins are not big enough to be too exclusive, socially or athletically. While no club sports are offered, Hollins gives interested students a chance to walk on to teams otherwise populated by mostly recruited athletes. For those uninterested in organized sports, Hollins has a gym equipped with a rock-climbing wall—donated by a

Hollins alum, a woman who climbed Mount Everest—a sauna, a pool, and a fencing studio that is also used for aerobics.

Sisterhood

Although sororities are prohibited by Hollins, the sense of sisterhood is campus-wide, and many campus activities still revolve around tradition. On Tinker Day, the day of the first autumn frost, students wake up to the sound of seniors banging on pots and pans as they run down underclassman hallways. Students head to breakfast in the dining halls "in the craziest outfits imaginable," and afterward ditch classes for the day to trek up nearby Tinker Mountain for a picnic buffet at the summit, where the day is spent performing songs and skits. Another popular tradition is Ring Night, when juniors are officially inducted as seniors. This three-day celebration culminates with juniors receiving gift baskets full of senior "necessities" such as pots and pans (for Tinker Day) and four bottles of champagne from their secret senior sisters. Why four bottles of champagne at this "one- to two-beer school?" Another tradition, of course. One of the champagne bottles is used for the women's first-step tradition. Only seniors are allowed to walk on the front quad grass, and, on first-step day, seniors take their first steps on the beautiful front quad while popping the cork of their first bottle of champagne.

With so many fun yet meaningful traditions and a strong sense of community and support, it is no wonder that students grow to love Hollins for both its strengths and its weaknesses. As one student noted, "This school wasn't necessarily my top choice, but looking back on it, Hollins really was my perfect school."—*Christine J. Kim*

FYI

If you come to Hollins, you'd better bring "something unusual to wear for Tinker Day."

What's the typical weekend schedule? "Most classes will end around noon on Fridays. About a third of the students will jump in their cars and head for JMU, VMI, or Virginia Tech. However, there's usually a party going on somewhere either Friday or Saturday, and these tend to follow all-day events like Arts Fest and the Hollins Theater shows. Sundays tend to be laid-back and quiet, with limited hours in the dining hall."

If I could change one thing about Hollins, "I'd alter the policies of the career development center to be more conducive to finding jobs rather than identifying possible career choices."

Three things every student at Hollins should do before leaving are "climb Tinker Mountain, see a Hollins dance performance, and participate in Ring Night."

James Madison University

Address: Sonner Hall, MSC 0101, Harrisonburg, VA 22807
Phone: 540-568-5681
E-mail address: admission@jmu.edu
Web site URL: www.jmu.edu
Year Founded: 1908
Private or Public: Public
Religious Affiliation: None
Location: Suburban
Number of Applicants: 19,245
Percent Accepted: 65%
Percent Accepted who enroll: 32%
Number Entering: 3,956
Number of Transfers Accepted each Year: 659
Middle 50% SAT range: M: 540–630, CR: 520–620, Wr: 520–620,
Middle 50% ACT range: 22–26
Early admission program EA/ED/None: EA

Percentage accepted through EA or ED: 46%
EA and ED deadline: 1-Nov
Regular Deadline: 15-Jan
Application Fee: $40
Full time Undergraduate enrollment: 16,916
Total enrollment: 18,454
Percent Male: 40%
Percent Female: 60%
Total Percent Minority or Unreported: 14%
Percent African-American: 4%
Percent Asian/Pacific Islander: 5%
Percent Hispanic: 2%
Percent Native-American: <1%
Percent International: 1%
Percent in-state/out of state: 71%/29%
Percent from Public HS: Unreported
Retention Rate: 91%
Graduation Rate 4-year: 66%

Graduation Rate 6-year: 81%
Percent Undergraduates in On-campus housing: 36%
Number of official organized extracurricular organizations: 328
3 Most popular majors: Finance, Health and Physical Education, Psychology
Student/Faculty ratio: 16:1
Average Class Size: 26
Percent of students going to grad school: 35%
Tuition and Fees: $9,229
In-State Tuition and Fees if different: $3,482
Cost for Room and Board: $7,690
Percent receiving financial aid out of those who apply, first year: 54%
Percent receiving financial aid among all students: 52%

In the midst of the stunning Shenandoah Valley lies a purple and gold gem, uncovered and raised from its modest beginnings as a Virginia teachers' school to become one of the leading schools in America. From the moment freshmen step onto James Madison University's campus, they are swept into the friendly bustle that defines the student body.

Academia Is Nuts (in a Good Way)

James Madison University offers a wide range of course offerings and lauded academic programs. Majors range from popular categories such as business and political science to the less popular (but nonetheless adored) social services program. Freshmen tend to attend larger lecture classes, while upperclassmen enjoy about a 16:1 student-professor ratio. Almost all classes, large or small, are taught by full professors who hold consistent office hours and make themselves extremely accessible. In fact, there are "a ton of professors whom you can run

into out on the town in bars and restaurants and they're almost always happy to chat."

Although some students complain about the general education requirements, there is no shortage of enthusiasm about particular departments. A senior describes the College of Integrated Science and Technology as "groundbreaking," a division with an entire portion of campus dedicated to it and a curriculum that incorporates biology, chemistry, physics, computer science, and technology. JMU features a fantastic education program, in which education majors can earn their masters in JMU's five-year program. Some Dukes (which is what students at James Madison are called) will admit that "people have a lot of trouble with Elementary Statistics," Macroeconomics, and College of Business 300 (COB 300, which includes four separate classes taken at once), but add that even these are recommendable and very worthwhile. Almost all Dukes agree that, no matter what you take, there is still plenty of time to immerse yourself in extracurriculars.

Outside the Classroom

As one student aptly stated, "You'd be hard-pressed to find someone here who's not involved in some sort of student activity." The student body offers over 300 active student-run groups. Not necessarily the most popular but one of the most famed among these is IN8, JMU's secret society. Every year, it gives out eight letters to students and faculty who have significantly impacted their society to let them know that their work does not go unnoticed. In addition, in 2003, they donated a human sundial, a spot in the middle of campus where a person stands on a particular month's mark and casts a shadow on plaques six or seven feet away that designate the time.

When it comes to nightlife, fraternities and sororities provide a nice opportunity to make friends and get involved in the "party scene." Greek life only involves about 12 percent of students, but the ones who go Greek love it. Men rush only one fraternity, while women rush all eight sororities and slowly narrow down their options. Other people get involved with groups such as religious organizations, student government, the yearbook committee, activist groups, a cappella groups, or the sailing club, to name a few.

> "[Dukes are] active and productive, and excited about what they're doing."

All sports at JMU are NCAA Division I. Football, which plays in the Colonial Athletic Association, and basketball provide nearly the strongest crowd draws, second only to the nationally acclaimed marching band. Although most Dukes do not attend all the games, everyone attends homecoming. The school annually provides a famous speaker to address a student body decked out in JMU's purple and gold, which proceeds to "tailgate all day and party all night." In general, students become involved in several activities over their four years and often still find time to work in local restaurants or as tutors, dining hall attendants, or teaching and information assistants. A stimulating environment succeeds in keeping Dukes, as one phrased it, "active and productive, and excited about what they're doing."

Relaxing Down Under

JMU is incredibly friendly; its social graces tend to alleviate what might otherwise be a stressful academic lifestyle. Additionally, the campus accommodates students' busy schedules exceedingly well. JMU provides plenty of student facilities, including one of the most popular lounges on campus, Taylor Down Under. Students can go to places like this and find access to computers, the Internet, billiards, board games, study areas, and comfortable futons ("Great for napping!"). The university also sends a constant flow of music over Taylor Down Under's PA system, interrupted only for common evening events such as "open mic nights," poetry readings, bands, comedy acts, and other entertainment. Other popularly frequented hangouts include the quad in the spring, where someone is always lying out doing homework or playing Frisbee, or even the on-campus dining halls, some of which stay open until 10 p.m. on weeknights.

Well-Catered

Students who linger in the dining halls find everything from all-you-can-eat buffet style meals to food courts and more specialized sandwich bars and salad bars. The school "keeps experimenting with the menu" and actively responding to student complaints to keep its students satisfied. Recently the dining halls relieved the threat of student uproar over the removal of a certain beloved chicken wrap. For a different taste, Chick-fil-A and an Einstein Bros. Bagels are located on campus, where students can use "dining dollars" that come with the standard 12-meal weekly plan. Of course, typical chain restaurants are scattered around Harrisonburg, especially after the recent addition of a new shopping center. Local favorites, however, include Mr. J's Bagels, known for its "AMAZING bagel sandwiches"; El Charro, a Mexican restaurant; and Luigi's, an Italian pizzeria. When they leave the table, students will be happy to find that no eatery is too far from home.

In the Hall of the Mountain King: The Suite Life

All freshmen and many sophomores live on campus in centrally located buildings, making "rolling out of bed three minutes before class starts incredibly possible (and done frequently)," according to one upperclassman veteran. In general, these residential halls vary from hall to suite style and offer warm, beautiful, and historical dorms. Many Dukes claim that "Old Campus," a group of dorms constructed between 1908 and 1948 with blue stone, stands out as the nicest housing in the area, especially since all of its buildings have been renovated during the past decade. For those not lucky enough (or not inclined) to live there, the "Village" is available, offering advantages of its own. Its nine residential halls are standard cinder block structures, including both standard freshman housing and interest-related accommodations. Students can live in leadership communities, biology-themed communities, substance-free communities, international halls (where international students are paired with American roommates), and more. All dorms have remained coed since the last all-girls dorm opened its doors to men. The system seems to produce fast friends: One senior praised, "I still live with five girls from my freshman hall."

On-campus housing is also available for upperclassmen, but most elect to enter the myriad of apartment and townhouse complexes that have sprouted around the school in response to the quickly growing student population. This growth has created what one apartment dweller termed a "mini satellite campus off campus," consisting of various buildings. The student body has approximately doubled to over 16,000 in the past 20 years, necessitating extra housing. Although parking spaces are generally scarce and the commute to class from the apartments is slightly longer than from on-campus housing, residents love where they live. Each of these complexes "has its own reputation and theme," providing off-campus essentials for their inhabitants.

Bust out the Party Hat

"Everyone from freshmen to super-seniors (5th years) show up at the apartment parties for mingling, dancing, flip cup, beer pong, and just some basic chatting over beer" when the weekend rolls around. Some Dukes start their nightlife on Wednesday or Thursday night, either in local bars or apartments. Mainstreet Bar and Grille, in particular, keeps some people dancing until 2 a.m. on Wednesday nights. Since no alcohol (JMU makes this very clear) is allowed in freshman dorms and no one underage can drink on campus, most partiers migrate to the apartments by Friday. Not everyone drinks, but those who do usually have the option to party hard: "At some universities, a cover is required by the owners of the house to pay for the alcohol, but at JMU, it's pretty much open and free to all, which is so nice to know that you're welcome everywhere." JMU students seem responsible about their habits, a trait best shown by the student-run "SafeRides" program that offers free taxi service to those who have been drinking.

Moreover, the school's "three strikes" program forces them to proceed with relative caution, especially with respect to local police or higher-up administrators. Residential assistants purportedly "are always there for you, and do what they need to do to keep us all safe but let us enjoy ourselves, too." Some of the less strict ones "have even been known to play beer pong with us," says a freshman, though this is rare. Dukes who would rather not party or drink can hit the student lounges, which stay open late, or go to a movie at the campus movie theater. Wherever students are, campus police, vigilant "campus cadets," and a "blue light system" (a series of blue lights all over campus, each within view from the last, that can be used to summon help or safety escorts) keep them safe all night.

The Bottom Line

As a recent student body president remarked in an interview, "I've never met a single person who left because they didn't like it here. The only ones who leave are the ones who think that maybe they wanted something different academically." As the school develops, however, this latter concern is becoming less and less prevalent. JMU provides a terrific liberal arts education and continues its history of producing successful alumni today, while fostering an inclusive and high-spirited atmosphere that complements its beautiful area. Most Dukes echo the testimony of one upperclassman: "If I had to choose all over again, I'd stick with JMU. Wouldn't change anything."
—*Hugh Sullivan*

FYI
If you come to JMU, you'd better bring "a friendly attitude."
What's the typical weekend schedule? "Go to bars on Wednesday and Thursdays, apartment parties on Friday. Saturday, work out during the day; go to a frat party at night. Sunday, sleep in and study!"
If I could change one thing about JMU, I would "move it closer to a major city. JMU does a good job of bringing stuff down, and Charlottesville isn't too far away, but I would prefer to have the D.C. nightlife available."
Three things that every student at JMU should do before graduating are "swim in Newman Lake (not as pleasant as it may sound), ring the bells in the bell tower, and find the hidden underground tunnels that were originally built so that women could avoid the cold weather between classes but have since been shut down. (The bell tower is rumored to be haunted on foggy nights by the ghost of the girl whose death in the tunnels caused the tunnels' closing.)"

Randolph College

Address: 2500 Rivermont Avenue, Lynchburg, VA 24503
Phone: 434-947-8100
E-mail address: admissions@randolph college.edu
Web site URL: www.randolphcollege.edu
Year Founded: 1891
Private or Public: Private
Religious Affiliation: Methodist
Location: Urban
Number of Applicants: 1,585
Percent Accepted: 83%
Percent Accepted who enroll: 11%
Number Entering: 144
Number of Transfers Accepted each Year: 53
Middle 50% SAT range: M: 490–600, **CR:** 500–630, **Wr:** Unreported
Middle 50% ACT range: 23–27

Early admission program EA/ED/None: EA
Percentage accepted through EA or ED: 73%
EA and ED deadline: 1-Dec
Regular Deadline: 1-April
Application Fee: $35; online application is free
Full time Undergraduate enrollment: 500
Total enrollment: 524
Percent Male: 18%
Percent Female: 82%
Total Percent Minority or Unreported: 36%
Percent African-American: 9%
Percent Asian/Pacific Islander: 3%
Percent Hispanic: 7%
Percent Native-American: 1%
Percent International: 11%
Percent in-state/out of state: 48%/52%
Percent from Public HS: 78%

Retention Rate: 70%
Graduation Rate 4-year: 66%
Graduation Rate 6-year: 66%
Percent Undergraduates in On-campus housing: 88%
Number of official organized extracurricular organizations: 40
3 Most popular majors: Biology, Political Science, Psychology
Student/Faculty ratio: 7:1
Average Class Size: 8
Percent of students going to grad school: 31%
Tuition and Fees: $27,890
In-State Tuition and Fees if different: No difference
Cost for Room and Board: $9,310
Percent receiving financial aid out of those who apply, first year: 83%
Percent receiving financial aid among all students: 96%

A Close-Knit Community

Randolph College, formerly Randolph-Macon Women's College, is beginning a new chapter of its 120-year history. In fall of 2007, this small liberal arts college admitted its first coeducational class. The school also began, in 2007, to fulfill its plans to release a new, enhanced curriculum. Yet with all these dramatic changes, the school insists that "the essential elements of the Randolph-Macon experience will remain constant."

Randolph College is described as a "gorgeous" college, set against the backdrop of the Virginia hills, and it is distinctive for its classic red-brick buildings and a matching red-brick wall that surrounds the entire campus. Students are required to live on campus for their full four years. "I like that everyone lives here," said one student. "We have such a wonderful sense of community, and it only takes five minutes to get from one part of campus to another." Most people have "no real complaints" about the living situation, as the rooms are larger than those at many other colleges and each of the dorm buildings has a unique attribute such as air conditioning, elevators, larger rooms, a better location, or extended quiet hours. Freshman dorms are assigned based on student preference forms, and upperclassmen draw for rooms in spring. Most of the dormitories are divided proportionally among the classes (except for the senior dorm and the mostly freshmen dorm) in order to facilitate and encourage interaction among upperclassmen and underclassmen. One senior commented, "My first year, I had so many upperclassmen coming into my room, welcoming me, letting me borrow books, telling me about professors, giving me tips, asking me about my clubs . . . people just take you under their wing!"

Another student commented, "It's really easy to meet people here because it's such a small school. There is only one dining hall and everyone has the same set meal plan, so sometimes people will stay at dinner for hours, just talking. Of course there are a couple of cliques, but there will be groups in any community and no one is exclusive."

Students say they met their friends through athletics, clubs, classes, or freshman orientation groups. "There are a ton of mixers," said one student. "You'd have to live in a hole not to have any friends at [Randolph]. And that's not possible to do here, either!" The college is very geographically diverse and boasts a large international student population, but ethnic diversity could use some improvement. "We could use more diversity, but I'm glad that we're at least as diverse as we are now," said one student. "It brings a lot to the classroom to have so many different vantage points."

From Homework to Happy Hour

The academics at Randolph are rigorous, to say the least. Students have a variety of requirements to fulfill, spanning such subjects as religion, philosophy, English, physical education, and a lab science. "Because of the liberal arts requirements, I get exposed to a lot of classes that may not be my strengths," commented one student. "But if you come in with an open mind and you push yourself to do well, they're really great." The most popular majors are psychology, politics, biology, and English, and if a student can't find a major that suits her among the list of more than 25 possibilities, she always has the op-

portunity to design her own major. Most students agree, "All the majors are difficult— [Randolph] definitely doesn't give anything out for free." Registration is based on seniority and usually people are satisfied with the system, but the popularity of certain majors (particularly biology), the limited selection of classes, and the small class size can sometimes make it difficult to get into certain courses. Class size varies from four or five students to 30, although the average is 12. Workload, too, varies and depends on the class, the professor, and the preparation of the students. While one described it as "pretty heavy compared to other colleges," another observed, "It's not too different from high school AP classes. It can be overwhelming at first, but it's definitely manageable." Said one student, "Standards are fairly high, but there's no animosity within the classroom. People just want to do their own personal best."

According to many students, grading can be stringent. "We have a saying here: 'Anywhere else it would have been an A,'" said one. "I don't know if that's true, or if that's just us complaining about it." Still, student-faculty relations are "amazing. There's a lot of interaction with professors, especially on independent research projects." Another said, "A lot of professors have students babysitting, house-sitting, pet-sitting, whatever!" Most professors have an open-door policy, where students can come by and talk or ask questions even if it's not during office hours. "Professors want students to do well," noted one junior. The faculty is also highly involved in student extracurricular life, participating in award shows or other activities and often attending a Macon Community Happy Hour. Overall, students appreciate their professors and their academic opportunities, believing that the rigor of the curriculum is "worth it, because we're working hard for our education and becoming stronger in the process."

We Like to Party?

The extracurricular activity at Randolph is centered around a wide variety of student clubs and organizations. "We're very involved in our clubs," said one student. "We're always out to save the world in one form or another." Several of the larger groups include Amnesty International, the Environmental Club, the Black Students Alliance, various religious organizations, language clubs, and the Macon Activities Council, which brings in speakers and musicians and organizes events such as horseback riding or whitewater rafting. There are also multiple drama productions, musical ensembles, and a whole host of other clubs. "We have upwards of 100 clubs for a student body of only 1,150 people, if that gives you any idea of how important clubs are to us," one student said.

> "You'd have to live in a hole not to have any friends at [Randolph]. And that's not possible to do here, either!"

Varsity athletics, however, has a slowly growing following, thanks to the college's recent infusion of males. In fact, nearly half of the male students are varsity athletes. "The people involved are really dedicated and the faculty is supportive, but I don't know how much attention the student body pays to the WildCats," said one student athlete. Intramural sports are not big; most students get their exercise by working out on their own, lifting weights or going running. A large majority of students have jobs on campus, especially since many of them participate in the work-study program.

As far as the weekend social scene is concerned, Randolph is not a party school. "We go off campus to party," one student said. "I'd say that on the weekends, almost half the campus goes home or goes to another college to party, while the other half stays behind to do work or club stuff." Another student said that weekend socializing can consist of a variety of activities such as drinking in people's rooms, going to a movie or out to dinner, going to see guest speakers or musicians, or going out to a club. "One club across the street has Wednesday college night, but generally, there's not a whole lot to do in Lynchburg," commented one sophomore. "Occasionally an organization on campus will host a bigger party, but for the most part people stick to smaller groups in rooms." One famous annual celebration is the "Never-Ending Weekend," with Friday night being the Tacky Party (the name is self-explanatory) and Saturday night being Fall Formal. Weekend activities in the surrounding town are limited, since Lynchburg "is not really a college town, so you have to drive to get to a movie theatre and most good restaurants." When asked to comment on the town's relationship with the college, one student responded, "We're definitely a separate community, but the town respects Randolph students and they have no real reason to complain about us because we're not a party school."

Daisy Chains and Pumpkin Parades

One particularly distinctive tradition at Randolph is the inter-class rivalry. Students identify themselves as "evens" or "odds," depending on the year of their graduation, and they enthusiastically participate in a vast collection of activities—such as water balloon fights and painting each other's banners—associated with the even-odd rivalry. "Sister classes" (freshmen/juniors and sophomores/seniors) have a strong connection, and they show their support for one another during Ring Week, when freshmen give small gifts to the juniors and create a scavenger hunt for them to find their class rings, and the Pumpkin Parade, where each senior receives a pumpkin carved by a sophomore. Right before graduation, sophomores make a huge daisy chain and pass it to the seniors. The class rivalry is even physically built into the school: a special staircase in the main lobby has one side for evens and one side for odds, and if a student goes up or down the wrong side, rumor has it that she won't graduate on time.

Randolph is certainly not for everyone. But for those who are willing to brave the tough academics and enjoy a somewhat quieter social scene, the college offers a vibrant community of dedicated, intelligent students who are working to better themselves and their society. One senior's final comment was, "It's a wonderful place. I've been exceedingly happy with what I've experienced there in the past four years."—*Lindsay Starck*

FYI
If you come to RC, you'd better bring "a whole lot of class spirit for the even-odd rivalry!"
What's the typical weekend schedule? "Relax, maybe party a bit or take a trip off-campus, then hit the books on Sunday."
If I could change one thing about RC, I'd "have more faculty available so that it's easier to get into popular or required classes."
Three things every student at RC should do before graduation are "join a club or several of them, ring the bell in Main Hall, and participate in the traditional Dell Run (running naked across the Greek-style ampitheater)."

S w e e t   B r i a r   C o l l e g e

Address: P.O. Box 1052
Sweet Briar, VA 24595
Phone: 800-381-6142
E-mail address:
admissions@sbc.edu
Web site URL: www.sbc.edu
Year Founded: 1901
Private or Public: Private
Religious Affiliation: None
Location: Rural
Number of Applicants: 607
Percent Accepted: 82%
**Percent Accepted who
enroll:** 38%
Number Entering: 164
**Number of Transfers
Accepted each Year:**
Unreported
Middle 50% SAT range: M:
480–590, **CR:** 510–620,
Wr: Unreported
Middle 50% ACT range:
23–28
**Early admission program
EA/ED/None:** None
**Percentage accepted
through EA or ED:** NA

EA and ED deadline: NA
Regular Deadline: 1-Feb
(rolling)
Application Fee: $40
**Full time Undergraduate
enrollment:** 639
Total enrollment: 745
Percent Male: 0%
Percent Female: 100%
**Total Percent Minority or
Unreported:** 13%
Percent African-American:
4%
**Percent Asian/Pacific
Islander:** 3%
Percent Hispanic: 4%
Percent Native-American:
1%
Percent International: 1%
**Percent in-state/out of
state:** 43%/57%
Percent from Public HS: 72%
Retention Rate: 78%
Graduation Rate 4-year:
70%
Graduation Rate 6-year:
72%

**Percent Undergraduates
in On-campus housing:**
90%
**Number of official organized
extracurricular
organizations:** 53
3 Most popular majors:
Biology, Business
Management, Political
Science/Government/
International Affairs
Student/Faculty ratio:
Unreported
Average Class Size: 13
**Percent of students going to
grad school:** 24%
Tuition and Fees: $28,860
**In-State Tuition and Fees if
different:** No difference
Cost for Room and Board:
$10,460
**Percent receiving financial
aid out of those who apply,
first year:** 90%
**Percent receiving financial
aid among all students:**
93%

Though small and rural, Sweet Briar College's quaint, historical campus seems to house the best of everything—except for men, of course. According to a locally printed bumper sticker, at Sweet Briar College, "women are leaders and men are *guests.*" That's an overstatement considering the male visitation privileges and security clearance they have to gain just to get on campus. They don't call Sweet Briar the "pink bubble" for nothing!

Workin' It
Don't think that all that pink means these girls aren't working hard. Academics are taken very seriously at Sweet Briar College. Writes one junior, "There is a lot of reading and paper writing, etc . . . and it can be really hard but we're all at Sweet Briar to gain an education and so we do what it takes." The girls are required to meet general education requirements including fulfilling certain knowledge areas and skill areas, but course options allow for students to do so according to their own interests. For

example, one junior took a course on the "History of Crime and Punishment in the West" to fulfill the Quantitative Reasoning requirement.

Sweet Briar girls agree that there are no "hard" or "easy" majors offered there. "Sweet Briar academics aren't for the faint of heart, no matter which major or minor you choose. We are a very small school . . . but it does ensure that none of our 40-something programs are weak." That may mean no coasting, but it also means that Sweet Briar students have full reign over their course options. Honors classes are available to all who are interested, and Sweet Briar offers certificate programs in Arts Management, Equine Studies, and Leadership. Furthermore, the average class size is 12 students. That kills all hopes of unnoticed absences on especially early—or late—mornings, but students have no trouble working their way into capped courses. All they have to do is ask nicely.

The workload can be heavy at Sweet Briar, but "girls learn to balance things quickly. Study parties are a popular and fun way to get work done, but have a little fun at the same time." Professors are also very accessible for outside help, and no classes are taught by TAs, so girls enjoy lots of one-on-one time with their instructors. Moreover, they are able to complete special projects researching the local history in nearby Amherst and Lynchburg. Twenty-one of Sweet Briar's 30 campus buildings are part of the "Sweet Briar College National Historic District" on the National Register of Historic Places.

Out on the Town

Social life at Sweet Briar is different than at other schools because girls go off campus to party. "The campus is pretty evenly split between the girls who like to go to other area schools and girls who like to stay around SBC on the weekends." Shopping, dining out, and movie-going are popular. Though drinking is not unheard of, the Sweet Briar honor code disallows underage drinking, ensuring that non-drinkers are satisfied by a myriad of alternatives. The Campus Events Organization plans concerts and events on the weekends, including two annual formal events, the "Fall Formal" and the "Junior Banquet." The CEO also organizes lectures and exhibitions on a weekly basis. Recent guests have included Salman Rushdie, Dance-Brazil, and the Roanoke Opera. Not bad for a small college town.

There's no Greek system at Sweet Briar College, but, as one T-shirt reads, "SBC: We're one big sorority." Tap Clubs are similar institutions, all but one of which are exclusive. Bum Chums and Ants 'N' Asses are the most popular, and many sponsor boathouse parties. However, on-campus cliques "change and morph frequently," so meeting new people is not a problem. In fact, most faces are familiar anyway on such a small campus.

According to a traditional jingle, "Diamonds are pretty and so are pearls, but nothing compares to Sweet Briar girls." It's not surprising, then, that boys come from nearby Hampden-Sydney to take Sweet Briar girls on dinner and movie dates in Lynchburg. Only about half of the student body is sexually active, however, so the jury's out on after-dinner activities. Says one junior, "a large percentage of the school is sexually active, but as educated women, I'm sure many, if not all of them make sure to use protection so STDs are not a perceived problem."

The Sweet Briar student body is "diverse in terms of personality types and back-

grounds" but not much else. One girl writes that "Sweet Briar students are stereotyped as preppy girls who wear pearls, pink and green, and Vera Bradley bags." Most girls dress more casually than expected, however, and would prefer that the campus as a whole were more diverse.

Dorms and Dining

Unless they're married or over 22, Sweet Briar students are required to live on campus or at home. Freshmen are divided into floors and halls based on their chosen "male visitation option," but upperclasswomen are automatically allowed visitors at all hours, unless enough students request otherwise. Meta Glass and Grammer Halls are for first-year students and are monitored by upperclasswomen called FYAs or First-Year Assistants, and even the upperclass dorms have Community Assistants (CAs). Dew is the worst dorm, and Manson has the best kitchen, but according to one student, "All of the dorms on campus are pretty nice . . . they all have nice big rooms and are really good compared to other college dorms I have seen." They had better be if there's no way out of them.

> **"It's like a four-year slumber party with great classes interspersed!"**

Along with a four-year residential plan comes a 21-meal fixed dining plan. Sweet Briar girls can eat in the dining hall or have wraps made at a station on the way to class. They can also purchase food from the "Bistro" or the "Café" at their expense, but the dining hall overlooks the mountain, so it's absolutely worth the time. "One could easily spend hours sitting in our dining hall and chatting, and I have on several occasions," says one student. Many student groups also hold meetings in the dining area. Girls who need a change of pace dine out at the Briar Patch in Amherst, or grab coffee at the Drowsy Poet.

Loving the Locals

Sweet Briar students can't say enough about their campus—almost as beautiful as the students. Writes one student, "[Sweet Briar] is the one college that I visited where I felt the pictures in the brochures didn't do it justice." The original campus buildings were built by Ralph Adams Cram, who also designed many of Princeton's buildings, and the recent ones emulate his style so that the architecture blends with the natural surroundings. "The campus feels very peaceful and is just a really pleasant place to be." At least there's something for these ladies to feast their eyes on.

The "Dell" is the grassy courtyard in the center of campus—a popular perch for students in search of a little sun. Other students, assured by the vigilance of the Campus Police, like to take walks around the "Dairy Loop." Those who want a break from nature can explore the shopping districts in Amherst and Lynchburg, both of which have healthy relationships with the College. Local elementary school students enjoy campus and gallery tours and science and art days given by Sweet Briar students. The girls also host a school supply drive and teach dance classes in town.

Down Time . . . Or Not

Sweet Briar girls don't take academics lightly, and the same goes for extracurriculars. One junior writes that "Sweet Briar students in general are extremely active in extracurricular activities, almost to the point of insanity." So when they're not in class, girls engage with respected groups like the student government, student newspaper, and intramurals. Tap Clubs are also popular, but more fun than structured. Girls who need a good football fix have to travel to nearby Hampden-Sydney or VMI to catch a boy in uniform. The Sweet Briar Equestrian Team, however, is well-supported and fitted with a recruiting office. Less competitive souls get their workouts in the recreational gym, swimming pool, or tennis court.

When they're not excelling in the classroom or on the IM fields, the Sweet Briar Vixens are participating in one of the college's many traditions—or hiding from them. Daisy, the daughter of the College's founder, is rumored to haunt the place. More wholesome rituals include "the Ring Game," which roots out those lucky girls who are engaged—yes, to be married—and the "Big/Little Sister" program, which partners juniors and freshmen, not to mention Scream Night, Lantern Bearing, Step Singing, and Founders' Day. Wherever they choose to expend their energies, the girls of Sweet Briar College are wed to their alma mater. Quirky traditions and an idyllic campus are their favorite parts. One student comments, "It's like a four-year slumber party with great classes interspersed!" Pillow fights, anyone?—*Lauren Ezell*

FYI
If you come to Sweet Briar, you better bring "a car."
What is a typical weekend schedule? "Whatever you want!"
If I could change one thing about Sweet Briar, I'd "make the student body more diverse."
Three things every student at Sweet Briar should do before graduating are "go sledding on a dining hall tray, walk the Dairy Loop, and admire just how beautiful the campus is."

University of Richmond

Address: 28 Westhampton Way, University of Richmond, VA 23173
Phone: 804-289-8640
E-mail address: admissions@richmond.edu
Web site URL: www.richmond.edu
Year Founded: 1830
Private or Public: Private
Religious Affiliation: None
Location: Suburban
Number of Applicants: 7,970
Percent Accepted: 32%
Percent Accepted who enroll: 29%
Number Entering: 787
Number of Transfers Accepted each Year: 108
Middle 50% SAT range: M: 590–680, CR: 580–680, Wr: 590–690
Middle 50% ACT range: 26–30
Early admission program EA/ED/None: ED I, ED II

Percentage accepted through EA or ED: 28%
EA and ED deadline: 15-Nov, 15-Jan
Regular Deadline: 15-Jan
Application Fee: $50
Full time Undergraduate enrollment: 2,735
Total enrollment: 3,445
Percent Male: 49%
Percent Female: 51%
Total Percent Minority or Unreported: 13%
Percent African-American: 6%
Percent Asian/Pacific Islander: 4%
Percent Hispanic: 3%
Percent Native-American: 1%
Percent International: Unreported
Percent in-state/out of state: 17%/83%
Percent from Public HS: 61%
Retention Rate: 91%

Graduation Rate 4-year: 82%
Graduation Rate 6-year: 87%
Percent Undergraduates in On-campus housing: 91%
Number of official organized extracurricular organizations: 275
3 Most popular majors: Business Administration, Accounting, International Studies
Student/Faculty ratio: 9:1
Average Class Size: 16
Percent of students going to grad school: 40%
Tuition and Fees: $38,850
In-State Tuition and Fees if different: No difference
Cost for Room and Board: $8,200
Percent receiving financial aid out of those who apply, first year: 75%
Percent receiving financial aid among all students: 42%

Located in a lush landscape near the James River, the University of Richmond offers arguably one of the most beautiful campuses in the country. But don't let the seemingly serene environment of UR fool you. Throughout their four years at UR, Richmond students are kept busy by a multitude of academic, social and extracurricular activities. When the freshmen arrive on campus, they will be pleasantly surprised by the welcoming and friendly atmosphere and quickly delve into the unique opportunities offered by UR.

Only at Richmond

Bloomberg Businessweek recently ranked the Robins School of Business as the 15th best undergraduate business program in the country. Thus it's no surprise that business is one of the most popular majors and students can choose to focus on accounting, business administration or economics. UR also offers a unique interdisciplinary major: leadership studies. Students apply in their second year for admission into the Jepson

School of Leadership Studies, where they will study a variety of subjects including economics, history, literature, philosophy, and psychology. While all the majors are challenging in their own rights, they are not overwhelming. "I haven't heard of any major being especially hard, but many of them are quite competitive," said a sophomore. "Pre-medicine biology, for example, has a laid out plan for all four years so it's hard if you do not start early." Sophomores can also design unique fields of study by creating their own interdisciplinary studies major.

Richmond students must complete the General Education curriculum, which covers art, history, language, natural sciences, social analysis, symbolic reasoning, and First Year Seminar courses. In addition, everyone at UR has to take The Core Course, which examines common human problem through a combination philosophy and literature. Prior to graduation, students must also complete three part Wellness classes that aim to promote academic success and healthy lifestyle. Another unique academic program UR offers is the Bonner Scholars Program, which pairs up students with local non-profit organizations and lets them engage in social issues that interest them. About 25 students in each class are selected as Bonner Scholars and they commit ten hours each week toward community service. In return, the students receive a renewable $2,500 scholarship.

Most Richmond students agree that classes are not easy. "There are no really easy classes in general, as you progress anywhere the classes get harder and more challenging," one junior said. Many students complain about the calculus courses, which are required for getting into the business school, as well as the lab sciences. One student describes the typical workload as "150 to 450 pages of reading a week and then a paper every other week with a couple of smaller assignments in between." With a student-faculty of 8:1, most students find it very easy to engage with the professors and receive help. "The teachers will help with papers or tell you where to go to get help," one freshman noted. The average class size is around 15 people and most classes are less than 20 people, which helps to foster discussions in an intimate environment. Getting into certain classes is competitive especially as a first year student. The basic classes always fill up quickly and you should always have alternates. Sometimes, the professors are willing to help out and accept students into closed classes.

Outside the Classrooms

Richmond students balance out their busy academic life by actively pursuing a myriad of student groups. The most popular groups are the 15 active fraternity and sorority chapters, with 37% of the undergraduates affiliated with a Greek group. "The dominant social scene is probably the frat parties, whether in a lodge (fraternity house) or at an apartment," one freshman explained. "However, you don't need to join the frat to go." People usually go out Thursday, Friday, and Saturday nights. The upperclassmen live in on-campus apartments, which also host a lot of parties on those nights. Students agree that while the majority of people drink, there are large numbers of people who do not and capable of finding other events to attend on the weekend.

But Greek life isn't the only activity that Richmond students are heavily involved with. UR boasts over 250 student-run clubs and organizations, covering a wide range of subjects from academics to sports to visual and performing arts. Time commitments toward these groups are entirely up to the students. "Extracurricular involvement depends on what groups you join and the time you have," one student said. "If you can't attend the meetings but still want to be part of the group, that works, too."

Like many other liberal arts colleges, sports do not play a very important role at UR and student enthusiasm is not very high. Football and basketball are probably the most popular ones. Tailgating, which is a social event by itself, during football season tends to bring out a lot of students, many of who never actually make it into the stadium or simply leave at half time. "There is pride amongst the people who attend the games, but outside the sports arenas, there is not an outstanding amount of pride for the sports teams," a freshman said.

> "The school surprised me in how welcoming it was to incoming freshmen and how well it helped people transition from high school to college."

Even though UR is located within the suburbs, it is close enough to Richmond that students can get off campus and explore the surroundings. The James River is a great spot for swimming and sunbathing in the afternoon as well as running and biking trails. However, many students choose to stay on campus and do not venture into the city too often despite free transportation services offered by the University. Many students have cars to escape the confines of the campus. "There is plenty to do without leaving the campus," one junior explained. "But if you do want to leave campus for a while, there are plenty of available."

On Campus Perks

In recent years, UR renovated several existing buildings and added a new residence hall as well as a planned business school building set to open this spring. The University expanded the Robins Stadium from a soccer and track complex to a multi-purpose stadium that will now serve the football, lacrosse, soccer and track and field teams. In 2006, the Gottwald Center for the Sciences, which hosts the biology, chemistry and physics departments, underwent a $37 million expansion that provided brand new equipments and facilities for students and faculties. As part of UR's effort to expand the internationalization of the school, the Carole Weinstein International Center was constructed and helps to match students with nearly 80 study abroad programs. "The International Center is very open and has many places to sit and relax," one freshman said.

The dining hall, affectionately known as "D-Hall," provides another place for friends to hang out. Though students are generally satisfied with the quality of food served at the Heilman Dining Center, many complain about the lack of variety. "The main dining hall has everything and nothing," one junior said. "There are many choices, but the choices do not change ever and get boring after a while." In addition to D-Hall, there are many other dining options on campus available to students. Tyler's Grill is great for a quick sandwich or breakfast snack, and it has a weekly special to change things up. One student compared the Grill to a "healthy McDonalds: very quick and tastes good." The Celllar offers great dinner choices with take-out options and also doubles as a bar, letting students to grab drinks without leaving the campus. There is a large selection of restaurants on Broad Street in downtown Richmond, about 20 minutes from campus driving.

The Weinstein Center for Recreation and Wellness is also a popular destination for students. It has a three-court gymnasium, an indoor track, six-lane swimming as well as racquet and squash courts. "The gym is clean, well-kept and extensive," one freshman said. Other student favorites include the Whitehurst building and the centrally located Commons, which spans across Westhampton Lake and provides a restaurant, a smoothie bar, TVs and game systems and play movies on the weekend.

A View to the Lake

While students have the option to move off campus, most choose stay in one of the 14 residence halls or the on-campus apartments. Freshmen are housed in single-sex dorms: Dennis, Marsh or Wood Halls for men and Lora Robins Court or Moore Hall for women. "The freshman dorms are really nice," one freshman said. "They get cleaned almost every day and are bigger than the dorms at many colleges I have seen." Several coed residence halls are also available to upperclassmen and learning communities, where all of the people live together because they are all interested in one topic. Freshmen are assigned dorms by the housing department while upperclassmen can either participate in a lottery for dorms or request a town house styled apartment. There are also RAs assigned to each freshmen residence and students said that they try to help out whenever they can and keep the hall running smoothly without becoming overly involved in people's lives. The Westhampton Lake divides the residence halls and legend has it that whoever kisses on the gazebo that connects the two sides of the lake are bound to marry each other.

There are also many traditions that students eagerly observe and participate in. At the beginning of the year, the freshmen class collectively participates in the honor code signing ceremonies—Proclamation for women and Investiture for men—that officially recognize them as members of the University. Held at a hotel in downtown Richmond, the annual Ring Dance is a formal event celebrating the junior women, who can bring family and friends as well as a date with them to the dance. During graduation weekend, the entire graduating class circles around the Westhampton Lake as part of a candlelight ceremony.

Richmond students are excited to be where they are and ready to take advantage of the plethora of opportunities available to them. Their enthusiasm for academics and extracurricular activities can be matched at very few places. As one freshman said, "The school surprised me in how welcoming it was to incoming freshmen and how well it helped people transition from high school to college."—*Jimin He*

FYI

If you come to UR, you'd better bring "comfortable shoes for walking around and knowledge of calculus."

What's the typical weekend schedule? "Generally people eat brunch between 12 and 1 pm. On Saturdays the football games are in the afternoon with tailgates before them. Then you go out Saturday night and wake up late on Sunday and do homework the rest of Sunday."

If I could change one thing about UR, it would be "making scheduling easier, especially for first year students."

University of Virginia

Address: PO Box 400160
Charlottesville, VA
22904-4160
Phone: 434-924-0311
E-mail address:
undergradadmission@
virginia.edu
Web site URL:
www.virginia.edu
Year Founded: 1819
Private or Public: Public
Religious Affiliation: None
Location: Urban
Number of Applicants:
17,798
Percent Accepted: 35%
**Percent Accepted who
enroll:** 52%
Number Entering: 3,246
**Number of Transfers
Accepted each Year:** 850
**Middle 50% SAT range: M:
620–730, CR: 600–710,
Wr: 600–710**
Middle 50% ACT range:
Unreported
**Early admission program
EA/ED/None:** None

**Percentage accepted
through EA or ED:** NA
EA and ED deadline: NA
Regular Deadline:
2-Jan
Application Fee: $60
**Full time Undergraduate
enrollment:** 15,078
Total enrollment: 22,533
Percent Male: 43%
Percent Female: 57%
**Total Percent Minority or
Unreported:** 42%
Percent African-American:
7%
**Percent Asian/Pacific
Islander:** 14%
Percent Hispanic: 5%
Percent Native-American:
<1%
Percent International: 6%
**Percent in-state/out of
state:** 72%/28%
Percent from Public HS:
75%
Retention Rate: 97%
Graduation Rate 4-year:
84%

Graduation Rate 6-year:
91%
**Percent Undergraduates
in On-campus housing:**
43%
**Number of official organized
extracurricular
organizations:** 604
3 Most popular majors:
Social Sciences,
Engineering,
Business/Marketing
Student/Faculty ratio: 15:1
Average Class Size: 16
**Percent of students
going to grad school:**
Unreported
Tuition and Fees: $29,798
**In-State Tuition and Fees if
different:** $9,505
Cost for Room and Board:
$7,820
**Percent receiving financial
aid out of those who apply,
first year:** 45%
**Percent receiving financial
aid among all students:**
25%

Founded in 1819 by Thomas Jefferson, the University of Virginia is rich with tradition and history dating back to its creation by the man who would become the third President of the United States. Since its founding, UVa has revolutionized the American university, as it was the first to offer courses of study in subjects such as philosophy, architecture, and political science. UVa's tradition of breaking tradition dictates that no student is a "freshman" or a "senior," but simply a first-year, second-year, third-year, or fourth-year. Students call their campus "the Grounds," and often refer to UVa as very simply "the University."

The University
The undergraduate program of The University of Virginia is divided into seven schools, including the Engineering School, the Architecture School, the Nursing School, the McIntire School of Commerce, the Curry School of Education, the Batten School of Leadership and Public Policy, and the College of Arts and

Sciences. Each of the University's schools has different requirements for graduation, and they are often specific to a student's major. The College of Arts and Sciences requires that students complete 120 credits to graduate, including 12 credits in sciences and mathematics, six in humanities, six in social sciences, three in history, and three in non-Western perspectives. Students as well must complete a foreign language requirement and a writing requirement. Upon entry to UVa, a small number of students, selected by the University from a pool of those specifically nominated by their high schools, are named Jefferson Scholars, and receive a full scholarship for four years of tuition, room, board, books, and other expenses. Echols Scholars, who get priority over the rest of the undergraduate body when scheduling courses, are also automatically selected during the admissions process. These students have the chance to create their own Interdisciplinary Major program, and are housed in the same first-year dormitories.

By far, the most popular major in the College is Economics, "mostly populated by those who were denied entry into the McIntire School of Commerce," as reported by one fourth-year. Some of the most difficult majors traditionally include Mechanical Engineering, Commerce, and Biochemistry. Another student illustrated this difficulty: "For example, to receive a C in Dr. Grisham's Biochemistry lecture class, he states that for every hour that students spend in class per week, they must work for a total of three hours outside of class. This totals to 9 hours outside of class for a C—you do the math." However, there are always "gut" classes, like every other university, as well as very popular classes "because the professor is just great." One more recent addition to the list of popular classes is "Gaga for Gaga," which one student described as "a legitimate class, despite accusations otherwise, where the students and professor use Lady Gaga as a launching point for discussing issues of gender and sexuality in modern society."

Students say that the workload for these classes is considerable but always manageable. "Just as any other large university, it takes a fair amount of self-discipline and initiative to stand out and do well at UVa. A student's workload is strictly dependent on his future aspirations and competitive drive," one student commented. One fourth-year student who transferred to UVa noted, "I had to get used to writing 20- to 45-page papers instead of five pages . . . but the workload obviously depends on the class and it's not very hard to adapt."

Students often find adapting to a high-work environment is easy because the professors are very helpful and readily accessible. One student said "professors are keen to the needs of their students and are very supportive." Faculty members are described as "friendly, available, and helpful." Professors are "very responsive to email" and provide very valuable help during office hours. The University strives to make the interaction between students and faculty closer and more active, and has implemented a program in which a student can "take any professor out to lunch and UVa funds will pick up your tab."

Amidst the tradition embedded in UVa culture, the University also promotes honor in all aspects of social and academic life through the Honor System. Student-governed, the Honor System places a lot of trust in the students, but treats all academic and behavioral infractions as equal under the infamous "single sanction": dismissal from the University. Some students find the code to be "frightening and fair." One student said, "Though cheating still exists at the University, the threat of expulsion and the effectiveness of honor trials in expelling students at UVa make doing so unattractive enough where it is kept to a minimum."

Wahoo!

Of course, UVa students must work hard to stand out in class, but all the hard work done during the week gives way to parties and release in this university that is more than 30 percent Greek.

> "People here just seem to have an air of integrity, and the Honor System is merely a reflection of the collective atmosphere."

While the mascot of UVa is officially the Cavaliers, the "Wahoo" has long been a popular name for those attending the University, and Charlottesville has earned the nickname "Hooville" from the presence of UVa's Wahoos. This moniker comes from name of the wahoo fish, which can supposedly drink its weight in water. "There is alcohol everywhere, and it's surprising how many UVa students actually do drink like a fish." However, one student said, "there are those who do not drink (including me) and they can still have fun, especially if they avoid the crazy-partier types."

With the prevalence of Greek life at the University, there is a party to be found every night of the weekend, but still most students restrict themselves to partying from Thursday through Saturday nights, spending the weeknights on coursework. For Wahoos, including one fourth-year athlete, who are not fans of fraternity parties, "there are over 10 bars open 7 days a week on the Corner (the popular name for a row of shops, bars, and eateries on the corner of a nearby block) in walking distance from any area on campus."

Grounds

On the Grounds, old, renovated, and new buildings retain "Thomas Jefferson's unique flair for architecture. UVa is a World Heritage Site for a reason. It's stunning and one of a kind," according to one first-year housed on UVa's campus.

First-years live on Grounds and are randomly assigned to the Old Dorms or the

New Dorms. Old Dorms—"small," non-air-conditioned two-person doubles—are "often highly sought after for their proximity to central Grounds, even though students no longer have a choice." New Dorms, which "despite renovations are not as new as the common name implies," are larger and suite-styled. One drawback of the New Dorms is their distance from the center of campus. However, they are rather close to the largest dining hall and "some lucky suites are air-conditioned." Each floor on Old Dorms and each pair of ten-person suites in New Dorms has an RA. Students say that their RAs are often rather relaxed, "but some are very strict about enforcing school policies."

After their first year, many students move off of Grounds, with 50 percent of second-years living off-campus. Many move to fraternity or sorority houses, and others move to one of the residential colleges. The residential colleges, including Hereford, Brown, and the International Residential College (IRC), "are social communities and tend to each have a basic principle, like 'odd' or 'artsy' or 'diverse,' that describes them very well." One resident of Brown described the college as "eccentric, quirky, fun, and friendly"—qualities of a community that are ensured by a long application requiring essays responding to such ridiculous topics as "Backpacking across Europe, you manage to irrevocably offend an entire village. In retaliation, an old gypsy woman puts a curse on you, making you fall in love with a refrigerator. Explain your newfound love to your parents with utmost sincerity." Hereford, while much farther from campus, is usually a very culturally and socially diverse community. Its residents request Hereford for the chance to live in a diverse community of their choosing, in lieu of the regular first-year housing which offers no choice between Old Dorms and New Dorms. In addition, "about half of the International Residential College's residents are international students and the other half American." IRC partners with local community service organizations so that its students can get more involved in local and global service.

Students who live on campus say that the dining hall food is "less than perfect, but still rather good: B+." The few complaints about dining facilities are centered on the sometimes long lines. There are three main dining halls, spaced roughly evenly on the Grounds. The newest, Observatory Hill Dining Hall, is right next to New Dorms, and is a "very social experience," according to one first-year.

Runk Dining Hall, which is rather far from much of Grounds "serves arguably the best food on Grounds." Students with meal plans can use "Plus Dollars" to shop at restaurants near campus, like Domino's and Starbucks, and can eat at on-Grounds food courts like Pavilion and Crossroads, which have restaurants like Chik-fil-A and Sbarro.

"After first year, some students do not opt in for a meal plan and either prepare or purchase their own meals in restaurants along the Corner or on campus," according to one student who described the life of students who live off-campus.

While the University's bus system "does a really great job of getting you around Grounds to wherever you need to be," many second-, third-, and fourth-years who live off-Grounds have cars. The few who do drive away from UVa on the weekends "go back home to visit their family in Virginia (since most are in-state)."

The "Conservative Stronghold"

Since UVa is a public university, it accepts primarily in-state students, and the "wealth in Northern Virginia in the suburbs of D.C. in counties such as Fairfax and Prince William" has led to a stereotype of the UVa student as white, "preppy, conservative, upper-middle class, wearing polo shirts and khaki pants." While some students see this as reality and are upset that "some people seem close-minded," others are refreshed to see Charlottesville as "one of the most open-minded places in all of Virginia," and find that in the University, there is "significant ethnic and cultural diversity despite the relative lack of geographic diversity." The latter students often find that the UVa community is "open and embracing" to those of different socio-economic backgrounds, as well as those of different sexual orientations and gender identities.

Wah-Hoo-Wah, Hoo-Rah-Ray, U-V-A!

The University of Virginia is rife with history and tradition, and this translates into intense devotion to and pride in the University's extracurricular activities, sports, and overall community. People are "very dedicated" to their extracurricular activities, which include debate in the Jefferson Society, volunteerism with the Madison House, writing for such publications as *The Cavalier Daily*, or university-wide organization of students and clubs with the University Judiciary Committee, the Honor Committee, and Student Council: "the Big Three." Besides some work-study jobs and "working in some capacity at a bar," most Wahoos are too busy with their academic life and their extracurricular life to have jobs.

Attending sports games and other athletic events is a huge way that students at UVa show school spirit. While "just about every sports team besides the football team does extremely well," especially men's and women's soccer, lacrosse, swimming, and tennis, one Cavaliers football fan said, "We dress up for no apparent reason but tradition, pre-game, and scream our hearts out even though we know we'll probably lose, and I think that says a lot about our school spirit." Besides the football games, "huge crowds show up for the champion soccer team's games and basketball games and get to see some great athletic success there as well."

Imbued in the tradition of the University are a great many secret societies. Most of these societies' operations are philanthropic in nature, but, according to one student, the different organizations of community-minded students "have different styles of secrecy." The IMPs are very public with their identities, but keep their generally altruistic actions well hidden from view. The Zs are very public about their community service, but choose to keep their identities secret until graduation. Members of the 7 Society, however, are secret until death. The philanthropy of these groups is carried out in very secretive and exciting ways, as one first year recounted that "at Convocation, the President of the University's address to all the first-years on the Lawn, the 7 Society planted letters in one speaker's hand and under the seventh seat in the seventh row, revealing that the society had donated several thousand dollars to the first-years' graduating class."

As a listen to UVa's de facto alma mater, "The Good Ole Song," will make clear, the sense of community and school pride that saturates the University is unquestionable. One Wahoo said that he would make the decision to choose UVa over other universities "every time, without question. The University is my home."—*Connor Moseley*

FYI

If you come to UVa, you'd better leave behind "the words 'freshman,' 'sophomore,' 'junior,' and 'senior.' "

If I could change one thing about UVa, "I'd change the time when first-years have to submit applications for their second-year housing—way too early in October or November, before people get to know each other and make good decisions."

Three things every student at UVa should do before graduating are "Streak the Lawn, make out in the tunnels below the Rotunda while it's raining, and give Dean Groves a high-five."

Virginia Polytechnic Institute & State University

Address: 201 Burruss Hall
Blacksburg, VA 24061
Phone: 540-231-6267
E-mail address:
vtadmiss@vt.edu
Web site URL: www.vt.edu
Year Founded: 1872
Private or Public: Public
Religious Affiliation: None
Location: Rural
Number of Applicants:
21,201
Percent Accepted: 61%
**Percent Accepted who
enroll:** 40%
Number Entering: 5,177
**Number of Transfers
Accepted each Year:** 1,358
Middle 50% SAT range: M:
580–680, CR: 540–640,
Wr: 540–630
Middle 50% ACT range:
Unreported
**Early admission program
EA/ED/None:** ED

**Percentage accepted
through EA or ED:** 51%
EA and ED deadline: 1-Nov
Regular Deadline: 15-Jan
Application Fee: $50
**Full time Undergraduate
enrollment:** 27,887
Total enrollment: 30,870
Percent Male: 58%
Percent Female: 42%
**Total Percent Minority or
Unreported:** 14%
Percent African-American:
3%
**Percent Asian/Pacific
Islander:** 8%
Percent Hispanic: 5%
Percent Native-American:
<1%
Percent International: 2%
**Percent in-state/out of
state:** 25%/75%
Percent from Public HS:
Unreported
Retention Rate: 91%

Graduation Rate 4-year: 52%
Graduation Rate 6-year: 53%
**Percent Undergraduates in
On-campus housing:** 39%
**Number of official organized
extracurricular
organizations:** 600
3 Most popular majors:
Engineering, University
Studies, Business
Student/Faculty ratio: 16:1
Average Class Size: 30
**Percent of students going to
grad school:** 21%
Tuition and Fees: $21,878
**In-State Tuition and Fees if
different:** $8,605
Cost for Room and Board:
$6,024
**Percent receiving financial
aid out of those who apply,
first year:** 36%
**Percent receiving financial
aid among all students:**
34%

Virginia Polytechnic Institute and State University, often referred to at VT or Virginia Tech, is home to more than 23,000 undergraduates. Located in Blacksburg, Virginia, the university draws much of its student body from Virginia. Here students not only get a great education, but they also are immersed with school spirit and surrounded by amazing food options.

Hokies Seek Academic Success

"The biggest thing for me that differentiates VT from other schools is our engineering fair." Every semester, VT gathers about 50 companies that are there to hire engineers for internships and co-ops. This allows students to bypass online searching for jobs, rather they just go and hand out resumes and schedule interviews on campus. Many have found paid summer internships through this event.

Students are excited by the span of classes to take. With nearly 3000 students World Regions is often regarded as one of the largest classes at VTech. Many students enjoyed this class and noted it as one of

their favorites courses taken. The class is popular with good reason—it's once a week, a core curriculum class, and with an interesting professor.

Other classes students interviewed highlighted include Intro to Acting, Human Sexuality, and Cryptography. Classes vary in how difficult they are to get into at VT. Some of the large classes that have over 2700 students and are easy to get into, while others like Intro to Acting, which is significantly smaller, is much more difficult.

Students are happy to be learning at VT. "I love going to class and learning new ways to think and considering new perspectives on things," a junior said. A sophomore noted that she felt she was getting a great education. While students pointed out they don't like the stress of exams, they feel prepared for the real world when they graduate. Hokies point out that the staff is very well qualified.

One of the downsides of a large school is that not all classes are taught by professors—some are taught by graduate students. "At first I didn't like that graduate students teach some of my classes, but I haven't found it to be a problem." Most students find faculty accessible. All teachers have "set office hours and are more than willing to make separate appointments if their office hours conflict with your schedule," a sophomore said.

Hokie Pride

Despite a large student body, they're all connected by school spirit. "We take our Hokie pride seriously," a junior said. Hokies have an immense amount of school pride. "I think by far Virginia Tech has the best school spirit out there," a sophomore said.

VT pride is also obvious in the surrounding Blacksburg area and alumni who continue to be Tech fans for life. "Once a Hokie, always a Hokie. I can say with full confidence that there is no other school like us and there is really nothing like being a Hokie," a junior said.

Everything relates back to our school's motto "Ut Prosim" which means that I may serve. A current junior described a visit to Virginia Tech her senior year of high school: "I was amazed at how many people were wearing Virginia Tech gear. It was literally a sea of maroon and orange." She said she felt an instant connection with other students. "Every time I step foot outside I realize how lucky I am to be here."

One of the dominant social scenes is at Hokie athletics when the whole community is involved and school spirit comes out in number and intensity. "The football games in Lane Stadium and the basketball games in Cassel Colosseum are intense with pride and everyone goes all out to support our Hokies," a sophomore said.

Greek life is also a major part of the social scene. Around 20% of Hokies participate in Greek life. Some students look to Greek organizations to provide parties. "Frats can host crazy parties," a sophomore said. There are also co-ed fraternities and the sororities that organize activities ranging from volunteering at animal shelters to going on cruises together.

Pomp and Circumstance

Virginia Tech abounds with traditions. One famous annual event is a huge snowball fight for the first snowfall. Corps play against Civilians. VTech is one of the few public universities that maintain a corps of cadets. "Despite the larger number of civilians, the Corps uses strategy and usually wins. It's really fun to have everyone out on the drill field in the snow!" a junior said.

Another tradition is jumping up and down to enter Sandman when the football team comes out. "Everyone is jumping and if you're not, you're forced to anyway because the entire stadium is shaking," a sophomore said. "I heard at the ACC Championship we shook the press box."

The big tradition at Virginia Tech for the juniors is the annual Ring Dance. Established by the Class of 1935, the dance has been held in subsequent years in the spring. There is a catered dinner banquet on the Friday before the dance, and then on Saturday the dance is held. The Corps of Cadets march in to form the Class' roman numerals, and dates exchange rings and see their rings for the first time. There is also a Military Ball and the Navy Ball for the Corps of Cadets every year.

There are annual parties for everybody, from the ballroom dancers to the salsa dancers to the grinders, a sophomore stated. "With such a large school if you have a .5% interest in a group, that's more than enough to host large events."

One Large Campus

Most Hokies enjoy the size of the campus and the students. "My favorite part of campus is the Drill Field," a junior said. "I think it is what makes our campus stand out. I love walking across it going to and from class, watching the Corps of Cadets marching and students wearing Maroon and Orange with pride."

> We are especially spirited. It's one of the reasons that I chose to come.

Others enjoy Lane Stadium because football games are the highlight of the year, while others revel in the size of the student population. "There's so many people that you just meet everyone and know there's still so many different people to meet."

Another benefit of a large campus is that there are clubs for everything—"Skydiving, skiing, snowboarding, surfing, chess, math, obscure Indian culture, renaissance, etc." There are also clubs for most majors.

There are also various singing groups: Juxtaposition (all male a capella), Solstice (all female a capella). "The VTU (Virginia Tech Union) arranges for the awesome concerts and entertainment we have at Tech," a junior said. Virginia Tech's clubs host many large events such as Relay For Life.

Though many VTech students come from Virginia, not many go home on weekends, as there is so much fun and events to go to at VTech. According to a sophomore, "No one goes home, unless sick or visiting others." Many students stay on campus because their friends are on campus and since sporting events are often on weekends.

Housing Options and Yummy Food

Freshmen are required to live on campus. Housing is selected in a lottery system based on seniority. There are special housing requests that you can opt into (i.e. the Galileo dorm is half full of engineers). After freshman year, most live off campus. There are around 5000 freshmen and approximately 9000 slots for on campus housing.

Dorms typically have 1 RA for each floor or hallway who serve as mentors. "They basically make sure you have a pleasant living experience on campus and that you stay out of trouble," a sophomore stated. The RAs are there for students to talk to, get advice from, and to enforce housing rules when needed.

The strictness of the RA is dependent on the RA. "I've heard stories of RAs who enforced curfew and made random checks, and I've heard of RAs who regularly took the kids out to parties," a sophomore said. "Personally, I still party with my RA."

Those in sororities and fraternities can live in the Oak Lane community, which is considered on campus housing but is more of a home with brothers or sisters. Food gets top marks at VT—it's rated #1 for campus food in the country. "Virginia Tech has the best dining service in the country, our food is unbelievable," a junior said. They have steak, lobster, and salmon options at the five main dining halls. There is also an additional express dining hall, kiosks, and a few small places here and there where students can get food.

"I can pretty much think of anything I want and I'll be able to get it at least one place campus," a sophomore said.

Hokies report there is a new dining hall being built on the academic side of campus for those who live off-campus and don't want to hike across the drill field to get food between classes.

To pay for the food, students sign up for a certain amount of money and it's put on a Hokie Passport. The food is priced and when students swipe their Hokie Passport, they get 50% off the price and the money is taken off their card.

With all Virginia Tech has to offer, it's no surprise students from all over the nation flock there to get an undergraduate education. The students are full of spirit and the school is so full of traditions, making VT a destination to learn and create friendships for life.—*Sharon Yin & Jenny Dai*

FYI

If you come to VT, you'd better leave behind "anything UVA related, there will be serious consequences!"

What is the typical weekend schedule? "Parties are usually on Friday and Saturday nights, studying and sleep in the time between."

Three things every student at VT should do before graduating: "go to a football game, Ring Dance, and live off-campus"

Washington & Lee University

Address: 204 West
Washington Avenue
Lexington, VA 24450-2116
Phone: 540-458-8710
E-mail address:
admissions@wlu.edu
Web site URL: www.wlu.edu
Year Founded: 1749
Private or Public: Private
Religious Affiliation: None
Location: Rural
Number of Applicants: 4,215
Percent Accepted: 27%
Percent Accepted who
enroll: 39%
Number Entering: 449
Number of Transfers
Accepted each Year: 17
Middle 50% SAT range: M:
650–730, CR: 650–740,
Wr: Unreported
Middle 50% ACT range:
28–32
Early admission program
EA/ED/None: ED
Percentage accepted
through EA or ED: 38%

EA and ED deadline:
15-Nov
Regular Deadline: 15-Jan
Application Fee: $50
Full time Undergraduate
enrollment: 1,752
Total enrollment: 2,155
Percent Male: 50%
Percent Female: 50%
Total Percent Minority or
Unreported: 10%
Percent African-American:
3%
Percent Asian/Pacific
Islander: 4%
Percent Hispanic: 2%
Percent Native-American:
1%
Percent International:
Unreported
Percent in-state/out of
state: 15%/85%
Percent from Public HS:
94%
Retention Rate: 94%
Graduation Rate 4-year:
Unreported

Graduation Rate 6-year:
Unreported
Percent Undergraduates
in On-campus housing:
61%
Number of official organized
extracurricular
organizations: Unreported
3 Most popular majors:
Social Science, Art, History
Student/Faculty ratio:
Unreported
Average Class Size: 23
Percent of students
going to grad school:
Unreported
Tuition and Fees: $37,412
In-State Tuition and Fees if
different: No difference
Cost for Room and Board:
$9,400
Percent receiving financial
aid out of those who apply,
first year: 73%
Percent receiving financial
aid among all students:
35%

As its name suggests, Washington and Lee University is steeped in history and shaped by two of America's greatest leaders, George Washington and Robert E. Lee.

Since it was founded in 1749, the board of trustees has renamed the institution three times before settling on its current name in 1870 after Lee's death. Though it is a traditional Southern institution with a dominating Greek life, Washington and Lee's student body has a lot of geographical diversity, which, as one sophomore from Texas put it, "not as Southern as I thought it would be." Located in a small town in Lexington, Virginia (about 3 1/2 hours southwest of Washington, D.C.), Washington and Lee is the central focus of the town, making Lexington a "quaint and safe" college town for all students. What distinguishes Washington and Lee over other small liberal arts schools are its traditions, most notably the "speaking tradition" and the Honor Code. Moreover, the size fosters a really strong sense of community. As one sophomore put it, "I feel like I know the names of almost everyone here."

Work Hard

Washington and Lee has a rigorous academic program which often requires students to spend quite a bit of time in the library. One student said that she has never been in a class with more than 30 people. She couldn't even imagine a class having more than 40 people. But because of these small classes, one sophomore noted that it puts pressure on kids to step up to the plate and participate. Instead of having a midterm and a final that makes up your grade for the term, students at Washington and Lee also have frequent homework and papers because teachers have time to grade students' work because they don't have that many students in their classes. Additionally, one student said, "most classes aren't curved because they don't want students to compete. That mentality discourages cut-throat competitiveness."

There are three terms at Washington and Lee (fall, winter and spring). During fall and winter terms, students usually take four classes. But during spring term, students immerse themselves into one class. According to one student, "everyone loves spring term." Students can also join the Journalism or Business school if they want to concentrate on one of those subjects. You don't need to apply for these schools, so anyone can do it. Students at Washington and Lee really value the constant communication with their professors. One sophomore said, "It's really easy to stay over the summer and do research with professors. You can make your own experience here because there are so many options." Though most students at Washington and Lee rave about the classroom life, one student did say that she was disappointed with all of the requirements for majors (the business major in particular).

Play Hard

After long days and nights in the library during the week, Washington and Lee students definitely know how to have fun. Like most Southern schools, the social life at Washington and Lee is centered around fraternities and sororities. "Almost everyone is in a frat or a sorority," one sophomore said. But another student added that "Greek life is very welcoming here. There are no closed parties. Anyone can walk into Frats." One freshman also said that upperclassmen are very welcoming to freshman at parties. While freshmen live in freshman dorms and eat in the dining hall, sophomores live in their fraternity's or sorority's houses and eat in their fraternity's or sorority's dining hall. But one student said "you can eat in whatever house you want. It's not exclusive."

Be a Gentleman

When Robert E. Lee became president of Washington and Lee in 1865, he established what is now known as the Honor Code in order to encourage men to "behave like gentlemen." Though the institution began admitting women in 1985, the Honor Code still has a huge presence at the school, dictating almost everything students do. While there are no written rules, no "dos" or "don'ts," an executive committee comprised entirely of students determines whether or not a student has violated the honor code. Violations can be anything from speeding to more serious offenses such as plagiarism and cheating, which lead directly to expulsion if the student is found guilty. While one student noted that the honor code "makes people cautious of working together on assignments," she added that this doesn't mean that Washington and Lee is a "cut-throat" environment. Because of the Honor Code's strong presence on campus, teachers often give students closed-book take-home tests and even allow students to pick up their final exams to complete at their own convenience. Once students turn in their assignments, they have to sign their name to ensure that they have upheld the Honor Code. Additionally, one freshman said, "There's a huge sense of trust on campus. You can leave anything anywhere without worrying that someone would take it." When asked how many people actually follow the Honor Code, a sophomore said, "definitely 99%." She added, "it works because you pick the school knowing about the Honor Code and you take pride in it."

> "There's a huge sense of trust on campus. You can leave anything anywhere without worrying that someone would take it."

Washington and Lee students also take pride in another aspect of chivalry known as the "speaking tradition." The small undergraduate population (around 1800 students) fosters a real sense of community that is strengthened by this tradition which encourages everyone to say hi to each other whenever you pass someone on a path or in the hallway. "Everyone is really friendly," one freshman said. "With this tradition, it's not weird to say hi to someone you don't know. It just works really well with our small school."

"Lex Vegas"

Well, Lexington, Virginia isn't exactly Las Vegas, but it definitely has its perks. One student described Lexington as a "historic town with plenty of good restaurants and shops." Another added that it's great for college kids because it has the basic necessities and it's really safe. A lot of Juniors and Seniors move off campus and live in apartments in Lexington. One sophomore also insisted that all students must explore Lexington and the surrounding area during their four years at Washington and Lee. "There are the Blue Ridge mountains and hiking and camping and tubing all really close to campus. It's one of the prettiest parts of the country." The Honor System also extends into the town. A sophomore said, "If you're ever short of money when you're buying something, stores and restaurants in the town trust that kids from Washington and Lee will always pay them back."—*Charlotte Dillon and Madeline McMahon*

FYI
If you come to Washington and Lee, you'd better leave "liberal points of view" behind.
What's the typical weekend schedule? "Pregame, party until 2, brunch on Sunday, work in the library."
Three things every student at Washington and Lee should do before graduating are "go to a sporting event; streak the Collonade; visit the Robert E. Lee chapel; go to homecoming."

Washington

Evergreen State College

Address: 2700 Evergreen Parkway NW, Olympia, WA 98505
Phone: 360-867-6170
E-mail address: admissions@evergreen.edu
Web site URL: www.evergreen.edu
Year Founded: 1967
Private or Public: Public
Religious Affiliation: None
Location: Urban
Number of Applicants: 1,989
Percent Accepted: 94%
Percent Accepted who enroll: 35%
Number Entering: 659
Number of Transfers Accepted each Year: 1,281
Middle 50% SAT range: M: 470–600, CR: 530–660, Wr: Unreported
Middle 50% ACT range: Unreported
Early admission program EA/ED/None: None

Percentage accepted through EA or ED: NA
EA and ED deadline: NA
Regular Deadline: 1-Mar
Application Fee: $50
Full time Undergraduate enrollment: 4,364
Total enrollment: 4,696
Percent Male: 54%
Percent Female: 46%
Total Percent Minority or Unreported: 32%
Percent African-American: 4%
Percent Asian/Pacific Islander: 5%
Percent Hispanic: 5%
Percent Native-American: 3%
Percent International: 1%
Percent in-state/out of state: 72%/28%
Percent from Public HS: Unreported
Retention Rate: 70%
Graduation Rate 4-year: 51%

Graduation Rate 6-year: 57%
Percent Undergraduates in On-campus housing: 22%
Number of official organized extracurricular organizations: 61
3 Most popular majors: Social Sciences, Humanities, Visual Performing Arts
Student/Faculty ratio: 22:1
Average Class Size: 25
Percent of students going to grad school: 21%
Tuition and Fees: $16,189
In-State Tuition and Fees if different: $5,329
Cost for Room and Board: $8,052
Percent receiving financial aid out of those who apply, first year: 67%
Percent receiving financial aid among all students: 54%

Founded in 1968 to balance the geographical distribution of public universities in the State of Washington, Evergreen State College is a liberal arts institution that caters mostly to undergraduates, though there are also a small number of postgraduates in the masters programs. It has a reputation of being politically liberal, which is certainly the case as most students are left leaning. However, a large part of its liberal reputation is also because Evergreen State was founded as an alternative institution, much different from other schools. The best-known feature of Evergreen State is that it does not give out grades. Instead, students receive narrative-style narratives by professors. Therefore, all students only get comments on their performances, not an actual letter or number. However, far beyond the grading system, Evergreen State is every bit different from most other colleges in the country.

Hard Working Yet No Grade

As an experimental college, Evergreen State already has a long history of doing things differently from others. The most intriguing part of the college, however, is still the unique grading system. After all, following years of laboring for a high GPA in high school, it may seem inconceivable for many college freshmen to find themselves without having to worry about scoring a certain number of points on a test. That is the beauty of Evergreen State. It allows students to focus on learning something from their classes instead of trying to get through tests and papers to obtain a reasonable score. Therefore, at Evergreen State, learning comes before grading. Although the lack of grading may seem simply strange, people at Evergreen State believe that it actually approaches what happens in the real world. Most employers do not give a single number to people to determine whether they should be retained, promoted, or fired. They take a broader view of what the employee has achieved. The same works at Evergreen. At the end of each course, professors meet with the student about his or her performance. They provide a detailed narrative of the student's work. In addition, the student also has the opportunity to provide self-evaluation of performance, not to mention offering critiques of the professors. "I think the evaluation process at Evergreen State is the best part of my experience," said one student. "There is less stress and more learning."

One of the reasons for the narrative evaluation is that courses are taken differently at Evergreen State. At the majority of universities, students major in a field by taking individual classes in a single department. Although there may be a few required courses, most students end up with a collection of individual classes without being able to make the linkage between them. Therefore, students enroll in programs, which are a series of classes on a theme, not a single topic. Professors from different disciplines would teach the program. Students will therefore have a better appreciation of how academic fields are actually interrelated.

Students can also create their own area of study called Learning Contracts, in which students, after completing a few prerequisites, can simply decide to study on their own. Of course, a faculty member follows the student closely to provide advice and to ensure that the person is actually doing the work.

Given the necessity for professors to provide individual comments and the type of close interaction needed during classes, academic programs at Evergreen State have fewer than 25 people per session. "I love being able to study in smaller groups," said one student. "Large lectures at other schools make you go to sleep, but here, everything is so interactive."

From the outset, there would seem to be little incentive for students to work hard. After all, there is no grading. However, it is important to point out that there is still a transcript, which will have commentaries by the professors. That is the way employers or graduate schools will evaluate the students. Therefore, it is still important for students to do their work and try to do the best they can in classes. "We actually work a lot," said one student. "When I first came here, I thought that we can all slack off. But then I realized that we have a demanding curriculum, and there is a lot of pressure from your peers to professors to do well and participate in class."

> **"Most people are liberal here, but it does not mean that we are completely intolerant of conservative ideas."**

Even though Evergreen State is a small college, there are also plenty of research opportunities, especially in environment-related fields. In addition, the school encourages students to undertake internships and acquire work experiences, some of which can be converted into academic credits.

The Capital of Washington

Olympia is a small city of about 42,000 people. Nevertheless, it is one of Washington's cultural centers and the state's capital. As is expected of state capitals, the city provides a large number of cultural activities, such as fine art and theater, and parks. "Olympia is a very nice city," said one student. "We are definitely not a big place like Seattle, but we have our own identities." The city also has a collection of restaurants and bars around campus, which are certainly valuable for students in search of something to do during weekends. Furthermore, as one student pointed out, as the state capital, Olympia "feels like a highly intellectual city."

Most students live off campus while attending Evergreen State. Many people choose to do so because they come from nearby areas and live at home—since it is a public university, the majority of students are from the state. At the same time, many people choose to live in the blocks surrounding the college to have a more independent experience. A considerable number of freshmen, however, choose to spend their first year on campus. The school designates specific buildings for freshmen so that they can meet each other and create a sense of first-year community. Students are placed into either singles or doubles.

The dinning services operate five locations, including two convenience stores. Most students agree that the food is satisfactory. "We don't have that many choices, but the food is good," said one student. "If you don't like it, you can always find other places around campus." The college has four dining plans for freshmen and five voluntary plans for other students, as well as faculty and staff.

The social activities often happen on campus. Since many off campus students can be spread out, dorms are excellent places to host parties. The school is not extremely severe in monitoring the students' party scene, as long as no one does anything outrageous within the dorms.

Outside of Classrooms

Evergreen State is certainly not known for its sports teams. It has nine varsity intercollegiate teams. "Sports teams are definitely not big here," said one student. "Some people go to the games once in a while, but not often." Student clubs, on the other hand, abound and provide excellent opportunities to acquire a new interest or simply meet new people. As to the belief that Evergreen State is extremely liberal, one student remarked, "Most people are liberal here, but it does not mean that we are completely intolerant of conservative ideas."

Evergreen State is very different from other colleges, and so are the student experiences. In many ways, attending Evergreen State is a slightly risky move. Some people may truly enjoy a school without grades and big lectures. Others may prefer a more traditional college experience. Nevertheless, for all those willing to try something novel, something different, Evergreen State may be the answer for you.—*Xiaohang Liu, Paul Treadgold*

FYI
If you come to Evergreen State, you'd better bring "an umbrella."
What is the typical weekend schedule? "Party in dorms, concerts in Olympia, and homework."
If I could change one thing about Evergreen State, I'd "make it rain less."

University of Puget Sound

Address: 1500 North Warner Street, Tacoma, WA 98416-1062
Phone: 800-396-7191
E-mail address: admission@ups.edu
Web site URL: www.ups.edu
Year Founded: 1888
Private or Public: Private
Religious Affiliation: None
Location: Suburban
Number of Applicants: 5,580
Percent Accepted: 65%
Percent Accepted who enroll: 19%
Number Entering: 748
Number of Transfers Accepted each Year: 173
Middle 50% SAT range: M: 570–670, CR: 570–680, Wr: 560–660
Middle 50% ACT range: 25–29
Early admission program EA/ED/None: ED I, ED II

Percentage accepted through EA or ED: Unreported
EA and ED deadline: 15-Nov, 2-Jan
Regular Deadline: 15-Jan
Application Fee: $50
Full time Undergraduate enrollment: 2,536
Total enrollment: 2,858
Percent Male: 42%
Percent Female: 58%
Total Percent Minority or Unreported: 17%
Percent African-American: 3%
Percent Asian/Pacific Islander: 9%
Percent Hispanic: 4%
Percent Native-American: 1%
Percent International: Unreported
Percent in-state/out of state: 30%/70%
Percent from Public HS: 75%
Retention Rate: 85%

Graduation Rate 4-year: 70%
Graduation Rate 6-year: 76%
Percent Undergraduates in On-campus housing: 59%
Number of official organized extracurricular organizations: Unreported
3 Most popular majors: Business, Psychology, English & International Political Economy
Student/Faculty ratio: 11:1
Average Class Size: 18
Percent of students going to grad school: 55%
Tuition and Fees: $33,975
In-State Tuition and Fees if different: No difference
Cost for Room and Board: $8,760
Percent receiving financial aid out of those who apply, first year: 83%
Percent receiving financial aid among all students: 60%

Located near the cities of Tacoma and Seattle and the natural landmarks of Mount Rainier and Puget Sound, University of Puget Sound gives its students a unique experience that is both urban and rural. With a variety of social and academic areas to explore, Puget Sound offers all the opportunities of a larger university while structuring its academics and extracurriculars around what is most important: a personal experience for each and every student.

A Unique Introduction

Students' holistic experiences at University of Puget Sound begin as soon as they step foot on campus. Puget Sound's unique three-part orientation is called Prelude, Passages and Perspectives. It introduces students to the environmental, academic, and community-oriented aspects of the university. Students are first given a taste, or "Prelude," of Puget Sound academics with a sample of a typical day of classes. Then, during "Passages," students are sent on a camping trip in Hood Canal, three hours away from campus. Through three days of hiking through the wilderness, watching the sunrise from the top of a mountain, and gathering around huge bonfires, students learn to appreciate the natural beauty surrounding Puget Sound and develop bonds with their fellow students. One student recounted, "There is a special kind of bonding that takes place when you spend three days backpacking in the wilderness without a shower." The third segment, "Perspectives: Urban Plunge," demonstrates Puget Sound's involvement with the Tacoma community. In "Perspectives," students engage in service projects ranging from cleaning the Puget Sound to working with mentally disabled people. These three components let students experience three important parts of a Puget Sound education: environment, academics and community.

Small College Treatment, Large College Selection

As a liberal arts college, University of Puget Sound encourages its students to explore numerous academic fields outside of their own majors. In order to fulfill the core requirements, which consist of eight different courses in different academic areas, students must take at least one core course every semester over their four years at Puget Sound. However, the university's unique core class system makes it simple to find classes that fulfill the core requirements and that interest students from every major by offering these classes in almost every department. For instance, one potential English major claimed, "I can fulfill my math core requirement with a class in the philosophy department."

Although the ways through which students can fulfill their core requirements are numerous, some students may find it difficult to get the exact classes that they want. Course scheduling for freshmen is a laborious process because some popular classes fill up quickly or are offered in only a couple of time slots. As a result, some students may find it difficult to "take the classes [they] need to take while fitting them into a feasible schedule."

Once students get into their desired classes, however, they are likely to find a unique and personal experience. The majority of courses at Puget Sound consist of classes with fewer than 25 students, and each student should expect to pay attention in every class. Because of the small class sizes, one student noted, "people attend class and pay attention to the discussion because, when there is no back row, sleeping is not an option." Similarly, students expect to receive personal attention from their professors. As one student reported, when she began to pay less attention in class, her professor e-mailed her, writing, "I noticed that your in-class participation has dropped off a little, and I wanted to say that I value your opinion very much and encourage you to talk." Eager to ensure that each of their students performs well, professors are available for assistance outside of class, by office hours, or by e-mail appointments. In addition, professors encourage students to meet with them on other subjects. For example, one student said, "I spent one afternoon going over a German test and the meeting ended with us talking about places in Washington to go spelunking."

Although teachers want their students to do well, good grades are by no means easily achieved at Puget Sound. One student says, "In one of my classes the professor told us that A's were reserved for perfect work only." However, getting good grades is not impossible. Students agree that professors grade fairly. One student said, "I have never felt cheated out of the grade I deserved, nor have I felt I've gotten good grades when I least deserved them."

Daring You to Try Something New

Extracurriculars at Puget Sound are numerous and diverse, from political clubs such as Young Democrats and Young Republicans to entertainment groups such as the Circus Club. Puget Sound is not a sports school—in the words of one student, "You won't find 10,000 students at the football games"—but on the whole its athletic teams are competitive. Among the most competitive of the Division III teams are the swim team–the women's team is ranked number one in the region—the women's soccer team, and the crew team. For those who would rather participate than observe, Puget Sound intramurals are extensive and popular as well.

The variety in Puget Sound's extracurriculars dares the University's students to try something new. One of the most popular extracurricular groups at Puget Sound is the Repertory Dance Group (RDG). A no-cut campus dance troupe that performs one show every semester, RDG is composed of expert and novice dancers and choreographers of every style. The most unique extracurricular activities at Puget Sound, however, take advantage of its proximity to natural reserves. One of the most popular activities is Puget Sound Outdoors, which organizes "reasonably priced outdoors trips like weekend backpacking trips, ski trips, rock climbing trips, etc." Puget Sound even has its own student-run equipment rental shop, the Expeditionary (affectionately called the Expy), which equips students for outdoor excursions from camping to cross-country skiing.

At Puget Sound, not only are students encouraged to try a variety of extracurriculars, but they are also given motivation to pursue them. The unique system of credits at Puget Sound awards 0.25 credits for certain co-curricular activities. For instance, students majoring in Communication Studies may earn activity credits for participating in competitive forensic programs like the National Parliamentary Debate Association (NPDA) debate.

Of Castles and Cafés

University of Puget Sound is located in a suburban neighborhood. Puget Sound has taken advantage of the area near the University and purchased houses surrounding the campus for student living. Consequently, many juniors and seniors live in these on-campus houses instead of dorms. However, off-campus housing in the neighborhood is also abundant.

On-campus housing is available in the form of themed houses and residence dorms, many of which have distinct personalities. For instance, Todd/Phibs is the unofficial "party dorm." Puget Sound's official themed dorms are not, as one student described it, the "look, all the potheads live together" unofficial kind. For example, Harrington features the official Healthy Options floor, and Schiff Hall houses the Outdoors dorm. Themed on-campus houses like the Comic House and House of Ramen line the famous "Theme Row."

Campus food at Puget Sound, like typical cafeteria food, can get tiring. However, students consistently boast of its variety. With sandwich lines and theme nights, there is usually something worth trying. Other on-campus restaurants, such as the Oppenheimer Café ("the OC"), Diversions Café, and the Cellar, which serves late-night pizza and ice cream, give students several dining and snacking options no matter what time of day or night they want to eat. Puget Sound is also very vegetarian-friendly and has been rated by PETA as one of the top 10 universities for most vegetarian options. For those who still want to dine off campus, there are numerous choices. Silk Thai offers delicious Thai cuisine. Farrelli's and Garlic Jim's pizza are popular, and cafés like the Mandolin and Rosewood Cafés serve delicious sandwiches and other simple fare. Puget Sound's proximity to Tacoma gives students ample opportunity to explore the city's best restaurants.

> "I spent one afternoon going over a German test and the meeting ended with us talking about places in Washington to go spelunking."

"Student opinion on campus security varies depending on who is asked. While some contend that they have "never felt unsafe on campus" and emphasize that there have been "no crimes and no thefts," others say that they feel uncomfortable walking alone at night. However, students know that security is always available to escort students both on and off campus.

Puget Sound 101: How to Change the World

Appropriate to its proximity to nature and its devotion to the outdoors, Puget Sound is a university that makes sustainability one of its priorities. For example, the university participates in numerous sustainable programs around campus, such as the vermicomposting program, which is run by Students for a Sustainable Campus in conjunction with Dining Services and turns the University's food waste into fertile soil by using red worms. Puget Sound's eco-friendly beliefs also manifest in its mascot. While the Puget Sound athletic teams are called the "Loggers," the university's official mascot has changed from a logger to a grizzly bear, "Grizz." As one student reports, "Grizz is our mascot, because at such an eco-friendly school, we felt a logger was too unsustainable . . . we take our sustainability very seriously." In addition to sustainability, Puget Sound students have been passionate about many other domestic and international issues, such as the 2008 presidential election and the genocide in Darfur.

As part of the "number one liberal college feeder into the Peace Corps," Puget Sound students are, as one student describes, "the ones who will change the world."

For the student who is passionate about resolving current issues, University of Puget Sound offers a personalized education and numerous opportunities to explore in academics, extracurriculars and life experience. As one student put it, Puget Sound is "for dedicated, intelligent, outdoorsy, active, passionate, open-minded people. [It] will give you a unique education [and] teach you to think in a forward, global way."—*Chaoran Chen*

FYI

If you come to UPS, you'd better bring "your hiking boots and rain slicker."
What's the typical weekend schedule? "Friday night, prepare for a hiking trip or find a party; Saturday night, watch a movie or hang out with friends; Sunday, wake up late and do homework."
If I could change one thing about UPS, I'd "find a way to encourage ethnic diversity on campus."
Three things every student at UPS should do before graduating are "spend a weekend in the mountains, devise a plan to steal the Hatchet, and participate in the Repertory Dance Group."

University of Washington

Address: 1410 Northeast Campus Parkway, Box 355852, Seattle, WA 98195
Phone: 206-543-2100
E-mail address: Visit website to submit questions
Web site URL: www.washington.edu
Year Founded: 1861
Private or Public: Public
Religious Affiliation: None
Location: Suburban
Number of Applicants: 17,777
Percent Accepted: 65%
Percent Accepted who enroll: 46%
Number Entering: 5,278
Number of Transfers Accepted each Year: 1,807
Middle 50% SAT range: M: 570–680, CR: 530–650, Wr: 530–640
Middle 50% ACT range: 23–29
Early admission program EA/ED/None: None

Percentage accepted through EA or ED: NA
EA and ED deadline: NA
Regular Deadline: 15-Jan
Application Fee: $50
Full time Undergraduate enrollment: 28,570
Total enrollment: 38,415
Percent Male: 45%
Percent Female: 55%
Total Percent Minority or Unreported: 53%
Percent African-American: 2%
Percent Asian/Pacific Islander: 31%
Percent Hispanic: 6%
Percent Native-American: 1%
Percent International: 9%
Percent in-state/out of state: 84%/16%
Percent from Public HS: Unreported
Retention Rate: 92%
Graduation Rate 4-year: 48%

Graduation Rate 6-year: 74%
Percent Undergraduates in On-campus housing: 20%
Number of official organized extracurricular organizations: 550
3 Most popular majors: Social Sciences, Biology, Business/Marketing
Student/Faculty ratio: 12:1
Average Class Size: 24
Percent of students going to grad school: Unreported
Tuition and Fees: $23,219
In-State Tuition and Fees if different: $6,802
Cost for Room and Board: $8,640
Percent receiving financial aid out of those who apply, first year: Unreported
Percent receiving financial aid among all students: Unreported

Nestled in the shadows of the Cascade and Olympic Mountain Ranges, the University of Washington embraces its Seattle location by combining the distinction of a prominent research institution with a "relaxed, West coast atmosphere."

Living in Husky Territory
Despite the rumors, Seattle is far from being the rain capital of the nation. In fact, Seattle's annual precipitation is actually less than that of Miami, Boston, New York, Philadelphia, and Washington D.C.! That being said, the city's rainy reputation stems from the dreary winter months, when for several weeks the region is enveloped in cloudy skies and light drizzle.

UW is a large university, enrolling nearly 43,000 undergraduate and graduate students on three campuses. The main location is in Seattle, Washington, with smaller campuses in Bothell and Tacoma. All three facilities serve an incredibly diverse student body, offering combinations of day and evening classes for either full-time or part-time students. Raved one junior, "The [Seattle] campus is absolutely gorgeous. We have over 700 acres of trees, grass, and amazing Gothic architecture. The people are amazing and it honestly doesn't rain that much!"

"UW is a very self-directed university," another student noted. "You need to know what you want in order to get it. Because it's so big, no one does it for you." With over 25,000 undergraduates on the Seattle campus alone, many incoming freshmen worry that they will become a nameless face in the crowd. However, current students repeatedly declared that friends are easy to find, and with "over 500 student groups, there's always something going on!"

> "The campus is absolutely gorgeous, the people are amazing, and it honestly doesn't rain that much!"

Most students begin to associate with a certain social circle early in their college experience. Social life at the UW, despite its diversity, is described as fairly segregated between the Greeks, the dorm kids, and the commuters. While the Greeks are sometimes described as "the rich white kids who wear Uggs and North Face jackets," the dominant campus fashion is decidedly practical: "fleeces, jeans, comfy stuff to stay dry and warm." One student cited the social groups as the main difference between underclassmen and upperclassmen; the older students tend to already have their social circles established, while the incoming freshmen are much more open to hanging out with whomever.

Dorm Life and Coffee Breaks
Most UW students live on campus for their freshman year. Hansee (all singles) and McCarty halls are the two most popular. There are also theme dorms based on a student's interests, each occupying one or two floors inside the larger buildings. "I lived in the Honors House for two years, which was all the honors students. There's also a substance-free dorm and an outdoor focus dorm," one student said. Even though the dorms are always full, UW is also "a huge commuter school."

When it comes to dining, Huskies claim that "we have the best campus food service in the country!" The meal plan is fairly simple, as students place a certain amount of money in their dining accounts to spend like cash. Even though there are dining halls all over campus, Huskies may also choose to take advantage of the "cheap, amazing ethnic food places" in the U-District. As is to be expected in the birthplace of Starbucks, "The coffee shops are good, and there are tons of cute little secret ones all over, so go search for them!"

Upperclassmen often move off-campus into the surrounding neighborhoods. The Greek system occupies the north neighborhood, with 27 frats and 16 sororities owning off-campus houses. The area ten or so blocks north, Ravenna, is "nice, a little quieter." Despite the slightly higher rent, the U-District is a vibrant, diverse neighborhood, filled with cheap eateries, popular hangouts, and cool stores.

With over 85 percent of the undergraduate student body hailing from Washington State, the campus can often feel empty on Saturdays when students go home for the weekends. Most do not have cars, as parking is expensive. The bus system is easy, efficient, and free for students because part of their tuition goes toward a bus pass that allows for free rides on all Seattle public transportation. With the Sea-Tac airport, the ferry docks, and the Amtrak train station only a bus ride away, most UW students find they can travel fairly conveniently.

Sleepless in Seattle
In keeping with the diverse student body, there are many options for nighttime activities,

though students listed a few particularly notable events. The residence halls throw a weeklong extravaganza called "Winterfest," complete with casino nights, dances, and bonfires. The annual "Powwow" and "Spring Cruise," in addition to the Greeks' annual Homecoming and "Anchor Splash" parties, also received high praise. On normal weekends, upperclassmen party more at bars or houses, while freshmen tend to flock to the larger frat parties.

UW's student body incorporates the complete spectrum of attitudes toward student drinking: some students go out every night of the week, while other students never touch alcohol. Students claim that, depending on one's social circle, there is not a lot of pressure to drink. Because the residence halls actually have a pretty strict alcohol and drug policy—including probation and mandatory alcohol counseling following certain offenses—most of the drinking takes place off campus. These regulations, however, are met with mixed reviews. According to one student, "If you get caught smoking pot by the campus police, you get in less trouble than you do for jaywalking."

Husky Fitness and Pride

Since Seattle has been named "the fittest city in the U.S." (according to rankings released by *Men's Fitness* in 2005), it comes as no surprise that the University of Washington is also recognized as one of the top athletic programs in the country. It is not unusual for the 10 men's and 11 women's varsity teams to earn national honors. If you are more inclined to cheer from the stands, Huskies hold the gold standard for the student cheering sections: "There is a lot of pride invested in being a Husky!" exclaimed a junior. All sports, except basketball and football, are free for students. During the fall, volleyball and football dominate the scene, as the "campus literally shuts down on football Saturday." During the annual Apple Cup, thousands of UW Huskies flock to the football stadium to cheer their school to victory over archrival Washington State. During the winter, die-hard basketball fans camp outside the gym for days before games even if they already have tickets—just to show their support! This student section is one of the best in the country; affectionately called the "Dawg Pack," this group of devoted fans even has its own locker in the men's locker room.

For the non-varsity athletes, there is a state-of-the-art gym called the "IMA." It has an elevated running track, a 5,000-square-foot weight room, over 300 machines, four basketball courts, racquetball, squash and tennis courts, a pool, saunas, and an indoor climbing wall. Free for all students, the gym also offers a diverse array of fitness classes, over 30 club sports, and the Dawg Bites Sports Café. Intramural sports are also a popular activity, ranging from very competitive to purely recreational. Examples include inner-tube basketball, ultimate Frisbee, rowing, and bowling.

There are over 550 student clubs on campus, ranging from living groups to multicultural societies to political associations to "just plain weird" groups. Students listed a medley of different organizations, including the Filipino American Student Association, the Amateur Porn Club, the Peanut Butter and Jelly Club, and Habitat for Humanity. Extremist or not, students dedicate a lot of time to their organizations, and social groups are often defined by extracurricular activities.

Many students also manage to balance their studies and a job—either on campus as RAs or tutors, or in the local "U-District" neighborhood as waiters or store clerks. Since Huskies love their coffee, 22 espresso stands on campus supply students with part-time jobs, hang-out places, and delicious, cheap coffee.

In the Classroom

With over 1,800 undergraduate courses offered every quarter, incoming freshmen might feel slightly overwhelmed. Freshmen may choose to join the FIG (Freshman Interest Group) program, where small groups of freshmen with similar academic interests share the same courses during their first quarter. The Honors Program is highly regarded, though a junior stressed that the program's diverse and interesting classes can be hard to get into.

Don't be surprised if many classes your freshman year are on the higher end of the student-to-faculty ratio. Said one sophomore, "My first quarter, all my classes had over 700 people in them, which was really daunting." Although the workload of a specific course almost directly corresponds with the difficulty of a class, a sophomore noted an important exception in the introductory classes. "The introductory grading can be very hard," she said, "as the main purpose of many of the intro classes is to 'weed out' those students who cannot handle the workload." However, once a student becomes more involved in a department, the focus is more on the material and the learning process. "I didn't expect the professors to be as open to students as they were," one student explained. "They really made an effort to get to know us, so it wasn't at all impersonal."

The academics at the UW are extremely varied, as the requirements for graduation differ from college to college. The most competitive programs include the business school, the architecture school, and the college of engineering. The science majors are also widely cited as being difficult, due to the UW's top-tier medical school and the large number of students who enroll for its stellar scientific research facilities. Many other majors do not have any prerequisites for admission or a competitive admissions process. Several students testified to the discrepancy between the science and the humanities programs: "I have friends who take communications and history classes and they can easily get 3.6's or 3.7," said a sophomore, "while science majors often have GPAs an entire point lower." Students recommended Comparative History of Ideas, International Studies, and Near Eastern Languages and Civilization as being unique and intriguing majors.

Among UW's 3,600-plus faculty are six Nobel Laureates, a National Book Award Winner, and 43 members of the National Academy of Sciences, not to mention many other widely renowned scholars and scientists. Freshman seminars offer incoming students the opportunity to establish a relationship with these faculty members while exploring their fields of study. But don't get too excited, a sophomore warns, as "in all honesty, the school is so big it is really hard to identify famous professors. There are celebrity profs, you just have to be part of the department to realize it." The competition for popular classes varies depending on the department, but as one student noted, "if you're a good enough student and stubborn enough, you can get into anything."

Even given the rare circumstance that a student does not find a niche on campus, Seattle and the surrounding area provide countless opportunities for adventure and entertainment. The school's proximity to both the Cascade Mountains and Puget Sound leads to many diverting weekend trips. Seattle itself is a fascinating city, home to Starbucks, Microsoft, Amazon.com, REI, and Nintendo. Clearly, the University of Washington and the surrounding area can cater to the interests of all 43,000 undergraduate and graduate students, whether athletes, baristas, scholars, or ski bums. One student's comment in particular emphasized the enthusiasm characteristic of all Huskies: "I love the UW. It's a fantastic education, I get exposed to a huge amount of cutting-edge research, and there are so many opportunities I don't know where to start!"

FYI

If you come to UW, you'd better bring "a raincoat."

What's the typical weekend schedule? "Friday: hit up a party or lay low with friends; Saturday: shop, cheer on the Huskies at the football game, go out; Sunday: sleep till noon, get up and study, study, study!"

If I could change one thing about UW, I'd "make the registration process during freshman and sophomore year easier to get the classes you need."

Three things every student at UW should do before graduating are "jump off the bridge that goes to nowhere, eat at Burger Hut at 2 a.m., and take the bus to class even though it's only a 10-minute walk."

Washington State University

Address: 370 Lighty Student Services Building, Pullman, WA 99164-1067	**Percentage accepted through EA or ED:** NA	**Graduation Rate 6-year:** 69%
Phone: 888-468-6978	**EA and ED deadline:** NA	**Percent Undergraduates in On-campus housing:** 35%
E-mail address: admissions@wsu.edu	**Regular Deadline:** Rolling	
Web site URL: www.wsu.edu	**Application Fee:** $50	**Number of official organized extracurricular organizations:** 200
Year Founded: 1890	**Full time Undergraduate enrollment:** 21,726	
Private or Public: Public	**Total enrollment:** 26,101	**3 Most popular majors:** Business, Social Sciences, Communication
Religious Affiliation: None	**Percent Male:** 47%	
Location: Rural	**Percent Female:** 53%	**Student/Faculty ratio:** 15:1
Number of Applicants: 12,478	**Total Percent Minority or Unreported:** 16%	**Average Class Size:** 16
Percent Accepted: 76%	**Percent African-American:** 2%	**Percent of students going to grad school:** 62%
Percent Accepted who enroll: 39%	**Percent Asian/Pacific Islander:** 6%	**Tuition and Fees:** $19,565
Number Entering: 3,668	**Percent Hispanic:** 6%	**In-State Tuition and Fees if different:** $8,489
Number of Transfers Accepted each Year: 3,728	**Percent Native-American:** 1%	**Cost for Room and Board:** $9,330
Middle 50% SAT range: M: 490–610, **CR:** 480–590, **Wr:** 460–570	**Percent International:** 3%	**Percent receiving financial aid out of those who apply, first year:** 52%
Middle 50% ACT range: 21–26	**Percent in-state/out of state:** 89%/11%	
Early admission program EA/ED/None: None	**Percent from Public HS:** 99%	**Percent receiving financial aid among all students:** 49%
	Retention Rate: 84%	
	Graduation Rate 4-year: 40%	

Going to Washington State University might only last a few years of your life, but being a Cougar is a lifetime commitment. It involves a ferocious pride for your school and a willingness to don crimson whenever physically possible.

"WSU has a ridiculous amount of school pride, to the point of violence," explained a freshman. She added, "I wouldn't be walking the streets wearing anything purple or gold during Apple Cup week," referring to the historic rivalry with the University of Washington.

Although the school's atmosphere of school pride and spirit may permeate the air as you walk around campus, there are other reasons why the overall experience is intoxicating, to say the least.

Academics? Oh yeah. . . .

Although simply being a cougar is an experience in itself, WSU academics are rigorous, high caliber, and stimulating. US News and World Report has consistently ranked WSU among the nation's top public research universities, and more than 200 fields of studies are offered. Perhaps most impressive is WSU's communications program, which is ranked by Radio and Television News Directors survey in the top four in the nation. The Communications major is one of the most popular majors on campus in addition to Agricultural Science, Sports Management, and Education.

Science classes are no joke—most students say pre-medicine classes are the toughest, while general education requirements can be the easiest "as long as you stay caught up on the reading," says one freshman.

Students say their least favorite part about Coug academics is the giant classes. "You're just a number at WSU," lamented one freshman. Still, professors are more than willing to help and provide resources outside of class. The New Student Programs helps orient students to their new environment and make a smooth transition into college. Freshmen say these programs have helped them adjust to WSU's rigorous academic demands.

Although the academic workload may be challenging and time consuming, going to WSU involves much more than just going to class.

Greeks and Athletes

It's the social life that distinguishes WSU from most other universities. One freshman, who said she was anxious about getting lost in such a big school, says she is surprised how she is "meeting so many people who are nice and welcoming." Another student said she is continually surprised with the school's welcoming environment and the constant stream of activities throughout the day.

> **"WSU has a ridiculous amount of school pride, to the point of violence."**

The Greek scene is very involved, though students stress it is not necessarily the dominant social activity on campus. There are ways for anybody to be involved as long as they are friendly. "It's very easy to meet people, join a club, and be social in classes," says one freshman.

"Thirsty Thursday"

Like most schools, Friday and Saturday nights are a popular time for people to go to fraternities, house parties, or watch movies in the dorms. However, a particularly interesting day is "thirsty" Thursday, when people usually party and walk up Greek Row. So is there much drinking on campus? Oh ya. But the only people who get blackout drunk are those guys whose only goal *is* to intoxicate themselves as quickly as possible. Some, but not all students describe binge drinking as a serious problem. Although drinking is present at most parties, students say there is not necessarily negative pressure to drink. However, since students describe drinking is a social event, most people choose to participate.

Careful though, because alcohol is only allowed in the dorms if you're over 21, and there are Residential Advisors (RAs) to make sure everything runs smoothly in the dorm. Students say that generally, RAs are very understanding.

Pullman: Middle of Nowhere

Fret not that eastern Washington is not very populated; amenities on campus are very accommodating. The newly renovated CUB (Compton Union Building) is one of the main places to meet people on campus, and the distinct clock tower glows crimson at night. There are advantages to a small town. "Everyone in town is a Coug, and [townspeople] love the college," said one freshman. And since Pullman is so small, students describe it as a very safe campus. WSU basically *is* Pullman. But don't expect you'll be living in a palace.

"The food is extremely mediocre," explained one freshman.

Pay attention to dorm policies: the earlier freshmen send in their confirmation to attend WSU, the higher they are ranked on the dorm choice priority list. There are older "hill halls" that are mostly either girl or boy dorms built in the 1900s, and newer dorms built around the 1960s that are coed. The dorms near Bohler Gym (the gym for athletes only) are usually full of athletes so they can get to their gym quickly.

All dorms are age diverse, so freshmen could be living close to seniors.

Extracoug activities

"Extracurricular activities are open to anyone willing to try out," said one freshman. Intramural sports, especially soccer and ultimate Frisbee, are both popular and competitive.

Many people have jobs on campus, especially in the dining halls.

Look to *The Daily Evergreen*, the campus newspaper, for daily news and sports updates. Because there are so many ways to be involved, most people are involved in some sort of club activity. The football team is always supported by the student body, regardless of their record.

Coming to WSU is more than an investment in your education—it's an investment in your life. Every day is an adventure, with new people and exciting activities. Perhaps most important, the people you meet at WSU will be your lifelong friends. Being a coug is for life.—*Mitchell Murdock*

FYI

If I could change one thing about WSU, I'd open up the Greek system to be more inviting to the rest of the school.

The typical weekend schedule: You wake up Saturday morning around 1:00 p.m. (don't worry, they serve breakfast until 2:00 on the weekends). Then, you talk to your friends about what the hell happened last night and then lay in bed all day in order to recover in time for Saturday night's activities. Eventually, get on your party clothes and walk up to Greek Row with your group of friends and get ready for a long night.

The biggest college-wide tradition is "the Apple Cup! Go Cougs!"

Whitman College

Address: 345 Boyer Avenue Walla Walla, WA 99362	**EA and ED deadline:** 15-Nov	**Graduation Rate 6-year:** 85%
Phone: 509-527-5176	**Regular Deadline:** 15-Jan	**Percent Undergraduates in On-campus housing:** 62%
E-mail address: admission@whitman.edu	**Application Fee:** $50	
Web site URL: www.whitman.edu	**Full time Undergraduate enrollment:** 1,458	**Number of official organized extracurricular organizations:** 60
Year Founded: 1883	**Total enrollment:** 1,458	
Private or Public: Private	**Percent Male:** 45%	**3 Most popular majors:** Biology, History, Political
Religious Affiliation: None	**Percent Female:** 55%	Science
Location: Rural	**Total Percent Minority or Unreported:** 19%	**Student/Faculty ratio:** 9:1
Number of Applicants: 3,096		**Average Class Size:** 16
Percent Accepted: 46%	**Percent African-American:** 2%	**Percent of students going to grad school:** Unreported
Percent Accepted who enroll: 28%	**Percent Asian/Pacific Islander:** 10%	**Tuition and Fees:** $34,880
Number Entering: 401	**Percent Hispanic:** 6%	**In-State Tuition and Fees if**
Number of Transfers Accepted each Year: 50	**Percent Native-American:** 1%	**different:** No difference
Middle 50% SAT range: M: 610–700, CR: 630–730, Wr: 620–710	**Percent International:** 3%	**Cost for Room and Board:** $8,820
	Percent in-state/out of state: 40%/60%	**Percent receiving financial aid out of those who apply, first year:** 70%
Middle 50% ACT range: 28–32	**Percent from Public HS:** 75%	
Early admission program EA/ED/None: ED	**Retention Rate:** 93%	**Percent receiving financial aid among all students:** 74%
Percentage accepted through EA or ED: 75%	**Graduation Rate 4-year:** 84%	

If you love nature, the outdoors, and learning, then Whitman College in Walla Walla, Washington is the place for you. With a generally laid-back attitude and overall liberal mindset, Whitman students can take advantage of the abundance of activities offered on campus, as well as enjoy the outdoors in the beautiful Pacific Northwest.

Welcoming "Whitties"

Students say that one of the greatest perks of a Whitman experience is going to school in Walla Walla. Whitman students (called "Whitties") say that Walla Walla is the perfect college town—small and friendly with lots to do. One student remarked, "The campus and surrounding areas are so safe . . . I can leave my purse and belongings in a public place and know that when I return they'll be sitting right where I left them." Another described the campus and Walla Walla as "incredibly safe. You wouldn't believe it. I can trust anyone on this campus."

At Whitman, it's not uncommon to say hi to or strike up a conversation with a stranger on the street. Freshmen at Whitman even said that the welcome they received on their first day at college was almost overwhelming. "Since it is a school of maybe 1,400 students, you end up meeting a lot of people pretty easily," one junior explained. "As far as friendliness goes, Whitman students are some of the friendliest people I have ever met." But the student population of Whitman is "not diverse." "There is not much diversity," and Whitties are "mostly white," with a very "small population of international students," one Whittie noted. Despite the lack of diversity, Whitties maintain that they are extremely accepting of any student. One Whittie summed up the student body by saying, "I was surprised by the kindness and acceptance I found here that I have never found anywhere else."

Love the Core

Many undergrads agree that one of the most important qualities of Whitman students is a "genuine interest in learning." Academics have always been central to life at Whitman, and many students say that the only thing Whitties love as much as the outdoors is learning.

> "I can leave my purse and belongings in a public place and know that when I return they'll be sitting right where I left them."

At the center of a Whitman education is the core curriculum. Students describe the Core program as one to "ensure some kind of exposure to all areas of the liberal arts." In addition to taking two semesters of Core classes ("Antiquity" and "Modernity") freshman year, Whitties are also required to fulfill a plethora of distributional requirements, including two social science classes, two humanities, two fine arts, two sciences, two alternative voices classes, and a quantitative analysis course before graduating.

While premed and the sciences are popular majors, they are also known to be the most difficult. Of course, it is possible to be "challenged by any program you pursue," although reportedly there is a fair amount of grade inflation. And students maintain that it is hard to do poorly at Whitman because so many academic resources are available outside of class.

Whitties rave about their professors, describing them as "highly regarded" and "very accessible." "I love the profs here . . . they

are highly accessible people, and very friendly and helpful," one junior said.

What About the Weekends?

Whitties report a great social scene on campus. Students say that unofficial on-campus parties, fraternity and sorority parties, and dances and events hosted by official Whitman clubs are the dominant activities for Friday and Saturday nights. One third of the student population is involved in Greek life. Sorority members live in the all-female Prentiss Hall. Frat parties are popular social events, but students report that they are "exclusive" or hard to get in to.

Students say that, "like any other college," alcohol is very present on campus. The school's alcohol policy "is very laid-back." Most students drink "in a private space that is somewhat contained (i.e., in one's room with the door closed). If an RA catches you drinking in public, they pour out your drink, and that is all," one Whittie warned. However, many students stress that there are "plenty of activities on campus if you don't drink." And students seem to agree that there are almost no drugs present on campus.

Whittie Winners

Whitties describe their campus as "beautiful." The campus is centered around Ankeny Field, which is pretty much "your typical college quad." Freshmen and sophomores live on campus and are required to have an on-campus meal plan. The biggest dorms on campus are Anderson and Jewitt Halls. There are also several smaller residence halls for juniors and seniors. In addition to the traditional dorm housing, Whitman also has many different theme houses, ranging from a volunteer house to a writing house, which, as one student described, "allow upperclassmen to live within a community of people with similar interests."

The meal plan at Whitman allows students to eat at two dining halls and the student center, Reid Campus Center. Students assert that Reid Center has better food than the halls, but the halls have "exceptional salad bars."

In terms of sports, jocks should take heed—Whitman has no football team or cheerleaders. However, students are quick to say that "tennis, cross country, and skiing are very popular." There is also a biking team that is growing in popularity. Whitman's new tennis facility and indoor pool are proclaimed by most to be "high quality."

Because of the lack of varsity sports, Whitman students take intramural sports very seriously. Some of the most popular are bowling, flag football, ultimate Frisbee, basketball, and soccer. And despite a high level of competition, Whitties say that IMs are "fun!"

Whitman draws much of its appeal from its beautiful Pacific Northwest surroundings. While Whitties hold a great appreciation for nature, they are quick to refute common stereotypes that Whitman students care more about their hiking boots than their grades or extracurriculars. In truth, while the typical Whitman student is outdoorsy and free-spirited, he or she is also friendly, accepting, hard-working, and high-achieving. One student summed up his experience at Whitman by saying, "Being a 'Whittie' is an amazing experience, and if this school is the right place for you as a person, it's the best place in the world."—*Becky Bicks*

FYI

If you come to Whitman, you'd better bring: "Hiking boots, a Frisbee, a spirit of adventure, and an open mind."

If I could change anything at Whitman, I'd "push the food service provider (Bon Appetit) to improve overall quality."

What's a typical weekend schedule? "Party on campus Saturday and sleep in and study on Sunday, or go on a camping trip Friday night and come back Sunday."

Three things everyone should do before graduating from Whitman are: "Run the Beer Mile, complete the Frisbee golf course, go on as many camping trips as possible."

West Virginia

Marshall University

Address: One John Marshall Drive, Huntington, WV 25655
Phone: 304-696-3160
E-mail address: admissions@marshall.edu
Web site URL: www.marshall.edu
Year Founded: 1837
Private or Public: Public
Religious Affiliation: None
Location: Suburban
Number of Applicants: 2,409
Percent Accepted: 83%
Percent Accepted who enroll: 83%
Number Entering: 1,661
Number of Transfers Accepted each Year: 762
Middle 50% SAT range: M: 440–560, CR: 450–560, Wr: 440–550
Middle 50% ACT range: 19–25
Early admission program EA/ED/None: None
Percentage accepted through EA or ED: NA

EA and ED deadline: NA
Regular Deadline: Rolling
Application Fee: $30
Full time Undergraduate enrollment: 8,904
Total enrollment: 13,562
Percent Male: 45%
Percent Female: 55%
Total Percent Minority or Unreported: 11%
Percent African-American: 6%
Percent Asian/Pacific Islander: 1%
Percent Hispanic: 2%
Percent Native-American: 1%
Percent International: 1%
Percent in-state/out of state: 74% / 26%
Percent from Public HS: Unreported
Retention Rate: 71%
Graduation Rate 4-year: 44%

Graduation Rate 6-year: Unreported
Percent Undergraduates in On-campus housing: Unreported
Number of official organized extracurricular organizations: 100
3 Most popular majors: Business, Education, Liberal Arts
Student/Faculty ratio: 19:1
Average Class Size: 25
Percent of students going to grad school: 27%
Tuition and Fees: $11,702
In-State Tuition and Fees if different: $4,598
Cost for Room and Board: $7,210
Percent receiving financial aid out of those who apply, first year: 68%
Percent receiving financial aid among all students: 44%

For the many West Virginia residents on campus, Marshall University can seem like a larger version of high school: a familiar environment surrounded by classmates they have known since kindergarten. While this can contribute to a lack of diversity on campus, Marshall is able to boast accessible professors, brand-new facilities, and a tight-knit community available to students who live both on and off campus.

One Class at a Time

All students must satisfy the requirements of the Marshall Plan, which is composed of a course or two in mathematics, science, computer literacy, writing, multicultural studies, international studies, and a senior capstone experience involving both oral and written presentations. Although the Plan is considered more annoying than demanding, many students would like to see changes to these general education requirements or at least a decrease in the time they must devote to them. Furthermore, several students, particularly those who commute, complained of not having enough time for electives. And at the same time, many of the "coolest" electives are only offered through the Marshall Community and Technical College. "I don't want to sacrifice the authenticity of regular Marshall courses for the coolness of the technical school ones," said one senior.

Although the Marshall Plan consumes large portions of students' academic hours, one psychology major said that he loves the freedom within his major. "You don't really have to take a lot of hours in your major," he said. Many students concentrate in business or nursing, but other departments also receive praise from students. "Take as many history classes as you can. Those have the best professors," one student said, while another described his first-year experience in the music department as "amazing." Science majors are generally regarded as more difficult, and those students not in the science departments bemoan a lack of opportunities in humanities and social sciences. The University seems to propel this perspective, having unveiled the Robert C. Byrd Biotechnology Science Center in 2006.

Nevertheless, students agree that the workload at Marshall is not strenuous. "I would definitely apply myself more if I were in a more intense academic environment," one senior said. Students said that many professors implement curves, and one freshman laughed when she was asked about the difficulty of the course load. "My favorite thing about Marshall is how easy my classes are," she said. "But Drinko Library is always packed."

However easy the classes are, Marshall University does attract talented students with not only the promise of intimate student-teacher interaction but also financial incentives. The University offers myriad scholarships, particularly for in-state students, based on ACT scores and cumulative GPA. There is also the prestigious Yeager Scholarship, which provides tuition, room and board, a semester abroad for foreign language study, a summer program at Oxford University in the United Kingdom, and convenient benefits like early registration for classes.

Living the Dream
Many West Virginia residents view Marshall and its rival, West Virginia University, as the only college options. The West Virginia state government encourages this idea with a scholarship called the PROMISE. The result is a student population that is overwhelmingly homogenous and can often make out-of-state students feel like outsiders. Most in-state students continue associating with their friends from high school, so it can be difficult for out-of-state students to acclimate. However, students say that the social scene at Marshall depends greatly on the living situations.

Marshall requires students to live in dorms for the first two years on campus. However, the two-year rule only applies to those living

outside of a 50-mile radius, so commuters have very different opinions of Marshall and its social scene. Students who live in the dorms rate Marshall as much more diverse, and they praise the quality of freshman dorms. When asked if rooms get better with seniority, one freshman said, "No, not at all." This is because Marshall recently constructed new buildings designed just for freshmen, and the additions are expected to attract more students to on-campus living.

> "The most political that the campus gets is during elections for Mr. and Miss Marshall."

There exists a thriving off-campus life as well. Many students live in designated off-campus apartments and enjoy more freedom than those who opt for dormitory living, probably because of the strict dry policy enforced by on-campus housing authorities.

Eat, Drink, and Be Merry
One student who had lived in the small city her entire life commented that "Huntington is the place to be if you want to go to church, go out to eat, or get totally drunk." Being located in what the Centers for Disease Control and Prevention recently named the unhealthiest city in America does have advantages. The city of Huntington recently constructed a complex called Pullman Square that caters to college students looking for both daytime and nighttime fun. Pullman Square offers restaurants, a movie theater, an independent bookstore, a comedy club, shops, and plenty of parking for all the commuters.

Students also frequent Huntington's numerous bars and nightclubs. One student spoke passionately about "quarter-pitcher night" at the Eager Beaver, while others never miss an opportunity to go "club-hopping" on Friday and Saturday nights. In addition, Marshall has a large Greek scene that provides weekend parties for the entire community.

Students praise the number of extracurricular options available to Marshall students. One freshman noticed that students are "very committed" to their extracurricular activities, particularly those that are entirely student-run. There are plenty of activities and resources available for religious students in particular, but those looking for political activism should search elsewhere. "The most political that the campus gets is during elections for Mr. and Miss Marshall," said one senior. The student newspaper, *The Parthenon*, is extremely popular on campus, and most students are kept up-to-date by reading it.

Sports also have a dominant presence on campus. Excitement abounds during football season, and students are dedicated to their football team, the "Thundering Herd," known to provide quality players to the NFL. The Marshall basketball program also gets significant attention, particularly during the Marshall-WVU game, which brings a large audience of both current students and alumni. "There is a ton of school pride," said one sophomore. "Go Herd!" he added.

"We Are Marshall"

Nothing better illustrates the closeness of the Marshall campus than the sentimentality associated with the plane crash that killed almost the entire football team, coaching staff, and some fans in November of 1970. Often called the "worst sports-related disaster in United States history," the tragedy continues to affect students, staff, and area residents. The Memorial Fountain that commemorates the catastrophe is not only considered one of the "prettiest" parts of campus, but also the most meaningful.

The overall atmosphere at Marshall University can be summed up by the school's motto, "We Are Marshall." This sentiment is a testimony to the enormous pride that students, faculty and alumni feel about their school. The recent renovations and additions demonstrate that Marshall is expanding, and many students see their school changing from being known as a commuter school to becoming a leading university in the near future.—*Lauren Oyler*

FYI

If you come to Marshall, you'd better bring "a ton of green clothes."

What is the typical weekend schedule? "On Wednesdays, it's quarter-pitcher night at Eager Beaver. Thursdays and Fridays are frat parties or clubbing. Saturday is football or basketball games. Then on Sunday, go to church and start studying."

If I could change one thing about Marshall, I'd "decrease the number of requirements of the Marshall Plan."

Three things every student at Marshall should do before graduating are "eat the peach pie at Harless, take advantage of the Marshall Artist Series, and see *We Are Marshall* to understand the school's history."

West Virginia University

Address: PO Box 6009 Morgantown, WV 26506-6009	**Percentage accepted through EA or ED:** NA	**Graduation Rate 6-year:** Unreported
Phone: 304-293-2121	**EA and ED deadline:** NA	**Percent Undergraduates**
E-mail address: go2wvu@mail.wvu.edu	**Regular Deadline:** Rolling	**in On-campus housing:** 25%
Web site URL: www.wvu.edu	**Application Fee:** $25	**Number of official organized**
Year Founded: 1867	**Full time Undergraduate enrollment:** 21,145	**extracurricular**
Private or Public: Public	**Total enrollment:** 26,740	**organizations:** 300
Religious Affiliation: None	**Percent Male:** 55%	**3 Most popular majors:** Business, Engineering,
Location: Rural	**Percent Female:** 45%	Health Professions
Number of Applicants: 15,094	**Total Percent Minority or Unreported:** 7%	**Student/Faculty ratio:** 23:1
Percent Accepted: 88%	**Percent African-American:** 3%	**Average Class Size:** 25
Percent Accepted who enroll: 39%	**Percent Asian/Pacific Islander:** 2%	**Percent of students going to grad school:** Unreported
Number Entering: 5,099	**Percent Hispanic:** 2%	**Tuition and Fees:** $15,770
Number of Transfers Accepted each Year: 1,495	**Percent Native-American:** 0%	**In-State Tuition and Fees if**
Middle 50% SAT range: M:	**Percent International:** 2%	**different:** No difference
480–580, **CR:** 470–560,	**Percent in-state/out of**	**Cost for Room and Board:**
Wr: Unreported	**state:** 54%/46%	$7,434
Middle 50% ACT range:	**Percent from Public HS:**	**Percent receiving financial**
20–28	Unreported	**aid out of those who apply,**
Early admission program	**Retention Rate:** 84%	**first year:** 69%
EA/ED/None: None	**Graduation Rate 4-year:** 56%	**Percent receiving financial aid among all students:** 86%

Vest Virginia University is better known for its football and basketball teams than academics, but this nationally ranked party school certainly offers much more than just a good time outside of classes.

All Play and No Work?

Despite its reputation as a party school, students at WVU actually do study. Popular majors include business, communications and journalism, and engineering, but many students take advantage of WVU's more esoteric programs, such as Exercise Physiology or Textiles, Apparel and Merchandising. By the time students are juniors, they apply to a specific college within the University, such as the Perley Isaac Reed School of Journalism, the College of Human Resources and Education, or the Eberly College of Arts and Sciences. WVU also offers over 60 minors, including a great variety of disciplines such as Native American Studies, Conservation Ecology, and Pest Management.

In addition to the broad range of majors and minors offered, WVU students love the large number of class choices. The only drawback is the size of classes. "All of my classes this semester are too big," said one sophomore majoring in chemistry. "I'm talking 250 or so students." Although the classes do become progressively smaller with seniority, many students feel that they have trouble choosing a major because "lecture hall classes are impossible to pay attention in."

Because the school is so large, many students receive relatively little advising. All students must complete the requirements of the General Education Curriculum (GEC), which ultimately takes up about one third of each student's course schedule. Although students are assigned an academic advisor, one freshman said she didn't even know she had to complete the GEC and "expected much more help with scheduling" from the advisors.

The Honors College at WVU provides a more intimate learning environment for students who have demonstrated academic prowess throughout high school. The Honors Program allows students to graduate with honors as well as take small classes that are unheard of for students not in the program. These courses, which are capped at 20 students, are offered in departments ranging from microbiology to theater. They make it possible for honors students to engage in discussions and debate with their professors and peers. Students in the Honors Program say that they don't know what they would do without the additional benefits of the program, which include better housing, priority course registration, and more easily available study abroad opportunities. In return, students must complete at least 24 credit hours of Honors courses and maintain a high GPA.

On the other hand, the Honors program at WVU reportedly lacks academic diversity. Students claim that the number of science majors in the Honors College is significantly disproportional to the number of science majors in the overall undergraduate population. "The only time I hear anyone talking about humanities is when they are trying to fill GECs," said one sophomore in the Honors College. This disparity contributes to the overarching belief around campus that social sciences and humanities are easy. "Whenever I'm at a party and tell people that I'm a biology major, people cringe," said one junior. "They usually follow up with something like 'Oh, that's so hard. I could never do that.'"

Country Roads

Located in the Mountain State, WVU's campus boasts great opportunities for hiking, which may be required to get to classes. West Virginia has two campuses, the Evansdale campus and the Downtown campus. To connect them, the University constructed a monorail system, called the Personal Rapid Transit (PRT) Personal Rapid Transit. While riding the PRT remains a uniquely Mountaineer experience, students' overall impressions of the PRT are negative. "The PRT is like a roller coaster for little children," one WVU junior said.

Running from 6:30 a.m. to 10:15 p.m. on weekdays, 9:30 a.m. to 5:00 p.m. on Saturdays, and closed on Sundays, the PRT schedule is not designed for convenience. It is also known to break down frequently, leaving students without cars stuck on their respective campuses. Even students who do have cars have trouble getting around because parking is "severely limited."

Instead of solving the parking or the PRT

problem, many students would prefer that the University somehow unify the two campuses, which are separated by about one and a half miles. While the Downtown campus is known as the heart and soul of WVU, the Evansdale campus has many necessary resources as well, including many athletic facilities, making transportation between the two campuses unavoidable. One freshman complained that the dual campus structure of WVU makes it "impossible to see anyone."

The West Virginia hills are also considered inconvenient by some students. There is even a Facebook group called "I Got 99 Problems and 82 of them are the Steps by the Life Science Building," dedicated to commiserating about the hilly terrain at WVU. However, the hills are also beloved by students. Active students utilize the area's natural landscape by hiking, walking, or jogging on trails located next to the Monongahela River. They can also make frequent visits to Coopers Rock State Forest, make use of the nearby ski resorts, and enjoy whitewater rafting.

Take Me Home

Ironically, the dorms at WVU are unwaveringly dry, even for students over the age of 21. The school's policy on alcohol in the dorms is strict: All students found drinking in the dorms will be written up and fined. Students looking to drink need not search far, however, for an off-campus house party or a bar. Because Greek life is not particularly important on campus, students say that the social scene at WVU truly revolves around Morgantown's bounty of bars and clubs, frequented by students every night of the week. On the other hand, the easy access can be problematic when finals approach. The dilemma of juggling the bustling social scene and academics contributes to WVU's relatively low freshman to sophomore retention rate, and one sophomore estimated that "probably 95 percent" of the student body drinks.

For those not looking to imbibe, WVU has WVUp All Night, a weekly event that takes place in the Mountainlair, the student union on the Downtown campus. Each Thursday, Friday, and Saturday night beginning at 7 p.m., the Mountainlair is transformed into Up All Night, where students can get free food, watch movies, go bowling, and enjoy myriad other activities. Although many students view Up All Night as a way to sober up after a long night of drinking, it is still lauded as one of the country's best weekend alternatives to the "college party scene."

The school also sponsors another entertainment event called FallFest. Every year the University welcomes students back to campus with a huge outdoor concert featuring several headlining bands. This event is so impressive that it even attracts students from rival Marshall University, whose students are often willing to make the two-and-a-half-hour drive from southern West Virginia to enjoy big-name acts at WVU.

> "'WVU is like being a kid trying to do a jigsaw puzzle at a carnival.'"

Sports are also an essential part of student life at WVU. With sports teams that consistently rank among the top 25 in the nation, loyal Mountaineer fans look forward to game days with passion. On Saturday mornings in the fall, fans in gold and blue shirts flock to the Pit for unforgettable tailgates before moving on to Milan Puskar Stadium, where they cheer on the Mountaineers in what is usually a spectacular football game. School spirit is also palpable during the basketball season, when Mountaineer fans religiously follow NCAA Division I rankings to see if their team prevails.

Students are envious of the "sweet" athletic facilities reserved for varsity athletes, but the Student Rec Center is more than adequate for non-athletes. Boasting everything from standard exercise equipment to a 50-foot climbing wall, badminton courts, and an elevated track, the Student Rec Center is home to WVU's intramurals, which are fairly popular among students.

To the Place I Belong

"My economics professor really said it best," commented one junior majoring in accounting. "He said 'WVU is like being a kid trying to do a jigsaw puzzle at a carnival.' You can get the education at WVU that you could get anywhere, but there is so much going on around you that it's really a test to see if you can concentrate, which is something I think is unique. It probably prepares you for the real world better than a lot of places in that sense." The majority of students are proud of their school and their Mountaineers. Students are known to sing along to John Denver's "Country Roads," which is usually done at sporting events. This is because, to them, WVU really is "home."—*Lauren Oyler*

FYI
If you come to West Virginia, you'd better bring "an appreciation for beer."
What is the typical weekend schedule? "Go out to bars or an off-campus party on Thursdays and Fridays, wake up early for a tailgate on Saturday, cheer on the Mountaineers, and have a victory celebration on Saturday night."
If I could change one thing about West Virginia, I'd "bring the two campuses together."
Three things every student at West Virginia should do before graduating are "walk down High Street to see all the crazy parties, go to a football game at Milan Puskar Stadium, and see Coopers Rock."

Wisconsin

Beloit College

Address: 700 College Street
Beloit, WI 53511
Phone: 608-363-2500
E-mail address:
admiss@beloit.edu
Web site URL:
www.beloit.edu
Year Founded: 1846
Private or Public: Private
Religious Affiliation: None
Location: Urban
Number of Applicants:
2,248
Percent Accepted: 63%
**Percent Accepted who
enroll:** 24%
Number Entering: 362
**Number of Transfers
Accepted each Year:**
25
**Middle 50% SAT range: M:
560–690, CR: 570–700,
Wr:** Unreported
Middle 50% ACT range:
25–30
**Early admission program
EA/ED/None:** EA

**Percentage accepted
through EA or ED:**
Unreported
EA and ED deadline: 1-Dec
Regular Deadline: 15-Jan
Application Fee: $35
**Full time Undergraduate
enrollment:** 1,388
Total enrollment: 1,388
Percent Male: 44%
Percent Female: 56%
**Total Percent Minority or
Unreported:** 13%
Percent African-American:
4%
**Percent Asian/Pacific
Islander:** 3%
Percent Hispanic: 4%
Percent Native-American:
<1%
Percent International:
Unreported
**Percent in-state/out of
state:** 22%/78%
Percent from Public HS:
78%
Retention Rate: 89%

Graduation Rate 4-year: 72%
Graduation Rate 6-year:
78%
**Percent Undergraduates in
On-campus housing:** 95%
**Number of official organized
extracurricular
organizations:** 95
3 Most popular majors:
Creative Writing, Sociology,
Anthropology/Political
Science
Student/Faculty ratio: 11:1
Average Class Size: 15
**Percent of students going to
grad school:** 40%
Tuition and Fees: $31,540
**In-State Tuition and Fees if
different:** No difference
Cost for Room and Board:
$6,696
**Percent receiving financial
aid out of those who apply,
first year:** 80%
**Percent receiving financial
aid among all students:**
62%

Founded in 1846 in territorial Wisconsin with just $7,000 and a desire to bring education to the Midwest, Beloit College has now become an internationally recognized college famed for its liberal arts education and its distinctive atmosphere. A few students may whine about the cold winters of Wisconsin, but the environment at Beloit is very welcoming. Strong academics with a focus on global relations and a thriving social life complete the beauty of a hip and enthusiastic campus.

Interdisciplinary Innovation
Although some students call the workload "challenging," most agree that it is quite rewarding, thoughtful, and interdisciplinary.

Beloiters also rave that their professors are accessible and helpful. One freshman said that her professor offered her class an opportunity to work and learn in Africa with the professor over the summer.

A First-Year Initiatives program brings all Beloit's freshmen together through interdisciplinary seminars and orientation programs. This is complemented by a Sophomore-Year Initiatives program that works with sophomores to overcome the dreaded "sophomore slump" and helps them to become more aware of their aims and goals in college. Beyond that, there are few academic requirements—two courses in natural sciences or math, two in social sciences, and two in humanities. Additionally, each student must complete three writing-focused classes and one interdisciplinary class. These requirements can be fulfilled through a variety of unique classes; the course catalogue has such offerings as Egyptian, History of Physics, Dinosaurs and Their Lost World, and even Film Music. "The requirements are good in that they offer structure, but they are quite flexible and can be tailored to your individual interests," one undergrad explained.

To help students through difficult classes, Beloit offers a number of resources. The Learning Support Services Center often tutors students either individually or in groups, and the Writing Center, where tutors "work with students on a collaborative basis" is open until 10 p.m. on school nights. Students agree that the workload is just as intense as that at any first-rate university, regardless of the department. Classics is said to be a somewhat easy major, but one junior pointed out that the sciences tend to be more challenging "because of time and difficulty. There is certainly less wiggle room in [science majors] to take classes you are interested in" outside the major. Beloit's specialties, international relations and anthropology, are fairly difficult, but both are popular and renowned majors. Anthropology, in particular, received rave reviews. One student gushed that "Indiana Jones was based on one of our archeology graduates named Roy Chapman [Andrews]. He donated all his artifacts to the school upon his death!" Luckily, living professors tend to be just as amazing. The reigning celebrity is Tom McBride of the English department, who is the creator of the annual "mindset lists" and is described as "very Texan" with a "loud teaching style." There is also an archaeology professor, Dan Shea, who "frequently takes students along on his digs in Chile," and Pablo Toral, a specialist on development and Latin America, a favorite of students.

The atmosphere at Beloit is intimate, considering that the college only has 1,300 undergraduates. Classes are usually smaller than 20 students and always under 30. Even the introductory survey classes are personal, although one philosophy major whined that they were "lacking in depth . . . but also unavoidable." Assignments, according to students, tend to go beyond the standard papers. One student recalled "performing the entire *Paradise Lost* in front of an audience for an English class," while another said, "In my African studies class we had to do oral presentations because African culture is more oral than ours."

Frisbee and Freak-Dancing

Beyond homework and classes, Beloit students keep busy. For those not writing for the *Round Table*, the school paper, school nights are devoted to homework and other extracurriculars. Sports are very low-key. When asked, a student said, "Sports? We have sports? Oh, yeah, intramurals. I've heard rumors of varsity sports but never witnessed them. Kind of like ghost stories." When it's warm enough, Frisbee is surprisingly common on the grounds. Extracurricular groups include Young Democrats, Young Republicans, the Gay-Straight Alliance, Black Students United, Voces Latinas, and even fencing.

> "Everything begins and ends here! We also have a rich history of hippiedom."

Thursday through Saturday nights, "everyone parties together on campus, which is awesome and friendly, but can always be awkward the next morning, since you know everyone," one female undergrad said. Freshmen tend to mix and mingle at larger and more formal functions, while upperclassmen parties are usually more private, "but they are still very much out in public with the rest of us mortals." The Greek scene, with only eight percent of men and six percent of women involved, is small but key to the party circuit. One fraternity member commented that "Greek life affects the community, but does not run it like at other schools. That's why I joined." All the parties have different themes, from a "Talking Heads" party to the soccer team's 70s-style "Playaz Ball" party, but students uniformly have a good time together. Beloit also organizes a Folk and Blues weekend every fall that brings a number of bands to campus for two nights.

As part of the hippie environment, people do respect what alcohol can do to the body. Most people who do drink end up at Aldrich residential hall. One girl who lives there said that "when I didn't drink, I didn't feel out of the loop, but sometimes I feel that drinkers can be really inconsiderate about others, especially when it's a Wednesday night." Students said that IDs are rarely checked, and private parties are very common and very open. There is a zero tolerance policy on drugs. However, since there is a large proportion of hippies on campus, "there is certainly a lot of pot here, but you have to look harder to find stronger drugs." Coed dorms make hooking up and sex fairly common. "Students at Beloit can't be described as polyamorous," said one student. "They are just plain amorous." Of course, "there are also a fair amount of committed couples of all preferences."

Wild, Wonderful Wisconsin

The campus is very idyllic, thanks to its scenic location in the woods of Wisconsin. Beloit's greatest claim to landscape fame is its Native American burial mounds, which no other college in the States has. One of the burial mounds is shaped like a turtle, from which was derived Beloit's unofficial turtle mascot. "We're freaking Beloit College," one student exclaimed. "Everything begins and ends here! We also have a rich history of hippiedom." The campus incorporates Georgian and colonial architecture, and the woods add natural beauty. The city of Beloit is fairly unexciting, but just seven dollars buys a bus ticket to Madison, which is 45 minutes away.

The campus residences are extraordinarily varied. One college radio announcer gave a quick rundown of the major dorms: "Peet is the stoner dorm. Aldrich is where the drunks go. 810 [College Street] is where soccer players usually live. Avoid the '64 halls—they were built to be riotproof and thus are ugly as sin. The worst dorm would be 609 Emerson, a freshman dorm with cinder block walls and dingy lighting."

The students, however, make up for the buildings. Of course, the student body can still easily fall into stereotypes: "You know those white kids with dreadlocks who are actually from the 'burbs of Chicago? A lot of those go here. A fair amount of indie kids/art students. But all the rest are pretty normal." There is some self-segregation, but the large number of international students really balances out the student body. A student government leader said, "I feel comfortable sitting with anybody" in the cafeterias.

From the campus to the classes to the night scene, there is a focus more on connections and understanding than just textbook learning at Beloit. It is "this emphasis on experiential learning and international perspectives," one freshman explained, "that makes Beloit truly excellent." Oh, yeah, and it's fun, too!—*Jeffrey Zuckerman*

FYI
If you come to Beloit, you better bring "lots of costumes because people here *love* theme parties."
What's the typical weekend schedule? "Friday night: party. Saturday: Sleep it off, do a little bit of homework. Party at night. Sunday: Do a lot of homework."
If I could change one thing about Beloit, I'd "get more diversity. Tons more. As in people who are not white and from Chicago."
Three things every student at Beloit should do before graduating are "study abroad, have tea at a professor's house, and dance their ass off at as many campus parties as possible."

Lawrence University

Address: P.O. Box 599
Appleton, WI 54912-0599
Phone: 800-227-0982
E-mail address:
excel@lawrence.edu
Web site URL:
www.lawrence.edu
Year Founded: 1847
Private or Public: Private
Religious Affiliation: None
Location: Suburban
Number of Applicants:
2,618
Percent Accepted: 59%
**Percent Accepted who
enroll:** 25%
Number Entering: 414
**Number of Transfers
Accepted each Year:** 68
Middle 50% SAT range: M:
610–720, CR: 590–720,
Wr: 610–690
Middle 50% ACT range:
27–31
**Early admission program
EA/ED/None:** EA and ED

**Percentage accepted
through EA or ED:** 39%
EA and ED deadline: 15-Nov
for EA, 1-Dec for ED
Regular Deadline: 15-Jan
Application Fee: $40
**Full time Undergraduate
enrollment:** 1,503
Total enrollment: 1,503
Percent Male: 46%
Percent Female: 54%
**Total Percent Minority or
Unreported:** Unreported
Percent African-American:
4%
**Percent Asian/Pacific
Islander:** 2%
Percent Hispanic: 1%
Percent Native-American:
<1%
Percent International:
Unreported
**Percent in-state/out of
state:** 27%/73%
Percent from Public HS:
Unreported

Retention Rate: 90%
Graduation Rate 4-year: 63%
Graduation Rate 6-year:
79%
**Percent Undergraduates in
On-campus housing:** 97%
**Number of official organized
extracurricular
organizations:** 130
3 Most popular majors:
Biology, History, English
Student/Faculty ratio: 9:1
Average Class Size: 15
**Percent of students going to
grad school:** 22%
Tuition and Fees: $33,264
**In-State Tuition and Fees if
different:** No difference
Cost for Room and Board:
$6,957
**Percent receiving financial
aid out of those who apply,
first year:** 66%
**Percent receiving financial
aid among all students:**
Unreported

L awrence University's 84 acres in Wisconsin barely contain the vibrancy and excitement of the 1,500 students that bring the school to life. Lawrence is renowned for its music conservatory, and a sizeable percentage of students choose to follow its five-year double-degree program for a Bachelor of Music and Bachelor of Arts. At the same time, the close, intimate atmosphere of its liberal arts curriculum provides the opportunity for budding English and Biology majors alike to shine. And as if that wasn't enough, Lawrence students regularly go on retreats to Björklunden (pronounced "Bee-york-lun-den"), an estate on the shore of Lake Michigan, for seminars and weekend trips and and to enjoy nature at its most beautiful. "I had my choice of so many schools," one sophomore said, "and I picked Lawrence because it had everything I could ask for."

So a Connie and a Bio major are in a Frosh Studies class . . .

The hallmark of any Lawrentian's education is the Freshman Studies program, which every professor teaches and all students take in their first year at school: "It's unique to Lawrence, because all the freshmen read the same works, which cross different disciplines . . . so the curriculum covers works mostly from literature but also from science and math, history, and of course music." One student mentioned looking at Martin Luther King Jr.'s "I Have a Dream" speech alongside John Coltrane's song "Alabama" and realizing with her classmates that the two texts shared the same rhythms and cadences: "It was just fascinating to uncover things like that, that you would never notice outside of the classroom!"

The distributional requirements are a writing-intensive and speaking-intensive class, a quantitative class, classes with elements of diversity, a lab science class, a humanities class, a social science class, a fine arts class, a semester of a foreign language (or its equivalent), and a year of Freshman Studies. An English major noticed that "especially with the 'diversity' classes, the distributional requirements encourage people to have a broad view of the foundations of our world. Dead white males have been powerful forces, yes, but there's so much more than that." Classes are on the small side, and one student said she was surprised when her roommate was in a chemistry lecture class with 60 students, "and I had just never heard of anything that big at Lawrence. Classes are usually closer to 15 or 20, but they get smaller as you take more advanced courses."

Lawrence's music conservatory adds a unique twist to the school, and a significant number of students take classes at the Con, as it is called. One student considering a degree in music spent her free hours in a new way: "My workload is a different kind because I'll practice for several hours every day rather than reading books and writing papers or working in a lab." Still, she added, the amount of work is not unreasonable: "I've heard about people pulling all-nighters, but usually it's their fault because they've been putting off something too long."

With such small classes, professors focus on students and strive to make the work interesting. "In Music Theory we each wrote our own four-part chorales and then had people in that class perform them on their respective instruments . . . Viola was a really popular instrument," said a viola player from that class. Geology classes have also gone out into Wisconsin's geologic deposits, and students have dug up rather sizeable artifacts.

Life in between Brewed Awakenings and Björklunden!

When Lawrentians are not hard at work (and most of them do have some time to relax on weeknights), they take the time to enjoy themselves. On weekend afternoons, people usually go to a coffee shop in Appleton "and pretend to work while socializing and enjoying the day." Most students are split between the smaller, cozier Brewed Awakenings and the slightly more posh Copper Rock with its high ceilings, exposed brick walls, and cool art. "On weekend nights, there's usually one or two main parties that have been advertised, usually at the theme house or frat house," so the campus tends to split into the "party" groups and the "relaxed" groups. When asked about parties, one underclassman said, "The Coop's Nearly Naked parties are really neat—the point is to be creative and dress in anything other than clothing. We've even had dresses made out of juice boxes."

True to Lawrence's focus on music, the all-around coolest frat on campus is Sinfonia, a music fraternity that is almost all brass and percussion, with a lot of jazz musicians. "They provide the music for all their parties, and I just think that's really cool," said a staff writer for the school paper.

"If I had to nail down a stereotypical Lawrence student," said the writer, "it would be a music nerd. Nice, yes, but nerdy. There are definitely jocks on campus, though, and both groups have their female counterparts." On a 1-to-10 scale, Lawrence students rate an eight for all-around attractiveness. Downer Commons, where most students tend to eat, has three rooms that segment the student body in an interesting way: "A lot of the huge jocks sit in the A room, probably because it's closer to the food. The 'cool and alternative' people, including the outdoorsy people, sit in B, because it gets the best sunlight. And people who want peace and quiet sit upstairs in C, but everybody talks to them because the soft-serve ice cream machine is upstairs!" Lucinda's Dining Hall, the smaller dining facility, is a dining hall with an amazing view of the Wisconsin landscape that Lawrence borders. A vending machine is being added to the Con, and "now Connies won't ever go outside the Con again," joked a musician.

> "I had my choice of so many schools and I picked Lawrence because it had everything I could ask for."

Almost all students live on campus, with a very small handful of super seniors, or fifth-year students in the double-degree program, living in apartments. A major part of dorm life is theme housing, "a hot-button issue every spring. The validity of the Swing (Dancing) House and SoundBoard House are the topics of much debate, in comparison to the CompSci House, the GLOW (Gay, Lesbian, or Whatever) House and the oft-discussed but never realized French House." While most floors are single-sex, "coed floors are creeping slowly onto campus." The Lawrence campus is small enough that news often spreads over Saturday and Sunday brunch at Downer.

On some weekends, for a change of pace, students can go to Björklunden to explore the beautiful 425-acre estate that the University owns along Lake Michigan on the Door County peninsula. There is a lodge, and often student concerts are performed there. Different student groups go each weekend, and some students manage to go two or three times per term. Many students would tell you that a memorable part of a weekend at Björklunden is the food. It's a weekend of nonstop eating, and the food is a nice break from cafeteria food. A notable treat is Chef Steve's famous bread pudding.

One Lawrence student said that, even in the cold of winter, "Lawrence is a bit like Lake Wobegon (which makes sense since we're pretty close to Minnesota), because all the women are strong, all the men are good looking, so all us students are above average." With such a tight-knit community, an intimate liberal arts curriculum, nightlife as cozy as the town of Appleton, and the wild beauty of Wisconsin all around, how could any student *not* pick Lawrence?—*Jeffrey Zuckerman*

FYI

If you come to Lawrence University, you'd better bring " 'an active love of music.' "

What is a typical weekend schedule? " 'Friday: dinner at the Coop, concert, dance party. Saturday: yoga, Farmer's Market, study until your friend's recital, dance party. Sunday: brunch, studying, and maybe another recital, SoundBoard at the coffeehouse in the evening.' "

If I could change one thing about Lawrence University, " 'I'd spend more time at Björklunden.' "

Three things every student at Lawrence University should do before graduating are " 'visit the cupola on top of Main Hall, answer phones all night during the Great Midwest Trivia Contest, and spend all Saturday attending student recitals.' "

Marquette University

Address: P.O. Box 1881 Milwaukee, WI 53201-1881
Phone: 414-288-7302
E-mail address: admissions@marquette.edu
Web site URL: www.marquette.edu
Year Founded: 1881
Private or Public: Private
Religious Affiliation: Roman Catholic-Jesuit
Location: Suburban
Number of Applicants: 19,500
Percent Accepted: 34%
Percent Accepted who enroll: 29%
Number Entering: 1,950
Number of Transfers Accepted each Year: 350
Middle 50% SAT range: M: 550–660, CR: 540–630, Wr: 530–640
Middle 50% ACT range: 24–29

Early admission program EA/ED/None: None
Percentage accepted through EA or ED: NA
EA and ED deadline: NA
Regular Deadline: 1-Dec
Application Fee: $0
Full time Undergraduate enrollment: 8,142
Total enrollment: 11,062
Percent Male: 48%
Percent Female: 52%
Total Percent Minority or Unreported: 17%
Percent African-American: 5%
Percent Asian/Pacific Islander: 4%
Percent Hispanic: 5%
Percent Native-American: 1%
Percent International: 2%
Percent in-state/out of state: 43% / 57%
Percent from Public HS: 54%
Retention Rate: 93%
Graduation Rate 4-year: 58%

Graduation Rate 6-year: 77%
Percent Undergraduates in On-campus housing: 51%
Number of official organized extracurricular organizations: 250
3 Most popular majors: Communication, Business, Biomedical Sciences/Journalism
Student/Faculty ratio: 15:1
Average Class Size: 16
Percent of students going to grad school: 41%
Tuition and Fees: $28,680
In-State Tuition and Fees if different: No difference
Cost for Room and Board: $9,680
Percent receiving financial aid out of those who apply, first year: 92%
Percent receiving financial aid among all students: 74%

The largest private university in the state of Wisconsin, Marquette University is also one of the most important Jesuit universities in the country. Marquette certainly has a strong Catholic character and incorporates theological classes into the university's curriculum. Of course, this does not mean that Marquette focuses on religious training. It is in fact a well-respected institution of higher learning in a large number of fields, ranking among the top 100 national universities by the *U.S. News & World Report*. Most students tend to have a very good academic and social experience, making it a great college choice.

A Different Approach to Learning

At the outset, Marquette is very similar to universities of similar scope. It is divided into 12 different colleges and schools. Of course, a number of them, such as the Schools of Law and Management, are only available to graduate students. However, the university certainly has a large selection of programs to satisfy almost any academic pursuit. Indeed, for undergraduates, the university offers a long list of programs in engineering, business, communications, health sciences, nursing, and liberal arts, not to mention a number of pre-professional curricula to help those planning for graduate school. "I think we do have a lot of choices at Marquette," said one student. "The College of Business Administration, especially, has a lot of options." The university has more than 100 majors offered, as well as a good selection of minors. The majors in communications and business are highly popular. For those who are not sure about majors, they are not alone. In fact, about 20 percent of students are unsure about the precise direction of their studies and need to take a number of classes at Marquette before deciding on a major.

What is different about Marquette is its Core of Common Studies, which is similar to most universities' general education requirements. In order to provide a well-rounded education, students must all complete courses in certain topics. Marquette, given its Catholic traditions, has a very extensive list of required fields, ranging from the usual mathematics and social sciences to areas such as rhetoric and theology. The idea of taking classes in theology may not be very amenable to a number of less than religious students, but these theology courses are in fact basic introductions to the Bible and the Christian faith. "The requirements in theology are not there to make you become a priest," said one student. "They can actually be really interesting in teaching you about the history of Catholicism." Furthermore, the university also requires classes about other cultures to establish better global understanding.

Students are generally satisfied with the class sizes at Marquette, which offers a combination of hundred-people lectures and small discussion-based seminars. According to students, both types of classes are important in a college education. "Going to a bigger lecture is totally different from sitting in a small class with twelve people," said one student. "I don't know which one is better, but you will definitely get a chance to do both at Marquette." Of course, freshmen tend to be stuck with larger classes, if only due to the large number of people enrolling in introductory courses.

> "I think Milwaukee is great. It is not really stressful like New York, but it has all the attractions of a big city, and Marquette is right in the center of it."

The workload is also manageable, but students should remember not to overload their schedule. "You should try to find a balance between easy and difficult classes," said one student. "If you are already taking two hard courses, you should choose a couple of easy ones to balance them out." Another issue is to find the equilibrium between extracurricular activities and academics. "Because we have so many organizations, you can be involved in too many of them and forget about your classes," said one student.

Students are also happy with their access to professors. They can go to office hours, and course instructors are happy to have informal chats with students on topics beyond academics. "Most professors are really helpful, and they can give you all kinds of advice on classes, careers, everything," said one student.

At the Center of Brew City

Marquette's location is one of the best assets of the university. Milwaukee is one of the 30 largest cities in the United States in terms of population. In addition, it is also a city of college students, serving as the location of more than a dozen colleges and universities. Marquette is very close to downtown Milwaukee, thus offering students the chance of having access to the numerous cultural activities of the city. In addition, given the high level of economic activities in Milwaukee, students have an easier time finding jobs and internships in the area that can accompany their studies. "I think Milwaukee is great," said one student. "It is not really stressful like New York, but it has all the attractions of a big city, and Marquette is right in the center of it."

Marquette offers nine different residential halls, most of which are modern high- to mid-rises, in accordance with an urban setting. The freshmen rooms tend to be small and cramped, but the quality of accommodations improve as students rise in seniority. "You have to be patient and wait until the last couple of years to have nicer housing," said one student. "But then again, you might no longer be living on campus after sophomore year." In fact, a large number of upperclassmen leave dorms to enjoy greater freedom in nearby off campus housing. There is more space and certainly fewer restrictions on student activities. "You can definitely find pretty good off-campus housing nearby at a reasonable price," said one student. "So there is less incentive to stay in dorms after freshman year."

Marquette operates five dining halls from early morning into late night. In addition, each residential hall has a store mostly used for snacks and drinks. "There is nothing great about the food," said one student. "But it is definitely good enough for you to get by on during the school year." For those who have difficulties with the dining services, it is important to remember that Marquette is in a city, and there are restaurants of all types around the university.

Weekend activities vary for students. Some people prefer fraternities and sororities, which hold big, theme parties. Others go to local bars and clubs. For those uninterested in drinking, there are plenty of shows and events to attend around Milwaukee, not to mention the proximity to Chicago. "There are so many things to do here," said one student. "I just wish I had more time during the weekends."

Like Pros

Marquette is known for one of the most successful men's basketball programs in the country. The Golden Eagles have produced a large number of players in the National Basketball Association and qualify for the NCAA Division I Tournament almost every year. The games are some of the best-attended college basketball events in the country. "Basketball is huge here," said one student. "When March comes around, everyone is infected with a basketball craze." In fact, the Golden Eagles play at Bradley Center, which is the home to none other than Milwaukee's professional team, the Bucks.

With the Golden Eagles, Marquette certainly has a great deal of school spirit. Of course, the university also derives pride from its Catholic tradition. Some students do complain that the university is not sufficiently diverse. Most students come from Wisconsin and the surrounding Midwestern states and are predominantly white. However, the university is certainly working toward making Marquette better known and more attractive to those outside of the region. Ultimately, the university has strong academics, good location, and fun social life, three great selling points to prospective students.—*Xiaohang Liu*

FYI

If you come to Marquette, you'd better bring "some winter clothing."

What is the typical weekend schedule? "Basketball games and frat parties."

Three things every student at Marquette should do before graduating are "go to mass, go to Chicago, and make sure that you show up to as many basketball games as possible. Some people would pay a fortune to see some of the games."

University of Wisconsin / Madison

Address: 716 Langdon Street Madison, WI 53706-1481

Phone: 608-262-3961

E-mail address: onwisconsin@admissions.wisc.edu

Web site URL: www.admissions.wisc.edu

Year Founded: 1848

Private or Public: Public

Religious Affiliation: None

Location: Urban

Number of Applicants: 25,522

Percent Accepted: 57%

Percent Accepted who enroll: 41%

Number Entering: 5,920

Number of Transfers Accepted each Year: 1,777

Middle 50% SAT range: M: 620–730, CR: 540–670, Wr: 570–670

Middle 50% ACT range: 26–30

Early admission program EA/ED/None: None

Percentage accepted through EA or ED: NA

EA and ED deadline: NA

Regular Deadline: 15-Nov, 1-Feb

Application Fee: $44

Full time Undergraduate enrollment: 27,680

Total enrollment: 42,041

Percent Male: 47%

Percent Female: 53%

Total Percent Minority or Unreported: 13%

Percent African-American: 3%

Percent Asian/Pacific Islander: 6%

Percent Hispanic: 3%

Percent Native-American: 1%

Percent International: 6%

Percent in-state/out of state: 66%/34%

Percent from Public HS: Unreported

Retention Rate: 93%

Graduation Rate 4-year: 49%

Graduation Rate 6-year: 80%

Percent Undergraduates in On-campus housing: 24%

Number of official organized extracurricular organizations: 700

3 Most popular majors: Political Science, Biology, Psychology

Student/Faculty ratio: 13:1

Average Class Size: 29

Percent of students going to grad school: Unreported

Tuition and Fees: $21,820

In-State Tuition and Fees if different: $7,570

Cost for Room and Board: $7,770

Percent receiving financial aid out of those who apply, first year: 54%

Percent receiving financial aid among all students: 32%

The University of Wisconsin-Madison, a school of 30,000 undergraduates, is one of the top public universities in the nation, known for stellar academics, a powerhouse football team, and a lively party environment. Students find Madison to be a perfect college town, despite the cold winter weather. Wisconsin challenges students to grow independent, taking the big school and breaking it down into small, Badger communities.

Work Hard

Wisconsin is divided up into nine schools and colleges, including the very strong School of Business and the liberal arts-style College of Letters and Science. With over 100 majors, it is not too difficult for students to find something they are interested in, whether it is the popular science, psychology, and business majors or the more wacky ones, like Dairy Science. Within the colleges there are various general education requirements, including two quantitative reasoning and communication classes for the College

of Letter and Science, but students don't find them too frustrating. "Most people do it anyway," one student noted.

Students with the most credits are given priority when choosing classes, meaning that it is sometimes difficult for underclassmen to get into the classes they want to take. However, with so many options to choose from, students don't think it's hard to find an interesting class.

Especially for freshmen, a majority of classes may be lectures, which can include more than 400 people. Often, the professors put the notes online, which students find enormously helpful. In one student's sociology class, there are 420 students, but the class is coupled with a 10-person discussion section to ensure maximum understanding. However, the same student shared her public speaking seminar with just 12 other students.

Professors, like any school, are largely good, but vary on the class. For some classes, they are very interesting, though on the other hand, some find it difficult to keep the lecture hall engaged. One student said her professor was "really into the class, always joking and having fun with everyone." However, students say the TAs are really good, which, according to one student, "is almost more important than the professor."

Wisconsin has a somewhat strange grading system. Students can obtain the following grades in their courses: A, A/B, B, B/C, C, D or F. This can be a detriment or a benefit depending on the person. For an A- student it is particularly frustrating, when a 91 on a test is counted the same as a 87.

Those seeking more of a challenge can apply for the College of Letters and Science honor program, which can involve honors in the liberal arts, honors in a specific major, or both. As a member of the honor program, students can test themselves academically and grow closer to professors. One freshman said she took a class with 17 other people from a professor who usually lectures to hundreds of students.

For freshmen, it is a big transition from high school. Yes there is more reading and the workload increases, but freshman receive an "overwhelming amount of independence," one student said. Because of big lectures and less one on one time with professors, students have to be more proactive with their college experience. "There's so much I don't know about still," said a freshman. "I have to figure things out on my own."

Play Hard

"Students study so much during the week," one student said. "We work really hard, and we earn it for the weekends." While for some, the weekend starts on Tuesdays, for many students Thursday night is the beginning of the fun. The bar scene is huge, even for minors: "Fake IDs are pretty crucial," one student said. "Don't expect to get away with any old one—it has to be good." Students also go to house parties, fraternities and sororities.

According to one student, Greek life isn't dominating on campus after they got in trouble a few years ago. Many students join fraternities or sororities to "make a school of 40,000 a little smaller," said one sorority member.

There are a few famous parties that take place throughout the year, but the two biggest are the Mifflin Street Block Party and the State Street Halloween Party. Mifflin occurs the week before finals and involves the complete takeover of the street. Halloween lasts at least three nights, meaning three nights of costumed brouhaha, with music, concerts, and tons of fun. The party takes place on State Street, which leads from Bascom Hill, a hub of Wisconsin academics, to the state capitol.

Life in Madison

Students consider Madison, the capital of Wisconsin, the perfect college town. "It's not a huge city, but it's a lot bigger than what I'm used to," said one Wisconsin native. "There's always so many different things going on." Another student added: "With Madison you get a small town college feel while still having that big time college experience." Madison is home to lots of concerts, many which take place at the Majestic Theater, and scores of restaurants serving all types of cuisine. For parents' weekend, Tornado is a great place to go, where you can find the "best steak of your life," one student said. After a night of late partying—or studying—students often head over to Ian's Pizza, which has lines out the door at two in the morning. "It's really nice that everything is close," one student said. "The capital is right here. The lake is right here. We have natural trails and a downtown with interesting food."

> "With Madison you get a small town college feel while still having that big time college experience."

With the state capitol right next to campus, Madison offers countless opportunities to get involved in local politics. Many student organizations are involved with lobbying (and following around) local politicians. One student said, "We're so close, so we have a big influence on the government." Many students, especially political science majors, take on an internship through the year to get a taste of civil service. Other internship opportunities arise from the sciences. As Wisconsin is a research-based college, lots of students are involved in medical internships, sometimes paid, which they keep throughout their college career. According to one student, about half of the students have jobs—including those paid internships—which can range from the ordinary (dining hall worker) to the more fun (scoring intramural sports).

Your own Wisconsin Community

Wisconsin has over 500 student organizations on campus, so there is always something to get involved in. Many students view clubs and extracurriculars as not only a way to pursue passions outside the classroom, but also to make Wisconsin feel smaller. "There are lots of options," one student said. "If you want it, it's here." One example of this is intramurals. There are dozens of IM sports to participate in, from volleyball to broomball to Ultimate Frisbee, and they are very low stress. One student noted: "They're as competitive as you want them to be. I have some friends who just have fun with them."

Most freshmen live in dorms, though upperclassmen generally move off campus. Students consider the dorms a smaller community and quickly bond with others on their floor. There are two areas of dorms: Lakeshore ("secluded, quiet, and nature-y") and Southeast (closer to downtown with more of a party reputation). Every year, there is a huge snowball fight between the two. "It's pretty intense," one freshman said.

Bucky Badger

In the early days of Wisconsin, the mascot at football games was a live badger. When it proved too dangerous and uncontrollable, an art student had an idea—she crafted a paper mache head for the original Bucky the Badger student costume. As a mascot for a Big Ten powerhouse football school, Bucky makes it to every game, but he is definitely not alone.

On Game Days, Wisconsin students wake up early, dress in red, and walk together to the huge Camp Randall Stadium. They are soon surrounded by "the entire town" of Madison natives; one student noted that "everyone comes to football games. They take a lot of pride in the school." The student section, a sea of red, stands up for the entire game. At the end of the third quarter, House of Pain's song, "Jump Around" begins to play. According to one freshman, "the entire student section goes up and down and goes absolutely nuts." The so-called fifth quarter is a continuation of the rumpus, which is an entire quarter of more jumping and singing about Wisconsin. "You finally feel like this huge school is coming together as one, with everyone in one location," one student said.

Sconnies and Coasties

When first arriving at Wisconsin, there is some tension between the Wisconsin natives ("Sconnies") and those from out-of-state ("Coasties"). One Coastie from Los Angeles mentioned an incident when she was trying out for the club water polo team, saying that "they look down on you when they see where you're from and what you're wearing." A Sconnie said that Coasties "bring more of a city atmosphere, party habits, and different clothes. They're a little more wild than Wisconsin people." Though there is some self-segregation, the two groups generally "mix pretty well." "I have lots of Coastie friends," one Wisconsin-native said.

"People are extremely friendly," said one student. "Every single flight home I've been on, I've met someone who went to Wisconsin. Everyone who goes there loves it and wants to talk about it." It is easy to make new friends, whether through dorms, classes, or extracurriculars.

The Polar Plunge

Standard dress, at least during winter, is a staple Wisconsin sweatshirt, Uggs, and a north face jacket. According to some, it is not that big of a deal. "I expected this freezing terrain. When I came, it was absolutely beautiful," one student said. However, some brave students undertake the polar plunge, jumping into the freezing cold water of Lake Mendota. Somewhere, apparently, there is a list of all students that ever accepted the challenge. "I hope I have it in me," one student said.

But despite the frigid winter months, students are generally happy they chose to be Badgers. "Madison has always been a dream school for me," one student said. Another noted, "I wanted to be in a school that had a big-spirited athletic environment while still excelling academically."

Students say that almost everyone at Wisconsin loves it, and it's easy to see why. Wisconsin is a perfect school for students looking to obtain a great education in a place where school pride, especially in athletics, is a dominant force. Though students have to be more independent academically and socially, they learn to break Wisconsin up into smaller communities, making great friends in the process. Spending four years at Wisconsin, students can get the parties, college town and fun of a traditional college experience.—*Mason Kroll*

FYI
Three things every student at Wisconsin should do before graduating are: "complete the polar plunge, storm the field, and go to a hockey game."

If you come to Wisconsin, you'd better bring "snowboots. Don't think your Uggs can last in the snow—you have to do a penguin waddle to keep dry."

If I could change one thing about Wisconsin, I'd "make there be less students per professor—you really have to go out and make an effort to talk to a professor."

Wyoming

Not many universities can claim a location at 7,200 feet. Amidst mountain ranges and grassy plains, the height only adds to the remote, yet urban setting of the University of Wyoming, one that most students come to love. With the University of Wyoming being the only big college in the state, the University continually draws fans to cheer for the brown and gold.

The State University

With just over 9,000 undergraduates claiming their loyalty to UW, many students feel that the size is perfect. One sophomore commented that the student body population is "the perfect size, enabling individual attention and creating an atmosphere for better learning, but also big enough to see unfamil-

iar faces." Like any university, the class sizes vary with specialization. While introductory courses can range anywhere from 200 to 500 students, the higher-level courses cater to crowds of 30 students or less.

At U of Wyoming, one will find most students looking to major in Business Administration or Education, but don't be fooled: Wyoming offers a variety of fun areas of study. "In order to fulfill the physical education requirement, I've known people who have taken Ballroom Dancing, Ballet, and even Tai Chi," one senior said. The University of Wyoming offers strong honors programs and boasts fantastic engineering and research science departments. In order to qualify for the honors program at Wyoming, high school students must have a minimum 3.7 GPA, at least a 1240 total score on the

SAT, or composite ACT scores of at least 28. Honor students are required to take five honors courses throughout their time at UW, two freshman year and one each of the three remaining years. One student at UW commented that the courseload is "pretty manageable, but continues to get more difficult as you go. The honors classes and the science courses are amongst the most challenging."

A Little Too Small

Similar to many campuses, most students at Wyoming usually move off campus after freshman year. For those students still on campus, their housing options include Wyoming's six dorm buildings located at the center of campus, "Prexy's Pasture." With the ability to move off campus, approximately 50 percent of sophomores do so along with almost all the juniors and seniors. "It's sort of a rite of passage to be able to live off campus. Although it's nice to live close to classes, living off campus is really liberating: no restrictions and no RAs," commented one Wyoming senior. As far as the architectural style of the University is concerned, students find it somewhat uninviting. The cement facades seem to emphasize the barren winter months. However, the University is undergoing "a lot of renovation and is committed to modernizing all of campus."

For those students still living on campus, the dining halls are one of Wyoming's best features: "The dining halls are all renovated and the food offered by UW is actually really good. There's a lot of variety and the food is pretty fresh," one freshman noted. Open until 10:30 p.m., the dining halls resemble more of a food court than a dining hall. Off-campus students don't have to miss out. Local businesses are able to serve Wyoming students through the use of their WyoOne ID cards. Thus, all students can take advantage of a late-night slice of pizza or cup of coffee with the swipe of a card.

A Separate Place

Students can feel a true sense of community in Laramie. With only 25,000 people occupying the small town, more than half are students. As great as a small-town community may feel, it can be a bit restricting. "Laramie is about a two-hour drive from anywhere. Most students will usually stay on campus," one sophomore said. But most students do have cars, so the possibility for escape is always there. When on campus, upperclassmen mostly hit the bar scene, with Lovejoy's

Bar and Grill and Altitude Chophouse & Brewery being two favorites. Underclassmen usually either attend the usual frat parties or make their way to the athletes' houses. Because many upperclassmen live off campus, the underclassmen "don't really intermingle regularly with juniors and seniors unless they are a part of the same team or organization," one junior said. The University of Wyoming has a strict policy against alcohol in the dorms and really tries to curb underage drinking, but "alcohol is very accessible" nonetheless. The big event all students can look forward to is the annual Beach Party that one on-campus frat puts on. "The frat actually drags sand in and transforms the entire house into a beach. It's pretty fun; everyone goes," one sophomore said.

> "I think the fact that the entire state of Wyoming is behind the university and all of its programs means a lot to the students here."

Although it is hard for some students to feel so isolated, Laramie has many other kinds of attractions, including its breathtaking scenery. The surrounding areas include everything from grassy plains to rocky climbing areas. With a mountainous landscape in the background, many students rock climb, hike, or even ski at Snowy Range or Happy Jack. On weekends, many students set aside a day to head up to the mountains and get some fresh air.

Saddle Up for the Gold and Brown

With an overall student body of over 12,000, many students find their niches in diverse activities. Varsity athletics are valued highly. With football and basketball bringing in the biggest crowds, other sports draw supportive crowds as well. "As a swimmer at Wyoming, I am proud to say that we bring in more spectators at home meets than any other school in our conference," remarked one junior. Wyoming also emphasizes an active lifestyle by providing 18 different club sports, involving nearly 6,000 students, faculty, and staff. UW's Half Acre Gym is a "hot spot to hang out and one of the most noteworthy buildings on campus." Life at UW is one of comfort. Many students will show up to class in sweats and sometimes pajamas. The general feel is that the atmosphere is easygoing and laid-back, but where school spirit is concerned, the Cowboys and Cowgirls find themselves very well supported.

Nowhere Else

Students across the nation have school pride; that's a given. But for students at the University of Wyoming, it's deeper than that. The community involvement is really treasured, and the people are friendly. "First and foremost, I go to the University of Wyoming. I think the fact that the entire state of Wyoming is behind the university and all of its programs means a lot to the students here. Also, I think that the small community brings the students here closer together."
—*Taylor Ritzel*

FYI

If you come to the University of Wyoming, you'd better bring a "'big winter coat and anything that protects you from the wind.'"

What is the typical weekend schedule? "'Party Fridays, sleep and climb Saturdays, party Saturday nights, and study on Sundays.'"

If I could change one thing about the University of Wyoming, I'd "'get rid of the wind. The weather can be really nice on any given day, but the wind ruins the day.'"

Three things every student at the University of Wyoming should do before graduating are "'ski at Snowy Range, attend a home UW football game, and hike Vedauwoo.'"

Canada

Despite Canada's image as a country of winter storms and glaciers, thousands of American students cross the border every year to seek an education from their country's northern neighbor. The reasons for this northbound move range from low tuition to beautiful landscape to high educational standards. Given the numerous advantages of attending Canadian universities, it is certainly worthwhile for American students to take a close look.

Money Matters

One important factor in choosing which college to attend is money. In that respect, Canadian universities, which are all public, have significant advantages over their American counterparts. The tuition rates at the most expensive schools are generally below $8,000 for Canadians. Even for American citizens, the average rate hovers below $20,000, much cheaper than the price tags of many universities in the United States, which are rapidly approaching $40,000.

Another major expense that students will face, the cost of living, depends greatly on location—living in Toronto is certainly more expensive than, say, Wolfville, Nova Scotia, but it is still cheaper than a number of cities in the United States. American students in need of financial aid can apply for Stafford loans from the federal government, even if they study in Canada. Both merit- and need-based scholarships are also available.

The low fees, however, come with a disadvantage. Funding for universities in Canada depends on the government. This means that they tend to have fewer resources than many private institutions in the United States. In general, however, the overall impact of tight government funding on the quality of education is minimal, especially for undergraduates.

A Whole Different Country

Each Canadian province maintains its own system of higher education. For example, in Quebec, most students attend a post-secondary program called a College of General and Vocational Education (CEGEP) prior to enrollment in universities, making the academic programs more specialized. In fact, unlike many American universities, which encourage students to study in a wide range of subjects, Canadian schools tend to place greater emphasis on career preparation.

Most American students studying in Canada choose to attend one of the major research universities, creating the perception that undergraduate education in Canada is always within large, impersonal institutions located in urban centers. While it is true that the better-known universities, such as McGill University and the University of Toronto, enroll tens of thousands of undergraduate and graduate students, there are plenty of smaller, predominantly undergraduate schools housing only a few thousand students, very similar to liberal arts colleges in the United States. Choices abound for those who would like to escape the noise of bustling cities and settle in the countryside.

One aspect of college life that Canada fails to offer is school spirit. Although students wear their college gear and cheer for their sports teams, their attachment to their schools is not as strong as in the United States, many students say. This is in part because intercollegiate sports are not as important in Canada. Youngsters who aspire to become professional athletes mostly rise through junior leagues instead of collegiate competitions. Furthermore, the large number of students in off-campus housing diminishes the sense of community in many universities.

Getting in

The admissions process in Canada places greater emphasis on grades and standardized test scores than do American universities. Although extracurricular activities and achievements outside of school are also considered, academic performance significantly outweighs everything else. Many schools even set cutoff limits for SAT scores and high school GPAs. Of course, this is not universal, and different schools have different policies regarding admissions.

Studying in Canada for non–Canadian citizens requires a student visa, which is easy to obtain once the student is admitted. Just like those in the United States, Canadian universities attract thousands of students from around the world every year. The cold weather and the differences in college life may turn away many American students, but given its quality of education and affordability, Canada is certainly a great destination for college students and deserves strong consideration.—*Xiaohang Liu*

Carleton University

Address: 1125 Colonel By Drive, 315 Robertson Hall Ottawa, ON K1S5B6 Canada	**Percentage accepted through EA or ED:** NA	**Graduation Rate 4-year:** Unreported
Phone: 613-520-3663	**EA and ED deadline:** NA	**Graduation Rate 6-year:** Unreported
E-mail address: liaison@admissions .carleton.ca	**Regular Deadline:** Rolling	**Percent Undergraduates in On-campus housing:** 15%
Web site URL: www.carleton.ca	**Application Fee:** $85 (Canadian dollars)	**Number of official organized extracurricular**
Year Founded: 1945	**Full time Undergraduate enrollment:** 20,746	**organizations:** 78
Private or Public: Private	**Total enrollment:** 23,161	**3 Most popular majors:** Unreported
Religious Affiliation: None	**Percent Male:** 50%	**Student/Faculty ratio:** 2:1
Location: Urban	**Percent Female:** 50%	**Average Class Size:** 9
Number of Applicants: 15,934	**Total Percent Minority or Unreported:** Unreported	**Percent of students going to grad school:** Unreported
Percent Accepted: 73%	**Percent African-American:** Unreported	**Tuition and Fees:** $14,936 Canadian
Percent Accepted who enroll: 43%	**Percent Asian/Pacific Islander:** Unreported	**In-State Tuition and Fees if different:** $4,794 Canadian
Number Entering: 5,000	**Percent Hispanic:** Unreported	**Cost for Room and Board:** $7,247 Canadian
Number of Transfers Accepted each Year: 830	**Percent Native-American:** Unreported	**Percent receiving financial aid out of those who apply, first year:** Unreported
Middle 50% SAT range: Unreported	**Percent International:** 8%	
Middle 50% ACT range: Unreported	**Percent in-state/out of state:** 1% from U.S.	**Percent receiving financial aid among all students:** Unreported
Early admission program EA/ED/None: None	**Percent from Public HS:** Unreported	
	Retention Rate: Unreported	

Located in Ottawa, Ontario, Carleton University combines the splendor of Canada's English-speaking capital city with the French-Canadian culture of nearby Québec. In addition to a treasure trove of national museums, government buildings, memorials, and celebrations of heritage, safe and scenic Ottawa offers trendy night spots, sidewalk cafés, hiking trails, the beautiful Rideau Canal that turns into the world's largest skating rink, and world-class research and development facilities in technology and medicine. Carleton students benefit from abundant opportunities for co-ops, internships, and real-world field experience as well as their school's challenging academic programs in a variety of areas.

Pre-Professionalism
Carleton is best known for its challenging professional programs in journalism, architecture, engineering, and public affairs. The school is one of only two universities in Canada to offer a degree in aerospace engi-

neering, and the program has been growing quickly in recent years. Students within this major choose to focus on aerodynamics, propulsion and vehicle performance; aerospace structures, systems, and vehicle design; aerospace electronics and systems; or space systems design, and everyone must complete a final independent project before graduation. Many students take advantage of the option to take an aerospace engineering co-op internship instead of classes during their fourth year of enrollment, although this decision stretches the time required for graduation to five years. Carleton's program in criminology and criminal justice is also quite popular, and the proximity of the Parliamentary and other governmental buildings in Canada's capital city allows for a unique experience in field placement for internships. Criminology majors can choose to intern with attorneys, policy analysts, police, or victim counselors, to name a few of the options that present an exceptional opportunity to learn about the discipline from a front-line, hands-on perspective. The University's College of the Humanities offers a four-year, interdisciplinary Bachelor of Humanities degree focusing on the great Western canon. There students read a veritable "who's who" list of the most well-known historical works in Western civilization, including selections by Plato, Homer, Virgil, Shakespeare, Molière, and Kant. Although well-rounded, this major does not necessarily come with the best reputation, as one non-humanities student admitted to hearing that the program is "easy" and "basically for people who have less of a clue about what they want to do with themselves than people studying the arts." Carleton also boasts one of the "best journalism programs in Canada," which prepares students to become premier journalists with an understanding of the responsibility of the press and which incorporates short apprenticeships as well as the possibility of specializing in print or broadcast media.

Carleton offers a program called ArtsOne for first-year students who have not yet chosen a major and who are undecided about which courses they should take when they arrive. This program, which offers several different sets, or "clusters," of four courses revolving around a particular theme, contributes to the eventual awarding of a Bachelor of Arts degree. One hundred students enroll in each cluster and thus take all of the same classes, providing a smaller peer group within the larger university and a way to establish a home base of friends.

Professors at Carleton can be "eccentric," "enthusiastic," and "witty," and students generally find them to be easily accessible and very helpful. The most popular professors understandably tend to be the most dynamic and engaging: Professor Matthew Yeager of the sociology and anthropology department, for example, asks his students to call him "Thunder" as a reflection of his unique, theatrical lecturing style (although as one student warned, "do not sit in the front rows, or even at the edge of any row, because he THUNDERS around the class!").

Students at Carleton are known for being welcoming and sociable and, according to one student, "it's easy to meet people because everyone at school is very friendly and willing to talk to people they don't know. Most people are in the same situation: they're in a new city where they don't know anyone and they are looking for friends to fill the loneliness of missing home." The school also prides itself on the carefully cultivated diversity within its student body and boasts a high rate of international enrollment with more than 140 different countries represented.

Tunnel Moles and Party Rats

Carleton offers underground, well-lit, heated tunnels that connect every building on campus and allow students to travel between their dorm rooms and classrooms in warmth and comfort as the outside temperatures drop to an average high of 21°F in January. The tunnels are appreciated by under- and upperclassmen alike, but as one student notes, this method of travel can become a way of life: "Some students living in the residence halls can go for months without actually seeing daylight! We call them tunnel-rats or tunnel-moles. But the tunnels do make going to school in one of the coldest cities (in this part of Canada) a lot easier." Luckily, the campus is fairly compact, and walking from one class to another takes only a few minutes.

"You don't mess with the R.A.s."

Housed in "institutional, modern and artsy style buildings," undergraduates at Carleton can choose between two major options for dorm life: "Suite Style" residence halls such as Leeds and Prescott come equipped with various kitchen appliances in each room, while "Traditional Style" dorms do not permit in-room cooking and instead require students to buy a meal plan and eat in the Residence Dining Hall or in the various additional on-campus food outlets. The Residence Advisors in each dorm can be pretty strict about upholding the rules; as one of their undergraduate charges put it, "you don't mess with the R.A.s." Most students move out of the residence halls, or "res," after their first year and relocate to apartments off campus. However, "there are a few lifers who love res too much to ever leave and go on to be Residence Advisors or just live in upper-year residences for the duration of their schooling."

The drinking age in Ontario is 19, and students who have reached this birthday milestone are permitted to bring alcohol into their rooms within the residence halls but must refrain from carrying it outside or into shared dorm spaces such as stairways, lobbies, and elevators. Binge drinking exists as at any other college, but it is not especially prevalent; marijuana use, on the other hand, is "a big thing," and students "see people smoking weed pretty much every day."

The weeknight social scene revolves around Carleton's on-campus pub, Oliver's. Oliver's tends to be extremely popular on Tuesdays and particularly Thursdays, when "everyone from different social circles attends and intermingles," providing an excellent opportunity for meeting new people. In contrast, weekends are "usually left for parties and other clubbing and bar experiences throughout the city." Because Carleton is located in the suburbs of Ottawa rather than in the middle of the city, "the social scene right around the school is a little lacking," but students can reach the downtown area very quickly thanks to the city's efficient transit system. Students also like to hang out in the food court in the recently renovated University Centre, particularly in the student-run Rooster's Coffeehouse, which offers an assortment of coffees and teas as well as a seating area in front of a wide-screen TV. Underclassmen who have not yet reached Ontario's drinking age often journey into Hull, Québec, about 15 to 20 minutes away by car, where the legal age of imbibing is only 18 and where "the bars are all scuzzy but promise a good time."

No Football? No Problem

Carleton does not have a varsity football team—it was disbanded in 1999—and instead, school pride rests with the successes of the "best men's basketball team in Canada," according to one enthusiastic student. Indeed, the Ravens seldom disappoint and have won many championships and titles, including the Canadian Interuniversity Sport (CIS) National Championship Tournament for five consecutive years between 2002 and 2007, as well as 2009. The school's rivalry with the nearby University of Ottawa keeps the competition heated when the two basketball teams meet on the court. Carleton also hosts varsity fencing, golf, hockey, rugby, and water polo, among many other sports, as well as a variety of intramurals, including flag football for the pigskin enthusiasts who bemoan the loss of the varsity team. The Physical Recreation Centre, the largest facility of its kind in Canada, features two gymnasiums, a 50-meter indoor pool, a cardio center, a fitness testing lab, squash and tennis courts, a yoga room, and the Ice House skating and hockey rink, and serves the student body with training programs and services to accommodate everyone from beginner athletes to professionals.

As with many universities located in colder climates, the CU Ski and Snowboard Club is a popular organization on campus. Every fall, this organization generally sponsors a big hip-hop show accompanied by ski and snowboard movie premieres that caters to "the hip-hop community, the ski and snowboard community, and the drinking community (party people)." Carleton also offers over 150 student-run organizations, including the sexagenarian weekly campus newspaper *The Charlatan*, the Sock 'n' Buskin Theatre Company, the community radio station CKCU-FM, and the Rideau River Residence Association (RRRA), which oversees students living on campus in the dorms. Generally, Carleton "frowns on frats and sororities," but they do exist off campus, and all Greek activities operate without University support.

Undergraduates at Carleton University generally exhibit enthusiasm and pride when discussing their alma mater and appreciate their school's efforts to keep them happy, from the underground tunnel system to the dedicated professors, from the friendly rivalry with the University of Ottawa to the co-op opportunities sponsored and arranged by the various academic departments. As one student summed up, "The atmosphere at Carleton is very positive. Everyone seems to really enjoy being at school and everyone is proud to be a student here."—*Kristin Knox*

FYI

If you come to Carleton, you'd better bring "a good supply of winter clothing."

What is the typical weekend schedule? "Attempt to do work on Saturday but instead choose to go to Ottawa and have fun. Then on Sunday you really try to get work done."

If I could change one thing about Carleton, I'd "take away dry frosh week (no drinking events)."

Three things every student at Carleton should do before graduating are "climb all the stairs in Dunton Tower (if you don't, you're doomed to be jobless forever!), jump in the Alumni Park fountain during convocation, and hang out at Oliver's."

McGill University

Address: 845 Sherbrooke Street West, Montreal, QC H3A-2T5 Canada

Phone: 514-398-3910

E-mail address: admissions@mcgill.ca

Web site URL: www.mcgill.ca

Year Founded: 1821

Private or Public: Public

Religious Affiliation: None

Location: Urban

Number of Applicants: 20,391

Percent Accepted: 54%

Percent Accepted who enroll: 43%

Number Entering: 4,781

Number of Transfers Accepted each Year: 933

Middle 50% SAT range: M: 640–720, **CR:** 640–740, **Wr:** 650–720

Middle 50% ACT range: 29–31

Early admission program EA/ED/None: None

Percentage accepted through EA or ED: NA

EA and ED deadline: NA

Regular Deadline: 15-Jan

Application Fee: $80 Canadian

Full time Undergraduate enrollment: 20,459

Total enrollment: 29,585

Percent Male: 40%

Percent Female: 60%

Total Percent Minority or Unreported: Unreported

Percent African-American: Unreported

Percent Asian/Pacific Islander: Unreported

Percent Hispanic: Unreported

Percent Native-American: Unreported

Percent International: 19%

Percent in-state/out of state: 9% from the U.S.

Percent from Public HS: Unreported

Retention Rate: 92%

Graduation Rate 4-year: 68%

Graduation Rate 6-year: 83%

Percent Undergraduates in On-campus housing: 11%

Number of official organized extracurricular organizations: 150

3 Most popular majors: Business/Commerce, Political Science, Psychology

Student/Faculty ratio: 16:1

Average Class Size: 15

Percent of students going to grad school: Unreported

Tuition and Fees: $15,420 Canadian

In-State Tuition and Fees if different: $1,868 Canadian within Quebec; $5,378 within Canada

Cost for Room and Board: $12,948 Canadian

Percent receiving financial aid out of those who apply, first year: Unreported

Percent receiving financial aid among all students: Unreported

I f you're looking for a truly international college experience, look no further than McGill University in Montreal, Quebec. While the Canadian university system is not well known in the United States, the caliber of students that McGill attracts from all over the world and its emphasis on undergraduate studies make it a top-tier international institution. Founded in 1821 by James McGill, a prominent Montreal merchant, this publicly funded university boasts a diverse student body, a cosmopolitan setting, and, as a result of recent efforts, top research facilities.

Parlez-vous français?

Located in Montreal, the second-largest French speaking city in the world, McGill is one of only three English-language universities in the province of Quebec. Most students do not consider McGill to be a "bilingual school." "If you want to immerse yourself in French, Montreal is a great place to start, but if you don't want to learn a word, it's not a problem," said a junior political science major. With the exception of the Faculty of Law, students are not required to speak or learn French. However, the influence and presence of French and francophone culture is integral to the McGill experience. As one senior said, "It's wonderful to hear a mix of French and English being spoken on campus since it truly gives the cultural experience I was looking for." Since 1964, students in all faculties have had the option to write exams and papers in either English or French. While less-than-perfect *français* is not a problem in the classroom, don't attempt to use developing language skills in the streets of Montreal: "If you try to speak French the Montrealers will respond in English—they know a fakie when they hear one."

Eleven Faculties

Given McGill's international campus culture, it is only fitting that McGill has a very diverse student body where international students are a significant presence. Close to 20 percent of McGill's student body is comprised of international students, a third of which are American. These students are attracted to McGill for its European feel, diverse culture, and the relatively reasonable tuition. Since 1996, McGill has been following the Ministry of Education, Leisure and Sports guidelines by exempting qualified international students from paying certain tuition fees. Due to this financial policy, more and more American students are expressing an interest in McGill and other Canadian schools close to the border.

In order to meet the interests of this diverse, multilingual student body, McGill has 13 different departments called faculties. Unlike most American universities, prospective students apply to each faculty, rather than applying to the university as a whole. Some of these faculties include the Schulich School of Music, the Faculty of Dentistry, and the Desautels Faculty of Management. A third of all students are enrolled in the Faculty of Arts, while the Centre for Continuing Education, the Faculty of Science, and the Faculty of Engineering all enroll around 10 percent each. Some students complain that the mandatory introductory classes in each of these faculties can result in 500-person lectures that are "impersonal" and "intimidating." However, one upperclassman claimed that "it gets better after those entry-level courses." Once students are done with the requirements, there are many thought-provoking and unique electives to choose from.

The "Rez"

McGill's main campus is situated in downtown Montreal by Mount Royal, a beautiful park enjoyed by students and denizens of Montreal for its walking trails. It is close to the metro stations of McGill and Peel, often filled with off-campus students. Once you enter through the Roddick Gates, you are surrounded by a refreshing mix of gray limestone architecture and trees, where it is easy to forget that you are in the bustling business district of Montreal.

The second campus, the Macdonald Campus, is home to the natural sciences such as the Faculty of Agricultural and Environmental Science and the School of Dietetics and Human Nutrition. The Macdonald Campus has a hands-on approach to learning and focuses on preparing students for careers in science and technology.

> "If you want to immerse yourself in French, Montreal is a great place to start, but if you don't want to learn a word, it's not a problem."

Unlike those at many American colleges, after their first year, McGill students do not stay in residence halls, colloquially known as "rez." Although accepted first-year students are guaranteed on-campus housing, due to the limited space, upperclassmen are expected to find housing off campus. A freshman at McGill reports that living in residence "is definitely a great way to meet people, but it can get pretty loud in the hallways sometimes." There are four main rezzes you can live in. Most freshmen live in Upper Rez (officially Bishop Mountain Residences). Royal Victoria College is a women's university turned women's-only residence hall. Solin Hall is an apartment-style residence four metro stops away from central campus. The most coveted residence is New Residence Hall. New Rez was originally a four-star hotel, and students describe it as being superior in décor, space, and food. "They have sushi, steak, whatever you want, basically," says one former inhabitant of New Rez.

Beware of the McGill Bubble

Finding off-campus housing can be a bit of a hassle for McGill students. Although there are many university-owned apartments, some students have trouble finding off-campus housing due to strict housing markets and rising rents in the areas near campus. The section of Montreal dubbed McGill Ghetto, an area east of the campus, seems to be growing in popularity among McGill students. Despite the complications of living off campus, most upperclassmen like living on their own: "Unlike a lot of U.S. schools, McGill really lets you be an adult. I am 21; I can make my own food."

Another reason why students love living off campus is because they can explore the city of Montreal. "There is really no shortage of things to do in Montreal!" gushed one literature major. The city provides something different for every taste. For those who enjoy bar- and club-hopping, the streets of St. Laurent, St. Denis, and Ste. Catherine are lively with students on the weekends. For those who prefer a more relaxing scene, there are many jazz venues and lounges to be discovered. Students describe the people of Montreal and McGill as very accepting and tolerant, and the city as very gay-friendly. Because the city and the university are so integrated, many students warn of getting caught in the "McGill Bubble." One senior said, "Since I am always surrounded by students, I don't have a sense of living in a 'real-world' community."

Because so many students live off campus, most of the weekend activities take place off campus as well. The drinking age in Quebec is 18, so throughout their McGill career, students have easy access to bars, pubs, and alcohol. There are also several on-campus events that are not to be missed. In the warmer month of September, students flock to the lower field to partake in the outdoor open-air pub commonly known as OAP. Another event fondly looked back on is Frosh, the first week of freshman year.

"Basically a week of non-stop drinking and debauchery," reminisced one sophomore.

A Society of Students

If McGill students mostly reside off campus, what do they do on campus? In a school with nearly 24,000 undergraduates, one of the ways in which McGill students form communities amongst themselves is through clubs. There are over 150 student clubs and organizations to choose from. Students can be involved in everything from performance art to political action. Through some of these clubs, McGill students contribute to the community as well. Healthy Minds is an organization devoted to visiting children in hospitals, and Santropol Roulant is a student-run organization that delivers over 100 hot meals a day to housebound senior citizens.

The core of all of these student activities is the University Centre on the main campus. The William Shatner University Centre is a place for students to hang out with their friends, watch TV, play foosball, and hold club meetings. Named after William Shatner, alumnus and actor of *Star Trek* fame, the facility includes a food court, a legal clinic, a pub, and a lounge, all run by the Students' Society of McGill University. The SSMU is a student union that not only serves as an umbrella organization for many student activities but also serves as the voice of the student body. "I appreciate the efforts that SSMU goes through to makes sure our needs and voices are heard by the administration," said one senior. "It definitely brings the McGill student body together."—*Lee Komeda*

FYI

If you come to McGill, " 'you'd better bring a Canadian phone, a strong liver, and a good work ethic.' "

What's the typical weekend schedule? " 'A lot of reading and essay writing but also a lot of fun! On Saturdays you can head down to St. Laurent, St. Denis, or Ste. Catherine streets to have dinner with friends, then go to a bar, club, or a relaxing lounge. On Sundays you can take in a gallery show, go to a concert, or stroll down to the Old Port for a glass of wine.' "

If I could change one thing about McGill, I'd " 'make the final examination dates part of the syllabus (we wait until November, which makes booking a ticket home for Christmas costly).' "

Three things every student at McGill should do before graduating are " 'get trashed during Frosh Week, go to Winter Carnival, enjoy OAP in September.' "

McMaster University

Address: Gilmour Hall Room 108, 1280 Main Street W. Hamilton, Ontario, L8S4L8 Canada
Phone Number(s): 905-525-9140
E-mail address: macadmit@mcmaster.ca
Web site URL: www.mcmaster.ca
Year Founded: 1887
Private or Public: Public
Religious affiliation: None
Location: Suburban
Number of Applicants: Unreported
Percent Accepted: Varies by Program
Percent Accepted who enroll: Varies by Program
Number Entering: Unreported
Number of Transfers Accepted each Year: Unreported
Middle 50% SAT range: Minimum score of 580 for Critical Reading and 520 for Math
Middle 50% ACT range: Minimum score of 27

Early admission program (EA/ED/None): None
Percentage accepted through EA or ED: NA
EA/ED deadline: NA
Regular Deadline: 9-Feb
Application Fee: Varies by Program
Full time Undergraduate enrollment: 20,600
Total enrollment: 27,337
Percent Male: Unreported
Percent Female: Unreported
Total Percent Minority or Unreported: Unreported
Percent African-American: Unreported
Percent Asian/Pacific Islander: Unreported
Percent Hispanic: Unreported
Percent Native-American: Unreported
Percent International: Unreported
Percent in-Country/out of Country: Unreported
Percent from Public HS: Unreported
Retention Rate: Varies by Program

Graduation Rate (4-year): Unreported
Graduation Rate (6-year): Unreported
Percent in On-campus housing: Unreported
Number of official organized extracurricular organizations: Unreported
3 Most popular majors: Vaires by Program
Student/Faculty ratio: Varies by Program
Average Class Size: Varies by Program
Percent of students going to grad school: Unreported
Tuition and Fees: CA$13,693–$20,611 for visa students
In Province Tuition and Fees (if different): Unreported
Cost for Room and Board: Dependent on residence and meal plan
Percent receiving Financial aid, first-year (out of those who apply): Unreported
Percent of Undergraduates Receiving Financial Aid: Unreported

Sprawling over 300 green acres and studded with ivy-covered Gothic buildings, McMaster is regarded as one of the top universities in Canada. The University is named after Senator William McMaster, who in 1887 bequeathed a large sum of money to found a "Christian school of learning." Today, the affectionately named "Mac" is home to nearly 23,000 students and stands as an undisputed center for ground-breaking research and innovation.

Bring on the Innovation!

If there is one thing that students agree on, it's the breathtaking variety of programs that McMaster offers, with majors ranging from anthropology and women's studies to software engineering and Italian. Both basic three-year programs and four-year "Honors Programs" are available. The Honors Programs usually require a higher GPA than their three-year counterparts, as well as an application.

McMaster is especially well-known for its health sciences, business, natural sciences, and engineering departments. Not surprisingly, these are also some of the most difficult programs. "Math is ridiculously hard," said one fourth-year behavioral science major. "Sometimes the introductory classes become very difficult because they are designed to weed out students." But most science majors agree that it's worth it. Kinesiology, the study of human bodily movement, is especially acclaimed among undergrads.

Even if you're not into the hard-core sciences, McMaster still offers a great range of humanities courses. The limited-enrollment Arts & Science program is touted by current students as a great way to get a broad-based liberal arts education. "The Arts & Science program offers a carefully constructed program drawing from both the sciences and humanities," explained one student. Approximately 60 students enroll in this program each year, and its small class sizes guarantee that the students get plenty of attention from their professors.

Outside of the Arts & Science program, McMaster's classes tend to be quite large, especially freshman year. "First year, 300 in a lecture, easily," said one fourth-year. "But when you get into upper-level classes, they become more and more specialized. One of my current classes has 10 students." Another student agreed, advising newcomers not to be intimidated by larger lectures. "First year is full of lectures, but we have tutorials once a week with a TA. One of my favorite classes was Intro to Psych, which is a huge, impersonal class in most colleges. At Mac, we had the professor on video lecture, and when it was done, the TA's there to answer questions for us. It was really interactive and cool." Indeed, for a large research university, students agreed that professors and TAs are readily available and easy to approach, often giving McMaster the feeling of a small liberal arts college.

"What defines McMaster really is the diversity of its students . . . [And we're] always on the cutting edge of teaching methods."

One of the more peculiar things about a McMaster education is its grading scale. Classes at McMaster grade on a zero to 12 scale, zero being fail, one being pass, and 12 being an A+. Students are required to have an average of seven (or a B in most colleges) in order to move up to the next level. In general, students seem to enjoy this method of grading, because it is more specific than simple letter grades. However, some lament that this results in a stricter curve, the disadvantages of which are especially felt within the science sectors.

McMaster is renowned, above all, for its innovative teaching. One of the most interesting facets is the "Inquiry" program, in which a student can form an inquiry problem and explore his or her chosen problem with the help of an instructor, called a "facilitator." The "Inquiry" program has been expanded to most disciplines at McMaster. While it's inventive, there are downsides. One student complained that "Inquiry" projects are more like "giant independent study

projects that most students put on the back burner until a few weeks before they're due." Others disagreed: "My two to three years of Inquiry have taught me an entirely different skill set compared to my traditional lecture-based courses," said one third-year health student. "It really depends on what kind of facilitator you have," explained another.

Just Like John Belushi

The stress of a McMaster education shakes off pretty quickly during the weekends. After all, this is the school that graduated Ivan Reitman, one of the producers of *National Lampoon's Animal House*. In fact, a popular campus tale is that Reitman based some of the wild antics in the movie on actual events that occurred on the McMaster campus. One science student reported, "The Engs (engineers) work hard, but they party pretty hard too!" Indeed, that seems to be the social attitude of this friendly college.

The "weekend" starts on Thursday night, even though most students have class on Friday. A big component of the McMaster social life is the lack of Greek societies, which are prohibited under college rules. Thursday nights usually consist of clubbing or bar-hopping. Most students head over to either Quarters, a popular all-ages-allowed on-campus bar and club, or Hess Village in Hamilton, home to places like Elixir and Funky Munky. Those who are not yet 19 frequent "keggers," even though kegs are technically not allowed in dormitories. Off-campus house parties are also popular. Friday is described by most students as "off day," but once Saturday rolls around, the McMaster students are back in true collegiate-partying form.

Since the legal drinking age is 19 in Ontario, drinking is a popular activity on campus. The students agree that the administration is very reasonable about the alcohol policy. Alcohol is allowed in dorm rooms, provided that the occupants are not under 19, and the alcohol doesn't come in the form of glass bottles or kegs. At Quarters, the alcohol policy is said to be strictly enforced. Beyond alcohol, pot is the drug of choice for students, but very few actually partake in the so-called "heavier" drugs.

Not all of the partying needs to involve alcohol, though. The McMaster Students Union holds a Charity Ball every single year, which draws hundreds of students in formal attire. Nearby downtown Hamilton is also home to great live music venues, malls, and movie theaters. In addition to all of this, annual faculty formals, Homecoming, and Frost Week (the first week back after Winter Break) are yearly events conducive to an exciting campus life. Incoming freshmen can expect to get their first taste of the McMaster social scene at Welcome Week (also known as Frosh Week), which is, according to one student, "just really one whole month of partying. I don't think there was one night my entire freshman year in which I didn't have fun." One notable Frosh Week tradition is the "Pajama Parade." The new first-years don their best sleepwear and walk five or six blocks in broad daylight. Upperclassmen take their lawn chairs out and sit right on the street, greeting them and shaking their hands as they go past. Some upperclassmen get a little more affectionate, bestowing kisses on the new members of Mac.

Marauding Through Student Life

McMaster offers a host of extracurricular activities for its students. Recent success in sports has made athletic activities very popular at Mac. "The whole college comes out for the football games!" one student enthused. "It seems like *everybody* knows somebody on the team." Beyond football, basketball, volleyball, and men's rugby are all highly regarded varsity teams. In addition to varsity, students can also participate in a range of intramural sports such as water polo. "Ultimate Frisbee is *huge* here," a third-year political science major said. However, be prepared for a bit of dedication. "Athletics can be a little cultish at Mac," one student admitted. "Be aware that if you're going out on your own, and you run into your team, they might very well ostracize you."

If sports are not your thing, though, there are a host of other extracurricular activities in which to participate. A glance down the sprawling list of clubs yields the Chinese Commerce Association, the Jane Austen Society, the Trampoline and Power Tumbling Club, the Ismaili Students Association, and Students for Literacy. The major student-run organization is the McMaster Students Union (MSU), which does everything from running the design and copy center to publishing *The Silhouette*, McMaster's weekly newspaper. However, the MSU's biggest job is to regulate all campus clubs. "The MSU is really meant to be the connection between the students and the McMaster administration," said one student. And to that extent, "They get the job done."

One of the most distinguishing features of McMaster is the diversity. "Mac is very culturally diverse," said one second-year. "It was a culture shock coming from a mostly white high school. Diversity is really promoted during Welcome Week in September. Mac does a good job of accepting everyone." Indeed, one of the biggest events on campus is Pangaea, a multicultural performance housed in a pavilion in which the campus groups get to showcase the food, beverages, history, and traditions of their cultures.

Home, Home in Westdale

McMaster students who apply for residence choose from apartment-style or traditional-style dorms (in the latter, you can choose a single, double, or triple). Mac has one female-only residence, and students can opt for substance-free floors or international-themed residences. Brandon Hall has a reputation for being the party dorm, but that is as far as the stereotypes go. "It really depends on who gets assigned to which dorm," one student explained.

About 4,500 undergraduate students live on campus every year, and 65 percent of dorm space is reserved for freshmen. Students often gush about their "residence." "It's a great experience. I lived on a French floor, and I met most of my friends through residence."

Freshman year, rooms are randomly assigned. McMaster's two apartment-style residence halls often go to the upperclassmen, international students, or students with medical issues. Priority for upperclassmen housing is given to those who make the Dean's Honor List (average of 9.5 or above) and students who show exemplary leadership in extracurricular activities. "However, even if you get DHL, you may not get your first pick of residence—for most, their first choice is Mary E. Keyes."

At McMaster, Community Advisors (CAs) are assigned to each dorm. One of their biggest responsibilities is holding the "Connections" program, in which new students are able to air grievances, agree on overnight guest policies, and generally communicate with their roommates. How large a role a CA has in a first-year's life varies. "Are there residential advisors?" one student asked half-jokingly. "Probably. But if we did [have one], I didn't have much contact with her." A second-year commerce major, on the other hand, cited "very good experiences with my CA. We are still friends and talk all the time."

Even though many students enjoy their time in residence, many others choose to live off-campus. Rents around campus are pretty inexpensive, and to some, it seems like a natural transition to share a house with several other classmates after their first year. All full-time students receive an eight-month bus pass free, which makes getting around a whole lot easier. A large number of students also commute from nearby Toronto and London.

But regardless of whether you live on campus or off, dining is an important aspect of campus life. McMaster offers 10 meal plans for students, and they operate on a debit-card (that is, à la carte) system. Students on a meal plan can use their plans in any of 18 locations, including Commons Marketplace, which offers a host of healthy-food options, and the East Meets West Bistro in the Mary E. Keyes Residence. Few individuals, if any, complain about the quality of food at this university. McMaster features the only completely vegetarian college cafeteria in Canada, the Bridges Café. "Food at McMaster is perhaps one of the best among Canadian universities," boasted one student.

If there is one area to complain about, however, it is perhaps the price of food on campus. Students who live in campus dorms are required to subscribe to a minimum meal plan. Those who live off can choose from two meal plans. "Sometimes, however, it's just easier and cheaper to bring a sandwich from home," said a commuting student.

A Little Bit of Green
Despite the fact that McMaster is commonly listed as a part of Hamilton, Ontario, students are more likely to identify with upper-class Westdale, the village in which McMaster is located. "Nobody says it, but Westdale really is a university town," explained one McMaster student. "Hamilton? There are some people who have spent four years here but have never gone into downtown Hamilton." Other students agreed, one third-year stating that "Hamilton's gotten a bad rap over the years, so I was actually a little bit apprehensive about coming to McMaster. But McMaster is pretty isolated—it's easy for it to become your entire life." Some argue that Hamilton has its charms, however. Surely it supplies McMaster with plenty of things to do in the form of bars, pubs, clubs and music venues. "Everybody should get out of Westdale at least once and hang out in downtown Hamilton. No, you will not get shot or robbed, and you'll find very interesting places to hang out or eat," advised one student.

Of course, some will need that little bit of encouragement to leave campus. Current students rave about McMaster's grounds: "McMaster's campus is really beautiful, with lots of greenery and pathways, a rock garden, and picnic tables." It also doesn't hurt that it's surrounded by a conservation area known as Cootes Paradise. McMaster's pedestrian-friendly atmosphere extends even well into the night, since safety does not really rate as a concern for students living on campus and in Westdale.

There is one complaint about McMaster's grounds, though. "Parking is a disaster!" exclaimed one commuter. Agreed another, "My advice to first-years—definitely don't bring a car if you're living on campus." —*Janet Xu*

FYI
If you come to McMaster, you'd better bring "a healthy liver! You're going to be working it to death."
What's the typical weekend schedule? "Going to clubs or bars on Thursdays, just hanging out with friends on Fridays, then going out again Saturday night. On Sundays, you wake up, hit yourself on the head, and then go straight to work."
If I could change one thing about McMaster, I'd change "the corporate atmosphere. They're cutting back on the humanities programs because they don't make enough money, which I don't think is fair."
Three things every student at McMaster should do before graduating are "live in residence, go to Quarters, and get involved in a sport."

Queen's University

Address: Gordon Hall, 74 Union Street, Kingston, ON K7L3N6 Canada
Phone: 613-533-2218
E-mail address: NA
Web site URL: www.queensu.ca
Year Founded: 1841
Private or Public: Public
Religious Affiliation: None
Location: Urban
Number of Applicants: 25,403
Percent Accepted: Unreported
Percent Accepted who enroll: Unreported
Number Entering: 3,246
Number of Transfers Accepted each Year: Unreported
Middle 50% SAT range: Unreported
Middle 50% ACT range: Unreported
Early admission program EA/ED/None: None
Percentage accepted through EA or ED: NA

EA and ED deadline: NA
Regular Deadline: 16-Feb
Application Fee: $135 Canadian
Full time Undergraduate enrollment: 16,038
Total enrollment: Unreported
Percent Male: 40%
Percent Female: 60%
Total Percent Minority or Unreported: Unreported
Percent African-American: Unreported
Percent Asian/Pacific Islander: Unreported
Percent Hispanic: Unreported
Percent Native-American: Unreported
Percent International: 9%
Percent in-state/out of state: 1% from U.S.
Percent from Public HS: Unreported
Retention Rate: Unreported
Graduation Rate 4-year: Unreported
Graduation Rate 6-year: Unreported

Percent Undergraduates in On-campus housing: Unreported
Number of official organized extracurricular organizations: 200
3 Most popular majors: Business/Commerce, General Sport and Fitness Administration/Management
Student/Faculty ratio: 16:1
Average Class Size: 26
Percent of students going to grad school: Unreported
Tuition and Fees: $5,001 Canadian
In-State Tuition and Fees if different: $15,980 Canadian
Cost for Room and Board: $10,110 Canadian
Percent receiving financial aid out of those who apply, first year: Unreported
Percent receiving financial aid among all students: Unreported

One of the earliest institutions of higher learning in Canada, Queen's University is also one of the most prestigious schools in the country. It is a research university of more than 20,000 undergraduates and postgraduates—a rather small number by Canadian standards—and provides top-notch education to all of its students. For American students, Queen's may not be as readily recognized as schools such as the University of Toronto or McGill University, but the quality of education and the number of research opportunities certainly rival many of its better known counterparts. Queen's is not situated in the great metropolises of Toronto or Montreal, but its location in Kingston, Ontario offers students both the sense of a college town and the conveniences of a decent-sized city.

The Faculty

The terms used in Canada to describe different divisions of a university can sometimes baffle American students. Whereas universities in the United States are often divided into separate schools and colleges, in Canada, this type of division is often known as faculty. For example, Queen's is divided into five separate faculties, the Faculty of Arts and Sciences, the Faculty of Applied Science, the Faculty of Law, the Faculty of Education, and the Faculty of Health Sciences. In addition, the university also has its School of Business, School of Graduate Studies and Research, and Theology College. As a result, students have easy access to a large number of courses in different fields. "I think Queen's does a really good job of making sure that there are classes for people of any interest," said one student.

Another difference between Canadian and American universities is the specificity of majors in Canada. While many colleges in the United States also have unique and specialized majors, Canadian undergraduate programs can be in a very specific field, such as

Commerce or Geographic Information Science. For American students who are mostly familiar with the limited number of majors available at liberal arts colleges, the undergraduate programs in Canada can surprise quite a few people at the beginning. However, this also means that the education often provides better professional training and more in-depth teaching of different topics, which can be highly valuable for students.

The number of students in a class varies greatly. In the introductory classes, hundreds of freshmen can be crammed into a single lecture hall. However, that is normal for both Canadian and American universities, especially those with relatively large student populations. The drawback is that it can be difficult to maintain concentration in those classes. "Paying attention in those classes or even showing up to some of them is a big challenge for me," said one student. Of course, students in higher level courses eventually find themselves in much smaller classes. Some of the classes for seniors can have fewer than a dozen students.

The grading system for Canadian schools is also different from the United States. Instead of the letter grading system of A, B, C, D, and F, Canadians use numbers from zero to 100. The good part is that it differentiates those within grades. For example, someone with an A in a class could be scoring 90 on tests, while another with the same letter grade can have 100 on everything. This way, the numerical system helps to better differentiate students. On the other hand, some students may become too concerned with a few points in their grade. "I don't really care about the difference between 80 and 82, but some people do, and I think they spend too much time trying just to raise one or two points," said one student.

The admissions process in Canada can also be unfamiliar to American students. Luckily, given the large number of Americans going north to seek a good education at a relatively affordable price, Queen's has its own special admissions process for American high school students, which is mostly similar to college applications in the United States. Unlike American schools that typically do not have minimum requirements, Queen's admissions office does provide numbers for the minimal GPA and standardized test scores. The combined critical reading and math scores on the SAT should be above 1,200, and students must maintain a high school grade of B-. If the student decides to use ACT, the score must be at least 26. In addition, the requirements are also different depending on the specific programs

to which the student is applying. Just to offer an idea on the admissions standards, the average grade of first-year students from Canada is 87 percent, equivalent of an A to A- in the letter grade system.

Limestone City

Kingston is known as the Limestone City for the simple fact that it has a large number of limestone buildings. The campus is therefore very beautiful with many historic, neo-gothic structures, not unlike many of the Ivy League institutions on the East Coast of the United States. The city approximates a suburban environment with most low rises and large open spaces. Kingston does have a college town atmosphere, however, given that most of the economic activities are linked to universities, government, or hospitals.

One issue for many students in choosing Canadian schools is the weather. For the majority of students, however, the weather is actually not bad at all, but that is mostly because they are Canadians who come from areas north of Kingston. According to an American student, "It is what I expected: cold and long winters, but then again it is not that different from places like Minnesota or the Midwest."

"Queen's does a really good job of making sure that there are classes for people of any interest."

The university offers 16 different residence buildings spread around campus, though the majority of them are located in the southwest corner of the university. The rooms are generally very small, but they do have the basic furniture needed by students. After freshman year, many students choose to live off campus. Most of the time, a group of friends get together and rent a small house in the area, generally at a reasonable price that is competitive with the price of rooms at the university. Queen's has three main dining halls as well as seven retail food outlets. The quality of food is not great, but that is expected of college dining. "I had siblings who went to different universities," said one student. "So I sort of knew that food in dining halls get repetitive very quickly."

Perhaps one thing for American students to look forward to in Canada is the legal drinking age of 19 instead of 21 in the United States. Alcohol is certainly part of college life in Canada, and most people have easy access to it given the low age limit. However, the school does have strict policies limiting alcohol on campus. Of course, a number of bars surround the university, so finding places to drink and socialize is certainly not difficult during weekends. As a result, parties typically occur outside of university residences and in off-campus housing.

A Canadian Ivy

Although hockey is certainly the most important sport in Canada, to the delight of American students, the Queen's football team does draw big and fervent crowds. In many ways, Queen's is quite similar to an Ivy League university. It has a great reputation both domestically and internationally. It provides top-notch academic opportunities to students, and it provides a historic college town atmosphere. While the tuition is much lower for Canadians than for Americans, Queen's still provides an excellent education at an affordable price. Therefore, it is certainly a school to consider for all those willing to brave the cold of Canadian winters.—*Xiaohang Liu*

FYI
If you come to Queen's, you'd better bring "a big coat."
What is the typical weekend schedule? "Relax after a long week."
If I could change one thing about Queen's, I'd "make it easier to get to Toronto."
Three things every student at Queen's should do before graduating are "Go to football games, join a club, and go to the music festival here."

University of British Columbia

Address: Room 2016, 1874 East Mall Vancouver, BC V6T 1Z1, Canada
Phone: 604-822-3014
E-mail address: NA
Web site URL: www.welcome.ubc.ca
Year Founded: 1908
Private or Public: Public
Religious Affiliation: None
Location: Urban
Number of Applicants: 18,773
Percent Accepted: 60%
Percent Accepted who enroll: 44%
Number Entering: 5,017
Number of Transfers Accepted each Year: Unreported
Middle 50% SAT range: Unreported
Middle 50% ACT range: Unreported
Early admission program EA/ED/None: None
Percentage accepted through EA or ED: NA

EA and ED deadline: NA
Regular Deadline: 28-Feb
Application Fee: $60 Canadian
Full time Undergraduate enrollment: 30,170
Total enrollment: 38,811
Percent Male: 47%
Percent Female: 53%
Total Percent Minority or Unreported: Unreported
Percent African-American: Unreported
Percent Asian/Pacific Islander: Unreported
Percent Hispanic: Unreported
Percent Native-American: Unreported
Percent International: 7%
Percent in-state/out of state: 2% from U.S.
Percent from Public HS: Unreported
Retention Rate: 92%
Graduation Rate 4-year: Unreported
Graduation Rate 6-year: Unreported

Percent Undergraduates in On-campus housing: 20%
Number of official organized extracurricular organizations: 250
3 Most popular majors: Biological and Physical Sciences, Computer and Information Sciences, Psychology
Student/Faculty ratio: 15:1
Average Class Size: 9
Percent of students going to grad school: 50%
Tuition and Fees: $5,168 Canadian
In-State Tuition and Fees if different: $23,690 Canadian
Cost for Room and Board: $6,650 Canadian
Percent receiving financial aid out of those who apply, first year: Unreported
Percent receiving financial aid among all students: Unreported

Students at the University of British Columbia will strongly urge you not to overlook the benefits of spending four years in a foreign country—even if it's only across the border in Canada. UBC's blend of stunning natural surroundings, thriving city life, and comprehensive academic offerings gives the Thunderbirds good reason to be proud of their global school.

Studying: Canadian Style

UBC is divided into several schools, or faculties, within which students may choose their majors. Some of the most popular are the Faculty of Arts, which encompasses much of the university's liberal arts programs, and the Faculty of Applied Sciences, which houses the Engineering departments and the School of Nursing. Other options include the Faculty of Forestry, the School of Human Kinetics, and the School of Journalism. "UBC really requires more of you than many other Canadian universities," one sophomore said. And although the general requirements are considered to be a nuisance, most students recognize the value of taking these core classes. In the Faculty of Arts, students must enroll in English, Literature, Science, and Language courses, although some of the requirements may be fulfilled by scores on standardized tests.

It may not be surprising that nearly all of the introductory-level courses at UBC consist of large lectures averaging 200 students a class, but students take comfort in the knowledge that these classes also feature small 15-person weekly discussion groups to go over the material. In addition, upper-level courses go down in size, and after their first years, most students can find themselves in classes of 50 or fewer people. Although students lamented that "it's easy with such big classes to get overlooked," professors generally make themselves very available through e-mail and office hours. For freshmen looking for a gentler transition to the large university scene, UBC offers the Coordinated Arts Program, in which 100 first years have three of their five classes with the same group of people. Signing up for classes can pose a problem, particularly for first and second years, who get last pick, but one student reassuringly said that "if you really want to take a course, just go to the professor and they'll sign you up." For all years, the order of course signups is determined by grade point average.

The sciences, particularly engineering, are generally considered to be more difficult, and students described them as requiring more of a continuous workload than liberal arts courses. Within the arts departments, the International Relations major has a competitive application process. Highly recommended courses include History 103, a comprehensive general history class starting in 1800, and Economics 101 and 102, taught by Robert Gateman, who writes his own textbook. Political Science professor Bruce Baum also gets high marks for "dressing up as Marx" during a lecture. Overall, UBC's position as a highly regarded research community makes its students proud—one sophomore observed that the serious discoveries that her professors are making "really trickle down to the undergraduates they teach, and we benefit from their work."

No Need for a Fake ID

In this large of a university, which has an undergraduate population of 30,000, making friends as a first year might seem like an overwhelming task. However, students meet the majority of their friends in their residence halls through a variety of residence-sponsored activities and simple proximity to a large number of varied and interesting personalities hailing from all over the globe. Events hosted in the dorms include Totem Park's annual "Meat Market," where scantily clad first years are the norm, and an assortment of theme parties such as "Graffiti Night," which features a black light and the opportunity to use highlighters to create fluorescent works of art on other students' shirts.

One of the advantages of going to school in Canada, as many students will inform you, is that the legal drinking age is only 19. This increased access to alcohol contributes to UBC's extensive bar and pub culture, a feature of the University's social life that is all the more exciting because of the city of Vancouver's renowned nightlife. However, undergraduates need not stray far to drink, since the school itself has a number of drinking establishments on campus. The most-frequented of these is the Pit Pub, which hosts "Pit Night" every Wednesday, an event that students describe as an opportunity to "get really drunk, fall over, and stumble home." A lot of drinking occurs in the residences, where the more lenient RA's "don't crack down on underage drinking, but they can be hard on drugs," at least in the dorms. One girl claimed that "the best pot comes from British Columbia" and that this is reflected in the student body's affinities, but other students countered that "while [marijuana use] is a definite part of the UBC culture for many students, it's not over the top." The importance of having events and activities close to the dorms comes into play when it's raining, which "can get very dreary and usually lasts for several months at a time."

The social scene at UBC is characterized as being "generally very friendly," although students commented on certain cliques that form, particularly around ethnic groups and substance users. Not surprisingly, the campus is "extremely liberal" politically, although conservative students said that the atmosphere is "not repressive." Even though it is a public school, many students are perceived to be upper middle class and relatively affluent, which a girl speculated may stem from the fact that "tuition fees are higher for international students." Over 5,000 international undergraduate and graduate students from over 140 countries attend UBC, which creates a unique campus atmosphere. One sophomore even stated that she "can walk all the way across campus and not hear any English," an experience that she attributed to UBC's extensive international recruiting programs.

An International City
UBC is unique in that it does not require first years to live on campus. Those freshmen who do choose to live in the residence complexes settle in either Totem Park or Place Vanier, living situations that are described as "incredibly convenient." Each dorm features an assortment of singles, doubles, triples, and quads, as well as a lounge, study area, small gym, cafeteria and mini-mart. Totem has a reputation for being the party dorm, while Vanier is seen as "nicer and more sedate." There is a wider variety of residences available to upperclassmen, including Walter Gage, featuring suites of six bedrooms and shared living space, and Fairview Crescent, which consists of townhouses. The distinct Ritsumeikan-UBC House, or "Rits," was built as a symbol of UBC's academic partnership with Ritsumeikan University in Japan, and offers not only four-bedroom suites with shared kitchen and living room, but also a Japanese-style tatami room for "relaxing and meditation."

There is one RA on each floor in Totem and Vanier, each overseeing about 50 students. How strict they are depends on the person, but general consensus is that people get away with a lot in the dorms. Students say UBC does not make its substance policies

clear, but the residences do have clear policies that forbid drinking in the hallway but allow it in the rooms. Drugs are not allowed in the dorms, although a single offense will not get you removed. When outside the residences, one junior girl claimed that "you can walk around campus with a joint and rarely get in trouble, and if you're drinking outside, campus security will just tell you to dump it out."

> **"I can walk all the way across campus and not hear any English."**

A large number of students choose to forgo UBC's provided housing, which only accommodates one-fifth of the undergraduate population, and instead look to off-campus options. Students who take this option claim that the advantages of these living situations, which vary in distance from campus and can be as far away as the other side of Vancouver, far outweigh the drawbacks, since the many attractions of the greater city are even more accessible, especially with the convenience of local public transportation. Students can purchase "U-Passes," which give them unlimited access to the Vancouver bus system, which runs until four in the morning.

Thunderbirds find plenty to do on and around campus. The Student Union Building, also known as the SUB, houses a food court, the Pit, a number of small food vendors and restaurants, the Norm Theatre, and even clothing vendors on its multiple levels. The availability of these alternate eating opportunities can be a relief for students who find the cafeteria fare everything from "monotonous and unhealthy" to "disgusting." Meal plan money may be redeemed at other on-campus eateries besides those in Totem and Vanier, but many students choose to cook their own food.

While campus architecture is described as "eclectic but not very attractive at times," the scenic area surrounding UBC more than makes up for it. A junior gushed that "you're surrounded by forest, looking out on the water, with mountains on the other side—it's incredibly picturesque." Right next to campus, down a flight of stairs, is the famous Wreck Beach, where clothing is optional. Many students spend their wintry weekends at the famous Whistler Resort skiing or snowboarding. The city of Vancouver, however, is one of the main reasons students choose UBC. According to a senior: "You could manage by staying strictly on campus all four years, but you'd be missing out on a whole world out there." From clubs and bars to pubs and restaurants, Vancouver seems to have everything in the way of culture and entertainment. Students' favorite joints to frequent include the Blarney Stone and the King's Head pub for drinks, Numero Uno Pizza for cheap late-night slices, and the many ethnic cuisine restaurants, since "you name a country and you can probably find a restaurant that serves its food somewhere in Vancouver."

Thunderbirds Are Go!

UBC's varsity sports are apparently played down since, as a sophomore commented, "I'm not sure anyone attends many of the games at all." While they may not be following their fellow Thunderbirds closely, the rest of campus is reported to be pretty active, with students running outside whenever it isn't raining, or using the Birdcoop Fitness Centre. Intramural sports are popular, as well. With over 300 student-run organizations, UBC students have plenty of choices. Many take advantage of nearby Whistler by joining the extremely popular "Ski and Board Club," which offers discount season passes to the slopes. Clubs centered around celebration of ethnic and cultural heritage are ubiquitous, due largely to the

number of international students, as well as to the significant population of recent immigrants to Canada. These groups "put on a lot of events, like beer gardens and mixers."

A much-appreciated aspect of student life at UBC is the University's fun annual events. These include Day of the Longboat, when students gather in teams of ten to participate in a frantic canoe race, and Arts County Fair, which is held on the last day of classes and offers a chance for students to unwind, listen to famous bands, and "basically start drinking around breakfast and keep it going all day." Daily surprises can include sightings of the many celebrities who film their projects in the Vancouver area, ranging from Jessica Alba to Al Pacino.

UBC offers its students the opportunity to live and study in a renowned research university setting bordered by a "wealth of natural beauty" and one of the most exciting cities on the West Coast, Vancouver. It may be large, but "everyone finds their place here in this laid-back community," which is made even more attractive by its affordability. Students described UBC as a "completely comprehensive university," promising that "no matter what program you go into, you're going to get a great education out of it." Those looking for a truly international university in the top tier of Canadian education might want to consider giving border-hopping a try.—*Kimberly Chow*

FYI

If you come to the University of British Columbia, you'd better bring: "a George Foreman Grill for when you get tired of the cafeteria food, and rain boots."

What's the typical weekend schedule? "Friday night, go to a residence party or a beer garden on campus. Saturday, play IM sports, go to Granville Island for its shopping market; at night go to downtown Vancouver for its pubs, bars, and clubs. Sunday, play some sports and cram in the studying."

If I could change one thing about UBC, I'd "increase school spirit and promote clubs and organizations more."

Three things every student at UBC should do before graduating are: "Jump off the 10-meter high dive in your underwear or naked, gather your friends and race on Day of the Longboat, and go up the clock tower and appreciate the stunning view."

University of Toronto

Address: 25 King's College Circle, Toronto, ON M5S 1A1 Canada
Phone: 416 978-2190
E-mail address: NA
Web site URL: www.utoronto.ca
Year Founded: 1827
Private or Public: Public
Religious Affiliation: None
Location: Suburban
Number of Applicants: 60,776
Percent Accepted: 67%
Percent Accepted who enroll: Unreported
Number Entering: Unreported
Number of Transfers Accepted each Year: Unreported
Middle 50% SAT range: Unreported
Middle 50% ACT range: Unreported
Early admission program EA/ED/None: None
Percentage accepted through EA or ED: NA

EA and ED deadline: NA
Regular Deadline: 1-Mar
Application Fee: $80 Canadian
Full time Undergraduate enrollment: 58,182
Total enrollment: Unreported
Percent Male: 45%
Percent Female: 55%
Total Percent Minority or Unreported: Unreported
Percent African-American: Unreported
Percent Asian/Pacific Islander: Unreported
Percent Hispanic: Unreported
Percent Native-American: Unreported
Percent International: 10%
Percent in-state/out of state: 3% from U.S.
Percent from Public HS: Unreported
Retention Rate: Unreported
Graduation Rate 4-year: Unreported
Graduation Rate 6-year: Unreported

Percent Undergraduates in On-campus housing: 30%
Number of official organized extracurricular organizations: 250
3 Most popular majors: Unreported
Student/Faculty ratio: Unreported
Average Class Size: Unreported
Percent of students going to grad school: Unreported
Tuition and Fees: Dependent on major
In-State Tuition and Fees if different: NA
Cost for Room and Board: $7,000
Percent receiving financial aid out of those who apply, first year: Unreported
Percent receiving financial aid among all students: Unreported

A prestigious institution with three picturesque campuses spread around Canada's most vivacious and culturally diverse city, the University of Toronto has a wide selection of academic, athletic, and entertainment resources both on and off campus. The school is well known for its innovative research and academic prowess and has the best course selection in the nation. While most students are generally proud of the school and pleased with their choice, the intense workload and academic pressure can be overwhelming for many.

Competition in the Classroom

The professors at the University of Toronto are some of the most respected academics and experts in their respective fields. Past and present faculty members have made major contributions to academia and research, including Sir Frederick Banting and J.J.R. Macleod, who won the Nobel Prize in 1923 for their discovery that insulin could

control diabetes, as well as geneticist Tak Mak, who was the first person to clone a T-cell gene.

A senior noted, however, that one of the drawbacks of having world-class professors is that the class sizes are usually extremely large with limited student-faculty interaction. With over 50,000 undergraduate students, "it's hard to avoid feeling like a number," a freshman said. Courses at Toronto are extremely challenging, with professors who are noted to have higher standards than those at most other Canadian universities. Some students feel lost in the large classes and find the competitive nature among students and the overall academic intensity to be stifling.

One student expressed a desire to have professors "grade on academic achievement rather than academic achievement as compared to the rest of a class." But despite the high stress that comes with the academic prestige of the university, students don't regret the choice of attending; one student called his experience "an unparalleled educational opportunity," and said that the hard work is always worth it. Students are also encouraged to utilize on-campus resources such as counseling, writing centers, and tutorials designed to help with rigorous course loads.

With the new waitlist feature that allows students to sign up for a maximum of six courses, including waitlisted courses, U of T students are finding it more difficult to enroll in their classes of choice. But prospects become brighter as students delve deeper into their majors. Class size diminishes and student-faculty interaction increases with each year.

Out of 16 total faculties, there are four main faculties at the U of T: applied science and engineering, music, arts and science, and physical education and health. Applicants to the University apply directly to the faculty of their choice. Co-op programs within faculties incorporate classroom teaching with real-world working experience, as students switch between university work and co-op jobs each semester. There are also specified tracks offered for students interested in science, as well as research opportunities that allow students to work side by side with their highly regarded professors.

The Toronto Triad

The University of Toronto is broken down into three campuses: the St. George Campus, the Mississauga Campus, and the Scarborough Campus. The St. George Campus is the oldest of the three, established in 1827, and is nestled in a park-like setting in the downtown area. This, the primary campus, hosts about 50,000 undergraduate and graduate students. The approximately 10,000 students at Mississauga are located west of downtown in a more modern environment, while the comparably sized student body of the Scarborough campus is part of a small, friendly academic community east of Toronto. Each regional section has its own student culture and campus pride, but a freshman expressed frustration with this division. "I'd have the three separate campuses together," she said. "There are rivalries between the campuses and I think U of T would be stronger as one."

Students explain that the buildings of all three campuses are aesthetically beautiful. One student said, "The buildings downtown are exquisite, old and new ones. The old ones are all so unique and detailed, and have such a history. The newer buildings also offer a modern type of uniqueness to the campus." The University has created a residential college system in order to create smaller communities within the overwhelmingly large student body. Seven of the nine colleges are located in the downtown campus, with the other residences located within the two smaller campuses.

> "It is an urban metropolis that allows for anyone to explore culture, passions, or interests."

A senior explained that the dorm situation is largely traditional, with students housed in doubles their first year and singles in the following years; some students, however, live in suites or townhouses. One student explained that Toronto "does have a large commuter community, with many upper year students opting to live off campus in houses or apartments in the downtown core." He added that some students live at home with their parents, which takes away from the student life aspect of the Toronto experience.

Opportunities for Involvement

The University of Toronto has over 400 officially recognized student clubs, and opportunities for involvement are endless. Each of Toronto's three campuses has its own radio station, and there are over fifteen student publications, including two main newspapers. Campus groups are an integral part of the student experience, from the Aeronautics Team to West Indian Student Association. Hart House is a social, cultural, and recreational facility centered on cultural programming such as arts and music, and is a popular hangout for students.

First-rate athletic facilities include courts, pools, tracks, dance studios, beach volleyball courts, a sports medicine clinic, and facilities for weight training, aerobics and martial arts. There are free instructional classes each week as well as intramural sports leagues.

Students embrace the vast size of the campus and the opportunities available there, although it can be intimidating at first. "It is an urban metropolis that allows for anyone to explore culture, passions, or interests," one senior said. "However, it can be alienating and overwhelming for newcomers." The cultural diversity and social acceptance at U of T is a perk for many. One student explained, "Social groups are really very non-cliquey, with many students open to meeting friends that they normally would not have associated with in high school."

The student body is diverse, with a multitude of international students and cultural events that expose students to different foods, traditions, and beliefs. One sophomore explained that he's met students from all over the map. "You really feel like you are part of the global village," he said.

In Search of a Social Scene

Students say that while there are a multitude of on-campus parties and events, the city is the best place for nightlife and weekend parties. "There's a lot to do in Toronto City," a student explained. "There are loads of activities going on all the time—parties, plays, shows, musicals, concerts . . ." Popular downtown clubs for the university crowd include Tonic and Joe. The Duke of Gloucester, on Yonge Street, is often regarded as the best student hangout close to campus.

The drinking age in Canada is 19, a perk for students who can legally drink two years earlier than they would have been able to in the States. "Clubs and bars are spread out all over downtown Toronto," one student said. "That's what life is here!" One student said that "for a break from campus, U of T students generally go to one of the many nearby pubs to down a pint." Students explain that the general trend is pubs on Thursdays, clubs on Saturdays.

The Greek scene and sports scene are not central to student life at Toronto, falling far below the emphasis placed on academics. One student explained, "Toronto school spirit is generally lacking. Although students are proud of their academic and extracurricular life, generally that isn't parlayed into a strong school spirit." A senior said that

many students at U of T spend much of their weekends studying, but there are opportunities for fun if schedules allow. Typical hangouts are Diablos at University College, the UnderStudy Café in the central campus area, and the Cat's Eye at Victoria College.

The city of Toronto is the largest in Canada and offers a plethora of resources for food, fun, and entertainment beyond those available to students at the University. Toronto has a wide variety of ballet, dance, opera, music, and theater companies. The world's first permanent IMAX movie theater is in Toronto, as well as an open-air venue for music concerts, a popular pedestrian village, and a theater district. The yearly outdoor Shakespeare performances and international film festivals draw people from around the world, and sports fans will not be disappointed, as Toronto is the only Canadian city with teams in the NHL, NBA, and MLB.

The city is brimming with clubs, restaurants, sporting events, festivals, theaters, and shops, and students don't run out of things to do in this multicultural and cosmopolitan city. Toronto's subway, bus, and streetcar systems are speedy and efficient, allowing students to get around town with general ease, and Toronto students have discounted rates to many events.

Despite student complaints about the "mountains of work," Toronto is said to hold the torch for education in Canada. With superior academics, distinguished professors, a wide range of on-campus organizations, and a city with endless opportunity for exploration and enjoyment, the Toronto experience is hard to compete with as long as you're willing to work.—*Catherine Cheney*

FYI

What is the typical weekend schedule? "It involves studying and essay writing. But when schedules are clear, pubs on Thursdays and clubs on Saturdays are popular social events, and allow for the much needed blowing off of steam."

If I could change one thing about Toronto, I'd "combine the three campuses."

Three things every student at the University of Toronto should do before graduating are: "Attend a toga party at St. Michael's College, visit the U of T art gallery, and attend the special lectures offered, particularly those offered by visiting academics."

University of Waterloo

Address: 200 University
Avenue West, Waterloo, ON
N2L 3G1 Canada
Phone: 519-888-4567
E-mail address:
admissions@uwaterloo.ca
Web site URL:
www.uwaterloo.ca
Year Founded: 1957
Private or Public: Public
Religious Affiliation: None
Location: Urban
Number of Applicants:
37,113
Percent Accepted:
Unreported
**Percent Accepted who
enroll:** Unreported
Number Entering: Unreported
**Number of Transfers
Accepted each Year:**
Unreported
Middle 50% SAT range:
Unreported
Middle 50% ACT range:
Unreported
**Early admission program
EA/ED/None:** None

**Percentage accepted
through EA or ED:** NA
EA and ED deadline: NA
Regular Deadline: 31-Mar
Application Fee: $105
Canadian
**Full time Undergraduate
enrollment:** 22,368
Total enrollment: 27,978
Percent Male: 42%
Percent Female: 58%
**Total Percent Minority or
Unreported:** Unreported
Percent African-American:
Unreported
**Percent Asian/Pacific
Islander:** Unreported
Percent Hispanic: Unreported
Percent Native-American:
Unreported
Percent International: 8%
**Percent in-state/out of
state:** 3% from U.S.
Percent from Public HS:
Unreported
Retention Rate: Unreported
Graduation Rate 4-year:
79%

Graduation Rate 6-year:
Unreported
**Percent Undergraduates in
On-campus housing:**
Unreported
**Number of official organized
extracurricular
organizations:** 150
3 Most popular majors:
Unreported
Student/Faculty ratio: 23:1
Average Class Size:
Unreported
**Percent of students going to
grad school:** Unreported
Tuition and Fees: Dependent
on major
**In-State Tuition and Fees if
different:** NA
Cost for Room and Board:
Dependent on residence
plan
**Percent receiving financial
aid out of those who apply,
first year:** Unreported
**Percent receiving financial
aid among all students:**
Unreported

Where else can you get great academics, great work experience, and great bratwurst, all at Canadian prices? According to students at the University of Waterloo, all are within close reach.

A Taste of the Real World

The University of Waterloo is well-known for its rigorous academic programs. Students keep busy fulfilling the minimum 40 classes required for graduation (10 per year), while double majors are even more demanding. Academic programs are structured around Waterloo's six faculties: applied health sciences, arts, engineering, environmental studies, mathematics, and science; each has its own set of requirements and expectations. In addition, there is also an Independent Studies Program for those looking for something more specialized. While math and engineering have an especially strong reputation (Waterloo has more students enrolled in math than any other school in the world), the other departments are equally demanding. There is little reported grade inflation, and professors are fairly accessible. One arts student, discussing the personal attention students receive, commented that he could not remember taking any English classes with more than 40 students per class, even freshman year.

One of Waterloo's biggest highlights is its well-developed, prestigious co-op program, where students divide the school year by alternating terms of school and employment. The co-op program is the largest of its kind in the world, with over half of the student body participating. As a result, Waterloo operates on a trimester system, with classes in session all year long to allow students in the co-op program to graduate within five years. Current undergrads highly recommend the program, saying, "not only can you get some much-needed cash, but you also get work experience, which is great for future employment." Being a part of the co-op system means having the opportunity to travel—not just to nearby Toronto, but to places outside of Canada as well. Students also report that coming back to school from the "real world" after working for a term provides a better perspective on classes and university life in general. One undergraduate said that "sometimes it's nice just to get away for a change of scenery and to refocus my energies."

Building Friendships

Waterloo has no on-campus housing requirements, but almost all first-year students live in the dorms. Many second-years also try to stay on campus, but a recent housing shortage has made this difficult. The university's eight on-campus residences (primarily for first-year students) can be categorized into two main communities—the "UW residences" and the "University college residences." Each dorm has a resident advisor, nicknamed a "don," who is an upperclassman. The UW residences consist of Village 1, Mackenzie King Village, UW Place, and Ron Eydt Village. The University college residences are Conrad Grebel, Renison, St. Jerome's, and St. Paul's. They are small religiously affiliated colleges with ties to the University. Many students are very enthusiastic about living within a residential college system. Offering both separate classes and housing spaces, the church colleges reportedly offer a "homier" atmosphere. Although each church college has a specific religious affiliation, students of any creed may apply for residence. Students say the church colleges have the most "spirit," and according to some, they also have better food—try Conrad Grebel for Mennonite cooking. Most students live in doubles, and on the whole, dorm rooms are small, but are the place where "we start to build lasting friendships so it isn't so bad—in a sense, we are all in it together."

Upperclassmen tend to live off campus—there is plenty of available housing conveniently near the school, and the cost of living is more affordable. By living off campus, students are able to avoid the meal plan, which freshmen are quick to call "a total rip-off." Many find tasty food off campus at popular places like East Side Mario's, Subway, and Campus Pizza, all located at University Plaza, which is open 24 hours a day.

Friendly, Outdoorsy Atmosphere

Students find the town of Waterloo, Ontario, a quiet kind of university town and are quick to differentiate it from nearby "gross, industrial, abandoned-factory-like" Kitchener. For the outdoorsy types, the area around Laurel Creek provides the perfect opportunity to jog, swim, and bike. For those eager to explore the social scene, the Student Life Centre organizes free movies and other recreational activities on campus and around Waterloo. The area is also famous for its great Oktoberfest celebration every year: people come from all over to sample the bratwurst, take in the dancing, and absorb the unique atmosphere of the festival. Students enthusiastically recommend the event, even if it means just taking a tour of the local breweries.

> "We really know how to go after what we want."

As for the night life, students often head to Bombshelter. The student-run bar and club, also known as "Bomber," features popular Wednesday night parties, concerts, and infamous hot wings ("Our wings are so hot you need to sign a waiver!"). Other than that, there are the usual weekend parties with plenty of alcohol available. Waterloo may have a reputation for being a studious school, but as one student commented, "even the engineering students know how to relax once in a while." Some students leave town on the weekends and head for Toronto, about an hour away, but most stay on campus, preferring to hang out with friends there.

Though not sanctioned by the University, fraternities and sororities do exist and are growing in size and number. Besides providing a social outlet, the groups organize a number of philanthropic events throughout the year. "Joining Kappa Kappa Gamma not only gave me the opportunity to do charity work, but it was also a great way to meet a fantastic group of smart, talented women," raved one fourth-year.

As a co-op school, the Waterloo campus is active year-round. Students on campus over the summer can attend the "huge" Canada Day party held on the first of July at Columbia Lake. The event features concerts, carnival games, and fireworks, giving students a chance to enjoy the warm summer weather.

IMs and More

Due to the co-op system, many students do not have a lot of time to pursue other extracurricular activities. However, clubs and organizations number about 150, and include an active student government, the Federation Orientation Committee (which runs frosh week) and *Imprint*, the main student newspaper. Intramurals are also strong, with a number of fine facilities available. Any student with interest can play, and the lack of pressure on the field makes the experience enjoyable. By comparison, varsity sports are more on the periphery of students' interest. One senior had "never even thought about going to a sporting event!"

Quest for the Pink Tie

Waterloo, like all universities, has its own colorful traditions. Among them is the quest for the pink tie, which occurs during freshman week at the start of the school year. Math students, or "mathies" as they are called, enjoy the week-long activities and get the coveted pink tie. Later, a huge pink tie is hung over the side of the math building, and this often adds to the touch of rivalry between the math and engineering departments. During frosh week, engineering students try to steal the giant pink tie, while mathies try to sneak out the "tool," the engineering faculty's prized possession. As one student said, "We love to scheme and plot, but it is really just fun and games."

A Place to Grow

Waterloo students take their academic demands very seriously. "There are lots of smart people, especially in the sciences and engineering," said one undergrad. Students head to the Dana Porter Library to study, and computer clusters are readily available on campus. While the academic atmosphere may not be cutthroat, some complain that there are people who study compulsively.
—*Laura Sullivan*

FYI
If you're coming to Waterloo, you'd better bring "cleats and shin guards so you can play in the intramurals."
What is the typical weekend schedule? "Eat, play sports, party, STUDY."
If I could change one thing about Waterloo, I'd "improve the architecture."
Three things that every Waterloo student should do before graduating are "go tubing in Laurel Creek, go out for a team (competitive or intramurals), and check out Oktoberfest."

University of Western Ontario

Address: 1151 Richmond
Street, London, ON N6A 3K7
Canada
Phone: 519-661-2111
E-mail address: NA
Web site URL: www.uwo.ca
Year Founded: 1878
Private or Public: Public
Religious Affiliation: None
Location: Suburban
Number of Applicants:
27,652
Percent Accepted: 59%
**Percent Accepted who
enroll:** 36%
Number Entering: 5,871
**Number of Transfers
Accepted each Year:**
Unreported
Middle 50% SAT range:
Unreported
Middle 50% ACT range:
Unreported
**Early admission program
EA/ED/None:** None
**Percentage accepted
through EA or ED:** NA
EA and ED deadline: NA

Regular Deadline: 1-Jun
Application Fee: $105
Canadian
**Full time Undergraduate
enrollment:** 20,524
Total enrollment: 24,943
Percent Male: 41%
Percent Female: 59%
**Total Percent Minority or
Unreported:** Unreported
Percent African-American:
Unreported
**Percent Asian/Pacific
Islander:** Unreported
Percent Hispanic:
Unreported
Percent Native-American:
Unreported
Percent International: 4%
**Percent in-state/out of
state:** 1% from U.S.
Percent from Public HS:
Unreported
Retention Rate: Unreported
Graduation Rate 4-year:
Unreported
Graduation Rate 6-year:
Unreported

**Percent Undergraduates in
On-campus housing:**
Unreported
**Number of official organized
extracurricular
organizations:** 100
3 Most popular majors:
Unreported
Student/Faculty ratio:
Unreported
Average Class Size:
Unreported
**Percent of students
going to grad school:**
Unreported
Tuition and Fees: $13,050
Canadian
**In-State Tuition and Fees if
different:** No difference
Cost for Room and Board:
$6,941 Canadian
**Percent receiving
financial aid out of
those who apply, first
year:** Unreported
**Percent receiving financial
aid among all students:**
Unreported

L ocated just under two hours from Toronto, Canada's largest city, which styles itself as "the center of the universe," the University of Western Ontario is one of the nation's most prestigious universities and a mecca in its own right. Outstanding professors, a beautiful campus, a world-renowned business school, and high-quality undergraduate programs draw many of Canada's top students to London, Ontario. The students here benefit not only from a highly respected degree but also from four years of "unparalleled fun."

Advancing Academics

The quality of the undergraduate academic experience at Western is, by most accounts, "steadily improving" as the administration tries to strengthen the school's academic credentials in order to attract top students. But though it is undeniably a "challenging" academic environment, for some students Western is "rightly known as a laid-back party school."

In general, classes are huge for most first-year students. Good professors are often found teaching underclassmen, but usually "there are about 500 of them crammed into a room at one time." Upper-level classes, however, tend to be a lot smaller. Says one student: "Western is not exactly well-known for its graduate and doctorate programs, so you definitely get the sense in third- and fourth-year classes that the professors are trying to woo you over to their discipline to build up the school's postgraduate reputation."

Of course, a student's impression of Western's academic experience depends greatly on which program he or she pursues. Western offers a competitive BA/HBA program in conjunction with its Richard Ivey School of Business, an internationally ranked management school. One student in the joint degree program described it as "very elite and 10 times harder than the rest of Western's undergraduate program." The University also boasts smaller, affiliate colleges, such as Huron College, which set their own academic programs and offer smaller classes. Students in other majors report varying degrees of overall satisfaction. A social science major would give Western academic experience a "five or six of ten," saying that there are "only a handful of amazing profs," and that "it's hard to get individual attention." An actuarial science major, on the other hand, reported receiving a lot of academic guidance during her first year.

Other students complain about a lack of grade inflation in certain departments. Many frustrated students find themselves with 67–75 percent when they feel that their work deserves better. However, one proactive student noted that approaching the professor and complaining about the TA's ineptitude often can result in a higher grade. Like many other big schools, Western is "a haven for finding loopholes."

A typical day at Western can stretch from early in the morning to late at night—one student reports having class from "9:00 a.m. to 10:00 p.m. with only a couple of hours of breaks in between." Engineering students sometimes have up to 35 hours of class a week. Ultimately, your schedule, your academic program, and your time at Western will be products of your ability to make the most of what the enormous school offers.

A Good Deal: Unless You're Hungry

Despite its sprawling size, Western retains a "tight, close-knit feel, even though it's a huge school," perhaps because London is so "tiny" and "in the middle of nowhere." Many say that London is "beautiful and cheap to live in" although "like elsewhere in Canada, the weather is pretty shitty."

All first-year, full-time students are guaranteed housing. There are two main kinds of residences, "suite-style" and "traditional." The suites are generally quite spacious, often featuring two bedrooms, two bathrooms, and a kitchen for four occupants. Rooms freshman year, says one student, are very clean. "We had a cleaning service every day and our own bathroom."

Residential life is extremely social. In fact, the largest dorm, Saugeen-Maitland Hall, nicknamed "the Zoo," is known as the ultimate party dorm. Both guys and girls can be "pretty skanky," says one student. Though not everyone shares that sentiment, many find that the dorms are the center of the campus social scene.

Food on campus is purchased on a pay-per-item basis, and though it is "generally pretty healthy," it can also be prohibitively expensive. Students living in residences get a substantial discount on the dining hall food. The meal plan allows students to purchase a debit card for use anywhere on campus and even in some London restaurants. Students praise the variety of offerings, including sundae and salad bars and pizza in some dining halls, but complain about the cost. Students living off campus—including most upperclassmen—more often take advantage of London's numerous eateries. There are many sushi places, and Starbucks shops abound. Says one student smugly, "the food around here is much better than at Queen's [University]," Western's chief rival and sport nemesis.

> **"I thought that everyone would go to class in their pajamas, but people really dress up here!"**

Students mainly describe the overall financial burden of attending Western as "reasonable," although "this school will nail you on expensive books—but you don't have to actually buy them unless you're a science major!" When the vast majority of upperclassmen move off campus, there is a wide variety of high-quality, relatively low-cost housing. As one student said, "$500 a month can get you a pretty nice place." And despite the higher tuition charges for international students and the current exchange rate, Western is still a bargain for Americans compared to U.S. schools of similar quality.

Primped and Primed

Students generally report that Western hosts a wide variety of people, and that every student can find their niche. Nevertheless, Western has a well-earned reputation as "Canada's private school" where many are the "children of wealthy families." There are "a lot of legacies," and "networking is really important here," says one student.

Another common observation about Western's student body is the *GQ*- and *Vogue*-worthy people who attend the University. There are some "very, very attractive women" who go here, and many students dress to impress. "I thought that everyone would go to class in their pajamas, but people really dress up here!" laments one student.

Like many other colleges, Western boasts an eccentric and resourceful group of engineering students. Recently a group of adept pranksters replicated a famous MIT stunt by disassembling a campus police car and re-assembling it on the roof of a tall building. Each year several engineering students show their school colors by dyeing themselves purple for Homecoming Week. For one unfortunate student, however, the ink proved indelible for months. Students can join many extracurricular activities during their time away from class. Charity fashion shows are quite popular. One student says that her sorority was "a great way to meet people and become involved early on." Improv groups, student media organizations, and pre-professional clubs are also abundant on campus.

Nightlife at Western revolves mainly around campus bars and clubs. Though some city natives complain that all the bars "resemble Cheers," most students report satis-faction with a bustling downtown scene. One bar even has a terrace that overlooks the library. Greek organizations can offer an important socializing venue for first-years, many of whom are not yet 19 and cannot drink in London unless they have a fake ID. The Greek community, however, is not affiliated with the University, and some students lament the hostile attitude on the part of the administration towards fraternities and sororities, which has inhibited their presence on campus from becoming more wide-spread.

In general, a "very collegial atmosphere" prevails on campus. For the motivated students willing to seek them out, Western offers many wonderful academic and social possibilities that, for many, verify its reputation as one of Canada's top schools.—*Sara Schlemm*

FYI

If you come to Western, you'd better bring an "ironing board," "fancy clothes," and "independence."

What's the typical weekend schedule? "Go to bars on Richmond Street or frat parties. There may even be a toga party!"

If I could change one thing about Western I'd change "the expensive on-campus food."

Three things every Western student should do before graduating are "climb to the top of University College tower, follow the football team to Queen's, go to Jack's (the only on-campus bar where 'everyone' goes)."

Index